Microsoft
WORD® 2010
COMPREHENSIVE

Microsoft® WORD® 2010
COMPREHENSIVE

Gary B. Shelly

Misty E. Vermaat

COURSE TECHNOLOGY
CENGAGE Learning™

SHELLY
CASHMAN
SERIES®

Australia • Brazil • Japan • Korea • Mexico • Singapore • Spain • United Kingdom • United States

COURSE TECHNOLOGY
CENGAGE Learning™

Microsoft® Word® 2010: Comprehensive
Gary B. Shelly, Misty E. Vermaat

Vice President, Publisher: Nicole Pinard

Executive Editor: Kathleen McMahon

Product Manager: Nada Jovanovic

Associate Product Manager: Aimee Poirier

Editorial Assistant: Angela Giannopoulos

Director of Marketing: Cheryl Costantini

Marketing Manager: Tristen Kendall

Marketing Coordinator: Adrienne Fung

Print Buyer: Julio Esperas

Director of Production: Patty Stephan

Senior Content Project Manager: Jill Braiewa

Development Editor: Lyn Markowicz

Copyeditor: Foxxe Editorial Services

Proofreader: Chris Clark

Indexer: Rich Carlson

QA Manuscript Reviewers: Chris Scriver,
  John Freitas, Serge Palladino, Susan Pedicini,
  Danielle Shaw

Art Director: Marissa Falco

Cover Designer: Lisa Kuhn, Curio Press, LLC

Cover Photo: Tom Kates Photography

Text Design: Joel Sadagursky

Compositor: PreMediaGlobal

For product information and technology assistance, contact us at
Cengage Learning Customer & Sales Support, 1-800-354-9706

For permission to use material from this text or product,
submit all requests online at **cengage.com/permissions**
Further permissions questions can be emailed to
permissionrequest@cengage.com

Library of Congress Control Number: 2010941782
ISBN-13: 978-1-4390-7900-3
ISBN-10: 1-4390-7900-5

Course Technology
20 Channel Center Street
Boston, MA 02210
USA

Microsoft and the Office logo are either registered trademarks or trademarks of Microsoft Corporation in the United States and/or other countries. Course Technology, a part of Cengage Learning, is an independent entity from the Microsoft Corporation, and not affiliated with Microsoft in any manner.

Cengage Learning is a leading provider of customized learning solutions with office locations around the globe, including Singapore, the United Kingdom, Australia, Mexico, Brazil, and Japan. Locate your local office at: **international.cengage.com/region**

Cengage Learning products are represented in Canada by Nelson Education, Ltd.

Visit our website **www.cengage.com/ct/shellycashman** to share and gain ideas on our textbooks!

To learn more about Course Technology,
visit **www.cengage.com/coursetechnology**

Purchase any of our products at your local college store or at our preferred online store **www.cengagebrain.com**

We dedicate this book to the memory of James S. Quasney (1940 – 2009), who for 18 years co-authored numerous books with Tom Cashman and Gary Shelly and provided extraordinary leadership to the Shelly Cashman Series editorial team. As series editor, Jim skillfully coordinated, organized, and managed the many aspects of our editorial development processes and provided unending direction, guidance, inspiration, support, and advice to the Shelly Cashman Series authors and support team members. He was a trusted, dependable, loyal, and well-respected leader, mentor, and friend. We are forever grateful to Jim for his faithful devotion to our team and eternal contributions to our series.

The Shelly Cashman Series Team

Printed in the United States of America
2 3 4 5 6 7 17 16 15 14 13 12 11

Microsoft WORD 2010 COMPREHENSIVE

Contents

Microsoft **Word 2010**

Appendices

What is the Microsoft® Office Specialist Program?

The Microsoft Office Specialist Program enables candidates to show that they have something exceptional to offer – proven expertise in certain Microsoft programs. Recognized by businesses and schools around the world, over 4 million certifications have been obtained in over 100 different countries. The Microsoft Office Specialist Program is the only Microsoft-approved certification program of its kind.

What is the Microsoft Office Specialist Certification?

The Microsoft Office Specialist certification validates through the use of exams that you have obtained specific skill sets within the applicable Microsoft Office programs and other Microsoft programs included in the Microsoft Office Specialist Program. The candidate can choose which exam(s) they want to take according to which skills they want to validate.

The available Microsoft Office Specialist Program exams include*:

- Using Windows Vista®
- Using Microsoft® Office Word 2007
- Using Microsoft® Office Word 2007 - Expert
- Using Microsoft® Office Excel® 2007
- Using Microsoft® Office Excel® 2007 - Expert
- Using Microsoft® Office PowerPoint® 2007
- Using Microsoft® Office Access® 2007
- Using Microsoft® Office Outlook® 2007
- Using Microsoft SharePoint® 2007

The Microsoft Office Specialist Program 2010 exams will include*:

- Microsoft Word 2010
- Microsoft Word 2010 Expert
- Microsoft Excel® 2010
- Microsoft Excel® 2010 Expert
- Microsoft PowerPoint® 2010
- Microsoft Access® 2010
- Microsoft Outlook® 2010
- Microsoft SharePoint® 2010

What does the Microsoft Office Specialist Approved Courseware logo represent?

The logo indicates that this courseware has been approved by Microsoft to cover the course objectives that will be included in the relevant exam. It also means that after utilizing this courseware, you may be better prepared to pass the exams required to become a certified Microsoft Office Specialist.

For more information:

To learn more about Microsoft Office Specialist exams, visit www.microsoft.com/learning/msbc

To learn about other Microsoft approved courseware from Cengage Learning, visit www.cengagebrain.com

*The availability of Microsoft Office Specialist certification exams varies by Microsoft program, program version and language. Visit www.microsoft.com/learning for exam availability.

Microsoft, Access, Excel, the Office Logo, Outlook, PowerPoint, SharePoint, and Windows Vista are either registered trademarks or trademarks of Microsoft Corporation in the United States and/or other countries. The Microsoft Office Specialist logo and the Microsoft Office Specialist Approved Courseware logo are used under license from Microsoft Corporation.

Preface

The Shelly Cashman Series® offers the finest textbooks in computer education. We are proud that since Mircosoft Office 4.3, our series of Microsoft Office textbooks have been the most widely used books in education. With each new edition of our Office books, we make significant improvements based on the software and comments made by instructors and students. For this Microsoft Word 2010 text, the Shelly Cashman Series development team carefully reviewed our pedagogy and analyzed its effectiveness in teaching today's Office student. Students today read less, but need to retain more. They need not only to be able to perform skills, but to retain those skills and know how to apply them to different settings. Today's students need to be continually engaged and challenged to retain what they're learning.

With this Microsoft Word 2010 text, we continue our commitment to focusing on the user and how they learn best.

Objectives of This Textbook

Microsoft Word 2010: Comprehensive is intended for a ten- to fifteen-week period in a course that teaches Word 2010 as the primary component. No experience with a computer is assumed, and no mathematics beyond the high school freshman level is required. The objectives of this book are:

- To offer a comprehensive presentation of Microsoft Word 2010
- To expose students to practical examples of the computer as a useful tool
- To acquaint students with the proper procedures to create documents suitable for coursework, professional purposes, and personal use
- To help students discover the underlying functionality of Word 2010 so they can become more productive
- To develop an exercise-oriented approach that allows learning by doing

New to This Edition

Microsoft Word 2010: Comprehensive offers a number of new features and approaches, which improve student understanding, retention, transference, and skill in using Word 2010. The following enhancements will enrich the learning experience:

- Office 2010 and Windows 7: Essential Concepts and Skills chapter presents basic Office 2010 and Windows 7 skills.

- Streamlined first chapter allows the ability to cover more advanced skills earlier.

- Chapter topic redistribution offers concise chapters that ensure complete skill coverage.

- New pedagogical elements enrich material, creating an accessible and user-friendly approach.

  - Break Points, a new boxed element, identify logical stopping points and give students instructions regarding what they should do before taking a break.

  - Within step instructions, Tab | Group Identifiers, such as (Home tab | Bold button), help students more easily locate elements in the groups and on the tabs on the Ribbon.

  - Modified step-by-step instructions tell the student what to do and provide the generic reason why they are completing a specific task, which helps students easily transfer given skills to different settings.

The Shelly Cashman Approach

A Proven Pedagogy with an Emphasis on Project Planning

Each chapter presents a practical problem to be solved, within a project planning framework. The project orientation is strengthened by the use of Plan Ahead boxes, which encourage critical thinking about how to proceed at various points in the project. Step-by-step instructions with supporting screens guide students through the steps. Instructional steps are supported by the Q&A, Experimental Step, and BTW features.

A Visually Engaging Book that Maintains Student Interest

The step-by-step tasks, with supporting figures, provide a rich visual experience for the student. Call-outs on the screens that present both explanatory and navigational information provide students with information they need when they need to know it.

Supporting Reference Materials (Appendices, Quick Reference)

The appendices provide additional information about the Application at hand and include such topics as project planning guidelines and certification. With the Quick Reference, students can quickly look up information about a single task, such as keyboard shortcuts, and find page references of where in the book the task is illustrated.

Integration of the World Wide Web

The World Wide Web is integrated into the Word 2010 learning experience by (1) BTW annotations; (2) BTW, Q&A, and Quick Reference Summary Web pages; and (3) the Learn It Online section for each chapter.

End-of-Chapter Student Activities

Extensive end-of-chapter activities provide a variety of reinforcement opportunities for students where they can apply and expand their skills.

Instructor Resources

The Instructor Resources include both teaching and testing aids and can be accessed via CD-ROM or at login.cengage.com

Instructor's Manual Includes lecture notes summarizing the chapter sections, figures and boxed elements found in every chapter, teacher tips, classroom activities, lab activities, and quick quizzes in Microsoft Word files.

Syllabus Easily customizable sample syllabi that cover policies, assignments, exams, and other course information.

Figure Files Illustrations for every figure in the textbook in electronic form.

PowerPoint Presentations A multimedia lecture presentation system that provides slides for each chapter. Presentations are based on chapter objectives.

Solutions To Exercises Includes solutions for all end-of-chapter and chapter reinforcement exercises.

Test Bank & Test Engine Test Banks include 112 questions for every chapter, featuring objective-based and critical thinking question types, and including page number references and figure references, when appropriate. Also included is the test engine, ExamView, the ultimate tool for your objective-based testing needs.

Data Files for Students Includes all the files that are required by students to complete the exercises.

Additional Activities for Students Consists of Chapter Reinforcement Exercises, which are true/false, multiple-choice, and short answer questions that help students gain confidence in the material learned.

> **Book Resources**
>
> 🔒 **Additional Faculty Files**
> 🔒 **Blackboard Testbank**
> 🔒 **Data Files**
> 🔒 **Instructor's Manual**
> 🔒 **Lecture Success System**
> 🔒 **PowerPoint Presentations**
> 🔒 **Solutions to Exercises**
> 🔒 **Syllabus**
> 🔒 **Test Bank and Test Engine**
> 🔒 **WebCT Testbank**
>
> **Chapter Reinforcement Exercises**
>
> **Student Downloads**

SAM: Skills Assessment Manager

SAM 2010 is designed to help bring students from the classroom to the real world. It allows students to train on and test important computer skills in an active, hands-on environment.

SAM's easy-to-use system includes powerful interactive exams, training, and projects on the most commonly used Microsoft Office applications. SAM simulates the Microsoft Office 2010 application environment, allowing students to demonstrate their knowledge and think through the skills by performing real-world tasks such as bolding word text or setting up slide transitions. Add in live-in-the-application projects, and students are on their way to truly learning and applying skills to business-centric documents.

Designed to be used with the Shelly Cashman Series, SAM includes handy page references so that students can print helpful study guides that match the Shelly Cashman textbooks used in class. For instructors, SAM also includes robust scheduling and reporting features.

Content for Online Learning

Course Technology has partnered with the leading distance learning solution providers and class-management platforms today. To access this material, instructors will visit our password-protected instructor resources available at login.cengage.com. Instructor resources include the following: additional case projects, sample syllabi, PowerPoint presentations per chapter, and more. For additional information or for an instructor user name and password, please contact your sales representative. For students to access this material, they must have purchased a WebTutor PIN-code specific to this title and your campus platform. The resources for students may include (based on instructor preferences), but are not limited to: topic review, review questions, and practice tests.

CourseNotes

Course Technology's CourseNotes are six-panel quick reference cards that reinforce the most important and widely used features of a software application in a visual and user-friendly format. CourseNotes serve as a great reference tool during and after the student completes the  course. CourseNotes are available for software applications such as Microsoft Office 2010, Word 2010, Excel 2010, Access 2010, PowerPoint 2010, and Windows 7. Topic-based CourseNotes are available for Best Practices in Social Networking, Hot Topics in Technology, and Web 2.0. Visit www.cengagebrain.com to learn more!

A Guided Tour

Add excitement and interactivity to your classroom with "*A Guided Tour*" product line. Play one of the brief mini-movies to spice up your lecture and spark classroom discussion. Or, assign a movie for homework and ask students to complete the correlated assignment that accompanies each topic. "*A Guided Tour*" product line takes the prep work out of providing your students with information about new technologies and applications and helps keep students engaged with content relevant to their lives; all in under an hour!

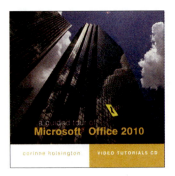

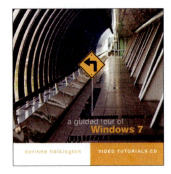

About Our Covers

The Shelly Cashman Series is continually updating our approach and content to reflect the way today's students learn and experience new technology. This focus on student success is reflected on our covers, which feature real students from Westfield State College using the Shelly Cashman Series in their courses, and reflect the varied ages and backgrounds of the students learning with our books. When you use the Shelly Cashman Series, you can be assured that you are learning computer skills using the most effective courseware available.

Textbook Walk-Through

The Shelly Cashman Series Pedagogy: Project-Based — Step-by-Step — Variety of Assessments

Plan Ahead boxes prepare students to create successful projects by encouraging them to think strategically about what they are trying to accomplish before they begin working.

Step-by-step instructions now provide a context beyond the point-and-click. Each step provides information on why students are performing each task, or what will occur as a result.

Explanatory callouts summarize what is happening on screen.

Navigational callouts in red show students where to click.

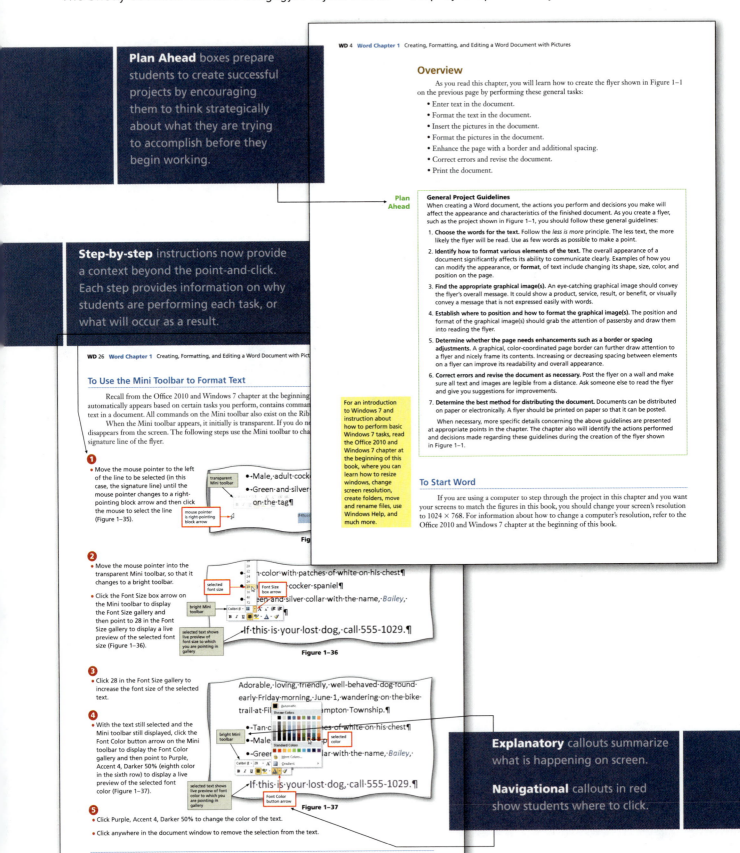

Overview

As you read this chapter, you will learn how to create the flyer shown in Figure 1–1 on the previous page by performing these general tasks:

• Enter text in the document.
• Format the text in the document.
• Insert the pictures in the document.
• Format the pictures in the document.
• Enhance the page with a border and additional spacing.
• Correct errors and revise the document.
• Print the document.

Plan Ahead

General Project Guidelines

When creating a Word document, the actions you perform and decisions you make will affect the appearance and characteristics of the finished document. As you create a flyer, such as the project shown in Figure 1–1, you should follow these general guidelines:

1. **Choose the words for the text.** Follow the *less is more* principle. The less text, the more likely the flyer will be read. Use as few words as possible to make a point.

2. **Identify how to format various elements of the text.** The overall appearance of a document significantly affects its ability to communicate clearly. Examples of how you can modify the appearance, or **format**, of text include changing its shape, size, color, and position on the page.

3. **Find the appropriate graphical image(s).** An eye-catching graphical image should convey the flyer's overall message. It could show a product, service, result, or benefit, or visually convey a message that is not expressed easily with words.

4. **Establish where to position and how to format the graphical image(s).** The position and format of the graphical image(s) should grab the attention of passersby and draw them into reading the flyer.

5. **Determine whether the page needs enhancements such as a border or spacing adjustments.** A graphical, color-coordinated page border can further draw attention to a flyer and nicely frame its contents. Increasing or decreasing spacing between elements on a flyer can improve its readability and overall appearance.

6. **Correct errors and revise the document as necessary.** Post the flyer on a wall and make sure all text and images are legible from a distance. Ask someone else to read the flyer and give you suggestions for improvements.

7. **Determine the best method for distributing the document.** Documents can be distributed on paper or electronically. A flyer should be printed on paper so that it can be posted.

When necessary, more specific details concerning the above guidelines are presented at appropriate points in the chapter. The chapter also will identify the actions performed and decisions made regarding these guidelines during the creation of the flyer shown in Figure 1–1.

For an introduction to Windows 7 and instruction about how to perform basic Windows 7 tasks, read the Office 2010 and Windows 7 chapter at the beginning of this book, where you can learn how to resize windows, change screen resolution, create folders, move and rename files, use Windows Help, and much more.

To Start Word

If you are using a computer to step through the project in this chapter and you want your screens to match the figures in this book, you should change your screen's resolution to 1024 × 768. For information about how to change a computer's resolution, refer to the Office 2010 and Windows 7 chapter at the beginning of this book.

To Use the Mini Toolbar to Format Text

Recall from the Office 2010 and Windows 7 chapter at the beginning automatically appears based on certain tasks you perform, contains comman text in a document. All commands on the Mini toolbar also exist on the Rib

When the Mini toolbar appears, it initially is transparent. If you do n disappears from the screen. The following steps use the Mini toolbar to cha signature line of the flyer.

1
• Move the mouse pointer to the left of the line to be selected (in this case, the signature line) until the mouse pointer changes to a right-pointing block arrow and then click the mouse to select the line (Figure 1–35).

transparent Mini toolbar

mouse pointer is right-pointing block arrow

• Male, adult cock
• Green and silver
  on the tag¶

Fig

2
• Move the mouse pointer into the transparent Mini toolbar, so that it changes to a bright toolbar.

• Click the Font Size box arrow on the Mini toolbar to display the Font Size gallery and then point to 28 in the Font Size gallery to display a live preview of the selected font size (Figure 1–36).

selected font size

Font Size box arrow

bright Mini toolbar

selected text shows live preview of font size to which you are pointing in gallery

color with patches of white on his chest¶
cocker spaniel¶
een and silver collar with the name, *Bailey*,
If this is your lost dog, call 555-1029.¶

Figure 1–36

3
• Click 28 in the Font Size gallery to increase the font size of the selected text.

4
• With the text still selected and the Mini toolbar still displayed, click the Font Color button arrow on the Mini toolbar to display the Font Color gallery and then point to Purple, Accent 4, Darker 50% (eighth color in the sixth row) to display a live preview of the selected font color (Figure 1–37).

Adorable, loving, friendly, well-behaved dog found early Friday morning, June 1, wandering on the bike trail at Fi___ ___ampton Township.¶

bright Mini toolbar

selected color

• Tan ___ ___es of white on his chest¶
• Male
• Green ___ ___ar with the name, *Bailey*,

selected text shows live preview of font color to which you are pointing in gallery

Font Color button arrow

If this is your lost dog, call 555-1029.¶

Figure 1–37

5
• Click Purple, Accent 4, Darker 50% to change the color of the text.

• Click anywhere in the document window to remove the selection from the text.

1

- With the shape still selected, click the More button (shown in Figure 3–6) in the Shape Styles gallery (Drawing Tools Format tab | Shape Styles group) to expand the gallery.

Q&A What if my shape is no longer selected?

Click the shape to select it.

- Point to Intense Effect - Brown, Accent 4 in the Shape Styles gallery to display a live preview of that style applied to the shape in the document (Figure 3–7).

Experiment

- Point to various styles in the Shape Styles gallery and watch the style of the shape change in the document.

2

- Click Intense Effect - Brown, Accent 4 in the Shape Styles gallery to apply the selected style to the shape.

Figure 3–7

Other Ways

1. Click Format Shape Dialog Box Launcher (Drawing Tools Format tab | Shape Styles group), click Picture Color in left pane	(Format Shape dialog box), select desired colors, click Close button	shortcut menu, click Picture Color in left pane (Format Shape dialog box), select desired colors, click Close button
	2. Right-click shape, click Format Shape on	

ion name to the shape. The following steps add text to a shape.

Figure 3–8

Selecting Text

In many of the previous steps, you have selected text. Table 1–3 summarizes the techniques used to select various items.

Table 1–3 Techniques for Selecting Text

Item to Select	Mouse	Keyboard (where applicable)
Block of text	Click at beginning of selection, scroll to end of selection, position mouse pointer at end of selection, hold down SHIFT key and then click; or drag through the text.	
Character(s)	Drag through character(s).	SHIFT+RIGHT ARROW or SHIFT+LEFT ARROW
Document	Move mouse to left of text until mouse pointer changes to a right-pointing block arrow and then triple-click.	CTRL+A
Graphic	Click the graphic.	
Line	Move mouse to left of line until mouse pointer changes to a right-pointing block arrow and then click.	HOME, then SHIFT+END or END, then SHIFT+HOME
Lines	Move mouse to left of first line until mouse pointer changes to a right-pointing block arrow and then drag up or down.	HOME, then SHIFT+DOWN ARROW or END, then SHIFT+UP ARROW
Paragraph	Triple-click paragraph; or move mouse to left of paragraph until mouse pointer changes to a right-pointing block arrow and then double-click.	CTRL+SHIFT+DOWN ARROW or CTRL+SHIFT+UP ARROW
Paragraphs	Move mouse to left of paragraph until mouse pointer changes to a right-pointing block arrow, double-click, and then drag up or down.	CTRL+SHIFT+DOWN ARROW or CTRL+SHIFT+UP ARROW repeatedly
Sentence	Press and hold down CTRL key and then click sentence.	
Word	Double-click the word.	CTRL+SHIFT+RIGHT ARROW or CTRL+SHIFT+LEFT ARROW
Words	Drag through words.	CTRL+SHIFT+RIGHT ARROW or CTRL+SHIFT+LEFT ARROW repeatedly

To Save an Existing Document with the Same File Name

You have made several modifications to the document since you last saved it. Thus, you should save it again. The following step saves the document again. For an example of the step listed below, refer to the Office 2010 and Windows 7 chapter at the beginning of this book.

1 Click the Save button on the Quick Access Toolbar to overwrite the previously saved file.

Break Point: If you wish to take a break, this is a good place to do so. You can quit Word now (refer to page WD 44 for instructions). To resume at a later time, start Word (refer to pages WD 4 and WD 5 for instructions), open the file called Found Dog Flyer (refer to page WD 45 for instructions), and continue following the steps from this location forward.

Inserting and Formatting Pictures in a Word Document

With the text formatted in the flyer, the next step is to insert digital pictures in the flyer and format the pictures. Flyers usually contain graphical images, such as a picture, to attract the attention of passersby. In the following pages, you will perform these tasks:

1. Insert the first digital picture into the flyer and then reduce its size.
2. Insert the second digital picture into the flyer and then reduce its size.
3. Change the look of the first picture and then the second picture.

Textbook Walk-Through

To Quit Word

The project now is complete. Thus, the following steps quit Word. For an example of the step listed below, refer to the Office 2010 and Windows 7 chapter at the beginning of this book.

1 If you have one Word document open, click the Close button on the right side of the title bar to close the document and quit Word; or if you have multiple Word documents open, click File on the Ribbon to open the Backstage view and then click Exit in the Backstage view to close all open documents and quit Word.

2 If a Microsoft Word dialog box appears, click the Save button to save any changes made to the document since the last save.

BTW

Printed Borders
If one or more of your borders do not print, click the Page Borders button (Page Layout tab | Page Background group), click the Options button (Borders and Shading dialog box), click the Measure from box arrow and click Text, change the four text boxes to 15 pt, and then click the OK button in each dialog box. Try printing the document again. If the borders still do not print, adjust the text boxes in the dialog box to a number smaller than 15 point.

Chapter Summary

In this chapter, you have learned how to enter text in a document, format text, insert a picture, format a picture, add a page border, and print a document. The items listed below include all the new Word skills you have learned in this chapter.

1. Start Word (WD 4)
2. Type Text (WD 6)
3. Display Formatting Marks (WD 7)
4. Insert a Blank Line (WD 7)
5. Wordwrap Text as You Type (WD 8)
6. Check Spelling and Grammar as You Type (WD 9)
7. Save a Document (WD 12)
8. Center a Paragraph (WD 14)
9. Select a Line (WD 15)
10. Change the Font Size of Selected Text (WD 16)
11. Change the Font of Selected Text (WD 17)
      (WD 18)
      (WD 19)

      (WD 26)

23. Bold Text (WD 28)
24. Change Theme Colors (WD 28)
25. Save an Existing Document with the Same File Name (WD 30)
26. Insert a Picture (WD 31)
27. Zoom the Document (WD 33)
28. Resize a Graphic (WD 34)
29. Resize a Graphic by Entering Exact Measurements (WD 36)
30. Apply a Picture Style (WD 37)
31. Apply Picture Effects (WD 38)
32. View One Page (WD 40)
33. Add a Page Border (WD 41)
34. Change Spacing before and after a Paragraph (WD 44)
35. Quit Word (WD 44)
36. Open a Document from Word (WD 45)
37. Insert Text in an Existing Document (WD 46)
38. Delete Text (WD 47)
39. Move Text (WD 47)
40. Change Document Properties (WD 49)
41. Print a Document (WD 51)

profile, your instructor may have assigned an autogradable f so, log into the SAM 2010 Web site at www.cengage.com/sam2010 nd start files.

BTW

Quick Reference
For a table that lists how to complete the tasks covered in this book using the mouse, Ribbon, shortcut menu, and keyboard, see the Quick Reference Summary at the back of this book, or visit the Word 2010 Quick Reference Web page (scsite.com/wd2010/qr).

Learn It Online

Test your knowledge of chapter content and key terms.

Instructions: To complete the Learn It Online exercises, start your browser, click the Address bar, and then enter the Web address **scsite.com/wd2010/learn**. When the Word 2010 Learn It Online page is displayed, click the link for the exercise you want to complete and then read the instructions.

Chapter Reinforcement TF, MC, and SA
A series of true/false, multiple choice, and short answer questions that test your knowledge of the chapter content.

Flash Cards
An interactive learning environment where you identify chapter key terms associated with displayed definitions.

Practice Test
A series of multiple choice questions that test your knowledge of chapter content and key terms.

Who Wants To Be a Computer Genius?
An interactive game that challenges your knowledge of chapter content in the style of a television quiz show.

Wheel of Terms
An interactive game that challenges your knowledge of chapter key terms in the style of the television show *Wheel of Fortune*.

Crossword Puzzle Challenge
A crossword puzzle that challenges your knowledge of key terms presented in the chapter.

Apply Your Knowledge

Reinforce the skills and apply the concepts you learned in this chapter.

Modifying Text and Formatting a Document
Note: To complete this assignment, you will be required to use the Data Files for Students. See the inside back cover of this book for instructions on downloading the Data Files for Students, or contact your instructor for information about accessing the required files.

Instructions: Start Word. Open the document, Apply 1-1 Buffalo Photo Shoot Flyer Unformatted, from the Data Files for Students. The document you open is an unformatted flyer. You are to modify text, format paragraphs and characters, and insert a picture in the flyer.

Perform the following tasks:
1. Delete the word, single, in the sentence of body copy below the headline.
2. Insert the word, Creeks, between the words, Twin Buffalo, in the sentence of body copy below the headline.
3. At the end of the signature line, change the period to an exclamation point.
4. Center the headline and the signature line.
5. Change the theme colors to the Aspect color scheme.
6. Change the font and font size of the headline to 48-point Impact, or a similar font. Change the case of the headline text to all capital letters. Apply the text effect called Gradient Fill – Orange, Accent 1, Outline – White to the headline.
7. Change the font size of body copy between the headline and the signature line to 20 point.
8. Use the Mini toolbar to change the font size of the signature line to 26 point.
9. Select the words, hundreds of buffalo, in the paragraph below the headline and underline them.

Extend Your Knowledge

Extend the skills you learned in this chapter and experiment with new skills. You may need to use Help to complete the assignment.

Modifying Text and Picture Formats and Adding Page Borders

Note: To complete this assignment, you will be required to use the Data Files for Students. See the inside back cover of this book for instructions on downloading the Data Files for Students, or contact your instructor for information about accessing the required files.

Instructions: Start Word. Open the document, Extend 1-1 TVC Cruises Flyer, from the Data Files for Students. You will enhance the look of the flyer shown in Figure 1–76. *Hint:* Remember, if you make a mistake while formatting the picture, you can reset it by clicking the Reset Picture button or Reset Picture button arrow (Picture Tools Format tab | Adjust group).

Perform the following tasks:
1. Use Help to learn about the following formats: remove bullets, grow font, shrink font, art page borders, decorative underline(s), picture bullets, picture border shading, shadow picture effects, and color saturation and tone.
2. Remove the bullet from the paragraph below the picture.

3. Select the text, 10 percent, and use the Grow Font button to increase its font size.
4. Add an art page border to the flyer. If the border is not in color, add color to it.
5. Change the solid underline below the word, cruises, to a decorative underline. Change

[add art page border]

NEED AN ESCAPE?

[change border color and add shadow effect; change color saturation and color tone]

[remove bullet]

Tango Vacation Club members receiv[e]
[use Grow Font button to increase font size] **a 10 percent discount for <u>cruises</u> booked during May. Select from a variety of destinations.**

An experience of a lifetime awaits you!

[change to picture bullets]
- **Ultimate relaxation**
- **Endless fun and entertainment**
- **Breathtaking scenery**
- **Friendly, attentive staff**
- **Clean facilities**

Interested? Call TVC at 555-102[9]

Figure 1–76

Make It Right

Analyze a document and correct all errors and/or improve the design.

Correcting Spelling and Grammar Errors

Note: To complete this assignment, you will be required to use the Data Files for Students. See the inside back cover of this book for instructions on downloading the Data Files for Students, or contact your instructor for information about accessing the required files.

Instructions: Start Word. Open the document, Make It Right 1-1 Karate Academy Flyer Unchecked, from the Data Files for Students. The document is a flyer that contains spelling and grammar errors, as shown in Figure 1–77. You are to correct each spelling (red wavy underline) and grammar error (green and blue wavy underlines) by right-clicking the flagged text and then clicking the appropriate correction on the shortcut menu.

If your screen does not display the wavy underlines, click File on the Ribbon and then click Options in the Backstage view. When the Word Options dialog box is displayed, click Proofing in the left pane, be sure the 'Hide spelling errors in this document only' and 'Hide grammar errors in this document only' check boxes do not contain check marks, and then click the OK button. If your screen still does not display the wavy underlines, redisplay the Word Options dialog box, click Proofing, and then click the Recheck Document button.

Change the document properties, including keywords, as specified by your instructor. Save the revised document with the name, Make It Right 1-1 Karate Academy Flyer, and then submit it in the format specified by your instructor.

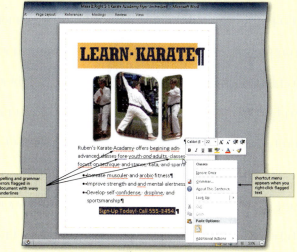

Figure 1–77

Textbook Walk-Through

In the Lab

Design and/or create a document using the guidelines, concepts, and skills presented in this chapter. Labs are listed in order of increasing difficulty.

Lab 1: Creating a Flyer with a Picture

Problem: As a part-time employee in the Student Services Center at school, you have been asked to prepare a flyer that advertises study habits classes. First, you prepare the unformatted flyer shown in Figure 1–78a, and then you format it so that it looks like Figure 1–78b. *Hint:* Remember, if you make a mistake while formatting the flyer, you can click the Undo button on the Quick Access Toolbar to undo your last action.

Note: To complete this assignment, you will be required to use the Data Files for Students. See the inside back cover of this book for instructions on downloading the Data Files for Students, or contact your instructor for information about accessing the required files.

Instructions: Perform the following tasks:
1. Start Word. Display formatting marks on the screen.
2. Type the flyer text, unformatted, as shown in Figure 1–78a, inserting a blank line between the headline and the body copy. If Word flags any misspelled words as you type, check their spelling and correct them.
3. Save the document using the file name, Lab 1-1 Study Habits Flyer.
4. Center the headline and the signature line.
5. Change the theme colors to Concourse.
6. Change the font size of the headline to 36 point and the font to Ravie, or a similar font. Apply the text effect called Gradient Fill – Dark Red, Accent 6, Inner Shadow.
7. Change the font size of body copy between the headline and the signature line to 20 point.
8. Change the font size of the signature line to 22 point. Bold the text in the signature line.

In the Lab Three all new in-depth assignments per chapter require students to utilize the chapter concepts and techniques to solve problems on a computer.

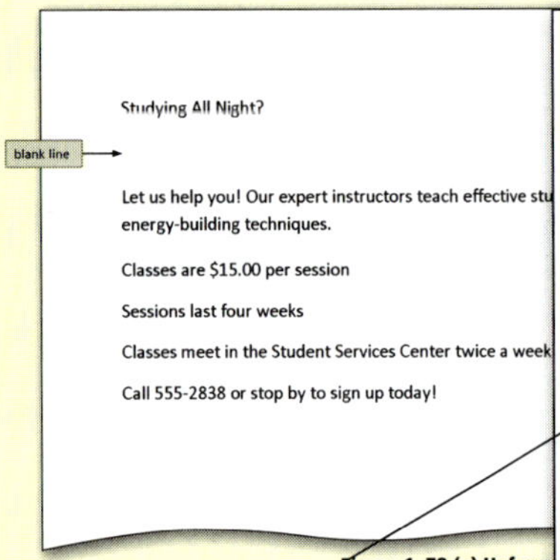

Studying All Night?

[blank line]

Let us help you! Our expert instructors teach effective stu... energy-building techniques.

Classes are $15.00 per session

Sessions last four weeks

Classes meet in the Student Services Center twice a week

Call 555-2838 or stop by to sign up today!

Figure 1–78 (a) Unform...

---

create a building block for Fair Grove Elementary School and insert the building block whenever you have to enter the school name. Resize table columns to fit contents. Check the spelling of the letter. Change the document properties, as specified by your instructor. Save the letter with Lab 3-3 Education Board Letter as the file name.

Cases and Places

Apply your creative thinking and problem solving skills to design and implement a solution.

Note: To complete these assignments, you may be required to use the Data Files for Students. See the inside back cover of this book for instructions on downloading the Data Files for Students, or contact your instructor for information about accessing the required files.

1: Create a Letter to a Potential Employer
Academic
As a student about to graduate, you are actively seeking employment in your field and have located an advertisement for a job in which you are interested. You decide to write a letter to the potential employer: Ms. Janice Tremont at Home Health Associates, 554 Mountain View Lane, Blue Dust, MO 64319.

The draft wording for the letter is as follows: I am responding to your advertisement for the nursing position in the *Blue Dust Press*. I have tailored my activities and education for a career in geriatric medicine. This month, I will graduate with concentrations in Geriatric Medicine (24 hours), Osteopathic Medicine (12 hours), and Holistic Nursing (9 hours). In addition to receiving my bachelor degree in nursing, I have enhanced my education by participating in the following activities: volunteered at Blue Dust's free health care clinic; attended several continuing education and career-specific seminars, including An Aging Populace, Care of the Homebound, and Special Needs of the Elderly; completed one-semester internship at Blue Dust Community Hospital in spring semester of 2012; completed Certified Nursing Assistant (CNA) program at Blue Dust Community College; and worked as nurse's aide for two years during college. I look forward to an interview so that we can discuss the position you offer and my qualifications. With my background and education, I am confident that I will make a positive contribution to Home Health Associates.

The letter should contain a letterhead that uses a shape and clip art, a table (use a table to present the areas of concentration), and a bulleted list (use a bulleted list to present the activities). Insert nonbreaking spaces in the newspaper name. Use the concepts and techniques presented in this chapter to create and format a letter according to the modified block style, creating appropriate paragraph breaks and rewording the draft as necessary. Use your personal information for contact information in the letter. Be sure to check the spelling and grammar of the finished letter. Submit your assignment in the format specified by your instructor.

2: Create a Letter Requesting Donations
Personal
As an alumnus of your historic high school, you are concerned that the building is being considered for demolition. You decide to write a letter to another graduate: Mr. Jim Lemon, 87 Travis Parkway, Vigil, CT 06802.

The draft wording for the letter is as follows: As a member of the class of 1988, you, like many others, probably have many fond memories of our alma mater, Vigil East High School. I recently learned that the building is being considered for demolition because of its age and structural integrity.

Cases & Places exercises call on students to create open-ended projects that reflect academic, personal, and business settings.

Continued >

STUDENT ASSIGNMENTS

Word Chapter 3

Microsoft

WORD® 2010

COMPREHENSIVE

Office 2010 and Windows 7: Essential Concepts and Skills

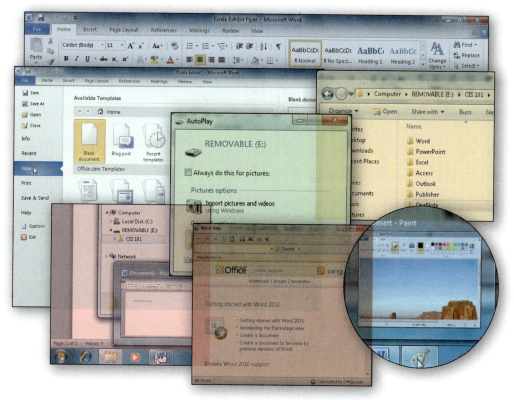

Objectives

You will have mastered the material in this chapter when you can:

- Perform basic mouse operations
- Start Windows and log on to the computer
- Identify the objects on the Windows 7 desktop
- Identify the programs in and versions of Microsoft Office
- Start a program
- Identify the components of the Microsoft Office Ribbon

- Create folders
- Save files
- Change screen resolution
- Perform basic tasks in Microsoft Office programs
- Manage files
- Use Microsoft Office Help and Windows Help

Office 2010 and Windows 7: Essential Concepts and Skills

Office 2010 and Windows 7

This introductory chapter uses Word 2010 to cover features and functions common to Office 2010 programs, as well as the basics of Windows 7.

Overview

As you read this chapter, you will learn how to perform basic tasks in Windows and Word by performing these general activities:

- Start programs using Windows.
- Use features in Word that are common across Office programs.
- Organize files and folders.
- Change screen resolution.
- Quit programs.

Introduction to the Windows 7 Operating System

Windows 7 is the newest version of Microsoft Windows, which is the most popular and widely used operating system. An **operating system** is a computer program (set of computer instructions) that coordinates all the activities of computer hardware such as memory, storage devices, and printers, and provides the capability for you to communicate with the computer.

The Windows 7 operating system simplifies the process of working with documents and programs by organizing the manner in which you interact with the computer. Windows 7 is used to run **application software**, which consists of programs designed to make users more productive and/or assist them with personal tasks, such as word processing.

Windows 7 has two interface variations, Windows 7 Basic and Windows 7 Aero. Computers with up to 1 GB of RAM display the Windows 7 Basic interface (Figure 1a). Computers with more than 1 GB of RAM also can display the Windows Aero interface (Figure 1b), which provides an enhanced visual appearance. The Windows 7 Professional, Windows 7 Enterprise, Windows 7 Home Premium, and Windows 7 Ultimate editions have the capability to use Windows Aero.

Using a Mouse

Windows users work with a mouse that has at least two buttons. For a right-handed user, the left button usually is the primary mouse button, and the right mouse button is the secondary mouse button. Left-handed people, however, can reverse the function of these buttons.

Figure 1(a) Windows 7 Basic interface

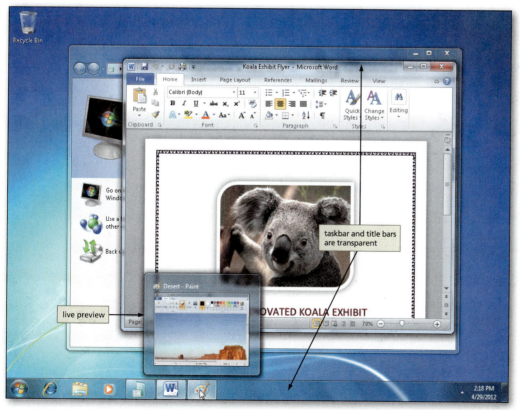

Figure 1(b) Windows 7 Aero interface

Table 1 explains how to perform a variety of mouse operations. Some programs also use keys in combination with the mouse to perform certain actions. For example, when you hold down the CTRL key while rolling the mouse wheel, text on the screen becomes larger or smaller based on the direction you roll the wheel. The function of the mouse buttons and the wheel varies depending on the program.

Table 1 Mouse Operations

Operation	Mouse Action	Example*
Point	Move the mouse until the pointer on the desktop is positioned on the item of choice.	Position the pointer on the screen.
Click	Press and release the primary mouse button, which usually is the left mouse button.	Select or deselect items on the screen or start a program or program feature.
Right-click	Press and release the secondary mouse button, which usually is the right mouse button.	Display a shortcut menu.
Double-click	Quickly press and release the left mouse button twice without moving the mouse.	Start a program or program feature.
Triple-click	Quickly press and release the left mouse button three times without moving the mouse.	Select a paragraph.
Drag	Point to an item, hold down the left mouse button, move the item to the desired location on the screen, and then release the left mouse button.	Move an object from one location to another or draw pictures.
Right-drag	Point to an item, hold down the right mouse button, move the item to the desired location on the screen, and then release the right mouse button.	Display a shortcut menu after moving an object from one location to another.
Rotate wheel	Roll the wheel forward or backward.	Scroll vertically (up and down).
Free-spin wheel	Whirl the wheel forward or backward so that it spins freely on its own.	Scroll through many pages in seconds.
Press wheel	Press the wheel button while moving the mouse.	Scroll continuously.
Tilt wheel	Press the wheel toward the right or left.	Scroll horizontally (left and right).
Press thumb button	Press the button on the side of the mouse with your thumb.	Move forward or backward through Web pages and/or control media, games, etc.

*Note: The examples presented in this column are discussed as they are demonstrated in this chapter.

Scrolling

Minimize Wrist Injury Computer users frequently switch between the keyboard and the mouse during a word processing session; such switching strains the wrist. To help prevent wrist injury, minimize switching. For instance, if your fingers already are on the keyboard, use keyboard keys to scroll. If your hand already is on the mouse, use the mouse to scroll.

A **scroll bar** is a horizontal or vertical bar that appears when the contents of an area may not be visible completely on the screen (Figure 2). A scroll bar contains **scroll arrows** and a **scroll box** that enable you to view areas that currently cannot be seen. Clicking the up and down scroll arrows moves the screen content up or down one line. You also can click above or below the scroll box to move up or down a section, or drag the scroll box up or down to move up or down to a specific location.

Shortcut Keys

In many cases, you can use the keyboard instead of the mouse to accomplish a task. To perform tasks using the keyboard, you press one or more keyboard keys, sometimes identified as

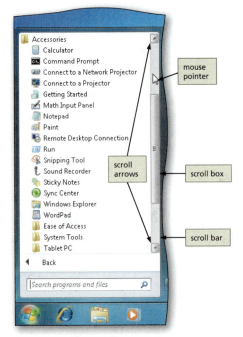

Figure 2

a **shortcut key** or **keyboard shortcut**. Some shortcut keys consist of a single key, such as the F1 key. For example, to obtain help about Windows 7, you can press the F1 key. Other shortcut keys consist of multiple keys, in which case a plus sign separates the key names, such as CTRL+ESC. This notation means to press and hold down the first key listed, press one or more additional keys, and then release all keys. For example, to display the Start menu, press CTRL+ESC, that is, hold down the CTRL key, press the ESC key, and then release both keys.

Starting Windows 7

It is not unusual for multiple people to use the same computer in a work, educational, recreational, or home setting. Windows 7 enables each user to establish a **user account**, which identifies to Windows 7 the resources, such as programs and storage locations, a user can access when working with a computer.

Each user account has a user name and may have a password and an icon, as well. A **user name** is a unique combination of letters or numbers that identifies a specific user to Windows 7. A **password** is a private combination of letters, numbers, and special characters associated with the user name that allows access to a user's account resources. A **user icon** is a picture associated with a user name.

When you turn on a computer, an introductory screen consisting of the Windows logo and copyright messages is displayed. The Windows logo is animated and glows as the Windows 7 operating system is loaded. After the Windows logo appears, depending on your computer's settings, you may or may not be required to log on to the computer. **Logging on** to a computer opens your user account and makes the computer available for use. If you are required to log on to the computer, the **Welcome screen** is displayed, which shows the user names of users on the computer (Figure 3). Clicking the user name or picture begins the process of logging on to the computer.

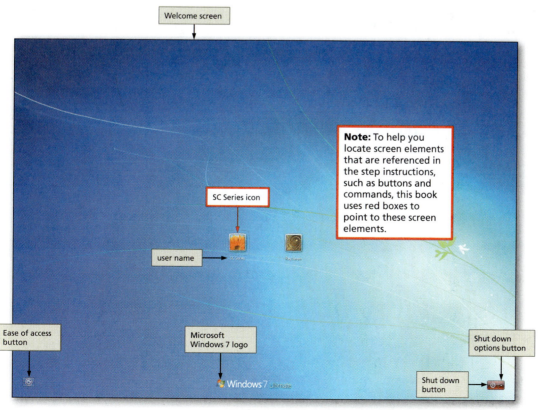

Figure 3

At the bottom of the Welcome screen is the 'Ease of access' button, Windows 7 logo, a Shut down button, and a 'Shut down options' button. The following list identifies the functions of the buttons and commands that typically appear on the Welcome screen:

- Clicking the 'Ease of access' button displays the Ease of Access Center, which provides tools to optimize your computer to accommodate the needs of the mobility-, hearing-, and vision-impaired users.
- Clicking the Shut down button shuts down Windows 7 and the computer.
- Clicking the 'Shut down options' button, located to the right of the Shut down button, displays a menu containing commands that perform actions such as restarting the computer, placing the computer in a low-powered state, and shutting down the computer. The commands available on your computer may differ.
  - The **Restart command** closes open programs, shuts down Windows 7, and then restarts Windows 7 and displays the Welcome screen.
  - The **Sleep command** waits for Windows 7 to save your work and then turns off the computer fans and hard disk. To wake the computer from the Sleep state, press the power button or lift a notebook computer's cover, and log on to the computer.
  - The **Shut down command** shuts down and turns off the computer.

To Log On to the Computer

After starting Windows 7, you might need to log on to the computer. The following steps log on to the computer based on a typical installation. You may need to ask your instructor how to log on to your computer. This set of steps uses SC Series as the user name. The list of user names on your computer will be different.

- Click the user icon (SC Series, in this case) on the Welcome screen (shown in Figure 3 on the previous page); depending on settings, this either will display a password text box (Figure 4) or will log on to the computer and display the Windows 7 desktop.

Q&A Why do I not see a user icon?

Your computer may require you to type a user name instead of clicking an icon.

Q&A What is a text box?

A text box is a rectangular box in which you type text.

Q&A Why does my screen not show a password text box?

Your account does not require a password.

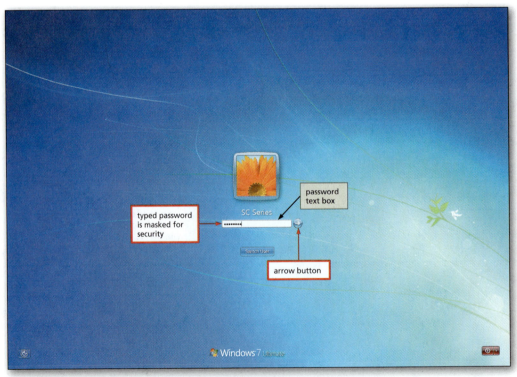

Figure 4

❷
- If Windows 7 displays a password text box, type your password in the text box and then click the arrow button to log on to the computer and display the Windows 7 desktop (Figure 5).

Q&A

Why does my desktop look different from the one in Figure 5?

The Windows 7 desktop is customizable, and your school or employer may have modified the desktop to meet its needs. Also, your screen resolution, which affects the size of the elements on the screen, may differ from the screen resolution used in this book. Later in this chapter, you learn how to change screen resolution.

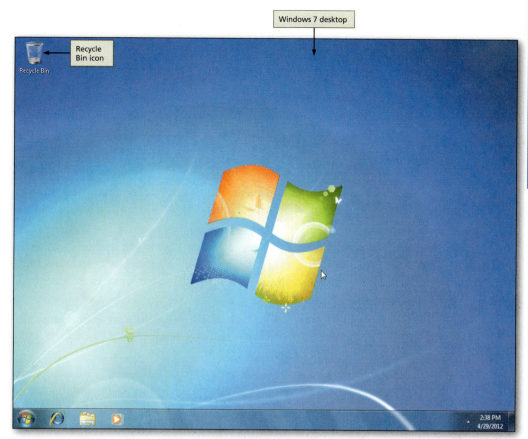

Figure 5

The Windows 7 Desktop

The Windows 7 desktop (Figure 5) and the objects on the desktop emulate a work area in an office. Think of the Windows desktop as an electronic version of the top of your desk. You can perform tasks such as placing objects on the desktop, moving the objects around the desktop, and removing items from the desktop.

When you start a program in Windows 7, it appears on the desktop. Some icons also may be displayed on the desktop. For instance, the icon for the **Recycle Bin**, the location of files that have been deleted, appears on the desktop by default. A **file** is a named unit of storage. Files can contain text, images, audio, and video. You can customize your desktop so that icons representing programs and files you use often appear on your desktop.

Introduction to Microsoft Office 2010

Microsoft Office 2010 is the newest version of Microsoft Office, offering features that provide users with better functionality and easier ways to work with the various files they create. These features include enhanced design tools, such as improved picture formatting tools and new themes, shared notebooks for working in groups, mobile versions of Office programs, broadcast presentation for the Web, and a digital notebook for managing and sharing multimedia information.

Microsoft Office 2010 Programs

Microsoft Office 2010 includes a wide variety of programs such as Word, PowerPoint, Excel, Access, Outlook, Publisher, OneNote, InfoPath, SharePoint Workspace, Communicator, and Web Apps:

- **Microsoft Word 2010**, or Word, is a full-featured word processing program that allows you to create professional-looking documents and revise them easily.

- **Microsoft PowerPoint 2010**, or PowerPoint, is a complete presentation program that allows you to produce professional-looking presentations.

- **Microsoft Excel 2010**, or Excel, is a powerful spreadsheet program that allows you to organize data, complete calculations, make decisions, graph data, develop professional-looking reports, publish organized data to the Web, and access real-time data from Web sites.

- **Microsoft Access 2010**, or Access, is a database management system that allows you to create a database; add, change, and delete data in the database; ask questions concerning the data in the database; and create forms and reports using the data in the database.

- **Microsoft Outlook 2010**, or Outlook, is a communications and scheduling program that allows you to manage e-mail accounts, calendars, contacts, and access to other Internet content.

- **Microsoft Publisher 2010**, or Publisher, is a desktop publishing program that helps you create professional-quality publications and marketing materials that can be shared easily.

- **Microsoft OneNote 2010**, or OneNote, is a note taking program that allows you to store and share information in notebooks with other people.

- **Microsoft InfoPath 2010**, or InfoPath, is a form development program that helps you create forms for use on the Web and gather data from these forms.

- **Microsoft SharePoint Workspace 2010**, or SharePoint, is collaboration software that allows you to access and revise files stored on your computer from other locations.

- **Microsoft Communicator** is communications software that allows you to use different modes of communications such as instant messaging, video conferencing, and sharing files and programs.

- **Microsoft Web Apps** is a Web application that allows you to edit and share files on the Web using the familiar Office interface.

Microsoft Office 2010 Suites

A **suite** is a collection of individual programs available together as a unit. Microsoft offers a variety of Office suites. Table 2 lists the Office 2010 suites and their components.

Programs in a suite, such as Microsoft Office, typically use a similar interface and share features. In addition, Microsoft Office programs use **common dialog boxes** for performing actions such as opening and saving files. Once you are comfortable working with these elements and this interface and performing tasks in one program, the similarity can help you apply the knowledge and skills you have learned to another Office program(s). For example, the process for saving a file in Word is the same in PowerPoint, Excel, and the other Office programs. While briefly showing how to use Word, this chapter illustrates some of the common functions across the Office programs and also identifies the characteristics unique to Word.

Table 2 Microsoft Office 2010 Suites					
	Microsoft Office Professional Plus 2010	Microsoft Office Professional 2010	Microsoft Office Home and Business 2010	Microsoft Office Standard 2010	Microsoft Office Home and Student 2010
Microsoft Word 2010	✔	✔	✔	✔	✔
Microsoft PowerPoint 2010	✔	✔	✔	✔	✔
Microsoft Excel 2010	✔	✔	✔	✔	✔
Microsoft Access 2010	✔	✔	✘	✘	✘
Microsoft Outlook 2010	✔	✔	✔	✔	✘
Microsoft Publisher 2010	✔	✔	✘	✔	✘
Microsoft OneNote 2010	✔	✔	✔	✔	✔
Microsoft InfoPath 2010	✔	✘	✘	✘	✘
Microsoft SharePoint Workspace 2010	✔	✘	✘	✘	✘
Microsoft Communicator	✔	✘	✘	✘	✘

Starting and Using a Program

To use a program, such as Word, you must instruct the operating system to start the program. Windows 7 provides many different ways to start a program, one of which is presented in this section (other ways to start a program are presented throughout this chapter). After starting a program, you can use it to perform a variety of tasks. The following pages use Word to discuss some elements of the Office interface and to perform tasks that are common to other Office programs.

Word

Word is a full-featured word processing program that allows you to create professional-looking documents and revise them easily. A document is a printed or electronic medium that people use to communicate with others. With Word, you can develop many types of personal and business documents, including flyers, letters, memos, resumes, reports, fax cover sheets, mailing labels, and newsletters. Word also provides tools that enable you to create Web pages and save these Web pages directly on a Web server.

Word has many features designed to simplify the production of documents and add visual appeal. Using Word, you easily can change the shape, size, and color of text. You also can include borders, shading, tables, images, pictures, charts, and Web addresses in documents.

While you are typing, Word performs many tasks automatically. For example, Word detects and corrects spelling and grammar errors in several languages. Word's thesaurus allows you to add variety and precision to your writing. Word also can format text, such as headings, lists, fractions, borders, and Web addresses, as you type.

To Start a Program Using the Start Menu

Across the bottom of the Windows 7 desktop is the **taskbar**. The taskbar contains the **Start button**, which you use to access programs, files, folders, and settings on a computer. A **folder** is a named location on a storage medium that usually contains related documents. The taskbar also displays a button for each program currently running on a computer.

Clicking the Start button displays the Start menu. The **Start menu** allows you to access programs, folders, and files on the computer and contains commands that allow you to start programs, store and search for documents, customize the computer, and obtain help about thousands of topics. A **menu** is a list of related items, including folders, programs, and commands. Each **command** on a menu performs a specific action, such as saving a file or obtaining help.

The following steps, which assume Windows 7 is running, use the Start menu to start the Microsoft Word 2010 program based on a typical installation. You may need to ask your instructor how to start Word for your computer. Although the steps illustrate starting the Word program, the steps to start any program are similar.

1

• Click the Start button on the Windows 7 taskbar to display the Start menu (Figure 6).

Q&A Why does my Start menu look different?

It may look different depending on your computer's configuration. The Start menu may be customized for several reasons, such as usage requirements or security restrictions.

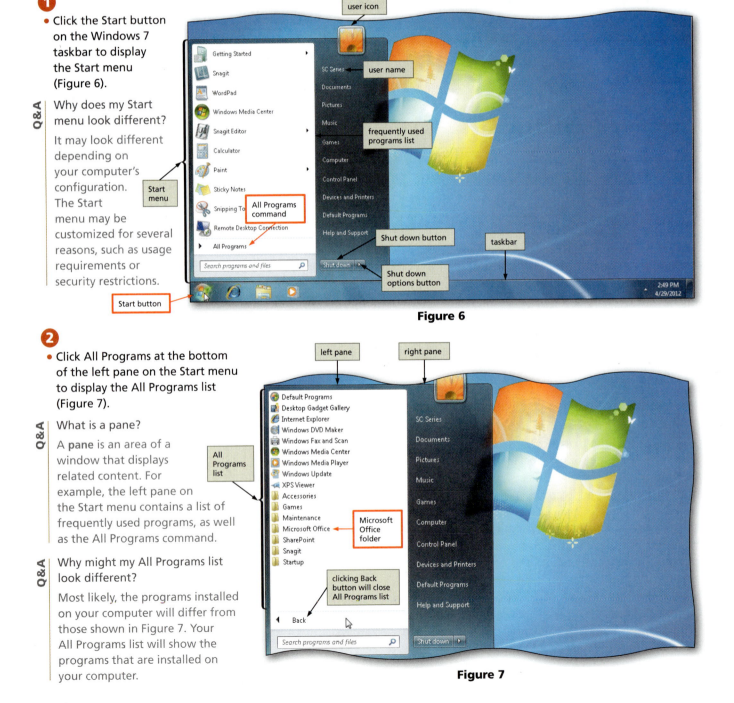

Figure 6

2

• Click All Programs at the bottom of the left pane on the Start menu to display the All Programs list (Figure 7).

Q&A What is a pane?

A **pane** is an area of a window that displays related content. For example, the left pane on the Start menu contains a list of frequently used programs, as well as the All Programs command.

Q&A Why might my All Programs list look different?

Most likely, the programs installed on your computer will differ from those shown in Figure 7. Your All Programs list will show the programs that are installed on your computer.

Figure 7

- If the program you wish to start is located in a folder, click or scroll to and then click the folder (Microsoft Office, in this case) in the All Programs list to display a list of the folder's contents (Figure 8).

Q&A

Why is the Microsoft Office folder on my computer?

During installation of Microsoft Office 2010, the Microsoft Office folder was added to the All Programs list.

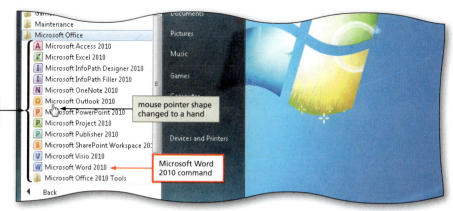

Figure 8

- Click, or scroll to and then click, the program name (Microsoft Word 2010, in this case) in the list to start the selected program (Figure 9).

Q&A

What happens when you start a program?

Many programs initially display a blank document in a program window, as shown in the Word window in Figure 9; others provide a means for you to create a blank document. A **window** is a rectangular area that displays data and information. The top of a window has a **title bar**, which is a horizontal space that contains the window's name.

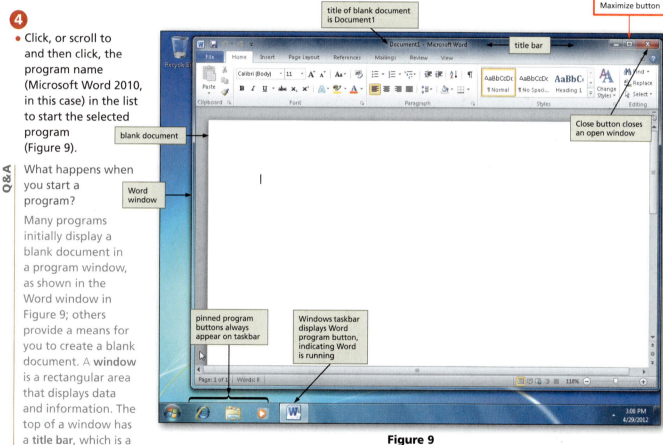

Figure 9

Q&A

Why is my program window a different size?

The Word window shown in Figure 9 is not maximized. Your Word window already may be maximized. The steps on the next page maximize a window.

Other Ways

1. Double-click program icon on desktop, if one is present

2. Click program name in left pane of Start menu, if present

3. Display Start menu, type program name in search box, click program name

4. Double-click file created using program you want to start

To Maximize a Window

Sometimes content is not visible completely in a window. One method of displaying the entire contents of a window is to **maximize** it, or enlarge the window so that it fills the entire screen. The following step maximizes the Word window; however, any Office program's window can be maximized using this step.

- If the program window is not maximized already, click the Maximize button (shown in Figure 9 on the previous page) next to the Close button on the window's title bar (the Word window title bar, in this case) to maximize the window (Figure 10).

Q&A What happened to the Maximize button?

It changed to a Restore Down button, which you can use to return a window to its size and location before you maximized it.

Q&A How do I know whether a window is maximized?

A window is maximized if it fills the entire display area and the Restore Down button is displayed on the title bar.

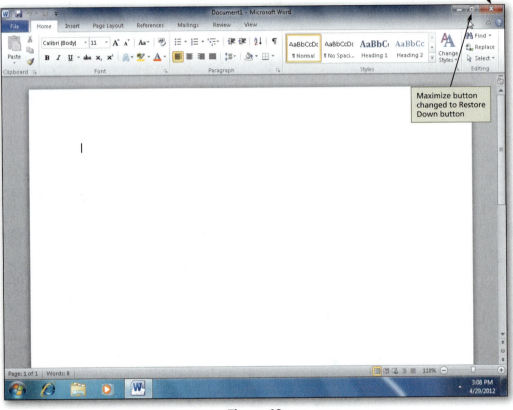

Figure 10

Other Ways
1. Double-click title bar
2. Drag title bar to top of screen

The Word Document Window, Ribbon, and Elements Common to Office Programs

The Word window consists of a variety of components to make your work more efficient and documents more professional. These include the document window, Ribbon, Mini toolbar, shortcut menus, and Quick Access Toolbar. Most of these components are common to other Microsoft Office 2010 programs; others are unique to Word.

You view a portion of a document on the screen through a **document window** (Figure 11). The default (preset) view is **Print Layout view**, which shows the document on a mock sheet of paper in the document window.

Scroll Bars You use a scroll bar to display different portions of a document in the document window. At the right edge of the document window is a vertical scroll bar. If a document is too wide to fit in the document window, a horizontal scroll bar also appears at the bottom of the document window. On a scroll bar, the position of the scroll box reflects the location of the portion of the document that is displayed in the document window.

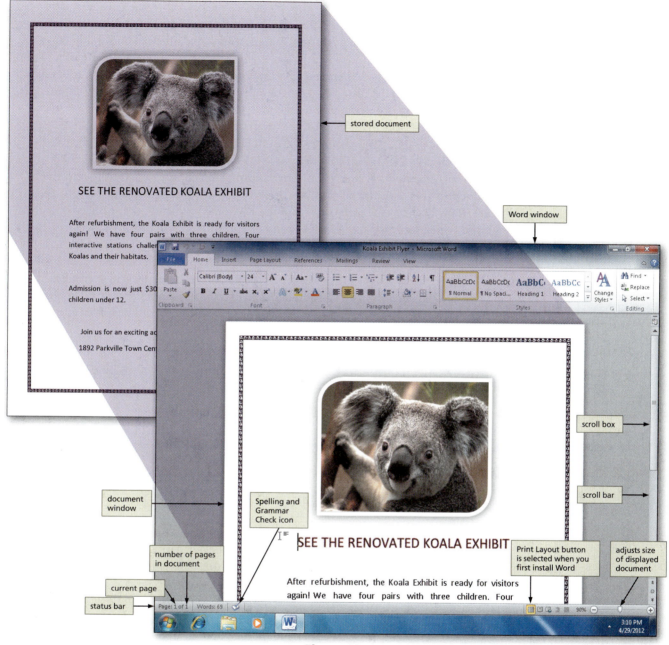

Figure 11

Status Bar The **status bar**, located at the bottom of the document window above the Windows 7 taskbar, presents information about the document, the progress of current tasks, and the status of certain commands and keys; it also provides controls for viewing the document. As you type text or perform certain tasks, various indicators and buttons may appear on the status bar.

The left side of the status bar in Figure 11 shows the current page followed by the total number of pages in the document, the number of words in the document, and an icon to check spelling and grammar. The right side of the status bar includes buttons and controls you can use to change the view of a document and adjust the size of the displayed document.

Ribbon   The Ribbon, located near the top of the window below the title bar, is the control center in Word and other Office programs (Figure 12). The Ribbon provides easy, central access to the tasks you perform while creating a document. The Ribbon consists of tabs, groups, and commands. Each **tab** contains a collection of groups, and each **group** contains related functions. When you start an Office program, such as Word, it initially displays several main tabs, also called default tabs. All Office programs have a **Home tab**, which contains the more frequently used commands.

In addition to the main tabs, Office programs display **tool tabs**, also called contextual tabs (Figure 13), when you perform certain tasks or work with objects such as pictures or tables. If you insert a picture in a Word document, for example, the Picture Tools tab and its related subordinate Format tab appear, collectively referred to as the Picture Tools Format tab. When you are finished working with the picture, the Picture Tools Format tab disappears from the Ribbon. Word and other Office programs determine when tool tabs should appear and disappear based on tasks you perform. Some tool tabs, such as the Table Tools tab, have more than one related subordinate tab.

Items on the Ribbon include buttons, boxes (text boxes, check boxes, etc.), and galleries (Figure 12). A **gallery** is a set of choices, often graphical, arranged in a grid or in a list. You can scroll through choices in an in-Ribbon gallery by clicking the gallery's scroll arrows. Or, you can click a gallery's More button to view more gallery options on the screen at a time.

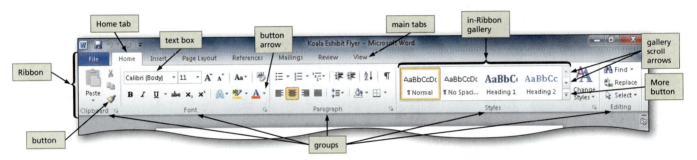

Figure 12

Some buttons and boxes have arrows that, when clicked, also display a gallery; others always cause a gallery to be displayed when clicked. Most galleries support **live preview**, which is a feature that allows you to point to a gallery choice and see its effect in the document — without actually selecting the choice (Figure 13).

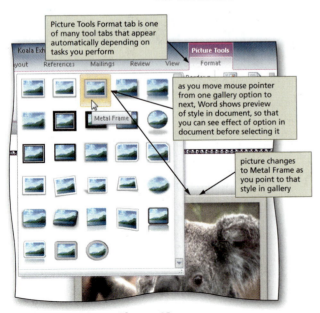

Figure 13

Some commands on the Ribbon display an image to help you remember their function. When you point to a command on the Ribbon, all or part of the command glows in shades of yellow and orange, and an Enhanced ScreenTip appears on the screen. An **Enhanced ScreenTip** is an on-screen note that provides the name of the command, available keyboard shortcut(s), a description of the command, and sometimes instructions for how to obtain help about the command (Figure 14). Enhanced ScreenTips are more detailed than a typical ScreenTip, which usually displays only the name of the command.

Some groups on the Ribbon have a small arrow in the lower-right corner, called a **Dialog Box Launcher**, that when clicked, displays a dialog box or a task pane with additional options for the group (Figure 15). When presented with a dialog box, you make selections and must close the dialog box before returning to the document. A **task pane**, in contrast to a dialog box, is a window that can remain open and visible while you work in the document.

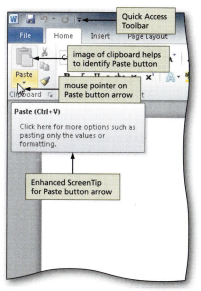

Figure 14

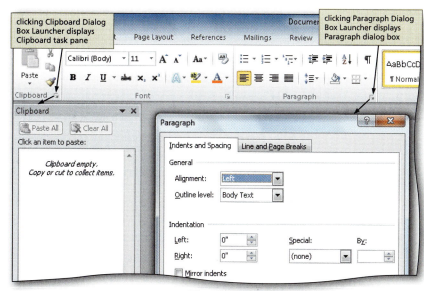

Figure 15

Mini Toolbar The **Mini toolbar**, which appears automatically based on tasks you perform, contains commands related to changing the appearance of text in a document. All commands on the Mini toolbar also exist on the Ribbon. The purpose of the Mini toolbar is to minimize mouse movement.

When the Mini toolbar appears, it initially is transparent (Figure 16a). If you do not use the transparent Mini toolbar, it disappears from the screen. To use the Mini toolbar, move the mouse pointer into the toolbar, which causes the Mini toolbar to change from a transparent to bright appearance (Figure 16b). If you right-click an item in the document window, Word displays both the Mini toolbar and a shortcut menu, which is discussed in a later section in this chapter.

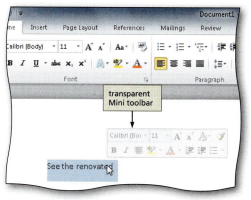

(a) transparent Mini toolbar

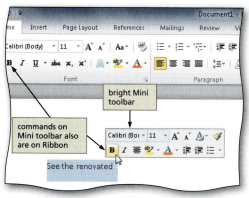

(b) bright Mini toolbar

Figure 16

Quick Access Toolbar The **Quick Access Toolbar**, located initially (by default) above the Ribbon at the left edge of the title bar, provides convenient, one-click access to frequently used commands (Figure 14). The commands on the Quick Access Toolbar always are available, regardless of the task you are performing. The Quick Access Toolbar is discussed in more depth later in the chapter.

KeyTips If you prefer using the keyboard instead of the mouse, you can press the ALT key on the keyboard to display **KeyTips**, or keyboard code icons, for certain commands

Figure 17

(Figure 17). To select a command using the keyboard, press the letter or number displayed in the KeyTip, which may cause additional KeyTips related to the selected command to appear. To remove KeyTips from the screen, press the ALT key or the ESC key until all KeyTips disappear, or click the mouse anywhere in the program window.

To Display a Different Tab on the Ribbon

When you start Word, the Ribbon displays eight main tabs: File, Home, Insert, Page Layout, References, Mailings, Review, and View. The tab currently displayed is called the **active tab**.

The following step displays the Insert tab, that is, makes it the active tab.

- Click Insert on the Ribbon to display the Insert tab (Figure 18).

🔍 **Experiment**

- Click the other tabs on the Ribbon to view their contents. When you are finished, click the Insert tab to redisplay the Insert tab.

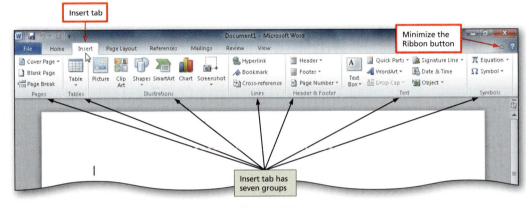

Figure 18

Q&A If I am working in a different Office program, such as PowerPoint or Access, how do I display a different tab on the Ribbon?

Follow this same procedure; that is, click the desired tab on the Ribbon.

To Minimize, Display, and Restore the Ribbon

To display more of a document or other item in the window of an Office program, some users prefer to minimize the Ribbon, which hides the groups on the Ribbon and displays only the main tabs. Each time you start an Office program, such as Word, the Ribbon appears the same way it did the last time you used that Office program. The chapters in this book, however, begin with the Ribbon appearing as it did at the initial installation of Word.

The following steps minimize, display, and restore the Ribbon in Word.

- Click the Minimize the Ribbon button on the Ribbon (shown in Figure 18) to minimize the Ribbon (Figure 19).

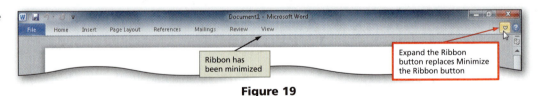

Figure 19

Q&A What happened to the groups on the Ribbon?

When you minimize the Ribbon, the groups disappear so that the Ribbon does not take up as much space on the screen.

Q&A What happened to the Minimize the Ribbon button?

The Expand the Ribbon button replaces the Minimize the Ribbon button when the Ribbon is minimized.

2

- Click Home on the Ribbon to display the Home tab (Figure 20).

Q&A

Why would I click the Home tab?

If you want to use a command on a minimized Ribbon, click the main tab to display the groups for that tab. After you select a command on the Ribbon, the groups will be hidden once again. If you decide not to use a command on the Ribbon, you can hide the groups by clicking the same main tab or clicking in the program window.

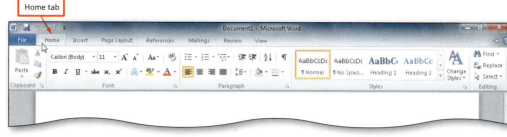

Figure 20

3

- Click Home on the Ribbon to hide the groups again (shown in Figure 19).

- Click the Expand the Ribbon button on the Ribbon (shown in Figure 19) to restore the Ribbon.

Other Ways

1. Double-click Home on the Ribbon
2. Press CTRL+F1

To Display and Use a Shortcut Menu

When you right-click certain areas of the Word and other program windows, a shortcut menu will appear. A **shortcut menu** is a list of frequently used commands that relate to the right-clicked object. When you right-click a scroll bar, for example, a shortcut menu appears with commands related to the scroll bar. When you right-click the Quick Access Toolbar, a shortcut menu appears with commands related to the Quick Access Toolbar. You can use shortcut menus to access common commands quickly. The following steps use a shortcut menu to move the Quick Access Toolbar, which by default is located on the title bar.

1

- Right-click the Quick Access Toolbar to display a shortcut menu that presents a list of commands related to the Quick Access Toolbar (Figure 21).

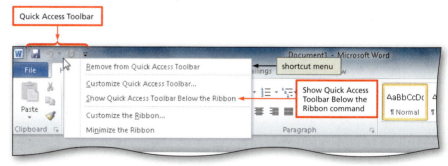

Figure 21

2

- Click Show Quick Access Toolbar Below the Ribbon on the shortcut menu to display the Quick Access Toolbar below the Ribbon (Figure 22).

Figure 22

3

- Right-click the Quick Access Toolbar to display a shortcut menu (Figure 23).

4

- Click Show Quick Access Toolbar Above the Ribbon on the shortcut menu to return the Quick Access Toolbar to its original position (shown in Figure 21 on the previous page).

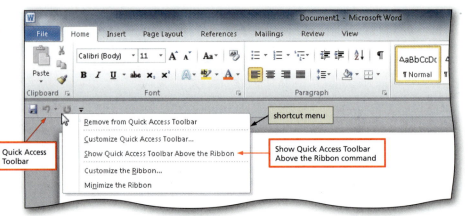

Figure 23

To Customize the Quick Access Toolbar

The Quick Access Toolbar provides easy access to some of the more frequently used commands in Office programs. By default, the Quick Access Toolbar contains buttons for the Save, Undo, and Redo commands. You can customize the Quick Access Toolbar by changing its location in the window, as shown in the previous steps, and by adding more buttons to reflect commands you would like to access easily. The following steps add the Quick Print button to the Quick Access Toolbar in the Word window.

1

- Click the Customize Quick Access Toolbar button to display the Customize Quick Access Toolbar menu (Figure 24).

Q&A Which commands are listed on the Customize Quick Access Toolbar menu?

It lists commands that commonly are added to the Quick Access Toolbar.

Q&A What do the check marks next to some commands signify?

Check marks appear next to commands that already are on the Quick Access Toolbar. When you add a button to the Quick Access Toolbar, a check mark will be displayed next to its command name.

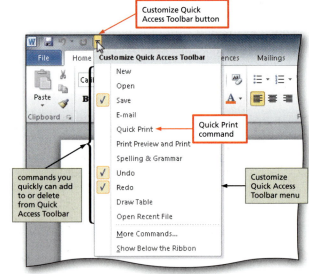

Figure 24

2

- Click Quick Print on the Customize Quick Access Toolbar menu to add the Quick Print button to the Quick Access Toolbar (Figure 25).

Q&A How would I remove a button from the Quick Access Toolbar?

You would right-click the button you wish to remove and then click Remove from Quick Access Toolbar on the shortcut menu. If you want your screens to match the screens in the remaining chapters in this book, you would remove the Quick Print button from the Quick Access Toolbar.

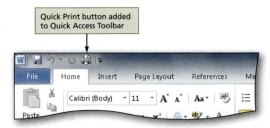

Figure 25

To Enter Text in a Document

The first step in creating a document is to enter its text by typing on the keyboard. By default, Word positions text at the left margin as you type. To begin creating a flyer, for example, you type the headline in the document window. The following steps type this first line of text, a headline, in a document.

- Type **SEE THE RENOVATED KOALA EXHIBIT** as the text (Figure 26).

Q&A What is the blinking vertical bar to the right of the text?

The insertion point. It indicates where text, graphics, and other items will be inserted in the document. As you type, the insertion point moves to the right, and when you reach the end of a line, it moves downward to the beginning of the next line.

Q&A What if I make an error while typing?

You can press the BACKSPACE key until you have deleted the text in error and then retype the text correctly.

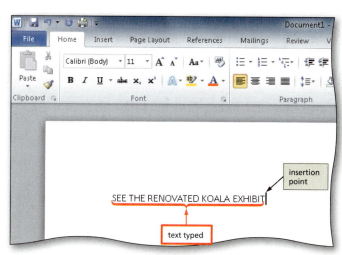

Figure 26

- Press the ENTER key to move the insertion point to the beginning of the next line (Figure 27).

Q&A Why did blank space appear between the entered text and the insertion point?

Each time you press the ENTER key, Word creates a new paragraph and inserts blank space between the two paragraphs.

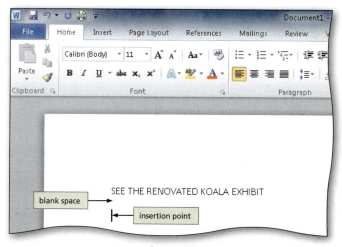

Figure 27

Saving and Organizing Files

While you are creating a document, the computer stores it in memory. When you save a document, the computer places it on a storage medium such as a hard disk, USB flash drive, or optical disc. A saved document is referred to as a file. A **file name** is the name assigned to a file when it is saved. It is important to save a document frequently for the following reasons:

- The document in memory might be lost if the computer is turned off or you lose electrical power while a program is running.
- If you run out of time before completing a project, you may finish it at a future time without starting over.

When saving files, you should organize them so that you easily can find them later. Windows 7 provides tools to help you organize files.

Organizing Files and Folders

A file contains data. This data can range from a research paper to an accounting spreadsheet to an electronic math quiz. You should organize and store these files in folders to avoid misplacing a file and to help you find a file quickly.

If you are a freshman taking an introductory computer class (CIS 101, for example), you may want to design a series of folders for the different subjects covered in the class. To accomplish this, you can arrange the folders in a hierarchy for the class, as shown in Figure 28.

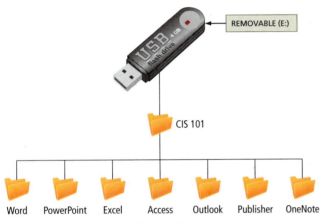

Figure 28

The hierarchy contains three levels. The first level contains the storage device, in this case a USB flash drive. Windows 7 identifies the storage device with a letter, and, in some cases, a name. In Figure 28, the USB flash drive is identified as REMOVABLE (E:). The second level contains the class folder (CIS 101, in this case), and the third level contains seven folders, one each for a different Office program that will be covered in the class (Word, PowerPoint, Excel, Access, Outlook, Publisher, and OneNote).

When the hierarchy in Figure 28 is created, the USB flash drive is said to contain the CIS 101 folder, and the CIS 101 folder is said to contain the separate Office folders (i.e., Word, PowerPoint, Excel, etc.). In addition, this hierarchy easily can be expanded to include folders from other classes taken during additional semesters.

The vertical and horizontal lines in Figure 28 form a pathway that allows you to navigate to a drive or folder on a computer or network. A **path** consists of a drive letter (preceded by a drive name when necessary) and colon, to identify the storage device, and one or more folder names. Each drive or folder in the hierarchy has a corresponding path.

Table 3 shows examples of paths and their corresponding drives and folders.

Table 3 Paths and Corresponding Drives and Folders	
Path	**Drive and Folder**
Computer ▶ REMOVABLE (E:)	Drive E (REMOVABLE (E:))
Computer ▶ REMOVABLE (E:) ▶ CIS 101	CIS 101 folder on drive E
Computer ▶ REMOVABLE (E:) ▶ CIS 101 ▶ Word	Word folder in CIS 101 folder on drive E

The following pages illustrate the steps to organize folders for a class and save a file in a folder:

1. Create a folder identifying your class.
2. Create a Word folder in the folder identifying your class.
3. Save a file in the Word folder.
4. Verify the location of the saved file.

To Create a Folder

When you create a folder, such as the CIS 101 folder shown in Figure 28, you must name the folder. A folder name should describe the folder and its contents. A folder name can contain spaces and any uppercase or lowercase characters, except a backslash (\), slash (/), colon (:), asterisk (*), question mark (?), quotation marks ("), less than symbol (<), greater than symbol (>), or vertical bar (|). Folder names cannot be CON, AUX, COM1, COM2, COM3, COM4, LPT1, LPT2, LPT3, PRN, or NUL. The same rules for naming folders also apply to naming files.

To store files and folders on a USB flash drive, you must connect the USB flash drive to an available USB port on a computer. The following steps create your class folder (CIS 101, in this case) on a USB flash drive.

1

- Connect the USB flash drive to an available USB port on the computer to open the AutoPlay window (Figure 29). (You may need to click the Windows Explorer program button on the taskbar to make the AutoPlay window visible.)

Q&A Why does the AutoPlay window not open?

Some computers are not configured to open an AutoPlay window. Instead, they might display the contents of the USB flash drive automatically, or you might need to access contents of the USB flash drive using the Computer window. To use the Computer window to display the USB flash drive's contents, click the Start button, click Computer on the Start menu, and then click the icon representing the USB flash drive and then proceed to Step 3 on the next page.

Q&A Why does the AutoPlay window look different from the one in Figure 29?

The AutoPlay window that opens on your computer might display different options. The type of USB flash drive, its contents, and the next available drive letter on your computer all will determine which options are displayed in the AutoPlay window.

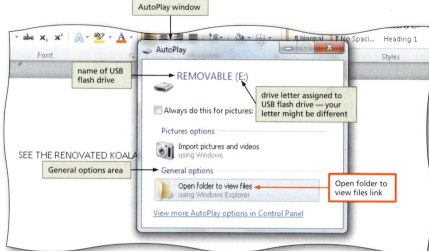

Figure 29

2

- Click the 'Open folder to view files' link in the AutoPlay window to open the USB flash drive window (Figure 30).

Q&A Why does Figure 30 show REMOVABLE (E:) for the USB flash drive?

REMOVABLE is the name of the USB flash drive used to illustrate these steps. The (E:) refers to the drive letter assigned by Windows 7 to the USB flash drive. The name and drive letter of your USB flash drive probably will be different.

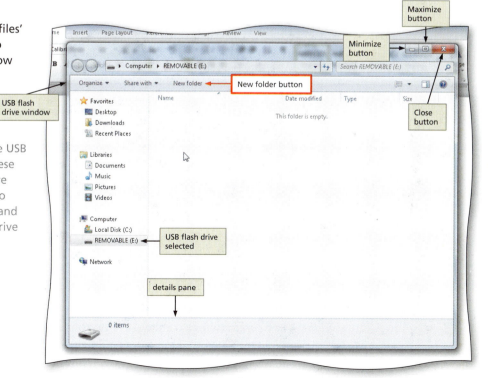

Figure 30

3

- Click the New folder button on the toolbar to display a new folder icon with the name, New folder, selected in a text box.

- Type `CIS 101` (or your class code) in the text box to name the folder.

- Press the ENTER key to create a folder identifying your class on the selected drive (Figure 31). If the CIS 101 folder does not appear in the navigation pane, double-click REMOVABLE (E:) in the navigation pane to display the folder just added.

Q&A

What happens when I press the ENTER key?

The class folder (CIS 101, in this case) is displayed in the File list, which contains the folder name, date modified, type, and size.

Q&A

Why is the folder icon displayed differently on my computer?

Windows might be configured to display contents differently on your computer.

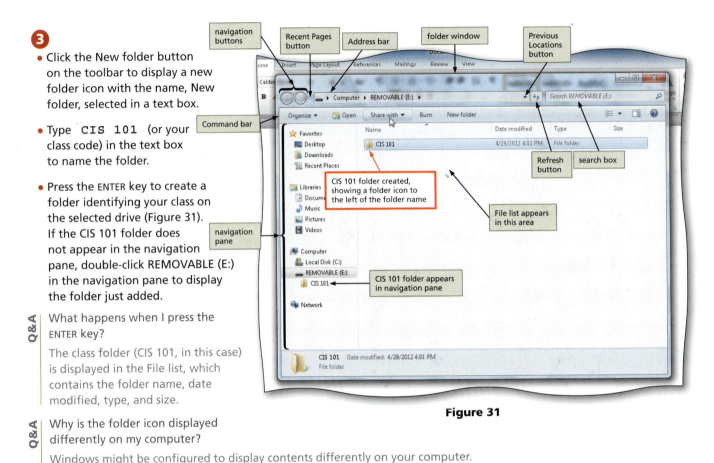

Figure 31

Folder Windows

The USB flash drive window (shown in Figure 31) is called a folder window. Recall that a folder is a specific named location on a storage medium that contains related files. Most users rely on **folder windows** for finding, viewing, and managing information on their computer. Folder windows have common design elements, including the following (Figure 31).

- The **Address bar** provides quick navigation options. The arrows on the Address bar allow you to visit different locations on the computer.
- The buttons to the left of the Address bar allow you to navigate the contents of the left pane and view recent pages. Other buttons allow you to specify the size of the window.
- The **Previous Locations button** saves the locations you have visited and displays the locations when clicked.
- The **Refresh button** on the right side of the Address bar refreshes the contents of the right pane of the folder window.
- The **search box** to the right of the Address bar contains the dimmed word, Search. You can type a term in the search box for a list of files, folders, shortcuts, and elements containing that term within the location you are searching. A **shortcut** is an icon on the desktop that provides a user with immediate access to a program or file.
- The **Command bar** contains five buttons used to accomplish various tasks on the computer related to organizing and managing the contents of the open window.
- The **navigation pane** on the left contains the Favorites area, Libraries area, Computer area, and Network area.

- The **Favorites area** contains links to your favorite locations. By default, this list contains only links to your Desktop, Downloads, and Recent Places.
- The **Libraries area** shows links to files and folders that have been included in a library.

A **library** helps you manage multiple folders and files stored in various locations on a computer. It does not store the files and folders; rather, it displays links to them so that you can access them quickly. For example, you can save pictures from a digital camera in any folder on any storage location on a computer. Normally, this would make organizing the different folders difficult; however, if you add the folders to a library, you can access all the pictures from one location regardless of where they are stored.

To Create a Folder within a Folder

With the class folder created, you can create folders that will store the files you create using Word. The following steps create a Word folder in the CIS 101 folder (or the folder identifying your class).

- Double-click the icon or folder name for the CIS 101 folder (or the folder identifying your class) in the File list to open the folder (Figure 32).

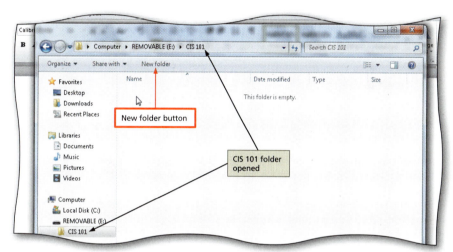

Figure 32

- Click the New folder button on the toolbar to display a new folder icon and text box for the folder.

- Type `Word` in the text box to name the folder.

- Press the ENTER key to create the folder (Figure 33).

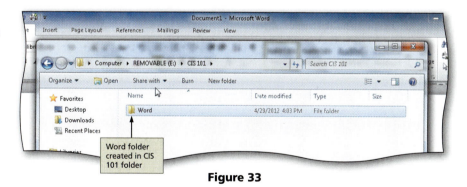

Figure 33

To Expand a Folder, Scroll through Folder Contents, and Collapse a Folder

Folder windows display the hierarchy of items and the contents of drives and folders in the right pane. You might want to expand a drive in the navigation pane to view its contents, scroll through its contents, and collapse it when you are finished viewing its contents. When a folder is expanded, it lists all the folders it contains. By contrast, a collapsed folder does not list the folders it contains. The steps on the next page expand, scroll through, and then collapse the folder identifying your class (CIS 101, in this case).

1

- Double-click the folder identifying your class (CIS 101, in this case) in the navigation pane, which expands the folder to display its contents and displays a black arrow to the left of the folder icon (Figure 34).

Q&A Why is the Word folder indented below the CIS 101 folder in the navigation pane?

It shows that the folder is contained within the CIS 101 folder.

Q&A Why did a scroll bar appear in the navigation pane?

When all contents cannot fit in a window or pane, a scroll bar appears. As described earlier, you can view areas currently not visible by (1) clicking the scroll arrows, (2) clicking above or below the scroll bar, and (3) dragging the scroll box.

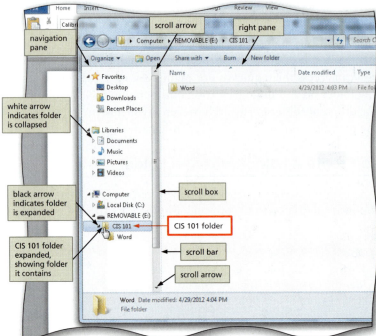

Figure 34

Experiment

- If your navigation pane has a scroll bar, click the down scroll arrow on the vertical scroll bar to display additional content at the bottom of the navigation pane.

- If your navigation pane has a scroll bar, click the scroll bar above the scroll box to move the scroll box to the top of the navigation pane.

- If your navigation pane has a scroll bar, drag the scroll box down the scroll bar until the scroll box is halfway down the scroll bar.

2

- Double-click the folder identifying your class (CIS 101, in this case) in the navigation pane to collapse the folder (Figure 35).

Figure 35

Other Ways
1. Point in navigation pane to display arrows, click white arrow to expand or click black arrow to collapse   2. Select folder to expand or collapse using arrow keys, press RIGHT ARROW to expand; press LEFT ARROW to collapse.

To Switch from One Program to Another

The next step is to save the Word file containing the headline you typed earlier. Word, however, currently is not the active window. You can use the program button on the taskbar and live preview to switch to Word and then save the document in the Word document window.

If Windows Aero is active on your computer, Windows displays a live preview window whenever you move your mouse on a button or click a button on the taskbar. If Aero is not supported or enabled on your computer, you will see a window title instead of a live preview. These steps use the Word program; however, the steps are the same for any active Office program currently displayed as a program button on the taskbar.

The next steps switch to the Word window.

1

- Point to the Word program button on the taskbar to see a live preview of the open document(s) or the window title(s) of the open document(s), depending on your computer's configuration (Figure 36).

2

- Click the program button or the live preview to make the program associated with the program button the active window (shown in Figure 27 on page OFF 19).

Q&A What if multiple documents are open in a program?

If Aero is enabled on your computer, click the desired live preview. If Aero is not supported or not enabled, click the window title.

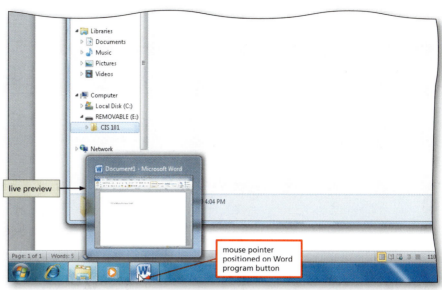

Figure 36

To Save a File in a Folder

Now that you have created the Word folder for storing files, you can save the Word document in that folder. The following steps save a file on a USB flash drive in the Word folder contained in your class folder (CIS 101, in this case) using the file name, Koala Exhibit.

1

- With a USB flash drive connected to one of the computer's USB ports, click the Save button on the Quick Access Toolbar to display the Save As dialog box (Figure 37).

Q&A Why does a file name already appear in the File name text box?

Word automatically suggests a file name the first time you save a document. The file name normally consists of the first few words contained in the document. Because the suggested file name is selected, you do not need to delete it; as soon as you begin typing, the new file name replaces the selected text.

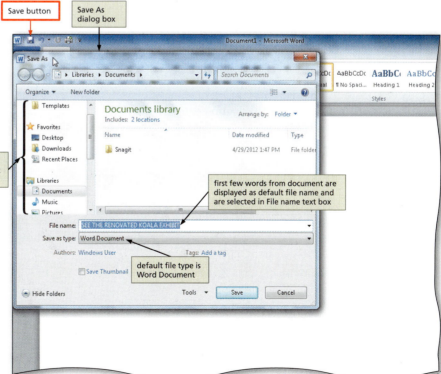

Figure 37

• Type **Koala Exhibit** in the File name text box (Save As dialog box) to change the file name. Do not press the ENTER key after typing the file name because you do not want to close the dialog box at this time (Figure 38).

Q&A

What characters can I use in a file name?

The only invalid characters are the backslash (\), slash (/), colon (:), asterisk (*), question mark (?), quotation mark ("), less than symbol (<), greater than symbol (>), and vertical bar (|).

• Navigate to the desired save location (in this case, the Word folder in the CIS 101 folder [or your class folder] on the USB flash drive) by performing the tasks in Steps 3a – 3c.

• If the navigation pane is not displayed in the dialog box, click the Browse Folders button to expand the dialog box.

• If Computer is not displayed in the navigation pane, drag the navigation pane scroll bar until Computer appears.

• If Computer is not expanded in the navigation pane, double-click Computer to display a list of available storage devices in the navigation pane.

• If necessary, scroll through the dialog box until your USB flash drive appears in the list of available storage devices in the navigation pane (Figure 39).

• If your USB flash drive is not expanded, double-click the USB flash drive in the list of available storage devices in the navigation pane to select that drive as the new save location and display its contents in the right pane.

• If your class folder (CIS 101, in this case) is not expanded, double-click the CIS 101 folder to select the folder and display its contents in the right pane.

Q&A

What if I do not want to save in a folder?

Although storing files in folders is an effective technique for organizing files, some users prefer not to store files in folders. If you prefer not to save this file in a folder, skip all instructions in Step 3c and proceed to Step 4.

• Click the Word folder to select the folder and display its contents in the right pane (Figure 40).

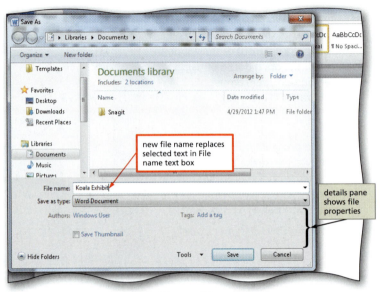

Figure 38

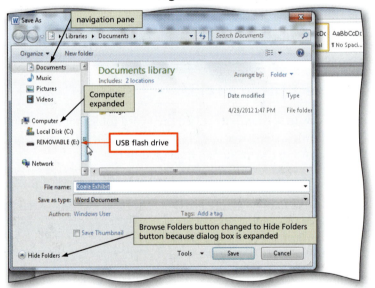

Figure 39

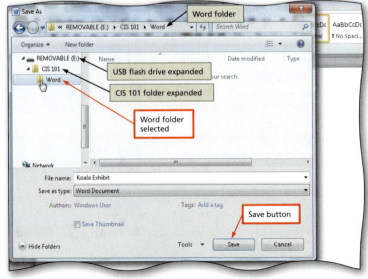

Figure 40

4

- Click the Save button (Save As dialog box) to save the document in the selected folder on the selected drive with the entered file name (Figure 41).

Q&A

How do I know that the file is saved?

While an Office program such as Word is saving a file, it briefly displays a message on the status bar indicating the amount of the file saved. In addition, the USB flash drive may have a light that flashes during the save process.

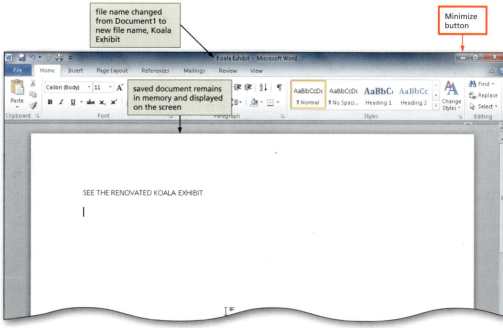

file name changed from Document1 to new file name, Koala Exhibit

Minimize button

saved document remains in memory and displayed on the screen

SEE THE RENOVATED KOALA EXHIBIT

Figure 41

Other Ways	
1. Click File on Ribbon, click Save, type file name, navigate to desired save location, click Save button	2. Press CTRL+S or press SHIFT+F12, type file name, navigate to desired save location, click Save button

Navigating in Dialog Boxes

Navigating is the process of finding a location on a storage device. While saving the Koala Exhibit file, for example, Steps 3a – 3c in the previous set of steps navigated to the Word folder located in the CIS 101 folder. When performing certain functions in Windows programs, such as saving a file, opening a file, or inserting a picture in an existing document, you most likely will have to navigate to the location where you want to save the file or to the folder containing the file you want to open or insert. Most dialog boxes in Windows programs requiring navigation follow a similar procedure; that is, the way you navigate to a folder in one dialog box, such as the Save As dialog box, is similar to how you might navigate in another dialog box, such as the Open dialog box. If you chose to navigate to a specific location in a dialog box, you would follow the instructions in Steps 3a – 3c on page OFF 26.

BTW

File Type
Depending on your Windows 7 settings, the file type .docx may be displayed immediately to the right of the file name after you save the file. The file type .docx is a Word 2010 document.

To Minimize and Restore a Window

Before continuing, you can verify that the Word file was saved properly. To do this, you will minimize the Word window and then open the USB flash drive window so that you can verify the file is stored on the USB flash drive. A **minimized window** is an open window hidden from view but that can be displayed quickly by clicking the window's program button on the taskbar.

In the following example, Word is used to illustrate minimizing and restoring windows; however, you would follow the same steps regardless of the Office program you are using.

The steps on the next page minimize the Word window, verify that the file is saved, and then restore the minimized window.

1

● Click the Minimize button on the program's title bar (shown in Figure 41 on the previous page) to minimize the window (Figure 42).

Q&A

Is the minimized window still available?

The minimized window, Word in this case, remains available but no longer is the active window. It is minimized as a program button on the taskbar.

● If necessary, click the Windows Explorer program button on the taskbar to open the USB flash drive window.

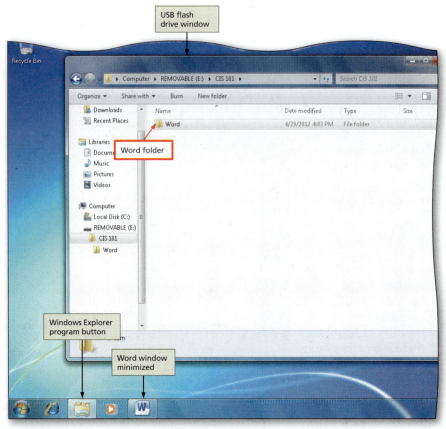

Figure 42

2

● Double-click the Word folder to select the folder and display its contents (Figure 43).

Q&A

Why does the Windows Explorer button on the taskbar change?

The button changes to reflect the status of the folder window (in this case, the USB flash drive window). A selected button indicates that the folder window is active on the screen. When the button is not selected, the window is open but not active.

3

● After viewing the contents of the selected folder, click the Word program button on the taskbar to restore the minimized window (as shown in Figure 41 on the previous page).

Other Ways

1. Right-click title bar, click Minimize on shortcut menu, click taskbar button in taskbar button area

2. Press WINDOWS+M, press WINDOWS+SHIFT+M

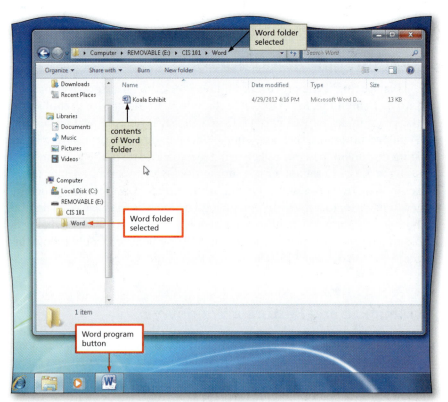

Figure 43

Screen Resolution

Screen resolution indicates the number of pixels (dots) that the computer uses to display the letters, numbers, graphics, and background you see on the screen. When you increase the screen resolution, Windows displays more information on the screen, but the information decreases in size. The reverse also is true: as you decrease the screen resolution, Windows displays less information on the screen, but the information increases in size.

Screen resolution usually is stated as the product of two numbers, such as 1024×768 (pronounced "ten twenty-four by seven sixty-eight"). A 1024×768 screen resolution results in a display of 1,024 distinct pixels on each of 768 lines, or about 786,432 pixels. Changing the screen resolution affects how the Ribbon appears in Office programs. Figure 44, for example, shows the Word Ribbon at screen resolutions of 1024×768 and 1280×800. All of the same commands are available regardless of screen resolution. Word, however, makes changes to the groups and the buttons within the groups to accommodate the various screen resolutions. The result is that certain commands may need to be accessed differently depending on the resolution chosen. A command that is visible on the Ribbon and available by clicking a button at one resolution may not be visible and may need to be accessed using its Dialog Box Launcher at a different resolution.

Comparing the two Ribbons in Figure 44, notice the changes in content and layout of the groups and galleries. In some cases, the content of a group is the same in each resolution, but the layout of the group differs. For example, the same gallery and buttons appear in the Styles groups in the two resolutions, but the layouts differ. In other cases, the content and layout are the same across the resolution, but the level of detail differs with the resolution. In the Clipboard group, when the resolution increases to 1280×800, the names of all the buttons in the group appear in addition to the buttons themselves. At the lower resolution, only the buttons appear.

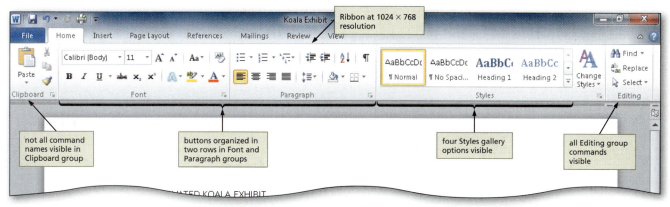

Figure 44 (a) Ribbon at Resolution of 1024 x 768

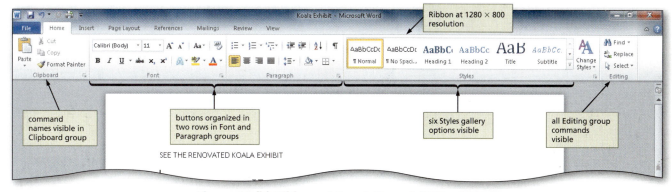

Figure 44 (b) Ribbon at Resolution of 1280 x 800

To Change the Screen Resolution

If you are using a computer to step through the chapters in this book and you want your screen to match the figures, you may need to change your screen's resolution. The figures in this book use a screen resolution of 1024×768. The following steps change the screen resolution to 1024×768. Your computer already may be set to 1024×768 or some other resolution. Keep in mind that many computer labs prevent users from changing the screen resolution; in that case, read the following steps for illustration purposes.

- Click the Show desktop button on the taskbar to display the Windows 7 desktop.

- Right-click an empty area on the Windows 7 desktop to display a shortcut menu that displays a list of commands related to the desktop (Figure 45).

Q&A

Why does my shortcut menu display different commands?

Depending on your computer's hardware and configuration, different commands might appear on the shortcut menu.

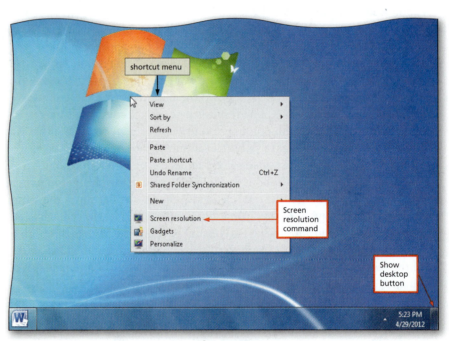

Figure 45

- Click Screen resolution on the shortcut menu to open the Screen Resolution window (Figure 46).

Figure 46

3

- Click the Resolution button in the Screen Resolution window to display the resolution slider.

 What is a slider?

A **slider** is an object that allows users to choose from multiple predetermined options. In most cases, these options represent some type of numeric value. In most cases, one end of the slider (usually the left or bottom) represents the lowest of available values, and the opposite end (usually the right or top) represents the highest available value.

4

- If necessary, drag the resolution slider until the desired screen resolution (in this case, 1024 × 768) is selected (Figure 47).

 What if my computer does not support the 1024 × 768 resolution?

Some computers do not support the 1024 × 768 resolution. In this case, select a resolution that is close to the 1024 × 768 resolution.

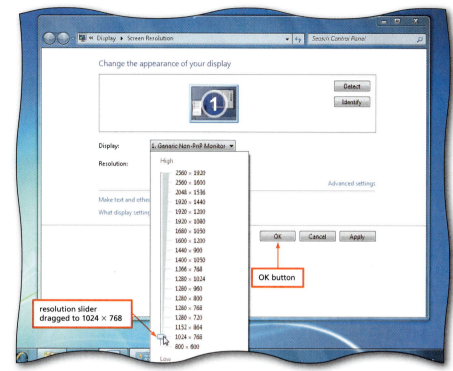

Figure 47

5

- Click an empty area of the Screen Resolution window to close the resolution slider.

- Click the OK button to change the screen resolution and display the Display Settings dialog box (Figure 48).

- Click the Keep changes button (Display Settings dialog box) to accept the new screen resolution.

 Why does a message display stating that the image quality can be improved?

Some computer monitors are designed to display contents better at a certain screen resolution, sometimes referred to as an optimal resolution.

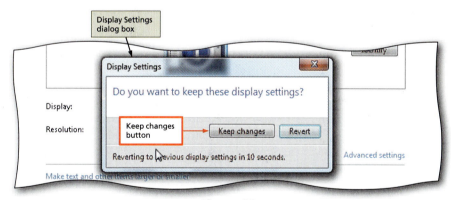

Figure 48

To Quit a Program with One Document Open

When you quit an Office program, such as Word, if you have made changes to a file since the last time the file was saved, the Office program displays a dialog box asking if you want to save the changes you made to the file before it closes the program window. The dialog box contains three buttons with these resulting actions: the Save button saves the changes and then quits the Office program, the Don't Save button quits the Office program without saving changes, and the Cancel button closes the dialog box and redisplays the file without saving the changes.

If no changes have been made to an open document since the last time the file was saved, the Office program will close the window without displaying a dialog box.

The following steps quit Word. You would follow similar steps in other Office programs.

- If necessary, click the Word program button on the taskbar to display the Word window on the desktop.
- Point to the Close button on the right side of the program's title bar, Word in this case (Figure 49).

Figure 49

- Click the Close button to close the document and quit Word.

 Q&A

What if I have more than one document open in Word?

You would click the Close button for each open document. When you click the last open document's Close button, Word also quits. As an alternative, you could click File on the Ribbon to open the Backstage view and then click Exit in the Backstage view to close all open documents and quit Word.

Q&A

What is the Backstage view?

The **Backstage view** contains a set of commands that enable you to manage documents and data about the documents. The Backstage view is discussed in more depth later in this chapter.

- If a Microsoft Word dialog box appears, click the Save button to save any changes made to the document since the last save.

> **Other Ways**
>
> 1. Right-click the Office program button on Windows 7 taskbar, click Close window or 'Close all windows' on shortcut menu
> 2. Press ALT+F4

Break Point: If you wish to take a break, this is a good place to do so. To resume at a later time, continue to follow the steps from this location forward.

Additional Common Features of Office Programs

The previous section used Word to illustrate common features of Office and some basic elements unique to Word. The following sections continue to use Word to present additional common features of Office.

In the following pages, you will learn how to do the following:

1. Start an Office program (Word) using the search box.
2. Open a document in an Office program (Word).
3. Close the document.
4. Reopen the document just closed.
5. Create a blank Office document from Windows Explorer and then open the file.
6. Save a document with a new file name.

To Start a Program Using the Search Box

The next steps, which assume Windows 7 is running, use the search box to start Word based on a typical installation; however, you would follow similar steps to start any program. You may need to ask your instructor how to start programs for your computer.

1

- Click the Start button on the Windows 7 taskbar to display the Start menu.

2

- Type **Microsoft Word** as the search text in the 'Search programs and files' text box and watch the search results appear on the Start menu (Figure 50).

Q&A

Do I need to type the complete program name or correct capitalization?

No, just enough of it for the program name to appear on the Start menu. For example, you may be able to type Word or word, instead of Microsoft Word.

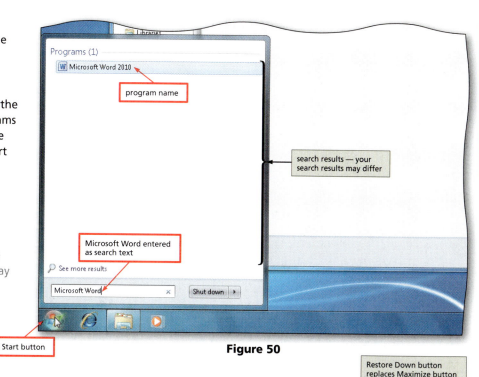

Figure 50

3

- Click the program name, Microsoft Word 2010 in this case, in the search results on the Start menu to start Word and display a new blank document in the Word window.

- If the program window is not maximized, click the Maximize button on its title bar to maximize the window (Figure 51).

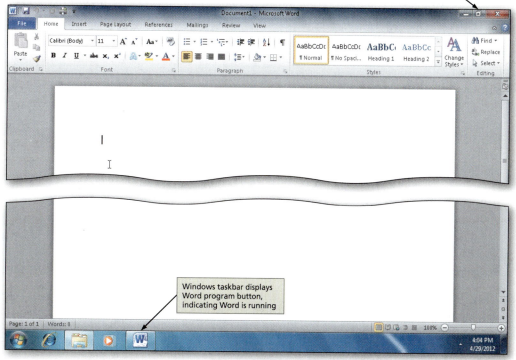

Figure 51

To Open an Existing File from the Backstage View

As discussed earlier, the Backstage view provides data about documents and contains a set of commands that assist you with managing documents. From the Backstage view in Word, for example, you can create, open, print, and save documents. You also can share documents, manage versions, set permissions, and modify document properties.

Assume you wish to continue working on an existing file, that is, a file you previously saved. The following steps use the Backstage view to open a saved file, specifically the Koala Exhibit file, from the USB flash drive.

1

- With your USB flash drive connected to one of the computer's USB ports, if necessary, click File on the Ribbon to open the Backstage view (Figure 52).

Q&A What is the purpose of the File tab?

The File tab is used to display the Backstage view for each Office program.

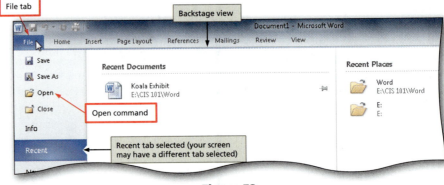

Figure 52

2

- Click Open in the Backstage view to display the Open dialog box (Figure 53).

3

- Navigate to the location of the file to be opened (in this case, the USB flash drive, then to the CIS 101 folder [or your class folder], and then to the Word folder). For detailed steps about navigating, see Steps 3a – 3c on page OFF 26.

Q&A What if I did not save my file in a folder?

If you did not save your file in a folder, the file you wish to open should be displayed in the Open dialog box before navigating to any folders.

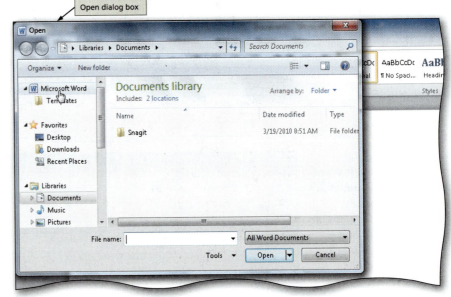

Figure 53

4

- Click the file to be opened, Koala Exhibit in this case, to select the file (Figure 54).

5

- Click the Open button (Open dialog box) to open the selected file and display the opened file in the current program window (shown in Figure 41 on page OFF 27).

Other Ways

1. Click File on the Ribbon, click Recent in Backstage view, double-click file
2. Press CTRL+O
3. Navigate to file in Windows Explorer, double-click file

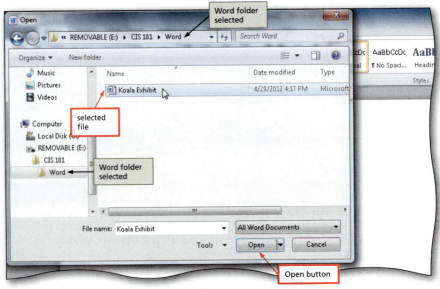

Figure 54

To Create a New Document from the Backstage View

You can create multiple documents at the same time in an Office program, such as Word. The following steps create a file, a blank document in this case, from the Backstage view.

1

- Click File on the Ribbon to open the Backstage view.

- Click the New tab in the Backstage view to display the New gallery (Figure 55).

Q&A

Can I create documents through the Backstage view in other Office programs?

Yes. If the Office program has a New tab in the Backstage view, the New gallery displays various options for creating a new file.

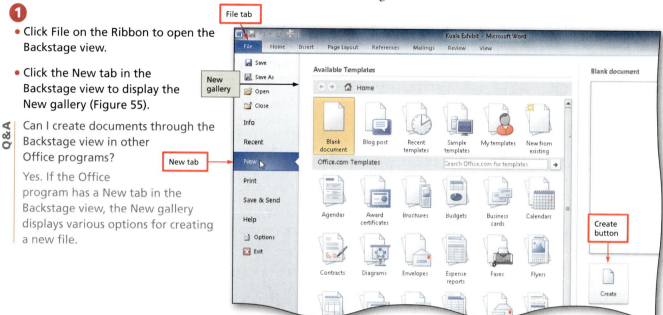

Figure 55

2

- Click the Create button in the New gallery to create a new document (Figure 56).

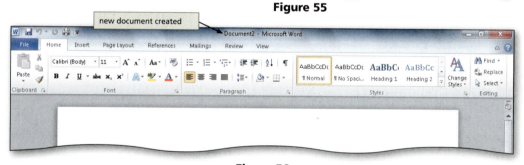

Figure 56

Other Ways
1. Press CTRL+N

To Enter Text in a Document

The next Word document identifies the names of the Koala Exhibit sponsors. The following step enters text in a document.

1 Type **List of Current Sponsors for the Koala Exhibit** and then press the ENTER key to move the insertion point to the beginning of the next line (Figure 57).

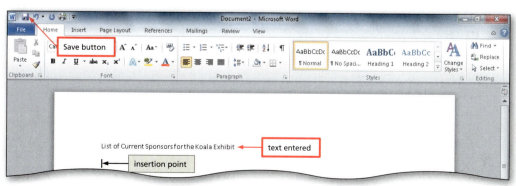

List of Current Sponsors for the Koala Exhibit

Figure 57

BTW

Customizing the Ribbon

In addition to customizing the Quick Access Toolbar, you can add items to and remove items from the Ribbon. To customize the Ribbon, click File on the Ribbon to open the Backstage view, click Options in the Backstage view, and then click Customize Ribbon in the left pane of the Options dialog box. More information about customizing the Ribbon is presented in a later chapter.

To Save a File in a Folder

The following steps save the second document in the Word folder in the class folder (CIS 101, in this case) on a USB flash drive using the file name, Koala Exhibit Sponsors.

1 With a USB flash drive connected to one of the computer's USB ports, click the Save button on the Quick Access Toolbar to display the Save As dialog box.

2 If necessary, type **Koala Exhibit Sponsors** in the File name text box to change the file name. Do not press the ENTER key after typing the file name because you do not want to close the dialog box at this time.

3 If necessary, navigate to the desired save location (in this case, the Word folder in the CIS 101 folder [or your class folder] on the USB flash drive).

4 Click the Save button (Save As dialog box) to save the document in the selected folder on the selected drive with the entered file name.

To Close a File Using the Backstage View

Sometimes, you may want to close an Office file, such as a Word document, entirely and start over with a new file. You also may want to close a file when you are finished working with it so that you can begin a new file. The following steps close the current active Word file (that is, the Koala Exhibit Sponsors document) without quitting the active program (Word in this case).

1
• Click File on the Ribbon to open the Backstage view (Figure 58).

2
• Click Close in the Backstage view to close the open file (Koala Exhibit Sponsors, in this case) without quitting the active program.

Q&A

What if Word displays a dialog box about saving?

Click the Save button if you want to save the changes, click the Don't Save button if you want to ignore the changes since the last time you saved, and click the Cancel button if you do not want to close the document.

Q&A

Can I use the Backstage view to close an open file in other Office programs, such as PowerPoint and Excel?

Yes.

Figure 58

To Open a Recent File Using the Backstage View

You sometimes need to open a file that you recently modified. You may have more changes to make such as adding more content or correcting errors. The Backstage view allows you to access recent files easily. The next steps reopen the Koala Exhibit Sponsors file just closed.

1

- Click File on the Ribbon to open the Backstage view.

- Click the Recent tab in the Backstage view to display the Recent gallery (Figure 59).

2

- Click the desired file name in the Recent gallery, Koala Exhibit Sponsors in this case, to open the file (shown in Figure 57 on page OFF 35).

Can I use the Backstage view to open a recent file in other Office programs, such as PowerPoint and Excel?

Yes, as long as the file name appears in the list of recent files in the Recent gallery.

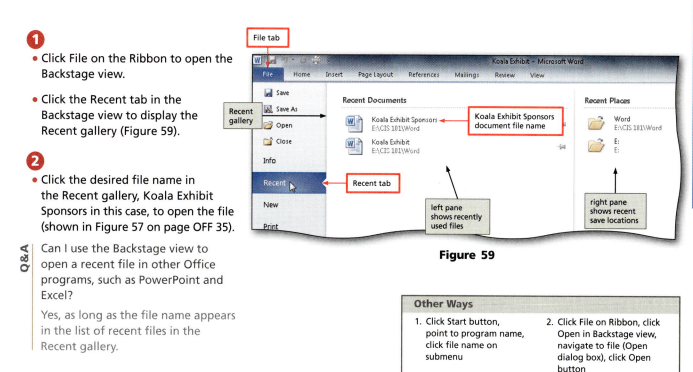

Figure 59

Other Ways
1. Click Start button, point to program name, click file name on submenu
2. Click File on Ribbon, click Open in Backstage view, navigate to file (Open dialog box), click Open button

To Create a New Blank Document from Windows Explorer

Windows Explorer provides a means to create a blank Office document without ever starting an Office program. The following steps use Windows Explorer to create a blank Word document.

1

- Click the Windows Explorer program button on the taskbar to make the folder window the active window in Windows Explorer.

- If necessary, navigate to the desired location for the new file (in this case, the Word folder in the CIS 101 folder [or your class folder] on the USB flash drive).

- With the Word folder selected, right-click an open area in the right pane to display a shortcut menu.

- Point to New on the shortcut menu to display the New submenu (Figure 60).

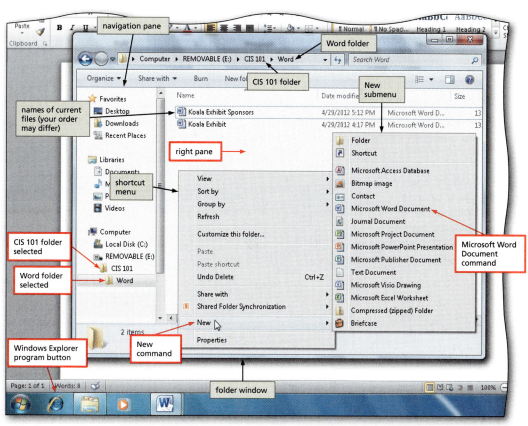

Figure 60

2

- Click Microsoft Word Document on the New submenu to display an icon and text box for a new file in the current folder window (Figure 61).

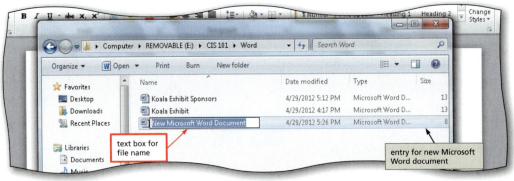

Figure 61

3

- Type **Koala Exhibit Volunteers** in the text box and then press the ENTER key to assign a name to the new file in the current folder (Figure 62).

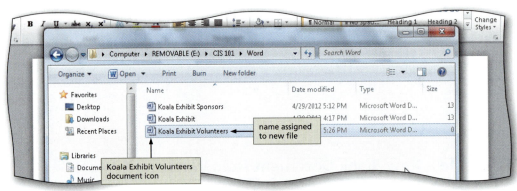

Figure 62

To Start a Program from Windows Explorer and Open a File

Previously, you learned how to start an Office program (Word) using the Start menu and the search box. Another way to start an Office program is to open an existing file from Windows Explorer, which causes the program in which the file was created to start and then open the selected file. The following steps, which assume Windows 7 is running, use Windows Explorer to start Word based on a typical installation. You may need to ask your instructor how to start Word for your computer.

1

- If necessary, display the file to open in the folder window in Windows Explorer (shown in Figure 62).

- Right-click the file icon or file name (Koala Exhibit Volunteers, in this case) to display a shortcut menu (Figure 63).

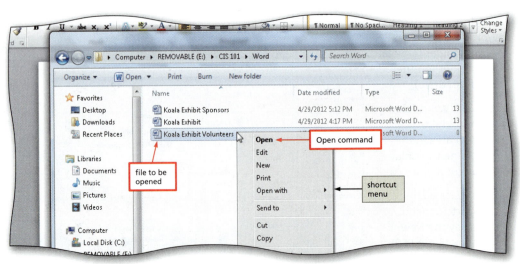

Figure 63

2

- Click Open on the shortcut menu to open the selected file in the program used to create the file, Microsoft Word in this case (Figure 64).

- If the program window is not maximized, click the Maximize button on the title bar to maximize the window.

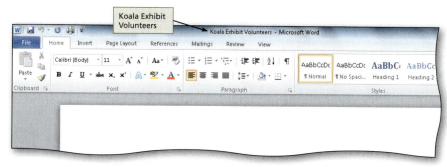

Figure 64

To Enter Text in a Document

The next step is to enter text in this blank Word document. The following step enters a line of text.

1 Type **Koala Exhibit Staff and Volunteers** and then press the ENTER key to move the insertion point to the beginning of the next line (shown in Figure 65).

To Save an Existing Document with the Same File Name

Saving frequently cannot be overemphasized. You have made modifications to the file (document) since you created it. Thus, you should save again. Similarly, you should continue saving files frequently so that you do not lose your changes since the time you last saved the file. You can use the same file name, such as Koala Exhibit Volunteers, to save the changes made to the document. The following step saves a file again.

1

- Click the Save button on the Quick Access Toolbar to overwrite the previously saved file (Koala Exhibit Volunteers, in this case) on the USB flash drive (Figure 65).

Q&A

Why did the Save As dialog box not appear?

Office programs, including Word, overwrite the document using the setting specified the first time you saved the document.

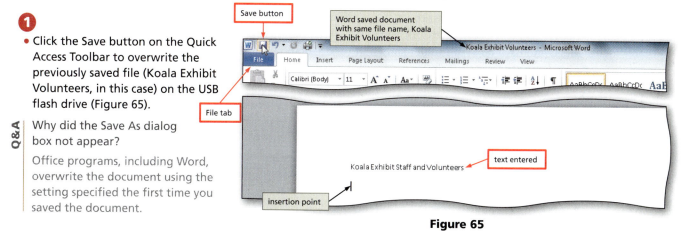

Figure 65

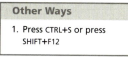

Other Ways

1. Press CTRL+S or press SHIFT+F12

To Use Save As to Change the Name of a File

You might want to save a file with a different name and even to a different location. For example, you might start a homework assignment with a data file and then save it with a final file name for submitting to your instructor, saving it to a location designated by your instructor. The following steps save a file with a different file name.

1 With your USB flash drive connected to one of the computer's USB ports, click File on the Ribbon to open the Backstage view.

2 Click Save As in the Backstage view to display the Save As dialog box.

3 Type **Koala Exhibit Staff and Volunteers** in the File name text box (Save As dialog box) to change the file name. Do not press the ENTER key after typing the file name because you do not want to close the dialog box at this time.

4 If necessary, navigate to the desired save location (the Word folder in the CIS 101 folder [or your class folder] on the USB flash drive, in this case).

5 Click the Save button (Save As dialog box) to save the file in the selected folder on the selected drive with the new file name.

BTW

Multiple Open Files
If the program button on the taskbar displays as a tiered stack, you have multiple files open in the program.

To Quit an Office Program

You are finished using Word. The following steps quit Word. You would use similar steps to quit other office programs.

1 Because you have multiple Word documents open, click File on the Ribbon to open the Backstage view and then click Exit in the Backstage view to close all open documents and quit Word.

2 If a dialog box appears, click the Save button to save any changes made to the file since the last save.

Moving, Renaming, and Deleting Files

Earlier in this chapter, you learned how to organize files in folders, which is part of a process known as **file management**. The following sections cover additional file management topics including renaming, moving, and deleting files.

To Rename a File

In some circumstances, you may want to change the name of, or rename, a file or a folder. For example, you may want to distinguish a file in one folder or drive from a copy of a similar file, or you may decide to rename a file to better identify its contents. The Word folder shown in Figure 66 contains the Word document, Koala Exhibit. The following steps change the name of the Koala Exhibit file in the Word folder to Koala Exhibit Flyer.

1
- If necessary, click the Windows Explorer program button on the taskbar to display the folder window in Windows Explorer.

- If necessary, navigate to the location of the file to be renamed (in this case, the Word folder in the CIS 101 [or your class folder] folder on the USB flash drive) to display the file(s) it contains in the right pane.

- Right-click the Koala Exhibit icon or file name in the right pane to select the Koala Exhibit file and display a shortcut menu that presents a list of commands related to files (Figure 66).

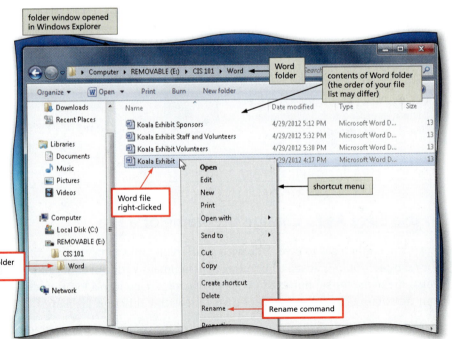

Figure 66

2

- Click Rename on the shortcut menu to place the current file name in a text box.

- Type **Koala Exhibit Flyer** in the text box and then press the ENTER key (Figure 67).

Q&A Are any risks involved in renaming files that are located on a hard disk?

If you inadvertently rename a file that is associated with certain programs, the programs may not be able to find the file and, therefore, may not execute properly. Always use caution when renaming files.

Q&A Can I rename a file when it is open?

No, a file must be closed to change the file name.

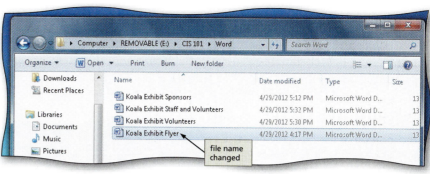

Figure 67

Other Ways

1. Select file, press F2, type new file name, press ENTER

To Move a File

At some time, you may want to move a file from one folder, called the source folder, to another, called the destination. When you move a file, it no longer appears in the original folder. If the destination and the source folders are on the same disk drive, you can move a file by dragging it. If the folders are on different disk drives, then you will need to right-drag the file. The following step moves the Koala Exhibit Volunteers file from the Word folder to the CIS 101 folder.

1

- In Windows Explorer, if necessary, navigate to the location of the file to be moved (in this case, the Word folder in the CIS 101 folder [or your class folder] on the USB flash drive).

- If necessary, click the Word folder in the navigation pane to display the files it contains in the right pane.

- Drag the Koala Exhibit Volunteers file in the right pane to the CIS 101 folder in the navigation pane and notice the ScreenTip as you drag the mouse (Figure 68).

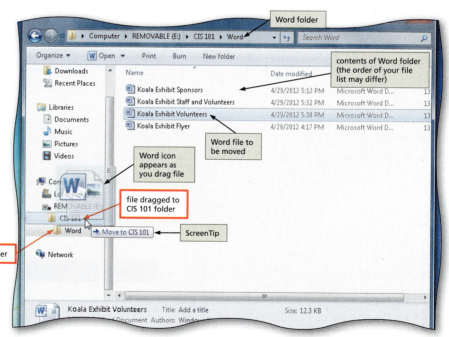

Figure 68

Other Ways

1. Right-click file, drag file to destination folder, click Move here

2. Right-click file to copy, click Cut on shortcut menu, right-click destination

    folder, click Paste on shortcut menu

3. Select file to copy, press CTRL+X, select destination folder, press CTRL+V

To Delete a File

A final task you may want to perform is to delete a file. Exercise extreme caution when deleting a file or files. When you delete a file from a hard disk, the deleted file is stored in the Recycle Bin where you can recover it until you empty the Recycle Bin. If you delete a file from removable media, such as a USB flash drive, the file is deleted permanently. The next steps delete the Koala Exhibit Volunteers file from the CIS 101 folder.

- In Windows Explorer, navigate to the location of the file to be deleted (in this case, the CIS 101 folder [or your class folder] on the USB flash drive).

- If necessary, click the CIS 101 folder in the navigation pane to display the files it contains in the right pane.

- Right-click the Koala Exhibit Volunteers icon or file name in the right pane to select the file and display a shortcut menu (Figure 69).

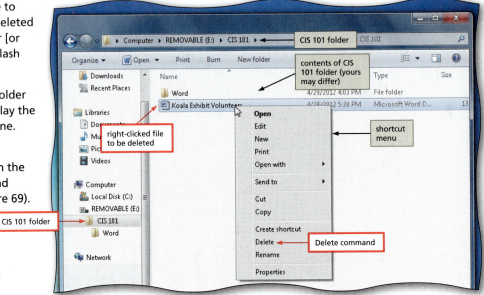

Figure 69

- Click Delete on the shortcut menu to display the Delete File dialog box (Figure 70).

- Click the Yes button (Delete File dialog box) to delete the selected file.

Q&A

Can I use this same technique to delete a folder?

Yes. Right-click the folder and then click Delete on the shortcut menu. When you delete a folder, all of the files and folders contained in the folder you are deleting, together with any files and folders on lower hierarchical levels, are deleted as well.

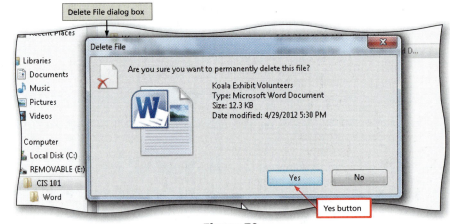

Figure 70

Other Ways

1. Select icon, press DELETE

Microsoft Office and Windows Help

At any time while you are using one of the Microsoft Office 2010 programs, such as Word, you can use Office Help to display information about all topics associated with the program. This section illustrates the use of Word Help. Help in other Office 2010 programs operates in a similar fashion.

In Office 2010, Help is presented in a window that has Web-browser-style navigation buttons. Each Office 2010 program has its own Help home page, which is the starting Help page that is displayed in the Help window. If your computer is connected to the Internet, the contents of the Help page reflect both the local help files installed on the computer and material from Microsoft's Web site.

To Open the Help Window in an Office Program

The following step opens the Word Help window. The step to open a Help window in other Office programs is similar.

- Start Word.

- Click the Microsoft Word Help button near the upper-right corner of the program window to open the Word Help window (Figure 71).

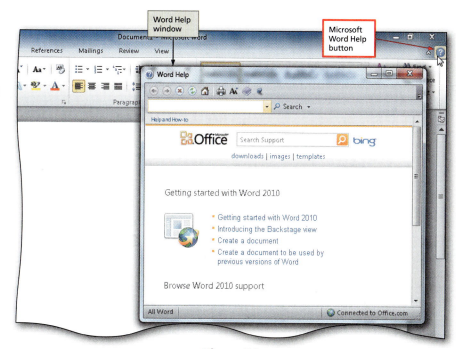

Figure 71

Other Ways
1. Press F1

Moving and Resizing Windows

Up to this point, this chapter has used minimized and maximized windows. At times, however, it is useful, or even necessary, to have more than one window open and visible on the screen at the same time. You can resize and move these open windows so that you can view different areas of and elements in the window. In the case of the Help window, for example, it could be covering document text in the Word window that you need to see.

To Move a Window by Dragging

You can move any open window that is not maximized to another location on the desktop by dragging the title bar of the window. The step on the next page drags the Word Help window to the top left of the desktop.

1

- Drag the window title bar (the Word Help window title bar, in this case) so that the window moves to the top left of the desktop, as shown in Figure 72.

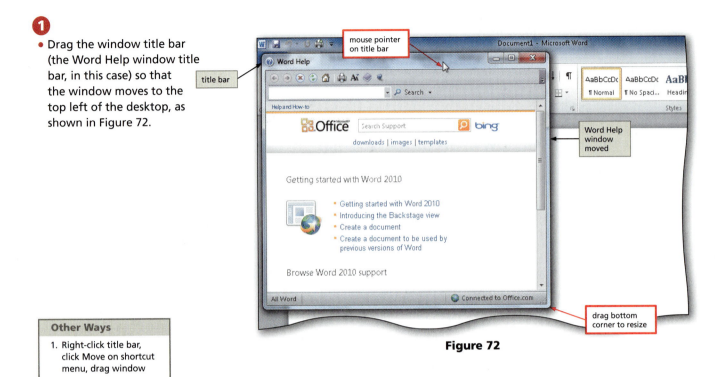

Figure 72

Other Ways

1. Right-click title bar, click Move on shortcut menu, drag window

To Resize a Window by Dragging

Sometimes, information is not visible completely in a window. A method used to change the size of the window is to drag the window borders. The following step changes the size of the Word Help window by dragging its borders.

1

- Point to the lower-right corner of the window (the Word Help window, in this case) until the mouse pointer changes to a two-headed arrow.

- Drag the bottom border downward to display more of the active window (Figure 73).

Q&A Can I drag other borders on the window to enlarge or shrink the window?

Yes, you can drag the left, right, and top borders and any window corner to resize a window.

Q&A Will Windows 7 remember the new size of the window after I close it?

Yes. When you reopen the window, Windows 7 will display it at the same size it was when you closed it.

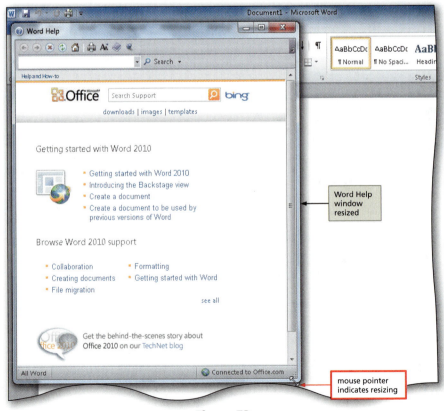

Figure 73

Using Office Help

Once an Office program's Help window is open, several methods exist for navigating Help. You can search for help by using any of the three following methods from the Help window:

1. Enter search text in the 'Type words to search for' text box.
2. Click the links in the Help window.
3. Use the Table of Contents.

To Obtain Help Using the 'Type words to search for' Text Box

Assume for the following example that you want to know more about the Backstage view. The following steps use the 'Type words to search for' text box to obtain useful information about the Backstage view by entering the word, Backstage, as search text.

1

- Type **Backstage** in the 'Type words to search for' text box at the top of the Word Help window to enter the search text.

- Click the Search button arrow to display the Search menu (Figure 74).

- If it is not selected already, click All Word on the Search menu, so that Help performs the most complete search of the current program (Word, in this case). If All Word already is selected, click the Search button arrow again to close the Search menu.

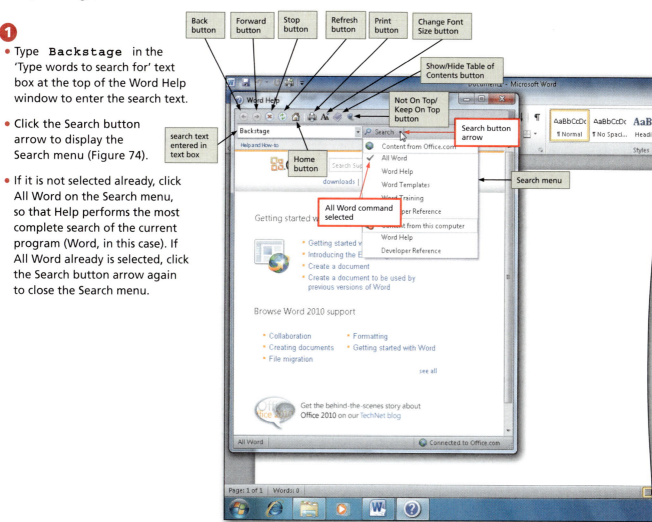

Figure 74

Why select All Word on the Search menu?

Selecting All Word on the Search menu ensures that Word Help will search all possible sources for information about your search term. It will produce the most complete search results.

2

- Click the Search button to display the search results (Figure 75).

Q&A Why do my search results differ?

If you do not have an Internet connection, your results will reflect only the content of the Help files on your computer. When searching for help online, results also can change as material is added, deleted, and updated on the online Help Web pages maintained by Microsoft.

Q&A Why were my search results not very helpful?

When initiating a search, be sure to check the spelling of the search text; also, keep your search specific, with fewer than seven words, to return the most accurate results.

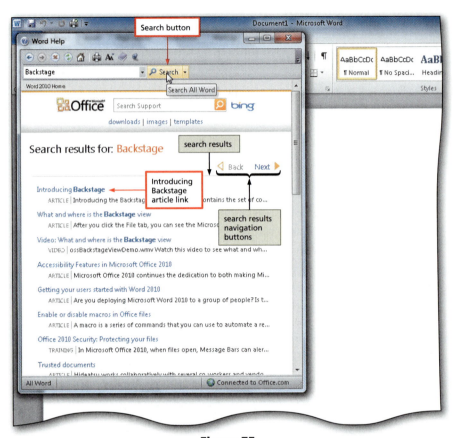

Figure 75

3

- Click the Introducing Backstage link to open the Help document associated with the selected topic (Figure 76).

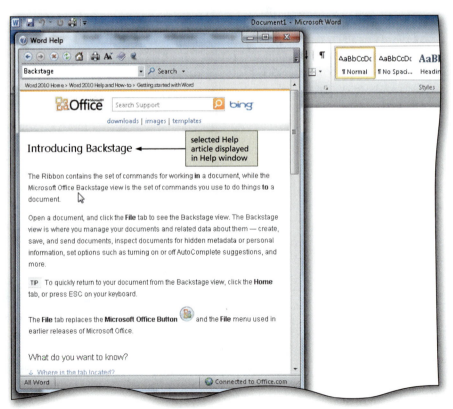

Figure 76

● Click the Home button on the toolbar to clear the search results and redisplay the Help home page (Figure 77).

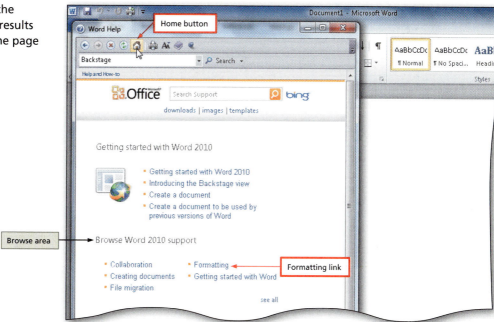

Figure 77

To Obtain Help Using the Help Links

If your topic of interest is listed in the Browse area of the Help window, you can click the link to begin browsing the Help categories instead of entering search text. You browse Help just as you would browse a Web site. If you know which category contains your Help information, you may wish to use these links. The following step finds the Formatting Help information using the category links from the Word Help home page.

● Click the Formatting link on the Help home page (shown in Figure 77) to display the Formatting page (Figure 78).

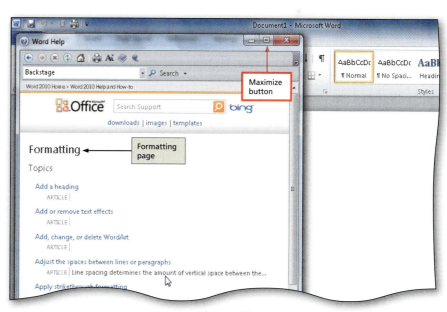

Figure 78

To Obtain Help Using the Help Table of Contents

A third way to find Help in Office programs is through the Help Table of Contents. You can browse through the Table of Contents to display information about a particular topic or to familiarize yourself with an Office program. The following steps access the Help information about themes by browsing through the Table of Contents.

- Click the Home button on the toolbar to display the Help home page.

- Click the Show Table of Contents button on the toolbar to display the Table of Contents pane on the left side of the Help window. If necessary, click the Maximize button on the Help title bar to maximize the window (Figure 79).

Q&A Why does the appearance of the Show Table of Contents button change?

When the Table of Contents is displayed in the Help window, the Hide Table of Contents button replaces the Show Table of Contents button.

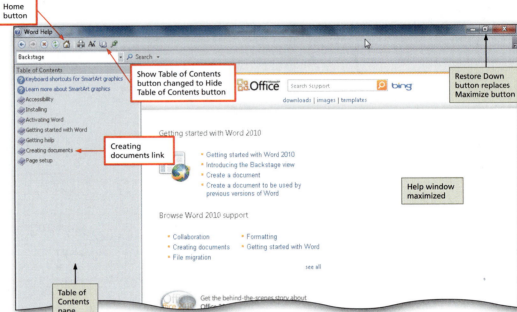

Figure 79

- Click the Creating documents link in the Table of Contents pane to view a list of Help subtopics.

- Click the Apply themes to Word documents link in the Table of Contents pane to view the selected Help document in the right pane (Figure 80).

- After reviewing the page, click the Close button to quit Help.

- Click Word's Close button to quit Word.

Figure 80

Q&A How do I remove the Table of Contents pane when I am finished with it?

The Show Table of Contents button acts as a toggle. When the Table of Contents pane is visible, the button changes to Hide Table of Contents. Clicking it hides the Table of Contents pane and changes the button to Show Table of Contents.

Obtaining Help while Working in an Office Program

Help in Office programs, such as Word, provides you with the ability to obtain help directly, without the need to open the Help window and initiate a search. For example, you may be unsure about how a particular command works, or you may be presented with a dialog box that you are not sure how to use.

Figure 81 shows one option for obtaining help while working in Word. If you want to learn more about a command, point to the command button and wait for the Enhanced ScreenTip to appear. If the Help icon appears in the Enhanced ScreenTip, press the F1 key while pointing to the command to open the Help window associated with that command.

Figure 82 shows a dialog box that contains a Help button. Pressing the F1 key while the dialog box is displayed opens a Help window. The Help window contains help about that dialog box, if available. If no help file is available for that particular dialog box, then the main Help window opens.

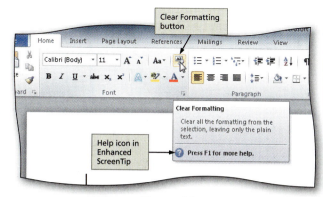

Figure 81

Using Windows Help and Support

One of the more powerful Windows 7 features is Windows Help and Support. **Windows Help and Support** is available when using Windows 7 or when using any Microsoft program running under Windows 7. This feature is designed to assist you in using Windows 7 or the various programs. Table 4 describes the content found in the Help and Support Center. The same methods used for searching Microsoft Office Help can be used in Windows Help and Support. The difference is that Windows Help and Support displays help for Windows 7, instead of for Microsoft Office.

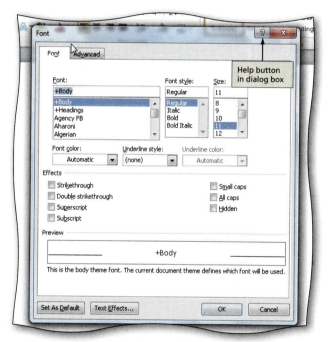

Figure 82

Table 4 Windows Help and Support Center Content Areas	
Area	**Function**
Find an answer quickly	This area contains instructions about how to do a quick search using the search box.
Not sure where to start?	This area displays three topics to help guide a user: How to get started with your computer, Learn about Windows Basics, and Browse Help topics. Clicking one of the options navigates to corresponding Help and Support pages.
More on the Windows Website	This area contains links to online content from the Windows Web site. Clicking the links navigates to the corresponding Web pages on the Web site.

To Start Windows Help and Support

The steps on the next page start Windows Help and Support and display the Windows Help and Support window, containing links to more information about Windows 7.

1

- Click the Start button on the taskbar to display the Start menu (Figure 83).

Q&A

Why are the programs that are displayed on the Start menu different?

Windows adds the programs you have used recently to the left pane on the Start menu. You have started Word while performing the steps in this chapter, so that program now is displayed on the Start menu.

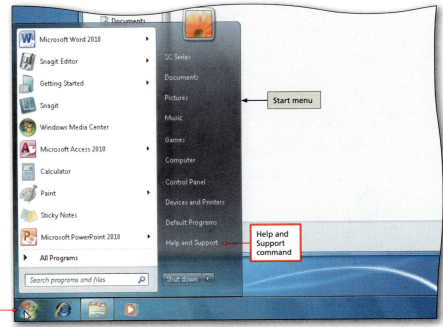

Figure 83

2

- Click Help and Support on the Start menu to open the Windows Help and Support window (Figure 84).

- After reviewing the Windows Help and Support window, click the Close button to quit Windows Help and Support.

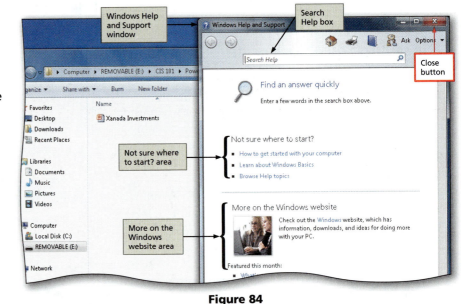

Figure 84

Other Ways

1. Press CTRL+ESC, press RIGHT ARROW, press UP ARROW, press ENTER
2. Press WINDOWS+F1

Chapter Summary

In this chapter, you learned about the Windows 7 interface. You started Windows 7, were introduced to the components of the desktop, and learned several mouse operations. You opened, closed, moved, resized, minimized, maximized, and scrolled a window. You used folder windows to expand and collapse drives and folders, display drive and folder contents, create folders, and rename and then delete a file.

You also learned some basic features of Microsoft Word 2010. As part of this learning process, you discovered the common elements that exist among Microsoft Office programs.

Microsoft Office Help was demonstrated using Word, and you learned how to use the Word Help window. You were introduced to the Windows 7 Help and Support Center and learned how to use it to obtain more information about Windows 7.

The items listed below include all of the new Windows 7 and Word 2010 skills you have learned in this chapter.

1. Log On to the Computer (OFF 6)
2. Start a Program Using the Start Menu (OFF 10)
3. Maximize a Window (OFF 12)
4. Display a Different Tab on the Ribbon (OFF 16)
5. Minimize, Display, and Restore the Ribbon (OFF 16)
6. Display and Use a Shortcut Menu (OFF 17)
7. Customize the Quick Access Toolbar (OFF 18)
8. Enter Text in a Document (OFF 19)
9. Create a Folder (OFF 20)
10. Create a Folder within a Folder (OFF 23)
11. Expand a Folder, Scroll through Folder Contents, and Collapse a Folder (OFF 23)
12. Switch from One Program to Another (OFF 24)
13. Save a File in a Folder (OFF 25)
14. Minimize and Restore a Window (OFF 27)
15. Change the Screen Resolution (OFF 30)
16. Quit a Program with One Document Open (OFF 31)
17. Start a Program Using the Search Box (OFF 32)
18. Open an Existing file from the Backstage View (OFF 33)
19. Create a New Document from the Backstage View (OFF 35)
20. Close a File Using the Backstage View (OFF 36)
21. Open a Recent File Using the Backstage View (OFF 36)
22. Create a New Blank Document from Windows Explorer (OFF 37)
23. Start a Program from Windows Explorer and Open a File (OFF 38)
24. Save an Existing Document with the Same File Name (OFF 39)
25. Rename a File (OFF 40)
26. Move a File (OFF 40)
27. Delete a File (OFF 42)
28. Open the Help Window in an Office Program (OFF 43)
29. Move a Window by Dragging (OFF 43)
30. Resize a Window by Dragging (OFF 44)
31. Obtain Help Using the 'Type words to search for' Text Box (OFF 45)
32. Obtain Help Using the Help Links (OFF 47)
33. Obtain Help Using the Help Table of Contents (OFF 48)
34. Start Windows Help and Support (OFF 49)

If you have a SAM 2010 user profile, your instructor may have assigned an autogradable version of this assignment. If so, log into the SAM 2010 Web site at www.cengage.com/sam2010 to download the instruction and start files.

Learn It Online

Test your knowledge of chapter content and key terms.

Instructions: To complete the Learn It Online exercises, start your browser, click the Address bar, and then enter the Web address **scsite.com/office2010/learn**. When the Office 2010 Learn It Online page is displayed, click the link for the exercise you want to complete and then read the instructions.

Chapter Reinforcement TF, MC, and SA
A series of true/false, multiple choice, and short answer questions that test your knowledge of the chapter content.

Flash Cards
An interactive learning environment where you identify chapter key terms associated with displayed definitions.

Practice Test
A series of multiple choice questions that test your knowledge of chapter content and key terms.

Who Wants To Be a Computer Genius?
An interactive game that challenges your knowledge of chapter content in the style of a television quiz show.

Wheel of Terms
An interactive game that challenges your knowledge of chapter key terms in the style of the television show *Wheel of Fortune*.

Crossword Puzzle Challenge
A crossword puzzle that challenges your knowledge of key terms presented in the chapter.

Apply Your Knowledge

Reinforce the skills and apply the concepts you learned in this chapter.

Creating a Folder and a Document

Instructions: You will create a Word folder and then create a Word document and save it in the folder.

Perform the following tasks:

1. Connect a USB flash drive to an available USB port and then open the USB flash drive window.
2. Click the New folder button on the toolbar to display a new folder icon and text box for the folder name.
3. Type **Word** in the text box to name the folder. Press the ENTER key to create the folder on the USB flash drive.
4. Start Word.
5. Enter the text shown in Figure 85.
6. Click the Save button on the Quick Access Toolbar. Navigate to the Word folder on the USB flash drive and then save the document using the file name, Apply 1 Class List.
7. If your Quick Access Toolbar does not show the Quick Print button, add the Quick Print button to the Quick Access Toolbar. Print the document using the Quick Print button on the Quick Access Toolbar. When you are finished printing, remove the Quick Print button from the Quick Access Toolbar.
8. Submit the printout to your instructor.
9. Quit Word.

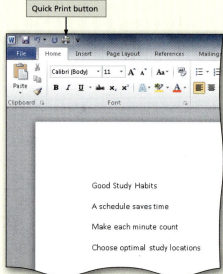

Figure 85

Extend Your Knowledge

Extend the skills you learned in this chapter and experiment with new skills. You will use Help to complete the assignment.

Using Help

Instructions: Use Word Help to perform the following tasks.

Perform the following tasks:

1. Start Word.
2. Click the Microsoft Word Help button to open the Word Help window (Figure 86).

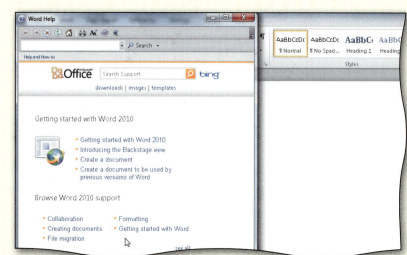

Figure 86

3. Search Word Help to answer the following questions.

    a. What are three features new to Word 2010?

    b. What type of training courses are available through Help?

    c. What are the steps to add a new group to the Ribbon?

    d. What are Quick Parts?

    e. What are document properties?

    f. What is a template?

    g. How do you print a document?

    h. What type of graphics can you insert in a document?

    i. What is cropping?

    j. What is the purpose of the Navigation Pane?

4. Submit the answers from your searches in the format specified by your instructor.

5. Quit Word.

Make It Right

Analyze a file structure and correct all errors and/or improve the design.

Organizing Vacation Photos

Note: To complete this assignment, you will be required to use the Data Files for Students. See the inside back cover of this book for instructions on downloading the Data Files for Students, or contact your instructor for information about accessing the required files.

Instructions: Traditionally, you have stored photos from past vacations together in one folder. The photos are becoming difficult to manage, and you now want to store them in appropriate folders. You will create the folder structure shown in Figure 87. You then will move the photos to the folders so that they will be organized properly.

1. Connect a USB flash drive to an available USB port to open the USB flash drive window.

2. Create the hierarchical folder structure shown in Figure 87.

3. Move one photo to each folder in the folder structure you created in Step 2. The five photos are available on the Data Files for Students.

4. Submit your work in the format specified by your instructor.

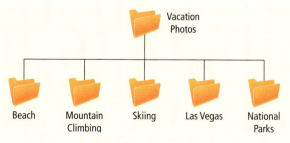

Figure 87

In the Lab

Use the guidelines, concepts, and skills presented in this chapter to increase your knowledge of Windows 7 and Word 2010. Labs are listed in order of increasing difficulty.

Lab 1: Using Windows Help and Support

Problem: You have a few questions about using Windows 7 and would like to answer these questions using Windows Help and Support.

Instructions: Use Windows Help and Support to perform the following tasks:

1. Display the Start menu and then click Help and Support to start Windows Help and Support.

2. Use the Help and Support Content page to answer the following questions.
   a. How do you reduce computer screen flicker?
   b. Which dialog box do you use to change the appearance of the mouse pointer?
   c. How do you minimize all windows?
   d. What is a VPN?

3. Use the Search Help text box in Windows Help and Support to answer the following questions.
   a. How can you minimize all open windows on the desktop?
   b. How do you start a program using the Run command?
   c. What are the steps to add a toolbar to the taskbar?
   d. What wizard do you use to remove unwanted desktop icons?

4. The tools to solve a problem while using Windows 7 are called **troubleshooters**. Use Windows Help and Support to find the list of troubleshooters (Figure 88), and answer the following questions.
   a. What problems does the HomeGroup troubleshooter allow you to resolve?
   b. List five Windows 7 troubleshooters that are not listed in Figure 88.

5. Use Windows Help and Support to obtain information about software licensing and product activation, and answer the following questions.
   a. What is genuine Windows?
   b. What is activation?
   c. What steps are required to activate Windows?
   d. What steps are required to read the Microsoft Software License Terms?
   e. Can you legally make a second copy of Windows 7 for use at home, work, or on a mobile computer or device?
   f. What is registration?

6. Close the Windows Help and Support window.

Figure 88

In the Lab

Lab 2: Creating Folders for a Pet Supply Store

Problem: Your friend works for Pete's Pet Supplies. He would like to organize his files in relation to the types of pets available in the store. He has five main categories: dogs, cats, fish, birds, and exotic. You are to create a folder structure similar to Figure 89.

Instructions: Perform the following tasks:

1. Connect a USB flash drive to an available USB port and then open the USB flash drive window.
2. Create the main folder for Pete's Pet Supplies.
3. Navigate to the Pete's Pet Supplies folder.
4. Within the Pete's Pet Supplies folder, create a folder for each of the following: Dogs, Cats, Fish, Birds, and Exotic.
5. Within the Exotic folder, create two additional folders, one for Primates and the second for Reptiles.
6. Submit the assignment in the format specified by your instructor.

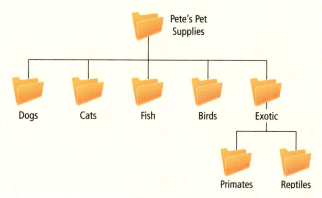

Figure 89

In the Lab

Lab 3: Creating Word Documents and Saving Them in Appropriate Folders

Problem: You are taking a class that requires you to complete three Word chapters. You will save the work completed in each chapter in a different folder (Figure 90).

Instructions: Create the folders shown in Figure 90. Then, using Word, create three small files to save in each folder.

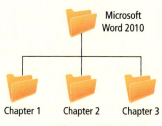

Figure 90

1. Connect a USB flash drive to an available USB port and then open the USB flash drive window.
2. Create the folder structure shown in Figure 90.
3. Navigate to the Chapter 1 folder.
4. Create a Word document containing the text, My Chapter 1 Word Document, and then save it in the Chapter 1 folder using the file name, Word Chapter 1 Document.
5. Navigate to the Chapter 2 folder.
6. Create another Word document containing the text, My Chapter 2 Word Document, and then save it in the Chapter 2 folder using the file name, Word Chapter 2 Document.
7. Navigate to the Chapter 3 folder.
8. Create another Word document containing the text, My Chapter 3 Word Document, and then save it in the Chapter 3 folder using the file name, Word Chapter 3 Document.
9. Quit Word.
10. Submit the assignment in the format specified by your instructor.

Cases and Places

Apply your creative thinking and problem solving skills to design and implement a solution.

Note: To complete these assignments, you may be required to use the Data Files for Students. See the inside back cover of this book for instructions on downloading the Data Files for Students, or contact your instructor for information about accessing the required files.

1: Creating Beginning Files for Classes

Academic

You are taking the following classes: Introduction to Engineering, Beginning Psychology, Introduction to Biology, and Accounting. Create folders for each of the classes. Use the following folder names: Engineering, Psychology, Biology, and Accounting, when creating the folder structure. In the Engineering folder, use Word to create a document with the name of the class and the class meeting location and time (MW 10:30 – 11:45, Room 317). In the Psychology folder, use Word to create a document containing the text, Behavioral Observations. In the Biology folder, use Word to create a document with the title Research. In the Accounting folder, create a Word document with the text, Tax Information. Use the concepts and techniques presented in this chapter to create the folders and files.

2: Using Help

Personal

Your parents enjoy working and playing games on their home computers. Your mother uses a notebook computer downstairs, and your father uses a desktop computer upstairs. They expressed interest in sharing files between their computers and sharing a single printer, so you offered to research various home networking options. Start Windows Help and Support, and search Help using the keywords, home networking. Use the link for installing a printer on a home network. Start Word and then type the main steps for installing a printer. Use the link for setting up a HomeGroup and then type the main steps for creating a HomeGroup in the Word document. Use the concepts and techniques presented in this chapter to use Help and create the Word document.

3: Creating Folders

Professional

Your boss at the bookstore where you work part-time has asked for help with organizing her files. After looking through the files, you decided upon a file structure for her to use, including the following folders: books, magazines, tapes, DVDs, and general merchandise. Within the books folder, create folders for hardback and paperback books. Within magazines, create folders for special issues and periodicals. In the tapes folder, create folders for celebrity and major release. In the DVDs folder, create a folder for book to DVD. In the general merchandise folder, create folders for novelties, posters, and games. Use the concepts and techniques presented in this chapter to create the folders.

1 Creating, Formatting, and Editing a Word Document with Pictures

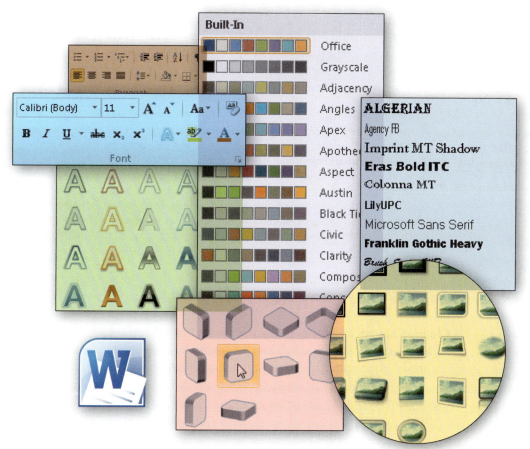

Objectives

You will have mastered the material in this chapter when you can:

- Enter text in a Word document
- Check spelling as you type
- Format paragraphs
- Format text
- Undo and redo commands or actions
- Change theme colors

- Insert digital pictures in a Word document
- Format pictures
- Add a page border
- Correct errors and revise a document
- Change document properties
- Print a document

1 | Creating, Formatting, and Editing a Word Document with Pictures

Introduction

To advertise a sale, promote a business, publicize an event, or convey a message to the community, you may want to create a flyer and hand it out in person or post it in a public location. Libraries, schools, religious organizations, grocery stores, coffee shops, and other places often provide bulletin boards or windows for flyers. These flyers announce personal items for sale or rent (car, boat, apartment); garage or block sales; services being offered (animal care, housecleaning, lessons); membership, sponsorship, or donation requests (club, religious organization, charity); and other messages such as a lost or found pet.

Project Planning Guidelines

> The process of developing a document that communicates specific information requires careful analysis and planning. As a starting point, establish why the document is needed. Once the purpose is determined, analyze the intended readers of the document and their unique needs. Then, gather information about the topic and decide what to include in the document. Finally, determine the document design and style that will be most successful at delivering the message. Details of these guidelines are provided in Appendix A. In addition, each project in this book provides practical applications of these planning considerations.

Project — Flyer with Pictures

Individuals and businesses create flyers to gain public attention. Flyers, which usually are a single page in length, are an inexpensive means of reaching the community. Many flyers, however, go unnoticed because they are designed poorly.

The project in this chapter follows general guidelines and uses Word to create the flyer shown in Figure 1–1. This colorful, eye-catching flyer announces that a dog has been found. The pictures of the dog, taken with a camera phone, entice passersby to stop and look at the flyer. The headline on the flyer is large and colorful to draw attention into the text. The body copy below the pictures briefly describes where and when the dog was found, along with a bulleted list that concisely highlights important identifying information. The signature line of the flyer calls attention to the contact phone number. The dog's name, Bailey, and signature line are in a different color so that they stand apart from the rest of the text on the flyer. Finally, the graphical page border nicely frames and complements the contents of the flyer.

Figure 1–1

Overview

As you read this chapter, you will learn how to create the flyer shown in Figure 1–1 on the previous page by performing these general tasks:

- Enter text in the document.
- Format the text in the document.
- Insert the pictures in the document.
- Format the pictures in the document.
- Enhance the page with a border and additional spacing.
- Correct errors and revise the document.
- Print the document.

Plan Ahead

> **General Project Guidelines**
>
> When creating a Word document, the actions you perform and decisions you make will affect the appearance and characteristics of the finished document. As you create a flyer, such as the project shown in Figure 1–1, you should follow these general guidelines:
>
> 1. **Choose the words for the text.** Follow the *less is more* principle. The less text, the more likely the flyer will be read. Use as few words as possible to make a point.
>
> 2. **Identify how to format various elements of the text.** The overall appearance of a document significantly affects its ability to communicate clearly. Examples of how you can modify the appearance, or **format**, of text include changing its shape, size, color, and position on the page.
>
> 3. **Find the appropriate graphical image(s).** An eye-catching graphical image should convey the flyer's overall message. It could show a product, service, result, or benefit, or visually convey a message that is not expressed easily with words.
>
> 4. **Establish where to position and how to format the graphical image(s).** The position and format of the graphical image(s) should grab the attention of passersby and draw them into reading the flyer.
>
> 5. **Determine whether the page needs enhancements such as a border or spacing adjustments.** A graphical, color-coordinated page border can further draw attention to a flyer and nicely frame its contents. Increasing or decreasing spacing between elements on a flyer can improve its readability and overall appearance.
>
> 6. **Correct errors and revise the document as necessary.** Post the flyer on a wall and make sure all text and images are legible from a distance. Ask someone else to read the flyer and give you suggestions for improvements.
>
> 7. **Determine the best method for distributing the document.** Documents can be distributed on paper or electronically. A flyer should be printed on paper so that it can be posted.
>
> When necessary, more specific details concerning the above guidelines are presented at appropriate points in the chapter. The chapter also will identify the actions performed and decisions made regarding these guidelines during the creation of the flyer shown in Figure 1–1.

For an introduction to Windows 7 and instruction about how to perform basic Windows 7 tasks, read the Office 2010 and Windows 7 chapter at the beginning of this book, where you can learn how to resize windows, change screen resolution, create folders, move and rename files, use Windows Help, and much more.

To Start Word

If you are using a computer to step through the project in this chapter and you want your screens to match the figures in this book, you should change your screen's resolution to 1024 × 768. For information about how to change a computer's resolution, refer to the Office 2010 and Windows 7 chapter at the beginning of this book.

The following steps, which assume Windows 7 is running, start Word based on a typical installation. You may need to ask your instructor how to start Word for your computer. For a detailed example of the procedure summarized below, refer to the Office 2010 and Windows 7 chapter.

1 Click the Start button on the Windows 7 taskbar to display the Start menu.

2 Type `Microsoft Word` as the search text in the 'Search programs and files' text box and watch the search results appear on the Start menu.

3 Click Microsoft Word 2010 in the search results on the Start menu to start Word and display a new blank document in the Word window.

4 If the Word window is not maximized, click the Maximize button next to the Close button on its title bar to maximize the window.

5 If the Print Layout button on the status bar is not selected (shown in Figure 1–2 on the next page), click it so that your screen is in Print Layout view.

Q&A What is Print Layout view?

The default (preset) view in Word is **Print Layout view**, which shows the document on a mock sheet of paper in the document window.

6 If Normal (Home tab | Styles group) is not selected in the Quick Style gallery (shown in Figure 1–2), click it so that your document uses the Normal style.

Q&A What is the Normal style?

When you create a document, Word formats the text using a particular style. The default style in Word is called the **Normal style**, which is discussed later in this book.

Q&A What if rulers appear on my screen?

Click the View Ruler button above the vertical scroll bar to hide the rulers, or click View on the Ribbon to display the View tab and then place a check mark in the Ruler check box.

Entering Text

The first step in creating a document is to enter its text. With the projects in this book, you enter text by typing on the keyboard. By default, Word positions text you type at the left margin. In a later section of this chapter, you will learn how to format, or change the appearance of, the entered text.

Choose the words for the text.
The text in a flyer is organized into three areas: headline, body copy, and signature line.

- The **headline** is the first line of text on the flyer. It conveys the product or service being offered, such as a car for sale or personal lessons, or the benefit that will be gained, such as a convenience, better performance, greater security, higher earnings, or more comfort; or it can contain a message such as a lost or found pet.

- The **body copy** consists of all text between the headline and the signature line. This text highlights the key points of the message in as few words as possible. It should be easy to read and follow. While emphasizing the positive, the body copy must be realistic, truthful, and believable.

- The **signature line**, which is the last line of text on the flyer, contains contact information or identifies a call to action.

Plan Ahead

BTW

For an introduction to Office 2010 and instruction about how to perform basic tasks in Office 2010 programs, read the Office 2010 and Windows 7 chapter at the beginning of this book, where you can learn how to start a program, use the Ribbon, save a file, open a file, quit a program, use Help, and much more.

BTW The Word Window The chapters in this book begin with the Word window appearing as it did at the initial installation of the software. Your Word window may look different depending on your screen resolution and other Word settings.

BTW Zooming If text is too small for you to read on the screen, you can zoom the document by dragging the Zoom slider on the status bar or clicking the Zoom Out or Zoom In buttons on the status bar. Changing the zoom has no effect on the printed document.

To Type Text

To begin creating the flyer in this chapter, type the headline in the document window. The following steps type this first line of text in the document.

1

● Type **Found Dog** as the headline (Figure 1–2).

Q&A What if I make an error while typing?

You can press the BACKSPACE key until you have deleted the text in error and then retype the text correctly.

Q&A Why did the Spelling and Grammar Check icon appear on the status bar?

When you begin typing text, the **Spelling and Grammar Check icon** appears on the status bar with an animated pencil writing on paper to indicate that Word is checking for spelling and grammar errors. When you stop typing, the pencil changes to a blue check mark (no errors) or a red X (potential errors found). Word flags potential errors in the document with a red, green, or blue wavy underline. Later in this chapter, you will learn how to fix flagged errors.

Home tab

document window

Normal style automatically selected when you first install Word

Styles group

View Ruler button shows or hides rulers

insertion point moves to the right as you type

Found Dog

text typed

mouse pointer's shape changes depending on task you are performing in Word and pointer's location on screen

Note: To help you locate screen elements that are referenced in the step instructions, such as buttons and commands, this book uses red boxes to point to these screen elements.

number of words in document

Spelling and Grammar Check icon contains a blue check mark, indicating the entered text contains no spelling or grammar errors

Print Layout button automatically selected when you first install Word

Zoom slider

Page: 1 of 1   Words: 2

Figure 1–2

2

● Press the ENTER key to move the insertion point to the beginning of the next line (Figure 1–3).

Q&A Why did blank space appear between the headline and the insertion point?

Each time you press the ENTER key, Word creates a new paragraph and inserts blank space between the two paragraphs. Later in this chapter, you will learn how to adjust the spacing between paragraphs.

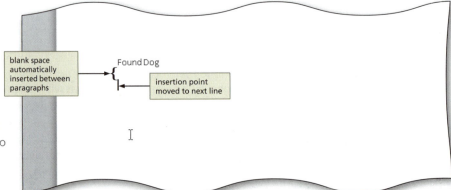

blank space automatically inserted between paragraphs

Found Dog

insertion point moved to next line

Figure 1–3

To Display Formatting Marks

To indicate where in a document you press the ENTER key or SPACEBAR, you may find it helpful to display formatting marks. A **formatting mark**, sometimes called a **nonprinting character**, is a character that Word displays on the screen but is not visible on a printed document. For example, the paragraph mark (¶) is a formatting mark that indicates where you press the ENTER key. A raised dot (·) shows where you press the SPACEBAR. Other formatting marks are discussed as they appear on the screen.

Depending on settings made during previous Word sessions, your Word screen already may display formatting marks (Figure 1–4). The following step displays formatting marks, if they do not show already on the screen.

- If the Home tab is not the active tab, click Home on the Ribbon to display the Home tab.

- If it is not selected already, click the Show/Hide ¶ button (Home tab | Paragraph group) to display formatting marks on the screen (Figure 1–4).

What if I do not want formatting marks to show on the screen?

You can hide them by clicking the Show/Hide ¶ button (Home tab | Paragraph group) again. It is recommended that you display formatting marks so that you visually can identify when you press the ENTER key, SPACEBAR, and other keys associated with nonprinting characters; therefore, most of the document windows presented in this book show formatting marks.

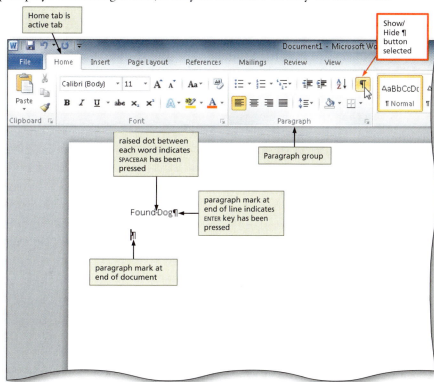

Figure 1–4

Other Ways

1. Press CTRL+SHIFT+*

To Insert a Blank Line

In the flyer, the digital pictures of the dog appear between the headline and body copy. You will not insert these pictures, however, until after you enter and format all text. Thus, you leave a blank line in the document as a placeholder for the pictures. To enter a blank line in a document, press the ENTER key without typing any text on the line. The following step inserts one blank line below the headline.

- Press the ENTER key to insert a blank line in the document (Figure 1–5).

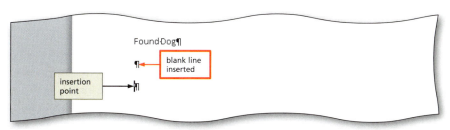

Figure 1–5

Wordwrap

Wordwrap allows you to type words in a paragraph continually without pressing the ENTER key at the end of each line. As you type, if a word extends beyond the right margin, Word also automatically positions that word on the next line along with the insertion point.

Word creates a new paragraph each time you press the ENTER key. Thus, as you type text in the document window, do not press the ENTER key when the insertion point reaches the right margin. Instead, press the ENTER key only in these circumstances:

1. To insert a blank line(s) in a document (as shown in the steps on the previous page)
2. To begin a new paragraph
3. To terminate a short line of text and advance to the next line
4. To respond to questions or prompts in Word dialog boxes, task panes, and other on-screen objects

To Wordwrap Text as You Type

The next step in creating the flyer is to type the body copy. The following step illustrates how the body copy text wordwraps as you enter it in the document.

1

- Type the first sentence of the body copy: `Adorable, loving, friendly, well-behaved dog found early Friday morning, June 1, wandering on the bike trail at Filcher Park in Hampton Township.`

Q&A

Why does my document wrap on different words?

The printer connected to a computer is one factor that can control where wordwrap occurs for each line in a document. Thus, it is possible that the same document could wordwrap differently if printed on different printers.

- Press the ENTER key to position the insertion point on the next line in the document (Figure 1–6).

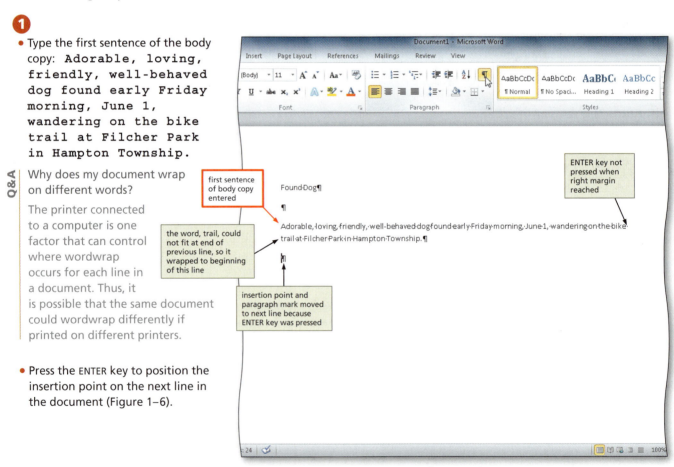

Figure 1–6

Spelling and Grammar Check

As you type text in a document, Word checks your typing for possible spelling and grammar errors. If all of the words you have typed are in Word's dictionary and your grammar is correct, as mentioned earlier, the Spelling and Grammar Check icon on the status bar displays a blue check mark. Otherwise, the icon shows a red X. In this case, Word flags the potential error in the document window with a red, green, or blue wavy underline. A red wavy underline means the flagged text is not in Word's dictionary (because it is a proper name or misspelled). A green wavy underline indicates the text may be incorrect grammatically. A blue wavy underline indicates the text may contain a contextual spelling error such as the misuse of homophones (words that are pronounced the same but that have different spellings or meanings, such as one and won). Although you can check the entire document for spelling and grammar errors at once, you also can check flagged errors as they appear on the screen.

A flagged word is not necessarily misspelled. For example, many names, abbreviations, and specialized terms are not in Word's main dictionary. In these cases, you can instruct Word to ignore the flagged word. As you type, Word also detects duplicate words while checking for spelling errors. For example, if your document contains the phrase, to the the store, Word places a red wavy underline below the second occurrence of the word, the.

BTW

Automatic Spelling Correction
As you type, Word automatically corrects some misspelled words. For example, if you type recieve, Word automatically corrects the misspelling and displays the word, receive, when you press the SPACEBAR or type a punctuation mark. To see a complete list of automatically corrected words, click File on the Ribbon to open the Backstage view, click Options in the Backstage view, click Proofing in the left pane (Word Options dialog box), click the AutoCorrect Options button, and then scroll through the list near the bottom of the dialog box.

To Check Spelling and Grammar as You Type

In the following steps, the word, patches, has been misspelled intentionally as paches to illustrate Word's check spelling as you type feature. If you are doing this project on a computer, your flyer may contain different misspelled words, depending on the accuracy of your typing.

1

• Type `Tan color with paches` and then press the SPACEBAR so that a red wavy line appears below the misspelled word (Figure 1–7).

Q&A

What if Word does not flag my spelling and grammar errors with wavy underlines?

To verify that the check spelling and grammar as you type features are enabled, click File on the Ribbon to open the Backstage view and then click Options in the Backstage view. When the Word Options dialog box is displayed, click Proofing in the left pane, and then ensure the 'Check spelling as you type' and 'Mark grammar errors as you type' check boxes contain check marks. Also ensure the 'Hide spelling errors in this document only' and 'Hide grammar errors in this document only' check boxes do not have check marks. Click the OK button.

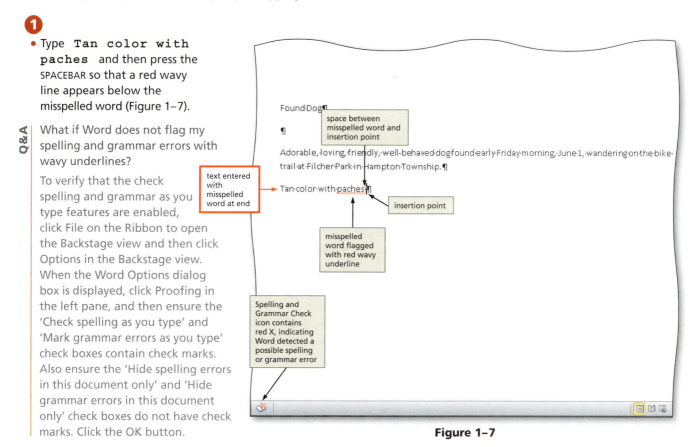

Figure 1–7

● Right-click the flagged word (paches, in this case) to display a shortcut menu that presents a list of suggested spelling corrections for the flagged word (Figure 1–8).

What if, when I right-click the misspelled word, my desired correction is not in the list on the shortcut menu?

You can click outside the shortcut menu to close the shortcut menu and then retype the correct word, or you can click Spelling on the shortcut menu to display the Spelling dialog box. Chapter 2 discusses the Spelling dialog box.

What if a flagged word actually is, for example, a proper name and spelled correctly?

Right-click it and then click Ignore All on the shortcut menu to instruct Word not to flag future occurrences of the same word in this document.

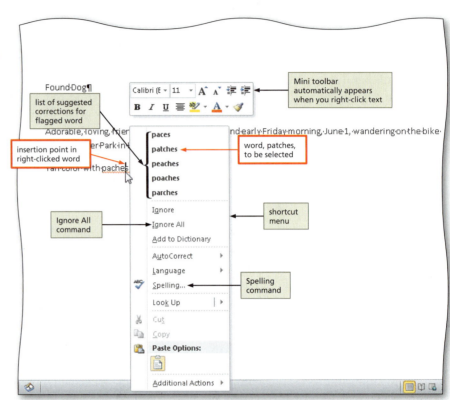

Figure 1–8

● Click patches on the shortcut menu to replace the misspelled word in the document with a correctly spelled word (Figure 1–9).

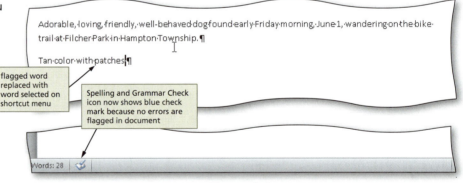

Figure 1–9

Other Ways

1. Click Spelling and Grammar Check icon on status bar, click desired word on shortcut menu

Character Widths

Many word processing documents use variable character fonts, where some characters are wider than others; for example, the letter w is wider than the letter i.

To Enter More Text

In the flyer, the text yet to be entered includes the remainder of the body copy, which will be formatted as a bulleted list, and the signature line. The next steps enter the remainder of text in the flyer.

1 Press the END key to move the insertion point to the end of the current line.

2 Type `of white on his chest` and then press the ENTER key.

3 Type `Male, adult cocker spaniel` and then press the ENTER key.

4 Type `Green and silver collar with the name, Bailey, on the tag` and then press the ENTER key.

5 Type the signature line in the flyer (Figure 1–10):
`If this is your lost dog, call 555-1029.`

three paragraphs of body copy entered, which will be formatted as a bulleted list → Tan·color·with·patches·of·white·on·his·chest¶

Male,·adult·cocker·spaniel¶

Green·and·silver·collar·with·the·name,·Bailey,·on·the·tag¶

signature line entered → If·this·is·your·lost·dog,·call·555-1029.¶

Figure 1–10

Navigating a Document

You view only a portion of a document on the screen through the document window. At some point when you type text or insert graphics, Word probably will **scroll** the top or bottom portion of the document off the screen. Although you cannot see the text and graphics once they scroll off the screen, they remain in the document.

You can use either the keyboard or the mouse to scroll to a different location in a document and/or move the insertion point around a document. When you use the keyboard, the insertion point automatically moves when you press the desired keys. For example, the previous steps used the END key to move the insertion point to the end of the current line. Table 1–1 outlines various techniques to navigate a document using the keyboard.

With the mouse, you can use the scroll arrows or the scroll box on the scroll bar to display a different portion of the document in the document window and then click the mouse to move the insertion point to that location. Table 1–2 explains various techniques for using the scroll bar to scroll vertically with the mouse.

BTW

Minimize Wrist Injury
Computer users frequently switch between the keyboard and the mouse during a word processing session; such switching strains the wrist. To help prevent wrist injury, minimize switching. For instance, if your fingers already are on the keyboard, use keyboard keys to scroll. If your hand already is on the mouse, use the mouse to scroll.

Table 1–1 Moving the Insertion Point with the Keyboard

Insertion Point Direction	Key(s) to Press	Insertion Point Direction	Key(s) to Press
Left one character	LEFT ARROW	Up one paragraph	CTRL+UP ARROW
Right one character	RIGHT ARROW	Down one paragraph	CTRL+DOWN ARROW
Left one word	CTRL+LEFT ARROW	Up one screen	PAGE UP
Right one word	CTRL+RIGHT ARROW	Down one screen	PAGE DOWN
Up one line	UP ARROW	To top of document window	ALT+CTRL+PAGE UP
Down one line	DOWN ARROW	To bottom of document window	ALT+CTRL+PAGE DOWN
To end of line	END	To beginning of document	CTRL+HOME
To beginning of line	HOME	To end of document	CTRL+END

Table 1–2 Using the Scroll Bar to Scroll Vertically with the Mouse

Scroll Direction	Mouse Action	Scroll Direction	Mouse Action
Up	Drag the scroll box upward.	Down one screen	Click anywhere below the scroll box on the vertical scroll bar.
Down	Drag the scroll box downward.	Up one line	Click the scroll arrow at the top of the vertical scroll bar.
Up one screen	Click anywhere above the scroll box on the vertical scroll bar.	Down one line	Click the scroll arrow at the bottom of the vertical scroll bar.

BTW

Organizing Files and Folders
You should organize and store files in folders so that you easily can find the files later. For example, if you are taking an introductory computer class called CIS 101, a good practice would be to save all Word files in a Word folder in a CIS 101 folder. For a discussion of folders and detailed examples of creating folders, refer to the Office 2010 and Windows 7 chapter at the beginning of this book.

To Save a Document

You have performed many tasks while creating this flyer and do not want to risk losing work completed thus far. Accordingly, you should save the document.

The following steps assume you already have created folders for storing your files, for example, a CIS 101 folder (for your class) that contains a Word folder (for your assignments). Thus, these steps save the document in the Word folder in the CIS 101 folder on a USB flash drive using the file name, Found Dog Flyer. For a detailed example of the procedure summarized below, refer to the Office 2010 and Windows 7 chapter at the beginning of this book.

1 With a USB flash drive connected to one of the computer's USB ports, click the Save button on the Quick Access Toolbar to display the Save As dialog box.

2 Type **Found Dog Flyer** in the File name text box to change the file name. Do not press the ENTER key after typing the file name because you do not want to close the dialog box at this time.

3 Navigate to the desired save location (in this case, the Word folder in the CIS 101 folder [or your class folder] on the USB flash drive).

4 Click the Save button (Save As dialog box) to save the document in the selected folder on the selected drive with the entered file name.

Formatting Paragraphs and Characters

With the text for the flyer entered, the next step is to **format**, or change the appearance of, its text. A paragraph encompasses the text from the first character in the paragraph up to and including its paragraph mark (¶). **Paragraph formatting** is the process of changing the appearance of a paragraph. For example, you can center or add bullets to a paragraph. Characters include letters, numbers, punctuation marks, and symbols. **Character formatting** is the process of changing the way characters appear on the screen and in print. You use character formatting to emphasize certain words and improve readability of a document. For example, you can color or underline characters. Often, you apply both paragraph and character formatting to the same text. For example, you may center a paragraph (paragraph formatting) and underline some of the characters in the same paragraph (character formatting).

Although you can format paragraphs and characters before you type, many Word users enter text first and then format the existing text. Figure 1–11a shows the flyer in this chapter before formatting its paragraphs and characters. Figure 1–11b shows the flyer after formatting. As you can see from the two figures, a document that is formatted is easier to read and looks more professional. The following pages discuss how to format the flyer so that it looks like Figure 1–11b.

Characters that appear on the screen are a specific shape and size. The **font**, or typeface, defines the appearance and shape of the letters, numbers, and special characters. In Word, the default font usually is Calibri (shown in Figure 1–12 on page WD 14). You can leave characters in the default font or change them to a different font. **Font size** specifies the size of the characters and is determined by a measurement system called points. A single **point** is about 1/72 of one inch in height. The default font size in Word typically is 11 (Figure 1–12). Thus, a character with a font size of 11 is about 11/72 or a little less than 1/6 of one inch in height. You can increase or decrease the font size of characters in a document.

A document **theme** is a set of unified formats for fonts, colors, and graphics. Word includes a variety of document themes to assist you with coordinating these visual elements in a document. The default theme fonts are Cambria for headings and Calibri for body text. By changing the document theme, you quickly can give your document a new look. You also can define your own document themes.

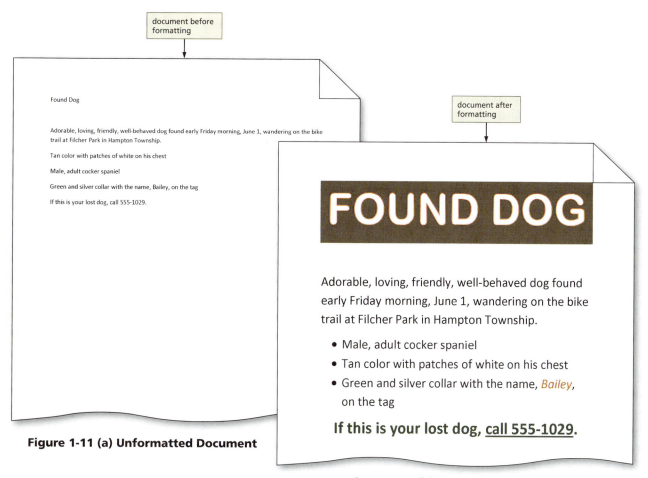

document before formatting

Found Dog

Adorable, loving, friendly, well-behaved dog found early Friday morning, June 1, wandering on the bike trail at Filcher Park in Hampton Township.

Tan color with patches of white on his chest

Male, adult cocker spaniel

Green and silver collar with the name, Bailey, on the tag

If this is your lost dog, call 555-1029.

document after formatting

FOUND DOG

Adorable, loving, friendly, well-behaved dog found early Friday morning, June 1, wandering on the bike trail at Filcher Park in Hampton Township.

- Male, adult cocker spaniel
- Tan color with patches of white on his chest
- Green and silver collar with the name, *Bailey*, on the tag

If this is your lost dog, <u>call 555-1029</u>.

Figure 1-11 (a) Unformatted Document

Figure 1-11 (b) Formatted Document

Identify how to format various elements of the text.

By formatting the characters and paragraphs in a document, you can improve its overall appearance. In a flyer, consider the following formatting suggestions.

- **Increase the font size of characters.** Flyers usually are posted on a bulletin board or in a window. Thus, the font size should be as large as possible so that passersby easily can read the flyer. To give the headline more impact, its font size should be larger than the font size of the text in the body copy. If possible, make the font size of the signature line larger than the body copy but smaller than the headline.

- **Change the font of characters.** Use fonts that are easy to read. Try to use only two different fonts in a flyer, for example, one for the headline and the other for all other text. Too many fonts can make the flyer visually confusing.

- **Change paragraph alignment.** The default alignment for paragraphs in a document is **left-aligned**, that is, flush at the left margin of the document with uneven right edges. Consider changing the alignment of some of the paragraphs to add interest and variety to the flyer.

- **Highlight key paragraphs with bullets.** A bulleted paragraph is a paragraph that begins with a dot or other symbol. Use bulleted paragraphs to highlight important points in a flyer.

- **Emphasize important words.** To call attention to certain words or lines, you can underline them, italicize them, or bold them. Use these formats sparingly, however, because overuse will minimize their effect and make the flyer look too busy.

- **Use color.** Use colors that complement each other and convey the meaning of the flyer. Vary colors in terms of hue and brightness. Headline colors, for example, can be bold and bright. Signature lines should stand out more than body copy but less than headlines. Keep in mind that too many colors can detract from the flyer and make it difficult to read.

Plan Ahead

To Center a Paragraph

The headline in the flyer currently is left-aligned (Figure 1–12). You want the headline to be **centered**, that is, positioned horizontally between the left and right margins on the page. Recall that Word considers a single short line of text, such as the two-word headline, a paragraph. Thus, you will center the paragraph containing the headline. The following steps center a paragraph.

1
• Click somewhere in the paragraph to be centered (in this case, the headline) to position the insertion point in the paragraph to be formatted (Figure 1–12).

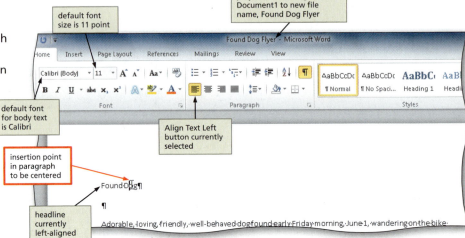

Figure 1–12

2
• Click the Center button (Home tab | Paragraph group) to center the paragraph containing the insertion point (Figure 1–13).

Q&A
What if I want to return the paragraph to left-aligned?

You would click the Center button again or click the Align Text Left button (Home tab | Paragraph group).

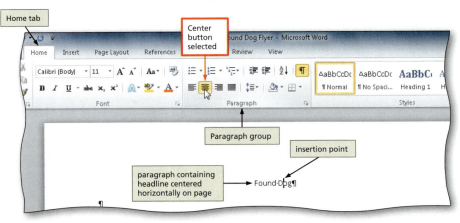

Figure 1–13

Other Ways

1. Right-click paragraph, click Center button on Mini toolbar

2. Right-click paragraph, click Paragraph on shortcut menu, click Indents and Spacing tab

(Paragraph dialog box), click Alignment box arrow, click Centered, click OK button

3. Click Paragraph Dialog Box Launcher (Home tab or Page Layout tab | Paragraph

group), click Indents and Spacing tab (Paragraph dialog box), click Alignment box arrow, click Centered, click OK button

4. Press CTRL+E

BTW

File Type
Depending on your Windows settings, the file type .docx may be displayed on the title bar immediately to the right of the file name after you save the file. The file type .docx is a Word 2010 document.

To Center Another Paragraph

In the flyer, the signature line is to be centered to match the paragraph alignment of the headline. The following steps center the signature line.

1 Click somewhere in the paragraph to be centered (in this case, the signature line) to position the insertion point in the paragraph to be formatted.

2 Click the Center button (Home tab | Paragraph group) to center the paragraph containing the insertion point (shown in Figure 1–14).

Formatting Single versus Multiple Paragraphs and Characters

As shown on the previous pages, to format a single paragraph, simply move the insertion point in the paragraph, to make it the current paragraph, and then format the paragraph. Similarly, to format a single word, position the insertion point in the word, to make it the current word, and then format the word.

To format multiple paragraphs or words, however, you first must select the paragraphs or words you want to format and then format the selection. If your screen normally displays dark letters on a light background, which is the default setting in Word, then selected text displays light letters on a dark background.

To Select a Line

The default font size of 11 point is too small for a headline in a flyer. To increase the font size of the characters in the headline, you first must select the line of text containing the headline. The following steps select a line.

1
- Move the mouse pointer to the left of the line to be selected (in this case, the headline) until the mouse pointer changes to a right-pointing block arrow (Figure 1–14).

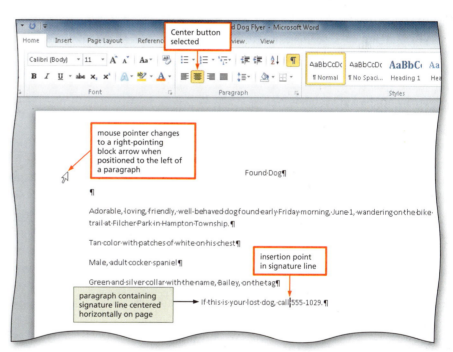

Figure 1–14

2
- While the mouse pointer is a right-pointing block arrow, click the mouse to select the entire line to the right of the mouse pointer (Figure 1–15).

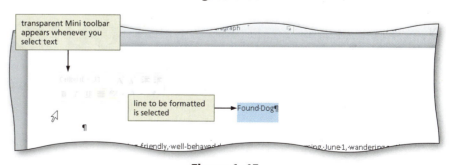

Figure 1–15

Other Ways	
1. Drag mouse through line	2. With insertion point at beginning of desired line, press SHIFT+DOWN ARROW

To Change the Font Size of Selected Text

The next step is to increase the font size of the characters in the selected headline. You would like the headline to be as large as possible and still fit on a single line, which in this case is 72 point. The following steps increase the font size of the headline from 11 to 72 point.

1

- With the text selected, click the Font Size box arrow (Home tab | Font group) to display the Font Size gallery (Figure 1–16).

Q&A Why are the font sizes in my Font Size gallery different from those in Figure 1–16?

Font sizes may vary depending on the current font and your printer driver.

Q&A What happened to the Mini toolbar?

The Mini toolbar disappears if you do not use it. These steps use the Font Size box arrow on the Home tab instead of the Font Size box arrow on the Mini toolbar.

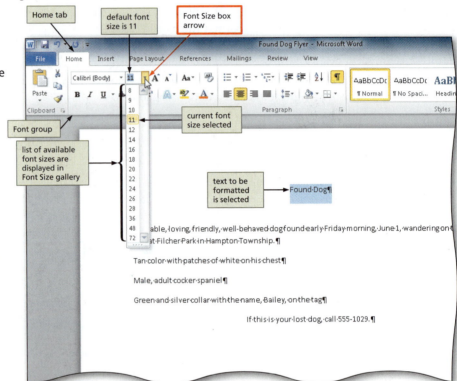

Figure 1–16

2

- Point to 72 in the Font Size gallery to display a live preview of the selected text at the selected point size (Figure 1–17).

 Experiment

- Point to various font sizes in the Font Size gallery and watch the font size of the selected text change in the document window.

3

- Click 72 in the Font Size gallery to increase the font size of the selected text.

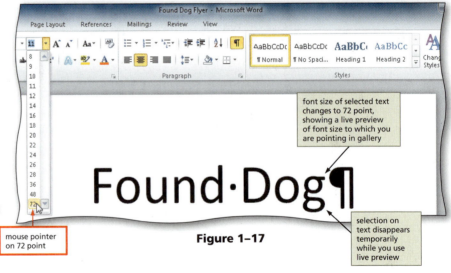

Figure 1–17

Other Ways

1. Click Font Size box arrow on Mini toolbar, click desired font size in Font Size gallery

2. Right-click selected text, click Font on shortcut menu, click Font tab (Font dialog box), select desired font size in Size list, click OK button

3. Click Font Dialog Box Launcher, click Font tab (Font dialog box), select desired font size in Size list, click OK button

4. Press CTRL+D, click Font tab (Font dialog box), select desired font size in Size list, click OK button

To Change the Font of Selected Text

The default theme font for headings is Cambria and for all other text, called body text in Word, is Calibri. Many other fonts are available, however, so that you can add variety to documents.

To draw more attention to the headline, you change its font so that it differs from the font of other text in the flyer. The following steps change the font of the headline from Calibri to Arial Rounded MT Bold.

1

- With the text selected, click the Font box arrow (Home tab | Font group) to display the Font gallery (Figure 1–18).

Will the fonts in my Font gallery be the same as those in Figure 1–18?

Your list of available fonts may differ, depending on the type of printer you are using and other settings.

What if the text is no longer selected?

Follow the steps on page WD 15 to select a line.

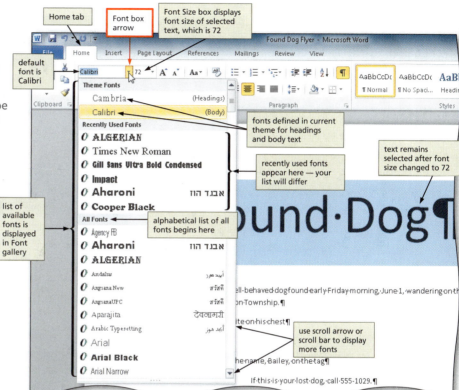

Figure 1–18

2

- Scroll through the Font gallery, if necessary, and then point to Arial Rounded MT Bold (or a similar font) to display a live preview of the selected text in the selected font (Figure 1–19).

 **Experiment**

- Point to various fonts in the Font gallery and watch the font of the selected text change in the document window.

3

- Click Arial Rounded MT Bold (or a similar font) to change the font of the selected text.

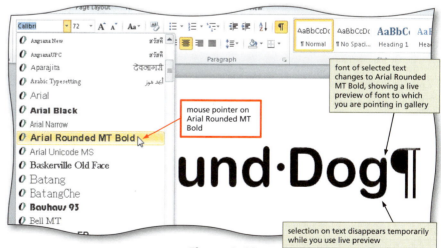

Figure 1–19

Other Ways

1. Click Font box arrow on Mini toolbar, click desired font in Font gallery

2. Right-click selected text, click Font on shortcut menu, click Font tab (Font dialog box), select desired font in Font list, click OK button

3. Click Font Dialog Box Launcher (Home tab | Font group), click Font tab (Font dialog box), select desired font in Font list, click OK button

4. Press CTRL+D, click Font tab (Font dialog box), select desired font in the Font list, click OK button

To Change the Case of Selected Text

The headline currently shows the first letter in each word capitalized, which sometimes is referred to as initial cap. To draw more attention to the headline, you would like the entire line of text to be capitalized, or in uppercase letters. The following steps change the headline to uppercase.

1
- With the text selected, click the Change Case button (Home tab | Font group) to display the Change Case gallery (Figure 1–20).

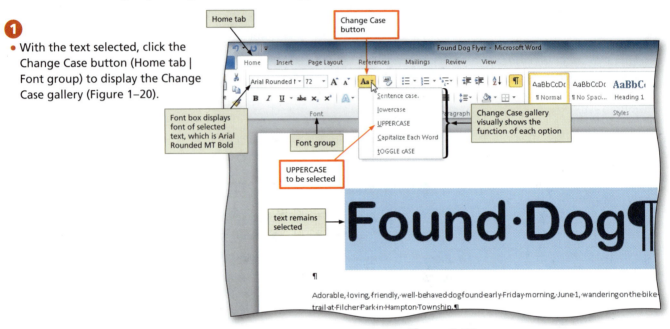

Figure 1–20

2
- Click UPPERCASE in the Change Case gallery to change the case of the selected text (Figure 1–21).

Q&A

What if a ruler appears on the screen or the mouse pointer shape changes?

Depending on the position of your mouse pointer and locations you click on the screen, a ruler may automatically appear or the mouse pointer shape may change. Simply move the mouse and the ruler should disappear and/or the mouse pointer shape will change.

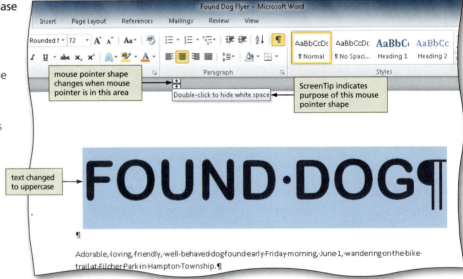

Figure 1–21

Other Ways
1. Right-click selected text, click Font on shortcut menu, click Font tab (Font dialog box), select All caps in Effects area, click OK button
2. Click Font Dialog Box Launcher (Home tab | Font group), click Font tab (Font dialog box), select All caps in Effects area, click OK button
3. Press SHIFT+F3 repeatedly until text is desired case

To Apply a Text Effect to Selected Text

You would like the text in the headline to be even more noticeable. Word provides many text effects to add interest and variety to text. The following steps apply a text effect to the headline.

- With the text selected, click the Text Effects button (Home tab | Font group) to display the Text Effects gallery (Figure 1–22).

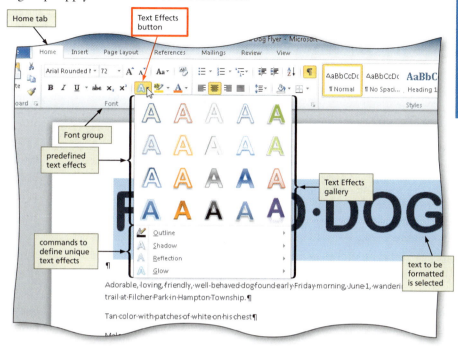

Figure 1–22

- Point to Fill – White, Gradient Outline – Accent 1 (first text effect in third row) to display a live preview of the selected text in the selected text effect (Figure 1–23).

 **Experiment**

- Point to various text effects in the Text Effects gallery and watch the text effects of the selected text change in the document window.

- Click Fill – White, Gradient Outline – Accent 1 to change the text effect of the selected text.

4

- Click anywhere in the document window to remove the selection from the selected text.

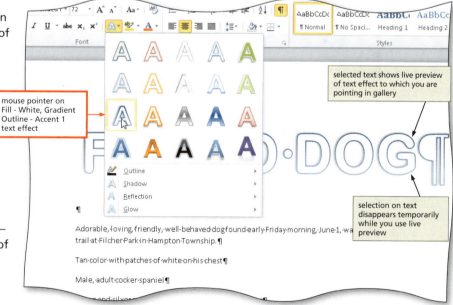

Figure 1–23

Other Ways
1. Right-click selected text, click Font on shortcut menu, click Font tab (Font dialog box), click Text Effects button, select desired text effects	(Format Text Effects dialog box), click Close button, click OK button 2. Click Font Dialog Box Launcher (Home tab | Font group), click Font	tab (Font dialog box), click Text Effects button, select desired text effects (Format Text Effects dialog box), click Close button, click OK button

To Shade a Paragraph

To make the headline of the flyer more eye-catching, you would like to shade it. When you **shade** text, Word colors the rectangular area behind any text or graphics. If the text to shade is a paragraph, Word shades the area from the left margin to the right margin of the current paragraph. To shade a paragraph, place the insertion point in the paragraph. To shade any other text, you must first select the text to be shaded. This flyer uses brown as the shading color for the headline. The following steps shade a paragraph.

- Click somewhere in the paragraph to be shaded (in this case, the headline) to position the insertion point in the paragraph to be formatted.

- Click the Shading button arrow (Home tab | Paragraph group) to display the Shading gallery (Figure 1–24).

Q&A What if I click the Shading button by mistake?

Click the Shading button arrow and proceed with Step 2.

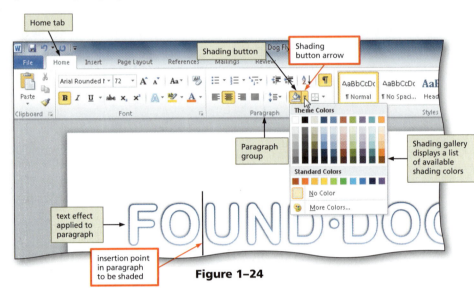

Figure 1–24

- Point to Orange, Accent 6, Darker 50% (rightmost color in the sixth row) to display a live preview of the selected shading color (Figure 1–25).

🔍 Experiment

- Point to various colors in the Shading gallery and watch the shading color of the current paragraph change.

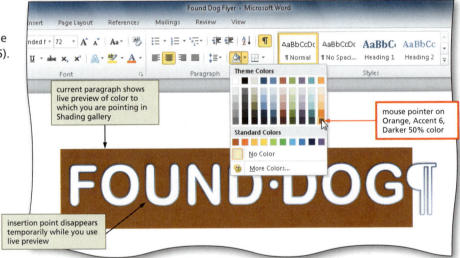

Figure 1–25

3
- Click Orange, Accent 6, Darker 50% to shade the current paragraph.

Q&A What if I apply a dark shading color to dark text?

When the font color of text is Automatic, it usually is black. If you select a dark shading color, Word automatically may change the text color to white so that the shaded text is easier to read.

Other Ways
1. Click Border button arrow (Home tab | Paragraph group), click Borders and Shading, click Shading   tab (Borders and Shading dialog box), click Fill box arrow, select desired color, click OK button

To Select Multiple Lines

The next formatting step for the flyer is to increase the font size of the characters between the headline and the signature line so that they are easier to read from a distance. To change the font size of the characters in multiple lines, you first must select all the lines to be formatted. The following steps select multiple lines.

- Move the mouse pointer to the left of the first paragraph to be selected until the mouse pointer changes to a right-pointing block arrow (Figure 1–26).

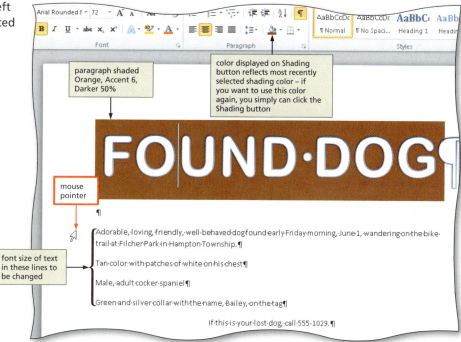

Figure 1–26

2

- Drag downward to select all lines that will be formatted (Figure 1–27).

Figure 1–27

Other Ways

1. With insertion point at beginning of desired line, press SHIFT+DOWN ARROW repeatedly until all lines are selected

To Change the Font Size of Selected Text

The characters between the headline and the signature line in the flyer currently are 11 point. To make them easier to read from a distance, this flyer uses 22 point for these characters. The steps on the next page change the font size of the selected text.

1 With the text selected, click the Font Size box arrow (Home tab | Font group) to display the Font Size gallery.

2 Click 22 in the Font Size gallery to increase the font size of the selected text.

3 Click anywhere in the document window to remove the selection from the text.

4 If necessary, scroll so that you can see all the text on the screen (Figure 1–28).

BTW

Formatting Marks
With some fonts, formatting marks do not display properly on the screen. For example, the raised dot that signifies a blank space between words may be displayed behind a character instead of in the blank space, causing the characters to look incorrect.

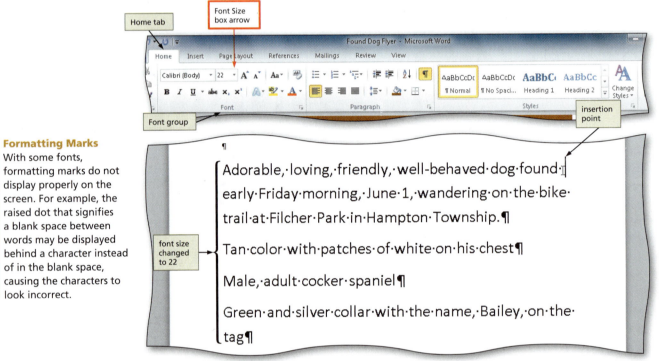

Figure 1–28

To Bullet a List of Paragraphs

The next step is to format as a bulleted list the three paragraphs of identifying information that are above the signature line in the flyer. A **bulleted list** is a series of paragraphs, each beginning with a bullet character.

To format a list of paragraphs with bullets, you first must select all the lines in the paragraphs. The following steps bullet a list of paragraphs.

1

- Move the mouse pointer to the left of the first paragraph to be selected until the mouse pointer changes to a right-pointing block arrow.

- Drag downward until all paragraphs that will be formatted with a bullet character are selected (Figure 1–29).

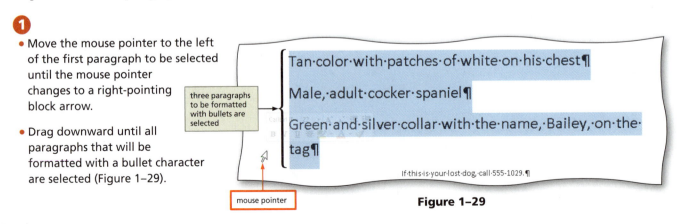

Figure 1–29

2

- Click the Bullets button (Home tab | Paragraph group) to place a bullet character at the beginning of each selected paragraph (Figure 1–30).

Q&A How do I remove bullets from a list or paragraph?

Select the list or paragraph and then click the Bullets button again.

Q&A What if I accidentally click the Bullets button arrow?

Press the ESCAPE key to remove the Bullets gallery from the screen and then repeat Step 2.

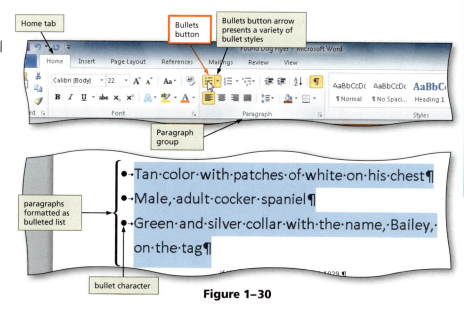

Figure 1–30

Other Ways

1. Right-click selected paragraphs, point to Bullets on shortcut menu, click desired bullet style

To Undo and Redo an Action

Word provides a means of canceling your recent command(s) or action(s). For example, if you format text incorrectly, you can undo the format and try it again. When you point to the Undo button, Word displays the action you can undo as part of a ScreenTip.

If, after you undo an action, you decide you did not want to perform the undo, you can redo the undone action. Word does not allow you to undo or redo some actions, such as saving or printing a document. The next steps undo the bullet format just applied and then redo the bullet format.

1

- Click the Undo button on the Quick Access Toolbar to reverse your most recent action (in this case, remove the bullets from the paragraphs) (Figure 1–31).

2

- Click the Redo button on the Quick Access Toolbar to reverse your most recent undo (in this case, place a bullet character on the paragraphs again) (shown in Figure 1–30).

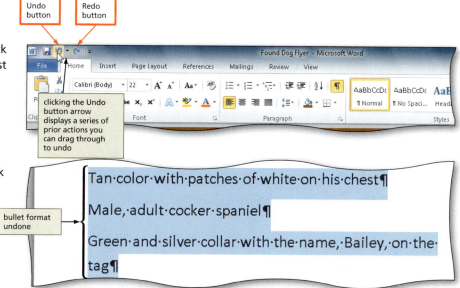

Figure 1–31

Other Ways

1. Press CTRL+Z to undo; press CTRL+Y to redo

To Italicize Text

The next step is to italicize the dog's name, Bailey, in the flyer to further emphasize it. **Italicized** text has a slanted appearance. As with a single paragraph, if you want to format a single word, you do not need to select it. Simply position the insertion point somewhere in the word and apply the desired format. The following step formats a word in italics.

- Click somewhere in the word to be italicized (Bailey, in this case) to position the insertion point in the word to be formatted.

- Click the Italic button (Home tab | Font group) to italicize the word containing the insertion point (Figure 1–32).

Q&A   How would I remove an italic format?

You would click the Italic button a second time, or you immediately could click the Undo button on the Quick Access Toolbar or press CTRL+Z.

Q&A   How can I tell what formatting has been applied to text?

The selected buttons and boxes on the Home tab show formatting characteristics of the location of the insertion point. With the insertion point in the word, Bailey, the Home tab shows these formats: 22-point Calibri italic font, bulleted paragraph.

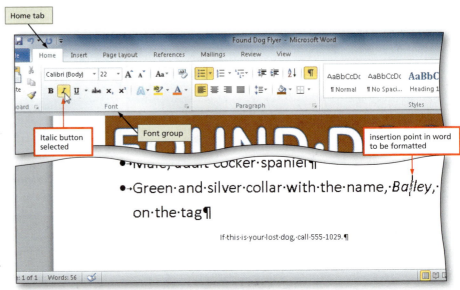

Figure 1–32

Other Ways		
1. Click Italic button on Mini toolbar	(Font dialog box), click Italic in Font style list, click OK button	Font group), click Font tab (Font dialog box), click Italic in Font style list, click OK button
2. Right-click selected text, click Font on shortcut menu, click Font tab	3. Click Font Dialog Box Launcher (Home tab |	4. Press CTRL+I

Plan Ahead

Use color.
When choosing color, associate the meaning of color to your message:

- Red expresses danger, power, or energy, and often is associated with sports or physical exertion.
- Brown represents simplicity, honesty, and dependability.
- Orange denotes success, victory, creativity, and enthusiasm.
- Yellow suggests sunshine, happiness, hope, liveliness, and intelligence.
- Green symbolizes growth, healthiness, harmony, blooming, and healing, and often is associated with safety or money.
- Blue indicates integrity, trust, importance, confidence, and stability.
- Purple represents wealth, power, comfort, extravagance, magic, mystery, and spirituality.
- White stands for purity, goodness, cleanliness, precision, and perfection.
- Black suggests authority, strength, elegance, power, and prestige.
- Gray conveys neutrality and thus often is found in backgrounds and other effects.

BTW

Q&As
For a complete list of the Q&As found in many of the step-by-step sequences in this book, visit the Word 2010 Q&A Web page (scsite.com/wd2010/qa).

To Color Text

To emphasize the dog's name even more, its color is changed to a shade of blue. The following steps change the color of the word, Bailey.

- With the insertion point in the word to format, click the Font Color button arrow (Home tab | Font group) to display the Font Color gallery (Figure 1–33).

Q&A What if I click the Font Color button by mistake?

Click the Font Color button arrow and then proceed with Step 2.

- Point to Blue, Accent 1, Darker 25% (fifth color in the fifth row) to display a live preview of the selected font color.

🔍 Experiment

- Point to various colors in the Font Color gallery and watch the color of the current word change.

Figure 1–33

3

- Click Blue, Accent 1, Darker 25% to change the color of the text (Figure 1–34).

Q&A How would I change the text color back to black?

You would position the insertion point in the word or select the text, click the Font Color button arrow (Home tab | Font group) again, and then click Automatic in the Font Color gallery.

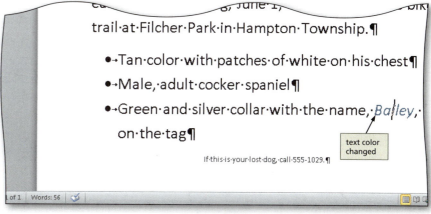

Figure 1–34

Other Ways

1. Click Font Color button arrow on Mini toolbar, click desired color

2. Right-click selected text, click Font on shortcut menu, click Font tab

   (Font dialog box), click Font color box arrow, click desired color, click OK button

3. Click Font Dialog Box Launcher (Home tab |

   Font group), click Font tab (Font dialog box), click Font color box arrow, click desired color, click OK button

To Use the Mini Toolbar to Format Text

Recall from the Office 2010 and Windows 7 chapter at the beginning of this book that the Mini toolbar, which automatically appears based on certain tasks you perform, contains commands related to changing the appearance of text in a document. All commands on the Mini toolbar also exist on the Ribbon.

When the Mini toolbar appears, it initially is transparent. If you do not use the transparent Mini toolbar, it disappears from the screen. The following steps use the Mini toolbar to change the color and font size of text in the signature line of the flyer.

- Move the mouse pointer to the left of the line to be selected (in this case, the signature line) until the mouse pointer changes to a right-pointing block arrow and then click the mouse to select the line (Figure 1–35).

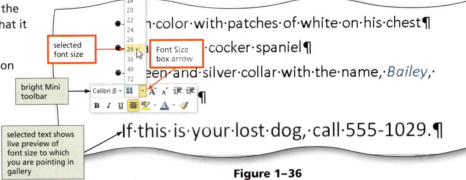

Figure 1–35

- Move the mouse pointer into the transparent Mini toolbar, so that it changes to a bright toolbar.

- Click the Font Size box arrow on the Mini toolbar to display the Font Size gallery and then point to 28 in the Font Size gallery to display a live preview of the selected font size (Figure 1–36).

Figure 1–36

- Click 28 in the Font Size gallery to increase the font size of the selected text.

- With the text still selected and the Mini toolbar still displayed, click the Font Color button arrow on the Mini toolbar to display the Font Color gallery and then point to Purple, Accent 4, Darker 50% (eighth color in the sixth row) to display a live preview of the selected font color (Figure 1–37).

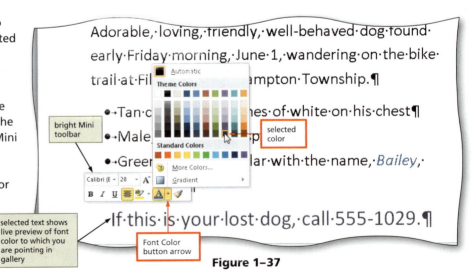

Figure 1–37

- Click Purple, Accent 4, Darker 50% to change the color of the text.

- Click anywhere in the document window to remove the selection from the text.

To Select a Group of Words

To emphasize the contact information (call 555-1029), these words are underlined in the flyer. To format a group of words, you first must select them. The following steps select a group of words.

- Position the mouse pointer immediately to the left of the first character of the text to be selected, in this case, the c in call (Figure 1–38).

Q&A

Why did the shape of the mouse pointer change?

The mouse pointer's shape is an I-beam when positioned in unselected text in the document window.

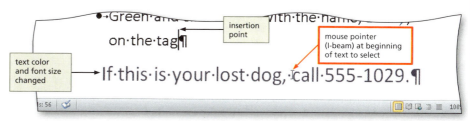

Figure 1–38

- Drag the mouse pointer through the last character of the text to be selected, in this case, the 9 in the phone number (Figure 1–39).

Q&A

Why did the mouse pointer shape change again?

When the mouse pointer is positioned in selected text, its shape is a left-pointing block arrow.

Figure 1–39

Other Ways

1. With insertion point at beginning of first word in group, press

   CTRL+SHIFT+RIGHT ARROW repeatedly until all words are selected

To Underline Text

Underlines are used to emphasize or draw attention to specific text. **Underlined** text prints with an underscore (_) below each character. In the flyer, the contact information, call 555-1029, in the signature line is emphasized with an underline. The following step formats selected text with an underline.

- With the text selected, click the Underline button (Home tab | Font group) to underline the selected text (Figure 1–40).

Q&A

How would I remove an underline?

You would click the Underline button a second time, or you immediately could click the Undo button on the Quick Access Toolbar.

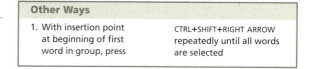

Figure 1–40

Other Ways

1. Right-click text, click Font on shortcut menu, click Font tab (Font dialog box), click Underline style box arrow, click desired

   underline style, click OK button

2. Click Font Dialog Box Launcher (Home tab | Font group), click Font tab

   (Font dialog box), click Underline style box arrow, click desired underline style, click OK button

3. Press CTRL+U

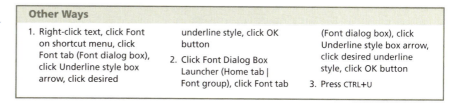

To Bold Text

Bold characters appear somewhat thicker and darker than those that are not bold. To further emphasize the signature line, it is bold in the flyer. To format the line, as you have learned previously, you select the line first. The following steps format the signature line bold.

1

- Move the mouse pointer to the left of the line to be selected (in this case, the signature line) until the mouse pointer changes to a right-pointing block arrow and then click the mouse to select the text to be formatted.

- With the text selected, click the Bold button (Home tab | Font group) to bold the selected text (Figure 1–41).

Q&A

How would I remove a bold format?

You would click the Bold button a second time, or you immediately could click the Undo button on the Quick Access Toolbar.

2

- Click anywhere in the document window to remove the selection from the screen.

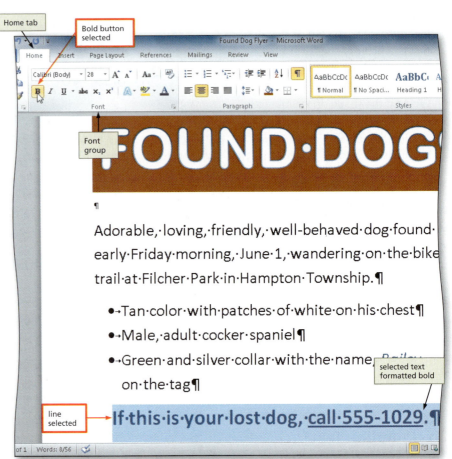

Figure 1–41

Other Ways

1. Click Bold button on Mini toolbar

2. Right-click selected text, click Font on shortcut menu, click Font tab (Font dialog box), click Bold in Font style list, click OK button

3. Click Font Dialog Box Launcher (Home tab | Font group), click Font tab (Font dialog box), click Bold in Font style list, click OK button

4. Press CTRL+B

To Change Theme Colors

A **color scheme** in Word is a document theme that identifies 12 complementary colors for text, background, accents, and links in a document. With more than 20 predefined color schemes, Word provides a simple way to select colors that work well together.

In the flyer, you want all the colors to convey honesty, dependability, and healing, that is, shades of browns and greens. In Word, the Aspect color scheme uses these colors. Thus, you will change the color scheme from the default, Office, to Aspect. The next steps change theme colors.

1

• Click the Change Styles button (Home tab | Styles group) to display the Change Styles menu.

• Point to Colors on the Change Styles menu to display the Colors gallery (Figure 1–42).

🔑 **Experiment**

• Point to various color schemes in the Colors gallery and watch the colors change in the document window.

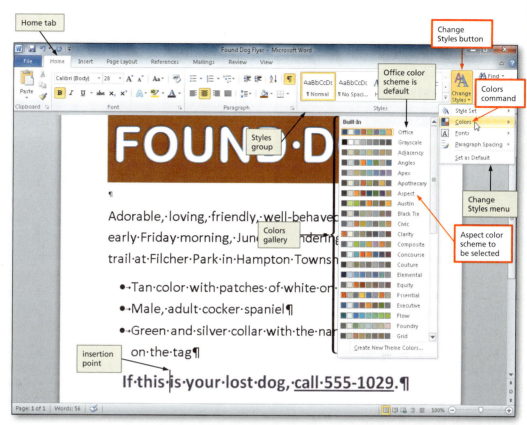

Figure 1–42

2

• Click Aspect in the Colors gallery to change the document theme colors (Figure 1–43).

Q&A

What if I want to return to the original color scheme?

You would click the Change Styles button again, click Colors on the Change Styles menu, and then click Office in the Colors gallery.

Figure 1–43

Other Ways

1. Click Theme Colors button (Page Layout tab | Themes group), select desired color scheme

Selecting Text

In many of the previous steps, you have selected text. Table 1–3 summarizes the techniques used to select various items.

Table 1–3 Techniques for Selecting Text		
Item to Select	**Mouse**	**Keyboard (where applicable)**
Block of text	Click at beginning of selection, scroll to end of selection, position mouse pointer at end of selection, hold down SHIFT key and then click; or drag through the text.	
Character(s)	Drag through character(s).	SHIFT+RIGHT ARROW or SHIFT+LEFT ARROW
Document	Move mouse to left of text until mouse pointer changes to a right-pointing block arrow and then triple-click.	CTRL+A
Graphic	Click the graphic.	
Line	Move mouse to left of line until mouse pointer changes to a right-pointing block arrow and then click.	HOME, then SHIFT+END or END, then SHIFT+HOME
Lines	Move mouse to left of first line until mouse pointer changes to a right-pointing block arrow and then drag up or down.	HOME, then SHIFT+DOWN ARROW or END, then SHIFT+UP AROW
Paragraph	Triple-click paragraph; or move mouse to left of paragraph until mouse pointer changes to a right-pointing block arrow and then double-click.	CTRL+SHIFT+DOWN ARROW or CTRL+SHIFT+UP ARROW
Paragraphs	Move mouse to left of paragraph until mouse pointer changes to a right-pointing block arrow, double-click, and then drag up or down.	CTRL+SHIFT+DOWN ARROW or CTRL+SHIFT+UP ARROW repeatedly
Sentence	Press and hold down CTRL key and then click sentence.	
Word	Double-click the word.	CTRL+SHIFT+RIGHT ARROW or CTRL+SHIFT+LEFT ARROW
Words	Drag through words.	CTRL+SHIFT+RIGHT ARROW or CTRL+SHIFT+LEFT ARROW repeatedly

To Save an Existing Document with the Same File Name

You have made several modifications to the document since you last saved it. Thus, you should save it again. The following step saves the document again. For an example of the step listed below, refer to the Office 2010 and Windows 7 chapter at the beginning of this book.

 Click the Save button on the Quick Access Toolbar to overwrite the previously saved file.

Break Point: If you wish to take a break, this is a good place to do so. You can quit Word now (refer to page WD 44 for instructions). To resume at a later time, start Word (refer to pages WD 4 and WD 5 for instructions), open the file called Found Dog Flyer (refer to page WD 45 for instructions), and continue following the steps from this location forward.

Inserting and Formatting Pictures in a Word Document

With the text formatted in the flyer, the next step is to insert digital pictures in the flyer and format the pictures. Flyers usually contain graphical images, such as a picture, to attract the attention of passersby. In the following pages, you will perform these tasks:

1. Insert the first digital picture into the flyer and then reduce its size.

2. Insert the second digital picture into the flyer and then reduce its size.

3. Change the look of the first picture and then the second picture.

Find the appropriate graphical image.

Plan
Ahead

To use a graphical image, also called a graphic, in a Word document, the image must be stored digitally in a file. Files containing graphical images are available from a variety of sources:

- Word includes a collection of predefined graphical images that you can insert in a document.

- Microsoft has free digital images on the Web for use in a document. Other Web sites also have images available, some of which are free, while others require a fee.

- You can take a picture with a digital camera or camera phone and **download** it, which is the process of copying the digital picture from the camera or phone to your computer.

- With a scanner, you can convert a printed picture, drawing, or diagram to a digital file.

   If you receive a picture from a source other than yourself, do not use the file until you are certain it does not contain a virus. A **virus** is a computer program that can damage files and programs on your computer. Use an antivirus program to verify that any files you use are virus free.

Establish where to position and how to format the graphical image.

Plan
Ahead

The content, size, shape, position, and format of a graphic should capture the interest of passersby, enticing them to stop and read the flyer. Often, the graphic is the center of attraction and visually the largest element on a flyer. If you use colors in the graphical image, be sure they are part of the document's color scheme.

To Insert a Picture

The next step in creating the flyer is to insert one of the digital pictures of the dog so that it is centered on the blank line below the headline. The picture, which was taken with a camera phone, is available on the Data Files for Students. See the inside back cover of this book for instructions on downloading the Data Files for Students, or contact your instructor for information about accessing the required files.

The following steps insert a centered picture, which, in this example, is located in the Chapter 01 folder in the Word folder in the Data Files for Students folder on a USB flash drive.

- Position the insertion point on the blank line below the headline, which is the location where you want to insert the picture.

- Click the Center button (Home tab | Paragraph group) to center the paragraph that will contain the picture.

- Click Insert on the Ribbon to display the Insert tab (Figure 1–44).

Figure 1–44

- With your USB flash drive connected to one of the computer's USB ports, click the Insert Picture from File button (Insert tab | Illustrations group) (shown in Figure 1-44) to display the Insert Picture dialog box (shown in Figure 1-45 on the next page).

3

- Navigate to the picture location (in this case, the Chapter 01 folder in the Word folder in the Data Files for Students folder on a USB flash drive). For a detailed example of this procedure, refer to Steps 3a – 3c in the To Save a File in a Folder section in the Office 2010 and Windows 7 chapter at the beginning of this book.

- Click Dog Picture 1 to select the file (Figure 1–45).

Q&A What if the picture is not on a USB flash drive?

Use the same process, but select the storage location containing the picture.

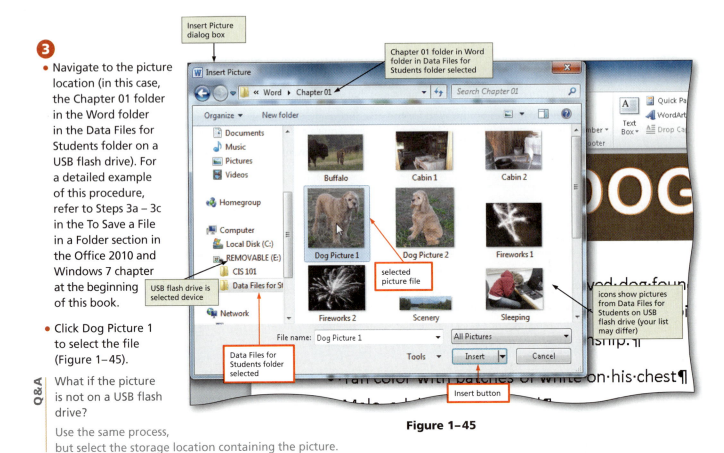

Figure 1–45

4

- Click the Insert button (Insert Picture dialog box) to insert the picture at the location of the insertion point in the document (Figure 1–46).

Q&A What are the symbols around the picture?

A selected graphic appears surrounded by a **selection rectangle**, which has small squares and circles, called **sizing handles**, at each corner and middle location.

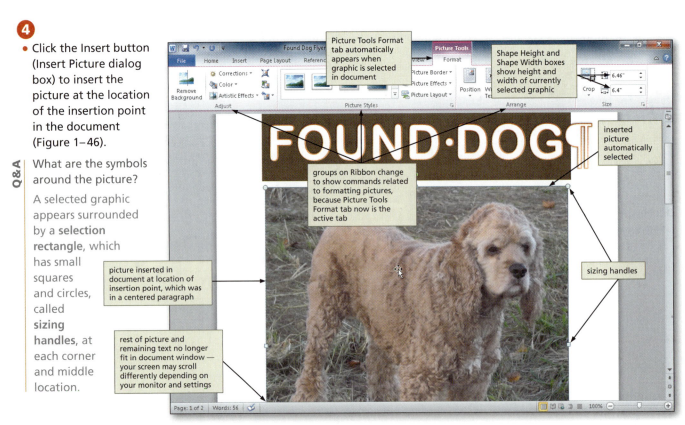

Figure 1–46

To Zoom the Document

The next step is to reduce the size of the picture so that both pictures will fit side-by-side on the same line. With the current picture size, the flyer now has expanded to two pages. The final flyer, however, should fit on a single page. In Word, you can change the zoom so that you can see the entire document (that is, both pages) on the screen at once. Seeing the entire document at once helps you determine the appropriate size for the picture. The following step zooms the document.

1

Experiment

- Repeatedly click the Zoom Out and Zoom In buttons on the status bar and watch the size of the document change in the document window.

- Click the Zoom Out or Zoom In button as many times as necessary until the Zoom button on the status bar displays 50% on its face (Figure 1–47).

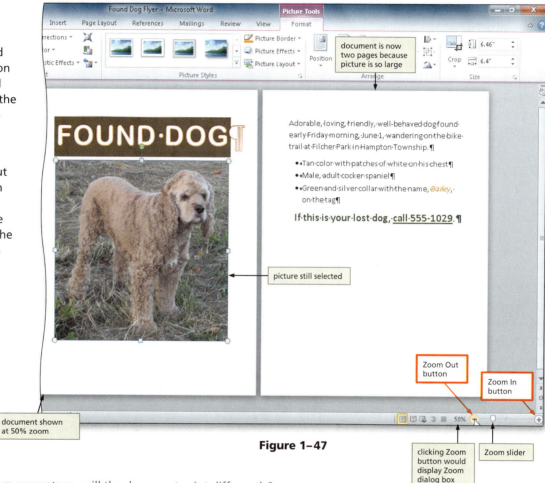

Figure 1–47

Q&A If I change the zoom percentage, will the document print differently?

Changing the zoom has no effect on the printed document.

Q&A Are there predefined zoom options?

Yes. Through the View tab | Zoom group or the Zoom dialog box, you can zoom to one page, two pages, many pages, page width, text width, and a variety of set percentages. Page width zoom places the edges of the page at the edges of the Word window, whereas Text width zoom places the contents of the page at the edges of the Word window.

Other Ways	
1. Drag Zoom slider on status bar	3. Click Zoom button (View tab | Zoom group), select desired zoom percent or type (Zoom dialog box), click OK button
2. Click Zoom button on status bar, select desired zoom percent or type (Zoom dialog box), click OK button	

To Resize a Graphic

The next step is to resize the picture so that both pictures will fit side-by-side on the same line below the headline. **Resizing** includes both enlarging and reducing the size of a graphic. In this flyer, you will reduce the size of the picture. With the entire document displayed in the document window, you will be able to see how the resized graphic will look on the entire page. The following steps resize a selected graphic.

1

- With the graphic still selected, point to the upper-right corner sizing handle on the picture so that the mouse pointer shape changes to a two-headed arrow (Figure 1–48).

What if my graphic (picture) is not selected?

To select a graphic, click it.

Figure 1–48

2

- Drag the sizing handle diagonally inward until the crosshair mouse pointer is positioned approximately as shown in Figure 1–49.

3

- Release the mouse button to resize the graphic, which in this case should have a height of about 2.74" and a width of about 2.73".

How can I see the height and width measurements?

Look in the Size group on the Picture Tools Format tab to see the height and width measurements of the currently selected graphic (shown in Figure 1–46 on page WD 32).

What if the graphic is the wrong size?

Repeat Steps 1, 2, and 3; or enter the desired height and width values in the Shape Height and Shape Width boxes (Picture Tools Format tab | Size group).

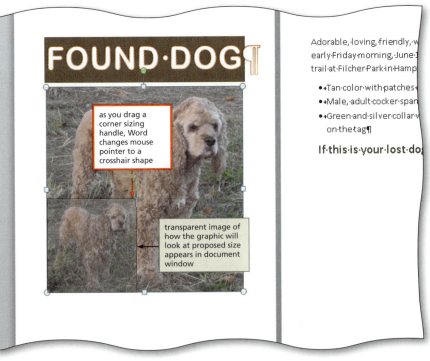

Figure 1–49

4

• Click to the right of the graphic to deselect it (Figure 1–50).

Q&A What happened to the Picture Tools Format tab?

When you click outside of a graphic or press a key to scroll through a document, Word deselects the graphic and removes the Picture Tools Format tab from the screen.

Q&A What if I want to return a graphic to its original size and start again?

With the graphic selected, click the Size Dialog Box Launcher (Picture Tools Format tab | Size group), click the Size tab (Layout dialog box), click the Reset button, and then click the OK button.

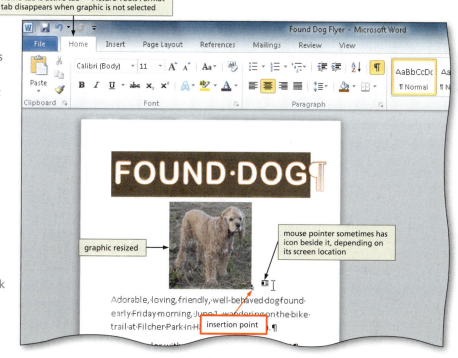

Figure 1–50

Other Ways		
1. Enter height and width of graphic in Shape Height and Shape Width boxes (Picture Tools Format tab | Size group)	2. Click Size Dialog Box Launcher (Picture Tools Format tab | Size group), click Size tab (Layout dialog box), enter desired	height and width values in boxes, click OK button

To Insert Another Picture

The next step is to insert the other digital picture of the dog immediately to the right of the current picture. This second picture also is available on the Data Files for Students. See the inside back cover of this book for instructions on downloading the Data Files for Students, or contact your instructor for information about accessing the required files.

The following steps insert another picture immediately to the right of the current picture.

1 With the insertion point positioned as shown in Figure 1–50, click Insert on the Ribbon to display the Insert tab.

2 With your USB flash drive connected to one of the computer's USB ports, click the Insert Picture from File button (Insert tab | Illustrations group) to display the Insert Picture dialog box.

3 If necessary, navigate to the picture location (in this case, the Word folder in the CIS 101 folder [or your class folder] on the USB flash drive). For a detailed example of this procedure, refer to Steps 3a – 3c in the To Save a File in a Folder section in the Office 2010 and Windows 7 chapter at the beginning of this book.

4 Click Dog Picture 2 to select the file.

5 Click the Insert button (Insert Picture dialog box) to insert the picture at the location of the insertion point in the document.

BTW

Word Help
At any time while using Word, you can find answers to questions and display information about various topics through Word Help. Used properly, this form of assistance can increase your productivity and reduce your frustrations by minimizing the time you spend learning how to use Word. For instruction about Word Help and exercises that will help you gain confidence in using it, read the Office 2010 and Windows 7 chapter at the beginning of this book.

To Resize a Graphic by Entering Exact Measurements

The next step is to resize the second picture so that it is the exact same size as the first picture. The height and width measurements of the first graphic are approximately 2.74" and 2.73", respectively. When a graphic is selected, its height and width measurements show in the Size group of the Picture Tools Format tab. The following steps resize a selected graphic by entering its desired exact measurements.

- With the second graphic still selected, click the Shape Height box (Picture Tools Format tab | Size group) to select the contents in the box and then type 2.74 as the height.

Q&A What if the Picture Tools Format tab no longer is displayed on my Ribbon?

Double-click the picture to display the Picture Tools Format tab.

Q&A What if the contents of the Shape Height box are not selected?

Triple-click the Shape Height box.

2

- Click the Shape Width box to select the contents in the box, type 2.73 as the width, and then click the picture to apply the settings.

- If necessary, scroll up to display the entire document in the window (Figure 1–51).

Q&A Why did my measurements change slightly?

Depending on relative measurements, the height and width values entered may change slightly.

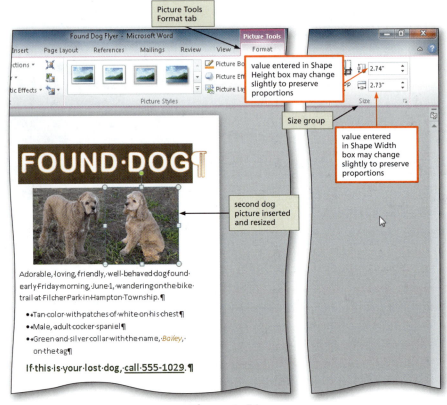

Figure 1–51

Other Ways
1. Right-click picture, enter shape height and width values in boxes on shortcut menu	2. Right-click picture, click Size and Position on shortcut menu, click Size tab (Layout dialog box), enter shape height and width values in boxes, click OK button

To Zoom the Document

You are finished resizing the graphics and no longer need to view the entire page in the document window. Thus, the following step changes the zoom back to 100 percent.

1 Click the Zoom In button on the status bar as many times as necessary until the Zoom button displays 100% on its face (shown in Figure 1–52).

To Apply a Picture Style

A **style** is a named group of formatting characteristics. Word provides more than 25 picture styles that enable you easily to change a picture's look to a more visually appealing style, including a variety of shapes, angles, borders, and reflections. The flyer in this chapter uses a style that applies soft edges to the picture. The following steps apply a picture style to a picture.

1

• Click the leftmost dog picture to select it (Figure 1–52).

Q&A

What is the green circle attached to the selected graphic?

It is called a rotate handle. When you drag a graphic's rotate handle, the graphic moves in either a clockwise or counterclockwise direction.

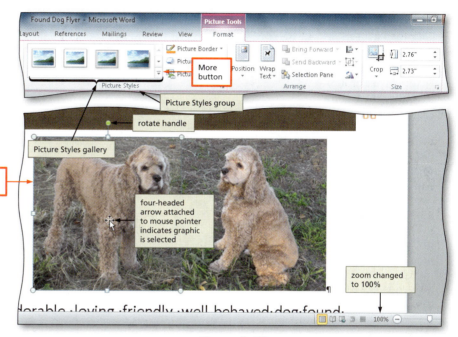

Figure 1–52

2

• Click the More button in the Picture Styles gallery (Picture Tools Format tab | Picture Styles group) (shown in Figure 1–52) to expand the gallery.

• Point to Soft Edge Rectangle in the Picture Styles gallery to display a live preview of that style applied to the picture in the document (Figure 1–53).

🔎 **Experiment**

• Point to various picture styles in the Picture Styles gallery and watch the style of the picture change in the document window.

3

• Click Soft Edge Rectangle in the Picture Styles gallery to apply the style to the selected picture.

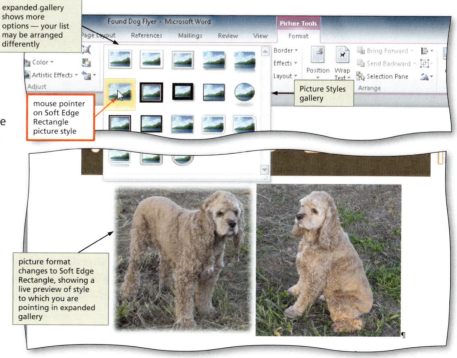

Figure 1–53

To Apply Picture Effects

Word provides a variety of picture effects so that you can further customize a picture. Effects include shadows, reflections, glow, soft edges, bevel, and 3-D rotation. The difference between the effects and the styles is that each effect has several options, providing you with more control over the exact look of the image.

In this flyer, the leftmost dog picture has a slight tan glow effect and is turned inward toward the center of the page. The following steps apply picture effects to the selected picture.

1

- Click the Picture Effects button (Picture Tools Format tab | Picture Styles group) to display the Picture Effects menu.

- Point to Glow on the Picture Effects menu to display the Glow gallery.

- Point to Tan, 5 pt glow, Accent color 6 in the Glow Variations area (rightmost glow in first row) to display a live preview of the selected glow effect applied to the picture in the document window (Figure 1–54).

Figure 1–54

Experiment

- Point to various glow effects in the Glow gallery and watch the picture change in the document window.

2

- Click Tan, 5 pt glow, Accent color 6 in the Glow gallery to apply the selected picture effect.

Q&A What if I wanted to discard formatting applied to a picture?

You would click the Reset Picture button (Picture Tools Format tab | Adjust group). To reset formatting and size, you would click the Reset Picture button arrow (Picture Tools Format tab | Adjust group) and then click Reset Picture & Size on the Reset Picture menu.

- Click the Picture Effects button (Picture Tools Format tab | Picture Styles group) to display the Picture Effects menu again.

- Point to 3-D Rotation on the Picture Effects menu to display the 3-D Rotation gallery.

- Point to Off Axis 1 Right in the Parallel area (second rotation in second row) to display a live preview of the selected 3-D effect applied to the picture in the document window (Figure 1–55).

🔎 **Experiment**

- Point to various 3-D rotation effects in the 3-D Rotation gallery and watch the picture change in the document window.

- Click Off Axis 1 Right in the 3-D Rotation gallery to apply the selected picture effect.

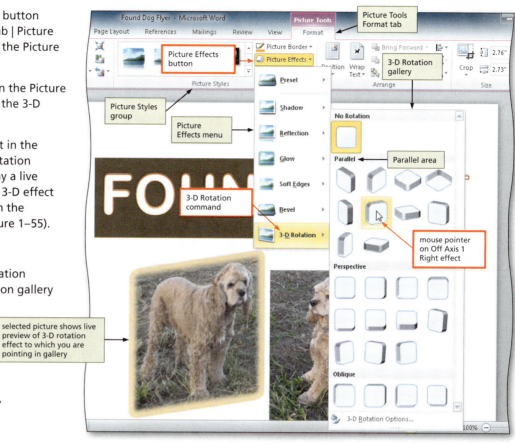

Figure 1–55

Other Ways
1. Right-click picture, click Format Picture on shortcut menu, select desired options (Format Picture   dialog box), click Close button   2. Click Format Shape Dialog Box Launcher (Picture   Tools Format tab | Picture Styles group), select desired options (Format Picture dialog box), click Close button

To Apply a Picture Style and Effects to Another Picture

In this flyer, the rightmost dog picture also uses the soft edge picture style, has a slight tan glow effect, and is turned inward toward the center of the page. The following steps apply the picture style and picture effects to the picture.

1 Click the rightmost dog picture to select it.

2 Click the More button in the Picture Styles gallery (Picture Tools Format tab | Picture Styles group) to expand the gallery and then click Soft Edge Rectangle in the Picture Styles gallery to apply the selected style to the picture.

3 Click the Picture Effects button (Picture Tools Format tab | Picture Styles group) to display the Picture Effects menu and then point to Glow on the Picture Effects menu to display the Glow gallery.

4 Click Tan, 5 pt glow, Accent color 6 (rightmost glow in first row) in the Glow gallery to apply the picture effect to the picture.

5 Click the Picture Effects button (Picture Tools Format tab | Picture Styles group) to display the Picture Effects menu again and then point to 3-D Rotation on the Picture Effects menu to display the 3-D Rotation gallery.

6 Click Off Axis 2 Left (rightmost rotation in second row) in the Parallel area in the 3-D Rotation gallery to apply the picture effect to the selected picture.

7 Click to the right of the picture to deselect it (Figure 1–56).

BTW

BTWs
For a complete list of the BTWs found in the margins of this book, visit the Word 2010 BTW Web page (scsite .com/wd2010/btw).

picture style and picture effects applied to picture

Figure 1–56

Enhancing the Page

BTW

Centering Page Contents Vertically
You can center page contents vertically between the top and bottom margins. To do this, click the Page Setup Dialog Box Launcher (Page Layout tab | Page Setup group), click the Layout tab (Page Setup dialog box), click the Vertical alignment box arrow, click Center in the list, and then click the OK button.

With the text and graphics entered and formatted, the next step is to look at the page as a whole and determine if it looks finished in its current state. As you review the page, answer these questions:

- Does it need a page border to frame its contents, or would a page border make it look too busy?
- Is the spacing between paragraphs and graphics on the page adequate? Do any sections of text or graphics look as if they are positioned too closely to the items above or below them?

You determine that a graphical, color-coordinated border would enhance the flyer. You also notice that the flyer would look more proportionate if it had a little more space above and below the pictures. The following pages make these enhancements to the flyer.

To View One Page

Earlier in this chapter, you changed the zoom using the Zoom Out and Zoom In buttons on the status bar. If you want to display an entire page as large as possible in the document window, Word can compute the correct zoom percentage for you. The next steps display a single page in its entirety in the document window as large as possible.

- Click View on the Ribbon to display the View tab.

- Click the One Page button (View tab | Zoom group) to display the entire page in the document window as large as possible (Figure 1–57).

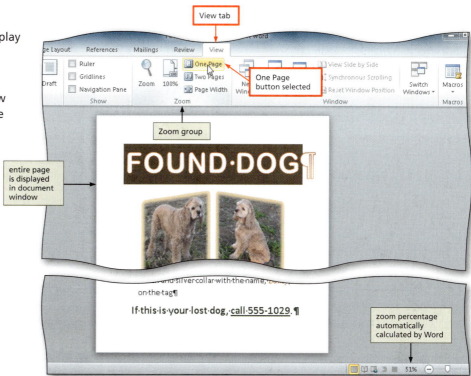

Figure 1–57

To Add a Page Border

In Word, you can add a border around the perimeter of an entire page. The flyer in this chapter has a light green dashed border. The following steps add a page border.

1

- Click Page Layout on the Ribbon to display the Page Layout tab.

- Click the Page Borders button (Page Layout tab | Page Background group) to display the Borders and Shading dialog box (Figure 1–58).

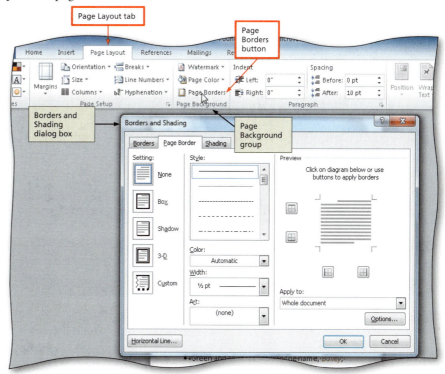

Figure 1–58

2

- Scroll through the Style list (Borders and Shading dialog box) and select the style shown in Figure 1–59.

- Click the Color box arrow to display a Color palette (Figure 1–59).

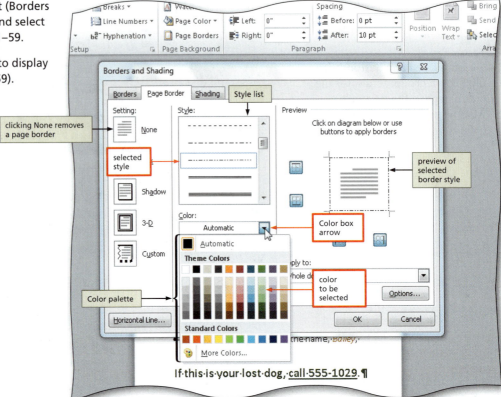

Figure 1–59

3

- Click Dark Green, Accent 4, Lighter 60% (eighth color in third row) in the Color palette to select the color for the page border.

- Click the Width box arrow and then click 3 pt to select the thickness of the page border (Figure 1–60).

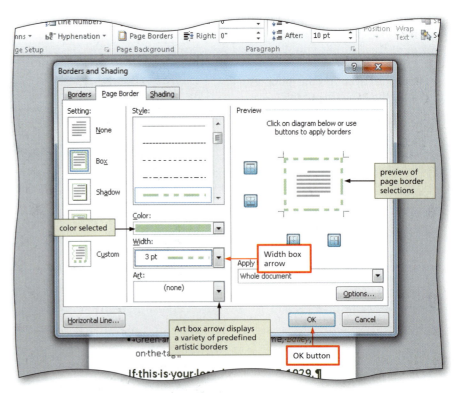

Figure 1–60

4

- Click the OK button to add the border to the page (Figure 1–61).

Q&A

What if I wanted to remove the border?

You would click None in the Setting list in the Borders and Shading dialog box.

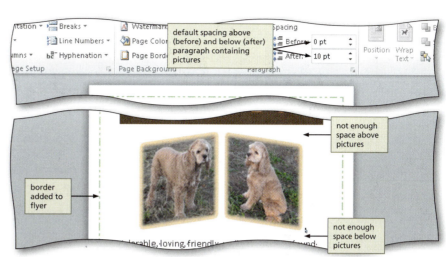

Figure 1–61

To Change Spacing before and after a Paragraph

The default spacing above (before) a paragraph in Word is 0 points and below (after) is 10 points. In the flyer, you want to increase the spacing above and below the paragraph containing the pictures. The following steps change the spacing above and below a paragraph.

1

- Position the insertion point in the paragraph to be adjusted, in this case, the paragraph containing the pictures.

- Click the Spacing Before box up arrow (Page Layout tab | Paragraph group) as many times as necessary until 24 pt is displayed in the Spacing Before box to increase the space above the current paragraph.

2

- Click the Spacing After box up arrow (Page Layout tab | Paragraph group) so that 12 pt is displayed in the Spacing After box to increase the space below the current paragraph (Figure 1–62).

- If the text flows to two pages, reduce the spacing above and below paragraphs as necessary.

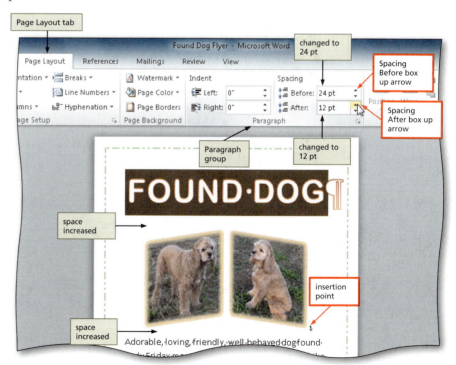

Figure 1–62

Other Ways

1. Right-click paragraph, click Paragraph on shortcut menu, click Indents and Spacing tab (Paragraph dialog box), enter spacing before and after values, click OK button

2. Click Paragraph Dialog Box Launcher (Home tab or Page Layout tab | Paragraph group), click Indents and Spacing tab (Paragraph dialog box), enter spacing before and after values, click OK button

To Save an Existing Document with the Same File Name

You have made several modifications to the document since you last saved it. Thus, you should save it again. The following step saves the document again. For an example of the step listed below, refer to the Office 2010 and Windows 7 chapter at the beginning of this book.

1 Click the Save button on the Quick Access Toolbar to overwrite the previously saved file.

To Quit Word

Although you still need to make some edits to this document, you want to quit Word and resume working on the project at a later time. Thus, the following steps quit Word. For a detailed example of the procedure summarized below, refer to the Office 2010 and Windows 7 chapter at the beginning of this book.

1 If you have one Word document open, click the Close button on the right side of the title bar to close the document and quit Word; or if you have multiple Word documents open, click File on the Ribbon to open the Backstage view and then click Exit in the Backstage view to close all open documents and quit Word.

2 If a Microsoft Word dialog box appears, click the Save button to save any changes made to the document since the last save.

BTW

Certification
The Microsoft Office Specialist (MOS) program provides an opportunity for you to obtain a valuable industry credential — proof that you have the Word 2010 skills required by employers. For more information, visit the Word 2010 Certification Web page (scsite.com/wd2010/cert).

Break Point: If you wish to take a break, this is a good place to do so. To resume at a later time, continue following the steps from this location forward.

Correcting Errors and Revising a Document

After creating a document, you may need to change it. For example, the document may contain an error, or new circumstances may require you to add text to the document.

Types of Changes Made to Documents

The types of changes made to documents normally fall into one of the three following categories: additions, deletions, or modifications.

Additions Additional words, sentences, or paragraphs may be required in a document. Additions occur when you omit text from a document and want to insert it later. For example, you may want to add your e-mail address to the flyer.

Deletions Sometimes, text in a document is incorrect or is no longer needed. For example, you may discover the dog's collar is just green. In this case, you would delete the words, and silver, from the flyer.

Modifications If an error is made in a document or changes take place that affect the document, you might have to revise a word(s) in the text. For example, the dog may have been found in Hampton Village instead of Hampton Township.

To Start Word

Once you have created and saved a document, you may need to retrieve it from your storage medium. For example, you might want to revise the document or print it. The following steps, which assume Windows 7 is running, start Word so that you can open and modify the flyer. You may need to ask your instructor how to start Word for your computer. For a detailed example of the procedure summarized below, refer to the Office 2010 and Windows 7 chapter at the beginning of this book.

1 Click the Start button on the Windows 7 taskbar to display the Start menu.

2 Type **Microsoft Word** as the search text in the 'Search programs and files' text box and watch the search results appear on the Start menu.

3 Click Microsoft Word 2010 in the search results on the Start menu to start Word and display a new blank document in the Word window.

4 If the Word window is not maximized, click the Maximize button next to the Close button on its title bar to maximize the window.

To Open a Document from Word

Earlier in this chapter, you saved your project on a USB flash drive using the file name, Found Dog Flyer. The following steps open the Found Dog Flyer file from the Word folder in the CIS 101 folder on the USB flash drive. For a detailed example of the procedure summarized below, refer to the Office 2010 and Windows 7 chapter at the beginning of this book.

1 With your USB flash drive connected to one of the computer's USB ports, click File on the Ribbon to open the Backstage view.

2 Click Open in the Backstage view to display the Open dialog box.

3 Navigate to the location of the file to be opened (in this case, the Word folder in the CIS 101 folder [or your class folder] on the USB flash drive). For a detailed example of this procedure, refer to Steps 3a – 3c in the To Save a File in a Folder section in the Office 2010 and Windows 7 chapter at the beginning of this book.

4 Click Found Dog Flyer to select the file to be opened.

5 Click the Open button (Open dialog box) to open the selected file and display the opened document in the Word window.

Q&A Could I have clicked the Recent tab to open the file?

Yes. Because the file was recently closed, it should appear in the Recent Documents list.

To Zoom the Document

While modifying the document, you prefer the document at 100 percent so that it is easier to read. Thus, the following step changes the zoom back to 100 percent.

1 If necessary, click the Zoom In button on the status bar as many times as necessary until the Zoom button displays 100% on its face (shown in Figure 1–63 on the next page).

To Insert Text in an Existing Document

Word inserts text to the left of the insertion point. The text to the right of the insertion point moves to the right and downward to fit the new text. The following steps insert the word, very, to the left of the word, early, in the flyer.

1
- Scroll through the document and then click to the left of the location of text to be inserted (in this case, the e in early) to position the insertion point where text should be inserted (Figure 1–63).

insertion point

Adorable, loving, friendly, well-behaved dog found early Friday morning, June 1, wandering on the bike trail at Filcher Park in Hampton Township.¶

- → Tan color with patches of white on his chest¶
- → Male, adult cocker spaniel¶
- → Green and silver collar with the name, *Bailey*, on the tag¶

If this is your lost dog, call 555-1029.¶

zoom is 100%

100%

Figure 1–63

2
- Type **very** and then press the SPACEBAR to insert the word to the left of the insertion point (Figure 1–64).

Q&A

Why did the text move to the right as I typed?

In Word, the default typing mode is **insert mode**, which means as you type a character, Word moves all the characters to the right of the typed character one position to the right.

Adorable, loving, friendly, well-behaved dog found very early Friday morning, June 1, wandering on the bike trail at Filcher Park in Hampton Township.¶

word inserted

- → Tan color with patches of white on his chest¶
- → Male, adult cocker spaniel¶
- → Green and silver collar with the name, *Bailey*, on the tag¶

If this is your lost dog, call 555-1029.¶

Figure 1–64

Deleting Text from a Document

It is not unusual to type incorrect characters or words in a document. As discussed earlier in this chapter, you can click the Undo button on the Quick Access Toolbar to undo a command or action immediately — this includes typing. Word also provides other methods of correcting typing errors.

To delete an incorrect character in a document, simply click next to the incorrect character and then press the BACKSPACE key to erase to the left of the insertion point, or press the DELETE key to erase to the right of the insertion point.

To Delete Text

To delete a word or phrase, you first must select the word or phrase. The following steps select the word, very, that was just added in the previous steps and then delete the selection.

- Position the mouse pointer somewhere in the word to be selected (in this case, very) and then double-click to select the word (Figure 1–65).

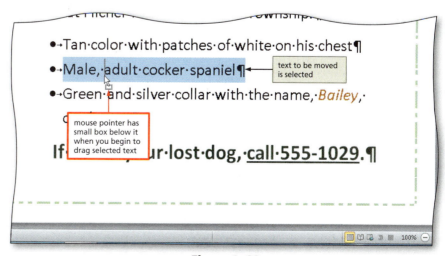

Adorable,·loving,·friendly,·well-behaved·dog·found·
very·early·Friday·morning,·June·1,·wandering·on·the·
bike·trail·at·Filcher·Park·in·Hampton·Township.¶

text to be deleted is selected

mouse pointer

Figure 1–65

- With the text selected, press the DELETE key to delete the selected text (shown in Figure 1–63).

To Move Text

While proofreading the flyer, you realize that the body copy would read better if the first two bulleted paragraphs were reversed. An efficient way to move text a short distance, such as reversing two paragraphs, is drag-and-drop editing. With **drag-and-drop editing**, you select the text to be moved and then drag the selected item to the new location and then *drop*, or insert, it there. Another technique for moving text is the cut-and-paste technique, which is discussed in the next chapter. The following steps use drag-and-drop editing to move text.

- Position the mouse pointer in the paragraph to be moved (in this case, the second bulleted item) and then triple-click to select the paragraph.

- With the mouse pointer in the selected text, press and hold down the mouse button, which displays a dotted insertion point and a small dotted box with the mouse pointer (Figure 1–66).

•→Tan·color·with·patches·of·white·on·his·chest¶

•→Male,·adult·cocker·spaniel¶ ← text to be moved is selected

•→Green·and·silver·collar·with·the·name,·*Bailey*,·

mouse pointer has small box below it when you begin to drag selected text

If·…·ur·lost·dog,·call·555-1029.¶

100%

Figure 1–66

- Drag the dotted insertion point to the location where the selected text is to be moved, as shown in Figure 1–67.

selected text to be dropped at location of dotted insertion point

Adorable,·loving,·friendly,·well-behaved·dog·found· early·Friday·morning,·June·1,·wandering·on·the·bike· trail·at·Filcher·Park·in·Hampton·Township.¶

- →Tan·color·with·patches·of·white·on·his·chest¶
- →Male,·adult·cocker·spaniel¶
- →Green·and·silver·collar·with·the·name,·*Bailey*,· on·the·tag¶

If·this·is·your·lost·dog,·call·555-1029.¶

Figure 1–67

- Release the mouse button to move the selected text to the location of the dotted insertion point (Figure 1–68).

Q&A What if I accidentally drag text to the wrong location?

Click the Undo button on the Quick Access Toolbar and try again.

Q&A Can I use drag-and-drop editing to move any selected item?

Yes, you can select words, sentences, phrases, and graphics and then use drag-and-drop editing to move them.

Q&A What is the purpose of the Paste Options button?

If you click the Paste Options button, a menu appears that allows you to change the format of the item that was moved. The next chapter discusses the Paste Options menu.

- Click anywhere in the document window to remove the selection from the bulleted item.

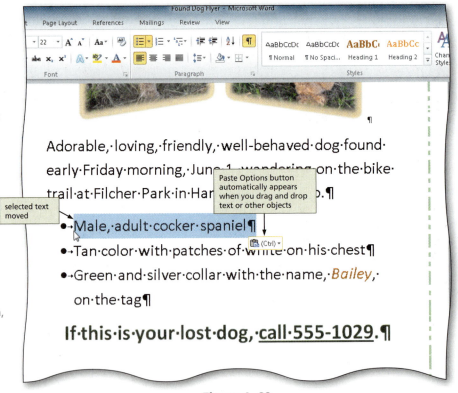

selected text moved

Paste Options button automatically appears when you drag and drop text or other objects

Figure 1–68

Other Ways

1. Click Cut button (Home tab | Clipboard group), click where text or object is to be pasted, click Paste button (Home tab | Clipboard group)

2. Right-click selected text, click Cut on shortcut menu, right-click where text or object is to be pasted, click Keep Source Formatting on shortcut menu

3. Press CTRL+X, position insertion point where text or object is to be pasted, press CTRL+V

Changing Document Properties

Word helps you organize and identify your files by using **document properties**, which are the details about a file. Document properties, also known as **metadata**, can include information such as the project author, title, subject, and keywords. A **keyword** is a word or phrase that further describes the document. For example, a class name or document topic can describe the file's purpose or content.

Document properties are valuable for a variety of reasons:

- Users can save time locating a particular file because they can view a document's properties without opening the document.

- By creating consistent properties for files having similar content, users can better organize their documents.

- Some organizations require Word users to add document properties so that other employees can view details about these files.

Five different types of document properties exist, but the more common ones used in this book are standard and automatically updated properties. **Standard properties** are associated with all Microsoft Office documents and include author, title, and subject. **Automatically updated properties** include file system properties, such as the date you create or change a file, and statistics, such as the file size.

BTW

Printing Document Properties
To print document properties, click File on the Ribbon to open the Backstage view, click the Print tab in the Backstage view to display the Print gallery, click the first button in the Settings area to display a list of options specifying what you can print, click Document Properties in the list to specify you want to print the document properties instead of the actual document, and then click the Print button in the Print gallery to print the document properties on the currently selected printer.

To Change Document Properties

The **Document Information Panel** contains areas where you can view and enter document properties. You can view and change information in this panel at any time while you are creating a document. Before saving the flyer again, you want to add your name and course information as document properties. The following steps use the Document Information Panel to change document properties.

1
- Click File on the Ribbon to open the Backstage view.

- If necessary, click the Info tab to display the Info gallery (Figure 1–69).

Q&A
How do I close the Backstage view?

Click File on the Ribbon or click the preview of the document in the Info gallery to return to the Word document window.

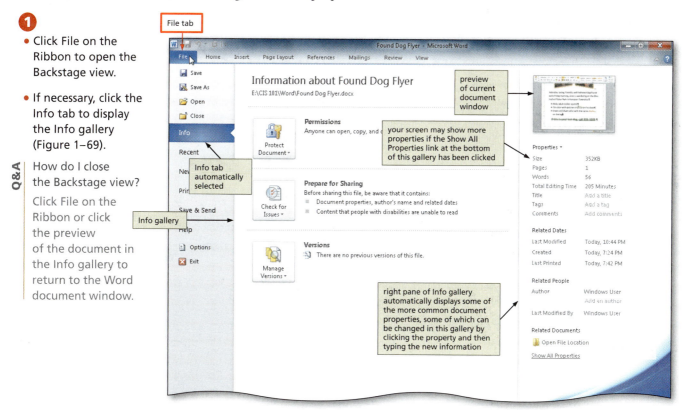

Figure 1–69

2

- Click the Properties button in the right pane of the Info gallery to display the Properties menu (Figure 1–70).

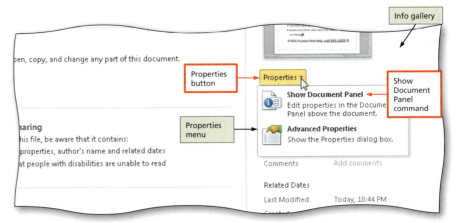

Figure 1–70

3

- Click Show Document Panel on the Properties menu to close the Backstage view and display the Document Information Panel in the Word document window (Figure 1–71).

Q&A

Why are some of the document properties in my Document Information Panel already filled in?

The person who installed Microsoft Office 2010 on your computer or network may have set or customized the properties.

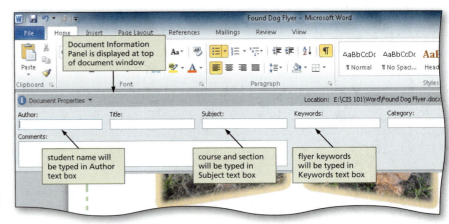

Figure 1–71

4

- Click the Author text box, if necessary, and then type your name as the Author property. If a name already is displayed in the Author text box, delete it before typing your name.

- Click the Subject text box, if necessary delete any existing text, and then type your course and section as the Subject property.

- If an AutoComplete dialog box appears, click its Yes button.

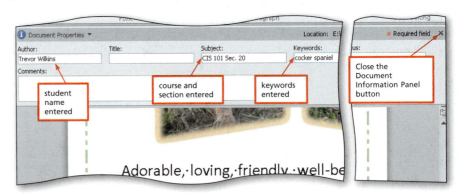

Figure 1–72

- Click the Keywords text box, if necessary delete any existing text, and then type **cocker spaniel** as the Keywords property (Figure 1–72).

Q&A

What types of document properties does Word collect automatically?

Word records details such as time spent editing a document, the number of times a document has been revised, and the fonts and themes used in a document.

5

- Click the Close the Document Information Panel button so that the Document Information Panel no longer is displayed.

Other Ways

1. Click File on Ribbon, click Info in Backstage view, if necessary click Show All Properties link in Info gallery, click property to change and then type new information, close Backstage view

To Save an Existing Document with the Same File Name

You are finished editing the flyer. Thus, you should save it again. The following step saves the document again. For an example of the step listed below, refer to the Office 2010 and Windows 7 chapter at the beginning of this book.

 Click the Save button on the Quick Access Toolbar to overwrite the previously saved file.

Printing a Document

After creating a document, you may want to print it. Printing a document enables you to distribute the document to others in a form that can be read or viewed but typically not edited. It is a good practice to save a document before printing it, in the event you experience difficulties printing.

Determine the best method for distributing the document.

The traditional method of distributing a document uses a printer to produce a hard copy. A **hardcopy** or **printout** is information that exists on a physical medium such as paper. For users that can receive fax documents, you can elect to print a hard copy on a remote fax machine. Hard copies can be useful for the following reasons:

- Many people prefer proofreading a hard copy of a document rather than viewing it on the screen to check for errors and readability.

- Hard copies can serve as reference material if your storage medium is lost or becomes corrupted and you need to recreate the document.

    Instead of distributing a hard copy of a document, users can choose to distribute the document as an electronic image that mirrors the original document's appearance. The electronic image of the document can be e-mailed, posted on a Web site, or copied to a portable storage medium such as a USB flash drive. Two popular electronic image formats, sometimes called fixed formats, are PDF by Adobe Systems and XPS by Microsoft. In Word, you can create electronic image files through the Print tab in the Backstage view, the Send & Save tab in the Backstage view, and the Save As dialog box. Electronic images of documents, such as PDF and XPS, can be useful for the following reasons:

- Users can view electronic images of documents without the software that created the original document (e.g., Word). Specifically, to view a PDF file, you use a program called Acrobat Reader, which can be downloaded free from Adobe's Web site. Similarly, to view an XPS file, you use a program called an XPS Viewer, which is included in the latest versions of Windows and Internet Explorer.

- Sending electronic documents saves paper and printer supplies. Society encourages users to contribute to **green computing**, which involves reducing the environmental waste generated when using a computer.

Plan Ahead

BTW

Conserving Ink and Toner
If you want to conserve ink or toner, you can instruct Word to print draft quality documents by clicking File on the Ribbon to open the Backstage view, clicking Options in the Backstage view to display the Word Options dialog box, clicking Advanced in the left pane (Word Options dialog box), scrolling to the Print area in the right pane, placing a check mark in the 'Use draft quality' check box, and then clicking the OK button. Then, use the Backstage view to print the document as usual.

To Print a Document

With the completed document saved, you may want to print it. Because this flyer is being posted, you will print a hard copy on a printer. The steps on the next page print a hard copy of the contents of the saved Found Dog Flyer document.

1

- Click File on the Ribbon to open the Backstage view.

- Click the Print tab in the Backstage view to display the Print gallery (Figure 1–73).

Q&A How can I print multiple copies of my document?

Increase the number in the Copies box in the Print gallery.

Q&A What if I decide not to print the document at this time?

Click File on the Ribbon to close the Backstage view and return to the Word document window.

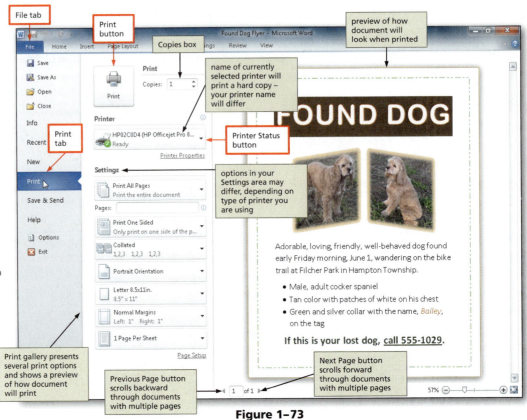

Figure 1–73

2

- Verify the printer name that appears on the Printer Status button will print a hard copy of the document. If necessary, click the Printer Status button to display a list of available printer options and then click the desired printer to change the currently selected printer.

3

- Click the Print button in the Print gallery to print the document on the currently selected printer.

- When the printer stops, retrieve the hard copy (Figure 1–74).

Q&A Do I have to wait until my document is complete to print it?

No, you can follow these steps to print a document at any time while you are creating it.

Q&A What if I want to print an electronic image of a document instead of a hard copy?

You would click the Printer Status button in the Print gallery and then select the desired electronic image option such as a Microsoft XPS Document Writer, which would create an XPS file.

Figure 1–74

Other Ways

1. Press CTRL+P, press ENTER

To Quit Word

The project now is complete. Thus, the following steps quit Word. For an example of the step listed below, refer to the Office 2010 and Windows 7 chapter at the beginning of this book.

1 If you have one Word document open, click the Close button on the right side of the title bar to close the document and quit Word; or if you have multiple Word documents open, click File on the Ribbon to open the Backstage view and then click Exit in the Backstage view to close all open documents and quit Word.

2 If a Microsoft Word dialog box appears, click the Save button to save any changes made to the document since the last save.

BTW

Printed Borders
If one or more of your borders do not print, click the Page Borders button (Page Layout tab | Page Background group), click the Options button (Borders and Shading dialog box), click the Measure from box arrow and click Text, change the four text boxes to 15 pt, and then click the OK button in each dialog box. Try printing the document again. If the borders still do not print, adjust the text boxes in the dialog box to a number smaller than 15 point.

Chapter Summary

In this chapter, you have learned how to enter text in a document, format text, insert a picture, format a picture, add a page border, and print a document. The items listed below include all the new Word skills you have learned in this chapter.

1. Start Word (WD 4)
2. Type Text (WD 6)
3. Display Formatting Marks (WD 7)
4. Insert a Blank Line (WD 7)
5. Wordwrap Text as You Type (WD 8)
6. Check Spelling and Grammar as You Type (WD 9)
7. Save a Document (WD 12)
8. Center a Paragraph (WD 14)
9. Select a Line (WD 15)
10. Change the Font Size of Selected Text (WD 16)
11. Change the Font of Selected Text (WD 17)
12. Change the Case of Selected Text (WD 18)
13. Apply a Text Effect to Selected Text (WD 19)
14. Shade a Paragraph (WD 20)
15. Select Multiple Lines (WD 21)
16. Bullet a List of Paragraphs (WD 22)
17. Undo and Redo an Action (WD 23)
18. Italicize Text (WD 24)
19. Color Text (WD 25)
20. Use the Mini Toolbar to Format Text (WD 26)
21. Select a Group of Words (WD 27)
22. Underline Text (WD 27)
23. Bold Text (WD 28)
24. Change Theme Colors (WD 28)
25. Save an Existing Document with the Same File Name (WD 30)
26. Insert a Picture (WD 31)
27. Zoom the Document (WD 33)
28. Resize a Graphic (WD 34)
29. Resize a Graphic by Entering Exact Measurements (WD 36)
30. Apply a Picture Style (WD 37)
31. Apply Picture Effects (WD 38)
32. View One Page (WD 40)
33. Add a Page Border (WD 41)
34. Change Spacing before and after a Paragraph (WD 44)
35. Quit Word (WD 44)
36. Open a Document from Word (WD 45)
37. Insert Text in an Existing Document (WD 46)
38. Delete Text (WD 47)
39. Move Text (WD 47)
40. Change Document Properties (WD 49)
41. Print a Document (WD 51)

If you have a SAM 2010 user profile, your instructor may have assigned an autogradable version of this assignment. If so, log into the SAM 2010 Web site at www.cengage.com/sam2010 to download the instruction and start files.

BTW

Quick Reference
For a table that lists how to complete the tasks covered in this book using the mouse, Ribbon, shortcut menu, and keyboard, see the Quick Reference Summary at the back of this book, or visit the Word 2010 Quick Reference Web page (scsite.com/wd2010/qr).

Learn It Online

Test your knowledge of chapter content and key terms.

Instructions: To complete the Learn It Online exercises, start your browser, click the Address bar, and then enter the Web address **scsite.com/wd2010/learn**. When the Word 2010 Learn It Online page is displayed, click the link for the exercise you want to complete and then read the instructions.

Chapter Reinforcement TF, MC, and SA
A series of true/false, multiple choice, and short answer questions that test your knowledge of the chapter content.

Flash Cards
An interactive learning environment where you identify chapter key terms associated with displayed definitions.

Practice Test
A series of multiple choice questions that test your knowledge of chapter content and key terms.

Who Wants To Be a Computer Genius?
An interactive game that challenges your knowledge of chapter content in the style of a television quiz show.

Wheel of Terms
An interactive game that challenges your knowledge of chapter key terms in the style of the television show *Wheel of Fortune*.

Crossword Puzzle Challenge
A crossword puzzle that challenges your knowledge of key terms presented in the chapter.

Apply Your Knowledge

Reinforce the skills and apply the concepts you learned in this chapter.

Modifying Text and Formatting a Document
Note: To complete this assignment, you will be required to use the Data Files for Students. See the inside back cover of this book for instructions on downloading the Data Files for Students, or contact your instructor for information about accessing the required files.

Instructions: Start Word. Open the document, Apply 1-1 Buffalo Photo Shoot Flyer Unformatted, from the Data Files for Students. The document you open is an unformatted flyer. You are to modify text, format paragraphs and characters, and insert a picture in the flyer.

Perform the following tasks:
1. Delete the word, single, in the sentence of body copy below the headline.
2. Insert the word, Creeks, between the words, Twin Buffalo, in the sentence of body copy below the headline.
3. At the end of the signature line, change the period to an exclamation point.
4. Center the headline and the signature line.
5. Change the theme colors to the Aspect color scheme.
6. Change the font and font size of the headline to 48-point Impact, or a similar font. Change the case of the headline text to all capital letters. Apply the text effect called Gradient Fill – Orange, Accent 1, Outline – White to the headline.
7. Change the font size of body copy between the headline and the signature line to 20 point.
8. Use the Mini toolbar to change the font size of the signature line to 26 point.
9. Select the words, hundreds of buffalo, in the paragraph below the headline and underline them.

10. Italicize the word, every, in the paragraph below the headline. Undo this change and then redo the change.

11. Select the three lines (paragraphs) of text above the signature line and add bullets to the selected paragraphs.

12. Switch the last two bulleted paragraphs. That is, select the Questions bullet and move it so that it is the last bulleted paragraph.

13. Bold the first word of each bulleted paragraph. Change the font color of these same three words to Dark Green, Accent 4, Darker 50%.

14. Bold the text in the signature line. Shade the signature line Dark Green, Accent 4, Darker 50%. If the font color does not automatically change to a lighter color, change it to a shade of white.

15. Change the zoom so that the entire page is visible in the document window.

16. Insert the picture of the buffalo centered on the blank line below the headline. The picture is called Buffalo and is available on the Data Files for Students. Apply the Snip Diagonal Corner, White picture style to the inserted picture. Apply the glow called Dark Green, 5 pt glow, Accent color 4 to the picture.

17. Change the spacing after the headline paragraph to 6 point.

18. The entire flyer now should fit on a single page. If it flows to two pages, resize the picture or decrease spacing before and after paragraphs until the entire flyer text fits on a single page.

19. Change the zoom to text width, then page width, then 100% and notice the differences.

20. Enter the text, Twin Creeks, as the keywords in the document properties. Change the other document properties, as specified by your instructor.

21. Click File on the Ribbon and then click Save As. Save the document using the file name, Apply 1-1 Buffalo Photo Shoot Flyer Formatted.

22. Print the document. Submit the revised document, shown in Figure 1–75, in the format specified by your instructor.

23. Quit Word.

BUFFALO PHOTO SHOOT — headline

Join us for nonstop hayrides through the natural habitat of hundreds of buffalo at Twin Creeks Buffalo Farm *every* weekend in May. — body copy

- **Cost**: $5 for adults and $2 for children
- **Hours**: 9:00 a.m. to 6:00 p.m. Saturdays and Sundays
- **Questions**: 555-2838

bulleted list

Don't Forget to Bring Your Camera! — signature line

Figure 1–75

Extend Your Knowledge

Extend the skills you learned in this chapter and experiment with new skills. You may need to use Help to complete the assignment.

Modifying Text and Picture Formats and Adding Page Borders

Note: To complete this assignment, you will be required to use the Data Files for Students. See the inside back cover of this book for instructions on downloading the Data Files for Students, or contact your instructor for information about accessing the required files.

Instructions: Start Word. Open the document, Extend 1-1 TVC Cruises Flyer, from the Data Files for Students. You will enhance the look of the flyer shown in Figure 1–76. *Hint:* Remember, if you make a mistake while formatting the picture, you can reset it by clicking the Reset Picture button or Reset Picture button arrow (Picture Tools Format tab | Adjust group).

Perform the following tasks:

1. Use Help to learn about the following formats: remove bullets, grow font, shrink font, art page borders, decorative underline(s), picture bullets, picture border shading, shadow picture effects, and color saturation and tone.

2. Remove the bullet from the paragraph below the picture.

3. Select the text, 10 percent, and use the Grow Font button to increase its font size.

4. Add an art page border to the flyer. If the border is not in color, add color to it.

5. Change the solid underline below the word, cruises, to a decorative underline. Change the color of the underline.

6. Change the style of the bullets to picture bullet(s).

7. Change the color of the picture border. Add a shadow picture effect to the picture.

8. Change the color saturation and color tone of the picture.

9. Change the document properties, including keywords, as specified by your instructor. Save the revised document with a new file name and then submit it in the format specified by your instructor.

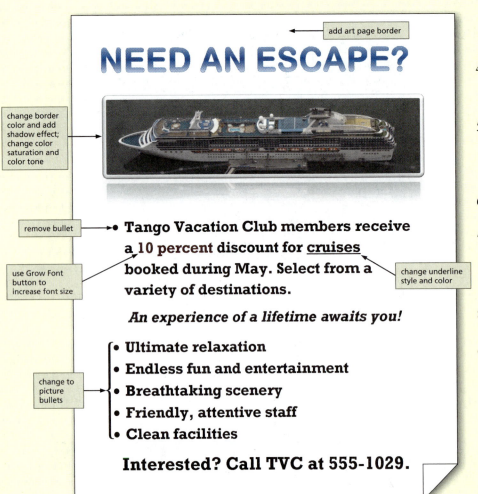

Figure 1–76

Make It Right

Analyze a document and correct all errors and/or improve the design.

Correcting Spelling and Grammar Errors

Note: To complete this assignment, you will be required to use the Data Files for Students. See the inside back cover of this book for instructions on downloading the Data Files for Students, or contact your instructor for information about accessing the required files.

Instructions: Start Word. Open the document, Make It Right 1-1 Karate Academy Flyer Unchecked, from the Data Files for Students. The document is a flyer that contains spelling and grammar errors, as shown in Figure 1–77. You are to correct each spelling (red wavy underline) and grammar error (green and blue wavy underlines) by right-clicking the flagged text and then clicking the appropriate correction on the shortcut menu.

   If your screen does not display the wavy underlines, click File on the Ribbon and then click Options in the Backstage view. When the Word Options dialog box is displayed, click Proofing in the left pane, be sure the 'Hide spelling errors in this document only' and 'Hide grammar errors in this document only' check boxes do not contain check marks, and then click the OK button. If your screen still does not display the wavy underlines, redisplay the Word Options dialog box, click Proofing, and then click the Recheck Document button.

   Change the document properties, including keywords, as specified by your instructor. Save the revised document with the name, Make It Right 1-1 Karate Academy Flyer, and then submit it in the format specified by your instructor.

Figure 1–77

In the Lab

Design and/or create a document using the guidelines, concepts, and skills presented in this chapter. Labs are listed in order of increasing difficulty.

Lab 1: Creating a Flyer with a Picture

Problem: As a part-time employee in the Student Services Center at school, you have been asked to prepare a flyer that advertises study habits classes. First, you prepare the unformatted flyer shown in Figure 1–78a, and then you format it so that it looks like Figure 1–78b. *Hint:* Remember, if you make a mistake while formatting the flyer, you can click the Undo button on the Quick Access Toolbar to undo your last action.

Note: To complete this assignment, you will be required to use the Data Files for Students. See the inside back cover of this book for instructions on downloading the Data Files for Students, or contact your instructor for information about accessing the required files.

Instructions: Perform the following tasks:

1. Start Word. Display formatting marks on the screen.

2. Type the flyer text, unformatted, as shown in Figure 1–78a, inserting a blank line between the headline and the body copy. If Word flags any misspelled words as you type, check their spelling and correct them.

3. Save the document using the file name, Lab 1-1 Study Habits Flyer.

4. Center the headline and the signature line.

5. Change the theme colors to Concourse.

6. Change the font size of the headline to 36 point and the font to Ravie, or a similar font. Apply the text effect called Gradient Fill – Dark Red, Accent 6, Inner Shadow.

7. Change the font size of body copy between the headline and the signature line to 20 point.

8. Change the font size of the signature line to 22 point. Bold the text in the signature line.

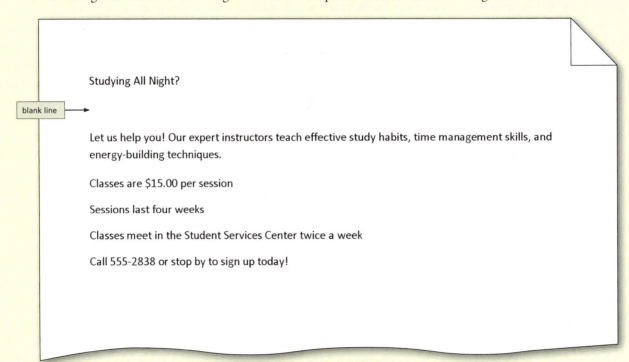

Studying All Night?

blank line

Let us help you! Our expert instructors teach effective study habits, time management skills, and energy-building techniques.

Classes are $15.00 per session

Sessions last four weeks

Classes meet in the Student Services Center twice a week

Call 555-2838 or stop by to sign up today!

Figure 1–78 (a) Unformatted Flyer

9. Change the font of the body copy and signature line to Rockwell, and change the color of the signature line to Dark Red, Accent 6.

10. Bullet the three lines (paragraphs) of text above the signature line.

11. Bold and capitalize the text, Let us help you!, and change its color to Dark Red, Accent 6.

12. Italicize the word, or, in the signature line.

13. Underline the text, Student Services Center, in the third bulleted paragraph.

14. Change the zoom so that the entire page is visible in the document window.

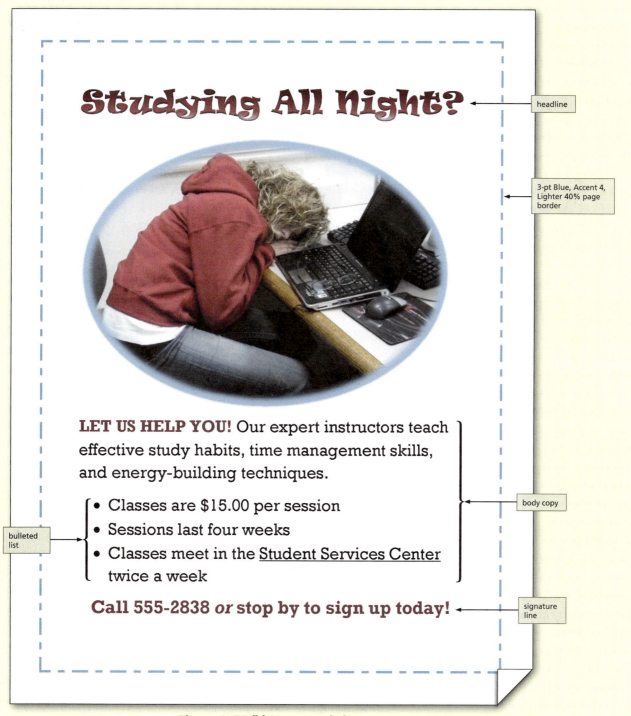

Figure 1–78 (b) Formatted Flyer

Continued >

In the Lab *continued*

15. Insert the picture centered on a blank line below the headline. The picture is called Sleeping and is available on the Data Files for Students.

16. Apply the Soft Edge Oval picture style to the inserted picture. Apply the glow effect called Blue, 5 pt glow, Accent color 4 to the picture.

17. The entire flyer should fit on a single page. If it flows to two pages, resize the picture or decrease spacing before and after paragraphs until the entire flyer text fits on a single page.

18. Add the page border shown in Figure 1–78b on the previous page.

19. Change the document properties, including keywords, as specified by your instructor. Save the flyer again with the same file name. Submit the document, shown in Figure 1–78b, in the format specified by your instructor.

In the Lab

Lab 2: Creating a Flyer with a Resized Picture

Problem: Your boss at Granger Camera House has asked you to prepare a flyer that announces the upcoming photography contest. You prepare the flyer shown in Figure 1–79. *Hint:* Remember, if you make a mistake while formatting the flyer, you can click the Undo button on the Quick Access Toolbar to undo your last action.

Note: To complete this assignment, you will be required to use the Data Files for Students. See the inside back cover of this book for instructions on downloading the Data Files for Students, or contact your instructor for information about accessing the required files.

Instructions: Perform the following tasks:

1. Start Word. Type the flyer text, unformatted. If Word flags any misspelled words as you type, check their spelling and correct them.

2. Save the document using the file name, Lab 1-2 Photography Contest Flyer.

3. Change the theme colors to the Apex color scheme.

4. Center the headline, the line that says RULES, and the signature line.

5. Change the font size of the headline to 36 point and the font to Stencil, or a similar font. Shade the headline paragraph Lavender, Background 2, Darker 50%. Apply the text effect called Fill – Lavender, Accent 6, Outline – Accent 6, Glow – Accent 6.

6. Change the font size of body copy between the headline and the signature line to 18 point.

7. Change the font size of the signature line to 24 point and the font to Stencil. Bold the text in the signature line. Change the font color of the text in the signature line to Gray-50%, Text 2.

8. Bullet the three paragraphs of text above the signature line.

9. Italicize the word, not.

10. Bold the word, landscape.

11. Underline the text, August 31.

12. Shade the line that says RULES to the Gray-50%, Text 2 color. If the font color does not automatically change to a lighter color, change it to White, Background 1.

13. Change the zoom so that the entire page is visible in the document window.

14. Insert the picture on a blank line below the headline. The picture is called Wind Power and is available on the Data Files for Students.

15. Resize the picture so that it is approximately 3.5" × 5.25". Apply the Rotated, White picture style to the inserted picture. Apply the glow effect called Lavender, 5 pt glow, Accent color 6 to the picture.

16. The entire flyer should fit on a single page. If it flows to two pages, resize the picture or decrease spacing before and after paragraphs until the entire flyer text fits on a single page.

17. Add the page border shown in Figure 1–79.

18. Change the document properties, including keywords, as specified by your instructor. Save the flyer again with the same file name. Submit the document, shown in Figure 1–79, in the format specified by your instructor.

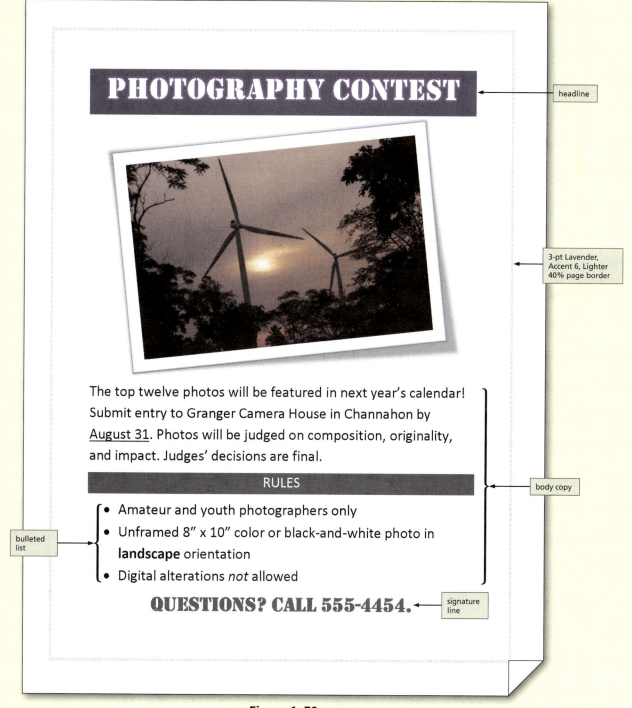

Figure 1–79

In the Lab

Lab 3: Creating a Flyer with Pictures

Problem: Your boss at Warner Depot has asked you to prepare a flyer that advertises its scenic train ride. You prepare the flyer shown in Figure 1–80.

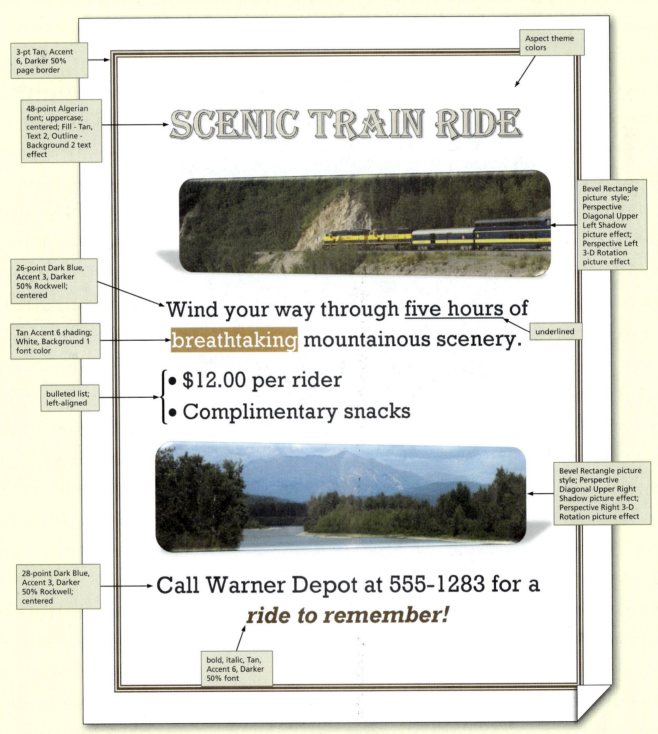

Figure 1–80

Note: To complete this assignment, you will be required to use the Data Files for Students. See the inside back cover of this book for instructions on downloading the Data Files for Students, or contact your instructor for information about accessing the required files.

Instructions: Start Word. Enter the text in the flyer, checking spelling as you type, and then format it as shown in Figure 1–80. The pictures to be inserted are called Train and Scenery and are available on the Data Files for Students. Adjust spacing before and after paragraphs and resize pictures as necessary so that the flyer fits on a single page.

Change the document properties, including keywords, as specified by your instructor. Save the document using the file name, Lab 1-3 Train Ride Flyer. Submit the document, shown in Figure 1–80, in the format specified by your instructor.

Cases and Places

Apply your creative thinking and problem solving skills to design and implement a solution.

Note: To complete these assignments, you may be required to use the Data Files for Students. See the inside back cover of this book for instructions on downloading the Data Files for Students, or contact your instructor for information about accessing the required files.

1: Design and Create a Spring Break Flyer

Academic

As secretary of your school's Student Government Association, you are responsible for creating and distributing flyers for spring break group outings. This year, you have planned a trip to Settlers Resort. The flyer should contain two digital pictures appropriately resized; the Data Files for Students contains two pictures called Cabin 1 and Cabin 2, or you can use your own digital pictures if they are appropriate for the topic of the flyer. The flyer should contain the headline, Feeling Adventurous?, and this signature line: Call Lyn at 555-9901 to sign up. The body copy consists of the following, in any order: Spring Break – Blast to the Past. Settlers Resort is like a page right out of a history textbook! Spend five days living in the 1800s. The bulleted list in the body copy is as follows: One-room cabins with potbelly stoves, Campfire dining with authentic meals, and Horseback riding and much more.

Use the concepts and techniques presented in this chapter to create and format this flyer. Be sure to check spelling and grammar. Submit your assignment in the format specified by your instructor.

2: Design and Create a Yard Sale Flyer

Personal

You are planning a yard sale and would like to create and post flyers around town advertising the upcoming sale. The flyer should contain two digital pictures appropriately resized; the Data Files for Students contains two pictures called Yard Sale 1 and Yard Sale 2, or you can use your own digital pictures if they are appropriate for the topic of the flyer. The flyer should contain the headline, Yard Sale!, and this signature line: Questions? Call 555-9820. The body copy consists of the following, in any order: Hundreds of items for sale. After 20 years, we are moving to a smaller house and are selling anything that won't fit. Everything for sale must go! The bulleted list in the body copy is as follows: When: August 7, 8, 9 from 9:00 a.m. to 7:00 p.m.; Where: 139 Ravel Boulevard; and What: something for everyone – from clothing to collectibles.

Use the concepts and techniques presented in this chapter to create and format this flyer. Be sure to check spelling and grammar. Submit your assignment in the format specified by your instructor.

Continued >

Cases and Places *continued*

3: Design and Create a Village Fireworks Flyer

Professional

As a part-time employee at the Village of Crestwood, your boss has asked you to create and distribute flyers for the upcoming fireworks extravaganza. The flyer should contain two digital pictures appropriately resized; the Data Files for Students contains two pictures called Fireworks 1 and Fireworks 2, or you can use your own digital pictures if they are appropriate for the topic of the flyer. The flyer should contain the headline, Light Up The Sky, and this signature line: Call 555-2983 with questions. The body copy consists of the following, in any order: Join Us! The Village of Crestwood will present its tenth annual Light Up The Sky fireworks extravaganza on August 8 at 9:00 p.m. during the end of summer celebration in Douglas Park. The bulleted list in the body copy is as follows: Pork chop dinners will be sold for $3.00 beginning at 6:00 p.m., Bring chairs and blankets, and Admission is free.

Use the concepts and techniques presented in this chapter to create and format this flyer. Be sure to check spelling and grammar. Submit your assignment in the format specified by your instructor.

2 Creating a Research Paper with Citations and References

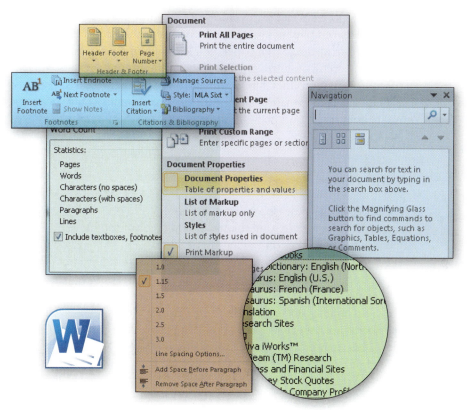

Objectives

You will have mastered the material in this chapter when you can:

- Describe the MLA documentation style for research papers
- Change line and paragraph spacing in a document
- Modify a style
- Use a header to number pages of a document
- Apply formatting using shortcut keys
- Modify paragraph indentation

- Insert and edit citations and their sources
- Add a footnote to a document
- Insert a manual page break
- Create a bibliographical list of sources
- Cut, copy, and paste text
- Find text and replace text
- Find a synonym
- Use the Research task pane to look up information

2 Creating a Research Paper with Citations and References

Introduction

In both academic and business environments, you will be asked to write reports. Business reports range from proposals to cost justifications to five-year plans to research findings. Academic reports focus mostly on research findings.

A **research paper** is a document you can use to communicate the results of research findings. To write a research paper, you learn about a particular topic from a variety of sources (research), organize your ideas from the research results, and then present relevant facts and/or opinions that support the topic. Your final research paper combines properly credited outside information along with personal insights. Thus, no two research papers — even if about the same topic — will or should be the same.

Project — Research Paper

When preparing a research paper, you should follow a standard documentation style that defines the rules for creating the paper and crediting sources. A variety of documentation styles exists, depending on the nature of the research paper. Each style requires the same basic information; the differences in styles relate to requirements for presenting the information. For example, one documentation style uses the term bibliography for the list of sources, whereas another uses references, and yet a third prefers the title works cited. Two popular documentation styles for research papers are the **Modern Language Association of America (MLA)** and **American Psychological Association (APA)** styles. This chapter uses the MLA documentation style because it is used in a wide range of disciplines.

The project in this chapter follows research paper guidelines and uses Word to create the short research paper shown in Figure 2–1. This paper, which discusses triangulation, follows the MLA documentation style. Each page contains a page number. The first two pages present the name and course information (student name, instructor name, course name, and paper due date), paper title, an introduction with a thesis statement, details that support the thesis, and a conclusion. This section of the paper also includes references to research sources and a footnote. The third page contains a detailed, alphabetical list of the sources referenced in the research paper. All pages include a header at the upper-right edge of the page.

BTW

APA Appendix
If your version of this book includes the Word APA Appendix and you are required to create a research paper using the APA documentation style instead of the MLA documentation style, the appendix shows the steps required to create the research paper in this chapter using the APA guidelines. If your version of this book does not include the Word APA Appendix, see print publications or search the Web for the APA guidelines.

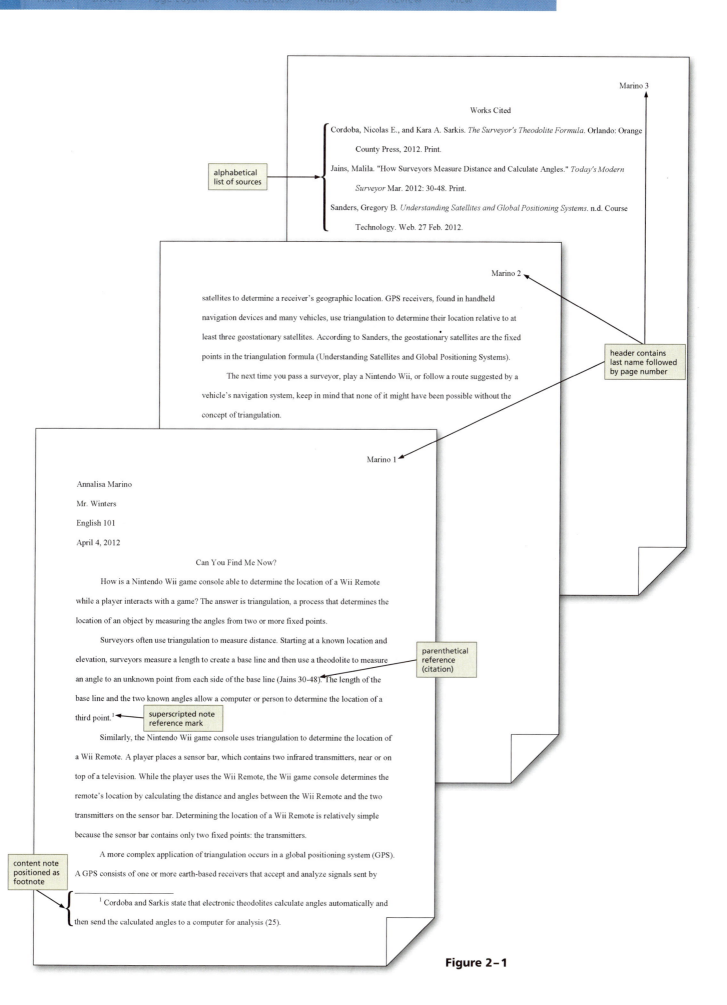

Figure 2–1

Overview

As you read through this chapter, you will learn how to create the research paper shown in Figure 2–1 on the previous page by performing these general tasks:

- Change the document settings.
- Type the research paper.
- Save the research paper.
- Create an alphabetical list of sources.
- Proof and revise the research paper.
- Print the research paper.

Plan Ahead

General Project Guidelines

When creating a Word document, the actions you perform and decisions you make will affect the appearance and characteristics of the finished document. As you create a research paper, such as the project shown in Figure 2–1, you should follow these general guidelines:

1. **Select a topic.** Spend time brainstorming ideas for a topic. Choose one you find interesting. For shorter papers, narrow the scope of the topic; for longer papers, broaden the scope. Identify a tentative thesis statement, which is a sentence describing the paper's subject matter.

2. **Research the topic and take notes.** Gather credible, relevant information about the topic that supports the thesis statement. Sources of research include books, magazines, newspapers, and the Internet. As you record facts and ideas, list details about the source: title, author, place of publication, publisher, date of publication, etc. When taking notes, be careful not to **plagiarize**. That is, do not use someone else's work and claim it to be your own. If you copy information directly, place it in quotation marks and identify its source.

3. **Organize your ideas.** Classify your notes into related concepts. Make an outline from the categories of notes. In the outline, identify all main ideas and supporting details.

4. **Write the first draft, referencing sources.** From the outline, compose the paper. Every research paper should include an introduction containing the thesis statement, supporting details, and a conclusion. Follow the guidelines identified in the required documentation style. Reference all sources of information.

5. **Create the list of sources.** Using the formats specified in the required documentation style, completely list all sources referenced in the body of the research paper in alphabetical order.

6. **Proofread and revise the paper.** If possible, proofread the paper with a fresh set of eyes, that is, at least one to two days after completing the first draft. Proofreading involves reading the paper with the intent of identifying errors (spelling, grammar, etc.) and looking for ways to improve the paper (wording, transitions, flow, etc.). Try reading the paper out loud, which helps to identify unclear or awkward wording. Ask someone else to proofread the paper and give you suggestions for improvements.

When necessary, more specific details concerning the above guidelines are presented at appropriate points in the chapter. The chapter also will identify the actions performed and decisions made regarding these guidelines during the creation of the research paper shown in Figure 2–1.

MLA Documentation Style

The research paper in this project follows the guidelines presented by the MLA. To follow the MLA documentation style, use 12-point Times New Roman, or a similar, font. Double-space text on all pages of the paper using one-inch top, bottom, left, and right margins. Indent the first word of each paragraph one-half inch from the left margin. At the right margin of each page, place a page number one-half inch from the top margin. On each page, precede the page number by your last name.

The MLA documentation style does not require a title page. Instead, place your name and course information in a block at the left margin beginning one inch from the top of the page. Center the title one double-spaced line below your name and course information.

In the text of the paper, place author references in parentheses with the page number(s) of the referenced information. The MLA documentation style uses in-text **parenthetical references** instead of noting each source at the bottom of the page or at the end of the paper. In the MLA documentation style, notes are used only for optional content or bibliographic notes.

If used, content notes elaborate on points discussed in the paper, and bibliographic notes direct the reader to evaluations of statements in a source or provide a means for identifying multiple sources. Use a superscript (raised number) both to signal that a note exists and to sequence the notes (shown in Figure 2-1 on page WD 67). Position notes at the bottom of the page as footnotes or at the end of the paper as endnotes. Indent the first line of each note one-half inch from the left margin. Place one space following the superscripted number before beginning the note text. Double-space the note text (shown in Figure 2–1).

The MLA documentation style uses the term **works cited** to refer to the bibliographic list of sources at the end of the paper. The works cited page alphabetically lists sources that are referenced directly in the paper. Place the list of sources on a separate numbered page. Center the title, Works Cited, one inch from the top margin. Double-space all lines. Begin the first line of each source at the left margin, indenting subsequent lines of the same source one-half inch from the left margin. List each source by the author's last name, or, if the author's name is not available, by the title of the source.

BTW

APA Documentation Style

In the APA documentation style, a separate title page is required instead of placing name and course information on the paper's first page. Double-space all pages of the paper with one-inch top, bottom, left, and right margins. Indent the first word of each paragraph one-half inch from the left margin. In the upper-right margin of each page, including the title page, place a running head that consists of the page number preceded by a brief summary of the paper title.

Changing Document Settings

The MLA documentation style defines some global formats that apply to the entire research paper. Some of these formats are the default in Word. For example, the default left, right, top, and bottom margin settings in Word are one inch, which meets the MLA documentation style. You will modify, however, the font, font size, line and paragraph spacing, and header formats as required by the MLA documentation style.

To Start Word

If you are using a computer to step through the project in this chapter and you want your screens to match the figures in this book, you should change your screen's resolution to 1024 × 768. For information about how to change a computer's resolution, refer to the Office 2010 and Windows 7 chapter at the beginning of this book.

For an introduction to Windows 7 and instruction about how to perform basic Windows 7 tasks, read the Office 2010 and Windows 7 chapter at the beginning of this book, where you can learn how to resize windows, change screen resolution, create folders, move and rename files, use Windows Help, and much more.

BTW

New Document Window
If you wanted to open a new blank document window, you could press CTRL+N or click File on the Ribbon to open the Backstage view, click the New tab to display the New gallery, click the Blank document button, and then click the Create button.

The following steps, which assume Windows 7 is running, start Word based on a typical installation. You may need to ask your instructor how to start Word for your computer. For a detailed example of the procedure summarized below, refer to the Office 2010 and Windows 7 chapter.

1 Click the Start button on the Windows 7 taskbar to display the Start menu.

2 Type **Microsoft Word** as the search text in the 'Search programs and files' text box and watch the search results appear on the Start menu.

3 Click Microsoft Word 2010 in the search results on the Start menu to start Word and display a new blank document in the Word window.

4 If the Word window is not maximized, click the Maximize button next to the Close button on its title bar to maximize the window.

5 If the Print Layout button on the status bar is not selected (shown in Figure 2–2), click it so that your screen is in Print Layout view.

6 If Normal (Home tab | Styles group) is not selected in the Quick Style gallery (shown in Figure 2–2), click it so that your document uses the Normal style.

7 If your zoom percent is not 100, click the Zoom Out or Zoom In button as many times as necessary until the Zoom button displays 100% on its face (shown in Figure 2–2).

BTW

Style Formats
To see the formats assigned to a particular style in a document, click the Styles Dialog Box Launcher (Home tab | Styles group) and then click the Style Inspector button in the Styles task pane. Position the insertion point in the style in the document and then point to the Paragraph formatting or Text level formatting areas in the Style Inspector task pane to display an Enhanced ScreenTip describing formats assigned to the location of the insertion point. You also can click the Reveal Formatting button in the Style Inspector task pane to display the Reveal Formatting task pane.

To Display Formatting Marks

As discussed in Chapter 1, it is helpful to display formatting marks that indicate where in the document you press the ENTER key, SPACEBAR, and other keys. The following steps display formatting marks.

1 If the Home tab is not the active tab, click Home on the Ribbon to display the Home tab.

2 If the Show/Hide ¶ button (Home tab | Paragraph group) is not selected already, click it to display formatting marks on the screen.

Styles

When you create a document, Word formats the text using a particular style. A **style** is a named group of formatting characteristics, including font and font size. The default style in Word is called the **Normal style**, which most likely uses 11-point Calibri font. If you do not specify a style for text you type, Word applies the Normal style to the text. In addition to the Normal style, Word has many other built-in, or predefined, styles that you can use to format text. Styles make it easy to apply many formats at once to text. You can modify existing styles and create your own styles. Styles are discussed as they are used in this book.

To Modify a Style

The MLA documentation style requires that all text in the research paper use 12-point Times New Roman, or a similar, font. If you change the font and font size using buttons on the Ribbon, you will need to make the change many times during the course of creating the paper because Word formats different areas of a document using the Normal style, which uses 11-point Calibri font. For example, body text, headers, and bibliographies all display text based on the Normal style. Thus, instead of changing the font and font size for each of these document elements, a more efficient technique would be to change the Normal style for this document to 12-point Times New Roman. By changing the Normal style, you ensure that all text in the document will use the format required by the MLA. The next steps change the Normal style.

1
- Right-click Normal in the Quick Style gallery (Home tab | Styles group) to display a shortcut menu related to styles (Figure 2–2).

Home tab

Show/Hide ¶ button selected

Normal style selected and right-clicked

Quick Style gallery

default font and font size for Normal style

Note: To help you locate screen elements that are referenced in the step instructions, such as buttons and commands, this book uses red boxes to point to these screen elements.

Paragraph group

Styles group

Modify command

shortcut menu

Print Layout button

zoom percent

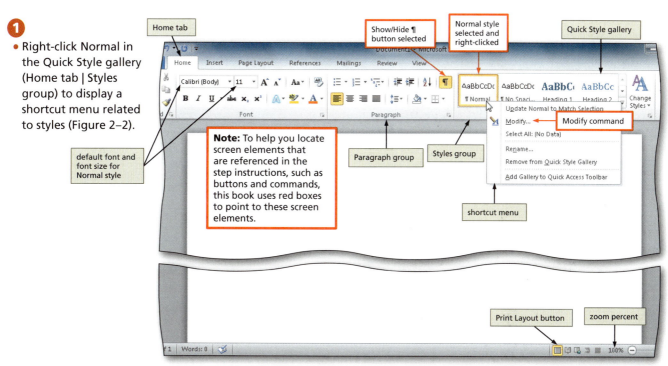

Figure 2–2

2
- Click Modify on the shortcut menu to display the Modify Style dialog box (Figure 2–3).

Modify Style dialog box

style name

current font for Normal style is Calibri

current font size for Normal style is 11 point

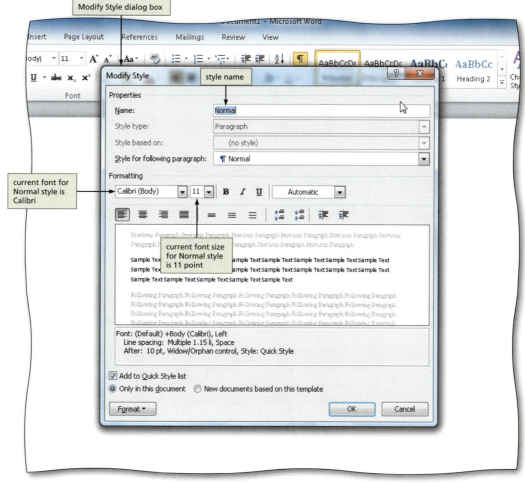

Figure 2–3

3

- Click the Font box arrow (Modify Style dialog box) to display the Font list. Scroll to and then click Times New Roman in the list to change the font for the style being modified.

- Click the Font Size box arrow (Modify Style dialog box) and then click 12 in the Font Size list to change the font size for the style being modified.

- Ensure that the 'Only in this document' option button is selected (Figure 2–4).

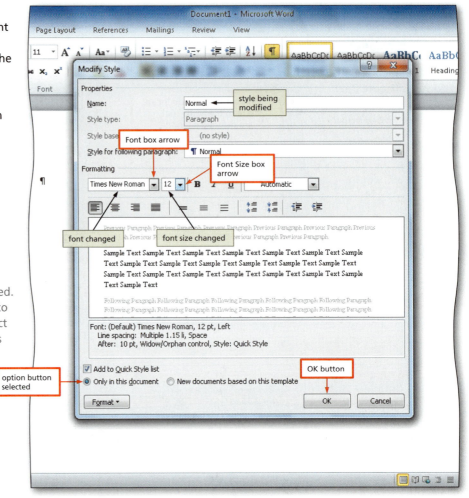

Q&A

Will all future documents use the new font and font size?

No, because the 'Only in this document' option button is selected. If you want all future documents to use a new setting, you would select the 'New documents based on this template' option button.

4

- Click the OK button (Modify Style dialog box) to update the Normal style to the specified settings.

Figure 2–4

Other Ways

1. Click Styles Dialog Box Launcher, click box arrow next to style name, click Modify on menu, change settings (Modify Style dialog box), click OK button

2. Press ALT+CTRL+SHIFT+S, click box arrow next to style name, click Modify on menu, change settings (Modify Style dialog box), click OK button

---

Adjusting Line and Paragraph Spacing

BTW

Line Spacing
If the top of a set of characters or a graphical image is chopped off, then line spacing may be set to Exactly. To remedy the problem, change line spacing to 1.0, 1.15, 1.5, 2.0, 2.5, 3.0, or At least (in the Paragraph dialog box), all of which accommodate the largest font or image.

Line spacing is the amount of vertical space between lines of text in a paragraph. **Paragraph spacing** is the amount of space above and below a paragraph. By default, the Normal style places 10 points of blank space after each paragraph and inserts a vertical space equal to 1.15 lines between each line of text. It also automatically adjusts line height to accommodate various font sizes and graphics.

The MLA documentation style requires that you **double-space** the entire research paper. That is, the amount of vertical space between each line of text and above and below paragraphs should be equal to one blank line. The next sets of steps adjust line spacing and paragraph spacing according to the MLA documentation style.

To Change Line Spacing

The lines of the research paper should be double-spaced, according to the MLA documentation style. In Word, you change the line spacing to 2.0 to double-space lines in a paragraph. The following steps change the line spacing to double.

1

- Click the Line and Paragraph Spacing button (Home tab | Paragraph group) to display the Line and Paragraph Spacing gallery (Figure 2–5).

What do the numbers in the Line and Paragraph Spacing gallery represent?

The default line spacing is 1.15 lines. The options 1.0, 2.0, and 3.0 set line spacing to single, double, and triple, respectively. Similarly, the 1.5 and 2.5 options set line spacing to 1.5 and 2.5 lines. All these options adjust line spacing automatically to accommodate the largest font or graphic on a line.

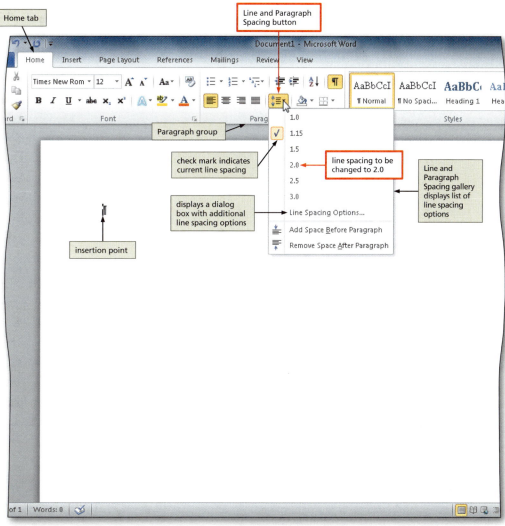

Figure 2–5

2

- Click 2.0 in the Line and Paragraph Spacing gallery to change the line spacing at the location of the insertion point.

Can I change the line spacing of existing text?

Yes. Select the text first and then change the line spacing as described in these steps.

Other Ways

1. Right-click paragraph, click Paragraph on shortcut menu, click Indents and Spacing tab (Paragraph dialog box), click Line spacing box arrow, click desired spacing, click OK button

2. Click Paragraph Dialog Box Launcher (Home tab or Page Layout tab | Paragraph group), click Indents and Spacing tab (Paragraph dialog box), click Line spacing box arrow, click desired spacing, click OK button

3. Press CTRL+2 for double-spacing

To Remove Space after a Paragraph

The research paper should not have additional blank space after each paragraph. The following steps remove space after a paragraph.

- Click the Line and Paragraph Spacing button (Home tab | Paragraph group) to display the Line and Paragraph Spacing gallery (Figure 2–6).

- Click Remove Space After Paragraph in the Line and Paragraph Spacing gallery so that no blank space appears after paragraphs.

Q&A

Can I remove space after existing paragraphs?

Yes. Select the paragraphs first and then remove the space as described in these steps.

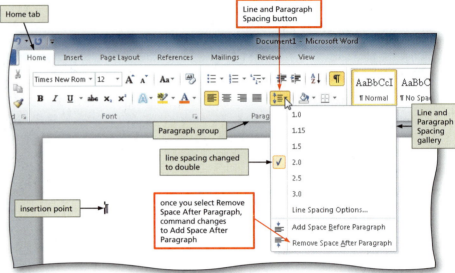

Figure 2–6

Other Ways

1. Click Spacing After box arrows (Page Layout tab | Paragraph group) until 0 pt is displayed

2. Right-click paragraph, click Paragraph on shortcut menu, click

   Indents and Spacing tab (Paragraph dialog box), click After box arrows until 0 pt is displayed, click OK button

3. Click Paragraph Dialog Box Launcher (Home

   tab or Page Layout tab | Paragraph group), click Indents and Spacing tab (Paragraph dialog box), click After box arrows until 0 pt is displayed, click OK button

To Update a Style to Match a Selection

To ensure that all paragraphs in the paper will be double-spaced and do not have space after the paragraphs, you want the Normal style to include the line and paragraph spacing changes made in the previous two sets of steps. You can update a style to reflect the settings of the location of the insertion point or selected text. Because no text has yet been typed in the research paper, you do not need to select text prior to updating the Normal style. The following steps update the Normal style.

- Right-click Normal in the Quick Style gallery (Home tab | Styles group) to display a shortcut menu (Figure 2–7).

- Click Update Normal to Match Selection on the shortcut menu to update the selected (or current) style to reflect the settings at the location of the insertion point.

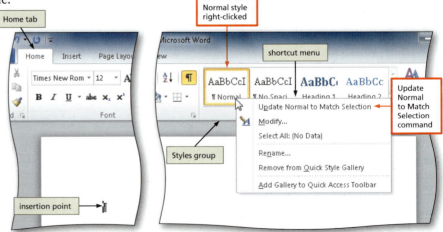

Other Ways

1. Right-click text, point to Styles on shortcut menu, click Update [style name] to Match Selection on submenu

Figure 2–7

Headers and Footers

A **header** is text and graphics that print at the top of each page in a document. Similarly, a **footer** is text and graphics that print at the bottom of every page. In Word, headers print in the top margin one-half inch from the top of every page, and footers print in the bottom margin one-half inch from the bottom of each page, which meets the MLA documentation style. In addition to text and graphics, headers and footers can include document information such as the page number, current date, current time, and author's name.

In this research paper, you are to precede the page number with your last name placed one-half inch from the upper-right edge of each page. The procedures on the following pages enter your name and the page number in the header, as specified by the MLA documentation style.

BTW

The Ribbon and Screen Resolution
Word may change how the groups and buttons within the groups appear on the Ribbon, depending on the computer's screen resolution. Thus, your Ribbon may look different from the ones in this book if you are using a screen resolution other than 1024 x 768.

To Switch to the Header

To enter text in the header, you instruct Word to edit the header. The following steps switch from editing the document text to editing the header.

1
- Click Insert on the Ribbon to display the Insert tab.

- Click the Header button (Insert tab | Header & Footer group) to display the Header gallery (Figure 2–8).

Q&A Can I use a built-in header for this research paper?

None of the built-in headers adheres to the MLA documentation style. Thus, you enter your own header content, instead of using a built-in header, for this research paper.

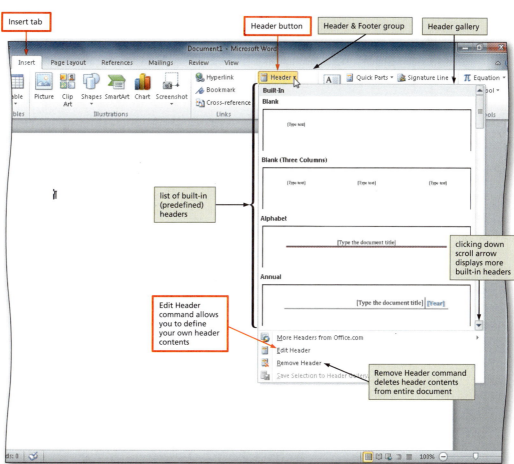

Figure 2–8

Q&A How would I remove a header from a document?

You would click Remove Header in the Header gallery (shown in Figure 2–8). Similarly, to remove a footer, you would click Remove Footer in the Footer gallery.

 **Experiment**
- Click the down scroll arrow in the Header gallery to see the available built-in headers.

2

- Click Edit Header in the Header gallery to switch from the document text to the header, which allows you to edit the contents of the header (Figure 2–9).

Q&A

How do I remove the Header & Footer Tools Design tab from the Ribbon?

When you are finished editing the header, you will close it, which removes the Header & Footer Tools Design tab.

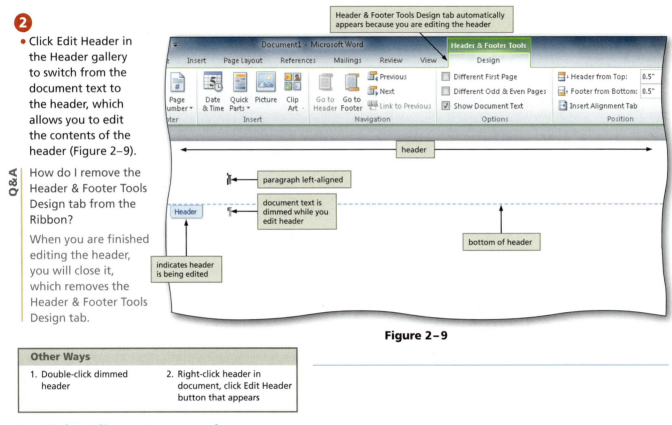

Figure 2–9

Other Ways

1. Double-click dimmed header

2. Right-click header in document, click Edit Header button that appears

To Right-Align a Paragraph

The paragraph in the header currently is left-aligned (Figure 2–9). Your last name and the page number should print **right-aligned**, that is, at the right margin. The following step right-aligns a paragraph.

1

- Click Home on the Ribbon to display the Home tab.

- Click the Align Text Right button (Home tab | Paragraph group) to right-align the current paragraph (Figure 2–10).

Q&A

What if I wanted to return the paragraph to left-aligned?

Click the Align Text Right button again, or click the Align Text Left button.

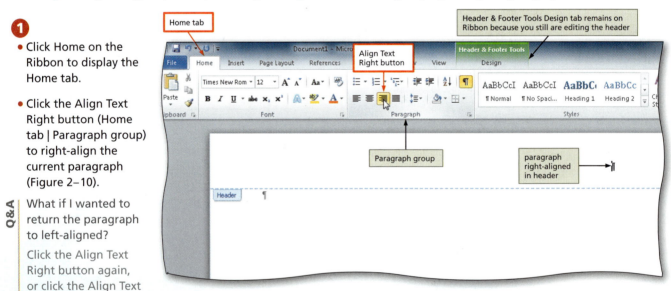

Figure 2–10

Other Ways

1. Right-click paragraph, click Paragraph on shortcut menu, click Indents and Spacing tab (Paragraph dialog box), click Alignment box arrow, click Right, click OK button

2. Click Paragraph Dialog Box Launcher (Home tab or Page Layout tab | Paragraph group), click Indents and Spacing tab (Paragraph dialog box), click Alignment box arrow, click Right, click OK button

3. Press CTRL+R

To Enter Text

The following steps enter your last name right-aligned in the header area.

 Click Design on the Ribbon to display the Header & Footer Tools Design tab.

2 Type **Marino** and then press the SPACEBAR to enter the last name in the header.

BTW

Footers
If you wanted to create a footer, you would click the Footer button (Insert tab | Header & Footer group) and then select the desired built-in footer or click Edit Footer to create a customized footer; you also could double-click the dimmed footer, or right-click the footer and then click the Edit Footer button that appears.

To Insert a Page Number

The next task is to insert the current page number in the header. The following steps insert a page number at the location of the insertion point.

1

• Click the Insert Page Number button (Header & Footer Tools Design tab | Header & Footer group) to display the Insert Page Number menu.

• Point to Current Position on the Insert Page Number menu to display the Current Position gallery (Figure 2–11).

Experiment

• Click the down scroll arrow in the Current Position gallery to see the available page number formats.

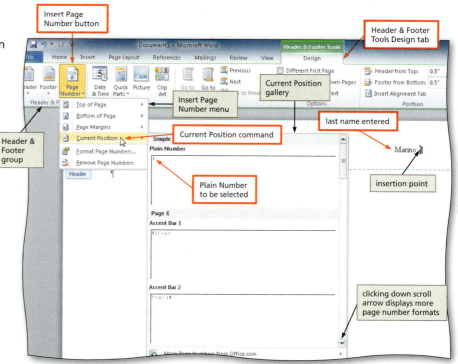

Figure 2–11

2

• If necessary, scroll to the top of the Current Position gallery. Click Plain Number in the Current Position gallery to insert an unformatted page number at the location of the insertion point (Figure 2–12).

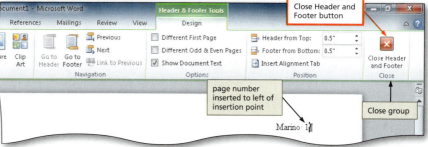

Figure 2–12

Other Ways		
1. Click Insert Page Number button (Insert tab | Header & Footer group)	2. Click Quick Parts button (Insert tab | Text group or Header & Footer Tools Design tab | Insert group),	click Field on Quick Parts menu, select Page in Field names list (Field dialog box), click OK button

To Close the Header

You are finished entering text in the header. Thus, the next task is to switch back to the document text. The following step closes the header.

- Click the Close Header and Footer button (Header & Footer Tools Design tab | Close group) (shown in Figure 2–12 on the previous page) to close the header and switch back to the document text (Figure 2–13).

Q&A

How do I make changes to existing header text?

Switch to the header using the steps described on pages WD 75 and WD 76, edit the header as you would edit text in the document window, and then switch back to the document text.

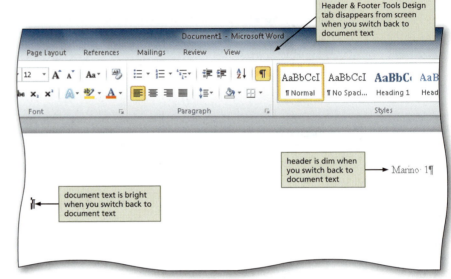

Figure 2–13

Other Ways

1. Double-click dimmed document text

Typing the Research Paper Text

The text of the research paper in this chapter encompasses the first two pages of the paper. You will type the text of the research paper and then modify it later in the chapter, so that it matches Figure 2–1 on page WD 67.

Plan Ahead

Write the first draft, referencing sources.
As you write the first draft of a research paper, be sure it includes the proper components, uses credible sources, and does not contain any plagiarized material.

- **Include an introduction, body, and conclusion.** The first paragraph of the paper introduces the topic and captures the reader's attention. The body, which follows the introduction, consists of several paragraphs that support the topic. The conclusion summarizes the main points in the body and restates the topic.

- **Evaluate sources for authority, currency, and accuracy.** Be especially wary of information obtained from the Web. Any person, company, or organization can publish a Web page on the Internet. Ask yourself these questions about the source:

  - Authority: Does a reputable institution or group support the source? Is the information presented without bias? Are the author's credentials listed and verifiable?

  - Currency: Is the information up to date? Are dates of sources listed? What is the last date revised or updated?

  - Accuracy: Is the information free of errors? Is it verifiable? Are the sources clearly identified?

(continued)

(continued)

**Plan
Ahead**

- **Acknowledge all sources of information; do not plagiarize.** Not only is plagiarism unethical, but it is considered an academic crime that can have severe punishments such as failing a course or being expelled from school.

  When you summarize, paraphrase (rewrite information in your own words), present facts, give statistics, quote exact words, or show a map, chart, or other graphical image, you must acknowledge the source. Information that commonly is known or accessible to the audience constitutes common knowledge and does not need to be acknowledged. If, however, you question whether certain information is common knowledge, you should document it — just to be safe.

To Enter Name and Course Information

As discussed earlier in this chapter, the MLA documentation style does not require a separate title page for research papers. Instead, place your name and course information in a block at the top of the page, below the header, at the left margin. The following steps enter the name and course information in the research paper.

1 Type `Annalisa Marino` as the student name and then press the ENTER key.

2 Type `Mr. Winters` as the instructor name and then press the ENTER key.

3 Type `English 101` as the course name and then press the ENTER key.

4 Type `April 4, 2012` as the paper due date and then press the ENTER key (Figure 2–14).

BTW

Date Formats
The MLA documentation style prefers the day-month-year (4 April 2012) or month-day-year (April 4, 2012) format.

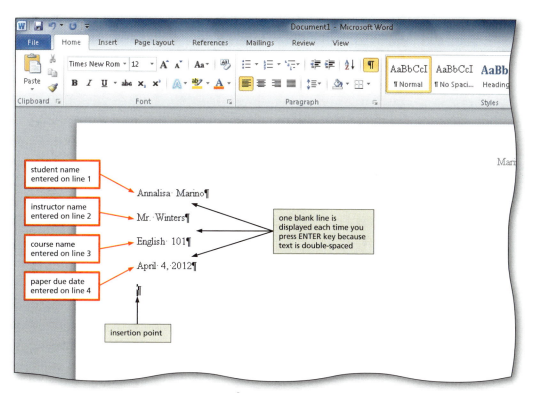

Figure 2–14

To Click and Type

The next step is to enter the title of the research paper centered between the page margins. In Chapter 1, you used the Center button (Home tab | Paragraph group) to center text and graphics. As an alternative, you can use Word's **Click and Type** feature to format and enter text, graphics, and other items. To use Click and Type, you double-click a blank area of the document window. Word automatically formats the item you type or insert according to the location where you double-clicked. The following steps use Click and Type to center and then type the title of the research paper.

 1

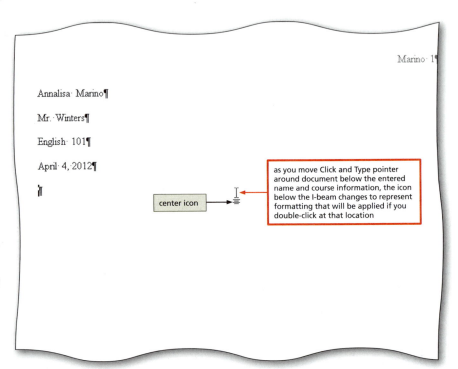

🔍 Experiment

- Move the mouse pointer around the document below the entered name and course information and observe the various icons that appear with the I-beam.

- Position the mouse pointer in the center of the document at the approximate location for the research paper title until a center icon appears below the I-beam (Figure 2–15).

Q&A

What are the other icons that appear in the Click and Type pointer?

A left-align icon appears to the right of the I-beam when the Click and Type pointer is in certain locations on the left side of the document window. A right-align icon appears to the left of the I-beam when the Click and Type pointer is in certain locations on the right side of the document window.

Figure 2–15

 2

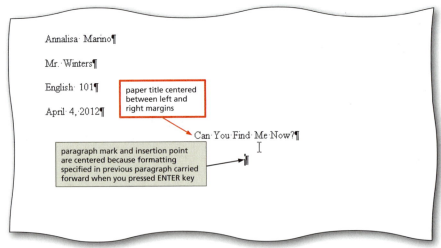

- Double-click to center the paragraph mark and insertion point between the left and right margins.

- Type **Can You Find Me Now?** as the paper title and then press the ENTER key to position the insertion point on the next line (Figure 2–16).

Figure 2–16

Shortcut Keys

Word has many **shortcut keys**, or keyboard key combinations, for your convenience while typing. Table 2–1 lists the common shortcut keys for formatting characters. Table 2–2 lists common shortcut keys for formatting paragraphs.

Table 2–1 Shortcut Keys for Formatting Characters

Character Formatting Task	Shortcut Keys	Character Formatting Task	Shortcut Keys
All capital letters	CTRL+SHIFT+A	Italic	CTRL+I
Bold	CTRL+B	Remove character formatting (plain text)	CTRL+SPACEBAR
Case of letters	SHIFT+F3	Small uppercase letters	CTRL+SHIFT+K
Decrease font size	CTRL+SHIFT+<	Subscript	CTRL+EQUAL SIGN
Decrease font size 1 point	CTRL+[	Superscript	CTRL+SHIFT+PLUS SIGN
Double-underline	CTRL+SHIFT+D	Underline	CTRL+U
Increase font size	CTRL+SHIFT+>	Underline words, not spaces	CTRL+SHIFT+W
Increase font size 1 point	CTRL+]		

Table 2–2 Shortcut Keys for Formatting Paragraphs

Paragraph Formatting	Shortcut Keys	Paragraph Formatting	Shortcut Keys
1.5 line spacing	CTRL+5	Justify paragraph	CTRL+J
Add/remove one line above paragraph	CTRL+0 (zero)	Left-align paragraph	CTRL+L
Center paragraph	CTRL+E	Remove hanging indent	CTRL+SHIFT+T
Decrease paragraph indent	CTRL+SHIFT+M	Remove paragraph formatting	CTRL+Q
Double-space lines	CTRL+2	Right-align paragraph	CTRL+R
Hanging indent	CTRL+T	Single-space lines	CTRL+1
Increase paragraph indent	CTRL+M		

To Format Text Using Shortcut Keys

The paragraphs below the paper title should be left-aligned, instead of centered. Thus, the next step is to left-align the paragraph below the paper title. When your fingers are already on the keyboard, you may prefer using shortcut keys to format text as you type it. The following step left-aligns a paragraph using the shortcut keys CTRL+L. (Recall from Chapter 1 that a notation such as CTRL+L means to press the letter L on the keyboard while holding down the CTRL key.)

 Press CTRL+L to left-align the current paragraph, that is, the paragraph containing the insertion point (shown in Figure 2–17 on the next page).

 Why would I use a keyboard shortcut instead of the Ribbon to format text?

Switching between the mouse and the keyboard takes time. If your hands are already on the keyboard, use a shortcut key. If your hand is on the mouse, use the Ribbon.

BTW

Shortcut Keys
To print a complete list of shortcut keys in Word, click the Microsoft Word Help button near the upper-right corner of the Word window, type **shortcut keys** in the 'Type words to search for' text box at the top of the Word Help window, press the ENTER key, click the Keyboard shortcuts for Microsoft Word link, click the Show All link in the upper-right corner of the Help window, click the Print button in the Help window, and then click the Print button in the Print dialog box.

For an introduction to Office 2010 and instruction about how to perform basic tasks in Office 2010 programs, read the Office 2010 and Windows 7 chapter at the beginning of this book, where you can learn how to start a program, use the Ribbon, save a file, open a file, quit a program, use Help, and much more.

To Save a Document

You have performed many tasks while creating this research paper and do not want to risk losing work completed thus far. Accordingly, you should save the document. The following steps assume you already have created folders for storing your files, for example, a CIS 101 folder (for your class) that contains a Word folder (for your assignments). Thus, these steps save the document in the Word folder in the CIS 101 folder on a USB flash drive using the file name, Triangulation Paper.

1 With a USB flash drive connected to one of the computer's USB ports, click the Save button on the Quick Access Toolbar to display the Save As dialog box.

2 Type `Triangulation Paper` in the File name text box to change the file name. Do not press the ENTER key after typing the file name because you do not want to close the dialog box at this time.

3 Navigate to the desired save location (in this case, the Word folder in the CIS 101 folder [or your class folder] on the USB flash drive).

4 Click the Save button (Save As dialog box) to save the document in the selected folder on the selected drive with the entered file name.

To Display the Rulers

According to the MLA documentation style, the first line of each paragraph in the research paper is to be indented one-half inch from the left margin. Although you can use a dialog box to indent paragraphs, Word provides a quicker way through the **horizontal ruler**. This ruler is displayed at the top edge of the document window just below the Ribbon. Word also provides a **vertical ruler** that is displayed along the left edge of the Word window. The following step displays the rulers because you want to use the ruler to indent paragraphs.

1

 Experiment

- Repeatedly click the View Ruler button on the vertical scroll bar to see the how this button is used to both show and hide the rulers.

- If the rulers are not displayed, click the View Ruler button on the vertical scroll bar to display the horizontal and vertical rulers on the screen (Figure 2–17).

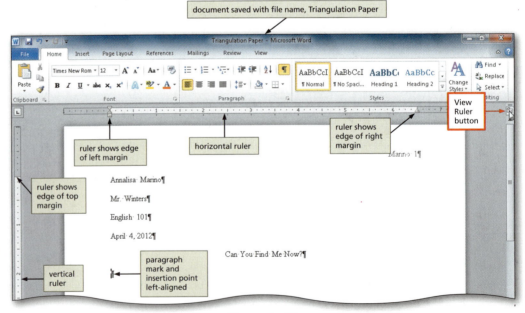

Figure 2–17

Q&A For what tasks would I use the rulers?

You can use the rulers to indent paragraphs, set tab stops, change page margins, and adjust column widths.

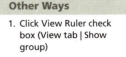

Other Ways

1. Click View Ruler check box (View tab | Show group)

To First-Line Indent Paragraphs

The first line of each paragraph in the research paper is to be indented one-half inch from the left margin. You can use the horizontal ruler, usually simply called the **ruler**, to indent just the first line of a paragraph, which is called a **first-line indent**.

The left margin on the ruler contains two triangles above a square. The **First Line Indent marker** is the top triangle at the 0" mark on the ruler (Figure 2–18). The bottom triangle is discussed later in this chapter. The small square at the 0" mark is the Left Indent marker. The **Left Indent marker** allows you to change the entire left margin, whereas the First Line Indent marker indents only the first line of the paragraph. The following steps first-line indent paragraphs in the research paper.

1

• With the insertion point on the paragraph mark below the research paper title, point to the First Line Indent marker on the ruler (Figure 2–18).

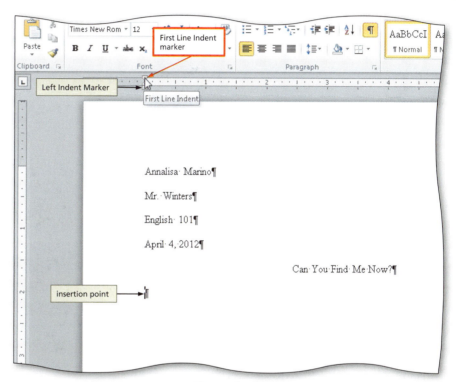

Figure 2–18

2

• Drag the First Line Indent marker to the .5" mark on the ruler to display a vertical dotted line in the document window, which indicates the proposed location of the first line of the paragraph (Figure 2–19).

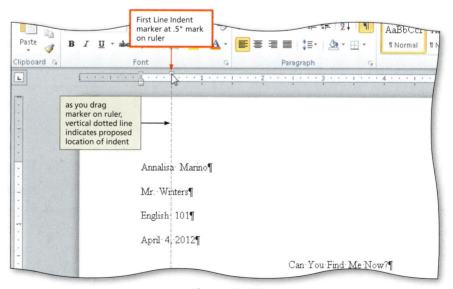

Figure 2–19

3

- Release the mouse button to place the First Line Indent marker at the .5" mark on the ruler, or one-half inch from the left margin (Figure 2–20).

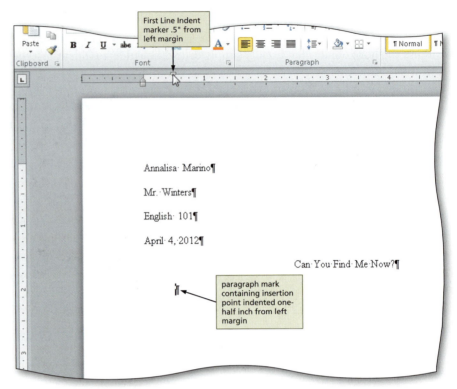

Figure 2–20

4

- Type **How is a Nintendo Wii console able to determine the location of a Wii Remote while a player interacts with a game?** and notice that Word automatically indented the first line of the paragraph by one-half inch (Figure 2–21).

Q&A

Will I have to set a first-line indent for each paragraph in the paper?

No. Each time you press the ENTER key, paragraph formatting in the previous paragraph carries forward to the next paragraph. Thus, once you set the first-line indent, its format carries forward automatically to each subsequent paragraph you type.

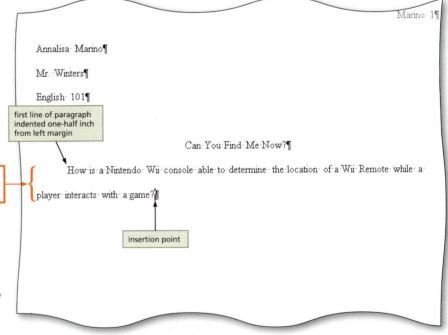

Figure 2–21

Other Ways

1. Right-click paragraph, click Paragraph on shortcut menu, click Indents and Spacing tab (Paragraph dialog box), click Special box arrow, click First line, click OK button

2. Click Paragraph Dialog Box Launcher (Home tab or Page Layout tab | Paragraph group), click Indents and Spacing tab (Paragraph dialog box), click Special box arrow, click First line, click OK button

3. Press TAB key at beginning of paragraph

To AutoCorrect as You Type

As you type, you may make typing, spelling, capitalization, or grammar errors. For this reason, Word provides an **AutoCorrect** feature that automatically corrects these kinds of errors as you type them in the document. For example, if you type ahve, Word automatically changes it to the correct spelling, have, when you press the SPACEBAR or a punctuation mark key such as a period or comma.

Word has predefined many commonly misspelled words, which it automatically corrects for you. The following steps intentionally misspell the word, the, as teh to illustrate the AutoCorrect feature.

- Press the SPACEBAR.

- Type the beginning of the next sentence, misspelling the word, the, as follows:
  The answer is triangulation, a process that determines teh (Figure 2–22).

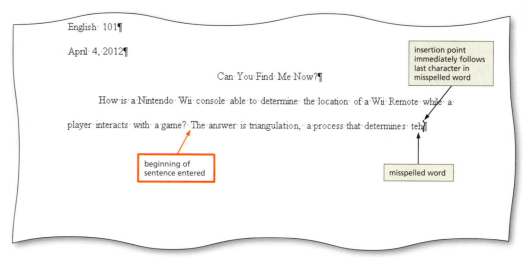

Figure 2–22

- Press the SPACEBAR and watch Word automatically correct the misspelled word.

- Type the rest of the sentence (Figure 2–23):
  location of an object by measuring the angles from two or more fixed points.

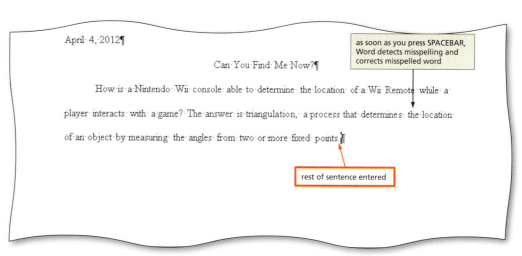

Figure 2–23

To Use the AutoCorrect Options Button

When you position the mouse pointer on text that Word automatically corrected, a small blue box appears below the text. If you point to the small blue box, Word displays the AutoCorrect Options button. When you click the **AutoCorrect Options button**, Word displays a menu that allows you to undo a correction or change how Word handles future automatic corrections of this type. The steps on the next page illustrate the AutoCorrect Options button and menu.

- Position the mouse pointer in the text automatically corrected by Word (the word, the, in this case) to display a small blue box below the automatically corrected word (Figure 2–24).

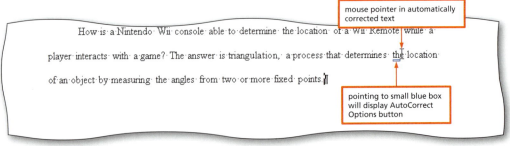

mouse pointer in automatically corrected text

pointing to small blue box will display AutoCorrect Options button

Figure 2–24

- Point to the small blue box to display the AutoCorrect Options button.

- Click the AutoCorrect Options button to display the AutoCorrect Options menu (Figure 2–25).

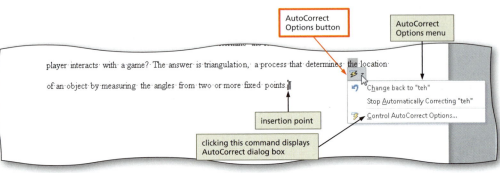

AutoCorrect Options button

AutoCorrect Options menu

insertion point

clicking this command displays AutoCorrect dialog box

Figure 2–25

- Press the ESCAPE key to remove the AutoCorrect Options menu from the screen.

Q&A

Do I need to remove the AutoCorrect Options button from the screen?

No. When you move the mouse pointer, the AutoCorrect Options button will disappear from the screen. If, for some reason, you wanted to remove the AutoCorrect Options button from the screen, you could press the ESCAPE key a second time.

To Create an AutoCorrect Entry

In addition to the predefined list of AutoCorrect spelling, capitalization, and grammar errors, you can create your own AutoCorrect entries to add to the list. For example, if you tend to mistype the word sensor as senser, you should create an AutoCorrect entry for it. The following steps create an AutoCorrect entry.

- Click File on the Ribbon to open the Backstage view (Figure 2–26).

File tab

Backstage view

Options command

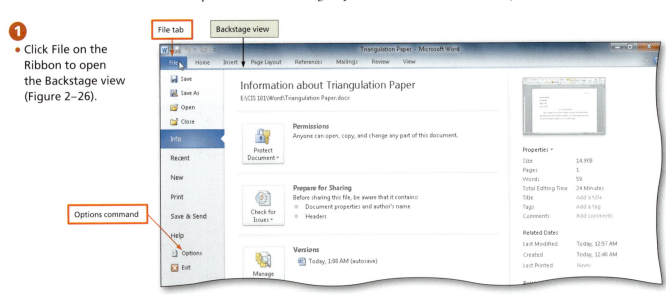

Figure 2–26

- Click Options in the Backstage view to display the Word Options dialog box.

- Click Proofing in the left pane (Word Options dialog box) to display proofing options in the right pane.

- Click the AutoCorrect Options button in the right pane to display the AutoCorrect dialog box.

- When Word displays the AutoCorrect dialog box, type **senser** in the Replace text box.

- Press the TAB key and then type **sensor** in the With text box (Figure 2–27).

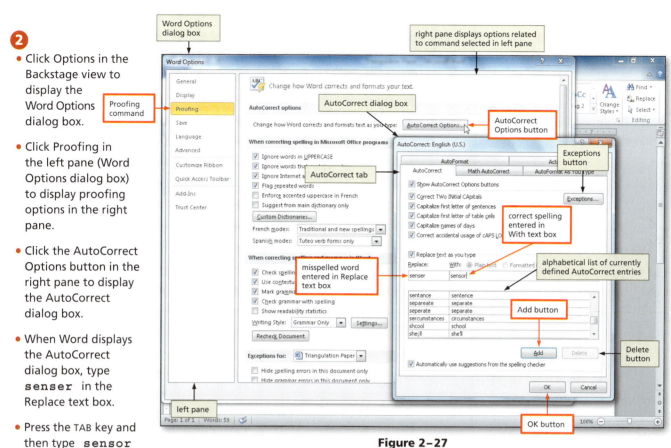

Figure 2–27

How would I delete an existing AutoCorrect entry?

You would select the entry to be deleted in the list of defined entries in the AutoCorrect dialog box and then click the Delete button.

- Click the Add button (AutoCorrect dialog box) to add the entry alphabetically to the list of words to correct automatically as you type. (If your dialog box displays a Replace button instead, click it and then click the Yes button in the Microsoft Word dialog box to replace the previously defined entry.)

- Click the OK button (AutoCorrect dialog box) to close the dialog box.

- Click the OK button (Word Options dialog box) to close the dialog box.

The AutoCorrect Dialog Box

In addition to creating AutoCorrect entries for words you commonly misspell or mistype, you can create entries for abbreviations, codes, and so on. For example, you could create an AutoCorrect entry for asap, indicating that Word should replace this text with the phrase, as soon as possible.

If, for some reason, you do not want Word to correct automatically as you type, you can turn off the 'Replace text as you type' feature by clicking Options in the Backstage view, clicking Proofing in the left pane (Word Options dialog box), clicking the AutoCorrect Options button in the right pane (Figure 2–27), removing the check mark from the 'Replace text as you type' check box, and then clicking the OK button in each open dialog box.

The AutoCorrect sheet in the AutoCorrect dialog box (Figure 2–27) contains other check boxes that correct capitalization errors if the check boxes are selected. If you

BTW

Automatic Corrections
If you do not want to keep a change automatically made by Word and you immediately notice the automatic correction, you can undo the change by clicking the Undo button on the Quick Access Toolbar or pressing CTRL+Z. You also can undo a correction through the AutoCorrect Options button, which was shown above.

type two capital letters in a row, such as TH, Word makes the second letter lowercase, Th. If you begin a sentence with a lowercase letter, Word capitalizes the first letter of the sentence. If you type the name of a day in lowercase letters, such as tuesday, Word capitalizes the first letter in the name of the day, Tuesday. If you leave the CAPS LOCK key on and begin a new sentence, such as aFTER, Word corrects the typing, After, and turns off the CAPS LOCK key. If you do not want Word to automatically perform any of these corrections, simply remove the check mark from the appropriate check box in the AutoCorrect dialog box.

Sometimes you do not want Word to AutoCorrect a particular word or phrase. For example, you may use the code WD. in your documents. Because Word automatically capitalizes the first letter of a sentence, the character you enter following the period will be capitalized (in the previous sentence, it would capitalize the letter i in the word, in). To allow the code WD. to be entered into a document and still leave the AutoCorrect feature turned on, you would set an exception. To set an exception to an AutoCorrect rule, click Options in the Backstage view, click Proofing in the left pane (Word Options dialog box), click the AutoCorrect Options button in the right pane, click the Exceptions button (Figure 2–27 on the previous page), click the appropriate tab in the AutoCorrect Exceptions dialog box, type the exception entry in the text box, click the Add button, click the Close button (AutoCorrect Exceptions dialog box), and then click the OK button in each of the remaining dialog boxes.

To Enter More Text

The next step is to continue typing text in the research paper up to the location of the in-text parenthetical reference. The following steps enter this text.

BTW

Spacing after Punctuation
Because word processing documents use variable character fonts, it often is difficult to determine in a printed document how many times someone has pressed the SPACEBAR between sentences. Thus, the rule is to press the SPACEBAR only once after periods, colons, and other punctuation marks.

1 With the insertion point positioned at the end of the first paragraph in the paper, as shown in Figure 2–25 on page WD 86, press the ENTER key, so that you can begin typing the text in the second paragraph.

2 Type `Surveyors often use triangulation to measure distance. Starting at a known location and elevation, surveyors measure a length to create a base line and then use a theodolite to measure an angle to an unknown point from each side of the base line` and then press the SPACEBAR.

Citations

Both the MLA and APA guidelines suggest the use of in-text parenthetical references (placed at the end of a sentence), instead of footnoting each source of material in a paper. These parenthetical references, called citations in Word, guide the reader to the end of the paper for complete information about the source.

Plan Ahead

Reference all sources.
During your research, be sure to record essential publication information about each of your sources. Following is a sample list of types of required information for the MLA documentation style.

- Book: full name of author(s), complete title of book, edition (if available), volume (if available), publication city, publisher name, publication year, publication medium

- Magazine: full name of author(s), complete title of article, magazine title, issue number (if available), date of magazine, page numbers of article, publication medium

- Web site: full name of author(s), title of Web site, Web site publisher or sponsor (if none, write N.p.), publication date (if none, write n.d.), publication medium, date viewed

Word provides tools to assist you with inserting citations in a paper and later generating a list of sources from the citations. With a documentation style selected, Word automatically formats the citations and list of sources according to that style. The process for adding citations in Word is as follows:

1. Modify the documentation style, if necessary.
2. Insert a citation placeholder.
3. Enter the source information for the citation.

You can combine Steps 2 and 3, where you insert the citation placeholder and enter the source information at once. Or, you can insert the citation placeholder as you write and then enter the source information for the citation at a later time. While creating the research paper in this chapter, you will use both methods.

To Change the Bibliography Style

The first step in inserting a citation is to be sure the citations and sources will be formatted using the correct documentation style, called the bibliography style in Word. The following steps change the specified documentation style.

1

- Click References on the Ribbon to display the References tab.

- Click the Bibliography Style box arrow (References tab | Citations & Bibliography group) to display a gallery of predefined documentation styles (Figure 2–28).

2

- Click MLA Sixth Edition in the Bibliography Style gallery to change the documentation style to MLA.

Q&A

What if I am using a different edition of a documentation style shown in the Bibliography Style gallery?

Select the closest one and then, if necessary, perform necessary edits before submitting the paper.

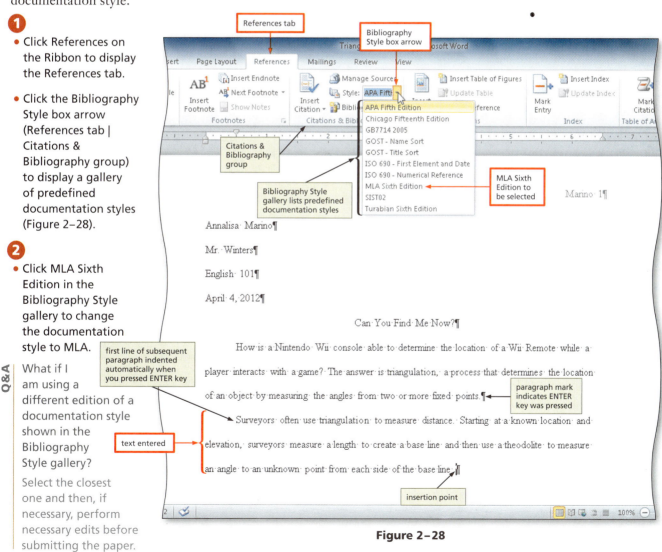

Figure 2–28

To Insert a Citation and Create Its Source

With the documentation style selected, the next task is to insert a citation placeholder and enter the source information for the citation. You can accomplish these steps at once by instructing Word to add a new source. The following steps add a new source for a magazine (periodical) article.

- Click the Insert Citation button (References tab | Citations & Bibliography group) to display the Insert Citation menu (Figure 2–29).

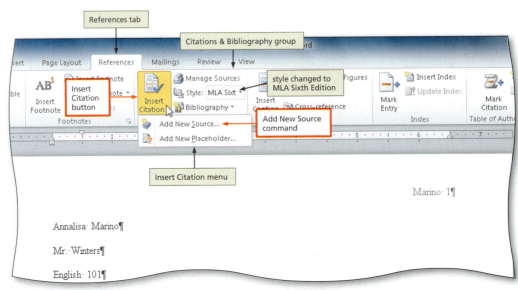

Figure 2–29

- Click Add New Source on the Insert Citation menu to display the Create Source dialog box (Figure 2–30).

Q&A What are the Bibliography Fields in the Create Source dialog box?

A **field** is a placeholder for data whose contents can change. You enter data in some fields; Word supplies data for others. In this case, you enter the contents of the fields for a particular source, for example, the author name in the Author field.

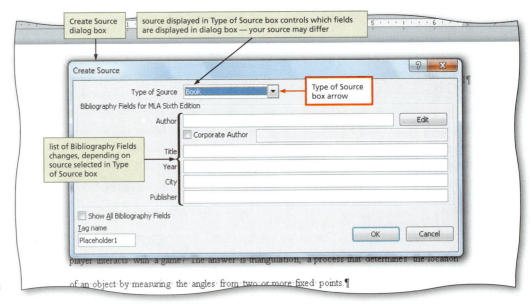

Figure 2–30

- Click the Type of Source box arrow and then click one of the source types in the list, so that you can see how the list of fields changes to reflect the type of source you selected.

- If necessary, click the Type of Source box arrow (Create Source dialog box) and then click Article in a Periodical, so that the list shows fields required for a magazine (periodical).

- Click the Author text box. Type `Jains, Malila` as the author.

- Click the Title text box. Type `How Surveyors Measure and Calculate Angles` as the article title.

- Press the TAB key and then type `Today's Modern Surveyor` as the periodical title.

- Press the TAB key and then type `2012` as the year.

- Press the TAB key and then type `Mar.` as the month.

- Press the TAB key twice and then type `30-48` as the pages (Figure 2–31).

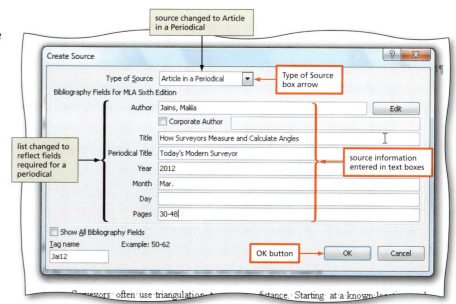

Figure 2–31

- Click the OK button to close the dialog box, create the source, and insert the citation in the document at the location of the insertion point (Figure 2–32).

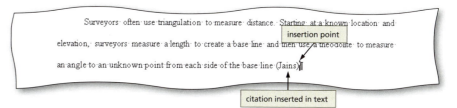

Figure 2–32

To Edit a Citation

In the MLA documentation style, if a source has page numbers, you should include them in the citation. Thus, Word provides a means to enter the page numbers to be displayed in the citation. The following steps edit a citation, so that the page numbers appear in it.

- Click somewhere in the citation to be edited, in this case somewhere in (Jains), which selects the citation and displays the Citation Options box arrow.

- Click the Citation Options box arrow to display the Citation Options menu (Figure 2–33).

What is the purpose of the tab to the left of the selected citation?

If, for some reason, you wanted to move a citation to a different location in the document, you would select the citation and then drag the citation tab to the desired location.

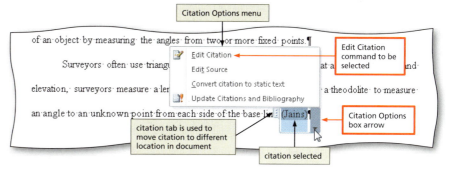

Figure 2–33

2
- Click Edit Citation on the Citation Options menu to display the Edit Citation dialog box.

- Type 30-48 in the Pages text box (Edit Citations dialog box) (Figure 2–34).

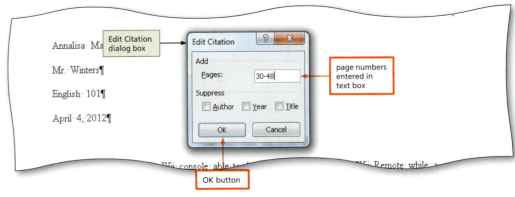

Figure 2–34

3
- Click the OK button to close the dialog box and add the page numbers to the citation in the document (Figure 2–35).

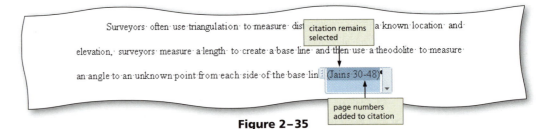

Figure 2–35

4
- Press the END key to move the insertion point to the end of the line, which also deselects the citation.

- Press the PERIOD key to end the sentence.

BTW

Edit a Source
To edit a source, click somewhere in the citation, click the Citation Options box arrow, and then click Edit Source on the Citation Options menu to display the Edit Source dialog box (which resembles the Create Source dialog box). Make necessary changes and then click the OK button.

To Enter More Text

The next step is to continue typing text in the research paper up to the location of the footnote. The following steps enter this text.

1 Press the SPACEBAR.

2 Type the next sentence (Figure 2–36): `The length of the base line and the two known angles allow a computer or person to determine the location of a third point.`

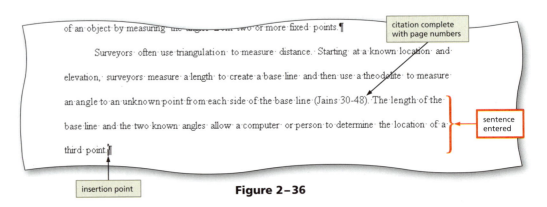

Figure 2–36

To Save an Existing Document with the Same File Name

You have made several modifications to the document since you last saved it. Thus, you should save it again. The following step saves the document again.

1 Click the Save button on the Quick Access Toolbar to overwrite the previously saved file.

Footnotes

As discussed earlier in this chapter, notes are optional in the MLA documentation style. If used, content notes elaborate on points discussed in the paper, and bibliographic notes direct the reader to evaluations of statements in a source or provide a means for identifying multiple sources. The MLA documentation style specifies that a superscript (raised number) be used for a **note reference mark** to signal that a note exists either at the bottom of the page as a **footnote** or at the end of the document as an **endnote**.

In Word, **note text** can be any length and format. Word automatically numbers notes sequentially by placing a note reference mark both in the body of the document and to the left of the note text. If you insert, rearrange, or remove notes, Word renumbers any subsequent note reference marks according to their new sequence in the document.

To Insert a Footnote Reference Mark

The following step inserts a footnote reference mark in the document at the location of the insertion point and at the location where the footnote text will be typed.

1

● With the insertion point positioned as shown in Figure 2–36, click the Insert Footnote button (References tab | Footnotes group) to display a note reference mark (a superscripted 1) in two places: (1) in the document window at the location of the insertion point and (2) at the bottom of the page where the footnote will be positioned, just below a separator line (Figure 2–37).

Q&A

What if I wanted notes to be positioned as endnotes instead of as footnotes?

You would click the Insert Endnote button (References tab | Footnotes group), which places the separator line and the endnote text at the end of the document, instead of the bottom of the page containing the reference.

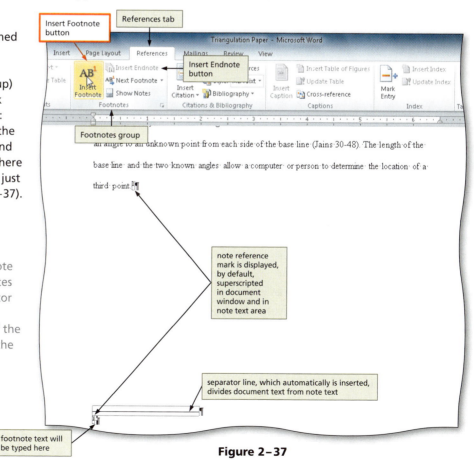

Figure 2–37

Other Ways
1. Press CTRL+ALT+F

To Enter Footnote Text

The following step types the footnote text to the right of the note reference mark below the separator line.

1 Type the footnote text up to the citation: `Cordoba and Sarkis state that electronic theodolites calculate angles automatically and then send the calculated angles to a computer for analysis` and then press the SPACEBAR.

To Insert a Citation Placeholder

Earlier in this chapter, you inserted a citation and its source at once. Sometimes, you may not have the source information readily available and would prefer entering it at a later time.

In the footnote, you will insert a placeholder for the citation and enter the source information later. The following steps insert a citation placeholder.

- With the insertion point positioned as shown in Figure 2–38, click the Insert Citation button (References tab | Citations & Bibliography group) to display the Insert Citation menu (Figure 2–38).

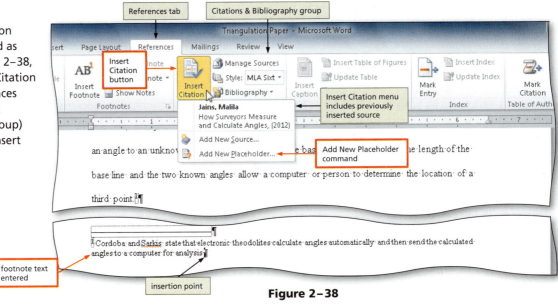

Figure 2–38

- Click Add New Placeholder on the Insert Citation menu to display the Placeholder Name dialog box.

- Type `Cordoba` as the tag name for the source (Figure 2–39).

Q&A

What is a tag name?

A tag name is an identifier that links a citation to a source. Word automatically creates a tag name when you enter a source. When you create a citation placeholder, enter a meaningful tag name, which will appear in the citation placeholder until you edit the source.

Figure 2–39

3

- Click the OK button (Placeholder Name dialog box) to close the dialog box and insert the entered tag name in the citation placeholder in the document.

- Press the PERIOD key to end the sentence.

Footnote Text Style

When you insert a footnote, Word formats it using the Footnote Text style, which does not adhere to the MLA documentation style. For example, notice in Figure 2–38 that the footnote text is single-spaced, left-aligned, and a smaller font size than the text in the research paper. According to the MLA documentation style, notes should be formatted like all other paragraphs in the paper.

You could change the paragraph formatting of the footnote text to first-line indent and double-spacing and then change the font size from 10 to 12 point. If you use this technique, however, you will need to change the format of the footnote text for each footnote you enter into the document.

A more efficient technique is to modify the format of the Footnote Text style so that every footnote you enter in the document will use the formats defined in this style.

To Modify a Style Using a Shortcut Menu

The Footnote Text style specifies left-aligned single-spaced paragraphs with a 10-point font size for text. To meet MLA documentation style, the footnotes should be double-spaced with a first line indent and a 12-point font size for text. The following steps modify the Footnote Text style.

1
- Right-click the note text in the footnote to display a shortcut menu related to footnotes (Figure 2–40).

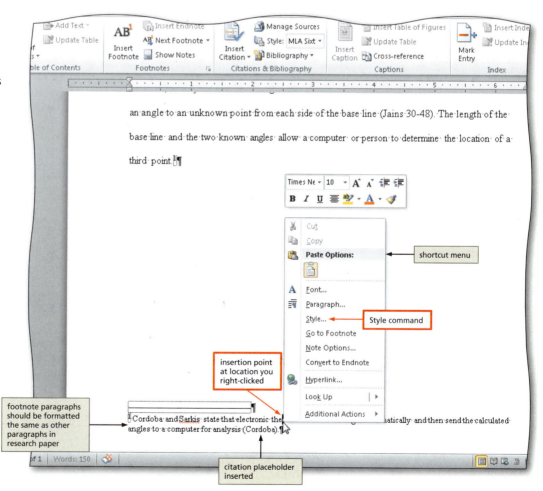

Figure 2–40

2

- Click Style on the shortcut menu to display the Style dialog box. If necessary, click the Category box arrow, click All styles in the Cagetory list, and then click Footnote Text in the Styles list.

- Click the Modify button (Style dialog box) to display the Modify Style dialog box.

- Click the Font Size box arrow (Modify Style dialog box) to display the Font Size list and then click 12 in the Font Size list to change the font size.

- Click the Double Space button to change the line spacing.

- Click the Format button to display the Format menu (Figure 2–41).

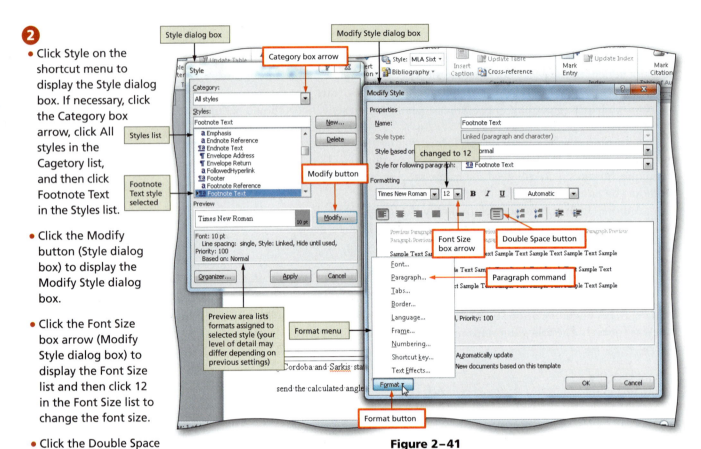

Figure 2–41

3

- Click Paragraph on the Format menu (Modify Style dialog box) to display the Paragraph dialog box.

- Click the Special box arrow (Paragraph dialog box) and then click First line (Figure 2–42).

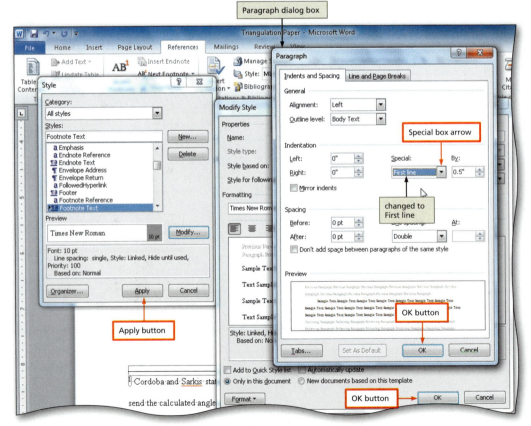

Figure 2–42

4
- Click the OK button (Paragraph dialog box) to close the dialog box.

- Click the OK button (Modify Style dialog box) to close the dialog box.

- Click the Apply button (Style dialog box) to apply the style changes to the footnote text (Figure 2–43).

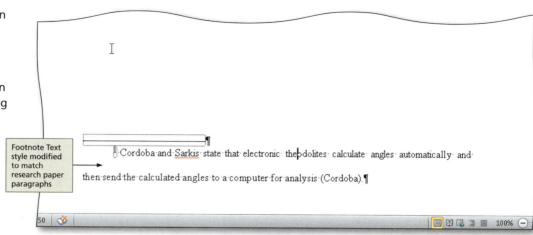

Figure 2–43

Q&A

Will all footnotes use this modified style?

Yes. Any future footnotes entered in the document will use a 12-point font with the paragraphs first-line indented and double-spaced.

Other Ways

1. Click Styles Dialog Box Launcher (Home tab | Styles group), point to style name in list, click style name box arrow, click Modify, change settings (Modify Style dialog box), click OK button

2. Click Styles Dialog Box Launcher (Home tab | Styles group), click Manage Styles button in task pane, select style name in list, click Modify button, change settings (Modify Style dialog box), click OK button in each dialog box

To Edit a Source

When you typed the footnote text for this research paper, you inserted a citation placeholder for the source. Assume you now have the source information and are ready to enter it. The following steps edit a source.

1
- Click somewhere in the citation placeholder to be edited, in this case (Cordoba), to select the citation placeholder.

- Click the Citation Options box arrow to display the Citation Options menu (Figure 2–44).

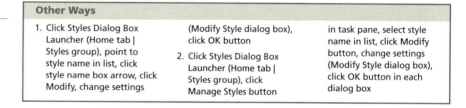

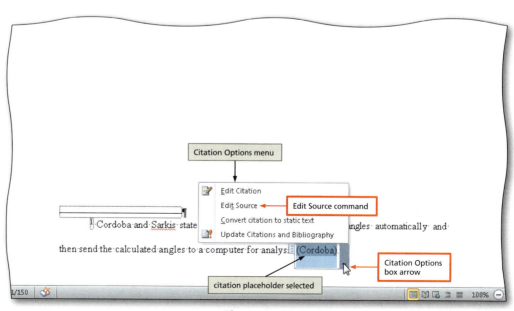

Figure 2–44

2

- Click Edit Source on the Citation Options menu to display the Edit Source dialog box.

- If necessary, click the Type of Source box arrow (Edit Source dialog box) and then click Book, so that the list shows fields required for a book.

- Click the Author text box. Type **Cordoba, Nicolas E.,; Sarkis, Kara A.** as the author.

Q&A

What if I do not know how to punctuate the author entry so that Word formats it properly?

Click the Edit button (Edit Source dialog box) to the right of the Author entry for assistance. For example, you should separate multiple author names with a semicolon as shown in this figure.

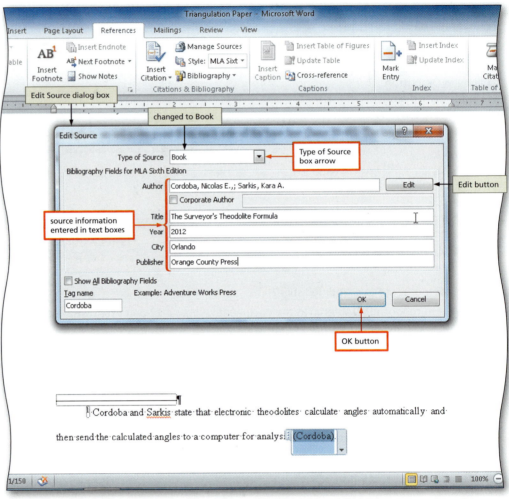

Figure 2–45

- Click the Title text box. Type **The Surveyor's Theodolite Formula** as the book title.

- Press the TAB key and then type **2012** as the year.

- Press the TAB key and then type **Orlando** as the city.

- Press the TAB key and then type **Orange County Press** as the publisher (Figure 2–45).

3

- Click the OK button to close the dialog box and create the source.

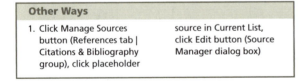

Other Ways

1. Click Manage Sources button (References tab | Citations & Bibliography group), click placeholder source in Current List, click Edit button (Source Manager dialog box)

BTW

Q&As
For a complete list of the Q&As found in many of the step-by-step sequences in this book, visit the Word 2010 Q&A Web page (scsite.com/wd2010/qa).

To Edit a Citation

In the MLA documentation style, if you reference the author's name in the text, you should not list it again in the parenthetical citation. Instead, just list the page number in the citation. To do this, you instruct Word to suppress author and title. The following steps edit the citation, suppressing the author and title but displaying the page numbers.

1 If necessary, click somewhere in the citation to be edited, in this case (Cordoba), to select the citation and display the Citation Options box arrow.

2 Click the Citation Options box arrow to display the Citation Options menu.

3 Click Edit Citation on the Citation Options menu to display the Edit Citation dialog box.

4 Type 25 in the Pages text box (Edit Citation dialog box).

5 Click the Author check box to place a check mark in it.

6 Click the Title check box to place a check mark in it (Figure 2–46).

7 Click the OK button to close the dialog box, remove the author name from the citation in the footnote, suppress the title from showing, and add a page number to the citation (shown in Figure 2-47 on page WD 101).

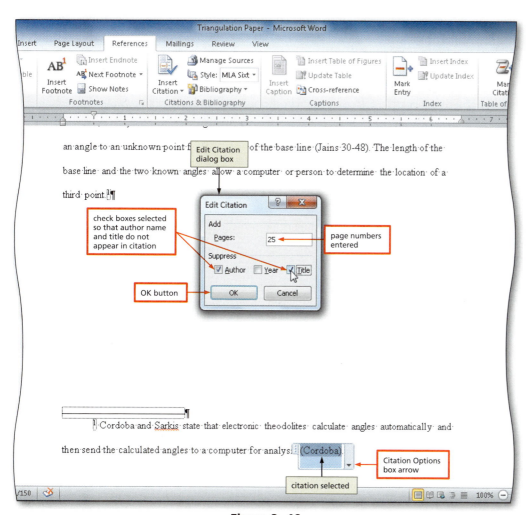

Figure 2–46

BTW

Footnote and Endnote Location
You can change the location of footnotes from the bottom of the page to the end of the text by clicking the Footnotes and Endnote Dialog Box Launcher (References tab | Footnotes group), clicking the Footnotes box arrow (Footnote and Endnote dialog box), and then clicking Below text. Similarly, clicking the Endnotes box arrow (Footnote and Endnote dialog box) enables you to change the location of endnotes from the end of the document to the end of a section. If you wanted to print just the footnotes or endnotes, you could position them at the end of the document on a separate page and then print that page.

BTW

Sending Footnotes or Endnotes to a PowerPoint Presentation
If you wanted footnotes and endnotes, or other headings, to be presented in a PowerPoint slide show, you would perform the following steps. Click the Customize Quick Access Toolbar button on the Quick Access Toolbar. Click More Commands on the Customize Quick Access Toolbar menu. Click the 'Choose commands from' box arrow (Word Options dialog box) and then click All Commands in the list. Scroll through the list of commands and then click Send to Microsoft PowerPoint to select the command. Click the Add button to add the selected command to the Customize Quick Access Toolbar list. Click the OK button to add the button to the Quick Access Toolbar. Then, click the Send to Microsoft PowerPoint button on the Quick Access Toolbar to create a PowerPoint presentation containing the endnotes and footnotes (it may also contain a few additional headings, which you can delete as needed).

Working with Footnotes and Endnotes

You edit footnote text just as you edit any other text in the document. To delete or move a note reference mark, however, the insertion point must be in the document text (not in the footnote text).

To delete a note, select the note reference mark in the document text (not in the footnote text) by dragging through the note reference mark and then click the Cut button (Home tab | Clipboard group). Or, click immediately to the right of the note reference mark in the document text and then press the BACKSPACE key twice, or click immediately to the left of the note reference mark in the document text and then press the DELETE key twice.

To move a note to a different location in a document, select the note reference mark in the document text (not in the footnote text), click the Cut button (Home tab | Clipboard group), click the location where you want to move the note, and then click the Paste button (Home tab | Clipboard group). When you move or delete notes, Word automatically renumbers any remaining notes in the correct sequence.

If you position the mouse pointer on the note reference mark in the document text, the note text is displayed above the note reference mark as a ScreenTip. To remove the ScreenTip, move the mouse pointer.

If, for some reason, you wanted to change the format of note reference marks in footnotes or endnotes (i.e., from 1, 2, 3, to A, B, C), you would click the Footnote & Endnote Dialog Box Launcher (References tab | Footnotes group) to display the Footnote and Endnote dialog box, click the Number format box arrow (Footnote and Endnote dialog box), click the desired number format in the list, and then click the Apply button.

If, for some reason, you wanted to convert footnotes to endnotes, you would click the Footnote & Endnote Dialog Box Launcher (References tab | Footnotes group) to display the Footnote and Endnote dialog box, click the Convert button (Footnote and Endnote dialog box), select the 'Convert all footnotes to endnotes' option button, click the OK button, and then click the Close button (Footnote and Endnote dialog box).

To Enter More Text

The next step is to continue typing text in the body of the research paper. The following steps enter this text.

1 Position the insertion point after the note reference mark in the document and then press the ENTER key.

2 Type the third paragraph of the research paper (Figure 2–47): `Similarly, the Nintendo Wii console uses triangulation to determine the location of a Wii Remote. A player places a sensor bar, which contains two infrared transmitters, near or on top of a television. While the player uses the Wii Remote, the Wii console determines the remote's location by calculating the distance and angles between the Wii Remote and the two transmitters on the sensor bar. Determining the location of a Wii Remote is relatively simple because the sensor bar contains only two fixed points: the transmitters.`

To Count Words

Often when you write papers, you are required to compose the papers with a minimum number of words. The minimum requirement for the research paper in this chapter is 325 words. You can look on the status bar and see the total number of words thus far in a document. For example, Figure 2–47 shows the research paper has 236 words, but you are not sure if that count includes the words in your footnote. The following steps display the Word Count dialog box, so that you can verify the footnote text is included in the count.

1

- Click the Word Count indicator on the status bar to display the Word Count dialog box.

- If necessary, place a check mark in the 'Include textboxes, footnotes and endnotes' check box (Word Count dialog box) (Figure 2–47).

Q&A

Why do the statistics in my Word Count dialog box differ from Figure 2–47?

Depending on the accuracy of your typing, your statistics may differ.

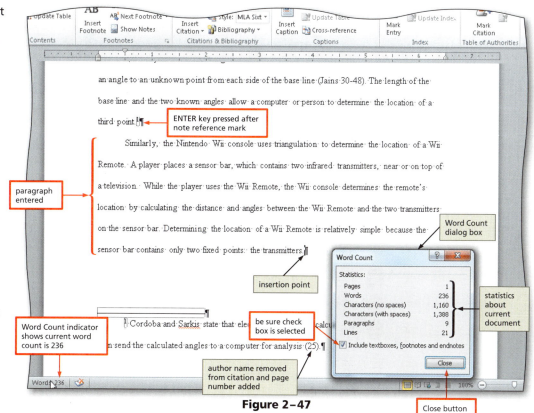

Figure 2–47

2

- Click the Close button to close the dialog box.

Q&A

Can I display statistics for just a section of the document?

Yes. Select the section and then click the Word Count indicator on the status bar to display statistics about the selected text.

Other Ways

1. Click Word Count button (Review tab | Proofing group)
2. Press CTRL+SHIFT+G

Automatic Page Breaks

As you type documents that exceed one page, Word automatically inserts page breaks, called **automatic page breaks** or **soft page breaks**, when it determines the text has filled one page according to paper size, margin settings, line spacing, and other settings. If you add text, delete text, or modify text on a page, Word recomputes the location of automatic page breaks and adjusts them accordingly.

Word performs page recomputation between the keystrokes, that is, in between the pauses in your typing. Thus, Word refers to the automatic page break task as **background repagination**. The steps on the next page illustrate Word's automatic page break feature.

To Enter More Text and Insert a Citation Placeholder

The next task is to type the fourth paragraph in the body of the research paper. The following steps enter this text and a placeholder.

1 With the insertion point positioned at the end of the third paragraph as shown in Figure 2–47 on the previous page, press the ENTER key.

2 Type the fourth paragraph of the research paper (Figure 2–48): `A more complex application of triangulation occurs in a global positioning system (GPS). A GPS consists of one or more earth-based receivers that accept and analyze signals sent by satellites to determine a receiver's geographic location. GPS receivers, found in handheld navigation devices and many vehicles, use triangulation to determine their location relative to at least three geostationary satellites. According to Sanders, the satellites are the fixed points in the triangulation formula` and then press the SPACEBAR.

Q&A

Why does the text move from the second page to the first page as I am typing?

Word, by default, will not allow the first line of a paragraph to be by itself at the bottom of a page (an orphan) or the last line of a paragraph to be by itself at the top of a page (a widow). As you type, Word adjusts the placement of the paragraph to avoid orphans and widows.

3 Click the Insert Citation button (References tab | Citations & Bibliography group) to display the Insert Citation menu. Click Add New Placeholder on the Insert Citation menu to display the Placeholder Name dialog box.

4 Type `Sanders` as the tag name for the source.

5 Click the OK button to close the dialog box and insert the tag name in the citation placeholder.

6 Press the PERIOD key to end the sentence.

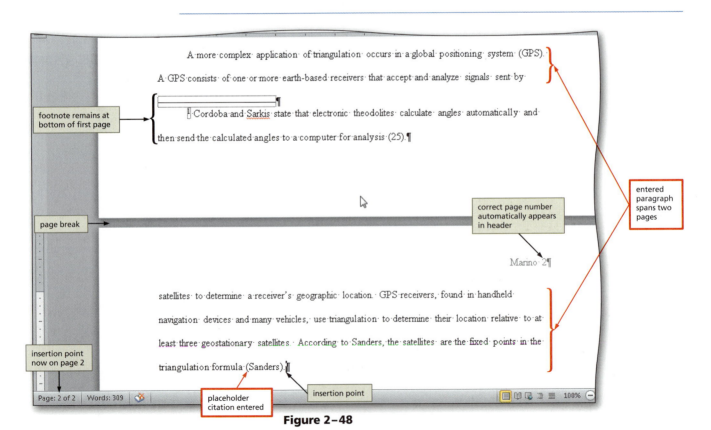

Figure 2–48

To Edit a Source

When you typed the fourth paragraph of the research paper, you inserted a citation placeholder, Sanders, for the source. You now have the source information, which is for a Web site, and are ready to enter it. The following steps edit the source for the Sanders citation placeholder.

1 Click somewhere in the citation placeholder to be edited, in this case (Sanders), to select the citation placeholder.

2 Click the Citation Options box arrow to display the Citation Options menu.

3 Click Edit Source on the Citation Options menu to display the Edit Source dialog box.

4 If necessary, click the Type of Source box arrow (Edit Source dialog box); scroll to and then click Web site, so that the list shows fields required for a Web site.

5 Place a check mark in the Show All Bibliography Fields check box to display more fields related to Web sites.

6 Click the Author text box. Type `Sanders, Gregory B.` as the author.

7 Click the Name of Web Page text box. Type `Understanding Satellites and Global Positioning Systems` as the Web page name.

8 Click the Production Company text box. Type `Course Technology` as the production company.

9 Click the Year Accessed text box. Type `2012` as the year accessed.

10 Press the TAB key and then type `Feb.` as the month accessed.

Q&A What if some of the text boxes disappear as I enter the Web site fields?

With the Show All Bibliography Fields check box selected, the dialog box may not be able to display all Web site fields at the same time. In this case, some may scroll up.

11 Press the TAB key and then type `27` as the day accessed (Figure 2–49).

Q&A Do I need to enter a Web address (URL)?

The latest MLA documentation style update does not require the Web address in the source.

12 Click the OK button to close the dialog box and create the source.

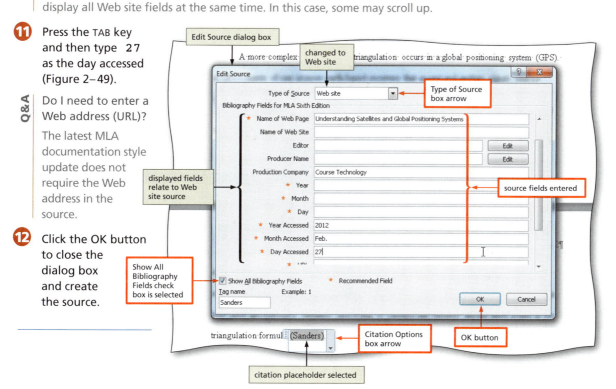

Figure 2–49

To Edit a Citation

As mentioned earlier, if you reference the author's name in the text, you should not list it again in the parenthetical citation. For Web site citations, when you suppress the author's name, the citation shows the Web site name because page numbers do not apply. The following steps edit the citation, suppressing the author and displaying the name of the Web site instead.

1 If necessary, click somewhere in the citation to be edited, in this case (Sanders), to select the citation and display the Citation Options box arrow.

2 Click the Citation Options box arrow and then click Edit Citation on the Citation Options menu to display the Edit Citation dialog box.

3 Click the Author check box (Edit Citation dialog box) to place a check mark in it (Figure 2–50).

4 Click the OK button to close the dialog box, remove the author name from the citation, and show the name of the Web site in the citation (shown in Figure 2–51).

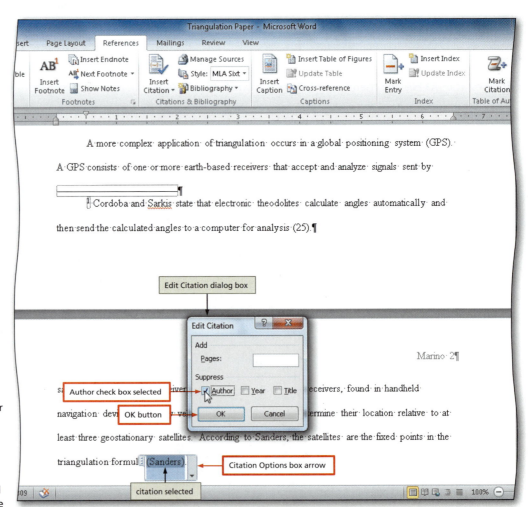

Figure 2–50

To Enter More Text

The next step is to type the last paragraph of text in the research paper. The following steps enter this text.

1 Press the END key to position the insertion point at the end of the fourth paragraph and then press the ENTER key.

2 Type the last paragraph of the research paper (Figure 2–51): `The next time you pass a surveyor, play a Nintendo Wii, or follow a route prescribed by a vehicle's navigation system, keep in mind that none of it might have been possible without the concept of triangulation.`

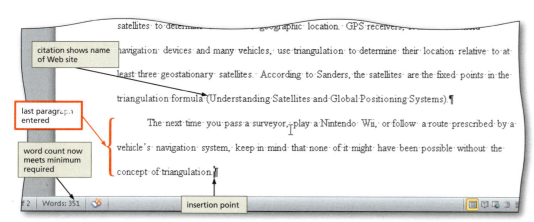

Figure 2–51

To Save an Existing Document with the Same File Name

You have made several modifications to the document since you last saved it. Thus, you should save it again. The following step saves the document again.

1 Click the Save button on the Quick Access Toolbar to overwrite the previously saved file.

Break Point: If you wish to take a break, this is a good place to do so. You can quit Word now (refer to page WD 125 for instructions). To resume at a later time, start Word (refer to page WD 70 for instructions), open the file called Triangulation Paper (refer to page WD 45 for instructions), and continue following the steps from this location forward.

Creating an Alphabetical Works Cited Page

According to the MLA documentation style, the **works cited page** is a list of sources that are referenced directly in a research paper. You place the list on a separate numbered page with the title, Works Cited, centered one inch from the top margin. The works are to be alphabetized by the author's last name or, if the work has no author, by the work's title. The first line of each entry begins at the left margin. Indent subsequent lines of the same entry one-half inch from the left margin.

Plan
Ahead

Create the list of sources.

A **bibliography** is an alphabetical list of sources referenced in a paper. Whereas the text of the research paper contains brief references to the source (the citations), the bibliography lists all publication information about the source. Documentation styles differ significantly in their guidelines for preparing a bibliography. Each style identifies formats for various sources, including books, magazines, pamphlets, newspapers, Web sites, television programs, paintings, maps, advertisements, letters, memos, and much more. You can find information about various styles and their guidelines in printed style guides and on the Web.

To Page Break Manually

The works cited are to be displayed on a separate numbered page. Thus, you must insert a manual page break following the body of the research paper so that the list of sources is displayed on a separate page. A **manual page break**, or **hard page break**, is one that you force into the document at a specific location.

Word never moves or adjusts manual page breaks. Word, however, does adjust any automatic page breaks that follow a manual page break. Word inserts manual page breaks immediately above or to the left of the location of the insertion point. The following step inserts a manual page break after the text of the research paper.

- Verify that the insertion point is positioned at the end of the text of the research paper, as shown in Figure 2–51 on the previous page.

- Click Insert on the Ribbon to display the Insert tab.

- Click the Page Break button (Insert tab | Pages group) to insert a manual page break immediately to the left of the insertion point and position the insertion point immediately below the manual page break (Figure 2–52).

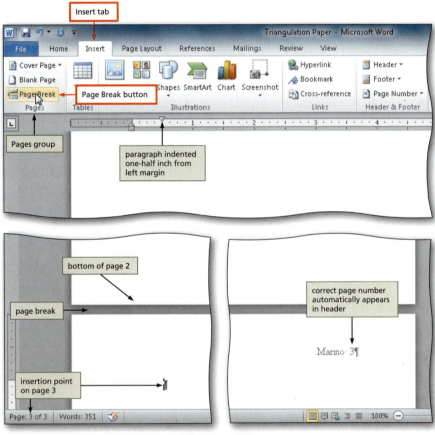

Figure 2–52

Other Ways

1. Press CTRL+ENTER

To Apply a Style

The works cited title is to be centered between the margins of the paper. If you simply issue the Center command, the title will not be centered properly. Instead, it will be one-half inch to the right of the center point because earlier you set the first-line indent for paragraphs to one-half inch.

To properly center the title of the works cited page, you could drag the First Line Indent marker back to the left margin before centering the paragraph, or you could apply the Normal style to the location of the insertion point. Recall that you modified the Normal style for this document to 12-point Times New Roman with double-spaced, left-aligned paragraphs that have no space after the paragraphs.

To apply a style to a paragraph, first position the insertion point in the paragraph and then apply the style. The following step applies the modified Normal style to the location of the insertion point.

1

- Click Home on the Ribbon to display the Home tab.

- With the insertion point on the paragraph mark at the top of page 3 (as shown in Figure 2–52) even if Normal is selected, click Normal in the Quick Style gallery (Home tab | Styles group) to apply the Normal style to the paragraph containing the insertion point (Figure 2–53).

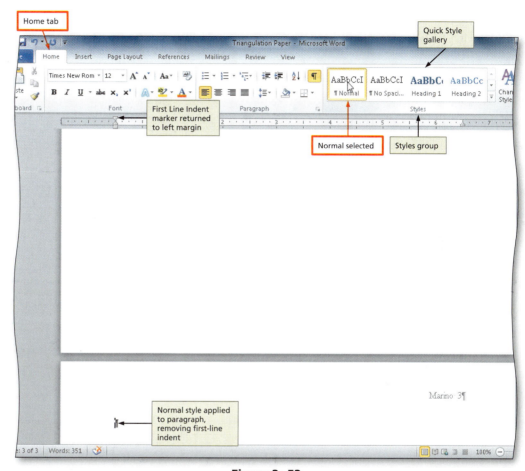

Figure 2–53

Other Ways	
1. Click Styles Dialog Box Launcher (Home tab | Styles group), click desired style in Styles task pane	2. Press CTRL+SHIFT+S, click Style Name box arrow in Apply Styles task pane, click desired style in list

To Center Text

The next step is to enter the title, Works Cited, centered between the margins of the paper. The following steps use shortcut keys to format the title.

1 Press CTRL+E to center the paragraph mark.

2 Type **Works Cited** as the title.

3 Press the ENTER key.

4 Press CTRL+L to left-align the paragraph mark (shown in Figure 2–54 on the next page).

BTW

BTWs
For a complete list of the BTWs found in the margins of this book, visit the Word 2010 BTW Web page (scsite.com/wd2010/btw).

To Create the Bibliographical List

While typing the research paper, you created several citations and their sources. Word can format the list of sources and alphabetize them in a **bibliographical list**, saving you time looking up style guidelines. That is, Word will create a bibliographical list with each element of the source placed in its correct position with proper punctuation, according to the specified style. For example, in this research paper, the book source will list, in this order, the author name(s), book title, publisher city, publishing company name, and publication year with the correct punctuation between each element according to the MLA documentation style. The following steps create an MLA-styled bibliographical list from the sources previously entered.

- Click References on the Ribbon to display the References tab.

- With the insertion point positioned as shown in Figure 2–54, click the Bibliography button (References tab | Citations & Bibliography group) to display the Bibliography gallery (Figure 2–54).

Q&A Will I select the Works Cited option from the Bibliography gallery?

No. The title it inserts is not formatted according to the MLA documentation style. Thus, you will use the Insert Bibliography command instead.

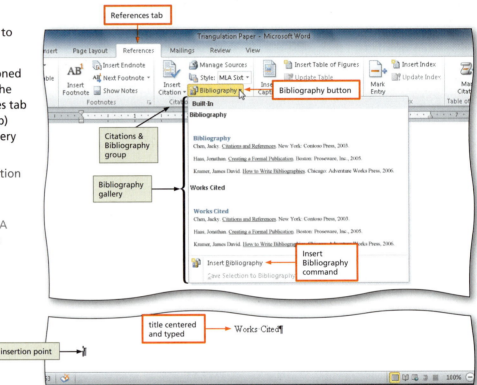

Figure 2–54

- Click Insert Bibliography in the Bibliography gallery to insert a list of sources at the location of the insertion point.

- If necessary, scroll to display the entire list of sources in the document window (Figure 2–55).

Q&A What is the n.d. in the last work?

The MLA documentation style uses the abbreviation n.d. for no date, for example, no date on the Web page.

Figure 2–55

TO FORMAT PARAGRAPHS WITH A HANGING INDENT

Notice in Figure 2–55 that the first line of each source entry begins at the left margin, and subsequent lines in the same paragraph are indented one-half inch from the left margin. In essence, the first line hangs to the left of the rest of the paragraph; thus, this type of paragraph formatting is called a **hanging indent**. The Bibliography style in Word automatically formats the works cited paragraphs with a hanging indent.

If you wanted to format paragraphs with a hanging indent, you would use one of the following techniques.

- With the insertion point in the paragraph to format, drag the **Hanging Indent marker** (the bottom triangle) on the ruler to the desired mark on the ruler (i.e., .5") to set the hanging indent at that location from the left margin.

or

- Right-click the paragraph to format, click Paragraph on shortcut menu, click Indents and Spacing tab (Paragraph dialog box), click Special box arrow, click Hanging, and then click the OK button.

or

- Click the Paragraph Dialog Box Launcher (Home tab or Page Layout tab | Paragraph group), click Indents and Spacing tab (Paragraph dialog box), click Special box arrow, click Hanging, and then click the OK button.

or

- With the insertion point in the paragraph to format, press CTRL+T.

To Modify a Source and Update the Bibliographical List

If you modify the contents of any source, the list of sources automatically updates because the list is a field. The following steps modify the title of the magazine article.

1

- Click the Manage Sources button (References tab | Citations & Bibliography group) to display the Source Manager dialog box.

- Click the source you wish to edit in the Current List, in this case the article by Jains, to select the source.

- Click the Edit button (Source Manager dialog box) to display the Edit Source dialog box.

- In the Title text box, insert the word, Distance, between the words, Measure and, in the title (Figure 2–56).

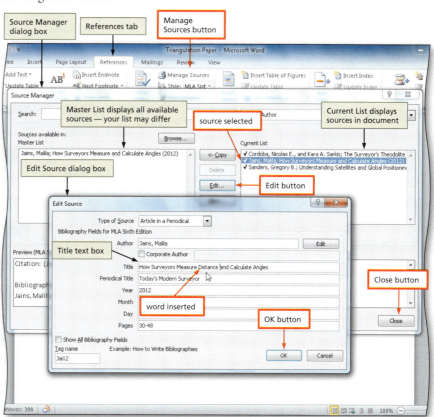

Figure 2–56

● Click the OK button (Edit Source dialog box) to close the dialog box.

● If a Microsoft Word dialog box appears, click its Yes button to update all occurrences of the source.

● Click the Close button (Source Manager dialog box) to update the list of sources in the document and close the dialog box (Figure 2–57).

Q&A What if the list of sources in the document is not updated automatically?

Click in the list of sources and then press the F9 key, which is the shortcut key to update a field.

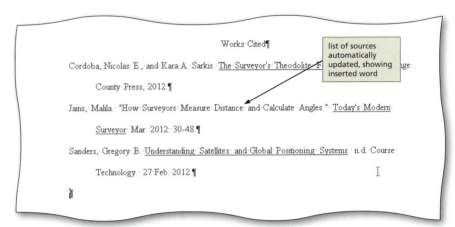

Figure 2–57

To Convert a Field to Regular Text

Word may use an earlier version of the MLA documentation style to format the bibliography. The latest guidelines for the MLA documentation style, for example, state that titles should be italicized instead of underlined, and each work should identify the source's publication medium (e.g., Print for printed media, Web for online media, etc.). If you format or add text to the bibliography, Word automatically will change it back to the Bibliography style's predetermined formats when the bibliography field is updated. To preserve modifications you make to the format of the bibliography, you can convert the bibliography field to regular text. Keep in mind, though, once you convert the field to regular text, it no longer is a field that can be updated. The following step converts a field to regular text.

● Click somewhere in the field to select it, in this case, somewhere in the bibliography (Figure 2–58).

Q&A What if the bibliography field is not shaded gray?

Click File on the Ribbon to open the Backstage view, click Options in the Backstage view, click Advanced in the left pane (Word Options dialog box), scroll to the 'Show document content' area, click the Field shading box arrow, click When selected, and then click the OK button.

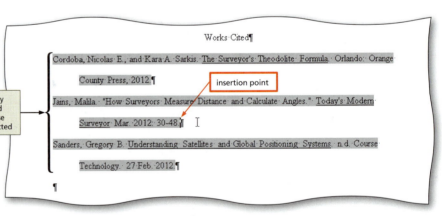

Figure 2–58

Q&A Why are all the words in the bibliography shaded?

The bibliography field consists of all text in the bibliography.

● Press CTRL+SHIFT+F9 to convert the selected field to regular text.

Q&A Why did the gray shading disappear?

The bibliography no longer is a field, so it is not shaded gray.

● Click anywhere in the document to remove the selection from the text.

To Format the Works Cited to the Latest MLA Documentation Style

As mentioned earlier, the latest the MLA documentation style guidelines state that titles should be italicized instead of underlined, and each work should identify the source's publication medium (e.g., Print, Web, Radio, Television, CD, DVD, Film, etc.). The following steps format and modify the Works Cited as specified by the latest MLA guidelines, if yours are not already formatted this way.

1 Drag through the book title, The Surveyor's Theodolite Formula, to select it.

2 Click Home on the Ribbon to display the Home tab. Click the Underline button (Home tab | Font group) to remove the underline from the selected text and then click the Italic button (Home tab | Font group) to italicize the selected text.

3 Select the magazine title, Today's Modern Surveyor. Remove the underline from the selected title and then italicize the selected title.

4 Select the Web page title, Understanding Satellites and Global Positioning Systems. Remove the underline from the selected title and then italicize the selected title.

5 After the period following the year in the first work, press the SPACEBAR and then type `Print.`

6 After the period following the page range in the second work, press the SPACEBAR and then type `Print.`

7 Before the date in the third work, type `Web.` and then press the SPACEBAR (Figure 2–59).

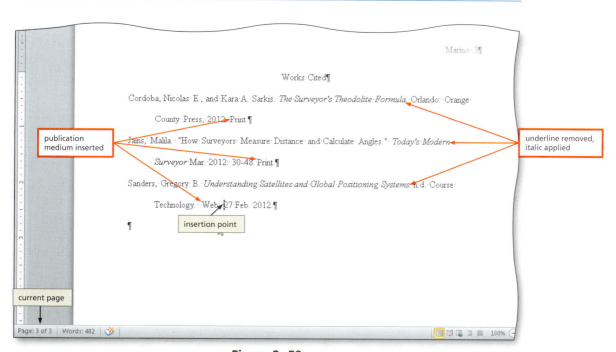

Figure 2–59

To Save an Existing Document with the Same File Name

You have made several modifications to the document since you last saved it. Thus, you should save it again. The following step saves the document again.

1 Click the Save button on the Quick Access Toolbar to overwrite the previously saved file.

Proofing and Revising the Research Paper

As discussed in Chapter 1, once you complete a document, you might find it necessary to make changes to it. Before submitting a paper to be graded, you should proofread it. While **proofreading**, look for grammatical errors and spelling errors. You also should ensure the transitions between sentences flow smoothly and the sentences themselves make sense.

Plan Ahead

Proofread and revise the paper.

As you proofread the paper, look for ways to improve it. Check all grammar, spelling, and punctuation. Be sure the text is logical and transitions are smooth. Where necessary, add text, delete text, reword text, and move text to different locations. Ask yourself these questions:

- Does the title suggest the topic?
- Is the thesis clear?
- Is the purpose of the paper clear?
- Does the paper have an introduction, body, and conclusion?
- Does each paragraph in the body relate to the thesis?
- Is the conclusion effective?
- Are all sources acknowledged?

To assist you with the proofreading effort, Word provides several tools. You can browse through pages, copy text, find text, replace text, insert a synonym, check spelling and grammar, and look up information. The following pages discuss these tools.

To Scroll Page by Page through a Document

The next step is to modify text on the second page of the paper. Currently, the third page is the active page (Figure 2–59 on the previous page). The following step scrolls up one page in the document.

1

- With the insertion point on the third page of the paper, click the Previous Page button on the vertical scroll bar to position the insertion point at the top of the previous page (Figure 2–60).

Q&A The button on my screen shows a ScreenTip different from Previous Page. Why?

By default, the functions of the buttons above and below the Select Browse Object button are Previous Page and Next Page, respectively. You can change the commands associated with these buttons by clicking the Select Browse Object button and then clicking the desired browse object. The Browse by Page command on the Select Browse Object menu, for example, changes the buttons back to Previous Page and Next Page.

Q&A How do I display the next page?

Click the Next Page button on the vertical scroll bar.

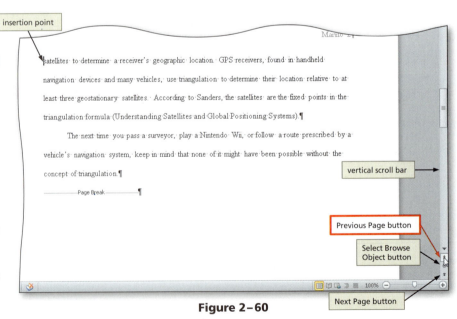

Figure 2–60

Other Ways	
1. Click Page Number indicator on status bar, click Page in 'Go to what' list (Find and Replace dialog box), type desired page number in	'Enter page number' text box, click Go To button
	2. Press CTRL+PAGE UP or CTRL+PAGE DOWN

Copying, Cutting, and Pasting

While proofreading the research paper, you decide it would read better if the word, geostationary, appeared in front of the word, satellites, in the last sentence of the fourth paragraph. You could type the word at the desired location, but because this is a difficult word to spell, you decide to use the Office Clipboard. The **Office Clipboard** is a temporary storage area that holds up to 24 items (text or graphics) copied from any Office program.

Copying is the process of placing items on the Office Clipboard, leaving the item in the document. **Cutting**, by contrast, removes the item from the document before placing it on the Office Clipboard. **Pasting** is the process of copying an item from the Office Clipboard into the document at the location of the insertion point.

To Copy and Paste

In the research paper, you copy a word from one sentence to another. The following steps copy and paste a word.

• Select the item to be copied (the word, geostationary, in this case).

• Click the Copy button (Home tab | Clipboard group) to copy the selected item in the document to the Office Clipboard (Figure 2–61).

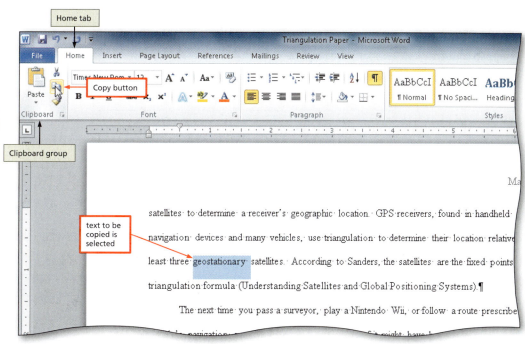

Figure 2–61

• Position the insertion point at the location where the item should be pasted (immediately to the left of the word, satellites, in this case) (Figure 2–62).

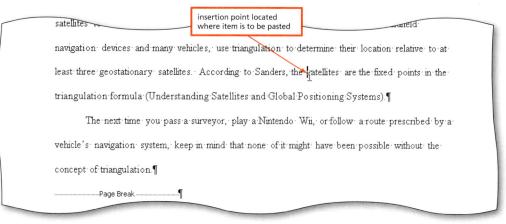

Figure 2–62

3

- Click the Paste button (Home tab | Clipboard group) to paste the copied item in the document at the location of the insertion point (Figure 2–63).

Q&A

What if I click the Paste button arrow by mistake?

Click the Paste button arrow again to remove the Paste menu.

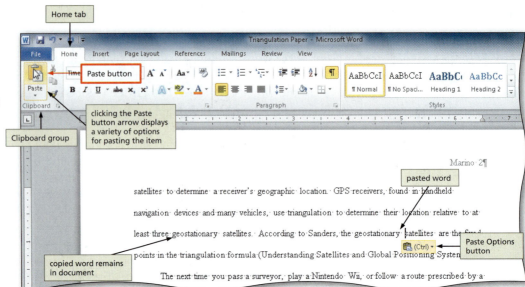

Figure 2–63

Other Ways
1. Right-click selected item, click Copy on shortcut menu, right-click where item is to be pasted, click Keep Source	Formatting in Paste Options area on shortcut menu 2. Select item, press CTRL+C, position insertion point	at paste location, press CTRL+V

To Display the Paste Options Menu

When you paste an item or move an item using drag-and-drop editing, which was discussed in the previous chapter, Word automatically displays a Paste Options button near the pasted or moved text (Figure 2–63). The Paste Options button allows you to change the format of a pasted item. For example, you can instruct Word to format the pasted item the same way as where it was copied, or format it the same way as where it is being pasted. The following steps display the Paste Options menu.

1

- Click the Paste Options button to display the Paste Options menu (Figure 2–64).

Q&A

What are the functions of the buttons on the Paste Options menu?

In general, the left button indicates the pasted item should look the same as it did in its original location. The second button formats the pasted text to match the rest of the item where it was pasted. The third button removes all formatting from the pasted item. The Set Default Paste command displays the Word Options dialog box. Keep in mind that the buttons shown on a Paste Options menu will vary, depending on the item being pasted.

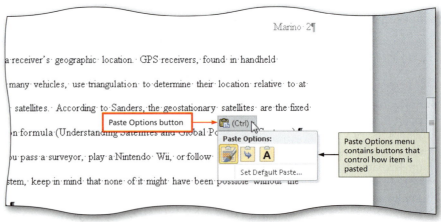

Figure 2–64

2

- Press the ESCAPE key to remove the Paste Options menu from the window.

To Find Text

While proofreading the paper, you would like to locate all occurrences of Wii console because you are contemplating changing this text to Wii game console. The following steps find all occurrences of specific text in a document.

1

● Click the Find button (Home tab | Editing group) to display the Navigation Pane (Figure 2–65).

What is the Navigation Pane?

The **Navigation Pane** is a window that enables you to search for text in a document, browse through pages in a document, or browse through headings in a document.

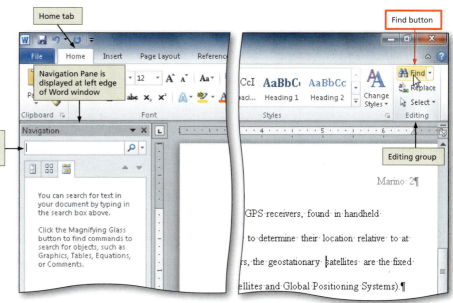

Figure 2–65

2

● Type `Wii console` in the Navigation Pane text box to display all occurrences of the typed text, called the search text, in the Navigation Pane and to highlight the occurrences of the search text in the document window (Figure 2–66).

3

 Experiment

● Type various search text in the Navigation Pane text box, and watch Word both list matches in the Navigation Pane and highlight matches in the document window. When you are finished experimenting, repeat Step 2.

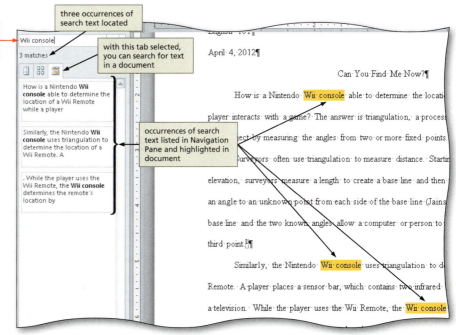

Figure 2–66

Other Ways

1. Click Find button arrow (Home tab | Editing group), click Find on Find menu, enter search text in Navigation Pane

2. Click Select Browse Object button on vertical scroll bar, click Find icon on Select Browse Object menu, enter search text (Find and Replace dialog box), click Find Next button

3. Click Page Number indicator on status bar, click Find tab (Find and Replace dialog box), enter search text, click Find Next button

4. Press CTRL+F

To Replace Text

You decide to change all occurrences of Wii console to Wii game console. To do this, you can use Word's find and replace feature, which automatically locates each occurrence of a word or phrase and then replaces it with specified text. The following steps replace all occurrences of Wii console with Wii game console.

- Click the Replace button (Home tab | Editing group) to display the Replace sheet in the Find and Replace dialog box.

- If necessary, type **Wii console** in the Find what text box (Find and Replace dialog box).

- Press the TAB key. Type **Wii game console** in the Replace with text box (Figure 2–67).

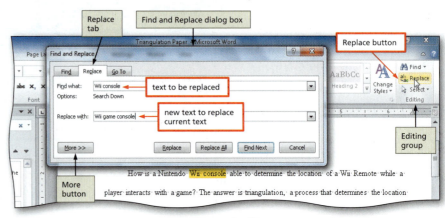

Figure 2–67

- Click the Replace All button to instruct Word to replace all occurrences of the Find what text with the Replace with text (Figure 2–68). If Word displays a dialog box asking if you want to continue searching from the beginning of the document, click the Yes button.

Q&A

Does Word search the entire document?

If the insertion point is at the beginning of the document, Word searches the entire document; otherwise, Word searches from the location of the insertion point to the end of the document and then displays a dialog box asking if you want to continue searching from the beginning. You also can search a section of text by selecting the text before clicking the Replace button.

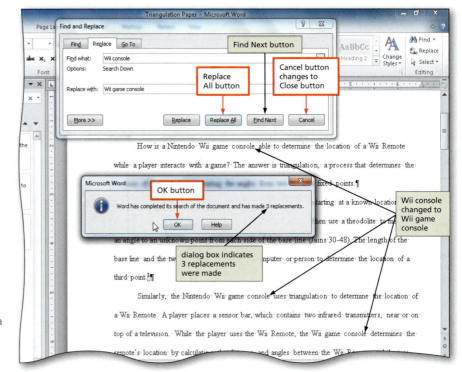

Figure 2–68

- Click the OK button (Microsoft Word dialog box) to close the dialog box.

- Click the Close button (Find and Replace dialog box) to close the dialog box.

Other Ways

1. Click Select Browse Object button on vertical scroll bar, click Find icon on Select Browse Object menu, click Replace tab

2. Click Page Number indicator on status bar, click Replace tab (Find and Replace dialog box)

3. Press CTRL+H

Find and Replace Dialog Box

The Replace All button (Find and Replace dialog box) replaces all occurrences of the Find what text with the Replace with text. In some cases, you may want to replace only certain occurrences of a word or phrase, not all of them. To instruct Word to confirm each change, click the Find Next button (Find and Replace dialog box) (Figure 2–68), instead of the Replace All button. When Word locates an occurrence of the text, it pauses and waits for you to click either the Replace button or the Find Next button. Clicking the Replace button changes the text; clicking the Find Next button instructs Word to disregard the replacement and look for the next occurrence of the Find what text.

If you accidentally replace the wrong text, you can undo a replacement by clicking the Undo button on the Quick Access Toolbar. If you used the Replace All button, Word undoes all replacements. If you used the Replace button, Word undoes only the most recent replacement.

BTW

Finding Formatting
To search for formatting or a special character, click the More button (shown in Figure 2–67) to expand the Find dialog box. To find formatting, use the Format button in the expanded Find dialog box. To find a special character, use the Special button.

To Go to a Page

The next step in revising the paper is to change a word on the second page of the document. You could scroll to the location in the document, or as mentioned earlier, you can use the Navigation Pane to browse through pages in a document. The following steps display the top of the second page in the document window and position the insertion point at the beginning of that page.

1
- Click the 'Browse the pages in your document' tab in the Navigation Pane to display thumbnail images of the pages in the document (Figure 2–69).

Q&A
What if the Navigation Pane is not on the screen anymore?

Click View on the Ribbon to display the View tab and then click Navigation Pane (View tab | Show group) to select the check box.

2
- Click the thumbnail of the second page, even if the second page already is selected, to display the top of the selected page in the top of the document window (shown in Figure 2–70 on the next page).

3
- Click the Close button in the Navigation Pane to close the pane.

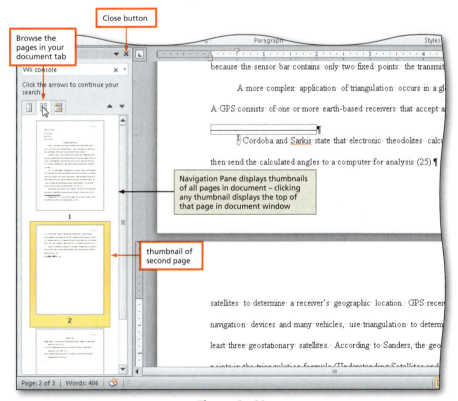

Close button

Browse the pages in your document tab

Navigation Pane displays thumbnails of all pages in document – clicking any thumbnail displays the top of that page in document window

thumbnail of second page

Figure 2–69

Other Ways

1. Click Find button arrow (Home tab | Editing group), click Go To on Find menu, click Go To tab (Find and Replace dialog box), enter page number, click Go To button

2. Click Select Browse Object button on vertical scroll bar, click Go To icon on Select Browse Object menu, enter page number (Find and Replace dialog box), click Go To button

3. Click Page Number indicator on status bar, click Go To tab (Find and Replace dialog box), enter page number, click Go To button

4. Press CTRL+G

To Find and Insert a Synonym

When writing, you may discover that you used the same word in multiple locations or that a word you used was not quite appropriate. In these instances, you will want to look up a **synonym**, or a word similar in meaning, to the duplicate or inappropriate word. A **thesaurus** is a book of synonyms. Word provides synonyms and a thesaurus for your convenience.

In this project, you would like a synonym for the word, prescribed, in the fourth paragraph of the research paper. The following steps find a suitable synonym.

- Locate and then right-click the word for which you want to find a synonym (in this case, prescribed) to display a shortcut menu related to the word you right-clicked.

- Point to Synonyms on the shortcut menu to display a list of synonyms for the word you right-clicked (Figure 2–70).

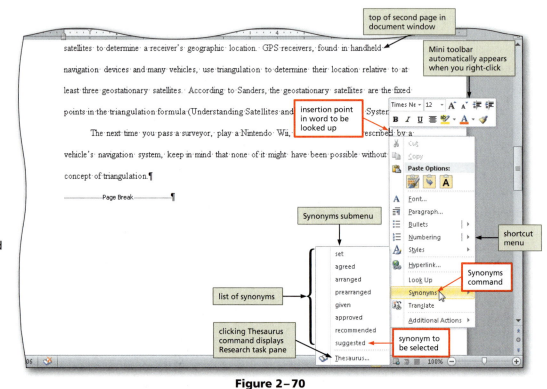

Figure 2–70

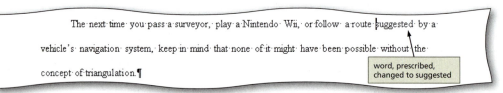

Figure 2–71

- Click the synonym you want (in this case, suggested) on the Synonyms submenu to replace the selected word in the document with the selected synonym (Figure 2–71).

Q&A What if the synonyms list on the shortcut menu does not display a suitable word?

You can display the thesaurus in the Research task pane by clicking Thesaurus on the Synonyms submenu. The Research task pane displays a complete thesaurus, in which you can look up synonyms for various meanings of a word. You also can look up an **antonym**, or word with an opposite meaning. The Research task pane is discussed later in this chapter.

Other Ways
1. Click Thesaurus (Review tab | Proofing group)   2. Press SHIFT+F7

To Check Spelling and Grammar at Once

As discussed in Chapter 1, Word checks spelling and grammar as you type and places a wavy underline below possible spelling or grammar errors. Chapter 1 illustrated how to check these flagged words immediately. As an alternative, you can wait and check the entire document for spelling and grammar errors at once. The next steps check spelling and grammar at once.

Note: In the following steps, the word, theodolite, has been misspelled intentionally as theadalight to illustrate the use of Word's check spelling and grammar at once feature. If you are completing this project on a personal computer, your research paper may contain different misspelled words, depending on the accuracy of your typing.

①

- Press CTRL+HOME because you want the spelling and grammar check to begin from the top of the document.

- Click Review on the Ribbon to display the Review tab.

- Click the Spelling & Grammar button (Review tab | Proofing group) to begin the spelling and grammar check at the location of the insertion point, which in this case, is at the beginning of the document.

- Click the desired spelling in the Suggestions list (theodolite, in this case) (Figure 2–72).

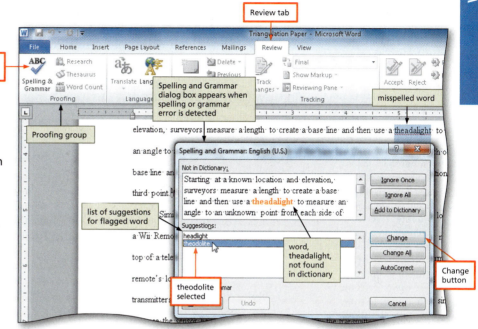

Figure 2–72

②

- With the word, theodolite, selected in the Suggestions list, click the Change button (Spelling and Grammar dialog box) to change the flagged word to the selected suggestion and then continue the spelling and grammar check until the next error is identified or the end of the document is reached (Figure 2–73).

③

- Click the Ignore All button (Spelling and Grammar dialog box) to ignore this and future occurrences of the flagged proper noun and then continue the spelling and grammar check until the next error is identified or the end of the document is reached.

④

- When the spelling and grammar check is finished and Word displays a dialog box, click its OK button.

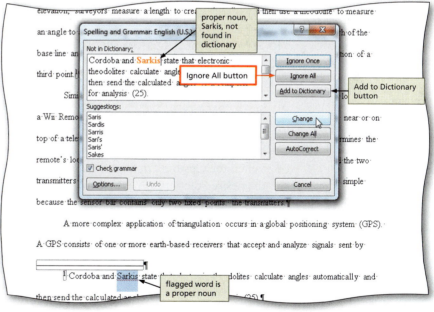

Figure 2–73

Q&A

Can I check spelling of just a section of a document?

Yes, select the text before starting the spelling and grammar check.

Other Ways
1. Click Spelling and Grammar Check icon on status bar, click Spelling on shortcut menu   2. Right-click flagged word, click Spelling on shortcut menu   3. Press F7

The Main and Custom Dictionaries

As shown in the steps on the previous page, Word may flag a proper noun as an error because the proper noun is not in its main dictionary. To prevent Word from flagging proper nouns as errors, you can add the proper nouns to the custom dictionary. To add a correctly spelled word to the custom dictionary, click the Add to Dictionary button (Spelling and Grammar dialog box) or right-click the flagged word and then click Add to Dictionary on the shortcut menu. Once you have added a word to the custom dictionary, Word no longer will flag it as an error.

TO VIEW OR MODIFY ENTRIES IN A CUSTOM DICTIONARY

To view or modify the list of words in a custom dictionary, you would follow these steps.

1. Click File on the Ribbon and then click Options in the Backstage view.
2. Click Proofing in the left pane (Word Options dialog box).
3. Click the Custom Dictionaries button.
4. When Word displays the Custom Dictionaries dialog box, place a check mark next to the dictionary name to view or modify. Click the Edit Word List button (Custom Dictionaries dialog box). (In this dialog box, you can add or delete entries to and from the selected custom dictionary.)
5. When finished viewing and/or modifying the list, click the OK button in the dialog box.
6. Click the OK button (Custom Dictionaries dialog box).
7. If the 'Suggest from main dictionary only' check box is selected in the Word Options dialog box, remove the check mark. Click the OK button (Word Options dialog box).

TO SET THE DEFAULT CUSTOM DICTIONARY

If you have multiple custom dictionaries, you can specify which one Word should use when checking spelling. To set the default custom dictionary, you would follow these steps.

1. Click File on the Ribbon and then click Options in the Backstage view.
2. Click Proofing in the left pane (Word Options dialog box).
3. Click the Custom Dictionaries button.
4. When the Custom Dictionaries dialog box is displayed, place a check mark next to the desired dictionary name. Click the Change Default button (Custom Dictionaries dialog box).
5. Click the OK button (Custom Dictionaries dialog box).
6. If the 'Suggest from main dictionary only' check box is selected in the Word Options dialog box, remove the check mark. Click the OK button (Word Options dialog box).

To Use the Research Task Pane to Look Up Information

From within Word, you can search through various forms of reference information. Earlier, this chapter discussed the Research task pane with respect to looking up a synonym in a thesaurus. Other services available in the Research task pane include a dictionary and, if you are connected to the Web, a search engine and other Web sites that provide information such as stock quotes, news articles, and company profiles.

Assume you want to know more about the word, geostationary. The following steps use the Research task pane to look up a definition of a word.

1
- Locate the word you want to look up.

- While holding down the ALT key, click the word you want to look up (in this case, geostationary) to open the Research task pane and display a dictionary entry for the ALT+clicked word. Release the ALT key.

2
- Click the Search for box arrow in the Research task pane to display a list of search locations (Figure 2–74).

Q&A Why does my Research task pane look different?

Depending on your settings and Microsoft's Web site search settings, your Research task pane may appear different from the figures shown here.

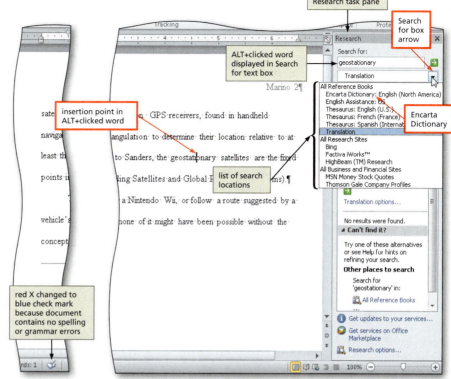

Figure 2–74

- Click Encarta Dictionary in the list to display a definition for the ALT+clicked word (Figure 2–75).

Q&A Can I copy information from the Research task pane into my document?

Yes, you can use the Copy and Paste commands. When using Word to insert material from the Research task pane or any other online reference, however, be careful not to plagiarize.

3
- Click the Close button in the Research task pane.

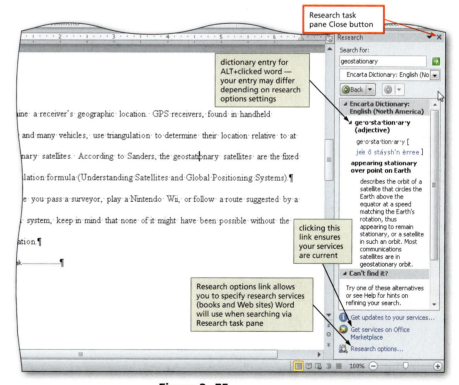

Figure 2–75

Other Ways

1. Click Research button (Review tab | Proofing group)

Grammar and Style Options

To set grammar and writing style options, click File on the Ribbon to open the Backstage view, click the Options button, and then click Proofing in the left pane (Word Options dialog box) to display a variety of spelling and grammar options that you can select or deselect by placing or removing check marks. To specify how Word checks grammar, click the Settings button in the right pane (Word Options dialog box) and then select the desired settings in the Grammar Settings dialog box.

Research Task Pane Options

When you install Word, it selects a series of services (reference books and Web sites) that it searches through when you use the Research task pane. You can view, modify, and update the list of services at any time.

Clicking the Research options link at the bottom of the Research task pane (shown in Figure 2–75 on the previous page) displays the Research Options dialog box, where you can view or modify the list of installed services. You can view information about any installed service by clicking the service in the list and then clicking the Properties button. To activate an installed service, click the check box to its left; likewise, to deactivate a service, remove the check mark. To add a particular Web site to the list, click the Add Services button, enter the Web address in the Address text box, and then click the Add button (Add Services dialog box). To update or remove services, click the Update/Remove button, select the service in the list, click the Update (or Remove) button (Update or Remove Services dialog box), and then click the Close button. You also can install parental controls through the Parental Control button (Research Options dialog box), for example, if you want to prevent minor children who use Word from accessing the Web.

To Change Document Properties

Before saving the research paper again, you want to add your name, course information, and some keywords as document properties. The following steps use the Document Information Panel to change document properties.

1 Click File on the Ribbon to open the Backstage view and, if necessary, select the Info tab.

2 Click the Properties button in the right pane of the Info gallery to display the Properties menu and then click Show Document Panel on the Properties menu to close the Backstage view and display the Document Information Panel in the Word document window.

3 Click the Author text box, if necessary, and then type your name as the Author property. If a name already is displayed in the Author text box, delete it before typing your name.

4 Click the Subject text box, if necessary delete any existing text, and then type your course and section as the Subject property.

5 Click the Keywords text box, if necessary delete any existing text, and then type **surveyor, Wii, GPS** as the Keywords property.

6 Click the Close the Document Information Panel button so that the Document Information Panel no longer is displayed.

Conserving Ink and Toner

If you want to conserve ink or toner, you can instruct Word to print draft quality documents by clicking File on the Ribbon to open the Backstage view, clicking Options in the Backstage view to display the Word Options dialog box, clicking Advanced in the left pane (Word Options dialog box), scrolling to the Print area in the right pane, placing a check mark in the 'Use draft quality' check box, and then clicking the OK button. Then, use the Backstage view to print the document as usual.

To Save an Existing Document with the Same File Name

You have made several modifications to the document since you last saved it. Thus, you should save it again. The following step saves the document again.

1 Click the Save button on the Quick Access Toolbar to overwrite the previously saved file.

To Print Document Properties

With the document properties entered and the completed document saved, you may want to print the document properties along with the document. The following steps print the document properties for the Triangulation Paper.

1
- Click File on the Ribbon to open the Backstage view and then click the Print tab in the Backstage view to display the Print gallery.

- Verify the printer name that appears on the Printer Status button will print a hard copy of the document. If necessary, click the Printer Status button to display a list of available printer options and then click the desired printer to change the currently selected printer.

- Click the first button in the Settings area to display a list of options specifying what you can print (Figure 2–76).

2
- Click Document Properties in the list to specify you want to print the document properties instead of the actual document.

- Click the Print button in the Print gallery to print the document properties on the currently selected printer (Figure 2–77).

Q&A

What if the currently updated document properties do not print on the hard copy?

Try closing the document, reopening the document, and then repeating these steps.

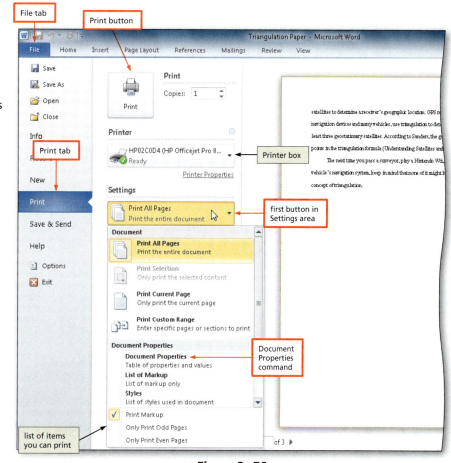

Figure 2–76

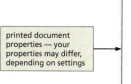

printed document properties — your properties may differ, depending on settings

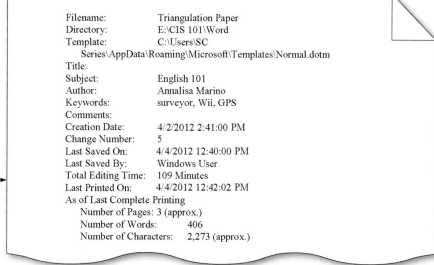

Filename:	Triangulation Paper
Directory:	E:\CIS 101\Word
Template:	C:\Users\SC
	Series\AppData\Roaming\Microsoft\Templates\Normal.dotm
Title:	
Subject:	English 101
Author:	Annalisa Marino
Keywords:	surveyor, Wii, GPS
Comments:	
Creation Date:	4/2/2012 2:41:00 PM
Change Number:	5
Last Saved On:	4/4/2012 12:40:00 PM
Last Saved By:	Windows User
Total Editing Time:	109 Minutes
Last Printed On:	4/4/2012 12:42:02 PM
As of Last Complete Printing	
Number of Pages: 3 (approx.)	
Number of Words:	406
Number of Characters:	2,273 (approx.)

Figure 2–77

Other Ways

1. Press CTRL+P, press ENTER

To Preview the Document and Then Print It

Before printing the research paper, you want to verify the page layouts. The following steps change the print option to print the document (instead of the document properties), preview the printed pages in the research paper, and then print the document.

- Position the insertion point at the top of the document because you want initially to view the first page in the document.

- Click File on the Ribbon to open the Backstage view and then click the Print tab in the Backstage view to display the Print gallery.

- Verify the printer name that appears on the Printer Status button will print a hard copy of the document. If necessary, select a different printer.

- Click the first button in the Settings area to display a list of options specifying what you can print (Figure 2–78).

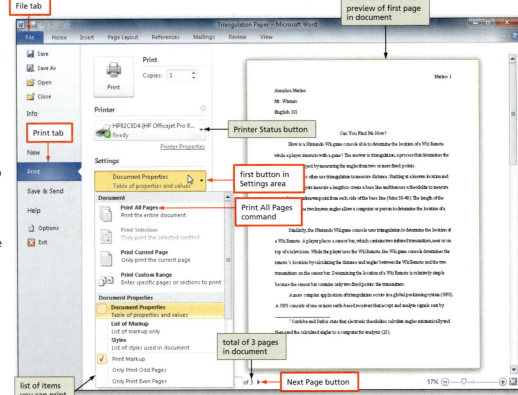

Figure 2–78

- Click Print All Pages in the list to specify you want to print all pages in the actual document.

- Click the Next Page button in the Print gallery to preview the second page of the research paper in the Print gallery.

- Click the Next Page button again to preview the third page of the research paper in the Print gallery (Figure 2–79).

- Click the Print button in the Print gallery to print the research paper on the currently selected printer (shown in Figure 2–1 on page WD 67).

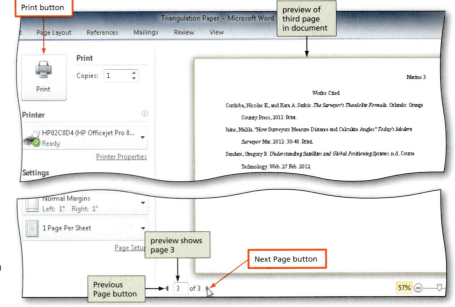

Figure 2–79

Other Ways

1. Press CTRL+P, press ENTER

To Quit Word

This project now is complete. The following steps quit Word. For a detailed example of the procedure summarized below, refer to the Office 2010 and Windows 7 chapter at the beginning of this book.

1 If you have one Word document open, click the Close button on the right side of the title bar to close the document and quit Word; or if you have multiple Word documents open, click File on the Ribbon to open the Backstage view and then click Exit in the Backstage view to close all open documents and quit Word.

2 If a Microsoft Word dialog box appears, click the Save button to save any changes made to the document since the last save.

BTW

Quick Reference
For a table that lists how to complete the tasks covered in this book using the mouse, Ribbon, shortcut menu, and keyboard, see the Quick Reference Summary at the back of this book, or visit the Word 2010 Quick Reference Web page (scsite.com/wd2010/qr).

Chapter Summary

In this chapter, you have learned how to change document settings, use headers to number pages, modify a style, insert and edit citations and their sources, add footnotes, create a bibliographical list of sources, and use the Research task pane. The items listed below include all the new Word skills you have learned in this chapter.

1. Modify a Style (WD 70)
2. Change Line Spacing (WD 73)
3. Remove Space after a Paragraph (WD 74)
4. Update a Style to Match a Selection (WD 74)
5. Switch to the Header (WD 75)
6. Right-Align a Paragraph (WD 76)
7. Insert a Page Number (WD 77)
8. Close the Header (WD 78)
9. Click and Type (WD 80)
10. Display the Rulers (WD 82)
11. First-Line Indent Paragraphs (WD 83)
12. AutoCorrect as You Type (WD 85)
13. Use the AutoCorrect Options Button (WD 85)
14. Create an AutoCorrect Entry (WD 86)
15. Change the Bibliography Style (WD 89)
16. Insert a Citation and Create Its Source (WD 90)
17. Edit a Citation (WD 91)
18. Insert a Footnote Reference Mark (WD 93)
19. Insert a Citation Placeholder (WD 94)
20. Modify a Style Using a Shortcut Menu (WD 95)
21. Edit a Source (WD 97)
22. Count Words (WD 101)
23. Page Break Manually (WD 106)
24. Apply a Style (WD 106)
25. Create the Bibliographical List (WD 108)
26. Format Paragraphs with a Hanging Indent (WD 109)
27. Modify a Source and Update the Bibliographical List (WD 109)
28. Convert a Field to Regular Text (WD 110)
29. Scroll Page by Page through a Document (WD 112)
30. Copy and Paste (WD 113)
31. Display the Paste Options Menu (WD 114)
32. Find Text (WD 115)
33. Replace Text (WD 116)
34. Go to a Page (WD 117)
35. Find and Insert a Synonym (WD 118)
36. Check Spelling and Grammar at Once (WD 118)
37. View or Modify Entries in a Custom Dictionary (WD 120)
38. Set the Default Custom Dictionary (WD 120)
39. Use the Research Task Pane to Look Up Information (WD 120)
40. Print Document Properties (WD 123)
41. Preview the Document and Then Print It (WD 124)

Learn It Online

Test your knowledge of chapter content and key terms.

Instructions: To complete the Learn It Online exercises, start your browser, click the Address bar, and then enter the Web address **scsite.com/wd2010/learn**. When the Word 2010 Learn It Online page is displayed, click the link for the exercise you want to complete and then read the instructions.

Chapter Reinforcement TF, MC, and SA
A series of true/false, multiple choice, and short answer questions that test your knowledge of the chapter content.

Flash Cards
An interactive learning environment where you identify chapter key terms associated with displayed definitions.

Practice Test
A series of multiple choice questions that test your knowledge of chapter content and key terms.

Who Wants To Be a Computer Genius?
An interactive game that challenges your knowledge of chapter content in the style of a television quiz show.

Wheel of Terms
An interactive game that challenges your knowledge of chapter key terms in the style of the television show *Wheel of Fortune*.

Crossword Puzzle Challenge
A crossword puzzle that challenges your knowledge of key terms presented in the chapter.

Apply Your Knowledge

Reinforce the skills and apply the concepts you learned in this chapter.

Revising Text and Paragraphs in a Document
Note: To complete this assignment, you will be required to use the Data Files for Students. See the inside back cover of this book for instructions on downloading the Data Files for Students, or contact your instructor for information about accessing the required files.

Instructions: Start Word. Open the document, Apply 2-1 Space Paragraph Draft, from the Data Files for Students. The document you open contains a paragraph of text. You are to revise the document as follows: move a word, move another word and change the format of the moved word, change paragraph indentation, change line spacing, find all occurrences of a word, replace all occurrences of a word with another word, locate a synonym, and edit the header.

Perform the following tasks:
1. Copy the word, exploration, from the first sentence and paste it in the last sentence after the word, space, so that it is the eighth word in the sentence.
2. Select the underlined word, safe, in the paragraph. Use drag-and-drop editing to move the selected word, safe, so that it is before the word, mission, in the same sentence. Click the Paste Options button that displays to the right of the moved word, safe. Remove the underline format from the moved sentence by clicking Keep Text Only on the Paste Options menu.
3. Display the ruler, if necessary. Use the ruler to indent the first line of the paragraph one-half inch.
4. Change the line spacing of the paragraph to double.
5. Use the Navigation Pane to find all occurrences of the word, sensors. How many are there?
6. Use the Find and Replace dialog box to replace all occurrences of the word, issues, with the word, problems. How many replacements were made?

7. Use Word to find the word, height. Use Word's thesaurus to change the word, height, to the word, altitude.

8. Switch to the header so that you can edit it. In the first line of the header, change the word, Draft, to the word, Modified, so that it reads: Space Paragraph Modified.

9. In the second line of the header, insert the page number (with no formatting) one space after the word, Page.

10. Change the alignment of both lines of text in the header from left-aligned to right-aligned. Switch back to the document text.

11. Change the document properties, as specified by your instructor.

12. Click File on the Ribbon and then click Save As. Save the document using the file name, Apply 2-1 Space Paragraph Modified.

13. Print the document properties and then print the revised document, shown in Figure 2–80.

14. Use the Research task pane to look up the definition of the word, NASA, in the paragraph. Handwrite the definition of the word on your printout, as well as your response to the question in #6.

15. Change the Search for box to All Research Sites. Print an article from one of the sites.

16. Display the Research Options dialog box and, on your printout, handwrite the currently active Reference Books, Research Sites, and Business and Financial Sites. If your instructor approves, activate one of the services.

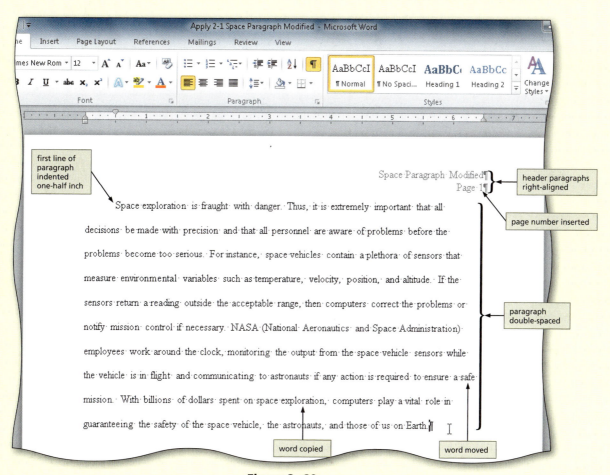

Figure 2–80

Extend Your Knowledge

Extend the skills you learned in this chapter and experiment with new skills. You may need to use Help to complete the assignment.

Working with References and Proofing Tools

Note: To complete this assignment, you will be required to use the Data Files for Students. See the inside back cover of this book for instructions on downloading the Data Files for Students, or contact your instructor for information about accessing the required files.

Instructions: Start Word. Open the document, Extend 2-1 Digital Camera Paper Draft, from the Data Files for Students. You will add another footnote to the paper, use the thesaurus, convert the document from MLA to APA documentation style, convert the footnotes to endnotes, modify the Endnote Text style, change the format of the note reference marks, and translate the document to another language (Figure 2–81).

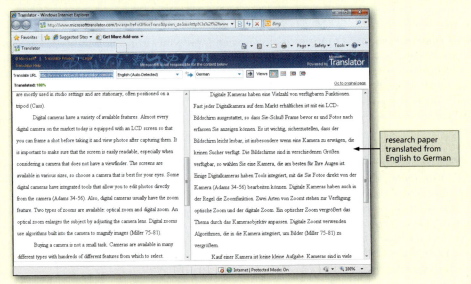

research paper translated from English to German

Figure 2–81

Perform the following tasks:

1. Use Help to learn more about footers, footnotes and endnotes, bibliography styles, AutoCorrect, and the Mini Translator.

2. Delete the footer from the document.

3. Insert a second footnote at an appropriate place in the research paper. Use the following footnote text: For instance, Adams states that you may be able to crop photos, change the brightness, or remove red eye effects.

4. Change the location of the footnotes from bottom of page to below text.

5. Use the Find and Replace dialog box to find the word, small, in the document and then replace it with a word of your choice.

6. Save the document with a new file name and then print it. On the printout, write the number of words, characters without spaces, characters with spaces, paragraphs, and lines in the document. Be sure to include footnote text in the statistics.

7. Select the entire document and then change the documentation style of the citations and bibliography from MLA to APA. Save the APA version of the document with a new file name and then print it. Compare the two versions. Circle the differences between the two documents.

8. Convert the footnotes to endnotes.

9. Modify the Endnote Text style to 12-point Times New Roman font, double-spaced text with a hanging-line indent.

10. Change the format of the note reference marks to capital letters (A, B, etc.).

11. Add an AutoCorrect entry that replaces the word, camora, with the word, camera. Add this sentence, A field camora usually is more than sufficient for most users., to the end of the second paragraph, misspelling the word camera to test the AutoCorrect entry. Delete the AutoCorrect entry that replaces camora with the word, camera.

12. Display readability statistics. What are the Flesch-Kincaid Grade Level, the Flesch Reading Ease score, and the percent of passive sentences?

13. Save the revised document with endnotes with a new file name and then print it. On the printout, write your response to the question in #12.

14. If you have an Internet connection, translate the research paper into a language of your choice using the Translate button (Review tab | Language group). Submit the translated document in the format specified by your instructor. Use the Mini Translator to hear how to pronounce three words in your paper.

Make It Right

Analyze a document and correct all errors and/or improve the design.

Inserting Missing Elements in an MLA-Styled Research Paper

Note: To complete this assignment, you will be required to use the Data Files for Students. See the inside back cover of this book for instructions on downloading the Data Files for Students, or contact your instructor for information about accessing the required files.

Instructions: Start Word. Open the document, Make It Right 2-1 Biometrics Paper Draft, from the Data Files for Students. The document is a research paper that is missing several elements. You are to insert these missing elements, all formatted according to the MLA documentation style: header with a page number, name and course information, paper title, footnote, and source information for a citation.

Perform the following tasks:

1. Insert a header with a page number (use your own last name), name and course information (your name, your instructor name, your course name, and today's date), and an appropriate paper title, all formatted according to the MLA documentation style.

2. The Jenkins citation placeholder is missing its source information (Figure 2–82). Use the following source information to edit the source: magazine article titled "Fingerprint Readers" written by Arthur D. Jenkins and Marissa K. Weavers, magazine name is *Security Today*, publication date is February 2012, article is on pages 55–60. Edit the citation so that it displays the author name and the page numbers of 55–56 for this reference.

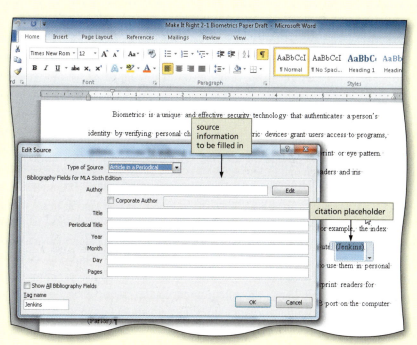

Figure 2–82

Continued >

Make It Right *continued*

3. Modify the source of the book authored by Carolina Doe, so that the publisher city is Chicago instead of Dallas.

4. Change the Footnote Text style to 12-point Times New Roman, double-spaced paragraphs with a first-line indent.

5. Insert the following footnote with the note reference at an appropriate place in the paper, formatted according to the MLA documentation style: Parlor states that one use of fingerprint readers is for users to log on to programs and Web sites via their fingerprint instead of entering a user name and password.

6. Use the Navigation Pane to display page 3. Use Word to insert the bibliographical list (bibliography). Convert the works cited to regular text. Change the underline format on the titles of the works to the italic format, and insert the correct publication medium for each work.

7. Change the document properties, as specified by your instructor. Save the revised document with the file name, Make It Right 2-1 Biometrics Paper Modified, and then submit it in the format specified by your instructor.

In the Lab

Design and/or create a document using the guidelines, concepts, and skills presented in this chapter. Labs are listed in order of increasing difficulty.

Lab 1: Preparing a Short Research Paper

Problem: You are a college student currently enrolled in an introductory business class. Your assignment is to prepare a short research paper (275–300 words) about video or computer games. The requirements are that the paper be presented according to the MLA documentation style and have three references. One of the three references must be from the Web. You prepare the paper shown in Figure 2–83 on pages WD 131 and WD 132, which discusses game controllers.

Instructions: Perform the following tasks:

1. Start Word. If necessary, display formatting marks on the screen.

2. Modify the Normal style to 12-point Times New Roman font.

3. Adjust line spacing to double.

4. Remove space below (after) paragraphs.

5. Update the Normal style to reflect the adjusted line and paragraph spacing.

6. Create a header to number pages.

7. Type the name and course information at the left margin. Center and type the title.

8. Set a first-line indent to one-half inch for paragraphs in the body of the research paper.

9. Type the research paper as shown in Figures 2–83a and 2–83b. Change the bibliography style to MLA. As you insert citations, enter their source information (shown in Figure 2–83c). Edit the citations so that they are displayed according to Figures 2–83a and 2–83b.

10. At the end of the research paper text, press the ENTER key and then insert a manual page break so that the Works Cited page begins on a new page. Enter and format the works cited title (Figure 2–83c). Use Word to insert the bibliographical list (bibliography). Convert the bibliography field to text. Change the underline format on the titles of the works to the italic format and insert the correct publication medium for each work (shown in Figure 2–83c).

(b) Page 2

Kimble 2

Game controllers are used primarily to direct movement and actions of on-screen objects. Two popular types are gamepads and motion-sensing game controllers. Games become more enjoyable every day with the use of new and exciting game controllers. What will be next?

(a) Page 1

Kimble 1

Harley Kimble

Ms. Longherst

English 101

April 30, 2012

From One Controller to Another

Video games and computer games use a game controller as the input device that directs movements and actions of on-screen objects. Two commonly used game controllers are gamepads and motion-sensing game controllers (Joyce). Game controllers not only enrich the gaming experience but also aid in the movements and actions of players.

A gamepad is held by the player with both hands, allowing the player to control the movement or actions of the objects in the video or computer games. Players press buttons on the gamepad, often with their thumbs, to carry out actions. Some gamepads have swiveling sticks that also can trigger events during game play (Cortez 20-24). Some gamepads include wireless capabilities; others connect via a cable directly to the game console or a personal computer.

Motion-sensing game controllers allow the user to guide on-screen elements or trigger events by moving a handheld input device in predetermined directions through the air. These controllers communicate with a game console or personal computer via wired or wireless technology. A variety of games, from sports to simulations, use motion-sensing game controllers. Some of these controllers, such as baseball bats and golf clubs, are designed for only one specific kind of game; others are general purpose. A popular, general-purpose, motion-sensing game controller is Nintendo's Wii Remote. Shaped like a television remote control and operated with one hand, the Wii Remote uses Bluetooth wireless technology to communicate with the Wii game console (Bloom 56-59).

Figure 2–83

Continued >

In the Lab *continued*

(c) Page 3

Kimble 3

Works Cited

Bloom, June. *The Gaming Experience*. New York: Buffalo Works Press, 2012. Print.

Cortez, Domiciano Isachar. "Today's Game Controllers." *Gaming, Gaming, Gaming* Jan. 2012:

12-34. Print.

Joyce, Andrea D. *What Gamers Want*. 15 Feb. 2012. Web. 28 Mar. 2012.

11. Check the spelling and grammar of the paper at once.

12. Change the document properties, as specified by your instructor. Save the document using Lab 2-1 Game Controllers Paper as the file name.

13. Print the research paper. Handwrite the number of words, paragraphs, and characters in the research paper above the title of your printed research paper.

In the Lab

Lab 2: Preparing a Research Report with a Footnote

Problem: You are a college student enrolled in an introductory English class. Your assignment is to prepare a short research paper in any area of interest to you. The requirements are that the paper be presented according to the MLA documentation style, contain at least one note positioned as a footnote, and have three references. One of the three references must be from the Internet. You prepare a paper about trends in agriculture (Figure 2–84).

Instructions: Perform the following tasks:

1. Start Word. Modify the Normal style to 12-point Times New Roman font. Adjust line spacing to double and remove space below (after) paragraphs. Update the Normal style to include the adjusted line and paragraph spacing. Create a header to number pages. Type the name and course information at the left margin. Center and type the title. Set a first-line indent for paragraphs in the body of the research paper.

2. Type the research paper as shown in Figures 2–84a and 2–84b. Insert the footnote as shown in Figure 2–84a. Change the Footnote Text style to the format specified in the MLA documentation style. Change the bibliography style to MLA. As you insert citations, use the source information listed below and on page WD 134:

   a. Type of Source: Article in a Periodical
      Author: Barton, Blake
      Title: Computers in Agriculture
      Periodical Title: Agriculture Today and Tomorrow
      Year: 2012
      Month: Feb.
      Pages 53–86
      Publication Medium: Print

(b) Page 2

Gander 2

Brewster, the discovery of pests might trigger a pesticide to discharge in the affected area

automatically (Agriculture: Expanding and Growing).

Many farmers use technology on a daily basis to regulate soil moisture and to keep their

crops pest free. With technology, farming can be much more convenient and efficient.

(a) Page 1

Gander 1

Samuel Gander

Mr. Dunham

English 102

April 25, 2012

Farming on a Whole New Level

Although people have worked in agriculture for more than 10,000 years, advances in

technology assist with maintaining and protecting land, crops, and animals. The demand to keep

food prices affordable encourages those working in the agriculture industry to operate as

efficiently as possible (Newman and Ruiz 33-47).

Almost all people and companies in this industry have many acres of land they must

maintain, and it is not always feasible for farmers to take frequent trips around the property to

perform basic tasks such as watering soil in the absence of rain. The number of people-hours

required to water soil manually on several thousand acres of land might result in businesses

spending thousands of dollars in labor and utility costs. If the irrigation process is automated,

sensors detect how much rain has fallen recently, as well as whether the soil is in need of

watering. The sensors then send this data to a computer that processes it and decides when and

how much to water.[1]

In addition to keeping the soil moist and reducing maintenance costs, computers also can

utilize sensors to analyze the condition of crops in the field and determine whether pests or

diseases are affecting the crops. If sensors detect pests and/or diseases, computers send a

notification to the appropriate individual to take corrective action. In some cases, according to

---

[1] Barton states that many automated home irrigation systems also are programmable and

use rain sensors (67-73).

Figure 2–84

Continued >

In the Lab *continued*

    b. Type of Source: Book
       Author: Newman, Albert D., and Carmen W. Ruiz
       Title: The Agricultural Industry Today
       Year: 2012
       City: New York
       Publisher: Alabama Press
       Publication Medium: Print

    c. Type of Source: Web site
       Author: Brewster, Letty
       Name of Web page: Agriculture: Expanding and Growing
       Year: 2012
       Month: Jan.
       Day: 3
       Publication Medium: Web
       Year Accessed: 2012
       Month Accessed: Feb.
       Day Accessed: 9

3. At the end of the research paper text, press the ENTER key once and insert a manual page break so that the Works Cited page begins on a new page. Enter and format the works cited title. Use Word to insert the bibliographical list. Convert the bibliography field to text. Change the underline format on the titles of the works to the italic format, and insert the correct publication medium for each work.

4. Check the spelling and grammar of the paper.

5. Save the document using Lab 2-2 Agriculture Paper as the file name.

6. Print the research paper. Handwrite the number of words, including the footnotes, in the research paper above the title of your printed research paper.

In the Lab

Lab 3: Composing a Research Paper from Notes

Problem: You have drafted the notes shown in Figure 2–85. Your assignment is to prepare a short research paper from these notes.

Instructions: Perform the following tasks:

1. Start Word. Review the notes in Figure 2–85 and then rearrange and reword them. Embellish the paper as you deem necessary. Present the paper according to the MLA documentation style.

    Create an AutoCorrect entry that automatically corrects the spelling of the misspelled word, digtal, to the correct spelling, digital. Set an AutoCorrect exception for CD., so that Word does not lowercase the next typed letter.

    Insert a footnote that refers the reader to the Web for more information. Enter citations and their sources as shown.

    Create the works cited page (bibliography) from the listed sources. Convert the bibliography field to text. Change the underline format on the titles of the works to the italic format, and insert the correct publication medium for each work.

2. If necessary, set the default dictionary. Add the word, Flickr, to the dictionary. Check the spelling and grammar of the paper.

3. Use the Research task pane to look up a definition of a word in the paper. Copy and insert the definition into the document as a footnote. Be sure to quote the definition and cite the source. *Hint:* Use a Web site as the type of source.

4. Save the document using Lab 2-3 Cloud Storage Paper as the file name. Print the research paper. Handwrite the number of words, including the footnotes, in the research paper above the title of the printed research paper.

Cloud Storage:

- When storing data using cloud storage, the user must locate the appropriate Web site. Some sites support only certain file types. Other sites provide more than just storage.
- Cloud storage is one of the many different features available on the Internet.
- Cloud storage allows users to store files on Web sites.
- Computer users may use this type of storage if they do not want to store their data locally on a hard disk or other type of media.

Different Web sites provide different types of cloud storage. Three are Google's Gmail, YouTube, and Windows Live SkyDrive (source: "Cloud Storage and the Internet," an article on pages 23-37 in March 2012 issue of *Internet Usage and Trends* by Leona Carter).

- Google's e-mail program, Gmail, is cloud storage that stores e-mail messages.
- YouTube is different from Gmail, however, because it stores only digital videos (source: pages 22-24 in a book called *Working with the Internet: Cloud Storage* by Robert M. Gaff, published at Jane Lewis Press in New York in 2012).
- Windows Live SkyDrive is a cloud storage provider that accepts any type of file. This type of Web site is used mainly for backup or additional storage space.

Some cloud storage Web sites also provide other services (source: a Web site titled *The Internet: Cloud Storage* by Rebecca A. Ford and Harry I. Garland of Course Technology dated January 2, 2012, viewed on March 7, 2012).

- Flickr provides cloud storage for digital photos and also enables users to manage their photos and share them with others.
- Facebook provides cloud storage for a number of different file types including digital photos, digital videos, messages, and personal information. Facebook also provides a means of social networking.
- Google Docs not only stores documents, spreadsheets, and presentations in its cloud, it also enables its users to create these documents.

Figure 2–85

Cases and Places

Apply your creative thinking and problem solving skills to design and implement a solution.

Note: To complete these assignments, you may be required to use the Data Files for Students. See the inside back cover of this book for instructions on downloading the Data Files for Students, or contact your instructor for information about accessing the required files.

1: Create a Research Paper about Preparing for a Career in the Computer Industry

Academic

As a student in an introductory computer class, your instructor has assigned a research paper that discusses educational options available for students pursuing a career in the computer industry. The source for the text in your research paper is in a file called Preparing for a Career in the Computer Industry, which is located on the Data Files for Students. In addition to this source, if your instructor requests, use the Research task pane to obtain information from another source. Include a note positioned as a footnote. Add an AutoCorrect entry to correct a word you commonly mistype.

Using the concepts and techniques presented in this chapter, along with the text in the file on the Data Files for Students, create and format this research paper according to the MLA documentation style. Be sure to check spelling and grammar of the finished paper. Submit your assignment in the format specified by your instructor.

2: Create a Research Paper about Computer Viruses

Personal

The computer you recently purchased included an antivirus program. Because you need practice writing research papers and you want to learn more about computer viruses, you decide to write a paper about computer viruses. The source for the text in your research paper is in a file called Computer Viruses, which is located on the Data Files for Students. In addition to this source, if your instructor requests, use the Research task pane to obtain information from another source. Include a note positioned as a footnote. Add an AutoCorrect entry to correct a word you commonly mistype.

Using the concepts and techniques presented in this chapter, along with the text in the file on the Data Files for Students, create and format this research paper according to the MLA documentation style. Be sure to check spelling and grammar of the finished paper. Submit your assignment in the format specified by your instructor.

3: Create a Research Paper about a Disaster Recovery Plan

Professional

Your boss has asked you to research the components of a disaster recovery plan. Because you learned in college how to write research papers, you decide to present your findings in a research paper. The source for the text in your research paper is in a file called Disaster Recovery Plan, which is located on the Data Files for Students. In addition to this source, if your instructor requests, use the Research task pane to obtain information from another source. Include a note positioned as a footnote. Add an AutoCorrect entry to correct a word you commonly mistype.

Using the concepts and techniques presented in this chapter, along with the text in the file on the Data Files for Students, create and format this research paper according to the MLA documentation style. Be sure to check spelling and grammar of the finished paper. Submit your assignment in the format specified by your instructor.

3 Creating a Business Letter with a Letterhead and Table

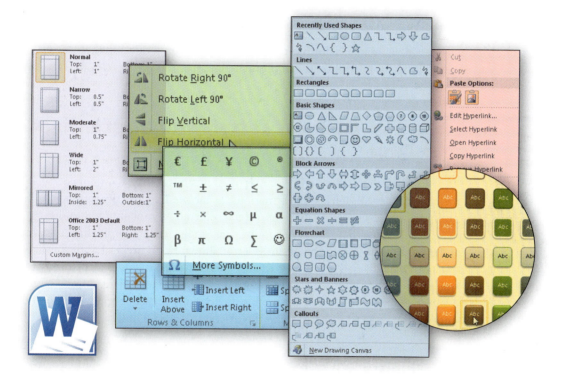

Objectives

You will have mastered the material in this chapter when you can:

- Change margins
- Insert and format a shape
- Change text wrapping
- Insert and format a clip art image
- Insert a symbol
- Add a border to a paragraph
- Clear formatting
- Convert a hyperlink to regular text

- Create a file from an existing file
- Apply a Quick Style
- Set and use tab stops
- Insert the current date
- Create, insert, and modify a building block
- Insert a Word table, enter data in the table, and format the table
- Address and print an envelope

3 | Creating a Business Letter with a Letterhead and Table

Introduction

In a business environment, people use documents to communicate with others. Business documents can include letters, memos, newsletters, proposals, and resumes. An effective business document clearly and concisely conveys its message and has a professional, organized appearance. You can use your own creative skills to design and compose business documents. Using Word, for example, you can develop the content and decide on the location of each item in a business document.

Project — Business Letter with a Letterhead and Table

At some time, you will prepare some type of business letter. Contents of business letters include requests, inquiries, confirmations, acknowledgements, recommendations, notifications, responses, invitations, offers, referrals, complaints, and more.

The project in this chapter follows generally accepted guidelines for writing letters and uses Word to create the business letter shown in Figure 3–1. This business letter to a potential advertiser (Wilcox Tractor Restorations) includes a custom letterhead, as well as all essential business letter components: date line, inside address, salutation, body, complimentary close, and signature block. To easily present the advertisement rates, this information appears in a table, and the discounts are in a bulleted list.

Overview

As you read through this chapter, you will learn how to create the business letter in Figure 3–1 by performing these general tasks:

- Design and create a letterhead.
- Compose a business letter.
- Print the business letter.
- Address and print an envelope.

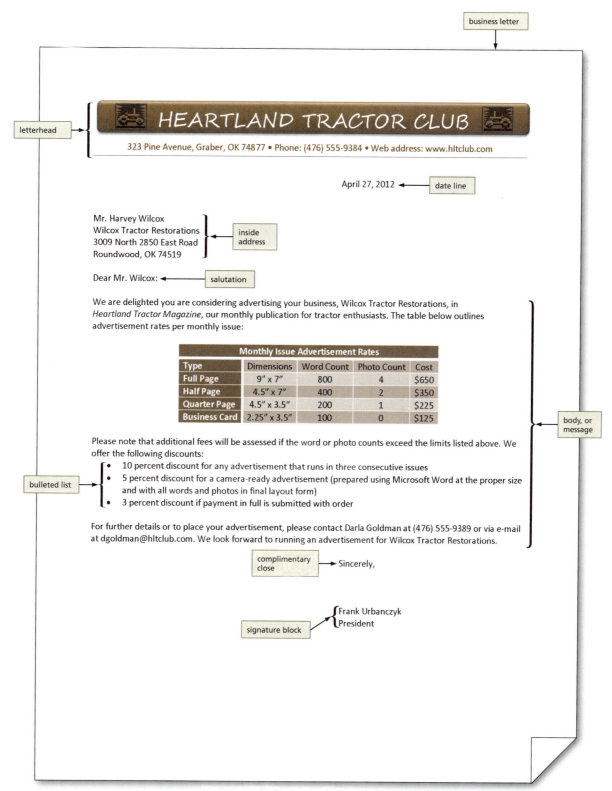

business letter

letterhead

HEARTLAND TRACTOR CLUB

323 Pine Avenue, Graber, OK 74877 • Phone: (476) 555-9384 • Web address: www.hltclub.com

April 27, 2012 ← date line

Mr. Harvey Wilcox
Wilcox Tractor Restorations
3009 North 2850 East Road
Roundwood, OK 74519

inside address

Dear Mr. Wilcox: ← salutation

We are delighted you are considering advertising your business, Wilcox Tractor Restorations, in *Heartland Tractor Magazine*, our monthly publication for tractor enthusiasts. The table below outlines advertisement rates per monthly issue:

Monthly Issue Advertisement Rates				
Type	Dimensions	Word Count	Photo Count	Cost
Full Page	9" x 7"	800	4	$650
Half Page	4.5" x 7"	400	2	$350
Quarter Page	4.5" x 3.5"	200	1	$225
Business Card	2.25" x 3.5"	100	0	$125

body, or message

Please note that additional fees will be assessed if the word or photo counts exceed the limits listed above. We offer the following discounts:

bulleted list

- 10 percent discount for any advertisement that runs in three consecutive issues
- 5 percent discount for a camera-ready advertisement (prepared using Microsoft Word at the proper size and with all words and photos in final layout form)
- 3 percent discount if payment in full is submitted with order

For further details or to place your advertisement, please contact Darla Goldman at (476) 555-9389 or via e-mail at dgoldman@hltclub.com. We look forward to running an advertisement for Wilcox Tractor Restorations.

complimentary close → Sincerely,

signature block → Frank Urbanczyk
President

Figure 3–1

Plan Ahead

General Project Guidelines

When creating a Word document, the actions you perform and decisions you make will affect the appearance and characteristics of the finished document. As you create a business letter, such as the project shown in Figure 3–1 on the previous page, you should follow these general guidelines:

1. **Determine how to create a letterhead.** A **letterhead** is the section of a letter that identifies an organization or individual. Often, the letterhead appears at the top of a letter. Although you can design and print a letterhead yourself, many businesses pay an outside firm to design and print their letterhead, usually on higher-quality paper. They then use the professionally preprinted paper for external business communications.

2. **If you do not have preprinted letterhead paper, design a creative letterhead.** Use text, graphics, formats, and colors that reflect the organization or individual. Include the organization's or individual's name, postal mailing address, and telephone number. If the organization or individual has an e-mail address and Web address, you may include those as well.

3. **Compose an effective business letter.** A finished business letter should look like a symmetrically framed picture with evenly spaced margins, all balanced below an attractive letterhead. The letter should be well-written, properly formatted, logically organized, and use visuals where appropriate. The content of a letter should contain proper grammar, correct spelling, logically constructed sentences, flowing paragraphs, and sound ideas. If possible, keep the length of a business letter to one page. Be sure to proofread the finished letter carefully.

When necessary, more specific details concerning the above guidelines are presented at appropriate points in the chapter. The chapter also will identify the actions performed and decisions made regarding these guidelines during the creation of the business letter shown in Figure 3–1.

For an introduction to Windows 7 and instruction about how to perform basic Windows 7 tasks, read the Office 2010 and Windows 7 chapter at the beginning of this book, where you can learn how to resize windows, change screen resolution, create folders, move and rename files, use Windows Help, and much more.

To Start Word and Display Formatting Marks

If you are using a computer to step through the project in this chapter and you want your screens to match the figures in this book, you should change your screen's resolution to 1024 × 768. For information about how to change a computer's resolution, refer to the Office 2010 and Windows 7 chapter at the beginning of this book.

The following steps start Word and display formatting marks.

1 Start Word. If necessary, maximize the Word window.

2 If the Print Layout button on the status bar is not selected (shown in Figure 3–2), click it so that your screen is in Print Layout view.

3 Change your zoom to 110% (or a percent where the document is large enough for you easily to see its contents).

4 If the Show/Hide ¶ button (Home tab | Paragraph group) is not selected already, click it to display formatting marks on the screen.

For an introduction to Office 2010 and instruction about how to perform basic tasks in Office 2010 programs, read the Office 2010 and Windows 7 chapter at the beginning of this book, where you can learn how to start a program, use the Ribbon, save a file, open a file, quit a program, use Help, and much more.

To Change Theme Colors

Recall that Word provides document themes that contain a variety of color schemes to assist you in selecting complementary colors in a document. In a letter, select a color scheme that adequately reflects the organization or person. The letter in this chapter uses the Executive color scheme. The following steps change theme colors.

1 Click the Change Styles button (Home tab | Styles group) to display the Change Styles menu and then point to Colors on the Change Styles menu to display the Colors gallery.

2 Click Executive in the Colors gallery to change the document theme colors to the selected color scheme.

To Change Margin Settings

Word is preset to use standard 8.5-by-11-inch paper, with 1-inch top, bottom, left, and right margins. If you change the default (preset) margin settings, the new margin settings affect every page in the document. If you wanted the margins to affect just a portion of the document, you would divide the document into sections (discussed in a later chapter), which enables you to specify different margin settings for each section.

The business letter in this chapter uses .75-inch left and right margins and 1-inch top and bottom margins, so that more text can fit from left to right on the page. The following steps change margin settings.

1

- Display the Page Layout tab.

- Click the Margins button (Page Layout tab | Page Setup group) to display the Margins gallery (Figure 3–2).

2

- Click Moderate in the Margins gallery to change the margins to the specified settings.

Q&A What if the margin settings I want are not in the Margins gallery?

You can click Custom Margins in the Margins gallery and then enter your desired margin values in the top, bottom, left, and right text boxes in the dialog box.

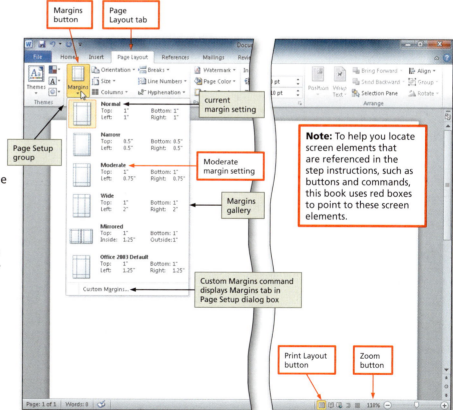

Figure 3–2

Creating a Letterhead

The cost of preprinted letterhead can be high. Thus, an alternative is to create your own letterhead and save it in a file. When you want to create a letter at a later time using the letterhead, simply create a new document from the letterhead file. In this chapter, you create a letterhead and then save it in a file for future use.

<table>
<tr>
<td>**Plan Ahead**</td>
<td>

Design a creative letterhead.
A letterhead often is the first section a reader notices on a letter. Thus, it is important the letterhead appropriately reflect the essence of the business or individual (i.e., formal, technical, creative, etc.). The letterhead should leave ample room for the contents of the letter. When designing a letterhead, consider its contents, placement, and appearance.

- **Contents of letterhead.** A letterhead should contain these elements:
  - Complete legal name of the individual, group, or company
  - Complete mailing address: street address including building, room, suite number, or post office box, along with city, state, and postal code
  - Telephone number(s) and fax number, if one exists

  Many letterheads also include a Web address, an e-mail address, and a logo or other image. If you use an image, select one that expresses your personality or goals.

- **Placement of elements in the letterhead.** Many letterheads center their elements across the top of the page. Others align some or all of the elements with the left or right margins. Sometimes, the elements are split between the top and bottom of the page. For example, a name and logo may be at the top of the page with the address at the bottom of the page.

- **Appearance of letterhead elements.** Use fonts that are easy to read. Give the organization or individual name impact by making its font size larger than the rest of the text in the letterhead. For additional emphasis, consider formatting the name in bold, italic, or a different color. Choose colors that complement each other and convey the goals of the organization or individual.

  When finished designing the letterhead, determine if a divider line would help to visually separate the letterhead from the remainder of the letter.

</td>
</tr>
</table>

The letterhead for the business letter in this chapter consists of the organization name, appropriate graphics, postal address, telephone number, and Web address. The name and graphics are enclosed in a rectangular shape (Figure 3–1 on page WD 139), and the contact information is below the shape. You will follow these general steps to create the letterhead for the business letter:

1. Insert and format a shape.
2. Enter and format the organization name in the shape.
3. Insert, format, and position the images in the shape.
4. Enter the contact information below the shape.
5. Add a border below the contact information.

To Insert a Shape

The first step is in creating the letterhead in this chapter is to draw a rectangular shape. Word has a variety of predefined shapes, which are a type of drawing object, that you can insert in documents. A **drawing object** is a graphic that you create using Word. Examples of shape drawing objects include rectangles, circles, triangles, arrows, flowcharting symbols, stars, banners, and callouts. The next steps insert a rounded rectangle shape.

1

- Display the Insert tab.

- Click the Shapes button (Insert tab | Illustrations group) to display the Shapes gallery (Figure 3–3).

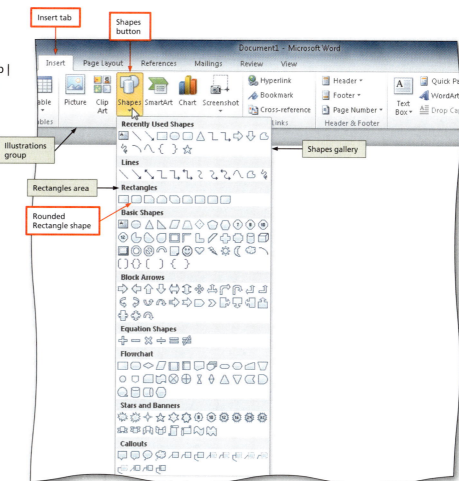

Figure 3–3

2

- Click the Rounded Rectangle shape in the Rectangles area of the Shapes gallery, which removes the gallery and changes the mouse pointer to the shape of a crosshair.

- Position the mouse pointer (a crosshair) by the insertion point in the document window, as shown in Figure 3–4, which is the location for the upper-left corner of the desired shape.

Q&A

What is the purpose of the crosshair mouse pointer?

In the document window, you will drag the crosshair mouse pointer from the upper-left corner to the lower-right corner to form the desired location and size of the shape.

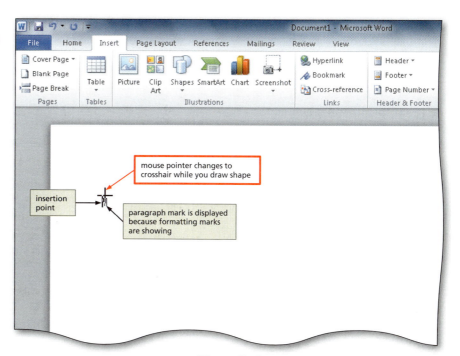

Figure 3–4

- Drag the mouse to the right and downward to form the boundaries of the shape, as shown in Figure 3–5. Do not release the mouse button.

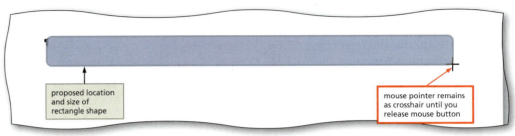

proposed location and size of rectangle shape

mouse pointer remains as crosshair until you release mouse button

Figure 3–5

- Release the mouse button so that Word draws the shape according to your drawing in the document window.

- Verify your shape is the same approximate height and width as the one in this project by clicking the Size button (Drawing Tools Format tab | Size group) and then, if necessary, changing the values in the Shape Height box and Shape Width boxes to 0.5" and 7", respectively (Figure 3–6). When finished, click the Size button again to remove the Shape Height and Shape Width boxes.

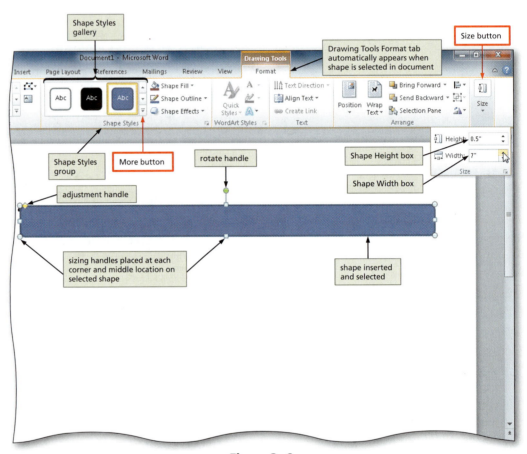

Shape Styles gallery

Size button

Drawing Tools Format tab automatically appears when shape is selected in document

Shape Styles group

More button

rotate handle

Shape Height box

Shape Width box

adjustment handle

sizing handles placed at each corner and middle location on selected shape

shape inserted and selected

Figure 3–6

What is the purpose of the rotate and adjustment handles?

When you drag an object's **rotate handle**, which is the green circle, Word rotates the object in the direction you drag the mouse. When you drag an object's **adjustment handle**, which is the yellow diamond, Word changes the object's shape.

What if I wanted to delete a shape and start over?

With the shape selected, you would press the DELETE key.

To Apply a Shape Style

Word provides a Shape Styles gallery, allowing you to change the appearance of the shape. Because the organization in this project, Heartland Tractor Club, supports many different tractor manufacturers, its letterhead should use a color that is not commonly associated with a particular tractor manufacturer. The next steps apply a shape style that uses a shade of brown.

1

- With the shape still selected, click the More button (shown in Figure 3–6) in the Shape Styles gallery (Drawing Tools Format tab | Shape Styles group) to expand the gallery.

Q&A What if my shape is no longer selected?

Click the shape to select it.

- Point to Intense Effect - Brown, Accent 4 in the Shape Styles gallery to display a live preview of that style applied to the shape in the document (Figure 3–7).

 Experiment

- Point to various styles in the Shape Styles gallery and watch the style of the shape change in the document.

2

- Click Intense Effect - Brown, Accent 4 in the Shape Styles gallery to apply the selected style to the shape.

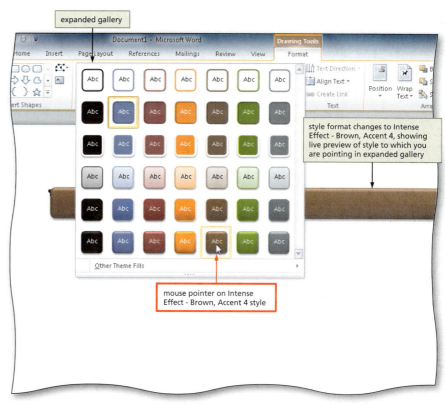

expanded gallery

style format changes to Intense Effect - Brown, Accent 4, showing live preview of style to which you are pointing in expanded gallery

mouse pointer on Intense Effect - Brown, Accent 4 style

Figure 3–7

Other Ways
1. Click Format Shape Dialog Box Launcher (Drawing Tools Format tab | Shape Styles group), click Picture Color in left pane	(Format Shape dialog box), select desired colors, click Close button 2. Right-click shape, click Format Shape on	shortcut menu, click Picture Color in left pane (Format Shape dialog box), select desired colors, click Close button

To Add Text to a Shape

The next step is to add the organization name to the shape. The following steps add text to a shape.

1

- Right-click the shape to display a shortcut menu and the Mini toolbar (Figure 3–8).

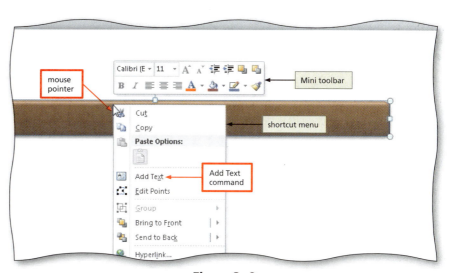

mouse pointer

Mini toolbar

shortcut menu

Add Text command

Cut
Copy
Paste Options:

Add Text
Edit Points
Group
Bring to Front
Send to Back
Hyperlink...

Figure 3–8

2
- Click Add Text on the shortcut menu to place an insertion point centered in the shape.

- Type **HEARTLAND TRACTOR CLUB** as the organization name in the shape (Figure 3–9).

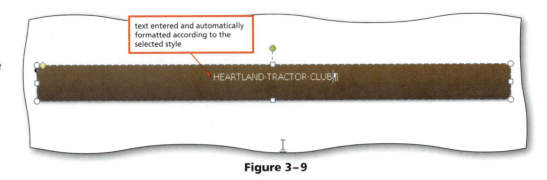

Figure 3–9

To Use the Grow Font Button to Increase Font Size

You want the font size of the organization name to be much larger in the shape. In previous chapters, you used the Font Size box arrow (Home tab | Font group) to change the font size of text. Word also provides a Grow Font button (Home tab | Font group), which increases the font size of selected text each time you click the button. The following steps use the Grow Font button to increase the font size of the organization name to 22 point.

1
- Drag through the organization name in the shape to select the text to be formatted.

2
- Display the Home tab.

- Repeatedly click the Grow Font button (Home tab | Font group) until the Font Size box displays 22 to increase the font size of the selected text (Figure 3–10).

Q&A What if I click the Grow Font button (Home tab | Font group) too many times, causing the font size to be too big?

Click the Shrink Font button (Home tab | Font group) until the desired font size is displayed.

Experiment
- Repeatedly click the Grow Font and Shrink Font buttons (Home tab | Font group) and watch the font size of the selected name change in the document window. When you are finished experimenting with these two buttons, set the font size to 22.

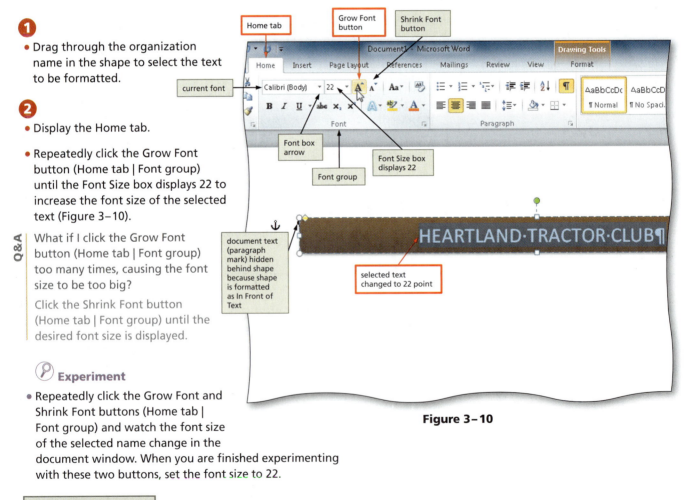

Figure 3–10

Other Ways
1. Press CTRL+SHIFT+>

To Change the Font of Selected Text

The font of the organization name currently is Calibri. To make the organization name stand out even more, change the font of the name in the letterhead to a font different from the rest of the letter. The following steps change the font of the selected text.

1 With the text selected, click the Font box arrow (Home tab | Font group) to display the Font gallery.

2 Scroll to and then click Segoe Script in the Font gallery to change the font of the selected text (shown in Figure 3–11 on the next page).

3 Click anywhere in the text in the shape to remove the selection and place the insertion point in the shape.

Floating versus Inline Objects

When you insert an object, such as a shape, in a document, Word inserts it as either an inline object or a floating object. An **inline object** is an object that is part of a paragraph. With inline objects, you change the location of the object by setting paragraph options, such as centered, right-aligned, and so on. A **floating object** is an object that can be positioned at a specific location in a document or in a layer over or behind text in a document. You have more flexibility with floating objects because you can position a floating object anywhere on the page.

In addition to changing an object from inline to floating and vice versa, Word provides several floating options. All of these options affect how text wraps with the object. Table 3–1 lists the various text wrapping options and explains the function of each one.

Table 3–1 Text Wrapping Options

Text Wrapping Option	Object Type	How It Works
In Line with Text	Inline	Object positioned according to paragraph formatting; for example, if paragraph is centered, object will be centered with any text in the paragraph.
Square	Floating	Text wraps around object, with text forming a box around the object.
Tight	Floating	Text wraps around object, with text forming to shape of the object.
Through	Floating	Object appears at beginning, middle, or end of text. Moving object changes location of text.
Top and Bottom	Floating	Object appears above or below text. Moving object changes location of text.
Behind Text	Floating	Object appears behind text.
In Front of Text	Floating	Object appears in front of text and may cover the text.

BTW

Positioning Objects
If you want to use the Square text wrapping option, you can specify where the object should be positioned on the page. To specify the position, select the object, click the Object Position button (Picture Tools Format tab | Arrange group), and then click the desired location in the Object Position gallery.

To Change an Object's Text Wrapping

When you insert a shape in a Word document, the default text wrapping is In Front of Text, which means the object will cover any text behind it. Because you want the letterhead above the contents of the letter, instead of covering the contents of the letter, you change the text wrapping for the shape to Top and Bottom. The following steps change a shape's text wrapping.

- Click the edge of the shape to select the shape.

- Display the Drawing Tools Format tab.

- Click the Wrap Text button (Drawing Tools Format tab | Arrange group) to display the Wrap Text gallery (Figure 3–11).

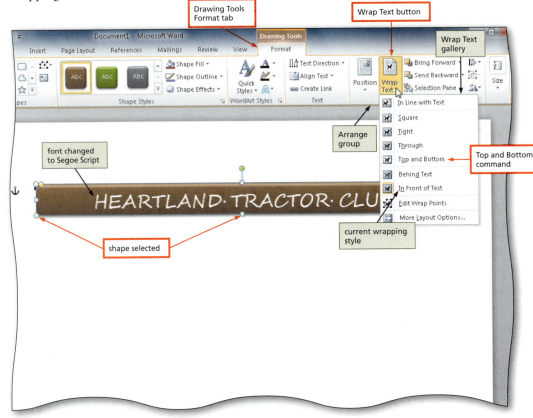

Figure 3–11

2

🔍 **Experiment**

- Point to various text wrapping options in the Wrap Text gallery and watch the shape configure to the selected wrapping option, which in this case, moves the paragraph mark to different locations in the document.

- Click Top and Bottom in the Wrap Text gallery so that the object does not cover the document text.

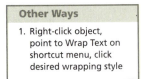

Other Ways

1. Right-click object, point to Wrap Text on shortcut menu, click desired wrapping style

To Insert Clip Art

Files containing graphical images, or graphics, are available from a variety of sources. In the Chapter 1 document, you inserted a digital picture taken with a camera phone. In this project, you insert **clip art**, which is a predefined graphic. In Microsoft Office programs, clip art is located in the **Clip Organizer**, which contains a collection of clip art, photos, animations, sounds, and videos.

The letterhead in this project contains clip art of a tractor (Figure 3–1 on page WD 139). Thus, the next steps insert a clip art image on the line below the shape in the document.

- Click the paragraph mark below the shape to position the insertion point where you want to insert the clip art image.

- Display the Insert tab.

- Click the Clip Art button (Insert tab | Illustrations group) to display the Clip Art pane (Figure 3–12).

Q&A

What is a pane?

Recall from the Office 2010 and Windows 7 chapter at the beginning of this book that a pane, or task pane, is a separate window that enables you to carry out some Word tasks more efficiently.

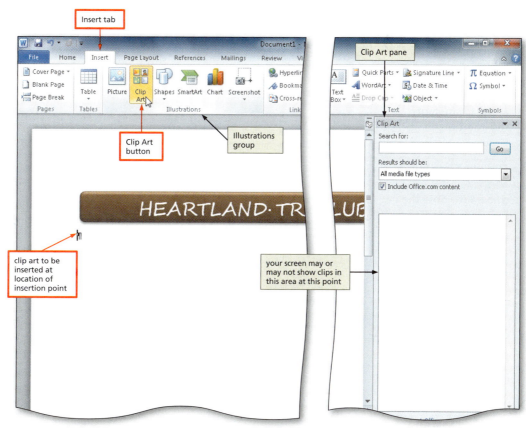

Figure 3–12

- If the Search for text box displays text, drag through the text to select it.

- Type **tractor** in the Search for text box to specify the search text, which in this case indicates the type of image you wish to locate.

- Click the Go button to display a list of clips that match the entered search text (Figure 3–13).

Q&A

Why is my list of clips different from Figure 3–13?

If your Include Office.com content check box is selected and you are connected to the Internet, the Clip Art pane displays clips from the Web as well as those installed on your hard disk.

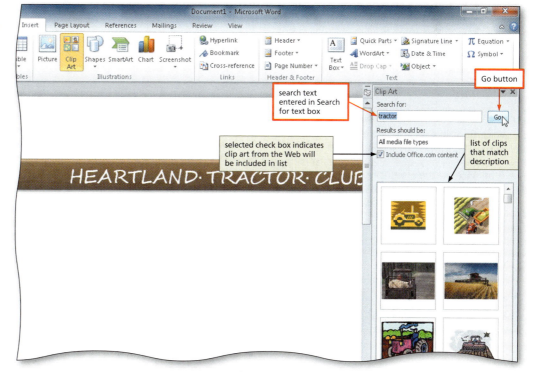

Figure 3–13

- Click the clip art of the yellow tractor to insert this clip art image in the document at the location of the insertion point (Figure 3–14).

- Click the Close button on the Clip Art pane title bar to close the task pane.

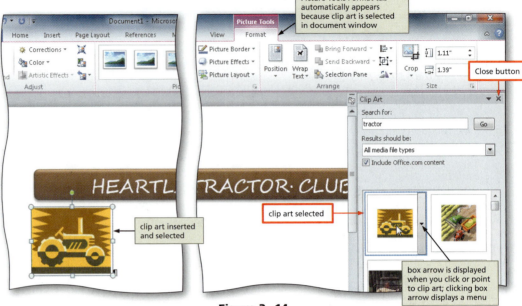

Figure 3–14

To Resize a Graphic to a Percent of the Original

In this project, the graphic is 35 percent of its original size. Instead of dragging a sizing handle to change the graphic's size, as you learned in Chapter 1, you can set exact size percentages. The following steps resize a graphic to a percent of the original.

- With the graphic still selected, click the Advanced Layout: Size Dialog Box Launcher (Picture Tools Format tab | Size group) to display the Layout dialog box.

Q&A What if the graphic is not selected or the Picture Tools Format tab is not on the Ribbon?

Click the graphic to select it or double-click the graphic to make the Picture Tools Format tab the active tab.

- In the Scale area (Layout dialog box), double-click the current value in the Height box to select it.

- Type 35 in the Height box and then press the TAB key to display the same percent value in the Width box (Figure 3–15).

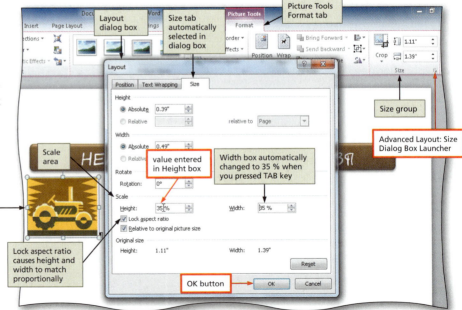

Figure 3–15

Q&A Why did Word automatically fill in the value in the Width box?

When the 'Lock aspect ratio' check box (Layout dialog box) is selected, Word automatically maintains the size proportions of the graphic.

Q&A How do I know to use 35 percent for the resized graphic?

The larger graphic consumed too much room on the page. Try various percentages to determine the size that works best in the letterhead design.

3
- Click the OK button to close the dialog box and resize the selected graphic (Figure 3–16).

graphic selected and resized to 35% of its original size

Figure 3–16

Other Ways
1. Right-click graphic, click Size and Position on shortcut menu, enter values (Layout dialog box), click OK button

To Change the Color of a Graphic

In Word, you can change the color of a graphic. The clip art currently consists of shades of yellow and brown. Because the clip art in this project will be placed in a rectangle shape, you prefer to use colors that blend better with the current color scheme. The following steps change the color of the graphic to a shade in the current color scheme that matches the color of the shape.

1
- With the graphic still selected (shown in Figure 3–16), click the Color button (Picture Tools Format tab | Adjust group) to display the Color gallery.

- Point to Orange, Accent color 3 Dark in the Color gallery (fourth color in second row) to display a live preview of that color applied to the selected graphic in the document (Figure 3–17).

 **Experiment**
- Point to various colors in the Color gallery and watch the color of the graphic change in the document.

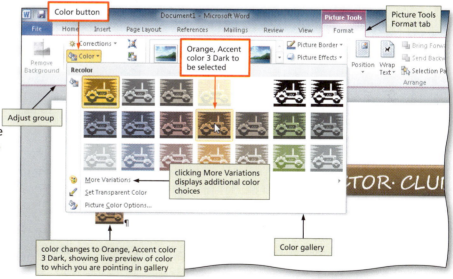

Color button

Picture Tools Format tab

Orange, Accent color 3 Dark to be selected

Adjust group

clicking More Variations displays additional color choices

color changes to Orange, Accent color 3 Dark, showing live preview of color to which you are pointing in gallery

Color gallery

Figure 3–17

2
- Click Orange, Accent color 3 Dark in the Color gallery to change the color of the selected graphic.

Q&A How would I change a graphic back to its original colors?

With the graphic selected, you would click No Recolor in the Color gallery (upper-left color).

Other Ways
1. Right-click graphic, click Format Picture on shortcut menu, click Picture Color button in left pane (Format Picture dialog box), select color, click Close button

To Set a Transparent Color in a Graphic

In Word, you can make one color in a graphic transparent, that is, remove the color. You would make a color transparent if you wanted to remove part of a graphic or see text or colors behind a graphic. In this project, you will remove the lighter brown from the edges of the tractor graphic so that when you move the graphic on the rectangular shape, the color of the shape can be seen in the transparent locations. The following steps set a transparent color in a graphic.

- With the graphic still selected, click the Color button (Picture Tools Format tab | Adjust group) to display the Color gallery (Figure 3–18).

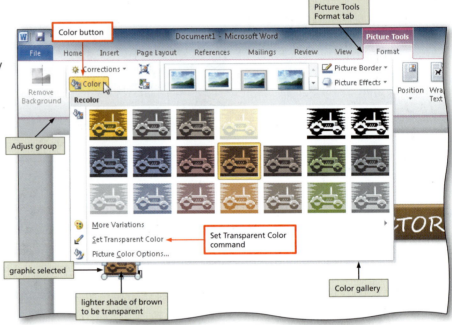

Figure 3–18

- Click Set Transparent Color in the Color gallery to display a pen mouse pointer in the document window.

- Position the pen mouse pointer in the graphic where you want to make the color transparent (Figure 3–19).

Q&A Can I make multiple colors in a graphic transparent?

No, you can make only one color transparent.

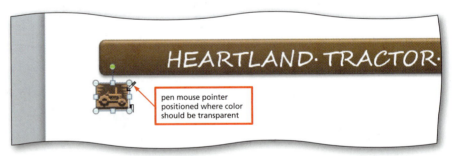

Figure 3–19

- Click the location in the graphic where you want the color to be transparent (Figure 3–20).

Q&A What if I make the wrong color transparent?

Click the Undo button on the Quick Access Toolbar, or press CTRL+Z, and then repeat these steps.

Figure 3–20

To Adjust the Brightness and Contrast of a Graphic

In Word, you can adjust the lightness (brightness) of a graphic and also contrast, which is the difference between the lightest and darkest areas of the graphic. The following steps decrease the brightness and contrast of the tractor graphic, each by 20%.

1

• With the graphic still selected (shown in Figure 3–20), click the Corrections button (Picture Tools Format tab | Adjust group) to display the Corrections gallery (Figure 3–21).

Q&A

Does live preview work in this gallery?

Yes, but the graphic is covered by the gallery in this case. To see the live preview, you would need to position the graphic so that you can see it while the gallery is displayed.

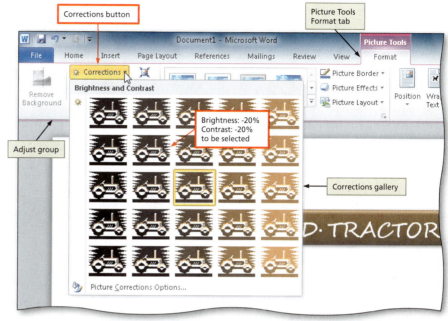

Figure 3–21

2

• Click Brightness: −20% Contrast: −20% in the Corrections gallery (second image in second row) to change the brightness and contrast of the selected graphic (Figure 3–22).

Q&A

Can I remove all formatting applied to a graphic and start over?

Yes. With the graphic selected, you would click the Reset Picture button (Picture Tools Format tab | Adjust group).

Figure 3–22

Other Ways

1. Right-click graphic, click Format Picture on shortcut menu, click Picture Corrections button in left pane (Format Picture dialog box), adjust settings, click Close button

To Change the Border Color on a Graphic

The tractor graphic currently has no border (outline). You would like the graphic to have a brown border. The following steps change the border color on a graphic.

 1

- Click the Picture Border button arrow (Picture Tools Format tab | Picture Styles group) to display the Picture Border gallery.

- Point to Brown, Accent 4, Darker 50% (eighth theme color from left in the sixth row) in the Picture Border gallery to display a live preview of that border color around the picture (Figure 3–23).

 **Experiment**

- Point to various colors in the Picture Border gallery and watch the border color on the picture change in the document window.

 2

- Click Brown, Accent 4, Darker 50% in the Picture Border gallery to change the picture border color.

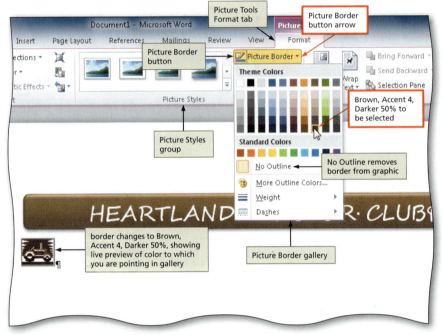

Figure 3–23

Q&A How would I remove a border from a graphic?

With the graphic selected, you would click the No Outline in the Picture Border gallery.

BTW

Clip Organizer
To make a Web clip available on your hard disk, point to the clip in the Clip Art pane, click its box arrow, click Make Available Offline, select the collection to store the clip (Copy to Collection dialog box) or click the New button to define a new collection, and then click the OK button. You can use the Clip Organizer to create, rename, or delete collections; add clips to a collection from the Web, a camera, or a scanner; delete, move, and copy clips; and search for existing clips. Start the Clip Organizer by clicking the Start button on the taskbar, clicking All Programs on the Start menu, clicking the Microsoft Office folder to its contents, clicking the Microsoft Office 2010 Tools folder to display its contents, and then clicking Microsoft Clip Organizer.

To Change an Object's Text Wrapping

The tractor graphic is to be positioned to the left of the organization name in the shape. Clip art, by default, is formatted as an inline graphic, which cannot be moved into a shape. To move the graphic in the shape so that it is not covered by any text, you format it as a floating object with In Front of Text wrapping. The following steps change a graphic's text wrapping.

1 If necessary, click the graphic to select it. If necessary, display the Picture Tools Format tab.

2 Click the Wrap Text button (Picture Tools Format tab | Arrange group) to display the Wrap Text gallery.

Q&A Do both the Picture Tools Format and Drawing Tools Format tabs have a Wrap Text button?

Yes. You can specify how to wrap text with both pictures and drawings.

3 Click In Front of Text in the Wrap Text gallery so that you can position the object on top of any item in the document, in this case, on top of the rectangular shape.

To Move a Graphic

The next step is to move the tractor graphic up so that it is positioned to the left of the text on the rectangle shape. The following steps move a graphic.

- Position the mouse pointer in the graphic so that the mouse pointer has a four-headed arrow attached to it (Figure 3–24).

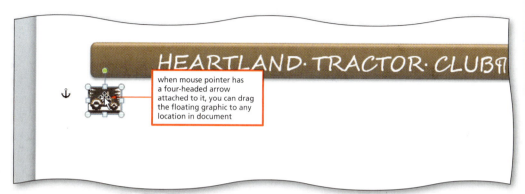

when mouse pointer has a four-headed arrow attached to it, you can drag the floating graphic to any location in document

Figure 3–24

- Drag the graphic to the location shown in Figure 3–25.

Q&A

What if I moved the graphic to the wrong location?

Repeat these steps. You can drag a floating graphic to any location in a document.

graphic moved to left of organization name

Figure 3–25

To Copy a Graphic

In this project, the same tractor graphic is to be placed to the right of the organization name in the shape. Instead of performing the same steps to insert and format another tractor graphic, you can copy the graphic to the Office Clipboard, paste the graphic from the Office Clipboard, and then move the graphic to the desired location.

You use the same steps to copy a graphic as you used in Chapter 2 to copy text. The following steps copy a graphic.

1 If necessary, click the graphic to select it.

2 Display the Home tab.

3 Click the Copy button, shown in Figure 3–26 on the next page, (Home tab | Clipboard group) to copy the selected item to the Office Clipboard.

To Use Paste Options

The next step is to paste the copied graphic in the document. The following steps paste a graphic using the Paste Options gallery.

 1

- Click the Paste button arrow (Home tab | Clipboard group) to display the Paste gallery.

Q&A What if I accidentally click the Paste button?

Click the Paste Options button below the graphic pasted in the document to display a Paste Options gallery.

- Point to the Keep Source Formatting button in the Paste gallery to display a live preview of that paste option (Figure 3–26).

Experiment

- Point to the two buttons in the Paste gallery and watch the appearance of the pasted graphic change.

Q&A What do the buttons in the Paste gallery mean?

The Keep Source Formatting button indicates the pasted graphic should have the same formats as it did in its original location. The second button removes all formatting from the graphic.

Q&A Why are these paste buttons different from the ones in Chapter 2?

The buttons that appear in the Paste gallery differ depending on the item you are pasting. Use live preview to see how the pasted object will look in the document.

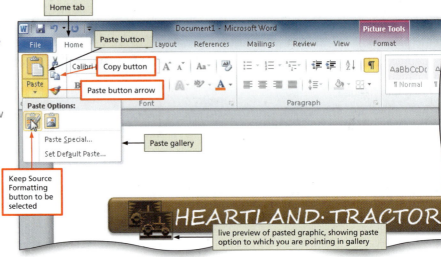

Figure 3–26

 2

- Click the Keep Source Formatting button in the Paste gallery to paste the object using the same formatting as the original.

To Move a Graphic

The next step is to move the second tractor graphic so that it is positioned to the right of the text in the rectangle shape. The following step moves a graphic.

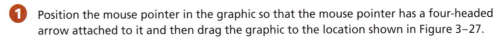

1 Position the mouse pointer in the graphic so that the mouse pointer has a four-headed arrow attached to it and then drag the graphic to the location shown in Figure 3–27.

Q&A Why does my graphic not look like it is positioned the same as the graphic on the left?

The paragraph mark at the end of the organization name may be obstructing your view. To determine if the graphic is positioned properly, you can temporarily turn off formatting marks by clicking the Show/Hide ¶ button (Home tab | Paragraph group).

Figure 3–27

To Flip a Graphic

The next step is to flip the clip art image on the right so that the tractor is facing the opposite direction. The following steps flip a graphic horizontally.

 1

- If necessary, display the Picture Tools Format tab.

- With the graphic still selected, click the Rotate button (Picture Tools Format tab | Arrange group) to display the Rotate gallery.

- Point to Flip Horizontal in the Rotate gallery to display a live preview of the selected rotate option applied to the selected graphic (Figure 3–28).

 Experiment

- Point to the rotate options in the Rotate gallery and watch the picture rotate in the document window.

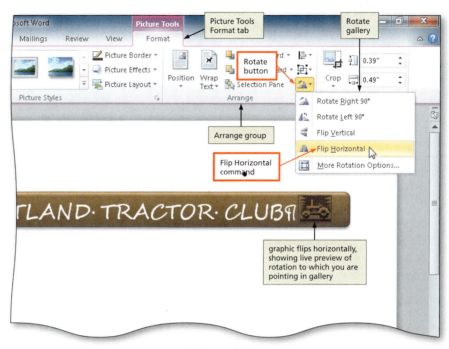

Figure 3–28

 2

- Click Flip Horizontal in the Rotate gallery, so that Word flips the graphic to display its mirror image.

Q&A Can I flip a graphic vertically?

Yes, you would click Flip Vertical in the Rotate gallery. You also can rotate a graphic clockwise or counterclockwise by clicking the Rotate Right 90° and Rotate Left 90° commands, respectively, in the Rotate gallery.

To Specify Formatting before Typing and Then Enter Text

The contact information for the organization in this project is located on the line below the organization name. The following steps format and then enter the postal address in the letterhead.

1 Position the insertion point on the line below the shape containing the organization name.

2 If necessary, display the Home tab. Click the Center button (Home tab | Paragraph group) to center the paragraph.

3 Click the Font Color button arrow (Home tab | Font group) to display the Font Color gallery and then click Orange, Accent 3, Darker 50% (seventh color in sixth row) in the Font Color gallery to change the font color.

4 Type `323 Pine Avenue, Graber, OK 74877` and then press the SPACEBAR (shown in Figure 3–29 on the next page).

BTW

Q&As

For a complete list of the Q&As found in many of the step-by-step sequences in this book, visit the Word 2010 Q&A Web page (scsite.com/wd2010/qa).

To Insert a Symbol from the Symbol Dialog Box

In the letterhead in this chapter, a small round dot separates the postal address and phone number, and the same type of dot separates the phone number and Web address information. This special symbol (the round dot) is not on the keyboard. Thus, Word provides a method of inserting dots and other symbols, such as letters in the Greek alphabet and mathematical characters.

The following steps insert a dot symbol, called a bullet symbol, between the postal address and phone number in the letterhead.

- If necessary, position the insertion point as shown in Figure 3–29.

- Display the Insert tab.

- Click the Insert Symbol button (Insert tab | Symbols group) to display the Insert Symbol gallery (Figure 3–29).

Q&A What if the symbol I want to insert already appears in the Symbol gallery?

You can click any symbol shown in the Symbol gallery to insert it in the document.

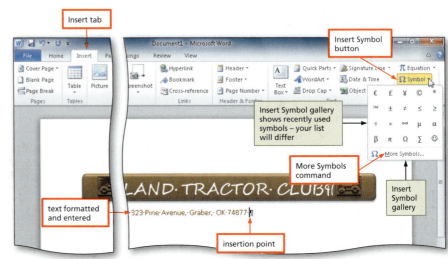

Figure 3–29

- Click More Symbols in the Insert Symbol gallery to display the Symbol dialog box.

- If the font in the Font box is not (normal text), click the Font box arrow (Symbol dialog box) and then scroll to (normal text) and click it to select this font.

- If the subset in the Subset box is not General Punctuation, click the Subset box arrow and then scroll to General Punctuation and click it to select this subset.

- In the list of symbols, if necessary, scroll to the bullet symbol shown in Figure 3–30 and then click the symbol to select it.

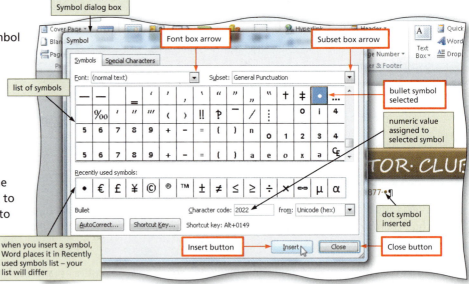

Figure 3–30

- Click the Insert button (Symbol dialog box) to place the selected symbol in the document to the left of the insertion point (Figure 3–30).

Q&A Why is the Symbol dialog box still open?

The Symbol dialog box remains open, allowing you to insert additional symbols.

- Click the Close button (Symbol dialog box) to close the dialog box.

To Insert a Symbol from the Symbol Gallery

In the letterhead, another bullet symbol separates the phone number from the Web address information. Once you insert a symbol using the Symbol dialog box, Word adds that symbol to the Symbol gallery so that it is more readily available. The following steps use the Symbol gallery to insert a bullet symbol between the phone number and Web address.

- Press the SPACEBAR, type **Phone: (476) 555-9384** and then press the SPACEBAR.

- Click the Insert Symbol button (Insert tab | Symbols group) to display the Insert Symbol gallery (Figure 3–31).

Q&A Why is the bullet symbol now in the Insert Symbol gallery?

When you insert a symbol from the Symbol dialog box, Word automatically adds the symbol to the Insert Symbol gallery.

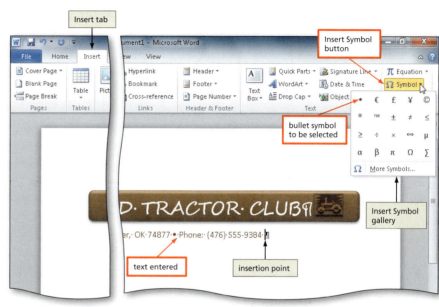

Figure 3–31

- Click the bullet symbol in the Insert Symbol gallery to insert the symbol at the location of the insertion point (shown in Figure 3–32).

To Enter Text

The following steps enter the Web address in the letterhead.

1. Press the SPACEBAR.
2. Type **Web Address: www.hltclub.com** to finish the text in the letterhead (Figure 3–32).

BTW

Inserting Special Characters
In addition to symbols, you can insert a variety of special characters including dashes, hyphens, spaces, apostrophes, and quotation marks. Click the Special Characters tab in the Symbols dialog box (Figure 3–30), click the desired character in the Character list, click the Insert button, and then click the Close button.

Figure 3–32

To Bottom Border a Paragraph

The letterhead in this project has a horizontal line that extends from the left margin to the right margin immediately below the address, phone, and Web address information, which separates the letterhead from the rest of the letter. In Word, you can draw a solid line, called a **border**, at any edge of a paragraph. That is, borders may be added above or below a paragraph, to the left or right of a paragraph, or in any combination of these sides. The following steps add a bottom border to the paragraph containing address, phone, and Web information.

- Display the Home tab.

- With the insertion point in the paragraph to border, click the Border button arrow (Home tab | Paragraph group) to display the Border gallery (Figure 3–33).

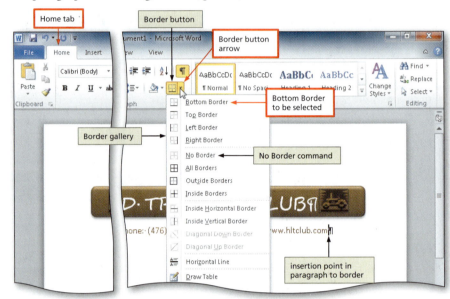

Figure 3–33

- Click Bottom Border in the Border gallery to place a border below the paragraph containing the insertion point (Figure 3–34).

Q&A If the face of the Border button displays the border icon I want to use, can I click the Border button instead of using the Border button arrow?

Yes.

Q&A How would I remove an existing border from a paragraph?

If, for some reason, you wanted to remove a border from a paragraph, you would position the insertion point in the paragraph, click the Border button arrow (Home tab | Paragraph group), and then click No Border in the Border gallery.

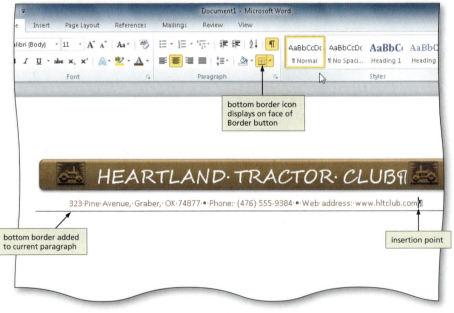

Figure 3–34

Other Ways

1. Click Page Borders button (Page Layout tab | Page Background group), click Borders tab (Borders and Shading dialog box), select desired border options, click OK button

To Clear Formatting

The next step is to position the insertion point below the letterhead, so that you can type the contents of the letter. When you press the ENTER key at the end of a paragraph containing a border, Word moves the border forward to the next paragraph. The paragraph also retains all current settings, such as the center format. Instead, you want the paragraph and characters on the new line to use the Normal style: black font with no border.

In Word, the term, **clear formatting**, refers to returning the formatting to the Normal style. The following steps clear formatting at the location of the insertion point.

- With the insertion point between the Web address and paragraph mark at the end of the line (as shown in Figure 3–34), press the ENTER key to move the insertion point and paragraph to the next line (Figure 3–35).

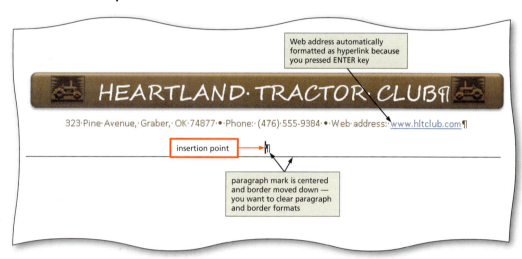

Figure 3–35

2

- Click the Clear Formatting button (Home tab | Font group) to apply the Normal style to the location of the insertion point (Figure 3–36).

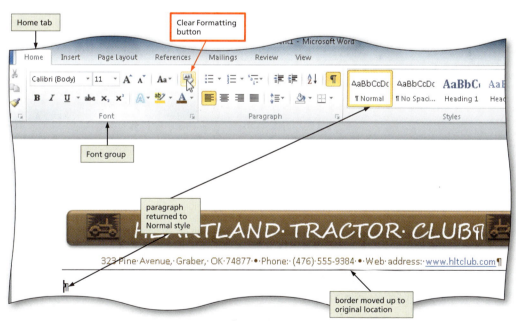

Figure 3–36

Other Ways
1. Click More button in Styles gallery (Home tab | Styles group), click Clear Formatting
2. Click Styles Dialog Box Launcher (Home tab | Styles group), click Clear All in Styles task pane
3. Select text, press CTRL+SPACEBAR, press CTRL+Q

AutoFormat as You Type

As you type text in a document, Word automatically formats some of it for you. For example, when you press the ENTER key or SPACEBAR after typing an e-mail address or Web address, Word automatically formats the address as a hyperlink, that is, colored blue and underlined. In Figure 3–35 on the previous page, for example, Word formatted the Web address as a hyperlink because you pressed the ENTER key at the end of the line. Table 3–2 outlines commonly used AutoFormat As You Type options and their results.

Table 3–2 Commonly Used AutoFormat As You Type Options		
Typed Text	**AutoFormat Feature**	**Example**
Quotation marks or apostrophes	Changes straight quotation marks or apostrophes to curly ones	"the" becomes "the"
Text, a space, one hyphen, one or no spaces, text, space	Changes the hyphen to an en dash	ages 20 - 45 becomes ages 20 – 45
Text, two hyphens, text, space	Changes the two hyphens to an em dash	Two types--yellow and red becomes Two types—yellow and red
Web or e-mail address followed by SPACEBAR or ENTER key	Formats Web or e-mail address as a hyperlink	www.scsite.com becomes www.scsite.com
Three hyphens, underscores, equal signs, asterisks, tildes, or number signs and then ENTER key	Places a border above a paragraph	--- This line becomes _____ This line
Number followed by a period, hyphen, right parenthesis, or greater than sign and then a space or tab followed by text	Creates a numbered list	1. Word 2. PowerPoint becomes 1. Word 2. PowerPoint
Asterisk, hyphen, or greater than sign and then a space or tab followed by text	Creates a bulleted list	* Home tab * Insert tab becomes • Home tab • Insert tab
Fraction and then a space or hyphen	Condenses the fraction entry so that it consumes one space instead of three	1/2 becomes ½
Ordinal and then a space or hyphen	Makes part of the ordinal a superscript	3rd becomes 3rd

BTW

AutoFormat Settings
Before you can use them, AutoFormat options must be enabled. To check if an AutoFormat option is enabled, click File on the Ribbon to open the Backstage view, click Options in the Backstage view, click Proofing in the left pane (Word Options dialog box), click the AutoCorrect Options button, click the AutoFormat As You Type tab, select the appropriate check boxes, and then click the OK button in each open dialog box.

To Convert a Hyperlink to Regular Text

The Web address in the letterhead should be formatted as regular text; that is, it should not be blue or underlined. Thus, the following steps remove the hyperlink format from the Web address in the letterhead.

1
- Right-click the hyperlink (in this case, the Web address) to display the Mini toolbar and a shortcut menu (Figure 3–37).

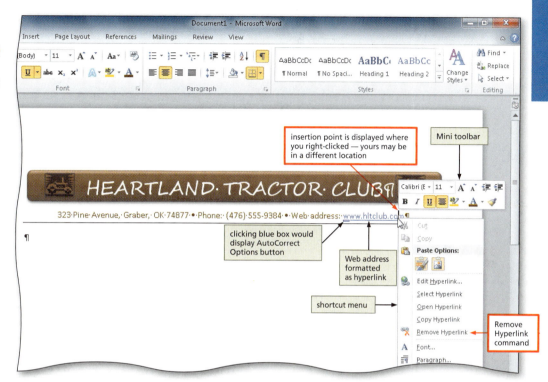

Figure 3–37

2
- Click Remove Hyperlink on the shortcut menu to remove the hyperlink format from the text.

- Position the insertion point on the paragraph mark below the border because you are finished with the letterhead (Figure 3–38).

Figure 3–38

Q&A

Could I have used the AutoCorrect Options button instead of the Remove Hyperlink command?

Yes. Alternatively, you could have pointed to the small blue box at the beginning of the hyperlink, clicked the AutoCorrect Options button, and then clicked Undo Hyperlink on the AutoCorrect Options menu.

Other Ways

1. With insertion point in hyperlink, click Hyperlink button (Insert tab | Links group), click Remove Link button

BTW

Saving a Template

As an alternative to saving the letterhead as a Word document, you could save it as a template. To do so, click File on the Ribbon to open the Backstage view, click the Save & Send tab to display the Save & Send gallery, click Change File Type, click Template in the right pane, click the Save As button, enter the template name (Save As dialog box), if necessary select the Templates folder, and then click the Save button in the dialog box. To use the template, click File on the Ribbon to open the Backstage view, click the New tab to display the New gallery, click My templates, and then double-click the template icon or name.

To Change Document Properties, Then Save and Close a File

The letterhead now is complete. Thus, you should save it in a file. The following steps assume you already have created folders for storing your files, for example, a CIS 101 folder (for your class) that contains a Word folder (for your assignments). Thus, these steps change document properties, save the file in the Word folder in the CIS 101 folder on a USB flash drive using the file name, Heartland Letterhead, and then close the file.

1. Click File on the Ribbon to open the Backstage view and then, if necessary, select the Info tab. Display the Properties menu and then click Show Document Panel on the Properties menu to close the Backstage view and display the Document Information Panel in the Word document window.

2. Enter your name in the Author property, and enter your course and section in the Subject property. Close the Document Information Panel.

3. With a USB flash drive connected to one of the computer's USB ports, click the Save button on the Quick Access Toolbar to display the Save As dialog box.

4. Type **Heartland Letterhead** in the File name text box to change the file name. Do not press the ENTER key after typing the file name because you do not want to close the dialog box at this time.

5. Navigate to the desired save location (in this case, the Word folder in the CIS 101 folder [or your class folder] on the USB flash drive).

6. Click the Save button (Save As dialog box) to save the file in the selected folder on the selected drive with the entered file name.

7. Click File on the Ribbon to open the Backstage view and then click Close in the Backstage view to close the document.

Break Point: If you wish to take a break, this is a good place to do so. To resume at a later time, start Word and continue following the steps from this location forward.

Creating a Business Letter

You have created a letterhead for the business letter. The next step is to compose the rest of the content in the business letter. The following pages use Word to create a business letter that contains a table and a bulleted list.

Plan Ahead

Compose an effective business letter.
When composing a business letter, you need to be sure to include all essential elements and to decide which letter style to use.

- **Include all essential letter elements, properly spaced and sized.** All business letters contain the same basic elements, including the date line, inside address, message, and signature block (shown in Figure 3–1 on page WD 139). If a business letter does not use a letterhead, then the top of the letter should include return address information in a heading.

- **Use proper spacing and formats for the contents of the letter below the letterhead.** Use a font that is easy to read, in a size between 8 and 12 point. Add emphasis with bold, italic, and bullets where appropriate, and use tables to present numeric information. Paragraphs should be single-spaced, with double-spacing between paragraphs.

- **Determine which letter style to use.** You can follow many different styles when creating business letters. A letter style specifies guidelines for the alignment and spacing of elements in the business letter.

To Create a New File from an Existing File

The top of the business letter in this chapter contains the letterhead, which you saved in a separate file. You could open the letterhead file and then save it with a new name, so that the letterhead file remains intact for future use. A more efficient technique is to create a new file from the letterhead file. Doing this enables you to save the document the first time using the Save button on the Quick Access Toolbar instead of requiring you to use the Save As command in the Backstage view. The following steps create a new file from an existing file.

1
- Click File on the Ribbon to open the Backstage view.

- Click the New tab in the Backstage view to display the New gallery (Figure 3–39).

Q&A

What are the templates in the New gallery?

A template is a document that includes prewritten text and/or formatting common to documents of the specified type. Word provides many templates to simplify the task of creating documents.

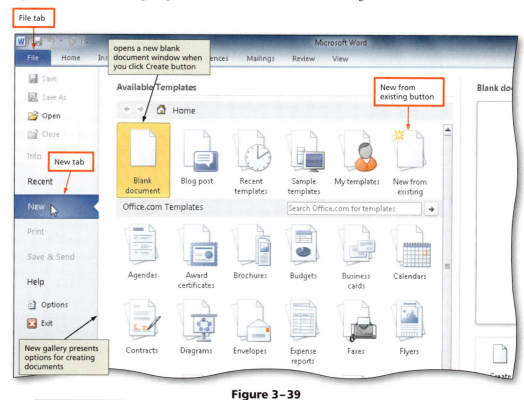

Figure 3–39

2
- Click the 'New from existing' button in the New gallery to display the New from Existing Document dialog box.

- If necessary, navigate to the location of the saved Heartland Letterhead file (in this case, the Word folder in the CIS 101 folder on the USB flash drive).

- Click Heartland Letterhead to select the file (Figure 3–40).

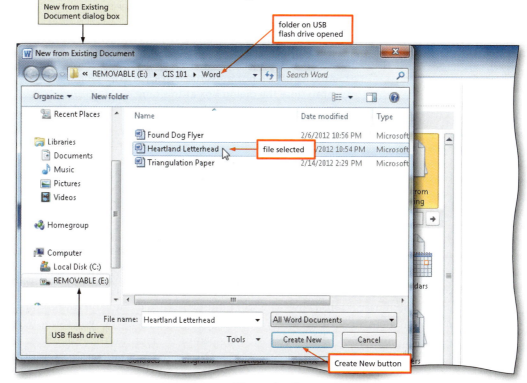

Figure 3–40

3

- Click the Create New button (New from Existing Document dialog box) to open a new document window that contains the contents of the selected file.

- If necessary, click the paragraph mark below the letterhead to position the insertion point at that location (Figure 3–41).

Figure 3–41

BTW

New Document Window

If you wanted to open a new blank document window, you could press CTRL+N or click File on the Ribbon to open the Backstage view, click the New tab to display the New gallery, click the Blank document button, and then click the Create button.

To Save a Document

Because you do not want to lose the letterhead at the top of this document, you should save the letter before continuing. The following steps assume you already have created folders for storing your files, for example, a CIS 101 folder (for your class) that contains a Word folder (for your assignments). Thus, these steps save the document in the Word folder in the CIS 101 folder on a USB flash drive using the file name, Heartland Advertisement Letter.

1 With a USB flash drive connected to one of the computer's USB ports, click the Save button on the Quick Access Toolbar to display the Save As dialog box.

2 Type **Heartland Advertisement Letter** in the File name text box to change the file name. Do not press the ENTER key after typing the file name because you do not want to close the dialog box at this time.

3 If necessary, navigate to the desired save location (in this case, the Word folder in the CIS 101 folder [or your class folder] on the USB flash drive).

4 Click the Save button (Save As dialog box) to save the document in the selected folder on the selected drive with the entered file name.

To Apply a Quick Style

Recall that the Normal style in Word places 10 points of blank space after each paragraph and inserts a vertical space equal to 1.15 lines between each line of text. The business letter should use single spacing for paragraphs and double spacing between paragraphs. Thus, you will modify the spacing for the paragraphs.

Word has many built-in, or predefined, styles called Quick Styles that you can use to format text. The No Spacing style, for example, defines line spacing to single and does not insert any additional blank space between lines when you press the ENTER key. To apply a quick style to a paragraph, you first position the insertion point in the paragraph and then apply the style. The next step applies the No Spacing quick style to a paragraph.

1

- With the insertion point positioned in the paragraph to be formatted, click No Spacing in the Quick Style gallery (Home tab | Styles group) to apply the selected style to the current paragraph (Figure 3–42).

Q&A

Will this style be used in the rest of the document?

Yes. The paragraph formatting, which includes the style, will carry forward to subsequent paragraphs each time you press the ENTER key.

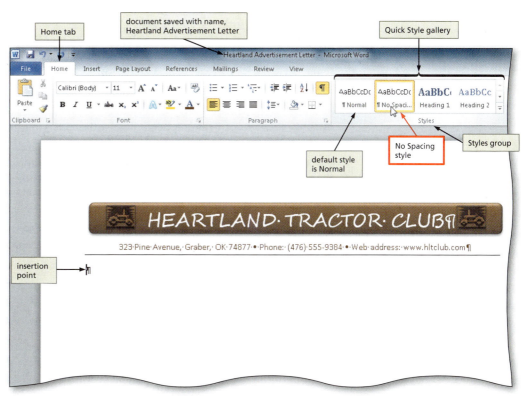

Figure 3–42

Other Ways	
1. Click Styles Dialog Box Launcher (Home tab | Styles group), click desired style in Styles task pane	2. Press CTRL+SHIFT+S, click Style Name box arrow in Apply Styles task pane, click desired style in list

Include all essential letter elements.

Be sure to include all essential business letter elements, properly spaced, in your letter.

- The **date line**, which consists of the month, day, and year, is positioned two to six lines below the letterhead.

- The **inside address**, placed three to eight lines below the date line, usually contains the addressee's courtesy title plus full name, job title, business affiliation, and full geographical address.

- The **salutation**, if present, begins two lines below the last line of the inside address. If you do not know the recipient's name, avoid using the salutation "To whom it may concern" — it is impersonal. Instead, use the recipient's title in the salutation, e.g., Dear Personnel Director. In a business letter, use a colon (:) at the end of the salutation; in a personal letter, use a comma.

- The body of the letter, the **message**, begins two lines below the salutation. Within the message, paragraphs are single-spaced with one blank line between paragraphs.

- Two lines below the last line of the message, the **complimentary close** is displayed. Capitalize only the first word in a complimentary close.

- Type the **signature block** at least four blank lines below the complimentary close, allowing room for the author to sign his or her name.

Plan Ahead

**Plan
Ahead**

Determine which letter style to use.
Three common business letter styles are the block, the modified block, and the modified semi-block. Each style specifies different alignments and indentations.

- In the block letter style, all components of the letter begin flush with the left margin.

- In the modified block letter style, the date, complimentary close, and signature block are positioned approximately one-half inch to the right of center or at the right margin. All other components of the letter begin flush with the left margin.

- In the modified semi-block letter style, the date, complimentary close, and signature block are centered, positioned approximately one-half inch to the right of center or at the right margin. The first line of each paragraph in the body of the letter is indented one-half to one inch from the left margin. All other components of the letter begin flush with the left margin.

The business letter in this project follows the modified block style.

Using Tab Stops to Align Text

A **tab stop** is a location on the horizontal ruler that tells Word where to position the insertion point when you press the TAB key on the keyboard. Word, by default, places a tab stop at every one-half inch mark on the ruler. These default tab stops are indicated at the bottom of the horizontal ruler by small vertical tick marks (shown in Figure 3–43). You also can set your own custom tab stops. Tab settings are a paragraph format. Thus, each time you press the ENTER key, any custom tab stops are carried forward to the next paragraph.

To move the insertion point from one tab stop to another, press the TAB key on the keyboard. When you press the TAB key, a **tab character** formatting mark appears in the empty space between the tab stops.

When you set a custom tab stop, you specify how the text will align at a tab stop. The tab marker on the ruler reflects the alignment of the characters at the location of the tab stop. Table 3–3 shows types of tab stop alignments in Word and their corresponding tab markers.

BTW

Tabs Dialog Box
You can use the Tabs dialog box to set, change the alignment of, and remove custom tab stops. To display the Tabs dialog box, click the Paragraph Dialog Box Launcher (Home tab or Page Layout tab | Paragraph group) and then click the Tabs button (Paragraph dialog box), or double-click a tab marker on the ruler. To set a custom tab stop, enter the desired position (Tabs dialog box) and then click the Set button. To change the alignment of a custom tab stop, click the tab stop position to be changed, click the new alignment, and then click the Set button. To remove an existing tab stop, click the tab stop position to be removed and then click the Clear button. To remove all tab stops, click the Clear All button in the Tabs dialog box.

Table 3–3 Types of Tab Stop Alignments			
Tab Stop Alignment	**Tab Marker**	**Result of Pressing TAB Key**	**Example**
Left Tab	L	Left-aligns text at the location of the tab stop	toolbar ruler
Center Tab	⊥	Centers text at the location of the tab stop	toolbar ruler
Right Tab	⌐	Right-aligns text at the location of the tab stop	toolbar ruler
Decimal Tab	⊥	Aligns text on decimal point at the location of the tab stop	45.72 223.75
Bar Tab	I	Aligns text at a bar character at the location of the tab stop	toolbar ruler

To Display the Ruler

One way to set custom tab stops is by using the horizontal ruler. Thus, the following step displays the ruler in the document window.

1 If the rulers are not displayed already, click the View Ruler button on the vertical scroll bar (shown in Figure 3–43).

Q&A What if the View Ruler button is not visible on the vertical scroll bar?

Display the View tab and then place a check mark in the Ruler check box.

To Set Custom Tab Stops

The first required element of the business letter is the date line, which in this letter is positioned two lines below the letterhead. The date line contains the month, day, and year, and begins four inches from the left margin, which is approximately one-half inch to the right of center. Thus, you should set a custom tab stop at the 4" mark on the ruler. The following steps set a left-aligned tab stop.

1

• With the insertion point on the paragraph mark below the border (shown in Figure 3–42 on page WD 167), press the ENTER key so that a blank line appears above the insertion point.

• If necessary, click the tab selector at the left edge of the horizontal ruler until it displays the type of tab you wish to use, which is the Left Tab icon in this case.

• Position the mouse pointer on the 4" mark on the ruler, which is the location of the desired custom tab stop (Figure 3–43).

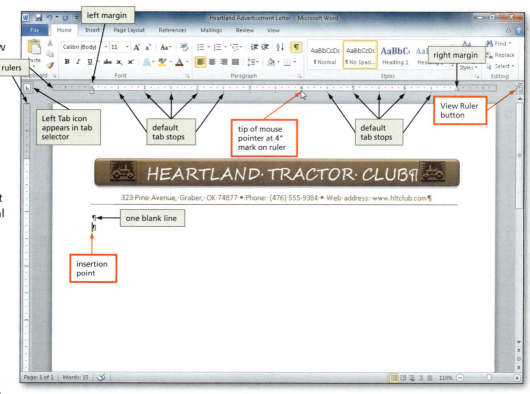

Figure 3–43

Q&A What is the purpose of the tab selector?

Before using the ruler to set a tab stop, ensure the correct tab stop icon appears in the tab selector. Each time you click the tab selector, its icon changes. The Left Tab icon is the default. For a list of the types of tab stops, see Table 3–3.

2

• Click the 4" mark on the ruler to place a tab marker at that location (Figure 3–44).

Q&A

What if I click the wrong location on the ruler?

You can move a custom tab stop by dragging the tab marker to the desired location on the ruler. Or, you can remove an existing custom tab stop by pointing to the tab marker on the ruler and then dragging the tab marker down and out of the ruler.

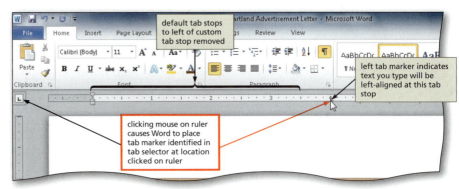

Figure 3–44

Q&A

What happened to all the default tab stops on the ruler?

When you set a custom tab stop, Word clears all default tab stops to the left of the newly set custom tab stop on the ruler.

Other Ways

1. Click Paragraph Dialog Box Launcher (Home tab or Page Layout tab | Paragraph group), click Tabs button (Paragraph dialog box), type tab stop position (Tabs dialog box), click Set button, click OK button

---

To Insert the Current Date in a Document

The next step is to enter the current date at the 4" tab stop in the document, as specified in the guidelines for a modified block style letter. In Word, you can insert a computer's system date in a document. The following steps insert the current date in the letter.

1

• Press the TAB key to position the insertion point at the location of the tab stop in the current paragraph.

• Display the Insert tab.

• Click the Insert Date and Time button (Insert tab | Text group) to display the Date and Time dialog box.

• Select the desired format (Date and Time dialog box), in this case April 27, 2012.

• If the Update automatically check box is selected, click the check box to remove the check mark (Figure 3–45).

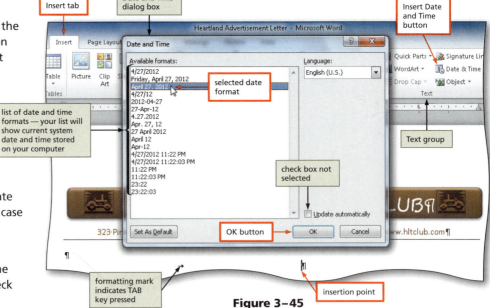

Figure 3–45

Q&A

Why should the Update automatically check box not be selected?

In this project, the date at the top of the letter always should show today's date (for example, April 27, 2012). If, however, you wanted the date always to change to reflect the current computer date (for example, showing the date you open or print the letter), then you would place a check mark in this check box.

2

- Click the OK button to insert the current date at the location of the insertion point (Figure 3–46).

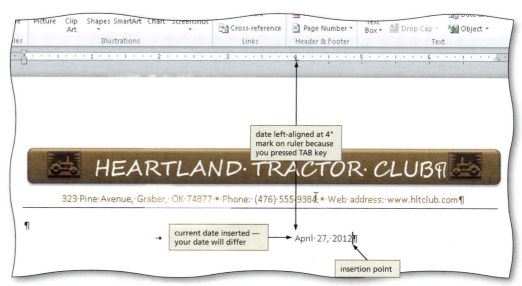

Figure 3–46

To Enter the Inside Address and Salutation

The next step in composing the business letter is to type the inside address and salutation. The following steps enter this text.

1 With the insertion point at the end of the date (shown in Figure 3–46), press the ENTER key three times.

2 Type **Mr. Harvey Wilcox** and then press the ENTER key.

3 Type **Wilcox Tractor Restorations** and then press the ENTER key.

4 Type **3009 North 2850 East Road** and then press the ENTER key.

5 Type **Roundwood, OK 74519** and then press the ENTER key twice.

6 Type **Dear Mr. Wilcox:** to complete the inside address and salutation entries (Figure 3–47).

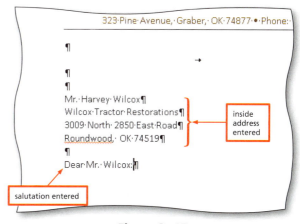

Figure 3–47

To Create a Building Block

If you use the same text or graphic frequently, you can store the text or graphic as a **building block** and then insert the stored building block entry in the open document, as well as in future documents. That is, you can create the entry once as a building block and then insert the building block when you need it. In this way, you avoid entering the text or graphics inconsistently or incorrectly in different locations throughout the same or multiple documents.

The steps on the next page create a building block for the prospective advertiser's name, Wilcox Tractor Restorations. Later, you will insert the building block in the document instead of typing the advertiser's name.

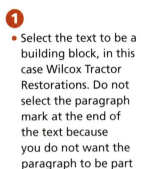

1

- Select the text to be a building block, in this case Wilcox Tractor Restorations. Do not select the paragraph mark at the end of the text because you do not want the paragraph to be part of the building block.

Q&A

Why is the paragraph mark not part of the building block?

Select the paragraph mark only if you want to store paragraph formatting, such as indentation and line spacing, as part of the building block.

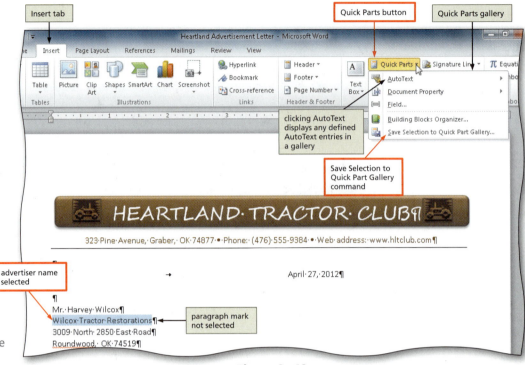

Figure 3–48

- Click the Quick Parts button (Insert tab | Text group) to display the Quick Parts gallery (Figure 3–48).

2

- Click Save Selection to Quick Part Gallery in the Quick Parts gallery to display the Create New Building Block dialog box.

- Type **wtr** in the Name text box (Create New Building Block dialog box) to replace the proposed building block name (Wilcox Tractor, in this case) with a shorter building block name (Figure 3–49).

3

- Click the OK button to store the building block entry and close the dialog box.

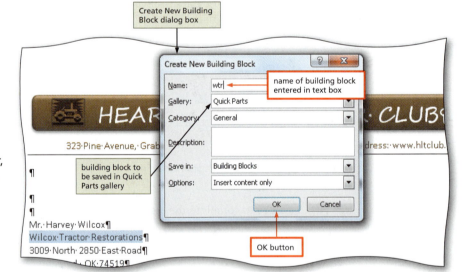

Figure 3–49

- If Word displays another dialog box, click the Yes button, to save changes to the building blocks.

Q&A

Will this building block be available in future documents?

When you quit Word, a dialog box may appear asking if you want to save changes to the "Building Blocks". Click the Save button if you want to use the new building block in future documents.

Other Ways

1. Select text, press ALT+F3

To Modify a Building Block

When you save a building block in the Quick Parts gallery, it is displayed at the top of the Quick Parts gallery. If the building block is a text entry, you can place it in the AutoText gallery instead, which also is accessible through the Quick Parts gallery.

When you point to the building block in the Quick Parts gallery, a ScreenTip displays the building block name. If you want to display more information when the user points to the building block, you can include a description as an Enhanced ScreenTip. The following steps modify a building block to include a description and change its category to AutoText.

1
- Click the Quick Parts button (Insert tab | Text group) to display the Quick Parts gallery.

- Right-click the Wilcox Tractor Restorations building block to display a shortcut menu (Figure 3–50).

Figure 3–50

2
- Click Edit Properties on the shortcut menu to display the Modify Building Block dialog box, filled in with information related to the selected building block.

- Click the Gallery box arrow (Modify Building Block dialog box) and then click AutoText to change the gallery in which the building block will be displayed.

- Type **Potential Advertiser** in the Description text box (Figure 3–51).

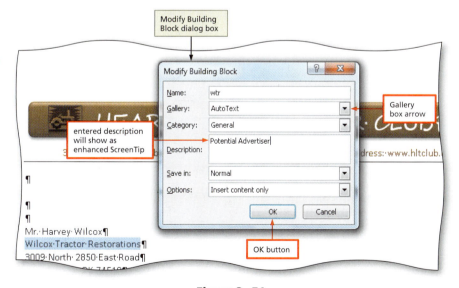

3
- Click the OK button to store the building block entry and close the dialog box.

- Click the Yes button when asked if you want to redefine the building block entry.

Figure 3–51

To Insert a Building Block

In the first sentence in the body of the letter, you want the prospective advertiser name, Wilcox Tractor Restorations, to be displayed. Recall that you stored a building block name of wtr for Wilcox Tractor Restorations. Thus, you will type the building block name and then instruct Word to replace a building block name with the stored building block entry. The following steps insert a building block.

- Click to the right of the colon in the salutation and then press the ENTER key twice to position the insertion point one blank line below the salutation.

- Type the beginning of the first sentence as follows, entering the building block name as shown: **We are delighted you are considering advertising your business, wtr** (Figure 3–52).

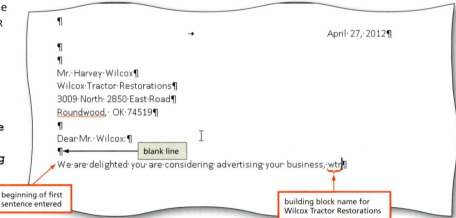

Figure 3–52

- Press the F3 key to instruct Word to replace the building block name (wtr) with the stored building block entry (Wilcox Tractor Restorations) (Figure 3–53).

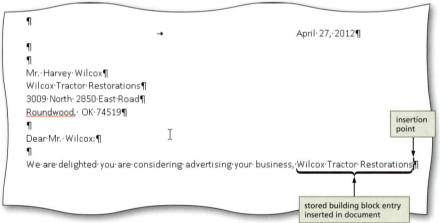

Figure 3–53

Other Ways

1. Click Quick Parts button (Insert tab | Text group), if necessary point to AutoText, click desired building block

Building Blocks versus AutoCorrect

In Project 2, you learned how to use the AutoCorrect feature, which enables you to insert and create AutoCorrect entries, similarly to how you created and inserted building blocks in this chapter. The difference between an AutoCorrect entry and a building block entry is that the AutoCorrect feature makes corrections for you automatically as soon as you press the SPACEBAR or type a punctuation mark, whereas you must instruct Word to insert a building block. That is, you enter the building block name and then press the F3 key, or click the Quick Parts button and select the building block from one of the galleries.

To Insert a Nonbreaking Space

Some compound words, such as proper nouns, dates, units of time and measure, abbreviations, and geographic destinations, should not be divided at the end of a line. These words either should fit as a unit at the end of a line or be wrapped together to the next line.

Word provides two special characters to assist with this task: the nonbreaking space and the nonbreaking hyphen. A **nonbreaking space** is a special space character that prevents two words from splitting if the first word falls at the end of a line. Similarly, a **nonbreaking hyphen** is a special type of hyphen that prevents two words separated by a hyphen from splitting at the end of a line.

The following steps insert a nonbreaking space between the words in the magazine name.

1

- With the insertion point at the end of the building block entry in the document (as shown in Figure 3–53), press the COMMA key and then press the SPACEBAR.

- Type **in** and then press the SPACEBAR. Press CTRL+I to turn on italics because magazine names should be italicized.

- Type **Heartland** as the first word in the magazine name and then press CTRL+SHIFT+SPACEBAR to insert a nonbreaking space after the entered word (Figure 3–54).

Figure 3–54

2

- Type **Tractor** and then press CTRL+SHIFT+SPACEBAR to insert another nonbreaking space after the entered word.

- Type **Magazine** and then press CTRL+I to turn off italics (Figure 3–55).

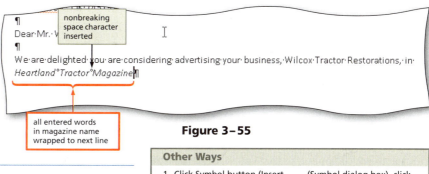

Figure 3–55

Other Ways
1. Click Symbol button (Insert tab | Symbols group), click More Symbols, click Special Characters tab (Symbol dialog box), click Nonbreaking Space in Character list, click Insert button, click Close button

To Enter Text

The next step in creating the letter is to enter the rest of the text in the first paragraph. The following steps enter this text.

1 Press the COMMA key and then press the SPACEBAR.

2 Type this text: **our monthly publication for tractor enthusiasts. The table below outlines advertisement rates per monthly issue:**

3 Press the ENTER key twice to place a blank line between paragraphs (shown in Figure 3–56 on the next page).

Q&A Why does my document wrap on different words?

Differences in wordwrap may relate to the printer connected to your computer. Thus, it is possible that the same document could wordwrap differently if associated with a different printer.

To Save an Existing Document with the Same File Name

You have made several modifications to the document since you last saved it. Thus, you should save it again. The following step saves the document again.

1 Click the Save button on the Quick Access Toolbar to overwrite the previously saved file.

Break Point: If you wish to take a break, this is a good place to do so. You can quit Word now. To resume at a later time, start Word, open the file called Heartland Advertisement Letter, and continue following the steps from this location forward.

Tables

The next step in composing the business letter is to place a table listing the rates for various types of advertisements (shown in Figure 3–1 on page WD 139). A Word **table** is a collection of rows and columns. The intersection of a row and a column is called a **cell**, and cells are filled with data.

The first step in creating a table is to insert an empty table in the document. When inserting a table, you must specify the total number of rows and columns required, which is called the **dimension** of the table. The table in this project has five columns. You often do not know the total number of rows in a table. Thus, many Word users create one row initially and then add more rows as needed. In Word, the first number in a dimension is the number of columns, and the second is the number of rows. For example, in Word, a 5 × 1 (pronounced "five by one") table consists of five columns and one row.

To Insert an Empty Table

The next step is to insert an empty table in the letter. The following steps insert a table with five columns and one row at the location of the insertion point.

1

- Scroll the document up so that you will be able to see the table in the document window.

- With the insertion point positioned as shown in Figure 3–56, click the Table button (Insert tab | Tables group) to display the Table gallery (Figure 3–56).

(magnifying glass icon) **Experiment**

- Point to various cells on the grid to see a preview of various table dimensions in the document window.

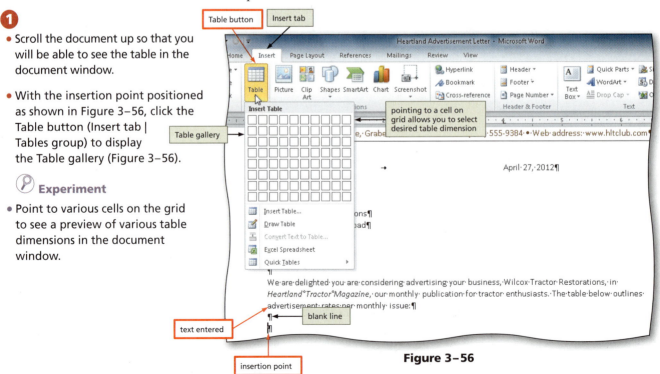

Figure 3–56

2

• Position the mouse pointer on the cell in the first row and fifth column of the grid to preview the desired table dimension (Figure 3–57).

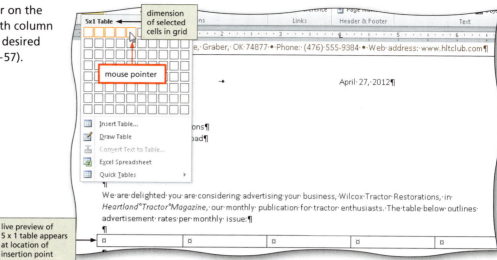

Figure 3–57

3

• Click the cell in the first row and fifth column of the grid to insert an empty table with one row and five columns in the document.

• If necessary, scroll the table up in the document window (Figure 3–58).

Q&A

What are the small circles in the table cells?

Each table cell has an **end-of-cell mark**, which is a formatting mark that assists you with selecting and formatting cells. Similarly, each row has an **end-of-row mark**, which you can use to add columns to the right of a table. Recall that formatting marks do not print on a hard copy. The end-of-cell marks currently are left-aligned, that is, positioned at the left edge of each cell.

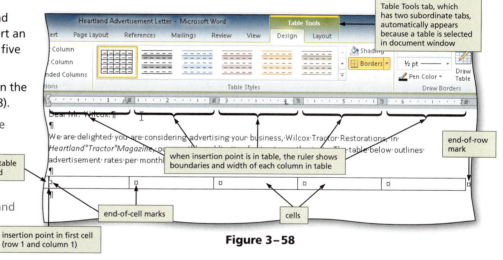

Figure 3–58

Other Ways
1. Click Table (Insert tab | Tables group), click Insert Table in Table gallery, enter   number of columns and rows (Insert Table dialog box), click OK button

To Enter Data in a Table

The next step is to enter data in the cells of the empty table. The data you enter in a cell wordwraps just as text wordwraps between the margins of a document. To place data in a cell, you click the cell and then type.

To advance rightward from one cell to the next, press the TAB key. When you are at the rightmost cell in a row, press the TAB key to move to the first cell in the next row; do not press the ENTER key. The ENTER key is used to begin a new paragraph within a cell. One way to add new rows to a table is to press the TAB key when the insertion point is positioned in the bottom-right corner cell of the table. The step on the next page enters data in the first row of the table and then inserts a blank second row.

1
- With the insertion point in the left cell of the table, type **Type** and then press the TAB key to advance the insertion point to the next cell.

- Type **Dimensions** and then press the TAB key to advance the insertion point to the next cell.

- Type **Word Count** and then press the TAB key to advance the insertion point to the next cell.

- Type **Photo Count** and then press the TAB key to advance the insertion point to the next cell.

- Type **Cost** and then press the TAB key to insert a second row at the end of the table and position the insertion point in the first column of the new row (Figure 3–59).

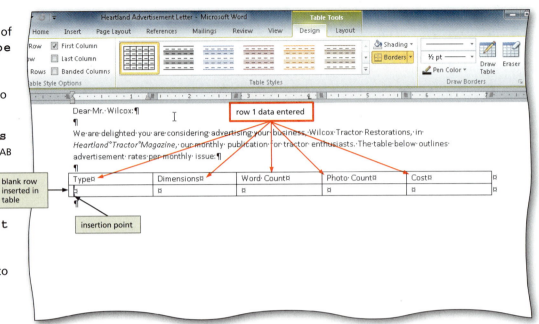

Figure 3–59

Q&A How do I edit cell contents if I make a mistake?
Click in the cell and then correct the entry.

To Enter Data in a Table

The following steps enter the remaining data in the table.

1 Type **Full Page** and then press the TAB key to advance the insertion point to the next cell. Type **9" x 7"** and then press the TAB key to advance the insertion point to the next cell. Type **800** and then press the TAB key to advance the insertion point to the next cell. Type **4** and then press the TAB key to advance the insertion point to the next cell. Type **$650** and then press the TAB key to insert a row at the end of the table and position the insertion point in the first column of the new row.

2 In the third row, type **Half Page** in the first column, **4.5" x 7"** as the dimensions, **400** as the word count, **2** as the photo count, and **$350** as the cost. Press the TAB key to position the insertion point in the first column of a new row.

3 In the fourth row, type **Quarter Page** in the first column, **4.5" x 3.5"** as the dimensions, **200** as the word count, **1** as the photo count, and **$225** as the cost. Press the TAB key.

4 In the fifth row, type **Business Card** in the first column, **2.25" x 3.5"** as the dimensions, **100** as the word count, **0** as the photo count, and **$125** as the cost (Figure 3–60).

BTW
Tables
For simple tables, such as the one just created, Word users often select the table dimension in the Table gallery to create the table. For a more complex table, such as one with a varying number of columns per row, Word has a Draw Table feature that allows users to draw a table in the document using a pencil pointer. To use this feature, click the Table button (Insert tab | Tables group) and then click Draw Table.

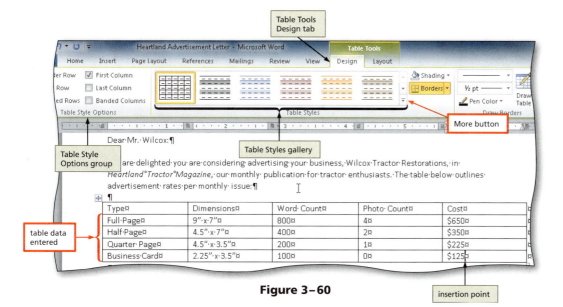

Figure 3–60

To Apply a Table Style

The next step is to apply a table style to the table. Word provides a Table Styles gallery, allowing you to change the basic table format to a more visually appealing style. Word provides a gallery of more than 90 table styles, which include a variety of colors and shading. The following steps apply a table style to the table in the letter.

1
• With the insertion point in the table, be sure the check marks match those in the Table Style Options group (Table Tools Design tab) as shown in Figure 3–60.

Q&A What if the Table Tools Design tab no longer is the active tab?

Click in the table and then display the Table Tools Design tab.

Q&A What do the options in the Table Style Options group mean?

When you apply table styles, if you want the top row of the table (header row), a row containing totals (total row), first column, or last column to be formatted differently, select those check boxes. If you want the rows or columns to alternate with colors, select Banded Rows or Banded Columns, respectively.

2
• Click the More button in the Table Styles gallery (shown in Figure 3–60) (Table Tools Design tab | Table Styles group) to expand the gallery.

• Scroll and then point to Medium Grid 3 - Accent 4 in the Table Styles gallery to display a live preview of that style applied to the table in the document (Figure 3–61).

 Experiment

• Point to various table styles in the Table Styles gallery and watch the format of the table change in the document window.

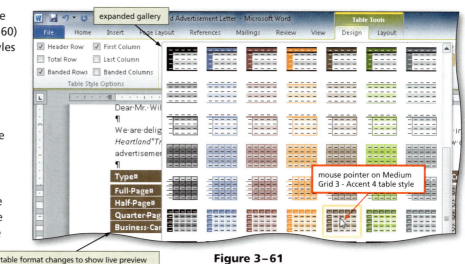

Figure 3–61

3

- Click Medium Grid 3 - Accent 4 in the Table Styles gallery to apply the selected style to the table (Figure 3–62).

Experiment

- Select and remove check marks from various check boxes in the Table Style Options group and watch the format of the table change in the document window. When finished experimenting, be sure the check marks match those shown in Figure 3–62.

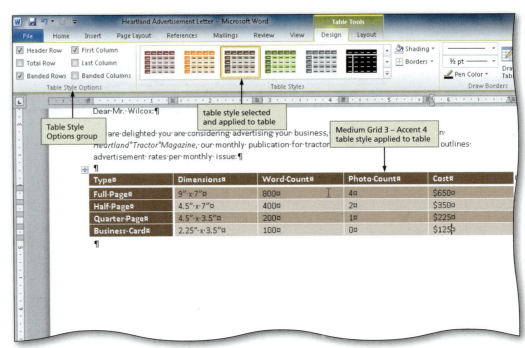

Figure 3–62

To Resize Table Columns to Fit Table Contents

The table in this project currently extends from the left margin to the right margin of the document. You want each column to be only as wide as the longest entry in the table. That is, the first column must be wide enough to accommodate the words, Business Card, and the second column should be only as wide as the title, Dimensions, and so on. The following steps instruct Word to fit the width of the columns to the contents of the table automatically.

1

- With the insertion point in the table, display the Table Tools Layout tab.

- Click the AutoFit button (Table Tools Layout tab | Cell Size group) to display the AutoFit menu (Figure 3–63).

Q&A

What causes the table move handle and table resize handle to appear and disappear from the table?

They appear whenever you position the mouse pointer in the table.

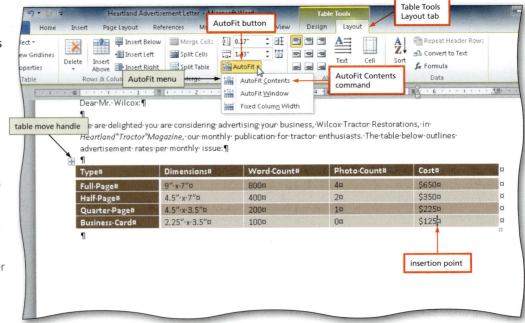

Figure 3–63

2

- Click AutoFit Contents on the AutoFit menu, so that Word automatically adjusts the widths of the columns based on the text in the table (Figure 3–64).

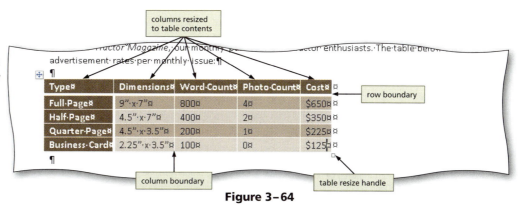

Figure 3–64

Q&A

Can I resize columns manually?

Yes, you can drag a **column boundary**, the border to the right of a column, until the column is the desired width. Similarly, you can resize a row by dragging the **row boundary**, the border at the bottom of a row, until the row is the desired height. You also can resize the entire table by dragging the **table resize handle**, which is a small square that appears when you point to a corner of the table (shown in Figure 3–63).

Other Ways

1. Right-click table, point to AutoFit on shortcut menu, click AutoFit to Contents

2. Double-click column boundary

Selecting Table Contents

When working with tables, you may need to select the contents of cells, rows, columns, or the entire table. Table 3–4 identifies ways to select various items in a table.

BTW

Resizing Table Columns and Rows
To change the width of a column or height of a row to an exact measurement, hold down the ALT key while dragging markers on the ruler. Or, enter values in the Table Column Width or Table Row Height text boxes (Table Tools Layout tab | Cell Size group).

Table 3–4 Selecting Items in a Table

Item to Select	Action
Cell	Point to left edge of cell and click when the mouse pointer changes to a small solid upward angled pointing arrow.
	Or, position insertion point in cell, click Select button (Table Tools Layout tab | Table group), and then click Select Cell on the Select menu.
Column	Point to border at top of column and click when the mouse pointer changes to a small solid downward-pointing arrow.
	Or, position insertion point in column, click Select button (Table Tools Layout tab | Table group), and then click Select Column on the Select menu.
Row	Point to the left of the row and click when mouse pointer changes to a right-pointing block arrow.
	Or, position insertion point in row, click Select button (Table Tools Layout tab | Table group), and then click Select Row on the Select menu.
Multiple cells, rows, or columns adjacent to one another	Drag through cells, rows, or columns.
Multiple cells, rows, or columns not adjacent to one another	Select first cell, row, or column (as described above) and then hold down CTRL key while selecting next cell, row, or column.
Next cell	Press TAB key.
Previous cell	Press SHIFT+TAB.
Table	Point somewhere in table and then click table move handle that appears in upper-left corner of table.
	Or, position insertion point in table, click Select button (Table Tools Layout tab | Table group), and then click Select Table on the Select menu.

BTW

Tab Character in Tables
In a table, the TAB key advances the insertion point from one cell to the next. To insert a tab character in a cell, you must press CTRL+TAB.

To Align Data in Cells

The next step is to change the alignment of the data in cells in the second, third, fourth, and fifth columns of the table. In addition to aligning text horizontally in a cell (left, center, or right), you can align it vertically within a cell (top, center, bottom). When the height of the cell is close to the same height as the text, however, differences in vertical alignment are not readily apparent, which is the case for this table. The following steps center data in cells.

● Select the cells in the second, third, fourth, and fifth columns using one of the techniques described in Table 3–4 on the previous page (Figure 3–65).

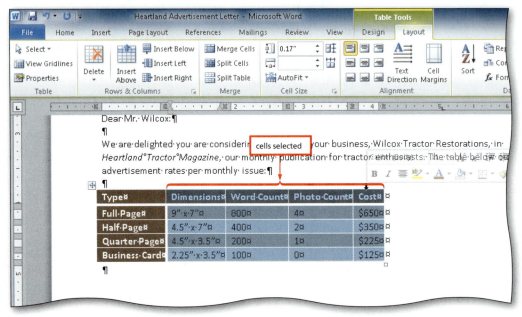

Figure 3–65

● Click the Align Top Center button (Table Tools Layout tab | Alignment group) to center the contents of the selected cells.

● Click in the table to remove the selection (Figure 3–66).

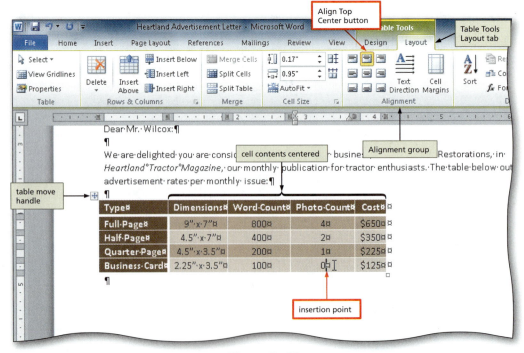

Figure 3–66

To Center a Table

When you first create a table, it is left-aligned, that is, flush with the left margin. In this letter, the table should be centered between the margins. To center a table, you first select the entire table. The following steps select and center a table using the Mini toolbar.

1

- Position the mouse pointer in the table so that the table move handle appears (shown in Figure 3–66).

What if the table move handle does not appear?

You also can select a table by clicking the Select button (Table Tools Layout tab | Table group) and then clicking Select Table on the menu.

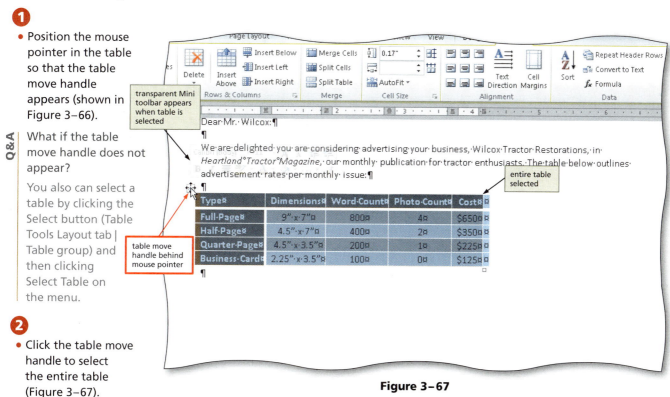

2

- Click the table move handle to select the entire table (Figure 3–67).

Figure 3–67

3

- Move the mouse pointer into the Mini toolbar, so that the toolbar changes to a bright toolbar. Click the Center button on the Mini toolbar to center the selected table between the left and right margins (Figure 3–68).

Could I have clicked the Center button on the Home tab?

Yes. If the command you want to use is

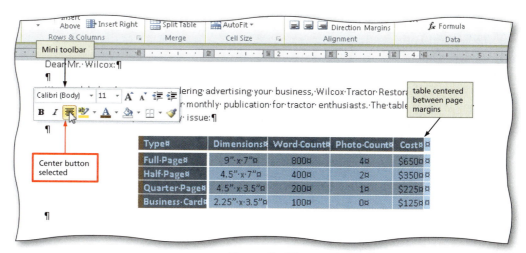

Figure 3–68

not on the currently displayed tab on the Ribbon and it is available on the Mini toolbar, use the Mini toolbar instead of switching to a different tab. This technique minimizes mouse movement.

To Insert a Row in a Table

The next step is to insert a row at the top of the table because you want to place a title on the table. As discussed earlier, you can insert a row at the end of a table by positioning the insertion point in the bottom-right corner cell and then pressing the TAB key. You cannot use the TAB key to insert a row at the beginning or middle of a table. Instead, you use the Insert Rows Above or Insert Rows Below command. The following steps insert a row in a table.

● Position the mouse pointer somewhere in the first row of the table because you want to insert a row above this row (Figure 3–69).

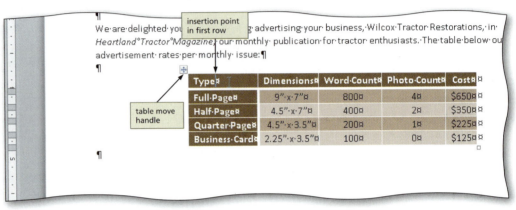

Figure 3–69

● Click the Insert Rows Above button (Table Tools Layout tab | Rows & Columns group) to insert a row above the row containing the insertion point and then select the newly inserted row (Figure 3–70).

Q&A | Do I have to insert rows above the row containing the insertion point?

No. You can insert below the row containing the insertion point by clicking the Insert Rows Below button (Table Tools Layout tab | Rows & Columns group).

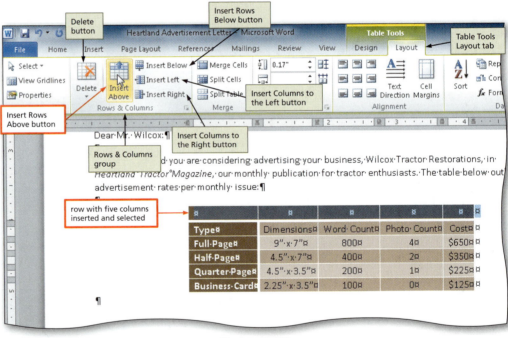

Figure 3–70

Q&A | Why did the colors in the second row change?

The table style specifies to format the Header row differently, which is the first row.

Other Ways

1. Right-click row, point to Insert on shortcut menu, click desired command on Insert submenu

TO INSERT A COLUMN IN A TABLE

If, instead of inserting rows, you wanted to insert a column in a table, you would perform the following steps.

1. Position the insertion point in the column to the left or right of where you want to insert the column.

2. Click the Insert Columns to the Left button (Table Tools Layout tab | Rows & Columns group) to insert a column to the left of the current column, or click the Insert Columns to the Right button (Table Tools Layout tab | Rows & Columns group) to insert a column to the right of the current column. Or you could right-click the table, point to Insert on the shortcut menu, and click Insert Columns to the Left or Insert Columns to the Right on the Insert submenu.

Deleting Table Data

If you want to delete row(s) or delete column(s) from a table, position the insertion point in the row(s) or column(s) to delete, click the Delete button (Table Tools Layout tab | Rows & Columns group), and then click Delete Rows or Delete Columns on the Delete menu. Or, select the row or column to delete, right-click the selection, and then click Delete Rows or Delete Columns on the shortcut menu.

To delete the contents of a cell, select the cell contents and then press the DELETE or BACKSPACE key. You also can drag and drop or cut and paste the contents of cells. To delete an entire table, select the table, click the Delete button (Table Tools Layout tab | Rows & Columns group), and then click Delete Table on the Delete menu. To delete the contents of a table and leave an empty table, you would select the table and then press the DELETE key.

To Merge Cells

The top row of the table is to contain the table title, which should be centered above the columns of the table. The row just inserted has one cell for each column, in this case, five cells (shown in Figure 3–70). The title of the table, however, should be in a single cell that spans all rows. Thus, the following steps merge the five cells into a single cell.

1

• With the cells to merge selected (as shown in Figure 3–70), click the Merge Cells button (Table Tools Layout tab | Merge group) to merge the five cells into one cell (Figure 3–71).

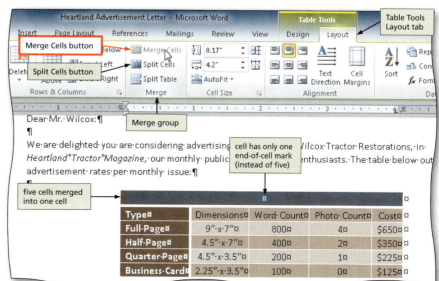

Figure 3–71

• Position the insertion point in the first row and then type **Monthly Issue Advertisement Rates** as the table title (Figure 3–72).

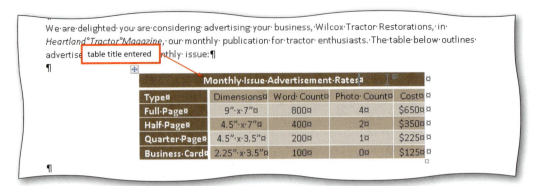

Figure 3–72

TO SPLIT TABLE CELLS

Instead of merging multiple cells into a single cell, sometimes you want to split a single cell into multiple cells. If you wanted to split cells, you would perform the following steps.

1. Position the insertion point in the cell to split.

2. Click the Split Cells button (Table Tools Layout tab | Merge group), or right-click the cell and then click Split Cells on the shortcut menu, to display the Split Cells dialog box.

3. Enter the number of columns and rows into which you want the cell split (Split Cells dialog box).

4. Click the OK button.

To Add More Text

The table now is complete. The next step is to enter text below the table. The following steps enter text.

1 Position the insertion point on the paragraph mark below the table and then press the ENTER key.

2 Type **Please note that additional fees will be assessed if the word or photo counts exceed the limits listed above. We offer the following discounts:** and then press the ENTER key (shown in Figure 3–73).

To Bullet a List as You Type

In Chapter 1, you learned how to apply bullets to existing paragraphs. If you know before you type that a list should be bulleted, you can use Word's AutoFormat As You Type feature to bullet the paragraphs as you type them (see Table 3–2 on page WD 162). The following steps add bullets to a list as you type.

1

• Press the ASTERISK key (*) as the first character on the line (Figure 3–73).

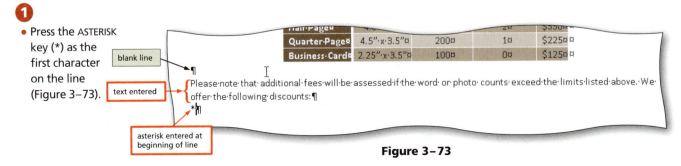

Figure 3–73

- Press the SPACEBAR to convert the asterisk to a bullet character.

What if I did not want the asterisk converted to a bullet character?

You could undo the AutoFormat by clicking the Undo button, pressing CTRL+Z, clicking the AutoCorrect Options button that appears to the left of the bullet character as soon as you press the SPACEBAR, and then clicking Undo Automatic Bullets on the AutoCorrect Options menu, or by clicking the Bullets button (Home tab | Paragraph group).

- Type `10 percent discount for any advertisement that runs in three consecutive issues` as the first bulleted item.

- Press the ENTER key to place another bullet character at the beginning of the next line (Figure 3–74).

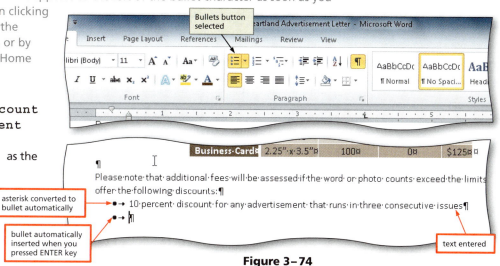

Figure 3–74

- Type `5 percent discount for a camera-ready advertisement (prepared using Microsoft Word at the proper size and with all words and photos in final layout form)` and then press the ENTER key.

- Type `3 percent discount if payment in full is submitted with order` and then press the ENTER key.

- Press the ENTER key to turn off automatic bullets as you type (Figure 3–75).

Why did automatic bullets stop?

When you press the ENTER key without entering any text after the automatic bullet character, Word turns off the automatic bullets feature.

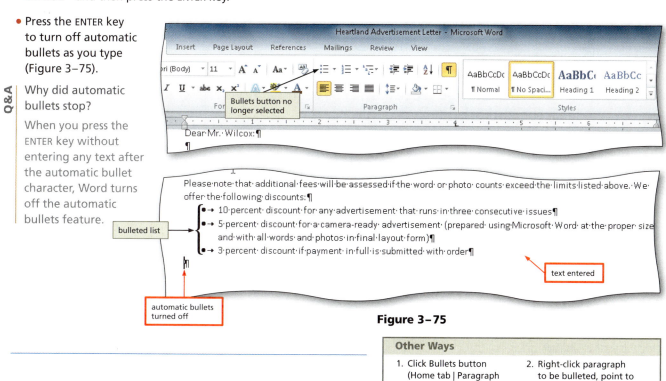

Figure 3–75

Other Ways
1. Click Bullets button (Home tab | Paragraph group)   2. Right-click paragraph to be bulleted, point to Bullets on shortcut menu, click desired bullet style

BTW

Certification
The Microsoft Office Specialist (MOS) program provides an opportunity for you to obtain a valuable industry credential — proof that you have the Word 2010 skills required by employers. For more information, visit the Word 2010 Certification Web page (scsite.com/wd2010/cert).

To Enter More Text

The following steps enter the remainder of text in the letter.

1 Press the ENTER key and then type the paragraph shown in Figure 3–76, making certain you use the building block name, wtr, to insert the advertiser name.

2 If necessary, remove the hyperlink from the e-mail address by right-clicking the e-mail address and then clicking Remove Hyperlink on the shortcut menu. Press the END key to position the insertion point at the end of the line.

3 Press the ENTER key twice. Press the TAB key to position the insertion point at the 4" mark on the ruler. Type `Sincerely,` and then press the ENTER key four times.

4 Press the TAB key to position the insertion point at the 4" mark on the ruler. Type `Frank Urbanczyk` and then press the ENTER key.

5 Press the TAB key to position the insertion point at the 4" mark on the ruler. Type `President` as the final text in the business letter (Figure 3–76).

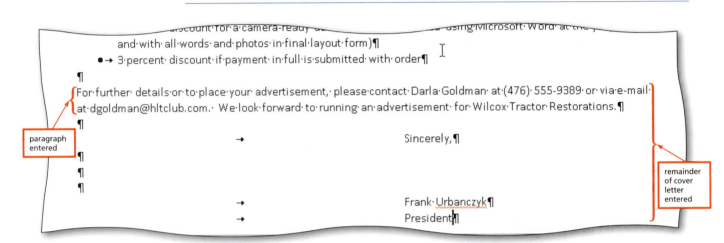

discount·for·a·camera-ready·ad ... using·Microsoft·Word·at·the·p

and·with·all·words·and·photos·in·final·layout·form)¶

●→ 3·percent·discount·if·payment·in·full·is·submitted·with·order¶

¶

For·further·details·or·to·place·your·advertisement,·please·contact·Darla·Goldman·at·(476)·555-9389·or·via·e-mail·at·dgoldman@hltclub.com.· We·look·forward·to·running·an·advertisement·for·Wilcox·Tractor·Restorations.¶

paragraph entered

¶

→   Sincerely,¶

¶

¶

¶

remainder of cover letter entered

→   Frank·Urbanczyk¶

→   President¶

Figure 3–76

To Change Document Properties, Save the Document Again, and Print It

BTW

Conserving Ink and Toner
If you want to conserve ink or toner, you can instruct Word to print draft quality documents by clicking File on the Ribbon to open the Backstage view, clicking Options in the Backstage view to display the Word Options dialog box, clicking Advanced in the left pane (Word Options dialog box), scrolling to the Print area in the right pane, placing a check mark in the 'Use draft quality' check box, and then clicking the OK button. Then, use the Backstage view to print the document as usual.

Before saving the letter again, you want to add your name and course and section as document properties. The following steps change document properties, save the document again, and then print the document.

1 Display the Document Information Panel in the Word document window. If necessary, enter your name in the Author property, and enter your course and section in the Subject property. Close the Document Information Panel.

2 Click the Save button on the Quick Access Toolbar to overwrite the previously saved file.

3 Open the Backstage view and then click the Print tab in the Backstage view to display the Print gallery.

4 Verify the printer name that appears on the Printer Status button will print a hard copy of the document. If necessary, click the Printer Status button to display a list of available printer options and then click the desired printer to change the currently selected printer.

5 Click the Print button in the Print gallery to print the letter on the currently selected printer (shown in Figure 3–1 on page WD 139).

Addressing and Printing Envelopes and Mailing Labels

BTW

BTWs
For a complete list of the BTWs found in the margins of this book, visit the Word 2010 BTW Web page (scsite.com/wd2010/btw).

With Word, you can print address information on an envelope or on a mailing label. Computer-printed addresses look more professional than handwritten ones.

To Address and Print an Envelope

The following steps address and print an envelope. If you are in a lab environment, check with your instructor before performing these steps.

- Scroll through the letter to display the inside address in the document window.

- Drag through the inside address to select it (Figure 3–77).

Figure 3–77

- Display the Mailings tab.

- Click the Create Envelopes button (Mailings tab | Create group) to display the Envelopes and Labels dialog box.

- If necessary, click the Envelopes tab (Envelopes and Labels dialog box) (Figure 3–78).

- Insert an envelope in your printer, as shown in the Feed area of the dialog box (your Feed area may be different depending on your printer).

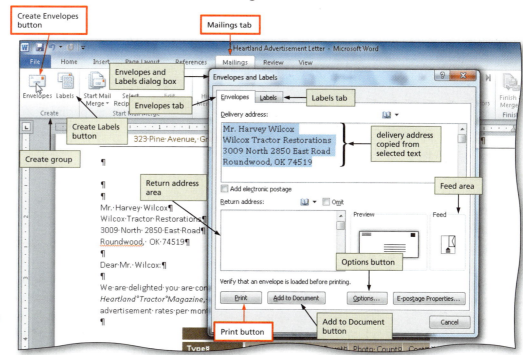

Figure 3–78

- Click the Print button (Envelopes and Labels dialog box) to print the envelope.

Envelopes and Labels

Instead of printing the envelope immediately, you can add it to the document by clicking the Add to Document button (Envelopes and Labels dialog box). To specify a different envelope or label type (identified by a number on the box of envelopes or labels), click the Options button (Envelopes and Labels dialog box).

Instead of printing an envelope, you can print a mailing label. To do this, click the Create Labels button (Mailings tab | Create group) (shown in Figure 3–78 on the previous page). Type the delivery address in the Delivery address box. To print the same address on all labels on the page, click 'Full page of the same label' in the Print area. Click the Print button (Envelopes and Labels dialog box) to print the label(s).

To Quit Word

This project now is complete. The following steps quit Word.

1 If you have one Word document open, click the Close button on the right side of the title bar to close the document and quit Word; or if you have multiple Word documents open, click File on the Ribbon to open the Backstage view and then click Exit in the Backstage view to close all open documents and quit Word.

2 If a Microsoft Word dialog box appears, click the Save button to save any changes made to the document since the last save.

3 If Word displays a dialog box asking if you want to save modified "Building Blocks", click the Save button.

Chapter Summary

In this chapter, you have learned how to use Word to change margins, insert and format a shape, change text wrapping, insert and format clip art, move and copy graphics, insert symbols, add a border, clear formatting, convert a hyperlink to regular text, create a file from an existing file, set and use tab stops, insert the current date, create and insert building blocks, insert and format tables, and address and print envelopes and mailing labels. The items listed below include all the new Word skills you have learned in this chapter.

1. Change Margin Settings (WD 141)
2. Insert a Shape (WD 142)
3. Apply a Shape Style (WD 144)
4. Add Text to a Shape (WD 145)
5. Use the Grow Font Button to Increase Font Size (WD 146)
6. Change an Object's Text Wrapping (WD 148)
7. Insert Clip Art (WD 148)
8. Resize a Graphic to a Percent of the Original (WD 150)
9. Change the Color of a Graphic (WD 151)
10. Set a Transparent Color in a Graphic (WD 152)
11. Adjust the Brightness and Contrast of a Graphic (WD 153)
12. Change the Border Color on a Graphic (WD 154)
13. Move a Graphic (WD 155)
14. Use Paste Options (WD 156)
15. Flip a Graphic (WD 157)
16. Insert a Symbol from the Symbol Dialog Box (WD 158)
17. Insert a Symbol from the Symbol Gallery (WD 159)
18. Bottom Border a Paragraph (WD 160)
19. Clear Formatting (WD 161)
20. Convert a Hyperlink to Regular Text (WD 163)
21. Create a New File from an Existing File (WD 165)
22. Apply a Quick Style (WD 166)
23. Set Custom Tab Stops (WD 169)
24. Insert the Current Date in a Document (WD 170)
25. Create a Building Block (WD 171)
26. Modify a Building Block (WD 173)
27. Insert a Building Block (WD 174)
28. Insert a Nonbreaking Space (WD 175)
29. Insert an Empty Table (WD 176)
30. Enter Data in a Table (WD 177)
31. Apply a Table Style (WD 179)
32. Resize Table Columns to Fit Table Contents (WD 180)
33. Align Data in Cells (WD 182)
34. Center a Table (WD 183)
35. Insert a Row in a Table (WD 184)
36. Insert a Column in a Table (WD 185)
37. Merge Cells (WD 185)
38. Split Table Cells (WD 186)
39. Bullet a List as You Type (WD 186)
40. Address and Print an Envelope (WD 189)

If you have a SAM 2010 user profile, your instructor may have assigned an autogradable version of this assignment. If so, log into the SAM 2010 Web site at www.cengage.com/sam2010 to download the instruction and start files.

Learn It Online

Test your knowledge of chapter content and key terms.

Instructions: To complete the Learn It Online exercises, start your browser, click the Address bar, and then enter the Web address `scsite.com/wd2010/learn`. When the Word 2010 Learn It Online page is displayed, click the link for the exercise you want to complete and then read the instructions.

Chapter Reinforcement TF, MC, and SA
A series of true/false, multiple choice, and short answer questions that test your knowledge of the chapter content.

Flash Cards
An interactive learning environment where you identify chapter key terms associated with displayed definitions.

Practice Test
A series of multiple choice questions that test your knowledge of chapter content and key terms.

Who Wants To Be a Computer Genius?
An interactive game that challenges your knowledge of chapter content in the style of a television quiz show.

Wheel of Terms
An interactive game that challenges your knowledge of chapter key terms in the style of the television show *Wheel of Fortune*.

Crossword Puzzle Challenge
A crossword puzzle that challenges your knowledge of key terms presented in the chapter.

Apply Your Knowledge

Reinforce the skills and apply the concepts you learned in this chapter.

Working with Tabs and a Table
Note: To complete this assignment, you will be required to use the Data Files for Students. See the inside back cover of this book for instructions on downloading the Data Files for Students, or contact your instructor for information about accessing the required files.

Instructions: Start Word. Create a new document from the file called Apply 3-1 Projected College Expenses Draft, located on the Data Files for Students. The document is a Word table that you are to edit and format. The revised table is shown in Figure 3–79.

Projected College Expenses

	Freshman	Sophomore	Junior	Senior
Room & Board	3390.00	3627.30	3881.21	4152.90
Tuition & Books	4850.50	5189.50	5552.72	5941.46
Entertainment	635.00	679.45	727.01	777.90
Cell Phone	359.88	365.78	372.81	385.95
Miscellaneous	325.00	347.75	372.09	398.14
Clothing	540.25	577.80	618.29	661.52
Total	$10,100.63	$10,787.58	$11,524.13	$12,317.87

Figure 3–79

Continued >

Apply Your Knowledge *continued*

Perform the following tasks:
1. In the line containing the table title, Projected College Expenses, remove the tab stop at the 1" mark on the ruler.

2. Set a centered tab at the 3" mark on the ruler.

3. Bold the characters in the title. Use the Grow Font button to increase their font size to 14. Change their color to Dark Blue, Text 2, Darker 25%.

4. In the table, delete the row containing the Food expenses.

5. Insert a new row at the bottom of the table. In the first cell of the new row, enter Total in the cell. Enter these values in the next three cells: Freshman – $10,100.63; Sophomore – $10,787.58; Senior – $12,317.87.

6. Insert a column between the Sophomore and Senior columns. Fill in the column as follows: Column Title – Junior; Room & Board – 3881.21; Tuition & Books – 5552.72; Entertainment – 727.01; Cell Phone – 372.81; Miscellaneous – 372.09; Clothing – 618.29; Total – $11,524.13.

7. In the Table Style Options group (Table Tools Design tab), these check boxes should have check marks: Header Row, Total Row, Banded Rows, and First Column. The Last Column and Banded Columns check boxes should not be selected.

8. Apply the Medium Grid 3 - Accent 2 style to the table.

9. Make all columns as wide as their contents (AutoFit Contents).

10. Center the cells containing the column headings.

11. Right-align all cells containing numbers in the table.

12. Center the table between the left and right margins of the page.

13. Change the document properties, as specified by your instructor.

14. Save the document using the file name, Apply 3-1 Projected College Expenses Modified and submit it in the format specified by your instructor.

Extend Your Knowledge

Extend the skills you learned in this chapter and experiment with new skills. You may need to use Help to complete the assignment.

Working with Formulas, Clip Art, Sorting, Picture Bullets, Tabs, and Mailing Labels
Note: To complete this assignment, you will be required to use the Data Files for Students. See the inside back cover of this book for instructions on downloading the Data Files for Students, or contact your instructor for information about accessing the required files.

Instructions: Start Word. Create a new document from the file called Extend 3-1 Herbals Letter Draft, located on the Data Files for Students. You will enter formulas in the table, change the clip art to Web clip art, change the table style, sort paragraphs, use picture bullets, move tabs, print mailing labels, and work with the Clip Organizer.

Perform the following tasks:
1. Use Help to learn about entering formulas, clip art from the Web, sorting, picture bullets, and printing mailing labels.

2. Use the Formula dialog box (Figure 3–80) to add formulas to the last column in the table so that the total due displays for each item; be sure to enter a number format so that the products are

displayed with dollar signs. Then, add formulas to the last row in the table so that the total quantity and total due are displayed, also with dollar signs. Write down the formulas that Word uses to find the product of values in the rows and to sum the values in a column.

3. Delete the current clip art images in the letterhead. Use the Clip Art pane to locate appropriate clip art from the Web, make the clip available offline, and insert an image on each side of the business name in the letterhead.

4. Change the table style. One at a time, select and deselect each check box in the Table Style Options group. Write down the function of each check box: Header Row, Total Row, Banded Rows, First Column, Last Column, and Banded Columns. Select the check boxes you prefer for the table.

5. Sort the paragraphs in the bulleted list.

6. Change the bullets in the bulleted list to picture bullets.

7. Move the tab stops in the date line, complimentary close, and signature block from the 3.5" mark to the 4" mark on the ruler.

8. Change the document properties, as specified by your instructor. Save the revised document and then submit it in the format specified by your instructor.

9. Print a single mailing label for the letter.

10. Print a full page of mailing labels, each containing the address shown in Figure 3–80.

11. If your instructor approves, start the Clip Organizer. How many collections appear? Expand the Office Collections. Copy one of the Academic clips to the Favorites folder in the My Collections folder. Locate the clip you made available offline in Step 3 and then preview it. What are five of its properties? Add a keyword to the clip. Delete the clip you made available offline.

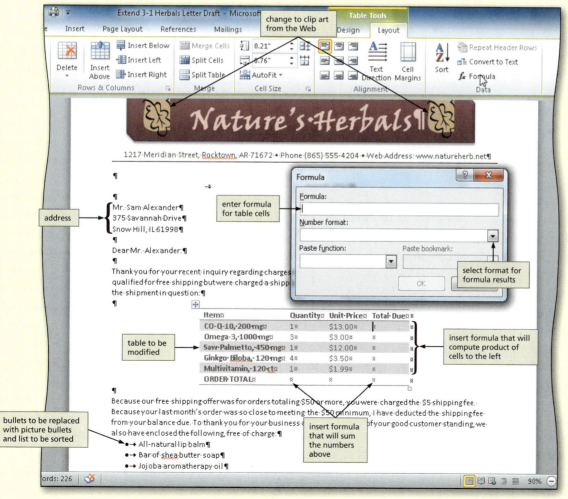

Figure 3–80

Make It Right

Analyze a document and correct all errors and/or improve the design.

Formatting a Business Letter

Note: To complete this assignment, you will be required to use the Data Files for Students. See the inside back cover of this book for instructions on downloading the Data Files for Students, or contact your instructor for information about accessing the required files.

Instructions: Start Word. Create a new document from the file called Make It Right 3-1 Scholarship Letter Draft, located on the Data Files for Students. The document is a business letter that is missing elements and is formatted poorly or incorrectly (Figure 3–81). You are to insert and format clip art in the letterhead, change the color of the text and graphic(s), insert symbols, remove a hyperlink, change the letter style from block to modified block, and format the table.

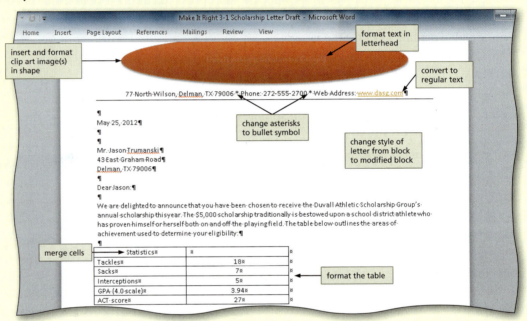

Figure 3–81

Perform the following tasks:

1. Increase the font size of the text in the letterhead. Change the color of the text in the letterhead.

2. Locate and insert at least one appropriate clip art image in the letterhead. If necessary, resize the graphic(s). Move the graphic(s) into the shape.

3. Change the color of the graphic to match the color of the text or shape. Adjust the brightness and contrast of the graphic. Format one color in the graphic as transparent. Change the picture border color.

4. Change the asterisks in the contact information to the dot symbol. Convert the Web address hyperlink to regular text.

5. The letter currently is the block letter style. It should be the modified block letter style. Format the appropriate paragraphs by setting custom tab stops and then positioning those paragraphs at the tab stops. Be sure to position the insertion point in the paragraph before setting the tab stop.

6. Merge the two cells in the first row of the table to one cell and then center the title in the cell. Center the entire table between the page margins. Apply a table style of your choice.

7. Change the document properties, as specified by your instructor. Save the revised document using the file name, Make It Right 3-1 Scholarship Letter Modified, and then submit it in the format specified by your instructor.

In the Lab

Design and/or create a document using the guidelines, concepts, and skills presented in this chapter. Labs are listed in order of increasing difficulty.

Lab 1: Creating a Letter with a Letterhead

Problem: As a consultant for DataLock Storage, you respond to queries from potential customers. One letter you prepare is shown in Figure 3–82.

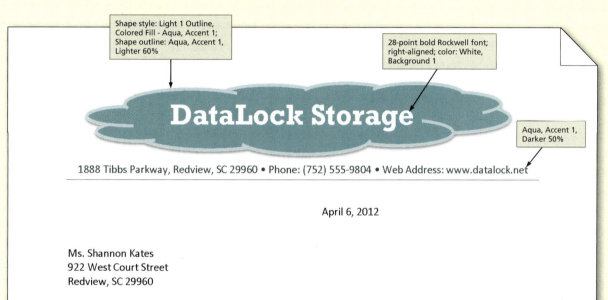

Figure 3–82

Continued >

In the Lab *continued*

Perform the following tasks:

1. Change the theme colors to Technic.

2. Create the letterhead shown at the top of Figure 3–82 on the previous page, following these guidelines:

   a. Insert the cloud shape at an approximate height of 0.95" and width of 5.85". Change text wrapping for the shape to Top and Bottom. Add the company name, DataLock Storage, to the shape. Format the shape and its text as indicated in the figure.

   b. Insert the bullet symbols as shown in the contact information. Remove the hyperlink format from the Web address. If necessary, clear formatting after entering the bottom border.

   c. Save the letterhead with the file name, Lab 3-1 Cloud Storage Letterhead.

3. Create the letter shown in Figure 3–82 using the modified block letter style, following these guidelines:

   a. Apply the No Spacing Quick Style to the document text (below the letterhead).

   b. Set a left-aligned tab stop at the 3.5" mark on the ruler for the date line, complimentary close, and signature block. Insert the current date.

   c. Bullet the list as you type it.

   d. Convert the e-mail address to regular text.

   e. Check the spelling of the letter. Change the document properties, as specified by your instructor. Save the letter with Lab 3-1 Cloud Storage Letter as the file name.

4. If your instructor permits, address and print an envelope or a mailing label for the letter.

In the Lab

Lab 2: Creating a Letter with a Letterhead and Table

Problem: As head librarian at Jonner Public Library, you are responsible for sending confirmation letters for class registrations. You prepare the letter shown in Figure 3–83.

Perform the following tasks:

1. Change the theme colors to Trek. Change the margins to 1" top and bottom and .75" left and right.

2. Create the letterhead shown at the top of Figure 3–83, following these guidelines:

   a. Insert the down ribbon shape at an approximate height of 1" and width of 7". Change text wrapping for the shape to Top and Bottom. Add the library name to the shape. Format the shape and its text as indicated in the figure.

   b. Insert the clip art image, resize it, change text wrapping to Top and Bottom, move it to the left of the shape, and format it as indicated in the figure. Copy the clip art image and move the copy of the image to the right of the shape, as shown in the figure. Flip the copied image horizontally.

   c. Insert the black small square symbols as shown in the contact information. Remove the hyperlink format from the Web address. If necessary, clear formatting after entering the bottom border.

   d. Save the letterhead with the file name, Lab 3-2 Library Letterhead.

3. Create the letter shown in Figure 3–83, following these guidelines:

   a. Apply the No Spacing Quick Style to the document text (below the letterhead).

   b. Set a left-aligned tab stop at the 4" mark on the ruler for the date line, complimentary close, and signature block. Insert the current date.

   c. Insert and center the table. Format the table as specified in the figure.

   d. Bullet the list as you type it. Convert the e-mail address to regular text.

   e. Check the spelling of the letter. Change the document properties, as specified by your instructor. Save the letter with Lab 3-2 Library Letter as the file name.

4. If your instructor permits, address and print an envelope or a mailing label for the letter.

Shape style: Colored
Fill - Orange, Accent 1

24-point bold
Harrington
font, centered

Clip art search
text: information;
Clip art color:
Orange, Accent
color 6 Light

Jonner Public Library

4992 Surrey Court, Jonner, MA 02198 ▪ 291-555-9454 ▪ Web Address: www.jpl.net

Orange, Accent 1,
Darker 50%

March 10, 2012

Mr. Brent Jackson
5153 Anlyn Drive
Jonner, MA 02198

Dear Mr. Jackson:

Thank you for registering online for our spring classes. As a library patron, you are aware that we offer a great deal more than books and magazines. The table below outlines the classes for which you have registered, along with the dates and locations:

Table style: Medium
Grid 3 - Accent 1; Table
style options: Header
Row and Banded
Columns

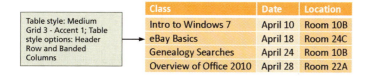

Class	Date	Location
Intro to Windows 7	April 10	Room 10B
eBay Basics	April 18	Room 24C
Genealogy Searches	April 24	Room 10B
Overview of Office 2010	April 28	Room 22A

Note that all classes, regardless of date, begin at 10:00 a.m. and last four hours. Although no materials or textbooks are required for the classes, you are strongly encouraged to bring the following items:

- Pens, pencils, or other writing implements
- Blank CD or DVD to store documents and notes created during class
- Notebook or loose-leaf binder for handwritten notes
- Your valid library card to verify enrollment eligibility

Please note that no food or drinks are allowed in any of our computer facilities. If you have any questions or would like to register for additional courses, please contact me at (291) 555-9454 or via e-mail at mtlawrence@jpl.net.

Again, thank you for your interest in and continued patronage of Jonner Public Library. We look forward to seeing you when your first class begins.

Sincerely,

Marcia Lawrence
Head Librarian

Figure 3–83

In the Lab

Lab 3: Creating a Letter with a Letterhead and Table

Problem: As president of the County Education Board, you communicate with schools in your district. One of the schools has just been awarded a four-star rating.

Instructions: Prepare the letter shown in Figure 3–84. Change the theme colors to Pushpin. Change the margins to 1" top and bottom and .75" left and right. Follow the guidelines in the modified semi-block letter style. Use proper spacing between elements of the letter. After entering the inside address,

Bevel shape: Intense Effect - Brown, Accent 3

28-point bold Comic Sans MS font, centered

Color: Red, Accent color 2 Light; Brightness: +20% Contrast: +20%

Brown, Accent 3, Darker 50%

County Education Board

53 State Avenue, Purlington, IN 46372 • Phone (751) 555-0412 • Web Address: www.ceb.com

March 31, 2012

Ms. Sarah Rosen, Principal
Fair Grove Elementary School
3373 Sherman Boulevard
Purlington, IN 46372

Dear Ms. Rosen:

We are delighted to announce that a four-star rating has been granted to Fair Grove Elementary School for the fifth consecutive year. As you know, this rating is the highest distinction a county school can receive. The table below outlines the county requirements compared with Fair Grove's overall figures:

Table style: Medium Grid 3 - Accent 3; Table style options: Header Row and First Column

Four-Star Ranking Requirements		
Area	Minimum Requirement	Fair Grove Figure
Attendance	95%	97.2%
Language Proficiency	90%	91.1%
Math Proficiency	90%	90.7%

To earn a four-star rating, schools must rank in the top 20 percent of the three areas shown in the table. Fair Grove Elementary School is one of only ten county schools to achieve this distinction. In addition to the academic performance and attendance figures, we recognize your other achievements, as follows:

- Nearly 80 percent of Fair Grove students are involved in extracurricular activities
- Operating expenses and budget are kept to a minimum, with no additional funds requested from county budget last year
- High rate of teacher retention and satisfaction
- Parental involvement and inclusion in coursework, volunteer projects, and unpaid positions (i.e., recreational sports league coaches, cafeteria monitors, chaperones, etc.)

The County Education Board extends its congratulations to you for a job well done. Please accept our thanks for your continuing role in shaping our county's future citizens.

Sincerely,

Walt Andreas
President

Figure 3–84

create a building block for Fair Grove Elementary School and insert the building block whenever you have to enter the school name. Resize table columns to fit contents. Check the spelling of the letter. Change the document properties, as specified by your instructor. Save the letter with Lab 3-3 Education Board Letter as the file name.

Cases and Places

Apply your creative thinking and problem solving skills to design and implement a solution.

Note: To complete these assignments, you may be required to use the Data Files for Students. See the inside back cover of this book for instructions on downloading the Data Files for Students, or contact your instructor for information about accessing the required files.

1: Create a Letter to a Potential Employer

Academic

As a student about to graduate, you are actively seeking employment in your field and have located an advertisement for a job in which you are interested. You decide to write a letter to the potential employer: Ms. Janice Tremont at Home Health Associates, 554 Mountain View Lane, Blue Dust, MO 64319.

The draft wording for the letter is as follows: I am responding to your advertisement for the nursing position in the *Blue Dust Press*. I have tailored my activities and education for a career in geriatric medicine. This month, I will graduate with concentrations in Geriatric Medicine (24 hours), Osteopathic Medicine (12 hours), and Holistic Nursing (9 hours). In addition to receiving my bachelor degree in nursing, I have enhanced my education by participating in the following activities: volunteered at Blue Dust's free health care clinic; attended several continuing education and career-specific seminars, including An Aging Populace, Care of the Homebound, and Special Needs of the Elderly; completed one-semester internship at Blue Dust Community Hospital in spring semester of 2012; completed Certified Nursing Assistant (CNA) program at Blue Dust Community College; and worked as nurse's aide for two years during college. I look forward to an interview so that we can discuss the position you offer and my qualifications. With my background and education, I am confident that I will make a positive contribution to Home Health Associates.

The letter should contain a letterhead that uses a shape and clip art, a table (use a table to present the areas of concentration), and a bulleted list (use a bulleted list to present the activities). Insert nonbreaking spaces in the newspaper name. Use the concepts and techniques presented in this chapter to create and format a letter according to the modified block style, creating appropriate paragraph breaks and rewording the draft as necessary. Use your personal information for contact information in the letter. Be sure to check the spelling and grammar of the finished letter. Submit your assignment in the format specified by your instructor.

2: Create a Letter Requesting Donations

Personal

As an alumnus of your historic high school, you are concerned that the building is being considered for demolition. You decide to write a letter to another graduate: Mr. Jim Lemon, 87 Travis Parkway, Vigil, CT 06802.

The draft wording for the letter is as follows: As a member of the class of 1988, you, like many others, probably have many fond memories of our alma mater, Vigil East High School. I recently learned that the building is being considered for demolition because of its age and structural integrity.

Continued >

Cases and Places *continued*

As a result, I have decided to call upon the many graduating classes of the school to band together and save the historic building from demolition. According to the documents I have reviewed and information from meetings I have attended, a minimum of $214,000 is necessary to save the school and bring it up to code. Once the repairs are made, I plan to start the process of having it declared an historic landmark. You can help by donating your time, skills, or money. We need skilled tradesmen, including carpenters, roofers, plumbers, and electricians, as well as laborers. In addition, we are asking for monetary donations, as follows, although donations in any amount will be accepted gladly: a donation of $100 categorizes you as a Save Our School Friend, $250 a Patron, and $500 a Benefactor. Once our monetary goal has been reached, the necessary repairs and replacements will be made as follows: Phase I: roof and exterior, Phase II: electrical and plumbing, and Phase III: interior walls, trim, flooring, and fixtures. I hope you will join our conservation efforts so that Vigil East High School will continue to stand proudly for many more years. If you have questions, please contact me at the phone number or e-mail address above. I hope to hear from you soon.

The letter should contain a letterhead that uses a shape and clip art, a table (use a table to present the Save Our School donor categories), and a bulleted list (use a bulleted list to present the phases). Use the concepts and techniques presented in this chapter to create and format a letter according to the modified block style, creating appropriate paragraph breaks and rewording the draft as necessary. Use your personal information for contact information in the letter and Save Our School as the text in the letterhead. Be sure to check spelling and grammar of the finished letter. Submit your assignment in the format specified by your instructor.

3: Create a Confirmation Letter

Professional

As coordinator for Condor Parks and Recreation, you send letters to confirm registration for activities. You write a confirmation letter to this registrant: Ms. Tracey Li, 52 West 15th Street, Harpville, KY 42194. Condor Parks and Recreation is located at 2245 Community Place, Harpville, KY 42194; phone number is (842) 555-0444; and Web address is www.condorparks.com.

The draft wording for the letter is as follows: Thank you for your interest in our new spring activities recently listed in the *Condor Daily Press*. The courses for which you have enrolled, along with their dates and times are Introductory Golf Clinic on May 5 – 6 from 4:00 – 6:00 p.m. at a cost of $25, Recreational League Volleyball on April 30 – May 28 from 7:30 – 9:00 p.m. at a cost of $130, Pilates on May 30 – June 27 from 8:00 – 9:00 p.m. at a cost of $75, and Intermediate Golf Clinic on June 9 – 10 from 12:00 – 2:00 p.m. at a cost of $30. By paying your annual $25 parks and recreation fee, you also are entitled to the following benefits: free access to racquetball and tennis courts, on a first-come-first-served basis; attendance at any park-sponsored events, including plays, musical performances, and festivals; and free parking at any parks and recreation facility. Please confirm your registration by calling me at [enter your phone number here] or via e-mail at [enter your e-mail address here]. Thank you for your interest in Condor Parks and Recreation offerings. We look forward to seeing you at upcoming events.

The letter should contain a letterhead that uses a shape and clip art, a table (use a table to present the courses enrolled), and a bulleted list (use a bulleted list to present the benefits). Insert nonbreaking spaces in the newspaper name. Use the concepts and techniques presented in this chapter to create and format a letter according to the modified block style, creating appropriate paragraph breaks and rewording the draft as necessary. Be sure to check spelling and grammar of the finished letter. Submit your assignment in the format specified by your instructor.

4 Creating a Document with a Title Page, Lists, Tables, and a Watermark

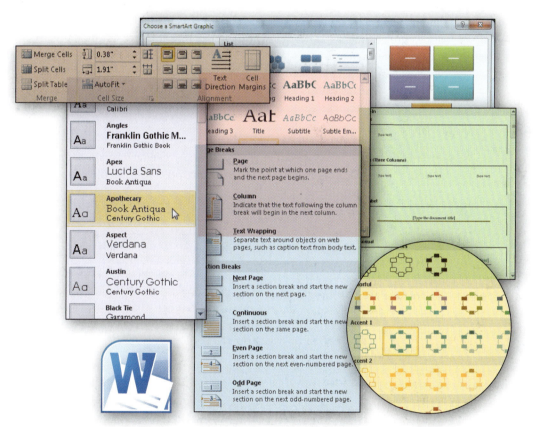

Objectives

You will have mastered the material in this project when you can:

- Border a paragraph
- Change paragraph indentation
- Insert and format a SmartArt graphic
- Apply character effects
- Insert a section break
- Insert a Word document in an open document
- Change theme fonts

- Insert formatted headers and footers
- Sort lists and tables
- Use the format painter
- Add picture bullets to a list
- Create a multilevel list
- Modify and format Word tables
- Sum columns in a table
- Create a watermark

4 | Creating a Document with a Title Page, Lists, Tables, and a Watermark

Introduction

During the course of your business and personal endeavors, you may want or need to provide a recommendation to a person or group of people for their consideration. You might suggest they purchase a product, such as vehicles or books, or contract a service, such as designing their Web page or remodeling their house. Or, you might try to convince an audience to take an action, such as signing a petition, joining a club, or donating to a cause. You may be asked to request funds for a new program or activity or to promote an idea, such as a benefits package to company employees or a budget plan to upper management. To present these types of recommendations, you may find yourself writing a proposal.

A proposal generally is one of three types: sales, research, or planning. A **sales proposal** sells an idea, a product, or a service. A **research proposal** usually requests funding for a research project. A **planning proposal** offers solutions to a problem or improvement to a situation.

Project Planning Guidelines

> The process of developing a document that communicates specific information requires careful analysis and planning. As a starting point, establish why the document is needed. Once the purpose is determined, analyze the intended readers of the document and their unique needs. Then, gather information about the topic and decide what to include in the document. Finally, determine the document design and style that will be most successful at delivering the message. Details of these guidelines are provided in Appendix A. In addition, each project in this book provides practical applications of these planning considerations.

Project — Sales Proposal

Sales proposals describe the features and value of products and services being offered, with the intent of eliciting a positive response from the reader. Desired outcomes include the reader accepting ideas, purchasing products, contracting services, volunteering time, contributing to a cause, or taking an action. A well-written proposal can be the key to obtaining the desired results.

The project in this chapter follows generally accepted guidelines for writing short sales proposals and uses Word to create the sales proposal shown in Figure 4–1. The sales proposal in this chapter is designed to persuade readers to join a health club. The proposal has a colorful title page to attract readers' attention. To add impact, the sales proposal has a watermark consisting of the text, GET FIT!, positioned behind the text and graphics on each page. It also uses lists and tables to summarize and highlight important data.

border

border

watermark

SmartArt graphic

Figure 4–1 (a) Title Page

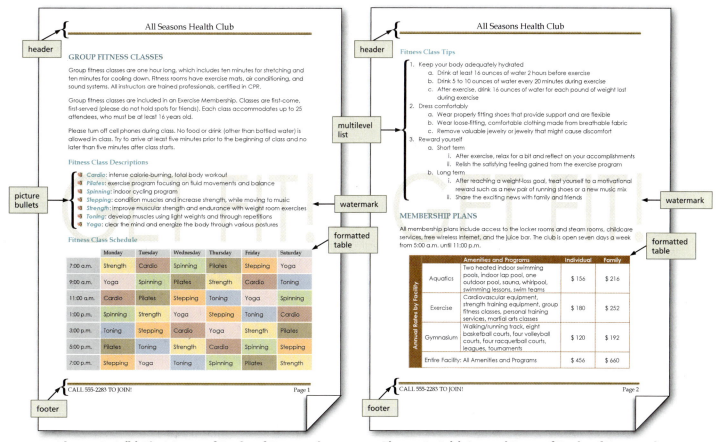

header

picture bullets

watermark

formatted table

footer

header

multilevel list

watermark

formatted table

footer

Figure 4–1 (b) First Page of Body of Proposal

Figure 4–1 (c) Second Page of Body of Proposal

Overview

As you read through this chapter, you will learn how to create the sales proposal shown in Figure 4–1 on the previous page by performing these general tasks:

- Create a title page.
- Save the title page.
- Insert a draft of the body of the sales proposal below the title page.
- Edit and enhance the draft of the body of the sales proposal.
- Save and print the sales proposal.

Plan Ahead

> **General Project Guidelines**
>
> When creating a Word document, the actions you perform and decisions you make will affect the appearance and characteristics of the finished document. As you create a sales proposal, such as the project shown in Figure 4–1, you should follow these general guidelines:
>
> 1. **Identify the nature of the proposal.** A proposal may be solicited or unsolicited. If someone else requests that you develop the proposal, it is solicited. Be sure to include all requested information in a solicited proposal. When you write a proposal because you recognize a need, the proposal is unsolicited. With an unsolicited proposal, you must gather information you believe will be relevant and of interest to the intended audience.
>
> 2. **Design an eye-catching title page.** The title page should convey the overall message of the sales proposal. Use text, graphics, formats, and colors that reflect the goals of the sales proposal. Be sure to include a title.
>
> 3. **Compose the text of the sales proposal.** Sales proposals vary in length, style, and formality, but all are designed to elicit acceptance from the reader. The sales proposal should have a neat, organized appearance. A successful sales proposal uses succinct wording and includes lists for textual messages. Write text using active voice, instead of passive voice. Assume that readers of unsolicited sales proposals have no previous knowledge about the topic. Be sure the goal of the proposal is clear. Establish a theme and carry it throughout the proposal.
>
> 4. **Enhance the sales proposal with appropriate visuals.** Use visuals to add interest, clarify ideas, and illustrate points. Visuals include tables, charts, and graphical images (i.e., photos, clip art).
>
> 5. **Proofread and edit the proposal.** Carefully review the sales proposal to be sure it contains no spelling, grammar, mathematical, or other errors. Check that transitions between sentences and paragraphs are smooth. Ensure that the purpose of the proposal is stated clearly. Ask others to review the proposal and give you suggestions for improvements.
>
> When necessary, more specific details concerning the above guidelines are presented at appropriate points in the chapter. The chapter also will identify the actions performed and decisions made regarding these guidelines during the creation of the sales proposal shown in Figure 4–1.

To Start Word

If you are using a computer to step through the project in this chapter and you want your screens to match the figures in this book, you should change your screen's resolution to 1024×768. The next steps, which assume Windows 7 is running, start Word based on a typical installation. You may need to ask your instructor how to start Word for your computer.

1 Click the Start button on the Windows 7 taskbar to display the Start menu.

2 Type `Microsoft Word` as the search text in the 'Search programs and files' text box and watch the search results appear on the Start menu.

3 Click Microsoft Word 2010 in the search results on the Start menu to start Word and display a new blank document in the Word window.

4 If the Word window is not maximized, click the Maximize button next to the Close button on its title bar to maximize the window.

5 If the Print Layout button on the status bar is not selected (shown in Figure 4–2 on page WD 207), click it so that your screen is in Print Layout view.

6 If your zoom percent is not 100, click the Zoom Out button or Zoom In button on the status bar as many times as necessary until the Zoom button displays 100% on its face (shown in Figure 4–2).

7 If the rulers are not displayed already, click the View Ruler button on the vertical scroll bar, or place a check mark in the Ruler check box (View tab | Show group), because you will use the rulers for several tasks in the creation of this project.

To Display Formatting Marks

It is helpful to display formatting marks that indicate where in the document you pressed the ENTER key, SPACEBAR, and other keys. The following steps display formatting marks.

1 If necessary, click Home on the Ribbon to display the Home tab.

2 If the Show/Hide ¶ button (Home tab | Paragraph group) is not selected already, click it to display formatting marks on the screen.

To Change Theme Colors

Word provides document themes that contain a variety of color schemes to assist you in selecting complementary colors in a document. You should select a color scheme that reflects the goals of a sales proposal. This proposal uses the Solstice color scheme. The following steps change theme colors.

1 Click the Change Styles button (Home tab | Styles group) to display the Change Styles menu and then point to Colors on the Change Styles menu to display the Colors gallery.

2 If necessary, scroll to and then click Solstice in the Colors gallery to change the document theme colors to the selected color scheme.

Creating a Title Page

A **title page** is a separate cover page that contains, at a minimum, the title of a document. For a sales proposal, the title page usually is the first page of the document. Solicited proposals often have a specific format for the title page. Guidelines for the title page of a solicited proposal may stipulate the margins, spacing, layout, and required contents such as title, sponsor name, author name, date, etc. With an unsolicited proposal, by contrast, you can design the title page in a way that best presents its message.

Plan Ahead

> **Design an eye-catching title page.**
> The title page is the first section a reader sees on a sales proposal. Thus, it is important that the title page appropriately reflects the goal of the sales proposal. When designing the title page, consider its text and graphics.
>
> - **Use concise, descriptive text.** The title page should contain a short, descriptive title that accurately reflects the message of the sales proposal. The title page also may include a theme or slogan. Do not place a page number on the title page.
>
> - **Identify appropriate fonts, font sizes, and colors for the text.** Use fonts that are easy to read. Avoid using more than three different fonts because too many fonts can make the title page visually confusing. Use larger font sizes to add impact to the title page. To give the title more emphasis, its font size should be larger than any other text on the title page. Use colors that complement each other and convey the meaning of the proposal.
>
> - **Use graphics to reinforce the goal.** Select simple graphics that clearly communicate the fundamental nature of the proposal. Possible graphics include shapes, pictures, and logos. Use colors that complement text colors. Be aware that too many graphics and colors can be distracting. Arrange graphics with the text so that the title page is attractive and uncluttered.

The title page of the sales proposal in this project (Figure 4–1a on page WD 203) contains a colorful title that is surrounded by a border with some shading, an artistic graphic with text, a colorful slogan, and the faded words, GET FIT!, in the background. The steps on the next several pages create this title page. The faded words, GET FIT!, are added to all pages at the end of the chapter.

To Format Characters

The title in the sales proposal should use a large font size and an easy-to-read font, and should be the focal point on the page. The following steps enter the title, All Seasons Health Club, with the first two words centered on the first line and the second two words centered on the second line.

BTW

Normal Style
If your screen settings differ from Figure 4–2, it is possible the default settings in your Normal style have been changed. Normal style settings are saved in a file called normal.dotm. To restore the original Normal style settings, quit Word and use Windows Explorer to locate the normal.dotm file (be sure that hidden files and folders are displayed, and include system and hidden files in your search — you may need to use Help to assist you with these tasks). Rename the normal.dotm file as oldnormal.dotm. After the normal.dotm file is renamed, it no longer will exist as normal.dotm. The next time you start Word, it will recreate a normal.dotm file using the original default settings.

1. Click the Center button (Home tab | Paragraph group) to center the paragraph that will contain the title.

2. Click the Font box arrow (Home tab | Font group). Scroll to and then click Berlin Sans FB Demi (or a similar font) in the Font gallery, so that the text you type will use the selected font.

3. Click the Font Size box arrow (Home tab | Font group) and then click 72 in the Font Size gallery, so that the text you type will use the selected font size.

4. Type **All Seasons** and then press the ENTER key to enter the first line of the title.

5. Click the Font Color button arrow (Home tab | Font group) and then click Red, Accent 3 (seventh color, first row) in the Font Color gallery, so that the text you type will use the selected font color.

6. Type **Health Club** as the second line of the title (shown in Figure 4–2).

To Border a Paragraph

When you click the Border button (Home tab | Paragraph group), Word applies the most recently defined border, or, if one has not been defined, it applies the default border to the current paragraph. To specify a border different from the most recently defined border, you use the Border button arrow (Home tab | Paragraph group).

In this project, the first line of the title in the sales proposal (All Seasons) has a 6-point red border around it. The following steps add a border to all edges of a paragraph.

1

- Position the insertion point in the paragraph to border, in this case, the first line of the document.

- Click the Border button arrow (Home tab | Paragraph group) to display the Border gallery (Figure 4–2).

Note: To help you locate screen elements that are referenced in the step instructions, such as buttons and commands, this book uses red boxes to point to these screen elements.

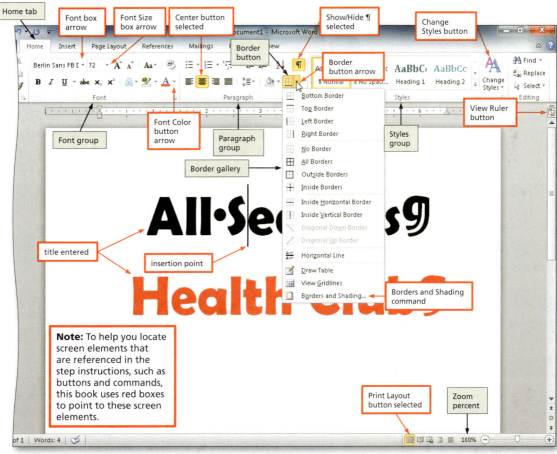

Figure 4–2

2

- Click Borders and Shading in the Border gallery to display the Borders and Shading dialog box.

- Click Box in the Setting area (Borders and Shading dialog box), which will place a border on each edge of the current paragraph.

- Click the Color box arrow and then click Red, Accent 3 (seventh color, first row) in the Color palette to specify the border color.

- Click the Width box arrow and then click 6 pt to specify the thickness of the border (Figure 4–3).

Q&A

What is the purpose of the buttons in the Preview area?

They are toggles that display and remove the top, bottom, left, and right borders from the diagram in the Preview area.

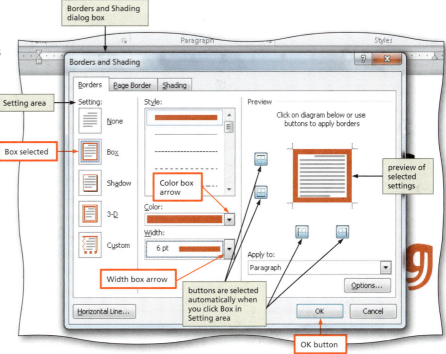

Figure 4–3

3

● Click the OK button (Borders and Shading dialog box) to place the border shown in the preview area of the dialog box around the current paragraph in the document (Figure 4–4).

Q&A

How would I remove an existing border from a paragraph?

Click the Border button arrow (Home tab | Paragraph group) and then click the border in the Border gallery that identifies the border you wish to remove, or click No Border to remove all borders.

Figure 4–4

Other Ways
1. Click Page Borders button (Page Layout tab | Page Background group), click Borders tab (Borders and Shading dialog box), select desired border, click OK button

To Shade a Paragraph and Change Font Color

To make the first line of the title of the sales proposal more eye-catching, it is shaded in aqua. When you shade a paragraph, Word shades the rectangular area behind any text or graphics in the paragraph from the left margin of the paragraph to the right margin. If the paragraph is surrounded by a border, Word shades inside the border. The following steps shade a paragraph and change font color.

1 With the insertion point in the paragraph to shade, the first line in this case (shown in Figure 4–4), click the Shading button arrow (Home tab | Paragraph group) to display the Shading gallery.

2 Click Aqua, Accent 1 (fifth color, first row) in the Shading gallery to shade the current paragraph (shown in Figure 4–5).

3 Drag through the words, All Seasons, in the first line of the title to select the text.

4 Click the Font Color button arrow (Home tab | Font group) to display the Font Color gallery and then click White, Background 1 (first color, first row) to change the color of the selected text (shown in Figure 4–5).

To Border Another Paragraph

To make the second line of the title of the sales proposal (Health Club) more eye-catching, it has a 6-point gold border around it. The following steps add a border to all edges of a paragraph.

1 Position the insertion point in the paragraph to border (in this case, the second paragraph containing the text, Health Club).

2 Click the Border button arrow (Home tab | Paragraph group) to display the Border gallery and then click Borders and Shading in the Border gallery to display the Borders and Shading dialog box.

3 Click Box in the Setting area (Borders and Shading dialog box), which will place a border on each edge of the current paragraph.

4 Click the Color box arrow and then click Gold, Accent 2 (sixth color, first row) in the Color palette to specify the border color.

5 If necessary, click the Width box arrow and then click 6 pt to specify the thickness of the border.

6 Click the OK button to place the defined border shown around the current paragraph in the document (Figure 4–5).

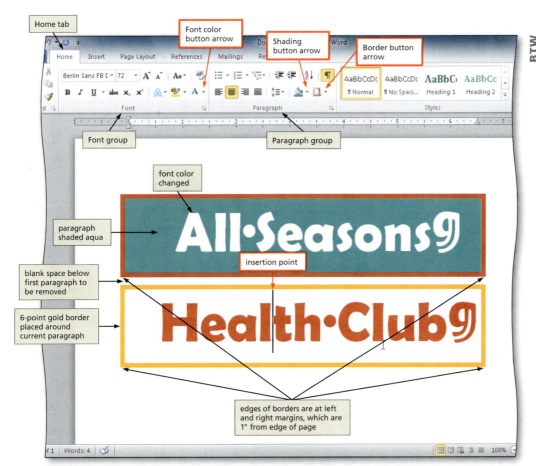

Figure 4–5

BTW

The Ribbon and Screen Resolution
Word may change how the groups and buttons within the groups appear on the Ribbon, depending on the computer's screen resolution. Thus, your Ribbon may look different from the ones in this book if you are using a screen resolution other than 1024 x 768.

To Change Spacing after a Paragraph

Currently, a small amount of blank space exists between the two paragraph borders because Word automatically places 10 points of blank space below paragraphs (shown in Figure 4–5 on the previous page). The following steps remove the blank space below the first paragraph.

1 Position the insertion point in the paragraph to be adjusted (in this case, the paragraph containing the text, All Seasons).

2 Display the Page Layout tab. Click the Spacing After box down arrow (Page Layout tab | Paragraph group) as many times as necessary until 0 pt is displayed in the Spacing After box to remove the space below the current paragraph (shown in Figure 4–6).

To Change Left and Right Paragraph Indent

The borders around the first and second paragraphs and the shading in the first paragraph currently extend from the left margin to the right margin (shown in Figure 4–5). In this project, the edges of the border and shading are closer to the text in the title. If you want the border and shading to start and end at a location different from the margin, you change the left and right paragraph indent.

The Increase Indent and Decrease Indent buttons (Home tab | Paragraph group) change the left indent by ½-inch, respectively. In this case, however, you cannot use these buttons because you want to change both the left and right indent. The following steps change the left and right paragraph indent.

1

- With the insertion point in the paragraph to indent (the first paragraph in this case), click the Indent Left box up arrow (Page Layout tab | Paragraph group) five times so that 0.5 " is displayed in the Indent Left box because you want to adjust the paragraph left indent by this amount.

- Click the Indent Right box up arrow (Page Layout tab | Paragraph group) five times so that 0.5 " is displayed in the Indent Right box because you want to adjust the paragraph right indent by this amount (Figure 4–6).

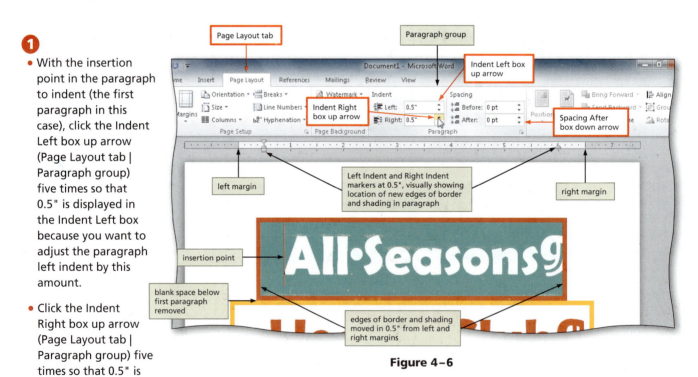

Figure 4–6

Experiment

- Repeatedly click the Indent Right and Indent Left box up and down scroll arrows (Page Layout tab | Paragraph group) and watch the left and right edges of the current paragraph change in the document window. When you have finished experimenting, set the left and right indent each to 0.5 ".

2

• Repeat Step 1 for the second paragraph, so that the paragraph containing the words, Health Club, also has a left and right indent of 0.5" (shown in Figure 4–7).

Other Ways		
1. Drag Left Indent and Right Indent markers on ruler	(Paragraph dialog box), set indentation values, click OK button	Indents and Spacing tab (Paragraph dialog box), set indentation values, click OK button
2. Click Paragraph Dialog Box Launcher (Home tab | Paragraph group), click Indents and Spacing tab	3. Right-click paragraph, click Paragraph on shortcut menu, click	

To Clear Formatting

The title is finished. When you press the ENTER key to advance the insertion point from the end of the second line to the beginning of the third line on the title page, the border is carried forward to line 3, and any text you type will be 72-point Berlin Sans FB Demi Red, Accent 3 font. The paragraphs and characters on line 3 should not have the same paragraph and character formatting as line 2. Instead, they should be formatted using the Normal style. The following steps clear formatting, which applies the Normal style formats to the location of the insertion point.

1 If necessary, press the END key to position the insertion point at the end of line 2, that is, after the b in Club.

2 Press the ENTER key.

3 Display the Home tab. Click the Clear Formatting button (Home tab | Font group) to apply the Normal style to the location of the insertion point (Figure 4–7).

Q&A Could I have clicked Normal in the Styles gallery instead of the Clear Formatting button?
Yes.

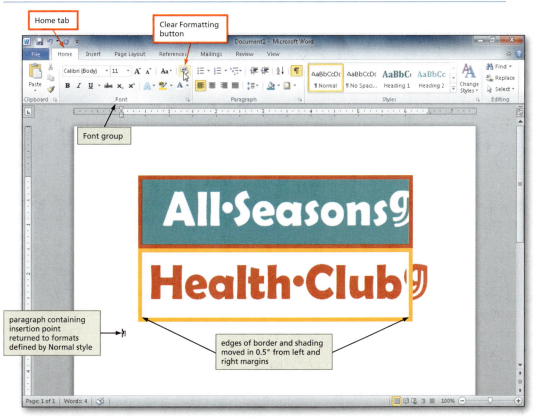

Figure 4–7

To Save a Document

You have performed many tasks while creating this proposal and do not want to risk losing work completed thus far. Accordingly, you should save the document. The following steps assume you already have created folders for storing your files, for example, a CIS 101 folder (for your class) that contains a Word folder (for your assignments). Thus, these steps save the document in the Word folder in the CIS 101 folder on a USB flash drive using the file name, All Seasons Title Page.

1 With a USB flash drive connected to one of the computer's USB ports, click the Save button on the Quick Access Toolbar to display the Save As dialog box.

2 Type `All Seasons Title Page` in the File name text box (Save As dialog box) to change the file name. Do not press the ENTER key after typing the file name because you do not want to close the dialog box at this time.

3 Navigate to the desired save location (in this case, the Word folder in the CIS 101 folder [or your class folder] on the USB flash drive).

4 Click the Save button (Save As dialog box) to save the document in the selected folder on the selected drive with the entered file name.

SmartArt Graphics

Microsoft Office 2010 includes **SmartArt graphics**, which are visual representations of information. Many different types of SmartArt graphics are available, allowing you to choose one that illustrates your message best. Table 4–1 identifies the purpose of some of the more popular types of SmartArt graphics. Within each type, Office provides numerous layouts. For example, you can select from more than 40 different layouts of the list type.

Table 4–1 SmartArt Graphic Types	
Type	**Purpose**
List	Shows nonsequential or grouped blocks of information.
Process	Shows progression, timeline, or sequential steps in a process or workflow.
Cycle	Shows continuous sequence of steps or events.
Hierarchy	Illustrates organization charts, decision trees, and hierarchical relationships.
Relationship	Compares or contrasts connections between concepts.
Matrix	Shows relationships of parts to a whole.
Picture	Uses images to present a message.
Pyramid	Shows proportional or interconnected relationships with the largest component at the top or bottom.

SmartArt graphics contain shapes. You can add text to shapes, add more shapes, or delete shapes. You also can modify the appearance of a SmartArt graphic by applying styles and changing its colors. The next several pages demonstrate the following general tasks to create the SmartArt graphic on the title page in this project:

1. Insert a SmartArt graphic.
2. Delete unneeded shapes from the SmartArt graphic.
3. Add text to the remaining shapes in the SmartArt graphic.
4. Change colors of the SmartArt graphic.
5. Apply a style to the SmartArt graphic.

BTW

BTWs
For a complete list of the BTWs found in the margins of this book, visit the Word 2010 BTW Web page (scsite.com/wd2010/btw).

To Insert a SmartArt Graphic

Below the title on the title page is a cycle SmartArt graphic. The following steps insert a SmartArt graphic centered below the title on the title page.

1

- With the insertion point on the blank paragraph below the title (shown in Figure 4–7 on page WD 211), click the Center button (Home tab | Paragraph group) so that the inserted SmartArt graphic will be centered below the title.

- Display the Insert tab.

- Click the Insert SmartArt Graphic button (Insert tab | Illustrations group) to display the Choose a SmartArt Graphic dialog box (Figure 4–8).

🔍 **Experiment**

- Click various SmartArt graphic types in the left pane of the dialog box and watch the related layout choices appear in the middle pane.

🔍 **Experiment**

- Click various layouts in the list of layouts in the middle pane to see the preview and description of the layout appear in the right pane of the dialog box.

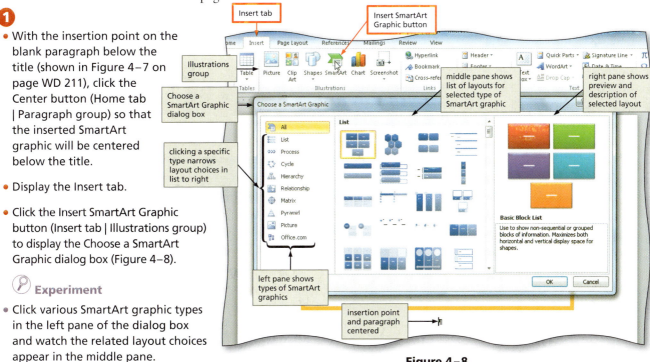

Figure 4–8

2

- Click Cycle in the left pane (Choose a SmartArt Graphic dialog box) to display the layout choices related to a cycle SmartArt graphic.

- Click Nondirectional Cycle in the middle pane, which displays a preview and description of the selected layout in the right pane (Figure 4–9).

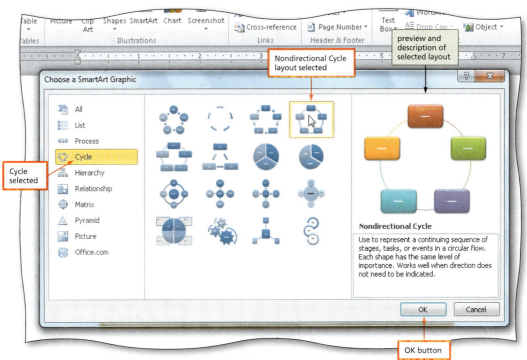

Figure 4–9

3

- Click the OK button to insert the Nondirectional Cycle SmartArt graphic in the document at the location of the insertion point (Figure 4–10).

Q&A

What if the Text Pane appears next to the SmartArt graphic?

Close the Text Pane by clicking its Close button or clicking the Text Pane button (SmartArt Tools Design tab | Create Graphic group).

Q&A

Can I change the layout of the inserted SmartArt graphic?

Yes. Click the More button in the Layouts gallery (SmartArt Tools Design tab | Layouts group) to display the list of layouts.

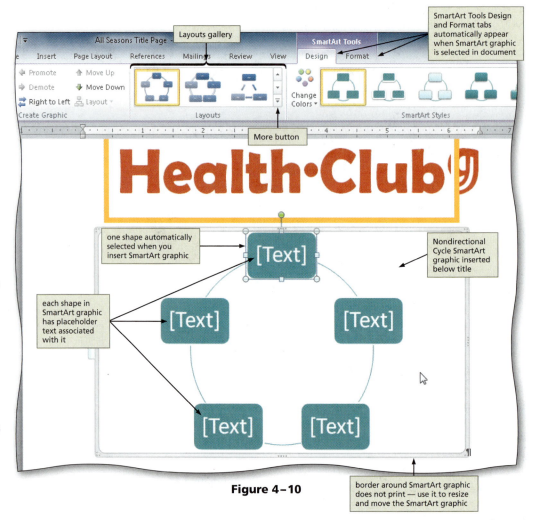

Figure 4–10

To Delete Shapes and Add Text to Shapes in a SmartArt Graphic

The Nondirectional Cycle SmartArt graphic initially has five shapes (shown in Figure 4–10). The SmartArt graphic in this project, however, has only three shapes, each one containing text that describes a type of facility at the health club: exercise, aquatics, and gymnasium. Each shape in the SmartArt graphic initially shows **placeholder text**, which indicates where text can be typed in a shape. The following steps delete two shapes in the SmartArt graphic and then add text to the remaining three shapes via their placeholder text.

1

- With any shape selected in the SmartArt graphic, press the DELETE key to delete the shape from the graphic and notice the other shapes resize and relocate in the graphic.

Q&A

What if a shape is no longer selected?

Click the edge of any shape to select the shape.

- Press the DELETE key again to delete another shape from the graphic, so that three shapes remain in the SmartArt graphic (Figure 4–11).

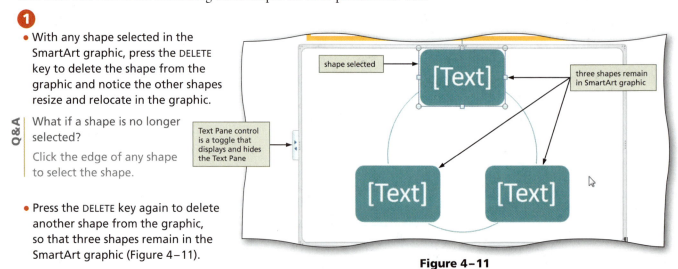

Figure 4–11

2

● With the top shape selected (shown in Figure 4–11), type **Exercise** to replace the placeholder text, [Text], with the entered text.

Q&A How do I edit placeholder text if I make a mistake?

Click the placeholder text to select it and then correct the entry.

Q&A What if my typed text is longer than the shape?

The font size of the text may be adjusted or the text may wordwrap within the shape.

3

● Click the lower-right shape to select it and then type **Aquatics** as the new text.

● Click the lower-left shape to select it and then type **Gymnasium** as the final text in the graphic (Figure 4–12).

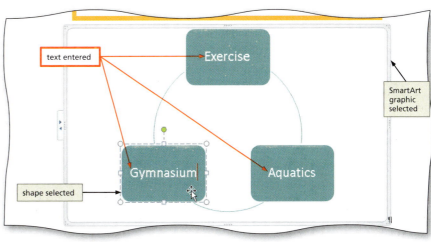

Figure 4–12

Other Ways

1. Click Text Pane control, enter text in Text Pane, close Text Pane

2. Click Text Pane button (SmartArt Tools Design

tab | Create Graphic group), enter text in Text Pane, click Text Pane button again

To Change Colors of a SmartArt Graphic

Word provides a variety of colors for a SmartArt graphic and the shapes in the graphic. In this project, the shapes are white inside, instead of blue, and the line connecting the shapes is red. The following steps change the colors of a SmartArt graphic.

1

● With the SmartArt graphic selected (shown in Figure 4–12), click the Change Colors button (SmartArt Tools Design tab | SmartArt Styles group) to display the Change Colors gallery.

Q&A What if the SmartArt graphic is not selected?

Click the SmartArt graphic to select it.

● Point to Colored Outline - Accent 3 in the Change Colors gallery to display a live preview of that color applied to the SmartArt graphic in the document (Figure 4–13).

 Experiment

● Point to various colors in the Change Colors gallery and watch the colors of the graphic change in the document window.

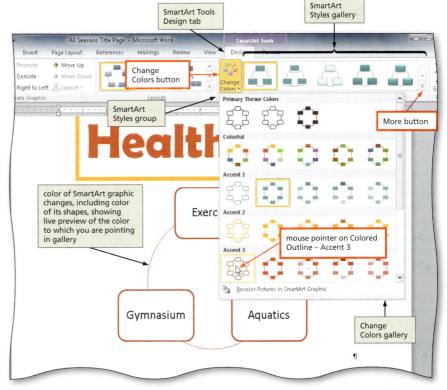

Figure 4–13

2

● Click Colored Outline - Accent 3 in the Change Colors gallery to apply the selected color to the SmartArt graphic.

BTW

Resetting Graphics
If you want to remove all formats from a SmartArt graphic and start over, you would click the Reset Graphic button (SmartArt Tools Design tab | Reset group).

TO ADD A SHAPE TO A SMARTART GRAPHIC

If, instead of deleting a shape, you wanted to add a shape to a SmartArt graphic, you would perform the following step.

1. With the SmartArt graphic selected, click the Add Shape button (SmartArt Tools Design tab | Create Graphic group) or click the Add Shape button arrow and then click the desired location for the shape on the Add Shape menu.

To Apply a SmartArt Style

The next step is to apply a SmartArt style to the SmartArt graphic. Word provides a SmartArt Styles gallery, allowing you to change the SmartArt graphic's format to a more visually appealing style. The following steps apply a SmartArt style to a SmartArt graphic.

- With the SmartArt graphic still selected, click the More button in the SmartArt Styles gallery (shown in Figure 4–13 on the previous page) to expand the SmartArt Styles gallery.

- Point to Powder in the 3-D area of the SmartArt Styles gallery to display a live preview of that style applied to the graphic in the document (Figure 4–14).

Experiment

- Point to various SmartArt styles in the SmartArt Styles gallery and watch the style of the graphic change in the document window.

- Click Powder in the SmartArt Styles gallery to apply the selected style to the SmartArt graphic.

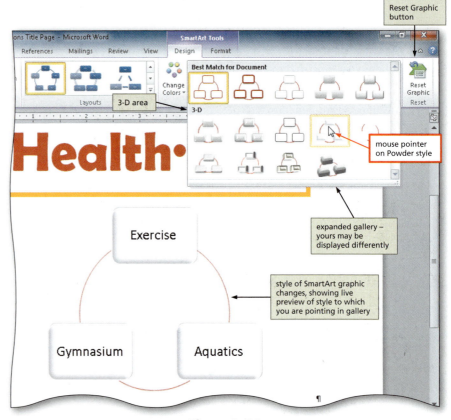

Figure 4–14

To Format Characters and Modify Character Spacing Using the Font Dialog Box

In this project, the next step is to enter and format the text at the bottom of the title page. This text is the theme of the proposal and is formatted so that it is noticeable. Its characters are 36-point bold, italic, aqua Book Antiqua. Each letter in this text is formatted in **small caps**, which are letters that look like capital letters but are not as tall as a typical capital letter. Also, you want extra space between each character so that the text spans the width of the page.

You could use buttons on the Home tab to apply some of these formats. The small caps effect and expanded spacing, however, are applied using the Font dialog box. Thus, the next steps apply all of the above-mentioned formats using the Font dialog box.

- Position the insertion point on the paragraph mark to the right of the SmartArt graphic and then press the ENTER key to position the insertion point centered below the SmartArt graphic.

- Type **Let us help you reach your fitness goals!**

- Select the sentence you just typed and then click the Font Dialog Box Launcher (Home tab | Font group) to display the Font dialog box. If necessary, click the Font tab in the dialog box to display the Font sheet.

- Scroll to and then click Book Antiqua in the Font list (Font dialog box) to change the font of the selected text.

- Click Bold Italic in the Font style list to bold and italicize the selected text.

- Scroll through the Size list and then click 36 to change the font size of the selected text.

- Click the Font color box arrow and then click Aqua, Accent 1 (fifth color, first row) in the Font color palette to change the color of the selected text.

- Click Small caps in the Effects area so that each character is displayed as a small capital letter (Figure 4–15).

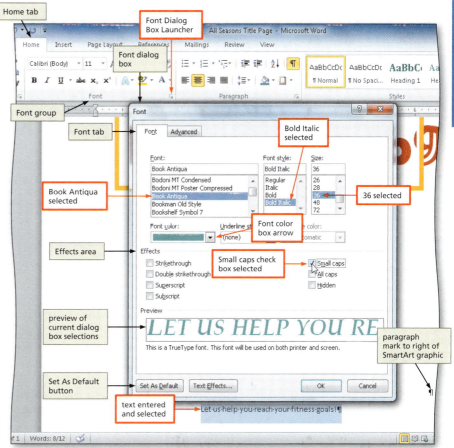

Figure 4–15

2

- Click the Advanced tab (Font dialog box) to display the Advanced sheet in the dialog box.

- Click the Spacing box arrow and then click Expanded to increase the amount of space between characters by 1 pt, which is the default.

- Click the Spacing By box up arrow until the box displays 4 pt because you want this amount of blank space to be displayed between each character (Figure 4–16).

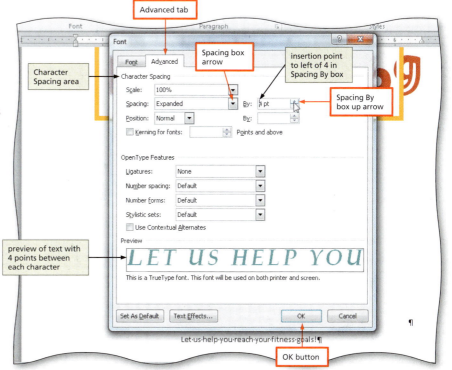

Figure 4–16

3

- Click the OK button to apply font changes to the selected text. If necessary, scroll so that the selected text is displayed completely in the document window.

- Click to remove the selection from the text (Figure 4–17).

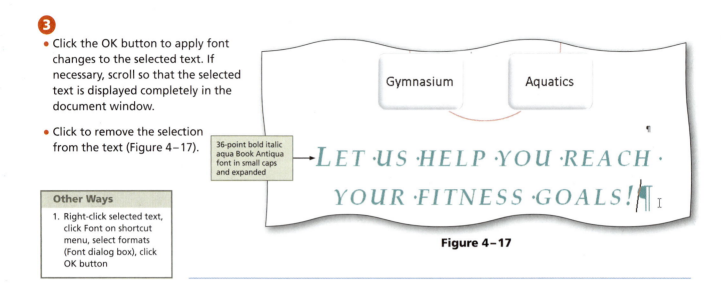

36-point bold italic aqua Book Antiqua font in small caps and expanded

Figure 4–17

Other Ways

1. Right-click selected text, click Font on shortcut menu, select formats (Font dialog box), click OK button

To Zoom One Page, Change Spacing before and after a Paragraph, and Set Zoom Level

The next step in creating the title page is to adjust spacing above and below the SmartArt graphic. You want to see the entire page while adjusting the spacing. Thus, the following steps zoom one page, increase spacing before and after the paragraph containing the SmartArt graphic, and then set the zoom level back to 100% because you will be finished with the title page.

1 Display the View tab. Click the One Page button (View tab | Zoom group) to display the entire page as large as possible centered in the document window.

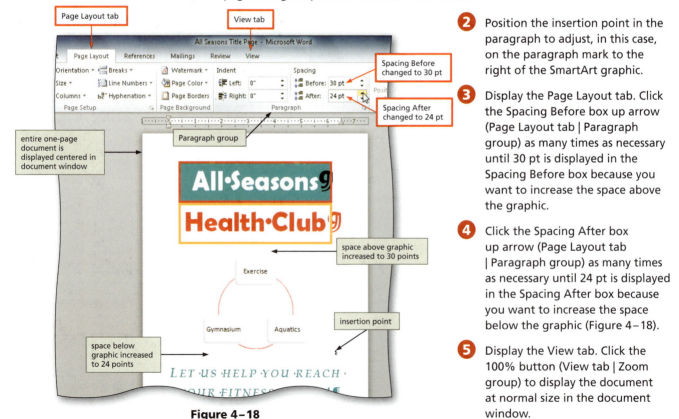

Figure 4–18

2 Position the insertion point in the paragraph to adjust, in this case, on the paragraph mark to the right of the SmartArt graphic.

3 Display the Page Layout tab. Click the Spacing Before box up arrow (Page Layout tab | Paragraph group) as many times as necessary until 30 pt is displayed in the Spacing Before box because you want to increase the space above the graphic.

4 Click the Spacing After box up arrow (Page Layout tab | Paragraph group) as many times as necessary until 24 pt is displayed in the Spacing After box because you want to increase the space below the graphic (Figure 4–18).

5 Display the View tab. Click the 100% button (View tab | Zoom group) to display the document at normal size in the document window.

To Save an Existing Document with the Same File Name

The title page for the sales proposal is complete. Thus, you should save it again. The following step saves the document again.

1 Click the Save button on the Quick Access Toolbar to overwrite the previously saved file.

Break Point: If you wish to take a break, this is a good place to do so. You can quit Word now. To resume at a later time, start Word, open the file called All Seasons Title Page, and continue following the steps from this location forward.

Inserting an Existing Document in an Open Document

Assume you already have prepared a draft of the body of the proposal and saved it with the file name, All Seasons Draft. You would like the draft to be displayed on a separate page following the title page.

Compose the sales proposal.
Be sure to include basic elements in your sales proposal:

- **Include an introduction, body, and conclusion.** The introduction could contain the subject, purpose, statement of problem, need, background, or scope. The body may include costs, benefits, supporting documentation, available or required facilities, feasibility, methods, timetable, materials, or equipment. The conclusion summarizes key points or requests an action.

- **Use headers and footers.** Headers and footers help to identify every page. A page number should be in either the header or footer. If the sales proposal ever becomes disassembled, the reader can use the headers and footers to determine the order and pieces of your proposal.

Plan Ahead

BTW

Inserting Documents
When you insert a Word document in another Word document, the entire inserted document is placed at the location of the insertion point. If the insertion point, therefore, is positioned in the middle of the open document when you insert another Word document, the open document continues after the last character of the inserted document.

In the following pages, you will insert the draft of the proposal below the title page and then edit the draft by deleting a page break, changing theme fonts, and applying Quick Styles.

To Save an Active Document with a New File Name

The current file name on the title bar is All Seasons Title Page, yet the document you will work on from this point forward in the chapter will contain both the title page and the body of the sales proposal. To keep the title page as a separate document called All Seasons Title Page, you should save the active document with a new file name. If you save the active document by clicking the Save button on the Quick Access Toolbar, Word will assign it the current file name. You want the active document to have a new file name. The following steps save the active document with a new file name.

1 With a USB flash drive connected to one of the computer's USB ports, click File on the Ribbon to open the Backstage view.

2 Click Save As in the Backstage view to display the Save As dialog box.

3 Type `All Seasons Sales Proposal` in the File name text box (Save As dialog box) to change the file name. Do not press the ENTER key after typing the file name because you do not want to close the dialog box at this time.

4 If necessary, navigate to the desired save location (in this case, the Word folder in the CIS 101 folder [or your class folder] on your USB flash drive).

5 Click the Save button (Save As dialog box) to save the document in the selected folder on the selected drive with the entered file name.

Sections

BTW

Section Numbers
If you want to display the current section number on the status bar, right-click the status bar to display the Customize Status Bar menu and then click Section on the Customize Status Bar menu. The section number appears at the left edge of the status bar. To remove the section number from the status bar, perform the same steps.

All Word documents have at least one section. A Word document can be divided into any number of sections. During the course of creating a document, you will create a new **section** if you need to change the top margin, bottom margin, page alignment, paper size, page orientation, page number position, or contents or position of headers, footers, or footnotes in just a portion of the document.

The next two pages of the sales proposal require page formatting different from that of the title page. The title page will not have a header or footer; the next two pages will have a header and footer.

When you want to change page formatting for a portion of a document, you create a new section in the document. Each section then may be formatted differently from the others. Thus, the title page formatted with no header or footer will be in one section, and the next two pages of the proposal that will have a header and footer will be in another section.

To Insert a Next Page Section Break

When you insert a section break, you specify whether the new section should begin on a new page. In this project, the title page is separate from the next two pages. Thus, the section break should contain a page break. The following steps insert a next page section break, which instructs Word to begin the new section on a new page in the document.

1

● Press CTRL+END to position the insertion point at the end of the title page, which is the location where you want to insert the next page section break.

● Display the Page Layout tab. Click the Insert Page and Section Breaks button (Page Layout tab | Page Setup group) to display the Insert Page and Section Breaks gallery (Figure 4–19).

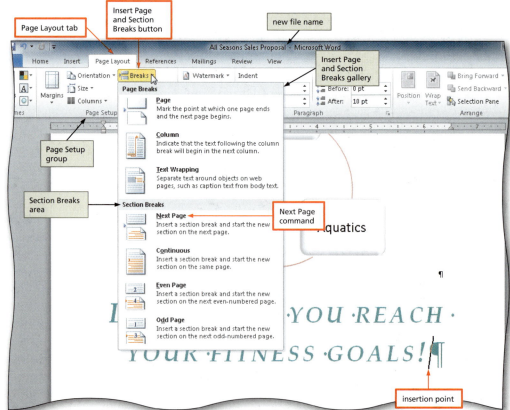

Figure 4–19

2

- Click Next Page in the Section Breaks area of the Insert Page and Section Breaks gallery to insert a next page section break in the document at the location of the insertion point. If necessary, scroll so that your screen matches Figure 4–20.

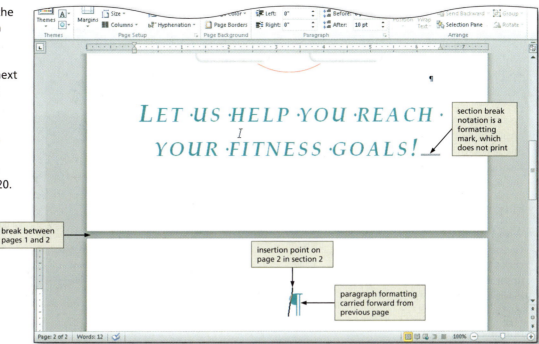

Figure 4–20

TO DELETE A SECTION BREAK

Word stores all section formatting in the section break. If you wanted to delete a section break and all associated section formatting, you would perform the following tasks.

1. Select the section break notation by dragging through it.
2. Right-click the selection to display a shortcut menu and then click Cut on the shortcut menu to delete the selection.

or

1. Position the insertion point immediately to the left or right of the section break notation.
2. Press the DELETE key to delete a section break to the right of the insertion point or press the BACKSPACE key to delete a section break to the left of the insertion point.

To Clear Formatting

When you create a section break, Word carries forward any formatting at the location of the insertion point to the next section. Thus, the current paragraph is formatted the same as the last line of the title page. In this project, the paragraphs and characters on the second page should return to the Normal style. Thus, the following step clears formatting.

1 Display the Home tab. With the insertion point positioned on the paragraph mark on the second page (shown in Figure 4–20), click the Clear Formatting button (Home tab | Font group) to apply the Normal style to the location of the insertion point (shown in Figure 4–21 on the next page).

BTW

Sections
To see the formatting associated with a section, double-click the section break notation or click the Page Setup Dialog Box Launcher (Page Layout tab | Page Setup group) to display the Page Setup dialog box. You can change margin settings and page orientation for a section in the Margins sheet. To change paper sizes for a section, click the Paper tab. The Layout tab allows you to change header and footer specifications and vertical alignment for the section. To add a border to a section, click the Borders button in the Layout sheet.

To Insert a Word Document in an Open Document

The next step is to insert the draft of the sales proposal at the top of the second page of the document. The draft is located on the Data Files for Students. See the inside back cover of this book for instructions on downloading the Data Files for Students, or contact your instructor for information about accessing the required files. The following steps insert an existing Word document in an open document.

1

- Be sure the insertion point is positioned on the paragraph mark at the top of page 2, which is the location where you want to insert the contents of the Word document.

- Display the Insert tab.

- With your USB flash drive connected to one of the computer's USB ports, click the Insert Object button arrow (Insert tab | Text group) to display the Insert Object menu (Figure 4–21).

Q&A What if I click the Insert Object button by mistake?

Click the Cancel button (Insert Object dialog box) and then repeat this step.

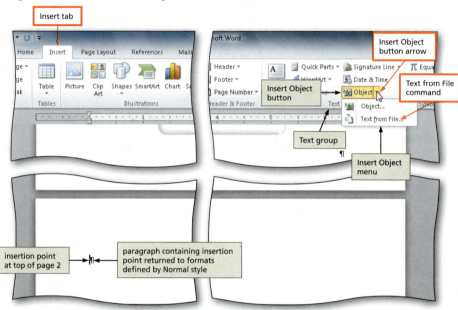

Figure 4–21

2

- Click Text from File on the Insert Object menu to display the Insert File dialog box.

- Navigate to the location of the file to be inserted (in this case, the Chapter 04 folder in the Word folder in the Data Files for Students folder on a USB flash drive).

- Click All Seasons Draft to select the file name (Figure 4–22).

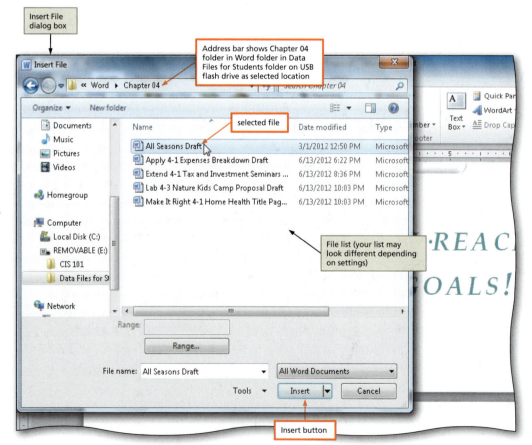

Figure 4–22

3

- Click the Insert button (Insert File dialog box) to insert the file, All Seasons Draft, in the open document at the location of the insertion point.

Q&A Where is the insertion point now?

When you insert a file in an open document, Word positions the insertion point at the end of the inserted document.

- Press SHIFT+F5 to position the insertion point on line 1 of page 2, which was its location prior to inserting the new Word document (Figure 4–23).

Q&A What is the purpose of SHIFT+F5?

The shortcut key, SHIFT+F5, positions the insertion point at your last editing location. Word remembers your last three editing locations, which means you can press this shortcut key repeatedly to return to one of your three most recent editing locations.

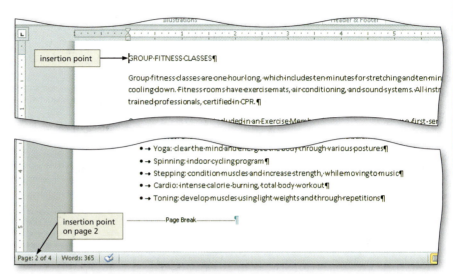

Figure 4–23

Other Ways
1. Click Insert Object button (Insert tab | Text group), click Create from File tab (Object dialog box), click	Browse button, locate file, click Insert button (Browse dialog box), click OK button (Object dialog box)

To Print Specific Pages in a Document

The title page is the first page of the proposal. The body of the proposal spans the second and third pages. The following steps print a hard copy of only the body of the proposal, that is, pages 2 and 3.

1

- Click File on the Ribbon to open the Backstage view and then click the Print tab in the Backstage view to display the Print gallery.

- Verify that the printer name that appears on the Printer Status button will print a hard copy of the document. If necessary, click the Printer Status button to display a list of available printer options and then click the desired printer to change the selected printer.

- Type 2–3 in the Pages text box in the Settings area of the Print gallery (Figure 4–24).

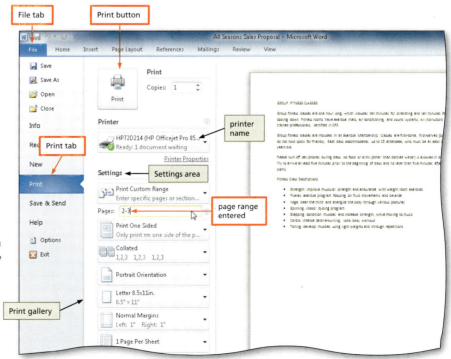

Figure 4–24

2

• Click the Print button to print the inserted draft of the sales proposal (Figure 4–25).

Q&A How would I print pages from a certain point to the end of a document?

You would enter the page number followed by a dash in the Pages text box. For example, 5- will print from page 5 to the end of the document. To print up to a certain page, put the dash first (e.g., -5 will print pages 1 through 5).

Q&A Why does my document wrap on different words than Figure 4–25?

Differences in wordwrap may be related to the printer used by your computer.

Q&A Why does my screen show the document has four pages?

You may have an extra blank page at the end of the document. This blank page will be deleted later in the chapter.

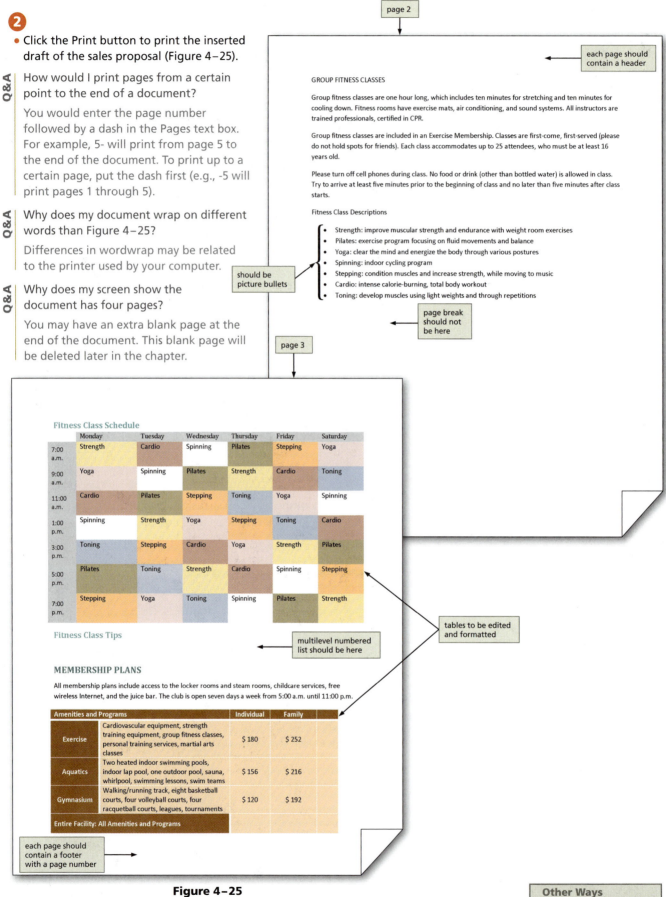

page 2

each page should contain a header

GROUP FITNESS CLASSES

Group fitness classes are one hour long, which includes ten minutes for stretching and ten minutes for cooling down. Fitness rooms have exercise mats, air conditioning, and sound systems. All instructors are trained professionals, certified in CPR.

Group fitness classes are included in an Exercise Membership. Classes are first-come, first-served (please do not hold spots for friends). Each class accommodates up to 25 attendees, who must be at least 16 years old.

Please turn off cell phones during class. No food or drink (other than bottled water) is allowed in class. Try to arrive at least five minutes prior to the beginning of class and no later than five minutes after class starts.

Fitness Class Descriptions

should be picture bullets

- Strength: improve muscular strength and endurance with weight room exercises
- Pilates: exercise program focusing on fluid movements and balance
- Yoga: clear the mind and energize the body through various postures
- Spinning: indoor cycling program
- Stepping: condition muscles and increase strength, while moving to music
- Cardio: intense calorie-burning, total body workout
- Toning: develop muscles using light weights and through repetitions

page break should not be here

page 3

Fitness Class Schedule

	Monday	Tuesday	Wednesday	Thursday	Friday	Saturday
7:00 a.m.	Strength	Cardio	Spinning	Pilates	Stepping	Yoga
9:00 a.m.	Yoga	Spinning	Pilates	Strength	Cardio	Toning
11:00 a.m.	Cardio	Pilates	Stepping	Toning	Yoga	Spinning
1:00 p.m.	Spinning	Strength	Yoga	Stepping	Toning	Cardio
3:00 p.m.	Toning	Stepping	Cardio	Yoga	Strength	Pilates
5:00 p.m.	Pilates	Toning	Strength	Cardio	Spinning	Stepping
7:00 p.m.	Stepping	Yoga	Toning	Spinning	Pilates	Strength

Fitness Class Tips

multilevel numbered list should be here

tables to be edited and formatted

MEMBERSHIP PLANS

All membership plans include access to the locker rooms and steam rooms, childcare services, free wireless Internet, and the juice bar. The club is open seven days a week from 5:00 a.m. until 11:00 p.m.

Amenities and Programs		Individual	Family	
Exercise	Cardiovascular equipment, strength training equipment, group fitness classes, personal training services, martial arts classes	$ 180	$ 252	
Aquatics	Two heated indoor swimming pools, indoor lap pool, one outdoor pool, sauna, whirlpool, swimming lessons, swim teams	$ 156	$ 216	
Gymnasium	Walking/running track, eight basketball courts, four volleyball courts, four racquetball courts, leagues, tournaments	$ 120	$ 192	
Entire Facility: All Amenities and Programs				

each page should contain a footer with a page number

Figure 4–25

Other Ways

1. Press CTRL+P; press ENTER

To Delete a Page Break

After reviewing the draft in Figure 4–25, you notice it contains a page break below the bulleted list. This page break should not be in the document. The following steps delete a page break.

1

- To select the page break notation, position the mouse pointer to the left of the page break and then click when the mouse pointer changes to a right-pointing arrow (Figure 4–26).

2

- Press the DELETE key to remove the page break from the document (shown in Figure 4–27 on the next page).

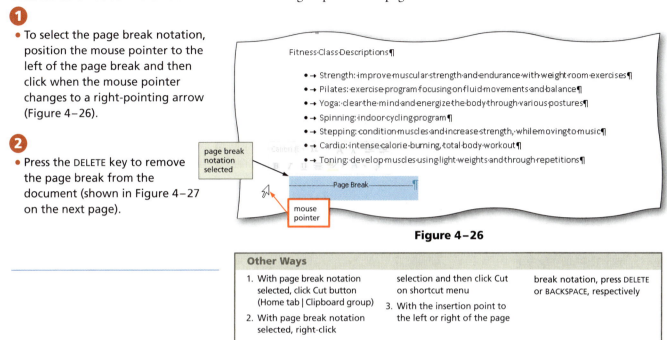

Figure 4–26

Other Ways
1. With page break notation selected, click Cut button (Home tab | Clipboard group) 2. With page break notation selected, right-click	selection and then click Cut on shortcut menu 3. With the insertion point to the left or right of the page	break notation, press DELETE or BACKSPACE, respectively

TO MODIFY THE DEFAULT FONT SETTINGS

You can change the default font so that the current document and all future documents use the new font settings. That is, if you quit Word, restart the computer, and restart Word, documents you create will use the new default font. If you wanted to change the default font from 11-point Calibri to another font, font style, font size, font color, and/or font effects, you would perform the following steps.

1. Display the Font dialog box.

2. Make desired changes to the font settings in the Font dialog box.

3. Click the Set As Default button (shown in Figure 4–15 on page WD 217) to change the default settings to those specified in Step 2.

4. When the Microsoft Word dialog box is displayed, select the desired option button and then click the Yes button.

TO RESET THE DEFAULT FONT SETTINGS

To change the font settings back to the default, you would follow the above steps, using the default font settings when performing Step 2. If you do not remember the default settings, you would perform the following steps to restore the original Normal style settings.

1. Quit Word.

2. Use Windows Explorer to locate the normal.dotm file (be sure that hidden files and folders are displayed and include system and hidden files in your search), which is the file that contains default font and other settings.

3. Rename the normal.dotm file to oldnormal.dotm file so that the normal.dotm file no longer exists.

4. Start Word, which will re-create a normal.dotm file using the original default settings.

BTW

Certification
The Microsoft Office Specialist (MOS) program provides an opportunity for you to obtain a valuable industry credential — proof that you have the Word 2010 skills required by employers. For more information, visit the Word 2010 Certification Web page (scsite.com/wd2010/cert).

To Change Theme Fonts

The next step is to change the font used for the text in the document because you want a different look for the text. If text is entered using the headings and body text fonts, you easily can change the font in the entire document by changing the font set. A **font set** defines one font for headings and another for body text. The Office font set uses the Cambria font for headings and the Calibri font for body text. In Word, you can select from more than 40 predefined, coordinated font sets to give the document's text a new look.

If you previously changed a font using buttons on the Ribbon or Mini toolbar, Word will not alter those when you change the font set because changes to the font set are not applied to individually changed fonts. This means the font of the title on the title page will remain as Berlin Sans FB Demi when you change the font set. The following steps change the font set to Apothecary, which uses the Book Antiqua font for headings and the Century Gothic font for body text.

 1

- Display the Home tab.

- Click the Change Styles button (Home tab | Styles group) to display the Change Styles menu.

- Point to Fonts on the Change Styles menu to display the Fonts gallery.

- Scroll through the Fonts gallery until Apothecary is displayed and then point to Apothecary to display a live preview of the selected font set (Figure 4–27).

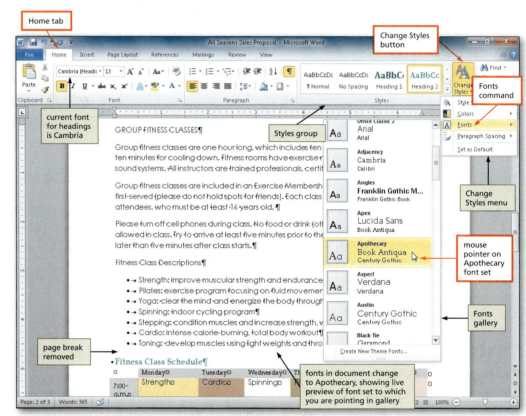

Figure 4–27

🔍 **Experiment**

- Point to various font sets in the Fonts gallery and watch the fonts of text in the document change.

 2

- Click Apothecary in the Fonts gallery to change the document theme fonts.

Q&A   What if I want to return to the original font set?

You would click the Change Styles button, click Fonts on the Change Styles menu, and then click Office in the Fonts gallery.

Other Ways

1. Click Theme Fonts button (Page Layout tab | Themes group), select desired font set

To Apply a Heading Quick Style

Word has many built-in, or predefined, styles called Quick Styles that you can use to format text. Three of the Quick Styles are for headings: Heading 1 for the major headings and Heading 2 and Heading 3 for minor headings. In the All Seasons Draft, all headings except for the first two were formatted using heading styles. The following steps apply the Heading 1 style to the paragraph containing the text, GROUP FITNESS CLASSES, and the Heading 2 style to the paragraph containing the text, Fitness Class Descriptions.

1 Position the insertion point in the paragraph to be formatted to the Heading 1 style, in this case, the first line on the second page with the text, GROUP FITNESS CLASSES.

2 Click Heading 1 in the Quick Style gallery (Home tab | Styles group) to apply the selected style to the paragraph containing the insertion point.

Q&A Why did a square appear on the screen near the left edge of the paragraph formatted with the Heading 1 style?

The square is a nonprinting character, like the paragraph mark, that indicates text to its right has a special paragraph format applied to it.

3 Position the insertion point in the paragraph to be formatted to the Heading 2 style, in this case, the line above the bulleted list with the text, Fitness Class Descriptions.

4 Click Heading 2 in the Quick Style gallery (Home tab | Styles group) to apply the selected style to the paragraph containing the insertion point (Figure 4–28).

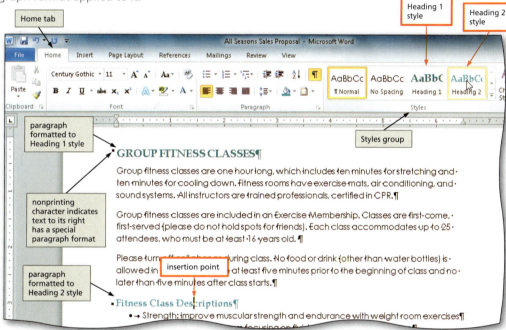

Figure 4–28

To Change Spacing before and after a Paragraph

The next step is to adjust spacing above and below the current paragraph, that is, the heading above the bulleted list. This paragraph is formatted using the Heading 2 style, which places 10 points of space above the paragraph and no space below the paragraph. You would like this paragraph, and all other paragraphs formatted using the Heading 2 style, to have 12 points of space above them and 6 points of space below them. Thus, the following steps adjust the spacing before and after a paragraph.

1 Display the Page Layout tab. Click the Spacing Before box up arrow (Page Layout tab | Paragraph group) so that 12 pt is displayed in the Spacing Before box.

2 Click the Spacing After box up arrow (Page Layout tab | Paragraph group) so that 6 pt is displayed in the Spacing After box.

To Update a Style to Match a Selection

You want all paragraphs formatted in the Heading 2 style in the proposal to use this adjusted spacing. Thus, the following steps update the Heading 2 style so that this adjusted spacing is applied to all Heading 2 paragraphs in the document.

1 If necessary, position the insertion point in the paragraph containing the style to be updated.

2 Display the Home tab. Right-click Heading 2 in the Quick Style gallery (Home tab | Styles group) to display a shortcut menu (Figure 4–29).

3 Click Update Heading 2 to Match Selection on the shortcut menu to update the Heading 2 style to reflect the settings at the location of the insertion point.

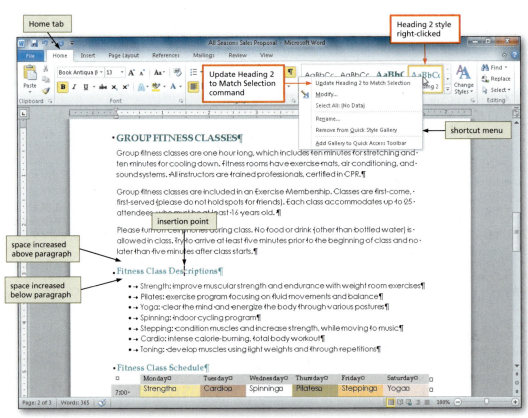

Figure 4–29

Creating Headers and Footers

A **header** is text that prints at the top of each page in the document. A **footer** is text that prints at the bottom of each page. In this proposal, you want the header and footer to appear on each page after the title page; that is, you do not want the header and footer on the title page. Recall that the title page is in a separate section from the rest of the sales proposal. Thus, the header and footer should not be in section 1, but they should be in section 2. The steps on the following pages explain how to create a header and footer in section 2 only.

BTW

Headers and Footers
If a portion of a header or footer does not print, it may be in a nonprintable area. Check the printer manual to see how close the printer can print to the edge of the paper. Then, click the Page Setup Dialog Box Launcher (Page Layout tab | Page Setup group), click the Layout tab (Page Setup dialog box), adjust the From edge text box to a value that is larger than the printer's minimum margin setting, click the OK button, and then print the document again.

To Insert a Formatted Header Different from the Previous Header

Word provides several built-in preformatted header designs for you to insert in documents. The following steps insert a formatted header in section 2 of the sales proposal.

1

- Display the Insert tab. Click the Header button (Insert tab | Header & Footer group) and then click Edit Header in the Header gallery to switch to the header for section 2.

- If the Link to Previous button (Header & Footer Tools Design tab | Navigation group) is selected, click it to deselect the button because you do not want the header in this section to be copied to the previous section (that is, the header should not be on the title page).

- Click the Header button (Header & Footer Tools Design tab | Header & Footer group) to display the Header gallery (Figure 4–30).

Experiment

- Scroll through the list of built-in headers to see the variety of available formatted header designs.

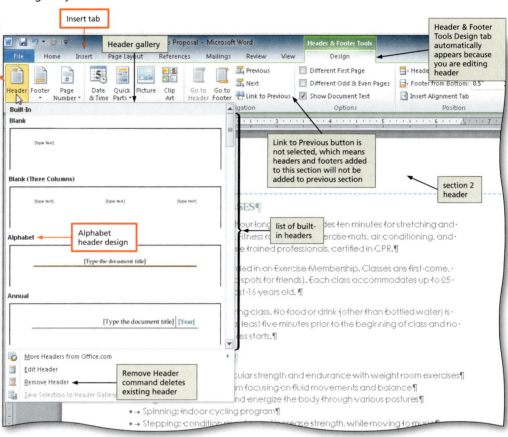

Figure 4–30

2

- Scroll to and then click the Alphabet header design in the Header gallery to insert the formatted header in the header of section 2, which contains a content control (Figure 4–31).

Q&A

What is a content control?

A **content control** is an object that contains instructions for filling in text and graphics.

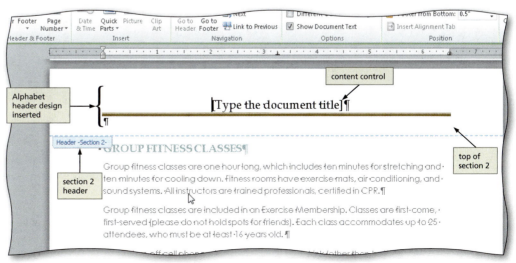

Figure 4–31

3
- Click the content control, Type the document title, to select it and then type **All Seasons Health Club** in the content control (Figure 4–32).

How would I delete a header?

You would click Remove Header in the Header gallery.

Figure 4–32

Other Ways

1. Click Header button (Insert tab | Header & Footer group), select desired header in list
2. Click Quick Parts button (Insert tab | Text group),

click Building Blocks Organizer on Quick Parts menu, select desired header (Building Blocks Organizer dialog box), click Insert button

To Insert a Formatted Footer

The next step is to insert the footer. Word provides the same built-in preformatted footer designs as header designs. The footer design that corresponds to the header just inserted contains text at the left margin and a page number at the right margin. The following steps insert a formatted footer in section 2 of the sales proposal that corresponds to the header just inserted.

1 Click the Footer button (Header & Footer Tools Design tab | Header & Footer group) to display the Footer gallery.

Linking Sections
If you wanted the same header or footer to appear in multiple sections, you would select the Link to Previous button (Header & Footer Tools Design tab | Navigation group).

2 Click the Alphabet footer design to insert the formatted footer in the footer of section 2.

3 Click the content control, Type text, and then type **CALL 555-2283 TO JOIN!** in the content control (Figure 4–33).

Why is the page number a 2?

The page number is 2 because, by default, Word begins numbering pages from the beginning of the document.

Page Numbers
If Word displays {PAGE} instead of the actual page number, press ALT+F9 to turn off field codes. If Word prints {PAGE} instead of the page number, open the Backstage view, click Options, click Advanced in the left pane, scroll to the Print area, remove the check mark from the 'Print field codes instead of their values' check box, and then click the OK button.

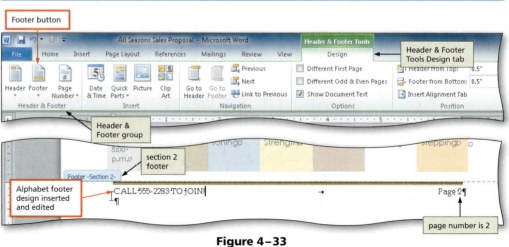

Figure 4–33

To Format Page Numbers to Start at a Different Number

On the page after the title page in the proposal, you want to begin numbering with a number 1, instead of a 2 as shown in Figure 4–33. Thus, you need to instruct Word to begin numbering the pages in section 2 with the number 1. The following steps format the page numbers so that they start at a different number.

- Click the Insert Page Number button (Header & Footer Tools Design tab | Header & Footer group) to display the Insert Page Number menu (Figure 4–34).

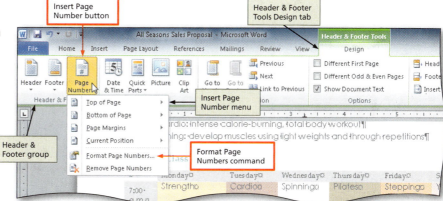

Figure 4–34

- Click Format Page Numbers on the Insert Page Number menu to display the Page Number Format dialog box.

- Click Start at in the Page numbering area (Page Number Format dialog box), which displays a 1 by default as the starting page number (Figure 4–35).

Q&A

Can I also change the look of the page number?

Yes. Click the Number format box arrow (Page Number Format dialog box) for a list of page number variations.

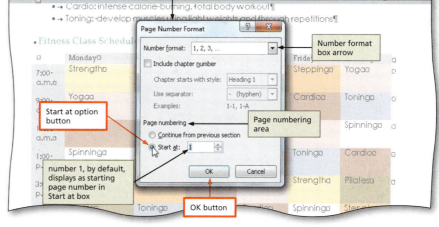

Figure 4–35

- Click the OK button to change the starting page number for section 2 to the number 1 (Figure 4–36).

- Click the Close Header and Footer button (Header & Footer Tools Design tab | Close group) to close the header and footer.

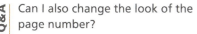

Other Ways

1. Click Insert Page Number (Insert tab | Header & Footer group), click Format Page Numbers on Insert Page Number menu, set page formats (Page Number Format dialog box), click OK button

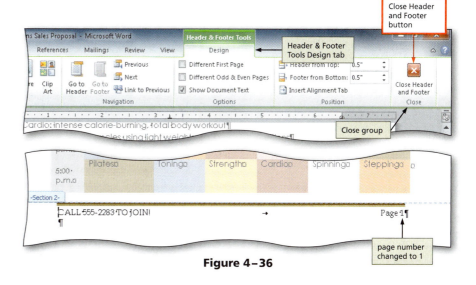

Figure 4–36

Editing and Formatting Lists

The finished sales proposal in this chapter has two lists: a bulleted list and a numbered list (shown in Figures 4–1b and 4–1c on page WD 203). The bulleted list is in alphabetical (sorted) order, the first word of each list item is emphasized, and the bullets are graphical instead of simple round dots. The numbered listed has multiple levels for each numbered item. The following pages illustrate steps used to edit and format the lists in the proposal:

1. Sort a list of paragraphs.
2. Format the first word in the first list item and then copy the format to the first word in each of the remaining list items.
3. Customize bullets in a list of paragraphs.
4. Create a multilevel numbered list.

To Sort Paragraphs

The next step is to alphabetize the paragraphs in the bulleted list. In Word, you can arrange paragraphs in alphabetic, numeric, or date order based on the first character in each paragraph. Ordering characters in this manner is called **sorting**. The following steps sort paragraphs.

1

- If necessary, scroll to display the paragraphs to be sorted.

- Drag through the paragraphs to be sorted, in this case, the bulleted list.

- Click the Sort button (Home tab | Paragraph group) to display the Sort Text dialog box (Figure 4–37).

Q&A

What does ascending mean?

Ascending means to sort in alphabetic, numeric, or earliest-to-latest date order.

2

- Click the OK button (Sort Text dialog box) to instruct Word to alphabetize the selected paragraphs (shown in Figure 4–38).

- Click anywhere to remove the selection from the text.

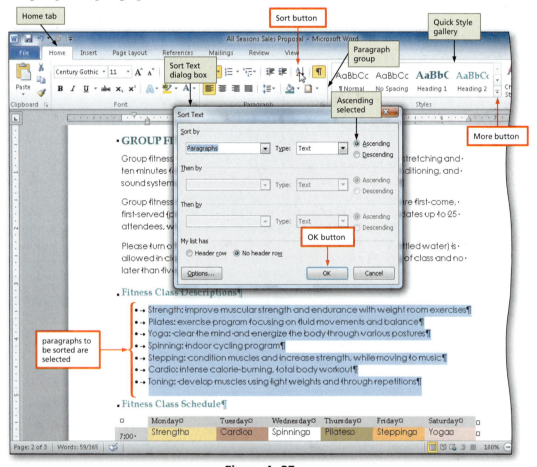

Figure 4–37

To Apply a Quick Style

The first word in each list item is formatted in bold, blue, and italic. Although you could apply formatting using buttons in the Font group on the Ribbon, it is more efficient to use the Intense Emphasis style. If you use a style and decide at a later time that you want to modify the formatting, you simply modify the style and Word will apply the changes to all text formatted with that style. Thus, the following steps format a word using a Quick Style.

1 Position the insertion point in the word to be formatted (in this case, the word, Cardio, in the first list item).

2 Click the More button in the Quick Style gallery (shown in Figure 4–37) to expand the gallery and then point to Intense Emphasis in the Quick Style gallery to see a live preview of the selected format applied to the word containing the insertion point in the document (Figure 4–38).

3 Click Intense Emphasis in the Quick Style gallery to apply the selected style to the word containing the insertion point.

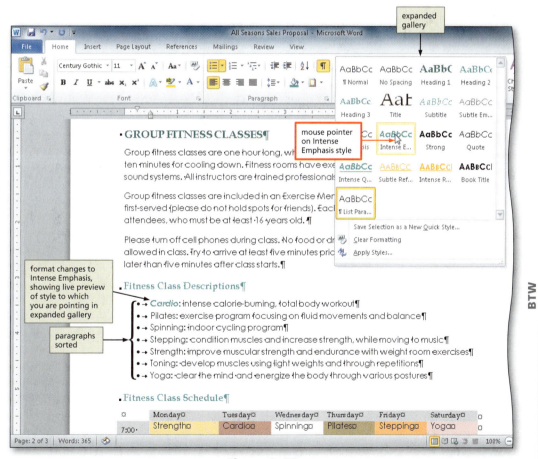

Figure 4–38

BTW

Format Painter
If you also want to copy paragraph formatting, such as alignment and line spacing, select the paragraph mark at the end of the paragraph prior to clicking the Format Painter button. If you want to copy only character formatting, such as fonts and font sizes, do not include the paragraph mark in your selected text.

To Use the Format Painter Button

The first word in each of the remaining list items is to be formatted the same as the first word in the first list item. Instead of selecting each word one at a time and then formatting it, you will copy the format from the first word to the remaining words. The steps on the next page copy formatting.

- Position the insertion point in the text that contains the formatting you wish to copy (in this case, the word, Cardio).

- Double-click the Format Painter button (Home tab | Clipboard group) to turn on the format painter.

Q&A Why double-click the Format Painter button?

To copy formats to only one other location, click the Format Painter button (Home tab | Clipboard group) once. If you want to copy formatting to multiple locations, however, double-click the Format Painter button so that the format painter remains active until you turn it off.

- Move the mouse pointer to where you want to copy the formatting (the word, Pilates, in this case) and notice that the format painter is active (Figure 4–39).

Q&A How can I tell if the format painter is active?

The mouse pointer has a paintbrush attached to it when the format painter is active.

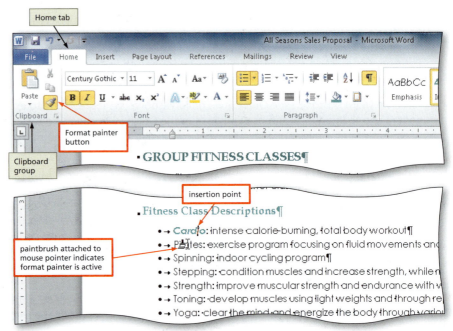

Figure 4–39

- Click the first word in the next list item (the word, Pilates, in this case) to paste the copied format to the selected text.

Q&A What if the Format Painter button no longer is selected?

Repeat Step 1.

- Repeat Step 2 for the remaining first words in the list items: Spinning, Stepping, Strength, Toning, and Yoga.

- Click the Format Painter button (Home tab | Clipboard group) to turn off the format painter (Figure 4–40).

Q&A How would I copy formatting to a group of words or paragraphs?

Instead of clicking the text, you would select it.

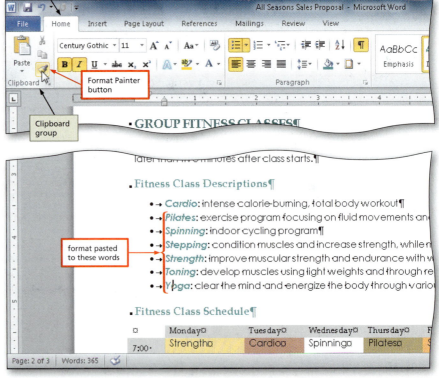

Figure 4–40

To Customize Bullets in a List

The bulleted list in the sales proposal draft uses default bullet characters, that is, the dot symbol. You want to use a more visually appealing picture bullet. The following steps change the bullets in a list from the default to picture bullets.

- Select all the paragraphs in the bulleted list.

- Click the Bullets button arrow (Home tab | Paragraph group) to display the Bullets gallery (Figure 4–41).

Q&A

Can I select any of the bullet characters in the Bullet Library area of the Bullets gallery?

Yes, but if you prefer a different bullet character, follow the rest of these steps.

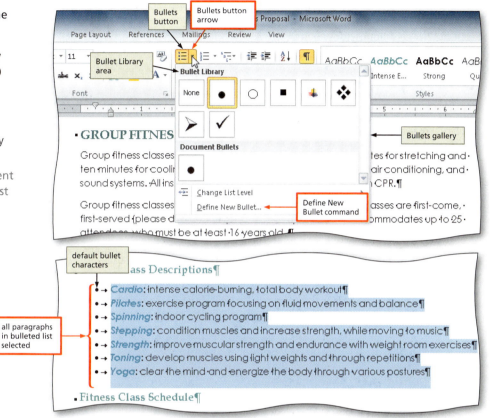

Figure 4–41

2

- Click Define New Bullet in the Bullets gallery to display the Define New Bullet dialog box.

- Click the Picture button (Define New Bullet dialog box) to display the Picture Bullet dialog box.

Experiment

- Scroll through the list of picture bullets (Picture Bullet dialog box) to see the available bullet characters.

- If necessary, scroll to the top of the list of picture bullets (Picture Bullet dialog box) and then select the picture bullet shown in Figure 4–42 (or a similar picture bullet).

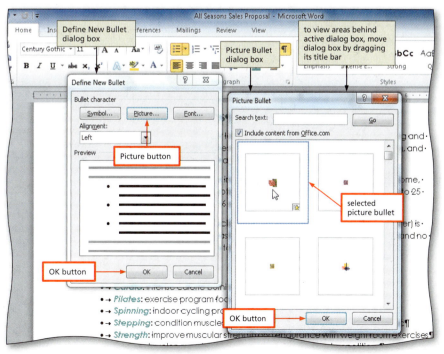

Figure 4–42

- Click the OK button (Picture Bullet dialog box) to close the dialog box and show a preview of the selected picture bullet in the Define New Bullet dialog box.

- Click the OK button (Define New Bullet dialog box) to change the bullets in the selected list to picture bullets.

- When the Word window is visible again, click in the selected list to remove the selection (Figure 4–43).

Figure 4–43

To Create a Multilevel Numbered List

The next step is to create a multilevel numbered list below the Fitness Class Tips heading on the last page of the sales proposal in this chapter (shown in Figure 4–1c on page WD 203). A **multilevel list** is a list that contains several levels of list items, with each lower level displaying a different numeric, alphabetic, or bullet character. In a multilevel list, the first level is displayed at the left edge of the list and subsequent levels are indented; that is, the second level is indented below the first, the third level is indented below the second level, and so on. The list is referred to as a numbered list if the first level contains numbers or letters and is referred to as a bulleted list if the first level contains a character other than a number or letter.

For the list in this project, the first level uses numbers (i.e., 1., 2., 3.), the second level uses lowercase letters (a., b., c.), and the third level uses lowercase Roman numerals (i.e., i., ii., iii.). The following steps create a multilevel numbered list.

1

- Position the insertion point at the location for the multilevel numbered list, which in this case is the blank line below the Fitness Class Tips heading on the last page of the sales proposal.

- Click the Numbering button (Home tab | Paragraph group) to format the current paragraph as a list item using the current number format, which in this case is an indented 1 followed by a period.

What if I wanted a different number format?

You would click the Numbering button arrow (Home tab | Paragraph group) and then select the desired number format in the Numbering gallery, or click the Define New Number Format command in the Numbering gallery to define your own number format.

- Type `Keep your body adequately hydrated` as a first-level list item and then press the ENTER key, which automatically places the next sequential number for the current level at the beginning of the next line (in this case, 2.) (Figure 4–44).

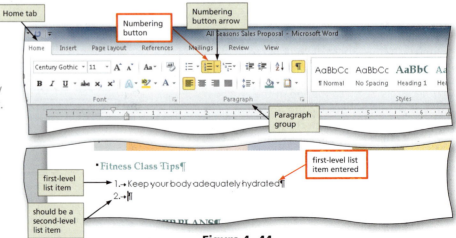

Figure 4–44

● Press the TAB key to demote the current list item (the 2.) to the next lower level, which is indented below the higher-level list item (in this case, converting 2. to a.).

Q&A

What if I wanted a different multilevel list format?

You would click the Multilevel List button (Home tab | Paragraph group) and then select the desired list style.

● Type the text for list item 1-a as shown in Figure 4–45 and then press the ENTER key, which automatically places the next sequential list item for the current level on the next line (in this case, b.).

● Type the text for list item 1-b as shown in Figure 4–45 and then press the ENTER key, which automatically places the next sequential list item on the next line (in this case, c.).

● Type the text for list item 1-c as shown in Figure 4–45 and then press the ENTER key, which automatically places the next sequential list item on the next line (Figure 4–45).

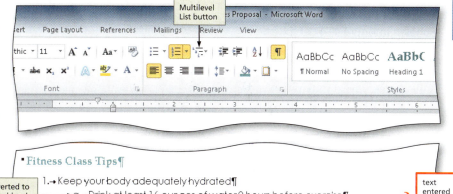

Figure 4–45

● Press SHIFT+TAB to promote the current-level list item to a higher-level list item (in this case, converting d. to 2.).

● Type **Dress comfortably** as a first-level list item and then press the ENTER key.

● Press the TAB key to demote the current level list item to a lower-level list item (in this case, converting 3. to a.).

● Type the text for list item 2-a as shown in Figure 4–46 and then press the ENTER key.

Figure 4–46

● Type the text for list item 2-b as shown in Figure 4–46 and then press the ENTER key.

● Type the text for list item 2-c as shown in Figure 4–46 and then press the ENTER key.

● Press SHIFT+TAB to promote the current-level list item to a higher-level list item (in this case, converting d. to 3.).

● Type **Reward yourself** as a first-level list item, press the ENTER key, and then press the TAB key to demote the current-level list item to a lower-level list item (in this case, converting 4. to a.).

● Type **Short term** as a second-level list item and then press the ENTER key (Figure 4–46).

5

- Press the TAB key to demote the current-level list item to a lower-level list item (in this case, converting b. to i.).

- Type the text for list item 3-a-i as shown in Figure 4–47 and then press the ENTER key.

- Type the text for list item 3-a-ii as shown in Figure 4–47 and then press the ENTER key.

- Press SHIFT+TAB to promote the current-level list item to a higher-level list item (in this case, converting iii. to b.).

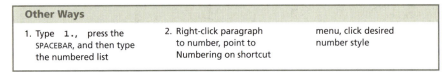

Figure 4–47

- Type **Long term** as a second-level list item and then press the ENTER key.

- Press the TAB key to demote the current-level list item to a lower-level list item (in this case, converting c. to i.).

- Type the text for list item 3-b-i as shown in Figure 4–47 and then press the ENTER key.

- Type the text for list item 3-b-ii as shown in Figure 4–47 to complete the multilevel list.

Q&A

Can I adjust the level of a list item after it is typed?

Yes. With the insertion point in the item to adjust, click the Increase Indent or Decrease Indent button (Home tab | Paragraph group), press TAB or SHIFT+TAB, right-click the list item, and then click the desired command on the shortcut menu, or point to Change List Level in the Bullets or Numbering gallery and then click the desired list level on the submenu.

Other Ways

1. Type **1.**, press the SPACEBAR, and then type the numbered list

2. Right-click paragraph to number, point to Numbering on shortcut menu, click desired number style

---

To Save an Existing Document with the Same File Name

You have made several modifications to the document since you last saved it. Thus, you should save it again. The following step saves the document again.

1 Click the Save button on the Quick Access Toolbar to overwrite the previously saved file.

Break Point: If you wish to take a break, this is a good place to do so. You can quit Word now. To resume at a later time, start Word, open the file called All Seasons Sales Proposal, and continue following the steps from this location forward.

Editing and Formatting Tables

The sales proposal draft contains two Word tables: the fitness class schedule table and the membership plans table (shown in Figure 4–25 on page WD 224). The fitness class schedule table shows the days and times for various fitness classes, and the membership plans table shows the costs of various membership plans. In this section, you will make several modifications to these two tables so that they appear as shown in Figure 4–1 on page WD 203.

Plan Ahead

Enhance the sales proposal with appropriate visuals.
Studies have shown that most people are visually oriented, preferring images to text. Use tables to clarify ideas and illustrate points. Be aware, however, that too many visuals can clutter a document.

The following pages explain how to modify the tables in the sales proposal draft:

1. Fitness Class Schedule Table
   a. Change the column width for the column containing the class times.
   b. Change row heights so that they are not so tall.
   c. Shade table cells containing Spinning classes.
   d. Change cell spacing.
   e. Change the column width of days of week columns.

2. Membership Plans Table
   a. Delete the extra column on the right edge of the table.
   b. Sort the table contents by facility.
   c. Split table cells so that the heading, Amenities and Programs, is above the second column.
   d. Display text in a cell vertically to the left of the table.
   e. Remove cell shading from the table.
   f. Add borders to the table.
   g. Sum columns in the table.

BTW

Table Wrapping
If you want text to wrap around a table, instead of displaying above and below the table, do the following: right-click the table and then click Table Properties on the shortcut menu or click the Table Properties button (Table Tools Layout tab | Table group), click the Table tab (Table Properties dialog box), click Around in the Text wrapping area, and then click the OK button.

To Show Gridlines

When a table contains no borders, it sometimes is difficult to see the individual cells in the table. To help identify the location of cells, you can display gridlines, which show cell outlines on the screen. Gridlines are formatting marks, which means the gridlines do not print. The following step shows gridlines.

1

- Display the table to be edited in the document window (in this case, the fitness class schedule table).

- Position the insertion point in any cell in the table.

- Display the Table Tools Layout tab.

- If gridlines are not displayed on the screen, click the View Table Gridlines button (Table Tools Layout tab | Table group) to show gridlines in the table (Figure 4–48).

Q&A

How do I turn table gridlines off?

Click the View Table Gridlines button again.

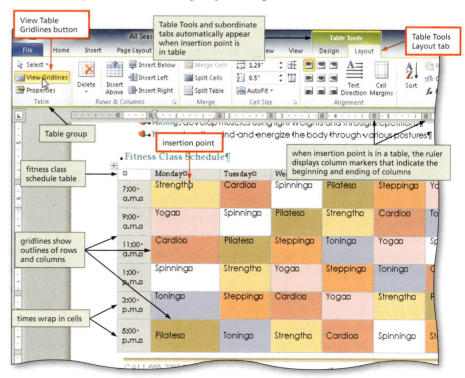

Figure 4–48

To Change Column Width

Notice in Figure 4–48 on the previous page that the leftmost column containing the class start times is not wide enough to fit the contents; that is, the times wrap in the cells. In this proposal, the times should appear on a single line that is just wide enough to accommodate the class start times. Thus, you will change the column width of just this single column. You can change column widths by entering a specific value on the Ribbon or in a dialog box, or by using a marker on the ruler or the column boundary. The following steps change column width by dragging a column's boundary.

- Position the mouse pointer on the column boundary to the right of the column to adjust (in this case, to the right of the first column) so that the mouse pointer changes to a double arrow split by two vertical bars (Figure 4–49).

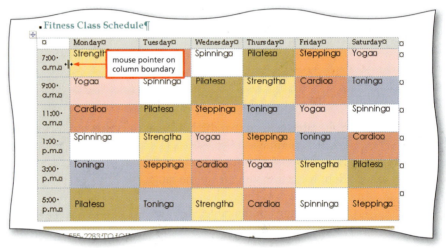

Figure 4–49

- Double-click the column boundary so that Word adjusts the column width according to the column contents. If all of the times still are not displayed on a single line, double-click the column boundary again so that all of the times show on a single line (Figure 4–50).

🔍 Experiment

- Practice changing this column's width using other techniques: drag the Move Table Column marker on the horizontal ruler to the right and then to the left. Click the Table Column Width box up and down arrows (Table Tools Layout tab | Cell Size group). When you have finished experimenting, type 1.29 in the Table Column Width box (Table Tools Layout tab | Cell Size group).

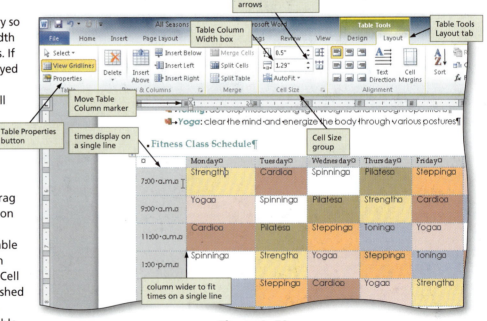

Figure 4–50

Other Ways

1. Drag Move Table Column marker on horizontal ruler to desired width

2. Enter desired value in Table Column Width box

(Table Tools Layout tab | Cell Size group)

3. Click Table Properties button (Table Tools Layout tab | Table group), click

Column tab, enter width, click OK button

To Hide White Space

The fitness class schedule table currently continues on the top of the next page in the document, and the headers and footers make it difficult to see the entire table at once. With the screen in Print Layout view, you can hide white space, which is the space that is displayed in the margins at the top and bottom of pages (including any headers and footers) and also the space between pages. The following steps hide white space, if your screen displays it.

1

- Position the mouse pointer in the document window in the space between the pages so that the mouse pointer changes to a Hide White Space button (Figure 4–51).

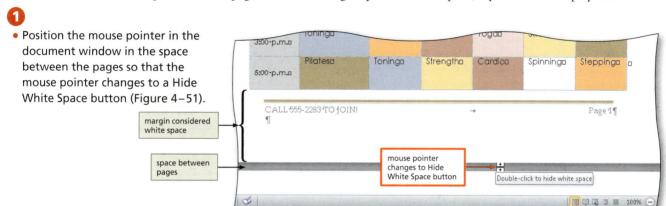

Figure 4–51

2

- While the mouse pointer is a Hide White Space button, double-click the mouse to hide white space, that is, the top and bottom margins and space between pages (Figure 4–52).

Q&A Does hiding white space have any effect on the printed document?

No.

Q&A How would I show white space again?

You would point to a line between two pages and double-click when the mouse pointer changes to a Show White Space button.

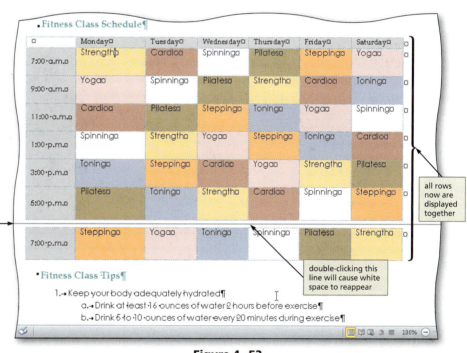

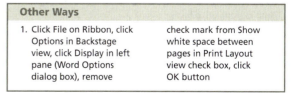

Figure 4–52

Other Ways

1. Click File on Ribbon, click Options in Backstage view, click Display in left pane (Word Options dialog box), remove check mark from Show white space between pages in Print Layout view check box, click OK button

To Change Row Height

The next step in this project is to narrow the height of the rows containing the classes. You change row height in the same ways you change column width. That is, you can change row height by entering a specific value on the Ribbon or in a dialog box, or by using a marker on the ruler or the row boundary. The latter two, however, work only for a single row at a time. The steps on the next page change row height by entering a value on the Ribbon.

1
• Select the rows to change (in this case, all the rows below the first row that contains the days of the week).

How do I select rows?

Point to the left of the first row and then drag downward when the mouse pointer changes to a right-pointing arrow.

2
• Click the Table Row Height box up or down arrows (Table Tools Layout tab | Cell Size group) as many times as necessary until the box displays 0.4" to change the row height to this value (Figure 4–53).

• Click anywhere to remove the selection from the table.

Figure 4–53

Other Ways

1. Click Table Properties button (Table Tools Layout tab | Table group), click Row tab (Table Properties dialog box), enter row height, click OK button

2. Right-click selected row, click Table Properties on shortcut menu, click Row tab, enter row height (Table Properties dialog box), click OK button

3. For a single row, drag row boundary (horizontal gridline at bottom of row in table) to desired height

4. Drag Adjust Table Row marker on vertical ruler to desired height

Page Breaks and Tables
If you do not want a page break to occur in the middle of a table, position the insertion point in the table, click the Table Properties button (Table Tools Layout tab | Table group), click the Row tab (Table Properties dialog box), remove the check mark from the 'Allow row to break across pages' check box, and then click the OK button. To force a table to break across pages at a particular row, click in the row that you want to appear on the next page and then press CTRL+ENTER.

To Align Data in Cells

The next step is to change the alignment of the data in cells that contain the class names. Recall that in addition to aligning text horizontally in a cell (left, center, or right), you can align it vertically within a cell (top, center, or bottom). Currently, the class names have a top left alignment (shown in Figure 4–53). In this project, they should be aligned center left so that they are more centered within the row height. The following steps change the alignment of data in cells.

1 Select the cells containing class names, as shown in Figure 4–54.

How do I select a series of cells?

Drag through the cells.

2 Click the Align Center Left button (Table Tools Layout tab | Alignment group) to center and left-align the contents of the selected cells (Figure 4–54).

3 Click anywhere to remove the selection from the table.

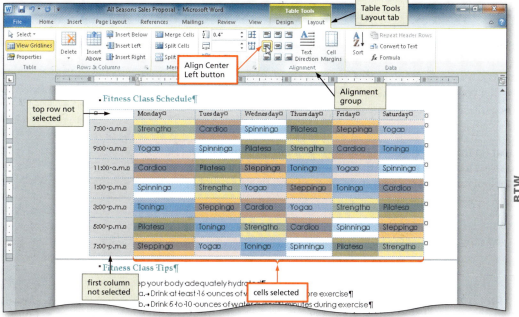

Figure 4-54

BTW

Table Headings
If a table continues on the next page, you can instruct Word to repeat the table headings at the top of the subsequent page(s) containing the table. To do this, select the first row in the table and then click the Repeat Header Rows button (Table Tools Layout tab | Data group).

To Shade a Table Cell

In this table, the cells containing the Spinning label are to be shaded light green. First, you will shade a single cell this color. Then, you will shade the remaining cells. The following steps shade a cell.

1

- Position the insertion point in the cell to shade (in this case, the cell containing Spinning on Monday at 1:00 p.m.).

- Display the Table Tools Design tab.

- Click the Shading button arrow (Table Tools Design tab | Table Styles group) to display the Shading gallery.

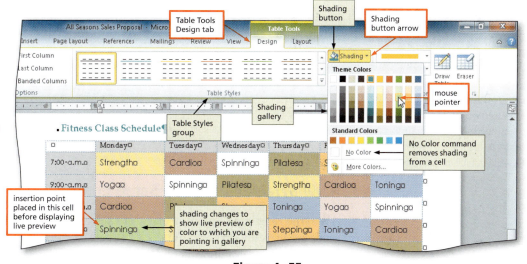

Figure 4-55

- Point to Green, Accent 4, Lighter 60% (eighth color, third row) in the Shading gallery to display a live preview of that shading color applied to the current cell in the table (Figure 4-55).

Experiment

- Point to various colors in the Shading gallery and watch the shading color of the current cell change.

2

- Click Green, Accent 4, Lighter 60% in the Shading gallery to apply the selected style to the current cell.

How do I remove shading from a cell?
Click the Shading button arrow and then click No Color in the Shading gallery.

To Select Nonadjacent Items

The next step is to select the rest of the cells containing Spinning: Tuesday at 9:00 a.m., Wednesday at 7:00 a.m., Thursday at 7:00 p.m., Friday at 5:00 p.m., and Saturday at 11:00 a.m. Word provides a method of selecting nonadjacent items, which are items such as text, cells, or graphics that are not next to each other, that is, not to the immediate right, left, top, or bottom. When you select nonadjacent items, you can format all occurrences of the items at once. The following steps select nonadjacent cells.

1
- Select the first cell to format (in this case, the cell containing Spinning on Saturday at 11:00 a.m.). Recall that to select a cell you position the mouse pointer on the left edge of the cell and then click when the pointer shape changes to an upward-pointing solid right arrow.

Q&A
Why start selecting at the right of the table and move to the left?

If you begin selecting from the left, the Mini toolbar may obstruct the view of the next cells you attempt to select.

2
- While holding down the CTRL key, select the next cell (in this case, the cell containing Spinning on Friday at 5:00 p.m.) to select the nonadjacent cell.

- While holding down the CTRL key, select the remaining nonadjacent cells (that is, Spinning on Thursday at 7:00 p.m., Spinning on Wednesday at 7:00 a.m., and Spinning on Tuesday at 9:00 a.m.), as shown in Figure 4–56.

Q&A
Do I follow the same procedure to select any nonadjacent item?

Yes. Select the first item and then hold down the CTRL key while selecting the remaining items.

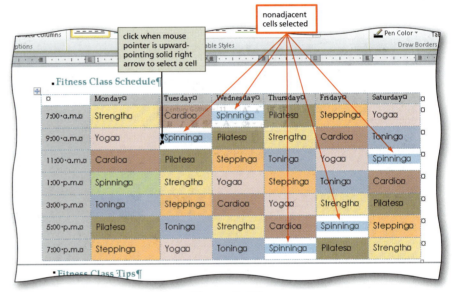

Figure 4–56

To Shade Selected Cells the Same Color

With the remaining Spinning class cells selected, the next step is to shade them the same color green as the first Spinning class. Because you earlier selected this color in the Shading gallery, this color appears on the face of the Shading button. Thus, you simply can click the Shading button to use the same color, which appears on the face of the button. The following steps shade selected cells with the current color.

1 With the cells selected, click the Shading button (Table Tools Design tab | Table Styles group) to shade the selected cells with the current color (in this case, Green, Accent 4, Lighter 60% (Figure 4–57).

Q&A
What if I accidentally click the Shading button arrow?

Press the ESC key to remove the gallery from the screen and then repeat Step 1.

Q&A
What if the current color on the Shading button is not the color I want?

Click the Shading button arrow and then click the desired color.

2 Click anywhere to remove the selection from the table.

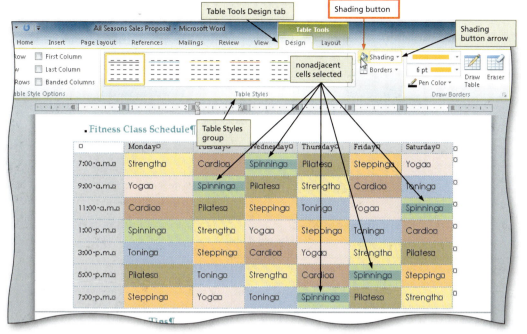

Figure 4–57

To Hide Gridlines

You no longer need to see the gridlines in the table. Thus, you can hide the gridlines. The following steps hide gridlines.

1 If necessary, position the insertion point in a table cell.

2 Display the Table Tools Layout tab.

3 Click the View Table Gridlines button (Table Tools Layout tab | Table group) to hide gridlines in the table on the screen.

To Change Cell Spacing

The next step in formatting the fitness class schedule table is to place a small amount of white space between every cell in the table. The following steps change spacing between cells.

1

• With the insertion point somewhere in the table, click the Cell Margins button (Table Tools Layout tab | Alignment group) to display the Table Options dialog box.

• Place a check mark in the 'Allow spacing between cells' check box and then click the up arrow once so that 0.02" is displayed in this box because you want to increase space between cells by this value (Figure 4–58).

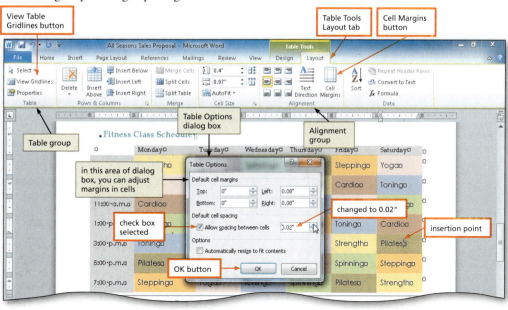

Figure 4–58

2
- Click the OK button (Table Options dialog box) to apply the cell spacing changes to the current table (Figure 4–59).

Figure 4–59

Other Ways

1. Click Table Properties button (Table Tools Layout tab | Table group), click Table tab (Table Properties dialog box), click Options button, select desired options (Table Options dialog box), click OK button in each dialog box

2. Right-click table, click Table Properties on shortcut menu, click Table tab (Table Properties dialog box), click Options button, select desired options (Table Options dialog box), click OK button in each dialog box

---

To Change Column Width

In reviewing the fitness class schedule table, you notice that the days of the week columns are different widths. Thus, the final step in formatting the fitness class schedule table is to change the column widths of the days of the week columns to the same width, specifically .95" so that the table does not extend so far into the margins. The following steps change column widths by specifying a value on the Ribbon.

1 Select the columns to be resized, in this case, all columns except the first.

2 Click the Table Column Width box (Table Tools Layout tab | Cell Size group) to select it.

3 Type **.95** in the Table Column Width box and then press the ENTER key to change the width of the selected table columns (Figure 4–60).

4 Click anywhere to remove the selection from the table.

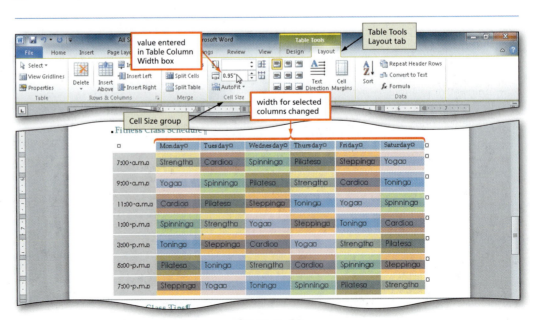

Figure 4–60

To Delete a Column

   With the fitness class schedule table finished, the next task is to format the membership plans table. The table in the draft of the proposal contains a blank column that should be deleted. The following steps delete a column from a table.

- Scroll to display the membership plans table in the document window.

- Position the insertion point in the column to be deleted (in this case, the rightmost column).

- Click the Delete button (Table Tools Layout tab | Rows & Columns group) to display the Delete menu (Figure 4–61).

- Click Delete Columns on the Delete menu to delete the column containing the insertion point.

Figure 4–61

Other Ways
1. Right-click column to delete, click Delete Cells on shortcut menu, click 'Delete entire column' (Delete Cells dialog box), click OK button	2. Select column, right-click selection, click Delete Columns on shortcut menu

TO DELETE A ROW

   If you wanted to delete a row, you would perform the following tasks.

1. Position the insertion point in the row to be deleted.

2. Click the Delete button (Table Tools Layout tab | Rows & Columns group) and then click Delete Rows on the Delete menu.

   or

1. Right-click the row to delete, click Delete Cells on the shortcut menu, click 'Delete entire row' (Delete Cells dialog box), and then click the OK button.

   or

1. Select the row to be deleted.

2. Right-click the selected row and then click Delete Rows on the shortcut menu.

BTW

Draw Table
If you want to draw the boundary, rows, and columns of a table, click the Table button on the Insert tab and then click Draw Table in the Table gallery. Use the pencil-shaped mouse pointer to draw the perimeter of the table and the inside rows and columns. Use the Eraser button (Table Tools Design tab | Draw Borders group) to erase lines in the table. To continue drawing, click the Draw Table button (Table Tools Design tab | Draw Borders group).

To Sort a Table

In the draft of this sales proposal, the membership plans are grouped by facility: exercise, aquatics, and gymnasium. These facilities should be listed in alphabetical order: aquatics, exercise, and then gymnasium. Thus, the next step is to sort rows in the table. Sorting tables is similar to sorting paragraphs. The following steps sort rows in a table.

1
- Select the rows to be sorted (in this case, the three middle rows).

Q&A What if I want to sort all rows in the table?

Place the insertion point anywhere in the table instead of selecting the rows.

- Click the Sort button (Table Tools Layout tab | Data group) to display the Sort dialog box (Figure 4–62).

Q&A What is the purpose of the Then by area (Sort dialog box)?

If you have multiple values for a particular column, you can sort by columns within columns. For example, if the table had a city column and a last name column, you could sort by last names within cities.

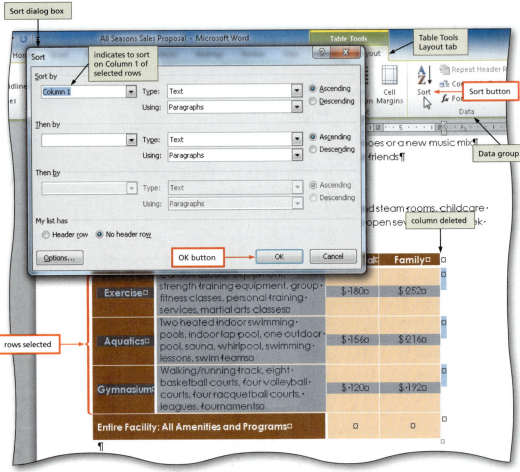

Figure 4–62

2
- Click the OK button (Sort dialog box) to instruct Word to alphabetize the selected rows.

- Click anywhere to remove the selection from the text (Figure 4–63).

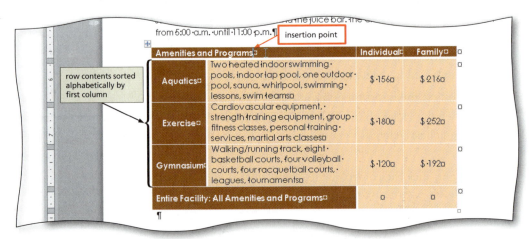

Figure 4–63

To Split Cells

The top, left cell of the table contains the text, Amenities and Programs. In the draft of the sales proposal, this row is above the first two columns in the table (the facilities and the descriptions of the facilities). This heading, Amenities and Programs, should be above the descriptions of the facilities, that is, above the second row. Thus, you will split the cell into two cells. The following steps split a single cell into two separate cells.

1

- Position the insertion point in the cell to split, in this case the top, left cell as shown in Figure 4–63.

- Click the Split Cells button (Table Tools Layout tab | Merge group) to display the Split Cells dialog box (Figure 4–64).

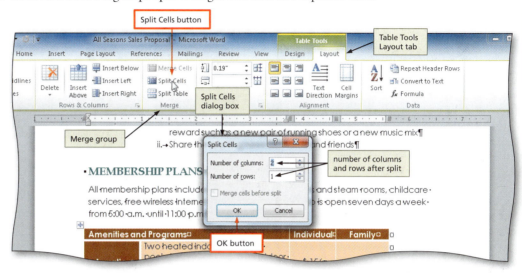

Figure 4–64

2

- Verify the number of columns and rows into which you want the cell split, in this case, 2 columns and 1 row.

- Click the OK button (Split Cells dialog box) to split the one cell into two columns (Figure 4–65).

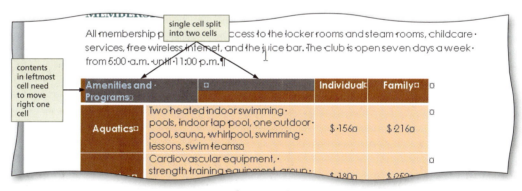

Figure 4–65

Other Ways

1. Right-click cell, click Split Cells on shortcut menu

To Move Cell Contents

When you split a cell into two cells, Word places the contents of the original cell in the leftmost cell after the split. In this case, the contents (Amenities and Programs) should be in the right cell. Thus, the following steps move cell contents.

1 Select the cell contents to be moved (in this case, Amenities and Programs).

2 Drag the cell contents to the desired location (in this case, the second cell in the first row) (shown in Figure 4–66 on the next page).

To Move a Cell Boundary

Notice in Figure 4–66 that the cell boundary to the left of the Amenities and Programs label does not line up with the boundary to the right of the facility types. This is because when you split a cell, Word divides the cell into evenly sized cells. If you want the boundary to line up with other column boundaries, drag it to the desired location. The following steps move a cell boundary.

- Position the mouse pointer on the cell boundary you wish to move so that the mouse pointer changes to a double arrow split by two vertical bars (Figure 4–66).

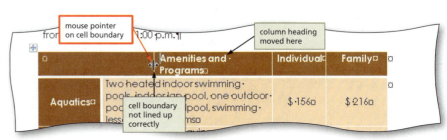

Figure 4–66

- Drag the cell boundary to the desired new location, in this case, to line up with the column boundary to its left, as shown in Figure 4–67.

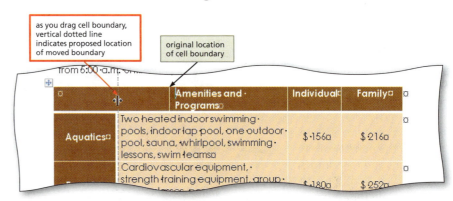

Figure 4–67

3

- When you release the mouse button, the cell boundary moves to the new location (Figure 4–68).

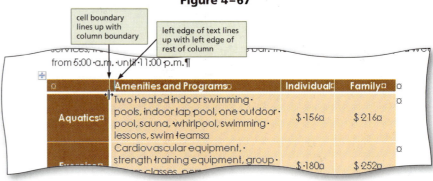

Figure 4–68

Other Ways

1. Drag Move Table Column marker on horizontal ruler to desired width

---

To Distribute Columns

The final step in formatting the membership plans table is to make the width of the individual and family columns uniform, that is, the same width. Instead of checking and adjusting the width of each column individually, you can make all columns uniform at the same time. The next step distributes selected columns.

1

- Select the columns to format, in this case, the two right columns.

- Click the Distribute Columns button (Table Tools Layout tab | Cell Size group) to make the width of the selected columns uniform (Figure 4–69).

Q&A

How would I make all columns in the table uniform?

Simply place the insertion point somewhere in the table before clicking the Distribute Columns button.

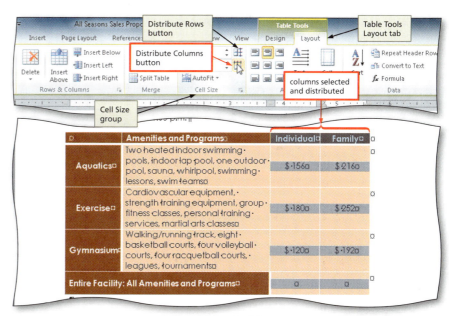

Figure 4–69

To Distribute Rows

If you wanted to make rows the same height, you would perform the following tasks.

1. Select the rows to format.

2. Click the Distribute Rows button (Table Tools Layout tab | Cell Size group) to make the width of the selected rows uniform.

To Insert a Column

In this project, the left edge of the membership plans table has a column that displays the label, Annual Rates by Facility. Thus, the following steps insert a column at the left edge of the table.

1 Position the insertion point somewhere in the first column of the table.

2 Click the Insert Columns to the Left button (Table Tools Layout tab | Rows & Columns group) to insert a column to the left of the column containing the insertion point (Figure 4–70).

3 Click anywhere in the table to remove the selection.

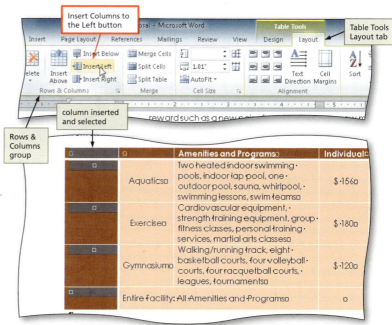

Figure 4–70

To Merge Cells and Enter Text

The label, Annual Rates by Facility, is to be displayed vertically to the left of the bottom four rows in the table. To display this text, the four cells should be merged into a single cell. The following steps merge cells and then enter text in the merged cell.

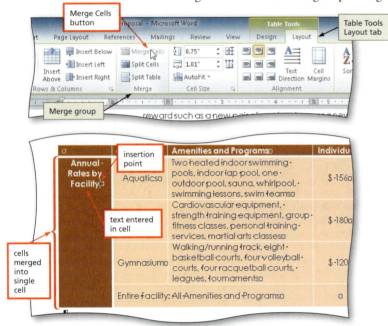

1 Select the cells to merge, in this case, the bottom four cells in the first column of the table.

2 Click the Merge Cells button (Table Tools Layout tab | Merge group) to merge the four selected cells into one cell.

3 Type **Annual Rates by Facility** in the merged cell.

4 If necessary, bold and center the entered text (Figure 4–71).

Figure 4–71

To Display Text in a Cell Vertically

The data you enter in cells is displayed horizontally by default. You can rotate the text so that it is displayed vertically. Changing the direction of text adds variety to your tables. The following step displays text vertically in a cell.

1

- Position the insertion point in the cell that contains the text to rotate (shown in Figure 4–71).

- Click the Text Direction button twice (Table Tools Layout tab | Alignment group) so that the text reads from bottom to top in the cell (Figure 4–72).

Q&A Why click the Text Direction button twice?

The first time you click the Text Direction button (Table Tools Layout tab | Alignment group), the text in the cell reads from top to bottom. The second time you click it, the text is displayed so that it reads from bottom to top (Figure 4–72). If you were to click the button a third time, the text would be displayed horizontally again.

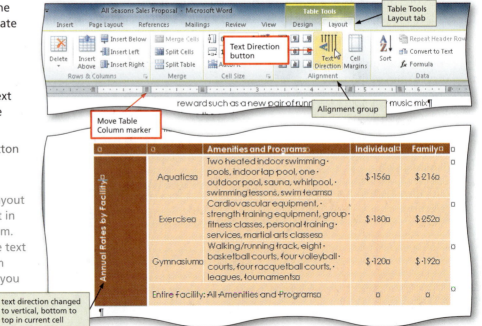

Figure 4–72

To Change Column Width

The cell containing the vertical text is too wide. Thus, the next step is to change the width of that column. If you drag the column boundary as you did earlier in the chapter, it will adjust the width of other columns in the table. If you want the other columns to remain their current widths, drag the Move Table Column marker on the ruler or hold down the CTRL key while dragging the column boundary. The following step changes column width using the ruler.

1 Drag the column's Move Table Column marker on the ruler to the left, as shown in Figure 4–73, to resize the column.

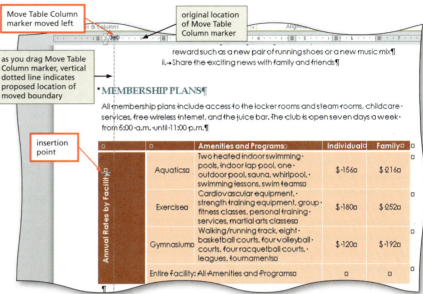

Figure 4–73

To Remove Cell Shading

In this table, only the first row and first column should have shading. Thus, the following steps remove shading from table cells.

1 Select the cells that should not contain shading (in this case, all of the cells below the first row and to the right of the first column).

2 Display the Table Tools Design tab. Click the Shading button arrow (Table Tools Design tab | Table Styles group) to display the Shading gallery (Figure 4–74).

3 Click No Color in the Shading gallery to remove the shading from the selected cells (shown in Figure 4–75 on the next page).

4 Click anywhere in the table to remove the selection.

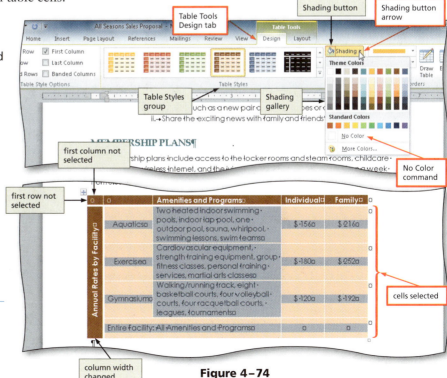

Figure 4–74

To Border a Table

The table in this project has a 1-point, brown border around all cells. Earlier in this chapter when you created the title page, the border line weight was changed to 6 point and the border color changed to gold. Because the table border should be 1 point and the color should be brown, you will use the Borders and Shading dialog box to change the line weight and color before adding the border to the table. The following steps add a border to a table.

- Position the insertion point somewhere in the table.

- Click the Borders button arrow (Table Tools Design tab | Table Styles group) to display the Borders gallery.

- Click Borders and Shading in the Borders gallery to display the Borders and Shading dialog box.

- Click All in the Setting area (Borders and Shading dialog box), which will place a border on every cell in the table.

- Click the Color box arrow and then click Brown, Accent 5 (ninth color, first row) in the Color palette to specify the border color.

- If necessary, click the Width box arrow and then click 1 pt to specify the thickness of the border (Figure 4–75).

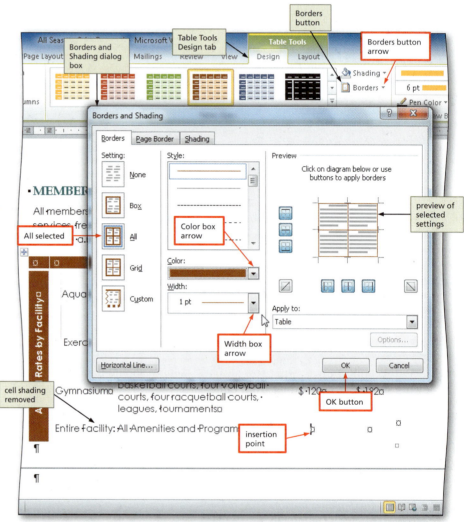

Figure 4–75

- Click the OK button to place the border shown in the preview area of the dialog box around the table cells in the document (shown in Figure 4–76).

To Sum Columns in a Table

In this project, the last row should display the sum (total) of the values in the last two columns: individual and family. Word can calculate the totals of rows and columns. You also can specify the format for how the totals will be displayed. The next steps sum the columns in a table.

1

- Position the insertion point in the cell to contain the sum (last row, second to last column).

2

- Display the Table Tools Layout tab.

- Click the Formula button (Table Tools Layout tab | Data group) to display the Formula dialog box.

Q&A What is the formula that shows in the Formula box, and can I change it?

Word places a default formula in the Formula box, depending on the location of the numbers in surrounding cells. In this case, because numbers are above the current cell, Word displays a formula that will add the numbers above the current cell. You can change the formula that Word proposes, or type a different formula. For example, instead of summing numbers you can multiply them.

- Click the Number format box arrow (Formula dialog box) and then click the desired format for the result of the computation, in this case, the format with the dollar sign (Figure 4–76).

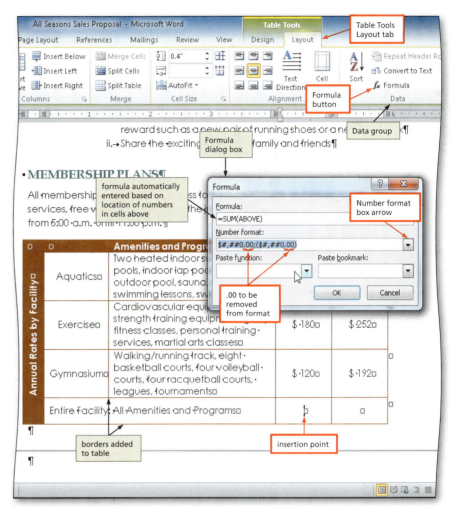

Figure 4–76

3

- Click the Number format box and then remove the two occurrences of .00 in the displayed format because you want the total to be displayed as a whole number, that is, with no cents (Figure 4–77).

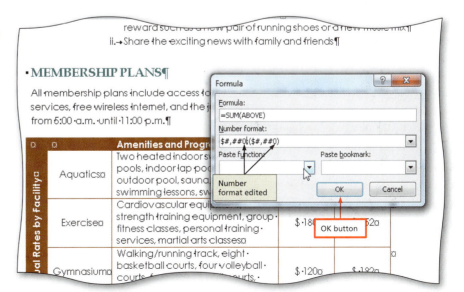

Figure 4–77

4

- Click the OK button (Formula dialog box) to place the sum of the numbers using the specified format in the current cell.

5

- Press the TAB key to move the insertion point to the next cell to sum.

- Repeat Steps 2, 3, and 4 to place the sum of the numbers using the specified format in the current cell (Figure 4–78).

Q&A Can I sum a row instead of a column?

Yes. You would position the insertion point in an empty cell at the right edge of the row before clicking the Formula button.

Q&A If I make a change to a number in a table, does Word automatically recompute the sum?

No. You will need to update the field by right-clicking it and then clicking Update Field on the shortcut menu, or selecting the field and then pressing the F9 key.

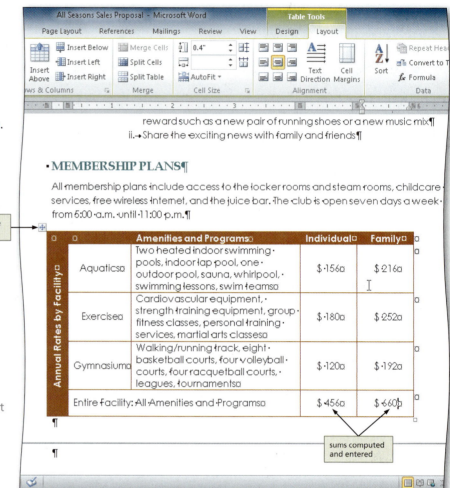

Figure 4–78

To Center a Table

The last step in formatting this table is to center it horizontally between the page margins. The following steps center a table.

1 Select the table.

2 Display the Home tab. Click the Center button (Home tab | Paragraph group) to center the selected table between the left and right margins.

3 Click anywhere to remove the selection from the table.

BTW

Moving Tables
If you wanted to move a table to a new location, you would point to the upper-left corner of the table until the table move handle appears (shown in Figure 4–78), point to the table move handle, and then drag the table move handle to move the entire table to a new location.

To Delete a Blank Paragraph and Show White Space

You notice an extra paragraph mark below the membership plans table that should be deleted because it is causing an extra blank page in the document. You also would like to show white space again, so that the headers and footers are visible in the document window. The following steps delete a blank paragraph and show white space.

1 Press CTRL+END to position the insertion point at the end of the document.

2 Press the BACKSPACE key to remove the extra blank paragraph and delete the blank page. If text spills onto a fourth page, remove space above paragraphs in the sales proposal until the entire proposal fits on three pages, as shown in Figure 4–1 on page WD 203.

3 Position the mouse pointer in the document window in the space below the current page or on the line between two pages so that the mouse pointer changes to a Show White Space button.

4 While the mouse pointer is a Show White Space button, double-click the mouse to show white space, that is, the top and bottom margins and space between pages (Figure 4–79).

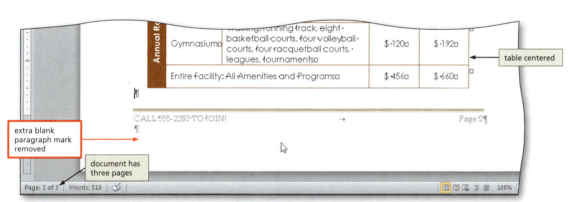

Figure 4–79

Creating a Watermark

The final task in this chapter is to create a watermark for the pages of the sales proposal. A **watermark** is text or a graphic that is displayed on top of or behind the text in a document. For example, a catalog may print the words, Sold Out, on top of sold-out items. The first draft of a five-year-plan may have the word, Draft, printed behind the text of the document. Some companies use their logos or other graphics as watermarks to add visual appeal to their documents.

To Zoom Two Pages

The following steps display two pages (the first two pages) in their entirety in the document window as large as possible, so that you can see the position of the watermark as you create it.

1 Press CTRL+HOME to position the insertion point at the beginning of the document.

2 Display the View tab. Click the Two Pages button (View tab | Zoom group) to display two entire pages in the document window as large as possible.

BTW

Quick Reference
For a table that lists how to complete the tasks covered in this book using the mouse, Ribbon, shortcut menu, and keyboard, see the Quick Reference Summary at the back of this book, or visit the Word 2010 Quick Reference Web page (scsite.com/wd2010/qr).

To Create a Watermark

In this project, the words, GET FIT!, are displayed behind all text and graphics as a watermark. The following steps create a watermark.

1

- Display the Page Layout tab.

- Click the Watermark button (Page Layout tab | Page Background group) to display the Watermark gallery (Figure 4–80).

2

- Click Custom Watermark in the Watermark gallery to display the Printed Watermark dialog box.

- Click Text watermark (Printed Watermark dialog box) so that you can enter the text and formats for the watermark.

- Delete the text, ASAP, and then type **GET FIT!** in the Text box.

- Click the Size box arrow to display a list of available watermark sizes. Scroll to and then click 144 as the watermark size.

- Click the Color box arrow and then click Tan, Background 2 (third color, first row) as the watermark color.

- Click Horizontal, so that the watermark appears horizontally on the page.

- Click the Apply button to show a preview of the watermark on the pages in the document window (Figure 4–81).

3

- Click the Close button (Printed Watermark dialog box) to close the dialog box.

Q&A How do I remove a watermark from a document?

Click the Watermark button (Page Layout tab | Page Background group) and then click Remove Watermark.

Q&A How do I create a picture watermark?

Click Picture watermark in the Printed Watermark dialog box (Figure 4–81), select the picture for the watermark, and then click the OK button.

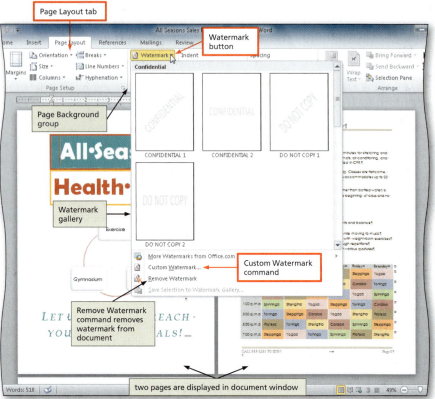

Figure 4–80

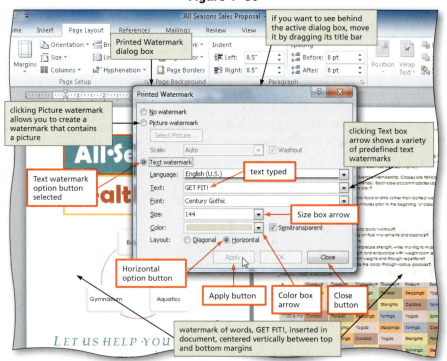

Figure 4–81

Other Ways

1. Click Quick Parts button (Insert tab | Text group), click Building Blocks

   Organizer on Quick Parts menu, select desired watermark (Building Blocks

   Organizer dialog box), click Insert button

To Check Spelling, Save, Print, and Quit Word

The following steps check the spelling of the document, save and print the document, and then quit Word.

1 Display the Review tab. Click the Spelling & Grammar button (Review tab | Proofing group) to begin the spelling and grammar check. Correct any misspelled words.

2 Save the sales proposal again with the same file name.

3 Print the sales proposal (shown in Figure 4–1 on page WD 203).

4 Quit Word.

BTW

Conserving Ink and Toner
If you want to conserve ink or toner, you can instruct Word to print draft quality documents by clicking File on the Ribbon to open the Backstage view, clicking Options in the Backstage view to display the Word Options dialog box, clicking Advanced in the left pane (Word Options dialog box), scrolling to the Print area in the right pane, placing a check mark in the 'Use draft quality' check box, and then clicking the OK button. Then, use the Backstage view to print the document as usual.

Chapter Summary

In this chapter, you learned how to add a border to a paragraph, change paragraph indentation, insert and format a SmartArt graphic, apply character effects, insert a section break, insert a Word document in an open document, change theme fonts, insert formatted headers and footers, sort lists and tables, modify and format existing Word tables, sum columns in a table, and insert a watermark. The items listed below include all the new Word skills you have learned in this chapter.

1. Border a Paragraph (WD 206)
2. Change Left and Right Paragraph Indent (WD 210)
3. Insert a SmartArt Graphic (WD 212)
4. Delete Shapes and Add Text to Shapes in a SmartArt Graphic (WD 214)
5. Change Colors of a SmartArt Graphic (WD 215)
6. Add a Shape to a SmartArt Graphic (WD 216)
7. Apply a SmartArt Style (WD 216)
8. Format Characters and Modify Character Spacing Using the Font Dialog Box (WD 216)
9. Insert a Next Page Section Break (WD 220)
10. Delete a Section Break (WD 221)
11. Insert a Word Document in an Open Document (WD 222)
12. Print Specific Pages in a Document (WD 223)
13. Delete a Page Break (WD 225)
14. Modify the Default Font Settings (WD 225)
15. Reset the Default Font Settings (WD 225)
16. Change Theme Fonts (WD 226)
17. Insert a Formatted Header Different from the Previous Header (WD 229)
18. Insert a Formatted Footer (WD 230)
19. Format Page Numbers to Start at a Different Number (WD 231)
20. Sort Paragraphs (WD 232)
21. Use the Format Painter Button (WD 233)
22. Customize Bullets in a List (WD 235)
23. Create a Multilevel Numbered List (WD 236)
24. Show Gridlines (WD 239)
25. Change Column Width (WD 240)
26. Hide White Space (WD 241)
27. Change Row Height (WD 241)
28. Shade a Table Cell (WD 243)
29. Select Nonadjacent Items (WD 244)
30. Change Cell Spacing (WD 245)
31. Delete a Column (WD 247)
32. Delete a Row (WD 247)
33. Sort a Table (WD 248)
34. Split Cells (WD 249)
35. Move a Cell Boundary (WD 250)
36. Distribute Columns (WD 250)
37. Distribute Rows (WD 251)
38. Display Text in a Cell Vertically (WD 252)
39. Border a Table (WD 254)
40. Sum Columns in a Table (WD 254)
41. Create a Watermark (WD 258)

 If you have a SAM 2010 user profile, your instructor may have assigned an autogradable version of this assignment. If so, log into the SAM 2010 Web site at www.cengage.com/sam2010 to download the instruction and start files.

Learn It Online

Test your knowledge of chapter content and key terms.

Instructions: To complete the Learn It Online exercises, start your browser, click the Address bar, and then enter the Web address **scsite.com/wd2010/learn**. When the Word 2010 Learn It Online page is displayed, click the link for the exercise you want to complete and then read the instructions.

Chapter Reinforcement TF, MC, and SA
A series of true/false, multiple choice, and short answer questions that test your knowledge of the chapter content.

Flash Cards
An interactive learning environment where you identify chapter key terms associated with displayed definitions.

Practice Test
A series of multiple choice questions that test your knowledge of chapter content and key terms.

Who Wants To Be a Computer Genius?
An interactive game that challenges your knowledge of chapter content in the style of a television quiz show.

Wheel of Terms
An interactive game that challenges your knowledge of chapter key terms in the style of the television show *Wheel of Fortune*.

Crossword Puzzle Challenge
A crossword puzzle that challenges your knowledge of key terms presented in the chapter.

Apply Your Knowledge

Reinforce the skills and apply the concepts you learned in this chapter.

Working with a Table
Note: To complete this assignment, you will be required to use the Data Files for Students. See the inside back cover of this book for instructions on downloading the Data Files for Students, or contact your instructor for information about accessing the required files.

Instructions: Start Word. Open the document, Apply 4-1 Expenses Breakdown Draft, from the Data Files for Students. The document contains a Word table that you are to modify. The modified table is shown in Figure 4–82.

Whitcomb Services					
Expenses Breakdown					
	1st Quarter	2nd Quarter	3rd Quarter	4th Quarter	Total
Advertising	6,444.22	5,398.99	6,293.49	6,009.29	$24,145.99
Maintenance	1,224.03	982.45	1,029.45	990.32	$4,226.25
Rent	2,200.00	2,200.00	2,200.00	2,200.00	$8,800.00
Salaries	6,954.34	7,300.28	6,887.39	7,102.83	$28,244.84
Supplies	1,932.76	1,727.84	1,623.26	1,887.54	$7,171.40
Total	$18,755.35	$17,609.56	$18,033.59	$18,189.98	$72,588.48

Figure 4–82

Perform the following tasks:

1. Show gridlines.
2. Delete the blank column between the 3rd and 4th Quarter columns.
3. Use the Distribute Rows command to evenly space all the rows in the table.
4. Use the Distribute Columns command to make the 1st, 2nd, 3rd, and 4th Quarter and Total columns evenly spaced.
5. Change the width of the 1st, 2nd, 3rd, and 4th Quarter and Total columns to 1".
6. Use the Formula button (Table Tools Layout tab | Data group) to place totals in the bottom row for the 1st, 2nd, 3rd, and 4th Quarter columns. The totals should be formatted to display dollar signs and cents.
7. Use the Formula button (Table Tools Layout tab | Data group) to place totals in the right column. Start in the bottom-right cell and work your way up the column.
8. Add a row to the top of the table. Merge all cells in the first row into a single cell. Enter the company name, Whitcomb Services, as the table title. Center the title.
9. Split the cell in the first row into two rows (one column). In the new cell below the company name, enter the text, Expenses Breakdown, as the subtitle.
10. Shade the first row Orange, Accent 6, Darker 25%. Shade the second row Orange, Accent 6, Lighter 40%.
11. Add a 1 pt, Orange, Accent 6, Darker 50% border to all cells in the table.
12. Hide gridlines.
13. Change the height of the row containing the quarter headings (row 3) to .01". Change the alignment of these headings to Align Top Center.
14. Change the height of all expense rows and the total row (rows 4 through 9) to 0.3".
15. Change the alignment of the cells in the first column to the left of all the dollar amounts to Align Center Left.
16. Change the alignment of the cells containing dollar amounts to Align Center Right.
17. Center the entire table across the width of the page.
18. Sort the rows containing the expenses.
19. Change the document properties as specified by your instructor.
20. Save the modified file with the file name, Apply 4-1 Expenses Breakdown Modified.
21. Submit the revised table in the format specified by your instructor.

Extend Your Knowledge

Extend the skills you learned in this chapter and experiment with new skills. You may need to use Help to complete the assignment.

Modifying Multilevel List Formats, Drawing Tables, and Creating Picture Watermarks

Note: To complete this assignment, you will be required to use the Data Files for Students. See the inside back cover of this book for instructions on downloading the Data Files for Students, or contact your instructor for information about accessing the required files.

Instructions: Start Word. Open the document, Extend 4-1 Tax and Investment Seminars Draft, from the Data Files for Students. You will define a new number format for the multilevel list, insert a picture watermark, and use Word's Draw Table feature to draw a table.

Continued >

Extend Your Knowledge *continued*

Perform the following tasks:

1. Use Help to learn about defining multilevel list number formats, picture watermarks, and Draw Table.

2. For each level in the multilevel list, define a new number format that is different from the format in the draft file. Be sure to change (at a minimum) the font, font size, and font color of the number format.

3. Insert a picture watermark using the Scales.wmf image on the Data Files for Students.

4. Below the multilevel list, draw the table shown in Figure 4–83. That is, use the Draw Table button to create the blank table.

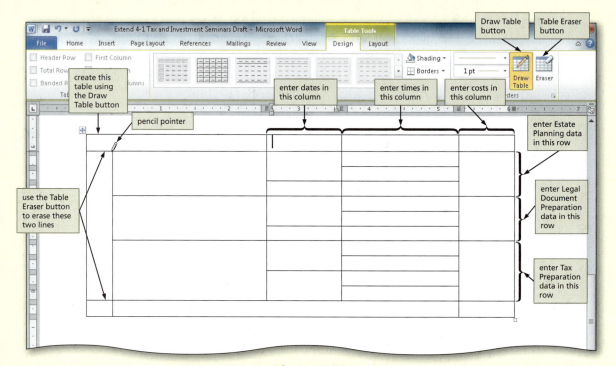

Figure 4–83

5. In the leftmost column of the table, enter the text, Seminar Topic, so that it displays vertically in the cell.

6. In the second column of the table, enter these labels in the second, third, and fourth rows: Estate Planning, Legal Document Preparation, and Tax Preparation.

7. In the top row, enter these headings in the last three columns: Date, Times, and Cost.

8. For Estate Planning, use this data for the table: Cost is $120; January 17 class times are 9:00 – 11:00 a.m. and 7:00 – 9:00 p.m.; January 31 class times are 1:00 – 3:00 p.m.

9. For Legal Document Preparation, use this data for the table: Cost is $140; January 10 class times are 9:00 – 11:30 a.m. and 7:30 – 10:00 p.m.; January 24 class times are 1:00 – 3:30 p.m.

10. For Tax Preparation, use this data for the table: Cost is $125; January 3 class times are 9:00 – 11:15 a.m. and 7:00 – 9:15 p.m.; January 10 class times are 1:00 – 3:15 p.m. and 5:00 – 7:15 p.m.

11. Enter the text, Special Offer: Attend all three seminars, in the bottom row. The cost for the bottom, right cell is $350.

12. Enhance the table as you deem appropriate.

13. Change the document properties, as specified by your instructor. Save the revised document using a new file name and then submit it in the format specified by your instructor.

Make It Right

Analyze a document and correct all errors and/or improve the design.

Formatting a Title Page

Note: To complete this assignment, you will be required to use the Data Files for Students. See the inside back cover of this book for instructions on downloading the Data Files for Students, or contact your instructor for information about accessing the required files.

Instructions: Start Word. Open the document, Make It Right 4-1 Home Health Title Page Draft, from the Data Files for Students. The document is a title page that is missing elements and that is not formatted ideally (Figure 4–84). You are to remove the header and footer, edit the border, change paragraph indents, modify the SmartArt graphic, change character spacing, and adjust font sizes.

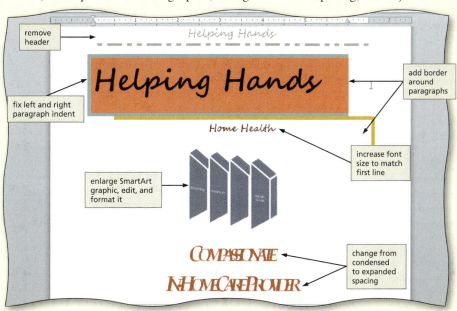

Figure 4–84

Perform the following tasks:

1. Remove the header and footer from the title page.

2. Modify the borders on the first and second lines so that they surround all edges of each paragraph.

3. Change the left and right paragraph indent of the first two lines (paragraphs) so that they have a 0.5" left and right indent.

4. Increase the font size of the text in the second line to match the font size of the text in the first line.

5. Increase the size of the SmartArt graphic on the title page. Delete the shape that has no text in it. Change the word, Maximum, to Optimum in the middle shape. Change the colors of the SmartArt graphic and then change the SmartArt style.

6. Change the zoom to one page.

7. Change the character spacing of the last two lines on the title page from condensed to expanded. The first of the two lines should be expanded more than the second of the two lines.

8. Increase font sizes so that the text is easy to read.

9. Add or remove space above or below paragraphs so that all contents of the title page fit on a single page. Change the zoom back to 100%.

10. Change the document properties, as specified by your instructor. Save the revised document with a new file name and then submit it in the format specified by your instructor.

In the Lab

Design and/or create a document using the guidelines, concepts, and skills presented in this chapter. Labs are listed in order of increasing difficulty.

Lab 1: Creating a Proposal with a SmartArt Graphic, a Bulleted List, and a Table

Problem: The owner of Reflections, a center for employee retreats, has hired you to prepare a sales proposal describing their facilities, which will be mailed to local businesses.

Instructions: Perform the following tasks:

1. Change the theme fonts to the Hardcover font set.
2. Create the title page as shown in Figure 4–85a. Be sure to do the following:
   a. Insert the SmartArt graphic, add text to it, and change its colors and style as specified.
   b. Change the fonts, font sizes, and font colors. Add the paragraph border. Indent the left and right edges of the title paragraph by 0.5 inches.
3. At the bottom of the title page, insert a next page section break. Clear formatting.

72-point Bradley Hand ITC bold font; color: Blue, Accent 1, Darker 25%

1½-pt triple line outside border; color: Olive Green, Accent 3, Darker 25%

SmartArt graphic – Type: Relationship Layout: Gear Colors: Colorful Range - Accent Colors 3 to 4 Style: Cartoon

36-point Perpetua Titling MT italic font; color: Purple, Accent 4, Darker 25%

Figure 4–85 (a) Title Page

4. Create the second page of the proposal as shown in Figure 4–85b.

   a. Insert the formatted header using the Alphabet design. The header should appear only on the second page (section) of the proposal. Format the header text as shown.

   b. Insert the formatted footer using the Alphabet design. The footer should appear only on the second page (section) of the proposal. Format the footer text as shown. Delete the page number.

   c. Format the headings using the heading styles as specified.

   d. Change the bullets in the bulleted list to purple picture bullets. Format the first word of one bulleted item as shown. Use the format painter to copy the formatting to the remaining initial words in the bulleted list.

   e. Create the table as shown. Border the table as specified. Distribute rows so that they are all the same height. Change the row height to 0.21 inches. Center the table. Left-align text in the first column, and center text in the second and third columns. Shade the table cells as specified.

5. Adjust spacing above and below paragraphs as necessary to fit all content as shown in the figure.

6. Check the spelling. Change the document properties, as specified by your instructor. Save the document with Lab 4-1 Employee Retreat Proposal as the file name.

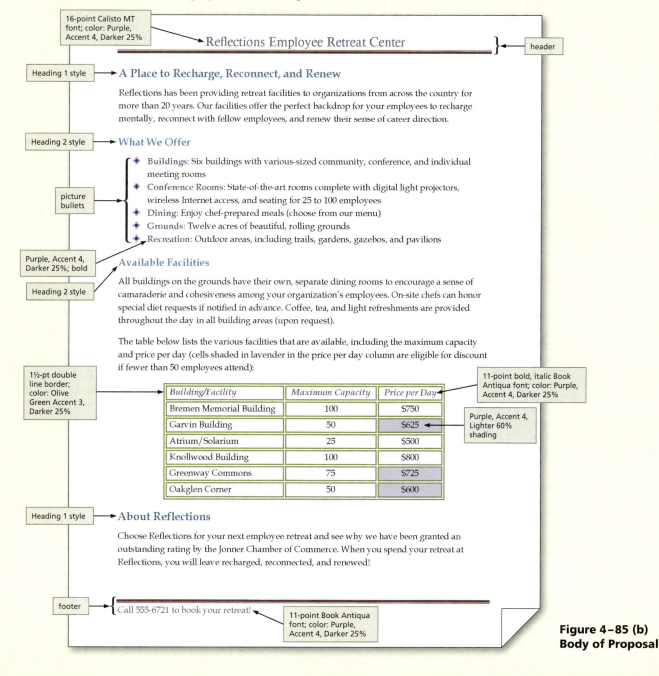

Figure 4–85 (b)
Body of Proposal

In the Lab

Lab 2: Creating a Proposal with a SmartArt Graphic, a Complex Table, and a Numbered List

Problem: The owner of the Wide Eye Java has hired you to prepare a sales proposal describing its monthly service in a first order confirmation.

Note: To complete this assignment, you will be required to use the Data Files for Students. See the inside back cover of this book for instructions on downloading the Data Files for Students, or contact your instructor for information about accessing the required files.

Instructions: Perform the following tasks:

1. Change the theme colors to the Horizon color scheme.
2. Change the theme fonts to the Pushpin font set.
3. Create the title page as shown in Figure 4–86a. Be sure to do the following:

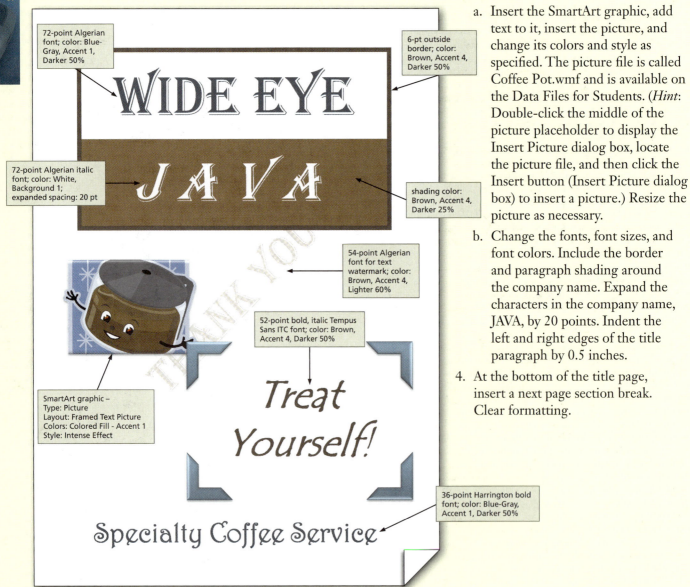

a. Insert the SmartArt graphic, add text to it, insert the picture, and change its colors and style as specified. The picture file is called Coffee Pot.wmf and is available on the Data Files for Students. (*Hint:* Double-click the middle of the picture placeholder to display the Insert Picture dialog box, locate the picture file, and then click the Insert button (Insert Picture dialog box) to insert a picture.) Resize the picture as necessary.

b. Change the fonts, font sizes, and font colors. Include the border and paragraph shading around the company name. Expand the characters in the company name, JAVA, by 20 points. Indent the left and right edges of the title paragraph by 0.5 inches.

4. At the bottom of the title page, insert a next page section break. Clear formatting.

Labels in figure:
- 72-point Algerian font; color: Blue-Gray, Accent 1, Darker 50%
- 6-pt outside border; color: Brown, Accent 4, Darker 50%
- 72-point Algerian italic font; color: White, Background 1; expanded spacing: 20 pt
- shading color: Brown, Accent 4, Darker 25%
- 54-point Algerian font for text watermark; color: Brown, Accent 4, Lighter 60%
- 52-point bold, italic Tempus Sans ITC font; color: Brown, Accent 4, Darker 50%
- SmartArt graphic – Type: Picture Layout: Framed Text Picture Colors: Colored Fill - Accent 1 Style: Intense Effect
- 36-point Harrington bold font; color: Blue-Gray, Accent 1, Darker 50%

Figure 4–86 (a) Title Page

5. Create the second page of the proposal as shown in Figure 4–86b.

   a. Insert the formatted header using the Alphabet design. The header should appear only on the second page of the proposal. Format the header text as shown.

   b. Format the headings using the heading styles specified. Adjust spacing before the Heading 1 style to 12 point and after to 6 point, and before and after the Heading 2 style to 6 point. Update both heading styles.

   c. Insert the formatted footer using the Alphabet design. The footer should appear only on the second page of the proposal. Delete the page number.

   d. Create the table as shown. Border the table as specified. Distribute rows so that they are all the same height. Change the row height to 0.2 inches. Align center left the text in the Item Description column, align center the text in the Quantity column and the Cost and Total headings, and align center right the dollar amounts in the Cost and Total columns. Center the table. Change the direction of the Food and Nonfood headings. Use a formula to compute the values in the total column (quantity times cost). Use another formula to sum the totals in the order total cell.

   e. Create the numbered list as shown.

6. Create a diagonal watermark with Thank You! as the text. Adjust spacing above and below paragraphs as necessary to fit all content as shown in the figure.

7. Check the spelling. Change the document properties, as specified by your instructor. Save the document with Lab 4-2 Coffee Service Proposal as the file name.

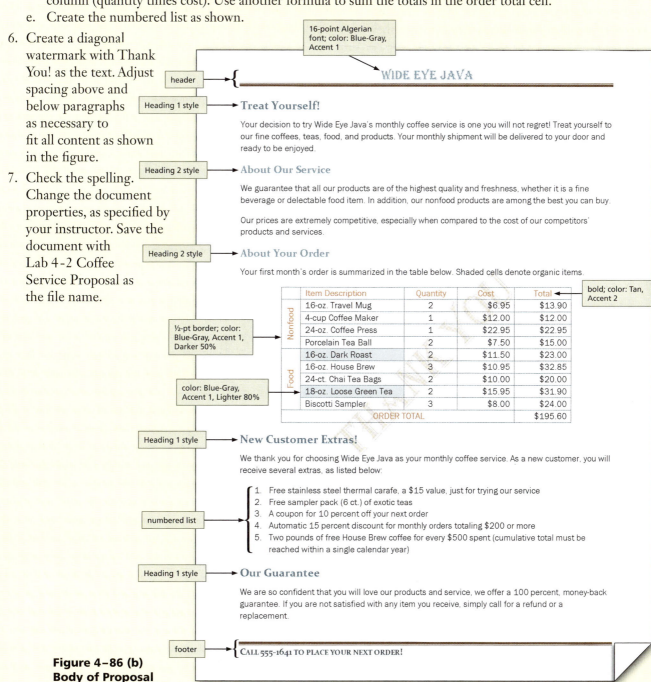

Figure 4–86 (b)
Body of Proposal

In the Lab

Lab 3: Enhancing a Draft of a Sales Proposal with a Title Page, a Bulleted List, Tables, and a Multilevel List

Problem: You work at Nature Kids Summer Camp. Your coworker has prepared a draft of a proposal about the upcoming summer camp. You decide to enhance the proposal by adding picture bullets, a multilevel list, and another table. You also prepare a title page that includes a SmartArt graphic.

Note: To complete this assignment, you will be required to use the Data Files for Students. See the inside back cover of this book for instructions on downloading the Data Files for Students, or contact your instructor for information about accessing the required files.

Instructions: Perform the following tasks:

1. Change the theme colors to the Solstice color scheme. Change the theme fonts to the Aspect font set.
2. Create a title page similar to the one shown in Figure 4–87a.

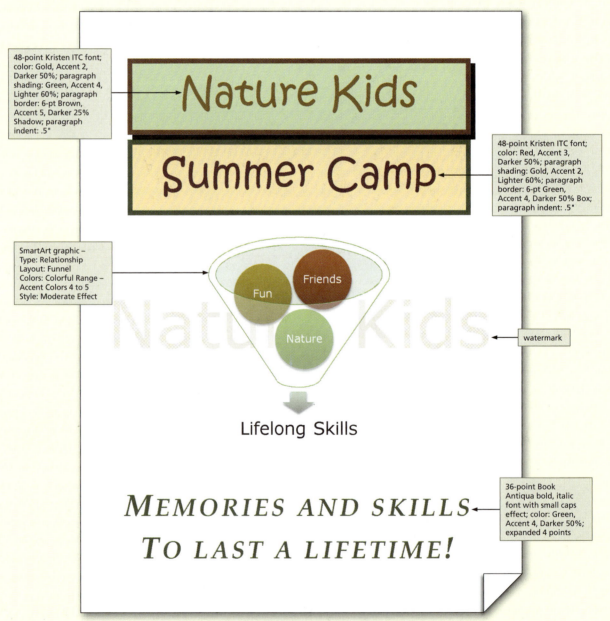

48-point Kristen ITC font; color: Gold, Accent 2, Darker 50%; paragraph shading: Green, Accent 4, Lighter 60%; paragraph border: 6-pt Brown, Accent 5, Darker 25% Shadow; paragraph indent: .5"

48-point Kristen ITC font; color: Red, Accent 3, Darker 50%; paragraph shading: Gold, Accent 2, Lighter 60%; paragraph border: 6-pt Green, Accent 4, Darker 50% Box; paragraph indent: .5"

SmartArt graphic – Type: Relationship Layout: Funnel Colors: Colorful Range – Accent Colors 4 to 5 Style: Moderate Effect

watermark

36-point Book Antiqua bold, italic font with small caps effect; color: Green, Accent 4, Darker 50%; expanded 4 points

Figure 4–87 (a) Title Page

3. Insert a next page section break. Insert the draft of the body of the proposal below the title page. The draft is called Lab 4-3 Nature Kids Camp Proposal Draft on the Data Files for Students.

4. Modify the first page of the body of the draft so that it looks like Figure 4–87b, by doing the following:

   a. Delete the page break above the Outdoor Activities heading.

   b. Insert a header and footer as shown. The footer should have a page number. Change the starting page number to 1.

   c. Change the style of bullet characters in the list to picture bullets. Format the first words in the bulleted item to the Intense Emphasis Quick Style. Use the format painter to copy the formatting to the remaining words. Sort the bulleted list.

   d. In the table below the bulleted list, shade cells similarly to the figure, adjust alignment of text in cells as shown, and change cell spacing to 0.02 inches between cells.

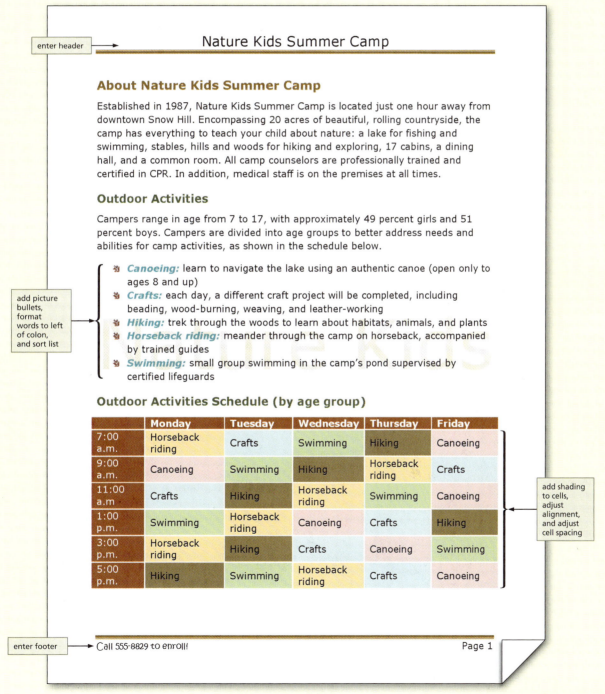

Figure 4–87 (b) Page 1

Continued >

In the Lab continued

5. Modify the second page of the body of the draft so that it looks like Figure 4–87c, by doing the following:

a. Create the multilevel list below the Camper Tips heading.

b. Create and format the table as shown below the Camp Fees paragraph.

6. Create the watermark as shown.

7. Check the spelling. Change the document properties, as specified by your instructor. Save the active document with the file name, Lab 4-3 Nature Kids Camp Proposal.

Nature Kids Summer Camp

Camper Tips

create this multilevel list

1. Bring only the items necessary, as outlined below:
   a. Bedding and linen (sleeping bag or blanket, pillow, and linen)
   b. Hygiene items, such as toothbrush and toothpaste, soap, shampoo, towels, and shower shoes
   c. Personal items, such as portable media players, cell phones, and handheld games, are discouraged strongly
2. Meals are provided, with light snacks available upon request
   a. Campers will be fed at assigned mealtimes, by age and cabin
   b. Healthy, balanced breakfasts, lunches, and dinners (please inform us of any special diet requests/restrictions)
3. Clothing recommendations are as follows:
   a. Footwear
      i. At least one pair each of hiking boots and tennis/running shoes
      ii. Extra socks (at least three extra pairs recommended)
      iii. Plastic or waterproof shoes for shower wear
   b. Clothing
      i. Comfortable clothing suitable for outdoor activity
      ii. Swimwear
      iii. Light jacket or sweatshirts for cool evenings

Camp Fees

The costs of attending this camp are outlined in the table below, along with cabin assignments by age group. All meals, lodging, and activities are included in the cost.

create this table

Age Group		Cabin Assignment	Cost
	7	Tadpole Grove Cabins #1, 3, 4, and 6	$425
	8 – 9	Arbor Grove Cabins #2, 5, 7, and 9	$400
	10 – 11	Campfire Hamlet Cabins #8, 10, and 11	$380
	12 – 14	Green Hollow Cabins #12, 13, and 15	$350
	15 – 17	Wilderness Circle Cabins #14, 16, and 17	$325
	Additional campers: Each sibling can attend for a flat fee, regardless of age group		$300

Call 555-8829 to enroll!   Page 2

Figure 4–87 (c) Page 2

Cases and Places

Apply your creative thinking and problem solving skills to design and implement a solution.

Note: To complete these assignments, you may be required to use the Data Files for Students. See the inside back cover of this book for instructions on downloading the Data Files for Students, or contact your instructor for information about accessing the required files.

1: Create a Proposal for Tutoring

Academic

As a part-time assistant in the tutoring center at your school, your boss has asked you to design a two-page sales proposal for the center that will be posted on campus. The title page is to contain the name, A+ Tutoring, formatted with a border and shading. Include an appropriate SmartArt graphic that conveys this message: Hard Work and Dedication Lead to Academic Success. Include the slogan, Building Successful Students.

The second page of the proposal should contain the following: heading — Help Is Here!; paragraph — Whether you need help in math, English, or a foreign language, A+ Tutoring is here to help. Conveniently located in the Student Services Building in room S-80, we offer extended hours and specialized tutoring in several different subjects.; heading — Prepare for Success; paragraph — The following are recommended materials and guidelines to help maximize your tutoring experience.; multilevel list — 1) Items to bring: although these items are not completely necessary, they have been found to be helpful during tutoring, 1a) Pens, pencils, highlighters, or other writing implements, 1b) Paper, notebooks, binders, 1c) Textbooks and any supplemental materials for subject (i.e., workbooks, handbooks, lab notes, assigned reading), 1d) Calculator, 2) Be prepared for your tutoring session, 2a) Have a list of questions ready for your tutor, 2b) Provide tutor with background information, 2bi) Is this subject your major?, 2bii) At what point or which topic caused you to fall behind?, 2biii) Do you plan to take additional courses in this subject?, 3) Choose a time slot for your tutoring session that allows you to be alert, punctual, and ready to learn; heading — Tutoring Hours; paragraph — The table below lists the tutoring hours available by subject.; table — row 1 column headings: Subject, Day, Time; row 2: Algebra, Monday – Friday, 9:00 a.m. – 1:00 p.m.; row 3: Calculus, Monday – Wednesday, 2:00 p.m. – 4:30 p.m.; row 4: Geometry, Monday, Tuesday, Friday, 8:00 a.m. – 11:30 a.m.; row 5: Spanish, Wednesday and Friday, 4:00 p.m. – 9:00 p.m.; row 6: German, Wednesday – Friday, 6:00 p.m. – 9:00 p.m.; row 7: French, Tuesday and Thursday, 9:00 a.m. – 2:00 p.m.; row 8: English Composition, Monday – Wednesday, 3:00 p.m. – 7:30 p.m.

Both pages should include the text watermark, Building Successful Students. Use the concepts and techniques presented in this chapter to create and format the sales proposal. Be sure to check the spelling and grammar of the finished document. Submit your assignment in the format specified by your instructor.

2: Create a Proposal for a Family Business

Personal

As a part-time helper with your family business, your sister has asked you to design a two-page sales proposal for the business that will be mailed to local residents. The title page is to contain the name, Steam n Fresh Carpet Cleaning, formatted with a border and shading. Include an appropriate SmartArt graphic with the text: Home, Office, Industrial. Include the slogan, Efficient and Thorough Carpet Cleaning.

The second page of the proposal should contain the following: heading — Why Choose Steam n Fresh?; paragraph — Steam n Fresh Carpet Cleaning is a family-owned business that has been in continuous operation for more than 30 years. We have four facilities in the greater Mitchelltown area, so we are never far from your home or business. And, whether it is your home or your business in need of our services, we have the equipment for the job.; heading — Your Customized Estimate; paragraph — As you requested in your e-mail query, below is an estimate to clean your facility. Note that the prices are discounted at 10 percent, per our online coupon offer.; table — row 1 column headings: Item, Cost; row 2: Air duct cleaning, $70; row 3: 3 offices @ $15 each, $45; row 4: 2 hallways @ $10 each, $20; row 5: Conference room, $25; row 6: 16 chairs @ $3 each, $48; row 7: Lunchroom, $40; row 8: Total, [use the formula command to compute the sum];

Continued >

Cases and Places *continued*

heading — Services Included; paragraph — Our technicians use an eco-friendly, biodegradable solution to clean your items. All furniture pieces (with the exception of large electronic items) are moved and replaced after the carpet beneath them has been cleaned. In addition, we use a patented brush attachment to clean next to the baseboard, which many other cleaners do not.; heading — Optional Services; paragraph — In addition to the standard services included, we offer the following optional services:; multilevel list — 1) Repair, 1a) Deep stain treatment and removal, 1b) Tears, burns, and other damage, 1c) Restretching, 1d) Odor removal, 2) Window coverings, 2a) Draperies of any fabric type or size (priced per panel; cost varies based on width and length of drapery), 2b) Mini and vertical blinds, shades, and other window coverings, 3) 24-hour emergency water damage and flood service.

Both pages should include the text watermark, Steam n Fresh. Use the concepts and techniques presented in this chapter to create and format the sales proposal. Be sure to check the spelling and grammar of the finished document. Submit your assignment in the format specified by your instructor.

3: Create a Proposal for a Construction Company

Professional

As a part-time assistant for Oak Ridge Builders, your boss has asked you to design a two-page sales proposal for the business that will mailed to residents of northwestern Indiana. The title page is to contain the name, Oak Ridge Builders, formatted with a border and shading. Include an appropriate SmartArt graphic that conveys this message: Quality, Design, and Affordability. Include the slogan, Building Better Homes for 50 Years!

The second page of the proposal should contain the following: heading — Select Lots Now Available in Windmere Estates; paragraph — Oak Ridge Builders has just acquired a substantial parcel of lots in the new, prestigious Windmere Estates subdivision. Let us build your new home on the lot of your choice. Windmere Estates offers the following:; bulleted list — Convenient location just 10 minutes from the interstate and approximately 20 minutes from downtown; Wooded lots with mature trees; Community pool, clubhouse, and park; Four-star school district; Reasonable neighborhood association fees provide snow removal, common area maintenance, and street signs; Wide, winding streets complete with sidewalks; heading — Available Lots; paragraph — All lots range from one-third to three-quarters of an acre. Discounts are available to buyers who wish to purchase a double lot. The table below lists the lots available for purchase (shaded lot numbers indicate wooded lot).; table — row 1 column headings: Lot Size, Price, Lot Number; row 2: One-third acre, $37,000, 80; row 3: One-third acre, $35,950, 58; row 4: One-half acre, $40,000, 56 (wooded lot); row 5: One-half acre, $40,000, 74; row 6: One-half acre, $45,000, 47 (wooded lot); row 7: Two-thirds acre, $46,000, 113; row 8: Two-thirds acre, $53,500, 94 (wooded lot); row 9: Three-quarter acre, $50,000, 98; row 10: Three-quarter acre, $57,000, 85 (wooded lot); row 11: Three-quarter acre, $62,000, 87 (wooded lot); heading — About Oak Ridge Builders; paragraph — At Oak Ridge Builders, we have been building affordable, quality housing in this area for more than 50 years. We offer a variety of floor plans, including ranch, bi-level and tri-level, and two-story homes, with or without basements. You can choose from one of our popular designs, or we can build from your plans. We also are happy to customize any floor plan to meet your needs.; paragraph — Take advantage of the various tax credits, discounts, and low interest rates available today. Let us help you build your dream home!

Both pages should include the text watermark, Phase 1 Now Open. Use the concepts and techniques presented in this chapter to create and format the sales proposal. Be sure to check the spelling and grammar of the finished document. Submit your assignment in the format specified by your instructor.

5 | Using a Template to Create a Resume and Sharing a Finished Document

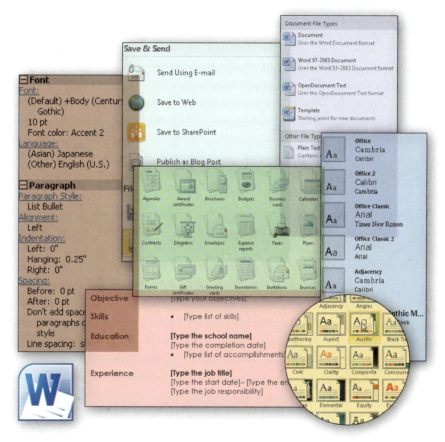

Objectives

You will have mastered the material in this chapter when you can:

- Use a template to create a document
- Change a document theme
- Fill in a document template
- Indent a paragraph
- Insert a building block
- Customize theme fonts
- Create a Quick Style

- Modify a style
- Save a Word document as a PDF or XPS document
- Send a Word document using e-mail
- Save a Word document as a Web page
- Format text as a hyperlink
- Add a background

5 | Using a Template to Create a Resume and Sharing a Finished Document

Introduction

Some people prefer to use their own creative skills to design and compose Word documents. Using Word, for example, you can develop the content and decide on the location of each item in a document. On occasion, however, you may have difficulty composing a particular type of document. To assist with the task of creating certain types of documents, such as resumes and letters, Word provides templates. A **template** is similar to a form with prewritten text; that is, Word prepares the requested document with text and/or formatting common to all documents of this nature. After Word creates a document from a template, you fill in the blanks or replace prewritten words in the document.

Once you have created a document, such as a resume, you often share it with others electronically via e-mail or on the Web.

Project — Resume

At some time, you will prepare a resume to send to prospective employers. In addition to some personal information, a **resume** usually contains the applicant's educational background and job experience. Employers review many resumes for each vacant position. Thus, you should design your resume carefully so that it presents you as the best candidate for the job.

The project in this chapter follows generally accepted guidelines for creating resumes and uses Word to create the resume shown in Figure 5–1. The resume for Riley Clarke, a recent graduate of a veterinary technology program, uses a Word template to present relevant information to a potential employer.

Overview

As you read through this chapter, you will learn how to create the resume shown in Figure 5–1 by performing these general tasks:

- Use a template to create a resume.
- Save and print the resume.
- Save the resume in a variety of formats.
- E-mail the resume.
- Save the resume as a Web page.
- Format the Web page.

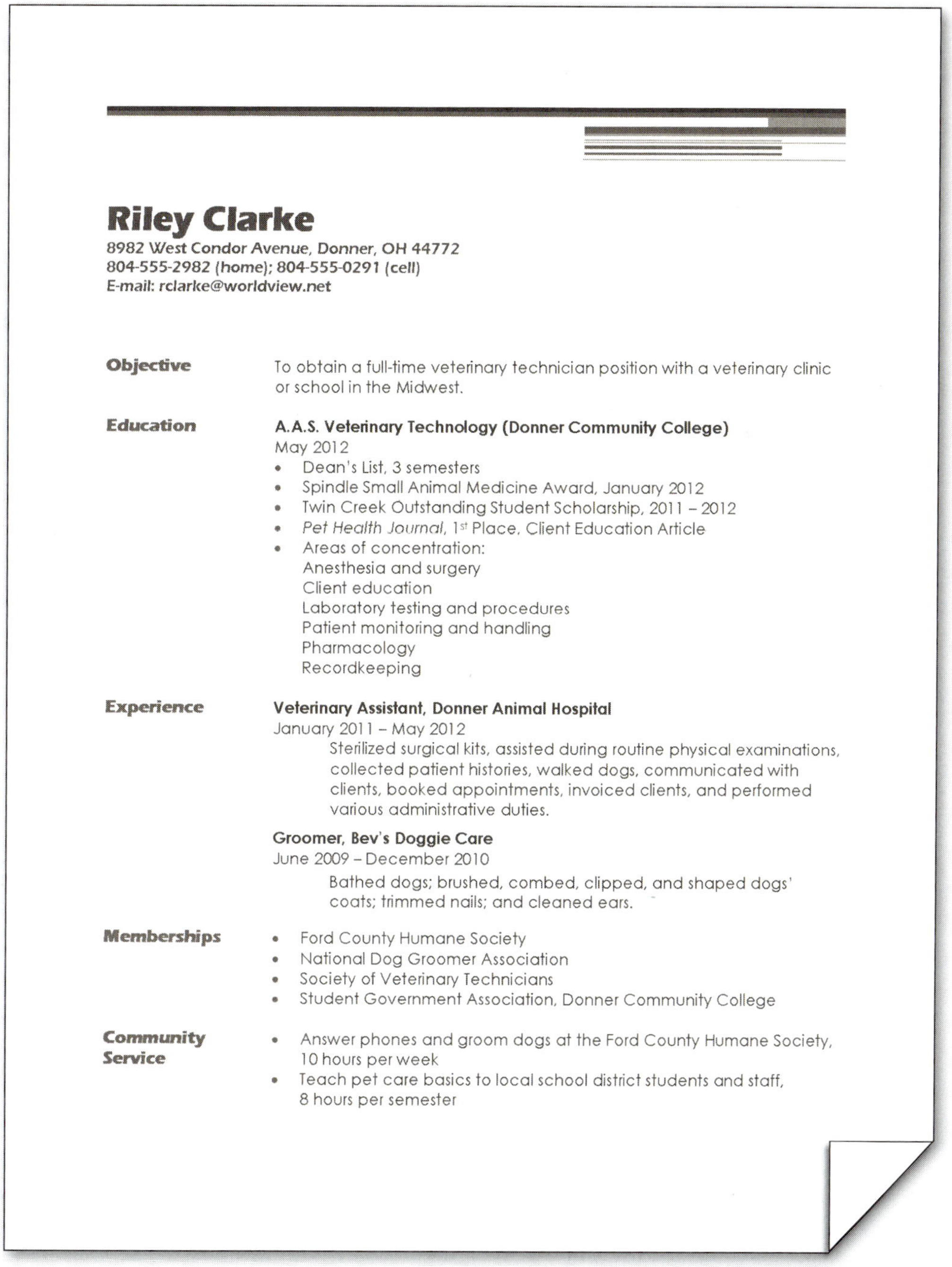

Riley Clarke
8982 West Condor Avenue, Donner, OH 44772
804-555-2982 (home); 804-555-0291 (cell)
E-mail: rclarke@worldview.net

Objective   To obtain a full-time veterinary technician position with a veterinary clinic
                     or school in the Midwest.

Education   **A.A.S. Veterinary Technology (Donner Community College)**
                     May 2012
                     - Dean's List, 3 semesters
                     - Spindle Small Animal Medicine Award, January 2012
                     - Twin Creek Outstanding Student Scholarship, 2011 – 2012
                     - *Pet Health Journal*, 1st Place, Client Education Article
                     - Areas of concentration:
                       Anesthesia and surgery
                       Client education
                       Laboratory testing and procedures
                       Patient monitoring and handling
                       Pharmacology
                       Recordkeeping

Experience   **Veterinary Assistant, Donner Animal Hospital**
                     January 2011 – May 2012
                             Sterilized surgical kits, assisted during routine physical examinations,
                             collected patient histories, walked dogs, communicated with
                             clients, booked appointments, invoiced clients, and performed
                             various administrative duties.

                     Groomer, Bev's Doggie Care
                     June 2009 – December 2010
                             Bathed dogs; brushed, combed, clipped, and shaped dogs'
                             coats; trimmed nails; and cleaned ears.

Memberships   - Ford County Humane Society
                     - National Dog Groomer Association
                     - Society of Veterinary Technicians
                     - Student Government Association, Donner Community College

Community   - Answer phones and groom dogs at the Ford County Humane Society,
Service   10 hours per week
                     - Teach pet care basics to local school district students and staff,
                       8 hours per semester

Figure 5–1

General Project Guidelines

When creating a Word document, the actions you perform and decisions you make will
affect the appearance and characteristics of the finished document. As you create a resume,
such as the project shown in Figure 5–1, you should follow these general guidelines:

1. **Craft a successful resume.** Your resume should present, at a minimum, your contact
   information, objective, educational background, and work experience to a potential
   employer. It should honestly present all your positive points. The resume should be
   error free. Ask someone else to proofread your resume and give you suggestions for
   improvements.

(continued)

**Plan
Ahead**

Plan Ahead

(continued)

2. **For electronic distribution, such as e-mail, ensure the document is in the proper format.** Save the resume in a format so that you can share it with others. Be sure that others will be able to open the resume using software on their computers and that the look of the resume will remain intact when recipients open the resume.

3. **Create a resume Web page from your resume Word document.** Save the Word document as a Web page. Improve the usability of the resume Web page by making your e-mail address a link to an e-mail program. Enhance the look of the Web page by adding, for example, a background color. Be sure to test your finished Web page document in at least one browser program to be sure it looks and works as you intended.

4. **Publish your resume Web page.** Once you have created a Web page, you can publish it. **Publishing** is the process of making a Web page available to others on a network, such as the Internet or a company's intranet. Many Internet access providers offer storage space on their Web servers at no cost to their subscribers. The procedures for using Microsoft Office to publish documents are discussed in Appendices B and C.

When necessary, more specific details concerning the above guidelines are presented at appropriate points in the chapter. The chapter also will identify the actions performed and decisions made regarding these guidelines during the creation of the resume shown in Figure 5–1 on the previous page.

To Start Word and Display Formatting Marks

If you are using a computer to step through the project in this chapter and you want your screens to match the figures in this book, you should change your screen's resolution to 1024 × 768. The following steps start Word and display formatting marks.

1 Start Word. If necessary, maximize the Word window.

2 If the Print Layout button on the status bar is not selected (as shown in Figure 5–4 on page WD 278), click it so that your screen is in Print Layout view.

3 Change your zoom to 100%.

4 If the Show/Hide ¶ button (Home tab | Paragraph group) is not selected already, click it to display formatting marks on the screen.

Using a Template to Create a Resume

Although you could compose a resume in a blank document window, this chapter shows how to use a template instead, where Word formats the resume with appropriate headings and spacing. You then customize the resume generated by the template by filling in blanks and by selecting and replacing text.

Plan Ahead

Craft a successful resume.
Two types of resumes are the chronological resume and the functional resume. A chronological resume sequences information by time, with the most recent listed first. This type of resume highlights a job seeker's job continuity and growth. A functional resume groups information by skills and accomplishments. This resume emphasizes a job seeker's experience and qualifications in specialized areas. Some resumes use a combination of the two formats. For an entry-level job search, experts recommend a chronological resume or a combination of the two types of resumes.

(continued)

(continued)

**Plan
Ahead**

When creating a resume, be sure to include necessary information and present it appropriately. Keep descriptions short and concise, using action words and bulleted lists.

- **Include necessary information.** Your resume should include contact information, a clearly written objective, educational background, and experience. Use your legal name and mailing address, along with your phone number and e-mail address, if you have one. Other sections you might consider including are memberships, skills, recognitions and awards, and/or community service. Do not include your Social Security number, marital status, age, height, weight, gender, physical appearance, health, citizenship, previous pay rates, reasons for leaving a prior job, current date, high-school information (if you are a college graduate), and references. Employers assume you will give references, if asked, and this information simply clutters a resume.

- **Present your resume appropriately.** For printed resumes, use a high-quality ink-jet or laser printer to print your resume on standard letter-size white or ivory paper. Consider using paper that contains cotton fibers for a professional look.

To Create a New Document from a Sample Template

Word installs a variety of sample templates for letters, fax cover sheets, reports, and resumes on your computer's hard disk. The sample templates are grouped in ten styles: Adjacency, Apothecary, Black Tie, Equity, Essential, Executive, Median, Oriel, Origin, and Urban. The sample templates in each style use similar formatting, themes, etc., enabling users to create a set of documents that complement one another, if desired. For example, if you create a letter and a resume using the same style, such as Urban, the two documents will have complementary colors, fonts, etc., and a similar look.

In this chapter, you will create a resume using the template with the Urban style. The following steps create a new document based on a sample (installed) template.

- Click File on the Ribbon to open the Backstage view.
- Click the New tab in the Backstage view to display the New gallery (Figure 5–2).

Q&A

What is the difference between Sample templates and Office.com Templates?

Sample templates are installed on your computer's hard disk, whereas Office.com templates are available on the Web. If you are connected to the Internet when you click the desired template in the Office.com Templates area of the New gallery, Word displays templates from the Web that you can download and use in Word.

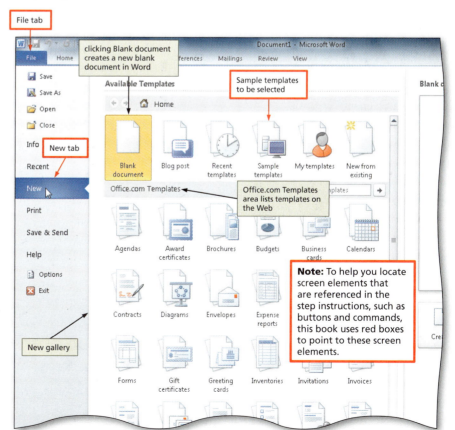

Figure 5–2

2

- Click Sample templates in the New gallery to display a list of templates installed on your computer's hard disk.

Experiment

- Click various installed templates in the Sample templates list and see a preview of the selected sample template in the right pane of the New gallery.

- Scroll through the Sample templates list and then click Urban Resume to select the template (Figure 5–3).

Q&A

How would I redisplay the original New gallery?

You would click the Back button in the New gallery. To return to the list in Figure 5–3, you would click the Forward button.

3

- Click the Create button to create a new document based on the selected template (Figure 5–4).

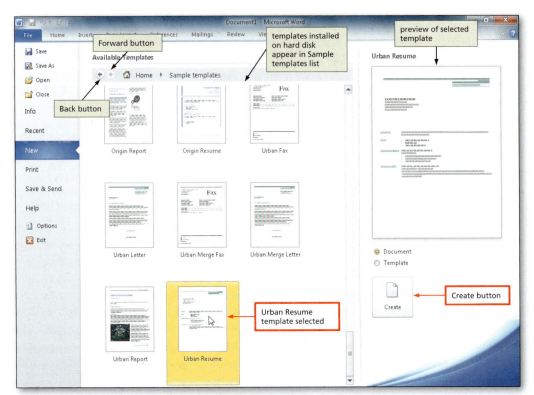

Figure 5–3

Figure 5–4

TO CREATE A NEW BLANK DOCUMENT

If, instead of a creating a new document from a sample template, you wanted to create a new blank document with the Word window open, you would perform the following steps.

1. Click File on the Ribbon to open the Backstage view.

2. Click the New tab to display the New gallery.

3. If necessary, click Blank document in the middle pane of the New gallery (shown in Figure 5–2 on page WD 277) and then click the Create button in the right pane to open a new blank document window in Word.

or

1. Press CTRL+N.

BTW

Q&As

For a complete list of the Q&As found in many of the step-by-step sequences in this book, visit the Word 2010 Q&A Web page (scsite.com/wd2010/qa).

To Change the Document Theme

A **document theme** is a coordinated combination of a color scheme, font set, and effects. In previous chapters, you have used a color scheme from one document theme and a font set from another document theme. In this chapter, the resume uses the Austin document theme, which uses the Austin color scheme and Austin font set. Instead of changing the color scheme and font set individually, Word provides a means of changing the entire document theme at once.

The document theme for the current resume is Urban. The following steps change the document theme to Austin.

1

- Display the Page Layout tab.

- Click the Themes button (Page Layout tab | Themes group) to display the Themes gallery.

- Point to Austin in the Themes gallery to display a live preview of that theme applied to the document (Figure 5–5).

🔎 **Experiment**

- Point to various themes in the Themes gallery and watch the color scheme and font set change in the document window.

2

- Click Austin in the Themes gallery to change the document theme.

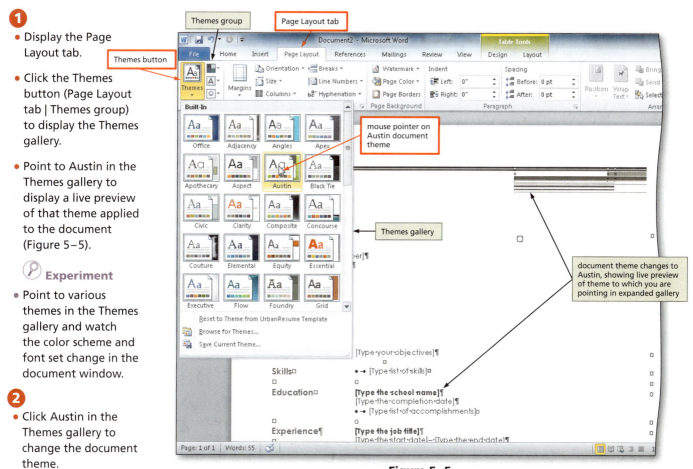

Figure 5–5

To Print the Resume

To see the entire resume created by the resume template using the Austin document theme, print the document shown in the Word window. The following steps print a document.

1 Click File on the Ribbon to open the Backstage view and then click the Print tab in the Backstage view to display the Print gallery.

2 Verify that the printer name on the Printer Status button will print a hard copy of the document. If necessary, change the selected printer.

3 Click the Print button to print the open document using the current document theme (Figure 5–6).

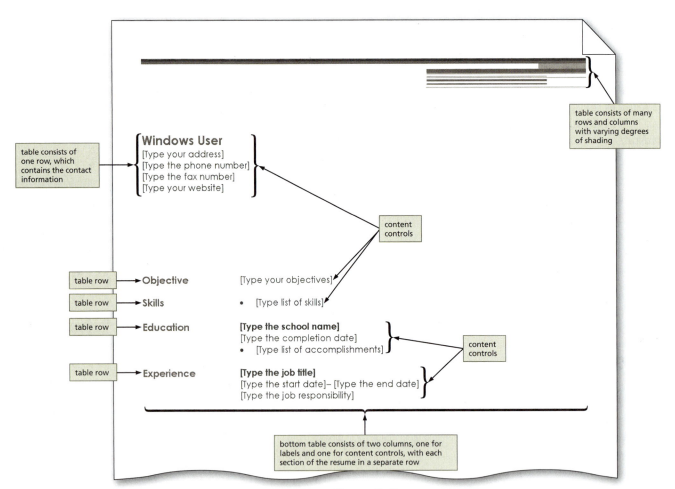

Figure 5–6

Resume Template

The resume created from the template, shown in Figure 5–6, consists of three separate tables. The table at the top of the document consists of many small rows with varying degrees of shading to give a decorative look to the resume. The second table contains content controls for the job seeker's contact information. The third table contains labels and content controls for the Objective, Skills, Education, and Experience sections of the resume.

A **content control** is an object that contains instructions for filling in text and graphics. To select a content control, you click it. As soon as you begin typing in the selected content control, your typing replaces the instructions in the control. Thus, you do not need to delete the selected instructions before you begin typing.

The following pages personalize the resume created by the resume template using these general steps:

1. Change the name at the top of the resume.
2. Fill in the contact information below the name.
3. Fill in the Objective section.
4. Move the Education and Experience sections above the Skills section.
5. Fill in the Education and Experience sections.
6. Add a row for the Community Service section.
7. Change the Skills labels to Membership and Community Service and fill in these sections.

To Change the Margin Settings

The resume template selected in this project uses .75-inch top, bottom, left, and right margins. You prefer a bit wider margin so that the text does not run so close to the edges of the page. Specifically, the resume in this chapter uses 1-inch top, bottom, left, and right margins. The following steps change the margin settings.

1 Click the Margins button (Page Layout tab | Page Setup group) to display the Margins gallery (Figure 5–7).

2 Click Normal in the Margins gallery to change the margins to the selected settings.

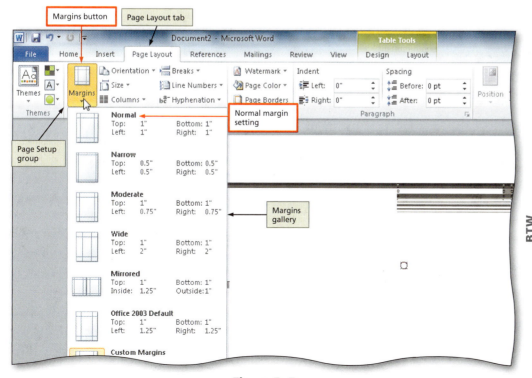

Figure 5–7

BTW

The Ribbon and Screen Resolution
Word may change how the groups and buttons within the groups appear on the Ribbon, depending on the computer's screen resolution. Thus, your Ribbon may look different from the ones in this book if you are using a screen resolution other than 1024 × 768.

To View Gridlines

When tables contain no borders, such as those in this resume, it can be difficult to see the individual cells in the table. To help identify the location of cells, you can display gridlines, which show cell outlines on the screen. The following steps show gridlines.

1 Position the insertion point in any table cell, in this case, the cell containing the Objective label.

2 Display the Table Tools Layout tab.

3 If it is not selected already, click the View Table Gridlines button (Table Tools Layout tab | Table group) to show gridlines in the tables (Figure 5–8).

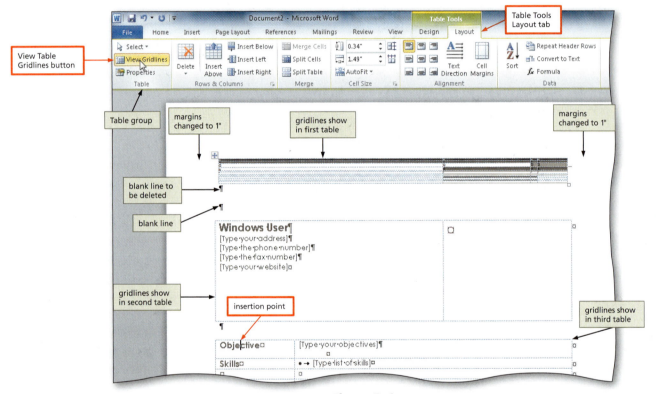

Figure 5–8

To Delete a Line

Two blank lines are above the name in the resume. In this project, to allow more space for the sections in the resume, you delete one of the blank lines above the name. The following steps delete a line.

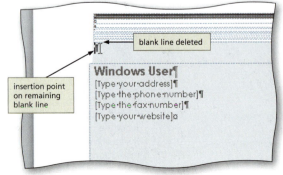

1 Position the insertion point on the first blank paragraph at the top of the resume.

2 Press the DELETE key to delete the blank line (Figure 5–9).

Q&A Why is the table containing the contact information shaded gray?

As you move the mouse pointer over the contact information, it may become shaded gray because the entire table is a building block. Recall that building blocks contain named text or graphics that you can reuse in documents.

Figure 5–9

To Modify Text in a Content Control

The next step is to select the text that the template inserted in the resume and replace it with personal information. The name area on your resume may contain a name, which Word copied from the Word Options dialog box, or it may contain the instruction, Type your name. This content control should contain the job seeker's name.

The following steps modify the text in a content control.

• If the name content control in your resume contains a name, triple-click the name content control to select it. If the name content control in your resume contains the instruction, Type your name, click the content control to select it (Figure 5–10).

Figure 5–10

• Type **Riley Clarke** as the name (Figure 5–11).

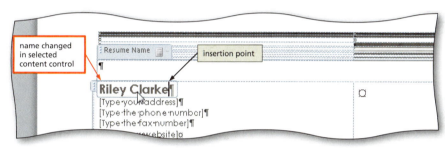

Figure 5–11

To Format a Content Control

The next step is to format the text in the name content control. In this project, the name is changed to a different color with a larger font size to give it more emphasis in the resume.

To modify text in a content control, select the content control and then modify the formats. That is, you do not need to select the text in the content control. The following step formats the name content control.

1

• If the name content control is not selected, click it.

Q&A

How can I tell if a content control is selected?

A selected content control is surrounded by a rounded rectangle.

• Click the Font Size box arrow (Home tab | Font group) and then click 22 in the Font Size gallery to increase the font size of the text in the selected content control.

• Click the Font Color button arrow (Home tab | Font group) and then click Brown, Accent 2, Darker 25% (sixth column, fifth row) in the Font Color gallery to change the font color of the text in the selected content control (Figure 5–12).

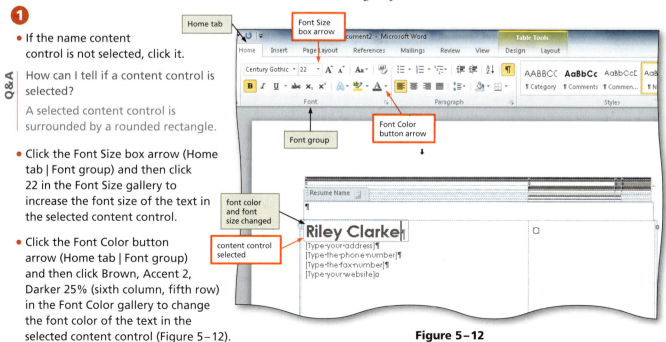

Figure 5–12

To Replace Placeholder Text

The next step is to select the placeholder text, Type your address, and replace it with your address. Word uses **placeholder text** to indicate where text can be typed. To replace placeholder text, you click it to select it and then type. The typed text automatically replaces the selected placeholder text. The following steps replace the placeholder text in the address content control.

- Click the content control with the placeholder text, Type your address, to select it (Figure 5–13).

Figure 5–13

- Type 8982 West Condor Avenue, Donner, OH 44772 as the address (Figure 5–14).

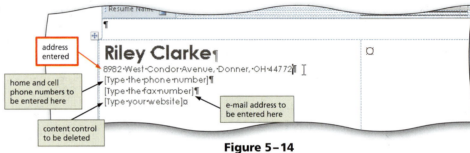

Figure 5–14

To Replace More Placeholder Text in Content Controls

The next step is to select the placeholder text in the phone number and fax number content controls in the resume and replace their instructions with personal information. You will enter home and cell phone numbers in the phone number placeholder text and an e-mail address in the fax number placeholder text (because you do not have a fax number). The following steps replace placeholder text.

1 Click the content control with the placeholder text, Type the phone number, to select it.

2 Type 804-555-2982 (home); 804-555-0291 (cell) as the home and cell phone numbers.

3 Click the content control with the placeholder text, Type the fax number, to select it.

4 Type E-mail: rclarke@worldview.net to enter the e-mail address in place of a fax number.

To Delete a Content Control

You do not have a Web site. Thus, the next step is to delete the website content control. The next steps delete a content control.

1

- Click the content control with the placeholder text, Type your website, to select it.

- Right-click the selected content control to display a shortcut menu (Figure 5–15).

2

- Click Remove Content Control on the shortcut menu to delete the selected content control, which also deletes the placeholder text contained in the content control.

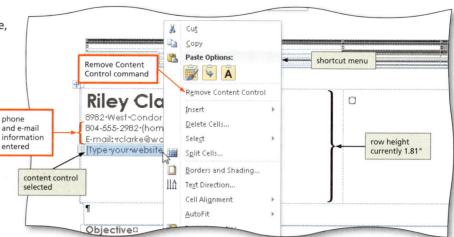

Figure 5–15

Other Ways	
1. With content control selected, click Cut button (Home tab | Clipboard group)	2. With content control selected, press CTRL+X or DELETE or BACKSPACE

To Change Row Height

The row containing the name and contact information currently is 1.81 inches tall (shown in Figure 5–15). This height places an excessively large gap between the e-mail address and Objective section on the resume. Thus, the next step is to reduce this row height to 1 inch. The following steps change row height.

1 With the insertion point in the row to adjust (shown in Figure 5–16), display the Table Tools Layout tab.

2 Click the Table Row Height box down arrow (Table Tools Layout tab \| Cell Size group) as many times as necessary until the box displays 1", to change the row height to the entered value (Figure 5–16).

BTW

Remove Content Control
If you discover that Word ignores entries in placeholder text due to certain settings, you can use the Remove Content Control command illustrated in the steps at the top of this page (shown in Figure 5–15) to convert values entered in placeholder text to regular text.

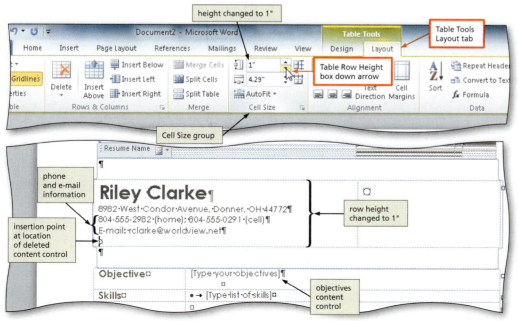

Figure 5–16

To Save the Resume

You have completed several tasks while creating this resume and do not want to risk losing work completed thus far. Accordingly, you should save the document. Thus, you should save it in a file. The following steps assume you already have created folders for storing your files, for example, a CIS 101 folder (for your class) that contains a Word folder (for your assignments). Thus, these steps save the document in the Word folder in the CIS 101 folder on a USB flash drive using the file name, Clarke Resume.

1 With a USB flash drive connected to one of the computer's USB ports, click the Save button on the Quick Access Toolbar to display the Save As dialog box.

2 Save the file in the desired location (in this case, the Word folder in the CIS 101 folder [or your class folder] on the USB flash drive) using the file name, Clarke Resume.

To Replace More Placeholder Text in Content Controls

The next step is to select the placeholder text in the objectives content control in the resume and replace it with personal information. The following steps replace placeholder text.

1 In the Objective section of the resume, select the content control with the placeholder text, Type your objectives (shown in Figure 5–16 on the previous page).

2 Type the objective: **To obtain a full-time veterinary technician position with a veterinary clinic or school in the Midwest.**

Q&A   Why is a blank line below the typed objective?

The resume template placed blank lines and blank rows throughout to separate sections of the resume.

To Move Table Rows

In the resume, you would like the Education and Experience sections immediately below the Objective sections. Because each section is in a separate row, the next step is to move the bottom three table rows (a blank table row separates the two sections) so that they are immediately below the row containing the Objective section.

You use the same procedure to move table rows as to move text. That is, select the rows to move and then drag them to the desired location. The following steps use drag-and-drop editing to move table rows.

1

- Select the rows to be moved, in this case, the last three rows in the table.

- With the mouse pointer in the selected table items, press and hold down the mouse button, which displays a dotted insertion point and a small dotted box with the mouse pointer.

- Drag the dotted insertion point to the location where the selected rows are to be moved, as shown in Figure 5–17.

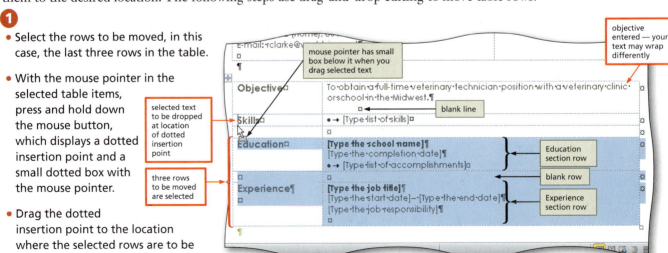

Figure 5–17

2

- Release the mouse button to move the selected rows to the location of the dotted insertion point (Figure 5–18).

Q&A What if I accidentally drag text to the wrong location?

Click the Undo button on the Quick Access Toolbar and try again.

Q&A What is the purpose of the Paste Options button?

If you click the Paste Options button, a menu appears that allows you to change the format of the rows that were moved.

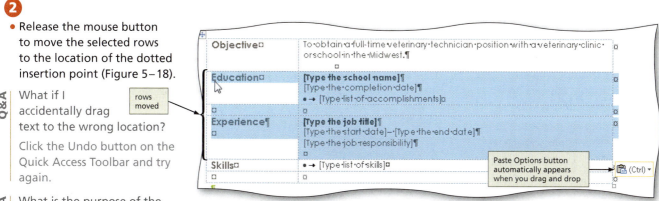

Figure 5–18

3

- Click anywhere to remove the selection from the rows.

Other Ways
1. Click Cut button (Home tab | Clipboard group), click where selected item is to be pasted, click Paste button (Home tab | Clipboard group)   2. Right-click selected text, click Cut on shortcut menu, right-click where selected item is to be pasted, click Keep Source Formatting on shortcut menu   3. Press CTRL+X, position insertion point where selected item is to be pasted, press CTRL+V

To Replace More Placeholder Text in Content Controls

The next step is to begin to enter text in the Education section of the resume. The following steps replace placeholder text.

1 In the Education section of the resume, select the content control with the placeholder text, Type the school name, and then type **A.A.S. Veterinary Technology (Donner Community College)** as the degree and school name.

2 Select the content control with the placeholder text, Type the completion date, and then type **May 2012** as the date.

3 Select the content control with the placeholder text, Type list of accomplishments.

4 Type **Dean's List, 3 semesters** as the first bulleted accomplishment and then press the ENTER key to place a bullet on the next line, ready for the next entry (shown in Figure 5–19 on the next page).

To Use AutoComplete

As you begin typing, Word may display a ScreenTip that presents a suggestion for the rest of the word or phrase you are typing. With its **AutoComplete** feature, Word predicts the word or phrase you are typing and displays its prediction in a ScreenTip. If the AutoComplete prediction is correct, you can instruct Word to finish your typing with its prediction, or you can ignore Word's prediction. Word draws its AutoComplete suggestions from its dictionary and from AutoText entries you create and save in the Normal template.

The steps on the next page use the AutoComplete feature as you type the next bulleted item in the Education section of the resume.

1

- Type **Spindle Small Animal Medicine Award, Janu** and notice the AutoComplete ScreenTip that appears on the screen (Figure 5–19).

Q&A Why would my screen not display the AutoComplete ScreenTip?

Depending on previous Word entries, you may need to type more characters in order for Word to predict a particular word or phrase accurately. Or, you may need to turn on AutoComplete by clicking File on the Ribbon to open the Backstage view, clicking Options in the Backstage view to display the Word Options dialog box; once this dialog box is displayed, click Advanced in the left pane (Word Options dialog box), place a check mark in the Show AutoComplete suggestions check box, and then click the OK button.

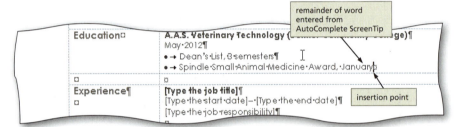

Figure 5–19

2

- Press the ENTER key to instruct Word to finish your typing with the word or phrase that appeared in the AutoComplete ScreenTip (Figure 5–20).

Q&A What if I do not want to use the text proposed in the AutoComplete ScreenTip?

Simply continue typing and the AutoComplete ScreenTip will disappear from the screen.

Figure 5–20

To Enter More Text

The following steps continue entering text in the Education section of the resume.

BTW

AutoFormat
Word automatically formats quotation marks, dashes, lists, fractions, ordinals, and other items depending on your typing and settings. To check if an AutoFormat option is enabled, click File on the Ribbon to open the Backstage view, click Options in the Backstage view, click Proofing in the left pane (Word Options dialog box), click the AutoCorrect Options button, click the AutoFormat As You Type tab, select the appropriate check boxes, and then click the OK button in each open dialog box.

1 With the insertion point following the y in January, press the SPACEBAR. Type **2012** and then press the ENTER key.

2 Type **Twin Creek Outstanding Student Scholarship, 2011 - 2012** and then press the ENTER key.

3 Type *Pet Health Journal*, 1st Place, Client Education Article (Figure 5–21).

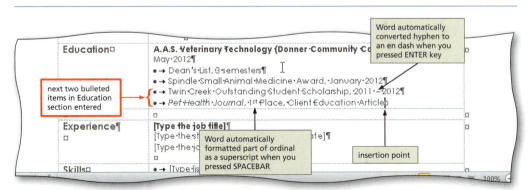

Figure 5–21

To Enter a Line Break

The next step in personalizing the resume is to enter the areas of concentration in the Education section. You want only the first line, which says, Areas of concentration:, to begin with a bullet. If you press the ENTER key on subsequent lines, Word automatically will carry forward the paragraph formatting, which includes the bullet. Thus, you will not press the ENTER key between each line. Instead, you will create a **line break**, which advances the insertion point to the beginning of the next physical line, ignoring any paragraph formatting. The following steps enter the areas of concentration using a line break, instead of a paragraph break, between each line.

1

- With the insertion point positioned as shown in Figure 5–21, press the ENTER key.

- If necessary, turn off italics. Type **Areas of concentration:** and then press SHIFT+ENTER to insert a line break character and move the insertion point to the beginning of the next physical line (Figure 5–22).

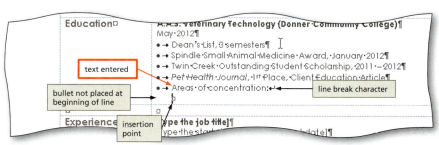

Figure 5–22

2

- Type **Anesthesia and surgery** and then press SHIFT+ENTER.

- Type **Client education** and then press SHIFT+ENTER.

- Type **Laboratory testing and procedures** and then press SHIFT+ENTER.

- Type **Patient monitoring and handling** and then press SHIFT+ENTER.

- Type **Pharmacology** and then press SHIFT+ENTER.

- Type **Recordkeeping** as the last entry. Do not press SHIFT+ENTER at the end of this line (Figure 5–23).

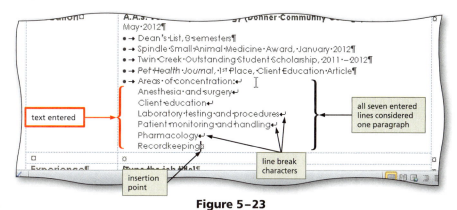

Figure 5–23

To Replace More Placeholder Text in Content Controls

The next step is to begin to enter text in the Experience section of the resume. The following steps replace placeholder text.

1 Scroll so that the bottom of the resume appears at the top of the document window.

2 In the Experience section of the resume, select the content control with the placeholder text, Type the job title, and then type **Veterinary Assistant, Donner Animal Hospital** as the job title and place of employment.

3 Select the content control with the placeholder text, Type the start date, and then type **January 2011** and then press the SPACEBAR.

4 Select the content control with the placeholder text, Type the end date, and then type **May 2012** as the end date.

BTW

Line Break Character
Line break characters do not print. A line break character is a formatting mark that indicates a line break at the end of the line.

5 Select the content control with the placeholder text, Type the job responsibility, and then type this text (Figure 5–24): `Sterilized surgical kits, assisted during routine physical examinations, collected patient histories, walked dogs, communicated with clients, booked appointments, invoiced clients, and performed various administrative duties.`

Figure 5–24

To Indent a Paragraph

In the resume, the lines below the job start date and end date that contain the job responsibilities are to be indented, so that the text in the Experience section is easier to read. The following steps indent the left edge of a paragraph.

1
- With the insertion point in the paragraph to indent, click the Increase Indent button (Home tab | Paragraph group) to indent the current paragraph one-half inch.

- To verify the paragraph is indented one-half inch, click the View Ruler button on the vertical ruler to display the rulers (Figure 5–25).

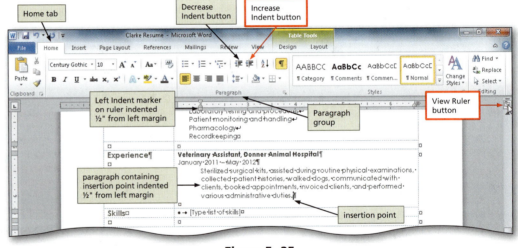

Figure 5–25

Q&A Why was the paragraph indented one-half inch?

Each time you click the Increase Indent button (Home tab | Paragraph group), the current paragraph is indented one-half inch. Similarly, clicking the Decrease Indent button (Home tab | Paragraph group) decreases the paragraph indent by one-half inch.

Experiment

- Repeatedly click the Increase Indent and Decrease Indent buttons (Home tab | Paragraph group) and watch the left indent of the current paragraph change. When you have finished experimenting, use the Increase Indent and Decrease Indent buttons until the paragraph is indented one-half inch.

2
- Click the View Ruler button on the vertical ruler to hide the rulers.

Other Ways

1. Drag Left Indent marker on horizontal ruler

2. Enter value in Indent Left text box (Page Layout tab | Paragraph group)

3. Click Paragraph Dialog Box Launcher (Home tab | Paragraph group), click Indents and Spacing tab (Paragraph dialog box),

set indentation in Left text box, click OK button

4. Right-click text, click Paragraph on shortcut menu, click Indents and

Spacing tab (Paragraph dialog box), set indentation in Left text box, click OK button

5. Press CTRL+M

To Insert a Building Block Using the Quick Parts Gallery

The Experience section of the resume in this chapter contains two jobs. The resume template, however, inserted content controls for only one job. Word has defined the sections and subsections of the resume as building blocks, which you can insert in the document. Recall that a building block contains named text or graphics that you can reuse in documents. In this case, the name of the building block you want to insert is called the Experience Subsection building block. The following steps insert a building block.

1
- Position the insertion point on the blank line below the first job entry.

- Display the Insert tab.

- Click the Quick Parts button (Insert tab | Text group) to display the Quick Parts gallery and then scroll through the Quick Parts gallery until Experience Subsection is displayed (Figure 5–26).

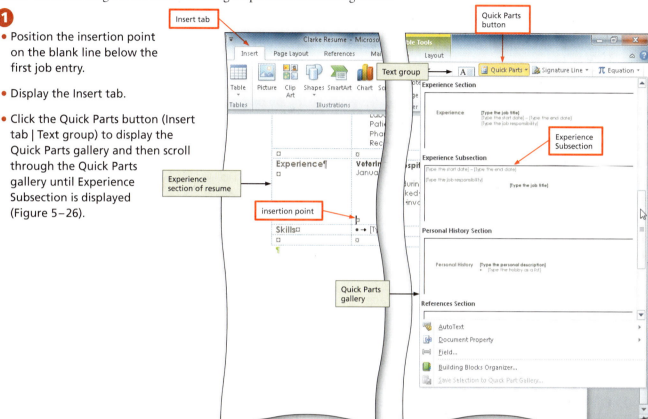

Figure 5–26

2
- Click Experience Subsection in the Quick Parts gallery to insert the building block in the document at the location of the insertion point.

- Press the BACKSPACE key to remove the extra blank space below the inserted building block (Figure 5–27).

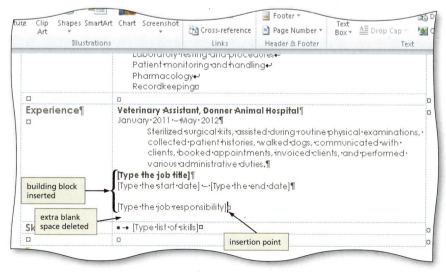

Figure 5–27

To Change Spacing before and after Paragraphs

The inserted Experience Subsection building block does not use the same paragraph spacing as the previous one in the resume. Thus, the next step is to adjust spacing before and after paragraphs in the inserted building block. The following steps change paragraph spacing.

1 Select the placeholder text, Type the end date, because you want to remove the space below this paragraph.

2 Display the Page Layout tab. If necessary, click the Spacing After box down arrow (Page Layout tab | Paragraph group) as many times as necessary until 0 pt is displayed in the Spacing After box because you want to decrease the space below the dates.

3 Select the placeholder text, Type the job title, because you want to increase the space before this paragraph.

4 Click the Spacing Before box up arrow (Page Layout tab | Paragraph group) as many times as necessary until 6 pt is displayed in the Spacing Before box because you want to increase the space above the job title.

To Replace More Placeholder Text in Content Controls and Change Paragraph Spacing

The next step is to enter the remainder of the text in the Experience section of the resume. The line spacing in the job description paragraph currently is 1.15 and should be 1 so that it matches the previous job description. The following steps replace placeholder text and change paragraph spacing.

1 In the Experience subsection of the resume, if necessary, select the content control with the placeholder text, Type the job title, and then type `Groomer, Bev's Doggie Care` as the job title and place of employment.

2 Select the content control with the placeholder text, Type the start date, and then type `June 2009` as the start date.

3 Select the content control with the placeholder text, Type the end date, and then type `December 2010` as the end date.

4 Select the content control with the placeholder text, Type the job responsibility, and then type this text: `Bathed dogs; brushed, combed, clipped, and shaped dogs' coats; trimmed nails; and cleaned ears.`

5 Display the Home tab. With the insertion point in the second job responsibility paragraph, click the Line and Paragraph Spacing button (Home tab | Paragraph group) to display the Line and Paragraph Spacing gallery and then, if necessary, click 1.0 in the gallery to change the line spacing of the current paragraph to single.

6 With the insertion point in the second job responsibility paragraph, click the Increase Indent button (Home tab | Paragraph group) to indent the current paragraph one-half inch (Figure 5–28).

BTW

BTWs
For a complete list of the BTWs found in the margins of this book, visit the Word 2010 BTW Web page (scsite.com/wd2010/btw).

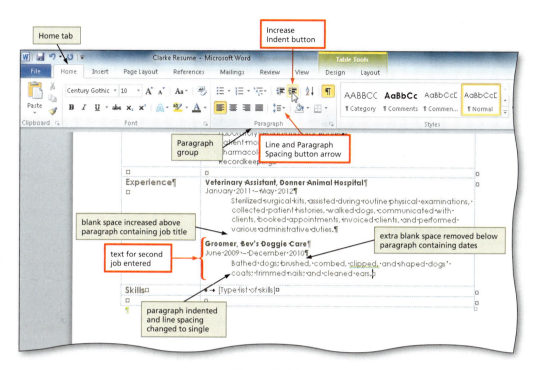

Figure 5–28

To Copy and Paste a Table Item

The last two sections of the resume in this chapter are the Memberships section and the Community Service section. Both of these sections contain a bulleted list. Currently, the resume ends with a Skills section, which contains a bulleted list. Thus, you create a copy of the Skills section so that you can then edit the two Skills sections to finish the resume for this chapter.

The Skills section currently is in one row. Because you want a blank space between the last two sections in the resume, you will copy the row containing the Skills section and then paste it below the blank row at the end of the table. You use the same procedure to copy table rows as to copy text. That is, select the rows to copy and then paste them at the desired location. The following steps copy table rows.

1

- Select the row to be copied, in this case, the row containing the Skills section in the resume.

- Click the Copy button (Home tab | Clipboard group) to copy the selected rows in the document to the Office Clipboard (Figure 5–29).

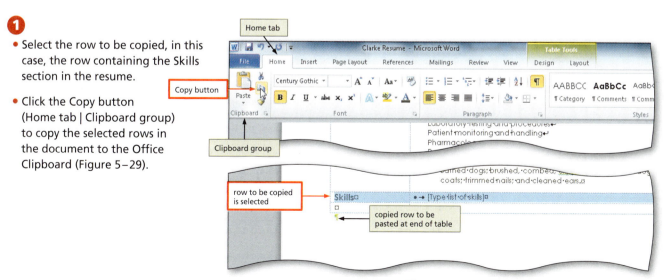

Figure 5–29

2

- Position the insertion point at the location where the copied row should be pasted, in this case, on the paragraph mark below the end of the table.

- Click the Paste button arrow (Home tab | Clipboard group) to display the Paste gallery.

Q&A
What if I click the Paste button by mistake?

Click the Undo button on the Quick Access Toolbar and then try again.

- Point to the Keep Original Table Formatting button in the Paste gallery to display a live preview of that paste option applied to the rows in the table (Figure 5–30).

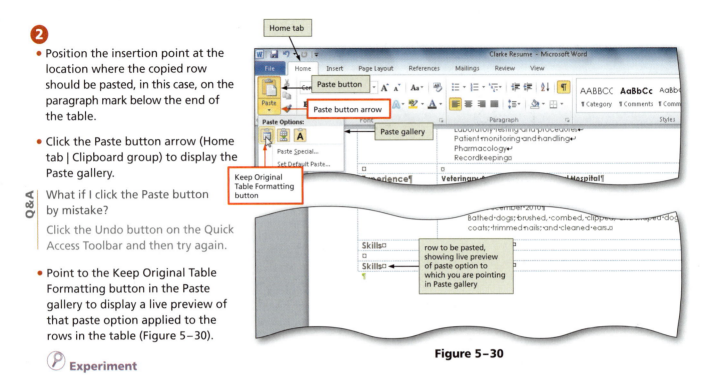

Figure 5–30

Experiment

- Point to the three options in the Paste gallery and watch the format of the pasted rows change in the document window.

3

- Click the Keep Original Table Formatting button in the Paste gallery to apply the selected option to the pasted table rows because you want the pasted rows to use the same formatting as the copied rows.

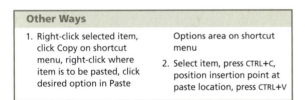

Other Ways	
1. Right-click selected item, click Copy on shortcut menu, right-click where item is to be pasted, click desired option in Paste	Options area on shortcut menu
	2. Select item, press CTRL+C, position insertion point at paste location, press CTRL+V

To Edit Text and Replace More Placeholder Text in Content Controls

The next step is to enter the remainder of the text in the resume, that is, the Memberships and Community Service sections. The following steps edit text and replace placeholder text.

1 Replace the first occurrence of the word, Skills, with `Memberships` as the new heading in the resume.

2 In the Memberships section of the resume, select the content control with the placeholder text, Type list of skills. Type `Ford County Humane Society` and then press the ENTER key.

3 Type `National Dog Groomer Association` and then press the ENTER key.

4 Type `Society of Veterinary Technicians` and then press the ENTER key.

5 Type `Student Government Association, Donner Community College` as the last membership entry.

6 In the last row of the table, replace the word, Skills, with `Community Service` as the new heading in the resume.

7 In the Community Service section of the resume, select the content control with the placeholder text, Type list of skills, and then type `Answer phones and groom dogs at the Ford County Humane Society,` and then press SHIFT+ENTER to insert a line break.

8 Type `10 hours per week` and then press the ENTER key.

9 Type `Teach pet care basics to local school district students and staff,` and then press SHIFT+ENTER to insert a line break.

10 Type `8 hours per semester` as the last community service entry.

11 Remove the bold format from the bulleted items in the Membership and Community Service sections at the bottom of the resume (Figure 5–31).

Figure 5–31

To Customize Theme Fonts

Recall that a font set defines one font for headings in a document and another font for body text. This resume currently uses the Austin font set, which specifies the Century Gothic font for both the headings and the body text. To add interest to the resume, the resume in this chapter creates a customized font set (theme font) so that the headings use the Eras Bold ITC font. Thus, the following steps create a customized theme font set with the name Resume Headings for this document.

1

• Click the Change Styles button (Home tab | Styles group) to display the Change Styles menu and then point to Fonts on the Change Styles menu to display the Fonts gallery (Figure 5–32).

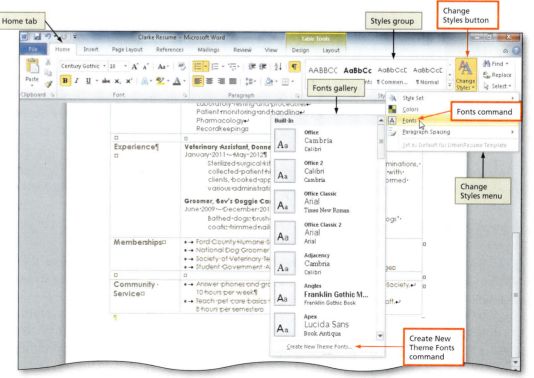

Figure 5–32

• Click Create New Theme Fonts in the Fonts gallery to display the Create New Theme Fonts dialog box.

• Click the Heading font box arrow (Create New Theme Fonts dialog box); scroll to and then click Eras Bold ITC (or a similar font).

Q&A

What if I wanted to change the font for body text, rather than or in addition to the font for headings?

You would click the Body font box arrow and then select the desired font for body text.

• Type **Resume Headings** as the name for the new theme font (Figure 5–33).

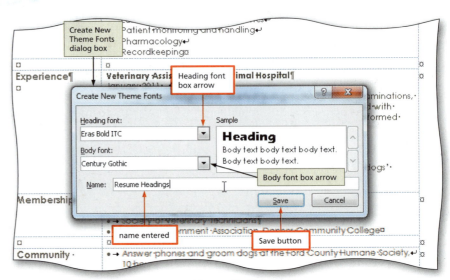

Figure 5–33

• Click the Save button (Create New Theme Fonts dialog box) to create the customized theme font with the entered name (Resume Headings, in this case) and apply the new heading fonts to the current document (Figure 5–34).

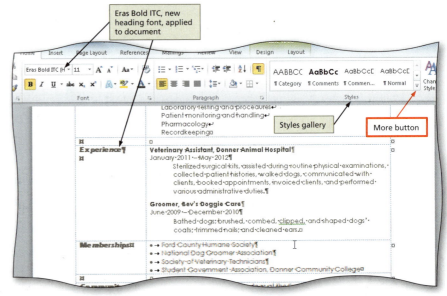

Figure 5–34

Other Ways
1. Click Theme Fonts button arrow (Page Layout tab | Themes group), click Create New Theme Fonts, select   fonts (Create New Theme Fonts dialog box), click Save button

To Create a Quick Style

Recall that a Quick Style is a predefined style that appears in the Styles gallery on the Ribbon. You have used styles in the Styles gallery to apply defined formats to text and have updated existing styles. You also can create your own Quick Styles.

In the resume for this chapter, you want to add more emphasis to the contact information. To illustrate creating a Quick Style, you will change the format of the address line and save the new format as a Quick Style. Then, you will apply the newly defined Quick Style to the lines containing the phone and e-mail information. The next steps format text in a paragraph and then create a Quick Style based on the formats in the selected paragraph.

- Scroll up so that the top of the resume is displayed in the document window.

- Select the line of text containing the address information at the top of the resume.

- Change the font of the selected text to Eras Demi ITC and change the font color to Brown, Accent 2, Darker 25% (fifth row, sixth column in the Font Color gallery).

- Click the More button (shown in Figure 5–34) in the Quick Styles gallery (Home tab | Styles group) to expand the gallery (Figure 5–35).

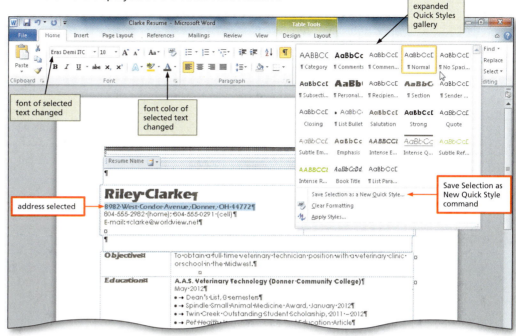

Figure 5–35

- Click Save Selection as a New Quick Style in the Quick Styles gallery to display the Create New Style from Formatting dialog box.

- Type **Resume Contact Information** in the Name text box (Create New Style from Formatting dialog box) (Figure 5–36).

③

- Click the OK button to create the new Quick Style and add it to the Styles gallery.

Q&A How can I see the style just created?

If the style name does not appear in the in-Ribbon Quick Styles gallery, click the More button on the Quick Styles gallery (Home tab | Styles group) to display the expanded Quick Styles gallery.

Figure 5–36

To Apply a Style

The next step is to apply the Quick Style just created to the lines containing the phone and e-mail information in the resume. The following steps apply a Quick Style.

① Select the text to which you want to apply the style, in this case, the lines of text containing the phone and e-mail information.

Other Ways

1. In some instances, right-click selected paragraph, click Save Selection as a New Quick Style on shortcut menu, enter name of new Quick Style (Create New Style from Formatting), click OK button

2 If the desired style name does not appear in the in-Ribbon Quick Styles gallery (in this case, Resume Contact Information), click the More button on the Quick Styles gallery (Home tab | Styles group) to expand the gallery and then point to Resume Contact Information in the Quick Style gallery to see a live preview of that style applied to the selected text in the document (Figure 5–37).

3 Click Resume Contact Information in the Quick Styles gallery to apply the selected style to the selected text in the document.

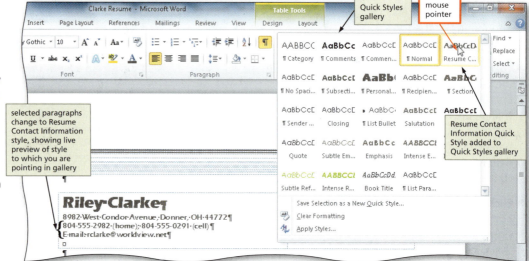

Figure 5–37

To Reveal Formatting

Sometimes, you want to know what formats were applied to certain text items in a document. For example, you may wonder what font, font size, font color, and other effects were applied to the bulleted paragraphs in the resume. To display formatting applied to text, use the Reveal Formatting task pane. The following steps show and then hide the Reveal Formatting task pane.

1

• Position the insertion point in the text for which you want to reveal formatting (in this case, the first bullet in the Education section).

• Press SHIFT+F1 to display the Reveal Formatting task pane, which shows formatting applied to the location of the insertion point in (Figure 5–38).

Experiment

• Click the Font collapse button to hide the Font formats. Click the Font expand button to redisplay the Font formats.

Q&A Why do some of the formats in the Reveal Formatting task pane appear as links?

Clicking a link in the Reveal Formatting task pane displays an associated dialog box, allowing you to change the format of the current text. For example, clicking the Font link in the Reveal Formatting task pane would display the Font dialog box. If you made changes in the Font dialog box and then clicked the OK button, Word would change the format of the current text.

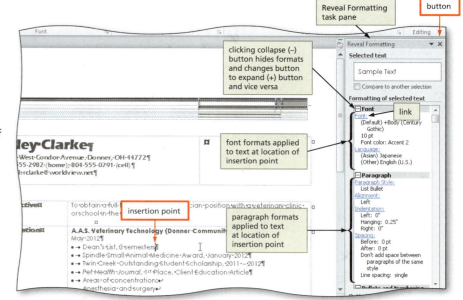

Figure 5–38

2

• Close the Reveal Formatting task pane by clicking its Close button.

To Modify a Style Using the Styles Dialog Box

The bulleted items in the resume currently have a different font color than the other text in the resume. You prefer that all text in the resume use the same font. The bulleted items are formatted according to the List Bullet style. Thus, the following steps modify the font color of the List Bullet style.

1

- Click somewhere in a bulleted list in the resume to position the insertion point in a paragraph formatted with the style to be modified.

- Click the Styles Dialog Box Launcher (Home tab | Styles group) to display the Styles task pane with the current style selected.

- If necessary, click List Bullet in the Styles task pane to select it and then click its box arrow to display the List Bullet menu (Figure 5–39).

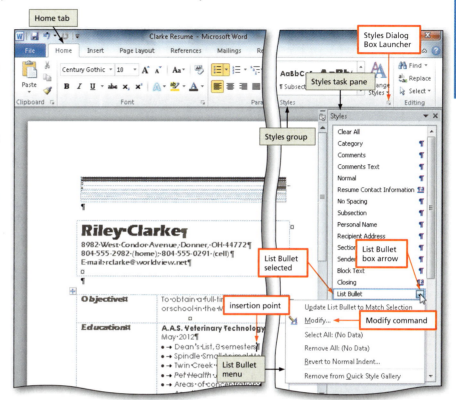

Figure 5–39

2

- Click Modify on the List Bullet menu to display the Modify Style dialog box.

- Click the Font Color button arrow (Modify Style dialog box) and then click Brown, Text 2 (first row, fourth column) in the Font Color gallery to change the font color of the current style.

- Place a check mark in the Automatically update check box so that any future changes you make to the style in the document will update the current style automatically (Figure 5–40).

Q&A

What is the purpose of the Format button in the Modify Style dialog box?

If the formatting you wish to change for the style is not available in the Modify Style dialog box, you can click the Format button and then select the desired command on the Format button menu to display a dialog box that contains additional formatting options.

Figure 5–40

3

- Click the OK button to close the dialog box and apply the style changes to the paragraphs in the document.

- Click the Close button on the Styles task pane title bar to close the task pane (Figure 5–41).

Q&A

What if the style is not updated?

Select a bulleted list paragraph in the resume; change the font color of the selected text to Brown, Text 2 using the Font Color button arrow (Home tab | Font group); click the More button in the Styles gallery (Home tab | Styles group); right-click List Bullet in the Styles gallery to display a shortcut menu; and then click Update List Bullet to Match Selection to update all similar styles in the document to the selected styles.

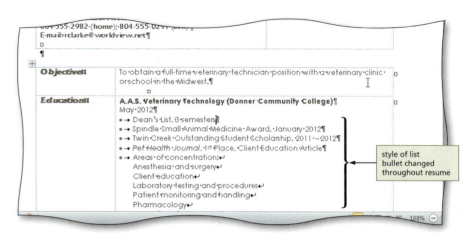

Figure 5–41

Other Ways

1. Right-click style name in Styles gallery (Home tab | Styles group), click Modify on shortcut menu, change settings (Modify Style dialog box), click OK button

2. Click Styles Dialog Box Launcher, click Manage Styles button, scroll to style and then select it (Manage Styles dialog box), click Modify button, change settings (Modify Style dialog box), click OK button in each dialog box

BTW

Conserving Ink and Toner

If you want to conserve ink or toner, you can instruct Word to print draft quality documents by clicking File on the Ribbon to open the Backstage view, clicking Options in the Backstage view to display the Word Options dialog box, clicking Advanced in the left pane (Word Options dialog box), scrolling to the Print area in the right pane, placing a check mark in the 'Use draft quality' check box, and then clicking the OK button. Then, use the Backstage view to print the document as usual.

To Save and Print the Document

The resume is complete. Thus, you should save it again. The following step saves the document again and prints it.

1 Click the Save button on the Quick Access Toolbar to overwrite the previously saved file.

2 Print the resume (shown in Figure 5–1 on page WD 275).

Online Templates

In addition to the sample templates installed on your computer's hard disk, you can access numerous online templates. Available online templates include agendas, award certificates, calendars, expense reports, fax cover letters, greeting cards, invitations, invoices, letters, meeting minutes, memos, and statements. When you select an online template, Word downloads (or copies) it from the Office.com Web site to your computer. Once it is downloaded, you can use the template directly from your computer.

TO CREATE A NEW DOCUMENT FROM AN ONLINE TEMPLATE

To create a new document based on an online template, you would follow these steps.

1. Open the Backstage view and then click the New tab in the Backstage view to display the New gallery.

2. Scroll through the list of templates and folders in the Office.com Templates area in the New gallery.

3. Click the desired folder or template.

4. Repeat Step 3 until you locate the desired template and then click that template.

5. Click the Download button in the New gallery to download the template and create a new document based on the downloaded template.

TO CREATE A NEW DOCUMENT FROM A TEMPLATE DOWNLOADED FROM OFFICE.COM

Word downloads a template from Office.com to the My templates folder on your computer. If you wanted to create another document using the downloaded template, you would do the following:

1. Open the Backstage view and then click the New tab in the Backstage view to display the New gallery.

2. Click My templates in the New gallery to display the New dialog box.

3. Click the desired template (New dialog box) and then click the OK button to create a new document based on the selected template.

> **Break Point:** If you wish to take a break, this is a good place to do so. You can quit Word now. To resume at a later time, start Word, open the file called Clarke Resume, and continue following the steps from this location forward.

Sharing a Document with Others

You may find the need to share Word documents with others electronically, such as via e-mail or via a USB flash drive. To ensure that others can read and/or open the files successfully, Word presents a variety of formats and tools to assist with sharing documents. This section uses the Clarke Resume created in this chapter to present a variety of these formats and tools.

> **For electronic distribution, such as e-mail, ensure the document is in the proper format.**
> When sharing a Word document with others, you cannot be certain that it will look or print the same on their computers as on your computer. For example, the document may wordwrap text differently on their computers. If others do not need to edit the document, that is, just view and/or print the document, you could save the file in a format that allows others to view the document as you see it. Two popular such formats are PDF and XPS.

Plan Ahead

PDF

PDF, which stands for Portable Document Format, is a file format created by Adobe Systems that shows all elements of a printed document as an electronic image. Users can view a PDF document without the software that created the original document. Thus, the PDF format enables users easily to share documents with others. To view, navigate, and print a PDF file, you use a program called **Adobe Reader**, which can be downloaded free from Adobe's Web site.

To Save a Word Document as a PDF Document and View the PDF Document in Adobe Reader

When you save a Word document as a PDF document, the original Word document remains intact; that is, Word creates a copy of the file in the PDF format. The steps on the next page save the Clarke Resume Word document as a PDF document and then open the Clarke Resume PDF document in Adobe Reader.

- Open the Backstage view and then click the Save & Send tab in the Backstage view to display the Save & Send gallery.

- Click Create PDF/XPS Document in the Save & Send gallery to display information about PDF/XPS documents in the right pane (Figure 5–42).

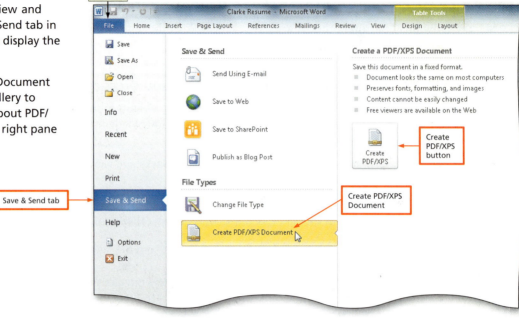

Figure 5–42

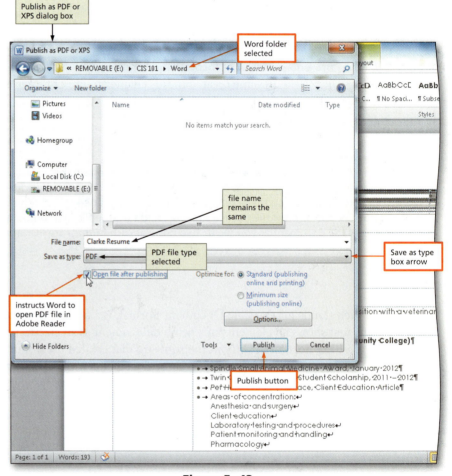

- Click the Create PDF/XPS button in the right pane to display the Publish as PDF or XPS dialog box.

- Navigate to the desired save location (in this case, the Word folder in the CIS 101 folder [or your class folder] on the USB flash drive) (Publish as PDF or XPS dialog box).

Q&A   Can the file name be the same for the Word document and the PDF document?

Yes. The file names can be the same because the file types are different: one is a Word document and the other is a PDF document.

- If necessary, click the 'Save as type' box arrow and then click PDF.

- If necessary, place a check mark in the 'Open file after publishing' check box so that Word will display the resulting PDF document in Adobe Reader (Figure 5–43).

Q&A   Why is my 'Open file after publishing' check box dimmed?

You do not have Adobe Reader installed on your computer. After installing Adobe Reader, repeat these steps.

Figure 5–43

3

- Click the Publish button to create the PDF document from the Word document and then, because the check box was selected, open the resulting PDF document in Adobe Reader.

- If necessary, click the Maximize button in the Adobe Reader window to maximize the window (Figure 5–44).

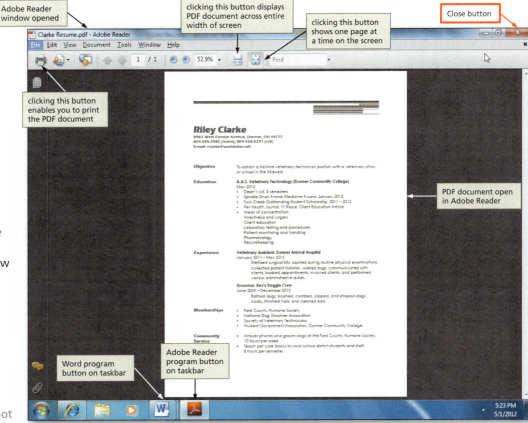

Q&A

Do I have to display the resulting PDF document in Adobe Reader?

No. If you do not want to display the document in Adobe Reader, you would not place a check mark in the 'Open file after publishing' check box in the Publish as PDF or XPS dialog box.

Q&A

Is the Clarke Resume Word document still open?

Yes. Word still is running with the Clark Resume document opened.

Figure 5–44

4

- Click the Close button on the Adobe Reader title bar to close the Clarke Resume.pdf document and quit Adobe Reader.

Other Ways

1. Press F12, click 'Save as type' box arrow (Save As dialog box), select PDF in list, click Save button

XPS

XPS, which stands for XML Paper Specification, is a file format created by Microsoft that shows all elements of a printed document as an electronic image. As with the PDF format, users can view an XPS document without the software that created the original document. Thus, the XPS format also enables users to share documents with others easily. Windows includes an XPS Viewer, which enables you to view, navigate, and print XPS files.

To Save a Word Document as an XPS Document and View the XPS Document in the XPS Viewer

When you save a Word document as an XPS document, the original Word document remains intact; that is, Word creates a copy of the file in the XPS format. The steps on the next page save the Clarke Resume Word document as an XPS document and then open the Clarke Resume XPS document in the XPS Viewer.

- Open the Backstage view and then click the Save & Send tab in the Backstage view to display the Save & Send gallery.

- Click Create PDF/XPS Document in the Save & Send gallery to display information about PDF/XPS documents in the right pane and then click the Create a PDF/XPS button to display the Publish as PDF or XPS dialog box.

- If necessary, navigate to the desired save location (in this case, the Word folder in the CIS 101 folder [or your class folder] on the USB flash drive) (Publish as PDF or XPS dialog box).

- If necessary, click the 'Save as type' box arrow and then click XPS Document.

- If necessary, place a check mark in the 'Open file after publishing' check box so that Word displays the resulting XPS document in the XPS Viewer (Figure 5–45).

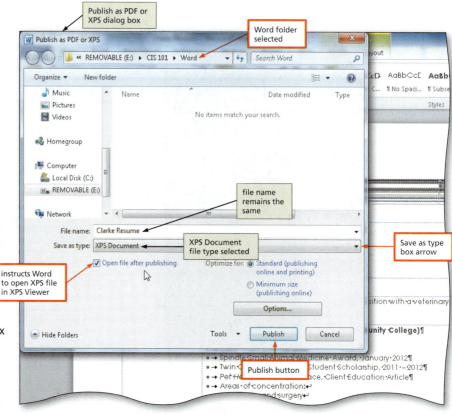

Figure 5–45

- Click the Publish button to create the XPS document from the Word document and then, because the check box was selected, open the resulting XPS document in the XPS Viewer.

Q&A What if I do not have an XPS Viewer?

The document will open in a browser window.

- If necessary, click the Maximize button in the XPS Viewer window to maximize the window (Figure 5–46).

Q&A Do I have to display the resulting XPS document in the XPS Viewer?

No. If you did not want to display the document in the XPS Viewer, you would not place a check mark in the 'Open file after publishing' check box in the Publish as PDF or XPS dialog box.

Q&A Is the Clarke Resume Word document still open?

Yes. Word still is running with the Clarke Resume document opened.

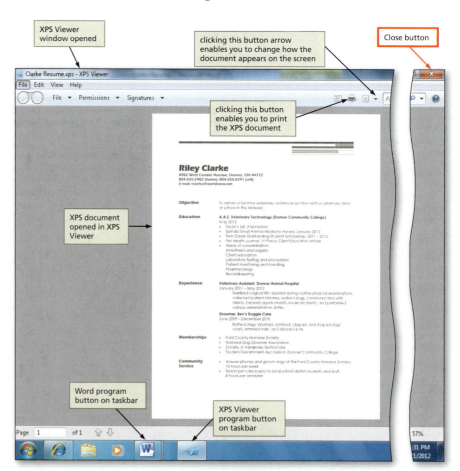

Figure 5–46

- Click the Close button on the XPS Viewer title bar to close the Clarke Resume.xps document and quit the XPS Viewer.

Other Ways
1. Press F12, click 'Save as type' box arrow (Save As dialog box), select XPS in list, click Save button

To Run the Compatibility Checker

Assume you have considered saving a document, such as your resume, in the Word 97-2003 format so that it can be opened by users with earlier versions of Microsoft Word. Before saving a document or template in an earlier Word format, however, you want to ensure that all of its elements (such as building blocks, content controls, and graphics) are compatible (will work with) earlier versions of Word. The following steps run the compatibility checker.

- Open the Backstage view and then click the Info tab in the Backstage view to display the Info gallery.
- Click the Check for Issues button in the Info gallery to display the Check for Issues menu (Figure 5–47).

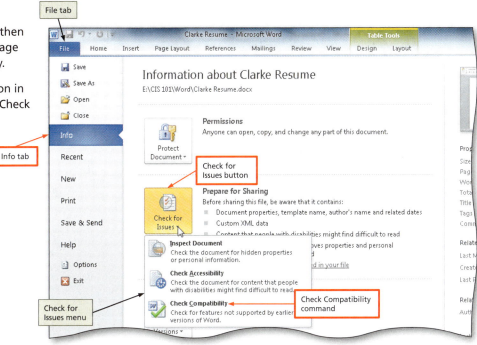

File tab

Info tab

Check for Issues button

Check for Issues menu

Check Compatibility command

Figure 5–47

- Click Check Compatibility on the Check for Issues menu to display the Microsoft Word Compatibility Checker dialog box, which shows any content that may not be supported by earlier versions of Word (Figure 5–48).

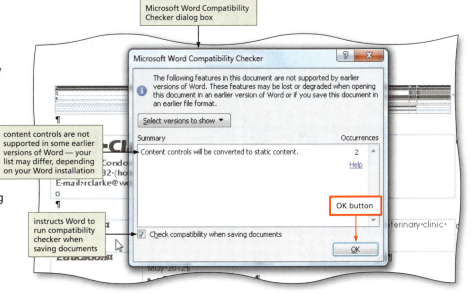

- Click the OK button (Microsoft Word Compatibility Checker dialog box) to close the dialog box.

Microsoft Word Compatibility Checker dialog box

content controls are not supported in some earlier versions of Word — your list may differ, depending on your Word installation

instructs Word to run compatibility checker when saving documents

OK button

Figure 5–48

To Save a Word 2010 Document in an Earlier Word Format

If you send a document created in Word 2010 to users who have a version of Word earlier than Word 2007, they will not be able to open the Word 2010 document because Word 2010 saves documents in a format that is not backward compatible with versions earlier than Word 2007. Word 2010 documents have a file type of .docx, and versions prior to Word 2007 have a .doc file type. To ensure that all Word users can open your Word 2010 document, you should save the document in a previous version format. The following steps save the Clarke Resume Word 2010 document in the Word 97-2003 format.

• Open the Backstage view and then click the Save & Send tab in the Backstage view to display the Save & Send gallery.

• Click Change File Type in the Save & Send gallery to display information in the right pane about various file types that can be opened in Word.

• Click Word 97-2003 in the right pane to specify the new file type (Figure 5–49).

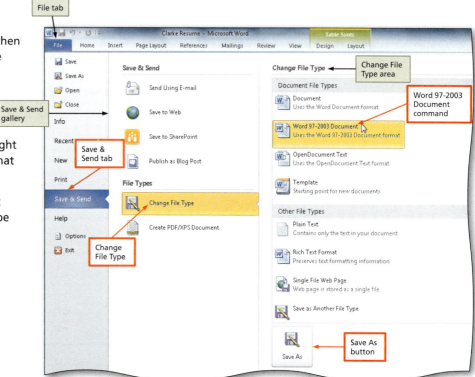

Figure 5–49

• Click the Save As button in the right pane to display the Save As dialog box.

• If necessary, navigate to the desired save location (in this case, the Word folder in the CIS 101 folder [or your class folder] on the USB flash drive) (Save As dialog box) (Figure 5–50).

Q&A

Can the file name be the same for the Word 2010 document and the Word 97-2003 document?

Yes. The file names can be the same because the file types are different: one is a Word document with a .docx extension, and the other is a Word document with a .doc extension. The next section discusses file types and extensions.

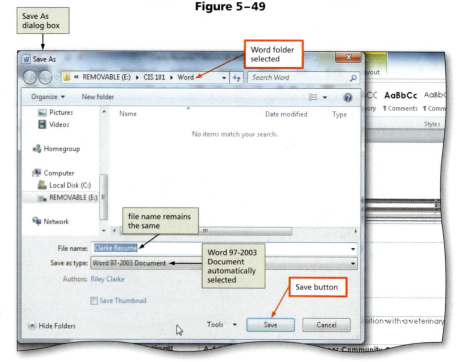

Figure 5–50

3

- Click the Save button, which may display the Microsoft Word Compatibility Checker dialog box before saving the document (Figure 5–51).

Q&A

My screen did not display the Microsoft Word Compatibility Checker dialog box. Why not?

If the 'Check compatibility when saving documents' check box is not selected (as shown in Figure 5–48 on page WD 305), Word will not check compatibility when saving a document.

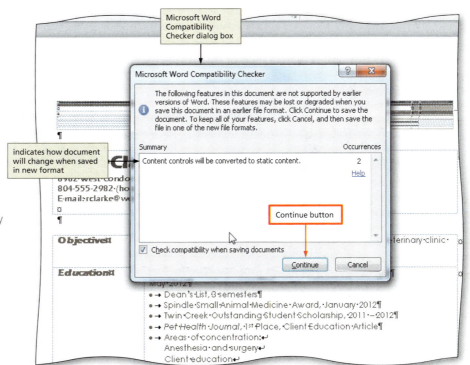

Microsoft Word Compatibility Checker dialog box

indicates how document will change when saved in new format

Continue button

Figure 5–51

4

- If the Microsoft Word Compatibility Checker dialog box is displayed, click its Continue button to save the document on the selected drive with the current file name in the specified format (Figure 5–52).

Q&A

Is the Clarke Resume Word 2010 document still open?

No. Word closed the original document (the Word 2010 Clarke Resume).

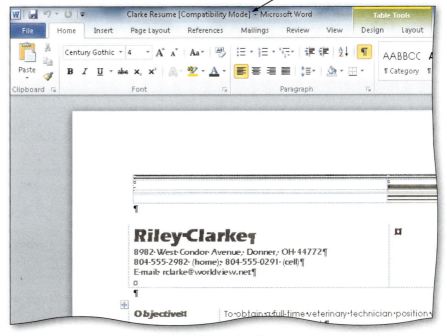

Compatibility Mode notation on title bar indicates document has been saved in a format different from Word 2010 format

Figure 5–52

Other Ways

1. Press F12, click 'Save as type' box arrow (Save As dialog box), select Word 97-2003 Document in list, click Save button

File Types

When saving documents in Word, you can select from a variety of file types that can be opened in Word using the Save & Send gallery in the Backstage view (shown in Figure 5–49) or by clicking the 'Save as type' box arrow in the Save As dialog box. To save in these varied formats (Table 5–1), you follow the same basic steps as just illustrated.

TO SAVE A WORD 2010 DOCUMENT AS A DIFFERENT FILE TYPE

To save a Word 2010 document as a different file type, you would follow these steps.

1. Open the Backstage view and then click the Save & Send tab in the Backstage view to display the Save & Send gallery.

2. Click Change File Type in the Save & Send gallery to display information in the right pane about various file types that can be opened in Word.

3. Click the desired file type in the right pane to display the Save As dialog box.

4. Navigate to the desired save location (in this case, the Word folder in the CIS 101 folder [or your class folder] on the USB flash drive) (Save As dialog box) and then click the Save button in the dialog box.

5. If the Microsoft Word Compatibility Checker dialog box appears and you agree with the changes that will be made to the document, click the Continue button (Microsoft Word Compatibility Checker dialog box) to save the document on the selected drive with the current file name in the specified format.

Table 5–1 File Types

File Type	File Extension	Windows Explorer Image	Description
Word Document	.docx		Format used for Word 2010 or Word 2007 documents
Word 97-2003 Document	.doc		Format used for documents created in versions of Word from Word 97 to Word 2003
Word Template	.dotx		Format used for Word 2010 or Word 2007 templates
Word 97-2003 Template	.dot		Format used for templates created in versions of Word from Word 97 and Word 2003
PDF	.pdf		Portable Document Format, which can be opened in Adobe Reader
XPS	.xps		XML Paper Specification, which can be opened in the XPS Viewer
Single File Web Page	.mht		HTML (Hypertext Markup Language) format that can be opened in a Web browser; all elements of the Web page are saved in a single file
Web Page	.htm		HTML (Hypertext Markup Language) format that can be opened in a Web browser; various elements of the Web page, such as graphics, saved in separate files and folders
Rich Text Format	.rtf		Format designed to ensure file can be opened and read in many programs; some formatting may be lost to ensure compatibility
Plain Text	.txt		Format where all or most formatting is removed from the document
OpenDocument Text	.odt		Format used by other word processing programs such as Google Docs and OpenOffice.org
Works 6 - 9	.wps		Format used by Microsoft Works

To Close a Document

You are finished with the Word 97-2003 format of the Clarke Resume. Thus, the next step is to close this document. The following steps close a document.

1 Open the Backstage view.

2 Click Close in the Backstage view to close the current open document.

To Open a Recent Document

You would like to reopen the Word 2010 format of the Clarke Resume. Thus, the next step is to open this document. Because it recently was open, the following steps open a document from Recent Documents.

1 Open the Backstage view and then, if necessary, click the Recent tab in the Backstage view to display the list of recent documents in the Recent gallery.

2 To be sure you open the Word 2010 format of the Clarke Resume, point to the file name and verify the file name is Clarke Resume.docx in the ScreenTip (Figure 5–53).

3 Click Clarke Resume (the Word 2010 format) in the Recent gallery to open the document in the Word document window.

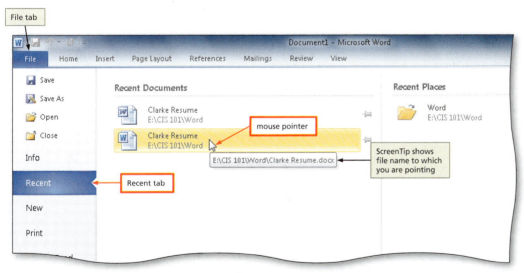

Figure 5–53

Plan Ahead

For electronic distribution, such as e-mail, ensure the document is in the proper format.
If you e-mail a document, such as your resume, consider that the recipient, such as a potential employer, may not have the same software you used to create the resume and, thus, may not be able to open the file. As an alternative, you could save the file in a format, such as a PDF or XPS, that can be viewed with a reader program. Many job seekers also post their resumes on the Web. Read Appendices B and C for ways to save Word documents on the Web.

To Send a Document Using E-Mail

In Word, you can e-mail the current document as an attachment, which is a file included with the e-mail message. The following steps e-mail the Clarke Resume, assuming you use Outlook as your default e-mail program.

- Open the Backstage view and then click the Save & Send tab in the Backstage view to display the Save & Send gallery.

- If necessary, click Send Using E-mail in the Save & Send gallery to display information in the right pane about various ways to e-mail a document from Word (Figure 5–54).

Q&A

What is the purpose of the Send as PDF and Send as XPS buttons?

Depending on which button you click, Word converts the current document either to the PDF or XPS format and then attaches the PDF or XPS document to the e-mail message.

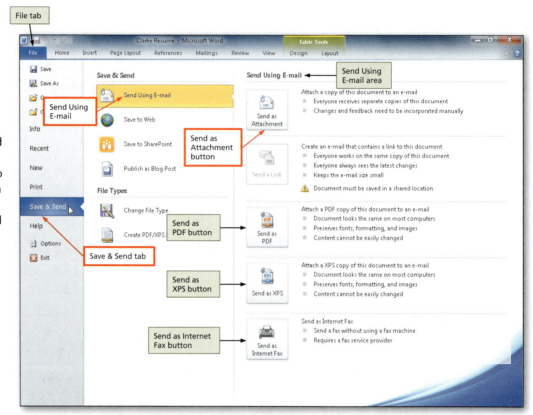

Figure 5–54

- Click the Send as Attachment button to start your default e-mail program (Outlook, in this case), which automatically attaches the active Word document to the e-mail message.

- Fill in the To text box with the recipient's e-mail address.

- Fill in the message text (Figure 5–55).

- Click the Send button to send the e-mail message along with its attachment to the recipient named in the To text box and close the e-mail window.

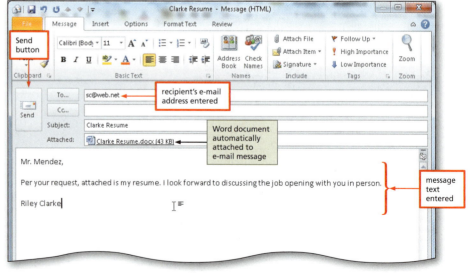

Figure 5–55

To Use the Document Inspector

Word includes a Document Inspector that checks a document for content you might not want to share with others, such as personal information. Before sharing a document with others, you may want to check for this type of content. If you wanted to use the Document Inspector, you would do the following:

1. Open the Backstage view and then click the Info tab in the Backstage view to display the Info gallery.

2. Click the Check for Issues button in the Info gallery to display the Check for Issues menu.

3. Click Inspect Document on the Check for Issues menu to display the Document Inspector dialog box.

4. Click the Inspect button (Document Inspector dialog box) to instruct Word to inspect the document.

5. Review the results (Document Inspector dialog box) and click the Remove All button(s) for any item that you do not want to be saved with the document.

6. When finished removing information, click the Close button to close the dialog box.

To Customize How Word Opens E-Mail Attachments

When a user sends you an e-mail message that contains a Word document as an attachment, Word may display the document in Full Screen Reading view. This view is designed to increase the readability and legibility of an on-screen document. Full Screen Reading view, however, does not represent how the document will look when it is printed. For this reason, many users prefer working in Print Layout view to read documents. To exit Full Screen Reading view, click the Close button in the upper-right corner of the screen.

If you wanted to customize how Word opens e-mail attachments, you would do the following.

1. Open the Backstage view and then click Options in the Backstage view to display the Word Options dialog box.

2. If necessary, click General in the left pane (Word Options dialog box).

3. If you want e-mail attachments to open in Full Screen Reading view, place a check mark in the Open e-mail attachments in Full Screen Reading view check box; otherwise, remove the check mark to open e-mail attachments in Print Layout view.

4. Click the OK button to close the dialog box.

Creating a Web Page from a Word Document

If you have created a document using Word, such as a resume, you can save it in a format that can be opened by a Web browser, such as Internet Explorer. When you save a file as a Web page, Word converts the contents of the document into **HTML** (Hypertext Markup Language), which is a set of codes that browsers can interpret. Some of Word's formatting features are not supported by Web pages. Thus, your Web page may look slightly different from the original Word document.

BTW

Internet Fax
If you do not have a stand-alone fax machine, you can send and receive faxes in Word by clicking the Send as Internet Fax button in the Backstage view (shown in Figure 5–54). To send or receive faxes using Word, you first must sign up with a fax service provider by clicking the OK button in the Microsoft Office dialog box that appears the first time you click the Send as Internet Fax button, which displays an Available Fax Services Web page. You also must ensure that either the Windows Fax printer driver or Windows Fax Services component is installed on your computer. When sending a fax, Word converts the document to an image file and attaches it to an e-mail message where you enter the recipient's fax number, name, subject, and message for the cover sheet, and then click the Send button to deliver the fax.

BTW

Saving as a Web Page
Because you might not have access to SkyDrive or a Web server, the Web page you create in this feature is saved on a USB flash drive rather than to SkyDrive or a Web server.

When saving a document as a Web page, Word provides you with three choices:

- The **single file Web page format** saves all of the components of the Web page in a single file that has a **.mht** extension. This format is particularly useful for e-mailing documents in HTML format.

- The **Web Page format** saves some of the components of the Web page in a folder, separate from the Web page. This format is useful if you need access to the individual components, such as images, that make up the Web page.

- The **filtered Web Page format** saves the file in Web page format and then reduces the size of the file by removing specific Microsoft Office formats. This format is useful if you want to speed up the time it takes to download a Web page that contains many graphics, video, audio, or animations.

The Web page created in this section uses the single file Web page format.

To Save a Word Document as a Web Page

The following steps save the Clarke Resume created earlier in this chapter as a Web page.

1

- With the Word 2010 format of the resume file open in the document window, open the Backstage view and then click the Save & Send tab in the Backstage view to display the Save & Send gallery.

- Click Change File Type in the Save & Send gallery to display information in the right pane about various file types that can be opened in Word.

- Click Single File Web Page in the right pane to specify a new file type (Figure 5–56).

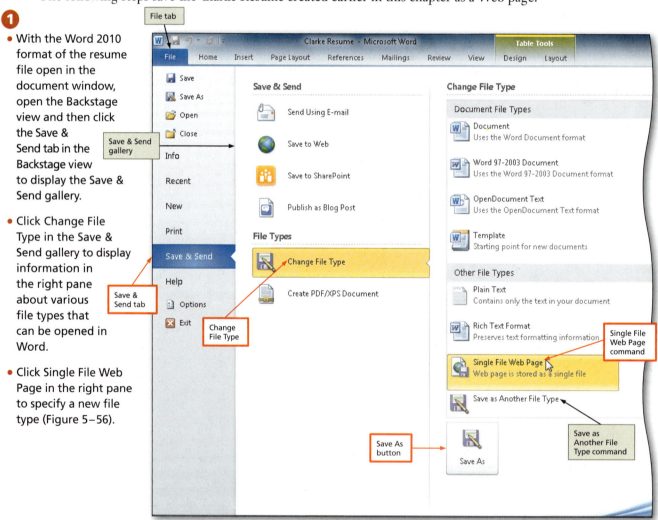

Figure 5–56

Q&A

What if I wanted to save the document as a Web Page instead of a Single File Web Page?

You would click Save as Another File Type in the Change File Type area, click the 'Save as type' box arrow in the Save As dialog box, and then click Web Page in the 'Save as type' list.

2

- Click the Save As button in the right pane to display the Save As dialog box.

- If necessary, navigate to the desired save location (in this case, the Word folder in the CIS 101 folder [or your class folder] on the USB flash drive) (Save As dialog box).

- Type **Clarke Resume Web Page** in the File name text box to change the file name.

- Click the Change Title button to display the Enter Text dialog box.

- Type **Clarke Resume** in the Page title text box (Enter Text dialog box) (Figure 5–57).

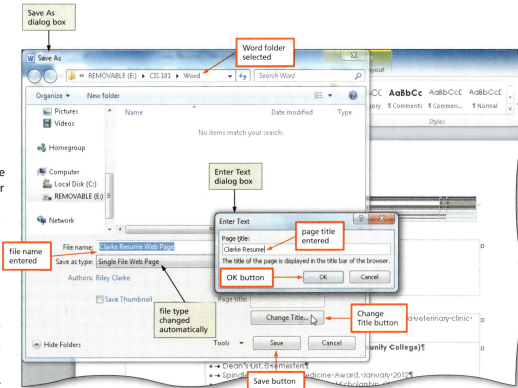

Figure 5–57

3

- Click the OK button (Enter Text dialog box) to close the dialog box.

- Click the Save button (Save As dialog box) to save the resume as a Web page and display it in the document window in Web Layout view (Figure 5–58).

- If the Microsoft Word Compatibility Checker dialog box appears, click its Continue button.

Q&A

Can I switch to Web Layout view at any time by clicking the Web Layout button?

Yes.

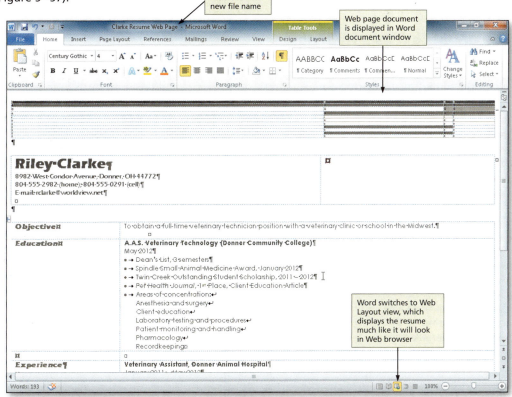

Figure 5–58

Other Ways

1. Press F12, click 'Save as type' box arrow (Save As dialog box), select Single File Web Page or Web Page in list, click Save button

Saving to the Web

If you have access to and can save files to a Web server or FTP server or have a SkyDrive or Windows Live account, then you can save the Web page from Word directly to the Web server, FTP server, or SkyDrive. To learn more about saving Web pages to a Web server or FTP site using Microsoft Office programs, refer to Appendix B. To learn more about saving to SkyDrive, refer to Appendix C.

TO SET A DEFAULT SAVE LOCATION

If you wanted to change the default location that Word uses when it saves a document, you would do the following.

1. Open the Backstage view and then click the Options in the Backstage view to display the Word Options dialog box.
2. Click Save in the left pane (Word Options dialog box) to display options for saving documents in the right pane.
3. In the 'Default file location' text box, type the new desired save location.
4. Click the OK button to close the dialog box.

Formatting and Testing a Web Page

On the Clarke Resume Web page in this chapter, the e-mail address is formatted as a hyperlink. Also, the background color of the Web page is brown. The following sections modify the Web page to include these enhancements and then test the finished Web page.

To Format Text as a Hyperlink

The e-mail address in the resume Web page should be formatted as a hyperlink. When a Web page visitor clicks the hyperlink-formatted e-mail address, his or her e-mail program starts automatically and opens an e-mail window with the e-mail address already filled in. The following steps format the e-mail address as a hyperlink.

1
• Select the e-mail address in the resume Web page (rclarke@worldview.net, in this case).

• Display the Insert tab.

• Click the Insert Hyperlink button (Insert tab | Links group) to display the Insert Hyperlink dialog box (Figure 5–59).

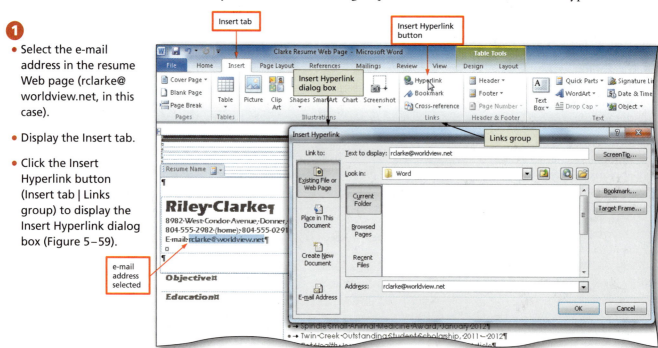

Figure 5–59

- Click E-mail Address in the Link to bar (Insert Hyperlink dialog box) so that the dialog box displays e-mail address settings instead of Web page settings.

- In the E-mail address text box, type `rclarke@worldview.net` to specify the e-mail address that the Web browser uses when a user clicks the hyperlink.

Q&A Can I change the text that automatically appeared in the 'Text to display' text box?

Yes. Word assumes that the hyperlink text should be the same as the e-mail address, so as soon as you enter the e-mail address, the same text is entered in the 'Text to display' text box.

- If the e-mail address in the 'Text to display' text box is preceded by the text, mailto:, delete this leading text because you want only the e-mail address to appear in the document.

- Click the ScreenTip button to display the Set Hyperlink ScreenTip dialog box.

- In the text box, type **Send e-mail message to Riley Clarke** (Set Hyperlink ScreenTip dialog box) to specify the text that will be displayed when a user points to the hyperlink (Figure 5–60).

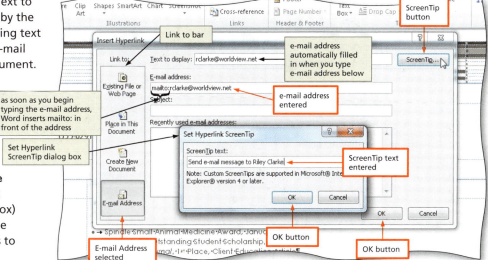

Figure 5–60

- Click the OK button in each dialog box to format the e-mail address as a hyperlink (Figure 5–61).

Q&A How do I know if the hyperlink works?

In Word, you can test the hyperlink by holding down the CTRL key while clicking the hyperlink. In this case, CTRL+clicking the e-mail address should open an e-mail window.

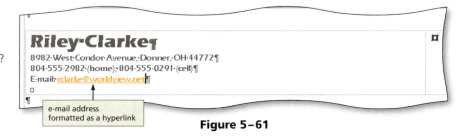

Figure 5–61

Other Ways

1. Right-click selected text, click Hyperlink on shortcut menu

2. Select text, press CTRL+K

TO EDIT A HYPERLINK

If you needed to edit a hyperlink, for example, to change its ScreenTip or its link, you would follow these steps.

1. Position the insertion point in the hyperlink.

2. Click the Insert Hyperlink button (Insert tab | Links group) or press CTRL+K to display the Edit Hyperlink dialog box.

or

1. Right-click the hyperlink to display a shortcut menu.

2. Click Edit Hyperlink on the shortcut menu to display the Edit Hyperlink dialog box.

To Add a Background Color

The next step is to add background color to the resume Web page so that it looks more eye-catching. This Web page uses a light shade of brown. The following steps add a background color.

 1

- Display the Page Layout tab.

- Click the Page Color button (Page Layout tab | Page Background group) to display the Page Color gallery.

- Point to Brown, Accent 5, Lighter 80% (ninth color in second row) in the Page Color gallery to display a live preview of the selected background color (Figure 5–62).

 **Experiment**

- Point to various colors in the Page Color gallery and watch the background color change in the document window.

 2

- Click Brown, Accent 5, Lighter 80% to change the background color to the selected color.

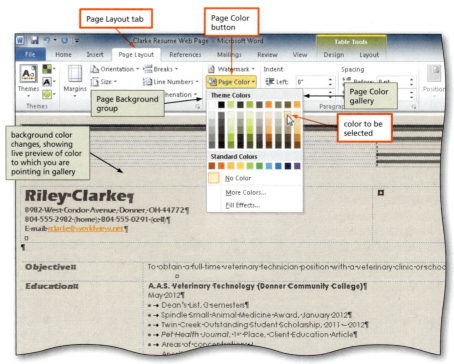

Figure 5–62

To Add a Pattern Fill Effect to a Background

When you changed the background color in the previous steps, Word placed a solid background color on the screen. For this resume Web page, the solid background color is a little too intense. To soften the background color, you can add patterns to it. The following steps add a pattern to the brown background.

 1

- Click the Page Color button (Page Layout tab | Page Background group) to display the Page Color gallery (Figure 5–63).

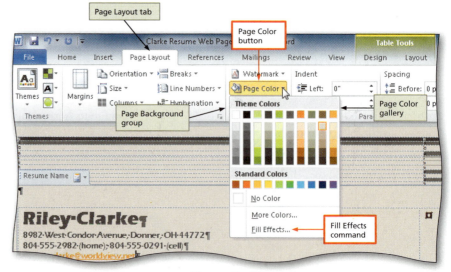

Figure 5–63

- Click Fill Effects in the Page Color gallery to display the Fill Effects dialog box.
- Click the Pattern tab (Fill Effects dialog box) to display the Pattern sheet in the dialog box.
- Click the Trellis pattern (seventh pattern in the fifth row) to select it (Figure 5–64).

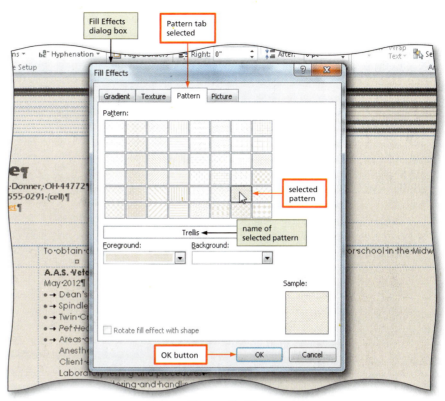

Figure 5–64

- Click the OK button to add the selected pattern to the current background color (Figure 5–65).

Figure 5–65

To Save an Existing Document and Quit Word

The Web page document now is complete. The following steps save the document again and quit Word.

 Click the Save button on the Quick Access Toolbar to overwrite the previously saved file.

2 Quit Word.

BTW

Background Colors
When you change the background color, it appears only on the screen and in documents that are viewed online, such as Web pages. Changing the background color has no affect on a printed document.

To Test a Web Page in a Web Browser

After creating and saving a Web page, you will want to test it in at least one browser to be sure it looks and works the way you intended. The steps on the next page use Windows Explorer to display the resume Web page in the Internet Explorer Web browser.

1

- Click the Windows Explorer program button on the Windows taskbar to open the Windows Explorer window.

- Navigate to the desired save location (in this case, the Word folder in the CIS 101 folder [or your class folder] on the USB flash drive) (Figure 5–66).

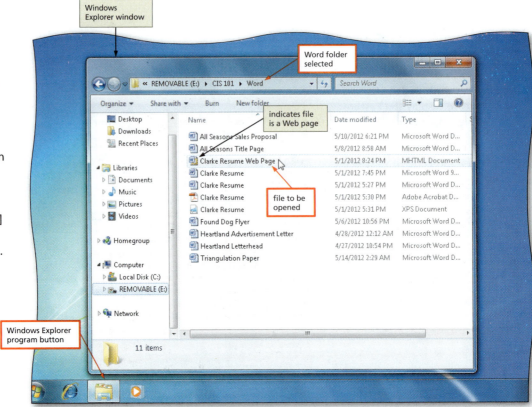

Figure 5–66

2

- Double-click the file name, Clarke Resume Web Page, to start the Internet Explorer Web browser and display the Web page file in the browser window (Figure 5–67).

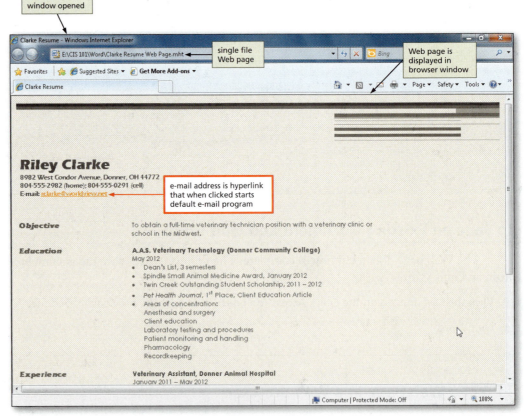

Figure 5–67

3

- With the Web page document displaying in the Web browser, click the e-mail address link to start the e-mail program with the e-mail address displayed in the e-mail window (Figure 5–68).

- If Internet Explorer displays a security dialog box, click its Allow button.

4

- Close all open windows.

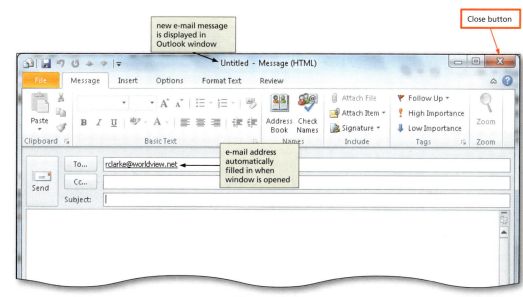

Figure 5–68

Chapter Summary

In this chapter, you learned how to use Word to use a template to create a document, change a document theme, fill in a document template, indent a paragraph, insert building blocks, customize theme fonts, create a Quick Style, modify a style, save a Word document in a variety of formats, insert a hyperlink, and add a background color. The items listed below include all the new Word skills you have learned in this chapter.

1. Create a New Document from a Sample Template (WD 277)
2. Create a New Blank Document (WD 279)
3. Change the Document Theme (WD 279)
4. Modify Text in a Content Control (WD 283)
5. Format a Content Control (WD 283)
6. Replace Placeholder Text (WD 284)
7. Delete a Content Control (WD 284)
8. Move Table Rows (WD 286)
9. Use AutoComplete (WD 287)
10. Enter a Line Break (WD 289)
11. Indent a Paragraph (WD 290)
12. Insert a Building Block Using the Quick Parts Gallery (WD 291)
13. Copy and Paste a Table Item (WD 293)
14. Customize Theme Fonts (WD 295)
15. Create a Quick Style (WD 296)
16. Reveal Formatting (WD 298)
17. Modify a Style Using the Styles Dialog Box (WD 299)
18. Create a New Document from an Online Template (WD 300)
19. Create a New Document from a Template Downloaded from Office.com (WD 301)
20. Save a Word Document as a PDF Document and View the PDF Document in Adobe Reader (WD 301)
21. Save a Word Document as an XPS Document and View the XPS Document in the XPS Viewer (WD 303)
22. Run the Compatibility Checker (WD 305)
23. Save a Word 2010 Document in an Earlier Word Format (WD 306)
24. Save a Word 2010 Document as a Different File Type (WD 308)
25. Send a Document Using E-Mail (WD 310)
26. Use the Document Inspector (WD 311)
27. Customize How Word Opens E-Mail Attachments (WD 311)
28. Save a Word Document as a Web Page (WD 312)
29. Set a Default Save Location (WD 314)
30. Format Text as a Hyperlink (WD 314)
31. Edit a Hyperlink (WD 315)
32. Add a Background Color (WD 316)
33. Add a Pattern Fill Effect to a Background (WD 316)
34. Test a Web Page in a Web Browser (WD 317)

Learn It Online

Test your knowledge of chapter content and key terms.

Instructions: To complete the Learn It Online exercises, start your browser, click the Address bar, and then enter the Web address **scsite.com/wd2010/learn**. When the Word 2010 Learn It Online page is displayed, click the link for the exercise you want to complete and then read the instructions.

Chapter Reinforcement TF, MC, and SA
A series of true/false, multiple choice, and short answer questions that test your knowledge of the chapter content.

Flash Cards
An interactive learning environment where you identify chapter key terms associated with displayed definitions.

Practice Test
A series of multiple choice questions that test your knowledge of chapter content and key terms.

Who Wants To Be a Computer Genius?
An interactive game that challenges your knowledge of chapter content in the style of a television quiz show.

Wheel of Terms
An interactive game that challenges your knowledge of chapter key terms in the style of the television show *Wheel of Fortune.*

Crossword Puzzle Challenge
A crossword puzzle that challenges your knowledge of key terms presented in the chapter.

Apply Your Knowledge

Reinforce the skills and apply the concepts you learned in this chapter.

Saving a Word Document as a Web Page and Other Formats
Note: To complete this assignment, you will be required to use the Data Files for Students. See the inside back cover of this book for instructions on downloading the Data Files for Students, or contact your instructor for information about accessing the required files.

Instructions: Start Word. Open the document, Apply 5-1 Computers in Health Care, from the Data Files for Students. You are to save the document as a single file Web Page (Figure 5–69), a PDF document, an XPS document, and in the Word 97-2003 format.

Perform the following tasks:

1. Save the document as a single file Web page using the file name, Apply 5-1 Computers in Health Care Web Page.

2. Add the background color Gold, Accent 2, Lighter 80% to the Web page document. Apply the Solid diamond pattern fill effect to the background. Save the file again.

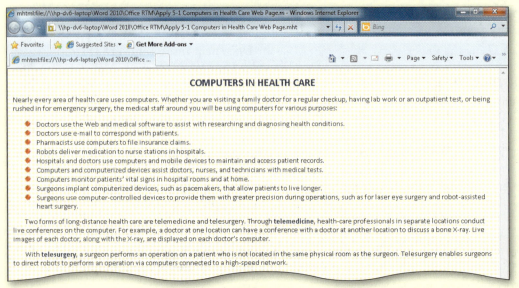

Figure 5–69

3. Use Internet Explorer to view the Web page (shown in Figure 5–69). Print the Web page. On the printout, identify how this document is different from the original Word document. Quit Internet Explorer and then close the Web page document in Word.

4. Open the original Apply 5-1 Computers in Health Care document. Save it as a PDF document and then view the PDF document in Adobe Reader. Submit the document as specified by your instructor. Quit Adobe Reader.

5. Using the original Apply 5-1 Computers in Health Care document, save the file as an XPS document and then view the XPS document in the XPS Viewer. Submit the document as specified by your instructor. Quit the XPS Viewer.

6. Using the original Apply 5-1 Computers in Health Care document, run the compatibility checker. Save the document in the Word 97-2003 format. Print the document. On the printout, write the issue(s) identified by the compatibility checker.

7. If your instructor allows, e-mail the document saved in #6 to his or her e-mail account.

Extend Your Knowledge

Extend the skills you learned in this chapter and experiment with new skills. You may need to use Help to complete the assignment.

Creating a Multi-File Web Page, Inserting a Screenshot, and Saving to the Web

Note: To complete this assignment, you will be required to use the Data Files for Students. See the inside back cover of this book for instructions on downloading the Data Files for Students, or contact your instructor for information about accessing the required files.

Instructions: Start Word. Open the document, Extend 5-1 Vincent Resume, from the Data Files for Students. You will save a Word document as a multi-file Web page and format it by inserting links, adding a texture fill effect as the background, and applying highlights to text. Then, you will take a screenshot of the Web page in your browser and insert the screenshot in a Word document.

Perform the following tasks:

1. Use Help to learn about saving as a Web page (not a single file Web page), hyperlinks, texture fill effects, text highlight color, screenshots, and saving to the Web.

2. Save the Extend 5-1 Vincent Resume file as a Web page (not as a single file Web page) using the file name, Extend 5-1 Vincent Resume Web Page.

3. Adjust the column widths in the resume table so that the resume fills the window. Convert the e-mail address to a hyperlink.

4. In the leftmost column, below the e-mail address, insert the Web address www.scsite.com and format it as a hyperlink so that when a user clicks the Web address, the associated Web page is displayed in the browser window.

5. Add a texture fill effect of your choice to the resume.

6. Apply a text highlight color of your choice to at least five words in the resume.

7. Change the document properties, as specified by your instructor. Save the document again. Test the Web page in Windows Explorer.

8. Take a screenshot(s) of Windows Explorer that shows all the files and folders created by saving the document as a Web page. Create a new Word document. Insert the screenshot(s) in the Word document. Insert callout shapes with text that points to and identifies the files and folders created by saving the document as a Web page. Change the document properties, as specified by your instructor. Save the document with the file name Extend 5-1 Vincent Resume Windows Explorer Files.

Continued >

Extend Your Knowledge *continued*

9. If you have access to a Web server, FTP site, or SkyDrive (Figure 5–70), save the Web page to the server, site, or online storage location (see Appendix B or C for instructions).

10. Submit the files in the format specified by your instructor.

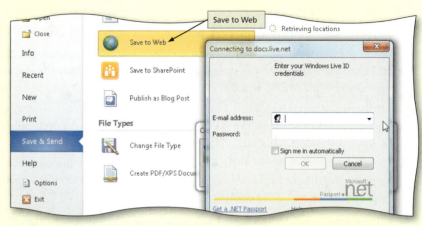

Figure 5–70

Make It Right

Analyze a document and correct all errors and/or improve the design.

Formatting a Resume Created from a Template

Note: To complete this assignment, you will be required to use the Data Files for Students. See the inside back cover of this book for instructions on downloading the Data Files for Students, or contact your instructor for information about accessing the required files.

Instructions: Start Word. Open the document, Make It Right 5-1 Buckman Resume Draft, from the Data Files for Students. The document is a resume created from a template that is formatted incorrectly (Figure 5–71). You are to change the margins, modify styles, adjust paragraph indent, modify a content control, remove a hyperlink format, and change the document theme.

Perform the following tasks:

1. Change the margins, and left and right indent, so that the resume text does not run into the orange borders on the right side of the page and text is balanced on the page.

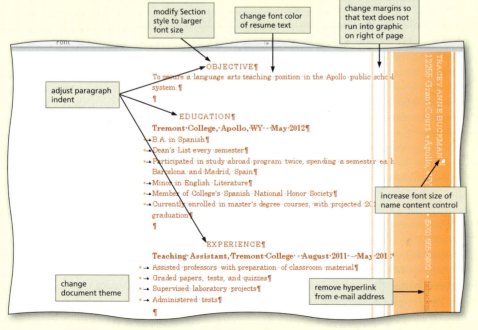

2. Modify the Normal style so that the text is a color other than red.

3. Fix the indent of the first three section headings (OBJECTIVE, EDUCATION, and EXPERIENCE) so that they are aligned with the text on the left, like the SKILLS heading.

4. Use the Reveal Formatting task pane to determine the font size of text in the Subsection style. Modify the Section style so that it uses a font size that is greater than the font size of the Subsection style.

Figure 5–71

5. Increase the font size of the name content control so that it is predominant in the color bar on the right side of the page.

6. Remove the hyperlink format from the e-mail address.

7. Change the document theme to one other than Oriel.

8. Change the document properties, as specified by your instructor. Save the revised document with the file name, Make It Right 5-1 Buckman Resume Modified, and then submit it in the format specified by your instructor.

In the Lab

Design and/or create a document using the guidelines, concepts, and skills presented in this chapter. Labs are listed in order of increasing difficulty.

Lab 1: Creating a Resume from a Template

Problem: You are an engineering student at Western College. As graduation is approaching quickly, you prepare the resume shown in Figure 5–72 using one of Word's resume templates.

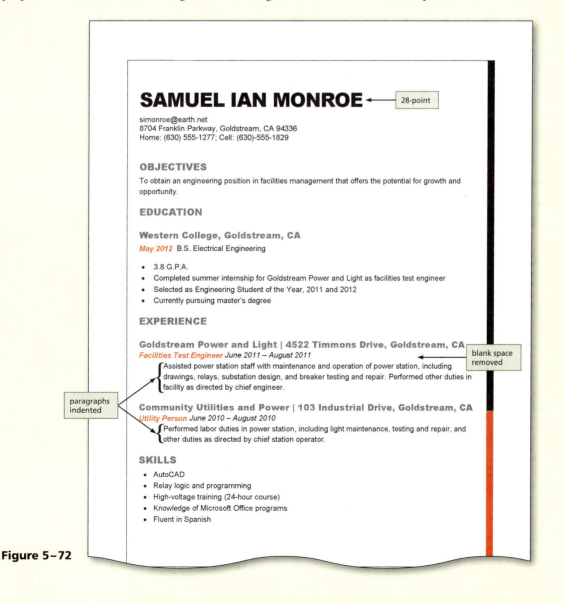

Figure 5–72

In the Lab *continued*

Perform the following tasks:

1. Use the Essential Resume template to create a resume.

2. If necessary, change the document theme to Essential.

3. Personalize the resume as shown in Figure 5–72 on the previous page. Following are some guidelines for some sections of the resume:

    a. Use your own name, e-mail address, postal address, and phone numbers, unless your instructor specifies to use the information shown in Figure 5–72. Delete the line containing the website content control.

    b. Insert an Experience Subsection building block so that you can enter the second job information.

    c. In the Experience section, indent the job responsibilities paragraphs one-half inch. Change the space after the job titles to 0 pt.

4. The entire resume should fit on a single page. If it flows to two pages, decrease spacing before and after paragraphs until the entire resume text fits on a single page.

5. Check the spelling of the resume. Change the document properties, as specified by your instructor. Save the resume with Lab 5-1 Monroe Resume as the file name and submit it in the format specified by your instructor.

In the Lab

Lab 2: Creating a Resume from a Template

Problem: You are a physical recreation and education student at Ward College. As graduation is approaching quickly, you prepare the resume shown in Figure 5–73 using one of Word's resume templates.

Perform the following tasks:

1. Use the Urban Resume template to create a resume.

2. Change the document theme to Perspective.

3. Personalize and format the resume as shown in Figure 5–73. Following are some guidelines for some sections of the resume:

    a. Change the Normal style font size to 11 point.

    b. Use your own name, postal address, phone numbers, and e-mail address, unless your instructor specifies to use the information shown in Figure 5–73.

    c. Change margins settings to Normal (1" top, bottom, left, and right).

    d. Reduce the row height of the row containing the name information to 1".

    e. Move rows containing the Education and Experience sections above the row containing the Skills section. Change the name, Skills, to the name, Community Service.

    f. In the Education section, enter line break characters between the areas of concentration.

    g. Insert an Experience Subsection building block so that you can enter the second job information. Indent the job responsibilities paragraphs one-half inch.

    h. Create a customized theme font set that uses Castellar for headings and Lucida Sans for Body text. Save the theme font with the name MacMahon Resume Fonts.

    i. Modify the Section style so that its text is not bold.

    j. Format the address line to 10-point Lucida Sans font with a font color of Brown, Accent 2, Darker 50%. Create a Quick Style called Contact Info using the format in the address line. Apply the Contact Info Quick Style to the phone and e-mail lines.

k. If necessary, format the second bulleted list the same as the first.

l. Adjust the spacing before and after paragraphs so that the resume looks like Figure 5–73.

4. The entire resume should fit on a single page. If it flows to two pages, decrease spacing before and after paragraphs until the entire resume text fits on a single page.

5. Check the spelling of the resume. Change the document properties, as specified by your instructor. Save the resume with Lab 5-2 MacMahon Resume as the file name, and submit it in the format specified by your instructor.

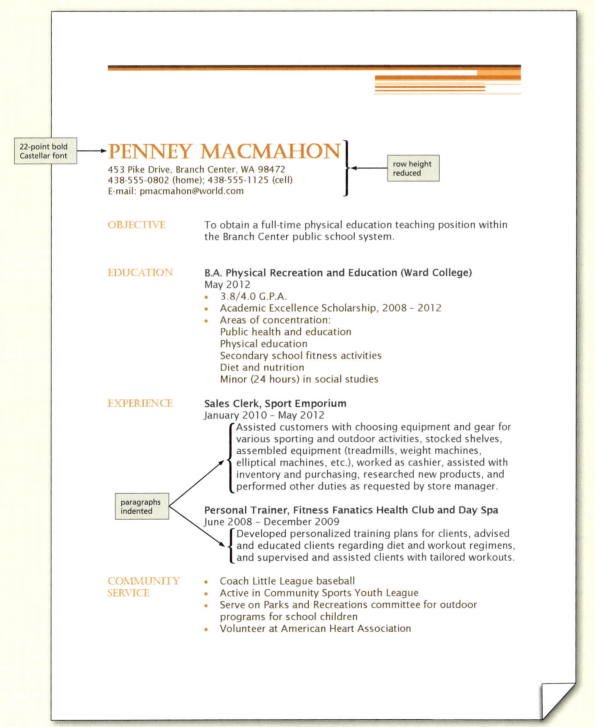

Figure 5–73

In the Lab

Lab 3: Creating a Resume from a Template and a Web Page from the Resume

Problem: You are a library and information science student at Benson College. As graduation is approaching quickly, you prepare the resume shown in Figure 5–74 using one of Word's resume templates.

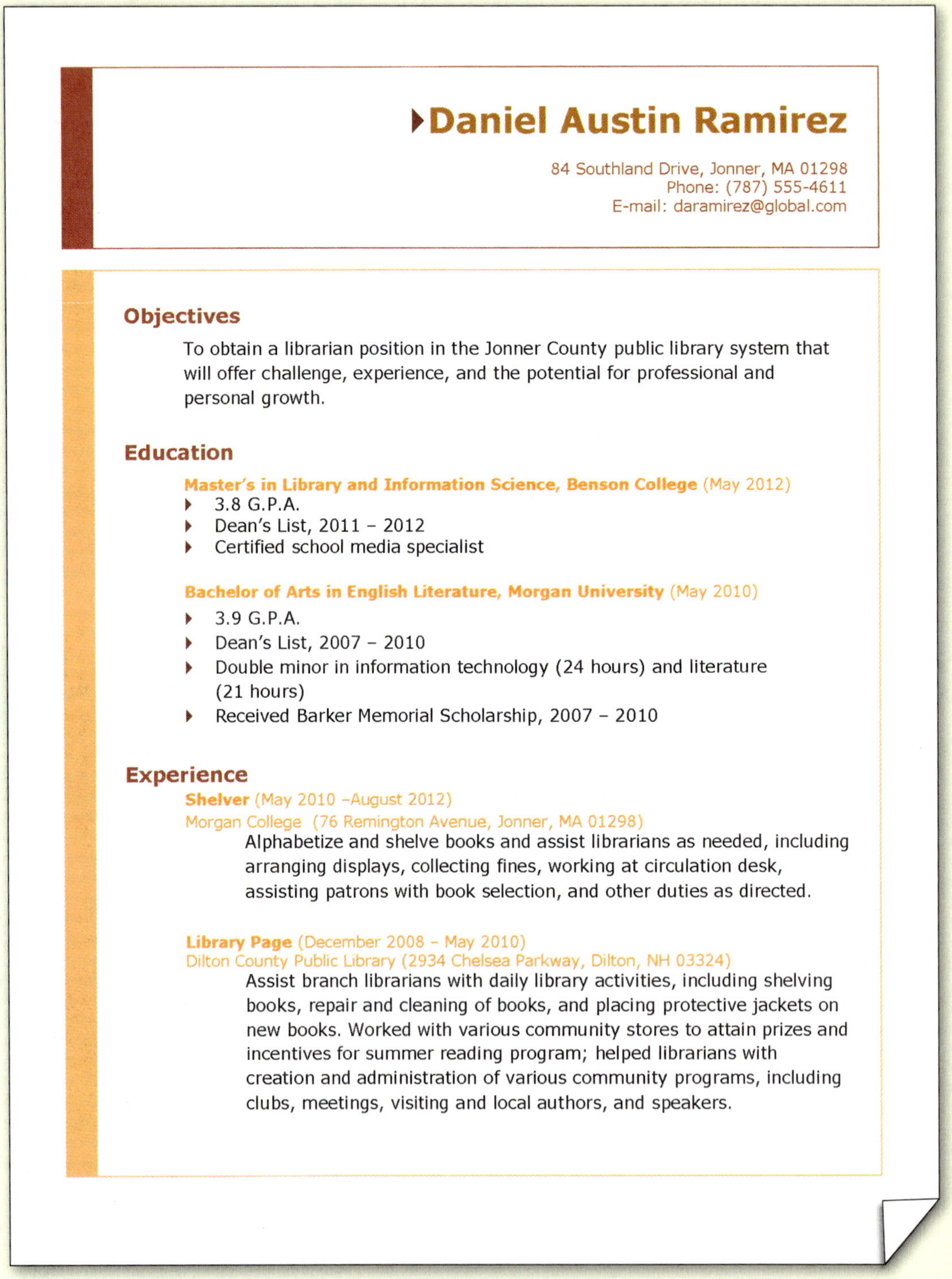

▶Daniel Austin Ramirez

84 Southland Drive, Jonner, MA 01298
Phone: (787) 555-4611
E-mail: daramirez@global.com

Objectives

To obtain a librarian position in the Jonner County public library system that will offer challenge, experience, and the potential for professional and personal growth.

Education

Master's in Library and Information Science, Benson College (May 2012)
▸ 3.8 G.P.A.
▸ Dean's List, 2011 – 2012
▸ Certified school media specialist

Bachelor of Arts in English Literature, Morgan University (May 2010)
▸ 3.9 G.P.A.
▸ Dean's List, 2007 – 2010
▸ Double minor in information technology (24 hours) and literature (21 hours)
▸ Received Barker Memorial Scholarship, 2007 – 2010

Experience

Shelver (May 2010 –August 2012)
Morgan College (76 Remington Avenue, Jonner, MA 01298)
Alphabetize and shelve books and assist librarians as needed, including arranging displays, collecting fines, working at circulation desk, assisting patrons with book selection, and other duties as directed.

Library Page (December 2008 – May 2010)
Dilton County Public Library (2934 Chelsea Parkway, Dilton, NH 03324)
Assist branch librarians with daily library activities, including shelving books, repair and cleaning of books, and placing protective jackets on new books. Worked with various community stores to attain prizes and incentives for summer reading program; helped librarians with creation and administration of various community programs, including clubs, meetings, visiting and local authors, and speakers.

Figure 5–74

Perform the following tasks:

1. Use the Origin Resume template to create a resume. Personalize and format the resume as shown in Figure 5–74. Change the document theme to Aspect. Use your own name, postal address, phone numbers, and e-mail address, unless your instructor specifies to use the information shown in Figure 5–74. View gridlines so that you can see the four tables in the resume. Delete the top and bottom decorative one-row tables. Adjust the margins, spacing before and after paragraphs, adjust table row sizes, and add or delete blank paragraphs so that the resume looks like Figure 5–74. Check the spelling of the resume. Change the document properties, as specified by your instructor. Save the resume with Lab 5-3 Ramirez Resume as the file name and submit it in the format specified by your instructor.

2. If your instructor permits, e-mail the final resume to his or her e-mail account.

3. Save the resume as a single file Web page using the file name Lab 5-3 Ramirez Resume Web Page. Change the page title to Daniel Austin Ramirez. Convert the e-mail address to a hyperlink. Apply the Orange, Accent 1, Lighter 80% background color to the document. Apply the Dashed downward diagonal pattern fill effect to the background color. Submit the file in the format specified by your instructor.

4. If you have access to a Web server, FTP site, or SkyDrive, save the Web page to the server, site, or online storage location (see Appendix B or C for instructions).

Cases and Places

Apply your creative thinking and problem solving skills to design and implement a solution.

Note: To complete these assignments, you may be required to use the Data Files for Students. See the inside back cover of this book for instructions on downloading the Data Files for Students, or contact your instructor for information about accessing the required files.

1: Create a Meeting Agenda and an Award Certificate

Academic

As a student assistant to the Office of Academic Affairs, you have been asked to create a meeting agenda for the upcoming council meeting, as well as an award certificate for the presentation of the Outstanding Student Award during the meeting. Browse through the Online Templates and download appropriate meeting agenda and award certificate templates and then use the text in the next two paragraphs for content. Use the concepts and techniques presented in this chapter to create and format the agenda and award certificate. Be sure to check the spelling and grammar of the finished documents. Submit your assignment in the format specified by your instructor.

Agenda information: The Excellence in Academics Council is holding a meeting on February 6, 2012, at 7:30 p.m. in the Nutonne College Community Room. Agenda items are as follows: Call to Order, Roll Call, Approval of Previous Meeting Minutes, Chairperson's Report (two items – Volunteer activities and Donor updates), Treasurer's Report (two items – New budgetary restrictions and Dues updates), Outstanding Student Award (two items: – Speech by Alana Sebastian, 2011 recipient, and Presentation of 2012 award to Derrick Jakes), Calendar, and Adjournment.

Award certificate information: The Outstanding Student 2012 is awarded on February 6, 2012, by Julianne Easton, President, Excellence in Academics Council, to Derrick Jakes for his hard work and dedication to his educational goals and for being an exceptional role model for young scholars.

2: Create a Calendar and an Invitation

Personal

To help organize your appointments and important dates, you use a calendar file. While filling in the calendar, you decide to schedule and host a family reunion for which you will need to send out

Continued >

Cases and Places *continued*

invitations. Browse through the Online Templates and download appropriate calendar and invitation templates and then use the information in the next two paragraphs for content. Use the concepts and techniques presented in this chapter to create and format the calendar and invitation. Be sure to check the spelling and grammar of the finished documents. Submit your assignment in the format specified by your instructor.

Calendar information: May 5 – Volleyball tournament at 3:00 p.m., May 8 – Algebra final at 10:00 a.m., May 9 – English final paper due by 11:59 p.m., May 15 – Grandpa's birthday, May 26 – Family reunion from 11:00 a.m. to ?? p.m., June 4 – First day of work!, June 9 – Dentist appointment at 9:00 a.m., June 14 – Lexy's birthday, June 16 – Volunteer Cook at Community Center from 6:00 – 9:00 a.m., and June 20 – Mom and Dad's anniversary (31st). If the template requires, insert an image(s) from the clip art gallery in the calendar.

Invitation information: You and your family are cordially invited to the Brogan Family Reunion, which will be held on May 26, 2012, from 11:00 a.m. to ?? p.m. at the Brogan Farm on 3392 W 2817 North Road, Donner Grove, New Hampshire. Main course and beverages will be provided. Please bring a dish to pass, swimsuits, and lawn chairs. If the template requires, insert an image(s) from the clip art gallery in the invitation.

3: Create a Fax Cover Letter and an Invoice

Professional

As a part-time employee at Milan Office Supplies, your boss has asked to you create a fax cover letter and an invoice for a customer. Browse through the Online Templates and download appropriate fax and invoice templates and then use the information in the next three paragraphs for content. Use the concepts and techniques presented in this chapter to create and format the fax cover letter and invoice. Be sure to check the spelling and grammar of the finished documents. Submit your assignment in the format specified by your instructor.

Milan Office Supplies is located at 808 Boyd Boulevard in Beachcombe, Florida 33115. Phone number is 774-555-6751, fax number is 774-555-6752, e-mail address is milan@earth.net; and slogan is *For the Well Stocked Office*. Customer is Stacy Listernik at Walsh Industries located at 247 Tremaine Industrial Parkway in Beachcombe, Florida 33115. Phone number is 774-555-0123 and fax number is 774-555-0124.

Fax message: Following is the duplicate invoice you requested. Thank you again for your prompt attention to this matter, and thank you for choosing Milan Office Supplies.

Invoice detail: Invoice number is 402 dated March 21, 2012. Salesperson is Samantha Hagen, job number 227-404, payment terms are due on receipt, and due date was March 1, 2012. Items purchased were 20 boxes of hanging folders with tabs at a price of $15.25 per box, 10 ink-jet cartridge refills at a price of $10.49 per cartridge, and 100 reams of 20# paper at a price of $3.19 per ream. All checks should be made payable to Milan Office Supplies.

6 Generating Form Letters, Mailing Labels, and a Directory

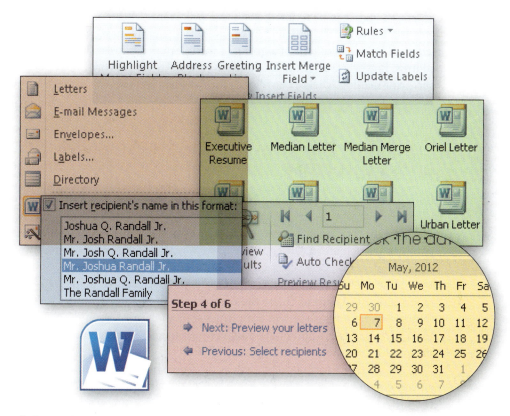

Objectives

You will have mastered the material in this chapter when you can:

- Explain the merge process
- Use the Mail Merge task pane and the Mailings tab on the Ribbon
- Use a letter template as the main document for a mail merge
- Create and edit a data source
- Insert merge fields in a main document
- Use an IF field in a main document

- Merge and print form letters
- Select records to merge
- Sort data records
- Address and print mailing labels and envelopes
- Change page orientation
- Merge all data records to a directory
- Convert text to a table

6 | Generating Form Letters, Mailing Labels, and a Directory

Introduction

People are more likely to open and read a personalized letter than a letter addressed as Dear Sir, Dear Madam, or To Whom It May Concern. Typing individual personalized letters, though, can be a time-consuming task. Thus, Word provides the capability of creating a form letter, which is an easy way to generate mass mailings of personalized letters. The basic content of a group of form letters is similar. Items such as name and address, however, vary from one letter to the next. With Word, you easily can address and print mailing labels or envelopes for the form letters.

Project — Form Letters, Mailing Labels, and a Directory

Both businesses and individuals regularly use form letters to communicate via the postal service or e-mail with groups of people. Types of form letter correspondence include announcements of sales to customers, notices of benefits to employees, invitations to the public to participate in a sweepstakes giveaway, and letters of job application to potential employers.

The project in this chapter follows generally accepted guidelines for writing form letters and uses Word to create the form letters shown in Figure 6–1. The form letters inform potential employers of your interest in a job opening at their organization. Each form letter states the potential employer's name and address, advertised job position, and the employer's type — a practice or a school.

To generate form letters, such as the ones shown in Figure 6–1, you create a main document for the form letter (Figure 6–1a), create or specify a data source (Figure 6–1b), and then merge, or *blend*, the main document with the data source to generate a series of individual letters (Figure 6–1c). In Figure 6–1a, the main document represents the portion of the form letter that repeats from one merged letter to the next. In Figure 6–1b, the data source contains the name, address, advertised job position, and employer type for different potential employers. To personalize each letter, you merge the potential employer data in the data source with the main document for the form letter, which generates or prints an individual letter for each potential employer listed in the data source.

Word provides two methods of merging documents: the Mail Merge task pane and the Mailings tab on the Ribbon. The Mail Merge task pane displays a wizard, which is a step-by-step progression that guides you through the merging process. The Mailings tab provides buttons and boxes you use to merge documents. This chapter illustrates both techniques.

Figure 6–1 (a) Main Document for the Form Letter

Figure 6–1 (b) Data Source

Title	First Name	Last Name	Organization Name	Address Line 1	Address Line 2	City	State	ZIP Code	Position	Employer Type
Ms.	Camille	Townsend	Sunbelt Veterinary Clinic	906 Center Street		Donner	OH	44772	Veterinary Technician	C
Mr.	Leon	Siefert	Bridgeton College	85 Parker Way	P.O. Box 3309	Bridgeton	OH	44710	Clinical Veterinary Technician I	S
Dr.	Natalia	Zajak	Zajak Animal Clinic	272 Mill Road	Unit 2B	Donner	OH	44772	Veterinary Assistant	C
Mr.	Hugo	Moreau	Ohio Animal Medicine College	3894 81st Street		Wilborn	OH	44752	Veterinary Technican I	S
Dr.	Min	Huan	Timber Creek Veterinary Center	55 Sycamore Avenue	P.O. Box 104	Timber Creek	OH	44729	Veterinary Technician	C

«AddressBlock» ← placeholder for address fields

form letter 1

5/11/2012

«GreetingLine» ← placeholder for salutation fields

I will graduate from Donner Community College this May with an Associate of Scien Veterinary Technology. My education, along with first-hand experience through pa and volunteer work, make me an ideal candidate for the «Position» position current at «Organization_Name».

merge field

job seeker (sender) name and address

Riley Clarke
8982 West Condor Avenue
Donner, OH 44772

As evidenced on the enclosed resume, my background matches the job requirem ough the Career Development Office at Donner Community College. My course erience have prepared me to assist during surgery and examinations, maintain provide hands-on education at your { IF Employer_Type = "C" "practice" "school"}.

merge field

Ms. Camille Townsend
Sunbelt Veterinary Clinic
906 Center Street
Donner, OH 44772

potential employer name and address in first data record

I will call you next week to see if we can set up a time to discuss my qualifications fu you, «Title» «Last_Name», for your time and consideration.

IF field

5/11/2012

merge fields

Dear Ms. Townsend:

position advertised in first data record

I will graduate from Donner Community College this May with an Associate of Science degree in Veterinary Technology. My education, along with first-hand experience through part-time jobs and volunteer work, make me an ideal candidate for the Veterinary Technician position currently available at Sunbelt Veterinary Clinic.

title and last name in first data record

Riley Clarke
8982 West C
Donner, OH

organization name in first data record

As evidenced on the enclosed resume, my background mat posted through the Career Development Office at Donner Community College. My coursework and experience have prepared me to assist during surgery and examinations, maintain records, and provide hands-on education at your practice.

Mr. Leon Siefert
Bridgeton College
85 Parker Way
P.O. Box 3309
Bridgeton, OH 44710

potential employer name and address in second data record

employer type in first data record

I will call you next week to see if we can set up a time to further. Thank you, Ms. Townsend, for your time and consideration.

5/11/2012

Sincerely,

Dear Mr. Siefert:

position advertised in second data record

Riley Clarke

I will graduate from Donner Community College this May with an Associate of Science Veterinary Technology. My education, along with first-hand experience through part-ti and volunteer work, make me an ideal candidate for the Clinical Veterinary Technician currently available at Bridgeton College.

Enclosure

title and last name in second data record

As evidenced on the enclosed resume, my backgrou ents through the Career Development Office at Donner Community College. My coursewo experience have prepared me to assist during surgery an ec provide hands-on education at your school.

organization name in second data record

I will call you next week to see if we can set up a time to discuss my qualifications further. Thank you, Mr. Siefert, for your time and consideration.

employer type in second data record

Figure 6–1 (c) Form Letters

Sincerely,

Riley Clarke

Enclosure

form letter 2

form letter 3

form letter 4

form letter 5

Overview

As you read through this chapter, you will learn how to create and generate the form letters shown in Figure 6–1 on the previous page, along with mailing labels, envelopes, and a directory, by performing these general tasks:

- Identify a template as the main document for the form letter.
- Type the contents of the data source.
- Compose the main document.
- Merge the data source with the main document to generate the form letters.
- Address and print mailing labels and envelopes using the data source.
- Create a directory, which displays the contents of the data source.

Plan Ahead

> **General Project Guidelines**
>
> When creating a Word document, the actions you perform and decisions you make will affect the appearance and characteristics of the finished document. As you create form letters, such as the project shown in Figure 6–1, and related documents, you should follow these general guidelines:
>
> 1. **Identify the main document for the form letter.** When creating form letters, you either can type the letter from scratch in a blank document window or use a letter template. A letter template saves time because Word prepares a letter with text and/or formatting common to all letters. Then, you customize the resulting letter by selecting and replacing prewritten text.
>
> 2. **Create or specify the data source.** The **data source** contains the variable, or changing, values for each letter. A data source can be an Access database table, an Outlook contacts list, or an Excel worksheet. If the necessary and properly organized data already exists in one of these Office programs, you can instruct Word to use the existing file as the data source for the mail merge. Otherwise, you can create a new data source using one of these programs.
>
> 3. **Compose the main document for the form letter.** A **main document** contains the constant, or unchanging, text, punctuation, spaces, and graphics. It should reference the data in the data source properly. The finished main document letter should look like a symmetrically framed picture with evenly spaced margins, all balanced below an attractive letterhead or return address. The content of the main document for the form letter should contain proper grammar, correct spelling, logically constructed sentences, flowing paragraphs, and sound ideas. Be sure to proofread it carefully.
>
> 4. **Merge the main document with the data source to create the form letters.** **Merging** is the process of combining the contents of a data source with a main document. You can print the merged letters on the printer or place them in a new document, which you later can edit. You also have the option of merging all data in a data source, or merging just a portion of it.
>
> 5. **Generate mailing labels and envelopes.** To generate mailing labels and envelopes for the form letters, follow the same process as for the form letters. That is, determine the appropriate data source, create the label or envelope main document, and then merge the main document with the data source to generate the mailing labels and envelopes.
>
> 6. **Create a directory of the data source.** A **directory** is a listing of the contents of the data source. To create a directory, follow the same process as for the form letters. That is, determine the appropriate data source, create the directory main document, and then merge the main document with the data source to create the directory.
>
> When necessary, more specific details concerning the above guidelines are presented at appropriate points in the chapter. The chapter also will identify the actions performed and decisions made regarding these guidelines during the creation of the form letters shown in Figure 6–1, and related documents.

To Start Word

If you are using a computer to step through the project in this chapter and you want your screens to match the figures in this book, you should change your computer's resolution to 1024 × 768. The following steps start Word and verify settings.

1 Start Word. If necessary, maximize the Word window.

2 If the Print Layout button on the status bar is not selected, click it so that your screen is in Print Layout view.

3 Change your zoom level to 100%.

4 If the Show/Hide ¶ button (Home tab | Paragraph group) is not selected already, click it to display formatting marks on the screen.

Identifying the Main Document for Form Letters

The first step in the mail merge process is to identify the type of document you are creating for the main document. Typical installations of Word support five types of main documents: letters, e-mail messages, envelopes, labels, and a directory. In this section of the chapter, you create letters as the main document. Later in this chapter, you will specify labels, envelopes, and a directory as the main document.

Identify the main document for the form letter.
Be sure the main document for the form letter includes all essential business letter elements. All business letters should contain a date line, inside address, message, and signature block. Many business letters contain additional items such as a special mailing notation(s), an attention line, a salutation, a subject line, a complimentary close, reference initials, and an enclosure notation.

Plan Ahead

To Identify the Main Document for the Form Letter Using the Mail Merge Task Pane

This project uses a letter template as the main document for the form letter. Word provides 10 styles of merge letter templates: Adjacency, Apothecary, Black Tie, Equity, Essential, Executive, Median, Oriel, Origin, and Urban. The letter in this chapter uses the Urban template so that it has a look similar to the accompanying resume created in Chapter 5, which also used an Urban template. The following steps use the Mail Merge task pane to identify the Urban Merge Letter template as the main document for a form letter.

1

- Click Mailings on the Ribbon to display the Mailings tab.

- Click the Start Mail Merge button (Mailings tab | Start Mail Merge group) to display the Start Mail Merge menu (Figure 6–2).

Q&A What is the function of the E-mail Messages option?

Instead of printing individual letters, you can send individual e-mail messages using e-mail addresses in the data source or using a Microsoft Outlook Contacts list.

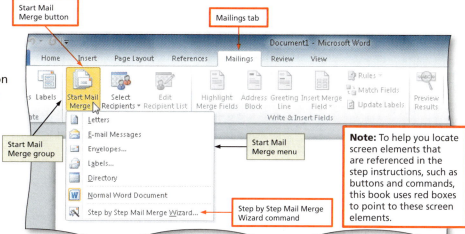

Figure 6–2

- Click Step by Step Mail Merge Wizard on the Start Mail Merge menu to display Step 1 of the Mail Merge wizard in the Mail Merge task pane (Figure 6–3).

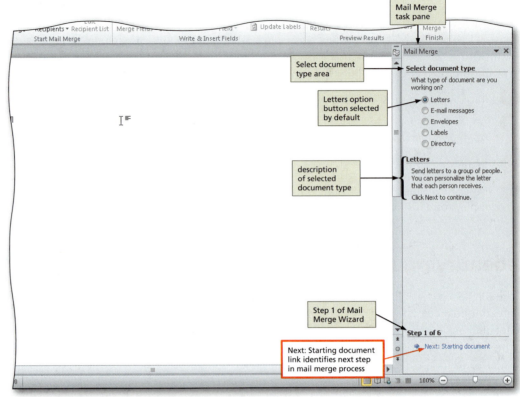

Figure 6–3

- Click the Next: Starting document link at the bottom of the Mail Merge task pane to display Step 2 of the Mail Merge wizard, which requests you select a starting document.

- Click 'Start from a template' in the 'Select starting document' area and then click the Select template link to display the Select Template dialog box.

- Click the Letters tab in the dialog box to display the Letters sheet; scroll to and then click Urban Merge Letter, which shows a preview of the selected template in the Preview area (Figure 6–4).

🔍 **Experiment**

- Click various Merge Letter templates in the Letters sheet and watch the preview change at the right edge of the dialog box. When you are finished experimenting, click the Urban Merge Letter template.

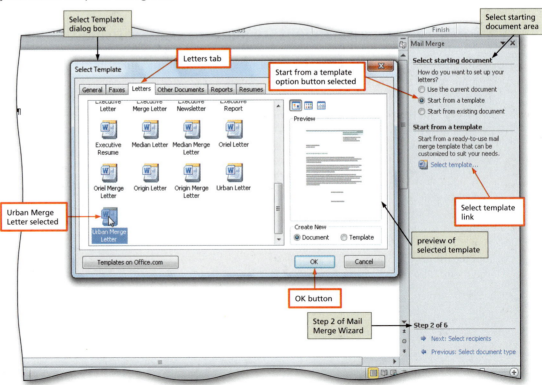

Figure 6–4

- Click the OK button to display a letter in the document window that is based on the Urban Merge Letter template (Figure 6–5).

Q&A Can I close the Mail Merge task pane?

Yes, you can close the Mail Merge task pane at any time by clicking its Close button. When you wish to continue with the merge process, you would repeat these steps and Word will resume the merge process at the correct step in the Mail Merge wizard.

Q&A Why does Windows User display as the sender name?

Word places the user name associated with your copy of Microsoft Word as the sender name. Windows User is the user name associated with this copy of Word.

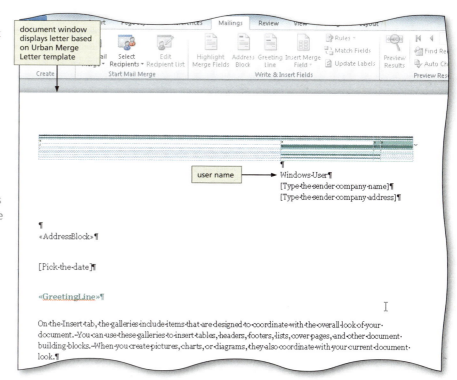

Figure 6–5

Other Ways	
1. Open Backstage view, click New, click Sample templates, click desired merge letter template, click Create button.	2. Click Start Mail Merge button (Mailings tab | Start Mail Merge group), click Letters

To Change the User Name and Initials

If you wanted to change the user name and initials associated with your copy of Microsoft Word, you would perform the following steps.

1. Open the Backstage view and then click Options to display the Word Options dialog box.
2. If necessary, click General in the left pane.
3. Enter your name in the User name text box.
4. Enter your initials in the Initials text box.
5. Click the OK button.

To Change the Document Theme

The form letter in this project uses the Austin document theme to match the theme used for the resume in Chapter 5. The following steps change the document theme.

1 Display the Page Layout tab.

2 Click the Themes button (Page Layout tab | Themes group) to display the Themes gallery and then click Austin in the Themes gallery to change the document theme.

BTW

The Ribbon and Screen Resolution
Word may change how the groups and buttons within the groups appear on the Ribbon, depending on the computer's screen resolution. Thus, your Ribbon may look different from the ones in this book if you are using a screen resolution other than 1024 × 768.

To Print the Document

The next step is to print the letter that Word generated, which is based on the Urban Merge Letter template.

1 Ready the printer. Open the Backstage view and then click the Print tab, if necessary select the desired printer, and then click the Print button to print the document that is based on the Urban Merge Letter template (Figure 6–6).

Q&A What are the content controls in the document?

A content control contains instructions for filling in areas of the document. To select a content control, click it. Later in this chapter, you will personalize the content controls.

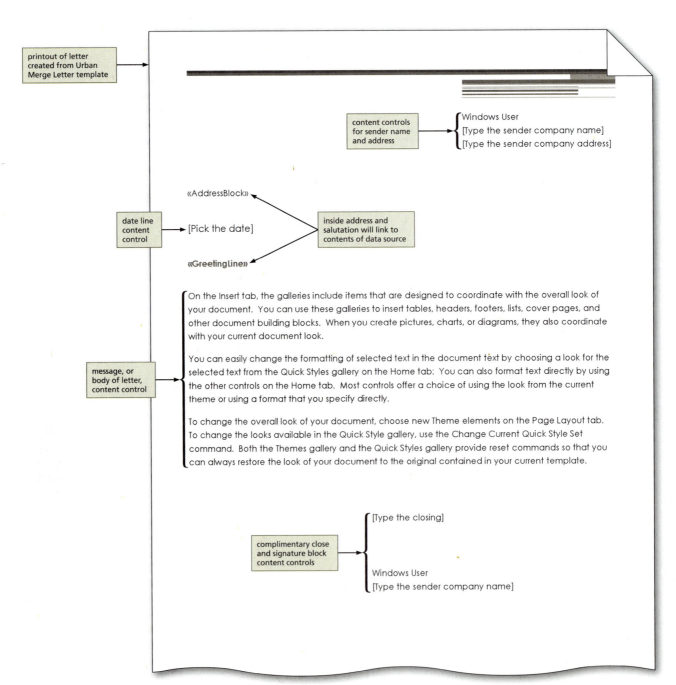

printout of letter created from Urban Merge Letter template

content controls for sender name and address

Windows User
[Type the sender company name]
[Type the sender company address]

«AddressBlock»

date line content control

[Pick the date]

inside address and salutation will link to contents of data source

«GreetingLine»

message, or body of letter, content control

On the Insert tab, the galleries include items that are designed to coordinate with the overall look of your document. You can use these galleries to insert tables, headers, footers, lists, cover pages, and other document building blocks. When you create pictures, charts, or diagrams, they also coordinate with your current document look.

You can easily change the formatting of selected text in the document text by choosing a look for the selected text from the Quick Styles gallery on the Home tab. You can also format text directly by using the other controls on the Home tab. Most controls offer a choice of using the look from the current theme or using a format that you specify directly.

To change the overall look of your document, choose new Theme elements on the Page Layout tab. To change the looks available in the Quick Style gallery, use the Change Current Quick Style Set command. Both the Themes gallery and the Quick Styles gallery provide reset commands so that you can always restore the look of your document to the original contained in your current template.

[Type the closing]

complimentary close and signature block content controls

Windows User
[Type the sender company name]

Figure 6–6

To Enter the Sender Information

The next step is to enter the sender information at the top of the letter. You will replace the name, Windows User, with the sender name. Then, you will delete the content control that contains the company name because the sender is an individual instead of a company. Note that any text you type in this content control also will appear in the signature block. Finally, you will enter the sender's address in the third content control. The following steps enter the sender information.

1 Triple-click the content control at the top of the letter that in this case, contains the name, Windows User, to select it.

2 Type `Riley Clarke` as the sender name.

3 Right-click the content control with the placeholder text, Type the sender company name, to display a shortcut menu and then click Remove Content Control on the shortcut menu to delete the content control.

Q&A What if my content control already displays a sender company name instead of placeholder text?

Select the text and then delete it.

4 Press the DELETE key to delete the blank line between the name and address content controls.

5 Click the content control with the placeholder text, Type the sender company address, to select it.

6 Type `8982 West Condor Avenue` as the sender street address.

7 Press the ENTER key and then type `Donner, OH 44772` as the sender city, state, and postal code.

To Change the Margin Settings

The Urban Merge Letter template uses .75-inch top, bottom, left, and right margins. You want the form letter to use 1-inch top, bottom, left, and right margins. The following steps change margin settings.

1 Click the Margins button (Page Layout tab | Page Setup group) to display the Margins gallery.

2 Click Normal in the Margins gallery to change the top, bottom, left, and right margins to 1 inch (Figure 6–7).

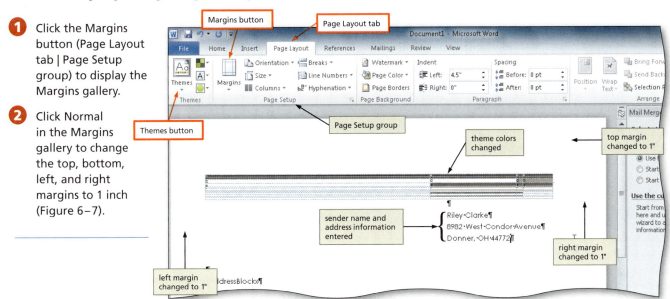

Figure 6–7

To Create a Folder while Saving

You have performed several tasks while creating this project and should save it. The following steps assume you already have created folders for storing files, for example, a CIS 101 folder (for your class) that contains a Word folder. You want to save this and all other documents created in this chapter in a folder called Job Hunting in the Word folder. This folder does not exist, so you must create it. Rather than creating the folder in Windows, you can create folders from Word. The following steps create a folder during the process of saving a document.

- With a USB flash drive connected to one of the computer's USB ports, click the Save button on the Quick Access Toolbar to display the Save As dialog box.

- Type **Clarke Cover Letter** in the File name text box (Save As dialog box) to change the file name. Do not press the ENTER key after typing the file name because you do not want to close the dialog box at this time.

- Navigate to the desired location for the new folder (in this case, the Word folder in the CIS 101 folder [or your class folder] on the USB flash drive).

- Click the New folder button (Save As dialog box) to display a new folder icon with the name New folder selected in the dialog box (Figure 6–8).

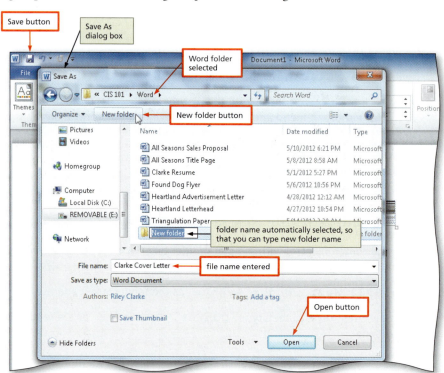

Figure 6–8

- Type **Job Hunting** as the new folder name and then press the ENTER key to create the new folder.

- Click the Open button to open the selected folder, in this case, the Job Hunting folder (Figure 6–9).

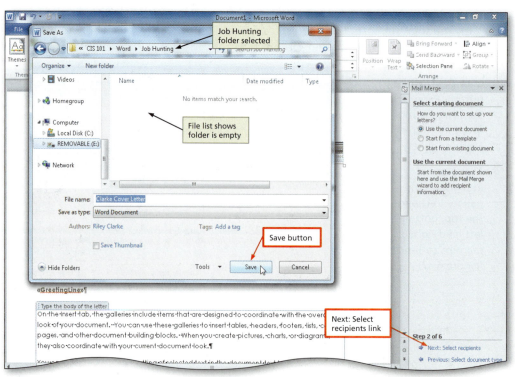

Figure 6–9

3
• Click the Save button (Save As dialog box) to save the current document in the selected folder on the selected drive.

Q&A Can I create a folder in any other dialog box?

Yes. Any dialog box that displays a File list, such as the Open and Insert File dialog boxes, also has the New folder button, allowing you to create a new folder in Word instead of using Windows for this task.

Other Ways
1. Press F12

Creating a Data Source

A data source is a file that contains the data that changes from one merged document to the next. As shown in Figure 6–10, a data source often is shown as a table that consists of a series of rows and columns. Each row is called a **record**. The first row of a data source is called the **header record** because it identifies the name of each column. Each row below the header row is called a **data record**. Data records contain the text that varies in each copy of the merged document. The data source for this project contains five data records. In this project, each data record identifies a different potential employer. Thus, five form letters will be generated from this data source.

Each column in the data source is called a **data field**. A data field represents a group of similar data. Each data field must be identified uniquely with a name, called a **field name**. For example, Position is the name of the data field (column) that contains the advertised job position. In this chapter, the data source contains 11 data fields with the following field names: Title, First Name, Last Name, Organization Name, Address Line 1, Address Line 2, City, State, ZIP Code, Position, and Employer Type.

First Name	Last Name	Organization Name	Address Line 1	Address Line 2	City	State	ZIP Code	Position	Type
Camille	Townsend	Sunbelt Veterinary Clinic	906 Center Street		Donner	OH	44772	Veterinary Technician	C
Leon	Siefert	Bridgeton College	85 Parker Way	P.O. Box 3309	Bridgeton	OH	44710	Clinical Veterinary Technician I	S
Natalia	Zajak	Zajak Animal Clinic	272 Mill Road	Unit 2B	Donner	OH	44772	Veterinary Assistant	C
Hugo	Moreau	Ohio Animal Medicine College	3894 81st Street		Wilborn	OH	44752	Veterinary Technican I	S
Min	Huan	Timber Creek Veterinary Center	55 Sycamore Avenue	P.O. Box 104	Timber Creek	OH	44729	Veterinary Technician	C

header record · field names · data records · data fields

Figure 6–10 Data Source

Create the data source.
When you create a data source, you will need to determine the fields it should contain. That is, you will need to identify the data that will vary from one merged document to the next. Following are a few important points about fields:

• For each field, you may be required to create a field name. Because data sources often contain the same fields, some programs create a list of commonly used field names that you may use.

• Field names must be unique; that is, no two field names may be the same.

• Fields may be listed in any order in the data source. That is, the order of fields has no effect on the order in which they will print in the main document.

• Organize fields so that they are flexible. For example, separate the name into individual fields: title, first name, and last name. This arrangement allows you to print a person's title, first name, and last name (e.g., Ms. Camille Townsend) in the inside address but only the title and last name in the salutation (Dear Ms. Townsend).

Plan Ahead

To Create a New Data Source

Word provides a list of 13 commonly used field names. This project uses 9 of the 13 field names supplied by Word: Title, First Name, Last Name, Company Name, Address Line 1, Address Line 2, City, State, and ZIP Code. This project does not use the other four field names supplied by Word: Country or Region, Home Phone, Work Phone, and E-mail Address. Thus, you will delete these four field names. Then, you will change the Company Name field name to Organization Name because organization better describes a school and a clinic (or practice). You also will add two new field names (Position and Employer Type) to the data source. The following steps create a new data source for a mail merge.

1

- Click the Next: Select recipients link at the bottom of the Mail Merge task pane (shown in Figure 6-9 on page WD 338) to display Step 3 of the Mail Merge wizard, which requests you select recipients.

- Click 'Type a new list' in the Select recipients area, which displays the 'Type a new list' area.

- Click the Create link to display the New Address List dialog box (Figure 6–11).

Q&A

When would I use the other two option buttons in the Select recipients area?

If a data source already was created, you would use the first option: Use an existing list. If you wanted to use your Outlook contacts list as the data source, you would choose the second option.

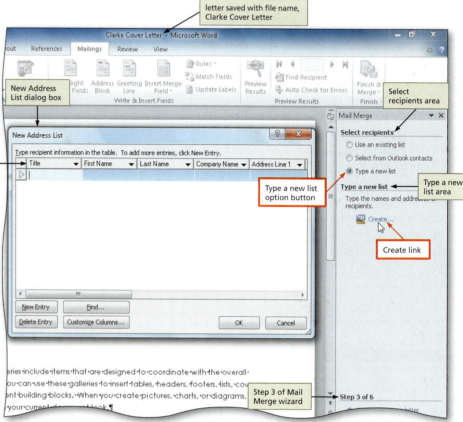

Figure 6–11

2

- Click the Customize Columns button (New Address List dialog box) to display the Customize Address List dialog box (Figure 6–12).

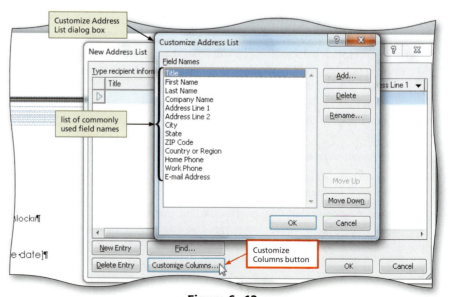

Figure 6–12

- Click Country or Region in the Field Names list to select the field to be deleted and then click the Delete button to display a dialog box asking if you are sure you want to delete the selected field (Figure 6–13).

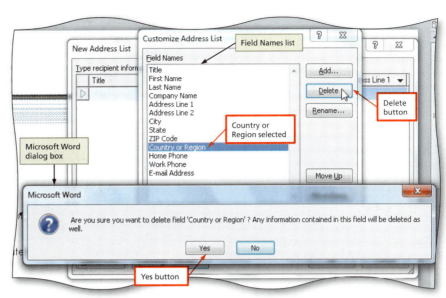

Figure 6–13

- Click the Yes button (Microsoft Word dialog box) to delete the field.

- Click Home Phone in the Field Names list to select the field. Click the Delete button (Customize Address List dialog box) and then click the Yes button (Microsoft Word dialog box) to delete the field.

- Use this same procedure to delete the Work Phone and E-mail Address fields.

- Click Company Name in the Field Names list to select the field to be renamed.

- Click the Rename button to display the Rename Field dialog box.

- Type **Organization Name** (Rename Field dialog box) in the To text box (Figure 6–14).

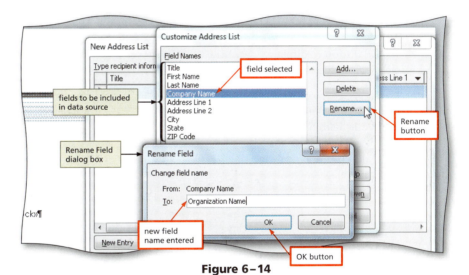

Figure 6–14

- Click the OK button to close the Rename Field dialog box and rename the selected field.

- Click the Add button to display the Add Field dialog box.

- Type **Position** in the 'Type a name for your field' text box (Add Field dialog box) (Figure 6–15).

Figure 6–15

8

- Click the OK button to close the Add Field dialog box and add the Position field name to the Field Names list immediately below the selected field (Figure 6–16).

Q&A Can I change the order of the field names in the Field Names list?

Yes. Select the field name and then click the Move Up or Move Down button to move the selected field in the direction of the button name.

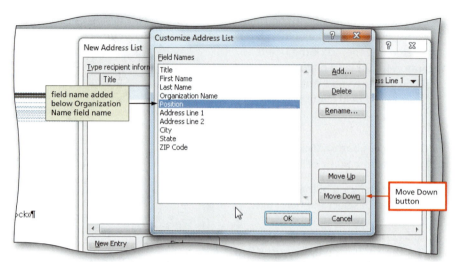

Figure 6–16

9

- With the Position field selected, click the Move Down button five times to position the selected field at the end of the Field Names list.

- Click the Add button to display the Add Field dialog box.

- Type **Employer Type** (Add Field dialog box) in the 'Type a name for your field' text box and then click the OK button to close the Add Field dialog box and add the Employer Type field name to the bottom of the Field Names list (Figure 6–17).

Q&A Could I add more field names to the list?

Yes. You would click the Add button for each field name you want to add.

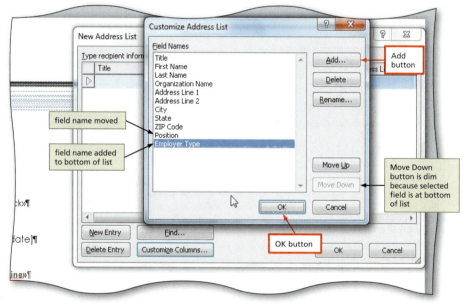

Figure 6–17

10

- Click the OK button to close the Customize Address List dialog box, which positions the insertion point in the Title text box for the first record (row) in the New Address List dialog box (Figure 6–18).

Figure 6–18

• Type **Ms.** and then press the TAB key to enter the title for the first data record.

• Type **Camille** and then press the TAB key to enter the first name.

• Type **Townsend** and then press the TAB key to enter the last name.

• Type **Sunbelt Veterinary Clinic** and then press the TAB key to enter the organization name.

• Type **906 Center Street** to enter the first address line (Figure 6–19).

Q&A What if I notice an error in an entry?

Click the entry and then correct the error as you would in the document window.

Q&A What happened to the rest of the Organization Name entry?

It is stored in the field, but you cannot see the entire entry because it is longer than the display area.

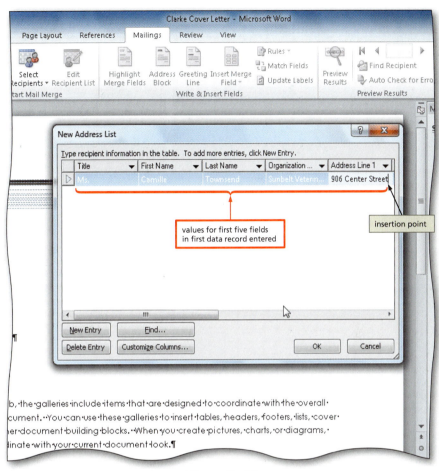

Figure 6–19

• Press the TAB key twice to leave the second address line empty.

• Type **Donner** and then press the TAB key to enter the city.

• Type **OH** and then press the TAB key to enter the state code.

• Type **44772** and then press the TAB key to enter the ZIP code.

• Type **Veterinary Technician** and then press the TAB key to enter the Position.

• Type **C** to enter the employer type (Figure 6–20).

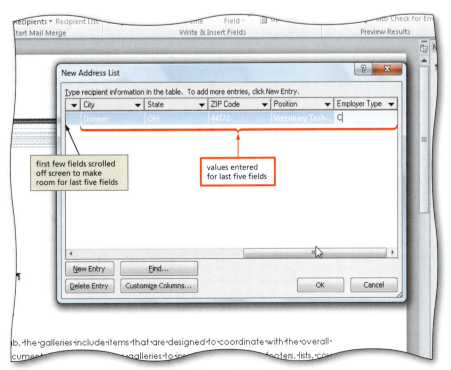

Figure 6–20

13
• Click the New Entry button to add a new blank record and position the insertion point in the Title field of the new record (Figure 6–21).

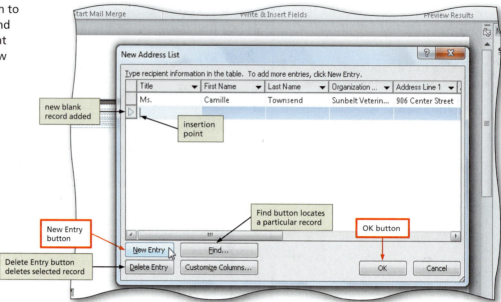

Figure 6–21

To Enter More Records

The following steps enter the remaining four records in the New Address List dialog box.

1 Type **Mr.** and then press the TAB key. Type **Leon** and then press the TAB key. Type **Siefert** and then press the TAB key. Type **Bridgeton College** and then press the TAB key.

2 Type **85 Parker Way** and then press the TAB key. Type **P.O. Box 3309** and then press the TAB key.

3 Type **Bridgeton** and then press the TAB key. Type **OH** and then press the TAB key. Type **44710** and then press the TAB key.

4 Type **Clinical Veterinary Technician** and then press the TAB key. Type **S** and then click the New Entry button.

Q&A

Instead of clicking the New Entry button, can I press the TAB key at the end of one row to add a new blank record?

Yes. Pressing the TAB key at the end of a row has the same function as clicking the New Entry button.

5 Type **Dr.** and then press the TAB key. Type **Natalia** and then press the TAB key. Type **Zajak** and then press the TAB key. Type **Zajak Animal Clinic** and then press the TAB key.

6 Type **272 Mill Road** and then press the TAB key. Type **Unit 2B** and then press the TAB key.

7 Type **Donner** and then press the TAB key. Type **OH** and then press the TAB key. Type **44772** and then press the TAB key.

8 Type **Veterinary Assistant** and then press the TAB key. Type **C** and then click the New Entry button.

9 Type **Mr.** and then press the TAB key. Type **Hugo** and then press the TAB key. Type **Moreau** and then press the TAB key. Type **Ohio Animal Medicine College** and then press the TAB key.

10 Type **3894 81st Street** and then press the TAB key twice.

11 Type **Wilborn** and then press the TAB key. Type **OH** and then press the TAB key. Type **44752** and then press the TAB key.

12 Type **Veterinary Technician I** and then press the TAB key. Type **S** and then click the New Entry button.

13 Type **Dr.** and then press the TAB key. Type **Min** and then press the TAB key. Type **Huan** and then press the TAB key. Type **Timber Creek Veterinary Center** and then press the TAB key.

14 Type **55 Sycamore Avenue** and then press the TAB key. Type **P.O. Box 104** and then press the TAB key.

15 Type **Timber Creek** and then press the TAB key. Type **OH** and then press the TAB key. Type **44729** and then press the TAB key.

16 Type **Veterinary Technician** and then press the TAB key. Type **C** and then click the OK button (shown in Figure 6–21), which displays the Save Address List dialog box (shown in Figure 6–22).

To Save a Data Source when Prompted by Word

When you click the OK button in the New Address List dialog box, Word displays the Save Address List dialog box so that you can save the data source. By default, the save location is the My Data Sources folder on your computer's hard disk. In this chapter, you save the data source to your USB flash drive. The following steps save the data source in the Job Hunting folder created earlier in this project.

1

• Type **Clarke Prospective Employers** in the File name text box (Save Address List dialog box) as the name for the data source. Do not press the ENTER key after typing the file name because you do not want to close the dialog box at this time.

• Navigate to the desired save location for the data source (in this case, the Job Hunting folder in the Word folder in the CIS 101 folder [or your class folder] on the USB flash drive) (Figure 6–22).

Q&A What is a Microsoft Office Address Lists file type?

It is a Microsoft Access database file. If you are familiar with Microsoft Access, you can open the Clarke Prospective Employers file in Access. You do not have to be familiar with Access or have Access installed on your computer, however, to continue with this mail merge process. Word simply stores a data source as an Access table because it is an efficient method of storing a data source.

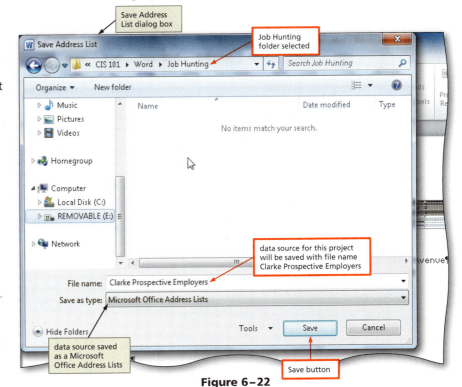

Figure 6–22

2
- Click the Save button (Save Address List dialog box) to save the data source in the selected folder using the entered file name and then display the Mail Merge Recipients dialog box (Figure 6–23).

Q&A

What if the fields in my Mail Merge Recipients list are in a different order?

The order of fields in the Mail Merge Recipients list has no effect on the mail merge process. If Word rearranges the order, you can leave them in the revised order.

3
- Click the OK button to close the Mail Merge Recipients dialog box.

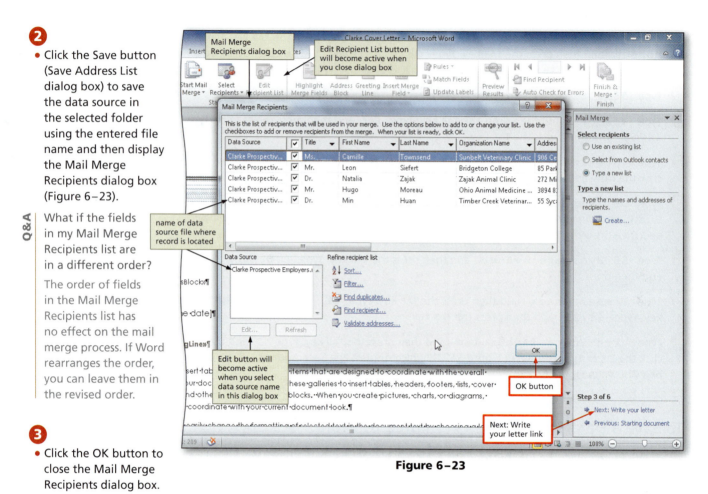

Figure 6–23

BTW

Saving Data Sources
Word, by default, saves a data source in the My Data Sources folder on your computer's hard disk. Likewise, when you open a data source, Word initially looks in the My Data Sources folder for the file. Because the data source files you create in Word are saved as Microsoft Access database file types, if you are familiar with Microsoft Access, you can open and view these files in Access.

Editing Records in the Data Source

All of the data records have been entered in the data source and saved with the file name, Clarke Prospective Employers. To add or edit data records in the data source, you would click the Edit Recipient List button (Mailings tab | Start Mail Merge group) to display the Mail Merge Recipients dialog box (shown in Figure 6–23). Click the data source name in the Data Source list and then click the Edit button (Mail Merge Recipients dialog box) to display the data records in a dialog box similar to the one shown in Figure 6–21 on page WD 344. Then, add or edit records as described in the previous steps. If you want to edit a particular record and the list of data records is long, you can click the Find button to locate an item, such as a last name, quickly in the list.

To delete a record, select it using the same procedure described in the previous paragraph. Then, click the Delete Entry button in the dialog box (Figure 6–21).

Using an Existing Data Source

Instead of creating a new data source, you can use an existing Microsoft Outlook Contacts list, an Access database table, an Excel table, or a Word table as a data source in a mail merge. To use an existing data source, select the appropriate option in the Select recipients area in the Mail Merge task pane or click the Select Recipients button (Mailings tab | Start Mail Merge group) and then click the desired option on the Select Recipients menu.

For a Microsoft Outlook Contacts list, click Select from Outlook contacts in the Mail Merge task pane or on the Select Recipients menu to display the Select Contacts dialog box. Next, select the contact folder you wish to import (Select Contacts dialog box) and then click the OK button.

For other existing data source types such as an Access database table, an Excel worksheet, or a Word table, click Use Existing List in the Mail Merge task pane or on the Select Recipients menu to display the Select Data Source dialog box. Next, select the file name of the data source you wish to use and then click the Open button.

With Access, you can use any field in the database in the main document. (Later in this chapter you use an existing Access database table as the data source.) For the merge to work properly with an Excel table or a Word table, you must ensure data is arranged properly and that the table is the only element in the file. The first row of the table should contain unique field names, and the table cannot contain any blank rows.

Composing the Main Document for the Form Letters

The next step in this project is to enter and format the text and fields in the main document for the form letters (shown in Figure 6–1a on page WD 331). You will follow these steps to compose the main document for the form letter.

1. Enter the date.
2. Edit the address block.
3. Edit the greeting line (salutation).
4. Enter text and insert merge fields.
5. Insert an IF field.
6. Merge the letters.

Compose the main document for the form letter.
This chapter uses a template for the main document for the form letter, where you select predefined content controls and replace them with personalized content, adjusting formats as necessary. As an alternative, some users prefer to enter the contents of the main document from scratch so that they can format the letter with business letter spacing while composing it according to the block, modified block, or semi-block letter style.

Plan Ahead

To Display the Next Step in the Mail Merge Wizard

The next step in the Mail Merge wizard is to write the letter. Because you are using a template to write the letter, you do not need to use the task pane for this step. If, however, you were not using a template, you could use this task pane to insert the AddressBlock and GreetingLine fields in the document. The following step displays the next step in the Mail Merge wizard.

1 Click the Next: Write your letter link at the bottom of the Mail Merge task pane (shown in Figure 6–23) to display Step 4 of the Mail Merge wizard in the Mail Merge task pane (shown in Figure 6–24 on the next page).

To Zoom the Document

So that the document is easier to read, you prefer it at 110 percent. Thus, the following step changes the zoom to 110%.

1 If necessary, click the Zoom In button on the status bar as many times as necessary until the Zoom button displays 110% on its face (shown in Figure 6–24).

BTWs
For a complete list of the BTWs found in the margins of this book, visit the Word 2010 BTW Web page (scsite.com/wd2010/btw).

To Enter the Date

The next step is to enter the date in the letter. You can click the date content control and type the correct date, or you can click the box arrow and select the date from a calendar. The following steps use the calendar to enter the date.

①

- If necessary, scroll to display the letter in the document window.

- Click the date content control to select it and then click its box arrow to display a calendar.

- Scroll through the calendar months until the desired month appears, May, 2012 in this case (Figure 6–24).

②

- Click 11 in the calendar to display 5/11/2012 in the date line of the form letter (shown in Figure 6–25).

- Click outside the content control to deselect it.

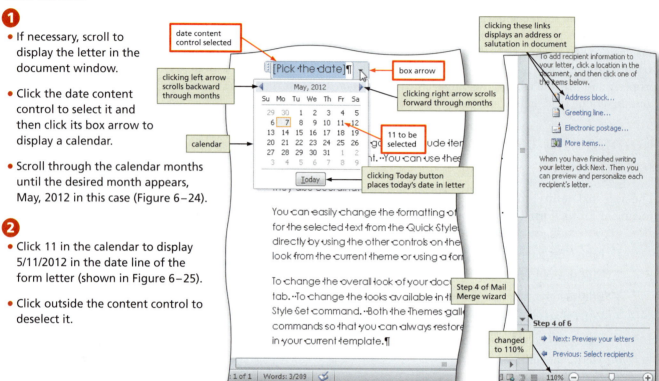

Figure 6–24

Merge Fields

In this form letter, the inside address appears below the date line, and the salutation is placed below the date line. The contents of the inside address and salutation are located in the data source. To link the data source to the main document, you insert the field names from the data source in the main document.

In the main document, field names linked to the data source are called **merge fields** because they merge, or combine, the main document with the contents of the data source. When a merge field is inserted in the main document, Word surrounds the field name with **merge field characters**, which are chevrons that mark the beginning and ending of a merge field. Merge field characters are not on the keyboard; therefore, you cannot type them directly in the document. Word automatically displays them when a merge field is inserted in the main document.

Most letters contain an address and salutation. For this reason, Word provides an AddressBlock merge field and a GreetingLine merge field. The **AddressBlock merge field** contains several fields related to an address: title, first name, middle name, last name, suffix, company, street address 1, street address 2, city, state, and ZIP code. When Word uses the AddressBlock merge field, it automatically looks for any fields in the associated data source that are related to an address and then formats the address block properly when you merge the data source with the main document. For example, if your inside address does not use a middle name, suffix, or company, Word omits these items from the inside address and adjusts the spacing so that the address prints correctly.

The Urban Mail Merge template automatically inserted the AddressBlock and GreetingLine merge fields in the form letter. If you wanted to insert these merge fields in a document, you would click the Address block link or the Greeting line link in the Mail Merge task pane or the associated buttons on the Mailings tab.

To View Merged Data in the Main Document

Instead of displaying merge fields, you can see how fields, such as the AddressBlock or GreetingLine fields, will look in the merged letters. The following step views merged data.

1

- If necessary, display the Mailings tab.

- Click the Preview Results button (Mailings tab | Preview Results group) to display the values in the current data record, instead of the merge fields (Figure 6–25).

Q&A

How can I tell which record is showing?

The current record number is displayed in the Preview Results group.

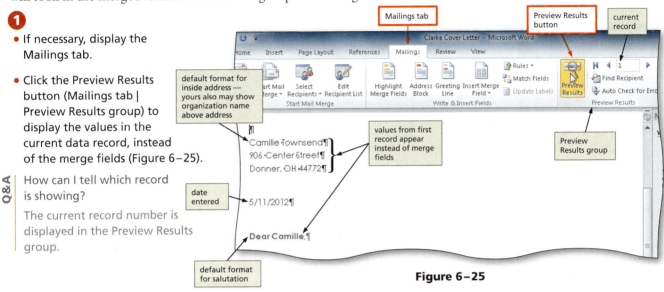

Figure 6–25

To Edit the AddressBlock Merge Field

The **AddressBlock merge field** contains text and fields related to the inside address. The default format for the inside address is the first name and last name on one line, followed by the street address on the next line, and then the city, state, and postal code on the next line. In this letter, you want the potential employer's title (i.e., Ms.) to appear to the left of the first name. You also want the organization name to appear above the street address, if it does not already. The following steps edit the AddressBlock merge field.

1

- Right-click the AddressBlock merge field to select it and display a shortcut menu and the Mini toolbar (Figure 6–26).

Q&A

Why does the AddressBlock merge field turn gray?

Word, by default, shades a field in gray when the field is selected. The shading displays on the screen to help you identify fields; the shading does not print on a hard copy. To select an entire field, double-click it.

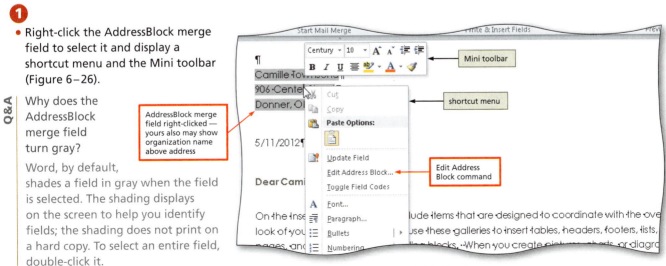

Figure 6–26

2

• Click Edit Address Block on the shortcut menu to display the Modify Address Block dialog box.

• Scroll through the list of recipient name formats (Modify Address Block dialog box) and then click the format, Mr. Joshua Randall Jr., in this list, because that format places the title to the left of the first name and last name.

🔍 **Experiment**

• Click various recipient name formats and watch the preview change in the dialog box. When finished experimenting, click the format: Mr. Joshua Randall Jr.

Q&A What causes the 'Insert company name' check box to be dimmed?

If your data source does not have a match to the Company Name in the AddressBlock merge field, this check box will be dimmed. Recall that earlier in this project the Company Name field was renamed as Organization Name, which may cause the fields to be unmatched.

• If your AddressBlock merge field does not show the Organization Name above the address, click the Match Fields button (Modify Address Block dialog box) to display the Match Fields dialog box (Figure 6–27); if the Organization Name appears in your AddressBlock merge field, proceed to Step 5.

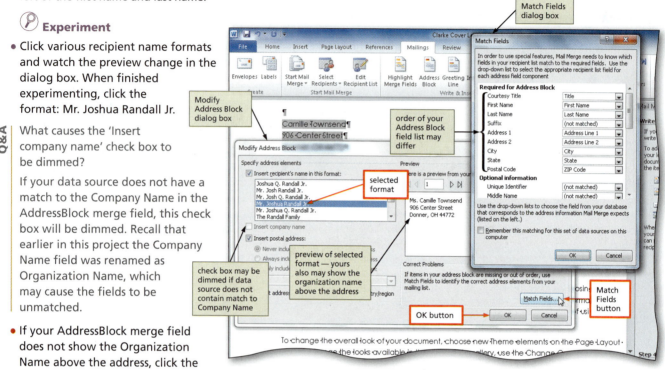

Figure 6–27

3

• If necessary, scroll through the Match Fields dialog box until Company appears.

• Click the Company box arrow (Match Fields dialog box) to display a list of fields in the data source and then click Organization Name to place that selected field as the match field.

• Click 'Remember this matching for this set of data sources on this computer' to place a check mark in the check box (Figure 6–28).

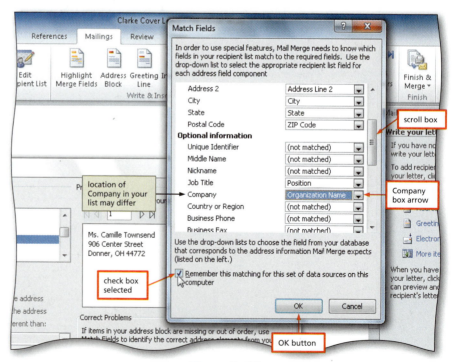

Figure 6–28

- Click the OK button (Match Fields dialog box) to close the dialog box, and notice the 'Insert company name' check box no longer is dimmed because the Company field now has a matched field in the data source.

- Click the 'Insert company name' check box to select it, and notice the preview area shows the organization name in the address (Figure 6–29).

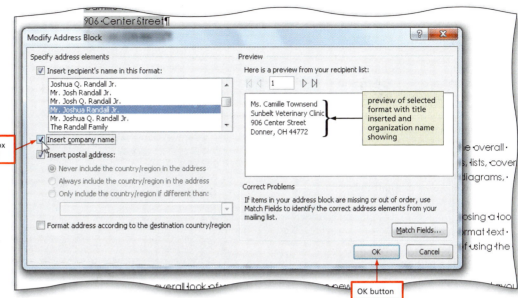

Figure 6–29

- Click the OK button (Modify Address Block dialog box) to modify the address block format.

To Edit the GreetingLine Merge Field

The **GreetingLine merge field** contains text and fields related to a salutation. The default greeting for the salutation is in the format, Dear Camille, followed by a comma. In this letter, you want a more formal salutation — Dear Ms. Townsend, followed by a colon. The following steps edit the GreetingLine merge field.

❶

- Right-click the GreetingLine merge field to select it and display a shortcut menu and the Mini toolbar (Figure 6–30).

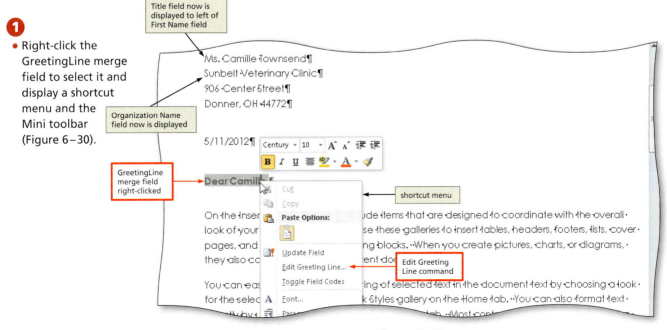

Figure 6–30

- Click Edit Greeting Line on the shortcut menu to display the Modify Greeting Line dialog box.

- Click the middle 'Greeting line format' box arrow; scroll to and then click the format, Mr. Randall, in this list because you want the title followed by the last name format.

- Click the rightmost 'Greeting line format' box arrow and then click the colon (:) in the list (Figure 6–31).

- Click the OK button to modify the greeting line format.

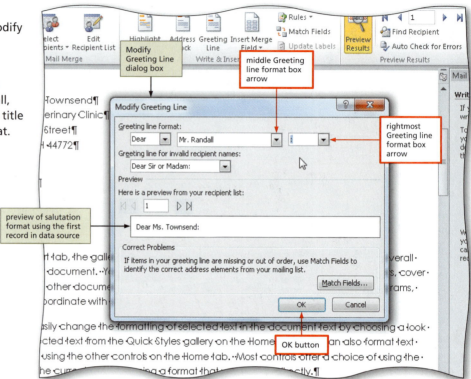

Figure 6–31

To View Merge Fields in the Main Document

Because you will be entering merge fields in the document next, you wish to display the merge fields instead of the merged data. The following step views merge fields instead of merged data.

1 Click the Preview Results button (Mailings tab | Preview Results group) to display the merge fields, instead of the values in the current data record (shown in Figure 6–32).

To Begin Typing the Body of the Form Letter

The next step is to begin typing the message, or body of the letter. This is to be located where Word displays the content control, Type the body of the letter, which contains three paragraphs of informational text. The following steps begin typing the letter in the location of the content control.

1 Click the body of the letter to select the content control (Figure 6–32).

2 With the content control selected, type `I will graduate from Donner Community College this May with an Associate of Science degree in Veterinary Technology. My education, along with first-hand experience through part-time jobs and volunteer work, make me an ideal candidate for the` and then press the SPACEBAR (shown in Figure 6–33).

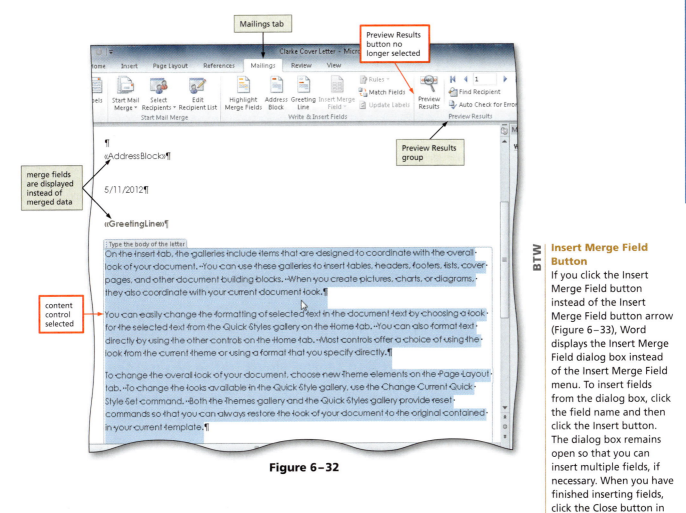

Figure 6–32

BTW

Insert Merge Field Button
If you click the Insert Merge Field button instead of the Insert Merge Field button arrow (Figure 6–33), Word displays the Insert Merge Field dialog box instead of the Insert Merge Field menu. To insert fields from the dialog box, click the field name and then click the Insert button. The dialog box remains open so that you can insert multiple fields, if necessary. When you have finished inserting fields, click the Close button in the dialog box.

To Insert a Merge Field in the Main Document

The second sentence in the first paragraph of the letter identifies the advertised job position. To instruct Word to use data fields from the data source, you insert merge fields in the main document for the form letter. The following steps insert a merge field at the location of the insertion point.

1
- Click the Insert Merge Field button arrow (Mailings tab | Write & Insert Fields group) to display the Insert Merge Field menu (Figure 6–33).

Q&A
What if I accidentally click the Insert Merge Field button instead of the button arrow?

Click the Cancel button in the dialog box and repeat Step 1.

Q&A
Why is the underscore character in some of the field names?

Word places an underscore character in place of the space in merge fields.

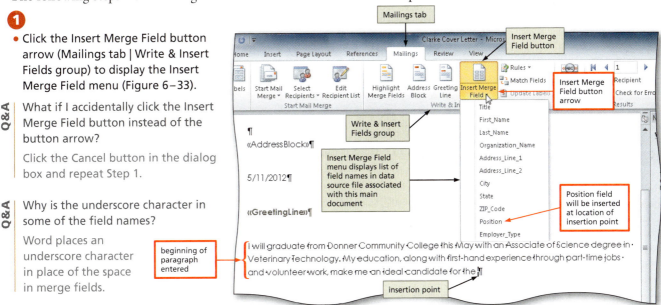

Figure 6–33

2

- Click Position on the Insert Merge Field menu to insert the selected merge field in the document at the location of the insertion point (Figure 6–34).

Q&A

Will the word, Position, and the chevron characters print when I merge the form letters?

No. When you merge the data source with the main document, the value in the Position field (e.g., Veterinary Technician) will print at the location of the merge field, Position.

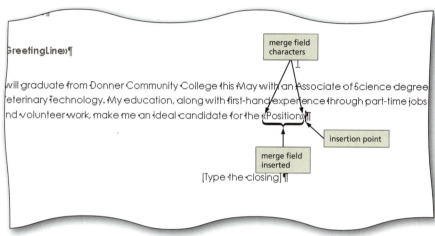

Figure 6–34

BTW

Merge Fields

When you insert fields in a document, the displayed fields may be surrounded by braces instead of chevrons, and extra instructions may appear between the braces. If this occurs, then field codes have been turned on. To turn off field codes so that they are not displayed, press ALT+F9.

To Enter More Text and Merge Fields in the Main Document

The next step is to enter the remainder of the first paragraph and part of the second paragraph, inserting the Organization Name merge field at the end of the first paragraph. The following steps enter more text and merge fields.

1 With the insertion point at the location shown in Figure 6–34, press the SPACEBAR. Type **position currently available at** and then press the SPACEBAR.

2 Click the Insert Merge Field button arrow (Mailings tab | Write & Insert Fields group) and then click Organization_Name on the Insert Merge Field menu to insert the selected merge field in the document.

3 Press the PERIOD key. Press the ENTER key. Type **As evidenced on the enclosed resume, my background matches the job requirements posted through the Career Development Office at Donner Community College. My coursework and experience have prepared me to assist during surgery and examinations, maintain records, and provide hands-on education at your** and then press the SPACEBAR (shown in Figure 6–35).

IF Fields

In addition to merge fields, you can insert Word fields that are designed specifically for a mail merge. An **IF field** is an example of a Word field. One form of the IF field is called an **If...Then:** If a condition is true, then perform an action. For example, If Mary owns a house, then send her information about homeowner's insurance. Another form of the IF field is called an **If...Then...Else:** If a condition is true, then perform an action; else perform a different action. For example, If John has an e-mail address, then send him an e-mail message; else send him the message via the postal service.

In this project, the form letter checks the employer's type. If the employer type is C (for clinic), then the letter should print the word, practice; else if the employer type is S (for school), then the letter should print the word, school. Thus, you will use an If...Then...Else: If the employer type is equal to C, then insert the word practice, else insert the word school.

The phrase that appears after the word If is called a rule or a condition. A **condition** consists of an expression, followed by a comparison operator, followed by a final expression.

Expression The expression in a condition can be a merge field, a number, a series of characters, or a mathematical formula. Word surrounds a series of characters with quotation marks ("). To indicate an empty, or null, expression, Word places two quotation marks together ("").

Comparison operator The comparison operator in a condition must be one of six characters: = (equal to or matches the text), <> (not equal to or does not match text), < (less than), <= (less than or equal to), > (greater than), or >= (greater than or equal to).

If the result of a condition is true, then Word evaluates the **true text**. If the result of the condition is false, Word evaluates the **false text** if it exists. In this project, the first expression in the condition is a merge field (Employer_Type); the comparison operator is equal to (=); and the second expression is the text "C". The true text is "practice". The false text is "school". The complete IF field is as follows:

BTW

IF Fields
The phrase, IF field, originates from computer programming. Do not be intimidated by the terminology. An IF field simply specifies a decision. Some programmers refer to it as an IF statement. Complex IF statements include one or more nested IF fields, which is a second IF field inside the true or false text of the first IF field.

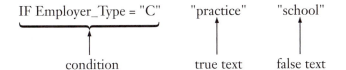

IF Employer_Type = "C"	"practice"	"school"
condition	true text	false text

To Insert an IF Field in the Main Document

The following steps insert this IF field in the form letter: If the employer type is C, then insert the text, practice; else insert the text, school.

1

- With the insertion point positioned as shown in Figure 6–35, click the Rules button (Mailings tab | Write & Insert Fields group) to display the Rules menu (Figure 6–35).

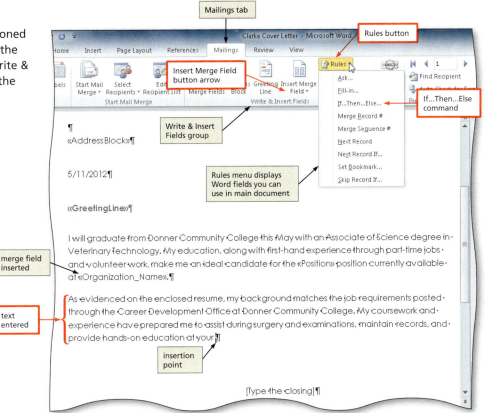

Figure 6–35

2

- Click If...Then...Else on the Rules menu to display the Insert Word Field: IF dialog box (Figure 6–36).

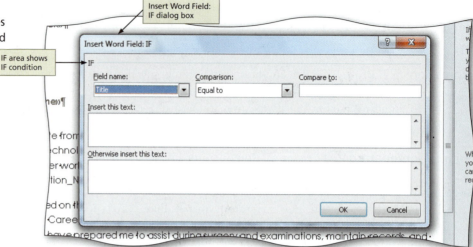

Figure 6–36

3

- Click the Field name box arrow to display the list of fields in the data source.

- Scroll through the list of fields in the Field name list and then click Employer_Type to select the field.

- Position the insertion point in the Compare to text box and then type C as the comparison text.

- Press the TAB key and then type **practice** as the true text.

- Press the TAB key and then type **school** as the false text (Figure 6–37).

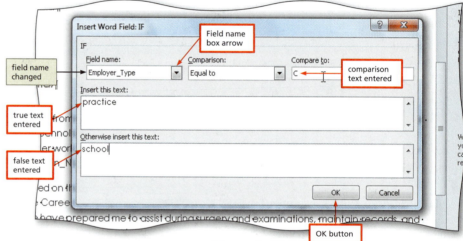

Figure 6–37

Q & A

Does the capitalization matter in the comparison text?

Yes. The text, C, is different from the text, c, in a comparison. Be sure to enter the text exactly as you entered it in the data source.

4

- Click the OK button to insert the IF field at the location of the insertion point (Figure 6–38).

Q & A

Why does the main document display the word, practice, instead of the IF field instructions?

The word, practice, is displayed because the first record in the data source has a employer type of C. Word, by default, evaluates the IF field using the current record and displays the results, called the **field results**, in the main document instead of displaying the IF field instructions. Later in the chapter, you will view the IF field instructions.

As evidenced on the enclosed resume, my background matches the job requirements posted through the Career Development Office at Donner Community College. My coursework and experience have prepared me to assist during surgery and examinations, maintain records, and provide hands-on education at your practice.

Figure 6–38

To Enter More Text and Merge Fields

The following steps enter the remainder of the form letter.

1 Press the PERIOD key to finish the sentence.

2 If necessary, scroll to display the bottom of the letter in the document window.

3 Press the ENTER key. Type `I will call you next week to see if we can set up a time to discuss my qualifications further. Thank you,` and then press the SPACEBAR.

4 Click the Insert Merge Field button arrow (Mailings tab | Write & Insert Fields group) and then click Title on the Insert Merge Field menu to insert the selected merge field in the document.

5 Press the SPACEBAR. Click the Insert Merge Field button arrow (Mailings tab | Write & Insert Fields group) and then click Last_Name on the Insert Merge Field menu to insert the selected merge field in the document.

6 Type `,  for your time and consideration.`

7 Select the closing content control and then type `Sincerely,` as the closing.

8 Right-click the content control with the placeholder text, Type the sender company name, to display a shortcut menu and then click Remove Content Control on the shortcut menu.

Q&A What if my content control already displays a sender company name instead of placeholder text?

Select the text and then delete it.

9 Press the ENTER key. Display the Home tab and then click the Decrease Indent button (Home tab | Paragraph group) six times to move the paragraph to the left margin. Type `Enclosure` as the last line of text in the letter (Figure 6–39).

BTW

Word Fields
In addition to the IF field, Word provides other fields that may be used in form letters. For example, the ASK and FILLIN fields prompt the user to enter data for each record in the data source. The SKIP RECORD IF field instructs the mail merge not to generate a form letter for a data record if a specific condition is met.

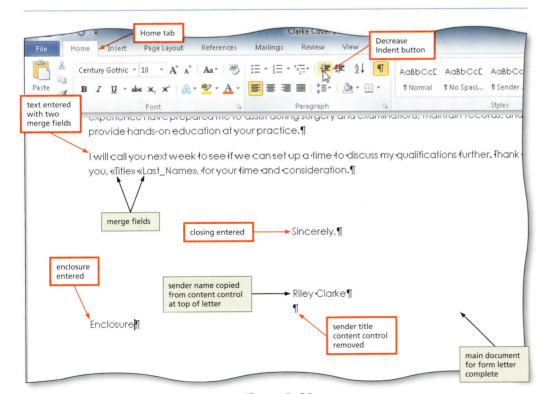

Figure 6–39

To Highlight Merge Fields

If you wanted to highlight all the merge fields in a document so that you could identify them quickly, you would perform the following steps.

1. Click the Highlight Merge Fields button (Mailings tab | Write & Insert Fields group) to highlight the merge fields in the document.

2. When finished viewing merge fields, click the Highlight Merge Fields button (Mailings tab | Write & Insert Fields group) again to remove the highlight from the merge fields in the document.

To Display a Field Code

The instructions in the IF field are not displayed in the document; instead, the field results are displayed for the current record (Figure 6–40). The instructions of an IF field are called **field codes**, and the default for Word is for field codes not to be displayed. Thus, field codes do not print or show on the screen unless you turn them on. You use one procedure to show field codes on the screen and a different procedure to print them on a hard copy.

You might want to turn on a field code to verify its accuracy or to modify it. Field codes tend to clutter the screen. Thus, most Word users turn them off after viewing them. The following steps show a field code on the screen.

- Scroll up to display the letter in the document window.

- Right-click the field results showing the word, practice, to display a shortcut menu (Figure 6–40).

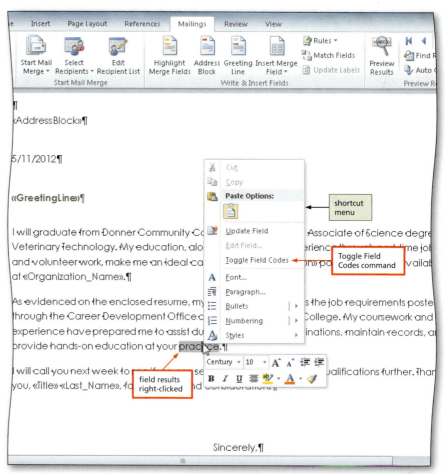

Figure 6–40

2

- Click Toggle Field Codes on the shortcut menu to display the field code instead of the field results for the IF field (Figure 6–41).

Q&A Will displaying field codes affect the merged documents?

No. Displaying field codes has no effect on the merge process.

Q&A What if I wanted to display all field codes in a document?

You would press ALT+F9. Then, to hide all the field codes, press ALT+F9 again.

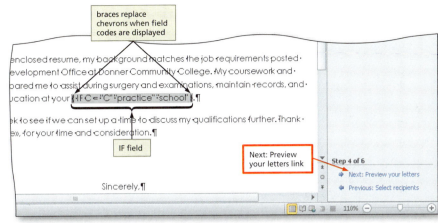

Figure 6–41

Other Ways

1. With insertion point in field, press SHIFT+F9

TO PRINT FIELD CODES IN THE MAIN DOCUMENT

When you merge or print a document, Word automatically converts field codes that show on the screen to field results. You may want to print the field codes version of the form letter, however, so that you have a hard copy of the field codes for future reference. When you print field codes, you must remember to turn off the field codes option so that merged documents print field results instead of field codes. If you wanted to print the field codes in the main document, you would perform the following steps.

1. Open the Backstage view and then click Options to display the Word Options dialog box.

2. Click Advanced in the left pane to display advanced options in the right pane and then scroll to the Print area in the right pane of the dialog box.

3. Place a check mark in the 'Print field codes instead of their values' check box.

4. Click the OK button to instruct Word to show field codes when the document prints.

5. Open the Backstage view, click the Print tab, and then click the Print button to print the document with all field codes showing.

6. Open the Backstage view and then click Options to display the Word Options dialog box.

7. Click Advanced in the left pane to display advanced options in the right pane and then scroll to the Print area in the right pane of the dialog box.

8. Remove the check mark from the 'Print field codes instead of their values' check box.

9. Click the OK button to instruct Word to show field results the next time you print the document.

To Save a Document Again

The main document for the form letter now is complete. Thus, you should save it again. The following step saves the document again.

1 Save the main document for the form letter again with the same file name, Clarke Cover Letter.

BTW

Converting Main Document Files
If you wanted to convert a mail merge main document to a regular Word document, you would open the main document, click the Start Mail Merge button (Mailings tab | Start Mail Merge group), and then click Normal Word Document on the Start Mail Merge menu.

Opening a Main Document

You open a main document as you open any other Word document (i.e., clicking Open in the Backstage view). If Word displays a dialog box indicating it will run an SQL command, click the Yes button (Figure 6–42).

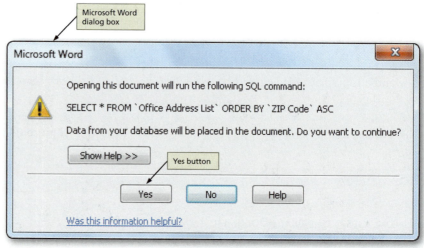

Figure 6–42

BTW

Data Source and Main Document Files
When you open a main document, if Word cannot locate the associated data source file or it does not display a dialog box with the Find Data Source button, then the data source may not be associated with the main document. To associate the data source with the main document, click the Select Recipients button (Mailings tab | Start Mail Merge group), click Use Existing List, and then locate the data source file. When you save the main document, Word will associate the data source with the main document.

When you open a main document, Word attempts to open the associated data source file, too. If the data source is not in exactly the same location (i.e., drive and folder) as when it originally was saved, Word displays a dialog box indicating that it could not find the data source (Figure 6–43). When this occurs, click the Find Data Source button to display the Open Data Source dialog box, which allows you to locate the data source file. (Word may display several dialog boxes requiring you to click an OK (or similar) button until the one shown in Figure 6–43 appears.)

Figure 6–43

> **Break Point:** If you wish to take a break, this is a good place to do so. You can quit Word now. To resume at a later time, start Word, open the file called Clarke Cover Letter, and continue following the steps from this location forward.

Merging the Data Source with the Main Document to Generate Form Letters

The next step in this project is to merge the data source with the main document to generate the form letters (shown in Figure 6–1c on page WD 331). You can generate the form letters to a new document or to a printer. You also can select certain records to merge and sort the records before merging. The following pages discuss these various ways to merge.

To Preview the Merged Letters

The next step in the Mail Merge wizard is to preview the letters. Earlier in this chapter, you previewed the letters using a button on the Ribbon. The following step uses the Mail Merge wizard to preview the letters.

1

- Click the Next: Preview your letters link at the bottom of the Mail Merge task pane (shown in Figure 6–41 on page WD 359) to display Step 5 of the Mail Merge wizard in the Mail Merge task pane (Figure 6–44).

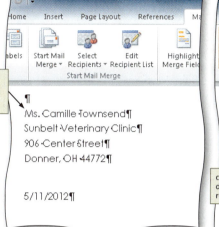

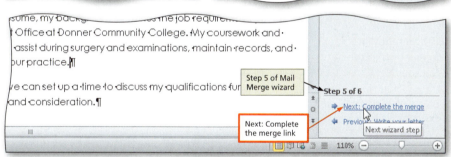

Figure 6–44

TO CHECK FOR ERRORS

Before merging documents, you can instruct Word to check for errors that might occur during the merge process. If you wanted to check for errors, you would perform the following steps.

1. Click the Auto Check for Errors button (Mailings tab | Preview Results group) to display the Checking and Reporting Errors dialog box.

2. Select the desired option and then click the OK button.

BTW

Locking Fields
If you wanted to lock a field so that its field results cannot be changed, click the field and then press CTRL+F11. To subsequently unlock a field so that it may be updated, click the field and then press CTRL+SHIFT+F11.

To Merge the Form Letters to a New Document

With the data source and main document for the form letter complete, the next step is to merge them to generate the individual form letters. You can merge the letters to a new document or to the printer. If you merge the documents to a new document, you can save the merged documents in a file in print them later or you can edit the contents of individual merged letters. Or, you can review the merged documents for accuracy and then close the file without saving it. The steps on the next page merge the form letters, sending the merged letters to a new document and then zoom the document window to display all merged documents at once.

- Click the Next: Complete the merge link at the bottom of the Mail Merge task pane (shown in Figure 6–44 on the previous page) to display Step 6 of the Mail Merge wizard in the Mail Merge task pane.

- Click the 'Edit individual letters' link in the Mail Merge task pane to display the Merge to New Document dialog box (Figure 6–45).

 What if I wanted to print the merged letters immediately instead of reviewing them first in a new document window?

You would click the Print link instead of the 'Edit individual letters' link.

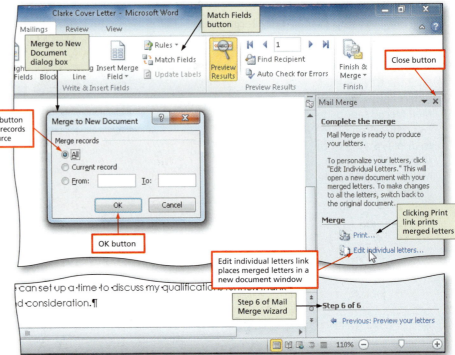

Figure 6–45

- If necessary, click All (Merge to New Document dialog box) so that all records in the data source are merged.

 Do I have to merge all records?

No. Through this dialog box, you can merge the current record or a range of record numbers.

- Click the OK button to merge the letters to a new document, in this case, five individual letters — one for each potential employer in the data source. (If Word displays a dialog box containing a message about locked fields, click its OK button.)

- To see all merged letters at once in the document window, display the View tab and then click the Zoom button (View tab | Zoom group) to display the Zoom dialog box.

- Click the Many pages button (Zoom dialog box) and then point to the third icon in the second row in the grid to specify the number of pages to be displayed in the document window at one time (Figure 6–46).

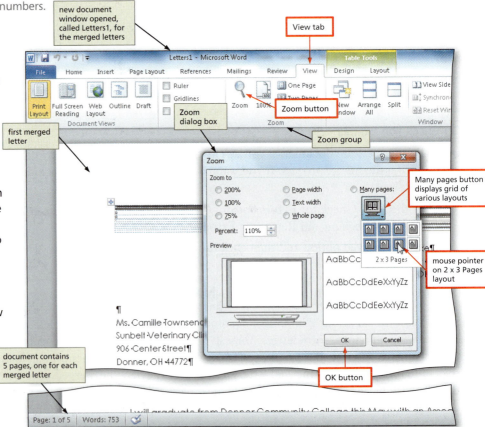

Figure 6–46

4
- Click the 2 × 3 Pages layout in the grid and then click the OK button to display the specified number of pages in the document window at once (Figure 6–47).

Q&A
Do I have to display all documents at once in the document window?

No. You can scroll through the documents instead, as you would in any other multipage document.

Q&A
Why does my screen show an extra blank page at the end?

You might have a blank record in the data source, or the spacing may cause an overflow to a blank page.

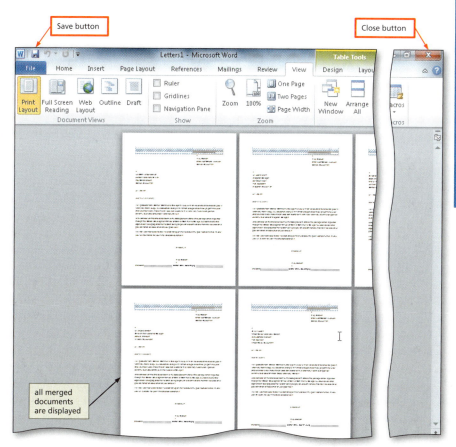

Save button

Close button

all merged documents are displayed

Figure 6–47

Other Ways

1. Click Finish & Merge button (Mailings tab | Finish group), click Edit Individual Documents

To Save the Merged Documents in a File and Close the Document Window

The following steps save the merged letters in a file and then close the document window containing the merged letters.

1 Click the Save button on the Quick Access Toolbar to display the Save As dialog box.

2 Type **Clarke Merged Letters** in the File name text box (Save As dialog box) as the name for the merged documents file. Do not press the ENTER key after typing the file name because you do not want to close the dialog box at this time.

3 If necessary, navigate to the desired save location for the merged documents file (in this case, the Job Hunting folder in the Word folder in the CIS 101 folder [or your class folder] on the USB flash drive).

4 Click the Save button (Save As dialog box) to save the document containing the merged letters in the selected folder using the entered file name.

Q&A
Do I have to save the document containing the merged letters?

No. You can scroll through the documents instead, as you would in any other multipage document, and then close the document without saving it.

5 Click the Close button on the right side of the document window to close the document.

6 Click the Close button on the Mail Merge task pane title bar (shown in Figure 6–45) because you are finished with the Mail Merge wizard.

BTW

Merging to E-Mail Messages
If you are merging to e-mail messages, you will click an Electronic Mail link in the Step 6 of 6 Mail Merge task pane to display a Merge to E-mail dialog box. Then, click the To box arrow (Merge to E-mail dialog box) and select the field name that contains e-mail addresses in the data source, enter the subject line for the e-mail messages, select the desired mail format, click All or another option in the Send records area, and then click the OK button to merge the messages to the e-mail addresses.

Correcting Errors in Merged Documents

If you notice errors in the merged form letters, edit the main document the same way you edit any other document. Then, save the changes and merge again. If the wrong field results print, Word may be mapping the fields incorrectly. To view fields, click the Match Fields button (Mailings tab | Write & Insert Fields group) (Figure 6–45 on page WD 362). Then, review the list of fields in the list. For example, Last Name should map to the Last Name field in the data source. If it does not, click the box arrow to change the name of the data source field.

If the fields are mapped correctly, the data in the data source may be incorrect. For a discussion about editing records in the data source, refer to page WD 346.

To Merge the Form Letters to the Printer

To print the merged documents, you could print the document just created that contains the five merged letters, or you can merge the form letters again and send them directly to the printer. The following steps merge the form letters and send them to the printer, using a button on the Ribbon.

- If necessary, display the Mailings tab.

- Click the Finish & Merge button (Mailings tab | Finish group) to display the Finish & Merge menu (Figure 6–48).

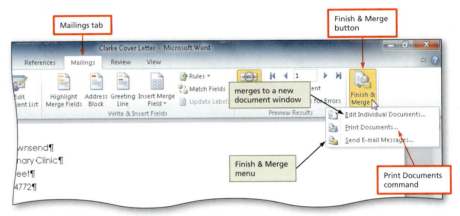

Figure 6–48

- Click Print Documents to display the Merge to Printer dialog box (Figure 6–49).

- If necessary, click All (Merge to Printer dialog box) and then click the OK button to display the Print dialog box.

- Click the OK button (Print dialog box) to print five separate letters, one for each potential employer in the data source, as shown in Figure 6–1c on page WD 331. (If Word displays a message about locked fields, click its OK button.)

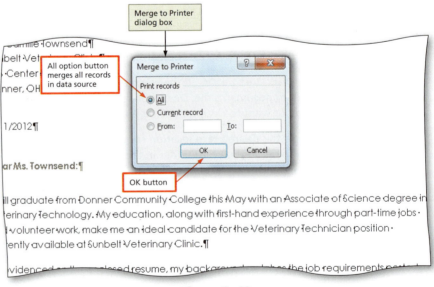

Figure 6–49

Other Ways

1. Print link in Mail Merge task pane

To Select Records to Merge

Instead of merging all of the records in the data source, you can choose which records to merge, based on a condition you specify. The dialog box in Figure 6–49 allows you to specify by record number which records to merge. Often, though, you want to merge based on the contents of a specific field. For example, you may want to merge and print only those employers whose employer type is S (for school). The following steps select records for a merge.

1

- Click the Edit Recipient List button (Mailings tab | Start Mail Merge group) to display the Mail Merge Recipients dialog box (Figure 6–50).

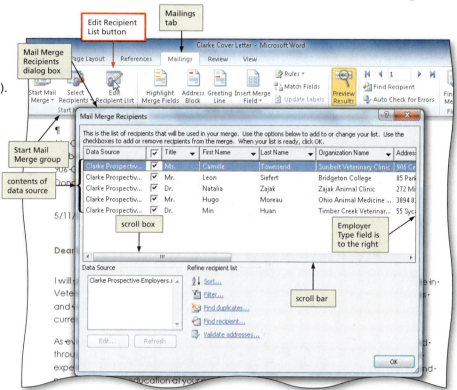

Figure 6–50

2

- Drag the scroll box to the right edge of the scroll bar (Mail Merge Recipients dialog box) so that the Employer Type field appears in the dialog box.

- Click the button arrow to the right of the field name, Employer Type, to display sort and filter criteria for the selected field (Figure 6–51).

Q&A

What are the filter criteria in the parentheses?

The (All) option clears any previously set filter criteria. The (Blanks) option selects records that contain blanks in that field, and the (Nonblanks) option selects records that do not contain blanks in that field. The (Advanced) option displays the Filter and Sort dialog box, which allows you to perform more advanced record selection operations.

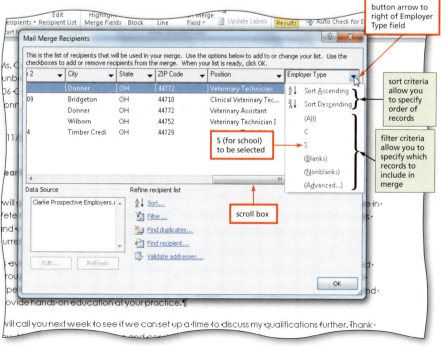

Figure 6–51

3

- Click S to reduce the number of data records displayed (Mail Merge Recipients dialog box) to two, because two potential employers are schools (Figure 6–52).

4

- Click the OK button to close the Mail Merge Recipients dialog box.

Q&A

What happened to the other three records that did not meet the criteria?

They still are part of the data source; they just are not appearing in the Mail Merge Recipients dialog box. When you clear the filter, all records will reappear.

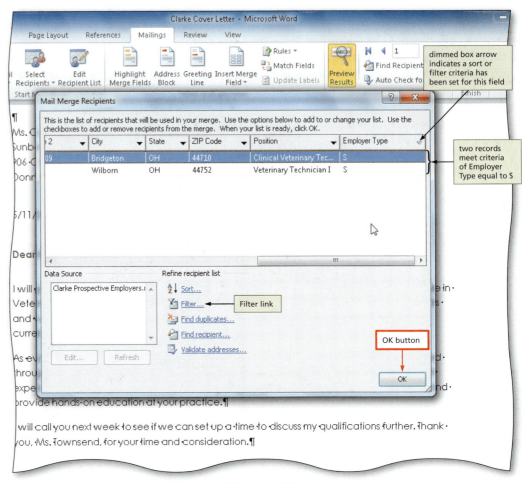

Figure 6–52

Other Ways

1. Click Filter link (Mail Merge Recipients dialog box), click Filter Records tab, enter filter criteria, click OK button

---

To Merge the Form Letters to the Printer

The next step is to merge the selected records. To do this, you follow the same steps described earlier. The difference is that Word will merge only those records that meet the criteria specified, that is, just those with an employer type of S. The following steps merge the filtered records to the printer.

1 Click the Finish & Merge button (Mailings tab | Finish group) to display the Finish & Merge menu.

2 Click Print Documents to display the Merge to Printer dialog box. If necessary, click All in the dialog box.

3 Click the OK button (Merge to Printer dialog box) to display the Print dialog box.

4 Click the OK button (Print dialog box) to print two separate letters, one for each potential employer whose employer type is S (Figure 6–53). (If Word displays a message about locked fields, click its OK button.)

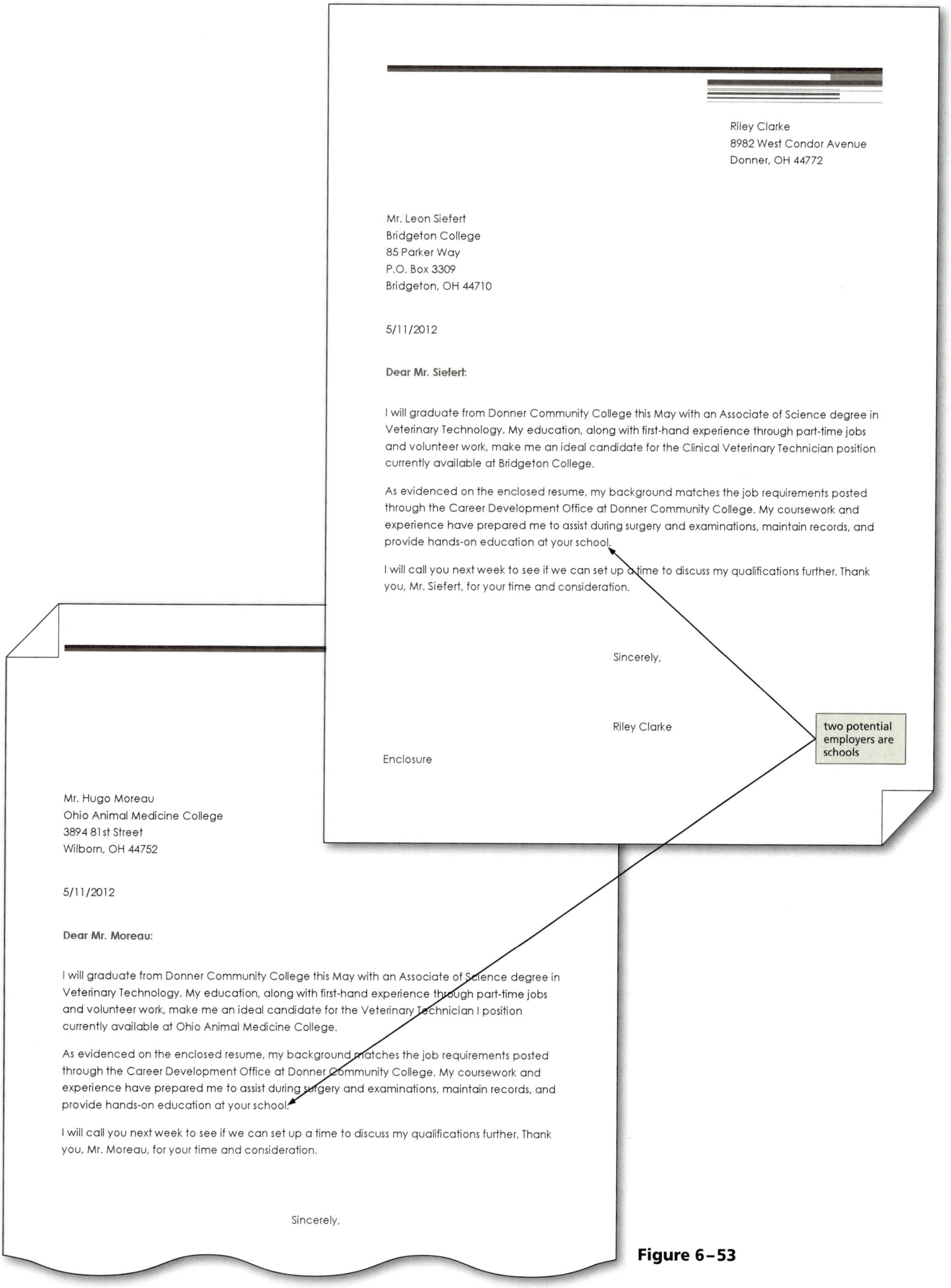

Riley Clarke
8982 West Condor Avenue
Donner, OH 44772

Mr. Leon Siefert
Bridgeton College
85 Parker Way
P.O. Box 3309
Bridgeton, OH 44710

5/11/2012

Dear Mr. Siefert:

I will graduate from Donner Community College this May with an Associate of Science degree in Veterinary Technology. My education, along with first-hand experience through part-time jobs and volunteer work, make me an ideal candidate for the Clinical Veterinary Technician position currently available at Bridgeton College.

As evidenced on the enclosed resume, my background matches the job requirements posted through the Career Development Office at Donner Community College. My coursework and experience have prepared me to assist during surgery and examinations, maintain records, and provide hands-on education at your school.

I will call you next week to see if we can set up a time to discuss my qualifications further. Thank you, Mr. Siefert, for your time and consideration.

Sincerely,

Riley Clarke

Enclosure

two potential employers are schools

Mr. Hugo Moreau
Ohio Animal Medicine College
3894 81st Street
Wilborn, OH 44752

5/11/2012

Dear Mr. Moreau:

I will graduate from Donner Community College this May with an Associate of Science degree in Veterinary Technology. My education, along with first-hand experience through part-time jobs and volunteer work, make me an ideal candidate for the Veterinary Technician I position currently available at Ohio Animal Medicine College.

As evidenced on the enclosed resume, my background matches the job requirements posted through the Career Development Office at Donner Community College. My coursework and experience have prepared me to assist during surgery and examinations, maintain records, and provide hands-on education at your school.

I will call you next week to see if we can set up a time to discuss my qualifications further. Thank you, Mr. Moreau, for your time and consideration.

Sincerely,

Figure 6–53

To Remove a Merge Condition

You should remove the merge condition so that future merges will not be restricted to potential employers with an employer type of S (for school). The following steps remove a merge condition.

1
- Click the Edit Recipient List button (Mailings tab | Start Mail Merge group) to display the Mail Merge Recipients dialog box.

2
- Click the Filter link (Mail Merge Recipients dialog box) to display the Filter and Sort dialog box.

- If necessary, click the Filter Records tab to display the Filter Records sheet (Figure 6–54).

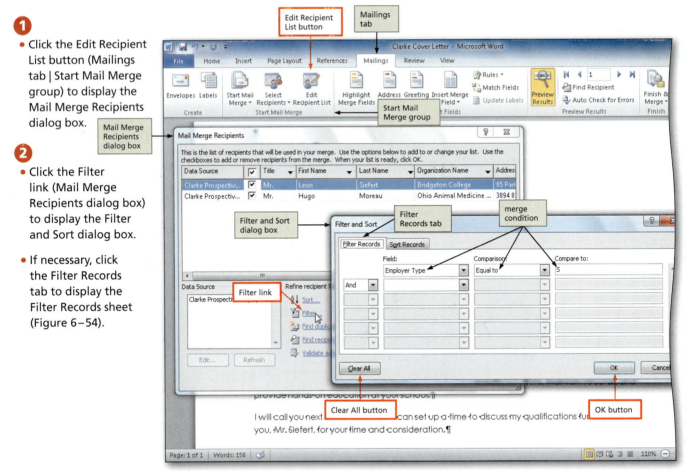

Figure 6–54

 Can I specify a merge condition in this dialog box instead of using the box arrow in the Mail Merge Recipients dialog box?

Yes.

3
- Click the Clear All button (Filter and Sort dialog box).

- Click the OK button in each of the two open dialog boxes to remove the merge condition.

To Sort the Data Records in a Data Source

If you mail the form letters using the U.S. Postal Service's bulk rate mailing service, the post office requires that you sort and group the form letters by ZIP code. Thus, the next steps sort the data records by ZIP code.

- Click the Edit Recipient List button (Mailings tab | Start Mail Merge group) to display the Mail Merge Recipients dialog box.

- Scroll to the right until the ZIP Code field shows in the dialog box.

- Click the button arrow to the right of the field name, ZIP Code, to display a menu of sort and filter criteria (Figure 6–55).

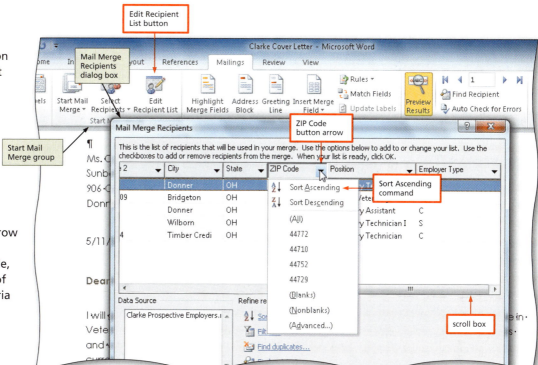

Figure 6–55

- Click Sort Ascending on the menu to sort the data source records in ascending (smallest to largest) order by ZIP Code (Figure 6–56).

- Click the OK button to close the Mail Merge Recipients dialog box.

Q&A

In what order would the form letters print if I merged them again now?

Word would print them in ZIP code order; that is, the record with ZIP code 44710 would print first, and the records with ZIP code 44772 would print last.

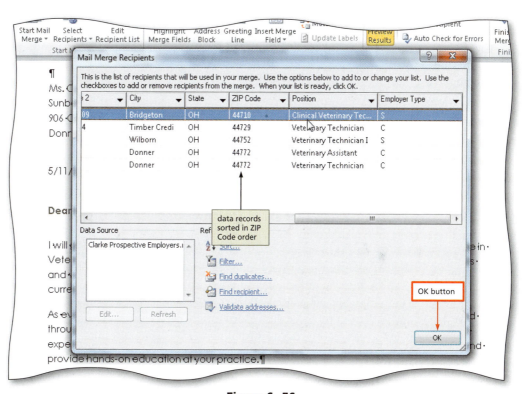

Figure 6–56

Other Ways
1. Click Filter link (Mail Merge Recipients dialog box), click Sort Records tab, enter sort criteria, click OK button

To Find and Display Data

If you wanted to find a particular record in the data source and display that record's data in the main document on the screen, you can search for a field value. The following steps find Zajak, which is a last name in the data source, and display that record's values in the form letter currently displaying on the screen.

1
- Click the Find Recipient button (Mailings tab | Preview Results group) to display the Find Entry dialog box.

- Type **Zajak** in the Find text box (Find Entry dialog box) as the search text.

- Click the Find Next button to display the record containing the entered text (Figure 6–57).

2
- Click the Cancel button (Find Entry dialog box) to close the dialog box.

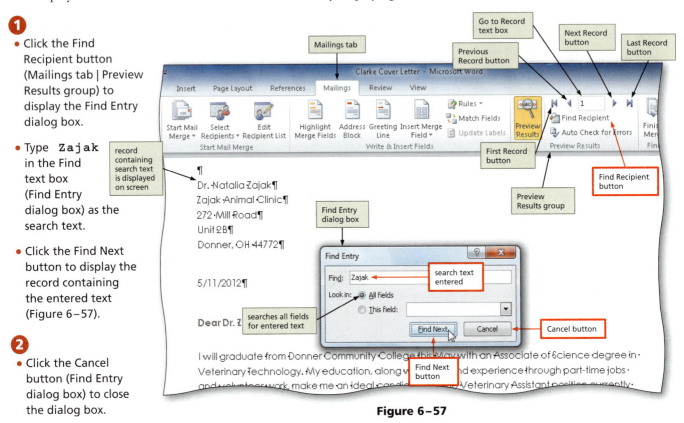

Figure 6–57

Displaying Data Source Records in the Main Document

When you are viewing merged data in the main document (Figure 6–57) — that is, the Preview Results button (Mailings tab | Preview Results group) is selected — you can click the Last Record button (Mailings tab | Preview Results group) to display the values from the last record in the data source, the First Record button (Mailings tab | Preview Results group) to display the values in record one, the Next Record button (Mailings tab | Preview Results group) to display the values in the next consecutive record number, or the Previous Record button (Mailings tab | Preview Results group) to display the values from the previous record number. You also can display a specific record by clicking the Go to Record text box (Mailings tab | Preview Results group), typing the record number you would like to be displayed in the main document, and then pressing the ENTER key.

To Close a Document

The cover letter is complete. Thus, the following steps close the document.

1 Open the Backstage view and then click Close.

2 If a Microsoft Word dialog box is displayed, click the Save button to save the changes.

Addressing Mailing Labels and Envelopes

Now that you have merged and printed the form letters, the next step is to print addresses on mailing labels to be affixed to envelopes for the form letters. The mailing labels will use the same data source as the form letter, Clarke Prospective Employers. The format and content of the mailing labels will be exactly the same as the inside address in the main document for the form letter. That is, the first line will contain the title and first name followed by the last name. The second line will contain the organization name, and so on. Thus, you will use the AddressBlock merge field in the mailing labels.

You follow the same basic steps to create the main document for the mailing labels as you did to create the main document for the form letters. The major difference is that the data source already exists because you created it earlier in this project.

BTW

Organizing Data
If you sort data records (pages WD 368 and WD 369) or select records to merge (pages WD 365 and WD 366), the merge process will generate mailing labels or envelopes using the specified criteria.

> **Generate mailing labels and envelopes.**
> An envelope should contain the sender's full name and address in the upper-left corner of the envelope. It also should contain the addressee's full name and address, positioned approximately in the vertical and horizontal center of the envelope. The address can be printed directly on the envelope or on a mailing label that is affixed to the envelope.

Plan Ahead

To Address and Print Mailing Labels Using an Existing Data Source

To address mailing labels, you specify the type of labels you intend to use. Word will request the label information, including the label vendor and product number. You can obtain this information from the box of labels. For illustration purposes in addressing these labels, the label vendor is Avery and the product number is J8158. The following steps address and print mailing labels using an existing data source.

Note: If your printer does not have the capability of printing mailing labels, skip these steps and proceed to the section titled, Merging All Data Records to a Directory, on page WD 378. If you are in a laboratory environment, ask your instructor if you should perform these steps or skip them.

1

- Open the Backstage view. Click the New tab in the Backstage view to display the New gallery. With Blank document selected, click the Create button to open a new blank document window.

- If necessary, change the zoom to 110%.

- Display the Mailings tab. Click the Start Mail Merge button (Mailings tab | Start Mail Merge group) and then click Step by Step Mail Merge Wizard on the Start Mail Merge menu to display Step 1 of the Mail Merge wizard in the Mail Merge task pane.

- Click Labels in the 'Select document type' area to specify labels as the main document type (Figure 6–58).

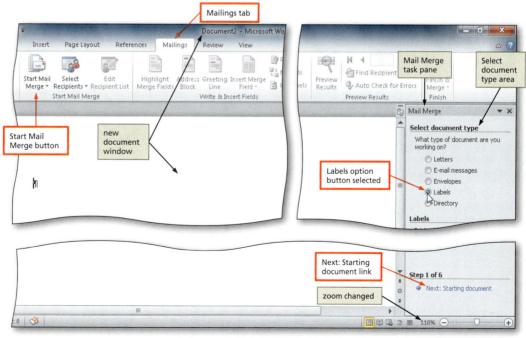

Figure 6–58

- Click the Next: Starting document link at the bottom of the Mail Merge task pane to display Step 2 of the Mail Merge wizard.

- In the Mail Merge task pane, click the Label options link to display the Label Options dialog box.

- Select the label vendor and product number (in this case, Avery A4/A5 and J8158), as shown in Figure 6–59.

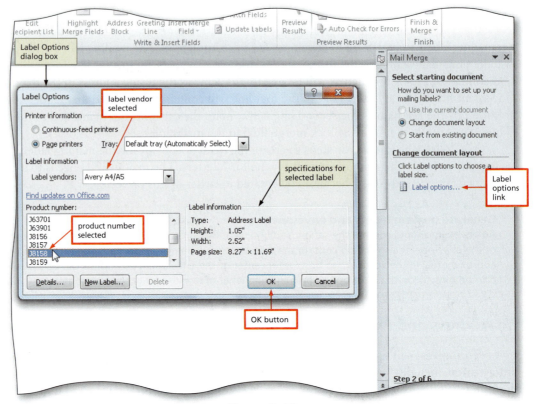

Figure 6–59

- Click the OK button (Label Options dialog box) to display the selected label layout as the main document (Figure 6–60).

- If necessary, scroll to display the left edge of the main document in the window.

- If gridlines are not displayed, click the View Table Gridlines button (Table Tools Layout tab | Table group) to show gridlines.

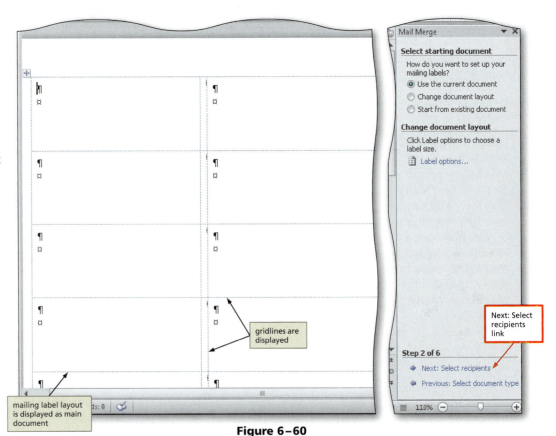

Figure 6–60

4

- Click the Next: Select recipients link at the bottom of the Mail Merge task pane to display Step 3 of the Mail Merge wizard, which allows you to select the data source.

- If necessary, click 'Use an existing list' in the Select recipients area.

- Click the Browse link to display the Select Data Source dialog box.

- If necessary, navigate to the location of the data source (in this case, the Job Hunting folder in the Word folder in the CIS 101 folder [or your class folder] on the USB flash drive).

- Click the file name, Clarke Prospective Employers, to select the data source you created earlier in the chapter (Figure 6–61).

Q&A

What is the folder initially displayed in the Select Data Source dialog box?

It is the default folder for storing data source files. Word looks in that folder first for an existing data source.

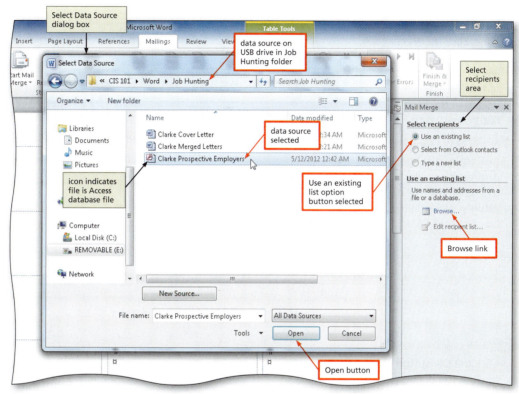

Figure 6–61

5

- Click the Open button to display the Mail Merge Recipients dialog box (Figure 6–62).

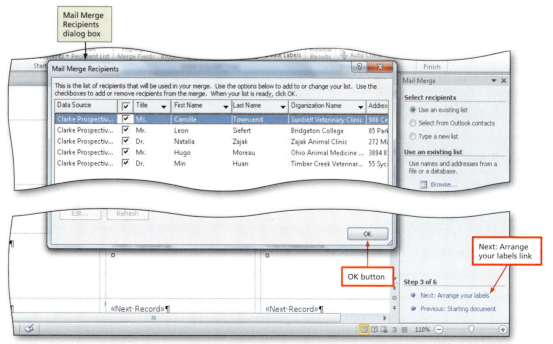

Figure 6–62

6

- Click the OK button (Mail Merge Recipients dialog box) to close the dialog box.

- At the bottom of the Mail Merge task pane, click the Next: Arrange your labels link to display Step 4 of the Mail Merge wizard in the Mail Merge task pane.

- In the Mail Merge task pane, click the Address block link to display the Insert Address Block dialog box (Figure 6–63).

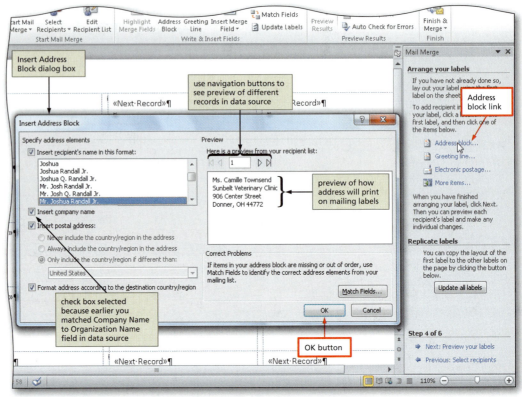

Figure 6–63

7

- Click the OK button to close the dialog box and insert the AddressBlock merge field in the first label of the main document (Figure 6–64).

Q&A

Do I have to use the AddressBlock merge field?

No. You can click the Insert Merge Field button (Mailings tab | Write & Insert Fields group) and then select the preferred fields for the mailing labels, organizing the fields as desired.

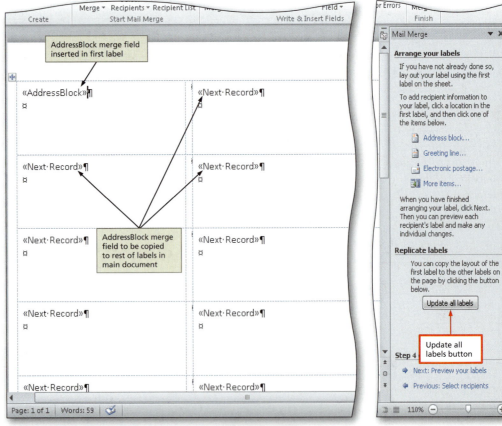

Figure 6–64

8

- Click the 'Update all labels' button in the Mail Merge task pane to copy the layout of the first label to the remaining label layouts in the main document (Figure 6–65).

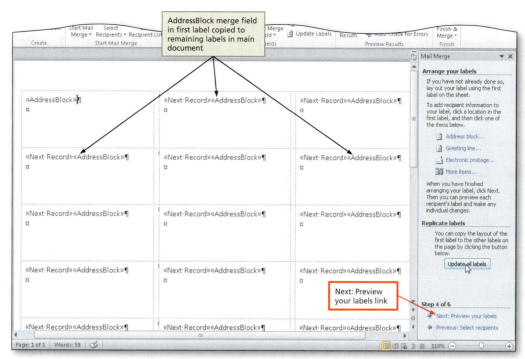

AddressBlock merge field in first label copied to remaining labels in main document

Next: Preview your labels link

Figure 6–65

9

- Click the Next: Preview your labels link at the bottom of the Mail Merge task pane to display Step 5 of the Mail Merge wizard, which shows a preview of the mailing labels in the document window.

- Because you do not want a blank space between each line in the printed mailing address, select the table containing the label layout (that is, click the table move handle in the upper-left corner of the table), display the Page Layout tab, change the Spacing Before and After boxes to 0 pt, and then click anywhere to remove the selection (Figure 6–66).

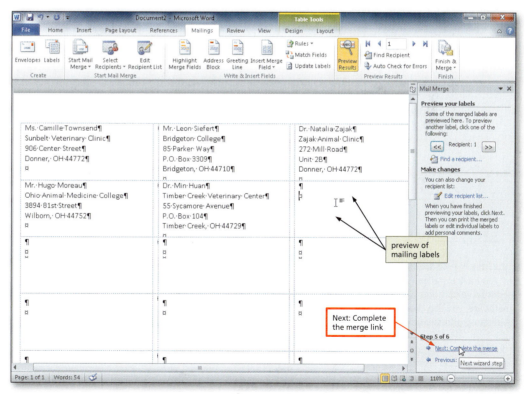

preview of mailing labels

Next: Complete the merge link

Figure 6–66

Q&A

What if the spacing does not change?

Drag through the labels and try changing the Spacing Before and After boxes to 0 again.

10

- Click the Next: Complete the merge link at the bottom of the Mail Merge task pane to display Step 6 of the Mail Merge wizard.

- In the Mail Merge task pane, click the Print link to display the Merge to Printer dialog box.

- If necessary, click All (Merge to Printer dialog box) so that all records in the data source will be included in the merge (Figure 6–67).

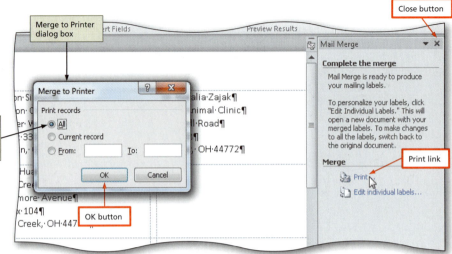

Figure 6–67

11

- If necessary, insert a sheet of blank mailing labels in the printer.

- Click the OK button to display the Print dialog box.

- Click the OK button (Print dialog box) to print the mailing labels (Figure 6–68).

12

- Click the Close button at the right edge of the Mail Merge task pane.

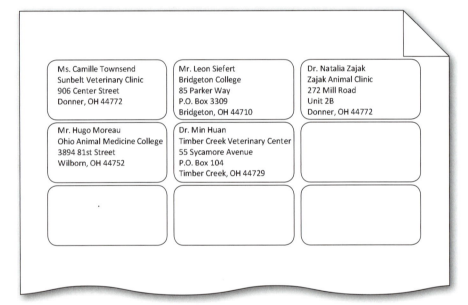

Ms. Camille Townsend
Sunbelt Veterinary Clinic
906 Center Street
Donner, OH 44772

Mr. Leon Siefert
Bridgeton College
85 Parker Way
P.O. Box 3309
Bridgeton, OH 44710

Dr. Natalia Zajak
Zajak Animal Clinic
272 Mill Road
Unit 2B
Donner, OH 44772

Mr. Hugo Moreau
Ohio Animal Medicine College
3894 81st Street
Wilborn, OH 44752

Dr. Min Huan
Timber Creek Veterinary Center
55 Sycamore Avenue
P.O. Box 104
Timber Creek, OH 44729

Figure 6–68

BTW

Validating Addresses
If you have installed address validation software, you can click the Validate addresses link in the Mail Merge Recipients dialog box to validate your recipients' addresses. If you have not yet installed address validation software and would like information about doing so, click the Validate addresses link in the Mail Merge Recipients dialog box and then click the Yes button in the Microsoft Word dialog box to display a related Microsoft Office Web page.

To Save the Mailing Labels

The following steps save the mailing labels.

1 With a USB flash drive connected to one of the computer's USB ports, click the Save button on the Quick Access Toolbar to display the Save As dialog box.

2 Type `Clarke Mailing Labels` in the File name text box to change the file name.

3 If necessary, navigate to the save location (in this case, the Job Hunting folder in the Word folder in the CIS 101 folder [or your class folder] on the USB flash drive).

4 Click the Save button (Save As dialog box) to save the document in the selected folder on the USB flash drive with the entered file name.

To Address and Print Envelopes Using an Existing Data Source

Instead of addressing mailing labels to affix to envelopes, your printer may have the capability of printing directly on envelopes. To print the address information directly on envelopes, follow the same basic steps as you did to address the mailing labels. The following steps address envelopes using an existing data source.

> **Note:** If your printer does not have the capability of printing envelopes, skip these steps and proceed to the section titled, Merging All Data Records to a Directory, on the next page. If you are in a laboratory environment, ask your instructor if you should perform these steps or skip them.

1 Open the Backstage view. Click the New tab in the Backstage view to display the New gallery. With Blank document selected, click the Create button to open a new blank document window.

2 Display the Mailings tab. Click the Start Mail Merge button (Mailings tab | Start Mail Merge group) and then click Step by Step Mail Merge Wizard on the Start Mail Merge menu to display Step 1 of the Mail Merge wizard in the Mail Merge task pane. Specify envelopes as the main document type by clicking Envelopes in the 'Select document type' area.

3 Click the Next: Starting document link at the bottom of the Mail Merge task pane to display Step 2 of the Mail Merge wizard. In the Mail Merge task pane, click the Envelope options link to display the Envelope Options dialog box.

4 Select the envelope size and then click the OK button (Envelope Options dialog box), which displays the selected envelope layout as the main document.

5 If your envelope does not have a preprinted return address, position the insertion point in the upper-left corner of the envelope layout and then type a return address.

6 Click the Next: Select recipients link at the bottom of the Mail Merge task pane to display Step 3 of the Mail Merge wizard, which allows you to select the data source. If necessary, click 'Use an existing list' in the Select recipients area. Click the Browse link to display the Select Data Source dialog box. If necessary, navigate to the location of the data source (in this case, the Job Hunting folder in the Word folder in the CIS 101 folder [or your class folder] on the USB flash drive). Click the file name, Clarke Prospective Employers, to select the data source you created earlier in the chapter. Click the Open button, which displays the Mail Merge Recipients dialog box, and then click the OK button to close the dialog box. At the bottom of the Mail Merge task pane, click the Next: Arrange your envelope link to display Step 4 of the Mail Merge wizard in the Mail Merge task pane.

7 Position the insertion point in the middle of the envelope. In the Mail Merge task pane, click the Address block link to display the Insert Address Block dialog box. Click the OK button to close the dialog box and insert the AddressBlock merge field in the envelope layout of the main document (Figure 6–69).

> **BTW**
>
> **AddressBlock Merge Field**
> Another way to insert the AddressBlock merge field in a document is to click the Address Block button (Mailings tab | Write & Insert Fields group). Instead of using the AddressBlock merge field, you can click the Insert Merge Field button (Mailings tab | Write & Insert Fields group) and then select the preferred fields for the envelope layout, organizing the fields as desired.

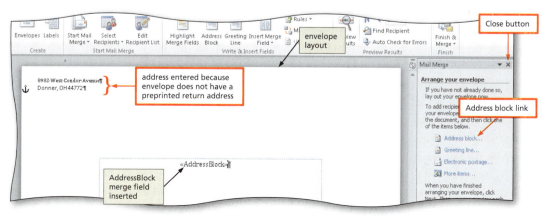

Figure 6–69

8 Click the Next: Preview your envelopes link at the bottom of the Mail Merge task pane to display Step 5 of the Mail Merge wizard, which shows a preview of an envelope in the document window.

9 Click the Next: Complete the merge link at the bottom of the Mail Merge task pane to display Step 6 of the Mail Merge wizard. In the Mail Merge task pane, click the Print link to display the Merge to Printer dialog box. If necessary, click All (Merge to Printer dialog box) so that all records in the data source will be included in the merge.

10 If necessary, insert blank envelopes in the printer. Click the OK button to display the Print dialog box. Click the OK button (Print dialog box) to print the addresses on the envelopes. Click the Close button at the right edge of the Mail Merge task pane.

To Save the Envelopes

The following steps save the envelopes.

1 With a USB flash drive connected to one of the computer's USB ports, click the Save button on the Quick Access Toolbar to display the Save As dialog box.

2 Type `Clarke Envelope Layout` in the File name text box to change the file name.

3 If necessary, navigate to the save location (in this case, the Job Hunting folder in the Word folder in the CIS 101 folder [or your class folder] on the USB flash drive).

4 Click the Save button (Save As dialog box) to save the document in the selected folder on the USB flash drive with the entered file name.

Merging All Data Records to a Directory

You may want to print the data records in the data source. Recall that the data source is saved as a Microsoft Access database table. Thus, you cannot open the data source in Word. To view the data source, you click the Edit Recipient List button (Mailings tab | Start Mail Merge group), which displays the Mail Merge Recipients dialog box. This dialog box, however, does not have a Print button.

One way to print the contents of the data source is to merge all data records in the data source into a single document, called a **directory**. That is, a directory does not merge each data record to a separate document; instead, a directory lists all records together in a single document. When you merge to a directory, the default organization of a directory places each record one after the next, similar to the look of entries in a telephone book.

The directory in this chapter is more organized with the rows and columns divided and field names placed above each column (shown in Figure 6–83 on page WD 385). To accomplish this look, the following steps are required:

1. Change the page orientation from portrait to landscape, so that each record fits on a single row.
2. Create a directory layout, placing a separating character between each merge field.
3. Merge the directory to a new document, which creates a list of all records in the data source.
4. Convert the directory to a table, using the separator character as the identifier for each new column.
5. Format the table containing the directory.
6. Sort the table by organization name within city, so that it is easy to locate a particular record.

To Create a New Blank Document

The following steps create a new blank document.

1 Open the Backstage view.

2 Click the New tab in the Backstage view to display the New gallery.

3 With Blank document selected, click the Create button to open a new blank document window (shown in Figure 6–70).

To Change Page Orientation

When a document is in **portrait orientation**, the short edge of the paper is the top of the document. You can instruct Word to lay out a document in **landscape orientation**, so that the long edge of the paper is the top of the document. The following steps change the orientation of the document from portrait to landscape, so that an entire record will fit on a single line in the directory.

1

• Display the Page Layout tab.

• Click the Page Orientation button (Page Layout tab | Page Setup group) to display the Page Orientation gallery (Figure 6–70).

2

• Click Landscape in the Page Orientation gallery to change the page orientation to landscape.

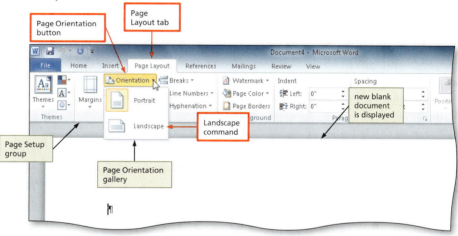

Figure 6–70

To Merge to a Directory

The next steps merge the data records in the data source to a directory. For illustration purposes, the following steps use the buttons on the Mailings tab rather than using the Mail Merge task pane to merge to a directory.

1

• Display the Mailings tab.

• Click the Start Mail Merge button (Mailings tab | Start Mail Merge group) to display the Start Mail Merge menu (Figure 6–71).

2

• Click Directory on the Start Mail Merge menu to select the main document type.

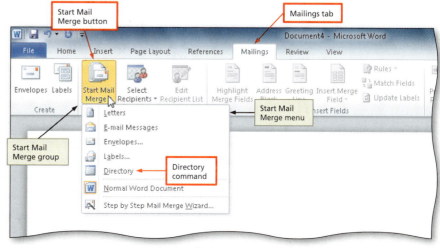

Figure 6–71

- Click the Select Recipients button (Mailings tab | Start Mail Merge group) to display the Select Recipients menu (Figure 6–72).

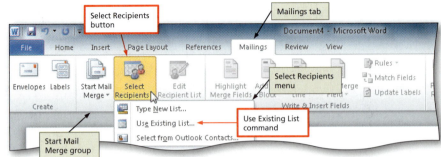

Figure 6–72

- Click Use Existing List on the Select Recipients menu to display the Select Data Source dialog box.

- If necessary, navigate to the location of the data source (in this case, the Job Hunting folder in the Word folder in the CIS 101 folder [or your class folder] on the USB flash drive).

- Click the file name, Clarke Prospective Employers, to select the data source you created earlier in the chapter (Figure 6–73).

- Click the Open button (Select Data Source dialog box) to associate the selected data source with the current main document.

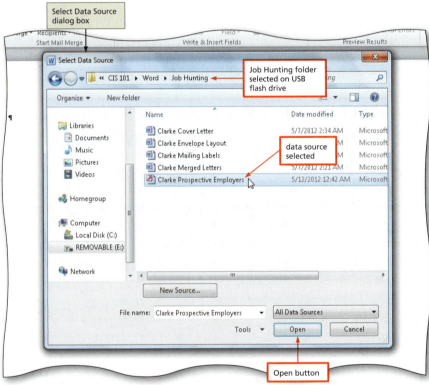

Figure 6–73

- Click the Insert Merge Field button arrow (Mailings tab | Write & Insert Fields group) to display the Insert Merge Field menu (Figure 6–74).

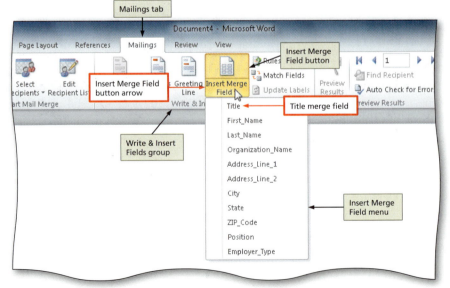

Figure 6–74

7

- Click Title on the Insert Merge Field menu to insert the merge field in the document.

- Press the COMMA (,) key to place a comma after the inserted merge field (Figure 6–75).

Why insert a comma after the merge field?

In the next steps, you will convert the entered merge fields to a table format with the records in rows and the fields in columns. To do this, Word divides the columns based on a character separating each field. In this case, you use the comma to separate the merge fields.

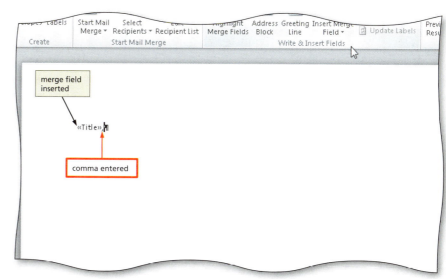

Figure 6–75

8

- Repeat Steps 6 and 7 for the First_Name, Last_Name, Organization_Name, Address_Line_1, Address_Line_2, City, State, and ZIP_Code fields on the Insert Merge Field menu, so that these fields in the data source appear in the main document separated by a comma, except do not type a comma after the last field: ZIP_Code.

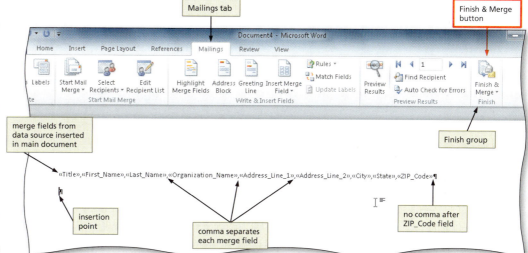

Figure 6–76

- Press the ENTER key (Figure 6–76).

Why press the ENTER key after entering the merge fields names?

This will place the first field in each record at the beginning of a new line.

To Merge to a New Document

The next step is to merge the data source and the directory main document to a new document, so that you can edit the resulting document. The following steps merge to a new document.

1 Click the Finish & Merge button (Mailings tab | Finish group) to display the Finish & Merge menu.

2 Click Edit Individual Documents on the Finish & Merge menu to display the Merge to New Document dialog box.

3 If necessary, click All (Merge to New Document dialog box).

4 Click the OK button to merge the data records to a directory in a new document window (Figure 6–77).

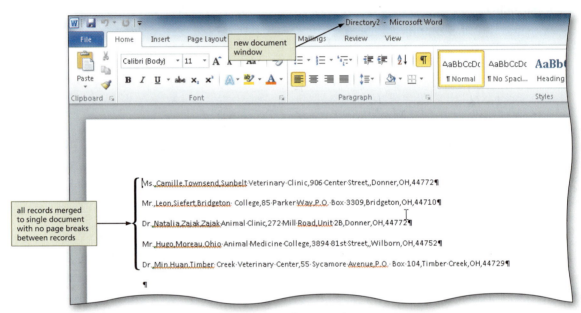

Figure 6–77

To Convert Text to a Table

You want each data record to be in a single row and each merge field to be in a column. That is, you want the directory to be in a table form. The following steps convert the text containing the merge fields to a table.

1

• Press CTRL+A to select the entire document, because you want all document contents to be converted to a table.

• Display the Insert tab.

• Click the Table button (Insert tab | Tables group) to display the Table gallery (Figure 6–78).

Q&A

Can I convert a section of a document to a table?

Yes, simply select the characters, lines, or paragraphs to be converted before displaying the Convert Text to Table dialog box.

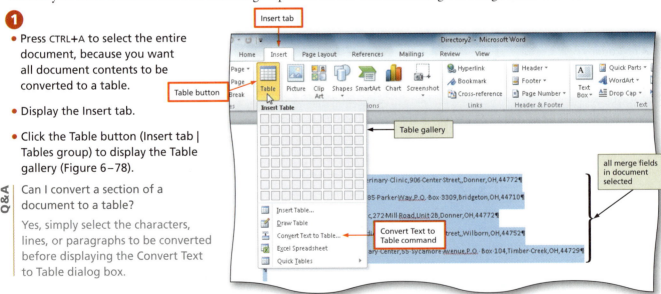

Figure 6–78

2

- Click Convert Text to Table in the Table gallery to display the Convert Text to Table dialog box.

- If necessary, type 9 in the Number of columns box (Convert Text to Table dialog box) to specify the number of columns for the resulting table.

- Click AutoFit to window, which instructs Word to fit the table and its contents to the width of the window.

- If necessary, click Commas to specify the character that separates the merge fields in the document (Figure 6–79).

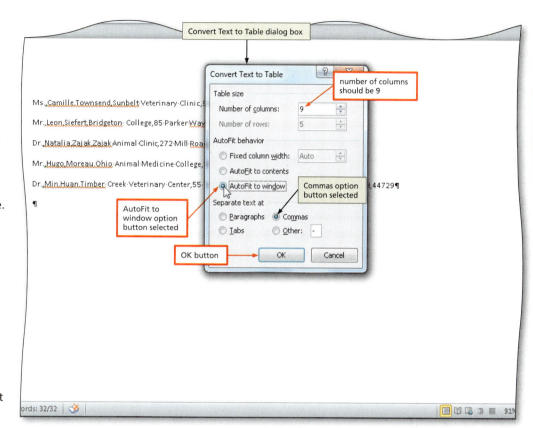

Figure 6–79

3

- Click the OK button to convert the selected text to a table (Figure 6–80).

Q&A

Can I format the table?

Yes. You can use any of the commands on the Table Tools Design and Layout tabs to change the look of the table.

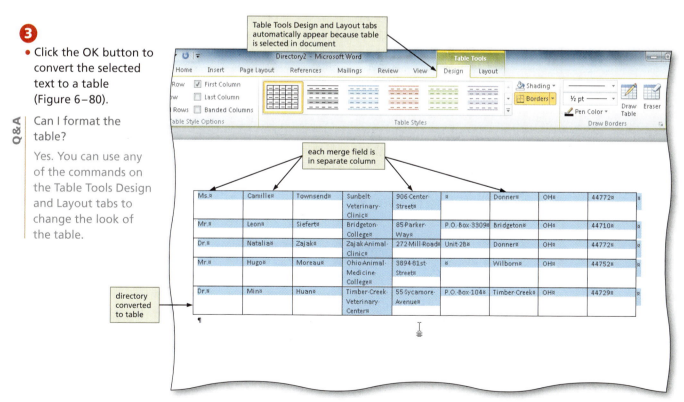

Figure 6–80

To Modify and Format a Table

The table would be more descriptive if the field names were displayed in a row above the actual data. The following steps add a row to the top of a table and format the data in the new row.

1 Add a row to the top of the table by positioning the insertion point in the first row of the table and then clicking the Insert Rows Above button (Table Tools Layout tab | Rows & Columns group).

2 Click in the first (leftmost) cell of the new row. Type **Title** and then press the TAB key. Type **First Name** and then press the TAB key. Type **Last Name** and then press the TAB key. Type **Organization Name** and then press the TAB key. Type **Address Line 1** and then press the TAB key. Type **Address Line 2** and then press the TAB key. Type **City** and then press the TAB key. Type **State** and then press the TAB key. Type **ZIP Code** as the last entry in the row.

3 Bold the contents of the first row.

4 Use the AutoFit Contents command to make all columns as wide as their contents (Figure 6–81).

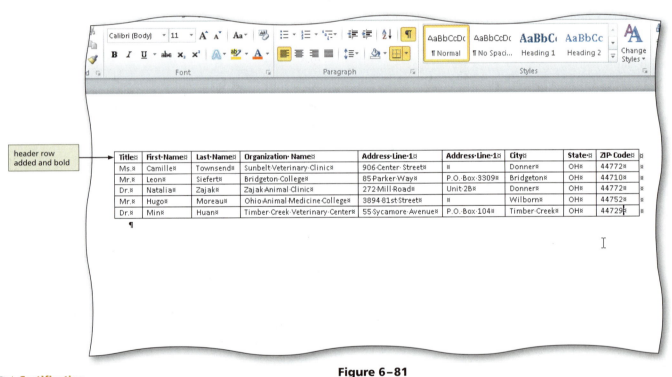

	Title¤	First·Name¤	Last·Name¤	Organization·Name¤	Address·Line·1¤	Address·Line·1¤	City¤	State·¤	ZIP·Code¤	¤
header row added and bold →	Ms.¤	Camille¤	Townsend¤	Sunbelt·Veterinary·Clinic¤	906·Center·Street¤	¤	Donner¤	OH¤	44772¤	¤
	Mr.¤	Leon¤	Siefert¤	Bridgeton·College¤	85·Parker·Way¤	P.O.·Box·3309¤	Bridgeton¤	OH¤	44710¤	¤
	Dr.¤	Natalia¤	Zajak¤	Zajak·Animal·Clinic¤	272·Mill·Road¤	Unit·2B¤	Donner¤	OH¤	44772¤	¤
	Mr.¤	Hugo¤	Moreau¤	Ohio·Animal·Medicine·College¤	3894·81st·Street¤	¤	Wilborn¤	OH¤	44752¤	¤
	Dr.¤	Min¤	Huan¤	Timber·Creek·Veterinary·Center¤	55·Sycamore·Avenue¤	P.O.·Box·104¤	Timber·Creek¤	OH¤	44729¤	¤

Figure 6–81

BTW

Certification
The Microsoft Office Specialist (MOS) program provides an opportunity for you to obtain a valuable industry credential — proof that you have the Word 2010 skills required by employers. For more information, visit the Word 2010 Certification Web page (scsite.com/wd2010/cert).

To Repeat Header Rows

If you had a table that exceeded a page in length and you wanted the header row (the first row) to appear at the top of the table on each continued page, you would perform the following steps.

1. Position the insertion point in the header row.

2. Click the Repeat Header Rows button (Table Tools Layout tab | Data group) to repeat the row containing the insertion point at the top of every page on which the table continues.

To Sort a Table by Multiple Columns

The next step is to sort the table. In this project, the table records are displayed in organization name within city. The following steps sort a table by multiple columns.

- Click the Sort button (Table Tools Layout tab | Data group) to display the Sort dialog box.

- Click the Sort by box arrow (Sort dialog box); scroll to and then click City in the list.

- Click the first Then by box arrow and then click Organization Name in the list.

- If necessary, click Header row so that the first row remains in its current location when the table is sorted (Figure 6–82).

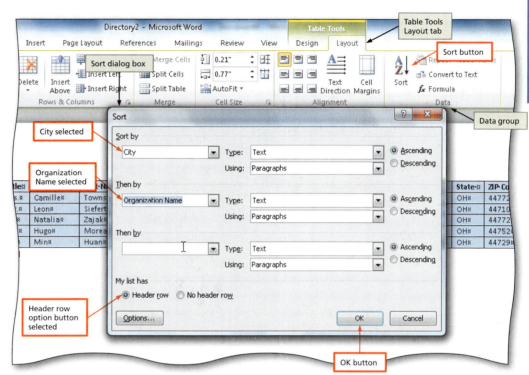

Figure 6–82

2

- Click the OK button to sort the records in the table in ascending Organization Name order within ascending City order (Figure 6–83).

- Position the insertion point below the table.

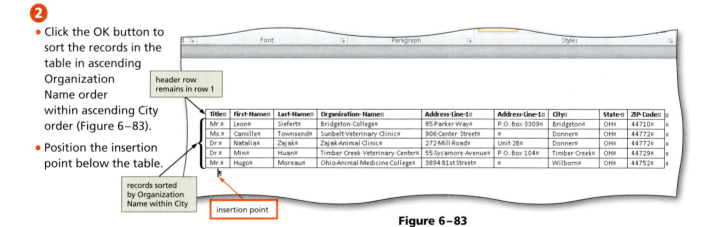

Figure 6–83

To Save and Print the Directory

The following steps save and print the directory.

1 With a USB flash drive connected to one of the computer's USB ports, click the Save button on the Quick Access Toolbar to display the Save As dialog box.

2 Type **Clarke Potential Employer Directory** in the File name text box to change the file name.

3 If necessary, navigate to the save location (in this case, the Job Hunting folder in the Word folder in the CIS 101 folder [or your class folder] on the USB flash drive).

4 Click the Save button (Save As dialog box) to save the document in the selected folder on the USB flash drive with the entered file name.

Q&A

If Microsoft Access is installed on my computer, can I use that to print the data source?

As an alternative to merging to a directory and printing the results, if you are familiar with Microsoft Access and it is installed on your computer, you can open and print the data source in Access.

To Quit Word

The following steps close all open documents and quit Word.

1 Open the Backstage view and then click Exit in the Backstage view to close all open documents and quit Word.

2 When Word asks if you want to save the document used to create the directory, click the Don't Save button. For all other documents, click the Save button to save the changes.

Chapter Summary

In this chapter, you have learned how to create and print form letters, create and edit a data source, address mailing labels and envelopes from a data source, and merge to a directory. The items listed below include all the new Word skills you have learned in this chapter.

1. Identify the Main Document for the Form Letter Using the Mail Merge Task Pane (WD 333)
2. Change the User Name and Initials (WD 335)
3. Create a Folder while Saving (WD 338)
4. Create a New Data Source (WD 340)
5. Save a Data Source when Prompted by Word (WD 345)
6. Enter the Date (WD 348)
7. View Merged Data in the Main Document (WD 349)
8. Edit the AddressBlock Merge Field (WD 349)
9. Edit the GreetingLine Merge Field (WD 351)
10. Insert a Merge Field in the Main Document (WD 353)
11. Insert an IF Field in the Main Document (WD 355)
12. Highlight Merge Fields (WD 358)
13. Display a Field Code (WD 358)
14. Print Field Codes in the Main Document (WD 359)
15. Preview the Merged Letters (WD 361)
16. Check for Errors (WD 361)
17. Merge the Form Letters to a New Document (WD 361)
18. Merge the Form Letters to the Printer (WD 364)
19. Select Records to Merge (WD 365)
20. Remove a Merge Condition (WD 368)
21. Sort the Data Records in a Data Source (WD 368)
22. Find and Display Data (WD 370)
23. Address and Print Mailing Labels Using an Existing Data Source (WD 371)
24. Address and Print Envelopes Using an Existing Data Source (WD 377)
25. Change Page Orientation (WD 379)
26. Merge to a Directory (WD 379)
27. Convert Text to a Table (WD 382)
28. Repeat Header Rows (WD 384)
29. Sort a Table by Multiple Columns (WD 385)

If you have a SAM 2010 user profile, your instructor may have assigned an autogradable version of this assignment. If so, log into the SAM 2010 Web site at www.cengage.com/sam2010 to download the instruction and start files.

Learn It Online

Test your knowledge of chapter content and key terms.

Instructions: To complete the Learn It Online exercises, start your browser, click the Address bar, and then enter the Web address `scsite.com/wd2010/learn`. When the Word 2010 Learn It Online page is displayed, click the link for the exercise you want to complete and then read the instructions.

Chapter Reinforcement TF, MC, and SA

A series of true/false, multiple choice, and short answer questions that test your knowledge of the chapter content.

Flash Cards

An interactive learning environment where you identify chapter key terms associated with displayed definitions.

Practice Test

A series of multiple choice questions that test your knowledge of chapter content and key terms.

Who Wants To Be a Computer Genius?

An interactive game that challenges your knowledge of chapter content in the style of a television quiz show.

Wheel of Terms

An interactive game that challenges your knowledge of chapter key terms in the style of the television show *Wheel of Fortune*.

Crossword Puzzle Challenge

A crossword puzzle that challenges your knowledge of key terms presented in the chapter.

Apply Your Knowledge

Reinforce the skills and apply the concepts you learned in this chapter.

Editing, Printing, and Merging with a Form Letter and Its Data Source

Note: To complete this assignment, you will be required to use the Data Files for Students. See the inside back cover of this book for instructions on downloading the Data Files for Students, or contact your instructor for information about accessing the required files.

Instructions: Start Word. Open the document, Apply 6-1 Fund Drive Letter, from the Data Files for Students. When you open the main document, if Word displays a dialog box about an SQL command, click the Yes button. If Word prompts for the name of the data source, select Apply 6-1 Donor List on the Data Files for Students.

The document is a main document for the Future Leaders Spring Fund Drive form letter. You are to edit the date content control and GreetingLine merge field, print the form letter, add a record to the data source, and merge the form letters to a file.

Perform the following tasks:
1. Edit the date content control so that it contains the date 4/9/2012.
2. Edit the GreetingLine merge field so that the salutation ends with a comma (,).
3. Save the modified main document for the form letter with the name Apply 6-1 Fund Drive Letter Modified.
4. Highlight the merge fields in the document. How many are there? Remove the highlight from the merge fields.
5. View merged data in the document. Use the navigation buttons in the Preview Results group to display merged data from various records in the data source. What is the last name shown in the first record? The third record? The fifth record? View merge fields (that is, turn off the view merged data).

Continued >

6. Print the main document for the form letter by opening the Backstage view, clicking the Print tab, and then clicking the Print button (Figure 6–84).

7. Add a record to the data source that contains your personal information. Type `$25` in the Amount field and `Scholarship` in the Fund field.

8. In the data source, change Shannon Goodman's last name to Milton.

9. Sort the data source by the Last Name field.

10. Save the main document for the form letter again.

11. Merge the form letters to a new document. Save the new document with the name Apply 6-1 Fund Drive Merged Letters.

12. If requested by your instructor, merge the form letters directly to the printer.

13. Submit the saved documents in the format specified by your instructor.

4/9/2012

Katie Aronson
5327 Gateway Boulevard
Four Points, IL 60232

«AddressBlock»

«GreetingLine»

Thank you for your generous gift to the Future Leaders Spring Fund Drive. For the past 30 years, Future Leaders has worked to benefit our community. Through local outreach programs, scholarship awards, and various projects, we have assisted people in our community. We appreciate your participation in making our efforts successful.

As you requested, your «Amount» gift will be applied to the «Fund» fund. All funds raised this year, regardless of where they are applied, will benefit residents of the greater Four Points area. A list of this year's sponsors will appear in next month's newsletter. We request that all changes or additions be processed by May 1, 2012 so that they will appear correctly in the newsletter.

Thank you again, «First_Name», for your support.

Sincerely,

Katie Aronson
Director
Future Leaders

Figure 6–84

Extend Your Knowledge

Extend the skills you learned in this chapter and experiment with new skills. You may need to use Help to complete the assignment.

Modifying a Data Source, Editing an IF Field, Inserting a Fill-In Field, and Formatting a Letter

Note: To complete this assignment, you will be required to use the Data Files for Students. See the inside back cover of this book for instructions on downloading the Data Files for Students, or contact your instructor for information about accessing the required files.

Instructions: Start Word. Open the document, Extend 6-1 Graduation Keepsakes Letter, from the Data Files for Students. When you open the main document, if Word displays a dialog box about an SQL command, click the Yes button. If Word prompts for the name of the data source, select Extend 6-1 Customers on the Data Files for Students.

The document is a main document for a Graduation Keepsakes form letter (Figure 6–85). You will change the margins, change the shape, add a field to the data source, modify an IF field, and add a Fill-in field.

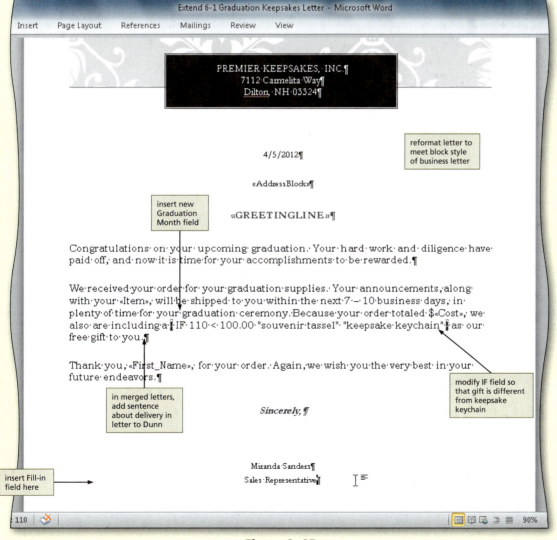

Figure 6–85

Continued >

Extend Your Knowledge *continued*

Perform the following tasks:

1. Use Help to learn about mail merge, IF fields, and Fill-in fields.

2. Add a field to the data source called Graduation Month. Enter field values for each record: Hernandez – May, Dunn – August, Quint – December, Lee – June, DeSantos – July.

3. Add another field to the data source called Major. Enter field values of your choice for each record.

4. In the second sentence in the second paragraph of the main document, insert the new field called Graduation Month, just before the words, graduation ceremony.

5. Edit the IF field so that the gift for orders greater than or equal to $100 is an item other than a keepsake keychain. *Hint*: Display the IF field code in the document window and edit the IF field directly in the document.

6. At the bottom of the document, insert a Fill-in field, so that you can type a different personalized note to each customer. When you merge the letters, type a note to each customer. The notes should be meaningful to the recipient, related to his or her major.

7. Merge the letters to a new document. Save the merged letters. At the end of the second paragraph in the letter to Dunn, type this sentence: In addition, we are upgrading your delivery method at no charge because of a manufacturer delay.

8. Print the main document for the form letter by opening the Backstage view, clicking the Print tab, and then clicking the Print button.

9. Print the form letter with field codes showing, that is, with the 'Print field codes instead of their values' check box selected in the Word Options dialog box. Be sure to deselect this check box after printing the field codes version of the letter. How does this printout differ from the one printed in Task #8?

10. Change the document properties, as specified by your instructor. Submit the merged letters in the format specified by your instructor.

11. If your instructor requests, create envelopes for each letter in the data source.

12. Reformat the letter so that it is properly spaced and sized according to the block style for business letters.

13. If you know Access and your instructor requests, create the data source in Access and then open the main document with the Access database file as the data source.

Make It Right

Analyze a document and correct all errors and/or improve the design.

Editing Merge Fields, Editing Data Source Records, and Specifying Filter Conditions

Note: To complete this assignment, you will be required to use the Data Files for Students. See the inside back cover of this book for instructions on downloading the Data Files for Students, or contact your instructor for information about accessing the required files.

Instructions: Start Word. Open the document, Make It Right 6-1 Registration Letter, from the Data Files for Students. When you open the main document, if Word displays a dialog box about an SQL command, click the Yes button. If Word prompts for the name of the data source, select Make It Right 6-1 Registrants on the Data Files for Students.

The document is a form letter that is missing fields and requires editing (Figure 6–86). You are to insert an AddressBlock merge field and a GreetingLine merge field, insert and delete merge fields, edit data source records, and filter records.

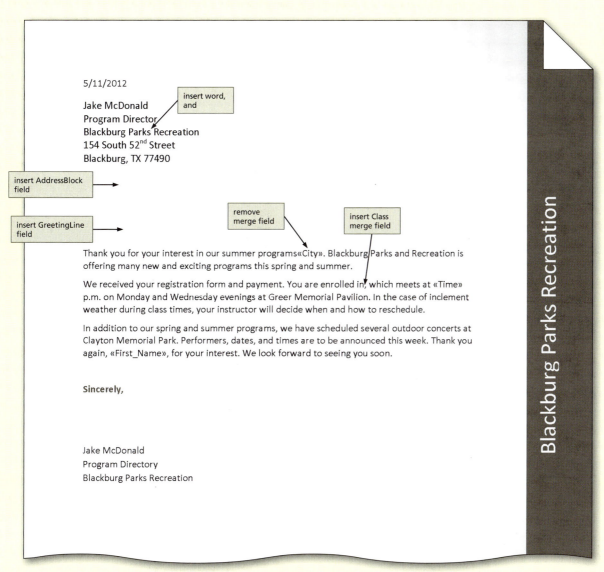

Figure 6–86

Perform the following tasks:

1. In the return address, change the text, Parks Recreation, to Parks and Recreation (insert the word, and). This update also should be reflected in the signature block.

2. Insert the AddressBlock merge field below the return address.

3. Insert the GreetingLine merge field below the AddressBlock. Use an appropriate salutation and punctuation.

4. In the second sentence in the second paragraph, insert the merge field, Class, before the comma.

5. In the first sentence, remove the City merge field.

6. In the data source, find the record whose last name is Abbott. Fix the State entry so that it reads, TX, and ZIP Code entry so that it reads 79006.

7. In the data source, find the misspelling Drivr and correct its spelling to Drive.

8. Change the document properties, as specified by your instructor. Save the revised document using the name Make It Right 6-1 Registration Letter Modified. Submit the letter in the format specified by your instructor.

Continued >

Make It Right *continued*

9. Specify that only recipients enrolled in Intermediate Tennis should be included in a merge. Merge these form letters to the printer. Clear the filter.

10. Identify another type of filter for this data source and merge those form letters to a new document. In the new document, type the filter you used. Submit the document in the format specified by your instructor.

11. Merge all the records to a new document in last name order. On a page at the end of the merged documents, type the if condition used in the letters. Submit the document in the format specified by your instructor.

In the Lab

Design and/or create a document using the guidelines, concepts, and skills presented in this chapter. Labs are listed in order of increasing difficulty.

Lab 1: Creating a Form Letter Using a Template, a Data Source, Mailing Labels, and a Directory

Problem: You are graduating this May and have prepared your resume (shown in Figure 5–72 on page WD 323 in Chapter 5). You decide to create a cover letter for your resume as a form letter that you will send to potential employers. The main document for the form letter is shown in Figure 6–87a.

Perform the following tasks:

1. Use the Essential Merge Letter template to begin creating the main document for the form letter. If necessary, change the document theme to Essential. Save the main document for the form letter with the file name, Lab 6-1 Monroe Cover Letter.

2. Type a new data source using the data shown in Figure 6–87b. Delete field names not used and add two field names: Position and Publication. Save the data source with the file name, Lab 6-1 Monroe Potential Employers.

3. Save the main document for the form letter again. Edit the AddressBlock and GreetingLine merge fields according to the sample formats shown in the figure. Insert the merge fields as shown in the figure. Delete the blank line at the top of the letter and the sender address in the signature block. Increase the blank space between the sender address and inside address. The entire letter should fit on a single page. *Hint*: The date is part of the footer.

4. Merge the form letters to a new document. Save the merged letters in a file called Lab 6-1 Monroe Merged Letters.

5. In a new document window, address mailing labels using the same data source you used for the form letters. Save the mailing label layout with the name, Lab 6-1 Monroe Mailing Labels. If required by your instructor, merge the mailing labels to the printer.

6. In a new document window, specify the main document type as a directory. Change the page layout to landscape orientation. Insert all merge fields in the document, separating each with a comma. Merge the directory layout to a new document window. Convert the list of fields to a Word table (the table will have 11 columns). Add a row to the top of the table and insert field names in the empty cells. Bold the text in the first row. Change the margins to narrow. Change the font size of all text in the table to 9 point. Apply the Light List - Accent 5 table style. Resize the table columns so that the table looks like Figure 6–87b. Sort the table in the directory by the Last Name field. Save the merged directory with the name, Lab 6-1 Monroe Merged Directory.

7. Submit all documents in the format specified by your instructor.

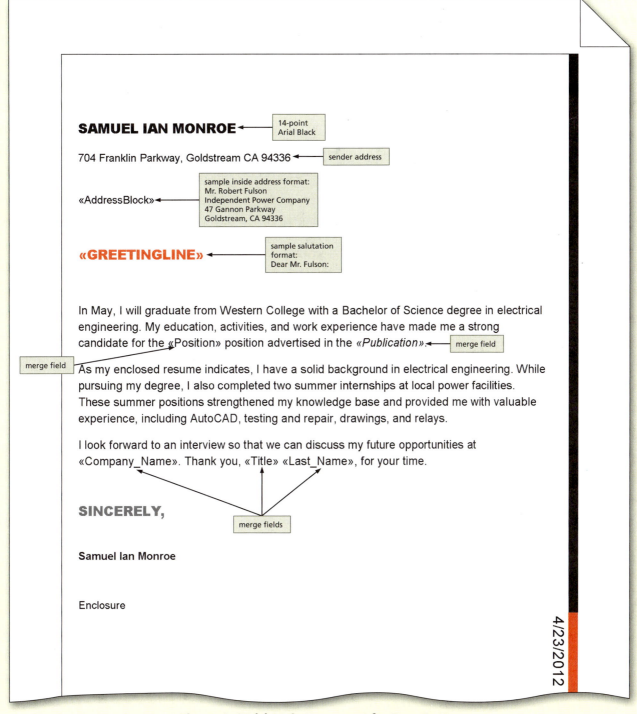

Figure 6–87 (a) Main Document for Form Letter

Title	First Name	Last Name	Company Name	Address Line 1	Address Line 2	City	State	ZIP Code	Position	Publication
Mr.	Robert	Fulson	Independent Power Company	47 Gannon Parkway		Goldstream	CA	94336	facilities engineer	Goldstream Press
Ms.	Nancy	Gross	Green Light Power	700 North 350 East		Goldstream	CA	94336	electrical engineer	Daily Journal
Mr.	Scott	Kazmierek	Frankfort Gas and Electric	7600 Penn Drive		Frankfort	CA	93225	engineering assistant	Frankfort Weekly
Mr.	Juan	Padilla	Arthur Power and Light	99 South Waterway	Building 4	Arthur	CA	94374	assistant facilities manager	Metropolitan News
Ms.	Shari	Warner	Electric Cooperative	322 Iverson Drive		Barrington	CA	94434	test engineer	Barrington Daily

Figure 6–87 (b) Data Source

In the Lab

Lab 2: Creating a Form Letter Using a Template with an IF Field, a Data Source, Mailing Labels, and a Directory

Problem: You are graduating this May and have prepared your resume (shown in Figure 5–73 on page WD 325 in Chapter 5). You decide to create a cover letter for your resume as a form letter that you will send to potential employers. The main document for the form letter is shown in Figure 6–88a. In the letter, the availability date will vary, depending on the job fair attended.

Perform the following tasks:

1. Use the Urban Merge Letter template to begin creating the main document for the form letter. Change the document theme to Perspective. Change the margins to Normal (1-inch top, bottom, left, and right). Save the main document for the form letter with the file name, Lab 6-2 MacMahon Cover Letter, in a folder called Lab 6-2 MacMahon Job Hunting. *Hint*: Create the folder while saving.

2. Type a new data source using the data shown in Figure 6–88b. Delete field names not used, rename the Company Name field as Organization Name, and add two field names: Job Fair and Position. Save the data source with the file name, Lab 6-2 MacMahon Potential Employers, in the Lab 6-2 MacMahon Job Hunting folder.

3. Save the main document for the form letter again. Edit the AddressBlock and GreetingLine merge fields according to the sample formats in the figure. Be sure to match the Organization Name field in the data source to the Company field in the Match Fields dialog box so that the organization name appears in each inside address. Insert the merge fields as shown in the figure. The IF field tests if Job Fair equal to Fairfax; if it is, then print the text, May 21; otherwise print the text, May 14. Delete the sender company name content control. The entire letter should fit on a single page.

4. Merge the form letters to a new document. Save the merged letters in a file called Lab 6-2 MacMahon Merged Letters in the Lab 6-2 MacMahon Job Hunting folder.

5. In a new document window, address mailing labels using the same data source you used for the form letters. Save the mailing label layout with the name, Lab 6-2 MacMahon Mailing Labels, in the Lab 6-2 MacMahon Job Hunting folder. If required by your instructor, merge the mailing labels to the printer.

6. If your printer allows and your instructor requests it, in a new document window, address envelopes using the same data source you used for the form letters. Save the envelopes with the file name, Lab 6-2 MacMahon Envelopes, in the folder named Lab 6-2 MacMahon Job Hunting. If required by your instructor, merge the envelopes to the printer.

7. In a new document window, specify the main document type as a directory. Change the page layout to landscape orientation. Insert all merge fields in the document, separating each with a comma. Merge the directory layout to a new document window. Convert the list of fields to a Word table (the table will have 11 columns). Add a row to the top of the table and insert field names in the empty cells. Bold the text in the first row. Change the margins to narrow. Apply the Light List - Accent 2 table style. Resize the table columns so that the table looks like Figure 6–88b. Center the table between the margins. Sort the directory by the Last Name field within Job Fair field. Save the merged directory with the name, Lab 6-2 MacMahon Merged Directory, in the folder named Lab 6-2 MacMahon Job Hunting.

8. Submit all documents in the format specified by your instructor.

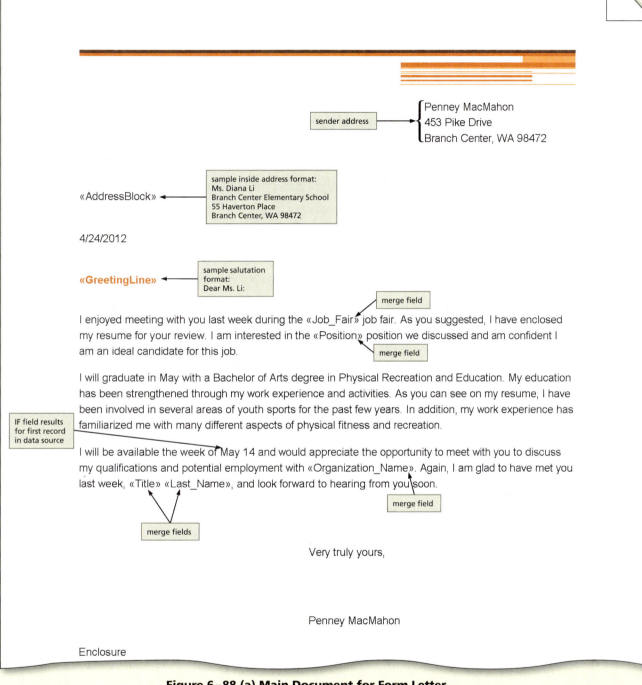

Figure 6–88 (a) Main Document for Form Letter

Title	First Name	Last Name	Organization Name	Address Line 1	Address Line 2	City	State	ZIP Code	Job Fair	Position
Mr.	Seth	Briggs	Branch Center Recreation Center	1274 Washington Avenue	P.O. Box 10	Branch Center	WA	98472	Branch Center	Recreation Director
Mr.	Dwayne	Jackman	Branch Center High School	8290 Morgan Parkway		Branch Center	WA	98472	Branch Center	Physical Education teacher
Ms.	Diana	Li	Branch Center Elementary School	55 Haverton Place		Branch Center	WA	98472	Campus Career Day	Physical Education teacher
Mr.	Stuart	Tan	Fairfax Parks and Recreation	500 Greenway Circle		Fairfax	WA	98446	Fairfax	Assistant Program Director
Ms.	Tammy	Walker	Fairfax Middle School	675 East 175th Street	Suite 15	Fairfax	WA	98446	Fairfax	Physical Education teacher

Figure 6–88 (b) Data Source

In the Lab

Lab 3: Designing a Data Source, Form Letter, and Directory from Sample Letters

Problem: You are graduating this May and have prepared your resume (shown in Figure 5–74 on page WD 326 in Chapter 5). Sample drafted letters for the cover letter are shown in Figure 6–89a and Figure 6–89b.

Perform the following tasks:

1. Review the letters in Figure 6–89 and determine the fields that should be in the data source. Write the field names down on a piece of paper.

2. Do not use a template to create this form letter. In Word, create a main document for the letters. Save the main document for the form letter with the file name, Lab 6-3 Ramirez Cover Letter.

Daniel Austin Ramirez
84 Southland Drive
Jonner, MA 01298

April 16, 2012

Ms. Beth Gupta
Jonner County Public Library
20 Oakton Parkway
North Branch
Jonner, MA 01298

Dear Ms. Gupta:

I have enclosed my resume in response to your advertisement for the Media Specialist position I saw advertised online. I will graduate in May with a Master's in Library and Information Science degree from Benson College.

Throughout my education, I worked in libraries, which has provided me with valuable experience and insight into the running and operation of a library. My coursework and media specialist certification, along with my library experience, make me an ideal candidate for the Media Specialist position.

I look forward to an interview, during which we can further discuss my qualifications for a position with Jonner County Public Library. Thank you, Ms. Gupta, for your consideration.

Sincerely,

Daniel Austin Ramirez

Enclosure

Figure 6–89 (a) Sample Merged Form Letter

3. Create a data source containing five records, consisting of data from the two letters shown in Figure 6–89 and then add three more records with your own data. Save the data source with the file name, Lab 6-3 Ramirez Potential Employers.

4. Merge the form letters to a new document or the printer, as specified by your instructor.

5. Merge the data source to a directory. Convert it to a Word table. Add an attractive border to the table and apply any other formatting you feel necessary. Submit the directory in the format specified by your instructor.

Daniel Austin Ramirez
84 Southland Drive
Jonner, MA 01298

April 16, 2012

Mr. Kirk Green
Jonner County Reference Library
3033 Cameron Boulevard
Jonner, MA 01298

Dear Mr. Green:

I have enclosed my resume in response to your advertisement for the Reference Librarian position I saw advertised in the newspaper. I will graduate in May with a Master's in Library and Information Science degree from Benson College.

Throughout my education, I worked in libraries, which has provided me with valuable experience and insight into the running and operation of a library. My coursework and media specialist certification, along with my library experience, make me an ideal candidate for the Reference Librarian position.

I look forward to an interview, during which we can further discuss my qualifications for a position with Jonner County Reference Library. Thank you, Mr. Green, for your consideration.

Sincerely,

Daniel Austin Ramirez

Enclosure

Figure 6–89 (b) Sample Merged Form Letter

Cases and Places

Apply your creative thinking and problem solving skills to design and implement a solution.

Note: To complete these assignments, you may be required to use the Data Files for Students. See the inside back cover of this book for instructions on downloading the Data Files for Students, or contact your instructor for information about accessing the required files.

1: Create a Form Letter for Dormitory Assignments

Academic

As assistant to the director of housing at Ronson University, you send letters to new students regarding dormitory assignments. Create the data source using the data in Figure 6–90.

Title	First Name	Last Name	Address Line 1	Address Line 2	City	State	ZIP Code	Dorm	Meal Plan	Cost
Ms.	Renee	Shelton	2008 Anderson Avenue	Apt. 12A	Rock Point	WI	42467	Billings Tower	A	$500
Ms.	Adriana	Pi	739 Clifton Place		Fort Benjamin	WI	42240	Goss Hall	B	$750
Mr.	Sam	Steinberg	586 Savannah Court		Rock Point	WI	42467	Court Quad	A	$500
Mr.	Marcus	Darien	3659 Haverston Lane	Unit 5	Darwin	WI	48472	Goss Hall	C	$975
Mr.	Derrick	Riley	65 East Fountain View		Darwin	WI	48472	Pfifer Courts	B	$750

Figure 6–90

Create a form letter using the following information: The school's address is 4541 North 175th Street, Fort Benjamin, WI 42240. After the salutation, the first paragraph in the main document should read: Congratulations again on your admission to Ronson University. We are delighted that you have chosen Ronson to pursue your educational goals. The second paragraph in the main document should read: We received your application for housing and have completed the dormitory assignments. As you requested, you have been assigned to «Dorm». Because you chose Meal Plan «Meal_Plan», a charge of «Cost» has been added to your tuition. A bill reflecting the total amount due will be mailed to you before May 1. The third paragraph in the main document should read: Ours is a vibrant, growing campus, and one on which we hope you will feel at home and welcome. We hope that your experience at Ronson will be enjoyable, memorable, and above all, rewarding. We look forward to seeing you, «First_Name», when classes begin in the fall!

Use your name in the signature block. If required by your instructor, address and print accompanying labels or envelopes for the form letters. Create a directory of the data source records. Use the concepts and techniques presented in this chapter to create and format the form letters, mailing labels or envelopes, and directory. The letter should include all essential elements, use proper spacing and formats for a business letter, and follow the guidelines of the block, modified block, or modified semi-block letter style. (*Hint:* You may need to use outside resources to obtain these guidelines.) Be sure to check the spelling and grammar of the finished documents. Submit your assignment in the format specified by your instructor.

2: Create a Form Letter for Children's Swimming Lessons

Personal

As a volunteer for Lincoln Community Pools, you send confirmation letters to parents regarding swimming lessons for their children. Create the data source using the data in Figure 6–91.

Title	First Name	Last Name	Address Line 1	Address Line 2	City	State	ZIP Code	Child Name	Class Time	Gender
Ms.	Lenore	Simms	500 Morris Street	Apt. 22	Four Points	IL	61922	Sophie	2:00 p.m.	her
Ms.	Tracy	Fenn	388 Chestnut Court		Aaron	IL	61933	Kyle	10:00 a.m.	his
Mr.	Morris	Feldman	709 East 500 South		Four Points	IL	61922	Stefan	2:00 p.m.	his
Ms.	Jane	Tu	430 Cloaken Court	Apt. 8	Aaron	IL	61933	Sarah	10:00 a.m.	her
Mr.	Ben	Skolman	2390 Darien Lane		Aaron	IL	61933	Benny	2:00 p.m.	his

Figure 6–91

Create a form letter using the following information: The center's address is 875 Fifteenth Street, Four Points, IL 61922. After the salutation, the first paragraph in the main document should read: Thank you for enrolling your child, «Child_Name», in our swimming lessons. Teaching your child to swim is both prudent and a priceless investment in your child's future safety. The second paragraph in the main document should read: As you requested, «Child_Name» has been placed in the «Class_Time» class, which meets on Monday, Wednesday, and Friday. The instructor for this time slot is Joe Sanchez. All of our swim instructors are Red Cross certified lifeguards, as well as experienced teachers and/or coaches. The third paragraph in the main document should read: An observation area is available for parents and caregivers who wish to stay during the lesson. Please bring a towel and, if your child requests or is accustomed to wearing them, goggles. All other items will be provided. We look forward to seeing «Child_Name» at «Gender» first lesson!

Use your name in the signature block. If required by your instructor, address and print accompanying labels or envelopes for the form letters. Create a directory of the data source records. Use the concepts and techniques presented in this chapter to create and format the form letters, mailing labels or envelopes, and directory. The letter should include all essential elements, use proper spacing and formats for a business letter, and follow the guidelines of the block, modified block, or modified semi-block letter style. (*Hint:* You may need to use outside resources to obtain these guidelines.) Be sure to check the spelling and grammar of the finished documents. Submit your assignment in the format specified by your instructor.

3: Create a Form Letter Confirming Ticket Sales

Professional

As ticket sales manager of Juniper Theatre Group, you send confirmation letters to customers. Create the data source using the data in Figure 6–92.

Title	First Name	Last Name	Address Line 1	Address Line 2	City	State	ZIP Code	Number of Tickets	Day	Date
Ms.	Alisha	Bright	6914 Leisure Lane		Goldstream	CA	94336	six	Friday	June 10
Mr.	Pete	Stanley	1210 Sunset Court	Apt. 21A	Condor	CA	95702	four	Saturday	June 4
Mr.	Rudy	Tan	5442 West 178th Street		Condor	CA	95702	two	Friday	June 3
Ms.	Carol	Athens	249 Westmore Place	Apt. 4L	Goldstream	CA	94336	two	Saturday	June 11
Ms.	Stacey	Rivera	148 Carver Street		Condor	CA	95702	four	Saturday	June 11

Figure 6–92

Continued >

Cases and Places *continued*

Create a form letter using the following information: The theatre's address is 407 Planters Avenue, Goldstream, CA 94336. After the salutation, the first paragraph in the main document should read: Thank you for your ticket purchase for *Romeo and Juliet*. We are excited about our new facility and are looking forward to our first production here. The second paragraph in the main document should read: Enclosed are the «Number_of_Tickets» tickets you ordered for the «Day», «Date» performance. We recommend that you arrive by 1:30 p.m. to allow ample time for seating. The third paragraph in the main document should read: Light refreshments and beverages will be available for purchase during Intermission. We hope you enjoy our new venue and what promises to be another spectacular production!

Use your name in the signature block. If required by your instructor, address and print accompanying labels or envelopes for the form letters. Create a directory of the data source records. Use the concepts and techniques presented in this chapter to create and format the form letters, mailing labels or envelopes, and directory. The letter should include all essential elements, use proper spacing and formats for a business letter, and follow the guidelines of the block, modified block, or modified semi-block letter style. (*Hint:* You may need to use outside resources to obtain these guidelines.) Be sure to check the spelling and grammar of the finished documents. Submit your assignment in the format specified by your instructor.

7 Creating a Newsletter with a Pull-Quote and Graphics

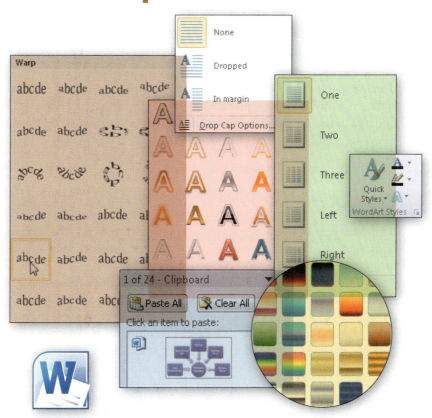

Objectives

You will have mastered the material in this chapter when you can:

- Insert and format WordArt
- Set custom margins
- Set custom tab stops
- Crop a graphic
- Rotate a graphic
- Format a document in multiple columns
- Justify a paragraph
- Hyphenate a document

- Format a character as a drop cap
- Insert a column break
- Insert and format a text box
- Copy and paste using a split window
- Balance columns
- Modify and format a SmartArt graphic
- Copy and paste using the Office Clipboard

7 | Creating a Newsletter with a Pull-Quote and Graphics

Introduction

Professional-looking documents, such as newsletters and brochures, often are created using desktop publishing software. With desktop publishing software, you can divide a document in multiple columns, wrap text around diagrams and other graphical images, change fonts and font sizes, add color and lines, and so on, to create an attention-grabbing document. Desktop publishing software, such as Microsoft Publisher, Adobe PageMaker, or QuarkXpress, enables you to open an existing word processing document and enhance it through formatting tools not provided in your word processing software. Word, however, provides many of the formatting features that you would find in a desktop publishing program. Thus, you can use Word to create eye-catching newsletters and brochures.

Project — Newsletter

A newsletter is a publication geared for a specific audience that is created on a recurring basis, such as weekly, monthly, or quarterly. The audience may be subscribers, club members, employees, customers, patrons, etc.

The project in this chapter uses Word to produce the two-page newsletter shown in Figure 7–1. The newsletter is a monthly publication, called *Savvy Shopper*. Each issue of *Savvy Shopper* contains a feature article and announcements. This month's feature article discusses tips for purchasing a notebook computer. The feature article spans the first two columns of the first page of the newsletter and then continues on the second page. The announcements, which are located in the third column of the first page, inform members about discounts, remind them about the upcoming meeting, and advise them of the topic of the next month's feature article.

The Savvy Shopper newsletter in this chapter incorporates the desktop publishing features of Word. The body of each page of the newsletter is divided in three columns. A variety of fonts, font sizes, and colors add visual appeal to the document. The first page has text wrapped around a pull-quote, and the second page has text wrapped around a graphic. Horizontal and vertical lines separate distinct areas of the newsletter, including a page border around the perimeter of each page.

The project in this chapter involves several steps requiring you to drag the mouse. If you drag to the wrong location, you may want to cancel an action. Remember that you always can click the Undo button on the Quick Access Toolbar to cancel your most recent action.

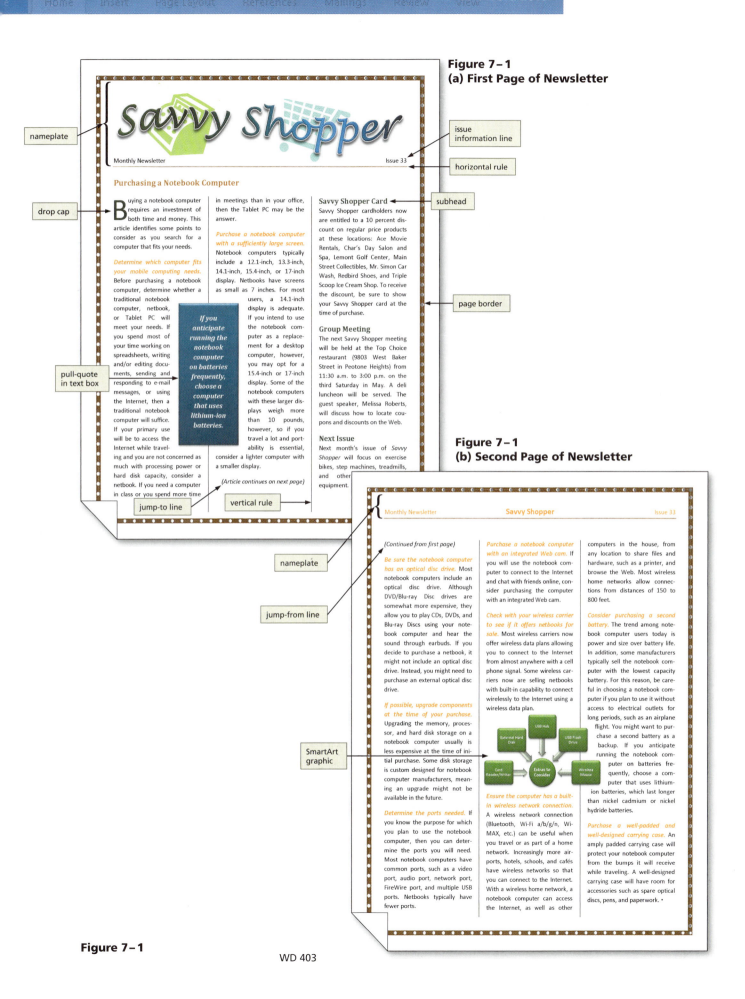

Figure 7–1
(a) First Page of Newsletter

Figure 7–1
(b) Second Page of Newsletter

nameplate

issue information line

horizontal rule

subhead

drop cap

page border

pull-quote in text box

jump-to line

vertical rule

nameplate

jump-from line

SmartArt graphic

Figure 7–1

Overview

As you read through this chapter, you will learn how to create the newsletter shown in Figure 7–1 on the previous page by performing these general tasks:

- Create the nameplate on the first page of the newsletter.
- Format the first page of the body of the newsletter.
- Create a pull-quote on the first page of the newsletter.
- Create the nameplate on the second page of the newsletter.
- Format the second page of the body of the newsletter.
- Print the newsletter.

Desktop Publishing Terminology

As you create professional-looking newsletters and brochures, you should be familiar with several desktop publishing terms. Figure 7–1 identifies these terms:

- A **nameplate**, or **banner**, is the portion of a newsletter that contains the title of the newsletter and usually an issue information line.
- The **issue information line** identifies the specific publication.
- A **ruling line**, usually identified by its direction as a **horizontal rule** or **vertical rule**, is a line that separates areas of the newsletter.
- A **subhead** is a heading within the body of the newsletter.
- A **pull-quote** is text that is *pulled*, or copied, from the text of the document and given graphical emphasis.

Plan Ahead

> **General Project Guidelines**
>
> When creating a Word document, the actions you perform and decisions you make will affect the appearance and characteristics of the finished document. As you create a newsletter, such as the project shown in Figure 7–1, you should follow these general guidelines:
>
> 1. **Create the nameplate.** The nameplate visually identifies the newsletter. Usually, the nameplate is positioned horizontally across the top of the newsletter, although some nameplates are vertical. The nameplate typically consists of text, graphics, and ruling lines.
>
> 2. **Determine content for the body of the newsletter.** Newsletters typically have one or more articles that begin on the first page. Include articles that are interesting to the audience. Incorporate color, appropriate fonts and font sizes, and alignment to provide visual interest. Use pull-quotes, graphics, and ruling lines to draw the reader's attention to important points. Avoid overusing visual elements — too many visuals can give the newsletter a cluttered look.
>
> 3. **Bind and distribute the newsletter.** Many newsletters are printed and mailed to recipients. Some are placed in public locations, free for interested parties. Others are e-mailed or posted on the Web for users to download. Printed newsletters typically are stapled at the top, along the side, or on a fold. For online newsletters, be sure the newsletter is in a format that most computer users will be able to open.
>
> When necessary, more specific details concerning the above guidelines are presented at appropriate points in the chapter. The chapter also will identify the actions performed and decisions made regarding these guidelines during the creation of the newsletter shown in Figure 7–1.

To Start Word

If you are using a computer to step through the project in this chapter and you want your screens to match the figures in this book, you should change your computer's resolution to 1024 × 768. The following steps start Word and verify settings.

1 Start Word. If necessary, maximize the Word window.

2 If the Print Layout button on the status bar is not selected, click it so that your screen is in Print Layout view.

3 Change your zoom level to 100%.

4 If the Show/Hide ¶ button (Home tab | Paragraph group) is not selected already, click it to display formatting marks on the screen.

5 If the rulers are not displayed already, click the View Ruler button on the vertical scroll bar to display the rulers because you will use the rulers to perform tasks in this chapter.

BTW

The Ribbon and Screen Resolution
Word may change how the groups and buttons within the groups appear on the Ribbon, depending on the computer's screen resolution. Thus, your Ribbon may look different from the ones in this book if you are using a screen resolution other than 1024 × 768.

To Set Custom Margins

Recall that Word is preset to use standard 8.5-by-11-inch paper, with 1-inch top, bottom, left, and right margins. In earlier chapters, you changed the margins by selecting predefined settings in the Margins gallery. For the newsletter in this chapter, all margins (left, right, top, and bottom) are .75 inches, which is not a predefined setting in the Margins gallery. Thus, the following steps set custom margins.

1

• Display the Page Layout tab.

• Click the Margins button (Page Layout tab | Page Setup group) to display the Margins gallery (Figure 7–2).

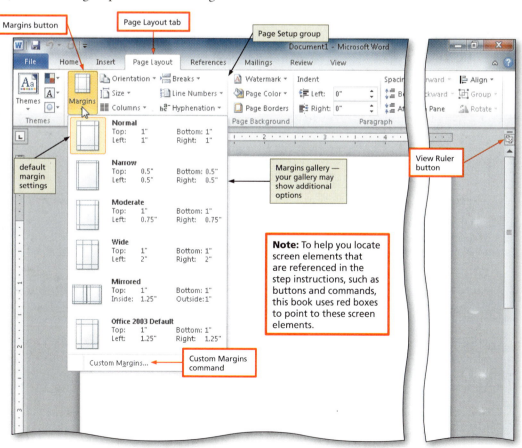

Figure 7–2

2

• Click Custom Margins in the Margins gallery to display the Page Setup dialog box. If necessary, click the Margins tab (Page Setup dialog box) to display the Margins sheet.

• Type **.75** in the Top box to change the top margin setting and then press the TAB key to position the insertion point in the Bottom box.

• Type **.75** in the Bottom box to change the bottom margin setting and then press the TAB key.

• Type **.75** in the Left box to change the left margin setting and then press the TAB key.

• Type **.75** in the Right box to change the right margin setting (Figure 7–3).

3

• Click the OK button to set the custom margins for this document.

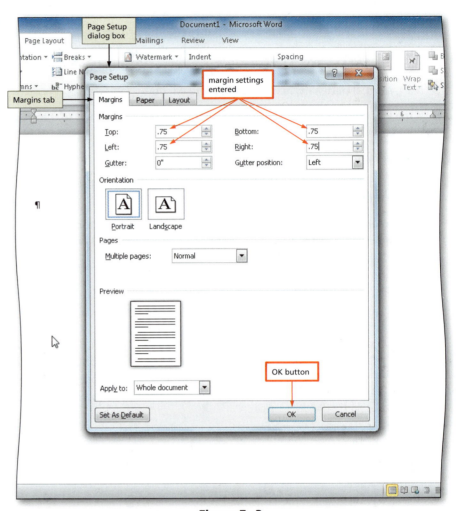

Figure 7–3

Other Ways

1. Position mouse pointer on margin boundary on ruler; when mouse pointer changes to two-headed arrow, drag margin boundaries on ruler

To Change Theme Colors

The newsletter in this chapter uses the Aspect color scheme. The following step changes the theme colors to the Aspect color scheme.

1 Click the Theme Colors button (Page Layout tab | Themes group) and then click Aspect in the Theme Colors gallery to change the document theme colors.

Creating the Nameplate

The nameplate on the first page of this newsletter consists of the information above the multiple columns (Figure 7–1a on page WD 403). In this project, the nameplate includes the newsletter title, Savvy Shopper, images of a cash register and a shopping cart, and the issue information line. The steps on the following pages create the nameplate for the first page of the newsletter in this chapter.

Create the nameplate.
The nameplate should catch the attention of readers, enticing them to read the newsletter. The nameplate typically consists of the title of the newsletter and the issue information line. Some also include a subtitle, a slogan, and a graphical image or logo. Guidelines for the newsletter title and other elements in the nameplate are as follows:

- Compose a title that is short, yet conveys the contents of the newsletter. In the newsletter title, eliminate unnecessary words such as these: the, newsletter. Use a decorative font in as large a font size as possible so that the title stands out on the page.

- Other elements on the nameplate should not compete in size with the title. Use colors that complement the title. Select easy-to-read fonts.

- Arrange the elements of the nameplate so that it does not have a cluttered appearance. If necessary, use ruling lines to visually separate areas of the nameplate.

The following pages use the steps outlined below to create the nameplate for the newsletter in this chapter.

1. Enter and format the newsletter title using WordArt.
2. Set custom tab stops for the issue information line.
3. Enter text in the issue information line.
4. Add a horizontal rule below the issue information line.
5. Insert and format the clip art images.

To Insert WordArt

In Chapter 3, you inserted a shape drawing object in a document. Recall that a drawing object is a graphic you create using Word. Another type of drawing object, called **WordArt**, enables you to create text with special effects such as shadowed, rotated, stretched, skewed, and wavy effects.

This project uses WordArt for the newsletter title, Savvy Shopper, to draw the reader's attention to the nameplate. The following steps insert WordArt.

1

- Display the Insert tab.

- Click the WordArt button (Insert tab | Text group) to display the WordArt gallery (Figure 7–4).

Q&A

Once I select a WordArt style, can I customize its appearance?

Yes. The next steps customize the WordArt style selected here.

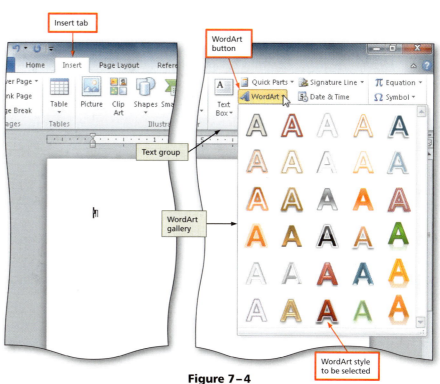

Figure 7–4

2

- Click Fill - Red, Accent 2, Matte Bevel in the WordArt gallery (third WordArt style in last row) to insert a drawing object in the document that is formatted according to the selected WordArt style, which contains the placeholder text, Your text here (Figure 7–5).

3

- Type **Savvy Shopper** to replace the selected placeholder text in the WordArt drawing object (shown in Figure 7–6).

Q&A What if my placeholder text is no longer selected?

Drag through it to select it.

Q&A How do I correct a mistake in the WordArt text?

You correct WordArt text using the same techniques you use to correct document text.

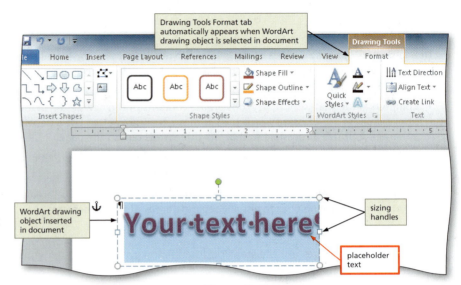

Figure 7–5

To Resize WordArt

You resize WordArt the same way you resize any other graphic. That is, you can drag its sizing handles or enter values in the Shape Height and Shape Width boxes. The next steps resize the WordArt drawing object.

1 With the WordArt drawing object selected, if necessary, display the Drawing Tools Format tab.

2 If necessary, click the Size button (Drawing Tools Format tab | Size group) to display the Shape Height and Shape Width boxes.

3 Change the value in the Shape Height box to 1.44 and the value in the Shape Width box to 7 (Figure 7–6).

4 If the Shape Height and Shape Width boxes display in a pop-up box because they do not fit on the Ribbon, click anywhere to remove the Shape Height and Shape Width boxes from the screen.

Figure 7–6

To Change the Font and Font Size of WordArt Text

You change the font and font size of WordArt text the same way you change the font and font size of any other text. That is, you select the text and then change its font and font size. The next steps change the font and font size of WordArt text.

1 Select the WordArt text, in this case, Savvy Shopper.

2 Change the font of the selected text to Lucida Handwriting.

3 Change the font size of the selected text to 48 point (shown in Figure 7–7).

To Change an Object's Text Wrapping

When you insert a drawing object in a Word document the default text wrapping is In Front of Text, which means the object will cover any text behind it. Because you want the nameplate above the rest of the newsletter, you change the text wrapping for the drawing object to Top and Bottom. The following steps change a drawing object's text wrapping.

1 If necessary, display the Drawing Tools Format tab.

2 With the WordArt drawing object selected, click the Wrap Text button (Drawing Tools Format tab | Arrange group) to display the Wrap Text gallery.

3 Click Top and Bottom in the Wrap Text gallery so that the WordArt drawing object will not cover the document text; in this case, the paragraph mark moves below the WordArt drawing object (Figure 7–7).

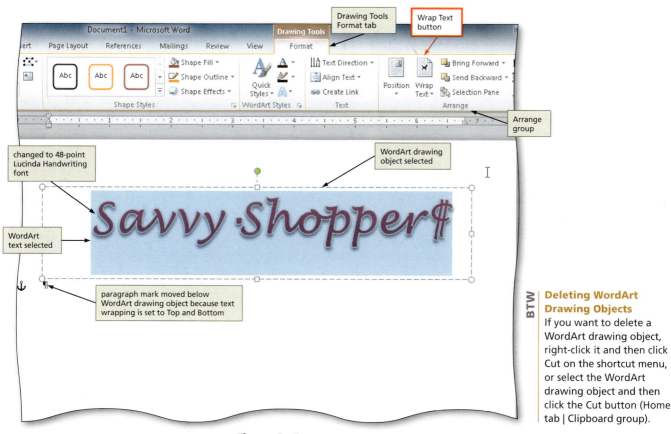

Figure 7–7

BTW

Deleting WordArt Drawing Objects
If you want to delete a WordArt drawing object, right-click it and then click Cut on the shortcut menu, or select the WordArt drawing object and then click the Cut button (Home tab | Clipboard group).

To Change the WordArt Fill Color

The next step is to change the color of the WordArt text so that it displays a green to blue gradient fill color. **Gradient** means the colors blend into one another. Word includes several built-in gradient fill colors, or you can customize one for use in drawing objects. The following steps change the fill color of the WordArt drawing object to a built-in gradient fill color and then customize the selected fill color.

- With the WordArt drawing object selected, click the Text Fill button arrow (Drawing Tools Format tab | WordArt Styles group) to display the Text Fill gallery.

Q&A

The Text Fill gallery did not display. Why not?

Be sure you click the Text Fill button arrow, which is to the right of the Text Fill button. If you mistakenly click the Text Fill button, Word places a default fill in the selected WordArt instead of displaying the Text Fill gallery.

- Point to Gradient in the Text Fill gallery to display the Gradient gallery (Figure 7–8).

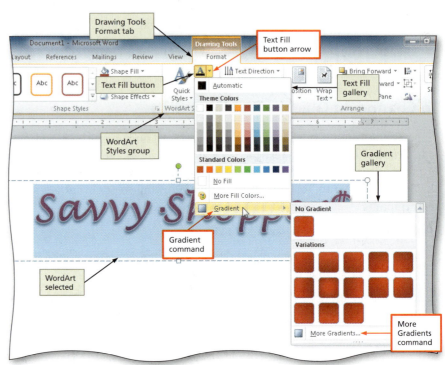

Figure 7–8

3

- Click More Gradients in the Gradient gallery to display the Format Text Effects dialog box. If necessary, click Text Fill in the left pane (Format Text Effects dialog box) and Gradient fill in the right pane (Figure 7–9).

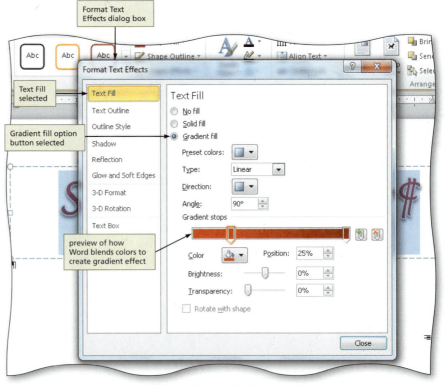

Figure 7–9

4

- In the right pane, click the Preset colors button to display a gallery of built-in gradient fill colors (Figure 7–10).

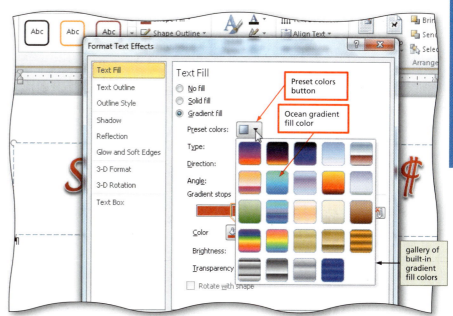

Figure 7–10

5

- Click Ocean (second row, second column) in the Preset colors gallery to select the built-in gradient color, which shows a preview in the Gradient stops area (Figure 7–11).

What is a gradient stop?

A gradient stop is the location where two colors blend. You can change the color of a stop so that Word changes the color of the blend. You also can add or delete stops, with a minimum of two stops and a maximum of ten stops per gradient fill color.

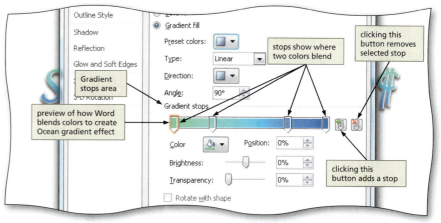

Figure 7–11

6

- If necessary, click the leftmost gradient stop to select it. Click the Color button to display a Color palette, from which you can select a color for the selected stop (Figure 7–12).

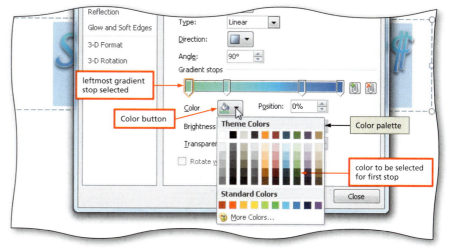

Figure 7–12

7

- Click Dark Green, Accent 4, Darker 25% (fifth row, eighth column) in the Color palette to change the color of the selected stop and the gradient between the selected stop and the next stop.

- Click the second gradient stop to select it. Click the Color box arrow to display a Color palette and then click Dark Green, Accent 4, Darker 50% (sixth row, eighth column) in the Color palette to change the color of the selected stop and the gradient between the selected stop and the next stop.

- Click the rightmost gradient stop to select it. Click the Color box arrow to display a Color palette and then click Dark Blue, Accent 3, Darker 50% (sixth row, seventh column) in the Color palette to change the color of the selected stop and the gradient between the selected stop and the next stop (Figure 7–13).

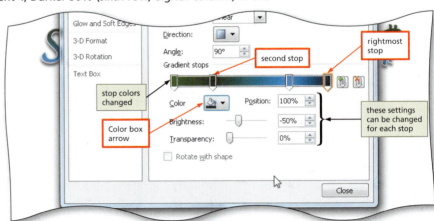

Figure 7–13

Q&A Can I move a gradient stop?

Yes. You can drag a stop to any location along the color bar. You also can adjust the position, brightness, and transparency of any selected stop.

8

- In the right pane, click the Direction button to display a gallery that shows a variety of directions for the gradient colors (Figure 7–14).

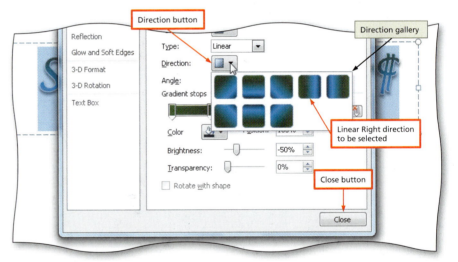

Figure 7–14

9

- Click Linear Right (first row, fourth column) in the Direction gallery to specify the colors should blend from left to right.

- Click the Close button in the dialog box to apply the selected gradient fill color to the selected drawing object.

- Click the paragraph mark below the WordArt drawing object to show its gradient fill colors (Figure 7–15).

Figure 7–15

To Change the WordArt Shape

Word provides a variety of shapes to make your WordArt more interesting. For the newsletter in this chapter, the WordArt has a wavy appearance. The following steps change the WordArt shape.

1
- Click the WordArt drawing object to select it.

- If necessary, display the Drawing Tools Format tab.

- Click the Text Effects button (Drawing Tools Format tab | WordArt Styles group) to display the Text Effects gallery.

- Point to Transform in the Text Effects gallery to display the Transform gallery.

- Point to Wave 1 (first effect, fifth row in Warp area) in the Transform gallery to display a live preview of that transform effect applied to the selected drawing object (Figure 7–16).

 Experiment
- Point to various text effects in the Transform gallery and watch the selected drawing object conform to that transform effect.

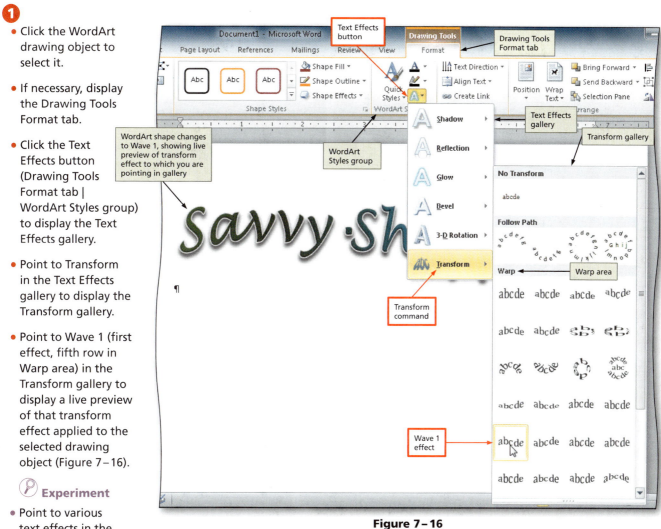

Figure 7–16

2
- Click the Wave 1 in the Transform gallery to change the shape of the WordArt drawing object.

To Set Custom Tab Stops Using the Tabs Dialog Box

The issue information line in this newsletter contains the text, Monthly Newsletter, at the left margin and the issue number at the right margin (shown in Figure 7–1a on page WD 403). In Word, a paragraph cannot be both left-aligned and right-aligned. If you click the Align Text Right button (Home tab | Paragraph group), for example, all text will be right-aligned. To place text at the right margin of a left-aligned paragraph, you set a tab stop at the right margin.

One method of setting custom tab stops is to click the ruler at the desired location of the tab stop, which you learned in an earlier chapter. You cannot click, however, at the right margin location. Thus, the steps on the next page use the Tabs dialog box to set a custom tab stop.

1

- Position the insertion point on the paragraph mark below the WordArt drawing object, which is the paragraph to be formatted with the custom tab stops.

- Click the Paragraph Dialog Box Launcher to display the Paragraph dialog box (Figure 7–17).

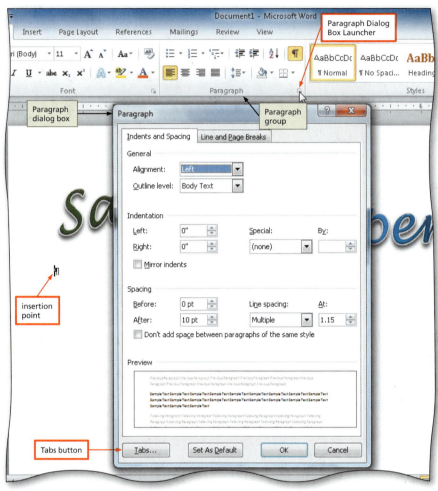

Figure 7–17

2

- Click the Tabs button (Paragraph dialog box) to display the Tabs dialog box.

- Type 7 in the Tab stop position text box (Tabs dialog box).

- Click Right in the Alignment area to specify alignment for text at the tab stop (Figure 7–18).

3

- Click the Set button (Tabs dialog box) to set a right-aligned custom tab stop.

- Click the OK button to place a right tab marker at the 7" mark on the ruler (shown in Figure 7–19).

Other Ways

1. Right-click paragraph, click Paragraph on shortcut menu, click Tabs button (Paragraph dialog box)

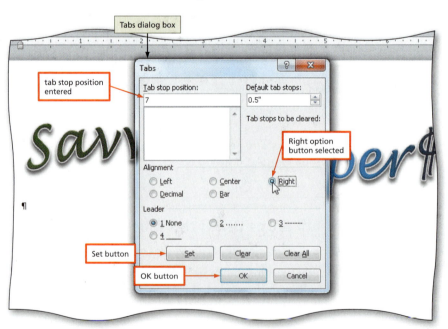

Figure 7–18

To Enter Text

The following steps enter the issue information line text.

1 With the insertion point on the paragraph below the WordArt, type **Monthly Newsletter** on line 2 of the newsletter.

2 Press the TAB key and then type **Issue 33** to complete the issue information line (Figure 7–19).

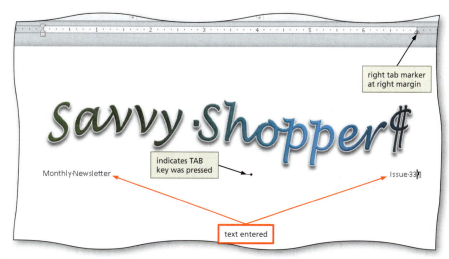

Figure 7–19

To Border One Edge of a Paragraph

In Word, you use borders to create ruling lines. As discussed in previous projects, Word can place borders on any edge of a paragraph; that is, Word can place a border on the top, bottom, left, and right edges of a paragraph.

One method of bordering paragraphs is by clicking the desired border in the Border gallery, which you learned in an earlier chapter. If you want to specify a particular border, for example, one with color, you use the Borders and Shading dialog box. In this newsletter, the issue information line has a ½-point double-line dark orange border below it. The following steps use the Borders and Shading dialog box to place a border below a paragraph.

1

• Click the Border button arrow (Home tab | Paragraph group) to display the Border gallery (Figure 7–20).

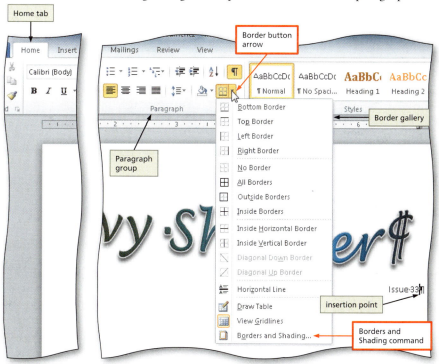

Figure 7–20

2

- Click Borders and Shading in the Border gallery to display the Borders and Shading dialog box.

- Click Custom in the Setting area (Borders and Shading dialog box) because you are setting just a bottom border.

- Scroll through the style list and click the style shown in Figure 7–21, which has two thin lines as the border.

- Click the Color button arrow and then click Orange, Accent 1, Darker 50% (fifth column, sixth row) in the Color gallery.

- Click the Bottom Border button in the Preview area of the dialog box to show a preview of the selected border style (Figure 7–21).

 Q&A What is the purpose of the buttons in the Preview area?

They are toggles that display and remove the top, bottom, left, and right borders from the diagram in the Preview area.

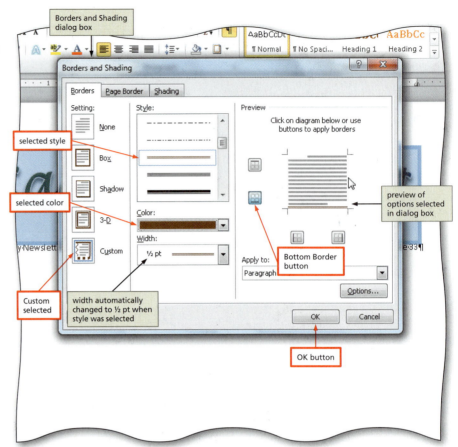

Figure 7–21

3

- Click the OK button to place the defined border on the paragraph containing the insertion point (Figure 7–22).

Q&A How would I change an existing border?

You first remove the existing border by clicking the Border button arrow (Home tab | Paragraph group) and then click the border in the Border gallery that identifies the border you wish to remove. Then, add a new border as described in these steps.

Figure 7–22

Other Ways

1. Click Page Borders (Page Layout tab | Page Background group), click Borders tab (Borders and Shading dialog box), select desired border, click OK button

Note: The following steps assume your computer is connected to the Internet. If it is not, go directly to the shaded steps on the next page that are titled To Insert a Graphic File from the Data Files for Students.

To Insert Clip Art from the Web

The next steps insert an image of a cash register from the Web in the nameplate.

1 Display the Insert tab. Click the Clip Art button (Insert tab | Illustrations group) to display the Clip Art pane.

2 Select any text that is displayed in the Clip Art pane and then type `cash register` in the Search for text box.

3 Be sure the Include Office.com content check box is selected and then click the Go button to display a list of clips that match the entered description.

4 Scroll to and then click the clip art of the cash register that matches the one in Figure 7–23 to insert the selected clip art image in the document at the location of the insertion point. (If the clip art image does not appear in the task pane, click the Close button on the Clip Art pane and then proceed to the shaded steps on the next page.)

5 Click the Close button on the Clip Art task pane title bar to close the task pane.

Q&A What if my clip art image is not in the same location as in Figure 7–23?

The clip art image may be in a different location, depending on the position of the insertion point when you inserted the image. In a later section, you will move the image to a different location.

BTW

Q&As
For a complete list of the Q&As found in many of the step-by-step sequences in this book, visit the Word 2010 Q&A Web page (scsite.com/wd2010/qa).

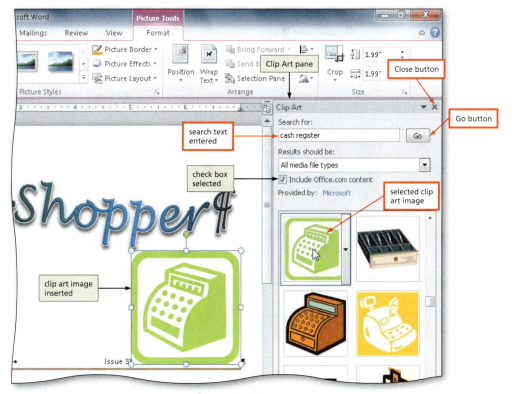

Figure 7–23

To Insert a Graphic File from the Data Files for Students

If you do not have access to the Internet, you can insert the clip art file in the Word document from the Data Files for Students. See the inside back cover of this book for instructions on downloading the Data Files for Students, or contact your instructor for information about accessing the required files. Perform these steps only if you were not able to insert the cash register clip art from the Web in the previous steps.

1 Display the Insert tab. Click the Insert Picture from File button (Insert tab | Illustrations group) to display the Insert Picture dialog box.

2 Navigate to the location of the picture to be inserted (in this case, the Chapter 07 folder in the Word folder in the Data Files for Students folder on a USB flash drive).

3 Click the Cash Register file (Insert Picture dialog box) to select the file.

4 Click the Insert button in the dialog box to insert the picture in the document at the location of the insertion point (shown in Figure 7–23 on the previous page).

To Crop a Graphic

The next step is to format the clip art image just inserted. You would like to remove the green rounded frame from the perimeter of the image. Word allows you to **crop**, or remove edges from, a graphic. The following steps crop a graphic.

- With the graphic selected, click the Crop button (Picture Tools Format tab | Size group), which places cropping handles on the image in the document.

Q&A What if I mistakenly click the Crop button arrow?

Clip the Crop button.

- Position the mouse pointer on the top-middle cropping handle so that it looks like an upside-down letter T (Figure 7–24).

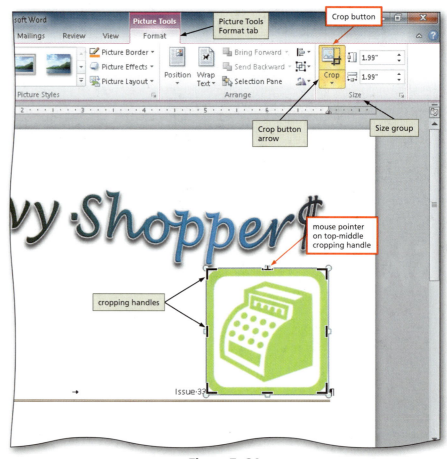

Figure 7–24

2
- Drag the top-middle cropping handle downward to the location of the mouse pointer shown in Figure 7–25 to remove the frame at the top of the image.

3
- Release the mouse button to crop the graphic to the location shown in Figure 7–25.

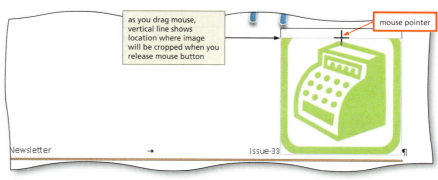

as you drag mouse, vertical line shows location where image will be cropped when you release mouse button

mouse pointer

Newsletter → Issue·33

Figure 7–25

4
- Position the mouse pointer on the left-middle cropping handle so that it looks like a sideways letter T and then drag the cropping handle inward until the frame at the left edge of the image disappears, as shown in Figure 7–26.

- Position the mouse pointer on the right-middle cropping handle so that it looks like a sideways letter T and then drag the cropping handle inward until the frame at the right edge of the image disappears, as shown in Figure 7–26.

- Position the mouse pointer on the bottom-middle cropping handle so that it looks like a letter T and then drag the cropping handle upward until the frame at the bottom edge of the image disappears, as shown in Figure 7–26.

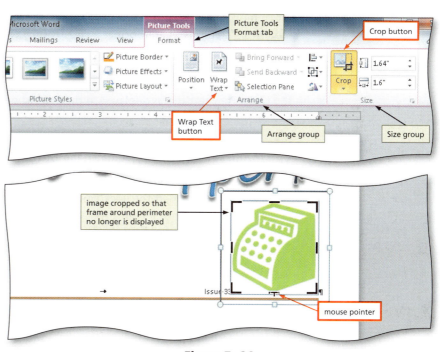

Picture Tools Format tab

Crop button

Wrap Text button

Arrange group

Size group

image cropped so that frame around perimeter no longer is displayed

Issue·33

mouse pointer

Figure 7–26

5
- Click the Crop button (Picture Tools Format tab | Size group) to deactivate the cropping tool, which removes the cropping handles from the selected image.

Other Ways

1. Right-click graphic, click Format Picture on shortcut menu, click Crop in left pane, enter values in text boxes, click Close button

To Change an Object's Text Wrapping

When you insert clip art in a Word document, the default text wrapping is In Line with Text, which means the object is part of the current paragraph. Because you want the clip art images behind the newsletter title, you change the text wrapping for the clip art image to Behind Text. The following steps change a drawing object's text wrapping.

 With the clip art image selected, click the Wrap Text button (Picture Tools Format tab | Arrange group) to display the Wrap Text gallery.

2 Click Behind Text in the Wrap Text gallery so that the clip art image is positioned behind text in the document.

To Move a Graphic

The clip art image needs to be moved up so that it is positioned behind the word, Savvy, in the newsletter title. The following step moves the graphic.

1 Point to the middle of the graphic, and when the mouse pointer has a four-headed arrow attached to it, drag the graphic to the location shown in Figure 7–27.

To Insert a Clip Art Image and Then Crop It, Change Its Text Wrapping, and Move It

The next step is to insert a clip art image of a shopping cart, crop it to remove the frame around the perimeter of the image, change its text wrapping to Behind Text, and then move it so that it is positioned behind the word, Shopper, in the nameplate. The following steps insert and format a clip art image.

1 Position the insertion point in the issue information line. Display the Insert tab. Click the Clip Art button (Insert tab | Illustrations group) to display the Clip Art pane.

2 Select any text that is displayed in the Clip Art pane and then type `shopping cart` in the Search for text box.

3 Be sure the Include Office.com content check box is selected and then click the Go button to display a list of clips that match the entered description.

4 Scroll to and then click the clip art of the shopping cart that matches the one in Figure 7–27 to insert the selected clip in the document at the location of the insertion point. (If the clip art image does not appear in the task pane, click the Close button on the Clip Art pane and then follow the shaded steps on page WD 418, inserting the picture called Shopping Cart. Then, proceed to Step 6 below.)

5 Click the Close button on the Clip Art pane title bar to close the pane.

6 With the graphic selected, click the Crop button (Picture Tools Format tab | Size group), which places cropping handles on the image in the document.

7 Drag each of the four cropping handles inward to remove the blue frame from the image, as shown in Figure 7–27.

8 Click the Crop button (Picture Tools Format tab | Size group) to deactive the cropping tool.

9 With the clip art image selected, click the Wrap Text button (Picture Tools Format tab | Arrange group) to display the Wrap Text gallery and then click Behind Text in the Wrap Text gallery so that the clip art image is positioned behind text in the document.

10 Point to the middle of the graphic, and when the mouse pointer has a four-headed arrow attached to it, drag the graphic to the location shown in Figure 7–27.

Figure 7–27

To Use the Selection Pane

The next step is to rotate the clip art images, but because they are positioned behind the text, it may be difficult to select them. The following step displays the Selection and Visibility task pane so that you easily can select items on the screen that are layered behind other objects.

- Click the Selection Pane button (Picture Tools Format tab | Arrange group) to display the Selection and Visibility task pane (Figure 7–28).

Experiment

- Click Text Box 1 in the Selection and Visibility task pane to select the WordArt drawing object. Click Picture 3 in the Selection and Visibility task pane to select the shopping cart image. Click Picture 2 in the Selection and Visibility task pane to select the cash register image.

Q&A

What are the displayed names in the Selection and Visibility task pane?

Word assigns names to each object in the document. The names displayed on your screen may differ.

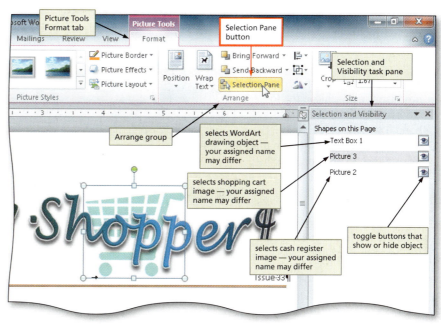

Figure 7–28

To Rotate a Graphic

The images of the cash register and shopping cart in this newsletter are slanted slightly to the right. In Word, you can rotate a graphic. The following steps rotate a graphic.

- If necessary, click Picture 3 in the Selection and Visibility task pane to select the image of the shopping cart.

- Position the mouse pointer on the graphic's rotate handle (Figure 7–29).

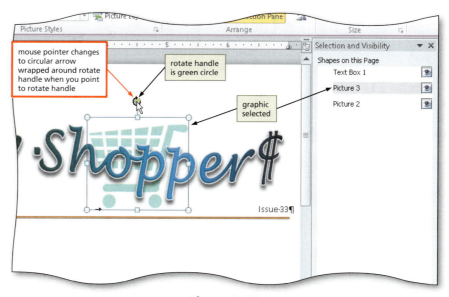

Figure 7–29

2

- Drag the rotate handle rightward and downward to rotate the graphic as shown in Figure 7–30.

Q&A

Can I drag the rotate handle in any direction?

You can drag the rotate handle clockwise or counterclockwise.

3

- Release the mouse button to position the graphic in the location where you dragged the rotate handle (shown in Figure 7–31). (You may need to rotate the graphic a few times to position it in the desired location.)

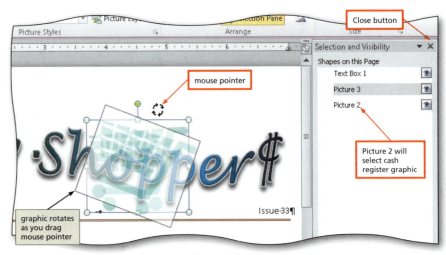

Figure 7–30

4

- Click Picture 2 in the Selection and Visibility task pane to select the image of the cash register.

- Position the mouse pointer on the graphic's rotate handle, in this case, the cash register's rotate handle.

- Drag the rotate handle rightward and downward to rotate the graphic as shown in Figure 7–31.

Figure 7–31

- If necessary, move the images or rotate them again or resize them so that they look the same as those shown in Figure 7–31 and then click the Close button on the Selection and Visibility task pane title bar to close the task pane.

- Click somewhere in the issue information to deselect the graphic (Figure 7–31).

To Save a Document

The nameplate now is complete. The next step is to save the newsletter because you have performed many steps thus far. The following steps save the newsletter.

1 With a USB flash drive connected to one of the computer's USB ports, click the Save button on the Quick Access Toolbar to display the Save As dialog box.

2 Type `Savvy Shopper Newsletter` in the File name text box to change the file name. Do not press the ENTER key because you do not want to close the dialog box at this time.

3 If necessary, navigate to the save location (in this case, the Word folder in the CIS 101 folder [or your class folder] on the USB flash drive).

4 Click the Save button (Save As dialog box) to save the document in the selected folder on the USB flash drive with the entered file name.

Break Point: If you wish to take a break, this is a good place to do so. You can quit Word now. To resume at a later time, start Word, open the file called Savvy Shopper Newsletter, and continue following the steps from this location forward.

Formatting the First Page of the Body of the Newsletter

The next step is to format the first page of the body of the newsletter. The body of the newsletter in this chapter is divided in three columns (Figure 7–1a on page WD 403). The first two columns contain the feature article, and the third column contains announcements. The characters in the paragraphs are aligned on both the right and left edges — similar to newspaper columns. The first letter in the first paragraph is much larger than the rest of the characters in the paragraph. A vertical rule separates the second and third columns. The steps on the following pages format the first page of the body of the newsletter using these desktop publishing features.

Plan Ahead

Determine the content for the body of the newsletter.
While content and subject matter of newsletters may vary, the procedures used to create newsletters are similar:

- **Write the body copy.** Newsletters should contain articles of interest and relevance to readers. Some share information, while others promote a product or service. Use active voice in body copy, which is more engaging than passive voice. Proofread the body copy to be sure it is error free. Check all facts for accuracy.

- **Organize body copy in columns.** Most newsletters arrange body copy in columns. The body copy in columns, often called **snaking columns** or newspaper-style columns, flows from the bottom of one column to the top of the next column.

- **Format the body copy.** Begin the feature article on the first page of the newsletter. If the article spans multiple pages, use a continuation line, called a jump or jump line, to guide the reader to the remainder of the article. The message at the end of the article on the first page of the newsletter is called a **jump-to line**, and a **jump-from line** marks the beginning of the continuation, which is usually on a subsequent page.

- **Maintain consistency.** Be consistent with placement of body copy elements in newsletter editions. If the newsletter contains announcements, for example, position them in the same location in each edition so that readers easily can find them.

- **Maximize white space.** Allow plenty of space between lines, paragraphs, and columns. Tightly packed text is difficult to read. Separate the text adequately from graphics, borders, and headings.

- **Incorporate color.** Use colors that complement those in the nameplate. Be careful not to overuse color. Restrict color below the nameplate to drop caps, subheads, graphics, and ruling lines. If you do not have a color printer, still change the colors because the colors will print in shades of black and gray, which add variety to the newsletter.

- **Select and format subheads.** Develop subheads with as few words as possible. Readers should be able to identify content of the next topic by glancing at a subhead. Subheads should be emphasized in the newsletter but should not compete with text in the nameplate. Use a larger, bold, or otherwise contrasting font for subheads so that they stand apart from the body copy. Use this same format for all subheads for consistency. Leave a space above subheads to visually separate their content from the previous topic. Be consistent with spacing above and below subheads throughout the newsletter.

- **Divide sections with vertical rules.** Use vertical rules to guide the reader through the newsletter.

- **Enhance the document with visuals.** Add energy to the newsletter and emphasis to important points with graphics, pull-quotes, and other visuals such as drop caps to mark beginning of an article. Use these elements sparingly, however, so that the newsletter does not have a crowded appearance. Fewer, large visuals are more effective than several smaller ones. If you use a graphic that you did not create, be sure to obtain permission to use it in the newsletter and give necessary credit to the creator of the graphic.

To Clear Formatting

The next step is enter the title of the feature article below the horizontal rule. To do this, you will position the insertion point at the end of the issue information line (after the 3 in Issue 33) and then press the ENTER key. Recall that the issue information line has a bottom border. When you press the ENTER key in a bordered paragraph, Word carries forward any borders to the next paragraph. Thus, after you press the ENTER key, you should clear formatting to format the new paragraph to the Normal style. The following steps clear formatting.

1 Click at the end of line 2 (the issue information line) so that the insertion point is immediately after the 3 in Issue 33. Press the ENTER key to advance the insertion point to the next line, which also moves the border down one line.

2 If necessary, display the Home tab. Click the Clear Formatting button (Home tab | Font group) to apply the Normal style to the location of the insertion point, which in this case moves the new paragraph below the border on the issue information line.

To Format Text as a Heading Style and Adjust Spacing before and after the Paragraph

Below the bottom border in the nameplate is the title of the feature article, Purchasing a Notebook Computer. The following steps apply the Heading 1 style to a paragraph and adjust the paragraph spacing.

1 With the insertion point on the paragraph mark below the border, click Heading 1 (Home tab | Styles group) to apply the Heading 1 style to the paragraph containing the insertion point.

2 Type `Purchasing a Notebook Computer` as the title of the feature article.

3 Display the Page Layout tab. Change the Spacing Before to 18 pt and the Spacing After to 12 pt (Figure 7–32).

Figure 7–32

Columns

When you begin a document in Word, it has one column. You can divide a portion of a document or the entire document in multiple columns. Within each column, you can type, modify, or format text.

To divide a portion of a document in multiple columns, you use section breaks. Word requires that a new section be created each time you alter the number of columns in a document. Thus, if a document has a nameplate (one column) followed by an article of three columns followed by an article of two columns, the document would be divided in three separate sections.

Organize body copy in columns.
Be consistent from page to page with the number of columns. Narrow columns generally are easier to read than wide ones. Columns, however, can be too narrow. A two- or three-column layout generally is appealing and offers a flexible design. Try to have between five and fifteen words per line. To do this, you may need to adjust the column width, the font size, or the leading (line spacing). Font size of text in columns should be no larger than 12 point but not so small that readers must strain to read the text.

Plan Ahead

To Insert a Continuous Section Break

In this chapter, the nameplate is one column and the body of the newsletter is three columns. Thus, you must insert a continuous section break below the nameplate. The term, continuous, means the new section should be on the same page as the previous section, which, in this case, means that the three columns of body copy will be positioned directly below the nameplate on the first page of the newsletter. The following steps insert a continuous section break.

- With the insertion point at the end of the feature article title (shown in Figure 7–32), press the ENTER key to position the insertion point below the article title.

- Click the Insert Page and Section Breaks button (Page Layout tab | Page Setup group) to display the Insert Page and Section Breaks gallery (Figure 7–33).

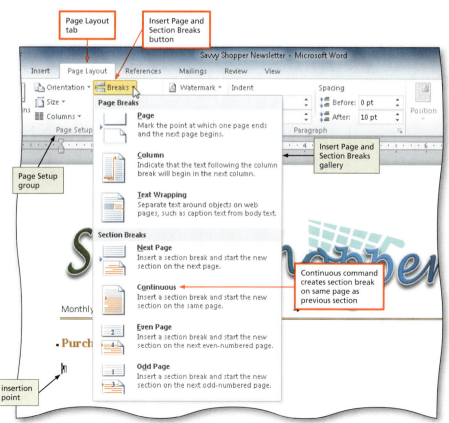

Figure 7–33

2

- Click Continuous in the Insert Page and Section Breaks gallery to insert a continuous section break above the insertion point (Figure 7–34).

Figure 7–34

To Change the Number of Columns

The document now has two sections. The nameplate is in the first section, and the insertion point is in the second section. The second section should be formatted to three columns. Thus, the following steps format the second section in the document to three columns.

1

- Click the Columns button (Page Layout tab | Page Setup group) to display the Columns gallery (Figure 7–35).

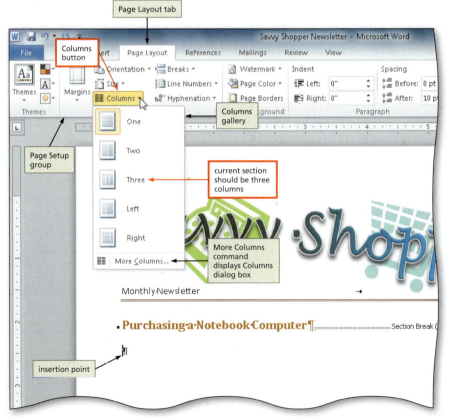

Figure 7–35

2

- Click Three in the Columns gallery to divide the section containing the insertion point in three evenly sized and spaced columns (Figure 7–36).

Q&A

What if I want columns of different widths?

You would click the More Columns command in the Columns gallery, which displays the Columns dialog box. In this dialog box, you can specify varying column widths and spacing.

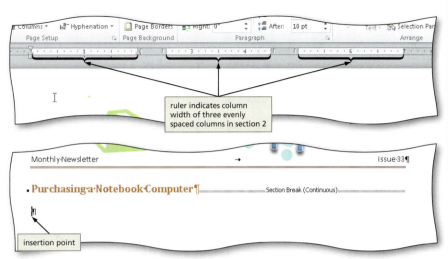

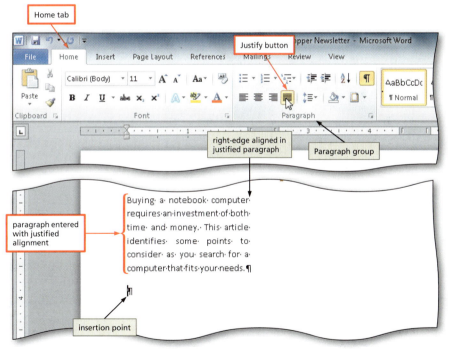

Figure 7–36

To Justify a Paragraph

The text in the paragraphs of the body of the newsletter is **justified**, which means that the left and right margins are aligned, like the edges of newspaper columns. The following step enters the first paragraph of the feature article using justified alignment.

1

- Display the Home tab.

- Click the Justify button (Home tab | Paragraph group) so that Word aligns both the left and right margins of typed text.

- Type the first paragraph of the feature article (Figure 7–37): `Buying a notebook computer requires an investment of both time and money. This article identifies some points to consider as you search for a computer that fits your needs.` and then press the ENTER key.

Q&A

Why do some words have extra space between them?

When a paragraph is formatted to justified alignment, Word places extra space between words so that the left and right edges of the paragraph are aligned. To remedy big gaps, sometimes called rivers, you can add or rearrange words, change the column width, change the font size, and so on.

Figure 7–37

Other Ways
1. Right-click paragraph, click Paragraph on shortcut menu, click Indents and Spacing tab (Paragraph dialog box), click Alignment box arrow, click Justified, click OK button 2. Click Paragraph Dialog Box Launcher (Home tab or Page Layout tab | Paragraph group), click Indents and Spacing tab (Paragraph dialog box), click Alignment box arrow, click Justified, click OK button 3. Press CTRL+J

To Insert a File in a Column of the Newsletter

Instead of typing the rest of the feature article in the newsletter in this chapter, the next step is to insert a file named Savvy Shopper Notebook Article in the newsletter. This file, which contains the remainder of the feature article, is located on the Data Files for Students. See the inside back cover of this book for instructions on downloading the Data Files for Students, or contact your instructor for information about accessing the required files.

The following steps insert the Savvy Shopper Notebook Article file in a column of the newsletter.

- Display the Insert tab.

- With the insertion point positioned in the left column as shown in Figure 7–37 on the previous page, click the Insert Object button arrow (Insert tab | Text group) to display the Insert Object menu.

- Click Text from File on the Insert Object menu to display the Insert File dialog box.

- Navigate to the location of the file to be inserted (in this case, the Chapter 07 folder in the Word folder in the Data Files for Students folder on a USB flash drive).

- Click Savvy Shopper Notebook Article to select the file (Figure 7–38).

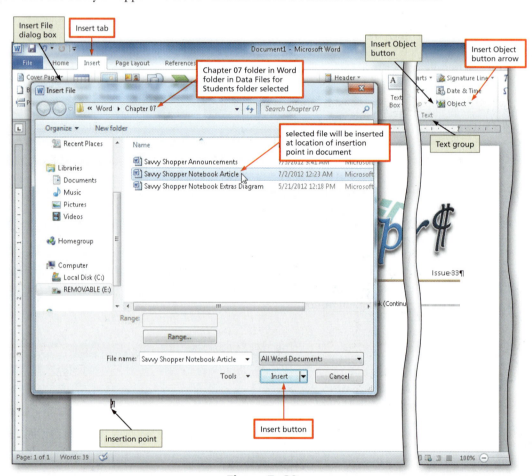

Figure 7–38

- Click the Insert button (Insert File dialog box) to insert the file, Savvy Shopper Notebook Article, in the current document at the location of the insertion point.

- Scroll to display the bottom of the first page in the document window so that you can see how the article fills the three columns on the first and second pages (Figure 7–39).

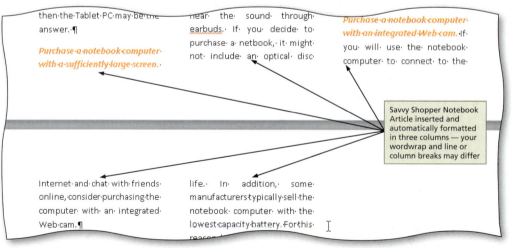

Figure 7–39

To Increase Column Width and Place a Vertical Rule between Columns

The columns in the newsletter currently contain many rivers due to the justified alignment in the narrow column width. To eliminate some of the rivers, you increase the size of the columns slightly in this newsletter. In newsletters, you often see a vertical rule separating columns. Through the Columns dialog box, you can change column width and add vertical rules. The following steps increase column widths and add vertical rules between columns.

1

- Position the insertion point somewhere in the feature article text.

- Display the Page Layout tab.

- Click the Columns button (Page Layout tab | Page Setup group) to display the Columns gallery (Figure 7–40).

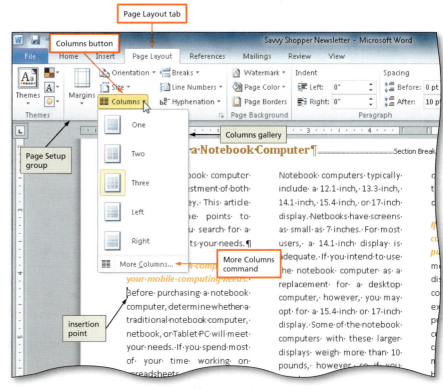

Figure 7–40

2

- Click More Columns in the Columns gallery to display the Columns dialog box.

- In the 'Width and spacing' area (Columns dialog box), click the Width box up arrow as many times as necessary until the Width box reads 2.1".

 How would I make the columns different widths?

You would remove the check mark from the 'Equal column width' check box and then set the individual column widths in the dialog box.

- Place a check mark in the Line between check box to select the check box (Figure 7–41).

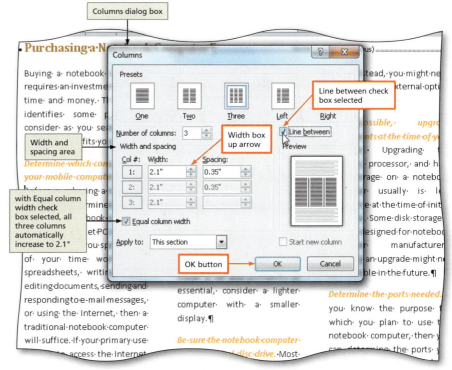

Figure 7–41

3

- Click the OK button to make the columns slightly wider and place a line (vertical rule) between each column in the document (Figure 7–42).

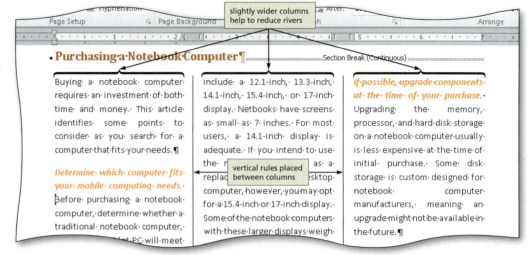

Figure 7–42

Other Ways

1. Double-click space between columns on ruler, enter settings (Columns dialog box), click OK button

2. To adjust column widths, drag column boundaries on ruler

3. To insert line, click Borders button arrow (Home tab | Paragraph group)

To Hyphenate a Document

To further eliminate some of the rivers in the columns of the newsletter, you could turn on Word's hyphenation feature so that words with multiple syllables are hyphenated at the end of lines instead of wrapped in their entirety to the next line. The following steps turn on the hyphenation feature.

1

- Click the Hyphenation button (Page Layout tab | Page Setup group) to display the Hyphenation gallery (Figure 7–43).

What is the difference between Automatic and Manual hyphenation?

Automatic hyphenation places hyphens wherever words can break at a syllable in the document. With manual hyphenation, Word displays a dialog box for each word it could hyphenate, enabling you to accept or reject the proposed hyphenation.

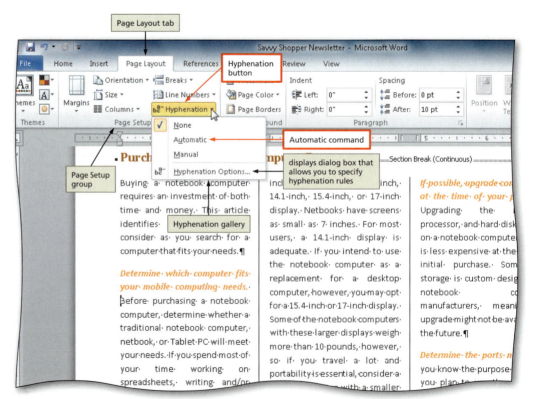

Figure 7–43

2
- Click Automatic in the Hyphenation gallery to hyphenate the document (Figure 7–44).

Q&A

Q&A What if I do not want a particular word hyphenated?

You can reword text and Word will automatically redo the hyphenation.

Figure 7–44

To Format a Character as a Drop Cap

The first character in the feature article in this newsletter, that is, the capital letter B, is formatted as a drop cap. A **drop cap** is a capital letter whose font size is larger than the rest of the characters in the paragraph. In Word, the drop cap can sink into the first few lines of text, or it can extend into the left margin, which often is called a stick-up cap. In this newsletter, the paragraph text wraps around the drop cap.

The following steps create a drop cap in the first paragraph of the feature article in the newsletter.

1
- Position the insertion point somewhere in the first paragraph of the feature article.

- Display the Insert tab.

- Click the Drop Cap button (Insert tab | Text group) to display the Drop Cap gallery (Figure 7–45).

Experiment

- Point to various commands in the Drop Cap gallery to see a live preview of the drop cap formats in the document.

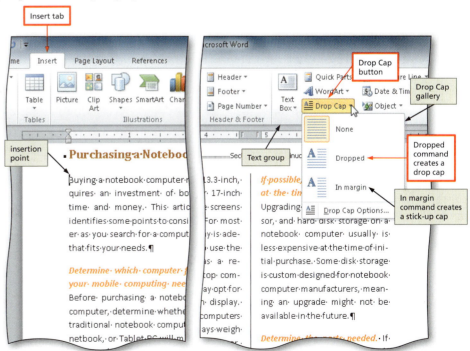

Figure 7–45

2

● Click Dropped in the Drop Cap gallery to format the first letter in the paragraph containing the insertion point (the B in Buying, in this case) as a drop cap and wrap subsequent text in the paragraph around the drop cap (Figure 7–46).

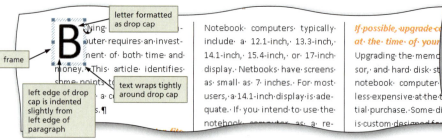

Figure 7–46

Q&A What is the outline around the drop cap in the document?

When you format a letter as a drop cap, Word places a frame around it. A **frame** is a container for text that allows you to position the text anywhere on the page. Word formats a frame for the drop cap so that text wraps around it. The frame also contains a paragraph mark nonprinting character to the right of the drop cap, which may or may not be visible on your screen.

To Format the Drop Cap

You will change the font color of the drop cap, move it left slightly, and reduce its size a bit. The following steps format the drop cap.

1 With the drop cap selected, display the Home tab, click the Font Color button arrow (Home tab | Font group), and then click Dark Green, Accent 4, Darker 50% (eighth color, sixth row) in the Font Color gallery to change the color of the drop cap.

Q&A What if my frame no longer is displayed?

Click the drop cap to select it. Then, click the blue selection rectangle to display the frame.

2 Position the mouse pointer on the drop cap frame until the mouse pointer has a four-headed arrow attached to it and then drag the drop cap left slightly so that the left edge of the letter aligns with the left edge of text.

Q&A What if the drop cap is not in the correct location?

Repeat Step 2.

3 Drag the sizing handles on the frame until the drop cap and the text in the paragraph look like Figure 7–47. If necessary, reposition the drop cap again.

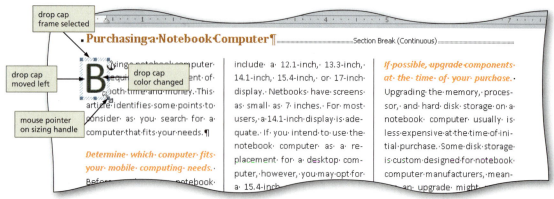

Figure 7–47

To Insert a Next Page Section Break

The third column on the first page of the newsletter is not a continuation of the feature article. The third column, instead, contains several member announcements. The feature article continues on the second page of the newsletter (shown in Figure 7–1b on page WD 403). Thus, you must insert a next page section break, which is a section break that also contains a page break, at the bottom of the second column so that the remainder of the feature article moves to the second page. The following steps insert a next page section break in the second column.

1
- Scroll to display the bottom of the second column of the first page of the newsletter in the document window. Position the insertion point at the location for the section break, in this case, to the left of the B in the paragraph beginning with the words, Be sure.

- Display the Page Layout tab.

- Click the Insert Page and Section Breaks button (Page Layout tab | Page Setup group) to display the Insert Page and Section Breaks gallery (Figure 7–48).

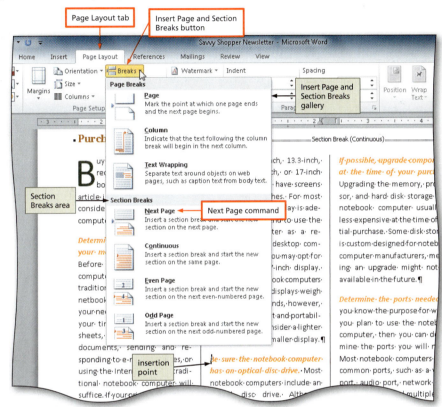

Figure 7–48

2
- In the Section Breaks area in the gallery, click Next Page to insert a next page section break, which positions the insertion point on the next page (Figure 7–49).

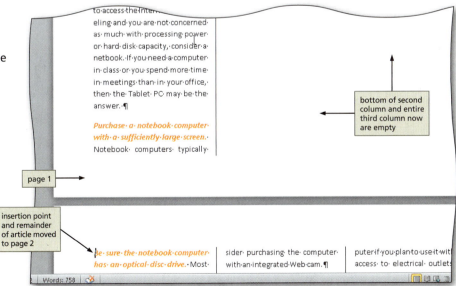

Figure 7–49

To Enter Text

The next step is to insert a jump-to line at the end of the second column, informing the reader where to look for the rest of the feature article. The following steps insert a jump-to line at the end of the text in the second column on the first page of the newsletter.

1 Scroll to display the end of the text in the second column of the first page of the newsletter and then position the insertion point between the paragraph mark and the section break notation.

2 Press the ENTER key twice to insert a blank line for the jump-to text above the section break notation.

3 Press the UP ARROW key to position the insertion point on the blank line. If the blank line is formatted in the Heading 1 style, click the Clear Formatting button (Home tab | Font group) so that the entered text follows the Normal style.

4 Press CTRL+R to right align the paragraph mark. Press CTRL+I to turn on the italic format. Type **(Article continues on next page)** as the jump-to text and then press CTRL+I again to turn off the italic format.

To Insert a Column Break

In the Savvy Shopper newsletters, for consistency, the member announcements always begin at the top of the third column. If you insert the Savvy Shopper Announcements at the current location of the insertion point, however, they will begin at the bottom of the second column.

For the member announcements to be displayed in the third column, you insert a **column break** at the bottom of the second column, which places the insertion point at the top of the next column. Thus, the following steps insert a column break at the bottom of the second column.

- Position the insertion point to the left of the paragraph mark on the line containing the next page section break, which is the location where the column break should be inserted.

- Click the Insert Page and Section Breaks button (Page Layout tab | Page Setup group) to display the Insert Page and Section Breaks gallery (Figure 7–50).

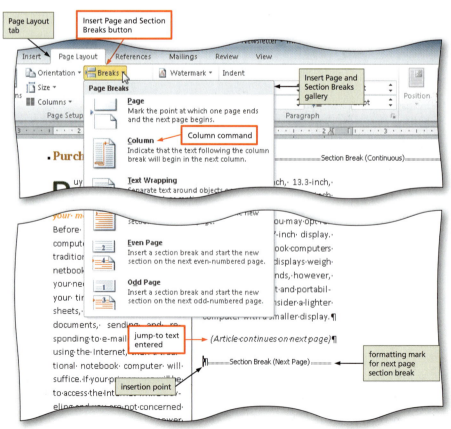

Figure 7–50

2

- Click Column in the Insert Page and Section Breaks gallery to insert a column break at the location of the insertion point and move the insertion point to the top of the next column (Figure 7–51).

Q&A What if I wanted to remove a column break?

You would double-click it to select it and then click the Cut button (Home tab | Clipboard group) or press the DELETE key.

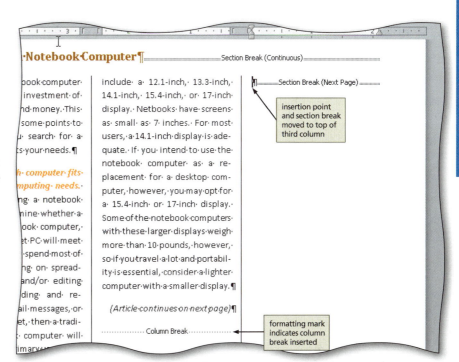

·Notebook·Computer·¶ ·····Section Break (Continuous)·····

book·computer·
investment·of·
nd·money.··This·
some·points·to·
u·search·for·a·
ts·your·needs.¶

h·computer·fits·
mputing·needs.·

ng·a·notebook·
nine·whether·a·
ook·computer,·
et·PC·will·meet·
·spend·most·of·
ng·on·spread-
and/or·editing·
ding·and·re-
ail·messages,·or·
et,·then·a·tradi-
·computer·will·
imaryw

include·a·12.1-inch,·13.3-inch,·14.1-inch,·15.4-inch,·or·17-inch·display.··Netbooks·have·screens·as·small·as·7·inches.··For·most·users,·a·14.1-inch·display·is·ade-quate.··If·you·intend·to·use·the·notebook·computer·as·a·re-placement·for·a·desktop·com-puter,·however,·you·may·opt·for·a·15.4-inch·or·17-inch·display.··Some·of·the·notebook·computers·with·these·larger·displays·weigh·more·than·10·pounds,·however,·so·if·you·travel·a·lot·and·portabil-ity·is·essential,·consider·a·lighter·computer·with·a·smaller·display.¶

(Article·continues·on·next·page)¶

················· Column Break ················

¶·····Section Break (Next Page)·····

insertion point and section break moved to top of third column

formatting mark indicates column break inserted

Figure 7–51

Other Ways

1. Press CTRL+SHIFT+ENTER

To Insert a File in a Column of the Newsletter

So that you do not have to enter the entire third column of announcements in the newsletter, the next step in the project is to insert the file named Savvy Shopper Announcements in the third column of the newsletter. This file contains the three announcements: the first about member discounts, the second about a group meeting, and the third about the topic of the next newsletter issue.

The Savvy Shopper Announcements file is located on the Data Files for Students. See the inside back cover of this book for instructions on downloading the Data Files for Students, or contact your instructor for information about accessing the required files. The following steps insert a file in a column of the newsletter.

1 With the insertion point at the top of the third column, display the Insert tab.

2 Click the Insert Object button arrow (Insert tab | Text group) to display the Insert Object menu and then click Text from File on the Object menu to display the Insert File dialog box.

3 Navigate to the location of the file to be inserted (in this case, the Chapter 07 folder in the Word folder in the Data Files for Students folder on a USB flash drive).

4 Click Savvy Shopper Announcements to select the file.

5 Click the Insert button (Insert File dialog box) to insert the file, Savvy Shopper Announcements, in the document at the location of the insertion point.

Q&A What if text from the announcements column spills onto the second page of the newsletter?

You will format text in the announcements column so that all of its text fits in the third column of the first page.

6 Press SHIFT+F5 to return the insertion point to the last editing location, in this case, the top of the third column on the first page of the newsletter (Figure 7–52).

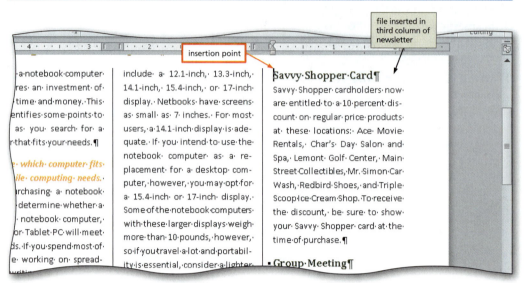

Figure 7–52

To Save a Document Again

You have performed several steps since the last save. Thus, you should save the newsletter again.

1 Save the newsletter again with the same file name, Savvy Shopper Newsletter.

Creating a Pull-Quote

A pull-quote is text pulled, or copied, from the text of the document and given graphical emphasis so that it stands apart and commands the reader's attention. The newsletter in this project copies text from the second page of the newsletter and places it in a pull-quote on the first page between the first and second columns (Figure 7–1a on page WD 403).

Plan Ahead

> **Enhance the document with pull-quotes.**
> Because of their bold emphasis, pull-quotes should be used sparingly in a newsletter. Pull-quotes are useful for breaking the monotony of long columns of text. Typically, quotation marks are used only if you are quoting someone directly. If you use quotation marks, use curly (or smart) quotation marks instead of straight quotation marks.

To create the pull-quote in this newsletter, follow this general procedure:

1. Create a **text box**, which is a container for text that allows you to position the text anywhere on the page.
2. Copy the text from the existing document to the Office Clipboard and then paste the text from the Office Clipboard to the text box.
3. Resize and format the text box.
4. Move the text box to the desired location.

To Insert a Text Box

The first step in creating the pull-quote is to insert a text box. A text box is like a frame; the difference is that a text box has more graphical formatting options than does a frame. Word provides a variety of built-in text boxes, saving you the time of formatting the text box. The following steps insert a built-in text box.

1
- Scroll to display the top portion of the newsletter in the document window and position the insertion point at an approximate location for the pull-quote (you will position the pull-quote at the exact location in a later step).

- Click the Text Box button (Insert tab | Text group) to display the Text Box gallery.

Experiment

- Scroll through the Text Box gallery to see the variety of available text box styles.

- Scroll to display Puzzle Quote in the Text Box gallery (Figure 7–53).

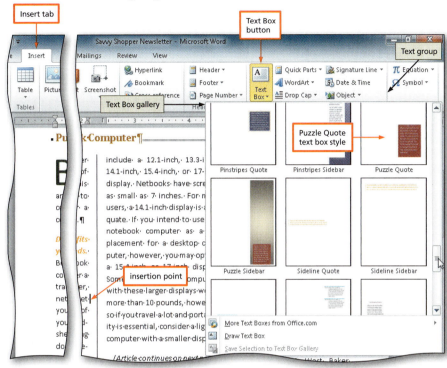

Figure 7–53

2
- Click Puzzle Quote in the Text Box gallery to insert that text box style in the document. If necessary, scroll to display the entire text box in the document window (Figure 7–54).

Q&A Does my text box need to be in the same location as Figure 7–54?

No. You will move the text box later.

Q&A The layout of the first page is not correct because of the text box. What do I do?

You will enter text in the text box and then position it in the correct location. At that time, the layout of the first page will be fixed.

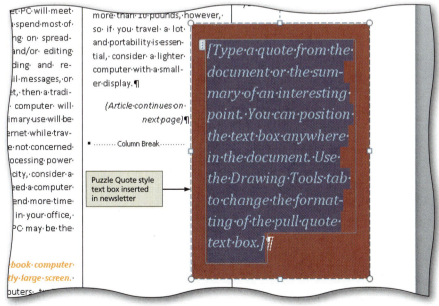

Figure 7–54

Other Ways	
1. Click Quick Parts button (Insert tab | Text group), click Building Blocks Organizer on Quick Parts	menu, select desired text box name in Building blocks list, click Insert button

To Split the Window

The text that you will copy for the pull-quote is on the second page of the newsletter and the pull-quote (text box) is on the first page of the newsletter. Thus, the next step is to copy the pull-quote text from the second page and then paste it on the first page. To simplify this process, you would like to view the pull-quote on the first page and the text to be copied on the second page on the screen at the same time. Word allows you to split the window in two separate panes, each containing the current document and having its own scroll bar. This enables you to scroll to and view two different portions of the same document at the same time. The following steps split the Word window.

1

• Position the mouse pointer on the split box at the top of the vertical scroll bar, which changes the mouse pointer to a resize pointer (Figure 7–55).

Q&A

What does the resize pointer look like?

The **resize pointer** consists of two small horizontal lines, each with a vertical arrow.

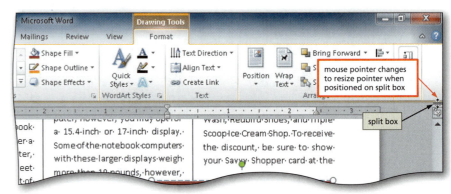

Figure 7–55

2

• Double-click the resize pointer to divide the document window in two separate panes — both the upper and lower panes display the current document (Figure 7–56).

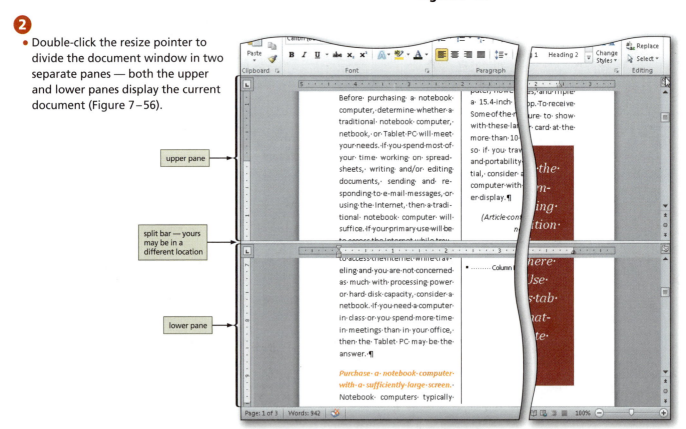

Figure 7–56

Other Ways

1. Click Split button (View tab | Window group), click at desired split location in window

2. Press ALT+CTRL+S, then ENTER

To Arrange All Open Word Documents on the Screen

If you have multiple Word documents open and want to view all of them at the same time on the screen, you can instruct Word to arrange all the open documents on the screen from top to bottom. If you wanted to arrange all open Word documents on the same screen, you would perform the following steps.

1. Click the Arrange All button (View tab | Window group) to display each open Word document on the screen.

2. To make one of the arranged documents fill the entire screen again, maximize the window by clicking its Maximize button or double-clicking its title bar.

To Copy and Paste Using Split Windows

The next step in creating the pull-quote is to copy text from the second page of the newsletter to the Clipboard and then paste the text into the text box. The item being copied is called the **source**. The location to which you are pasting is called the **destination**. Thus, the source is text in the body copy of the newsletter, and the destination is the text box. The following steps copy and then paste the text.

1

- In the upper pane, if necessary, scroll to display a portion of the text box.

- In the lower pane, scroll to display text to be copied, as shown in Figure 7–57, and then select the following text: If you anticipate running the notebook computer on batteries frequently, choose a computer that uses lithium-ion batteries

- Click the Copy button (Home tab | Clipboard group) to copy the selected text to the Clipboard (Figure 7–57).

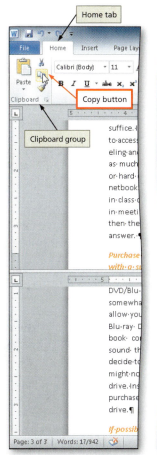
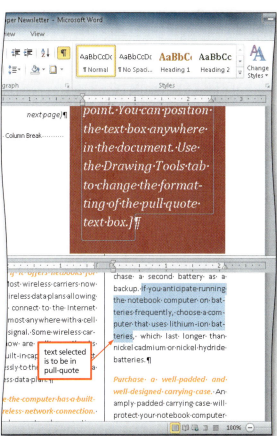

Figure 7–57

2

- In the upper pane, click the text in the text box to select it.

- Click the Paste button arrow (Home tab | Clipboard group) to display the Paste button menu.

Q&A What if I click the Paste button by mistake?

Click the Paste Options button to the right of the pasted text in the text box to display the Paste Options menu.

- Point to the Merge Formatting button on the Paste button menu and notice the text box shows a live preview of the selected paste option (Figure 7–58).

Q&A Why select the Merge Formatting button on the Paste button menu?

You want the pasted text to use the formats that were in the text box (the destination) instead of the formats of the copied text (the source).

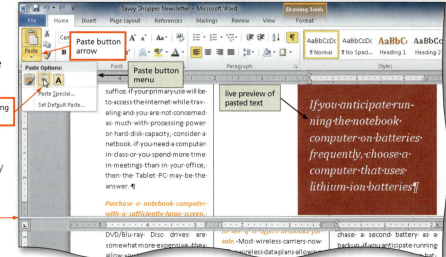

Figure 7–58

3

- Click the Merge Formatting button on the Paste button menu to paste the copied text into the text box.

Other Ways
1. Select text to copy, press CTRL+C; select destination for pasted text, press CTRL+V

To Remove a Split Window

The next step is to remove the split window so that you can continue formatting the second page of the newsletter. The following step removes a split window.

1 Double-click the split bar (shown in Figure 7–58), or click the Remove Split button (View tab | Window group), or press ALT+SHIFT+C, to remove the split window and return to a single Word window on the screen.

To Format Text in the Text Box

The next steps format the text in the pull-quote to color the text and change line spacing to 1.15.

1 If necessary, scroll to display the text box in the document window.

2 Press the PERIOD key to end the sentence in the text box.

3 Select the text in the text box.

4 Center the text in the text box.

5 Change the font size to 12 point.

6 Bold the text in the text box.

7 Click in the text box to deselect the text but leave the text box selected.

BTW

Rotating Text Box Text
To rotate text in a text box, select the text box, click the Text Direction button (Drawing Tools Format tab | Text group), and then click the desired direction on the Text Direction menu.

To Resize a Text Box and Insert a Line Break Character

The next step in formatting the pull-quote is to resize the text box. You resize a text box the same way as any other object. That is, you drag its sizing handles or enter values in the height and width boxes through the Size button (Drawing Tools Format tab | Size group). You do not want any hyphenated words in the text box. Once the text box is resized, you insert a line break character to eliminate any hyphenated words. The following steps resize the text box and insert a line break character.

1 Drag the sizing handles so that the pull-quote looks about the same size as Figure 7–59.

2 Verify the pull-quote dimensions by clicking the Size button (Drawing Tools Format tab | Size group) to display the Shape Height and Shape Width boxes and, if necessary, change the value in the Shape Height box to 3.28 and the Shape Width box to 1.45.

3 If the word, anticipate, is hyphenated in the resized pull-quote, position the insertion point to the left of the a in anticipate and then press SHIFT+ENTER to insert a line break character, which places the word on the next line and removes the hyphen (Figure 7–59).

BTW

Saving to the Text Box Gallery
To save a text box you have created and formatted so that it appears as a selection in the Text Box gallery, do the following: select the text box, click the Text Box button (Insert tab | Text group), click Save Selection to Text Box Gallery, type a name and description (Create New Building Block dialog box), and then click the OK button.

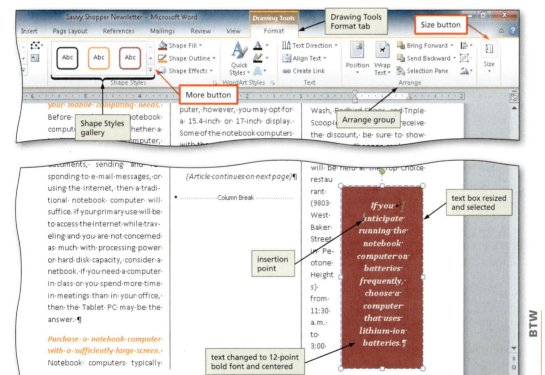

Figure 7–59

To Apply a Shape Style to a Text Box

The next step in formatting the pull-quote is to apply a shape style to the text box to coordinate its colors with the rest of the newsletter. The following steps apply a shape style to a text box.

1 With the text box still selected, click the More button (shown in Figure 7–59) in the Shape Styles gallery (Drawing Tools Format tab | Shape Styles group) to expand the gallery.

BTW

Text Box Styles
Like other drawing objects or pictures, text boxes can be formatted or have styles applied. You can change the fill in a text box by clicking the Shape Fill button (Drawing Tools Format tab | Shape Styles group), add an outline to a text box by clicking the Shape Outline button (Drawing Tools Format tab | Shape Styles group), and apply an effect such as shadow or 3-D effects by clicking the Shape Effects button (Drawing Tools Format tab | Shape Styles group).

2 Point to Intense Effect - Dark Blue, Accent 3 (fourth style, last row) in the Shape Styles gallery to display a live preview of that style applied to the text box (Figure 7–60).

3 Click to Intense Effect - Dark Blue, Accent 3 in the Shape Styles gallery to apply the selected style to the shape.

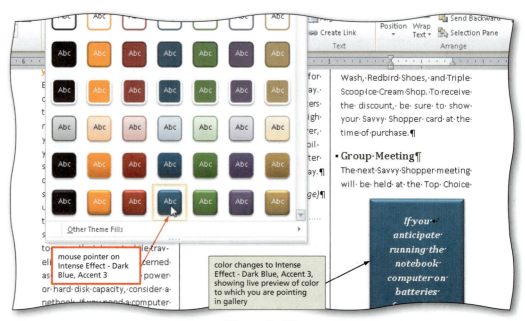

mouse pointer on Intense Effect - Dark Blue, Accent 3

color changes to Intense Effect - Dark Blue, Accent 3, showing live preview of color to which you are pointing in gallery

Figure 7–60

To Position a Text Box

The final step is to position the pull-quote text box between the first and second columns of the newsletter. The following step moves the text box to the desired location.

1

• With the text box still selected, drag the text box to its new location (Figure 7–61). You may need to drag and/or resize the text box a couple of times so that it looks similar to this figure.

• Click outside the text box to remove the selection.

Why does my text wrap differently around the text box?

Differences in wordwrap often relate to the printer used by your computer. Thus, your document may wordwrap around the text box differently.

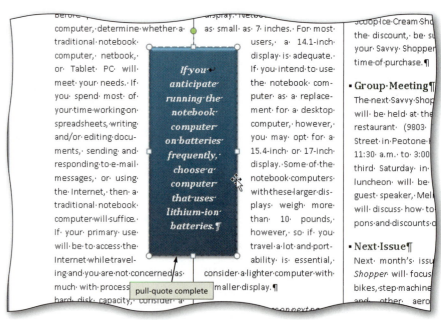

pull-quote complete

Figure 7–61

To Save a Document Again

You have performed several steps since the last save. You should save the newsletter again.

1 Save the newsletter again with the same file name, Savvy Shopper Newsletter.

Break Point: If you wish to take a break, this is a good place to do so. You can quit Word now. To resume at a later time, start Word, open the file called Savvy Shopper Newsletter, and continue following the steps from this location forward.

Formatting the Second Page of the Newsletter

The second page of the newsletter (Figure 7–1b on page WD 403) continues the feature article that began in the first two columns on the first page. The nameplate on the second page is less elaborate than the one on the first page of the newsletter. In addition to the text in the feature article, page two contains a graphic. The following pages format the second page of the newsletter in this project.

Create the nameplate.
The top of the inner pages of a newsletter may or may not have a nameplate. If you choose to create one for your inner pages, it should not be the same as, or compete with, the one on the first page. Inner page nameplates usually contain only a portion of the nameplate from the first page of a newsletter.

Plan Ahead

To Change Column Formatting

The document currently is formatted in three columns. The nameplate at the top of the second page, however, should be in a single column. The next step, then, is to change the number of columns at the top of the second page from three to one.

As discussed earlier in this project, Word requires a new section each time you change the number of columns in a document. Thus, you first must insert a continuous section break and then format the section to one column so that the nameplate can be entered on the second page of the newsletter. The following steps insert a continuous section break and then change the column format.

1

- If you have a blank page between the first and second pages of the newsletter, position the insertion point to the left of the paragraph mark at the end of the third column on the first page of the newsletter and then press the DELETE key to delete the blank line causing the overflow.

- Scroll through the document and then position the mouse pointer at the upper-left corner of the second page of the newsletter (to the left of B in Be).

- Display the Page Layout tab.

- Click the Insert Page and Section Breaks button (Page Layout tab | Page Setup group) to display the Insert Page and Section Breaks gallery (Figure 7–62).

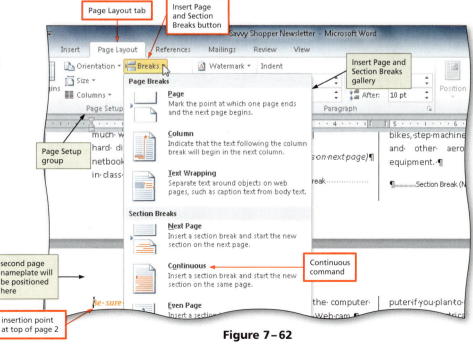

Figure 7–62

2

• Click Continuous in the Insert Page and Section Breaks gallery to insert a continuous section break above the insertion point.

• Press the UP ARROW key to position the insertion point to the left of the continuous section break just inserted.

• Click the Columns button (Page Layout tab | Page Setup group) to display the Columns gallery (Figure 7–63).

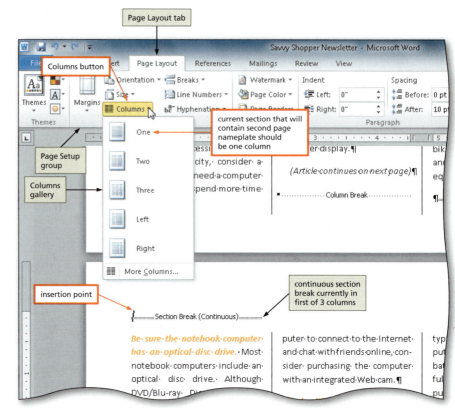

Figure 7–63

3

• Click One in the Columns gallery to format the current section to one column, which now is ready for the second page nameplate (Figure 7–64).

Q&A

Can I change the column format of existing text?

Yes. If you already have typed text and would like it to be formatted in a different number of columns, select the text, click the Columns button (Page Layout tab | Page Setup group), and then click the number of columns desired in the Columns gallery. Word automatically creates a new section for the newly formatted columns.

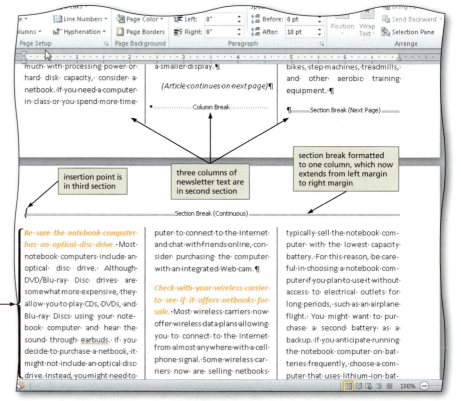

Figure 7–64

To Set Custom Tab Stops Using the Tabs Dialog Box

The nameplate on the second page of the newsletter contains the text, Monthly Newsletter, at the left margin, the newsletter title in the center, and the issue number at the right margin (shown in Figure 7–1a on page WD 403). To properly align the text in the center and at the right margin, you will set custom tab stops at these locations. The following steps set custom tab stops.

1 Press the ENTER key twice and then position the insertion point on the first line of the second page of the newsletter, which is the paragraph to be formatted with the custom tab stops.

2 Click the Paragraph Dialog Box Launcher (Page Layout tab | Paragraph group) to display the Paragraph dialog box and then click the Tabs button (Paragraph dialog box) to display the Tabs dialog box.

3 Type   3.5   in the Tab stop position text box (Tabs dialog box), click Center in the Alignment area to specify the tab stop alignment, and then click the Set button to set the custom tab stop.

4 Type   7   in the Tab stop position text box (Tabs dialog box), click Right in the Alignment area to specify the tab stop alignment, and then click the Set button to set the custom tab stop (Figure 7–65).

5 Click the OK button to place tab markers at the specified locations using the specified alignments.

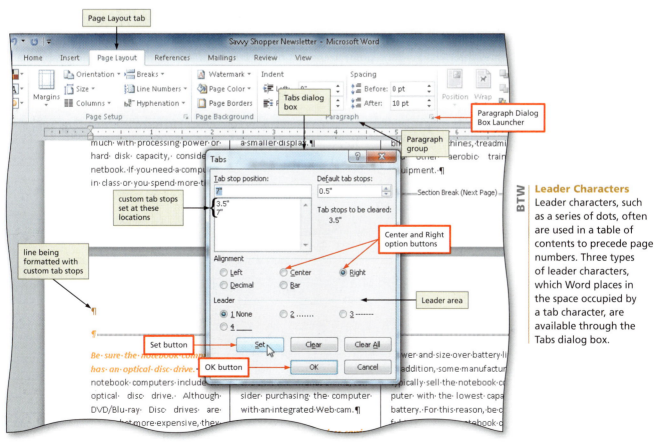

BTW

Leader Characters
Leader characters, such as a series of dots, often are used in a table of contents to precede page numbers. Three types of leader characters, which Word places in the space occupied by a tab character, are available through the Tabs dialog box.

Figure 7–65

To Format and Enter Text and Add a Border

The following steps enter the newsletter title at the top of the second page in the third section.

1 With the insertion point on the first line of the second page of the newsletter, display the Home tab and then, if necessary, click the Bold and Italic buttons (Home tab | Font group) to remove those formats. Type **Monthly Newsletter** at the left margin.

2 Press the TAB key to advance the insertion point to the centered tab stop. Increase the font size to 14 point and then click the Bold button (Home tab | Font group) to bold the text. Type **Savvy Shopper** at the centered tab stop.

3 Press the TAB key to advance the insertion point to the right-aligned tab stop. Reduce the font size to 11 point and then click the Bold button (Home tab | Font group) to turn off the bold format. Type **Issue 33** at the right-aligned tab stop.

4 Click the Borders button arrow (Home tab | Paragraph group) to display the Borders gallery and then click Bottom Border in the list (shown in Figure 7–66).

Q&A Why is the border formatted already?

When you define a custom border, Word uses that custom border the next time you click the Border button in the Border gallery.

To Enter Text

The second page of the feature article on the second page of this newsletter begins with a jump-from line (the continued message) immediately below the nameplate. The following steps enter the jump-from line.

1 Position the insertion point to the left of the B in Be at the top of the first column on the second page and then press the ENTER key.

2 Press the UP ARROW key to move the insertion point to the blank line.

3 Click the Clear Formatting button (Home tab | Font group) to remove formatting from the location of the insertion point.

4 Press CTRL+I to turn on the italic format.

5 Type **(Continued from first page)** and then press CTRL+I to turn off the italic format (Figure 7–66).

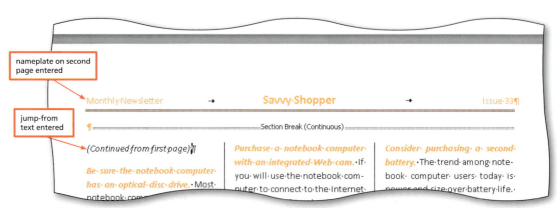

Figure 7–66

To Balance Columns

Currently, the text on the second page of the newsletter completely fills up the first and second columns and almost fills the third column. The text in the three columns should consume the same amount of vertical space. That is, the three columns should be balanced. To balance columns, you insert a continuous section break at the end of the text. The following steps balance columns.

 1

- Scroll to the bottom of the text in the third column on the second page of the newsletter and then position the insertion point at the end of the text.

- If an extra paragraph mark is below the last line of text, press the DELETE key to remove the extra paragraph mark.

- Display the Page Layout tab.

- Click the Insert Page and Section Breaks button (Page Layout tab | Page Setup group) to display the Insert Page and Section Breaks gallery (Figure 7–67).

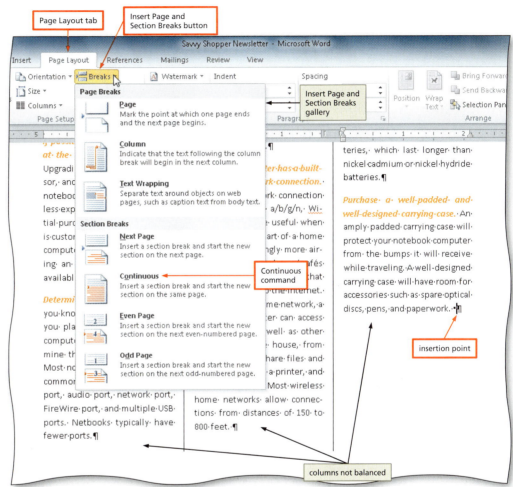

Figure 7–67

 2

- Click Continuous in the Insert Page and Section Breaks gallery to insert a continuous section break, which balances the columns on the second page of the newsletter (Figure 7–68).

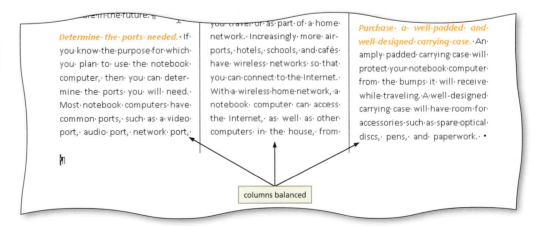

Figure 7–68

To Save a Document Again

You have performed several steps since the last save. Thus, you should save the newsletter again.

1 Save the newsletter again with the same file name, Savvy Shopper Newsletter.

Modifying and Formatting a SmartArt Graphic

Recall from Chapter 4 that Microsoft Office 2010 includes **SmartArt graphics**, which are visual representations of ideas. Many different types of SmartArt graphics are available, allowing you to choose one that illustrates your message best.

In this newsletter, a SmartArt graphic is positioned on the second page, in the second and third columns. Because the columns are small in the newsletter, it is best to work with a SmartArt graphic in a separate document window so that you easily can see all of its components. When finished editing the graphic, you can copy and paste it in the newsletter. You will follow these steps for the SmartArt graphic in this newsletter:

1. Open the document that contains the SmartArt graphic for the newsletter.
2. Modify the layout of the graphic.
3. Add a shape and text to the graphic.
4. Format a shape and the graphic.
5. Copy and paste the graphic in the newsletter.
6. Resize the graphic and position it in the desired location.

To Open a Document from Word

The first draft of the SmartArt graphic is in a file called Savvy Shopper Notebook Extras Diagram on the Data Files for Students. See the inside back cover of this book for instructions on downloading the Data Files for Students, or contact your instructor for information about accessing the required files. The following steps open the Savvy Shopper Notebook Extras Diagram file.

1 With your USB flash drive connected to one of the computer's USB ports, open the Backstage view and then click Open to display the Open dialog box.

2 Navigate to the location of the file to be opened (in this case, the Chapter 07 folder in the Word folder in the Data Files for Students folder on a USB flash drive).

3 Click Savvy Shopper Notebook Extras Diagram to select the file name.

4 Click the Open button (Open dialog box) to open the selected file.

5 Click the graphic to select it and display the SmartArt Tools Design and Format tabs (Figure 7–69).

Q&A Is the Savvy Shopper Newsletter file still open?

Yes. Leave it open because you will copy the modified diagram to the second page of the newsletter.

BTW

Certification
The Microsoft Office Specialist (MOS) program provides an opportunity for you to obtain a valuable industry credential — proof that you have the Word 2010 skills required by employers. For more information, visit the Word 2010 Certification Web page (scsite.com/wd2010/cert).

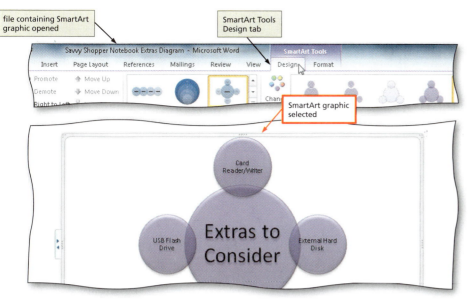

Figure 7–69

To Change the Layout of a SmartArt Graphic

The SmartArt graphic currently uses the Radial Venn layout. This newsletter uses the Converging Radial layout. The following step changes the layout of an existing SmartArt graphic.

1

- If necessary, display the SmartArt Tools Design tab.

- Scroll through the layouts in the Layouts gallery until Converging Radial appears (that is, click the up or down scroll arrows to scroll through the in-Ribbon gallery) and then click Converging Radial to change the layout of the SmartArt graphic (Figure 7–70).

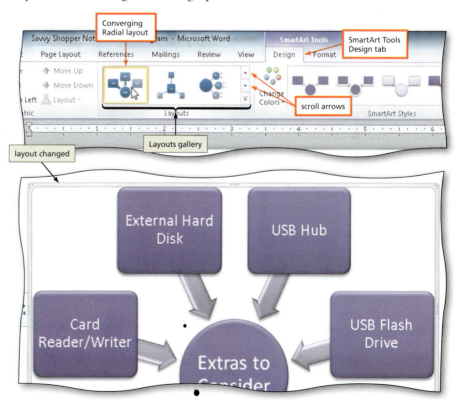

Figure 7–70

Other Ways	
1. Right-click the selected graphic, click Change Layout on shortcut menu, select desired layout	(Choose a SmartArt Graphic dialog box), click OK button

To Add a Shape to a SmartArt Graphic

The current SmartArt graphic has four perimeter shapes. This newsletter has a fifth shape. The following step adds a shape to a SmartArt graphic.

1 With the diagram selected, click the Add Shape button (SmartArt Tools Design tab | Create Graphic group) to add a shape to the SmartArt graphic (Figure 7–71).

Q&A Why did my screen display a menu instead of adding a shape?

You clicked the Add Shape button arrow instead of the Add Shape button. Clicking the Add Shape button adds the shape automatically; clicking the Add Shape button arrow displays a menu allowing you to specify the location of the shape.

Q&A How do I delete a shape?

Select the shape by clicking it and then press the DELETE key, or right-click the shape and then click Cut on the shortcut menu.

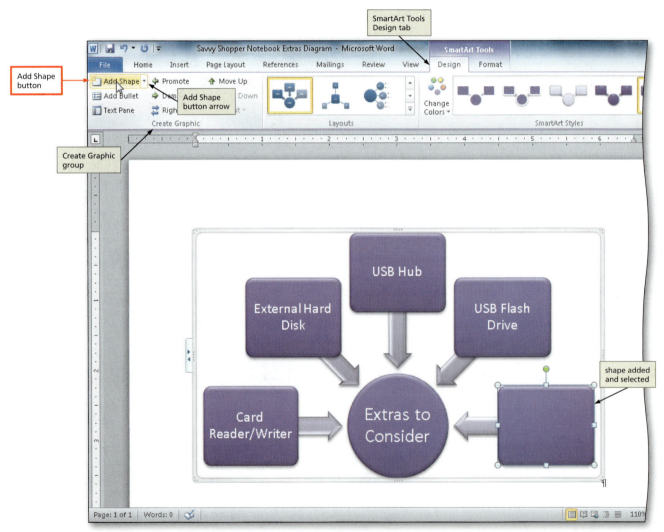

Figure 7–71

To Add Text to a SmartArt Graphic through the Text Pane

In Chapter 4, you added text directly to the shapes in a SmartArt graphic. In this project, you enter the text through the Text Pane. The following steps use the Text Pane to add text to a shape.

1
- Click the Text Pane button (SmartArt Tools Design tab | Create Graphic group) to display the Text Pane to the left of the SmartArt graphic.

2
- In the Text Pane, if necessary, position the insertion point to the right of the bullet that has no text to its right.

- Type **Wireless Mouse** as the text for the shape (Figure 7–72).

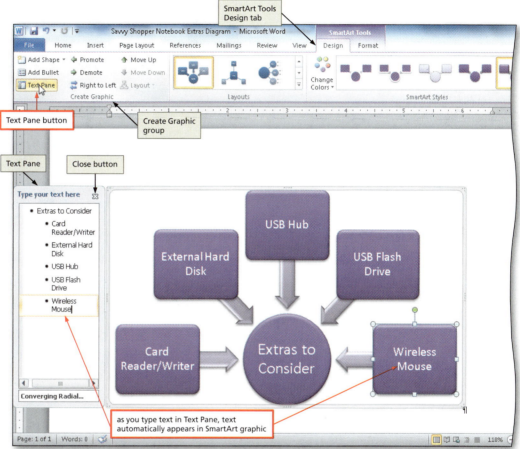

Figure 7–72

3
- Click the Text Pane button (SmartArt Tools Design tab | Create Graphic group) to close the Text Pane.

Q&A Can I instead close the Text Pane by clicking the Close button on the Text Pane?

Yes.

BTW

Demoting Text Pane Text
Instead of pressing the TAB key in the Text Pane, you could click the Demote button (SmartArt Tools Design tab | Create Graphic group) to increase (or move to the right) the indent for a bullet. You also can click the Promote button (SmartArt Tools Design tab | Create Graphic group) to decrease (or move to the left) the indent for a bullet.

To Adjust a Shape's Size

You want the circle shape to be slightly smaller in the SmartArt graphic. The following steps reduce the size of a shape in a SmartArt graphic.

1
- Click the circle shape in the middle of the SmartArt graphic to select it.

2
- Display the SmartArt Tools Format tab.

- Click the Smaller button (SmartArt Tools Format tab | Shapes group) to reduce the size of the selected shape (Figure 7–73).

Q&A Can I increase the size of a shape?

Yes. Select the shape and then click the Larger button (SmartArt Tools Format tab | Shapes group). You also can change a shape by clicking the Change Shape button (SmartArt Tools Format tab | Shapes group).

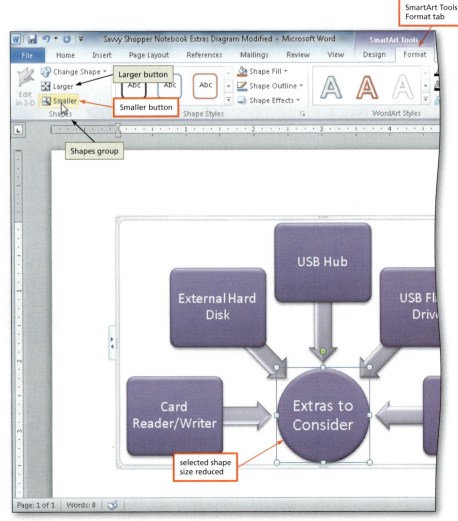

Figure 7–73

To Format SmartArt Graphic Text

To format text in an entire SmartArt graphic, select the graphic and then apply the format. The following steps bold the text in the SmartArt graphic.

1 If necessary, double-click the graphic to select it.

2 Display the Home tab. Click the Bold button (Home tab | Font group) to bold the text in the SmartArt graphic (shown in Figure 7–74 on page WD 454).

TO MODIFY THEME EFFECTS

If you wanted to change the look of graphics such as SmartArt graphics, you could perform the following steps to change the theme effects.

1. Click the Theme Effects button (Page Layout tab | Themes group).
2. Click the desired effect in the Theme Effects gallery.

TO SAVE CUSTOMIZED THEMES

When you modify the theme effects, theme colors, or theme fonts, you can save the modified theme for future use. If you wanted to save a customized theme, you would perform the following steps.

1. Click the Themes button (Page Layout tab | Themes group) to display the Themes gallery.
2. Click Save Current Theme in the Themes gallery.
3. Enter a theme name in the File name text box.
4. Click the Save button to add the saved theme to the Themes gallery.

To Save an Active Document with a New File Name

To preserve the contents of the original Savvy Shopper Notebook Extras Diagram file, you should save the active document with a new file name. The following steps save the active document with a new file name.

1 With the USB flash drive containing the Savvy Shopper Notebook Extras Diagram file connected to one of the computer's USB ports, open the Backstage view and then click Save As to display the Save As dialog box.

2 Navigate to the location of the file to be saved (in this case, the Word folder in the CIS 101 folder [or your class folder] on a USB flash drive).

3 Save the document with the file name, Savvy Shopper Notebook Extras Diagram Modified.

Copying and Pasting

The next step is to copy the SmartArt graphic from this document window and then paste it in the newsletter. To copy from one document and paste into another, you can use the Office Clipboard. Through the Office Clipboard, you can copy multiple items from any Office document and then paste them into the same or another Office document by following these general guidelines:

1. Items are copied *from* a **source document**. If the source document is not the active document, display it in the document window.
2. Display the Office Clipboard task pane and then copy items from the source document to the Office Clipboard.
3. Items are copied *to* a **destination document**. If the destination document is not the active document, display the destination document in the document window.
4. Paste items from the Office Clipboard to the destination document.

BTW

BTWs
For a complete list of the BTWs found in the margins of this book, visit the Word 2010 BTW Web page (scsite.com/wd2010/btw).

To Copy a SmartArt Graphic Using the Office Clipboard

You can copy multiple items to the Office Clipboard through the Clipboard task pane and then paste them later. The following step copies the SmartArt graphic to the Office Clipboard.

- Click the Clipboard Dialog Box Launcher (Home tab | Clipboard group) to display the Clipboard task pane.

- If the Office Clipboard in the Clipboard task pane is not empty, click the Clear All button in the Clipboard task pane.

- With the SmartArt graphic selected in the document window, click the Copy button (Home tab | Clipboard group) to copy the selected text to the Clipboard (Figure 7–74).

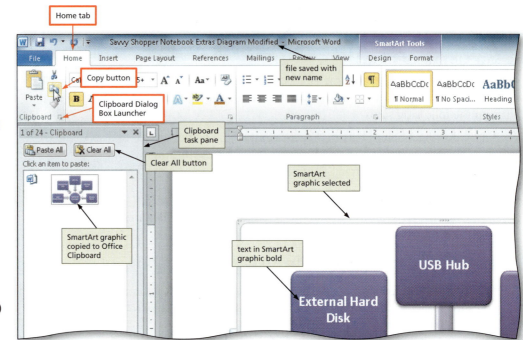

Figure 7–74

Other Ways

1. With Clipboard task pane displayed, right-click selected item, click Copy on shortcut menu

2. With Clipboard task pane displayed and item to copy selected, press CTRL+C

To Switch from One Open Document to Another

The steps below switch from the open Savvy Shopper Notebook Extras Diagram Modified document (the source document) to the open Savvy Shopper Newsletter document (the destination document).

- Point to the Word program button on the taskbar to display a live preview of the open documents or window titles of the open documents, depending on your computer's configuration (Figure 7–75).

- Click the live preview of the Savvy Shopper Newsletter on the Windows taskbar to display the selected document in the document window (shown in Figure 7–76).

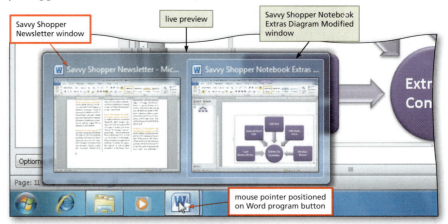

Figure 7–75

Other Ways

1. Click Switch Windows button (View tab | Window group), click document name

2. Press ALT+TAB

To Paste from the Office Clipboard

The next step is to paste the copied SmartArt graphic into the destination document, in this case, the newsletter document. The following steps paste from the Office Clipboard.

- If the Clipboard task pane is not displayed on the screen, display the Home tab and then click the Clipboard Dialog Box Launcher (Home tab | Clipboard group) to display the Clipboard task pane.

- Click the SmartArt graphic entry in the Office Clipboard to paste it in the document at the location of the insertion point (Figure 7–76).

Q&A Does the destination document have to be a different document?

No. The source and destination documents can be the same document.

Q&A What is the function of the Paste All button?

If you have multiple items in the Office Clipboard, it pastes all items in a row, without any characters between them, at the location of the insertion point or selection.

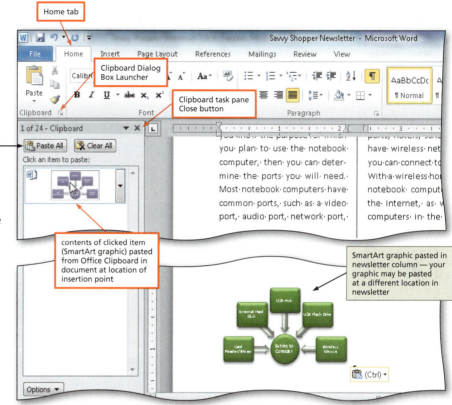

Figure 7–76

- Click the Close button in the Clipboard task pane.

Other Ways
1. With Clipboard task pane displayed, right-click selected item, click Paste on shortcut menu   2. With Clipboard task pane displayed, press CTRL+V

To Format a Graphic as Floating

The text in the newsletter should wrap tightly around the graphic; that is, the text should conform to the graphic's shape. Thus, the next step is to change the graphic from inline to floating with a wrapping style of tight. The following steps format the graphic as floating with tight wrapping.

1. If necessary, double-click the SmartArt graphic to select it.

2. Display the SmartArt Tools Format tab.

3. With the SmartArt graphic selected, click the Arrange button (SmartArt Tools Format tab | Arrange group) and then click the Wrap Text button on the Arrange menu to display the Wrap Text menu.

4. Click Tight on the Wrap Text menu to change the graphic from inline to floating with tight wrapping.

BTW

Clipboard Task Pane and Office Clipboard Icon
You can control when the Clipboard task pane appears on the Word screen and the Office Clipboard icon appears in the notification area on the taskbar. To do this, first display the Clipboard task pane by clicking the Clipboard Dialog Box Launcher. Next, click the Options button at the bottom of the Clipboard task pane and then click the desired option on the menu. For example, if you want to be able to display the Clipboard task pane by clicking the Office Clipboard icon on the Windows taskbar, click the Show Office Clipboard Icon on Taskbar command on the Options menu.

BTW

Space around Graphics

The space between a graphic and the text, which sometimes is called the run-around, should be at least 1/8" and should be the same for all graphics in a document. Adjust the run-around of a selected floating graphic by doing the following: click the Arrange button (SmartArt Tools Format tab | Arrange group), click the Object Position button, click More Layout Options on the Object Position menu, click the Text Wrapping tab (Layout dialog box), adjust the values in the 'Distance from text' boxes, and then click the OK button.

To Resize and Position the SmartArt Graphic

The next task is to increase the size of the SmartArt graphic and then position it in the second and third columns on the second page. The following steps resize and then position the graphic.

 Drag the sizing handles outward until the graphic is approximately the same size as shown in Figure 7–77, which has a height of 2.3" and a width of 2.8".

2 Point to the frame on the graphic and when the mouse has a four-headed arrow attached to it, drag the graphic to the location shown in Figure 7–77. You may have to drag the graphic a couple of times to position it similarly to the figure.

3 If the newsletter spills onto a third page, reduce the size of the SmartArt graphic. You may need to delete an extra paragraph mark at the end of the document, as well.

To Layer the SmartArt Graphic in Front of Text

Notice in Figure 7–77 that the ruling line covers the SmartArt graphic. In Word, you can layer objects on top of or behind other objects. The following steps layer the SmartArt graphic on top of all text.

1

- If necessary, click the SmartArt graphic to select it. Click the Arrange button (SmartArt Tools Format tab | Arrange group) to display the Arrange menu.

- Click the Bring Forward button arrow to display the Bring Forward menu (Figure 7–77).

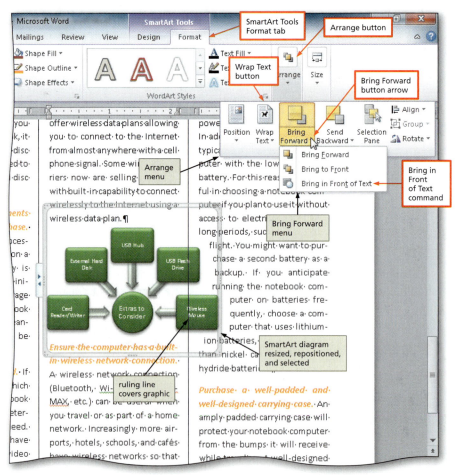

Figure 7–77

- Click Bring in Front of Text on the Bring Forward menu to position the selected object on top of all text, which in this case, positions the SmartArt graphic on top of the border (Figure 7–78).

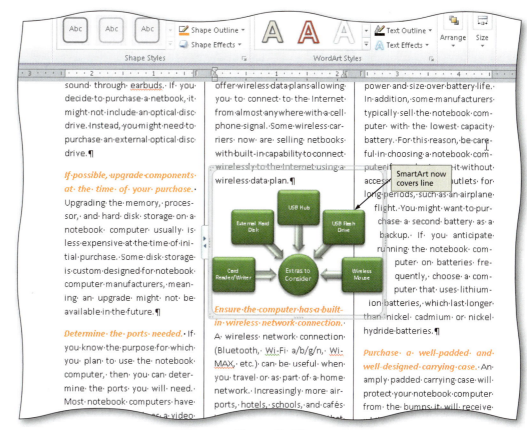

- Click outside the graphic so that it no longer is selected.

Figure 7–78

Finishing the Newsletter

With the text and graphics in the newsletter entered and formatted, the next step is to view the newsletter as a whole and determine if it looks finished in its current state. To give the newsletter a finished appearance, you will add a border to its edges.

To Zoom Two Pages

The last step in formatting the newsletter is to place a border around its edges. You can place both pages in the document window at once so that you can see all the page borders applied. The following steps zoom two pages.

1. Display the View tab.

2. Click the Two Pages button (View tab | Zoom group) to display both entire pages of the newsletter in the document window (shown in Figure 7–79 on the next page).

BTW

Quick Reference
For a table that lists how to complete the tasks covered in this book using the mouse, Ribbon, shortcut menu, and keyboard, see the Quick Reference Summary at the back of this book, or visit the Word 2010 Quick Reference Web page (scsite.com/wd2010/qr).

To Add an Art Page Border

This newsletter has orange art border around the perimeter of each page. The steps on the next page add a page border around the pages of the newsletter.

- Display the Page Layout tab.

- Click the Page Borders button (Page Layout tab | Page Background group) to display the Borders and Shading dialog box. If necessary, click the Page Border tab.

Q&A

What if I cannot select the Page Borders button because it is dimmed?

Click somewhere in the newsletter to make the newsletter the active document and then repeat Step 1.

- Click Box in the Setting area (Borders and Shading dialog box) to specify a border on all four sides.

- Click the Art box arrow, scroll to and then click the art border shown in Figure 7–79.

- Click the Width box down arrow until the box displays 8 pt.

- Click the Color box arrow and then click Orange, Accent 1, Darker 50% (sixth row, fifth column) on the palette (Figure 7–79).

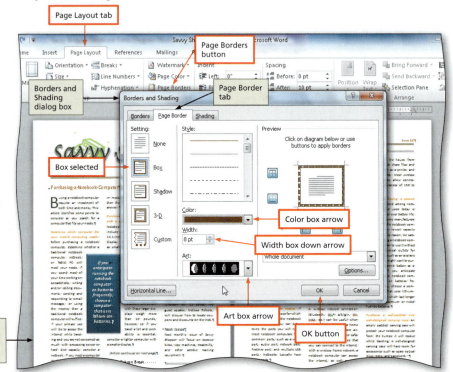

Page Layout tab

Page Borders button

Borders and Shading dialog box

Page Border tab

Box selected

Color box arrow

Width box down arrow

Art box arrow

OK button

both pages are displayed in document window

Figure 7–79

- Click the OK button to place the defined border on each page of the newsletter (Figure 7–80).

border added

Figure 7–80

To Save and Print the Document, Then Quit Word

The newsletter now is complete. You should save the document, print it, and then quit Word.

1 Save the newsletter again with the same file name.

2 Print the newsletter (shown in Figure 7–1 on page WD 403).

Q&A What if an error message appears about margins?

Depending on the printer you are using, you may need to set the margins differently for this project.

Q&A What if one or more of the borders do not print?

Click the Page Borders button (Page Layout tab | Page Background group), click the Options button (Borders and Shading dialog box), click the Measure from box arrow and click Text, change the four text boxes to 15 pt, and then click the OK button in each dialog box. Try printing the document again. If the borders still do not print, adjust the text boxes in the dialog box to a number smaller than 15 point.

3 Quit Word, closing all open documents.

BTW

Conserving Ink and Toner
If you want to conserve ink or toner, you can instruct Word to print draft quality documents by clicking File on the Ribbon to open the Backstage view, clicking Options in the Backstage view to display the Word Options dialog box, clicking Advanced in the left pane (Word Options dialog box), scrolling to the Print area in the right pane, placing a check mark in the 'Use draft quality' check box, and then clicking the OK button. Then, use the Backstage view to print the document as usual.

Chapter Summary

In this chapter, you have learned how to create a professional-looking newsletter using Word's desktop publishing features such as WordArt, columns, horizontal and vertical rules, and pull-quotes. The items listed below include all the new Word skills you have learned in this chapter.

1. Set Custom Margins (WD 405)
2. Insert WordArt (WD 407)
3. Change the WordArt Fill Color (WD 410)
4. Change the WordArt Shape (WD 413)
5. Set Custom Tab Stops Using the Tabs Dialog Box (WD 413)
6. Border One Edge of a Paragraph (WD 415)
7. Crop a Graphic (WD 418)
8. Use the Selection Pane (WD 421)
9. Rotate a Graphic (WD 421)
10. Insert a Continuous Section Break (WD 425)
11. Change the Number of Columns (WD 426)
12. Justify a Paragraph (WD 427)
13. Insert a File in a Column of the Newsletter (WD 428)
14. Increase Column Width and Place a Vertical Rule between Columns (WD 429)
15. Hyphenate a Document (WD 430)
16. Format a Character as a Drop Cap (WD 431)
17. Insert a Next Page Section Break (WD 433)
18. Insert a Column Break (WD 434)
19. Insert a Text Box (WD 437)
20. Split the Window (WD 438)
21. Arrange All Open Word Documents on the Screen (WD 439)
22. Copy and Paste Using Split Windows (WD 439)
23. Remove a Split Window (WD 440)
24. Position a Text Box (WD 442)
25. Change Column Formatting (WD 443)
26. Balance Columns (WD 447)
27. Change the Layout of a SmartArt Graphic (WD 449)
28. Modify Theme Effects (WD 453)
29. Save Customized Themes (WD 453)
30. Add Text to a SmartArt Graphic through the Text Pane (WD 451)
31. Adjust a Shape's Size (WD 452)
32. Copy a SmartArt Graphic Using the Office Clipboard (WD 454)
33. Switch from One Open Document to Another (WD 454)
34. Paste from the Office Clipboard (WD 455)
35. Layer the SmartArt Graphic in Front of Text (WD 456)
36. Add an Art Page Border (WD 457)

Learn It Online

Test your knowledge of chapter content and key terms.

Instructions: To complete the Learn It Online exercises, start your browser, click the Address bar, and then enter the Web address `scsite.com/wd2010/learn`. When the Word 2010 Learn It Online page is displayed, click the link for the exercise you want to complete and then read the instructions.

Chapter Reinforcement TF, MC, and SA
A series of true/false, multiple choice, and short answer questions that test your knowledge of the chapter content.

Flash Cards
An interactive learning environment where you identify chapter key terms associated with displayed definitions.

Practice Test
A series of multiple choice questions that test your knowledge of chapter content and key terms.

Who Wants To Be a Computer Genius?
An interactive game that challenges your knowledge of chapter content in the style of a television quiz show.

Wheel of Terms
An interactive game that challenges your knowledge of chapter key terms in the style of the television show *Wheel of Fortune*.

Crossword Puzzle Challenge
A crossword puzzle that challenges your knowledge of key terms presented in the chapter.

Apply Your Knowledge

Reinforce the skills and apply the concepts you learned in this chapter.

Working with Desktop Publishing Elements of a Newsletter

Note: To complete this assignment, you will be required to use the Data Files for Students. See the inside back cover of this book for instructions on downloading the Data Files for Students, or contact your instructor for information about accessing the required files.

Instructions: Start Word. Open the document, Apply 7-1 Career Finders Newsletter Draft, from the Data Files for Students. The document contains a newsletter that you are to modify (Figure 7–81).

Perform the following tasks:

1. Change the WordArt shape to Chevron Down.
2. Change the column width of the columns in the body of the newsletter to 2.2".
3. Add a vertical rule (line) between each column.
4. Insert a column break immediately to the left of the R in the Resources heading.
5. Change the style of the pull-quote (text box) to Light 1 Outline, Colored Fill - Tan, Accent 5.
6. Format the first paragraph with a drop cap.
7. Change the alignment of the paragraph containing the drop cap from left-aligned to justified.
8. Change the layout of the SmartArt graphic to Vertical Process.
9. Use the Text Pane to add the text, Continuing Education, to the bottom shape in the SmartArt graphic.
10. If necessary, move the SmartArt graphic and the pull-quote so that they are positioned similarly to the ones in Figure 7–81.
11. Change the document properties as specified by your instructor.
12. Save the modified file with the file name, Apply 7-1 Career Finders Newsletter Modified.
13. Submit the revised newsletter in the format specified by your instructor.

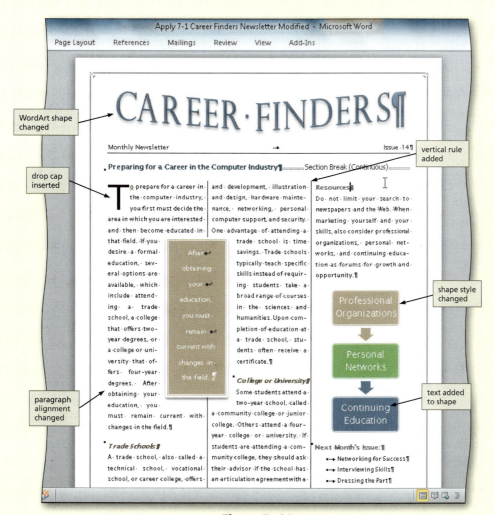

Figure 7–81

Extend Your Knowledge

Extend the skills you learned in this chapter and experiment with new skills. You may need to use Help to complete the assignment.

Adding a Table to a Newsletter and Enhancing a Nameplate

Note: To complete this assignment, you will be required to use the Data Files for Students. See the inside back cover of this book for instructions on downloading the Data Files for Students, or contact your instructor for information about accessing the required files.

Instructions: Start Word. Open the document, Extend 7-1 Classroom Chatter Newsletter Draft, from the Data Files for Students. You will add a table to the bottom of the newsletter, change the format of the WordArt, format the drop cap, adjust the hyphenation rules, move the page border closer to the text, clear tabs, and insert leader characters.

Perform the following tasks:

1. Use Help to review how to create and format a table, if necessary, and to learn about WordArt options, borders, hyphenation, and tabs.

Continued >

Extend Your Knowledge *continued*

2. Insert a continuous section break at the end of the third column of the newsletter to balance the columns. Change the number of columns in the new section from three to one. Change the style of the paragraph in the new section to No Spacing. Use the Insert Table command on the Insert Table menu (Insert tab | Table group) to display the Insert Table dialog box and then use the dialog box to insert a table that has five rows and four columns. Then, merge the cells in the first row. Enter the data in the table as shown in Figure 7–82. Format the table using a table style of your preference.

3. Change the WordArt to a style to use at least two WordArt style text effects. Change the color of the WordArt text outline. Change the color of the WordArt text fill color.

4. Add a shape fill color to the text box surrounding the WordArt.

5. Add a drop cap to the first paragraph in the body of the newsletter. Change the number of lines to drop from three to two lines.

6. Change the hyphenation rules to limit consecutive hyphens to two and the hyphenation zone to .3".

7. Change the page border so that the border is closer to the text.

8. If the newsletter flows to two pages, reduce the size of elements such as WordArt or pull-quote or the table, or adjust spacing above or below paragraphs so that the newsletter fits on a single page. Make any other necessary adjustments to the newsletter.

9. Clear the tabs in the issue information line in the nameplate. Use the Tabs dialog box to insert a right-aligned tab stop at the 6.5" mark. Fill the tab space with a leader character of your choice.

10. Change the document properties as specified by your instructor.

11. Save the revised document with a new file name and then submit it in the format specified by your instructor.

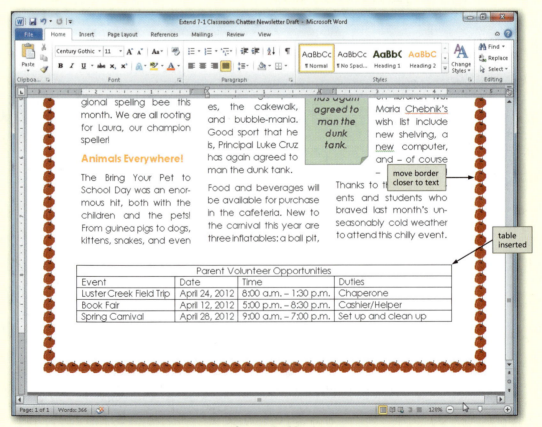

Figure 7–82

Make It Right

Analyze a document and correct all errors and/or improve the design.

Formatting a Newsletter

Note: To complete this assignment, you will be required to use the Data Files for Students. See the inside back cover of this book for instructions on downloading the Data Files for Students, or contact your instructor for information about accessing the required files.

Instructions: Start Word. Open the document, Make It Right 7-1 IT Club Newsletter Draft, from the Data Files for Students. The document is a newsletter whose elements are not formatted properly (Figure 7–83). You are to edit and format the WordArt, format the clip art image and columns, change tab stop alignment, change paragraph alignment, add a drop cap, format the pull-quote (text box), and add a border.

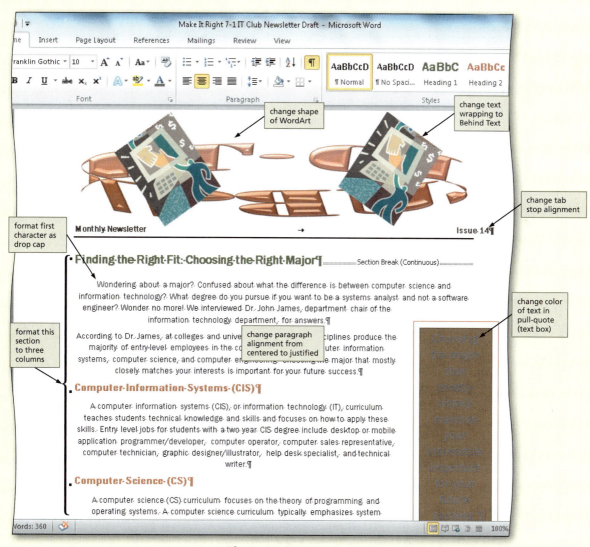

Figure 7–83

Continued >

Make It Right *continued*

Perform the following tasks:

1. Change the shape of the WordArt so that the text is more readable.

2. Format the clip art images in the nameplate to Behind Text. Crop the clip art images so that most of the dollar signs on their right edge are not visible. (*Hint:* Use the Selection and Visibility task pane to select each image.) If necessary, adjust the location and size of the clip art images so that they have a pleasing appearance in the nameplate.

3. Change the alignment of the custom tab stop at the 6.5" mark in the issue information line from centered to right-aligned.

4. Change the number of columns in the body of the newsletter from one to two.

5. Change all paragraphs of text from centered to justified paragraph alignment.

6. Format the first letter in the first paragraph of text as a drop cap. Color the drop cap.

7. Change the color of the text in the pull-quote (text box) so that it is easier to read. Position the pull-quote at the right edge of the newsletter.

8. Add an attractive border around the edge of the newsletter. Do not use the default single line, black border.

9. If the newsletter flows to two pages, reduce the size of elements such as WordArt or clip art or the pull-quote, or adjust spacing above or below paragraphs so that the newsletter fits on a single page. Make any other necessary adjustments to the newsletter.

10. Change the document properties, as specified by your instructor. Save the revised document with a new file name and then submit it in the format specified by your instructor.

In the Lab

Design and/or create a document using the guidelines, concepts, and skills presented in this chapter. Labs are listed in order of increasing difficulty.

Lab 1: Creating a Newsletter with a SmartArt Graphic and an Article on File

Note: To complete this assignment, you will be required to use the Data Files for Students. See the inside back cover of this book for instructions on downloading the Data Files for Students, or contact your instructor for information about accessing the required files.

Problem: You are an editor of the newsletter, *The Common Bond.* The next edition is due out in one week (Figure 7–84). The text for the feature articles in the newsletter is in a file on the Data Files for Students. You need to create the nameplate and the SmartArt graphic.

Perform the following tasks:

1. Change all margins to .75 inches. Depending on your printer, you may need different margin settings. Change the theme colors and theme fonts as specified in the figure.

2. Create the nameplate using the formats identified in Figure 7–84. Create the title using WordArt. Set a right-aligned custom tab stop at the right margin. Use the Clip Art task pane to locate the image shown. Resize the image to the size shown in the figure. Format the image as Behind Text, rotate it, and then position it as shown.

3. Below the nameplate, enter the heading News and Events, as shown in the figure.

4. Create a continuous section break below the heading, News and Events.

5. Format section 2 to three columns.

6. Insert the Lab 7-1 Common Bond Article file, which is located on the Data Files for Students, in section 2 below the nameplate.

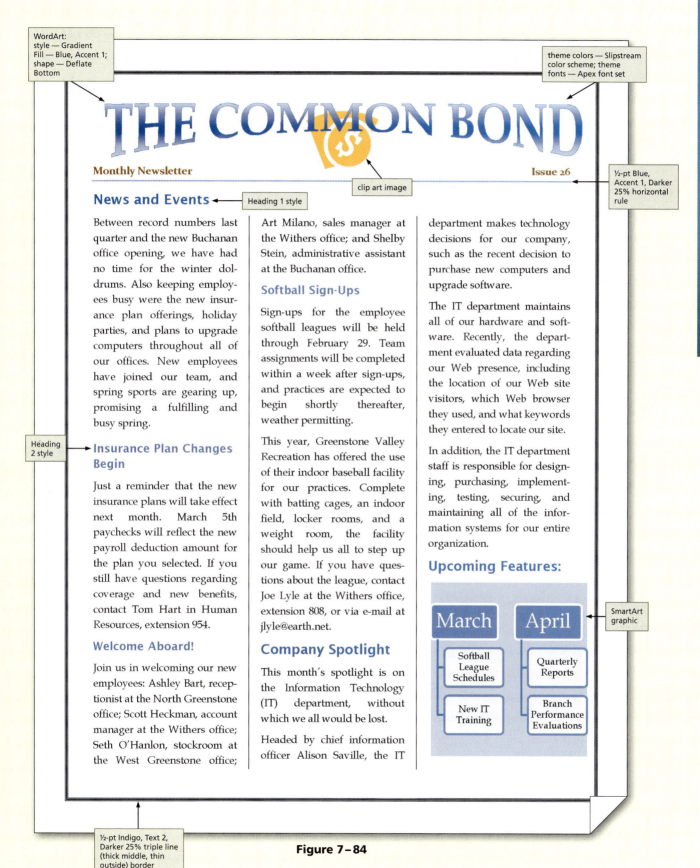

WordArt:
style — Gradient
Fill — Blue, Accent 1;
shape — Deflate
Bottom

theme colors — Slipstream
color scheme; theme
fonts — Apex font set

THE COMMON BOND

Monthly Newsletter **Issue 26**

clip art image

½-pt Blue,
Accent 1, Darker
25% horizontal
rule

News and Events

Heading 1 style

Between record numbers last quarter and the new Buchanan office opening, we have had no time for the winter doldrums. Also keeping employees busy were the new insurance plan offerings, holiday parties, and plans to upgrade computers throughout all of our offices. New employees have joined our team, and spring sports are gearing up, promising a fulfilling and busy spring.

Heading 2 style

Insurance Plan Changes Begin

Just a reminder that the new insurance plans will take effect next month. March 5th paychecks will reflect the new payroll deduction amount for the plan you selected. If you still have questions regarding coverage and new benefits, contact Tom Hart in Human Resources, extension 954.

Welcome Aboard!

Join us in welcoming our new employees: Ashley Bart, receptionist at the North Greenstone office; Scott Heckman, account manager at the Withers office; Seth O'Hanlon, stockroom at the West Greenstone office;

Art Milano, sales manager at the Withers office; and Shelby Stein, administrative assistant at the Buchanan office.

Softball Sign-Ups

Sign-ups for the employee softball leagues will be held through February 29. Team assignments will be completed within a week after sign-ups, and practices are expected to begin shortly thereafter, weather permitting.

This year, Greenstone Valley Recreation has offered the use of their indoor baseball facility for our practices. Complete with batting cages, an indoor field, locker rooms, and a weight room, the facility should help us all to step up our game. If you have questions about the league, contact Joe Lyle at the Withers office, extension 808, or via e-mail at jlyle@earth.net.

Company Spotlight

This month's spotlight is on the Information Technology (IT) department, without which we all would be lost.

Headed by chief information officer Alison Saville, the IT

department makes technology decisions for our company, such as the recent decision to purchase new computers and upgrade software.

The IT department maintains all of our hardware and software. Recently, the department evaluated data regarding our Web presence, including the location of our Web site visitors, which Web browser they used, and what keywords they entered to locate our site.

In addition, the IT department staff is responsible for designing, purchasing, implementing, testing, securing, and maintaining all of the information systems for our entire organization.

Upcoming Features:

March	April
Softball League Schedules	Quarterly Reports
New IT Training	Branch Performance Evaluations

SmartArt
graphic

½-pt Indigo, Text 2,
Darker 25% triple line
(thick middle, thin
outside) border

Figure 7–84

Continued >

STUDENT ASSIGNMENTS

In the Lab *continued*

7. Format the newsletter according to Figure 7–84 on the previous page. Columns should have a width of 2.1" with spacing of 0.35". Place a vertical rule between the columns.

8. Use Word's automatic hyphenation feature to hyphenate the document.

9. Insert a continuous section break at the end of the document to balance the columns.

10. Format the subheads, News and Events, Company Spotlight, and Upcoming Features, using the Heading 1 style, and the remaining headings using the Heading 2 style.

11. Open a new document window and create the SmartArt graphic shown in Figure 7–84. Use the Hierarchy List layout. Add the text shown in the figure. Make the bottom four shapes larger. Save the graphic with the file name, Lab 7-1 Common Bond Features. Use the Office Clipboard to copy and paste the SmartArt graphic in the bottom-right column of the newsletter. (*Hint:* Copy the graphic in the Lab 7-1 Common Bond Features window and then switch to the Lab 7-1 Common Bond Newsletter window, so that you can paste the graphic in the newsletter.) Resize the pasted graphic to fill the column. Apply the Indigo, Text 2, Lighter 80% fill color to the graphic (shape). Note that your graphic may look slightly different from the figure due to variations in the shape size.

12. Add the page border as shown in the figure.

13. If the document does not fit on a single page, adjust spacing above and below paragraphs.

14. Arrange both documents (the graphic and the newsletter) on the screen. Scroll through both open windows. Maximize the newsletter window.

15. Save the document with Lab 7-1 Common Bond Newsletter as the file name and then submit it in the format specified by your instructor.

In the Lab

Lab 2: Creating a Newsletter with a Pull-Quote (Text Box) and an Article on File

Note: To complete this assignment, you will be required to use the Data Files for Students. See the inside back cover of this book for instructions on downloading the Data Files for Students, or contact your instructor for information about accessing the required files.

Problem: You are responsible for the monthly preparation of *The Shutterbug*, a newsletter for photography enthusiasts. The next edition discusses upcoming digital cameras (Figure 7–85). This article already has been prepared and is on the Data Files for Students. You need to create the nameplate and the pull-quote.

Perform the following tasks:

1. Change all margins to .75 inches. Depending on your printer, you may need different margin settings.

2. Create the nameplate using the formats identified in Figure 7–85. Create the title using WordArt. Set a right-aligned custom tab stop at the right margin. Use the Clip Art task pane to locate the images shown, or similar images. Resize the images as shown in the figure. Format the images as Behind Text, rotate the left image, and position the images as shown.

3. Below the nameplate, enter the heading Overview of Digital Cameras, as shown in the figure.

4. Create a continuous section break below the heading.

5. Format section 2 to three columns.

6. Insert the Lab 7-2 The Shutterbug Article file, which is located on the Data Files for Students, in section 2 below the nameplate.

WordArt: style — Gradient Fill — Red, Accent 1, Outline — White, Glow, Accent 2 font — 48-point Berlin Sans FB Demi; shape — Triangle Up

document theme — Civic

The Shutterbug

Monthly Newsletter   Volume 28

Overview of Digital Cameras

Heading 1 style

Digital cameras allow users to take pictures and store the photographed images digitally, as an alternative to traditional film. Because digital cameras with new and improved features regularly are introduced to the marketplace, you should know how to compare the differences among various available cameras. Two important factors to consider are the type of camera you need and its resolution.

Heading 2 style modified to Brown, Accent 4, Darker 50%

Types of Cameras

Three basic types of digital cameras are studio cameras, field cameras, and point-and-shoot cameras. The most expensive and highest quality of the three types of digital cameras is a studio camera, which is a stationery camera used for professional studio work. Used often by photojournalists, the field camera is a portable camera that has many lenses

and other attachments. As with the studio camera, a field camera can be expensive. A point-and-shoot camera is more affordable than its counterparts. It is lightweight, and it provides acceptable quality photographic images for everyday users.

Resolution

Resolution, which is the number of horizontal and vertical pixels, is one factor that affects the quality of digital photos. A pixel, short for picture element, is the smallest element in an electronic image. The more pixels the camera uses to capture a picture, the better the

If you never plan to print any photos larger than 8 x 10", you do not need a camera with a resolution greater than 5 megapixels.

quality of the picture. For a good quality printed photo, you should have a 5 MP (megapixel, or million pixels) camera.

Many consumers mistakenly believe that the digital camera with the highest resolution is the best camera for their needs. A higher resolution increases quality and clarity of the pictures, as well as the size at which you can print the photos before noticing degradation in quality. If you never plan to print any photos larger than 8 x 10", you do not need a camera with a resolution greater than 5 megapixels.

On the Horizon

- Photography exhibit at Frankfort Heritage Museum, March 19 – April 6
- Lecture series by local photographer, Adam Schenkler, Mondays 8:00 – 9:00 p.m. in May
- Matting and Framing workshop, Frame It Right!, Wednesday, May 9, 7:30 – 9:00 p.m.

text box

14-point bold, italic font

8-pt Red, Accent 1, Darker 50% art border

Figure 7–85

Continued >

In the Lab *continued*

7. Format the newsletter according to Figure 7–85 on the previous page. Columns should have a width of 2" with spacing of 0.5". Place a vertical rule between the columns. Modify the Heading 2 style as indicated in the figure.

8. Use Word's automatic hyphenation feature to hyphenate the document.

9. Insert a continuous section break at the end of the document to balance the columns.

10. Add the page border as shown in the figure.

11. Insert a Mod Quote text box for the pull-quote. The text for the pull-quote is in the third column of the article. Split the window. Use the split window to copy the text and then paste it in the text box. Remove the split window. Change the fill color (shape fill) of the text box to Fill - Red, Accent 1. Resize the text box so that it is similar in size to Figure 7–85. Position the text box as shown in Figure 7–85.

12. If the document does not fit on a single page, adjust spacing above and below paragraphs.

13. Save the newsletter using Lab 7-2 The Shutterbug Newsletter as the file name and submit it in the format specified by your instructor.

In the Lab

Lab 3: Creating a Newsletter from Scratch

Problem: You work part-time for the city of Frankfort, which publishes a quarterly newsletter. Figure 7–86 shows the contents of the next issue.

Perform the following tasks:

1. Change all margins to .75 inches. Depending on your printer, you may need different margin settings.

2. Create the nameplate using the formats identified in Figure 7–86. Create the title using WordArt. Set a right-aligned custom tab stop at the right margin. Use the Clip Art task pane to locate the image shown, or a similar image. Resize the image as shown in the figure. Format the image as Behind Text, rotate the image, and position the image as shown.

3. Create a continuous section break below the nameplate. Format section 2 to two columns. Enter the text in section 2 using justified paragraph formatting.

4. Insert a Braces Quote 2 text box for the pull-quote. Copy the text for the pull-quote from the newsletter and then paste it in the text box. Change the fill of the text box to Gold, Background 2, Lighter 40%. Resize and position the text box so that it is similar in size and location to Figure 7–86.

5. Insert the table shown at the bottom of the right column in the newsletter and format it as indicated in the figure.

6. Make any additional formatting required in the newsletter so that it looks like the figure. The entire newsletter should fit on a single page.

7. Save the document with Lab 7-3 Frankfort Heritage Newsletter as the file name and then submit it in the format specified by your instructor.

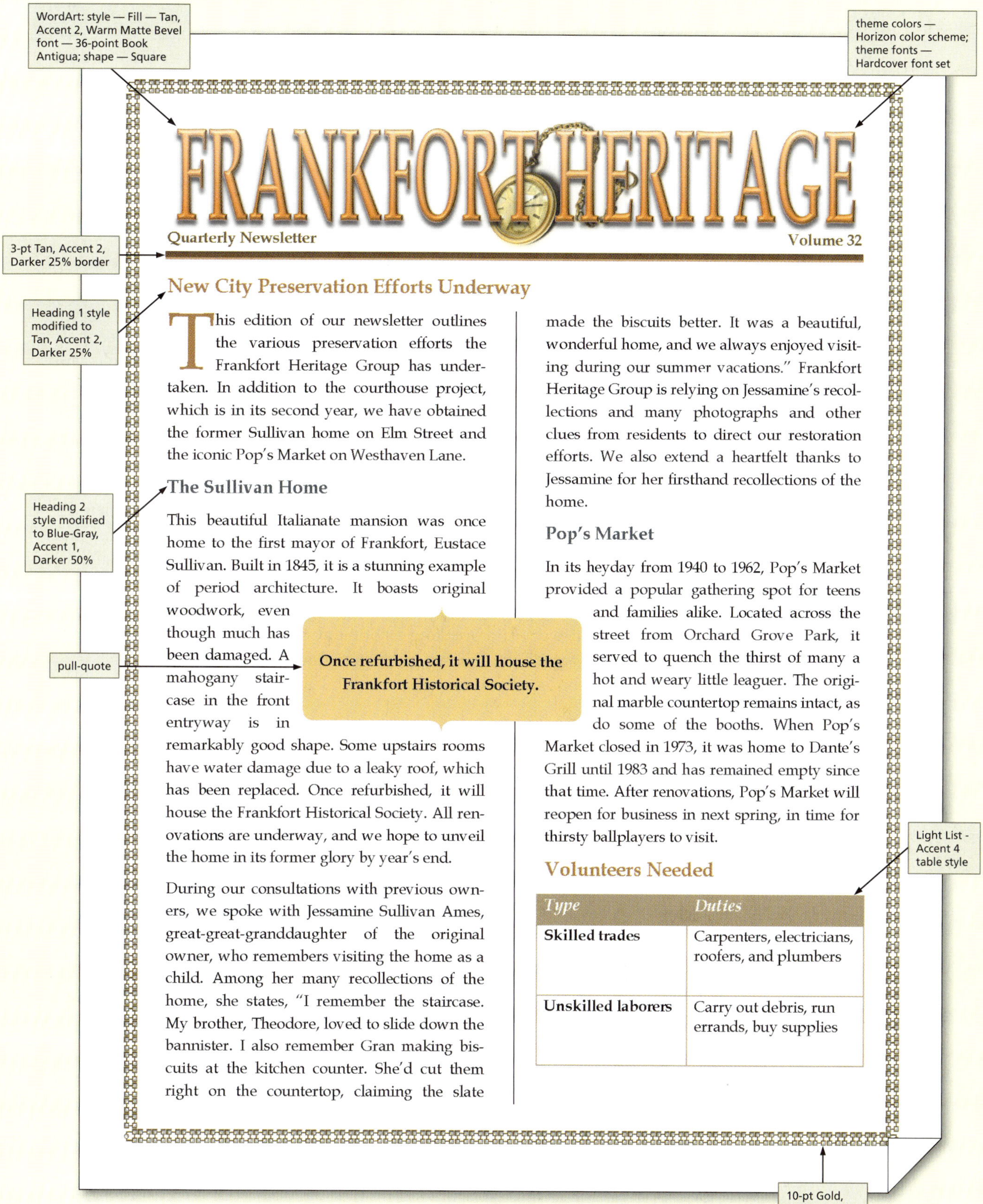

WordArt: style — Fill — Tan, Accent 2, Warm Matte Bevel font — 36-point Book Antigua; shape — Square

theme colors — Horizon color scheme; theme fonts — Hardcover font set

FRANKFORT HERITAGE

Quarterly Newsletter   Volume 32

3-pt Tan, Accent 2, Darker 25% border

New City Preservation Efforts Underway

Heading 1 style modified to Tan, Accent 2, Darker 25%

This edition of our newsletter outlines the various preservation efforts the Frankfort Heritage Group has undertaken. In addition to the courthouse project, which is in its second year, we have obtained the former Sullivan home on Elm Street and the iconic Pop's Market on Westhaven Lane.

The Sullivan Home

Heading 2 style modified to Blue-Gray, Accent 1, Darker 50%

This beautiful Italianate mansion was once home to the first mayor of Frankfort, Eustace Sullivan. Built in 1845, it is a stunning example of period architecture. It boasts original woodwork, even though much has been damaged. A mahogany staircase in the front entryway is in remarkably good shape. Some upstairs rooms have water damage due to a leaky roof, which has been replaced. Once refurbished, it will house the Frankfort Historical Society. All renovations are underway, and we hope to unveil the home in its former glory by year's end.

pull-quote

> Once refurbished, it will house the Frankfort Historical Society.

During our consultations with previous owners, we spoke with Jessamine Sullivan Ames, great-great-granddaughter of the original owner, who remembers visiting the home as a child. Among her many recollections of the home, she states, "I remember the staircase. My brother, Theodore, loved to slide down the bannister. I also remember Gran making biscuits at the kitchen counter. She'd cut them right on the countertop, claiming the slate made the biscuits better. It was a beautiful, wonderful home, and we always enjoyed visiting during our summer vacations." Frankfort Heritage Group is relying on Jessamine's recollections and many photographs and other clues from residents to direct our restoration efforts. We also extend a heartfelt thanks to Jessamine for her firsthand recollections of the home.

Pop's Market

In its heyday from 1940 to 1962, Pop's Market provided a popular gathering spot for teens and families alike. Located across the street from Orchard Grove Park, it served to quench the thirst of many a hot and weary little leaguer. The original marble countertop remains intact, as do some of the booths. When Pop's Market closed in 1973, it was home to Dante's Grill until 1983 and has remained empty since that time. After renovations, Pop's Market will reopen for business in next spring, in time for thirsty ballplayers to visit.

Volunteers Needed

Light List - Accent 4 table style

Type	Duties
Skilled trades	Carpenters, electricians, roofers, and plumbers
Unskilled laborers	Carry out debris, run errands, buy supplies

10-pt Gold, Background 2, Darker 50% art border

Figure 7–86

Cases and Places

Apply your creative thinking and problem solving skills to design and implement a solution.

Note: To complete these assignments, you may be required to use the Data Files for Students. See the inside back cover of this book for instructions on downloading the Data Files for Students, or contact your instructor for information about accessing the required files.

1: Create a Newsletter about Research and Learning Web Sites

Academic

As a part-time assistant for the English department at your school, you have been assigned the task of creating a newsletter that covers research and learning Web sites, which will be distributed to all enrolled students.

Content to be covered in the newsletter related to research includes the following: A recent Web usability survey conducted by the Nielsen Norman Group found that 88 percent of people who connect to the Internet use a search engine as their first online action. Search engines require users to type words and phrases that characterize the information being sought. Bing, Google, and AltaVista are some of the more popular search engines. The key to effective searching on the Web is composing search queries that narrow the search results and place the more relevant Web sites at the top of the results list. Keep up with the latest computer and related product developments by viewing online dictionaries and encyclopedias that add to their collections on a regular basis. Shopping for a new computer can be a daunting experience, but many online guides can help you select the components that best fit your needs and budget. If you are not confident in your ability to solve a problem alone, turn to online technical support. Web sites often provide streaming how-to video lessons, tutorials, and real-time chats with experienced technicians. Hardware and software reviews, price comparisons, shareware, technical questions and answers, and breaking technology news are found on comprehensive portals. Popular research Web sites include the following: A9.com, AccessMyLibrary, AltaVista, Answers.com, Ask, Bing, ChaCha, CNET, eHow, Google, HotBot, Librarians' Internet Index, PC911, Switchboard, Webopedia, and ZDNet.

Content to be covered in the newsletter related to learning includes the following: While you may believe your education ends when you finally graduate from college, learning is a lifelong process. You can increase your technological knowledge by visiting several Web sites with tutorials about building your own Web sites, the latest news about the Internet, and resources for visually impaired users. The HowStuffWorks Web site has won numerous awards for its clear, comprehensive articles that demystify aspects of our everyday life. It includes ratings and reviews of products written by Consumer Guide editors. A consortium of colleges maintains the Internet Public Library, which includes subject collections, reference materials, and a reading room filled with magazines and books. Volunteer librarians will answer your personal questions asked in its Ask an IPL Librarian form. Popular learning Web sites include the following: AT&T Knowledge Network Explorer, Bartleby: Great Books Online, BBC Learning, CBT Nuggets, HowStuffWorks, Internet Public Library, Learn the Net, ScienceMaster, Search Engine Watch, and Wiredguide.

The newsletter should present the above content as text and graphics. It should contain at least two of these graphical elements: a clip art image from the Web, a SmartArt graphic, a pull-quote, or a table. Enhance the newsletter with a drop cap, WordArt, color, ruling lines, and a page border. Be sure to use appropriate desktop publishing elements including a nameplate, columns of text, balanced columns, and a variety of font sizes, font colors, and shading. Use the concepts and techniques presented in this chapter to create and format the newsletter. Be sure to check spelling and grammar of the finished newsletter. Submit your assignment in the format specified by your instructor.

2: Create a Newsletter about Shopping and Health Web Sites

Personal

As a part-time assistant for the local community center, you have been assigned the task of creating a newsletter that covers shopping and health Web sites, which will be distributed to all center visitors.

Content to be covered in the newsletter related to shopping includes the following: From groceries to clothing to computers, you can buy just about everything you need with just a few clicks of your mouse. More than one-half of Internet users will make at least one online purchase this year. Books, computer software and hardware, and music are the hottest commodities. The two categories of Internet shopping Web sites are those with physical counterparts, such as Walmart and Fry's Electronics, and those with only a Web presence, such as Amazon and Buy. Another method of shopping for the items you need, and maybe some you really do not need, is to visit auction Web sites. Categories include antiques and collectibles, automotive, computers, electronics, music, sports, sports cards and memorabilia, and toys. Online auction Web sites can offer unusual items, including Star Wars memorabilia or a round of golf with Jack Nicklaus. Popular shopping Web sites include the following: Auctions: craigslist, eBay, Sotheby's, uBid, and U.S. Treasury - Seized Property Auctions; Books and Music: Amazon, Barnes & Noble, and BookFinder; Computers and Electronics: BestBuy, Buy, and Fry's Electronics; Miscellaneous: drugstore, Google Product Search, SmashBuys, and Walmart.

Content to be covered in the newsletter related to health includes the following: More than 75 million consumers use the Internet yearly to search for health information, so using the Web to store personal medical data is a natural extension of the Internet's capabilities. Internet health services and portals are available to store your personal health history, including prescriptions, lab test results, doctor visits, allergies, and immunizations. Google Health allows users to create a health profile, import medical records, and locate medical services and doctors. Web sites such as healthfinder.gov provide free wellness information to consumers. Wise consumers, however, verify the online information they read with their personal physician. In minutes, you can register with a health Web site by choosing a user name and password. Then, you create a record to enter your medical history. You also can store data for your emergency contacts, primary care physicians, specialists, blood type, cholesterol levels, blood pressure, and insurance plan. No matter where you are in the world, you and medical personnel can obtain records via the Internet or fax machine. Popular learning Web sites include the following: Medical History: Google Health, Lifestar, Medem, PersonalMD, Practice Solutions, Records for Living, Inc - Personal Health and Living Management, and WebMD; General Health: Consumer and Patient Health Information Section (CAPHIS), Centers for Disease Control and Prevention, family-doctor, healthfinder, KidsHealth, LIVESTRONG.COM, MedlinePlus, and PE Central: Health and Nutrition Web Sites.

The newsletter should present the above content as text and graphics. It should contain at least two of these graphical elements: a clip art image from the Web, a SmartArt graphic, a pull-quote, or a table. Enhance the newsletter with a drop cap, WordArt, color, ruling lines, and a page border. Be sure to use appropriate desktop publishing elements including a nameplate, columns of text, balanced columns, and a variety of font sizes, font colors, and shading. Use the concepts and techniques presented in this chapter to create and format the newsletter. Be sure to check spelling and grammar of the finished newsletter. Submit your assignment in the format specified by your instructor.

3: Create a Newsletter about Career Search and Travel Web Sites

Professional

As a board member of your alumni association, you have been assigned the task of creating a newsletter that covers career search and travel Web sites, which will be distributed to all newly inducted members.

Content to be covered in the newsletter related to career search includes the following: While your teachers give you valuable training to prepare you for a career, they rarely teach you how to begin that career. You can broaden your horizons by searching the Internet for career information and job openings. First, examine some of the job search Web sites. These resources list thousands of openings

Continued >

Cases and Places *continued*

in hundreds of fields, companies, and locations. For example, the USAJOBS Web site allows you to find information for federal jobs. This information may include the training and education required, salary data, working conditions, job descriptions, and more. In addition, many companies advertise careers on their Web sites. When a company contacts you for an interview, learn as much about it and the industry as possible before the interview. Popular career search Web sites include the following: Job Search: BestJobsUSA, CareerBuilder, Careerjet, CareerNET, CAREERXCHANGE, CollegeGrad.com, EmploymentGuide.com, Job.com, Job Bank USA, JobWeb, Monster, USAJOBS, VolunteerMatch, and Yahoo! HotJobs; Company/Industry Information: Careers.org, Forbes, Fortune, Hoover's, and Occupational Outlook Handbook.

Content to be covered in the newsletter related to travel includes the following: When you are ready to arrange your next travel adventure or just want to explore destination possibilities, the Internet provides ample resources to set your plans in motion. To discover exactly where your destination is on this planet, cartography Web sites, including MapQuest and Yahoo! Maps, allow you to pinpoint your destination. View your exact destination using satellite imagery with Google Maps and Bing Maps. Some excellent starting places are general travel Web sites such as Expedia Travel, Cheap Tickets, Orbitz, and Travelocity. Many airline Web sites allow you to reserve hotel rooms, activities, and rental cars while booking a flight. These all-encompassing Web sites have tools to help you find the lowest prices and details about flights, car rentals, cruises, and hotels. Comprehensive online guidebooks can provide useful details about maximizing your vacation time while saving money. Popular learning Web sites include the following: General Travel: CheapTickets, Expedia Travel, Kayak, Orbitz, SideStep, and Travelocity; Cartography: Bing Maps, Google Maps, MapQuest, Maps.com, and Yahoo! Maps; Travel and City Guides: Frommer's Travel Guides, GoPlanit, U.S.-Parks US National Parks Travel Guide, and Virtual Tourist.

The newsletter should present the above content as text and graphics. It should contain at least two of these graphical elements: a clip art image from the Web, a SmartArt graphic, a pull-quote, or a table. Enhance the newsletter with a drop cap, WordArt, color, ruling lines, and a page border. Be sure to use appropriate desktop publishing elements including a nameplate, columns of text, balanced columns, and a variety of font sizes, font colors, and shading. Use the concepts and techniques presented in this chapter to create and format the newsletter. Be sure to check spelling and grammar of the finished newsletter. Submit your assignment in the format specified by your instructor.

8 Using Document Collaboration and Integration Tools

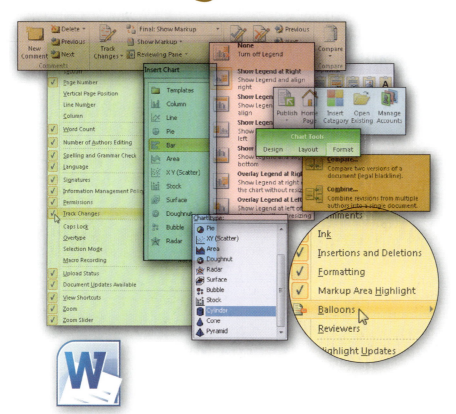

Objectives

You will have mastered the material in this chapter when you can:

- Insert, edit, view, and delete comments

- Track changes

- Review tracked changes

- Compare documents and combine documents

- Create and edit a chart using Microsoft Graph

- Link an Excel worksheet to a Word document

- Break a link

- Create and edit a chart using Office 2010 Chart Tools

- View and scroll through side-by-side documents

- Create a new document for a blog post

- Insert a quick table

- Publish a blog post

8 | Using Document Collaboration and Integration Tools

Introduction

Word provides the capability for users to work with other users, or **collaborate**, on a document. For example, you can show edits made to a document so that others can review the edits. You also can merge edits from multiple users or compare two documents to determine the differences between them.

From Word, you also can interact with other programs and incorporate the data and objects from those programs in a Word document. For example, you can create a chart of a Word table using an embedded charting program or using the advanced charting features of Microsoft Office 2010, all while working in Word. You also can link an Excel worksheet in a Word document or publish a blog post from Word.

Project Planning Guidelines

> The process of developing a document that communicates specific information requires careful analysis and planning. As a starting point, establish why the document is needed. Once the purpose is determined, analyze the intended readers of the document and their unique needs. Then, gather information about the topic and decide what to include in the document. Finally, determine the document design and style that will be most successful at delivering the message. Details of these guidelines are provided in Appendix A. In addition, each chapter in this book provides practical applications of these planning considerations.

Project — Memo with Chart

A memo is an informal document that businesses use to correspond with others. Memos often are internal to an organization, for example, to employees or coworkers.

The project in this chapter uses Word to produce the memo shown in Figure 8–1. First, you open an existing document that contains the memo and the Word table. Next, you insert comments and edit the document, showing the changes so that other users can review the changes. The changes appear on the screen with options that allow the author of the document to accept or reject the changes and delete the comments. Then, you chart the Word table using **Microsoft Graph**, which is a charting program included with Word (Figure 8–1a). As an alternative, if you have Microsoft Excel installed on your computer, you can use the Chart Tools tab in Word to create a chart (Figure 8–1b).

In this chapter, you also learn how to link an Excel worksheet to a Word document and create a document for a blog post.

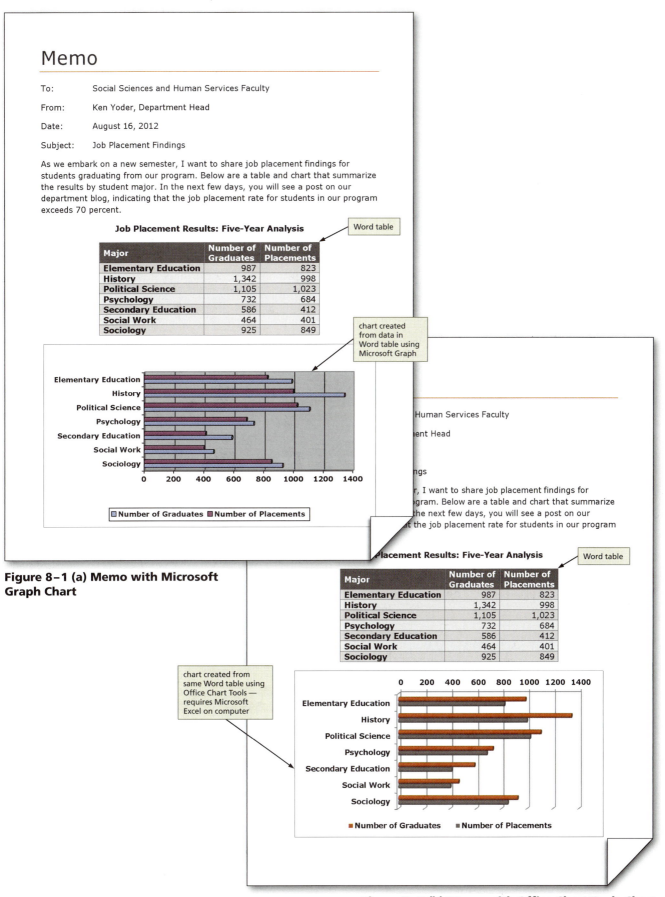

Memo

To:	Social Sciences and Human Services Faculty
From:	Ken Yoder, Department Head
Date:	August 16, 2012
Subject:	Job Placement Findings

As we embark on a new semester, I want to share job placement findings for students graduating from our program. Below are a table and chart that summarize the results by student major. In the next few days, you will see a post on our department blog, indicating that the job placement rate for students in our program exceeds 70 percent.

Job Placement Results: Five-Year Analysis — Word table

Major	Number of Graduates	Number of Placements
Elementary Education	987	823
History	1,342	998
Political Science	1,105	1,023
Psychology	732	684
Secondary Education	586	412
Social Work	464	401
Sociology	925	849

chart created from data in Word table using Microsoft Graph

Figure 8–1 (a) Memo with Microsoft Graph Chart

Human Services Faculty

...ent Head

...ngs

...r, I want to share job placement findings for ...ogram. Below are a table and chart that summarize ...the next few days, you will see a post on our ...at the job placement rate for students in our program

Placement Results: Five-Year Analysis — Word table

Major	Number of Graduates	Number of Placements
Elementary Education	987	823
History	1,342	998
Political Science	1,105	1,023
Psychology	732	684
Secondary Education	586	412
Social Work	464	401
Sociology	925	849

chart created from same Word table using Office Chart Tools — requires Microsoft Excel on computer

Figure 8–1 (b) Memo with Office Chart Tools Chart

Overview

As you read through this chapter, you will learn how to create the memo with the chart shown in Figure 8–1 on the previous page by performing these general tasks:

- Insert comments and track changes in the memo with the table.
- Review the comments and tracked changes.
- Chart the Word table using Graph.
- Link an Excel worksheet to a Word document and convert the worksheet to a Word table.
- Chart the Word table using Word's Chart Tools tab.
- Create and publish a blog post.

Plan Ahead

General Project Guidelines

When creating a Word document, the actions you perform and decisions you make will affect the appearance and characteristics of the finished document. As you collaborate on a document and integrate Word with other programs to create a document, such as the project shown in Figure 8–1, you should follow these general guidelines:

1. **If sharing documents, be certain received files and copied objects are virus free.** Do not open files created by others until you are certain they do not contain a virus or other malicious program. Use an antivirus program to verify that any files you use are free of viruses and other potentially harmful programs.

2. **If necessary, determine how to copy an object.** You have a variety of options for copying an object created in another Office program to a Word document. Your intended use of the Word document will help determine the best method for copying the object.

3. **Enhance a document with appropriate visuals.** Use visuals to add interest, clarify ideas, and illustrate points. Visuals include tables, charts, and graphical images (i.e., pictures or clip art).

4. **If desired, post communications on a blog.** Word provides tools enabling you to create and publish a blog post.

When necessary, more specific details concerning the above guidelines are presented at appropriate points in the chapter. The chapter also will identify the actions performed and decisions made regarding these guidelines during the creation of the documents shown in Figure 8–1.

To Start Word

BTW

The Ribbon and Screen Resolution
Word may change how the groups and buttons within the groups appear on the Ribbon, depending on the computer's screen resolution. Thus, your Ribbon may look different from the ones in this book if you are using a screen resolution other than 1024 x 768.

If you are using a computer to step through the project in this chapter and you want your screens to match the figures in this book, you should change your computer's resolution to 1024 × 768. The following steps start Word and verify settings.

1 Start Word. If necessary, maximize the Word window.

2 If the Print Layout button on the status bar is not selected, click it so that your screen is in Print Layout view.

3 Change your zoom level to 100%.

4 If the Show/Hide ¶ button (Home tab | Paragraph group) is not selected already, click it to display formatting marks on the screen.

Reviewing a Document

Word provides many tools that allow users to **collaborate** on a document. One set of collaboration tools within Word allows you to track changes in a document and review the changes. That is, one computer user can create a document and another user(s) can make changes and insert comments in the same document. Those changes then appear on the screen with options that allow the originator (author) to accept or reject the changes and delete the comments. With another collaboration tool, you can compare and/or merge two or more documents to determine the differences between them.

To illustrate Word collaboration tools, this section follows these general steps:

1. Open a document to be reviewed.
2. Insert comments in the document for the originator (author).
3. Track changes in the document.
4. View and delete the comments.
5. Accept and reject the tracked changes. For illustration purposes, you assume the role of originator (author) of the document in this step.
6. Compare the reviewed document to the original to view the differences.
7. Merge the original document with the reviewed document and with another reviewer's suggestions.

To Create a New File from an Existing File

Assume your coworker has created a draft of a memo and is sending it to you for review. To preserve the original memo, you create a file from the original. The file, called Job Placement Memo Findings Draft, is located on the Data Files for Students. See the inside back cover of this book for instructions on downloading the Data Files for Students, or contact your instructor for information about accessing the required files. The following steps create a new file from an existing file and then display its contents in the document window.

1 Click File on the Ribbon to open the Backstage view.

2 Click the New tab in the Backstage view to display the New gallery.

3 Click the 'New from existing' button in the New gallery to display the New from Existing Document dialog box.

4 Locate and then select the file with the name, Job Placement Findings Memo Draft.

5 Click the Create New button (New from Existing Document dialog box) to open a new document window that contains the contents of the selected file.

6 If necessary, change the zoom to 100% and scroll so that all document contents are visible in the document window.

To Insert a Comment

Reviewers often use comments to communicate suggestions, tips, and other messages to the author of a document. A **comment** is a note inserted in a document. Comments do not affect the text of the document.

After reading through the Job Placement Findings Memo Draft document, you have two comments for the originator (author) of the document. The first comment requests that the author insert a graph in the document. The steps on the next page insert this comment in the document.

1

- Position the insertion point at the location where the comment should be located (in this case, in the second sentence of the memo immediately to the left of the t in the word, table).

- Display the Review tab (Figure 8–2).

- If the Display for Review setting (Review tab | Tracking group) is not Final: Show Markup, click the Display for Review box arrow (Review tab | Tracking group) and then click Final: Show Markup to instruct Word to display the document with all proposed edits shown as markup.

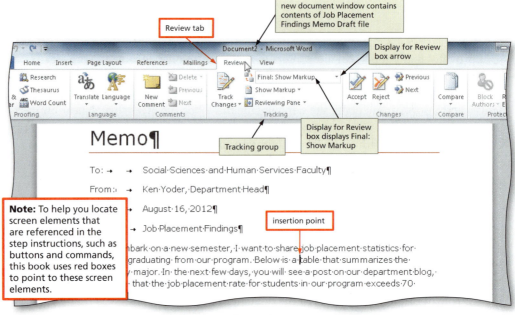

Figure 8–2

Q&A What are the other options in the Display for Review list?

Markup means that proposed changes are highlighted. The Final option displays the proposed edits as part of the final document, instead of as markup. The two Original options show the document before changes, either with or without markup.

2

- Click the Insert Comment button (Review tab | Comments group) to display a comment balloon in the Markup Area in the document window and place comment marks around the commented text in the document window (Figure 8–3).

Q&A What if the Markup Area does not appear with the comment balloon?

The balloons setting has been turned off. Click the Show Markup button (Review tab | Tracking group), point to Balloons on the Show Markup menu, and then click Show Only Comments and Formatting in Balloons, which is the default setting.

Figure 8–3

Q&A Why do comment marks surround selected text?

A comment is associated with text. If you do not select text on which you wish to comment, Word automatically selects the text to the right or left of the insertion point for the comment.

3

- In the comment balloon, type **Add a graph of the data below the table.** as the comment.

- If necessary, scroll to the right so that the entire comment is visible on the screen (Figure 8–4).

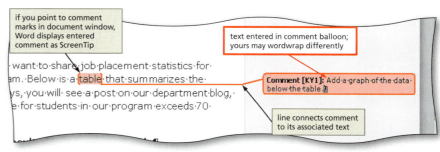

Figure 8–4

Other Ways

1. Press CTRL+ALT+M

To Insert Another Comment

The second comment you want to insert in the document is to request that the blog post also contain the August calendar. Because you want the comment associated with several words, you select the text before inserting the comment. The following steps insert another comment in the document.

1 Select the text where the comment should be located (in this case, the text, post on our department blog, in the last sentence of the memo).

2 Click the Insert Comment button (Review tab | Comments group) to display another comment balloon in the Markup Area in the document window.

3 In the new comment balloon, type **Post this note with the August calendar.** as the comment (Figure 8–5).

Q&A Can I see the name of the reviewer that entered a comment?

Yes. Point to the comment marks in the document window to display a ScreenTip that identifies the reviewer's name, the date and time the comment was entered, as well as the text of the comment itself.

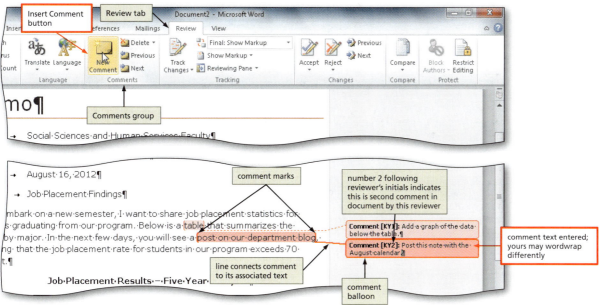

Figure 8–5

To Change Reviewer Information

Word uses predefined settings for the reviewer's initials and/or name that appear in the document window, the comment balloon, and the Reviewing Pane. If the reviewer's name or initials are not correct, you would change them by performing the following steps.

1a. Click the Track Changes button arrow (Review tab | Tracking group) to display the Track Changes menu. Click Change User Name on the Track Changes menu to display the Word Options dialog box.

or

1b. Open the Backstage view and then click Options to display the Word Options dialog box. If necessary, click General in the left pane.

2. Enter the correct name in the User name text box, and enter the correct initials in the Initials text box.

3. Click the OK button to change the reviewer information.

To Edit a Comment in a Comment Balloon

You modify comments in a comment balloon by clicking inside the comment balloon and editing the same way you edit text in the document window. In this project, you change the word, graph, to the word, chart, in the first comment. The following steps edit a comment in a balloon.

1 Click the first comment balloon to select it.

Q&A How can I tell if a comment is selected?

A selected comment appears in a brighter color than the rest of the comments.

2 Position the insertion point at the location of the text to edit (in this case, to the left of the g in graph in the first comment) (Figure 8–6).

3 Replace the word, graph, with the word, chart, to edit the comment (shown in Figure 8–7).

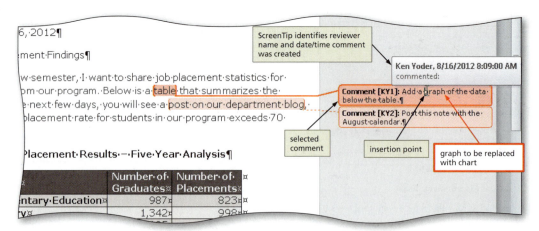

Figure 8–6

To Reply to a Comment

To reply to an existing comment, you select the comment and then follow the same steps that you would to insert a comment. The next steps reply to the first comment in the document.

1

- If necessary, click the comment to which you wish to reply so that the comment is selected (in this case, the first comment).

2

- Click the Insert Comment button (Review tab | Comments group) to display a reply comment balloon to the selected comment balloon.

3

- In the new comment balloon, type `Use horizontal bars or cylinders to plot the number of graduates and number of placements.` as the comment (Figure 8–7).

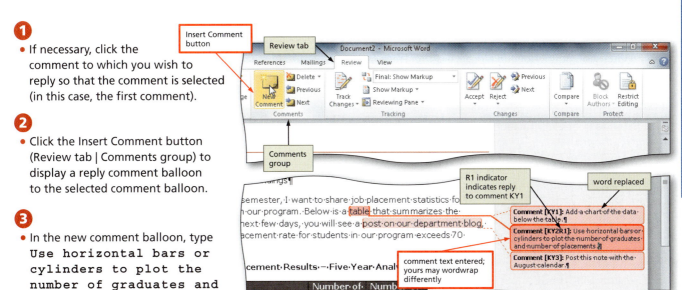

Figure 8–7

To Customize the Status Bar

You can customize the items that appear on the status bar. Recall that the status bar presents information about a document, the progress of current tasks, the status of certain commands and keys, and controls for viewing. Some indicators and buttons appear and disappear as you type text or perform certain commands. Others remain on the status bar at all times.

One indicator that does not appear by default is the Track Changes indicator. The following steps customize the status bar to show the Track Changes indicator.

1

- If the status bar does not show a desired item (in this case, the Track Changes indicator), right-click anywhere on the status bar to display the Customize Status Bar menu.

2

- Click the item on the Customize Status Bar menu that you want to show (in this case, Track Changes) to place a check mark beside the item, which also immediately may show as an indicator on the status bar (Figure 8–8).

Q&A

Can I show or hide any of the items listed in the Customize Status Bar menu?

Yes, click the item to display or remove its check mark.

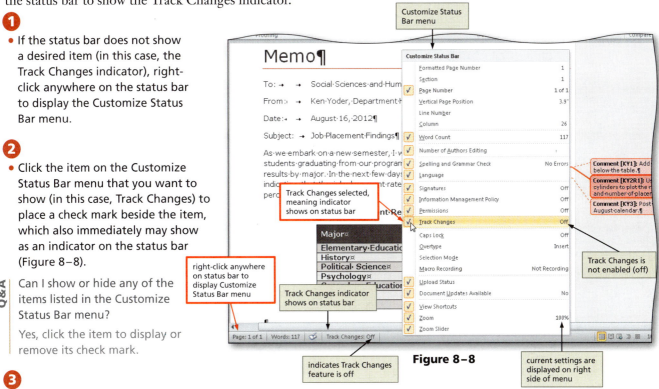

Figure 8–8

3

- Press the ESCAPE key to remove the Customize Status Bar menu from the screen.

To Enable Tracked Changes

When you edit a document that has the Track Changes feature enabled, Word marks all text or graphics that you insert, delete, or modify and refers to the revisions as **markups** or **revision marks**. An author can identify the changes a reviewer has made by looking at the markups in a document. The author also has the ability to accept or reject any change that a reviewer has made to a document.

To track changes in a document, you must enable (turn on) the Track Changes feature. The following step enables tracked changes.

- If the Track Changes indicator on the status bar shows that the Track Changes feature is off, click the Track Changes indicator on the status bar to enable the Track Changes feature (Figure 8–9).

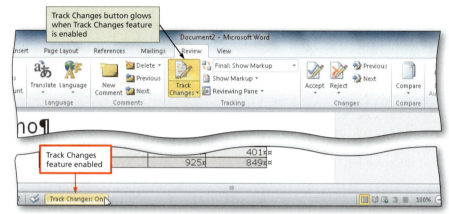

Figure 8–9

Other Ways
1. Click Track Changes button (Review tab | Tracking group)	Tracking group), click Track Changes
2. Click Track Changes button arrow (Review tab |	3. Press CTRL+SHIFT+E

To Track Changes

You have four suggested changes for the current document:

1. Insert the words, and chart, before the word, table, in the second sentence so that it reads: . . . a table and chart.

2. Delete the letter s at the end of the word, summarizes.

3. Change the word, statistics, to the word, findings, in the first sentence so that it reads: . . . job placement statistics.

4. Insert the word, student, before the word, job, in the last sentence so that it reads: . . . the student job placement rate.

The following steps track these changes as you enter them in the document. (Other edits required in this document will be made by another reviewer later in the chapter.)

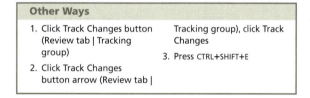

- Position the insertion point immediately to the left of the word, that, in the second sentence of the memo to position the insertion point at the location for the tracked change.

- Type **and chart** and then press the SPACEBAR to insert the typed text as a tracked change (Figure 8–10).

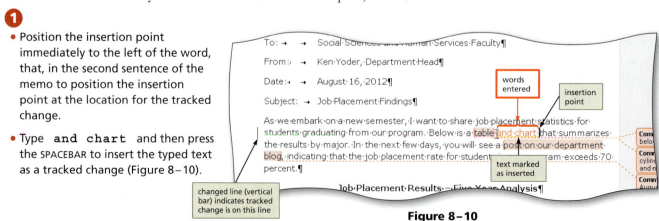

Figure 8–10

Q&A Why is the inserted text in color and underlined?

When the Track Changes feature is enabled, Word marks (signals) all text inserts by underlining them and changing their color, and marks all deletions by striking through them and changing their color.

2

- In the same sentence, delete the s at the end of the word, summarizes (so that it reads: summarize), to mark the letter for deletion (Figure 8–11).

Figure 8–11

3

- In the next sentence, position the insertion point immediately to the left of the word, job. Type **student** and then press the SPACEBAR to insert the typed text as a tracked change.

- In the first sentence, double-click the word, statistics, to select it.

- Type **findings** as the replacement text, which tracks a deletion and an insertion change (Figure 8–12).

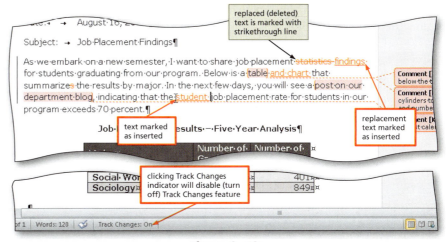
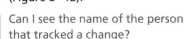

Figure 8–12

Q&A Can I see the name of the person that tracked a change?

Yes. If you point to a tracked change in the document window, Word displays a ScreenTip that identifies the reviewer's name and the type of change made by that reviewer.

TO CHANGE HOW MARKUPS AND COMMENTS ARE DISPLAYED

The tracked changes entered in the previous steps appeared inline instead of in markup balloons. Inline means that the inserts are underlined and the deletions are shown as strikethroughs. The default Word setting displays comments and formatting changes in balloons and all other changes inline. If you wanted all changes and comments to appear in balloons or all changes and comments to appear inline, you would perform the following steps.

1. Click the Show Markup button (Review tab | Tracking group) to display the Show Markup menu and then point to Balloons on the Show Markup menu.

2. If you want all revisions and comments to appear in balloons, click Show Revisions in Balloons on the Balloons submenu. If you want all revisions and comments to appear inline, click Show All Revisions Inline on the Balloons submenu. If you want to use the default Word setting, click Show Only Comments and Formatting in Balloons on the Balloons submenu.

To Disable Tracked Changes

When you have finished tracking changes, you should disable (turn off) the Track Changes feature so that Word stops marking your revisions. You follow the same steps to disable tracked changes as you did to enable them; that is, the indicator or button or keyboard shortcut function as a toggle, turning the Track Changes feature on or off each time the command is issued. The following step disables tracked changes.

1 To turn the Track Changes feature off, click the Track Changes indicator on the status bar (shown in Figure 8–12 on the previous page), or click the Track Changes button (Review tab | Tracking group), or press CTRL+SHIFT+E.

To Use the Reviewing Pane

As an alternative to reading through tracked changes in the document window and comment balloons in the Markup Area, some users prefer to view tracked changes and comments in the **Reviewing Pane**. The Reviewing Pane can be displayed either at the left edge (vertically) or the bottom (horizontally) of the screen. The following steps display the Reviewing Pane on the screen.

- Click the Reviewing Pane button arrow (Review tab | Tracking group) to display the Reviewing Pane menu (Figure 8–13).

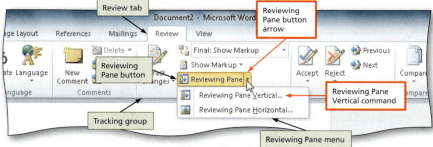

Figure 8–13

- Click Reviewing Pane Vertical on the Reviewing Pane menu to display the Reviewing Pane on the left side of the Word window.

Q&A

What if I click the Reviewing Pane button instead of the button arrow?

Word displays the Reviewing Pane in its most recent location, that is, either vertically on the left side of the screen or horizontally on the bottom of the screen.

- Click the Show Markup button (Review tab | Tracking group) to display the Show Markup menu.

- Point to Balloons on the Show Markup menu to display the Balloons submenu (Figure 8–14).

Q&A

Why click the Show Markup button and point to the Balloons command?

Because the Reviewing Pane shows all comments, you do not need the Markup Area to display comment balloons. Thus, you will display all revisions inline.

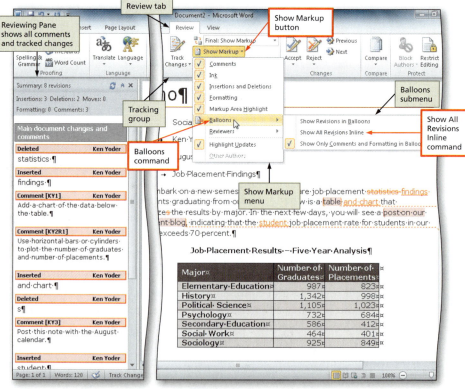

Figure 8–14

4
- Click Show All Revisions Inline on the Balloons submenu to remove the Markup Area from the Word window and place all markups inline (Figure 8–15).

Q&A Can I edit revisions in the Reviewing Pane?

Yes. Simply click in the Reviewing Pane and edit the text the same way you edit in the document window.

5
- Click the Close button in the Reviewing Pane to close the pane.

Q&A Can I also click the Reviewing Pane button to close the pane?

Yes.

- Click the Show Markup button (Review tab | Tracking group) to display the Show Markup menu, point to Balloons on the Show Markup menu, and then click Show Only Comments and Formatting in Balloons, so that the Markup Area reappears.

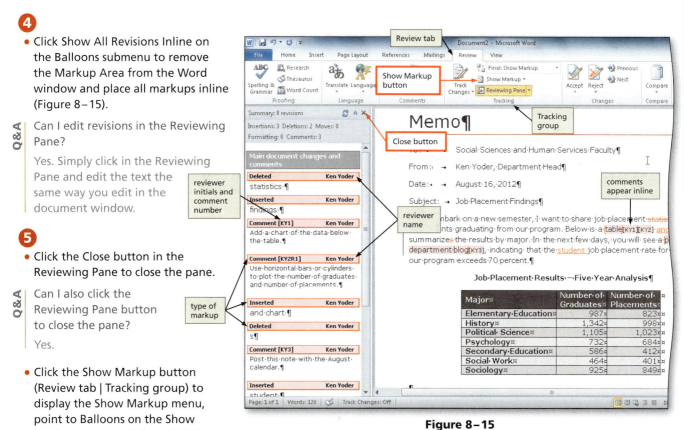

Figure 8–15

TO PRINT MARKUPS

When you print a document with comments and tracked changes, Word chooses the zoom percentage and page orientation that will best display the comments on the printed document. You can print the document with its markups, which looks similar to how the Word window shows the markups on the screen, or you can print just the list of the markups. If you wanted to print markups, you would perform the following steps.

1. Open the Backstage view and then click the Print tab in the Backstage view to display the Print gallery.

2. Click the first button in the Settings area to display a list of options specifying what you can print. To print the document with the markups, if necessary, place a check mark to the left of Print Markup in the Document Properties area. To print just the markups (without printing the document), click List of Markup in the Document Properties area.

3. Click the Print button.

To Save a Document

You are finished reviewing the document. The next step is to save it because you have performed many steps thus far. The following steps save a document.

1 With a USB flash drive connected to one of the computer's USB ports, click the Save button on the Quick Access Toolbar to display the Save As dialog box.

2 Type `Job Placement Findings Memo with Comments and Tracked Changes` in the File name text box to change the file name. Do not press the ENTER key because you do not want to close the dialog box at this time.

BTW

BTWs
For a complete list of the BTWs found in the margins of this book, visit the Word 2010 BTW Web page (scsite.com/wd2010/btw).

3 If necessary, navigate to the save location (in this case, the Word folder in the CIS 101 folder [or your class folder] on the USB flash drive).

4 Click the Save button (Save As dialog box) to save the document in the selected folder on the USB flash drive with the entered file name.

BTW

Locating Comments by Reviewer
You can find a comment from a specific reviewer through the Go To dialog box. Click the Find button arrow (Home tab | Editing group) and then click Go To or press CTRL+G to display the Go To sheet in the Find and Replace dialog box. Click Comment in the 'Go to what' list (Find and Replace dialog box). Select the reviewer whose comments you wish to find and then click the Next button. You also can click the Select Browse Object button on the vertical scroll bar and then click the Browse by Comment icon to scroll through comments.

Reviewing Tracked Changes and Comments

After tracking changes and entering comments in a document, you send the document to the originator for his or her review. For demonstration purposes in this chapter, you assume the role of originator and review the tracked changes and comments in the document.

To do this, be sure the markups are displayed on the screen. Click the Show Markup button (Review tab | Tracking group) and verify that Comments, Insertions and Deletions, and Formatting each have a check mark beside them. Ensure the Display for Review (Review tab | Tracking group) is Final: Show Markup; if it is not, click the Display for Review box arrow (Review tab | Tracking group) and then click Final: Show Markup.

The default Display for Review view is Final: Show Markup. This option shows the final document with tracked changes. To see how a document will look if you accept all the changes, without actually accepting them, click the Display for Review button arrow (Review tab | Tracking group) and then click Final. If you print this view of the document, it will print how the document will look if you accept all the changes. To see how the document looked before any changes were made, click the Display for Review button arrow (Review tab | Tracking group) and then click Original. The Original: Show Markup option shows the original document with tracked changes. When you have finished reviewing the various options, if necessary, click the Display for Review button arrow (Review tab | Tracking group) and then click Final: Show Markup.

To View Comments and Delete a Comment

The next step is to read the comments in the marked-up document. You could scroll through the document and read each comment that appears in the Markup Area, but you might overlook one or more comments using this technique. A more efficient method is to use the Review tab to review the comments one at a time. The following steps view comments in the document.

1

• Press CTRL+HOME to position the insertion point at the beginning of the document, so that Word begins searching for comments from the top of the document.

• Click the Next Comment button (Review tab | Comments group), which causes Word to locate and select the first comment in the document (Figure 8–16).

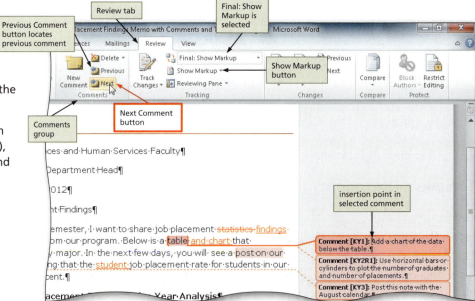

Figure 8–16

2

- Read through the comment and then click the Delete Comment button (Review tab | Comments group) to remove the comment balloon from the Markup Area (Figure 8–17).

Q&A What if I accidentally click the Delete Comment button arrow?

Click Delete on the Delete Comment menu.

3

- Click the Next Comment button (Review tab | Comments group) to locate and select the next comment in the document.

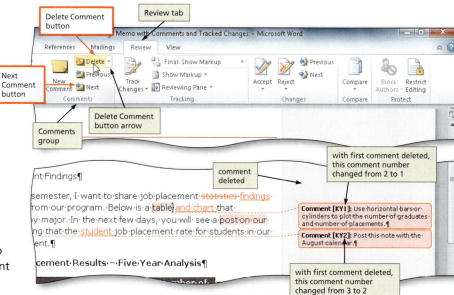

Figure 8–17

4

- Continue to repeat Step 3 until Word displays a dialog box asking if you want to continue searching from the beginning of the document for additional comments and then click the No button (because you started the comment search from the beginning of the document).

Other Ways
1. Right-click comment, click Delete Comment on shortcut menu

To Delete All Comments

Assume you now wish to delete all the comments in the document at once because you have read them all. The following steps delete all comments at once.

1

- Click the Delete Comment button arrow (Review tab | Comments group) to display the Delete Comment menu (Figure 8–18).

2

- Click Delete All Comments in Document on the Delete Comment menu to remove all comments from the document, which also closes the Markup Area (shown in Figure 8–19 on the next page).

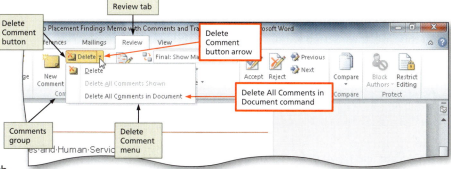

Figure 8–18

To Review Tracked Changes

The next step is to review the tracked changes in the marked-up document. As with the comments, you could scroll through the document and point to each markup to read it, but you might overlook one or more changes using this technique. A more efficient method is to use the Review tab to review the changes one at a time, deciding whether to accept, modify, or delete each change. The steps on the next page review the changes in the document.

1

- Press CTRL+HOME to position the insertion point at the beginning of the document, so that Word begins the review of tracked changes from the top of the document.

- Click the Next Change button (Review tab | Changes group), which causes Word to locate and select the first markup in the document (in this case, the deleted word, statistics) (Figure 8–19).

Q&A

What if my document also had contained comments?

When you click the Next Change button (Review tab | Changes group), Word locates the next tracked change or comment, whichever appears first.

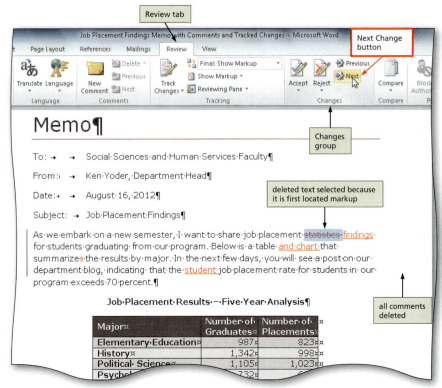

Figure 8–19

2

- Because you agree with this change, click the Accept and Move to Next button (Review tab | Changes group) to accept the deletion of the word, statistics, and instruct Word to locate and select the next markup (in this case, the inserted word, findings) (Figure 8–20).

Q&A

What if I accidentally click the Accept and Move to Next button arrow (Review tab | Changes group)?

Click Accept and Move to Next on the Accept and Move to Next menu.

Q&A

What if I wanted to accept the change but not search for the next tracked change?

You would click Accept and Move to Next button arrow and then click Accept Change on the Accept and Move to Next menu.

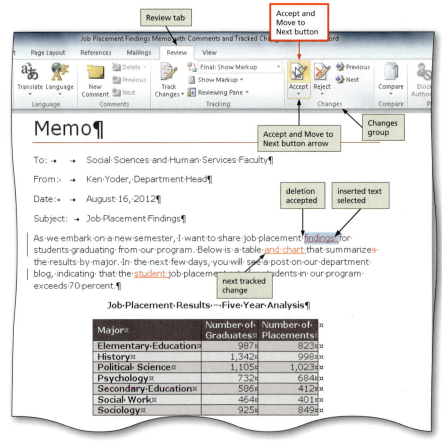

Figure 8–20

3

- Click the Accept and Move to Next button (Review tab | Changes group) to accept the insertion of the word, findings, and instruct Word to locate and select the next markup (in this case, the inserted words, and chart).

- Click the Accept and Move to Next button (Review tab | Changes group) to accept the insertion of the words, and chart, and instruct Word to locate and select the next markup (in this case, the deleted letter s).

- Click the Accept and Move to Next button (Review tab | Changes group) to accept the deletion of the letter s, and instruct Word to locate and select the next markup (in this case, the inserted word, student) (Figure 8–21).

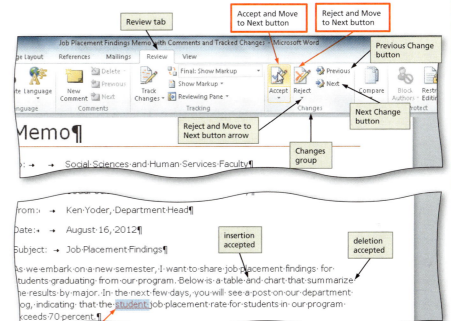

Figure 8–21

4

- Because you do not agree with this change, click the Reject and Move to Next button (Review tab | Changes group) to reject the marked deletion, and instruct Word to locate and select the next markup.

Q&A What if I accidentally click the Reject and Move to Next button arrow (Review tab | Changes group)?

Click Reject and Move to Next on the Reject and Move to Next menu.

Q&A What if I wanted to reject the change but not search for the next tracked change?

You would click the Reject and Move to Next button arrow (Review tab | Changes group) and then click Reject Change on the Reject and Move to Next menu.

Q&A What if I did not want to accept or reject a change but wanted to locate the next tracked change?

You would click the Next Change button (Review tab | Changes group) to locate the next tracked change or comment. Likewise, to locate the previous tracked change or comment, you would click the Previous Change button (Review tab | Changes group).

BTW

Q&As
For a complete list of the Q&As found in many of the step-by-step sequences in this book, visit the Word 2010 Q&A Web page (scsite.com/wd2010/qa).

5

- Click the OK button in the dialog box that appears, which indicates the document contains no more comments or tracked changes.

Other Ways

1. Right-click comment or tracked change, click desired command on shortcut menu

TO ACCEPT OR REJECT ALL TRACKED CHANGES

If you wanted to accept or reject all tracked changes in a document at once, you would perform the following steps.

1. To accept all tracked changes, click the Accept and Move to Next button arrow (Review tab | Comments group) to display the Accept and Move to Next menu and then click Accept All Changes in Document on the menu.

or

1. To reject all tracked changes, click the Reject and Move to Next button arrow (Review tab | Comments group) to display the Reject and Move to Next menu and then click Reject All Changes in Document on the menu.

Changing Tracking Options

If you wanted to change the color and markings reviewers use for tracked changes and comments or change how balloons are displayed, use the Track Changes Options dialog box (Figure 8–22). To display the Track Changes Options dialog box, click the Track Changes button arrow (Review tab | Tracking group) and then click Change Tracking Options on the Track Changes menu.

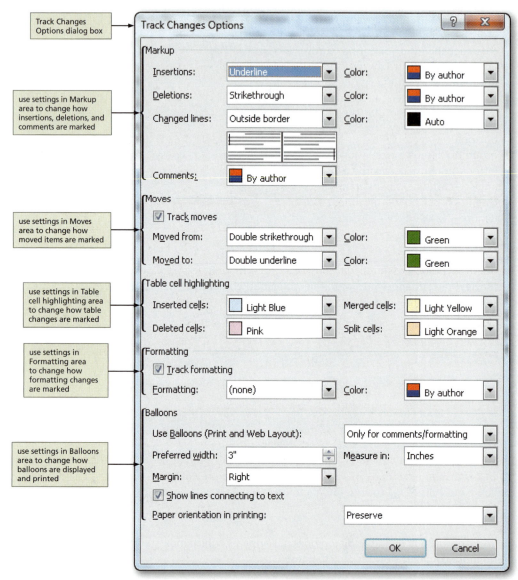

Figure 8–22

Mark as Final
If you wanted to mark a document as final so that users could not make further edits to it, you would perform these steps. Open the Backstage view, display the Info gallery, click the Protect Document button, and then click Mark as Final. This makes the document a read-only file, which prevents any further edits.

- To change how insertions, deletions, and comments are marked, modify the settings in the Markup area of the Track Changes Options dialog box.
- To change how moved items are marked, modify the settings in the Moves area of the Track Changes Options dialog box.
- To change how table changes are marked, modify the settings in the 'Table cell highlighting' area of the Track Changes Options dialog box.
- To change how formatting changes are marked, modify the settings in the Formatting area of the Track Changes Options dialog box.
- To change how balloons are displayed and printed, modify the settings in the Balloons area of the Track Changes Options dialog box.

To Save an Active Document with a New File Name and Close the File

The current file name is Job Placement Findings Memo with Comments and Tracked Changes. Because you would like to keep the document with comments and tracked changes, as well as the current one, you will save the current document with a new file name. The following steps save the active document with a new file name.

1 With a USB flash drive connected to one of the computer's USB ports, open the Backstage view and then click Save As in the Backstage view to display the Save As dialog box.

2 Type `Job Placement Findings Memo Reviewed` in the File name text box to change the file name. Do not press the ENTER key after typing the file name.

3 Navigate to the Word folder on your USB flash drive so that you can save your file in that location.

4 Click the Save button (Save As dialog box) to save the document on the selected drive with the entered file name.

5 Open the Backstage view and then click Close to close the document.

6 If necessary, click the Word program button on the taskbar to redisplay the Word window.

To Compare Documents

With Word, you can compare two documents to each other, which allows you easily to identify any differences between the two files. Word displays the differences between the documents as tracked changes for your review. By comparing files, you can verify that two separate files have the same or different content. If no tracked changes are found, then the two documents are identical.

Assume you want to compare the original Job Placement Findings Memo Draft document with the Job Placement Findings Memo Reviewed document so that you can identify the changes made to the document. The following steps compare two documents.

1

- Display the Review tab.

- Click the Compare button (Review tab | Compare group) to display the Compare menu (Figure 8–23).

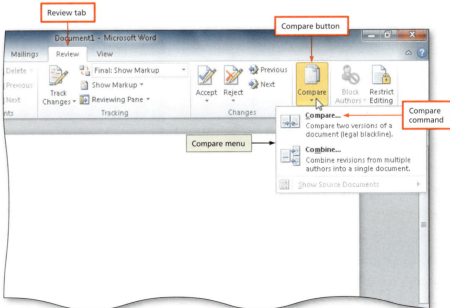

Figure 8–23

- Click Compare on the Compare menu to display the Compare Documents dialog box.

- Click the Original document box arrow (Compare Documents dialog box) and then click the file, Job Placement Findings Memo Draft, in the Original document list to select the first file to compare and place the file name in the Original document box.

Q&A What if the file is not in the Original document list?

Click the Open button to the right of the Original document box arrow, locate the file, and then click the Open button (Open dialog box).

- Click the Revised document box arrow (Compare Documents dialog box) and then click the file, Job Placement Findings Memo Reviewed, in the Revised document list to select the second file to compare and place the file name in the Revised document box.

Q&A What if the file is not in the Revised document list?

Click the Open button to the right of the Original document box arrow, locate the file, and then click the Open button (Open dialog box).

- If a More button appears in the dialog box, click it to expand the dialog box, which changes the More button to a Less button.

- If necessary, in the 'Show changes in' area, click New document so that tracked changes are marked in a new document. Ensure that all your settings in the expanded dialog box (below the Less button) match those in Figure 8–24.

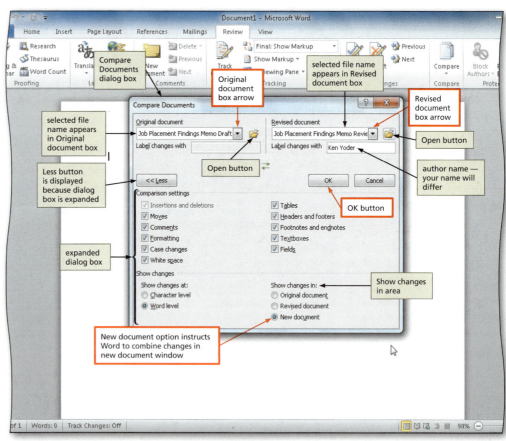

Figure 8–24

3

- Click the OK button to open a new document window and display the differences between the two documents as tracked changes in a new document window (Figure 8–25).

Q&A What if the original and source documents do not appear on the screen with the compared document?

Click the Compare button (Review tab | Compare group) to display the Compare menu, point to Show Source Documents on the Compare menu, and then click Show Both on the Show Source Documents submenu.

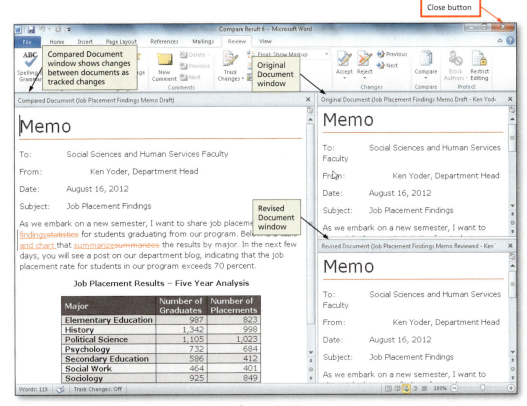

Figure 8–25

Q&A What if the Reviewing Pane appears on the screen?

Click its Close button.

 Experiment

- Click the Next Change button (Review tab | Changes group) to display the first tracked change in the compared document. Continue clicking the Next Change or Previous Change buttons. You can accept or reject changes in the compared document using the same steps described earlier in the chapter.

 Experiment

- Scroll through the Compared Document window and watch the Original Document window and Revised Document window scroll synchronously.

4

- When you have finished comparing the documents, click the Close button in the document window (shown in Figure 8–25), and then click the Don't Save button when Word asks if you want to save the compare results.

BTW

Compare and Merge
If you wanted to compare two documents and merge the changes into an existing document instead of into a new document, you would click Original document (Compare Documents dialog box) to merge into the original document or click Revised document (Compare Documents dialog box) to merge into the revised document (Figure 8–24), and then click the OK button.

To Combine Revisions from Multiple Authors

Often, multiple reviewers will send you their markups (tracked changes) for the same original document. Using Word, you can combine the tracked changes from multiple reviewers' documents into a single document, two documents at a time, until all documents are combined. Combining documents allows you to review all markups from a single document, from which you can accept and reject changes and read comments. Each reviewer's markups are shaded in a different color to help you visually differentiate among multiple reviewers' markups.

Assume you have you want to combine the original Job Placement Findings Memo Draft document with the Job Placement Findings Memo with Comments and Tracked Changes document and also with a document called Job

Placement Findings Memo — EA Review, which is on the Data Files for Students. See the inside back cover of this book for instructions on downloading the Data Files for Students, or contact your instructor for information about accessing the required files. The next steps combine these three documents, two at a time. The latter file identifies a grammar error, recommends alternate punctuation in the table title, and suggests the insertion of a word in one of the sentences. The following steps combine documents.

- Click the Compare button (Review tab | Compare group) to display the Compare menu (Figure 8–26).

- Click Combine on the Compare menu to display the Combine Documents dialog box.

- Click the Original document box arrow (Combine Documents dialog box) and then click the file, Job Placement Findings Memo Draft, in the Original document list to select the first file to combine and place the file name in the Original document box.

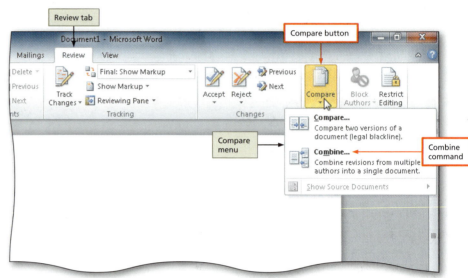

Figure 8–26

Q&A What if the file is not in the Original document list?

Click the Open button to the right of the Original document box arrow, locate the file, and then click the Open button (Open dialog box).

- Click the Revised document box arrow (Combine Documents dialog box) and then click the file, Job Placement Findings Memo with Comments and Tracked Changes, in the Revised document list to select the second file to combine and place the file name in the Revised document box.

Q&A What if the file is not in the Revised document list?

Click the Open button to the right of the Revised document box arrow, locate the file, and then click the Open button (Open dialog box).

- If a More button appears in the dialog box, click it to expand the dialog box, which changes the More button to a Less button.

- In the 'Show changes in' area, if necessary, click Original document so that tracked changes are marked in the original document (Job Placement Findings Memo Draft). Ensure that all your settings in the expanded dialog box (below the Less button) match those in Figure 8–27.

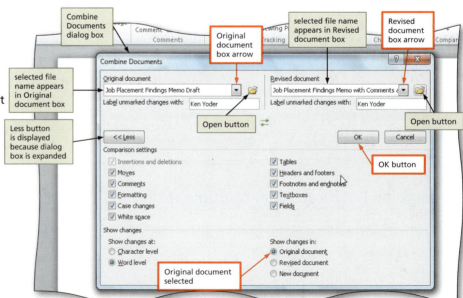

Figure 8–27

3

- Click the OK button to combine the Job Placement Findings Memo Draft document with the Job Placement Findings Memo with Comments and Tracked Changes document and display the differences between the two documents as tracked changes in the original document.

- Click the Compare button again (Review tab | Compare group) and then click Combine on the Compare menu to display the Combine Documents dialog box.

- Locate and display the file name, Job Placement Findings Memo Draft, in the Original document text box (Combine Documents dialog box) to select the first file and place the file name in the Original document box.

- Click the Open button to the right of the Revised document box arrow (Combine Documents dialog box) to display the Open dialog box.

- Locate the file name, Job Placement Findings Memo - EA Review, in the Data Files for Students and then click the Open button (Open dialog box) to display the selected file name in the Revised document box (Combine Documents dialog box).

- If a More button appears in the Combine Documents dialog box, click it to expand the dialog box.

- If necessary, in the 'Show changes in' area, click Original document so that tracked changes are marked in the original document (Job Placement Findings Memo Draft). Ensure that all your settings in the expanded dialog box (below the Less button) match those in Figure 8–28.

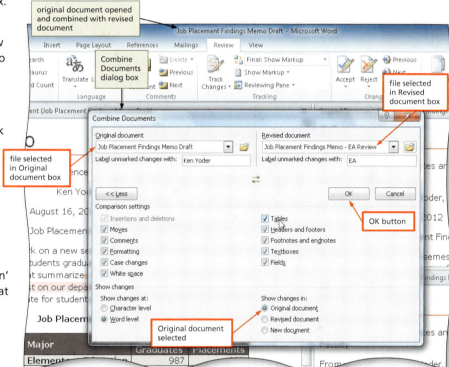

Figure 8–28

4

- Click the OK button to combine the Job Placement Findings Memo – EA Review document with the currently combined document and display the differences among the three documents as tracked changes in the original document (Figure 8–29).

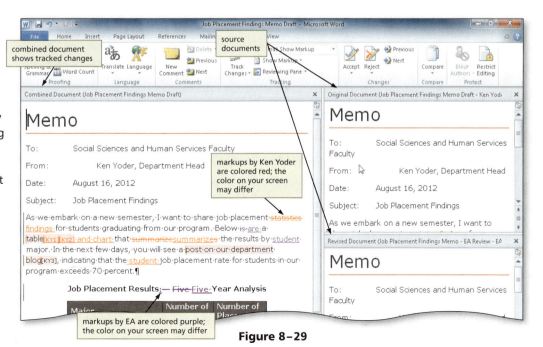

Figure 8–29

Q&A What if my screen does not display the original and source documents?

Click the Compare button (Review tab | Compare group) to display the Compare menu, point to Show Source Documents on the Compare menu, and then click Show Both on the Show Source Documents submenu.

 **Experiment**

- Click the Next Change button (Review tab | Changes group) to display the first tracked change in the combined document. Continue clicking the Next Change or Previous Change buttons. You can accept or reject changes in the combined document using the same steps described earlier in the chapter.

To Show Tracked Changes and Comments by a Single Reviewer

In the documents just combined, you previously have seen all the Ken Yoder (red) markups. The EA document had these additional markups (in purple): replace the word, is, with the word, are, in the second sentence; insert the word, student, in the second sentence; and change the punctuation in the table title. Instead of looking through a document for a particular reviewer's markups, you can show markups by reviewer. The following steps show the markups by the reviewer named EA by removing those by Ken Yoder.

1
- Click the Show Markup button (Review tab | Tracking group) to display the Show Markup menu and then point to Reviewers on the Show Markup menu to display the Reviewers submenu (Figure 8–30).

Q&A What if my Reviewers submenu differs?

Your submenu may have additional or different reviewer names or colors, depending on your Word settings.

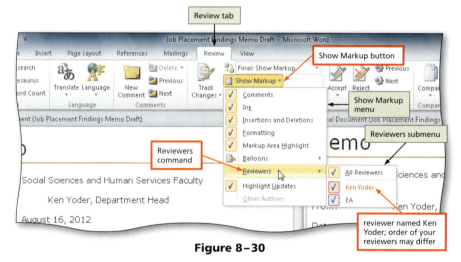

Figure 8–30

2
- Click Ken Yoder on the Reviewers submenu to hide the selected reviewer's markups and leave other markups on the screen (in this case, markups by EA) (Figure 8–31).

Q&A Are the Ken Yoder reviewer markups deleted?

No. They are hidden from view.

 **Experiment**

- Practice hiding and showing reviewer's markups in this document.

3
- Redisplay all reviewer comments by clicking the Show Markup button (Review tab | Tracking group), pointing to Reviewers, and then clicking All Reviewers on the Reviewers submenu.

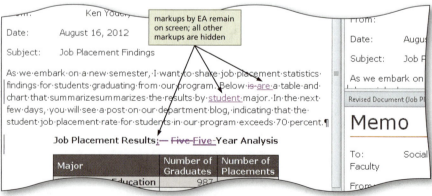

Figure 8–31

To Customize the Status Bar

You are finished working with tracked changes in this chapter. The following steps remove the Track Changes indicator from the status bar.

1 Right-click anywhere on the status bar to display the Customize Status Bar menu.

2 Remove the check mark to the left of Track Changes on the Status Bar menu, which removes the Track Changes indicator from the status bar.

3 Press the ESCAPE key to remove the Customize Status Bar menu from the screen.

To Close the Document without Saving It

The next step is to close the combined document without saving it.

1 Open the Backstage view and then click Close.

2 When Word displays the dialog box, click the Don't Save button.

BTW

Document Inspector
If you wanted to ensure that all comments were removed from a document, you could use the document inspector. Open the Backstage view, display the Info gallery, click the Check for Issues button, and then click Inspect Document. Place a check mark in the Comments, Revisions, Versions, and Annotations check box and then click the Inspect button (Document Inspector dialog box). If any comments are located, click the Remove All button.

Break Point: If you wish to take a break, this is a good place to do so. You can quit Word now. To resume at a later time, start Word and continue following the steps from this location forward.

Charting a Word Table Using Microsoft Graph

You easily can chart in a Word table using an embedded charting program called **Microsoft Graph**, or simply **Graph**. Graph has its own menus and commands because it is a program embedded in Word. Using Graph commands, you can modify the appearance of the chart after you create it.

In the following pages, you will insert a chart of the Job Placement Statistics Word table using Microsoft Graph and then format the chart as follows:

1. Graph by column instead of row.
2. Move the legend to a different location.
3. Resize the chart.
4. Change the chart type.
5. Change the font size of text in the chart.
6. Reverse the order of labels on the category axis (y-axis).

To Create a New File from an Existing File

The next step is to open the Job Placement Findings Memo file that contains the final wording so that you can create a chart of its Word table. This file, called Job Placement Findings Memo with Table, is located on the Data Files for Students. See the inside back cover of this book for instructions on downloading the Data Files for Students, or contact your instructor for information about accessing the required files.

To preserve the contents of the file on the Data Files for Students, create a new file from the existing file. The steps on the next page create a new file from an existing file.

1 Open the Backstage view and then click the New tab in the Backstage view to display the New gallery.

2 Click the 'New from existing' button in the New gallery to display the New from Existing Document dialog box.

3 Locate and then select the file with the name, Job Placement Findings Memo with Table.

4 Click the Create New button (New from Existing Document dialog box) to open a new document window that contains the contents of the selected file.

5 If necessary, change the zoom to 100% and scroll so that all document contents are visible in the document window.

To Chart a Table Using Graph

To chart a Word table, first select the rows and columns in the table to be charted. In this project, you chart the entire table. The following steps chart a table.

- Center the paragraph mark below the table so that the inserted chart will be centered.

- Select the table to be charted.

Q&A How do I select a table?

Point somewhere in the table and then click the table move handle that appears in the upper-left corner of the table, or position the insertion point in a table cell, click the Select button (Table Tools Layout tab | Table group) and then click Select Table on the Select menu.

- Display the Insert tab.

- Click the Insert Object button (Insert tab | Text group) to display the Object dialog box.

Q&A What if I accidentally click the Insert Object button arrow (Insert tab | Text group)?

Click Object on the Object menu.

- If necessary, click the Create New tab (Object dialog box).

- Scroll to and then select Microsoft Graph Chart in the Object type list to specify the object being inserted (Figure 8–32).

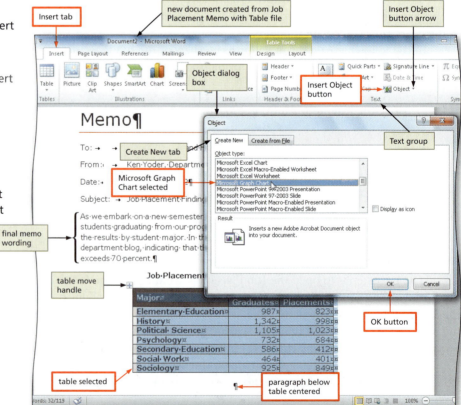

Figure 8–32

2

- Click the OK button to start the Microsoft Graph program, which creates a chart of the selected table (Figure 8–33).

Q&A What are the requirements for the format of a table that can be charted using Graph?

The first row and left column of the table or selected cells in the table must contain text labels, and the other cells in the selected cells must contain numbers.

- Close the Datasheet window by clicking the View Datasheet button on the Standard toolbar.

Q&A What is the Datasheet window?

Graph places the contents of the table in a **Datasheet window**, also

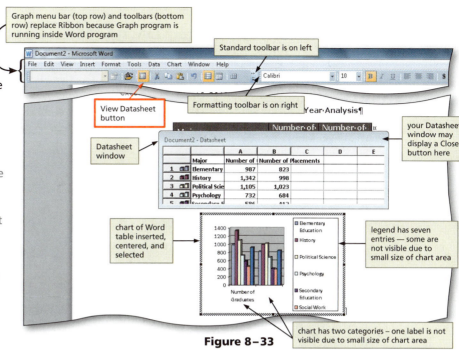

Figure 8–33

called a **datasheet**. Graph then charts the contents of the datasheet. Although you can modify the contents of the datasheet, it is not necessary in this project. Thus, the datasheet is closed.

Q&A If my Datasheet window displays a Close button, can I click the Close button to close the Datasheet window?

Yes.

To Graph by Column Using Graph

The first step in changing the chart is to reverse how the data is categorized in the chart and in the legend. The **legend** is a box that identifies the colors assigned to categories in the chart. The current graph (shown in Figure 8–33) has two categories, one for each column in the table (Number of Graduates and Number of Placements) with seven entries in each category, one for each row in the first column of the table (i.e., Elementary Education, History, etc.). For the chart in this chapter, you want the reverse, that is, seven categories, one for each row in the first column of the table with two entries in each category, one for each column in the first row of the table. The following step changes the chart from by row to by column so that the categories are the Number of Graduates and Number of Placements instead of majors.

1

- Click the By Column button on the Standard toolbar to plot the data by column instead of by row (Figure 8–34).

Q&A What if Microsoft Graph is no longer active; that is, what if the Word Ribbon is displayed instead of the Graph menus and toolbars?

While working in Graph, you may inadvertently click somewhere outside the chart, which quits Graph and returns to Word. If this occurs, simply double-click the chart to return to Graph.

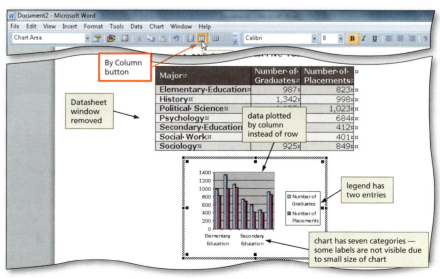

Figure 8–34

Other Ways

1. Click Series in Columns on Data menu

To Move Legend Placement in a Chart Using Graph

The next step in changing the chart is to move the legend so that it is displayed below the chart instead of to the right of the chart. The following steps move the legend in the chart.

1

• Click the Chart Objects box arrow on the Standard toolbar to display the Chart Objects menu, which contains a list of objects on the chart that you can format (Figure 8–35).

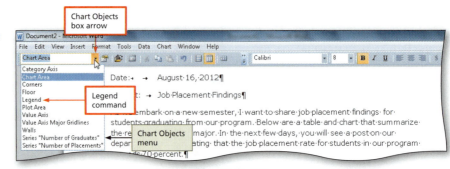

Figure 8–35

2

• Click Legend in the list to select the chart object to format.

• Click the Format Legend button on the Standard toolbar to display the Format Legend dialog box.

• If necessary, click the Placement tab (Format Legend dialog box).

• Click Bottom in the Placement area to specify the location for the legend (Figure 8–36).

3

• Click the OK button to place the legend in the selected location (shown in Figure 8–37).

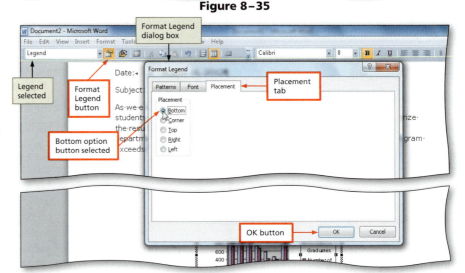

Figure 8–36

Other Ways

1. Right-click legend, click Format Legend on shortcut menu

To Resize a Chart

The next step is to resize the chart so that it is bigger. You resize a chart the same way you resize any other graphical object. That is, you drag the chart's sizing handles. The following steps resize the chart.

1

• Scroll as necessary so that blank space appears below the chart to make room for dragging the chart corner to a larger size.

• Point to the bottom-right sizing handle on the chart and drag downward and to the right as shown in Figure 8–37.

2

• Release the mouse button to resize the chart (shown in Figure 8–38).

• If the chart moves to a second page, resize the chart smaller so that it fits at the bottom of the first page.

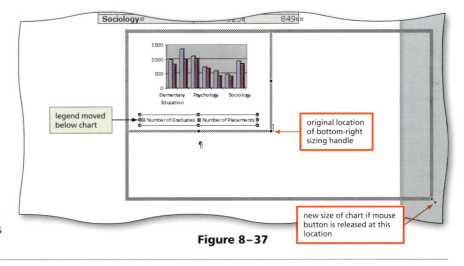

Figure 8–37

To Change the Chart Type Using Graph

The next task is to change the chart type so that the columns have a cylindrical shape instead of a rectangular shape and are displayed horizontally instead of vertically. Changing the direction of the columns will relocate the category names from the x-axis to the y-axis. The following steps change the chart type.

1

• Click Chart on the menu bar to display the Chart menu (Figure 8–38).

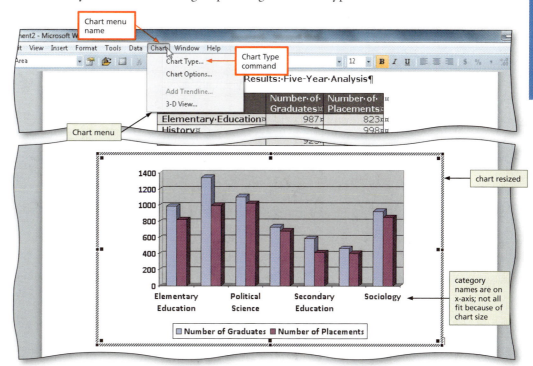

Figure 8–38

2

• Click Chart Type on the Chart menu to display the Chart Type dialog box.

• If necessary, click the Standard Types tab (Chart Type dialog box).

• In the Chart type list, scroll to and then select Cylinder to select the type of chart.

• In the Chart sub-type list, click the first sub-type in the second row to select the chart sub-type (in this case, Bar with a cylindrical shape) (Figure 8–39).

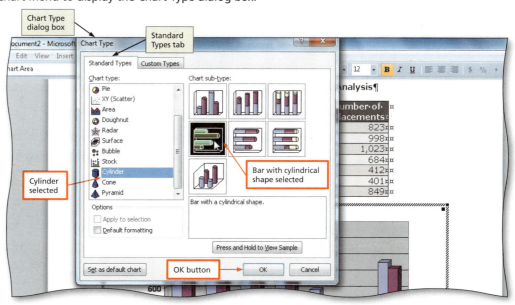

Figure 8–39

3

• Click the OK button to change the chart type (shown in Figure 8–40 on the next page).

Other Ways

1. Right-click white space in chart, click Chart Type on shortcut menu

To Format Text in the Chart Area Using Graph

Currently, the category names are not all visible on the y-axis because their font size is too big. Thus, the next task is to reduce the font size and change the font of text in the chart area. The following steps format the chart area.

- Click the Chart Objects box arrow on the Standard toolbar to display the Chart Objects menu.

- Click Chart Area in the list to specify the object to be formatted.

- Click the Format Chart Area button on the Standard toolbar to display the Format Chart Area dialog box.

Q&A

Did the function of the button to the right of the Chart Object box arrow change?

Yes. When you select an object to format on the Chart Objects menu, the function and name of the button to the right of the Chart Objects box arrow change to match the selected object.

- If necessary, click the Font tab (Format Chart Area dialog box).

- Select Verdana as the font and 10 as the font size (Figure 8–40).

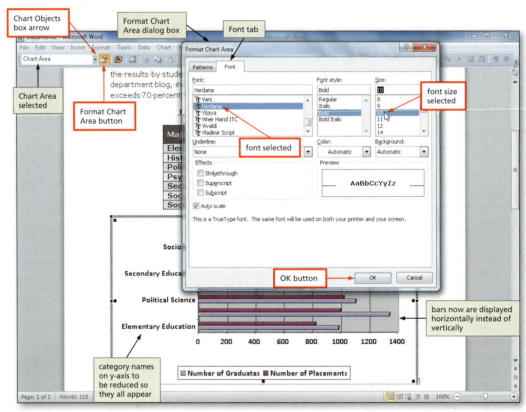

Figure 8–40

- Click the OK button to change the font and font size of the text in the chart area (shown in Figure 8–41).

- If necessary, resize the chart or reduce the font size of text in the chart area further so that all category names appear on the y-axis and the chart fits at the bottom of the page.

Other Ways

1. Right-click near inside edge of chart border, click Format Chart Area on shortcut menu

To Format an Axis Using Graph

Currently, the category names on the y-axis are in reverse order of the row labels in the table; that is, the category names are in alphabetical order from bottom to top, and the row labels in the table are in alphabetical order from top to bottom. The next task is to reverse the order of the categories in the chart. The next steps format an axis.

1

● Click the Chart Objects box arrow on the Standard toolbar to display the Chart Objects menu.

● Click Category Axis in the list to specify the object to be formatted.

● Click the Format Axis button on the Standard toolbar to display the Format Axis dialog box.

● If necessary, click the Scale tab (Format Axis dialog box).

● Place a check mark in the 'Categories in reverse order' check box to reverse the order of categories on the y-axis (Figure 8–41).

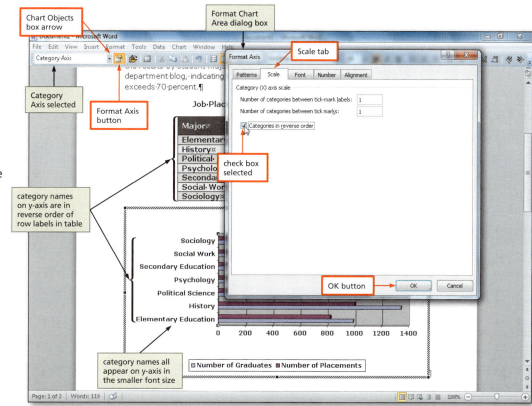

Figure 8–41

2

● Click the OK button to format the category axis as specified (shown in Figure 8–42 on the next page).

Other Ways

1. Right-click axis, click Format Axis on shortcut menu

To Quit Graph and Return to Word

The modified chart is finished. The next step is to quit Graph and return to Word. In Word, you place an outside border on the chart to give it a finished look. The following steps quit Graph and add a border to the chart.

1

● Click somewhere outside the chart to quit the Graph program and return to Word.

● If necessary, scroll to display the chart in the document window.

Q&A What if I want to modify an existing chart after I quit Graph?

You would double-click the chart to restart the Graph program. When you are finished making changes to the chart, click anywhere outside the chart to return to Word.

- Display the Home tab.

- Click the chart to select it.

- Click the Border button arrow (Home tab | Paragraph group) and then click Borders and Shading in the Border gallery to display the Borders and Shading gallery.

- Click Box (Borders and Shading dialog box) and then click the OK button to place a border around the chart.

- Click to the right of the chart to deselect it (Figure 8–42).

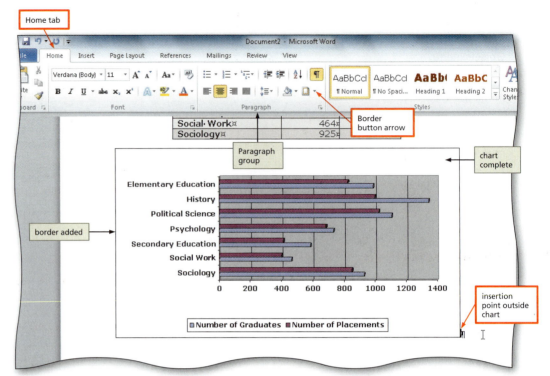

Figure 8–42

To Save a Document

You are finished charting the Word table using Graph. The next step is to save the document. Do not close the document because you will use it again later in the chapter. The following steps save a document.

1 With a USB flash drive connected to one of the computer's USB ports, click the Save button on the Quick Access Toolbar to display the Save As dialog box.

2 Type `Job Placement Memo with Table and Graph Chart` in the File name text box to change the file name. Do not press the ENTER key because you do not want to close the dialog box at this time.

3 If necessary, navigate to the save location (in this case, the Word folder in the CIS 101 folder [or your class folder] on the USB flash drive).

4 Click the Save button (Save As dialog box) to save the document in the selected folder on the USB flash drive with the entered file name.

Linking an Excel Worksheet to a Word Document

With Microsoft Office, you can copy part or all of a document created in one Office program to a document created in another Office program. The item being copied is called the **object**. For example, you could copy an Excel worksheet (the object) that is located in an Excel workbook (the source file) to a Word document (the destination file). That is, an object is copied from a source to a destination.

You can use one of three techniques to copy objects from one program to another: copy and paste, embed, or link.

- **Copy and paste**. When you copy an object and then paste it, the object becomes part of the destination document. You edit a pasted object using editing features of the destination program. For example, when you select an Excel worksheet in an Excel workbook, click the Copy button (Home tab | Clipboard group) in Excel, and then click the Paste button (Home tab | Clipboard group) in Word, the Excel worksheet becomes a Word table.

- **Embed**. When you embed an object, like a pasted object, it becomes part of the destination document. The difference between an embedded object and a pasted object is that you edit the contents of an embedded object using the editing features of the source program. The embedded object, however, contains static data; that is, any changes made to the object in the source program are not reflected in the destination document. If you embed an Excel worksheet in a Word document, the Excel worksheet remains as an Excel worksheet in the Word document. When you edit the Excel worksheet from within the Word document, you will use Excel editing features.

- **Link**. A linked objcct, by contrast, does not become a part of the destination document even though it appears to be a part of it. Rather, a connection is established between the source and destination documents so that when you open the destination document, the linked object appears as part of it. When you edit a linked object, the source program starts and opens the source document that contains the linked object. For example, when you edit a linked worksheet, Excel starts and displays the Excel workbook that contains the worksheet; you then edit the worksheet in Excel. Unlike an embedded object, if you open the Excel workbook that contains the Excel worksheet and then edit the Excel worksheet, the linked object will be updated in the Word document, too.

BTW

Linked Objects
When you open a document that contains linked objects, Word displays a dialog box asking if you want to update the Word document with data from the linked file. Click the Yes button only if you are certain the linked file is from a trusted source; that is, you should be confident that the source file does not contain a virus or other potentially harmful program before you instruct Word to link the source file to the destination document.

Determine how to copy an object.
You can copy and paste, embed, or link an object created in another Office program to a Word document.

- If you simply want to use the object's data and have no desire to use the object in the source program, then copy and paste the object.

- If you want to use the object in the source program but you want the object's data to remain static if it changes in the source file, then embed the object.

- If you want to ensure that the most current version of the object appears in the destination file, then link the object. If the source file is large, such as a video clip or a sound clip, link the object to keep the size of the destination file smaller.

Plan Ahead

The steps in this section show how to link an Excel worksheet (the object), which is located in an Excel workbook (the source file), to a Word document (the destination file). The Word document is similar to the same memo used in the previous section, except that it does not contain the table. To link the worksheet to the memo, you will follow these general steps:

1. Start Excel and open the Excel workbook that contains the object (worksheet) to be linked.

2. Select the object (worksheet) in Excel and then copy the selected object to the Clipboard.

3. Switch to Word and then link the copied object into the document.

Note: The steps in this section assume you have Microsoft Excel installed on your computer. If you do not have Excel, read the steps in this section without performing them.

To Create a New File from an Existing File

The first step in this section is to open the memo that is to contain link to the Excel worksheet object. The memo file, named Job Placement Findings Memo without Table, is located on the Data Files for Students. See the inside back cover of this book for instructions on downloading the Data Files for Students, or contact your instructor for information about accessing the required files.

To preserve the contents of the file on the Data Files for Students, create a new file from the existing file. The following steps create a new file from an existing file and then display its contents in the document window.

1 Open the Backstage view and then click the New tab in the Backstage view to display the New gallery.

2 Click the 'New from existing' button in the New gallery to display the New from Existing Document dialog box.

3 Locate and then select the file with the name, Job Placement Findings Memo without Table.

4 Click the Create New button (New from Existing Document dialog box) to open a new document window that contains the contents of the selected file.

5 If necessary, change the zoom to 100% and scroll so that all document contents are visible in the document window.

Excel Basics

The Excel window contains a rectangular grid that consists of columns and rows. A column letter above the grid identifies each column. A row number on the left side of the grid identifies each row. The intersection of each column and row is a cell. A cell is referred to by its unique address, which is the coordinates of the intersection of a column and a row. To identify a cell, specify the column letter first, followed by the row number. For example, cell reference A1 refers to the cell located at the intersection of column A and row 1 (Figure 8–43).

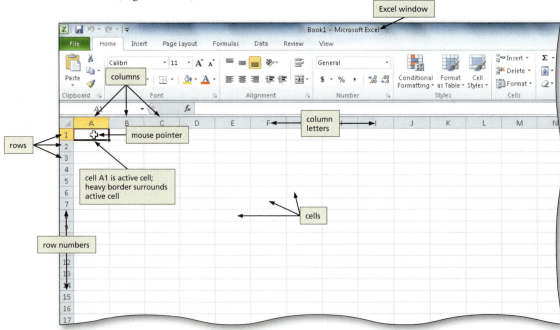

Figure 8–43

To Start Excel and Open an Excel Workbook

The Excel worksheet to be linked to the memo is in an Excel workbook called Job Placement Table in Excel, which is located on the Data Files for Students. See the inside back cover of this book for instructions on downloading the Data Files for Students, or contact your instructor for information about accessing the required files.

The following steps start Excel and open a workbook. (Do not quit Word or close the open Word document before starting these steps.)

1 Click the Start button on the Windows 7 taskbar to display the Start menu.

2 Type **Microsoft Excel** as the search text in the 'Search programs and files' text box and watch the search results appear on the Start menu.

3 Click Microsoft Excel 2010 in the search results on the Start menu to start Excel and display a new blank workbook in the Excel window.

4 If the Excel window is not maximized, click the Maximize button on its title bar to maximize the window.

5 Open the Backstage view and then click Open in the Backstage view to display the Open dialog box.

6 Navigate to the location of the file to be opened (in this case, the Job Placement Table in Excel file, on the Data Files for Students).

7 Click Job Placement Findings Table in Excel to select the file name and then click the Open button (Open dialog box) to open the selected file and display the opened workbook in the Excel window.

BTW

Opening Word Documents with Links
When you open a document that contains a linked object, Word attempts to locate the source file associated with the link. If Word cannot find the source file, open the Backstage view, display the Info tab, then click Edit Links to Files at the bottom of the right pane to display the Links dialog box. Next, select the appropriate source file in the list, click the Change Source button, locate the source file, and then click the OK button (Links dialog box).

To Link an Excel Worksheet in a Word Document

The next step is to copy the Excel worksheet to the Clipboard and then link the Excel worksheet to the Word document. The following steps link an Excel worksheet to a Word document.

1

• In the Excel window, drag through the cells in the range A1 through C8 to select them.

• In the Excel window, click the Copy button (Home tab | Clipboard group) to copy the selected cells to the Clipboard (Figure 8–44).

Q&A What if I click the Copy button arrow by mistake?

Click Copy on the Copy menu.

Q&A What is the dotted line around the selected cells?

Excel surrounds copied cells with a moving marquee to help you visually identify the copied cells.

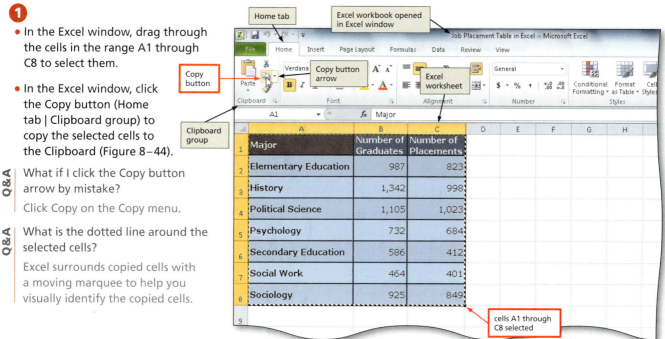

Figure 8–44

2

- Point to the Word program button on the taskbar to display a live preview of the open documents or window titles of the open documents, depending on your computer's configuration, and then click the live preview of the memo without the table to switch to Word and display the selected document in the Word document window.

- Position the insertion point on the paragraph mark below the paragraph.

- In Word, click the Paste button arrow (Home tab | Clipboard group) to display the Paste gallery.

Q&A
What if I accidentally click the Paste button instead of the Paste button arrow?

Click the Undo button on the Quick Access Toolbar and then click the Paste button arrow.

- Point to the Link & Keep Source Formatting button in the Paste gallery to display a live preview of that paste option (Figure 8–45).

Experiment

- Point to the various buttons in the Paste gallery to display a live preview of each paste option.

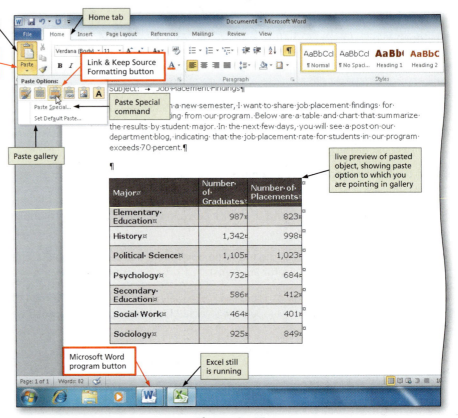

Figure 8–45

3

- Click the Link & Keep Source Formatting button in the Paste gallery to paste and link the object at the location of the insertion point in the document.

Q&A
What if I wanted to copy an object instead of link it?

To copy an object, you would click the Keep Source Formatting button in the Paste gallery. To convert the object to a picture so that you can use tools on Word's Picture Tools tab to format it, you would click the Picture button in the Paste gallery.

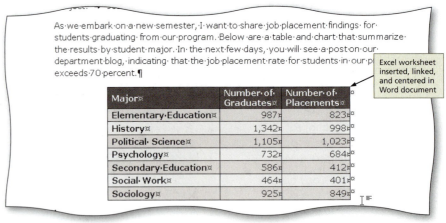

Figure 8–46

- Select and then center the linked Excel table using the same technique you use to select and center a Word table.

- Resize the linked Excel table by dragging its resize handle (in the lower-right corner) until the table is approximately the same size as Figure 8–46.

Q&A
What if I wanted to delete the linked worksheet?

You would select the linked worksheet and then press the DELETE key.

Other Ways

1. Click Paste button arrow (Home tab | Clipboard group), click Paste Special, click Paste link (Paste Special dialog box), click Microsoft Excel Worksheet Object, click OK button

2. To link an entire source file, click the Insert Object button (Insert tab | Text group), click Create from File tab (Object dialog box), locate file, click 'Link to file' check box, click OK button

TO EMBED AN EXCEL WORKSHEET IN A WORD DOCUMENT

If you wanted to embed an Excel worksheet in a Word document, instead of link it, you would perform the following steps.

1. Start Excel.

2. In Excel, select the worksheet cells to embed and then click the Copy button (Home tab | Clipboard group) to copy the selected cells to the Clipboard.

3. Switch to Word. In Word, click the Paste button arrow (Home tab | Clipboard group) to display the Paste gallery and then click the Paste Special command in the Paste gallery to display the Paste Special dialog box.

4. Select the Paste option button (Paste Special dialog box), which indicates the object will be embedded.

5. Select Microsoft Excel Worksheet Object as the type of object to embed.

6. Click the OK button to embed the contents of the Clipboard in the Word document at the location of the insertion point.

TO EDIT A LINKED OBJECT

At a later time, you may find it necessary to change the data in the Excel worksheet. Any changes you make to the Excel worksheet while in Excel will be reflected in the Excel worksheet in the Word document because the objects are linked to the Word document. If you wanted to edit a linked object, such as an Excel worksheet, you would perform these steps.

1. In the Word document, right-click the linked Excel worksheet, point to Linked Worksheet Object on the shortcut menu, and then click Edit Link on the Linked Worksheet Object submenu to start the Excel program and open the source file that contains the linked worksheet.

2. In Excel, make changes to the Excel worksheet.

3. Click the Save button on the Quick Access Toolbar to save the changes.

4. Quit Excel.

5. If necessary, redisplay the Word window.

6. If necessary, to update the worksheet with the edited Excel data, click the Excel worksheet in the Word document and then press the F9 key or right-click the linked object and then click Update Link on the shortcut menu to update the linked object with the revisions made to the source file.

BTW

Editing Embedded Objects
If you wanted to edit an embedded object in the Word document, you would double-click the object to display the source program's interface in the destination program. For example, double-clicking an embedded Excel worksheet in a Word document displays the Excel Ribbon in the Word window. To redisplay the Word Ribbon in the Word window, double-click outside the embedded object.

Enhance a document with appropriate visuals.
If you share a Word document that contains a linked object, such as an Excel worksheet, users will be asked by Word if they want to update the links when they open the Word document. If users are unfamiliar with links, they will not know how to answer the question. Further, if they do not have the source program, such as Excel, they may not be able to open the Word document. When sharing documents, it is recommended you convert links to a regular Word object, that is, break the link.

Plan Ahead

To Break a Link

To convert a linked or embedded object to a Word object, you break the link. That is, you break the connection between the source file and the destination file. When you break a linked object, such as an Excel worksheet, the linked object becomes a Word object, a Word table in this case. The steps on the next page break the link to the Excel worksheet.

1

- Right-click the linked object (the linked Excel worksheet, in this case) to display a shortcut menu.

- Point to Linked Worksheet Object on the shortcut menu to display the Linked Worksheet Object submenu (Figure 8–47).

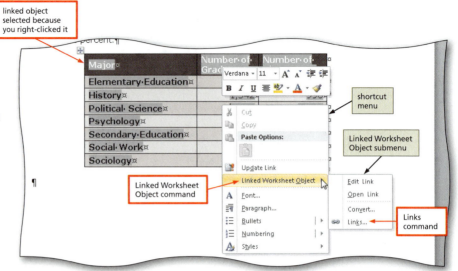

Figure 8–47

2

- Click Links on the Linked Worksheet Object submenu to display the Links dialog box.

- If necessary, click the source file listed in the dialog box to select it (Links dialog box).

- Click the Break Link button, which displays a dialog box asking if you are sure you want to break the selected links (Figure 8–48).

3

- Click the Yes button in the dialog box to remove the source file from the list (break the link).

Q&A

How can I verify the link is broken?

Right-click the table in the Word document. If the shortcut menu does not contain a Linked Worksheet Object command, a link does not exist for the object. Or, when you double-click the table, Excel should not open an associated workbook.

Figure 8–48

Other Ways

1. Select link, press CTRL+SHIFT+F9

To Close the Document without Saving It

The next step is to close the document without saving it. The following steps close the Word document and the Excel window.

1 Open the Backstage view and then click Close.

2 When Word displays the dialog box, click the Don't Save button.

3 Right-click the Excel program button on the taskbar and then click Close window on the shortcut menu.

4 If necessary, click the Word program button on the taskbar to redisplay the Word window, which contains the Job Placement Findings Memo with Table and Graph Chart.

Charting a Word Table Using Office 2010 Chart Tools

If you have Microsoft Excel installed on your computer and you know the basics of Excel, you can use the advanced data charting capabilities of Microsoft Office 2010 through your Microsoft Word program. The advanced data charting capabilities are accessed through Word's Chart Tools tabs, which has a similar look and functionality to Excel's charting functionality.

So that you can compare these chart tools with Microsoft Graph's charting capabilities, this section creates a chart similar to the one created earlier in the chapter using Microsoft Graph. In the following pages, you will insert and format a chart of the Job Placement Statistics Word table using the Chart Tools tab in Word, which utilizes Microsoft Excel. You will follow these general steps to insert and then format the chart using Office Chart Tools:

1. Create a chart of the table.
2. Resize the chart.
3. Move the legend to a different location.
4. Add an outline to the chart.
5. Reverse the order of labels on the category axis (y-axis).
6. Change the font size of text in the chart.

Note: The steps in this section assume you have Microsoft Excel installed on your computer. If you do not have Excel, read these steps without performing them.

To Create a New File from an Existing File

The next step is to open the Job Placement Findings Memo file that contains the final wording so that you can create a chart of its Word table. This file, called Job Placement Findings Memo with Table, is located on the Data Files for Students. See the inside back cover of this book for instructions on downloading the Data Files for Students, or contact your instructor for information about accessing the required files.

To preserve the contents of the file on the Data Files for Students, create a new file from the existing file. The following steps create a new file from an existing file and then display its contents in the document window.

1 Open the Backstage view and then click the New tab in the Backstage view to display the New gallery.

2 Click the 'New from existing' button in the New gallery to display the New from Existing Document dialog box.

3 Locate and then select the file with the name, Job Placement Findings Memo with Table.

4 Click the Create New button (New from Existing Document dialog box) to open a new document window that contains the contents of the selected file.

5 If necessary, change the zoom to 100% and scroll so that all document contents are visible in the document window.

To Chart a Table Using Office Chart Tools

To chart a table using the advanced charting capabilities of Office, you insert a default chart and fill in or copy the data to the associated Excel window that automatically opens after you insert the chart. The steps on the next page insert a default chart and then copy the data to be charted from the Word table in the Word document to the Excel window.

1

- Select the table to be charted.
- Click the Copy button (Home tab | Clipboard group) to copy the selected table to the Clipboard.
- Center the paragraph mark below the table so that the inserted chart will be centered. Leave the insertion point on this paragraph mark because the chart will be inserted at the location of the insertion point.
- Display the Insert tab.
- Click the Insert Chart button (Insert tab | Illustrations group) to display the Insert Chart dialog box.

Q&A

What if the Microsoft Graph program starts instead?

You do not have Microsoft Excel installed on your computer. Read through the remaining steps without performing them. See the section earlier in this chapter for steps related to creating a chart using Microsoft Graph.

- Click Bar in the left pane (Insert Chart dialog box) to display the available types of bar charts in the right pane.

Experiment

- Click the various types of charts in the left pane and watch the subtypes appear in the right pane. When finished experimenting, click Bar in the left pane.

- Click Clustered Horizontal Cylinder in the right pane to select the chart type (Figure 8–49).

2

- Click the OK button so that Word creates a default clustered horizontal cylinder bar chart in the Word document, starts Excel, and splits the screen with the Word window in the left half and the Excel window with the data for the chart in the right half (Figure 8–50).

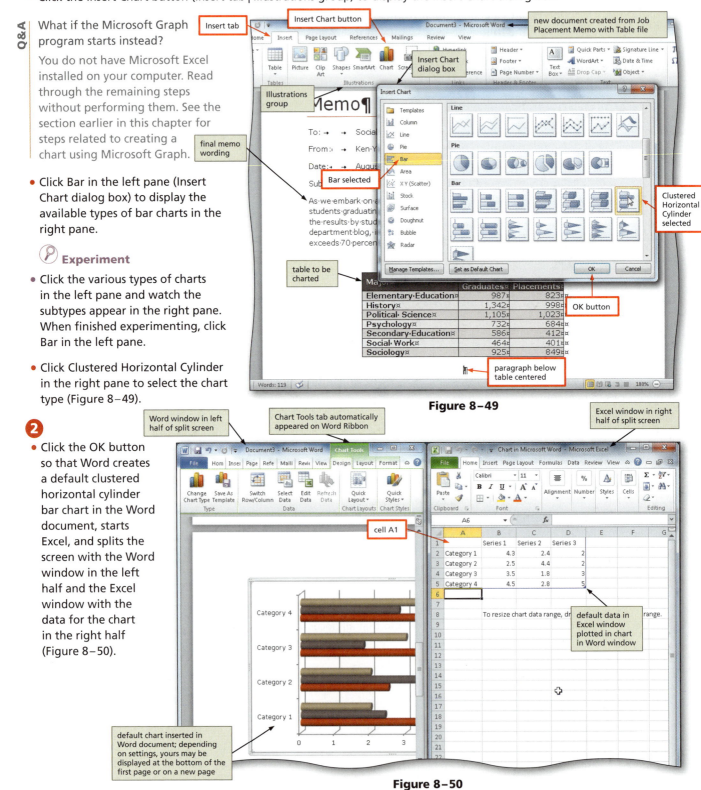

Figure 8–49

Figure 8–50

Q&A Why did Excel start?

To use the advanced charting capabilities of Office, the data to be plotted in a chart in the Word document is entered in an Excel worksheet, so the Excel program starts automatically.

Q&A What are the requirements for the format of a table that can be charted?

The Excel window shows the layout for the selected chart type. In this case, the categories are in the rows and the entries are in the columns.

3

- In the Excel window, click cell A1 to select it.

- In the Excel window, click the Paste button (Home tab | Clipboard group) to paste the contents of the Clipboard starting in the upper-left corner of the worksheet, and notice that the chart in the Word window automatically changes to reflect the new data (Figure 8–51).

Q&A What if I accidentally click the Paste button arrow?

Click the Keep Source Formatting button in the Paste gallery.

- If an Excel dialog box appears indicating cells will shift down, click its OK button.

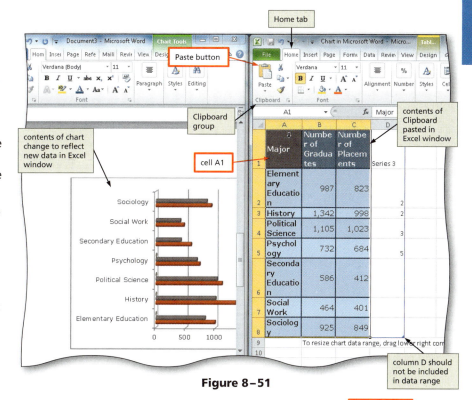

Figure 8–51

4

- In the Excel window, drag the lower-right corner of the blue outline to the left so that it ends at column C (Figure 8–52).

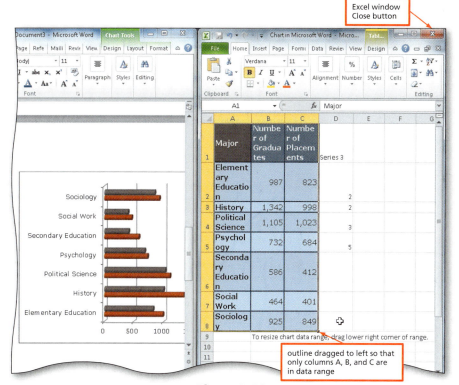

Figure 8–52

5

- In the Excel window, click the Close button to close the Excel window and show a maximized Word window with the chart (Figure 8–53).

Q&A

How would I edit the chart data, if necessary?

Click the Edit Data button (Chart Tools Design tab | Data group) to reopen the Excel window. When you are finished editing the data, close the Excel window.

Q&A

How would I change the chart type, if necessary?

With the chart selected, click the Change Chart Type button (Chart Tools Design tab | Type group) to display the Change Chart Type dialog box, select the desired chart type, and then click the OK button.

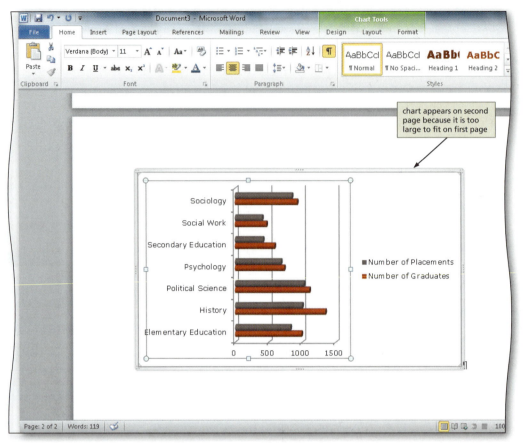

Figure 8–53

To Resize a Chart

The next step is to resize the chart so that it is smaller and fits at the bottom of the first page. You resize a chart the same way you resize any other graphical object. That is, you select it and then you drag a corner in the direction in which you want to resize. The following steps resize the chart.

1 Click the chart to select it.

2 Position the mouse pointer on a corner of the chart until it changes to a double-headed arrow and then drag inward a bit so that the chart fits on the bottom of the first page (shown in Figure 8–54).

3 If the chart does not fit at the bottom of the first page, repeat Step 2.

To Move the Legend Placement Using Office Chart Tools

The next step in changing the chart is to move the legend so that it is displayed below the chart instead of to the right of the chart. The next steps move the legend using Office Chart Tools.

1

• Display the Chart Tools Layout tab.

• Click the Legend button (Chart Tools Layout tab | Labels group) to display the Legend gallery (Figure 8–54).

2

• Click Show Legend at Bottom in the Legend gallery to place the legend in the selected location (shown in Figure 8–55).

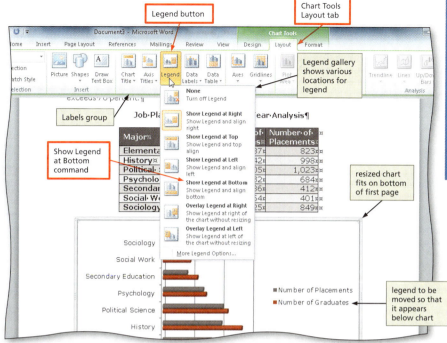

Figure 8–54

To Add an Outline to a Chart Using Office Chart Tools

The next task is to add a border to the chart. Because the chart is considered a shape object, you add an outline to the chart using the same technique you use to add an outline to a shape. The following steps add a black outline to the chart.

1

• Display the Chart Tools Format tab.

• Click the Shape Outline button arrow (Chart Tools Format tab | Shape Styles group) to display the Shape Outline gallery and then click Black, Text 1 (second color, first row) in the Shape Outline gallery to change the outline color.

• Click the Shape Outline button arrow (Chart Tools Format tab | Shape Styles group) again, point to Weight in the Shape Outline gallery to display the Weight gallery, and then point to ¼ pt to display a live preview of the selected weight (Figure 8–55).

2

• Click ¼ pt in the Weight gallery to apply the selected weight to the outline.

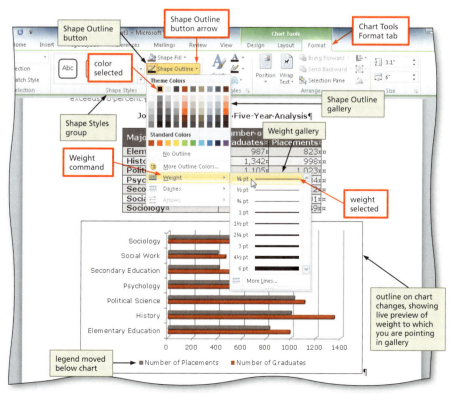

Figure 8–55

To Format an Axis Using Office Chart Tools

Currently, the category names on the y-axis are in reverse order of the row labels in the table; that is, category names are in alphabetical order from bottom to top and the row labels in the table are in alphabetical order from top to bottom. The next task is to reverse the order of the categories in the chart. The following steps format an axis.

1
• Click the Chart Elements box arrow (Chart Tools Format tab | Current Selection group) to display the Chart Elements gallery, which contains a list of objects on the chart that you can format (Figure 8–56).

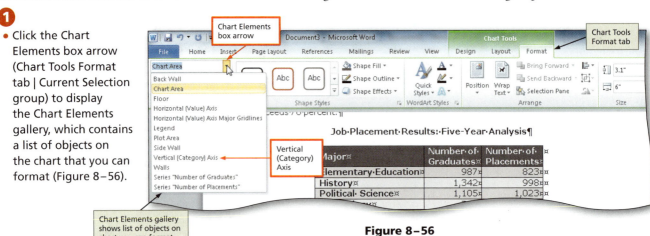

Figure 8–56

2
• Click Vertical (Category) Axis in the list to specify the object to be formatted.

• Click the Format Selection button (Chart Tools Format tab | Current Selection group) to display the Format Axis dialog box.

Q&A
Does the Format Selection button display the dialog box associated with the currently selected object in the Chart Elements box?

Yes.

• If necessary, click Axis Options in the left pane (Format Axis dialog box).

• Place a check mark in the 'Categories in reverse order' check box to indicate that the categories on the y-axis should be displayed in the reverse order (Figure 8–57).

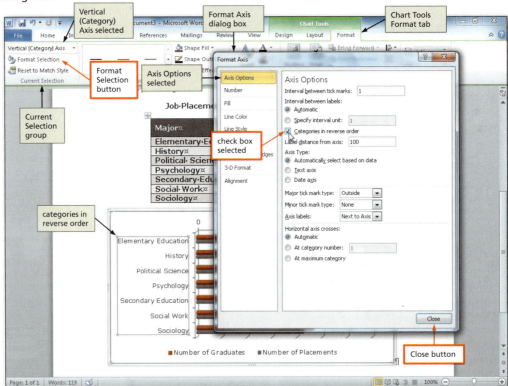

Figure 8–57

3
• Click the Close button to format the category axis as specified (shown in Figure 8–58).

Q&A
Why did the x-axis move from the bottom of the chart to the top?

When you reverse the categories, the x-axis automatically moves from the bottom of the chart to the top of the chart.

Other Ways

1. Right-click axis, click Chart Elements box arrow on Mini toolbar, click Vertical (Category) Axis in gallery

To Format Text in the Chart Area

The text in the chart should be bold. You format chart text the same way you format document text, that is, through the Font group on the Home tab. The following steps format the text in the chart area.

1 Click the outside edge of the chart to select the entire chart.

2 Display the Home tab.

3 Click the Bold button (Home tab | Font group) to bold the text in the chart (Figure 8–58).

4 If necessary, widen the chart so that all labels on the x-axis appear.

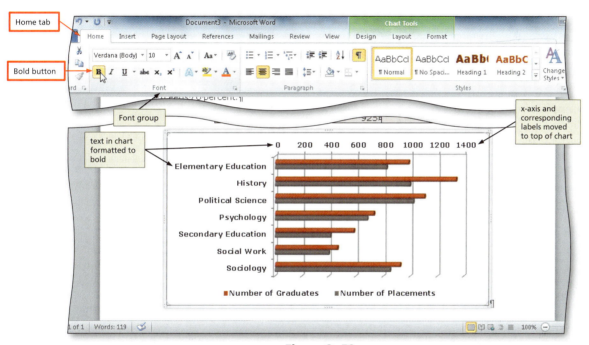

Figure 8–58

To Save a Document

You are finished charting the Word table using advanced charting capabilities of Office 2010. Thus, the following steps save the document.

1 With a USB flash drive connected to one of the computer's USB ports, click the Save button on the Quick Access Toolbar to display the Save As dialog box.

2 Type **Job Placement Memo with Table and Chart Tools Chart** in the File name text box to change the file name. Do not press the ENTER key because you do not want to close the dialog box at this time.

3 If necessary, navigate to the save location (in this case, the Word folder in the CIS 101 folder [or your class folder] on the USB flash drive).

4 Click the Save button (Save As dialog box) to save the document in the selected folder on the USB flash drive with the entered file name.

BTW

Save a Chart as a Template
To save a chart you create as a template, select the chart, click the Save As Template button (Chart Tools Design tab | Type group), type a file name in the File name box (Save Chart Template dialog box), and then click the Save button. To use the saved template, click the Change Chart Type button (Chart Tools Design tab | Type group), click Templates (Change Chart Type dialog box), click the desired saved template, and then click the OK button.

To View and Scroll through Documents Side by Side

You would like to see the how the chart created using Graph differs from the chart created using the Office Chart Tools. Word provides a way to display two documents side by side, each in a separate window. By default, the two documents scroll synchronously, that is, together. If necessary, you can turn off synchronous scrolling so that you can scroll through each document individually. The steps on the next page display documents side by side.

- Point to the Word program button on the taskbar to verify that the two documents to be displayed side by side are open (Figure 8–59).

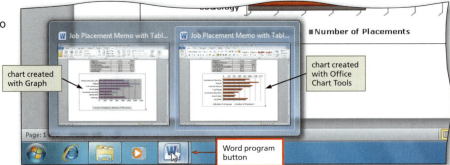

Figure 8–59

- Click the live preview of the document containing the chart created with Graph and then scroll to the top of the document because you want to begin viewing from the top of the document.

- Point to the Word program button on the taskbar and then click the live preview of the document containing the chart created with Office Chart Tools and then scroll to the top of the document because you want to begin viewing from the top of the document.

- Display the View tab (Figure 8–60).

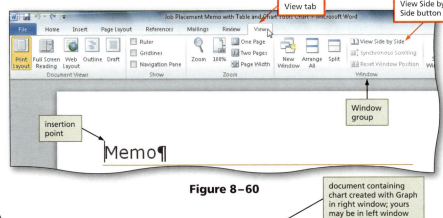

Figure 8–60

- Click the View Side by Side button (View tab | Window group) to display each open window side by side (Figure 8–61).

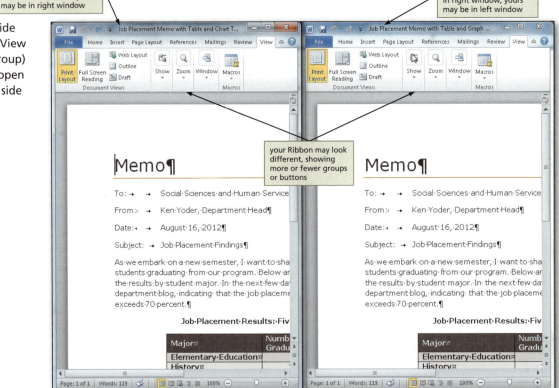

Figure 8–61

4

- Scroll to the bottom of one of the windows and notice how both windows (documents) scroll together.

Q&A | Can I scroll through one window separately from the other?

By default, synchronous scrolling is active when you display windows side by side. If you want to scroll separately through the windows, simply turn off synchronous scrolling.

5

- If necessary, display the View tab (in either window) and then, if necessary, click the Window button to display the Window group.

- Click the Synchronous Scrolling button (View tab | Window group) to turn off synchronous scrolling (Figure 8–62).

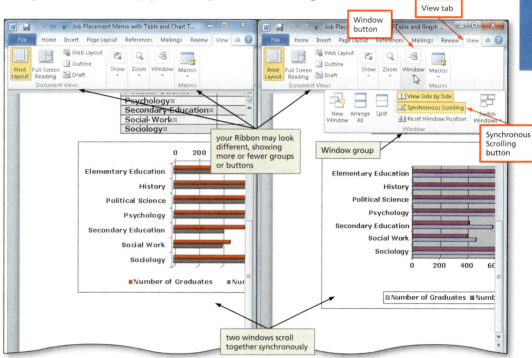

Figure 8–62

6

- Scroll to the top of the window on the right and notice that the window on the left does not scroll because you turned off synchronous scrolling (Figure 8–63).

7

- Click the View Side by Side button (View tab | Window group) to turn off side-by-side viewing and display each window in the full screen.

- Close each open Word document, saving them if prompted.

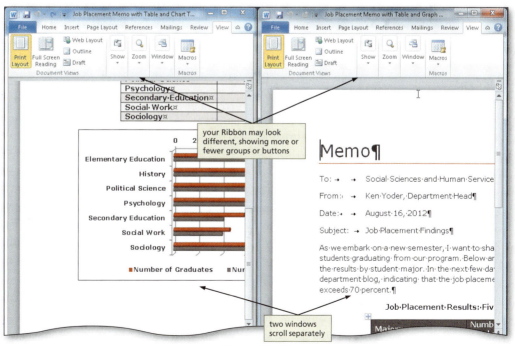

Figure 8–63

Creating a Blog Post

A **blog**, short for **Weblog**, is an informal Web site consisting of date- or time-stamped articles, or **posts**, in a diary or journal format, usually listed in reverse chronological order. Blogs reflect the interests, opinions, and personalities of the author, called the **blogger**, and sometimes of the site visitors as well.

Blogs have become an important means of worldwide communications. Businesses create blogs to communicate with employees, customers, and vendors. Teachers create blogs to collaborate with other teachers and students, and home users create blogs to share aspects of their personal life with family, friends, and others.

This section of the chapter creates a blog post and then publishes it to a registered blog account at WordPress, which is a blogging service on the Web. The blog post is a communication from the Department of Social Sciences and Human Services that welcomes students to the new semester and shows the August calendar.

Plan Ahead

> **Post communications on a blog.**
> When creating a blog post, you should follow these general guidelines:
>
> 1. **Create a blog account on the Web.** Many Web sites exist that allow users to set up a blog free or for a fee. Blogging services that work with Word 2010 include Windows Live Spaces, Blogger, SharePoint blog, Community Server, TypePad, and WordPress. For illustration purposes in this chapter, a free blog account was created at WordPress.com.
>
> 2. **Register your blog account in Word.** Before you can use Word to publish a blog post, you must register your blog account in Word. This step establishes a connection between Word and your blog account. The first time you create a new blog post, Word will ask if you want to register a blog account. You can click the Register Later button if you want to learn how to create a blog post without registering a blog account.
>
> 3. **Create a blog post.** Use Word to enter the text and any graphics in your blog post. Some blogging services accept graphics directly from a Word blog post. Others require that you use a picture hosting service to store pictures you use in a blog post.
>
> 4. **Publish a blog post.** When you publish a blog post, the blog post in the Word document is copied to your account at the blogging service. Once the post is published, it appears at the top of the blog Web page. You may need to click the Refresh button in the browser window to display the new post.

TO REGISTER A BLOG ACCOUNT

Once you set up a blog account with a blog provider, you must register it in Word so that you can publish your Word post on the blog account. Examples of blog providers are Windows Live Spaces, Blogger, SharePoint blog, Community Server, TypePad, and WordPress. To register a blog account, with WordPress for example, you would perform the following steps.

1. Click the Manage Accounts button (Blog Post tab | Blog group) to display the Blog Accounts dialog box.

2. Click the New button (Blog Accounts dialog box) to display the New Blog Account dialog box.

3. Click the Blog box arrow (New Blog Account dialog box) to display a list of blog providers and then select your provider in the list.

4. Click the Next button to display the New [Provider] Account dialog box (i.e., a New WordPress Account dialog box would appear if you selected WordPress as the provider).

5. In the Blog Post URL text box, replace the <Enter your blog URL here> with the Web address for your blog account. (Note that your dialog box may differ, depending on the provider you select.)

Q&A

What is a URL?

A URL (Uniform Resource Locator), often called a Web address, is the unique address for a Web page. For example, the Web address for a WordPress blog account might be smith.wordpress.com; in that case, the complete blog post URL would read as http://smith.wordpress.com/xhlrpc.php in the text box.

6. In the 'Enter account information' area, enter the user name and password you use to access your blog account.

Q&A

Should I click the Remember Password check box?

If you do not select this check box, Word will prompt you for a password each time you publish to the blog account.

7. If your blog provider does not allow pictures to be stored, click the Picture Options button, select the correct option for storing your posted pictures, and then click the OK button (Picture Options dialog box).

8. Click the OK button to register the blog account.

9. When Word displays a dialog box indicating the account registration was successful, click the OK button.

To Create a Blank Document for a Blog Post

The first step in this section is to create a document formatted for a blog post. The following steps create a new blank Word document for a blog post.

1

- Open the Backstage view.

- Click the New tab in the Backstage view to display the New gallery.

- Click the Blog post button in the Available Templates area to select the document type (Figure 8–64).

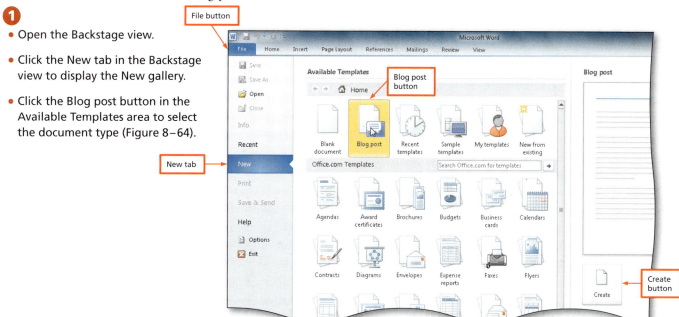

Figure 8–64

2

- Click the Create button in the New gallery to create a new blank document for a blog post (Figure 8–65).

Q&A
What if a Register a Blog Account dialog box appears?

Click the Register Later button to skip the registration process at this time. Or, if you have a blog account, you can click the Register Now button and follow the instructions to register your account.

Q&A
Why did the Ribbon change?

When creating a blog post, the Ribbon in Word changes to display only the tabs required to create and publish a blog post.

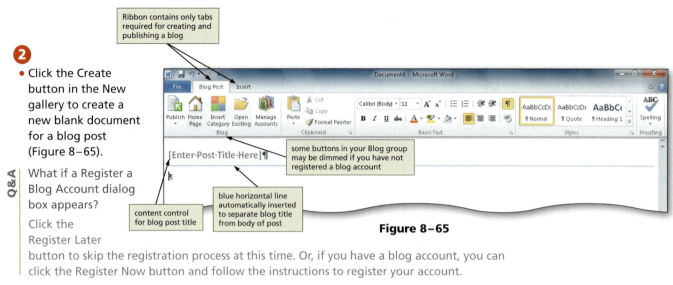

Ribbon contains only tabs required for creating and publishing a blog

some buttons in your Blog group may be dimmed if you have not registered a blog account

content control for blog post title

blue horizontal line automatically inserted to separate blog title from body of post

[Enter·Post·Title·Here]¶

Figure 8–65

To Enter Text

The next step is to enter the blog post title and text in the blog post. The following steps enter text in the blog post.

1 Click the Enter Post Title Here content control and then type `Social Sciences and Human Services Department Blog` as the title.

2 Position the insertion point below the blue horizontal line and then type these four lines of text:

`Welcome to a new semester!`

`Check here often for department updates.`

`Exciting news for current students - our job placement rate exceeds 70 percent in all majors!`

`August calendar:`

3 Press the ENTER key (Figure 8–66).

Q&A
Can I format text in the blog post?

Yes, you can use the Basic Text and other groups on the Ribbon to format the post. You also can check spelling using the Proofing group.

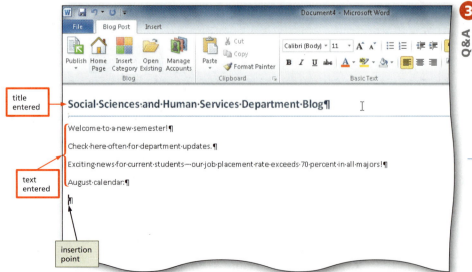

title entered

Social·Sciences·and·Human·Services·Department·Blog¶

Welcome·to·a·new·semester!¶

Check·here·often·for·department·updates.¶

Exciting·news·for·current·students—our·job·placement·rate·exceeds·70·percent·in·all·majors!¶

August·calendar:¶

text entered

insertion point

Figure 8–66

To Insert a Quick Table

The next step is to insert the August calendar in the blog. Word provides several quick tables, which are preformatted table styles that you can customize. Calendar formats are one type of quick table. The following steps insert a quick table.

1

- Display the Insert tab.

- With the insertion point positioned as shown in Figure 8–66, click the Table button (Insert tab | Tables group) to display the Table gallery.

- Point to Quick Tables in the Table gallery to display the Quick Tables gallery (Figure 8–67).

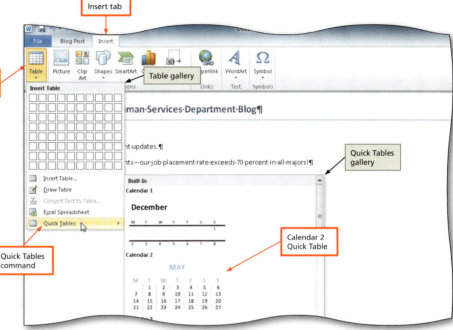

Figure 8–67

2

- Click Calendar 2 to insert the selected Quick Table in the document at the location of the insertion point (Figure 8–68).

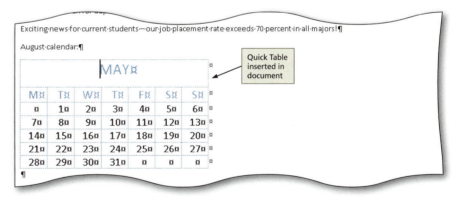

Figure 8–68

To Edit and Format a Table

The calendar in the blog post should show the month of August with a first day of the month starting on Wednesday. The following steps edit the table and apply a quick style.

1 Change the month in the first cell of the table from May to August.

2 Edit the contents of the cells in the table so that the first day of the month starts on a Wednesday and the 31 (the last day of the month) is on a Friday.

3 For the dates of August 14 through August 17, press the ENTER key after the date in each cell and then type `Open Registration` as additional text.

4 For the date of August 21, press the ENTER key after the date in the cell and then type `Classes Begin; Late Registration` as additional text.

5 For the dates of August 22 through August 24, press the ENTER key after the date in each cell and then type `Late Registration` as additional text.

6 If necessary, display the Table Tools Design tab.

7 Remove the check mark from the First Column check box (Table Tools Design tab | Table Style Options group) because you do not want the first column in the table formatted differently.

8 Apply the Medium Grid 2 – Accent 6 table style to the table (Figure 8–69).

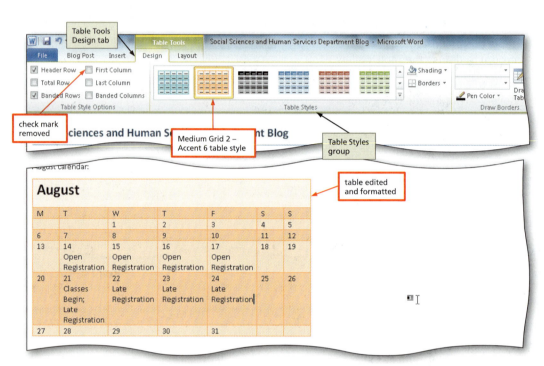

Figure 8–69

Note: If you have not registered a blog account, read the next series of steps without performing them.

To Insert a Category

In this chapter, the blog post is associated with the Current Students, Faculty, and Staff categories. These categories already have been created in the blog account that was registered with Word. The following steps associate this blog post with the categories in the registered blog account.

1

- Display the Blog Post tab.

- Click the Insert Category button (Blog Post tab | Blog group) to insert the Category drop-down list content control in the blog post (Figure 8–70).

- If Word displays a dialog box about sending information, click its Yes button.

Figure 8–70

● Click the 'Choose a category or
type a new one' box arrow in
the document to display a list
of categories associated with
the registered blog account
(Figure 8–71).

Q&A What if the list contains no
categories?

Either your blog account is not
registered or your account does not
have any categories. In this case, read Step 3 without performing it.

Social Sciences and Human Services Department Blog

Category   [Choose a category or type a new one] ◄── box arrow

Welcome to   Blogroll
               Current Students
Check here o   Faculty   list of categories associated
               Former Students   with registered blog account —
Exciting news   Prospective Students your list will differ   I majors!
               Staff
August calendar: none

Figure 8–71

● Click Current Students (or a category in your list), so that this blog post is listed in the
selected category when you publish the blog post.

4
● Repeat Steps 1, 2, and 3 for the Faculty and Staff categories (or two additional categories in
your list), so this blog post is listed in the selected categories when you publish the blog post
(shown in Figure 8–72).

To Save a Document

You are finished entering and formatting the content of the blog post. Thus, the
following steps save the blog post.

1 With a USB flash drive connected to one of the computer's USB ports, click the Save button
on the Quick Access Toolbar to display the Save As dialog box.

2 Type `Social Sciences and Human Services Department Blog` in
the File name text box to change the file name. Do not press the ENTER key because you do
not want to close the dialog box at this time.

3 If necessary, navigate to the save location (in this case, the Word folder in the CIS 101
folder [or your class folder] on the USB flash drive).

4 Click the Save button (Save As dialog box) to save the document in the selected folder on
the USB flash drive with the entered file name.

To Publish a Blog Post

The next step in this chapter is to publish the blog post, so that it appears at the top of the Web page
associated with this blog account. The following step publishes the blog post.

● Click the Publish button
(Blog Post tab | Blog
group), which causes
Word to display a
brief message that it
is contacting the blog
provider and then
display a message on the
screen that the post was
published (Figure 8–72).

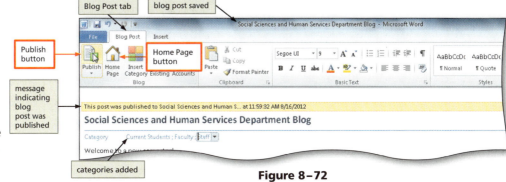

Blog Post tab   blog post saved

Publish button   Home Page button

message indicating blog post was published

This post was published to Social Sciences and Human S... at 11:59:32 AM 8/16/2012

Social Sciences and Human Services Department Blog

Category   Current Students ; Faculty ; Staff

categories added

Figure 8–72

To Display a Blog Web Page in a Web Browser Window

You can view a blog account associated with Word if you want to verify a post was successful. The following step displays the current blog account's Web page in a browser window.

1

- Click the Home Page button (Blog Post tab | Blog group) (shown in Figure 8–72), which starts the default browser (Internet Explorer, in this case) and displays the Web page associated with the registered blog account in the browser window. You may need to click the Refresh button in your browser window to display the most current Web page contents (Figure 8–73).

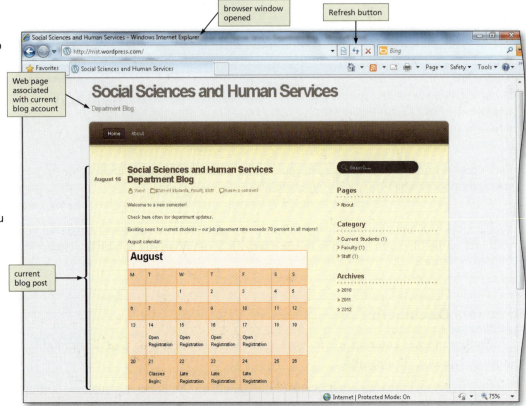

Figure 8–73

Q&A

What if the wrong Web page is displayed?

You may have multiple blog accounts registered with Word. To select a different blog account registered with Word, switch back to Word, click the Manage Accounts button (Blog Post tab | Blog group), click the desired account (Blog Accounts dialog box), and then click the Close button. Then, repeat Step 1.

BTW

Deleting Blog Posts
If you want to delete a blog post from your blog account, log in to your blog account and then follow the instructions from your blog provider to delete a post from your blog.

TO OPEN AN EXISTING BLOG POST

If you wanted to open an existing blog post to modify or view it in Word, you would perform the following steps.

1. Click the Open Existing button (Blog Post tab | Blog group) to display the Open Existing Post dialog box.
2. Select the title of the post you wish to open and then click the OK button (Open Existing Post dialog box).

To Quit Word

You are finished with the project in this chapter. Thus, the following steps close the open browser window and quit Word.

1 Close your browser window.

2 Quit Word.

BTW

Quick Reference
For a table that lists how to complete the tasks covered in this book using the mouse, Ribbon, shortcut menu, and keyboard, see the Quick Reference Summary at the back of this book, or visit the Word 2010 Quick Reference Web page (scsite.com/wd2010/qr).

Chapter Summary

In this chapter, you have learned how to insert comments, track changes, review tracked changes, compare documents and combine documents, chart a table and format the chart using Graph, link or embed an Excel worksheet to a Word document, chart a table and format the chart using Office 2010 Chart Tools, and create and publish a blog post. The items listed below include all the new Word skills you have learned in this chapter.

1. Insert a Comment (WD 477)
2. Change Reviewer Information (WD 480)
3. Reply to a Comment (WD 480)
4. Customize the Status Bar (WD 481)
5. Enable Tracked Changes (WD 482)
6. Track Changes (WD 482)
7. Change How Markups Are Displayed (WD 483)
8. Use the Reviewing Pane (WD 484)
9. Print Markups (WD 485)
10. View Comments and Delete a Comment (WD 486)
11. Delete All Comments (WD 487)
12. Review Tracked Changes (WD 487)
13. Accept or Reject All Tracked Changes (WD 489)
14. Compare Documents (WD 491)
15. Combine Revisions from Multiple Authors (WD 493)
16. Show Tracked Changes and Comments by a Single Reviewer (WD 496)
17. Chart a Table Using Graph (WD 498)
18. Graph by Column Using Graph (WD 499)
19. Move Legend Placement in a Chart Using Graph (WD 500)
20. Resize a Chart (WD 500)
21. Change the Chart Type Using Graph (WD 501)
22. Format Text in the Chart Area Using Graph (WD 502)
23. Format an Axis Using Graph (WD 502)
24. Quit Graph and Return to Word (WD 503)
25. Link an Excel Worksheet in a Word Document (WD 507)
26. Embed an Excel Worksheet in a Word Document (WD 509)
27. Edit a Linked Object (WD 509)
28. Break a Link (WD 509)
29. Chart a Table Using Office Chart Tools (WD 511)
30. Move the Legend Placement Using Office Chart Tools (WD 514)
31. Add an Outline to a Chart Using Office Chart Tools (WD 515)
32. Format an Axis Using Office Chart Tools (WD 516)
33. View and Scroll through Documents Side by Side (WD 517)
34. Register a Blog Account (WD 520)
35. Create a Blank Document for a Blog Post (WD 521)
36. Insert a Quick Table (WD 523)
37. Insert a Category (WD 524)
38. Publish a Blog Post (WD 525)
39. Display a Blog Web Page in a Web Browser Window (WD 526)
40. Open an Existing Blog Post (WD 526)

If you have a SAM 2010 user profile, your instructor may have assigned an autogradable version of this assignment. If so, log into the SAM 2010 Web site at www.cengage.com/sam2010 to download the instruction and start files.

Learn It Online

Test your knowledge of chapter content and key terms.

Instructions: To complete the Learn It Online exercises, start your browser, click the Address bar, and then enter the Web address `scsite.com/wd2010/learn`. When the Word 2010 Learn It Online page is displayed, click the link for the exercise you want to complete and then read the instructions.

Chapter Reinforcement TF, MC, and SA

A series of true/false, multiple choice, and short answer questions that test your knowledge of the chapter content.

Flash Cards

An interactive learning environment where you identify chapter key terms associated with displayed definitions.

Practice Test

A series of multiple choice questions that test your knowledge of chapter content and key terms.

Who Wants To Be a Computer Genius?

An interactive game that challenges your knowledge of chapter content in the style of a television quiz show.

Wheel of Terms

An interactive game that challenges your knowledge of chapter key terms in the style of the television show *Wheel of Fortune*.

Crossword Puzzle Challenge

A crossword puzzle that challenges your knowledge of key terms presented in the chapter.

Apply Your Knowledge

Reinforce the skills and apply the concepts you learned in this chapter.

Working with Comments and Tracked Changes

Note: To complete this assignment, you will be required to use the Data Files for Students. See the inside back cover of this book for instructions on downloading the Data Files for Students, or contact your instructor for information about accessing the required files.

Instructions: Start Word. Create a new document from the file called, Apply 8-1 Organizations and Their IT Departments Draft, from the Data Files for Students. The document includes two paragraphs of text that contain tracked changes and comments. You are to insert additional tracked changes and comments, accept and reject tracked changes, delete comments, and compare documents.

Perform the following tasks:

1. If necessary, customize the status bar so that it displays the Track Changes indicator.

2. Enable (turn on) tracked changes.

3. If approved by your instructor, change the user name and initials so that your name and initials are displayed in the tracked changes and comments.

4. Use the Review tab to navigate to the first comment. Follow the instruction in the comment. Be sure tracked changes are on when you add the required text to the document.

5. When you have finished making the change, reply to the comment with a new comment that includes a message stating you completed the requested task. What color are the WU markups? What color are your markups?

6. Navigate to the remaining comments and read through each one.

7. With tracked changes on, make the change specified in the third comment so that the sentence reads: Employees in the IT department work together as a team to meet the …

8. Insert the following comment for the word, taxes, in the second sentence in the first paragraph: Should the word, taxes, be capitalized?

9. With tracked changes on, change the word, employ, in the first sentence to the word, use.

10. Edit the comment entered in Step 8 to add the words, first letter of the, immediately to the right of the word, the, in the comment so that it reads: Should the first letter of the word, taxes, be capitalized?

11. Print the document with tracked changes.

12. Print just the tracked changes.

13. Save the document with the file name, Apply 8-1 Organizations and Their IT Departments Reviewed (Figure 8–74).

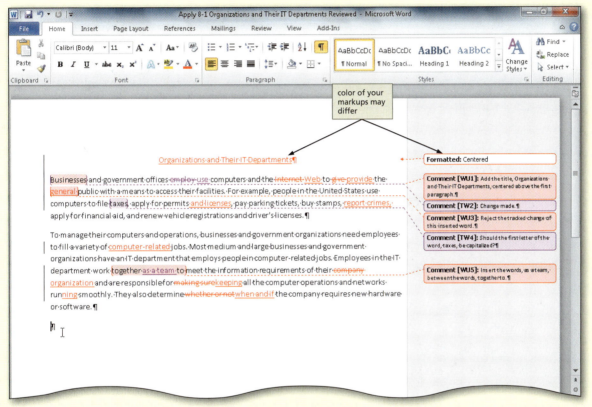

Figure 8–74

14. Show only your tracked changes in the document. Show all users' tracked changes in the document.

15. Reject the deletion of the word, general, in the first sentence.

16. Delete the second comment.

17. Accept all the remaining edits in the document.

18. Delete all the remaining comments.

19. Disable (turn off) tracked changes. Remove the Track Changes indicator from the status bar.

20. Change the document properties as specified by your instructor.

21. Save the modified file with a new file name, Apply 8-1 Organizations and Their IT Departments Final.

22. Submit the documents as specified by your instructor.

Extend Your Knowledge

Extend the skills you learned in this chapter and experiment with new skills. You may need to use Help to complete the assignment.

Working with Advanced Office Charting Tools

Note: To complete this assignment, you will be required to use the Data Files for Students. See the inside back cover of this book for instructions on downloading the Data Files for Students, or contact your instructor for information about accessing the required files.

Instructions: Start Word. Create a new document from the file called, Extend 8-1 Facility Usage Memo Draft, from the Data Files for Students. You will use the advanced data charting capabilities of Office to create and format a pie chart.

If you do not have Excel on your computer, do not follow the steps below; instead, use Graph to create a chart similar to the one described and enter the data for the chart in the Graph Datasheet.

Perform the following tasks:

1. Use Help to review and expand your knowledge about the advanced data charting capabilities of Office 2010, specifically creating and formatting a chart.

2. Insert a Pie in 3-D pie chart centered below the paragraph in the memo. In the Excel window, enter a title of Number of Attendees and this data for the pie chart: Cardio, 215; Pilates, 235; Spinning, 191; Stepping, 155; Strength, 104; Toning, 201, as shown in Figure 8–75.

3. Move the legend to the top of the chart.

4. Place data labels on the outside end of the chart, and include a percentage and a legend key in each label.

5. Add an outline to the chart.

6. Change the chart style to one other than Style 2.

7. Explode one of the pie slices out from the chart.

8. Rotate the chart.

9. Make any other desired formatting changes to the chart.

10. Change the document properties as specified by your instructor.

11. Save the document using a name of your choice.

12. Edit the data in the chart as follows: change the number of attendees in Strength to 210 and the number in Toning to 105. Save the revised document.

13. Submit both documents in the format specified by your instructor.

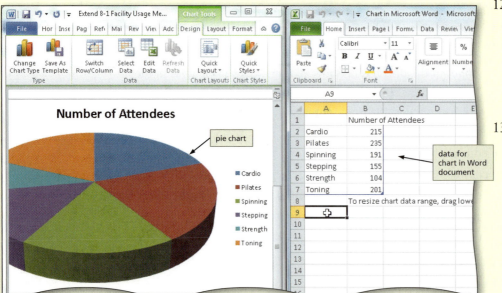

Figure 8–75

Make It Right

Analyze a document and correct all errors and/or improve the design.

Editing and Formatting a Quick Table and a Chart

Note: To complete this assignment, you will be required to use the Data Files for Students. See the inside back cover of this book for instructions on downloading the Data Files for Students, or contact your instructor for information about accessing the required files.

Instructions: Start Word. Create a new document from the file called, Make It Right 8-1 Donation Results Memo Draft, from the Data Files for Students. The document is a memo that is missing a table and whose chart is not formatted properly. You are to insert, format, and edit a Quick Table and edit a chart created using Microsoft Graph.

Perform the following tasks:

1. Immediately above the chart, insert the Tabular List Quick Table. Change the values in the header row and first four table rows as follows: Header row, first column: Donation Category; Header row, second column: Total Pledged; first data row, first column: Scholarships; first data row, second column: $13,750; second data row, first column: Laboratories; second data row, second column: $8,925; third data row, first column: Faculty Support; third data row, second column: $7,730; fourth data row, first column: Curriculum Development; fourth data row, second column: $7,665 (Figure 8–76). Delete the last four rows in the chart.

2. Apply a table style of your choice. Right-align the dollar values. Resize columns as appropriate.

3. Double-click the chart to start the Graph application. Make the following changes to the chart:

   a. Edit the Total Pledged amounts in the Datasheet window to match the values in the table in the document.
   b. Resize the chart so that all data is readable.
   c. Delete the legend.
   d. Change the chart type to something other than area.
   e. Format the numbers on the y-axis to show dollar signs with no decimals.
   f. Change the color of the data series. *Hint:* Series "Total Pledged" on Chart Objects menu.
   g. Change the color of the plot area.
   h. Add a chart title, category (x) axis title, and value (y) axis title. Add color to each of these titles. *Hint:* Use the Chart Options dialog box.

4. Change the document properties as specified by your instructor. Save the modified file with a new file name, Make It Right 8-1 Donation Results Memo Final. Submit the document in the format specified by your instructor.

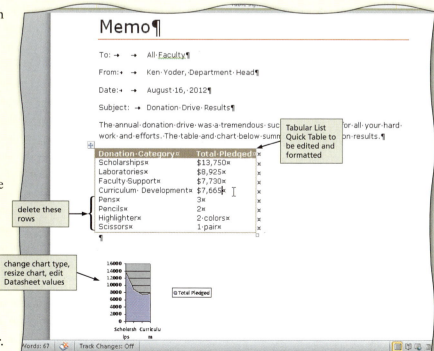

Figure 8–76

In the Lab

Design and/or create a document using the guidelines, concepts, and skills presented in this chapter. Labs are listed in order of increasing difficulty.

Lab 1: Creating a Memo with a Chart Using Microsoft Graph

Problem: Your supervisor has asked you to prepare a memo that contains a table and chart detailing the results of recent fund-raising events. You prepare the document shown in Figure 8–77.

Perform the following tasks:

1. Change the theme colors to Adjacency.
2. Enter all text in the memo and create the table, formatted as indicated in the figure.
3. Insert a chart of the entire table using Microsoft Graph. Format the chart as follows so that it appears like the figure:

   a. Graph by column instead of row.
   b. Move the legend so that it appears below the chart.
   c. Resize the chart.
   d. Change the chart type to cylinder (near the bottom of the Chart type list in the Chart Type dialog box).
   e. Change the font size of text in the chart to 11-point bold.
   f. After quitting Graph, place a border around the chart.
   g. Adjust spacing above and below paragraphs as necessary.

4. Check the spelling of the memo. Change the document properties as specified by your instructor. Save the document with the file name, Lab 8-1 Event Attendance Memo, and then submit it in the format specified by your instructor.

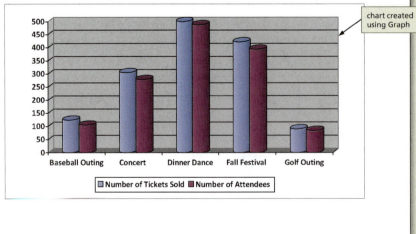
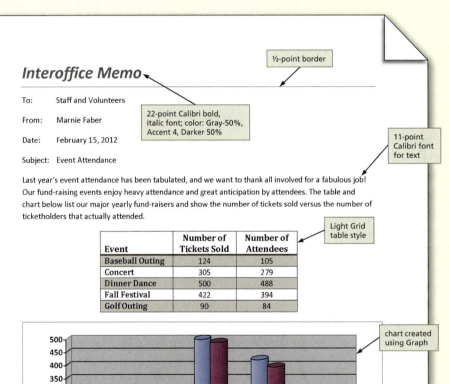

Figure 8–77

In the Lab

Lab 2: Creating a Memo with an Excel Table and Chart Using Office 2010 Chart Tools

Note: To complete this assignment, you will be required to use the Data Files for Students. See the inside back cover of this book for instructions on downloading the Data Files for Students, or contact your instructor for information about accessing the required files.

Problem: Your supervisor has asked you to prepare a memo that contains an Excel table and a chart detailing sales for the past six months. Thus, this lab requires that Excel be installed on your computer. You prepare the document shown in Figure 8–78.

Perform the following tasks:

1. Change the theme colors to Austin.
2. Enter all text in the memo, formatted as indicated in the figure.
3. Link the worksheet in the Lab 8-2 Sales Figures Table workbook, which is on the Data Files for Students, to the Word memo below the paragraph.
4. Save the document with the file name, Lab 8-2 Sales Figures Memo with Linked Excel Table.
5. Break the link between the Excel table in the Word document and the Excel worksheet in the Excel workbook. Center the linked table. If necessary, resize the linked table so that it looks like the one in Figure 8–78.
6. Insert a Line with Markers chart of the entire table using the Office Chart Tools, centered below the table. Format the chart as follows so that it appears like the figure:
   a. Move the legend so that it appears below the chart.
   b. Add a ¼-point Brown, Accent 2 outline around the chart.
   c. Resize the chart.
   d. Format the Vertical (Value) Axis so that the Minimum value is Fixed 80.0.
   e. Adjust spacing above and below paragraphs as necessary.
7. Check the spelling of the memo. Change the document properties as specified by your instructor. Save the revised

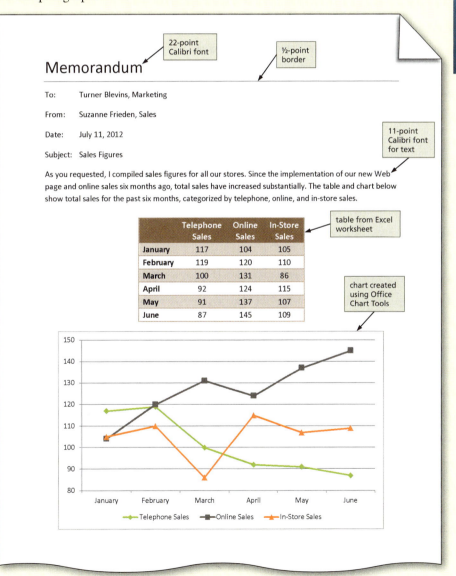

document with the file name, Lab 8-2 Sales Figures Memo with Chart Tools Chart. Submit the documents in the format specified by your instructor.

Figure 8–78

In the Lab

Lab 3: Working with Comments and Tracked Changes

Note: To complete this assignment, you will be required to use the Data Files for Students. See the inside back cover of this book for instructions on downloading the Data Files for Students, or contact your instructor for information about accessing the required files.

Problem: Your supervisor has asked you to prepare a draft of a memo, showing all tracked changes and comments. You mark up the document shown in Figure 8–79.

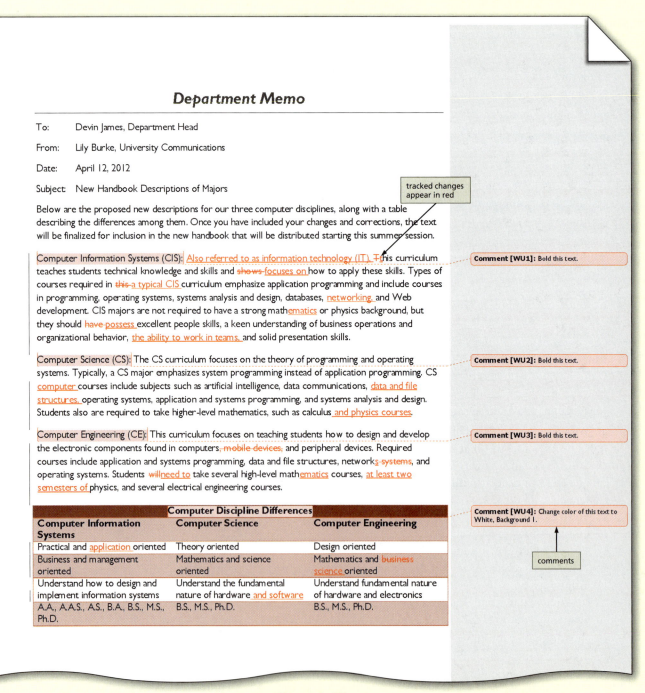

Figure 8–79

Perform the following tasks:

1. Create a new document from the file called, Lab 8-3 Handbook Descriptions Memo Draft, from the Data Files for Students.

2. Insert the comments and track all changes shown in Figure 8–79.

3. Save the document with the file name, Lab 8-3 Handbook Descriptions Memo with Markups.

4. Make the changes indicated in the comments and then delete the comments in the document.

5. Accept all tracked changes in the document.

6. Save the document with the file name, Lab 8-3 Handbook Descriptions Memo Final.

7. Compare the Lab 8-3 Handbook Descriptions Memo Draft file (original document) with the Lab 8-3 Handbook Descriptions Memo Final file (revised document). Save the compare result with the file name, Lab 8-3 Handbook Descriptions Memo Compared.

8. Close all windows and then open the Lab 8-3 Handbook Descriptions Memo Compared file. Print the document with markups. Use the Review tab to review each change. Close the document without saving.

Cases and Places

Apply your creative thinking and problem solving skills to design and implement a solution.

Note: To complete these assignments, you may be required to use the Data Files for Students. See the inside back cover of this book for instructions on downloading the Data Files for Students, or contact your instructor for information about accessing the required files.

1: Create a Memo to Students and a Blog Post

Academic

As a library assistant at your school, you have been asked to create a memo about recent class enrollment numbers. You are to write the memo to all library staff from Milton Wallis, Director, with a subject of Class Enrollment Numbers. Use today's date. The memo should contain a table and chart as specified below.

The wording for the text in the memo is as follows: For the past two years, our library has offered instruction courses to our students. These courses have been extremely popular. In the last six months, enrollment has increased rather substantially, especially in the computer courses. The table and chart below illustrate the enrollment numbers last year as contrasted with the enrollment so far this year.

The data for the table is as follows: Course Titles: Searching the Web, Using Word, Using PowerPoint, Using Excel, and Using Access. May 2011 Enrollments for each of these courses were 34, 42, 30, 18, and 20, respectively. May 2012 Enrollments were 45, 58, 41, 25, and 24. Create a chart of all table data using either Graph or the Office Chart Tools.

Use the concepts and techniques presented in this chapter to create and format the memo and its text, table, and chart. Be sure to check the spelling and grammar of the finished memo.

If you have permission and your instructor requests it, create a blog account on the Web. Register your blog account in Word. Display the blog account's Web page in a browser window. Use Word to create a blog post that contains the title Class Enrollment Numbers and the post: In the last six months, enrollment has increased rather substantially, especially in the computer courses! Insert the table created above in the blog post. Publish the blog post to your Web blog account. Display the updated blog Web page in a browser window.

Submit your memo and blog post in the format specified by your instructor.

Continued >

Cases and Places *continued*

2: Create a Memo Requesting Volunteers and a Blog Post

Personal

As volunteer coordinator for your village hall, you have been asked to create a memo requesting volunteers. You are to write the memo to all volunteers from Shentelle Stevens with a subject of Volunteers Needed. Use today's date. The memo should contain a table and chart as specified below.

The wording for the text in the memo is as follows: All volunteer hours for the past year have been compiled. Recently, we have noticed an increased demand for our services. The following table and chart outline the various areas in which we offer assistance/outreach and the number of volunteers for each service area. Numbers are based on the previous year's numbers compared to today.

The data for the table is as follows: Services: Food pantry, After-school care, Sports leagues, Elder care, Resale shop, and Beautification. Volunteers last year for each of these services were 53, 52, 193, 104, 33, and 78, respectively. Current volunteers are 54, 52, 205, 110, 40, and 84. Create a chart of all table data using either Graph or the Office Chart Tools.

Use the concepts and techniques presented in this chapter to create and format the memo and its text, table, and chart. Be sure to check the spelling and grammar of the finished memo.

If you have permission and your instructor requests it, create a blog account on the Web. Register your blog account in Word. Display the blog account's Web page in a browser window. Use Word to create a blog post that contains the title Volunteers Needed and the post: We have noticed an increased demand for our services! Insert the table created above in the blog post. Publish the blog post to your Web blog account. Display the updated blog Web page in a browser window.

Submit your memo and blog post in the format specified by your instructor.

3: Create a Memo to Employees and a Blog Post

Professional

As assistant to the manager of a video store chain, you have been asked to create a memo about rental numbers. You are to write the memo to all counter staff from Jose Rangel, Manager, with a subject of First Quarter Rentals. Use today's date. The memo should contain a table and chart as specified below.

The wording for the text in the memo is as follows: The video rental figures for the first quarter have been compiled. The table and chart below illustrate the total number of items rented in each genre. It appears our volume has increased, even taking into account the holiday season. Keep up the good work!

The data for the table is as follows: Genre: Horror, Comedy, Romance, Drama, Animated, and Suspense. The number of rentals for each of these genres was 553, 624, 498, 655, 702, and 508, respectively. The number of customers was 443, 598, 303, 499, 402, and 301. Create a chart of all table data using either Graph or the Office Chart Tools.

Use the concepts and techniques presented in this chapter to create and format the memo and its text, table, and chart. Be sure to check the spelling and grammar of the finished memo.

If you have permission and your instructor requests it, create a blog account on the Web. Register your blog account in Word. Display the blog account's Web page in a browser window. Use Word to create a blog post that contains the title First Quarter Rentals and the post: It appears our volume has increased! Insert the table created above in the blog post. Publish the blog post to your Web blog account. Display the updated blog Web page in a browser window.

Submit your memo and blog post in the format specified by your instructor.

9 Creating a Reference Document with a Table of Contents and an Index

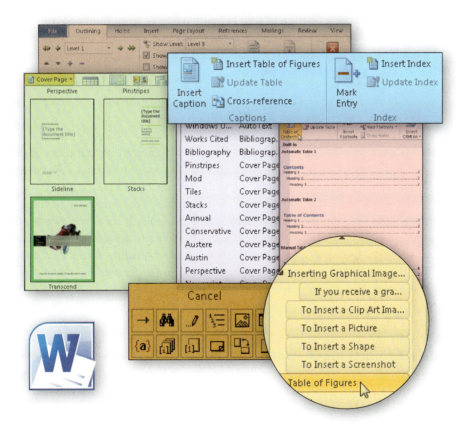

Objectives

You will have mastered the material in this chapter when you can:

- Insert a screenshot
- Add and modify a caption
- Create a cross-reference
- Use the Building Blocks Organizer
- Use the Navigation Pane
- Link text boxes
- Compress pictures
- Work in Outline view

- Work with a master document and subdocuments
- Insert a cover page
- Create and modify a table of contents
- Create and update a table of figures
- Build, modify, and update an index
- Create alternating footers
- Add bookmarks

9 | Creating a Reference Document with a Table of Contents and an Index

Introduction

During the course of your academic studies and professional activities, you may find it necessary to compose a document that is many pages or even hundreds of pages in length. When composing a long document, you must ensure that the document is organized so that a reader easily can locate material in that document. Sometimes a document of this nature is called a **reference document**.

Project — Reference Document

A reference document is any multipage document organized so that users easily can locate material and navigate through the document. Examples of reference documents include user guides, term papers, pamphlets, manuals, proposals, and plans.

The project in this chapter uses Word to produce the reference document shown in Figure 9–1. This reference document, titled the *Using Word Series*, is a multipage information guide that is distributed by Trenton College to students and staff. Notice that the inner margin between facing pages has extra space to allow duplicated copies of the document to be bound (i.e., stapled or fastened in some manner) — without the binding covering the words.

The *Using Word Series* reference document begins with a title page designed to entice the target audience to open the document and read it. Next is the copyright page, followed by the table of contents. The document then describes how to insert four types of graphical images in a Word document: clip art, picture, shape, and screenshot. The end of this reference document has a table of figures and an index to assist readers in locating information contained within the document. A miniature version of the *Using Word Series* reference document is shown in Figure 9–1; for a more readable view, visit scsite.com/wd2010/ch9.

The section of the *Using Word Series* reference document that is titled, Inserting Graphical Images First Draft, is a draft document that you will modify. The draft document is located on the Data Files for Students. See the inside back cover of this book for instructions on downloading the Data Files for Students, or contact your instructor for information about accessing the required files. After editing the content, you will incorporate a final version in the reference document.

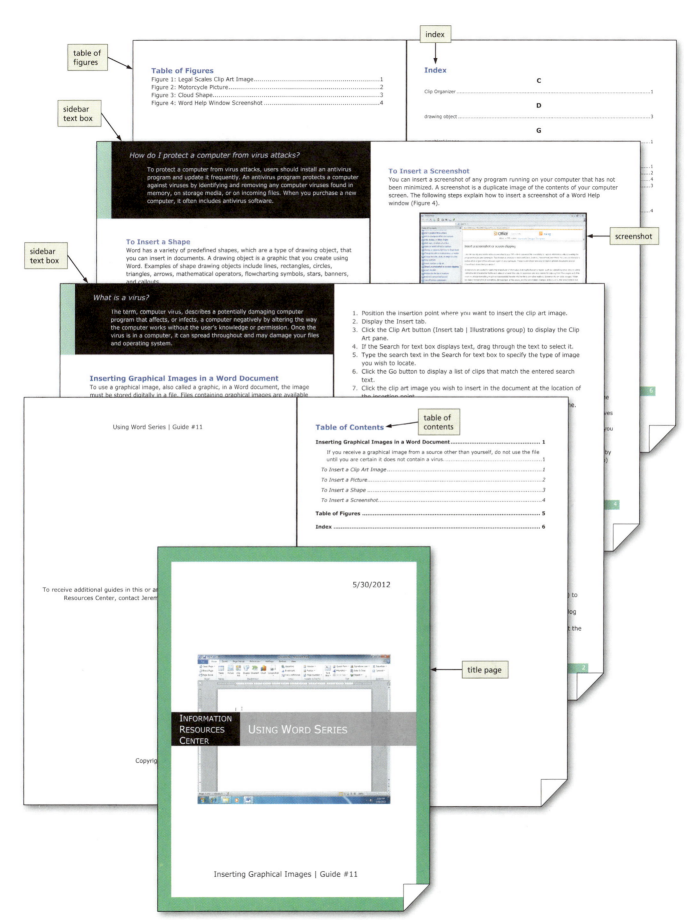

Figure 9–1

Overview

As you read through this chapter, you will learn how to create the reference document shown in Figure 9–1 on the previous page by performing these general tasks:

- Modify the draft document.
- Create a master document for the reference document.
- Organize the reference document with a table of contents, a table of figures, and an index.
- Print the reference document.

Plan Ahead

General Project Guidelines

When creating a Word document, the actions you perform and decisions you make will affect the appearance and characteristics of the finished document. As you create a reference document, such as the project shown in Figure 9–1, you should follow these general guidelines:

1. **Prepare a document to be included in a longer document.** If a document contains multiple illustrations (figures), each figure should have a caption. In addition, each figure should be referenced from within the text. Any term to be included in an index should be marked as an index entry.

2. **Include elements common to a reference document.** Most reference documents contain a title page, a table of contents, and an index. The title page entices passersby to take a copy of the document. By placing a table of contents at the beginning of the document and an index at the end, you help a reader locate topics within the document. If a document contains several illustrations, you also should include a table of figures.

3. **Prepare the document for distribution.** The reference document in Figure 9–1 prints on nine separate sheets of paper. When it is duplicated or printed back-to-back, however, the document uses only five sheets of paper. The top of the first sheet of paper shows the title page, and the back of the same sheet contains the copyright information; the top of the second sheet of paper shows the table of contents, and so on. The copyright and table of contents pages are called facing pages when duplicated in this manner. Be sure to allow enough room in the margins for binding (i.e., stapling) the document.

   For long documents that will be viewed online, incorporate bookmarks and/or hyperlinks so that a user can navigate quickly and easily through the document while viewing it on a computer.

   When necessary, more specific details concerning the above guidelines are presented at appropriate points in the chapter. The chapter also will identify the actions performed and decisions made regarding these guidelines during the creation of the reference document shown in Figure 9–1.

To Start Word

If you are using a computer to step through the project in this chapter and you want your screens to match the figures in this book, you should change your computer's resolution to 1024 × 768. The following steps start Word and verify settings.

1 Start Word. If necessary, maximize the Word window.

2 If the Print Layout button on the status bar is not selected, click it so that your screen is in Print Layout view.

3 If the rulers are displayed on the screen, click the View Ruler button at the top of the vertical scroll bar to remove the rulers from the Word window.

Preparing a Document to Be Included in a Reference Document

Before including the Inserting Graphical Images First Draft document in a longer document, you will make several modifications to the document:

1. Create a new file from the draft document.
2. Insert a screenshot.
3. Add captions to the images in the document.
4. Insert references to the figures in the text.
5. Mark an index entry.
6. Insert text boxes that contain information about computer viruses.
7. Compress the pictures.
8. Add a predefined draft watermark to the document.

The following pages outline these changes.

Plan Ahead

Prepare a document to be included in a longer document.
Ensure that reference elements in a document, such as captions and index entries, are formatted properly and entered consistently.

- **Captions.** A **caption** is text that appears outside of an illustration, usually below it. If the illustration is identified with a number, the caption may include the word, Figure, along with the illustration number (i.e., Figure 1). In the caption, separate the figure number from the text of the figure by a space or punctuation mark such as a period or colon (Figure 1: Legal Scales Clip Art Image).

- **Index Entries.** If your document will include an index, read through the document and mark any terms or headings that you want to appear in the index. Include any term that the reader may want to locate quickly. Omit figures from index entries if the document will have a table of figures; otherwise, include figures in the index if appropriate.

To Create a New Document from an Existing File

The draft document that you will insert in the reference document is called Inserting Graphical Images First Draft. To preserve the original draft document, you create a file from the original document. The draft document is located on the Data Files for Students. See the inside back cover of this book for instructions on downloading the Data Files for Students, or contact your instructor for information about accessing the required files.

The following steps create a new document from an existing file and then display its contents in the document window.

1 Click File on the Ribbon to open the Backstage view.

2 Click the New tab in the Backstage view to display the New gallery.

3 Click the 'New from existing' button in the New gallery to display the New from Existing Document dialog box.

4 Locate and then select the file with the name, Inserting Graphical Images First Draft.

5 Click the Create New button (New from Existing Document dialog box) to open a new document window that contains the contents of the selected file.

BTW

The Ribbon and Screen Resolution
Word may change how the groups and buttons within the groups appear on the Ribbon, depending on the computer's screen resolution. Thus, your Ribbon may look different from the ones in this book if you are using a screen resolution other than 1024 × 768.

6 If the Show/Hide ¶ button (Home tab | Paragraph group) is selected, click it to hide formatting marks.

Q&A What if some formatting marks still appear after clicking the Show/Hide ¶ button?

Open the Backstage view, click the Options button in the Backstage view to display the Word Options dialog box, click Display in the left pane (Word Options dialog box), remove the check mark from the Hidden text check box, and then click the OK button.

7 To see all three pages of the document at once, display the View tab, click the Zoom button (View tab | Zoom group), click the Many pages button (Zoom dialog box), click 1 × 3 Pages in the grid, and then click the OK button (Figure 9–2).

8 When you have finished viewing the document, click the 100% button (View tab | Zoom group) to show the document at 100 percent in the document window.

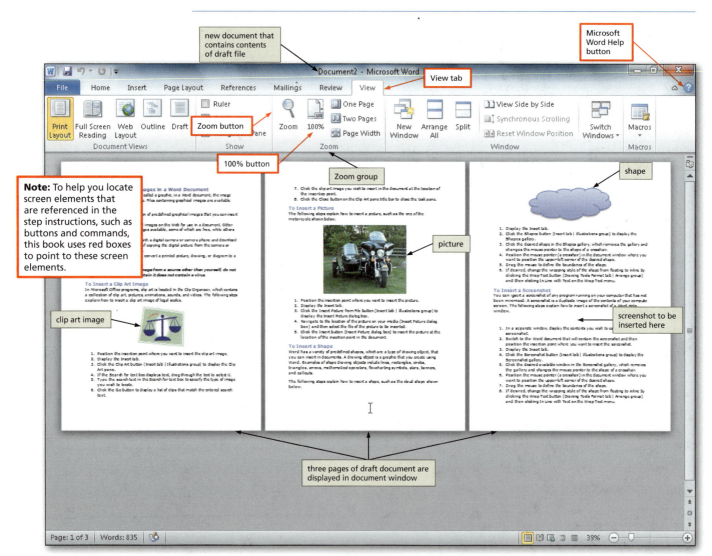

Figure 9–2

To Insert a Screenshot

A **screenshot** is a duplicate image of the contents of your computer screen. You can insert a screenshot of any program running on your computer, provided the program has not been minimized.

The draft document is missing a screenshot of a Word Help window. To insert a screenshot, you first must display the screen of which you want a screenshot in a window on your computer. The next steps insert a screenshot in a document.

1

- Display the contents you wish to capture in a screenshot (in this case, click the Microsoft Word Help button to open the Help window, click the Pictures and Clip Art link in the Table of Contents pane, click the 'Insert a screenshot or screen clipping' link, and then scroll to display the Word help information in the right pane. If necessary, maximize the Word Help window.)

- Point to the Word program button on the taskbar to display a live preview of the open documents or window titles of the open documents, depending on your computer's configuration (Figure 9–3).

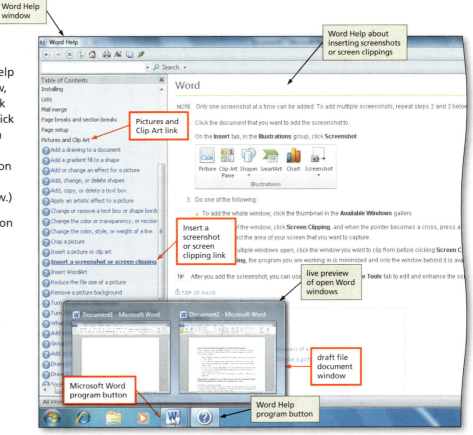

Figure 9–3

2

- Click the live preview of the draft file document window to switch to Word and display the selected document in the Word document window.

- Position the insertion point in the document where the screenshot should be inserted (in this case, on the centered blank line above the numbered list in the To Insert a Screenshot section at the bottom of the draft document).

- Display the Insert tab.

- Click the Screenshot button (Insert tab | Illustrations group) to display the Available Windows gallery (Figure 9–4).

 Q&A

What is a screen clipping?

A screen clipping is a section of a window. When you select Screen Clipping in the Available Windows gallery, the window turns opaque so that you can drag through the part of the window to be included in the document.

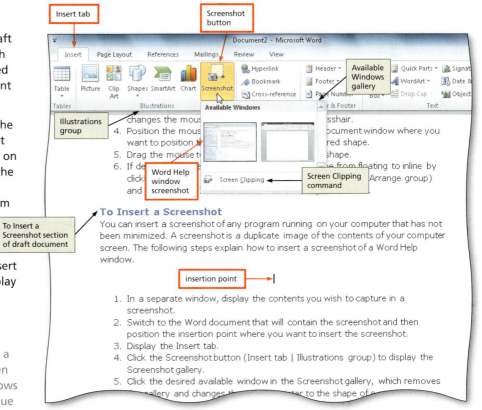

To Insert a Screenshot

You can insert a screenshot of any program running on your computer that has not been minimized. A screenshot is a duplicate image of the contents of your computer screen. The following steps explain how to insert a screenshot of a Word Help window.

insertion point

1. In a separate window, display the contents you wish to capture in a screenshot.
2. Switch to the Word document that will contain the screenshot and then position the insertion point where you want to insert the screenshot.
3. Display the Insert tab.
4. Click the Screenshot button (Insert tab | Illustrations group) to display the Screenshot gallery.
5. Click the desired available window in the Screenshot gallery, which removes the gallery and changes the mouse pointer to the shape of a

Figure 9–4

3

- Click the Word Help window screenshot in the Available Windows gallery to insert the selected screenshot in the Word document at the location of the insertion point.

- Click the Shape Height and Shape Width box down arrows (Picture Tools Format tab | Size group) as many times as necessary to resize the screenshot to approximately 3.4" tall by 4.75" wide (Figure 9–5).

Q&A What if my text appears on a separate page from the screenshot?

Depending on settings, the text may move to the next page.

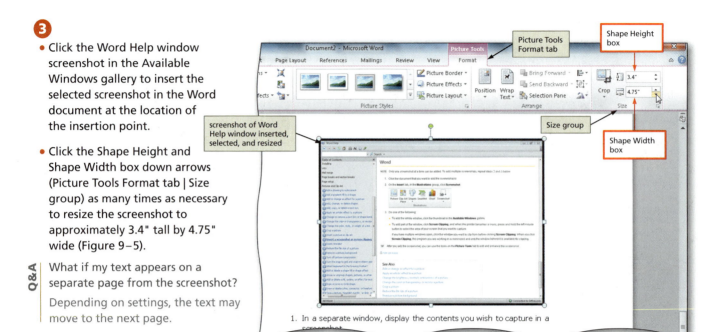

Figure 9–5

To Add a Caption

In this reference document, the captions contain the word, Figure, followed by the figure number, a colon, and a figure description. In Word, you can add a caption to an equation, a figure, and a table. If you move, delete, or add captions in a document, Word renumbers remaining captions in the document automatically. The Inserting Graphical Images document contains four images: a clip art image, a picture, a shape, and a screenshot. All of these images should have captions. The following steps add a caption to a graphic, specifically, the screenshot.

1

- If the screenshot is not selected already, click it to select the graphic for which you want a caption.

- Display the References tab.

- Click the Insert Caption button (References tab | Captions group) to display the Caption dialog box with a figure number automatically assigned to the selected graphic (Figure 9–6).

Q&A Why is the figure number a 1?

No other captions have been assigned in this document yet. When you insert a new caption, or move or delete items containing captions, Word automatically updates caption numbers throughout the document.

Q&A What if the Caption text box has the label Table or Equation instead of Figure?

Click the Label box arrow (Caption dialog box) and then click Figure.

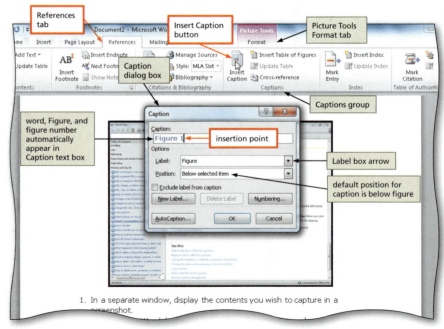

Figure 9–6

2

- Press the COLON (:) key and then press the SPACEBAR in the Caption text box (Caption dialog box) to place separating characters between the figure number and description.

- Type **Help Window Screenshot** as the figure description (Figure 9–7).

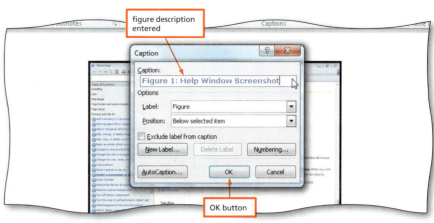

Figure 9–7

3

- Click the OK button to insert the caption below the selected graphic.

- If necessary, scroll to display the caption in the document window (Figure 9–8).

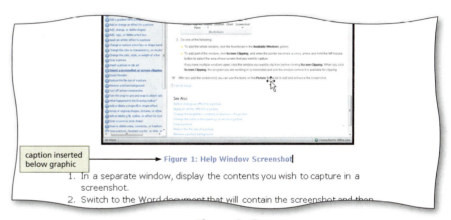

Figure 9–8

Caption Numbers

Each caption number contains a field. In Word, a **field** is a placeholder for data that can change in a document. Examples of fields you have used in previous projects are page numbers, merge fields, IF fields, and the current date. You update caption numbers using the same technique used to update any other field. That is, to update all caption numbers, select the entire document and then press the F9 key or right-click the field and then click Update Field on the shortcut menu. When you print a document, Word updates the caption numbers automatically, regardless of whether the document window displays the updated caption numbers.

To Hide White Space

White space is the space displayed in the margins at the top and bottom of pages (including any headers and footers) and also space between pages. To make it easier to see the text in this document as you scroll through it, the following step hides white space.

1 Position the mouse pointer in the document window in the space between the pages and then double-click when the mouse pointer changes to a Hide White Space button to hide white space.

BTW

Captions
If a caption appears with extra characters inside curly braces ({}), Word is displaying field codes instead of field results. Press ALT+F9 to display captions correctly as field results. If Word prints fields codes for captions, click File on the Ribbon to open the Backstage view, click Options in the Backstage view to display the Word Options dialog box, scroll to the Print section (Word Options dialog box), remove the check mark from the 'Print field codes instead of their values' check box, click the OK button, and then print the document again.

To Create a Cross-Reference

In reference documents, the text should reference each figure specifically and, if appropriate, explain the contents of the figure. The next step in this project is to add a reference to the new figure.

Because figures may be inserted, deleted, or moved, you may not know the actual figure number in the final document. For this reason, Word provides a method of creating a **cross-reference**, which is a link to an item such as a heading, caption, or footnote in a document. By creating a cross-reference to the caption, the text that mentions the figure will be updated whenever the caption to the figure is updated. The following steps create a cross-reference.

- At the end of the last sentence below the To Insert a Screenshot heading, position the insertion point to the left of the period, press the SPACEBAR, and then press the LEFT PARENTHESIS key.

- Click the Cross-reference button (References tab | Captions group) to display the Cross-reference dialog box (Figure 9–9).

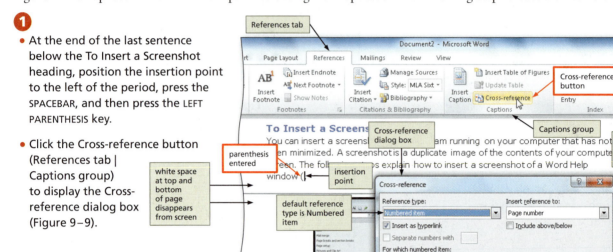

Figure 9–9

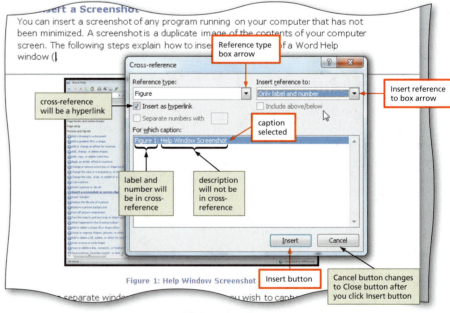

- Click the Reference type box arrow (Cross-reference dialog box) to display the Reference type list; scroll to and then click Figure, which displays a list of figures from the document in the 'For which caption' list (which, at this point, is only one figure).

- If necessary, click Figure 1: Help Window Screenshot in the 'For which caption' list to select the caption to reference.

- Click the 'Insert reference to' box arrow and then click 'Only label and number' to instruct Word that the cross-reference in the document should list just the label, Figure, followed by the figure number (Figure 9–10).

Figure 9–10

- Click the Insert button to insert the cross-reference in the document at the location of the insertion point.

Q&A

What if my cross-reference is shaded in gray?

The cross-reference is a field. Depending on your Word settings, fields may appear shaded in gray to help you identify them on the screen.

4

- Click the Close button (Cross-reference dialog box).

- Press the RIGHT PARENTHESIS key to close off the cross-reference (Figure 9–11).

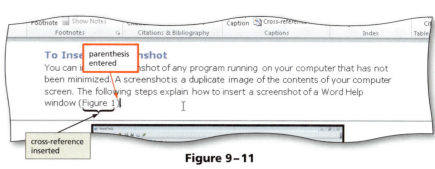

Figure 9–11

Q&A

How do I update a cross-reference if a caption is added, deleted, or moved?

In many cases, Word automatically updates a cross-reference in a document if the item to which it refers changes. To update a cross-reference manually, select the cross-reference and then press the F9 key, or right-click the cross-reference and then click Update Field on the shortcut menu.

To Use the Select Browse Object Menu

Often, you would like to bring a certain page, graphic, or other part of a document into view in the document window. To accomplish this, you could scroll through the document to find a desired page, graphic, or part of the document. Instead of scrolling through the document, however, you can use Word to go to a specific location via the Select Browse Object menu.

The next step in this chapter is to add a caption to another graphic in the document. Thus, the following steps display the previous graphic using the Select Browse Object menu.

1

- Click the Select Browse Object button on the vertical scroll bar to display the Select Browse Object menu (Figure 9–12).

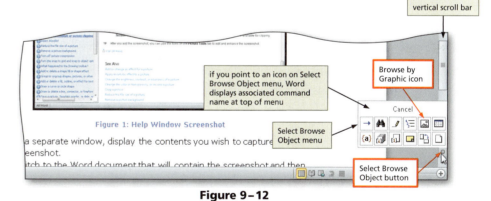

Figure 9–12

2

- Click the Browse by Graphic icon to set the browse object to the selected item (in this case, screenshot graphic).

- Click the Previous Graphic button on the vertical scroll bar to display the previous graphic in the document window (which is the cloud shape in this case) (Figure 9–13).

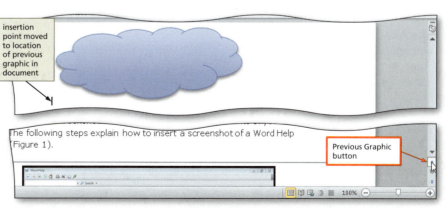

Figure 9–13

Q&A

Did the function of the button change?

Yes. By default, it is the Previous Page button and its color is black. Depending on the icon you click on the Select Browse Object menu, the function of the buttons above and below the Select Browse Object button on the vertical scroll bar changes and their color changes to blue.

Other Ways
1. Click Page Number indicator on status bar, click desired object in 'Go to what' list, click Previous or Next button (Find and Replace dialog box) 2. Press ALT+CTRL+HOME

Select Browse Object Menu

In addition to Browse by Graphic, the Select Browse Object menu provides many other options that enable you to go to various parts of a document. Other icons in the Select Browse Object menu enable you to go directly to the menu item selected: edit, heading, graphic, table, field, endnote, footnote, comment, section, and page. The top-left icons, Go To and Find, display the Go To sheet and Find sheet, respectively, in the Find and Replace dialog box if you prefer to use this dialog box to go to objects in a document.

To Add Captions and Create Cross-References

The previous steps added a caption to the screenshot graphic and then created a cross-reference to that caption. The following steps add captions to the remaining three graphics in the document (that is, the shape, the picture, and the clip art).

1 Click the cloud shape to select the graphic for which you want to add a caption.

2 Click the Insert Caption button (References tab | Captions group) to display the Caption dialog box with a figure number automatically assigned to the selected graphic.

3 Press the COLON (:) key and then press the SPACEBAR in the Caption text box (Caption dialog box) to place separating characters between the figure number and description.

4 Type `Cloud Shape` as the figure description and then click the OK button to insert the caption below the selected graphic.

5 At the end of the last sentence above the graphic, change the word, below, to the word, in, and then press the SPACEBAR.

6 Click the Cross-reference button (References tab | Captions group) to display the Cross-reference dialog box, if necessary, click Figure 1: Cloud Shape in the 'For which caption' list to select the caption to reference, click the Insert button to insert the cross-reference at the location of the insertion point, and then click the Close button in the Cross-reference dialog box.

Q&A

Why did I not need to change the settings for the reference type and reference to in the dialog box?

Word retains the previous settings in the dialog box.

7 Click the Previous Graphic button on the vertical scroll bar to display the previous graphic in the document window (which is the motorcycle picture in this case).

8 Click the motorcycle picture to select the graphic for which you want to add a caption.

9 Repeat Steps 2 and 3, type `Motorcycle Picture` as the figure description, and then click the OK button to insert the caption below the selected graphic.

10 At the end of the last sentence above the graphic, change the word, below, to the word, in, and then press the SPACEBAR.

11 Click the Cross-reference button (References tab | Captions group) to display the Cross-reference dialog box, if necessary, click Figure 1: Motorcycle Picture in the 'For which caption' list to select the caption to reference, click the Insert button to insert the cross-reference at the location of the insertion point, and then click the Close button in the Cross-reference dialog box.

12 Click the Previous Graphic button on the vertical scroll bar to display the previous graphic in the document window (which is the legal scales clip art image in this case).

13 Click the legal scales clip art image to select the graphic for which you want to add a caption.

14 Repeat Steps 2 and 3, type `Legal Scales Clip Art Image` as the figure description, and then click the OK button to insert the caption below the selected graphic.

15 At the end of the last sentence below the To Insert a Clip Art Image heading, position the insertion point to the left of the period, press the SPACEBAR, and then press the LEFT PARENTHESIS key.

16 Click the Cross-reference button (References tab | Captions group) to display the Cross-reference dialog box, if necessary, click Figure 1: Legal Scales Clip Art Image in the 'For which caption' list to select the caption to reference, click the Insert button to insert the cross-reference at the location of the insertion point, and then click the Close button in the Cross-reference dialog box.

17 Press the RIGHT PARENTHESIS key to enclose the cross-reference (Figure 9–14).

BTWs

BTW

For a complete list of the BTWs found in the margins of this book, visit the Word 2010 BTW Web page (scsite.com/wd2010/btw).

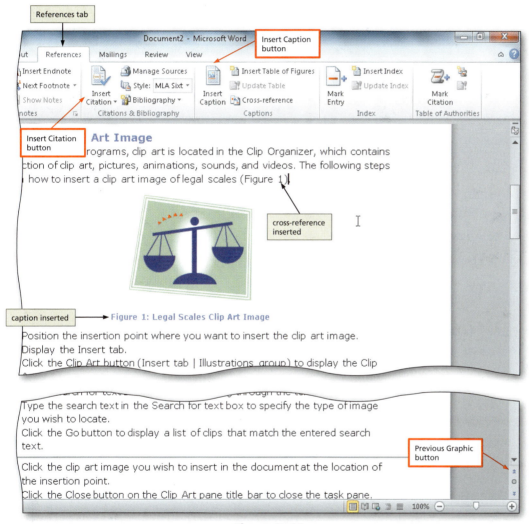

Figure 9–14

To Mark an Index Entry

The last page of the reference document in this project is an index, which lists important terms discussed in the document along with each term's corresponding page number. For Word to generate the index, you first must mark any text you wish to appear in the index. When you mark an index entry, Word creates a field that it uses to build the index. Index entry fields are hidden and are displayed on the screen only when you show formatting marks, that is, when the Show/Hide ¶ button (Home tab | Paragraph group) is selected.

In this document, you want the words, graphical image, in the first sentence below the Inserting Graphical Images in a Word document heading to be marked as an index entry. The steps on the next page mark an index entry.

1

- Select the text you wish to appear in the index (the words, graphical image, in the first sentence of the document in this case).

- Click the Mark Entry button (References tab | Index group) to display the Mark Index Entry dialog box (Figure 9–15).

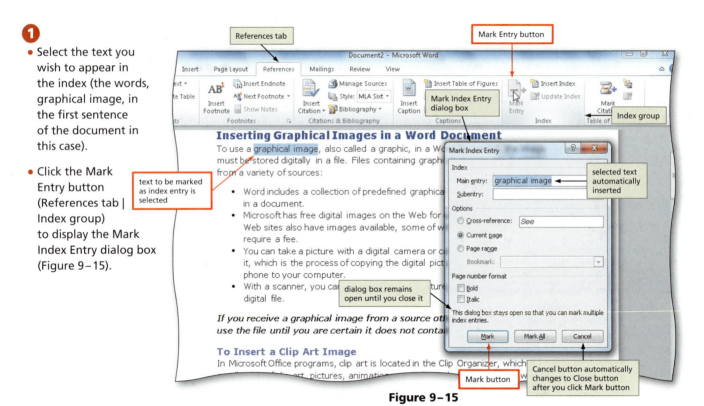

Figure 9–15

2

- Click the Mark button (Mark Index Entry dialog box) to mark the selected text in the document as an index entry.

Q&A

Why do formatting marks now appear on the screen?

When you mark an index entry, Word automatically shows formatting marks (if they are not showing already) so that you can see the index entry field. Notice that the marked index entry begins with the letters, XE.

- Click the Close button in the Mark Index Entry dialog box (Figure 9–16).

Q&A

How could I see all index entries marked in a document?

With formatting marks displaying, you could scroll through the document, scanning for all occurrences of XE, or you could use the Navigation Pane (that is, place a check mark in the Navigation Pane check box (View tab | Show group)) to find all occurrences of XE.

index entry field inserted as formatting mark in document

·Inserting·Graphical·Images·in·a·Word·Document¶

To·use·a·graphical·image{·XE·"graphical·image"·},·also·called·a·graphic{·XE·"graphic"·}·in·a·Word·document,·the·image·must·be·stored·digitally·in·a·file.·Files·containing·graphical·images·are·available·from·a·variety·of·sources:¶

- → Word·includes·a·collection·of·predefined·graphical·images·that·you·can·insert·in·a·document.¶
- → Microsoft·has·free·digital·images·on·the·Web·for·use·in·a·docu... Web·sites·also·have·images·available,·some·of·which·are·free,· require·a·fee.¶
- → You·can·ta... ...ital·camera·or·camera...

other index entry fields in document show onscreen when formatting marks are displayed

If·you·receive·a·graphical·image·from·a·source·other·than·yourself,·do·not· use·the·file·until·you·are·certain·it·does·not·contain·a·virus.·¶

·To·Insert·a·Clip·Art·Image{·XE·"insert·a·clip·art·image"·}¶

In·Microsoft·Office·programs,·clip·art·is·located·in·the·Clip·Organizer{·XE·"Clip·Organizer"·},·which·contains·a·collection·of·clip·art,·pictures,·animations,·sounds,·and·videos.·The·following·steps·explain·how·to·insert·a·clip·art·image·of·legal·scales·(Figure·1).¶

Figure 9–16

Other Ways

1. Select text, press ALT+SHIFT+X

To Mark Multiple Index Entries

Word leaves the Mark Index Entry dialog box open until you close it, which allows you to mark multiple index entries without having to reopen the dialog box repeatedly. To mark multiple index entries, you would perform the following steps.

1. With the Mark Index Entry dialog box displayed, click in the document window; scroll to and then select the next index entry.

2. If necessary, click the Main entry text box (Mark Index Entry dialog box) to display the selected text in the Main entry text box.

3. Click the Mark button.

4. Repeat Steps 1 through 3 for all entries. When finished, click the Close button in the dialog box.

To Hide Formatting Marks

To remove the clutter of index entry fields from the document, you should hide formatting marks. The following step hides formatting marks.

1 If the Show/Hide ¶ button (Home tab | Paragraph group) is selected, click it to hide formatting marks.

Q&A What if the index entries still appear after clicking the Show/Hide ¶ button?

Open the Backstage view, click the Options button in the Backstage view to display the Word Options dialog box, click Display in the left pane (Word Options dialog box), remove the check mark from the Hidden text check box, and then click the OK button.

To Show White Space

For the remainder of creating this project, you would like to see headers, footers, and margins. Thus, you should show white space. The following step shows white space.

1 Position the mouse pointer in the document window in the space between the pages and then double-click when the mouse pointer changes to a Show White Space button to show white space.

Building Blocks

Word includes many predefined **building blocks**, which are reusable formatted objects that are stored in galleries. Examples of building blocks include cover pages, headers, footers, page numbers, text boxes, and watermarks. When you inserted a formatted header in a previous chapter, for instance, you were working with a building block.

You can see a list of every available building block in the **Building Blocks Organizer**. From the Building Blocks Organizer, you can sort building blocks, change their properties, or insert them in a document. The project in this chapter uses a text box building block, specifically the Transcend Sidebar building block. The next pages follow these general steps to insert and format the building block.

1. Sort the building blocks in the Building Block Organizer.

2. Insert the Transcend Sidebar text box building block in the document.

3. Enter text in the text box.

4. Insert another Transcend Sidebar text box building block in the document.

5. Link the two text boxes together so that the text flows automatically from one text box to the other.

BTW

Index Entries
Index entries may include a switch, which is a slash followed by a letter inserted after the field text. Switches include \b to apply bold formatting to the entry's page number, \f to define an entry type, \i to make the entry's page number italic, \r to insert a range of page numbers, \t to insert specified text in place of a page number, and \y to specify that the subsequent text defines the pronunciation for the index entry. A colon in an index entry precedes a subentry keyword in the index.

BTW

Building Blocks
Many of the objects that you can insert through the Building Blocks gallery are available as built-in objects in galleries on the Ribbon. Some examples are cover pages in the Cover Page gallery (Insert tab | Pages group), equations in the Equations gallery (Insert tab | Symbols group), footers in the Footer gallery (Insert tab | Header & Footer group), headers in the Header gallery (Insert tab | Header & Footer group), page numbers in the various page number galleries (Insert tab | Header & Footer group), text boxes in the Text Box gallery (Insert tab | Text group), and watermarks in the Watermark gallery (Page Layout tab | Page Background group).

To Sort Building Blocks and Insert a Sidebar Text Box Building Block Using the Building Blocks Organizer

A **sidebar text box** is a text box that runs across the top or bottom of a page or along the edge of the right or left of a page. As an alternative to inserting a text box using the Text Box gallery, you can insert a text box (or any building block) using the Building Blocks Organizer.

To easily locate building blocks in the Building Blocks Organizer, you can sort its contents by name, gallery, category, template, behavior, or description. The following steps sort the Building Blocks Organizer by gallery, so that all the text box building blocks are grouped together, and then insert the Transcend Sidebar building block in the document on the current page.

①

- Be sure the insertion point is on page 1 of the document because building blocks are inserted on the current page.

Q&A

Does the insertion point need to be at the top of the page?

No. The insertion point can be anywhere on the page for which you want to insert the building block.

- Display the Insert tab.

- Click the Quick Parts button (Insert tab | Text group) to display the Quick Parts menu (Figure 9–17).

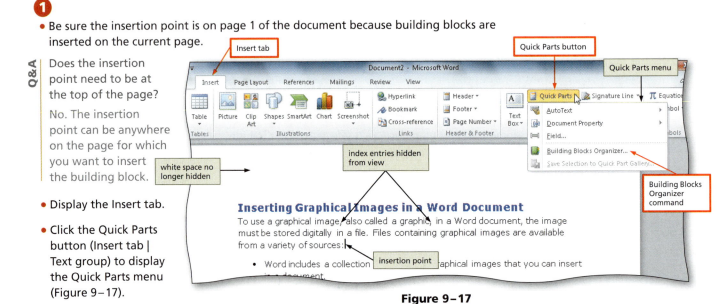

Figure 9–17

②

- Click Building Blocks Organizer on the Quick Parts menu to display the Building Blocks Organizer dialog box.

🔑 **Experiment**

- Drag the horizontal scroll box in the Building Blocks Organizer dialog box to the right so that you can look at all the columns. When finished, drag the horizontal scroll box back to the left in the Building Blocks Organizer dialog box.

- Click the Gallery heading (Building Blocks Organizer dialog box) in the Building blocks list to sort the building blocks by gallery (Figure 9–18).

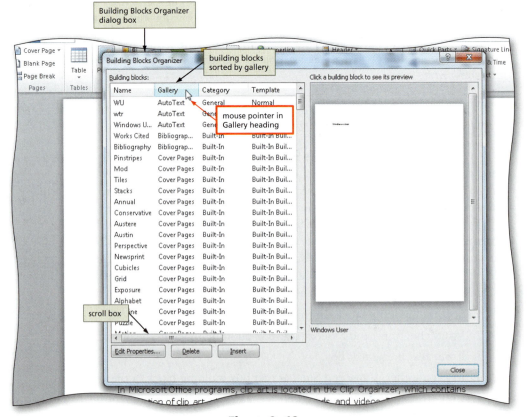

Figure 9–18

3

- Position the mouse pointer between the Name and Gallery column headings and double-click when the mouse pointer changes to a two-headed arrow, so that you can see the entire name in the first column of the list.

Experiment

- Click various names in the Building blocks list and notice that a preview of the selected building block appears in the dialog box.

- Scroll through the Building blocks list to the Text Boxes group in the Gallery column and then click Transcend Sidebar to select it (Figure 9–19).

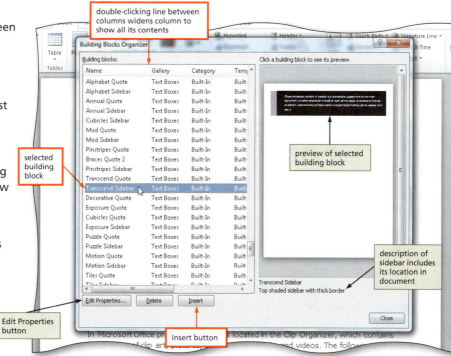

Figure 9–19

4

- Click the Insert button (Building Blocks Organizer dialog box) to insert the selected building block in the document on the current page (Figure 9–20).

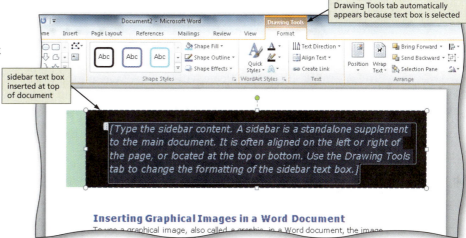

Figure 9–20

TO EDIT PROPERTIES OF BUILDING BLOCK ELEMENTS

Properties of a building block include its name, gallery, category, description, location where it is saved, and how it is inserted in the document. If you wanted to change any of these building block properties for a particular building block, you would perform these steps.

1. Click the Quick Parts button (Insert tab | Text group) to display the Quick Parts menu.

2. Click Building Blocks Organizer on the Quick Parts menu to display the Building Blocks Organizer dialog box.

3. Select the building block you wish to edit (Building Blocks Organizer dialog box).

4. Click the Edit Properties button (shown in Figure 9–19) to display the Modify Building Block dialog box.

5. Edit any property (Modify Building Block dialog box) and then click the OK button. Close the Building Blocks Organizer dialog box.

BTW

Equations

Word includes several predefined mathematical equations that you can insert in a document and then edit, if desired. You insert an equation, such as the quadratic equation, using the Building Blocks Organizer. Or, you can click the Equation button (Insert tab | Symbols group) to display the Equation Tools Design tab, which enables you to insert and customize equations. For practice with the Equation Tools Design tab, complete the Extend Your Knowledge exercise on page WD 597.

BTW

Protected View
To keep your computer safe from potentially dangerous files, Word automatically opens certain files in a restricted mode, called Protected View. To see the Protected View settings, click File on the Ribbon to open the Backstage view, click the Options button to display the Word Options dialog box, click Trust Center in the left pane and then click the Trust Center Settings button in the right pane to display the Trust Center dialog box, which shows the current Protected View settings.

To Enter and Format Text in the Sidebar Text Box

The next step is to enter the text in the sidebar text box. The following steps enter text in the text box.

1 If necessary, click the sidebar text box to select it.

2 Show formatting marks so that you can see paragraphs as you type them.

3 Type `What is a virus?` and then press the ENTER key.

4 Type the following paragraph: `The term, computer virus, describes a potentially damaging computer program that affects, or infects, a computer negatively by altering the way the computer works without the user's knowledge or permission. Once the virus is in a computer, it can spread throughout and may damage your files and operating system.`

5 Press the ENTER key. Type `How do I protect a computer from virus attacks?` and then press the ENTER key.

6 Type the following paragraph: `To protect a computer from virus attacks, users should install an antivirus program and update it frequently. An antivirus program protects a computer against viruses by identifying and removing any computer viruses found in memory, on storage media, or on incoming files. When you purchase a new computer, it often includes antivirus software.`

7 Position the insertion point in the second paragraph because you want to change the style of this paragraph.

8 Display the Home tab. Click the More button (Home tab | Styles group) to display the Styles gallery. Click List Paragraph in the Styles gallery to apply the selected style to the current paragraph in the document.

9 Apply the List Paragraph style to the last paragraph in the text box also (Figure 9–21).

10 Hide formatting marks.

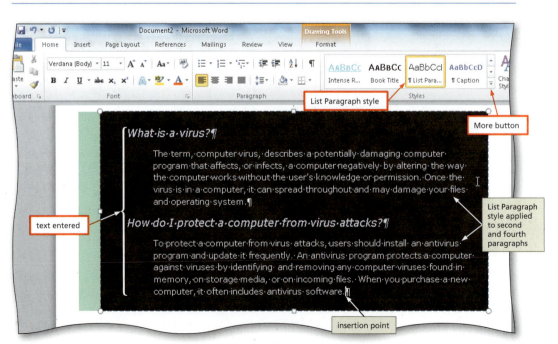

Figure 9–21

To Use the Navigation Pane to Go to a Page

The text box above the Inserting Graphical Images in a Word Document heading is too long. Instead of one long text box, this project splits the text box across the top of two pages, specifically, the first and third pages of this document. The following steps use the Navigation Pane to display page 3 in the document window so that you can insert another text box on that page.

1 Display the View tab. Place a check mark in the Navigation Pane check box (View tab | Show group) to display the Navigation Pane at the left edge of the Word window.

2 Click the 'Browse the pages in your document' tab in the Navigation Pane to display thumbnail images of the pages in the document.

3 Click the thumbnail of the third page in the Navigation Pane to display the top of the selected page in the top of the document window.

4 Position the insertion point near the middle of the third page (Figure 9–22).

5 Leave the Navigation Pane open for use in the next several steps.

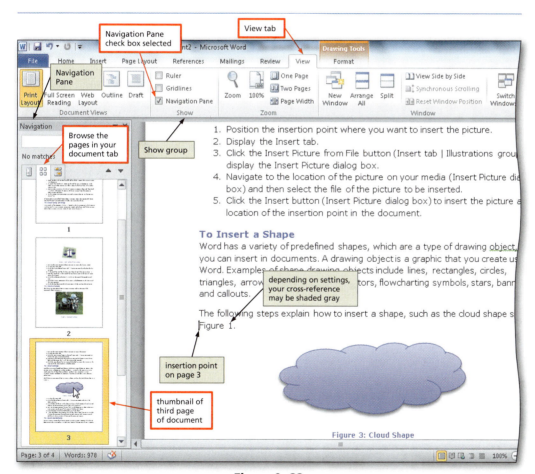

Figure 9–22

To Insert a Building Block

The steps on the next page insert a Transcend Sidebar text box building block at the top of the third page in the document.

1 Ensure that the insertion point is near the middle of the third page in the document.

Why position the insertion point near the middle of the page?

You want to ensure the text box will be positioned at the top of the third page after linking the two text boxes together. Because the content of the first and second text boxes will be shared, the content currently at the top of page three may move to page two after you link the text boxes.

2 Display the Insert tab.

3 Click the Quick Parts button (Insert tab | Text group) to display the Quick Parts menu and then click Building Blocks Organizer on the Quick Parts menu to display the Building Blocks Organizer dialog box.

4 Locate and select the Transcend Sidebar building block and then click the Insert button (Building Blocks Organizer dialog box) to insert the text box on the current page in the document.

5 Press the DELETE key to delete the current contents from the text box (Figure 9–23).

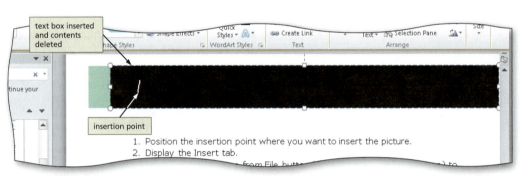

Figure 9–23

To Link Text Boxes

Word allows you to link two separate text boxes, so that the text automatically flows from one text box into the other. To link text boxes, the second text box must be empty. The following steps link text boxes.

- Click the thumbnail of the first page in the Navigation Pane to display the top of the selected page in the document window.

- If necessary, scroll up to display the text box. Click the text box at the top of the first page to select it.

- Display the Drawing Tools Format tab.

- Click the Create Link button (Drawing Tools Format tab | Text group), which changes the mouse pointer to the shape of a cup.

- Move the mouse pointer in the document window to see its new shape (Figure 9–24).

Figure 9–24

- Scroll through the document to display the second text box on the third page in the document window.

Q&A Can I use the Navigation Pane to go to the second text box?

No. If you click in the Navigation Pane, the link process will stop and the mouse pointer will return to its default shape.

- Position the mouse pointer in the empty text box, so that the mouse pointer shape changes to a pouring cup (Figure 9–25).

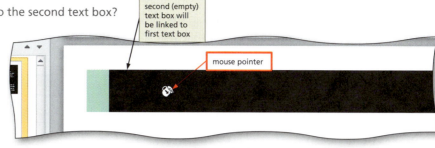

Figure 9–25

- Click the empty text box to link it to the first text box, which causes text from the first text box to flow into the second (linked) text box (Figure 9–26).

Q&A How would I remove a link?

Select the text box in which you created the link and then click the Break Link button (Drawing Tools Format tab | Text group).

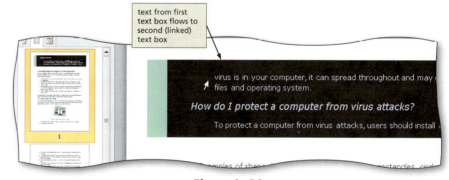

Figure 9–26

- Use the Navigation Pane to display the first page in the document window.
- If necessary, scroll to display the first text box in the document window and then select the text box.
- Resize the text box by dragging its bottom-middle sizing handle until the amount of text that is displayed in the text box is similar to Figure 9–27.

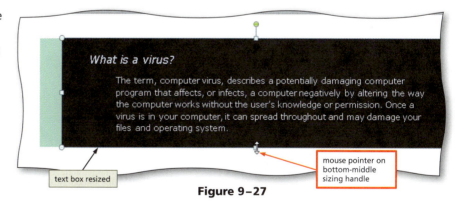

Figure 9–27

- Use the Navigation Pane to display the third page in the document window.
- If necessary, scroll to display the second text box in the document window and then select the text box.
- Resize the text box by dragging its bottom-middle sizing handle until the amount of text that is displayed in the text box is similar to Figure 9–28.

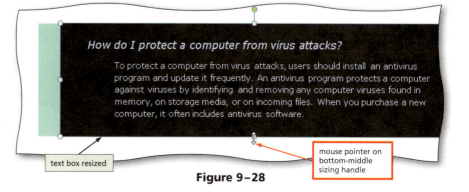

Figure 9–28

- Close the Navigation Pane.

To Compress Pictures

Pictures and other graphics in Word documents can increase the size of these files. If you plan to e-mail a Word document or post it for downloading, you may want to reduce its file size to speed up file transmission time. In Word, you can compress pictures, which reduces the size of the Word document. Compressing the pictures in Word does not cause any loss in their original quality. The following steps compress pictures in the document.

- Double-click a picture in the document to select it, such as the image of the legal scales, so that the Picture Tools Format tab appears.

- Click the Compress Pictures button (Picture Tools Format tab | Adjust group) to display the Compress Pictures dialog box.

- If the 'Apply only to this picture' check box (Compress Pictures dialog box) contains a check mark, remove the check mark so that all pictures in the document are compressed.

- If necessary, click 'Print (220 ppi): excellent quality on most printers and screens' in the Target output area to specify how images should be compressed (Figure 9–29).

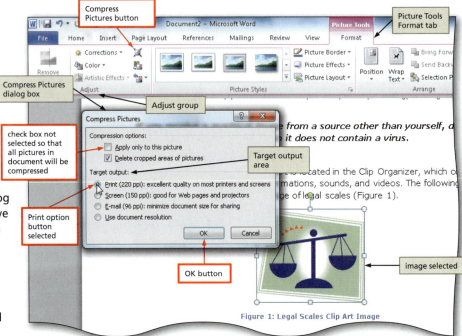

Figure 1: Legal Scales Clip Art Image

Figure 9–29

- Click the OK button to compress all pictures in the document.

Q&A Can I compress a single picture?

Yes. Select the picture and then place a check mark in the 'Apply only to this picture' check box (Compress Pictures dialog box).

Other Ways

1. Click the Tools button in the Save As dialog box, click Compress Pictures on Tools menu

---

BTW

Compressing Pictures
Selecting a lower ppi (pixels per inch) in the Target output area (Compress Picture dialog box) creates a smaller document file but also lowers the quality of the images.

BTW

Clip Organizer Photos
The Clip Organizer contains a collection of clip art, photos, animations, sounds, and video. You can follow these steps to compress any of the photos in the Clip Organizer.

To Save Pictures in Other Formats

You can save any graphic in a document as a picture file for use in other documents or programs. If you wanted to save a graphic in a Word document, you would perform these steps.

1. Right-click the graphic to display a shortcut menu.

2. Click Save as Picture on the shortcut menu to display the File Save dialog box.

3. In the navigation pane, select the location for the saved graphic.

4. Click the 'Save as type' box arrow and then select the graphic type.

5. Click the Save button (File Save dialog box) to save the graphic in the specified location using the specified graphic type.

To Change the Symbol Format in a Bulleted List

The project in this chapter uses a square bullet instead of the default round bullet. Word provides several predefined bullet symbols for use in bulleted lists. The steps on the next page change the symbol in a bulleted list.

- Navigate to the first page and then select the bulleted list for which you want to change the bullet symbol, as shown in Figure 9–30.

- Click the Bullets button arrow (Home tab | Paragraph group) to display the Bullets gallery (Figure 9–30).

- Click the square bullet symbol in the Bullet Library area to change the bullet symbol on the selected bulleted list.

- Click anywhere to remove the selection from the text.

Q&A Can I select any bullet symbol in the Bullet Library area?

Yes. You also can click the Define New Bullet command in the Bullets gallery if the bullet symbol you desire is not shown in the Bullet Library area.

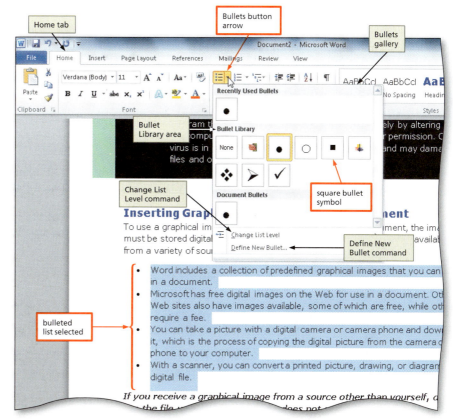

Figure 9–30

BTW

Bullets
You can select from a variety of other bullet symbols or change the font attributes of a bullet by clicking the Define New Bullet command and then clicking the Symbol button or Font button in the Define New Bullet dialog box. You also can change the level of a bullet by clicking the Change List Level command in the Bullets gallery.

To Insert a Building Block (a Watermark)

A watermark is text or a graphic that is displayed on top of or behind the text in a document. In a previous chapter, you created a watermark using the Watermark button (Page Layout tab | Page Background group). Word includes several predefined watermarks as Building Blocks. The following steps insert a watermark of the word, Draft, in the document to alert users who open the file that the document is a draft.

1 Display the Insert tab.

2 Click the Quick Parts button (Insert tab | Text group) to display the Quick Parts menu and then click Building Blocks Organizer on the Quick Parts menu to display the Building Blocks Organizer dialog box.

3 Locate and select the DRAFT 1 watermark building block and then click the Insert button (Building Blocks Organizer dialog box) to insert the watermark on all pages of the document (Figure 9–31).

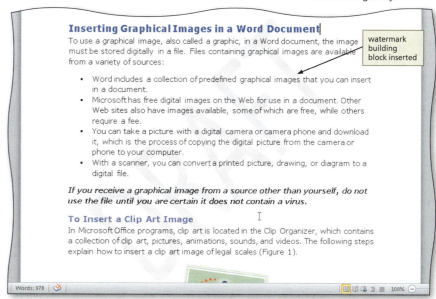

Figure 9–31

TO REMOVE A WATERMARK

If you wanted to remove a watermark, you would perform these steps.

1. Click the Watermark button (Page Layout tab | Page Background group) to display the Watermark gallery.

2. Click Remove Watermark in the Watermark gallery.

To Save a Document

You are finished for now with the draft document. The next step is to save it because you have performed many steps thus far. The following steps save a document.

1 With a USB flash drive connected to one of the computer's USB ports, click the Save button on the Quick Access Toolbar to display the Save As dialog box.

2 Type `Inserting Graphical Images Final Draft` in the File name text box to change the file name. Do not press the ENTER key because you do not want to close the dialog box at this time.

3 If necessary, navigate to the save location (in this case, the Word folder in the CIS 101 folder [or your class folder] on the USB flash drive).

4 Click the Save button (Save As dialog box) to save the document in the selected folder on the USB flash drive with the entered file name.

To Close a Document

The following steps close the open Word document and the Word Help window.

1 Open the Backstage view and then click Close to close the Inserting Graphical Images Final Draft file.

2 Display the Word Help window and close it.

TO RECOVER UNSAVED DOCUMENTS (DRAFT VERSIONS)

If you accidently quit Word without saving a document, you may be able to recover the unsaved document, called a **draft version**, in Word. If you wanted to recover an unsaved document, you would perform these steps.

1. Start Word.

2. Open the Backstage view and then, if necessary, click the Recent tab to display the Recent gallery. Click the Recover Unsaved Documents button to display an Open dialog box that lists unsaved files retained by Word.

or

2. Open the Backstage view and then, if necessary, click the Info tab to display the Info gallery. Click the Manage Versions button to display the Manage Versions menu. Click Recover Unsaved Documents on the Manage Versions menu to display an Open dialog box that lists unsaved files retained by Word.

3. Select the file to recover and then click the Open button to display the unsaved file in the Word window.

4. To save the document, click the Save As button on the Message Bar.

TO DELETE ALL UNSAVED DOCUMENTS (DRAFT VERSIONS)

If you wanted to delete all unsaved documents, you would perform these steps.

1. Start Word.
2. Open the Backstage view and then, if necessary, click the Info tab to display the Info gallery.
3. Click the Manage Versions button to display the Manage Versions menu.
4. Click Delete All Unsaved Documents on the Manage Versions menu.
5. When Word displays a dialog box asking if you are sure you want to delete all copies of unsaved files, click the Yes button to delete all unsaved documents.

Break Point: If you wish to take a break, this is a good place to do so. You can quit Word now. To resume at a later time, start Word and continue following the steps from this location forward.

Working with a Master Document

When you are creating a document that includes other files, you may want to create a master document to organize the documents. A **master document** is simply a document that contains links to one or more other documents, each of which is called a **subdocument**. In addition to subdocuments, a master document can contain its own text and graphics.

In this project, the master document file is named Using Word Series – Guide #11. This master document file contains a link to one subdocument: Inserting Graphical Images Final. The master document also contains other items: a title page, a copyright page, a table of contents, a table of figures, and an index. The following pages create this master document and insert the necessary elements in the document to create the finished Using Word Series – Guide #11 document.

Outlines

To create a master document, you must be in Outline view. You then enter the headings of the document as an outline using Word's built-in heading styles. In an outline, the major heading is displayed at the left margin with each subordinate, or lower-level, heading indented. In Word, the built-in Heading 1 style is displayed at the left margin in outline view. Heading 2 style is indented below Heading 1 style, Heading 3 style is indented further, and so on. (Outline view works similarly to multilevel lists.)

You do not want to use a built-in heading style for the paragraphs of text within the document because when you create a table of contents, Word places all lines formatted using the built-in heading styles in the table of contents. Thus, the text below each heading is formatted using the Body Text style.

Each heading should print at the top of a new page. Because you might want to format the pages within a heading differently from those pages in other headings, you insert next page section breaks between each heading.

To Add Entries in Outline View

The Using Word Series – Guide #11 document contains these three major headings: Inserting Graphical Images in a Word Document, Table of Figures, and Index. The heading, Inserting Graphical Images in a Word Document, is not entered in the outline; instead, it is part of the subdocument inserted in the master document.

BTW

Master Documents
Master documents can be used when multiple people prepare different sections of a document or when a document contains separate elements such as the chapters in a book. If multiple people in a network need to work on the same document simultaneously, individual people each can work on a section (subdocument); all subdocuments can be stored together collectively in a master document on the network server.

The first page of the outline (the copyright page) does not contain a heading; instead it contains three paragraphs of body text, which you enter directly in the outline. The Inserting Graphical Images in a Word Document content is inserted from the subdocument. You will instruct Word to create the content for the Table of Figures and Index later in this chapter. The following steps create an outline that contains headings and body text to be used in the master document.

- If necessary, display a new blank document window (open the Backstage view, click the New tab, if necessary, click the Blank document button, and then click the Create button).

- Click the Outline button on the status bar, which displays the Outlining tab on the Ribbon and switches to Outline view.

- Be sure the Show Text Formatting check box is selected (Outlining tab | Outline Tools group) (Figure 9–32).

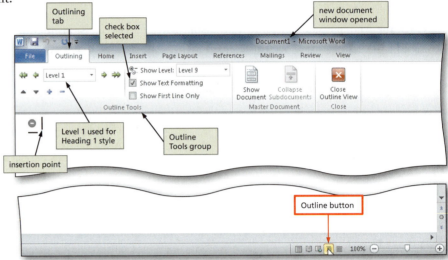

Figure 9–32

2

- Click the Demote to Body Text button (Outlining tab | Outline Tools group), so that you can enter the paragraphs of text for the copyright page.

- Type `Using Word Series | Guide #11` as the first paragraph in the outline and then press the ENTER key.

- Type `To receive additional guides in this or any other series by Trenton's Information Resources Center, contact Jeremy Rivers at jrivers@trenton.edu.` as the second paragraph in the outline and then press the ENTER key.

Q&A Why is only my first line of text in the paragraph displayed?

Remove the check mark from the Show First Line Only check box (Outlining tab | Outline Tools group).

- Right-click the e-mail address that converted to a hyperlink and then click Remove Hyperlink on the shortcut menu.

- Type `Copyright 2012` as the third paragraph and then press the ENTER key.

- Click the Promote to Heading 1 button (Outlining tab | Outline Tools group) because you are finished entering body text and will enter the remaining headings in the outline next (Figure 9–33).

Q&A Could I press SHIFT+TAB instead of clicking the Promote to Heading 1 button?

Yes.

Figure 9–33

3

- Display the Page Layout tab.

- Click the Insert Page and Section Breaks button (Page Layout tab | Page Setup group) and then click Next Page in the Section Breaks area on the Insert Page and Section Breaks gallery because you want to enter a next page section break before the next heading.

4

- Type **Table of Figures** and then press the ENTER key.

- Repeat Step 3.

5

- Type **Index** as the last entry (Figure 9–34).

Q&A Why do the outline symbols contain a minus sign?

The minus sign means the outline level does not have any subordinate levels. If an outline symbol contains a plus sign, it means the outline level has subordinate levels.

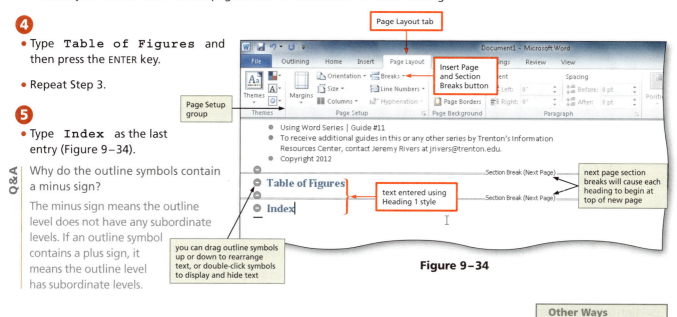

Figure 9–34

Other Ways

1. Click Outline View button (View tab | Document Views group)

To Show First Line Only

To make an outline more readable, users often instruct Word to display just the first line of each paragraph of body text. The following step displays only the first line of body text paragraphs.

1

- Display the Outlining tab.

- Place a check mark in the Show First Line Only check box (Outlining tab | Outline Tools group), so that Word displays only the first line of each paragraph (Figure 9–35).

Q&A How would I redisplay all lines of the paragraphs of body text?

Remove the check mark from the Show First Line Only check box (Outlining tab | Outline Tools group).

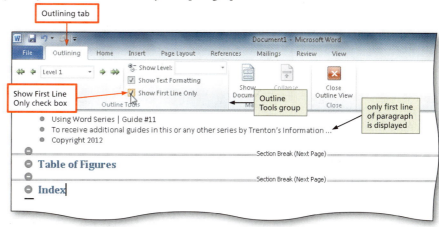

Figure 9–35

To Save a Document

The next step is to save the master document because you have performed many steps thus far. The following steps save a document.

1 With a USB flash drive connected to one of the computer's USB ports, click the Save button on the Quick Access Toolbar to display the Save As dialog box.

2 Type `Using Word Series - Guide #11` in the File name text box to change the file name. Do not press the ENTER key because you do not want to close the dialog box at this time.

3 If necessary, navigate to the save location (in this case, the Word folder in the CIS 101 folder [or your class folder] on the USB flash drive).

4 Click the Save button (Save As dialog box) to save the document in the selected folder on the USB flash drive with the entered file name.

To Insert a Subdocument

The next step is to insert a subdocument in the master document. Word places the first line of text in the subdocument at the first heading level because it is defined using the Heading 1 style. The subdocument to be inserted is the Inserting Graphical Images Final file, which is located on the Data Files for Students. See the inside back cover of this book for instructions on downloading the Data Files for Students, or contact your instructor for information about accessing the required files.

The following steps insert a subdocument in a master document.

- Display the Home tab. If formatting marks do not appear, click the Show/Hide ¶ button (Home tab | Paragraph group).

- Position the insertion point where you want to insert the subdocument (on the section break above the Table of Figures heading).

- Display the Outlining tab. Click the Show Document button (Outlining tab | Master Document group) so that all commands in the Master Document group appear.

2

- With the USB flash drive that contains the Inserting Graphical Images Final file connected to one of the computer's USB ports, click the Insert Subdocument button (Outlining tab | Master Document group) to display the Insert Subdocument dialog box.

- Locate and select the Inserting Graphical Images Final file (Insert Subdocument dialog box) (Figure 9–36).

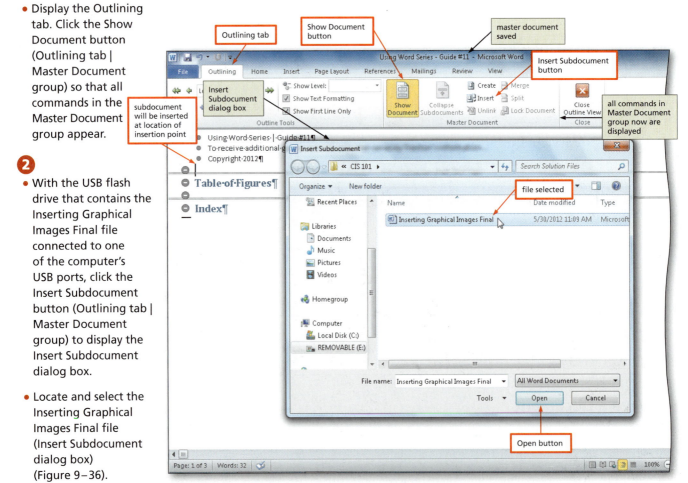

Figure 9–36

3

- Click the Open button (Insert Subdocument dialog box) to insert the selected file as a subdocument.

- If Word displays a dialog box about styles, click the No to All button.

- Press CTRL+HOME to position the insertion point at the top of the document (Figure 9–37).

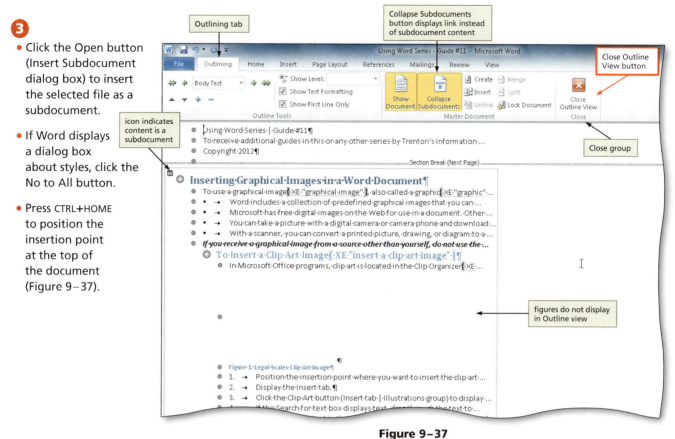

Figure 9–37

Master Documents and Subdocuments

When you open the master document, the subdocuments initially are collapsed; that is, they are displayed as hyperlinks (Figure 9–38). To work with the contents of a master document after you open it, switch to Outline view and then expand the subdocuments by clicking the Expand Subdocuments button.

BTW

Locked Subdocuments
If a lock icon is displayed next to a subdocument's name, either the master document is collapsed or the subdocument is locked. If the master document is collapsed, simply click the Expand Subdocuments button (Outlining tab | Master Document group). If the subdocument is locked, you will be able to display the contents of the subdocument but will not be able to modify it.

Figure 9–38

You can open a subdocument in a separate document window and modify it. To open a collapsed subdocument, click the hyperlink. To open an expanded subdocument, double-click the subdocument icon to the left of the document heading (shown in Figure 9–37).

If, for some reason, you wanted to remove a subdocument from a master document, you would expand the subdocuments, click the subdocument icon to the left of the subdocument's first heading, and then press the DELETE key. Although Word removes the subdocument from the master document, the subdocument file remains on disk.

Occasionally, you may want to convert a subdocument to part of the master document — breaking the connection between the text in the master document and the subdocument. To do this, expand the subdocuments, click the subdocument icon, and then click the Unlink button (Outlining tab | Master Document group).

To Hide Formatting Marks

To remove the clutter of index entry fields from the document, you should hide formatting marks. The following step hides formatting marks.

 Display the Home tab. If the Show/Hide ¶ button (Home tab | Paragraph group) is selected, click it to hide formatting marks.

To Exit Outline View

You are finished organizing the master document. Thus, you can exit Outline view. The following step exits Outline view.

- Display the Outlining tab.

- Click the Close Outline View button (shown in Figure 9–37 on the previous page) (Outlining tab | Close group) to redisplay the document in Print Layout view.

- If necessary, press CTRL+HOME to display the top of the document (Figure 9–39).

Experiment

- Scroll through the document to familiarize yourself with the sections. When finished, display the top of the subdocument in the document window.

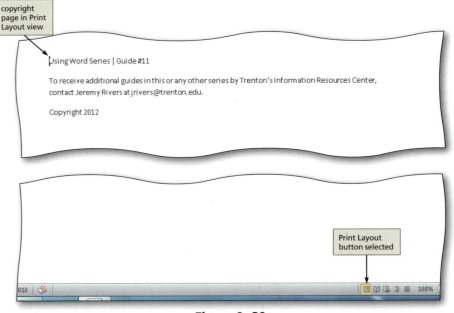

Figure 9–39

To Save a Document Again

The following step saves the master document again with the same file name.

1 Save the master document again with the same file name, Using Word Series - Guide #11.

Organizing a Reference Document

Reference documents are organized and formatted so that users easily can navigate through and read the document. The reference document in this chapter includes the following elements: a copyright page, a title page, a table of contents, a table of figures, an index, alternating footers, and a gutter margin. This section illustrates the tasks required to include these elements.

Include elements common to a reference document.
Be sure to include all essential information on the title page, table of contents, table of figures or list of tables (if one exists), and index.

- **Title Page.** A title page should contain, at a minimum, the title of the document. Some also contain the author, a subtitle, an edition or volume number, and the date written.

- **Table of Contents.** The table of contents should list the title (heading) of each chapter or section and the starting page number of the chapter or section. You may use a leader character, such as a dot or hyphen, to fill the space between the heading and the page number. Sections preceding the table of contents are not listed in it — only list material that follows the table of contents.

- **Table of Figures or List of Tables.** If you have multiple figures or tables in a document, consider identifying all of them in a table of figures or a list of tables. The format of the table of figures or list of tables should match the table of contents.

- **Index.** The index usually is set in two columns or one column. The index can contain any item a reader might want to look up, such as a heading or a key term. If the document does not have a table of figures or list of tables, also include figures and tables in the index.

Plan Ahead

To Change the Document Theme Colors and Font Set

The following steps change the document theme colors and font set for the master document.

1 If necessary, display the Home tab. Click the Change Styles button (Home tab | Styles group) to display the Change Styles menu and then point to Colors on the Change Styles menu to display the Colors gallery.

2 Scroll to and then click Slipstream in the Colors gallery to change the document theme colors to the selected color scheme.

3 Click the Change Styles button (Home tab | Styles group) to display the Change Styles menu and then point to Fonts on the Change Styles menu to display the Fonts gallery.

4 Scroll to and then click Aspect in the Fonts gallery to change the document theme fonts to the selected font set.

BTW

Style Sets
In addition to providing document themes to help you coordinate colors and fonts in a document, Word provides style sets. A **style set** consists of a group of frequently used styles formatted so that they look pleasing when used together. To use a style set other than the default, click the Change Styles button (Home tab | Styles group), point to Style Set on the Change Styles menu, and then select the desired style set in the gallery. To change the style set back to the original, select Default in the Style Set gallery.

To Insert a Cover Page

The reference document in this chapter includes a title page. Word has many predefined cover page formats that you can use for the title page in a document. The steps on the next page insert a cover page.

- Display the Insert tab.

- Click the Cover Page button (Insert tab | Pages group) to display the Cover Page gallery.

🔍 **Experiment**

- Scroll through the Cover Page gallery to see the variety of available predefined cover pages.

- Scroll to the bottom of the Cover Page gallery (Figure 9–40).

Q&A Does it matter where I position the insertion point before inserting a cover page?

No. By default, Word inserts the cover page as the first page in a document.

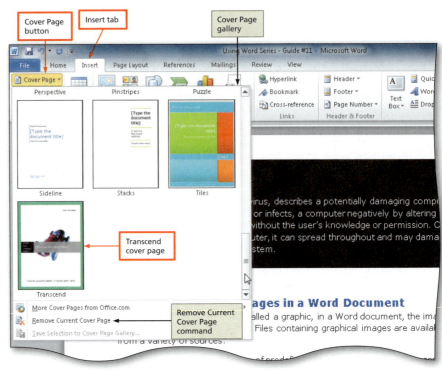

Figure 9–40

- Click Transcend in the Cover Page gallery to insert the selected cover page as the first page in the current document.

- Display the View tab. Click the One Page button (View tab | Zoom group) to display the entire cover page in the document window (Figure 9–41).

Q&A Does the cover page have to be the first page?

No. You can right-click the desired cover page and then click the desired location from the submenu.

Q&A How would I delete a cover page?

You would click the Cover Page button (Insert tab | Pages group) and then click Remove Current Cover Page in the Cover Page gallery.

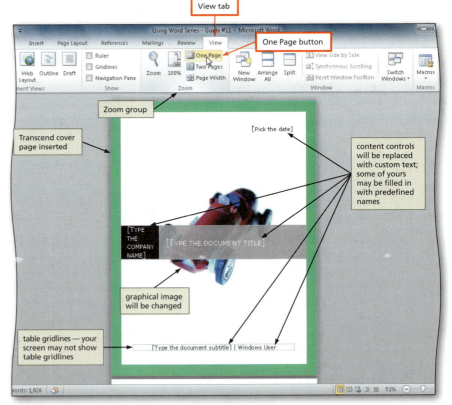

Figure 9–41

Other Ways

1. Click Quick Parts button (Insert tab | Text group), click Building Blocks Organizer, select desired cover page building block (Building Blocks Organizer dialog box), click Insert button, click Close button

To Enter Text in Content Controls

The next step is to select content controls on the cover page and replace their instructions or text with the title page information. Keep in mind that the content controls present suggested text. Depending on settings on your computer, some content controls already may contain customized text, which you will change. You can enter any appropriate text in any content control. The following steps enter title page text on the cover page.

1 Click the date content control to select it and then click its box arrow to display a calendar. Scroll through the calendar months until the desired month appears, May, 2012 in this case. Click 30 in the calendar to display 5/30/2012 as the date on the cover page.

2 Click the content control with the instruction, Type the company name. Type **Information Resources Center** as the name.

3 Click the content control with the instruction, Type the document title. Type **Using Word Series** in the content control.

4 Click the content control with the instruction, Type the document subtitle. Type **Inserting Graphical Images** in the content control.

5 Replace the text in the user name content control, Windows User in this case, with the text **Guide #11** (Figure 9–42).

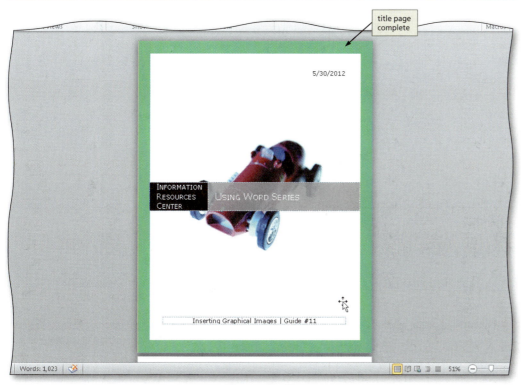

Figure 9–42

To Change a Picture

The current picture of the car on the cover page should be replaced with a screenshot of a Word screen. The screenshot is saved with the name, Word Screen, on the Data Files for Students. See the inside back cover of this book for instructions on downloading the Data Files for Students, or contact your instructor for information about accessing the required files.

The steps on the next page change a picture.

- Right-click the picture to be changed (in this case, the picture of the car) to display a shortcut menu (Figure 9–43).

- Click Change Picture on the shortcut menu to display the Insert Picture dialog box.

- Navigate to the location of the new picture file (in this case, the file named, Word Screen) and then select the file (Insert Picture dialog box).

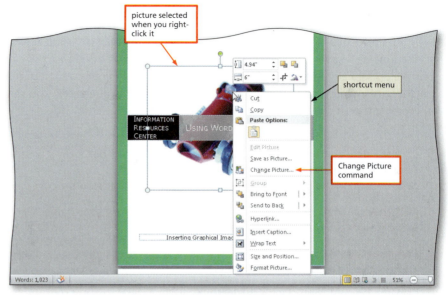

Figure 9–43

- Click the Insert button (Insert Picture dialog box) to replace the selected picture in the document with the new picture file (Figure 9–44).

- Change the zoom level to 100%.

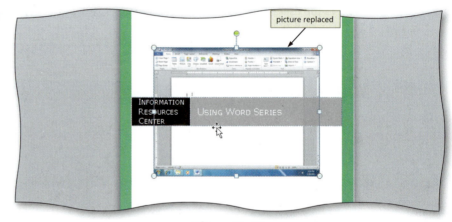

Figure 9–44

Other Ways

1. Click Change Picture button (Picture Tools Format tab | Adjust group)

To Center Text

The next step is to center the text on the copyright page. The following steps center text.

1. Scroll to display the copyright page text in the document window.

2. Select the text on the copyright page and then center it.

3. Deselect the text.

To Insert a Continuous Section Break and Change the Margins in the Section

The margins on the copyright page are wider than the rest of the document. To change margins for a page, the page must be in a separate section. The next steps insert a continuous section break and then change the margins.

① Position the insertion point at the location for the section break, in this case, to the left of U in Using on the copyright page.

② Display the Page Layout tab. Click the Insert Page and Section Breaks button (Page Layout tab | Page Setup group) to display the Insert Page and Section Breaks gallery.

③ Click Continuous in the Insert Page and Section Breaks gallery to insert a continuous section break to the left of the insertion point.

④ Click the Margins button (Page Layout tab | Page Setup group) to display the Margins gallery and then click Wide in the Margins gallery to change the margins on the copyright page to the selected settings (Figure 9–45).

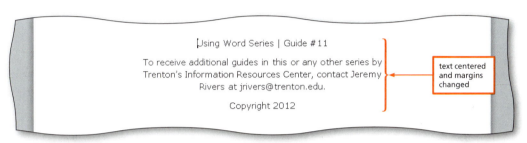

Using Word Series | Guide #11

To receive additional guides in this or any other series by Trenton's Information Resources Center, contact Jeremy Rivers at jrivers@trenton.edu.

Copyright 2012

text centered and margins changed

Figure 9–45

To Adjust Vertical Alignment on a Page

You can instruct Word to center the contents of a page vertically using one of two options: place an equal amount of space above and below the text on the page, or evenly space each paragraph between the top and bottom margins. The copyright page in this project uses the latter, which is called justified vertical alignment. The following steps vertically center text on a page.

①

• Click the Page Setup Dialog Box Launcher (Page Layout tab | Page Setup group) to display the Page Setup dialog box.

• Click the Layout tab (Page Setup dialog box) to display the Layout sheet.

• Click the Vertical alignment box arrow and then click Justified (Figure 9–46).

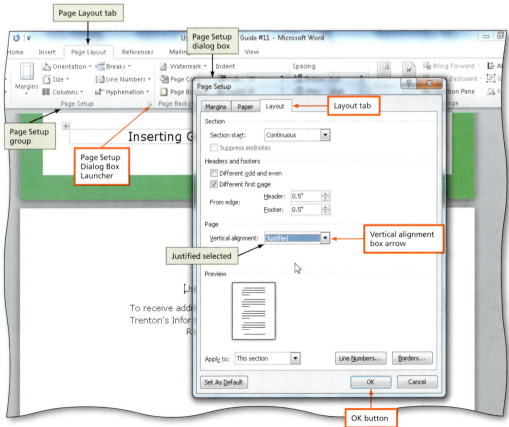

Figure 9–46

2

- Click the OK button to justify the text in the current section.

- To see the entire justified page, display the View tab and then click the One Page button (View tab | Zoom group) (Figure 9–47).

3

- Change the zoom back to 100%.

Q&A

What are the other vertical alignments?

Top, the default, aligns contents starting at the top margin on the page. Center places all contents centered vertically on the page, and Bottom places contents at the bottom of the page.

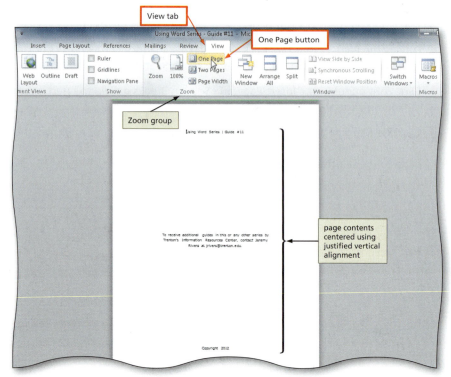

Figure 9–47

To Insert a Blank Page

In the reference document in this chapter, the table of contents is on a page between the copyright page and the first page of the subdocument. Thus, the following step inserts a blank page.

1

- Position the insertion point to the left of the word, Inserting, on the first page of the subdocument (as shown in Figure 9–48).

- Display the Insert tab.

- Click the Blank Page button (Insert tab | Pages group) to insert a blank page at the location of the insertion point.

- If necessary, scroll to display the blank page in the document window (Figure 9–48).

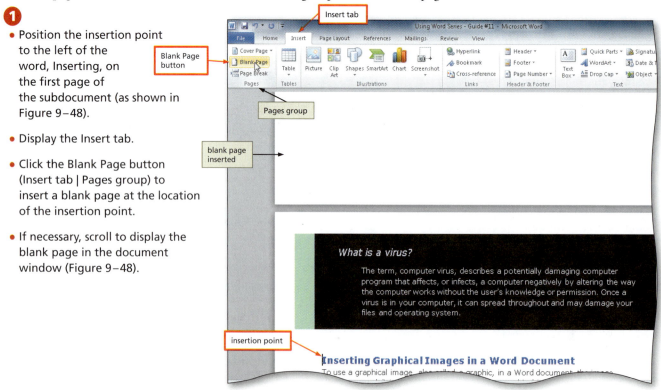

Figure 9–48

To Create a Table of Contents

A table of contents lists all headings in a document and their associated page numbers. When you use Word's built-in heading styles (for example, Heading 1, Heading 2, and so on), you can instruct Word to create a table of contents from these headings. In the reference document in this chapter, the heading of each section uses the Heading 1 style, and subheadings use the Heading 2 style.

Word has many predefined table of contents formats. The following steps use a predefined building block to create a table of contents.

1
- Position the insertion point at the top of the blank page 3, which is the location for the table of contents. (If necessary, show formatting marks so that you can easily see the paragraph at the top of the page.)
- Ensure that formatting marks do not show.

Q&A Why should I hide formatting marks?

Formatting marks, especially those for index entries, sometimes can cause wrapping to occur on the screen that will be different from how the printed document will wrap. These differences could cause a heading to move to the next page. To ensure that the page references in the table of contents reflect the printed pages, be sure that formatting marks are hidden when you create a table of contents.

- Display the References tab.
- Click the Table of Contents button (References tab | Table of Contents group) to display the Table of Contents gallery (Figure 9–49).

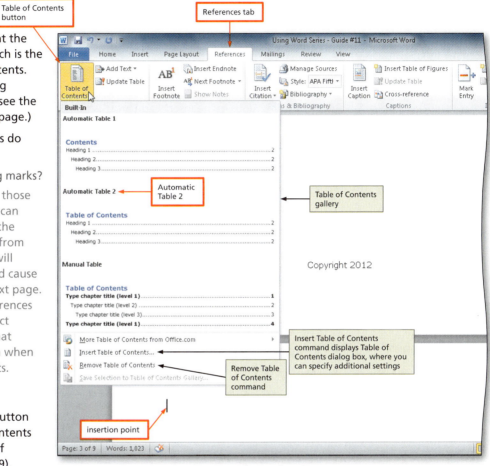

Figure 9–49

2
- Click Automatic Table 2 in the Table of Contents gallery to insert the table of contents at the location of the insertion point (Figure 9–50).

Q&A How would I delete a table of contents?

You would click the Table of Contents button (References tab | Table of Contents group) and then click Remove Table of Contents in the Table of Contents gallery.

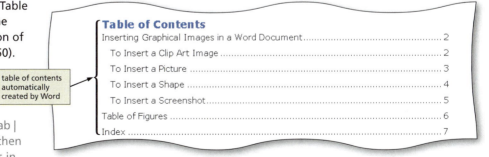

Figure 9–50

Other Ways

1. Click Table of Contents button (References tab | Table of Contents group), click Insert Table of Contents, select table of contents options, click OK button

2. Click Quick Parts button (Insert tab | Text group), click Building Blocks Organizer, select desired table of contents building block (Building Blocks Organizer dialog box), click Insert button, click Close button

BTW

Table of Contents Styles
If you wanted to change the level associated with each style used in a table of contents, click the Options button in the Table of Contents dialog box (shown in Figure 9–62 on page WD 579), enter the desired level number in the text box beside the appropriate heading or other styled item, and then click the OK button. To change the formatting associated with a style, click the Modify button in the Table of Contents dialog box.

To Insert a Continuous Section Break and Change the Starting Page Number in the Section

The table of contents should not be the starting page number; instead, the subdocument should be the starting page number in the document. To change the starting page number, the page must be in a separate section. The following steps insert a continuous section break and then change the starting page number for the table of contents.

1 Position the insertion point at the location for the section break, in this case, to the left of I in Inserting Graphical Images in a Word Document.

2 Display the Page Layout tab. Click the Insert Page and Section Breaks button (Page Layout tab | Page Setup group) to display the Insert Page and Section Breaks gallery.

3 Click Continuous in the Insert Page and Section Breaks gallery to insert a continuous section break to the left of the insertion point.

4 Position the insertion point in the table of contents.

5 Display the Insert tab. Click the Page Number button (Insert tab | Header & Footer group) to display the Page Number menu and then click Format Page Numbers on the Page Number menu to display the Page Number Format dialog box.

6 Click the Start at box down arrow (Page Number Format dialog box) until 0 is displayed in the Start at box (Figure 9–51).

7 Click the OK button to change the starting page for the current section.

BTW

Certification
The Microsoft Office Specialist (MOS) program provides an opportunity for you to obtain a valuable industry credential — proof that you have the Word 2010 skills required by employers. For more information, visit the Word 2010 Certification Web page (scsite.com/wd2010/cert).

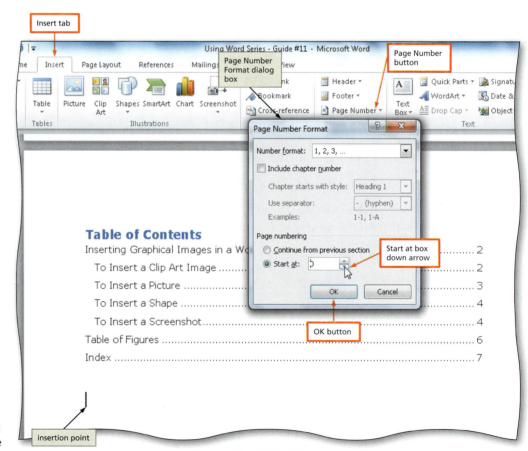

Figure 9–51

To Update Page Numbers in a Table of Contents

When you change a document, you should update the associated table of contents. The starting page number change will affect the page numbers in the table of contents. Thus, the following steps update the page numbers in the table of contents.

- If necessary, click the table of contents to select it.

Q&A

Why does the ScreenTip say 'CTRL+Click to follow link'?

Each entry in the table of contents is a link. If you hold down the CTRL key while clicking an entry in the table of contents, Word will display the associated heading in the document window.

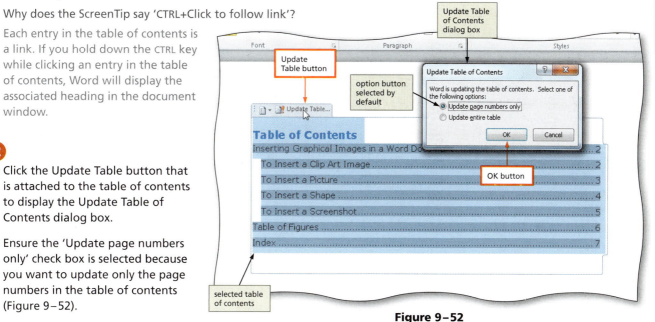

Figure 9–52

- Click the Update Table button that is attached to the table of contents to display the Update Table of Contents dialog box.

- Ensure the 'Update page numbers only' check box is selected because you want to update only the page numbers in the table of contents (Figure 9–52).

- Click the OK button (Update Table of Contents dialog box) to update the page numbers in the table of contents (Figure 9–53).

- Click outside the table of contents to remove the selection from the table.

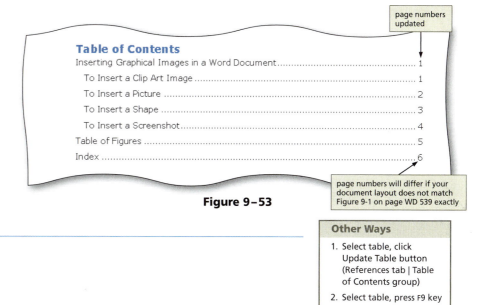

Figure 9–53

Other Ways

1. Select table, click Update Table button (References tab | Table of Contents group)
2. Select table, press F9 key

To Find a Format

In the document, you formatted a sentence of text as bold italic. To find this text in the document, you could scroll through the document until it is displayed on the screen. A more efficient way is to find the bold, italic format using the Find and Replace dialog box. The steps on the next page find a format.

- If necessary, display the Home tab.

- Click the Find button arrow (Home tab | Editing group) to display the Find menu (Figure 9–54).

Figure 9–54

- Click Advanced Find on the Find menu to display the Find and Replace dialog box.

- If Word displays a More button in the Find and Replace dialog box, click it so that it changes to a Less button and expands the dialog box.

- Click the Format button (Find and Replace dialog box) to display the Format menu (Figure 9–55).

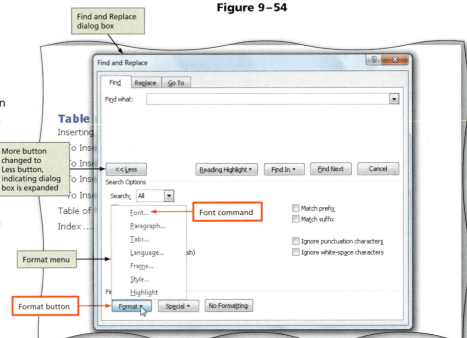

Figure 9–55

③

- Click Font on the Format menu to display the Find Font dialog box. If necessary, click the Font tab (Find Font dialog box) to display the Font sheet.

- Click Bold Italic in the Font style list because that is the format you wish to find (Figure 9–56).

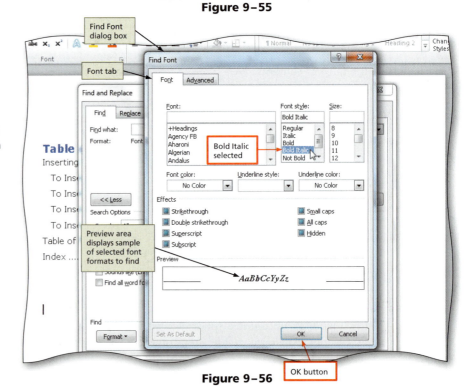

Figure 9–56

4

- Click the OK button to close the Find Font dialog box.

- Be sure no text is in the Find what text box (or click the Find what box arrow and then click [Formatting Only]).

- Be sure all check boxes in the Search Options area are cleared.

- When the Find and Replace dialog box is active again, click its Find Next button to locate and highlight in the document the first occurrence of the specified format (Figure 9–57).

Q&A How do I remove a find format?

You would click the No Formatting button in the Find and Replace dialog box.

5

- Click the Cancel button (Find and Replace dialog box) because the located occurrence is the one you wanted to find.

Q&A Can I search for (find) special characters such as page breaks?

Yes. To find special characters, you would click the Special button in the Find and Replace dialog box.

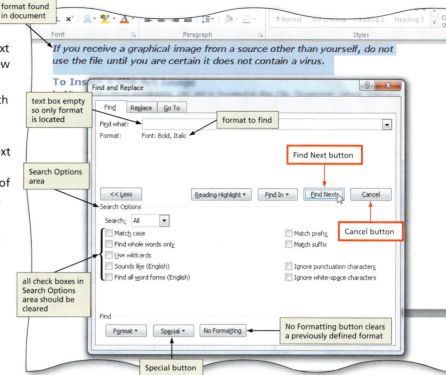

Figure 9–57

To Format Text as a Heading

Occasionally, you may want to add a paragraph of text, which normally is not formatted using a heading style, to a table of contents. To add the text, format it as a heading style. The following steps format a paragraph of text as a Heading 3 style.

1 With the paragraph still selected (shown in Figure 9–57), if necessary, display the Home tab.

2 Click the More button (Home tab | Styles group) to display the Styles gallery. Click Heading 3 in the Styles gallery to apply the selected style to the current paragraph in the document. Click outside the paragraph to deselect it (Figure 9–58).

BTW

Find and Replace
The expanded Find and Replace dialog box allows you to specify how Word locates search text. For example, selecting the Match case check box instructs Word to find the text exactly as you typed it, and selecting the 'Find whole words only' check box instructs Word to ignore text that contains the search text (i.e., the word, then, contains the word, the).

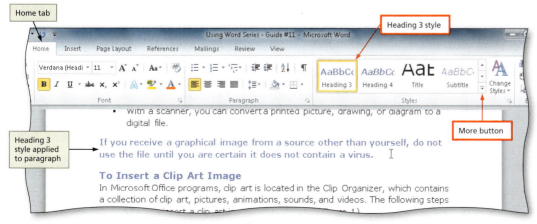

Figure 9–58

TO RETAIN FORMATTING WHEN ADDING TEXT TO THE TABLE OF CONTENTS
If you wanted to retain formatting of text when adding it to the table of contents, you would perform the following steps.

1. Position the insertion point in the paragraph of text that you want to add to the table of contents.

2. Click the Add Text button (References tab | Table of Contents group) to display the Add Text menu.

3. Click the desired level on the Add Text menu, which adds the format of the selected style to the selected paragraph and adds the paragraph of text to the table of contents.

To Update the Entire Table of Contents

The text changed to the Heading 3 style should appear in the table of contents. The following steps update the entire table of contents.

 1

- Display the table of contents in the document window.

- Click the table of contents to select it.

- Click the Update Table button that is attached to the table of contents to display the Update Table of Contents dialog box.

- Click the 'Update entire table' option button (Update Table of Contents dialog box) because you want to update the entire table of contents (Figure 9–59).

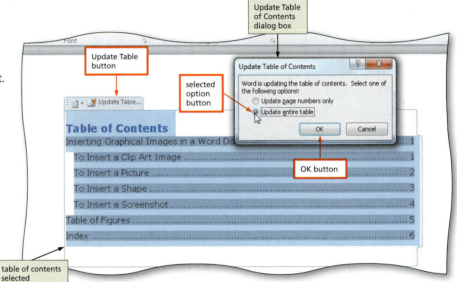

Figure 9–59

 2

- Click the OK button (Update Table of Contents dialog box) to update the entire table of contents (Figure 9–60).

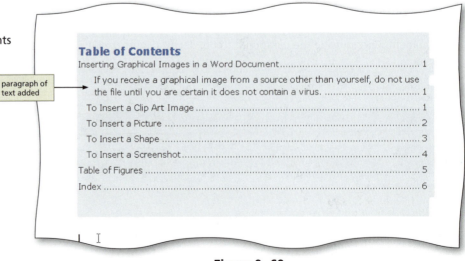

Figure 9–60

Other Ways

1. Select table, click Update Table button (References tab | Table of Contents group)

2. Select table, press F9 key

To Change the Format of a Table of Contents

You can change the format of the table of contents to any of the predefined table of contents styles or to custom settings. The following steps set the format, page number alignment, and tab leader character for a table of contents.

 1

- Display the References tab.

- Click the Table of Contents button (References tab | Table of Contents group) to display the Table of Contents gallery (Figure 9–61).

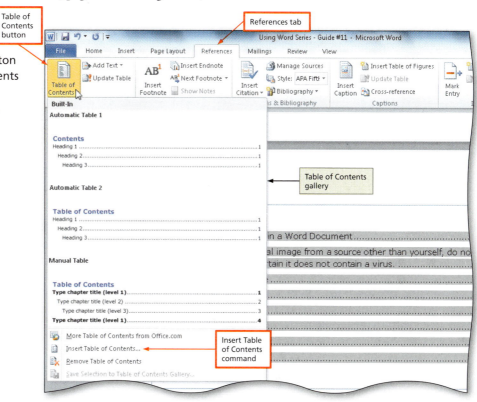

Figure 9–61

2

- Click Insert Table of Contents in the Table of Contents gallery to display the Table of Contents dialog box.

- Click the Formats box arrow (Table of Contents dialog box) and then click Simple to change the format style for the table of contents.

- Place a check mark in the 'Right align page numbers' check box so that the page numbers appear at the right margin in the table of contents.

- Click the Tab leader box arrow and then click the first leader type in the list so that the selected leader characters appear between the heading name and the page numbers in the table of contents (Figure 9–62).

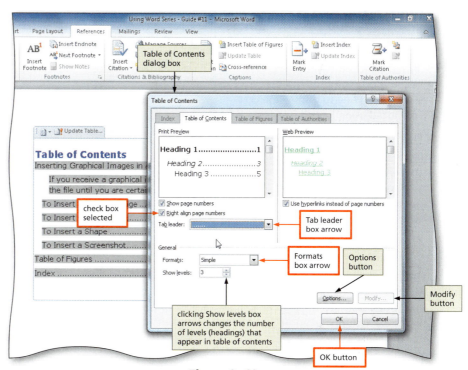

Figure 9–62

3

- Click the OK button to modify the table of contents according to the specified settings. When Word displays a dialog box asking if you want to replace the selected table of contents, click the Yes button (Figure 9–63).

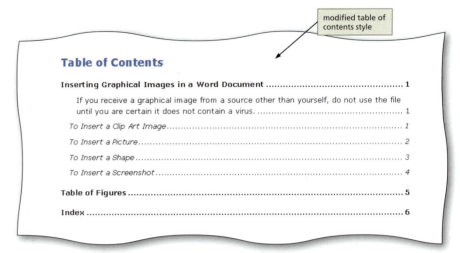

Figure 9–63

To Use the Navigation Pane to Go to a Heading in a Document

When you use Word's built-in heading styles in a document, you can use the Navigation Pane to go to headings in a document quickly. When you click a heading in the Navigation Pane, Word displays the page associated with that heading in the document window. The following step uses the Navigation Pane to display an associated heading in the document window.

1

- Display the View tab. Place a check mark in the Navigation Pane check box (View tab | Show group) to display the Navigation Pane at the left edge of the Word window.

- If necessary, click the 'Browse the headings in your document' tab in the Navigation Pane to display the text formatted using Heading styles.

- Click the Table of Figures heading in the Navigation Pane to display the top of the selected page in the top of the document window (Figure 9–64).

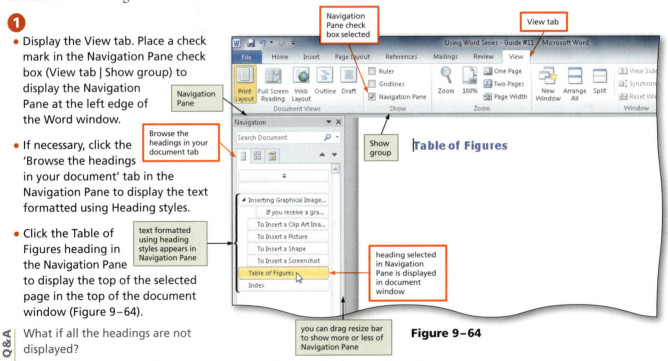

Figure 9–64

Q&A What if all the headings are not displayed?

Right-click a heading in the Navigation Pane and then click Expand All on the shortcut menu to ensure that all headings are displayed. If a heading still is not displayed, verify that the heading is formatted with a heading style. To display or hide subheadings below a heading in the Navigation Pane, click the triangle to the left of the heading. If a heading is too wide for the Navigation Pane, you can point to the heading to display a ScreenTip that shows the complete title.

To Create a Table of Figures

At the end of the reference document is a table of figures, which lists all figures and their corresponding page numbers. Word generates this table of figures from the captions in the document. The following steps create a table of figures.

1

- Ensure that formatting marks are not displayed.

- Position the insertion point at the end of the Table of Figures heading and then press the ENTER key, so that the insertion point is on the line below the heading.

- Display the References tab.

- Click the Insert Table of Figures button (References tab | Captions group) to display the Table of Figures dialog box.

- Be sure that all settings in your dialog box match those in Figure 9–65.

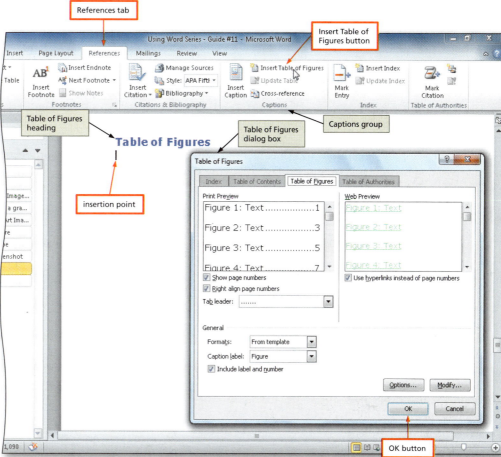

Figure 9–65

2

- Click the OK button to create a table of figures at the location of the insertion point (Figure 9–66).

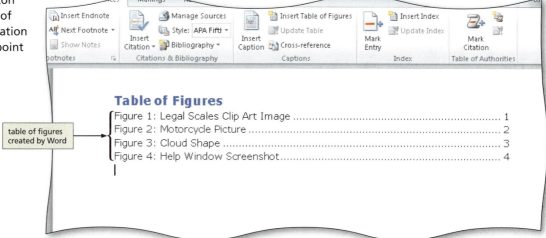

Figure 9–66

TO CHANGE THE FORMAT OF THE TABLE OF FIGURES

If you wanted to change the format of the table of figures, you would perform the following steps.

1. Click the table of figures to select it.
2. Click the Insert Table of Figures button (References tab | Captions group) to display the Table of Figures dialog box.
3. Change settings in the dialog box as desired.
4. Click the OK button (Table of Figures dialog box) to apply the changed settings.
5. Click the OK button when Word asks if you want to replace the selected table of figures.

To Edit a Caption and Update the Table of Figures

When you modify captions in a document or move illustrations to a different location in the document, you will have to update the table of figures. The following steps change the Figure 4 caption and then update the table of figures.

- Click the heading, To Insert a Screenshot, in the Navigation Pane to display the selected heading in the document window.

- Insert the text, Word, in the Figure 4 caption so that it reads: Word Help Window Screenshot (Figure 9–67).

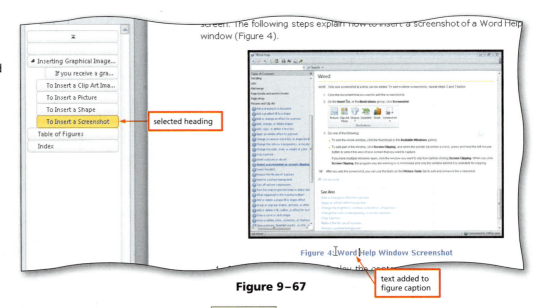

Figure 9–67

- Click the heading, Table of Figures, in the Navigation Pane to display the Table of Figures heading in the document window.

- Click the table of figures to select it.

- Click the Update Table of Figures button (References tab | Captions group) to display the Update Table of Figures dialog box.

- Click 'Update entire table' (Update Table of Figures dialog box), so that Word updates the contents of the entire table of figures instead of updating only the page numbers (Figure 9–68).

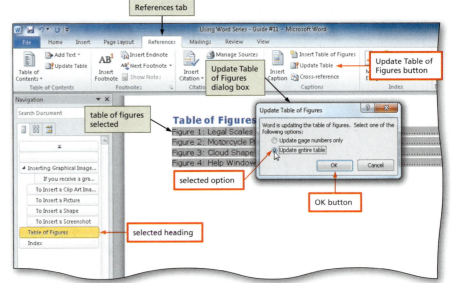

Figure 9–68

3
- Click the OK button to update the table of figures (Figure 9–69).

Q&A

Are the entries in the table of figures links?

Yes. As with the table of contents, you can CTRL+click any entry in the table of figures and Word will display the associated figure in the document window.

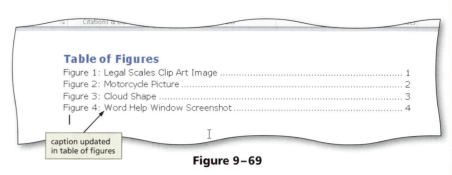

Table of Figures

caption updated
in table of figures

Figure 9–69

Other Ways

1. Select table, press F9 key

To Build an Index

The reference document in this chapter ends with an index. For Word to generate the index, you first must mark any text you wish to appear in the index. Earlier, this chapter showed how to mark index entries.

Once all index entries are marked, Word can build the index from the index entry fields in the document. Recall that index entry fields begin with XE, which appears on the screen when formatting marks are displayed. When index entry fields show on the screen, the document's pagination probably will be altered because of the extra text in the index entries. Thus, be sure to hide formatting marks before building an index. The following steps build an index.

1
- Click the heading, Index, in the Navigation Pane to display the Index heading in the document window.

- Click to the right of the Index heading and then press the ENTER key, so that the insertion point is on the line below the heading.

- Ensure that formatting marks are not displayed.

- Click the Insert Index button (References tab | Index group) to display the Index dialog box.

- If necessary, click the Formats box arrow in the dialog box and then click Classic in the list to change the index format.

- Place a check mark in the 'Right align page numbers' check box.

- Click the Tab leader box arrow and then click the first leader character in the list to specify the leader character to be displayed between the index entry and the page number.

- Click the Columns box down arrow until the number of columns is 1 to change the number of columns in the index (Figure 9–70).

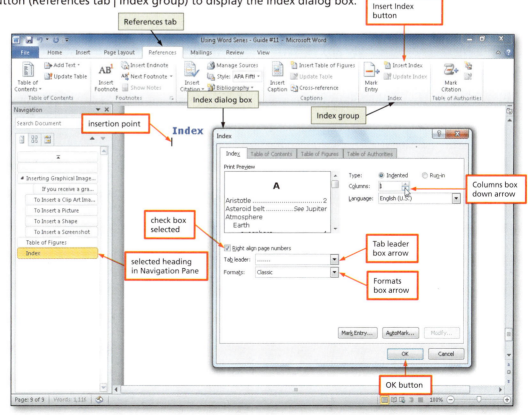

Figure 9–70

2

- Click the OK button (Index dialog box) to create an index at the location of the insertion point (Figure 9–71).

How would I change the language used in the index?

Click the Language box arrow (Index dialog box) and then click the desired language.

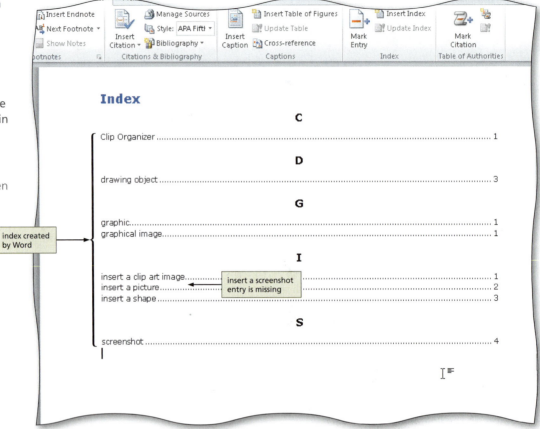

Figure 9–71

Navigation Pane
You can drag any heading in the Navigation Pane to reorganize document content. For example, you could drag the To Insert a Screenshot heading upward in the Navigation Pane so that its content appears earlier in the document.

To Mark Another Index Entry

Notice in Figure 9–71 that the 'insert a screenshot' index entry is missing. The following steps mark an index entry in the Insert a Screenshot section.

1 Click the heading, To Insert a Screenshot, in the Navigation Pane to display the selected heading in the document window.

2 Select the words, Insert a Screenshot, in the heading.

3 Click the Mark Entry button (References tab | Index group) to display the Mark Index Entry dialog box.

4 Type `insert a screenshot` in the Main Entry text box so that the entry is all lowercase (Figure 9–72).

5 Click the Mark button to mark the entry.

6 Close the dialog box.

7 Hide formatting marks.

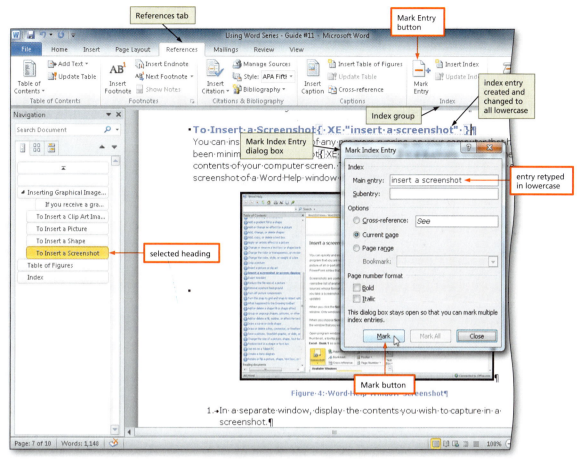

Figure 9–72

TO EDIT AN INDEX ENTRY

At some time, you may want to change an index entry after you have marked it. For example, you may forget to lowercase the entry for the headings. If you wanted to change an index entry, you would perform the following steps.

1. Display formatting marks.

2. Locate the XE field for the index entry you wish to change (i.e., { XE "Insert a Screenshot" }).

3. Change the text inside the quotation marks (i.e., { XE "insert a screenshot" }).

4. Update the index as described in the steps on the next page.

TO DELETE AN INDEX ENTRY

If you wanted to delete an index entry, you would perform the following steps.

1. Display formatting marks.

2. Select the XE field for the index entry you wish to delete (i.e., { XE "insert a screenshot" }).

3. Press the DELETE key.

4. Update the index as described in the steps on the next page.

BTW

Field Codes
If your index, table of contents, or table of figures displays odd characters inside curly braces ({}), then Word is displaying field codes instead of field results. Press ALT+F9 to display the index or table correctly.

To Update an Index

After marking a new index entry, you must update the index. The following step updates an index.

- Click the heading, Index, in the Navigation Pane to display the selected heading in the document window.

- In the document window, click the index to select it.

- If necessary, display the References tab.

- Click the Update Index button (References tab | Index group) to update the index (Figure 9–73).

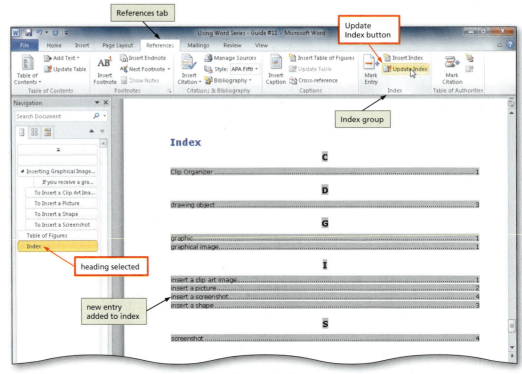

Figure 9–73

Other Ways

1. Select index, press F9 key

TO CHANGE THE FORMAT OF THE INDEX

If you wanted to change the format of the index, you would perform the following steps.

1. Click the index to select it.

2. Click the Insert Index button (References tab | Index group) to display the Index dialog box.

3. Change settings in the dialog box as desired. If you want to modify the style used for the index, click the Modify button.

4. Click the OK button (Index dialog box) to apply the changed settings.

5. Click the OK button when Word asks if you want to replace the selected index.

TO DELETE AN INDEX

If you wanted to delete an index, you would perform the following steps.

1. Click the index to select it.

2. Press SHIFT+F9 to display field codes.

3. Drag through the entire field code, including the braces, and then press the DELETE key.

BTW

Table of Authorities
See Appendix E for additional instructions related to creating a table of authorities.

Table of Authorities

In addition to creating an index, table of figures, and table of contents, you can use Word to create a table of authorities. Legal documents often include a **table of authorities** to list references to cases, rules, statutes, etc. To create a table of authorities, mark the citations first and then build the table of authorities.

The procedures for marking citations, editing citations, creating the table of authorities, changing the format of the table of authorities, and updating the table of authorities are the same as those for indexes. The only difference is you use the buttons in the Table of Authorities group instead of the buttons in the Index group.

To Create Alternating Footers Using a Footer Building Block

The *Using Word Series* documents are designed so that they can be duplicated back-to-back. That is, the document prints on nine separate pages. When they are duplicated, however, pages one and two are printed on opposite sides of the same sheet of paper. Thus, the nine-page document when printed back-to-back uses only five sheets of paper.

In many books and documents that have facing pages, the page number is always on the same side of the page — often on the outside edge. In Word, you accomplish this task by specifying one type of header or footer for even-numbered pages and another type of header or footer for odd-numbered pages. The following steps create alternating footers beginning on the fourth page of the document (the beginning of the subdocument), using the building block for even page footers on odd pages (so that page numbers are on the outside edge) and vice versa.

- Use the Navigation Pane to display the page with the heading, Inserting Graphical Images in a Word Document.

- Display the Insert tab.

- Click the Footer button (Insert tab | Header & Footer group) and then click Edit Footer to display the footer area.

- Be sure the Link to Previous button (Header & Footer Design tab | Navigation group) is not selected.

- Place a check mark in the Different Odd & Even Pages check box (Header & Footer Tools Design tab | Options group), so that you can enter a different footer for odd and even pages.

- If necessary, click the Show Next button (Header & Footer Tools Design tab | Navigation group) to display the desired footer page (in this case, the Odd Page Footer – Section 4).

- Click the Quick Parts button (Header & Footer Tools Design tab | Insert group) to display the Quick Parts menu and then click Building Blocks Organizer on the Quick Parts menu to display the Building Blocks Organizer dialog box.

- Locate and select the Transcend (Even Page) building block (Figure 9–74) and then click the Insert button (Building Blocks Organizer dialog box) to insert the footer on all odd pages of the document from this point forward.

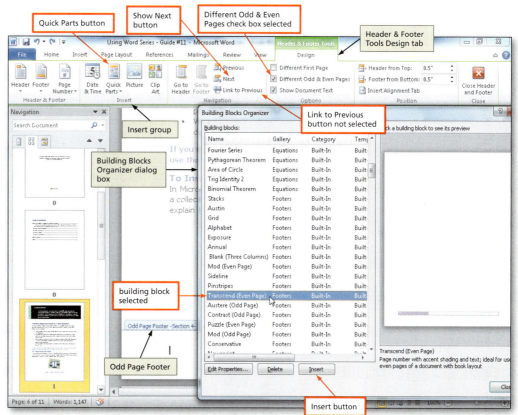

Figure 9–74

3

- Click the Show Next button to display the next footer, in this case, Even Page Footer -Section 4-.

- Be sure the Link to Previous button (Header & Footer Design tab | Navigation group) is not selected.

- Click the Quick Parts button (Header & Footer Tools Design tab | Insert group) to display the Quick Parts menu and then click Building Blocks Organizer on the Quick Parts menu to display the Building Blocks Organizer dialog box.

- Locate and select the Transcend (Odd Page) building block and then click the Insert button (Building Blocks Organizer dialog box) to insert the footer on all even pages of the document from this point forward (Figure 9–75).

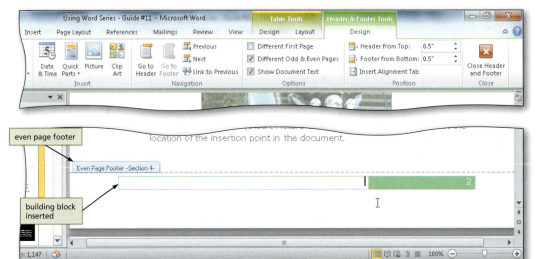

Can I create alternating headers?

Yes. Follow the same basic procedure, except insert a header building block or header text.

Figure 9–75

To Insert a Date in a Footer

You can insert the current date and time in a header or footer using a button on the Header & Footer Tools Design tab. The following steps insert the current date in a footer.

1

- With the insertion point in the even page footer, left-align the insertion point.

- Type **Guide #11|** and then press the SPACEBAR.

- If necessary, display the Header & Footer Tools Design tab.

- Click the Insert Date and Time button (Header & Footer Tools Design tab | Insert group) to display the Date and Time dialog box.

- Select the desired date and time format (Figure 9–76).

Can I insert a date and time in a header?

Yes. Follow the same basic procedure, except in a header.

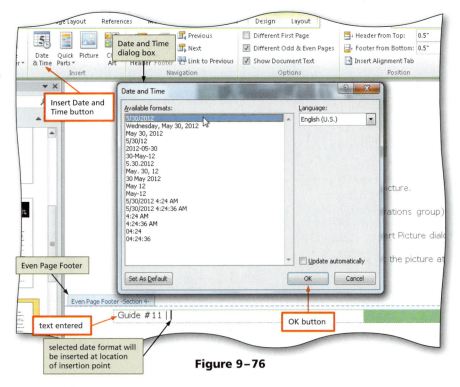

Figure 9–76

2

- Click the OK button to insert the selected date and time format in the document at the location of the insertion point (Figure 9–77).

Q&A What if my page numbers are not correct?

The page breaks will be adjusted later in the chapter.

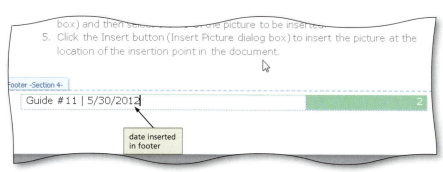

Figure 9–77

<table>
<tr><td>BTW</td><td>**Header and Footer Margins**

If you want the margin of the header or footer to be different from the default of one-half inch, you would adjust the margin in the Header Position from Top or Footer Position from Bottom boxes (Header & Footer Tools Design tab | Position group) or in the Layout sheet of the Page Setup dialog box through the Page Setup Dialog Box Launcher (Page Layout tab | Page Setup group). You also can specify alignment of items in the header or footer by clicking the Insert Alignment Tab button (Header & Footer Tools Design tab | Position group) and then clicking the desired alignment in the Alignment Tab dialog box.</td></tr>
</table>

To Enter Text and the Date in a Footer

The following steps insert text and the current date in the odd page footer.

1 Click the Show Previous button (Header & Footer Tools Design tab | Navigation group) to display the previous footer, in this case, the odd page footer for section 4.

2 Position the insertion point in the rightmost cell and then right-align the insertion point.

3 If necessary, display the Header & Footer Tools Design tab.

4 Click the Insert Date and Time button (Header & Footer Tools Design tab | Insert group) to display the Date and Time dialog box, select the desired date and time format (in this case, 5/30/2012), and then click the OK button to insert the selected date and time format in the document at the location of the insertion point.

5 Press the SPACEBAR and then type   `|Guide #11` as the text in the footer (Figure 9–78).

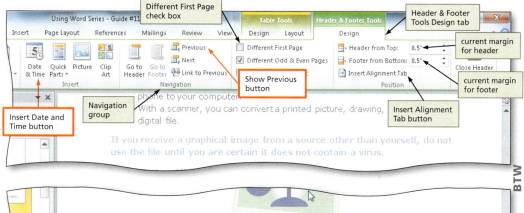

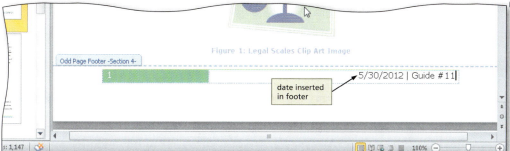

Figure 9–78

<table>
<tr><td>BTW</td><td>**Different First Page**

If you wanted only the first page of a document to have a different header or footer, you would place a check mark in the Different First Page check box (Header & Footer Tools Design tab | Options group). Doing so instructs Word to create a First Page Header or First Page Footer that can contain content that differs from the rest of the headers or footers.</td></tr>
</table>

To Set a Gutter Margin

The reference document in this chapter is designed so that the inner margin between facing pages has extra space to allow printed versions of the documents to be bound (such as stapled) — without the binding covering the words. This extra space in the inner margin is called the **gutter margin**. The following steps set a three-quarter-inch left and right margin and a one-half-inch gutter margin.

- Display the Page Layout tab.
- Click the Margins button (Page Layout tab | Page Setup group) and then click Custom Margins to display the Page Setup dialog box.
- Type .75 in the Left box, .75 in the Right box, and .5 in the Gutter box (Page Setup dialog box).
- Click the Apply to box arrow and then click Whole document (Figure 9–79).

- Click the OK button (Page Setup dialog box) to set the new margins for the entire document.

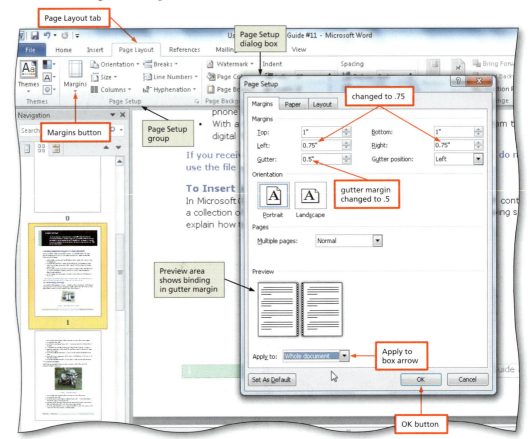

Figure 9–79

To Check the Layout of the Printed Pages

To view the layout of all the pages in the document, the following steps display all the pages as they will print.

1 Open the Backstage view.

2 Click the Print tab to display all pages of the document in the right pane, as shown in Figure 9–80. (If all pages are not displayed, change the Zoom level to 10%.)

Q&A Why do blank pages appear in the middle of the document?

When you insert even and odd headers or footers, Word may add pages to fill the gaps.

3 Click File on the Ribbon to close the Backstage view.

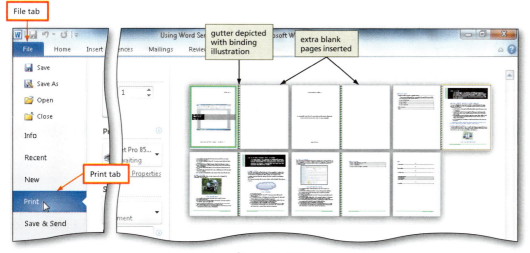

Figure 9–80

To Switch to Draft View

To adjust the blank pages automatically inserted in the printed document by Word, you change the continuous section break at the top of the document to an odd page section break. To see section breaks easily, switch to Draft view. The following step switches to Draft view.

1

- Click the Draft button on the status bar to switch to Draft view.

- Scroll to the top of the document and notice how different the document looks in Draft view (Figure 9–81).

Q&A

What happened to the graphics, footers, and other items?

They do not appear in Draft view because Draft view is designed to make editing text in a document easier.

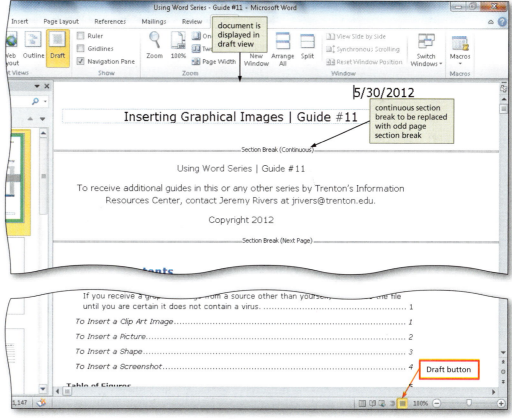

Figure 9–81

Other Ways

1. Click Draft View button (View tab | Document Views group)

BTW

Q&As
For a complete list of the Q&As found in many of the step-by-step sequences in this book, visit the Word 2010 Q&A Web page (scsite.com/wd2010/qa).

To Insert an Odd Page Section Break

To fix the extra pages in the printed document, replace the continuous section break at the end of the title page with an odd page section break. With an odd page section break, Word starts the next section on an odd page instead of an even page.

1 Select the continuous section break at the bottom of the title page and then press the DELETE key to delete the selected section break.

2 If necessary, display the Page Layout tab.

3 To insert an odd page section break, click the Insert Page and Section Breaks button (Page Layout tab | Page Setup group) and then click Odd Page in the Section Breaks area in the Insert Page and Section Breaks gallery (Figure 9–82).

Q&A Can I insert even page section breaks?

Yes. To instruct Word to start the next section on an even page, click Even Page in the Insert Page and Section Breaks gallery.

4 Click the Print Layout button on the status bar to switch to Print Layout view.

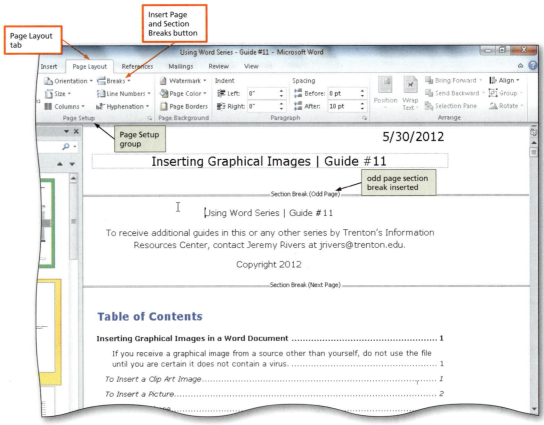

Figure 9–82

To Add a Bookmark

To assist users in navigating through a document online, you can add bookmarks. A **bookmark** is an item in a document that you name for future reference. For example, you could bookmark the headings in the document, so that users easily could jump to these areas of the document. The next steps add a bookmark.

- Display the To Insert a Clip Art Image heading in the document window and then select the heading.

- Display the Insert tab.

- Click the Bookmark button (Insert tab | Links group) to display the Bookmark dialog box.

- Type **ClipArt** in the Bookmark name text box (Figure 9–83).

Q&A

What are the rules for bookmark names?

Bookmark names can contain only letters, numbers, and the underscore character (_). They also must begin with a letter and cannot contain spaces.

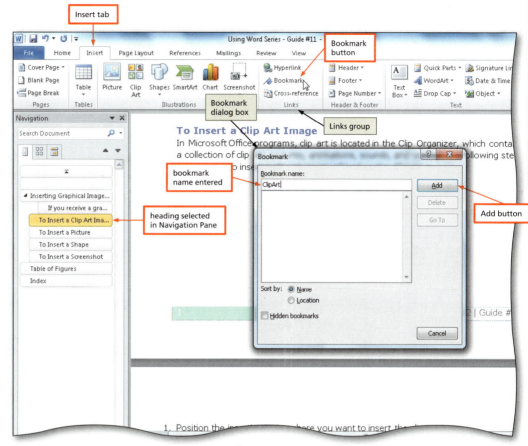

Figure 9–83

- Click the Add button (Bookmark dialog box) to add the bookmark name to the list of existing bookmarks in the document.

3

- Repeat Steps 1 and 2 for these headings in the document: To Insert a Picture, To Insert a Shape, To Insert a Screenshot (use bookmark names Picture, Shape, and Screenshot).

TO GO TO A BOOKMARK

Once you have added bookmarks, you can jump to them by performing these steps.

1. Click the Bookmark button (Insert tab | Links group) to display the Bookmark dialog box (Figure 9–83).

2. Click the bookmark name in the list (Bookmark dialog box) and then click the Go To button.

   or

1. Press the F5 key to display the Go To sheet in the Find and Replace dialog box.

2. Click Bookmark in the list (Find and Replace dialog box), select the bookmark name, and then click the Go To button.

BTW

Quick Reference
For a table that lists how to complete the tasks covered in this book using the mouse, Ribbon, shortcut menu, and keyboard, see the Quick Reference Summary at the back of this book, or visit the Word 2010 Quick Reference Web page (scsite.com/wd2010/qr).

BTW

Link to Graphic
If you wanted to link a graphic in a document to a Web page, you would click the Hyperlink button (Insert tab | Links group), enter the Web address in the Address text box (Insert Hyperlink dialog box), and then click the OK button. To display the Web page associated with the graphic, you CTRL+click the graphic.

BTW

Conserving Ink and Toner
If you want to conserve ink or toner, you can instruct Word to print draft quality documents by clicking File on the Ribbon to open the Backstage view, clicking Options in the Backstage view to display the Word Options dialog box, clicking Advanced in the left pane (Word Options dialog box), scrolling to the Print area in the right pane, placing a check mark in the 'Use draft quality' check box, and then clicking the OK button. Then, use the Backstage view to print the document as usual.

TO INSERT A HYPERLINK

Instead of or in addition to bookmarks in online documents, you can insert hyperlinks that link one part of a document to another. If you wanted to insert a hyperlink that links to a heading or bookmark in the document, you would follow these steps.

1. Select the text to be a hyperlink.
2. Click the Insert Hyperlink button (Insert tab | Links group) to display the Insert Hyperlink dialog box.
3. In the Link to bar, click Place in This Document, so that Word displays all the headings and bookmarks in the document.
4. Click the heading or bookmark to which you want to link.
5. Click the OK button (Insert Hyperlink dialog box).

To Save and Print a Document and Then Quit Word

The reference document for this project now is complete. Save the document, print it, and then quit Word.

1 Save the document with the same file name.

2 Print the finished document (shown in Figure 9–1 on page WD 539).

3 Quit Word.

Chapter Summary

In this chapter, you have learned how to insert a screenshot, add captions, create cross-references, use the Building Blocks Organizer, work with master documents and subdocuments, and create a table of contents, a table of figures, and an index. The items listed below include all the new Word skills you have learned in this chapter.

1. Insert a Screenshot (WD 542)
2. Add a Caption (WD 544)
3. Create a Cross-Reference (WD 546)
4. Use the Select Browse Object Menu (WD 547)
5. Mark an Index Entry (WD 549)
6. Mark Multiple Index Entries (WD 551)
7. Sort Building Blocks and Insert a Sidebar Text Box Building Block Using the Building Blocks Organizer (WD 552)
8. Edit Properties of Building Block Elements (WD 553)
9. Link Text Boxes (WD 556)
10. Compress Pictures (WD 558)
11. Save Pictures in Other Formats (WD 558)
12. Change the Symbol Format in a Bulleted List (WD 558)
13. Remove a Watermark (WD 560)
14. Recover Unsaved Documents (Draft Versions) (WD 560)
15. Delete All Unsaved Documents (Draft Versions) (WD 561)
16. Add Entries in Outline View (WD 561)
17. Show First Line Only (WD 563)
18. Insert a Subdocument (WD 564)
19. Exit Outline View (WD 566)
20. Insert a Cover Page (WD 567)
21. Change a Picture (WD 569)
22. Adjust Vertical Alignment on a Page (WD 571)
23. Insert a Blank Page (WD 572)
24. Create a Table of Contents (WD 573)
25. Update Page Numbers in a Table of Contents (WD 575)

26. Find a Format (WD 575)
27. Retain Formatting when Adding Text to the Table of Contents (WD 578)
28. Update the Entire Table of Contents (WD 578)
29. Change the Format of a Table of Contents (WD 579)
30. Use the Navigation Pane to Go to a Heading in a Document (WD 580)
31. Create a Table of Figures (WD 581)
32. Change the Format of the Table of Figures (WD 582)
33. Edit a Caption and Update the Table of Figures (WD 582)
34. Build an Index (WD 583)

35. Edit an Index Entry (WD 585)
36. Delete an Index Entry (WD 585)
37. Update an Index (WD 586)
38. Change the Format of the Index (WD 586)
39. Delete an Index (WD 586)
40. Create Alternating Footers Using a Footer Building Block (WD 587)
41. Insert a Date in a Footer (WD 588)
42. Set a Gutter Margin (WD 590)
43. Switch to Draft View (WD 591)
44. Add a Bookmark (WD 592)
45. Go to a Bookmark (WD 593)
46. Insert a Hyperlink (WD 594)

If you have a SAM 2010 user profile, your instructor may have assigned an autogradable version of this assignment. If so, log into the SAM 2010 Web site at www.cengage.com/sam2010 to download the instruction and start files.

Learn It Online

Test your knowledge of chapter content and key terms.

Instructions: To complete the Learn It Online exercises, start your browser, click the Address bar, and then enter the Web address **scsite.com/wd2010/learn**. When the Word 2010 Learn It Online page is displayed, click the link for the exercise you want to complete and then read the instructions.

Chapter Reinforcement TF, MC, and SA
A series of true/false, multiple choice, and short answer questions that test your knowledge of the chapter content.

Flash Cards
An interactive learning environment where you identify chapter key terms associated with displayed definitions.

Practice Test
A series of multiple choice questions that test your knowledge of chapter content and key terms.

Who Wants To Be a Computer Genius?
An interactive game that challenges your knowledge of chapter content in the style of a television quiz show.

Wheel of Terms
An interactive game that challenges your knowledge of chapter key terms in the style of the television show *Wheel of Fortune*.

Crossword Puzzle Challenge
A crossword puzzle that challenges your knowledge of key terms presented in the chapter.

Apply Your Knowledge

Reinforce the skills and apply the concepts you learned in this chapter.

Working with Outline View

Note: To complete this assignment, you will be required to use the Data Files for Students. See the inside back cover of this book for instructions on downloading the Data Files for Students, or contact your instructor for information about accessing the required files.

Instructions: Start Word. Open the document, Apply 9–1 Certification Outline Draft, from the Data Files for Students. The document is an outline for a paper. You are to modify the outline in Outline view. The final outline is shown in Figure 9–84.

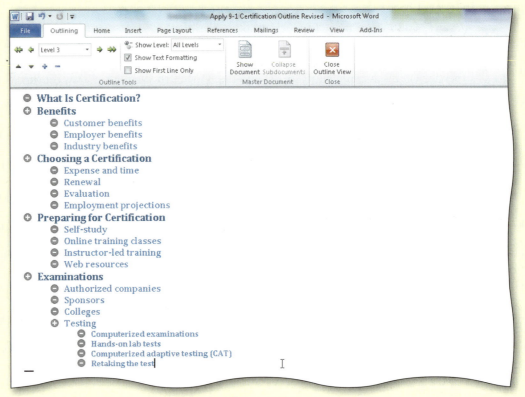

Figure 9–84

Perform the following tasks:

1. If necessary, switch to Outline view.

2. Use the Move Up button (Outlining tab | Outline Tools group) to move the What Is Certification? item up one line.

3. In the Choosing a Certification section, use the Move Down button (Outlining tab | Outline Tools group) to move the Employment projections item down one line.

4. Collapse the Examinations item and then expand the Examinations item.

5. Demote the last four items in the outline (Computerized examinations, Hands-on lab tests, Computerized adaptive testing (CAT), and Retaking the test) so that they are Level 3 instead of Level 2.

6. Promote the Evaluation item so that it is Level 2 instead of Level 3.

7. Change the word, courses, in the Online training courses item to the word, classes, so that it reads: Online training classes.

8. Insert an item, called Employer benefits, as a Level 2 item below the Customer benefits item.

9. Delete the item called In-class training.

10. Promote the Benefits item to Heading 1 (Level 1).

11. Remove the check mark in the Show Text Formatting check box (Outlining tab | Outline Tools group). Place the check mark in the check box again. What is the purpose of this check box?

12. Change the document properties as specified by your instructor.

13. Save the revised file with the file name, Extend 9–1 Certification Outline Revised.

14. Submit the revised document in the format specified by your instructor.

Extend Your Knowledge

Extend the skills you learned in this chapter and experiment with new skills. You may need to use Help to complete the assignment.

Working with Equations

Note: To complete this assignment, you will be required to use the Data Files for Students. See the inside back cover of this book for instructions on downloading the Data Files for Students, or contact your instructor for information about accessing the required files.

Instructions: Start Word. Open the document, Extend 9–1 Formulas Draft, from the Data Files for Students. The document is the start of a study guide containing formulas (Figure 9–85). You will insert additional formulas in a document.

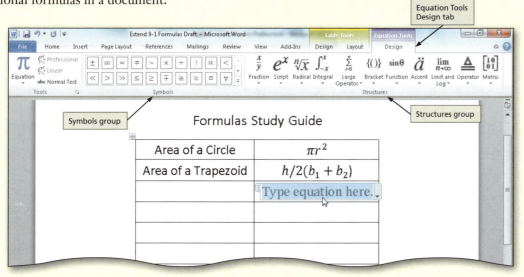

Figure 9–85

Perform the following tasks:

1. Use Help to expand your knowledge about inserting and formatting equations.

2. Add at least eight more formulas to the study guide. The formulas can relate to any academic subject: algebra, geometry, trigonometry, calculus, physics, statistics, finance, chemistry, etc. Insert one formula from the Building Blocks Organizer. Insert at least seven more using the Equation Tools Design tab: type one using symbols in the Symbols gallery and use at least two different structures in the Structures group. Add a column to the table that indicates how you entered the formula (i.e., Building Blocks Organizer, Radical button in Structures group, Symbols gallery, etc.).

Continued >

Extend Your Knowledge *continued*

3. Apply a table style of your choice to the table. Center the table.

4. Locate a Web site that has helpful information related to the formulas in your table. Insert a screenshot of the Web site below the table.

5. Change the document properties as specified by your instructor.

6. Save the revised file with the file name, Extend 9–1 Formulas Revised.

7. Submit the revised document in the format specified by your instructor.

Make It Right

Analyze a document and correct all errors and/or improve the design.

Formatting a Reference Document

Note: To complete this assignment, you will be required to use the Data Files for Students. See the inside back cover of this book for instructions on downloading the Data Files for Students, or contact your instructor for information about accessing the required files.

Instructions: Start Word. Open the document, Make It Right 9–1 Green Computing Draft, from the Data Files for Students. The document is a reference document whose elements are not formatted properly (Figure 9–86). You are to edit, modify, and update the table of contents and index; insert and delete section breaks; change bullet symbols; add bookmarks; and add a header and footer with a page number.

Perform the following tasks:

1. Display the Navigation Pane so that you can use it to go to specific headings and pages as referenced in this exercise.

2. Change the title, Green Computing, on the cover page to a color that is easier to see.

3. Insert a next page section break between the table of contents and the Green Computing heading. Change the Green Computing heading from a Heading 2 style to a Heading 1 style.

4. Change the starting page number of the table of contents page to 0 and the page with the Green Computing heading to 1. Update the table of contents. Change the format of the table of contents to Automatic Table 2.

5. Change the format of the index to a format other than From template. Right-align the page numbers and place a tab leader character between the index entries and the page numbers.

6. The document currently contains seven index entries. Read through the document and mark at least 15 more entries. Lowercase the G in the Green computing index entry so that it reads: green computing. Update the index.

7. Switch to Draft view and delete the next page section break above the Reducing Environmental Impact heading. Switch back to Print Layout view. Update the table of contents again, adjusting starting page numbers as necessary.

8. Change the symbol in both bulleted lists to one other than the dot symbol.

9. Insert a bookmark for each heading in the document.

10. Use the Go To command to practice locating bookmarks in the document.

11. Use the Building Blocks Organizer to add a built-in footer to the document, starting on the page after the table of contents. Add the same style of built-in header to the document. Fill in the appropriate text in the header and footer. Be sure to include a page number.

12. Change the document properties, as specified by your instructor. Save the revised document with a new file name and then submit it in the format specified by your instructor.

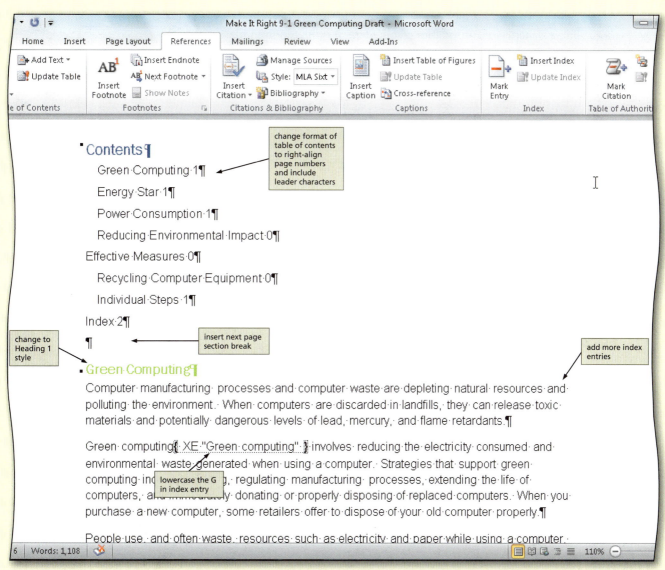

Figure 9–86

In the Lab

Design and/or create a document using the guidelines, concepts, and skills presented in this chapter. Labs are listed in order of increasing difficulty.

Lab 1: Creating a Reference Document with a Cover Page, a Table of Contents, and an Index

Note: To complete this assignment, you will be required to use the Data Files for Students. See the inside back cover of this book for instructions on downloading the Data Files for Students, or contact your instructor for information about accessing the required files.

Problem: As a lab assistant in the Computer Systems department at your school, you have been asked to prepare a guide outlining formatting procedures. A miniature version of this document is shown in Figure 9–87. For a more readable view, visit scsite.com/wd2010/ch9 or see your instructor. A draft of the body of the document is on the Data Files for Students.

Perform the following tasks:

1. Open the document, Lab 9–1 Formatting Documents Draft, from the Data Files for Students. Save the document with a new file name, Lab 9–1 Formatting Documents Final.

2. Create a title page by inserting the Mod style cover page. Use the following information on the title page: title – Enhancing Documents; subtitle – Formatting Made Easy; date – *use today's date*; author – *use your name*.

3. Insert a blank page between the title page and the heading, Formatting Documents.

4. Create a table of contents on the blank page using the Automatic Table 1 style. Insert a continuous section break at the end of the table of contents. Change the starting page number on the table of contents to 0. Update the table of contents.

5. Use the Building Blocks Organizer to insert the Conservative footer on all pages but the title page and the table of contents page. If necessary, adjust the cell width so that the label, Page, and the page number fit on the same line.

6. Mark the following terms in the document as index entries: border, character formatting, font, font size, font style, page color, page formatting, paragraph formatting, sans serif font, serif font, and watermark.

7. Build an index for the document. Remember to hide formatting marks prior to building the index. Use the From template format using one column, with right-aligned page numbers and leader characters.

8. Change the document properties, as specified by your instructor. Save the document again and then submit it in the format specified by your instructor.

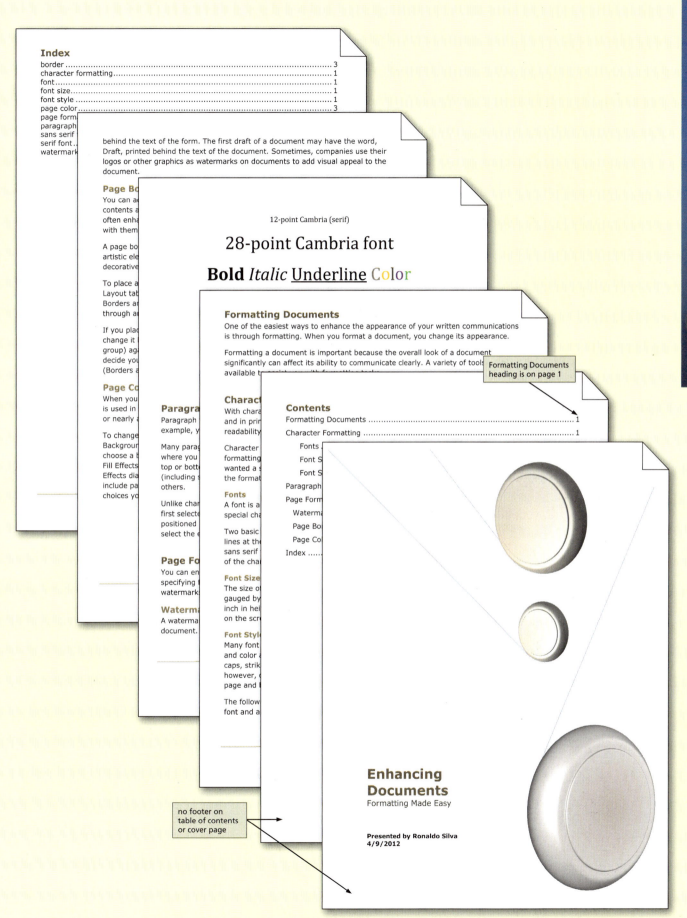

Index

behind the text of the form. The first draft of a document may have the word,
Draft, printed behind the text of the document. Sometimes, companies use their
logos or other graphics as watermarks on documents to add visual appeal to the
document.

Page Bo
You can a
contents a
often enha
with them

A page bo
artistic ele
decorative

To place a
Layout tab
Borders ar
through ar

If you plac
change it
group) aga
decide you
(Borders a

Page Co
When you
is used in
or nearly a

To change
Backgroun
choose a
Fill Effects
Effects dia
include pa
choices yo

12-point Cambria (serif)

28-point Cambria font

Bold *Italic* Underline Color

Formatting Documents
One of the easiest ways to enhance the appearance of your written communications
is through formatting. When you format a document, you change its appearance.

Formatting a document is important because the overall look of a document
significantly can affect its ability to communicate clearly. A variety of tools
available to assist you with formatting tasks.

Formatting Documents
heading is on page 1

Charact
With chara
and in prin
readability

Character
formatting
wanted a s
the format

Fonts
A font is a
special cha

Two basic
lines at the
sans serif
of the char

Font Size
The size o
gauged by
inch in hei
on the scr

Font Styl
Many font
and color a
caps, strik
however,
page and

The follow
font and a

Paragra
Paragraph
example, y

Many parag
where you
top or bott
(including s
others.

Unlike char
first selecte
positioned
select the e

Page Fo
You can en
specifying
watermark

Waterma
A waterma
document.

Contents

no footer on
table of contents
or cover page

Enhancing
Documents
Formatting Made Easy

Presented by Ronaldo Silva
4/9/2012

Figure 9–87

In the Lab

Lab 2: Creating a Reference Document with a Cover Page, a Table of Contents, a Table of Figures, and an Index

Note: To complete this assignment, you will be required to use the Data Files for Students. See the inside back cover of this book for instructions on downloading the Data Files for Students, or contact your instructor for information about accessing the required files.

Problem: As part of your internship duties, you have been tasked with creating an instructional document that discusses starting and shutting down your computer. A miniature version of this document is shown in Figure 9–88. For a more readable view, visit scsite.com/wd2010/ch9 or see your instructor. A draft of the body of the document is on the Data Files for Students.

Perform the following tasks:

1. Open the document, Lab 9–2 Starting and Shutting Down a Computer Draft, from the Data Files for Students. Save the document with a new file name, Lab 9–2 Starting and Shutting Down a Computer Final. If necessary, change the theme colors to Newsprint and theme fonts to Slipstream.

2. Create a title page by inserting the Newsprint style cover page. Use the following information on the title page: title – Basic Computer Functions; subtitle – Starting and Shutting Down Your Computer; abstract – IT Department; date – Spring 2012.

3. Insert a blank page between the title page and the heading, Starting a Computer.

4. Create a table of contents on the blank page using the Automatic Table 2 style. Insert a continuous section break at the end of the table of contents. Change the starting page number on the table of contents to 0. Update the table of contents.

5. Insert the Newsprint header on all pages but the title page (that is, different first page). Insert the Newsprint footer on all pages after the Table of Contents. Enter the text, IT Department, in the Author content control.

6. Start Windows Help and locate the help topic titled 'Turning off your computer properly'. Maximize the Help window. Switch back to Word and insert the Help window screenshot centered at the end of the Word document. Add two shape callouts to the figure in the Help window. The first callout should connect to the Restart command and read as follows: performs a warm boot. The second callout should connect to the Hibernate command and read as follows: puts computer in a low-power consumption state.

7. Add the following caption to the figures: first figure – Figure 1: Power Button; second figure – Figure 2: Hard Disk; third figure – Figure 3: Windows Help Information.

8. Replace the occurrences of xx in the document with cross-references to the figure captions.

9. Change the format of the numbered list so that the numbers are followed by a parenthesis instead of a period.

10. On the page containing the end of the numbered list, insert an Austere Sidebar text box using the Building Blocks Organizer. Change the text box shape style to Colored Fill - Brown, Accent 3. Change the font to the Normal style. The text for the text box is as follows: As the POST executes, LEDs (tiny lights) flicker on devices such as the disk drives and keyboard. Beeps also may sound, and messages may appear on the screen.

11. At the end of the document, create a table of figures on a separate page. Use the From template format.

12. Mark the following terms in the document as index entries (use the Navigation Pane to search for each term): basic input/output system, BIOS, boot disk, boot drive, booting, cold boot, hibernate, kernel, memory resident, nonresident, power-on self test (POST), recovery disk, registry, Sleep mode, Startup folder, system files, and warm boot.

13. Build an index for the document. Remember to hide formatting marks prior to building the index. Use the From template format, one column with right-aligned page numbers.

14. Save the document again and then submit it in the format specified by your instructor.

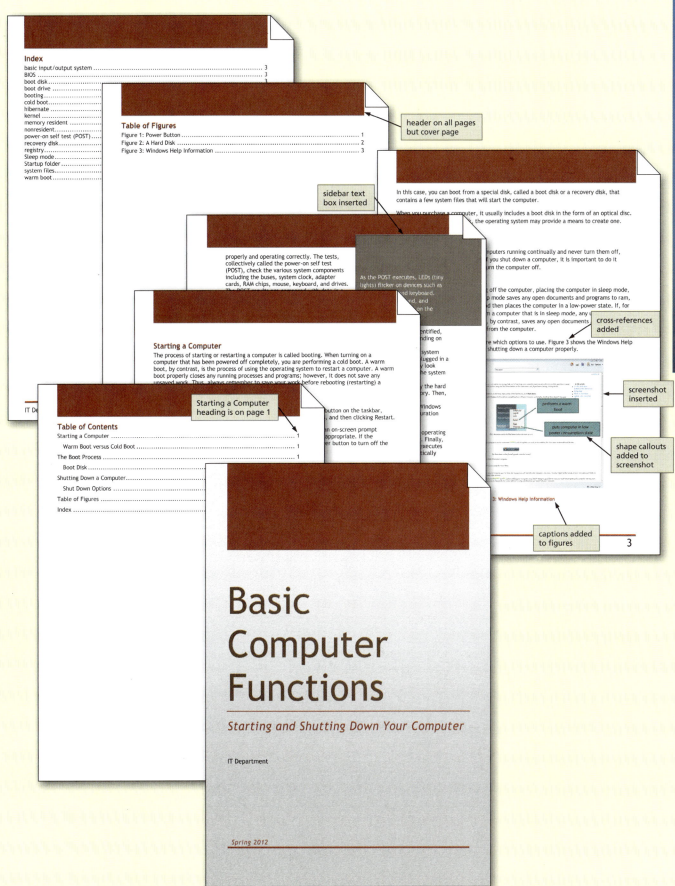

header on all pages but cover page

sidebar text box inserted

In this case, you can boot from a special disk, called a boot disk or a recovery disk, that contains a few system files that will start the computer.

When you purchase a computer, it usually includes a boot disk in the form of an optical disc. ... the operating system may provide a means to create one.

... computers running continually and never turn them off, ... you shut down a computer, it is important to do it ... urn the computer off.

... off the computer, placing the computer in sleep mode, ... p mode saves any open documents and programs to ram, ... and then places the computer in a low-power state. If, for ... m a computer that is in sleep mode, any ... by contrast, saves any open documents ... from the computer.

... re which options to use. Figure 3 shows the Windows Help ... shutting down a computer properly.

cross-references added

properly and operating correctly. The tests, collectively called the power-on self test (POST), check the various system components including the buses, system clock, adapter cards, RAM chips, mouse, keyboard, and drives.

As the POST executes, LEDs (tiny lights) flicker on devices such as ... and keyboard. ... and, and ... on the

... entified, ... nding on

... system ... lugged in a ... y look ... the system

... y the hard ... ry. Then,

Starting a Computer
The process of starting or restarting a computer is called booting. When turning on a computer that has been powered off completely, you are performing a cold boot. A warm boot, by contrast, is the process of using the operating system to restart a computer. A warm boot properly closes any running processes and programs; however, it does not save any unsaved work. Thus, always remember to save your work before rebooting (restarting) a

Starting a Computer heading is on page 1

... button on the taskbar, ... and then clicking Restart.

... an on-screen prompt ... appropriate. If the ... r button to turn off the

... operating ... Finally, ... executes ... tically

performs a warm boot

puts computer in low power consumption state

screenshot inserted

shape callouts added to screenshot

3: Windows Help Information

captions added to figures

3

Basic Computer Functions

Starting and Shutting Down Your Computer

IT Department

Spring 2012

Figure 9–88

Continued >

In the Lab

Lab 3: Using a Master Document and Subdocument for a Reference Document

Note: To complete this assignment, you will be required to use the Data Files for Students. See the inside back cover of this book for instructions on downloading the Data Files for Students, or contact your instructor for information about accessing the required files.

Problem: Your supervisor at your part-time job has asked you to prepare a guide about LCD Monitors. A miniature version of this document is shown in Figure 9–89. For a more readable view, visit scsite .com/wd2010/ch9 or see your instructor. The document is a master document with one subdocument. The subdocument is on the Data Files for Students.

Perform the following tasks:

1. Open the file Lab 9–3 LCD Monitors Subdocument Draft, from the Data Files for Students. Save the document with the file name, Lab 9–3 LCD Monitors Subdocument Final. If necessary, change the theme colors to Equity and theme fonts to Austin.

2. Insert a Sideline Sidebar text box on the page with the LCD Quality heading. Enter this text in the text box: `What type of video content do users view on display devices?` Press the ENTER key. Type: `Music videos and newscasts are the two most widely viewed types of video content on display devices. These are followed by sports, Internet TV, and films.` Press the ENTER key. Type: `Which screen resolution is the most popular today?` Press the ENTER key. Type: `A recent study shows that more than 93 percent of computer users configure their display devices with a 1024 x 768 resolution or higher.`

3. On the next page, insert another Sideline Sidebar text box. Link the two text boxes together. Resize each text box so that each one contains just one question and answer. Save and close the document.

4. Create a new document. If necessary, change theme colors and fonts as specified in Step 1. In Outline view, type `Copyright 2012` as the first line formatted as Body Text, and the remaining lines containing the headings Table of Figures and Index. Insert a next page section break between each heading.

5. Save the master document with the file name, Lab 9–3 LCD Monitors Master Document.

6. Between the Copyright line and Table of Figures headings, insert the subdocument named Lab 9–3 LCD Monitors Subdocument Final.

7. Switch to Print Layout view.

8. Create a cover page by inserting the Pinstripes style cover page. Use the following information on the title page: title – LCD Monitors; date – *use today's date*; company – Information Technology Department; author – *use your name*. Delete the subtitle placeholder.

9. Format the copyright page with a vertical alignment of Bottom.

10. Insert a blank page between the copyright page and the heading, Display Devices.

11. Create a table of contents on the blank page using the Distinctive style, right-aligned page numbers, and dots for leader characters.

12. At the end of the document, create a table of figures on the page with the Table of Figures heading, formatted as Heading 1. Use the Formal format with right-aligned page numbers and a tab leader character.

13. Build an index for the document. Remember to hide formatting marks prior to building the index. Use the Formal format in two columns with right-aligned page numbers.

14. Beginning on the fourth page (with the heading, Display Devices), create alternating footers. Use the Transcend (Even Page) footer style for the odd page footer. Use the Transcend (Odd Page) footer style for the even page footer. Insert the current date in the footer (right-aligned on odd pages and left-aligned on even pages). The cover page, copyright page, or table of contents should not contain the footer.

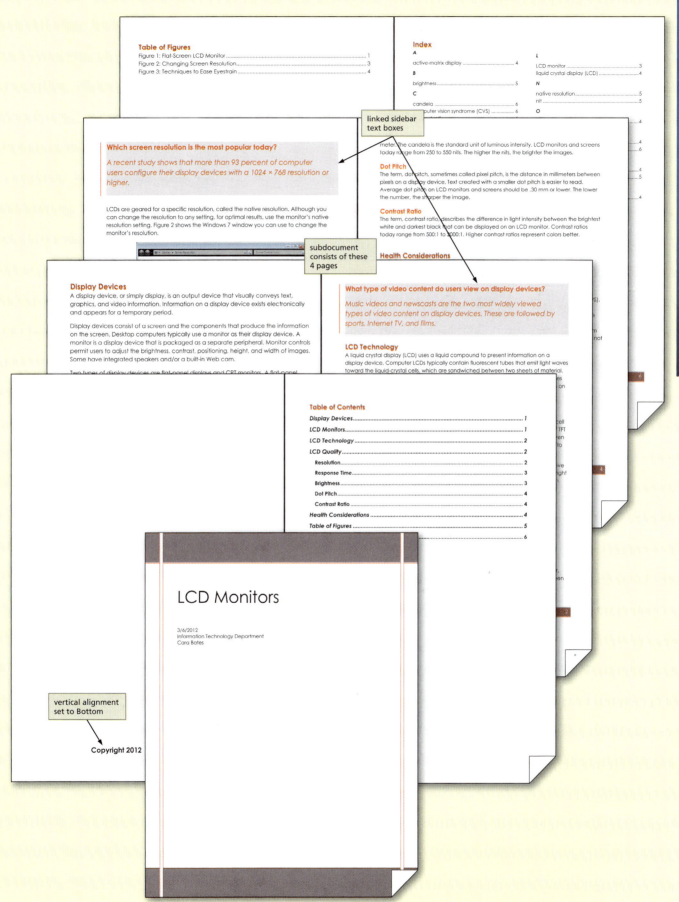

Figure 9–89

Continued >

In the Lab *continued*

15. For the entire document, set the left and right margins to .75" and set a gutter margin of .5".

16. Insert a bookmark for each Heading 2 in the document.

17. Compress the pictures in the document.

18. Save the document again and then submit it in the format specified by your instructor.

19. Make any additional adjustments so that the document looks like Figure 9–89.

20. Save the document again. Print the document (if your printer can print on both sides of a page, print the document back-to-back).

Cases and Places

Apply your creative thinking and problem solving skills to design and implement a solution.

Note: To complete these assignments, you may be required to use the Data Files for Students. See the inside back cover of this book for instructions on downloading the Data Files for Students, or contact your instructor for information about accessing the required files.

1: Create a Reference Document about Analysis and Design Approaches

Academic

In your Systems Analysis and Design class, you have been asked to create a reference document that discusses analysis and design approaches. You decide to use master and subdocuments. The subdocument you created is a file named, Case 9–1 – Detailed Analysis Draft (Figure 9–90), that is located on the Data Files for Students. In the subdocument, mark at least 20 terms as index entries and insert a Draft watermark building block. Save the subdocument file using a different file name.

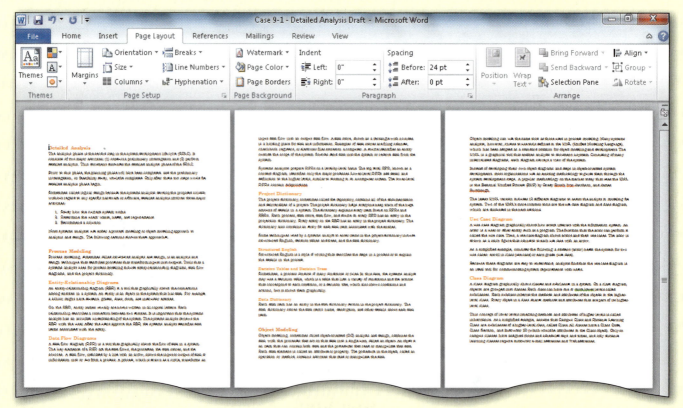

Figure 9–90

Create a master document that contains the subdocument file. The master document also should have a title page (cover page), a table of contents, and an index. Format the document with header and footer building blocks. Be sure to remove the watermark. Use the concepts and techniques presented in this chapter to organize and format the document.

2: Create a Reference Document about Hard Disks

Personal

Because several family members and friends have been asking you recently about the type of hard disks they should purchase with or for their computers, you decide to create a reference document that discusses hard disks. You decide to use master and subdocuments. The subdocument you created is a file named, Case 9–2 – Hard Disks Draft (Figure 9–91), that is located on the Data Files for Students. In the subdocument, mark at least 20 terms as index entries and insert a Draft watermark building block. Save the subdocument file using a different file name. Create a master document that contains the subdocument file. The master document also should have a title page (cover page), a table of contents, and an index. Format the document with header and footer building blocks. Be sure to remove the watermark. Use the concepts and techniques presented in this chapter to organize and format the document.

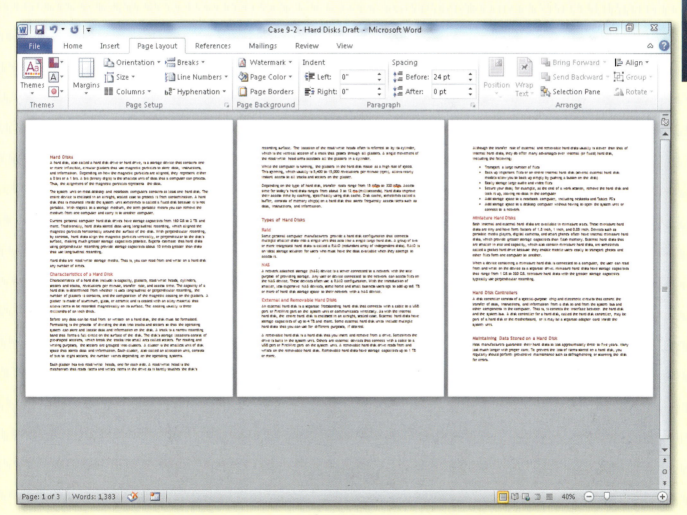

Figure 9–91

Continued >

Cases and Places continued

3: Create a Reference Document about Networks

Professional

As an assistant at a local computer installation and repair store, your supervisor has asked you to create a reference document that discusses types of networks. You decide to use master and subdocuments. The subdocument is a file named, Case 9–3 – Networks Draft (Figure 9–92), that is located on the Data Files for Students. In the subdocument, mark at least 20 terms as index entries and insert a Draft watermark building block. Save the subdocument file using a different file name. Create a master document that contains the subdocument file. The master document also should have a title page (cover page), a table of contents, and an index. Format the document with header and footer building blocks. Be sure to remove the watermark. Use the concepts and techniques presented in this chapter to organize and format the document.

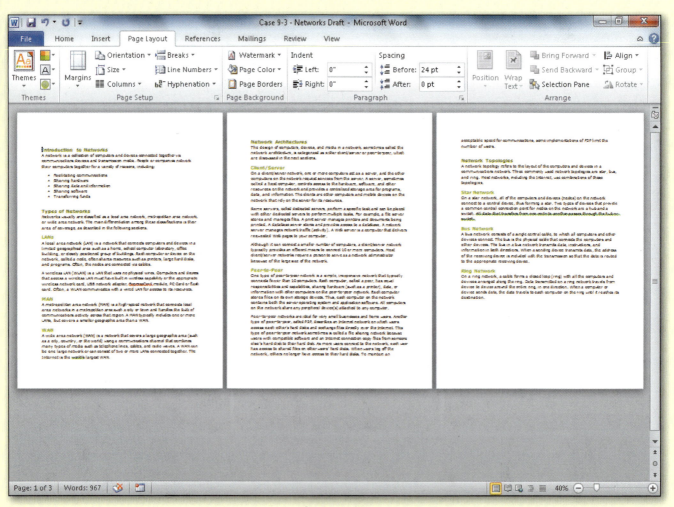

Figure 9–92

10 | Creating a Template for an Online Form

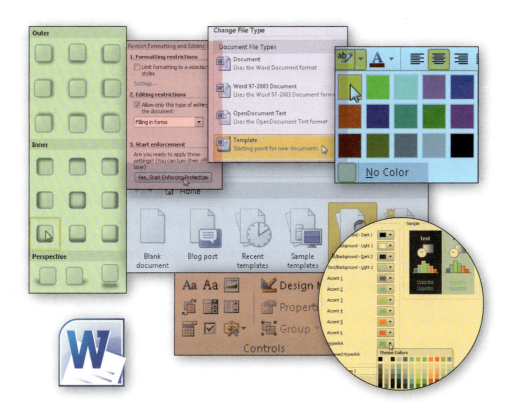

Objectives

You will have mastered the material in this chapter when you can:

- Design an online form
- Save a document as a template
- Change paper size
- Insert a borderless table in a form
- Show the Developer tab
- Insert plain text, drop-down list, check box, rich text, combo box, and date picker content controls

- Edit placeholder text
- Change properties of content controls
- Insert and format a rectangle shape
- Customize a theme
- Protect a form
- Open a new document based on a template
- Fill in a form

10 | Creating a Template for an Online Form

Introduction

During your personal and professional life, you undoubtedly have filled in countless forms. Whether a federal tax form, a time card, a job application, an order, a deposit slip, a request, or a survey, a form is designed to collect information. In the past, forms were printed; that is, you received the form on a piece of paper, filled it in with a pen or pencil, and then returned it manually. With an **online form**, you use a computer to access, fill in, and then return the form. In Word, you easily can create an online form for distribution electronically; you also can fill in that same form using Word.

Project — Online Form

Today, people are concerned with using resources efficiently. To minimize paper waste, protect the environment, enhance office efficiency, and improve access to data, many businesses have moved toward a paperless office. Thus, online forms have replaced many paper forms. You access online forms at a Web site, on your company's intranet, or from your inbox if you receive the form via e-mail.

The project in this chapter uses Word to produce the online form shown in Figure 10–1. Grant's Recycling Service is a new recycling facility interested in community feedback for their upcoming services. Instead of sending a survey via the postal service, Grant's Recycling Service will e-mail the survey to community members whose e-mail addresses are on file with the village hall. Upon receipt of the online form (a survey), the recipient fills in the form, saves it, and then e-mails it back to Grant's Recycling Service.

Figure 10–1a shows how the form is displayed on a user's screen initially; Figure 10–1b shows the form partially filled in by one user; and Figure 10–1c shows how this user filled in the entire form.

The data entry area of the form contains three text boxes (First Name, Last Name, and Other Recycled Items), one drop-down list box (Recycling Services), seven check boxes (Aluminum, Cardboard, Glass, Paper, Plastic, Yard Waste, and Other), a combination text box/drop-down list box (Yard Waste Frequency), and a date picker (Today's Date).

The form is designed so that it fits completely within a Word window that is set at a predefined zoom level, which prevents a user from having to scroll while filling in the form. The data entry area of the form is enclosed by a rectangle that has a shadow inside its bottom and left edges. The line of text above the data entry area is covered with the color yellow, giving it the look of text that has been marked with a highlighter pen.

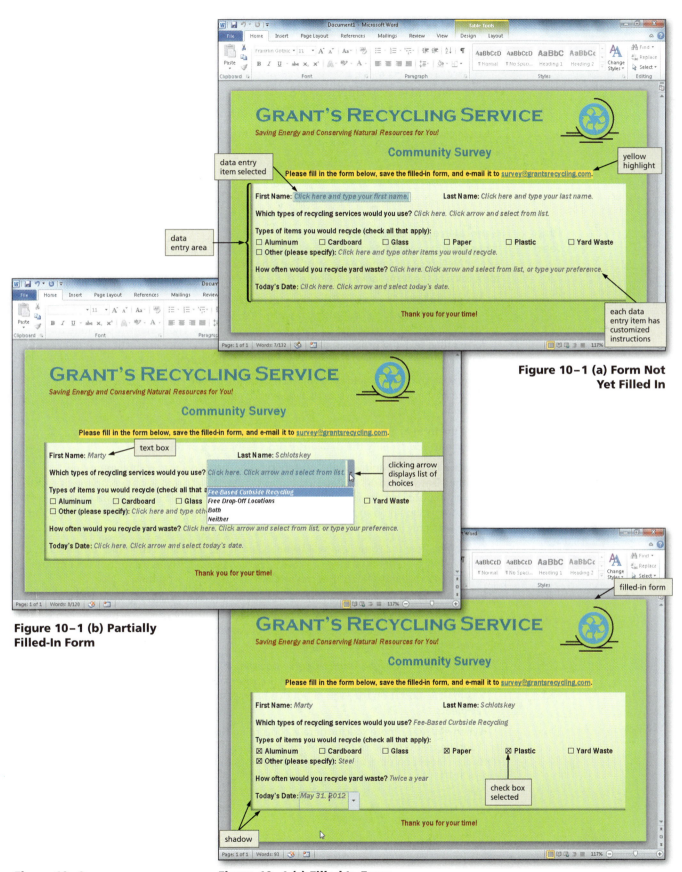

Figure 10–1 (a) Form Not Yet Filled In

Figure 10–1 (b) Partially Filled-In Form

Figure 10–1 (c) Filled-In Form

Figure 10–1

Overview

As you read through this chapter, you will learn how to create the online form shown in Figure 10–1 on the previous page by performing these general tasks:

- Save a document as a template.
- Set document formats.
- Enter text, graphics, and content controls in the form.
- Protect the form.
- Use the form.

Plan Ahead

> **General Project Guidelines**
>
> When creating a Word document, the actions you perform and decisions you make will affect the appearance and characteristics of the finished document. As you create an online form, such as the form shown in Figure 10–1, you should follow these general guidelines:
>
> 1. **Design the form.** To minimize the time spent creating a form while at the computer, you should sketch the form on a piece of paper first. Design a well-thought-out draft of the form — being sure to include all essential form elements. These elements include the form's title, text and graphics, data entry fields, and data entry instructions. A **data entry field** is a placeholder for data that a user enters in the form.
>
> 2. **Determine the correct field type for each data entry field.** For each data entry field, decide its specifications, such as its type and/or a list of possible values that it can contain.
>
> 3. **Save the form as a template.** By saving a form as a Word template, instead of as a Word document, you simplify the data entry process for users of the form.
>
> 4. **Create a functional and visually appealing form.** Use colors that complement one another. Draw the user's attention to important sections. Arrange data entry fields in logical groups on the form and in an order that users would expect. Data entry instructions should be succinct and easy to understand. Ensure that users can change and enter data only in designated areas of the form.
>
> 5. **Determine how the form data will be analyzed.** If the data entered in the form will be analyzed by a program outside of Word, create the data entry fields so that the entries are stored in separate fields that can be shared with other programs.
>
> 6. **Test the form.** Be sure that the form works as you intended. Fill in the form as if you are a user. Have others fill in the form to be sure it is organized in a logical manner and is easy to understand and complete. If any errors or weaknesses in the form are identified, correct them and test the form again.
>
> 7. **Publish or distribute the form.** Not only does an online form reduce the need for paper, it saves the time spent making copies of the form and distributing it. When the form is complete, post it on the Web or your company's intranet, or e-mail it to targeted recipients.
>
> When necessary, more specific details concerning the above guidelines are presented at appropriate points in the chapter. The chapter also will identify the actions performed and decisions made regarding these guidelines during the creation of the online form shown in Figure 10–1.

To Start Word

If you are using a computer to step through the project in this chapter and you want your screens to match the figures in this book, you should change your computer's resolution to 1024 × 768. The following steps start Word and verify settings.

1 Start Word. If necessary, maximize the Word window.

2 If the Print Layout button on the status bar is not selected, click it so that your screen is in Print Layout view.

3 Change your zoom level to 100%.

4 If the rulers are displayed on the screen, click the View Ruler button at the top vertical scroll bar to remove the rulers from the Word window because you will not use the rulers in this project.

5 If the Show/Hide ¶ button (Home tab | Paragraph group) is not selected already, click it to display formatting marks on the screen.

Saving a Document as a Template

A **template** is a file that contains the definition of the appearance of a Word document, including items such as default font, font size, margin settings, and line spacing; available styles; and even placement of text. Every Word document you create is based on a template. When you select the Blank document button in the New gallery of the Backstage view, Word creates a document based on the Normal template. Word also provides other templates for more specific types of documents such as memos, letters, and resumes. Creating a document based on these templates can improve your productivity because Word has defined much of the document's appearance for you.

In this chapter, you create an online form. If you create and save an online form as a Word document, users will be required to open that Word document to display the form on the screen. Next, they will fill in the form. Then, to preserve the content of the original form, they will have to save the form with a new file name. If they accidentally click the Save button on the Quick Access Toolbar during the process of filling in the form, Word will replace the original blank form with a filled-in form.

If you create and save the online form as a template instead, users will open a new document window that is based on that template. This displays the form on the screen as a brand new Word document; that is, the document does not have a file name. Thus, the user fills in the form and then clicks the Save button to save his or her filled-in form. By creating a Word template for the form, instead of a Word document, the original template for the form remains intact when the user clicks the Save button.

To Save a Document as a Template

The steps on the next page save a new blank document as a template, which will be used to create the online form shown in Figure 10–1 on page WD 611.

1

- If necessary, open a new blank document in the Word window.

- With a USB flash drive connected to one of the computer's USB ports, open the Backstage view and then click the Save & Send tab in the Backstage view to display the Save & Send gallery.

- Click Change File Type in the Save & Send gallery to display information in the right pane about various file types that can be opened in Word.

- Click Template in the right pane to specify the file type for the current document (Figure 10–2).

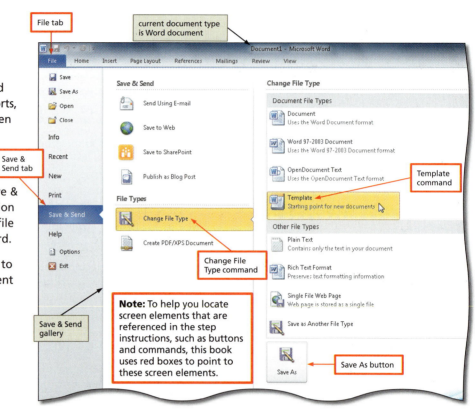

Figure 10–2

2

- Click the Save As button to display the Save As dialog box with the file type automatically changed to Word Template.

Q&A

How does Word differentiate between a saved Word template and a saved Word document?

Files typically have a file name and a file extension. The file extension identifies the file type. The source program often assigns a file type to a file. A Word document has an extension of .docx, whereas a Word template has an extension of .dotx. Thus, a file named July Report.docx is a Word document, and a file named Fitness Form.dotx is a Word template.

- Type **Recycling Survey** in the File name text box to change the file name.

- If necessary, navigate to the desired save location (in this case, the Word folder in the CIS 101 folder [or your class folder] on the USB flash drive) (Figure 10–3).

3

- Click the Save button (Save As dialog box) to save the document as a Word template with the entered file name.

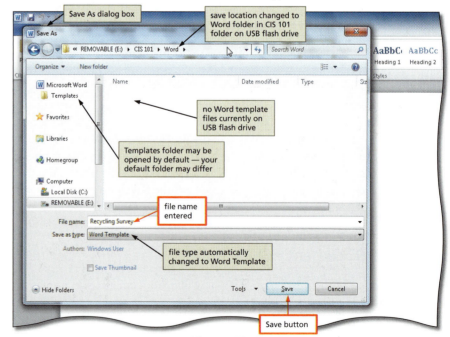

Figure 10–3

Other Ways	
1. Press F12; change document type to Word Template	2. Open Backstage view, click Save As, change document type to Word Template

Changing Document Settings

To enhance the look of the form, you change several default settings in Word:

1. Display the page as wide as possible in the document window to maximize the amount of space for text and graphics on the form.

2. Change the size of the paper so that it fits completely within the document window.

3. Adjust the margins so that as much text as possible will fit in the document.

4. Change the document theme fonts to the Grid font set and the theme colors to the Slipstream color scheme.

5. Change the page color to green.

The following pages make these changes to the document.

 BTW

The Ribbon and Screen Resolution
Word may change how the groups and buttons within the groups appear on the Ribbon, depending on the computer's screen resolution. Thus, your Ribbon may look different from the ones in this book if you are using a screen resolution other than 1024 × 768.

To Zoom Page Width

In the online form in this chapter, the form is to appear as wide as possible in the document window. When you change the zoom to page width, Word extends the edges of the page to the edge of the document window. The following step sets the zoom to page width.

- Display the View tab.

- Click the Page Width button (View tab | Zoom group) to change the zoom to page width (Figure 10–4).

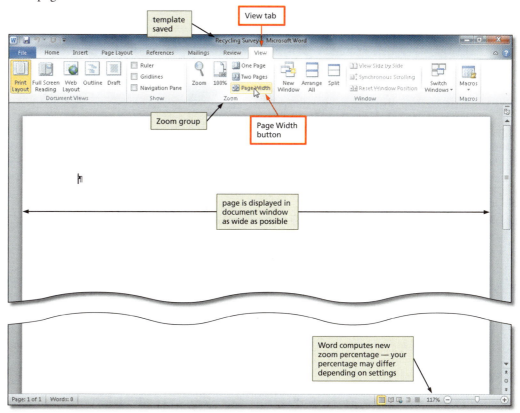

Figure 10–4

To Change Paper Size

For the online form in this chapter, all edges of the paper appear in the document window. Currently, the top, left, and right edges are displayed in the document window. To display the bottom edge also, change the height of the paper from 11 inches to 4.75 inches. The steps on the next page change paper size.

1

- Display the Page Layout tab.

- Click the Page Size button (Page Layout tab | Page Setup group) to display the Page Size gallery (Figure 10–5).

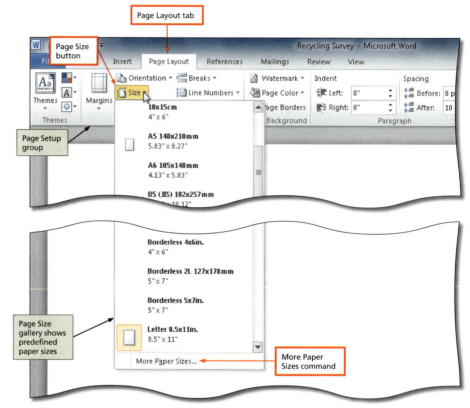

Figure 10–5

2

- Click More Paper Sizes in the Page Size gallery to display the Paper sheet in the Page Setup dialog box.

- In the Height box (Page Setup dialog box), type **4.75** as the new height (Figure 10–6).

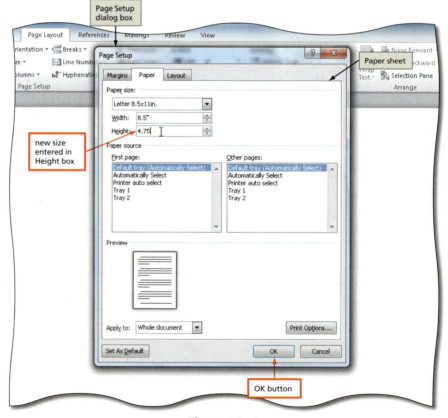

Figure 10–6

3

- Click the OK button to change the paper size to the entered measurements, which in this case, are 8.5 inches wide by 4.75 inches tall (Figure 10–7).

Q&A What if the height of my document does not match the figure?

You may need to show white space. To do this, position the mouse pointer above the top of the page below the Ribbon and then double-click when the mouse pointer changes to a Show White Space button. Or, your screen resolution may be different; if so, you may need to adjust the page height or width values.

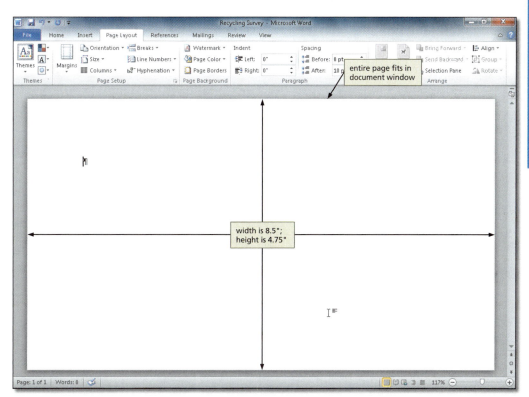

Figure 10–7

To Set Custom Margins

Recall that Word is preset to use 1-inch top, bottom, left, and right margins. To maximize the space for the contents of the form, this chapter sets the left and right margins to .5 inches, the top margin to .25 inches, and the bottom margin to 0 inches. The following steps set custom margins.

1 Click the Margins button (Page Layout tab | Page Setup group) to display the Margins gallery.

2 Click Custom Margins in the Margins gallery to display the Margins sheet in the Page Setup dialog box.

3 Type .25 in the Top box (Page Setup dialog box) to change the top margin setting and then press the TAB key to position the insertion point in the Bottom box.

4 Type 0 (zero) in the Bottom box to change the bottom margin setting and then press the TAB key.

Q&A Why set the bottom margin to zero?

This allows you to place form contents at the bottom of the page, if necessary.

5 Type .5 in the Left box to change the left margin setting and then press the TAB key.

6 Type `.5` in the Right box to change the right margin setting (Figure 10–8).

7 Click the OK button to set the custom margins for this document.

Q&A What if Word displays a dialog box indicating margins are outside the printable area?

Click the Ignore button because this is an online form that is not intended for printing.

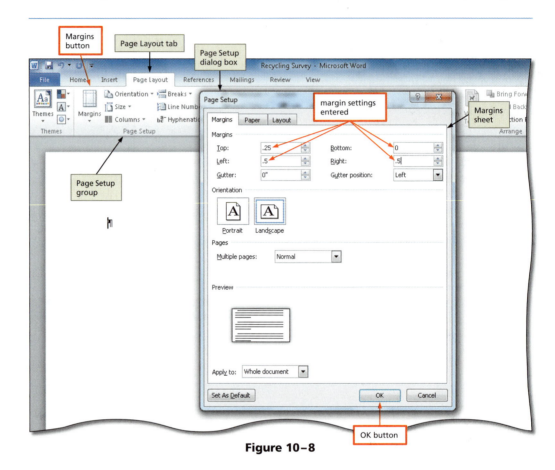

Figure 10–8

BTW

Set a Theme as a Default
If you wanted to change the default theme, you would select the theme you want to be the default theme, or select the color scheme, font set, and theme effects you would like to use as the default. Then, click the Change Styles button (Home tab | Styles group) and click Set as Default in the Change Styles gallery, which uses the current settings as the new default.

To Change the Theme Colors and Fonts

The following steps change the theme colors to Slipstream and the theme fonts to Grid.

1 Click the Theme Colors button (Page Layout tab | Themes group); scroll to and then click Slipstream in the Theme Colors gallery to change the color scheme.

2 Click the Theme Fonts button (Page Layout tab | Themes group); scroll to and then click Grid in the Theme Fonts gallery to change the font set.

To Change the Page Color

The next step is to change the page color of the online form so that it is visually appealing. This online form uses a shade of green. The following steps change the page color.

1 Click the Page Color button (Page Layout tab | Page Background group) to display the Page Color gallery.

2 Point to Green, Accent 3 (seventh color in the first row) to display a live preview of the selected page color (Figure 10–9).

3 Click Green, Accent 3 to change the page color to the selected color.

Q&A Do page colors print?

When you change the page color, it appears only on the screen. Changing the page color has no effect on a printed document.

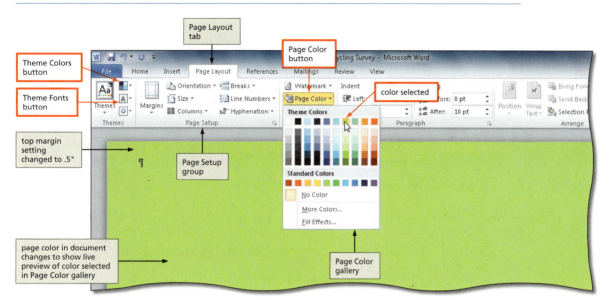

Figure 10–9

Enter Content in the Online Form

The next step in creating the online form in this chapter is to enter the text, graphics, and content controls in the document. The following pages describe this process.

To Enter and Format Text

The following steps enter the text at the top of the online form.

1 Type `Grant's Recycling Service` and then press the ENTER key.

2 Type `Saving Energy and Conserving Natural Resources for You!` and then press the ENTER key.

3 Type `Community Survey` and then press the ENTER key.

4 Type `Please fill in the form below, save the filled-in form, and e-mail it to survey@grantsrecycling.com.` and then press the ENTER key.

Q&A Why did the e-mail address change color?

In this document theme, the color for a hyperlink is a shade of blue. When you pressed the ENTER key, Word automatically formatted the hyperlink in this color.

5 Format the characters on the first line to 28-point Copperplate Gothic Bold font with the color of Turquoise, Accent 2, Darker 50%, and remove space after the paragraph (spacing after should be 0 point).

6 Format the characters on the second line to italic with the color of Orange, Accent 5, Darker 50%.

7 Format the characters on the third line to 18-point bold font with the color of Turquoise, Accent 2, Darker 50%, and center the text on the line.

8 Center the text on the fourth line and increase the spacing after this line to 18 point.

9 Position the insertion point on the blank line below the text (Figure 10–10).

GRANT'S·RECYCLING·SERVICE¶

Saving·Energy·and·Conserving·Natural·Resources·for·You!¶

Community·Survey¶

Please·fill·in·the·form·below,·save·the·filled-in·form,·and·e-mail·it·to·survey@grantsrecycling.com.¶

text entered and formatted

insertion point on blank line below text

space after changed to 0 point

space after changed to 18 point

text automatically formatted as hyperlink

Figure 10–10

To Insert Clip Art and Scale It

The next step is to insert a recycle image in the form. Because the graphic's original size is too large, you will scale it to 70 percent of its original size. The following steps insert and scale a graphic.

1 Display the Insert tab. Click the Clip Art button (Insert tab | Illustrations group) to display the Clip Art pane.

2 In the Clip Art pane, if necessary, click the Search for text box. Type **recycle** in the Search for text box. (If necessary, click the 'Results should be' box arrow and then place a check mark in the Illustrations check box so that Word displays illustrations in the search results.)

3 Click the Go button to display a list of clips that match the entered description.

4 Click the recycle clip art that matches the one in Figure 10–11 (or a similar image).

5 Close the Clip Art pane.

Q&A What if my clip art image is not in the same location as in Figure 10–11?

The clip art image may be in a different location, depending on the position of the insertion point when you inserted the image. In a later section, you will move the image to a different location.

6 With the graphic still selected, click the Size Dialog Box Launcher (Picture Tools Format tab | Size group) to display the Size sheet in the Layout dialog box.

Q&A What if the Picture Tools Format tab is not the active tab on my Ribbon?

Double-click the graphic or click the Picture Tools Format tab on the Ribbon.

7 Change the value in the Height box in the Scale area (Layout dialog box) to 70% and then, if necessary, press the TAB key to automatically change the width to the same value (Figure 10–11).

Q&A Why does the width value change to match the height value?

When the 'Lock aspect ratio' check box is selected, Word automatically keeps the proportion of the height and width the same.

8 Click the OK button (Layout dialog box) to close the dialog box and resize the selected clip art image to the specified size.

Figure 10–11

To Format a Graphic's Text Wrapping

Word inserted the clip art image as an inline graphic, that is, as part of the current paragraph. In this online form, the graphic should be positioned to the right of the company name (shown in Figure 10–1 on page WD 611). Thus, the graphic should be a floating graphic instead of an inline graphic. The text in the online form should not wrap around the graphic. Thus, the graphic should float in front of the text. The following steps change the graphic's text wrapping to In Front of Text.

1 With the graphic selected, click the Wrap Text button (Picture Tools Format tab | Arrange group) to display the Wrap Text menu (Figure 10–12).

2 Click In Front of Text on the Wrap Text menu to change the graphic from inline to floating with the selected wrapping style.

BTW

Ordering Graphics
If you have multiple graphics displaying on the screen and would like them to overlap, you can change their stacking order by using commands on the Bring Forward and Send Backward menus. The Bring to Front command on the Bring Forward menu displays the selected object at the top of the stack, and the Send to Back command on the Send Backward menu displays the selected object at the bottom of the stack. The Bring Forward and Send Backward commands each move the graphic forward or backward one layer in the stack. These commands also are available through the shortcut menu that is displayed when you right-click a graphic.

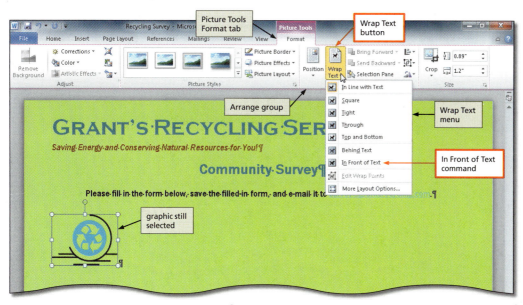

Figure 10–12

To Move a Graphic

The final step associated with the graphic is to move it so that it is positioned on the right side of the online form. The following step moves a graphic.

1 Point inside the selected graphic, and when the mouse pointer has a four-headed arrow attached to it, drag the graphic to the location shown in Figure 10–13.

Figure 10–13

To Use a Table to Control Layout

The first line of data entry in the form consists of the First Name content control, which begins at the left margin, and the Last Name content control, which begins at the center point of the same line. At first glance, you might decide to set a tab stop at each content control location. This, however, can be a complex task. For example, to place two content controls evenly across a row, you must calculate the location of each tab stop. If you insert a 2 × 1 table instead, Word automatically calculates the size of two evenly spaced columns. Thus, to enter multiple content controls on a single line, insert a table to control layout.

In this online form, the line containing the First Name and Last Name content controls will be a 2 × 1 table, that is, a table with two columns and one row. By inserting a 2 × 1 table, Word automatically positions the second column at the center point. When you insert a table, Word automatically surrounds it with a border. Because you are using the tables solely to control layout, you do not want the table borders visible. The following steps insert a 2 × 1 table in the form and remove its border.

1

- Position the insertion point where the table should be inserted, in this case, on the blank paragraph mark below the text on the form.

- Display the Insert tab. Click the Table button (Insert tab | Tables group) to display the Table gallery (Figure 10–14).

Figure 10–14

2

- Click the cell in the first row and second column of the grid to insert an empty 2 × 1 table at the location of the insertion point.

- Select the table.

Q&A How do I select a table?

Point somewhere in the table and then click the table move handle that appears in the upper-left corner of the table, or position the insertion point in a table cell, click the Select button (Table Tools Layout tab | Table group) and then click Select Table on the Select menu.

- Click the Borders button arrow (Table Tools Design tab | Table Styles group) to display the Borders gallery (Figure 10–15).

3

- Click No Border in the Borders gallery to remove the borders from the table.

Figure 10–15

4

- Click the first cell of the table to remove the selection (Figure 10–16).

Q&A My screen does not display the end-of-cell marks. Why not?

Display formatting marks by clicking the Show/Hide ¶ button (Home tab | Paragraph group).

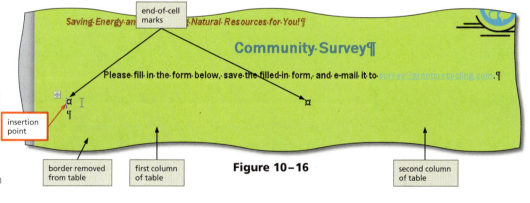

Figure 10–16

Other Ways	
1. Click Table button (Insert tab | Tables group), click Insert Table in Table	gallery, enter number of columns and rows, click OK button

To Show Table Gridlines

When you remove the borders from a table, you no longer can see the individual cells in the table. To help identify the location of cells, you can display **gridlines**, which show cell outlines on the screen. The following steps show gridlines.

1 If necessary, position the insertion point in a table cell.

2 Display the Table Tools Layout tab.

BTW

Q&As
For a complete list of the Q&As found in many of the step-by-step sequences in this book, visit the Word 2010 Q&A Web page (scsite.com/wd2010/qa).

3 Click the View Table Gridlines button (Table Tools Layout tab | Table group) to show table gridlines on the screen (Figure 10–17).

Q&A Do table gridlines print?

No. Gridlines are formatting marks that show only on the screen. Gridlines help users easily identify cells, rows, and columns in borderless tables.

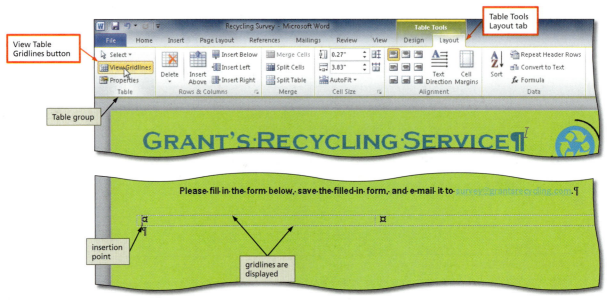

Figure 10–17

Content Controls

To add data entry fields in a Word form, you insert content controls. Word includes eight different content controls you can insert in your online forms. Table 10–1 outlines the use of each of these controls.

Table 10–1 Content Controls		
Type	**Icon**	**Use**
Rich Text	Aa	User enters text and, if desired, may format the entered text.
Plain Text	Aa	User enters text, which may not be formatted.
Picture	🖼	User inserts drawing, shape, picture, clip art, or SmartArt graphic.
Combo Box	▦	User types text entry or selects one item from a list of choices.
Drop-Down List	▦	User selects one item from a list of choices.
Date Picker	📅	User interacts with a calendar to select a date or types a date in the placeholder.
Check Box	☑	User selects or deselects a check box.
Building Block Gallery	🗔	User selects a built-in building block from gallery.

Determine the correct field type for each data entry field.

Word uses content controls for data entry fields. For each data entry field, decide which content control best maps to the type of data the field will contain. The field specifications for the fields in this chapter's online form are listed below:

- The First Name, Last Name, and Other data entry fields will contain text. The first two will be plain text content controls and the last will be a rich text content control.

- The Recycling Services data entry field must contain one of these four values: Fee-Based Curbside Recycling, Free Drop-Off Locations, Both, Neither. This field will be a drop-down list content control.

- The Aluminum, Cardboard, Glass, Paper, Plastic, Yard Waste, and Other data entry fields will be check boxes that the user can select or deselect.

- The Yard Waste Frequency data entry field can contain one of these three values: Twice a year, Four times a year, and Monthly. In addition, users should be able to enter their own value in this data entry field if none of these three values is applicable. A combo box content control will be used for this field.

- The Today's Date data entry field should contain only a valid date value. Thus, this field will be a date picker content control.

The following pages insert content controls in the online form.

To Show the Developer Tab

To create a form in Word, you use buttons on the Developer tab. Because it allows you to perform more advanced tasks not required by everyday Word users, the Developer tab does not appear on the Ribbon by default. The following steps display the Developer tab on the Ribbon.

1
- Open the Backstage view (Figure 10–18).

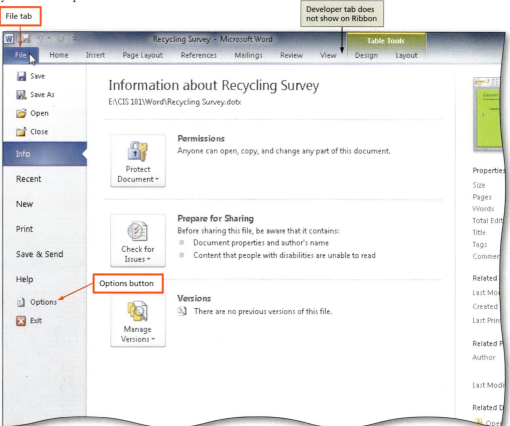

Figure 10–18

2
- Click the Options button in the Backstage view to display the Word Options dialog box.
- Click Customize Ribbon in the left pane (Word Options dialog box).
- Place a check mark in the Developer check box in the Main Tabs list (Figure 10–19).

Q&A What are the plus symbols to the left of each tab name?

Clicking the plus symbol expands to show the groups. You can show or hide groups on a tab on the Ribbon by selecting or deselecting the group check box.

Q&A Can I show or hide any tab in this list?

Yes. Place a check mark in the check box to show the tab, or remove the check mark to hide the tab.

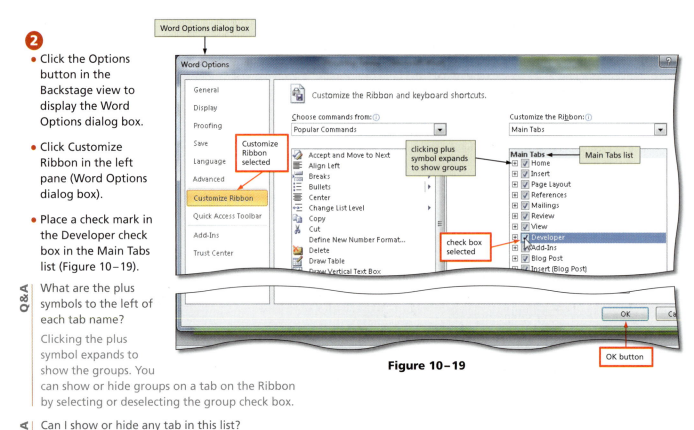

Figure 10–19

3
- Click the OK button to show the Developer tab on the Ribbon (Figure 10–20).

Q&A How do I remove the Developer tab from the Ribbon?

Follow these same steps, except remove the check mark from the Developer check box (Word Options dialog box).

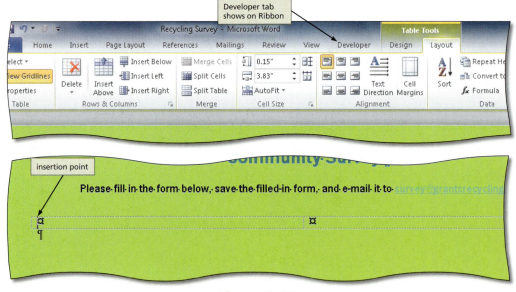

Figure 10–20

To Insert a Plain Text Content Control

The first item that a user enters in the Community Survey is his or her first name. Because the first name entry contains text that the user should not format, this online form uses a plain text content control for the First Name data entry field. The label, First Name, is displayed to the left of the plain text content control. To improve readability, a colon or some other character often separates a label from the content control. The next steps enter the label, First Name:, followed by a plain text content control.

- With the insertion point in the first cell of the table as shown in Figure 10–20, type **First Name:** as the label for the content control.

- Press the SPACEBAR (Figure 10–21).

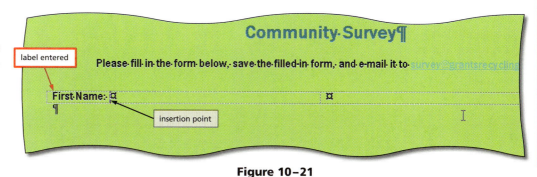

Figure 10–21

- Display the Developer tab.

- Click the Plain Text Content Control button (Developer tab | Controls group) to insert a plain text content control at the location of the insertion point (Figure 10–22).

Q&A Is the plain text content control similar to the content controls that I have used in templates installed with Word, such as in the letter, memo, and resume templates?

Yes. The content controls you insert through the Developer tab have the same functionality as the content controls in the templates installed with Word.

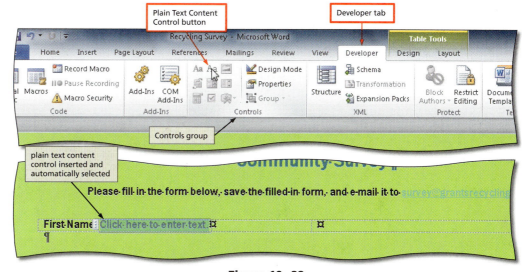

Figure 10–22

To Edit Placeholder Text

A content control displays **placeholder text**, which instructs the user how to enter values in the content control. The default placeholder text for a plain text content control is the instruction, Click here to enter text. You can change the wording in the placeholder text so that it is more instructional or applicable to the current form. The following steps edit the placeholder text for the plain text content control just entered.

- With the plain text content control selected (shown in Figure 10–22), click the Design Mode button (Developer tab | Controls group) to turn on design mode, which displays tags at the beginning and ending of the placeholder text (Figure 10–23).

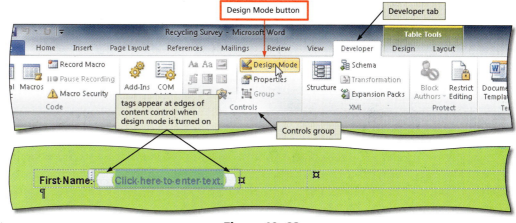

Figure 10–23

- If necessary, click the placeholder text to position the insertion point in it (Figure 10–24).

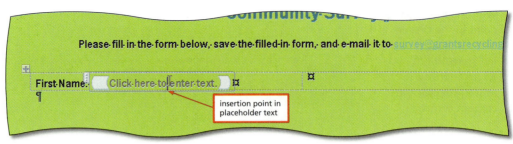

Figure 10–24

- Edit the placeholder text so that it contains the text, Click here and type your first name., as the instruction (Figure 10–25).

 What if the placeholder text wraps to the next line?

Because of the tags at each edge of the placeholder text, the entered text may wrap in the table cell. Once you turn off design mode, the placeholder text should fit on a single line.

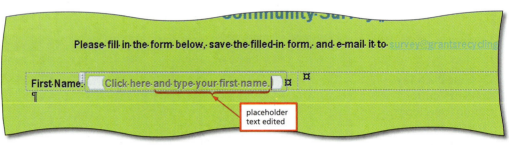

Figure 10–25

- Click the Design Mode button (Developer tab | Controls group) to turn off design mode (Figure 10–26).

 What if I notice an error in the placeholder text?

Follow these steps to turn on design mode, correct the error, and then turn off design mode.

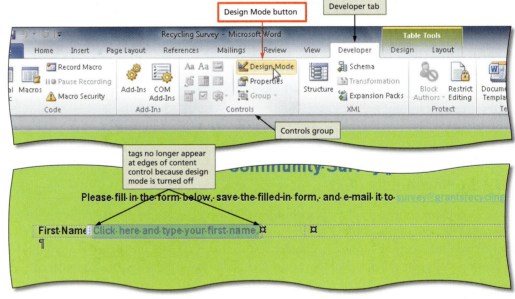

Figure 10–26

To Change the Properties of a Plain Text Content Control

When you click a content control in a Word installed template, the content control may display an identifier in its top-left corner. For templates that you create, you can instruct Word to display this identifier, called the title, by changing the properties of the content control. You also can apply a style to the content control to define how text will look as a user types data or makes selections, and you can lock the content control so that a user cannot delete the content control during the data entry process. The next steps change the properties of a plain text content control.

1

- With content control selected, click the Control Properties button (Developer tab | Controls group) to display the Content Control Properties dialog box (Figure 10–27).

How do I know the content control is selected?

A selected content control is surrounded by an outline. It also may be shaded.

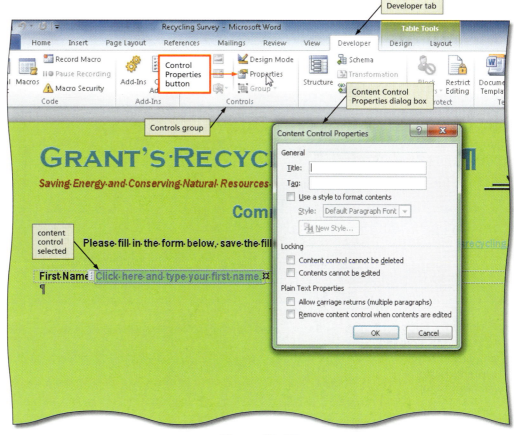

Figure 10–27

2

- Type **First Name** in the Title text box (Content Control Properties dialog box).

- Place a check mark in the 'Use a style to format contents' check box so that the Style box becomes active.

- Click the Style box arrow to display the Style list (Figure 10–28).

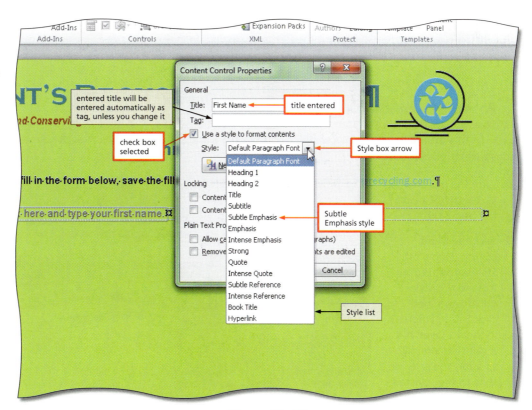

Figure 10–28

3

- Click Subtle Emphasis to select the style for the content control.

- Place a check mark in the 'Content control cannot be deleted' check box so that the user cannot delete the content control (Figure 10–29).

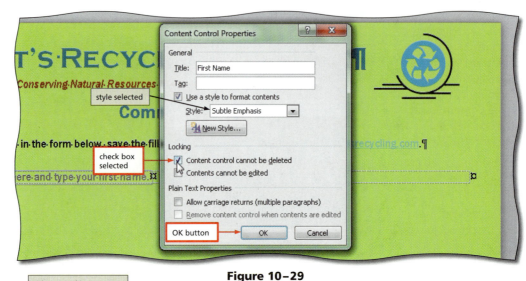

Figure 10–29

4

- Click the OK button to assign the modified properties to the content control (Figure 10–30).

 Q&A Why is the placeholder text not formatted to the selected style, Subtle Emphasis, in this case?

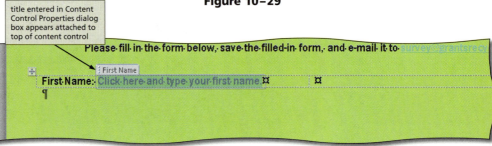

Figure 10–30

When you apply a style to a content control, as described in these steps, the style is applied to the text the user types during the data entry process. To change the appearance of the placeholder text, apply a style using the Home tab as shown in the next steps.

To Format Placeholder Text

In this online form, the placeholder text has the same style applied to it as the content control. The following steps format placeholder text.

1 With the placeholder text selected, display the Home tab.

2 Click the More button (Home tab | Styles group) to expand the Styles gallery and then click Subtle Emphasis in the list (even if it is selected already) to apply the selected style to the selected placeholder text (Figure 10–31).

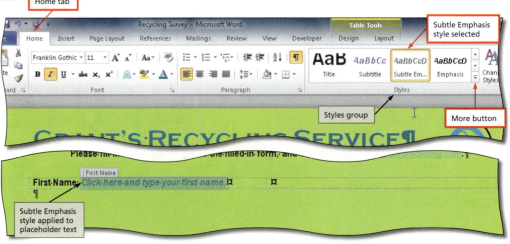

Figure 10–31

To Insert Another Plain Text Content Control and Edit Its Placeholder Text

The second item that a user enters in the Community Survey is his or her last name. The steps for entering the last name content control are similar to those for the first name because the last name also is a plain text content control. The following steps enter the label, Last Name:, and then insert a plain text content control and edit its placeholder text.

1 Position the insertion point in the second cell (column) in the table.

2 With the insertion point in the second cell of the table, type **Last Name:** as the label for the content control and then press the SPACEBAR.

3 Display the Developer tab. Click the Plain Text Content Control button (Developer tab | Controls group) to insert a plain text content control at the location of the insertion point.

4 With the plain text content control selected, click the Design Mode button (Developer tab | Controls group) to turn on design mode.

5 If necessary, click the placeholder text to position the insertion point in it.

6 Edit the placeholder text so that it contains the text, Click here and type your last name., as the instruction (Figure 10–32).

7 Click the Design Mode button (Developer tab | Controls group) to turn off design mode.

Figure 10–32

To Change the Properties of a Plain Text Content Control

The next step is to change the title, style, and locking properties of the Last Name content control, just as you did for the First Name content control. The following steps change properties of a plain text content control.

1 With content control selected, click the Control Properties button (Developer tab | Controls group) to display the Content Control Properties dialog box.

2 Type **Last Name** in the Title text box (Content Control Properties dialog box).

3 Place a check mark in the 'Use a style to format contents' check box to activate the Style box.

4 Click the Style box arrow and then select Subtle Emphasis in the list to specify the style for the content control.

5 Place a check mark in the 'Content control cannot be deleted' check box (Figure 10–33).

6 Click the OK button to assign the properties to the content control.

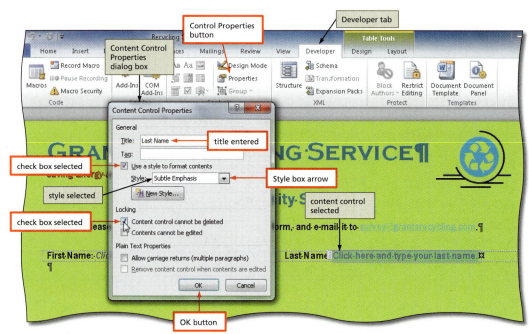

Figure 10–33

To Format Placeholder Text

As with the placeholder text for the first name, the placeholder text for the last name should use the Subtle Emphasis style. The following steps format placeholder text.

1 With the last name placeholder text selected, display the Home tab.

2 Click the More button (Home tab | Styles group) to expand the Styles gallery and then click Subtle Emphasis in the list (even if it is selected already) to apply the selected style to the selected placeholder text.

To Add Space before a Paragraph

The next step in creating this online form is to add space before a paragraph so that the space below the table is consistent with the space between other elements on the form. The following steps add space before a paragraph.

1 Position the insertion point on the blank line below the table.

2 Click the Line and Paragraph Spacing button (Home tab | Paragraph group) to display the Line and Paragraph Spacing gallery (Figure 10–34).

3 Click Add Space Before Paragraph in the Line and Paragraph Spacing gallery to place a blank line between the table and the paragraph.

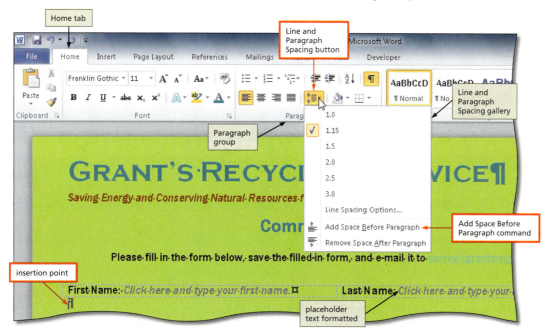

Figure 10–34

To Insert a Drop-Down List Content Control

In the online form in this chapter, the user selects from one of these four choices for the Recycling Services content control: Fee-Based Curbside Recycling, Free Drop-Off Locations, Both, or Neither. To present a set of choices to a user in the form of a drop-down list, from which the user selects one, insert a drop-down list content control. To view the set of choices, the user clicks the arrow at the right edge of the content control. The following steps insert a drop-down list content control.

1

• With the insertion point positioned on the blank paragraph mark below the First Name content control, type **Which types of recycling services would you use?** and then press the SPACEBAR.

2

• Display the Developer tab.

• Click the Drop-Down List Content Control button (Developer tab | Controls group) to insert a drop-down list content control at the location of the insertion point (Figure 10–35).

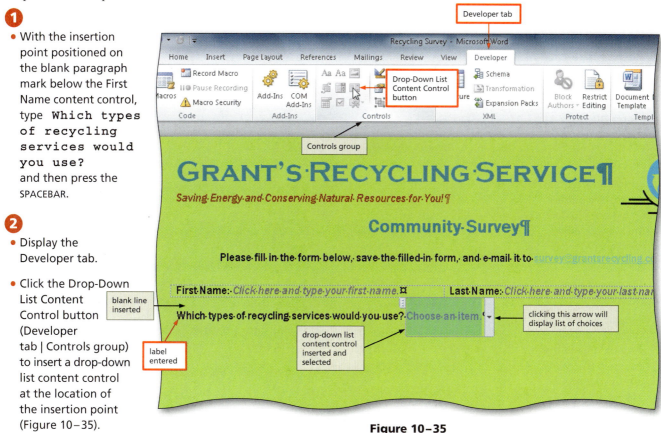

Figure 10–35

To Edit Placeholder Text

The following steps edit the placeholder text for the drop-down list content control.

1 With the drop-down list content control selected, click the Design Mode button (Developer tab | Controls group) to turn on design mode.

2 If necessary, click the placeholder text to position the insertion point in it.

3 Edit the placeholder text so that it contains this instruction: Click here. Click arrow and select from list.

4 Click the Design Mode button (Developer tab | Controls group) to turn off design mode.

To Change the Properties of a Drop-Down List Content Control

In addition to identifying a title, selecting a style, and locking the drop-down list content control, you specify the choices that will be displayed when a user clicks the arrow to the right of the content control. The following steps change the properties of a drop-down list content control.

• With the drop-down list content control selected, click the Control Properties button (Developer tab | Controls group) to display the Content Control Properties dialog box.

• Type **Recycling Services** in the Title text box (Content Control Properties dialog box).

• Place a check mark in the 'Use a style to format contents' check box to activate the Style box.

• Click the Style box arrow and then select Subtle Emphasis in the list to specify the style for the content control.

• Place a check mark in the 'Content control cannot be deleted' check box.

• In the Drop-Down List Properties area, click 'Choose an item.' to select it (Figure 10–36).

• Click the Remove button (Content Control Properties dialog box) to delete the 'Choose an item' entry.

Q&A Why delete the 'Choose an item' entry?

If you leave it in the list, it will appear as the first item in the list when the user clicks the content control arrow. You do not want it in the list, so you delete it.

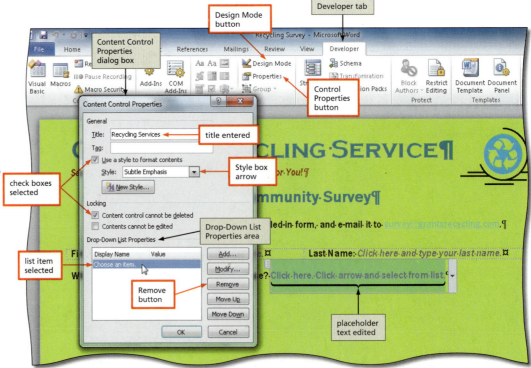

Figure 10–36

Q&A Can I delete any entry in a drop-down list using the Remove button?

Yes, select the entry in this dialog box and then click the Remove button. You also can rearrange the order of entries in a list by selecting the entry and then clicking the Move Up or Move Down button.

3

- Click the Add button to display the Add Choice dialog box.

- Type **Fee-Based Curbside Recycling** in the Display Name text box (Add Choice dialog box).

- Press the TAB key and then type **Curbside** in the Value text box (Figure 10–37).

 Q&A What is the difference between a display name and a value?

Often, they are the same, which is why when you type the display name, Word automatically enters the same text in the Value text box. Sometimes, however, you may want to store a shorter or different value, such as in this example. Using shorter values makes it easier for separate programs to analyze and interpret entered data.

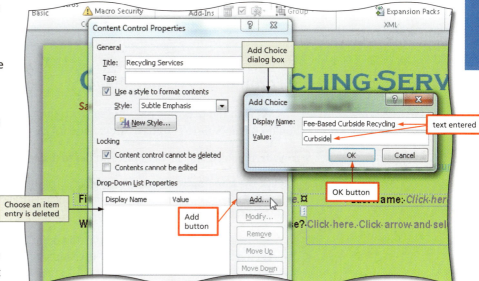

Figure 10–37

4

- Click the OK button (Add Choice dialog box) to add the entered display name and value to the list of choices in the Drop-Down List Properties area (Content Control Properties dialog box).

5

- Click the Add button to display the Add Choice dialog box.

- Type **Free Drop-Off Locations** in the Display Name text box.

- Press the TAB key and then type **Drop-Off** in the Value text box.

- Click the OK button to add the entry to the list.

- Click the Add button to display the Add Choice dialog box.

- Type **Both** in the Display Name text box.

- Click the OK button to add the entry to the list.

- Click the Add button to display the Add Choice dialog box.

- Type **Neither** in the Display Name text box.

- Click the OK button to add the entry to the list (Figure 10–38).

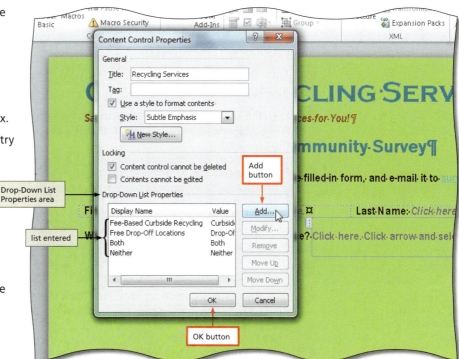

Figure 10–38

6

- Click the OK button (Content Control Properties dialog box) to change the content control properties.

Q&A

What if I want to change an entry in the drop-down list?

You would select the drop-down list content control, click the Control Properties button (Developer tab | Controls group) to display the Content Control Properties dialog box, select the entry to change, click the Modify button, adjust the entry, and then click the OK button.

To Format Placeholder Text

As with the previous placeholder text, the placeholder text for the recycling services should use the Subtle Emphasis style. The following steps format placeholder text.

1 With the Recycling Services placeholder text selected, display the Home tab.

2 Click the More button (Home tab | Styles group) to expand the Styles gallery and then click Subtle Emphasis in the list (even if it is selected already) to apply the selected style to the selected placeholder text.

3 Press the END key to position the insertion point at the end of the current line and then press the ENTER key to position the insertion point below the Recycling Services content control.

To Enter Text and Use a Table to Control Layout

The next step is to enter the user instructions for the check box content controls and insert a 6 × 1 borderless table so that six evenly spaced check boxes can be displayed horizontally below the check box instructions. The following steps enter text and insert a borderless table.

1 With the insertion point positioned on the paragraph below the Recycling Services content control, click Normal in the Styles list (Home tab | Styles group) to format the current paragraph to the Normal style.

2 Type **Types of items you would recycle (check all that apply):** as the instruction.

3 Click the Line and Paragraph Spacing button (Home tab | Paragraph group) and then click Remove Space After Paragraph so that the check boxes will appear one physical line below the instructions.

4 Press the ENTER key to position the insertion point on the line below the check box instructions.

5 Display the Insert tab. Click the Table button (Insert tab | Tables group) to display the Table gallery and then click the cell in the first row and sixth column of the grid to insert an empty 6 × 1 table at the location of the insertion point.

6 Select the table.

7 Click the Borders button arrow (Table Tools Design tab | Table Styles group) to display the Borders gallery and then click No Border in the Borders gallery to remove the borders from the table.

8 Click the first cell of the table to remove the selection (shown in Figure 10–39).

To Insert a Check Box Content Control

In the online form in this chapter, the user can select up to seven check boxes: Aluminum, Cardboard, Glass, Paper, Plastic, Yard Waste, and Other. The following step inserts the first check box content control.

1

- Position the insertion point at the location for the check box content control, in this case, the leftmost cell in the 6 × 1 table.

- Display the Developer tab.

- Click the Check Box Content Control button (Developer tab | Controls group) to insert a check box content control at the location of the insertion point (Figure 10–39).

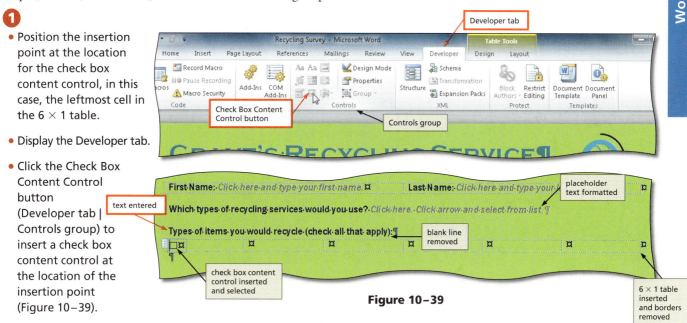

Figure 10–39

To Change the Properties of a Check Box Content Control

The next step is to change the title and locking properties of the content control. The following steps change properties of a check box content control.

1 With content control selected, click the Control Properties button (Developer tab | Controls group) to display the Content Control Properties dialog box.

2 Type **Aluminum** in the Title text box (Content Control Properties dialog box).

3 Place a check mark in the 'Content control cannot be deleted' check box (Figure 10–40).

4 Click the OK button to assign the properties to the selected content control.

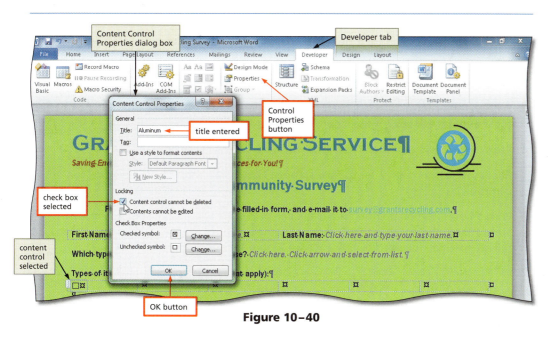

Figure 10–40

To Add a Label to a Check Box Content Control

The following steps add a label to the right of a check box content control.

1 With content control selected, press the END key twice to position the insertion point after the inserted check box content control.

2 Press the SPACEBAR and then type **Aluminum** as the check box label (Figure 10–41).

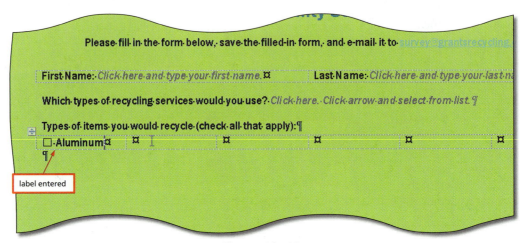

Figure 10–41

To Insert Additional Check Box Content Controls

The following steps insert the remaining check box content controls and their labels.

1 Press the TAB key to position the insertion point in the next cell, which is the location for the next check box content control.

2 Click the Check Box Content Control button (Developer tab | Controls group) to insert a check box content control at the location of the insertion point.

3 With content control selected, click the Control Properties button (Developer tab | Controls group) to display the Content Control Properties dialog box.

4 Type **Cardboard** in the Title text box (Content Control Properties dialog box).

5 Place a check mark in the 'Content control cannot be deleted' check box and then click the OK button to assign the properties to the selected content control.

6 With content control selected, press the END key twice to position the insertion point after the inserted check box content control.

7 Press the SPACEBAR and then type **Cardboard** as the check box label.

8 Repeat Steps 1 through 7 for the Glass, Paper, Plastic, and Yard Waste check box content controls.

9 Position the insertion point on the blank line below the 6 × 1 table and then repeat Steps 1 through 7 for the Other check box content control, which has the label, Other (please specify):, followed by the SPACEBAR (Figure 10–42).

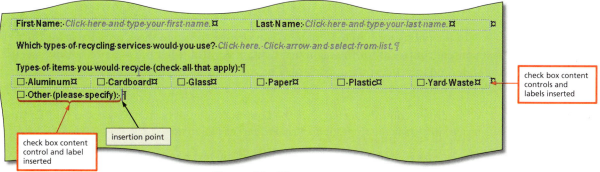

Figure 10–42

To Insert a Rich Text Content Control

The next step is to insert the content control that enables users to type in any other types of items they would recycle. Because you want to allow users to format the text they enter in this content control, you use the rich text content control. The difference between a plain text and rich text content control is that the users can format text as they enter it in the rich text content control. The following step inserts a rich text content control.

1
- If necessary, position the insertion point at the location for the rich text content control (shown in Figure 10–42).

- Click the Rich Text Content Control button (Developer tab | Controls group) to insert a rich text content control at the location of the insertion point (Figure 10–43).

Figure 10–43

To Edit Placeholder Text

The following steps edit placeholder text for the rich text content control.

1 With the rich text content control selected, click the Design Mode button (Developer tab | Controls group) to turn on design mode.

2 If necessary, click the placeholder text to position the insertion point in it.

3 Edit the placeholder text so that it contains the text, Click here and type other items you would recycle., as the instruction.

4 Click the Design Mode button (Developer tab | Controls group) to turn off design mode.

To Change the Properties of a Rich Text Content Control

In the online form in this chapter, you change the same three properties for the rich text content control as for the plain text content control. That is, you enter a title, specify the style, and lock the content control. The following steps change the properties of the rich text content control.

1 With content control selected, click the Control Properties button (Developer tab | Controls group) to display the Content Control Properties dialog box.

2 Type **Other Recycled Items** in the Title text box (Content Control Properties dialog box).

3 Place a check mark in the 'Use a style to format contents' check box to activate the Style box.

4 Click the Style box arrow and then select Subtle Emphasis in the list to specify the style for the content control.

5 Place a check mark in the 'Content control cannot be deleted' check box (Figure 10–44).

6 Click the OK button to assign the properties to the content control.

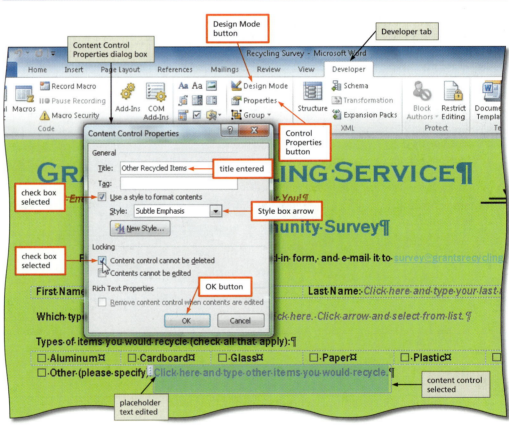

Figure 10–44

To Format Placeholder Text and Add Space before a Paragraph

The placeholder text for the Other Recycled Items text entry should use the Subtle Emphasis style, and the space below the check boxes should be consistent with the space between other elements on the form. The next steps format placeholder text and add space before a paragraph.

1 With the Other Recycled Items placeholder text selected, display the Home tab.

2 Click the More button (Home tab | Styles group) to expand the Styles gallery and then click Subtle Emphasis in the list (even if it is selected already) to apply the selected style to the selected placeholder text.

3 Press the END key to position the insertion point on the paragraph mark after the Other Recycled Items content control and then press the ENTER key to position the insertion point below the Other Recycled Items content control.

4 With the insertion point positioned on the paragraph below the Other Recycled Items content control, click Normal in the Styles list (Home tab | Styles group) to format the current paragraph to the Normal style.

5 Click the Line and Paragraph Spacing button (Home tab | Paragraph group) to display the Line and Paragraph Spacing gallery and then click Add Space Before Paragraph in the gallery to place a blank line between the check boxes and the current paragraph.

To Insert a Combo Box Content Control

In the online form in this chapter, users can type their own entry in the Yard Waste Frequency content control or select from one of these three choices: Twice a year, Four times a year, or Monthly. In Word, a combo box content control allows a user to type text or select from a list. The following steps insert a combo box content control.

1

- With the insertion point positioned on the blank paragraph mark, type **How often would you recycle yard waste?** and then press the SPACEBAR.

2

- Display the Developer tab.

- Click the Combo Box Content Control button (Developer tab | Controls group) to insert a combo box content control at the location of the insertion point (Figure 10–45).

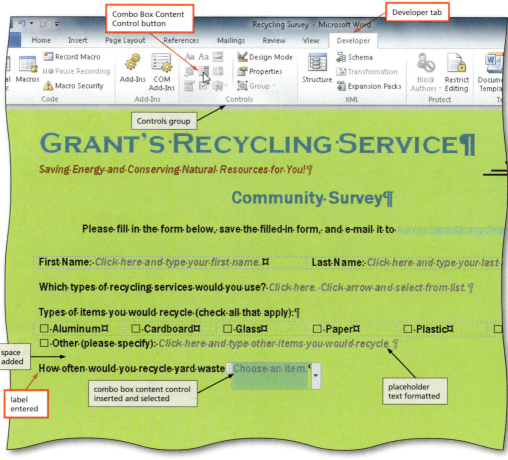

Figure 10–45

To Edit Placeholder Text

The following steps edit the placeholder text for the combo box content control.

① With the combo box content control selected, click the Design Mode button (Developer tab | Controls group) to turn on design mode.

② If necessary, scroll to page 2 to display the combo box content control.

Q&A Why did the content control move to another page?

Because design mode displays tags, the content controls and placeholder text are not displayed in their proper positions on the screen. When you turn off design mode, the content controls will return to their original locations and the extra page should disappear.

③ If necessary, click in the placeholder text to position the insertion point in it.

④ Edit the placeholder text so that it contains this instruction (Figure 10–46): Click here. Click arrow and select from list, or type your preference.

⑤ Click the Design Mode button (Developer tab | Controls group) to turn off design mode.

⑥ Scroll to display the top of the form in the document window.

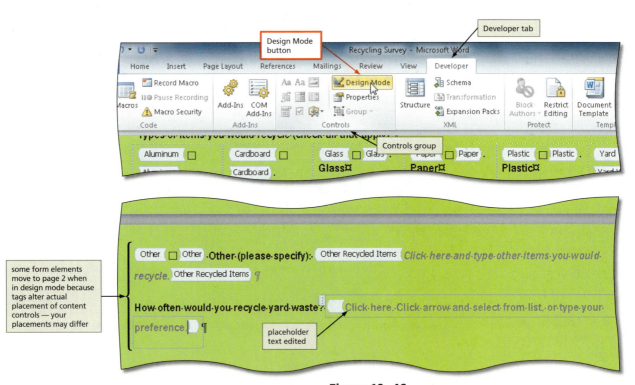

Figure 10–46

To Change the Properties of a Combo Box Content Control

You follow similar steps to enter the list for a combo box content control as you do for the drop-down list content control. The next steps change the properties of a combo box content control.

1

- With content control selected, click the Control Properties button (Developer tab | Controls group) to display the Content Control Properties dialog box.

- Type **Yard Waste Frequency** in the Title text box (Content Control Properties dialog box).

- Place a check mark in the 'Use a style to format contents' check box to activate the Style box.

- Click the Style box arrow and then select Subtle Emphasis in the list to specify the style for the content control.

- Place a check mark in the 'Content control cannot be deleted' check box.

- In the Drop-Down List Properties area, click 'Choose an item.' to select it (Figure 10–47).

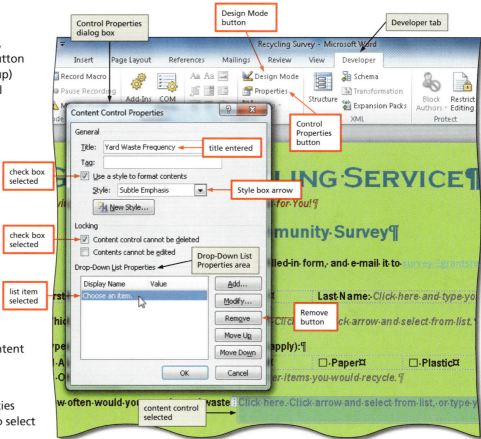

Figure 10–47

2

- Click the Remove button (Content Control Properties dialog box) to delete the selected entry.

3

- Click the Add button to display the Add Choice dialog box.

- Type **Twice a year** in the Display Name text box (Add Choice dialog box).

- Click the OK button to add the entered display name to the list of choices in the Drop-Down List Properties area (Content Control Properties dialog box).

- Click the Add button and add **Four times a year** to the list.

- Click the Add button and add **Monthly** to the list (Figure 10–48).

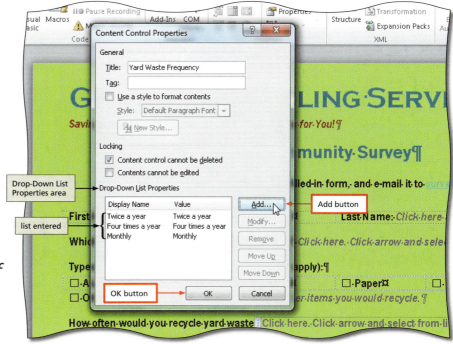

Figure 10–48

4

- Click the OK button (Content Control Properties dialog box) to change the content control properties.

Q&A How do I make adjustments to entries in the list?

Follow the same procedures as you use to make adjustments to entries in a drop-down list content control.

To Format Placeholder Text

As with the previous placeholder text, the placeholder text for the yard waste frequency should use the Subtle Emphasis style. The following steps format placeholder text.

1 With the Yard Waste Frequency placeholder text selected, display the Home tab.

2 Click the More button (Home tab | Styles group) to expand the Styles gallery and then click Subtle Emphasis in the list (even if it is selected already) to apply the selected style to the selected placeholder text.

3 Press the END key to position the insertion point at the end of the current line and then press the ENTER key to position the insertion point below the Yard Waste Frequency content control.

4 Click Normal in the Styles list (Home tab | Styles group) to format the current paragraph to the Normal style.

To Insert a Date Picker Content Control

The last item that users enter in the Community Survey is today's date. To assist users with entering dates, Word provides a date picker content control, which displays a calendar when the user clicks the arrow to the right of the content control. Users also can enter a date directly in the content control without using the calendar. The following steps enter the label, Today's Date:, and a date picker content control.

- With the insertion point below the Yard Waste Frequency content control, type **Today's Date:** as the label for the content control and then press the SPACEBAR.

- Display the Developer tab.

- Click the Date Picker Content Control button (Developer tab | Controls group) to insert a date picker content control at the location of the insertion point (Figure 10–49).

Figure 10–49

To Edit Placeholder Text

The following steps edit the placeholder text for the date picker content control.

1 With the date picker content control selected, click the Design Mode button (Developer tab | Controls group) to turn on design mode.

2 If necessary, scroll to page 2 to display the date picker content control.

3 If necessary, click in the placeholder text to position the insertion point in it.

4 Edit the placeholder text so that it contains this instruction: Click here. Click arrow and select today's date.

5 Click the Design Mode button (Developer tab | Controls group) to turn off design mode.

6 Scroll to display the top of the form in the document window.

To Change the Properties of a Date Picker Content Control

In addition to identifying a title for a date picker content control, specifying a style, and locking the control, you can specify how the date will be displayed when the user selects it from the calendar. The following steps change these properties of a date picker content control.

1

• With content control selected, click the Control Properties button (Developer tab | Controls group) to display the Content Control Properties dialog box.

• Type **Today's Date** in the Title text box.

• Place a check mark in the 'Use a style to format contents' check box to activate the Style box.

• Click the Style box arrow and then select Subtle Emphasis in the list to specify the style for the content control.

• Place a check mark in the 'Content control cannot be deleted' check box.

• In the 'Display the date like this' area, click the desired format in the list (Figure 10–50).

2

• Click the OK button to change the content control properties.

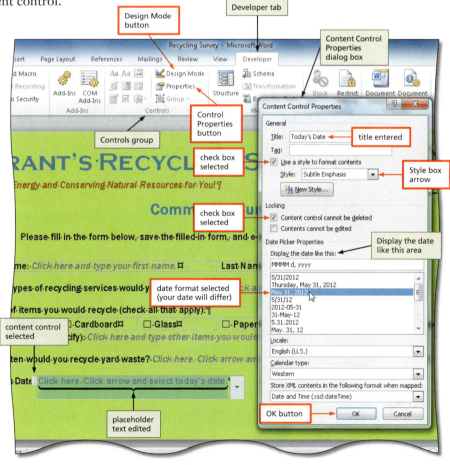

Figure 10–50

To Format Placeholder Text

As with the previous placeholder text, the placeholder text for today's date should use the Subtle Emphasis style. The following steps format placeholder text.

1 With the today's date placeholder text selected, display the Home tab.

2 Click the More button (Home tab | Styles group) to expand the Styles gallery and then click Subtle Emphasis in the list (even if it is selected already) to apply the selected style to the selected placeholder text.

3 Press the END key to position the insertion point at the end of the current line and then press the ENTER key to position the insertion point below the Today's Date content control.

4 Click Normal in the Styles list (Home tab | Styles group) to format the current paragraph to the Normal style.

To Enter and Format Text

The following steps enter and format the line of text at the bottom of the online form.

1 Be sure the insertion point is on the line below the Today's Date content control.

2 Center the paragraph mark.

3 Format the text to be typed with the color of Orange, Accent 5, Darker 50%.

4 Type `Thank you for your time!`

5 Change the space before the paragraph to 24 point (Figure 10–51).

6 If the text flows to a second page, reduce spacing before paragraphs in the form so that all lines fit on a single page.

Figure 10–51

BTW

BTWs
For a complete list of the BTWs found in the margins of this book, visit the Word 2010 BTW Web page (scsite.com/wd2010/btw).

To Hide Gridlines and Formatting Marks

Because you are finished with the tables in this form and will not enter any additional tables, you will hide the gridlines. You also are finished with entering and formatting text on the screen. To make the form easier to view, you hide formatting marks, which can clutter the screen. The following steps hide gridlines and formatting marks.

1 If necessary, position the insertion point in a table cell.

2 Display the Table Tools Layout tab.

3 Click the View Table Gridlines button (Table Tools Layout tab | Table group) to hide table gridlines.

4 If necessary, display the Home tab.

5 If the Show/Hide ¶ button (Home tab | Paragraph group) is selected, click it to remove formatting marks from the screen.

To Save an Existing Template with the Same File Name

You have made several modifications to the template since you last saved it. Thus, you should save it again. The following step saves the template again.

1 Click the Save button on the Quick Access Toolbar to overwrite the previously saved file.

Break Point: If you wish to take a break, this is a good place to do so. You can quit Word now. To resume at a later time, start Word, open the file called Recycling Survey, and continue following the steps from this location forward.

To Draw a Rectangle

The next step is to emphasize the data entry area of the form. The data entry area includes all the content controls in which a user enters data. To call attention to this area of the form, this online form places a rectangle around the data entry area, changes the style rectangle, and then adds a shadow to the rectangle. The following steps draw the rectangle, and subsequent steps format the rectangle.

1

- Position the insertion point on the last line in the document (shown in Figure 10–51).

- Display the Insert tab.

- Click the Shapes button (Insert tab | Illustrations group) to display the Shapes gallery (Figure 10–52).

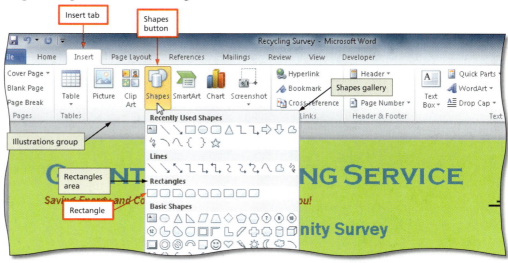

Figure 10–52

- Click Rectangle in the Rectangles area of the Shapes gallery, so that you can draw a rectangle on the screen.

- Position the crosshair mouse pointer as shown in Figure 10–53.

Figure 10–53

- Drag the mouse pointer downward and rightward to form a rectangle around the data entry area, as shown in Figure 10–54.

Figure 10–54

- Release the mouse button to draw the rectangle shape on top of the data entry area (Figure 10–55).

Q&A

What happened to all the text in the data entry area?

When you draw a shape in a document, Word initially places the shape in front of, or on top of, any text in the same area. You can change the stacking order of the shape so that it is displayed behind the text. Thus, the next steps move the shape behind text.

Figure 10–55

To Send a Graphic behind Text

You want the rectangle shape graphic to be positioned behind the data entry area text, so that you can see the text in the data entry area along with the shape. The following steps send a graphic behind text.

• If necessary, display the Drawing Tools Format tab.

• With the rectangle shape selected, click the Send Backward button arrow (Drawing Tools Format tab | Arrange group) to display the Send Backward menu (Figure 10–56).

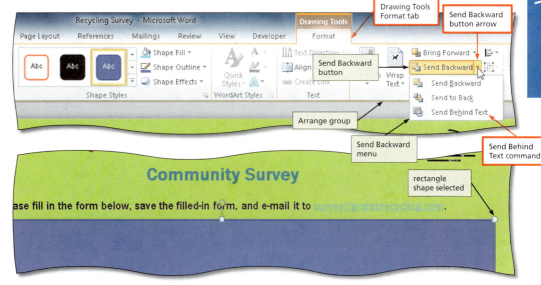

Q&A The Send Backward menu did not appear. Why not?

You clicked the Send Backward button instead of the Send Backward button arrow. Repeat Step 1.

Figure 10–56

• Click Send Behind Text on the Send Backward menu to position the rectangle shape behind the text (Figure 10–57).

Q&A What if I want a shape to cover text?

You would click the Bring Forward button arrow (Drawing Tools Format tab | Arrange group) and then click Bring in Front of Text on the Bring Forward menu.

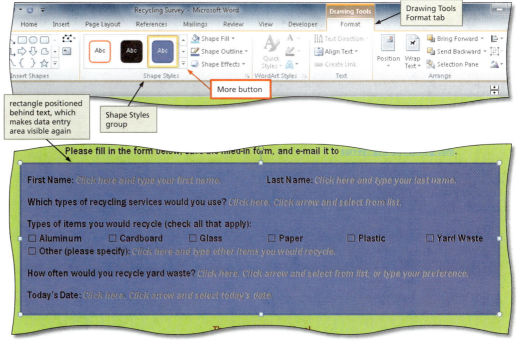

Figure 10–57

Other Ways

1. Right-click graphic, point to Send to Back on shortcut menu, click Send Behind Text on submenu

Shape Styles
Like other drawing objects or pictures, shapes can be formatted or have styles applied. You can change the fill in a shape by clicking the Shape Fill button (Drawing Tools Format tab | Shape Styles group), add an outline or border to a shape by clicking the Shape Outline button (Drawing Tools Format tab | Shape Styles group), and apply an effect such as shadow or 3-D effects by clicking the Shape Effects button (Drawing Tools Format tab | Shape Styles group).

To Apply a Shape Style

The next step is to apply a shape style to the rectangle, so that it is more colorful. Word's Shape Styles gallery allows you to change the look of the shape to a more visually appealing style. The following steps apply a style to the rectangle.

1 With the shape still selected, click the More button in the Shape Styles gallery (Drawing Tools Format tab | Shape Styles group) (shown in Figure 10–57 on the previous page) to expand the Shape Styles gallery.

2 Point to Subtle Effect - Green, Accent 3 in the Shape Styles gallery (fourth effect in fourth row) to display a live preview of that style applied to the rectangle shape in the document (Figure 10–58).

3 Click Subtle Effect - Green, Accent 3 in the Shape Styles gallery to apply the selected style to the selected shape.

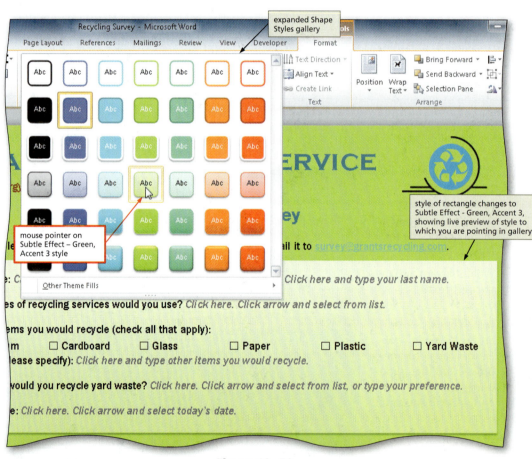

Figure 10–58

To Add a Shadow to a Shape

To further offset the data entry area of the form, this online form has a shadow inside the left and bottom edges of the rectangle shape. The next steps add a shadow to a shape.

- With the shape still selected, click the Shape Effects button (Drawing Tools Format tab | Shape Styles group) to display the Shape Effects menu.

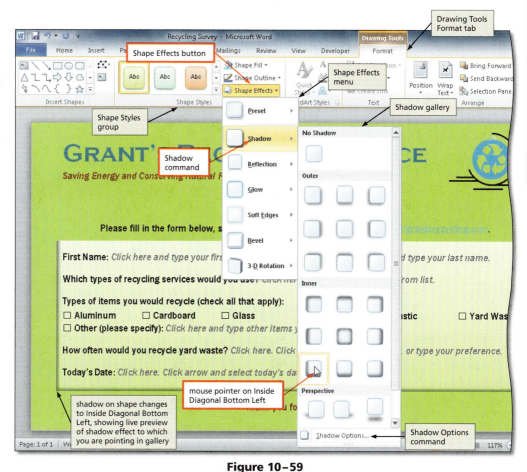

- Point to Shadow on the Shape Effects menu to display the Shadow gallery.

- Point to Inside Diagonal Bottom Left in the Shadow gallery to display a live preview of that shadow effect applied to the selected shape in the document (Figure 10–59).

Figure 10–59

Experiment

- Point to various shadows in the Shadow gallery and watch the shadow on the selected shape change.

- Click Inside Diagonal Bottom Left in the Shadow gallery to apply the selected shadow to the selected shape.

Q&A

Can I change the color of a shadow?

Yes. Click Shadow Options in the Shadow gallery.

To Highlight Text

You want to emphasize the fourth line of text on the form that contains instructions related to completing the form. To emphasize text in an online document, you can highlight it. **Highlighting** alerts a reader to online text's importance, much like a highlighter pen does on a printed page. Word provides 15 colors you can use to highlight text, including the traditional yellow and green, as well as some nontraditional highlight colors such as gray, dark blue, and dark red.

The steps on the next page highlight the fourth line of text in the color yellow.

BTW

Highlighter
If you click the Text Highlight Color button without first selecting any text, the highlighter remains active until you turn it off. This allows you to continue selecting text that you want to be highlighted. To deactivate the highlighter, click the Text Highlight Color button and then click Stop Highlighting on the Text Highlight Color menu, or press the ESC key.

1

- Select the text to be highlighted, which, in this case, is the fourth line of text.

Why is the selection taller than usual?

Earlier in this project you increased the space after this paragraph. The selection includes this vertical space.

- If necessary, display the Home tab.

- Click the Text Highlight Color button arrow (Home tab | Font group) to display the Text Highlight Color gallery (Figure 10–60).

The Text Highlight Color gallery did not appear. Why not?

You clicked the Text Highlight Color button instead of the Text Highlight Color button arrow. Click the Undo button on the Quick Access Toolbar and then repeat Step 1.

What if the icon on the Text Highlight Color button already displays the color I want to use?

You can click the Text Highlight Color button instead of the button arrow.

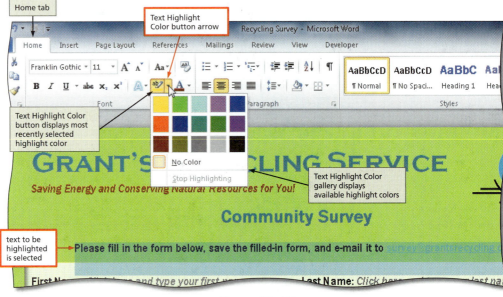

Figure 10–60

2

- Point to Yellow in the Text Highlight Color gallery to display a live preview of this highlight color applied to the selected text (Figure 10–61).

🔍 **Experiment**

- Point to various colors in the Text Highlight Color gallery and watch the highlight color on the selected text change.

3

- Click Yellow in the Text Highlight Color gallery to highlight the selected text in the selected highlight color.

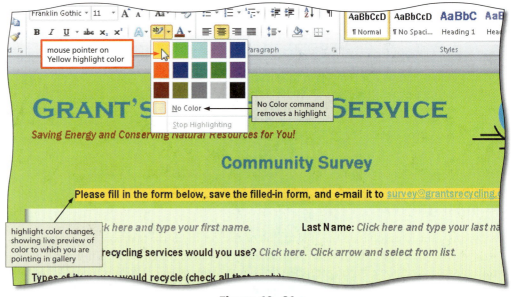

Figure 10–61

How would I remove a highlight from text?

Select the highlighted text, click the Text Highlight Color button arrow, and then click No Color in the Text Highlight Color gallery.

Other Ways

1. Click Text Highlight Color button arrow (Home tab | Font group), select desired color, select text to be highlighted in document, select any additional text to be highlighted, click Text Highlight Color button to turn off highlighting

To Customize a Theme Color and Save It with a New Theme Name

The final step in formatting the online form in this chapter is to change the color of the hyperlink. You would like the hyperlink to be darker, to match the company name. A document theme has 12 predefined colors for various on-screen objects including text, backgrounds, and hyperlinks. You can change any of the theme colors. The following steps customize the Slipstream theme, changing its designated theme color for hyperlinks.

1

- Display the Page Layout tab.

- Click the Theme Colors button (Page Layout tab | Themes group) to display the Theme Colors gallery (Figure 10–62).

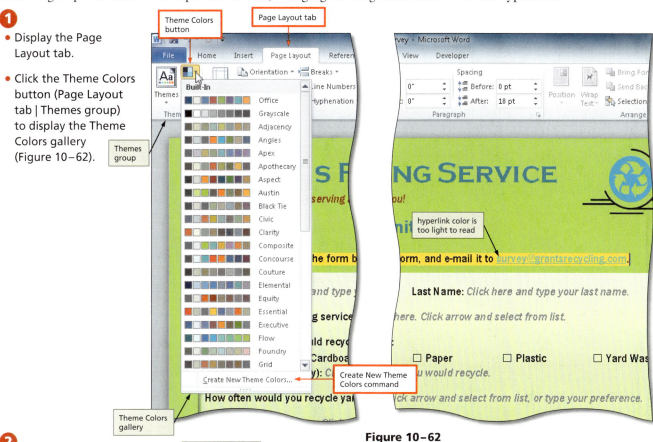

Figure 10–62

2

- Click Create New Theme Colors in the Theme Colors gallery to display the Create New Theme Colors dialog box.

- Click the Hyperlink button (Create New Theme Colors dialog box) to display the Theme Colors gallery (Figure 10–63).

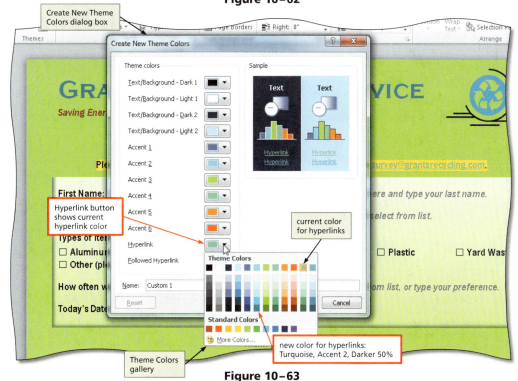

Figure 10–63

3

- Click Turquoise, Accent 2, Darker 50% in the Hyperlink column (sixth color in sixth row) as the new hyperlink color.

- Type **Recycling Survey** in the Name text box (Figure 10–64).

Q&A What if I wanted to reset all the original theme colors?

You would click the Reset button (Create New Theme Colors dialog box) before clicking the Save button.

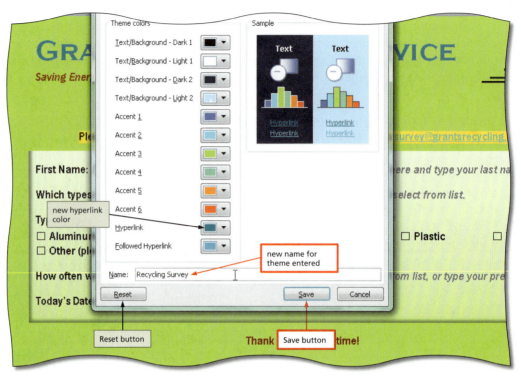

Figure 10–64

4

- Click the Save button (Create New Theme Colors dialog box) to save the modified theme with the name, Recycling Survey, which will be positioned at the top of the Theme Colors gallery for future access (Figure 10–65).

Q&A What if I do not enter a name for the modified theme?

Word assigns a name that begins with the letters, Custom, followed by a number (i.e., Custom8).

Figure 10–65

Other Ways

1. Make changes to theme colors, fonts, and/or effects; click Themes button (Page Layout tab | Themes group), click Save Current Theme in Themes gallery

To Protect a Form

It is crucial that you protect a form before making it available to users. When you **protect a form**, you are allowing users to enter data only in designated areas — specifically, the content controls. The following steps protect the online form.

- Display the Developer tab.

- Click the Restrict Editing button (Developer tab | Protect group) to display the Restrict Formatting and Editing task pane (Figure 10–66).

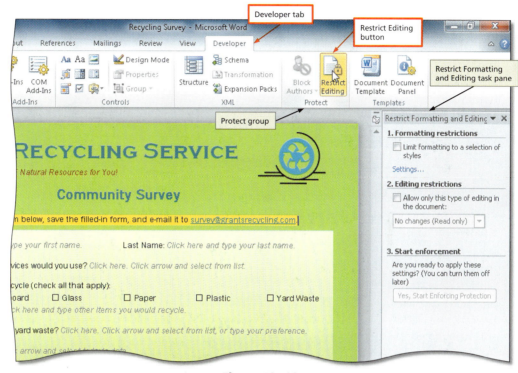

Figure 10–66

- In the Editing restrictions area, place a check mark in the 'Allow only this type of editing in the document' check box and then click its box arrow to display a list of the types of allowed restrictions (Figure 10–67).

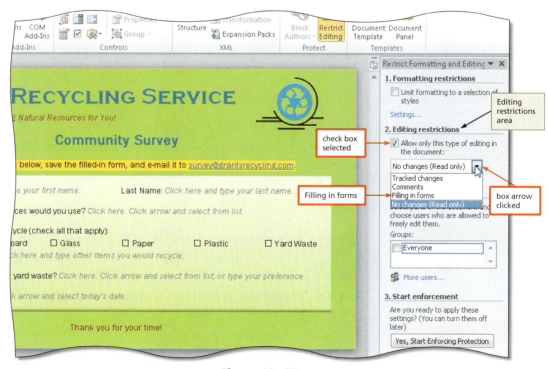

Figure 10–67

3

- Click 'Filling in forms' in the list to instruct Word that the only editing allowed in this document is to the content controls.

- In the Start enforcement area, click the Yes, Start Enforcing Protection button, which displays the Start Enforcing Protection dialog box (Figure 10–68).

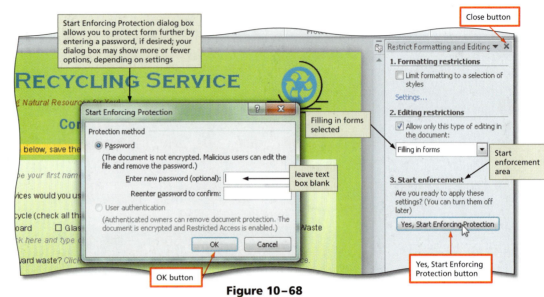

Figure 10–68

4

- Click the OK button (Start Enforcing Protection dialog box) to protect the document without a password.

Q&A What if I enter a password?

If you enter a password, only a user who knows the password will be able to unprotect the document.

- Close the Restrict Formatting and Editing task pane to show the protected form (Figure 10–69).

Figure 10–69

Protecting Documents

In addition to protecting a form so that it only can be filled in, Word provides several other options in the Restrict Formatting and Editing task pane.

To Set Formatting Restrictions

If you wanted to restrict users from making certain types of formatting changes to a document, you would perform the following steps.

1. Click the Restrict Editing button (Developer tab | Protect group) to display the Restrict Formatting and Editing task pane.

2. Place a check mark in the 'Limit formatting to a selection of styles' check box in the Formatting restrictions area.

3. Click the Settings link and then select the types of formatting you want to allow (Formatting Restrictions dialog box).

4. Click the OK button.

5. Click the Yes, Start Enforcing Protection button, enter a password if desired, and then click the OK button (Start Enforcing Protection dialog box).

TO SET EDITING RESTRICTIONS TO TRACKED CHANGES OR COMMENTS OR NO EDITS

If you wanted to restrict users' edits to allow only tracked changes, allow only comments, or not allow any edits (that is, make the document read only), you would perform the following steps.

1. Click the Restrict Editing button (Developer tab | Protect group) to display the Restrict Formatting and Editing task pane.

2. Place a check mark in the 'Allow only this type of editing in the document' check box in the Editing restrictions area, click the box arrow, and then click the desired option — that is, Tracked changes, Comments, or No changes (Read only) — to specify the types of edits allowed in the document.

3. Click the Yes, Start Enforcing Protection button, enter a password if desired, and then click the OK button (Start Enforcing Protection dialog box).

To Hide the Developer Tab

You are finished using the commands on the Developer tab. Thus, the following steps hide the Developer tab from the Ribbon.

1 Open the Backstage view and then click the Options button in the Backstage view to display the Word Options dialog box.

2 Click Customize Ribbon in the left pane (Word Options dialog box).

3 Remove the check mark from the Developer check box in the Main Tabs list.

4 Click the OK button to remove the Developer tab from the Ribbon.

To Save the Template Again

The online form template for this project now is complete. Thus, the following steps save the template and quit Word.

1 Click the Save button on the Quick Access Toolbar to overwrite the previously saved file.

2 Quit Word.

Working with an Online Form

When you create a template, you use the Open command in the Backstage view to open the template so that you can modify it. After you have created a template, you then can make it available to users. Users do not open templates with the Open command in Word. Instead, a user opens a new Word document that is based on the template, which means the title bar displays the default file name, Document1 (or a similar name) rather than the template name. When Word opens a document that is based on a template, the document window contains any text and formatting associated with the template. Word provides a variety of templates such as those for memos, letters, fax cover sheets, and resumes. If a user accesses a letter template, for example, Word opens the contents of a basic letter in a new document window.

BTW

Password-Protecting Documents
You can save documents with a password to keep unauthorized users from accessing files. To do this, type the password in the Start Enforcing Protection dialog box (shown in Figure 10–68); or open the Backstage view, click Save As, click the Tools button (Save As dialog box), click General Options on the Tools menu, type the password in the appropriate text box (General Options dialog box), type the password again (Confirm Password dialog box), and then click the OK button and Save button (Save As dialog box). As you type a password in the text box, Word displays a series of dots instead of the actual characters so that others cannot see your password as you type it.

Be sure to keep the password confidential. Choose a password that is easy to remember and that no one can guess. Do not use any part of your first or last name, Social Security number, birthday, and so on. Use a password that is at least six characters long, and if possible, use a mixture of numbers and letters.

To Use Windows Explorer to Open a New Document That Is Based on a Template

When you save the template to a USB flash drive, as instructed earlier in this chapter, a user can open a new document that is based on the template through Windows Explorer. This allows the user to work with a new document instead of risking the chance of altering the original template. The following steps open a new Word document that is based on the Recycling Survey template.

1

- Click the Windows Explorer program button on the Windows taskbar to open the Windows Explorer window.

- Navigate to the location of the saved template (in this case, the Word folder in the CIS 101 folder [or your class folder] on the USB flash drive) (Figure 10–70).

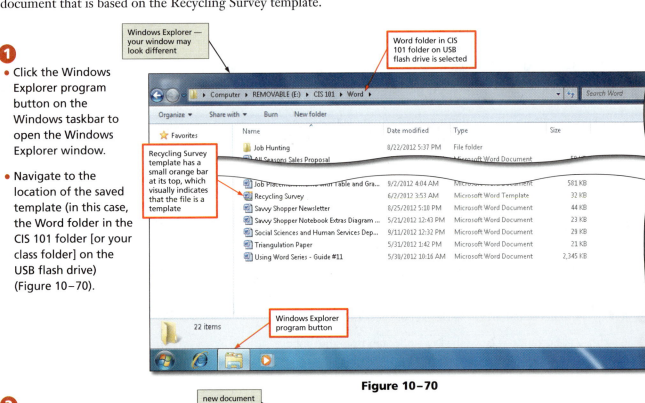

Figure 10–70

2

- Double-click the Recycling Survey file in the Windows Explorer window, which starts Word and opens a new document window that is based on the contents of the selected template (Figure 10–71).

BTW

Internet Explorer vs. Windows Explorer
Internet Explorer is a Web browser included with the Windows operating system. Windows Explorer is a file manager that is included with the Windows operating system. It enables you to perform functions related to file management, such as displaying a list of files, organizing files, and copying files.

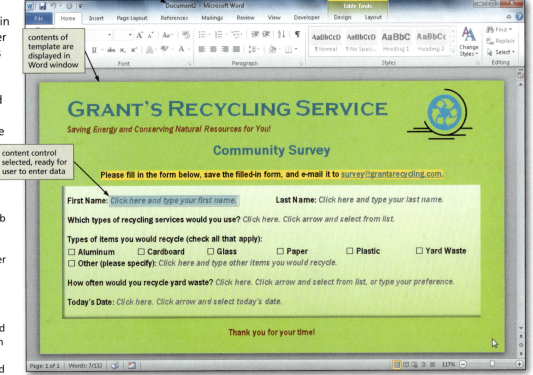

Figure 10–71

To Fill In a Form and Save It

The next step is to enter data in the form. To advance from one content control to the next, a user can click the content control or press the TAB key. To move to a previous content control, a user can click it or press SHIFT+TAB. The following steps fill in the Recyling Survey form.

- With the First Name content control selected, type **Marty** and then press the TAB key.

- Type **Schlotskey** in the Last Name content control.

- Press the TAB key to select the Recycling Services content control and then click its arrow to display the list of choices (shown in Figure 10–1b on page WD 611).

- Click Fee-Based Curbside Recycling in the list.

- Click the Aluminum, Paper, Plastic, and Other check boxes to select them.

- Type **Steel** in the Other Recycled Items content control.

- Click the Yard Waste Frequency content control and then click its arrow to display the list of choices (Figure 10–72).

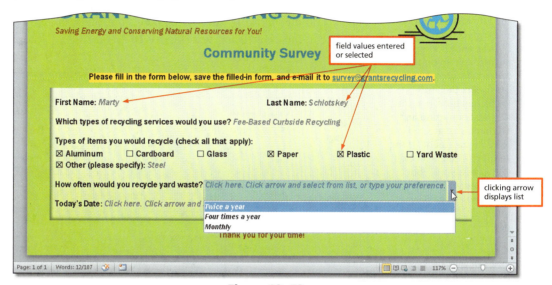

Figure 10–72

- Select 'Twice a year' in the list.

- Click the Today's Date arrow to display the calendar (Figure 10–73).

- Click May 31, 2012 in the calendar to complete the data entry (shown in Figure 10–1c on page WD 611).

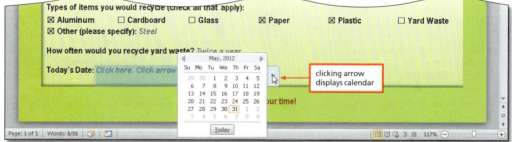

Figure 10–73

- Click the Save button on the Quick Access Toolbar and then save the file on your USB flash drive with the file name, Schlotskey Survey. If Word asks if you want to also save changes to the document template, click the No button.

Q&A

Can I print the form?

You can print the document as you print any other document. Keep in mind, however, that the colors used were designed for viewing online. Thus, different color schemes would have been selected if the form had been designed for a printout.

Protected Documents
If you open an existing form that has been protected, Word will not allow you to modify the form's appearance until you unprotect it. To unprotect a document, display the Restrict Formatting and Editing task pane by clicking the Restrict Editing button (Developer tab | Protect group) or opening the Backstage view, displaying the Info gallery, clicking the Protect Document button, and clicking Restrict Editing on the Protect Document menu. Then, click the Stop Protection button in the Restrict Formatting and Editing task pane and close the task pane. If the form has been protected with a password, you will be asked to enter the password when you attempt to unprotect the document.

Linking a Form to a Database
If you want to use or analyze the data that a user enters into a form in an Access database or an Excel worksheet, you could save the form data in a comma-delimited text file. This file separates each data item with a comma and places quotation marks around text data items. Then, you can use Access or Excel to import the comma-delimited text file for use in the respective program. To save form data, open the Backstage view and then click Save As in the Backstage view to display the Save As dialog box. Click the Tools button (Save As dialog box) and then click Save Options on the Tools menu to display the Word Options dialog box. Click Advanced in

Working with Templates

If you want to modify the template, open it by clicking the Open command in the Backstage view, clicking the template name, and then clicking the Open button in the dialog box. Then, you must **unprotect the form** by clicking the Restrict Editing button (Developer tab | Protect group) and then clicking the Stop Protection button in the Restrict Formatting and Editing task pane.

When you created the template in this chapter, you saved it on a USB flash drive. In environments other than an academic setting, you would not save the template on a USB flash drive. Instead, you would save it in the Templates folder (shown in Figure 10–3 on page WD 614). When you save a template in the Templates folder, you can locate the template by opening the Backstage view, clicking the New tab to display the New gallery, and then clicking the My templates button in the New gallery, which displays the template in the New dialog box (Figure 10–74).

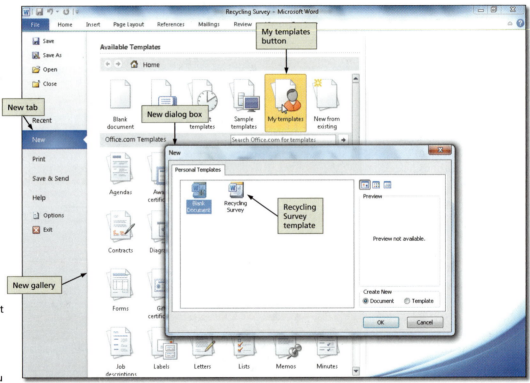

Figure 10–74

To Quit Word

The following steps quit Word and close the Windows Explorer window.

1 Quit Word. (If Word asks if you want to save the modified styles, click the Don't Save button.)

2 If the Windows Explorer window is still open, close it.

the left pane (Word Options dialog box), scroll to the Save area in the right pane, place a check mark in the 'Save form data as delimited text file' check box, and then click the OK button. Next, be sure the file type is Plain Text (Save As dialog box) and click the Save button. You can import the resulting comma-delimited file in an Access database or an Excel worksheet. To convert successfully, you should use the legacy controls (i.e., text form field, check box form field, etc.), which are available through the Legacy Tools button (Developer tab | Controls group). To use Word 2010 content controls, see Appendix E for instructions about working with XML.

Chapter Summary

In this chapter, you have learned how to create an online form. Topics covered included saving a document as a template, changing paper size, using a table to control layout, showing the Developer tab, inserting content controls, editing placeholder text, changing properties of content controls, and protecting a form. The items listed below include all the new Word skills you have learned in this chapter.

1. Save a Document as a Template (WD 613)
2. Zoom Page Width (WD 615)
3. Change Paper Size (WD 615)
4. Use a Table to Control Layout (WD 622)
5. Show the Developer Tab (WD 625)
6. Insert a Plain Text Content Control (WD 626)
7. Edit Placeholder Text (WD 627)
8. Change the Properties of a Plain Text Content Control (WD 628)
9. Insert a Drop-Down List Content Control (WD 633)
10. Change the Properties of a Drop-Down List Content Control (WD 634)
11. Insert a Check Box Content Control (WD 637)
12. Insert a Rich Text Content Control (WD 639)
13. Insert a Combo Box Content Control (WD 641)
14. Change the Properties of a Combo Box Content Control (WD 642)
15. Insert a Date Picker Content Control (WD 644)
16. Change the Properties of a Date Picker Content Control (WD 645)
17. Draw a Rectangle (WD 647)
18. Send a Graphic behind Text (WD 649)
19. Add a Shadow to a Shape (WD 650)
20. Highlight Text (WD 651)
21. Customize a Theme Color and Save It with a New Theme Name (WD 653)
22. Protect a Form (WD 655)
23. Set Formatting Restrictions (WD 656)
24. Set Editing Restrictions to Tracked Changes or Comments or No Edits (WD 657)
25. Use Windows Explorer to Open a New Document That Is Based on a Template (WD 658)
26. Fill In a Form and Save It (WD 659)

 If you have a SAM 2010 user profile, your instructor may have assigned an autogradable version of this assignment. If so, log into the SAM 2010 Web site at www.cengage.com/sam2010 to download the instruction and start files.

Learn It Online

Test your knowledge of chapter content and key terms.

Instructions: To complete the Learn It Online exercises, start your browser, click the Address bar, and then enter the Web address `scsite.com/wd2010/learn`. When the Word 2010 Learn It Online page is displayed, click the link for the exercise you want to complete and then read the instructions.

Chapter Reinforcement TF, MC, and SA
A series of true/false, multiple choice, and short answer questions that test your knowledge of the chapter content.

Flash Cards
An interactive learning environment where you identify chapter key terms associated with displayed definitions.

Practice Test
A series of multiple choice questions that test your knowledge of chapter content and key terms.

Who Wants To Be a Computer Genius?
An interactive game that challenges your knowledge of chapter content in the style of a television quiz show.

Wheel of Terms
An interactive game that challenges your knowledge of chapter key terms in the style of the television show *Wheel of Fortune*.

Crossword Puzzle Challenge
A crossword puzzle that challenges your knowledge of key terms presented in the chapter.

Apply Your Knowledge

Reinforce the skills and apply the concepts you learned in this chapter.

Filling In an Online Form

Note: To complete this assignment, you will be required to use the Data Files for Students. See the inside back cover of this book for instructions on downloading the Data Files for Students, or contact your instructor for information about accessing the required files.

Instructions: In this assignment, you access a template through Windows Explorer. The template is located on the Data Files for Students. The template contains an online form (Figure 10–75). You are to fill in the form, save it, and print it.

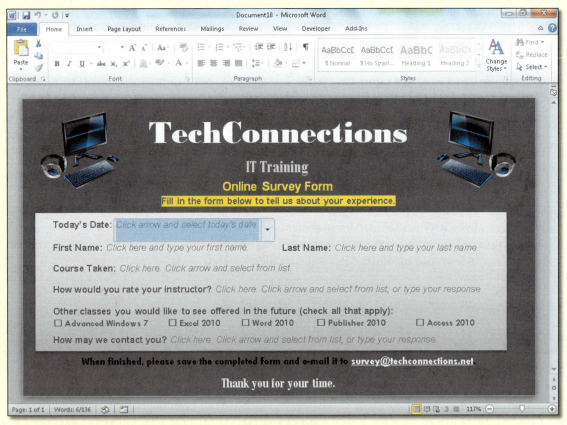

Figure 10–75

Perform the following tasks:

1. Start Windows Explorer. Double-click the Apply 10-1 TechConnections Survey template in Windows Explorer.

2. When Word displays a new document based on the Apply 10-1 TechConnections Survey template, if necessary, hide formatting marks and change the zoom to page width. Your screen should look like Figure 10–75.

3. Click the Today's Date content control arrow, click May 31, 2012 in the calendar and then press the TAB key.

4. With the First Name content control selected, type **Ashley** and then press the TAB key.

5. With the Last Name content control selected, type **Ohla** and then press the TAB key.

6. Click the Course Taken content control arrow and then click Overview of Office 2010 in the list. Press the TAB key.

7. Click the Rating content control arrow and then click Very Good in the list.

8. Click the Advanced Windows 7 check box.

9. Click the Contact content control to select it. Click the Contact content control arrow and then review the list. Press the ESCAPE key because none of these choices meets your criteria. Type **text message** as the contact method.

10. Save the file with the name Apply 10-1 Ohla Form. Print the form. Close the document.

11. Open the Apply 10-1 TechConnections Survey template from the Data Files for Students.

12. Unprotect the Apply 10-1 TechConnections Survey template.

13. Save the template with a new name, Apply 10-1 TechConnections Survey Modified.

14. Change the Today's Date content control to the format d-MMM-yy (i.e., 31-May-12).

15. Protect the modified template.

16. Save the modified template. Submit the revised template in the format specified by your instructor.

Extend Your Knowledge

Extend the skills you learned in this chapter and experiment with new skills. You may need to use Help to complete the assignment.

Working with Picture Content Controls, Grouping Objects, Themes, and Passwords

Note: To complete this assignment, you will be required to use the Data Files for Students. See the inside back cover of this book for instructions on downloading the Data Files for Students, or contact your instructor for information about accessing the required files.

Instructions: Start Word. Open the document, Extend 10-1 College Survey Draft, from the Data Files for Students. You will add a picture content control in a text box and then format the text box, group the graphical images, change the text highlight color, change the shadow color, change the shape fill, change theme colors, reset theme colors, save a modified theme, and protect a form with a password.

Perform the following tasks:
1. Use Help to review and expand your knowledge about these topics: picture content controls, text boxes, grouping objects, shadows, shape fill effects, changing theme colors, and protecting forms with passwords.

2. Add a simple text box to the empty space in the right side of the data entry area. Resize the text box so that it fits completely in the data entry area.

Continued >

Extend Your Knowledge *continued*

3. In the text box, type the label, Student ID Photo:, and then above the label, insert a picture content control. Resize the picture content control so that it fits in the text box and then center both the picture and label in the text box (Figure 10–76). Remove the border from the text box.

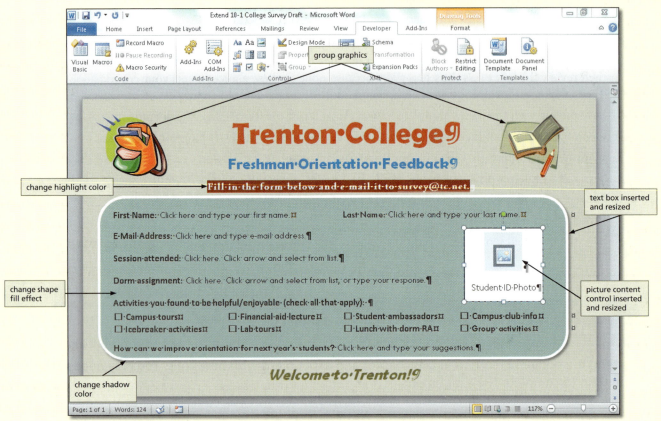

Figure 10–76

4. Change the fill effect in the rectangle shape to a texture of your choice.

5. Group the two graphics at the top of the form together. Move the grouped graphics. Return them to their original location.

6. Change the text highlight color of the third line of text to a color other than Dark Red. If necessary, change the text color so that you can read the text in the new highlight color.

7. Change the color of the shadow on the rectangle to a color other than the default.

8. Change the theme colors for Accent 1. Reset the theme colors.

9. Change the theme colors for Text/Background - Dark 2 and Hyperlink. Save the modified theme colors.

10. Make any necessary formatting changes to the form.

11. Protect the form with a password.

12. Change the document properties as specified by your instructor.

13. Save the revised document with a new file name.

14. Test the form. When filling in the form, use your own student ID or the picture called Student ID Photo on the Data Files for Students for the picture content control.

15. Submit the online form in the format specified by your instructor.

Make It Right

Analyze a document and correct all errors and/or improve the design.

Formatting an Online Form

Note: To complete this assignment, you will be required to use the Data Files for Students. See the inside back cover of this book for instructions on downloading the Data Files for Students, or contact your instructor for information about accessing the required files.

Instructions: Start Word. Open the document, Make It Right 10-1 Salon Survey Draft, from the Data Files for Students. The document is an online form containing unformatted elements (Figure 10–77).

You are to change the graphic's wrapping style; change the page color; change fonts, font sizes, font colors, and text highlight color; remove the table border; edit placeholder text; change content control properties; draw a rectangle and format it; and protect the form.

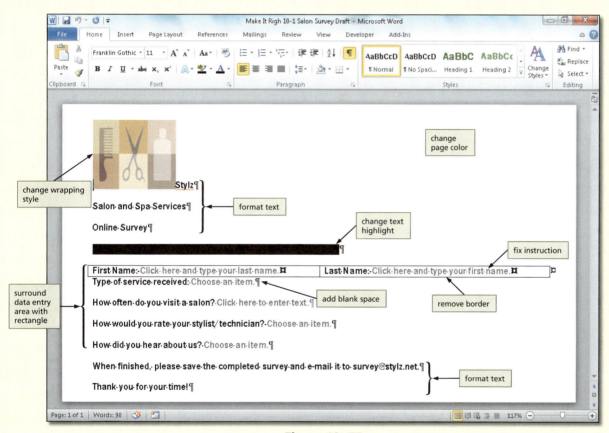

Figure 10–77

Perform the following tasks:

1. Change the graphic's wrapping style from inline to floating. Resize the graphic as necessary.

2. Change the page color to a color of your choice (other than white).

3. On the fourth line of text, change the text highlight color so that the text is visible.

4. Change the font, font size, and font color for the first four lines and last two lines of text. Center the six lines.

5. Remove the border from the 2 × 1 table that surrounds the First Name and Last Name content controls. Show table gridlines. Add a blank space below the table.

Continued >

Make It Right *continued*

6. Fix the placeholder text for the First Name content control so that it reads: Click here and type your first name. Similarly, fix the placeholder text for the Last Name content control. For the remaining placeholder text, change the instructions so that they are more meaningful.

7. For the Frequency of Visits content control, change the properties as follows: add a title and set the locking so that the content control cannot be deleted.

8. In the Rating content control, fix the spelling of the option, Unsatisfactory.

9. Draw a rectangle around the data entry area. Format the rectangle so that it is behind the text. Add a shape style and a shadow to the rectangle.

10. Make any necessary adjustments to the form so that it fits on a single page. Hide table gridlines. Protect the form.

11. Change the document properties as specified by your instructor.

12. Save the revised form with a new file name. Test the form. Submit the form in the format specified by your instructor.

In the Lab

Design and/or create a document using the guidelines, concepts, and skills presented in this chapter. Labs are listed in order of increasing difficulty.

Lab 1: Creating an Online Form with Plain Text and Drop-Down List Content Controls

Problem: You work as a part-time assistant at the Performing Arts Center. Your supervisor has asked you to prepare an online survey, shown in Figure 10–78.

Perform the following tasks:

1. Save a blank document as a template, called Lab 10-1 Theatre Survey, for the online form.

2. If necessary, change the view to page width.

3. Change the paper size to a width of 8.5 inches and a height of 4.75 inches.

4. Change the margins as follows: top - 0.25", bottom - 0", left - 0.5", and right - 0.5".

5. Change the theme fonts to Opulent. Change the theme colors to Apex.

6. Change the page color to Lavender, Accent 6, Lighter 40%.

7. Enter and format the company name, business tag line, and form title as shown in Figure 10–78 (or with similar fonts). Insert the clip art image (which is installed by default with Word) using the word, mask, as the search text. Change the wrapping style of the graphic to In Front of Text. If necessary, resize the graphic and move to the location shown.

8. Enter the instructions above the data entry area and highlight the line Bright Green.

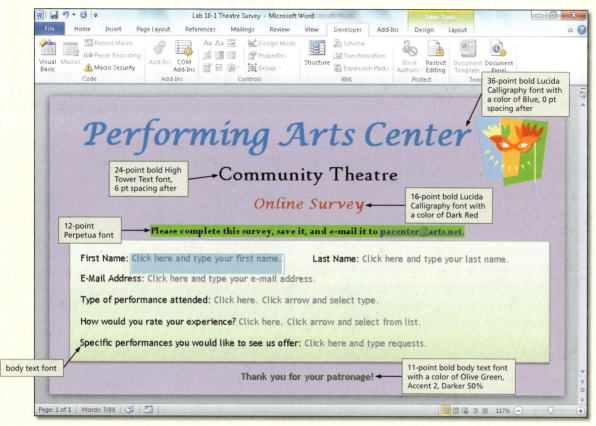

Figure 10–78

9. In the data entry area, enter the labels as shown in Figure 10–78 and the content controls as follows: First Name, Last Name, E-Mail Address, and Requests are plain text content controls. Performance is a drop-down list content control with these choices: Children's, Drama, Comedy, Experimental, Musical, and Ballet. Rating is a drop-down list content control with these choices: Excellent, Good, Fair, and Unsatisfactory.

10. Edit the placeholder text of all content controls to match Figure 10–78. Change the properties of the content controls so that each contains a title and has locking set so that the content control cannot be deleted.

11. Enter the line below the data entry area as shown in Figure 10–78.

12. Adjust spacing above and below paragraphs as necessary so that all contents fit on a single screen.

13. Draw a rectangle around the data entry area. Change the shape style of the rectangle to Subtle Effect - Olive Green, Accent 2. Apply the Offset Bottom shadow to the rectangle.

14. Protect the form.

15. Save the form again and submit it in the format specified by your instructor.

16. Access the template through Windows Explorer. Fill in the form using personal data and then submit it in the format specified by your instructor.

In the Lab

Lab 2: Creating an Online Form with Plain Text, Drop-Down List, Combo Box, and Rich Text Content Controls

Problem: You work part-time for Capital Investments, Inc. Your supervisor has asked you to prepare a request for information form, shown in Figure 10–79.

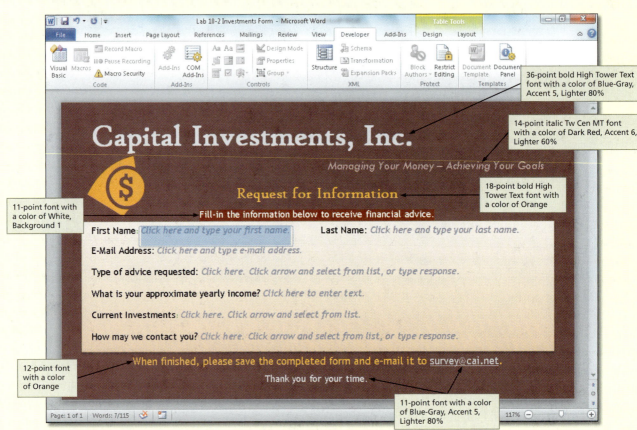

Figure 10–79

Perform the following tasks:

1. Save a blank document as a template, called Lab 10-2 Investments Form, for the online form.

2. If necessary, change the view to page width.

3. Change the paper size to a width of 8.5 inches and a height of 4.75 inches.

4. Change the margins as follows: top - 0.25", bottom - 0", left - 0.5", and right - 0.5".

5. Change the theme fonts to Slipstream. Change the theme colors to Clarity.

6. Change the page color to Dark Red, Accent 6.

7. Enter and format the company name, business tag line, and form title as shown in Figure 10–79 (or with similar fonts). Insert the clip art image (which is installed by default with Word) using the word, money, as the search text. Change the wrapping style of the graphic to In Front of Text. If necessary, resize the graphic. Move the graphic to the location shown.

8. Enter the instructions above the data entry area and highlight the line dark red.

9. In the data entry area, enter the labels as shown in Figure 10–79 and the content controls as follows: First Name, Last Name, and E-Mail Address are plain text content controls. Request is a combo box content control with these choices: Retirement Planning, Risk Assessment, College/ Educational Funds, Portfolio Review, and Account Monitoring. Income is a rich text content

control. Investments is a drop-down list content control with these choices: Savings, IRA/Roth/401k, Stock Holdings, Bonds, CDs, None, and Other. Contact is a combo box content control with these choices: Telephone, E-Mail, Appointment, U.S. Mail, and No contact.

10. Format the placeholder text to Subtle Emphasis. Edit the placeholder text of all content controls to match Figure 10–79. Change the properties of the content controls so that each contains a title, uses the Subtle Emphasis style, and has locking set so that the content control cannot be deleted.

11. Enter the two lines below the data entry area as shown in Figure 10–79.

12. Adjust spacing above and below paragraphs as necessary so that all contents fit on the screen.

13. Change the theme color for the hyperlink color to Blue-Gray, Accent 5, Lighter 80%.

14. Draw a rectangle around the data entry area. Change the shape style of the rectangle to Subtle Effect - Brown, Accent 2. Apply Offset Diagonal Bottom Right shadow to the rectangle.

15. Protect the form.

16. Save the form again and submit it in the format specified by your instructor.

17. Access the template through Windows Explorer. Fill in the form using personal data and submit it in the format specified by your instructor.

In the Lab

Lab 3: Creating an Online Form with Plain Text, Drop-Down List, Combo Box, Rich Text, Check Box, and Date Picker Content Controls

Problem: You work part-time for Monrovia Country Club. Your supervisor has asked you to prepare a member survey (Figure 10–80).

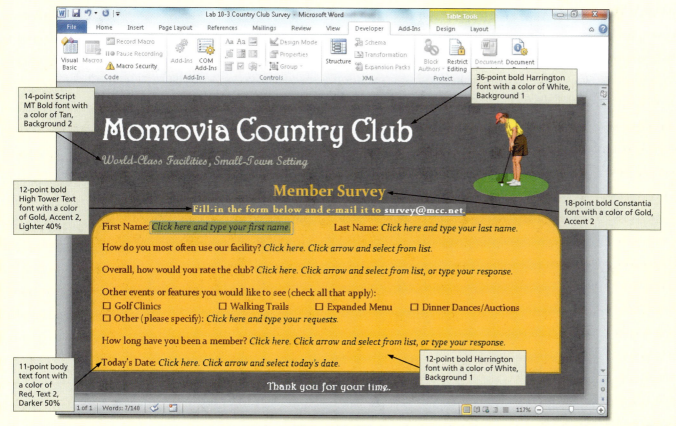

Figure 10–80

Continued >

Perform the following tasks:

1. Save a blank document as a template, called Lab 10-3 Country Club Survey, for the online form.

2. If necessary, change the view to page width.

3. Change the paper size to a width of 8.5 inches and a height of 4.75 inches.

4. Change the margins as follows: top - 0.25", bottom - 0", left - 0.5", and right - 0.5".

5. Change the theme fonts to Paper. Change the theme colors to Essential.

6. Change the page color to Gray-50%, Accent 1, Darker 25%.

7. Enter and format the company name, business tag line, and form title as shown in Figure 10–80 on the previous page (or with similar fonts). Insert the clip art image (which is installed by default with Word) using the word, golf, as the search text. Change the wrapping style of the graphic to In Front of Text. If necessary, resize the graphic and move it to the location shown.

8. Enter the instructions above the data entry area and highlight the line Gray-50%.

9. In the data entry area, enter the labels as shown in Figure 10–80 and the content controls as follows: First Name and Last Name are plain text content controls. Usage is a drop-down list content control with these choices: Golf, Tennis, Swimming, Racquetball, and Dining. Rating is a combo box content control with these choices: Excellent, Very Good, Good/Sufficient, Fair, and Poor. Golf Clinics, Walking Trails, Expanded Menu, Dinner Dances/Auctions, and Other are check boxes. Requests is a rich text content control. Membership is a combo box content control with these choices: Less than a year, 1-3 years, 3-5 years, and More than 5 years. Today's Date is a date picker content control.

10. Format the placeholder text to Emphasis. Edit the placeholder text of all content controls to match Figure 10–80. Change the properties of the content controls so that each contains a title, uses the Emphasis style, and has locking specified so that the content control cannot be deleted.

11. Change the theme color for the hyperlink color to White, Text 1. Save the modified theme.

12. Enter the line below the data entry area as shown in Figure 10–80.

13. Change the color of labels in the data entry area as shown in the figure.

14. Adjust spacing above and below paragraphs as necessary so that all contents fit on the screen.

15. Draw a Round Same Side Corner Rectangle around the data entry area. Change the shape style of the rectangle to Colored Fill - Gold, Accent 2.

16. Protect the form.

17. Save the form again and submit it in the format specified by your instructor.

18. Access the template through Windows Explorer. Fill in the form using personal data and submit it in the format specified by your instructor.

Cases and Places

Apply your creative thinking and problem solving skills to design and implement a solution.

Note: To complete these assignments, you may be required to use the Data Files for Students. See the inside back cover of this book for instructions on downloading the Data Files for Students, or contact your instructor for information about accessing the required files.

1: Create an Online Form for the Student Tutoring Center

Academic

As an assistant in the tutoring center, you have been asked to create an online student survey. Create a template that contains the business name (Student Tutoring Center), the business tag line (Achieving Academic Excellence), and appropriate clip art. The third line should have the text, Online Survey. The fourth line should be highlighted and should read: Tell us about your experience at our facility. The data entry area should contain the following. First Name and Last Name are plain text content controls within a table. A combo box content control with the label, Subject in which you most recently received tutoring:, has these choices: Math, English (Language), English (Literature), History, Foreign Language, and Science. A drop-down list content control with the label, How would you rate your experience?, has these choices: Excellent, Good, Fair, and Unsatisfactory. A rich text content control has the label, Other subjects you would like to see offered. The following instruction should appear above five check boxes: Times of day you would use the tutoring center (check all that apply); the check boxes are 9:00 – 11:00 a.m., 11:00 – 1:00 p.m., 1:00 – 3:00 p.m., 3:00 – 5:00 p.m., and 5:00 – 7:00 p.m. Today's Date is a date picker content control. Below the data entry area, place this line: When finished, please save the completed survey and e-mail it to studenttutors@campus.net. On the last line, include the text: Thank you for using the Student Tutoring Center.

Use the concepts and techniques presented in this chapter to create and format the online form. Use meaningful placeholder text for all content controls. (For example, the placeholder text for the First Name plain text content control could be as follows: Click here and then type your first name.) Draw a rectangle around the data entry area of the form. Add a shadow to the rectangle. Apply a style to the placeholder text. Assign names, styles, and locking to each content control. Protect the form, test it, and submit it in the format specified by your instructor.

2: Create an Online Form for a Children's Party Place

Personal

Your aunt owns a children's party business and has asked you to assist her in preparing an online form. Create a template that contains the business name (Cool Kidz Parties), the business tag line (Give your child a party to remember!), and appropriate clip art. The third line should have the text, Request for Information Form. The fourth line should be highlighted and should read: Fill in the form below to receive information. The data entry area should contain the following. First Name and Last Name are plain text content controls within a table. A drop-down list content control with the label, Who are we celebrating?, has these choices: Boy, Girl, Both. A combo box content control with the label, Type of party theme, has these choices: Pirate, Royalty, Clowns, Movie Character(s), Western, and Superhero. The following instruction should appear above nine check boxes: Services you would like us to provide (check all that apply); the check boxes are Paper goods, Set up/clean up, Entertainers, Animals, Balloons, Cake/ice cream, Beverages, DJ/music, and Other (please specify). A rich text content control should be positioned beside the Other (please specify) check box. Today's Date is a date picker content control. Below the data entry area, place this line: When complete, save this form and e-mail it to info@coolkidz.net.

Continued >

Cases and Places *continued*

Use the concepts and techniques presented in this chapter to create and format the online form. Use meaningful placeholder text for all content controls. (For example, the placeholder text for the First Name plain text content control could be as follows: Click here and then type your first name.) Draw a rectangle around the data entry area of the form. Add a shadow to the rectangle. Apply a style to the placeholder text. Assign names, styles, and locking to each content control. Protect the form, test it, and submit it in the format specified by your instructor.

3: Create an Online Form for an Environment-Friendly Business

Professional

You work part-time for a chain that sells all-natural products. Your boss has asked you to create an online survey. Create a template that contains the business name (Naturally Good), the business tag line (Get Healthy…Stay Healthy), and appropriate clip art. The third line should have the text, Online Survey. The fourth line should be highlighted and should read: Fill in the form below to tell us about you. The data entry area should contain the following. First Name and Last Name are plain text content controls within a table. A drop-down list content control with the label, How did you make your last purchase?, has these choices: Telephone, In-store, Kiosk, and Catalog. The following instruction should appear above nine check boxes: Product lines you would like to see offered/expanded (check all that apply); the check boxes are Herbals, Vitamins, Sugar-free, Gluten-free, Organics, Books, Green cleaning, Cosmetics, and Other (please specify). A rich text content control should be positioned beside the Other (please specify) check box. A combo box content control with the label, What is your age range?, has these choices: 18–25, 26–35, 36–50, and 51–70. Today's Date is a date picker content control. Below the data entry area, place this line: When finished, please save the completed form and e-mail it to survey@naturally.net. On the last line, include the text: Thank you for your time.

Use the concepts and techniques presented in this chapter to create and format the online form. Use meaningful placeholder text for all content controls. (For example, the placeholder text for the First Name plain text content control could be as follows: Click here and then type your first name.) Draw a rectangle around the data entry area of the form. Add a shadow to the rectangle. Apply a style to the placeholder text. Assign names, styles, and locking to each content control. Protect the form, test it, and submit it in the format specified by your instructor.

11 Enhancing an Online Form, Using Macros, and Adding Digital Signatures

Objectives

You will have mastered the material in this chapter when you can:

- Unprotect a document
- Specify macro settings
- Convert a table to text
- Insert and edit a field
- Create a character style
- Apply and modify fill effects
- Change a shape

- Remove a background from a graphic
- Apply an artistic effect to a graphic
- Insert and format a text box
- Record and execute a macro
- Customize the Quick Access Toolbar
- Edit a macro's VBA code
- Add a digital signature

11 | Enhancing an Online Form, Using Macros, and Adding Digital Signatures

Introduction

Word provides many tools that allow you to improve the appearance, functionality, and security of your documents. This chapter discusses tools used to perform the following tasks:

- Modify text and content controls.
- Enhance with color, shapes, effects, and graphics.
- Automate a series of tasks with a macro.
- Secure a document with digital signatures.

Project — Online Form Revised

This chapter uses Word to add macros and a digital signature to and improve the visual appearance of the online form created in Chapter 10, producing the online form shown in Figure 11–1a. This project begins with the Recycling Survey online form created in Chapter 10. Thus, you will need the online form template created in Chapter 10 to complete this project. (If you did not create the template, see your instructor for a copy.)

This project modifies the fonts and font colors of the text in the Recycling Survey online form and enhances the contents of the form to include a texture fill effect, a picture fill effect, and a text box and picture grouped together. The date in the form automatically displays the computer's system date, instead of requiring the user to enter the date.

This form also includes macros to automate tasks. A **macro** is a set of commands and instructions grouped together to allow a user to accomplish a task automatically. One macro allows the user to hide formatting marks and the ruler by pressing a shortcut key or clicking a button on the Quick Access Toolbar. Another macro specifies how the form is displayed initially on a user's Word screen. As shown in Figure 11–1b, when a document contains macros, Word may generate a security warning. If you are sure the macros are from a trusted source and free of viruses, then enable the content. Otherwise, do not enable the content, which protects your computer from potentially harmful viruses or other malicious software.

Figure 11–1 (a) Modified and Enhanced Online Form

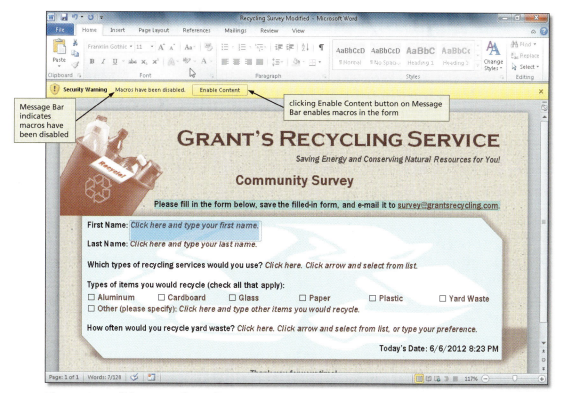

Figure 11–1 (b) Macros in Online Form Generate Security Warning

Overview

As you read through this chapter, you will learn how to create the online form shown in Figure 11–1 on the previous page, and make a document more secure, by performing these general tasks:

- Modify text and content controls on an existing online form.
- Enhance the look of an online form with color, shapes, effects, and graphics.
- Add macros to automate tasks.
- Add a digital signature to a document.

Plan Ahead

General Project Guidelines

When creating a Word document, the actions you perform and decisions you make will affect the appearance and characteristics of the finished document. As you enhance an online form, such as the project shown in Figure 11–1, and add macros and digital signatures, you should follow these general guidelines:

1. **Save the form to be modified as a macro-enabled template.** If you plan to include macros in a template for a form, be sure to save the template as a macro-enabled template. Basic Word templates cannot store macros.

2. **Enhance the visual appeal of a form.** Arrange data entry fields in logical groups on the form and in an order that users would expect. Draw the user's attention to important sections. Use colors and images that complement one another.

3. **Add macros to automate tasks.** In Word, a macro consists of VBA code. **VBA**, which stands for **Visual Basic for Applications**, is a powerful programming language included with Word that allows users to customize and extend the capabilities of Word. Word can generate the VBA code associated with a macro automatically, or you can write the VBA code yourself. To add macros, you do not need a computer programming background. To write VBA code, however, you should be familiar with computer programming.

4. **Determine how the form data will be analyzed.** If the data entered in the form will be analyzed by a program outside of Word, create the data entry fields so that the entries are stored in a format that can be shared with other programs.

When necessary, more specific details concerning the above guidelines are presented at appropriate points in the chapter. The chapter also will identify the actions performed and decisions made regarding these guidelines during the creation of the form in this chapter.

To Start Word

If you are using a computer to step through the project in this chapter and you want your screens to match the figures in this book, you should change your computer's resolution to 1024 × 768. The following steps start Word and verify settings.

1 Start Word. If necessary, maximize the Word window.

2 If the Print Layout button on the status bar is not selected, click it so that your screen is in Print Layout view.

3 If the rulers are displayed on the screen, click the View Ruler button at the top vertical scroll bar to remove the rulers from the Word window because you will not use the rulers in this project.

4 If the Show/Hide ¶ button (Home tab | Paragraph group) is selected, click it to hide formatting marks because you will not use them in this project.

5 If the edges of the page do not extend to the edge of the document window, display the View tab and then click the Page Width button (View tab | Zoom group) to zoom page width.

To Save a Macro-Enabled Template

The project in this chapter contains macros. To provide added security to templates, a basic Word template cannot store macros. Word instead provides a specific type of template, called a **macro-enabled template**, in which you can store macros. Thus, the first step in this chapter is to open the Recycling Survey template created in Chapter 10 and save it as a macro-enabled template. (If you did not create the template, see your instructor for a copy.)

The following steps open an existing Word template and then save it with a new file name as a Word macro-enabled template.

1
- Open the template named Recycling Survey created in Chapter 10.

2
- Open the Backstage view and then click Save As to display the Save As dialog box.

- Type `Recycling Survey Modified` in the File name text box (Save As dialog box) to change the file name.

- Click the Save as type box arrow to display the list of available file types and then click Word Macro-Enabled Template in the list to change the file type (Figure 11–2).

3
- Click the Save button (Save As dialog box) to save the file using the entered file name as a macro-enabled template.

Q&A How does Word differentiate between a Word template and a Word macro-enabled template?

A Word template has an extension of .dotx, whereas a Word macro-enabled template has an extension of .dotm. Also, the icon for a macro-enabled template contains an exclamation point.

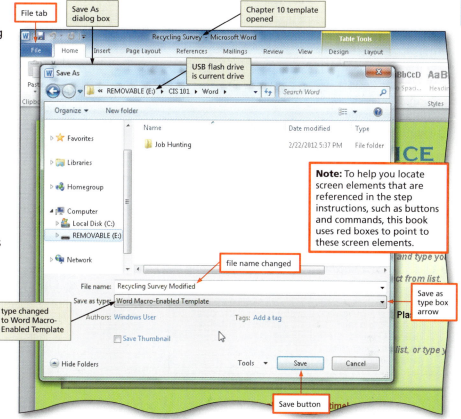

Figure 11–2

To Show the Developer Tab

Many of the tasks you will perform in this chapter use commands on the Developer tab. Thus, the following steps show the Developer tab on the Ribbon.

1 Open the Backstage view and then click the Options button in the Backstage view to display the Word Options dialog box.

2 Click Customize Ribbon in the left pane (Word Options dialog box).

3 If it is not selected already, place a check mark in the Developer check box in the Main Tabs list.

4 Click the OK button to show the Developer tab on the Ribbon.

To Unprotect a Document

The Recycling Survey Modified template is protected. Recall that Chapter 10 showed how to protect a form so that users could enter data only in designated areas, specifically, the content controls. Before this form can be modified, it must be unprotected. Later in this project, after you have completed the modifications, you will protect it again. The following steps unprotect a document.

1

- Display the Developer tab.

- Click the Restrict Editing button (Developer tab | Protect group) to display the Restrict Formatting and Editing task pane (Figure 11–3).

2

- Click the Stop Protection button in the Restrict Formatting and Editing task pane to unprotect the form.

- Click the Close button in the Restrict Formatting and Editing task pane to close the task pane.

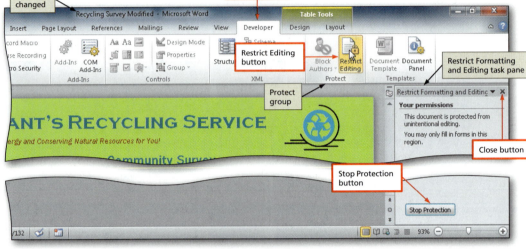

Figure 11–3

Other Ways

1. Click File on Ribbon, click Info tab in Backstage view, click Protect Document button, click Restrict Editing on Protect Document menu, click Stop Protection button in Restrict Formatting and Editing task pane

---

Plan Ahead

Protecting a Computer from Macro Viruses.

A **computer virus** is a type of malicious software, or malware, which is a potentially damaging computer program that affects, or infects, a computer negatively by altering the way the computer works without the user's knowledge or permission. Currently, more than one million known viruses and other malicious programs exist. The increased use of networks, the Internet, and e-mail has accelerated the spread of computer viruses and other malicious programs.

- To combat these threats, most computer users run an **antivirus program** that searches for viruses and other malware and destroys the malicious programs before they infect the computer. Macros are a known carrier of viruses and other malware. For this reason, you can specify a macro setting in Word to reduce the chance your computer will be infected with a macro virus. These macro settings allow you to enable or disable macros. An **enabled macro** is a macro that Word will execute, and a **disabled macro** is a macro that is unavailable to Word.

- As shown in Figure 11–1b on page WD 675, you can instruct Word to display a security warning on a Message Bar if it opens a document that contains a macro(s). If you are confident of the source (author) of the document and macros, enable the macros. If you are uncertain about the reliability of the source of the document and macros, then do not enable the macros.

Macro Viruses

A macro virus is a type of computer virus that is stored in a macro within a file, template, or add-in. For the best protection against macro viruses, purchase and install an antivirus program.

To Specify Macro Settings in Word

This chapter shows how to create macros. When you open the online form in this chapter, you want the macros enabled. At the same time, your computer should be protected from potentially harmful macros. Thus, you will specify a macro setting that allows you to enable macros each time you open this chapter's online form or any document that contains a macro from an unknown source. The following steps specify macro settings.

- Click the Macro Security button (Developer tab | Code group) to display the Trust Center dialog box.

- If it is not selected already, click the 'Disable all macros with notification' option button (Trust Center dialog box), which causes Word to alert you when a document contains a macro so that you can decide whether to enable the macro(s) (Figure 11–4).

- Click the OK button to close the dialog box.

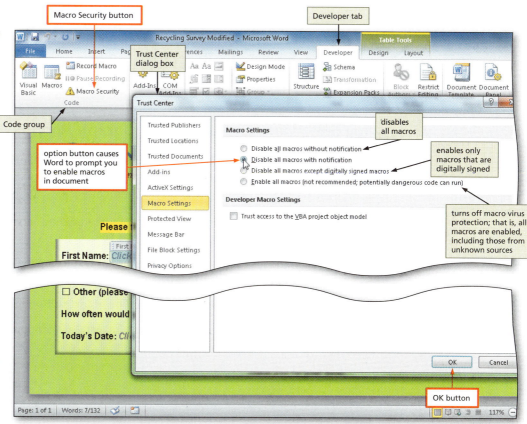

Figure 11–4

Other Ways
1. Click File on Ribbon, click Options button, click Trust Center in left pane (Word Options dialog box), click Trust Center Settings button in right pane, click Macro Settings in left pane (Trust Center dialog box), select desired setting, click OK button in each dialog box

Modifying Text and Form Content Controls

The form created in Chapter 10 is enhanced in this chapter by performing these steps:

1. Delete the current clip art image, and change the document theme.
2. Change the fonts, colors, and alignments of the first four lines of text.
3. Convert the 2 × 1 table containing the First Name and Last Name content controls to text so that each of these content controls is on a separate line.
4. Delete the date picker content control and replace it with a date field.
5. Modify the color of the hyperlink and the check box labels.

The following pages apply these changes to the form.

BTW

Save a New Theme
If you have changed the color scheme and font set and want to save this combination for future use, save it as a new theme by clicking the Themes button (Page Layout tab | Themes group), clicking Save Current Theme, entering a theme name in the File name box, and then clicking the Save button (Save Current Theme dialog box).

To Delete a Graphic and Change the Document Theme

The online form in this chapter has a different clip art image and uses the Grid document theme. The following steps delete the current clip art image and change the document theme.

1 Click the recycling clip art image to select it and then press the DELETE key to delete the selected clip art image.

2 Display the Page Layout tab. Click the Themes button (Page Layout tab | Themes group) and then click Grid in the Themes gallery to change the document theme.

To Format Text and Change Paragraph Alignment

The next step in modifying the online form for this chapter is to change the formats of the company name, business tag line, form name, and form instructions. The following steps format text and change paragraph alignment.

1 Change the color of the first line of text, Grant's Recycling Service, and third line of text, Community Survey, to Tan, Accent 1, Darker 50%.

2 Right-align the first, second, and fourth lines of text (company name, business tag line, and form instructions).

3 Change the highlight color on the fourth line of text to Turquoise.

4 Right-align the line of text containing the Today's Date content control (Figure 11–5).

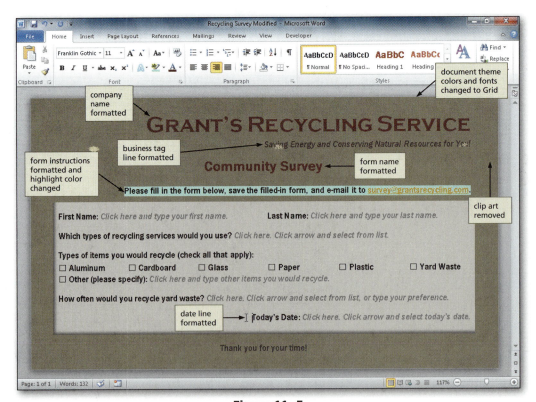

Figure 11–5

To Change the Properties of a Plain Text Content Control

In this online form, the First Name and Last Name content controls are on separate lines. In Chapter 10, you selected the 'Content control cannot be deleted' check box in the Content Control Properties dialog box so that users could not delete the content control accidentally while filling in the form. With this check box selected, however, you cannot move a content control from one location to another on the form. Thus, the following steps change the locking properties of the First Name and Last Name content controls so that you can rearrange them.

1 Display the Developer tab.

2 Click the First Name content control to select it.

3 Click the Control Properties button (Developer tab | Controls group) to display the Content Control Properties dialog box.

4 Remove the check mark from the 'Content control cannot be deleted' check box (Content Control Properties dialog box) (Figure 11–6).

5 Click the OK button to assign the modified properties to the content control.

6 Click the Last Name content control to select it and then click the Control Properties button (Developer tab | Controls group) to display the Content Control Properties dialog box.

7 Remove the check mark from the 'Content control cannot be deleted' check box (Content Control Properties dialog box), and then click the OK button to assign the modified properties to the content control.

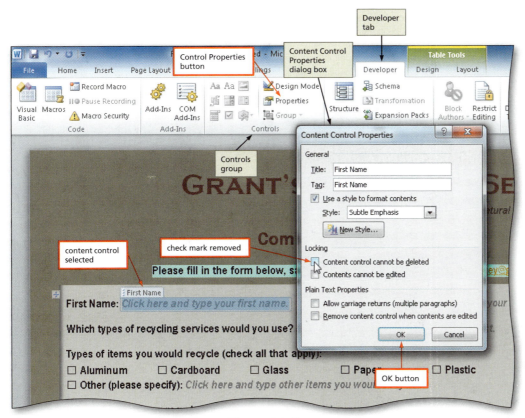

Figure 11–6

To Convert a Table to Text

The First Name and Last Name content controls currently are in a 2 × 1 table. In this online form, these content controls are on separate lines, one below the other. That is, they are not in a table. The following steps convert the table to regular text, placing a paragraph break at the location of the second column.

- Position the insertion point somewhere in the table.

- Display the Table Tools Layout tab.

- Click the Convert to Text button (Table Tools Layout tab | Data group) to display the Convert Table To Text dialog box.

- Click Paragraph marks (Convert Table To Text dialog box), which will place a paragraph mark at the location of each new column in the table (Figure 11–7).

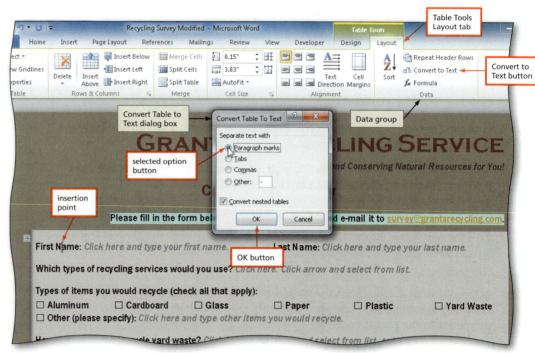

Figure 11–7

- Click the OK button to convert the table to text, separating each column with the specified character, a paragraph mark in this case (Figure 11–8).

Q&A
Why did the Last Name content control move below the First Name content control?

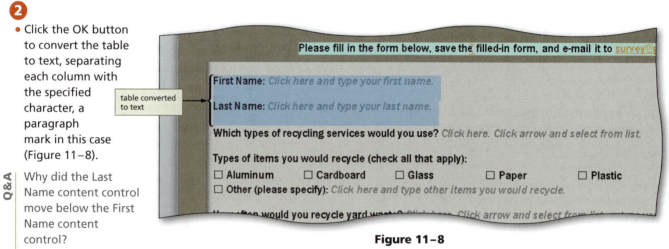

Figure 11–8

The 'Separate text with' area (Convert Table To Text dialog box) controls how the table is converted to text. The Paragraph marks setting converts each column in the table to a line of text below the previous line. The Tabs setting places a tab character where each column was located, and the Commas setting places a comma where each column was located.

3

- Click anywhere to remove the selection from the text.

To Change the Properties of a Plain Text Content Control

You are finished moving the First Name and Last Name content controls. The following steps reset the locking properties of these content controls.

1 Display the Developer tab.

2 Click the First Name content control to select it and then click the Control Properties button (Developer tab | Controls group) to display the Content Control Properties dialog box.

3 Place a check mark in the 'Content control cannot be deleted' check box (Content Control Properties dialog box) and then click the OK button to assign the modified properties to the content control.

4 Repeat Steps 2 and 3 for the Last Name content control.

To Adjust Paragraph Spacing and Resize the Rectangle Shape

With the First Name and Last Name content controls on separate lines, the thank you line moved to a second page, and the rectangle outline in the data entry area now is too short to accommodate the text. The following steps adjust paragraph spacing and extend the rectangle shape downward so that it surrounds the entire data entry area.

1 Position the insertion point in the fourth line of text on the form (the form instructions) and then adjust the spacing after to 12 pt (Page Layout tab | Paragraph group).

2 Position the insertion point in the last line of text on the form (the thank you line, which may be positioned on a second page) and then adjust the spacing before to 18 pt (Page Layout tab | Paragraph group).

3 Scroll to display the entire form in the document window. If necessary, reduce spacing after other paragraphs so that the entire form fits in a single document window.

4 Click the rectangle shape to select it.

5 Position the mouse pointer on the bottom-middle sizing handle of the rectangle shape.

6 Drag the bottom-middle sizing handle downward so that the shape includes the bottom content control, in this case, the Today's Date content control (Figure 11–9).

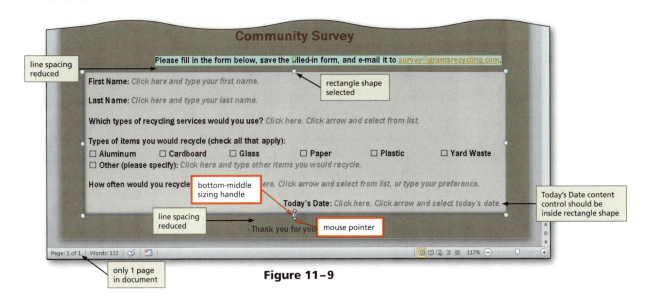

Figure 11–9

To Change the Properties of a Date Picker Content Control

In this online form, instead of the user entering the current date, the computer's system date will be filled in automatically by Word. Thus, the Today's Date content control is not needed and can be deleted. To delete the content control, you first will need to remove the check mark from the 'Content control cannot be deleted' check box in the Content Control Properties dialog box. The following steps change the locking properties of the Today's Date content control and then delete the content control.

1 Display the Developer tab.

2 Click the Today's Date content control to select it.

3 Click the Control Properties button (Developer tab | Controls group) to display the Content Control Properties dialog box.

4 Remove the check mark from the 'Content control cannot be deleted' check box (Content Control Properties dialog box) (Figure 11–10).

5 Click the OK button to assign the modified properties to the content control.

6 Even if it appears selected, click the Today's Date content control title to select it again and then press the DELETE key to delete it.

BTW

Q&As
For a complete list of the Q&As found in many of the step-by-step sequences in this book, visit the Word 2010 Q&A Web page (scsite.com/wd2010/qa).

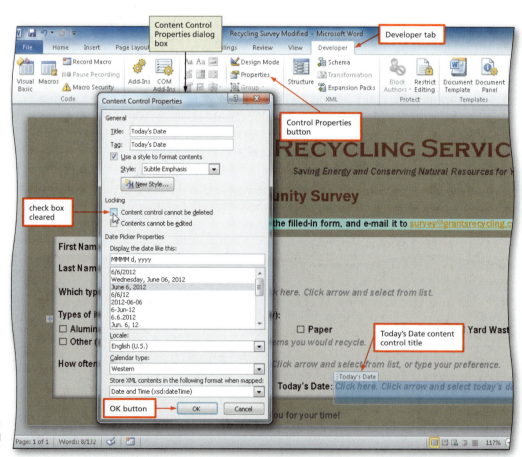

Figure 11–10

To Insert a Date Field

The next step is to instruct Word to display the current date and time at the location of the insertion point. The current date and time is a field. Recall that a field is a set of codes that instructs Word to perform a certain action. The following steps insert the date and time as a field in the form at the location of the insertion point.

1
- Display the Insert tab.

- With the insertion point positioned as shown in Figure 11–11, which is the location for the date and time, click the Quick Parts button (Insert tab | Text group) to display the Quick Parts menu.

Figure 11–11

2
- Click Field on the Quick Parts menu to display the Field dialog box.

- Scroll through the Field names list (Field dialog box) and then click Date, which displays the Date formats list in the Field properties area.

- Click the date in the format of 6/6/2012 2:30:26 PM in the Date formats list to select a date format — your date and time will differ (Figure 11–12).

Q&A What controls the date that appears?

Your current computer date appears in this dialog box. The format for the selected date shows in the Date formats box. In this case, the format for the selected date is M/d/yyyy h:mm:ss am/pm, which displays the date as month/day/year hours:minutes:seconds AM/PM.

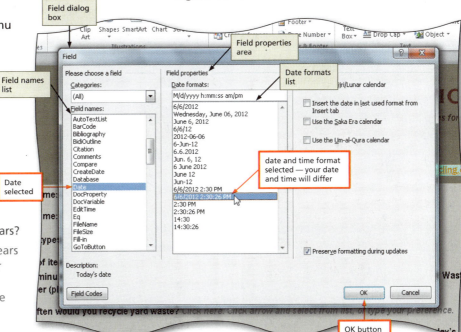

Figure 11–12

3
- Click the OK button to insert the current date and time at the location of the insertion point (Figure 11–13).

Q&A How do I delete a field?

Select it and then press the DELETE key or click the Cut button (Home tab | Clipboard group), or right-click it and then click Cut on the shortcut menu.

Figure 11–13

Other Ways		
1. Click Insert Date and Time button (Insert tab | Text group), select date format	(Date and Time dialog box), place check mark	in Update automatically check box, click OK button

To Edit a Field

After you see the date and time in the form, you decide not to include the seconds in the time. That is, you want just the hours and minutes to be displayed. Thus, the following steps edit the field.

- Right-click the date field to display a shortcut menu (Figure 11–14).

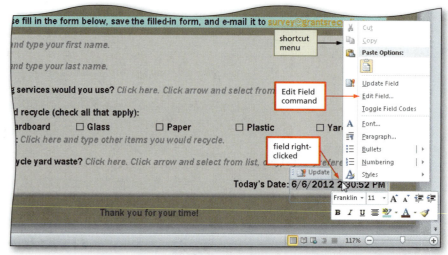

Figure 11–14

- Click Edit Field on the shortcut menu to display the Field dialog box.

- If necessary, scroll through the Field names list (Field dialog box) and then click Date to display the Date formats list in the Field properties area.

- Select the desired date format, in this case 6/6/2012 2:35 PM (Figure 11–15).

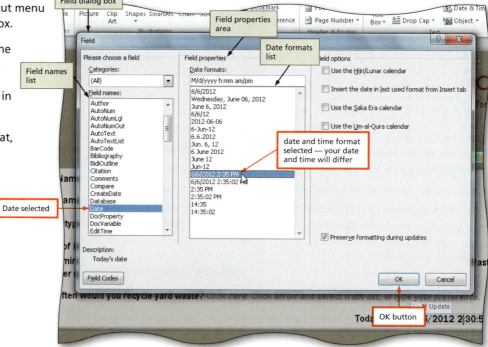

Figure 11–15

❸

- Click the OK button to insert the edited field at the location of the insertion point (Figure 11–16).

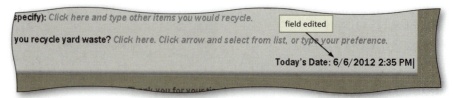

Figure 11–16

To Modify a Style Using the Styles Task Pane

The new text highlight color of the form instructions makes it difficult to see the hyperlink. In this online form, the hyperlink should be the same color as the company name so that the hyperlink is noticeable. The Hyperlink style is not in the Styles gallery. To modify a style that is not in the Styles gallery, you can use the Styles task pane. The following steps modify a style using the Styles task pane.

- Position the insertion point in the hyperlink in the form.

- Display the Home tab.

- Click the Styles Dialog Box Launcher (Home tab | Styles group) to display the Styles task pane.

- If necessary, click Hyperlink in the list of styles in the task pane to select it and then click the Hyperlink box arrow to display the Hyperlink menu (Figure 11–17).

Q&A

What if the style I want to modify is not in the list?

Click the Manage Styles button at the bottom of the task pane, locate the style, and then click the Modify button in the dialog box.

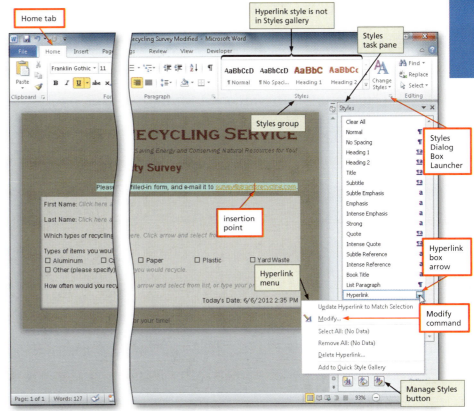

Figure 11–17

- Click Modify on the Hyperlink menu to display the Modify Style dialog box.

- Click the Font Color box arrow (Modify Style dialog box) to display the Font Color gallery (Figure 11–18).

Figure 11–18

3

- Click Tan, Accent 1, Darker 50% (fifth color in sixth row) as the new hyperlink color.

- Click the OK button to close the dialog box. Close the Styles task pane (Figure 11–19).

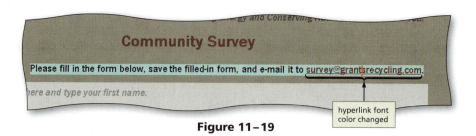

Figure 11–19

To Modify a Style

In this online form, the placeholder text is to be the same color as the company name. Currently, the placeholder text is formatted using the Subtle Emphasis style, which uses a shade of gray as the font color. Thus, the following steps modify the color of the Subtle Emphasis style.

1 Scroll through the Quick Styles gallery (Home tab | Styles group) to locate the Subtle Emphasis Quick Style.

2 Right-click Subtle Emphasis in the Quick Styles gallery to display a shortcut menu and then click Modify on the shortcut menu to display the Modify Style dialog box.

3 Click the Font Color box arrow (Modify Style dialog box) to display the Font Color gallery (Figure 11–20).

4 Click Tan, Accent 1, Darker 50% (fifth color in sixth row) as the new color.

5 Click the OK button to change the color of the style, which automatically changes the color of every item formatted using this style in the document.

Hidden Styles
Some styles are hidden, which means they do not appear in the Styles task pane. You can display all styles, including hidden styles, by clicking the Manage Styles button in the Styles task pane (Figure 11–21), which displays the Manage Styles dialog box. Click the Edit tab, if necessary, and then locate the style name in the 'Select a style to edit' list.

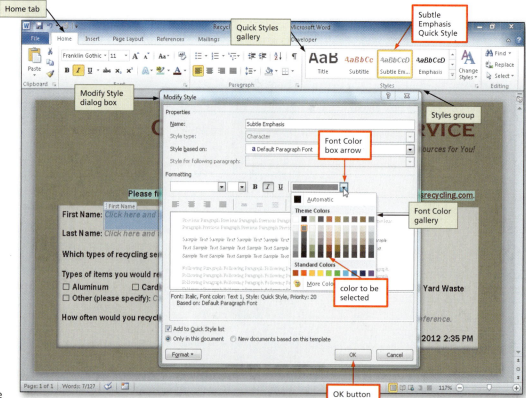

Figure 11–20

To Create a Character Style

In this online form, the check box labels are to be the same color as the company name. You could select each of the check box labels and then format them. A more efficient technique is to create a character style. If you decide to modify the formats of the check box labels at a later time, you simply change the formats assigned to the style. All characters in the document based on that style will change automatically.

The following steps create a character style called Check Box Labels.

• Position the insertion point in one of the check box labels.

• Click the Styles Dialog Box Launcher (Home tab | Styles group) to display the Styles task pane.

• Click the Manage Styles button in the Styles task pane to display the Manage Styles dialog box (Figure 11–21).

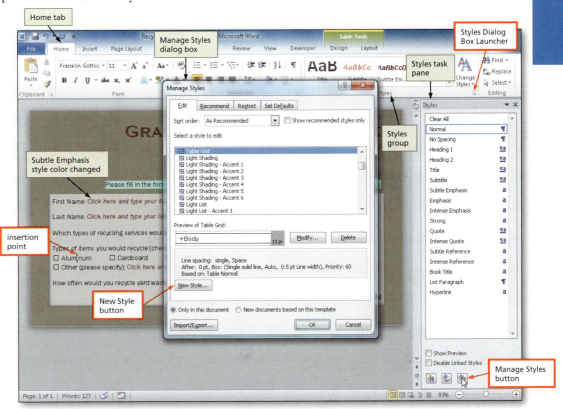

Figure 11–21

② • Click the New Style button (Manage Styles dialog box) to display the Create New Style from Formatting dialog box.

• Type **Check Box Labels** in the Name text box (Create New Style from Formatting dialog box) as the name of the new style.

• Click the Style type box arrow and then click Character so that the new style does not contain any paragraph formats.

• Click the Font Color box arrow to display the Font Color gallery and then click Tan, Accent 1, Darker 50% (fifth color in sixth row) as the new color (Figure 11–22).

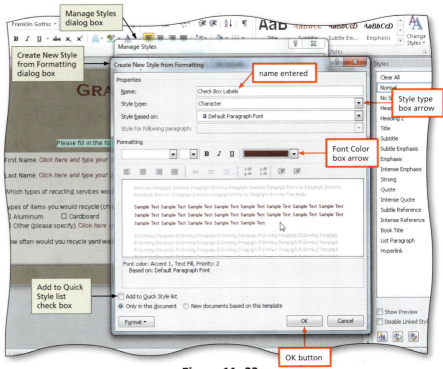

Figure 11–22

3

- Click the OK button in each open dialog box to create the new character style, Check Box Labels in this case, and insert the new style name in the Styles task pane (Figure 11–23).

Q&A

What if I wanted the style added to the Quick Styles gallery?

You would place a check mark in the Add to Quick Style list check box (Create New Style from Formatting dialog box), shown in Figure 11–22 on the previous page.

Figure 11–23

BTW

Character Styles
In the Styles task pane, character styles display a lowercase letter a to the right of the style name, and paragraph styles show a paragraph mark. With a character style, Word applies the formats to the selected text. With a paragraph style, Word applies the formats to the entire paragraph.

To Apply a Style

The next step is to apply the Check Box Labels style just created to the check box labels in the form. The following steps apply a style.

1 Position the insertion point in the Aluminum check box label and then click Check Box Labels in the Styles task pane to apply the style to the word containing the insertion point.

2 Repeat Step 1 for these check box labels: Cardboard, Glass, Paper, and Plastic.

3 Select the text, Yard Waste, and then click Check Box Labels in the Styles task pane to apply the style to the selected text.

Q&A

Why select Yard Waste instead of positioning the insertion point in the text?

To format a single word, you place the insertion point in the word. To format multiple words at once, select the words and then format them.

4 Repeat Step 3 for the label, Other (please specify):, as shown in Figure 11–24.

5 Close the Styles task pane.

6 Click anywhere to remove the selection from the check box label.

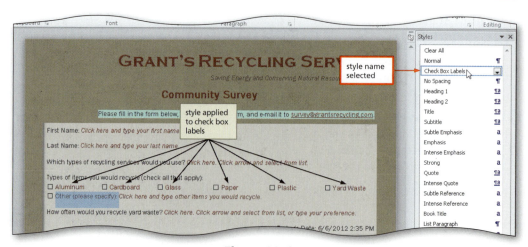

Figure 11–24

To Save an Existing Template with the Same File Name

You have made several modifications to the template since you last saved it. Thus, you should save it again. The following step saves the template again.

 Click the Save button on the Quick Access Toolbar to overwrite the previously saved file.

Break Point: If you wish to take a break, this is a good place to do so. You can quit Word now. To resume at a later time, start Word, open the file called Recycling Survey Modified, and continue following the steps from this location forward.

Enhancing with Color, Shapes, Effects, and Graphics

You will enhance the form created in Chapter 10 by performing these steps:

1. Apply a texture fill effect for the page color.
2. Change the appearance of the shape.
3. Change the color of a shadow on the shape.
4. Fill the rectangle with a picture.
5. Insert a picture, remove its background, and apply an artistic effect.
6. Insert and format a text box.
7. Group the picture and the text box together.

The following pages apply these changes to the form.

To Use a Fill Effect for the Page Color

Instead of a simple color for the background page color, this online form uses a texture for the page color. Word provides a gallery of 24 predefined textures you can use as a page background. These textures resemble various wallpaper patterns. The following steps change the page color to a texture fill effect.

1

- Display the Page Layout tab.

- Click the Page Color button (Page Layout tab | Page Background group) to display the Page Color gallery (Figure 11–25).

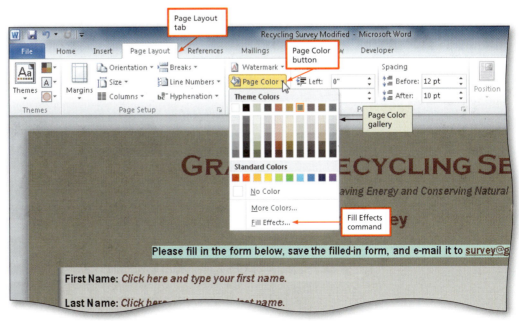

Figure 11–25

- Click Fill Effects in the Page Color gallery to display the Fill Effects dialog box.

- Click the Texture tab (Fill Effects dialog box) to display the Texture sheet.

- Click the Recycled paper texture in the Texture gallery to select the texture (Figure 11–26).

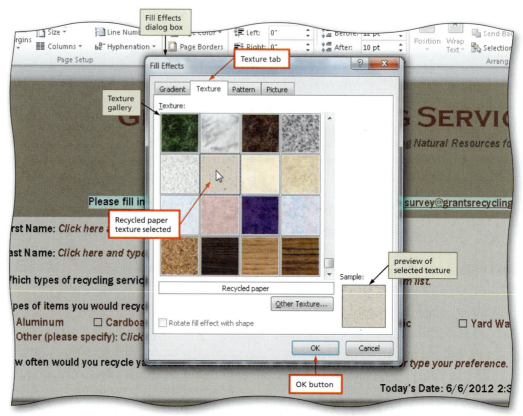

Figure 11–26

- Click the OK button to apply the selected texture as the page color in the document (Figure 11–27).

How would I remove a texture page color?

You would click the Page Color button (Page Layout tab | Page Background group) and then click No Color in the Page Color gallery.

Figure 11–27

To Change a Shape

This online form uses a variation of the standard rectangle shape. The following steps change a shape.

1

- Click the rectangle shape to select it.

- Display the Drawing Tools Format tab.

- Click the Edit Shape button (Drawing Tools Format tab | Insert Shapes group) to display the Edit Shape menu.

- Point to Change Shape on the Edit Shape menu to display the Change Shape gallery (Figure 11–28).

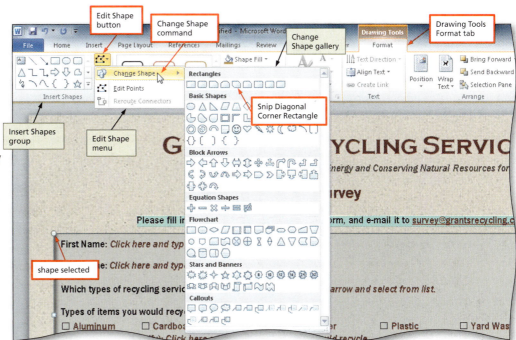

Figure 11–28

2

- Click Snip Diagonal Corner Rectangle in the Rectangles area in the Change Shape gallery to change the selected shape (Figure 11–29).

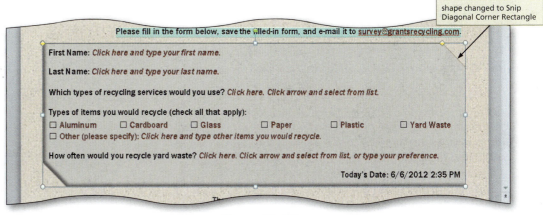

Figure 11–29

To Apply a Glow Shape Effect

The next step is to apply a glow effect to the rectangle shape. You can apply the same effects to shapes as to pictures. That is, you can apply shadows, reflections, glows, soft edges, bevels, and 3-D rotations to pictures and shapes. The following steps apply a shape effect.

1 With the rectangle shape selected, click the Shape Effects button (Drawing Tools Format tab | Shape Styles group) to display the Shape Effects menu.

2 Point to Glow on the Shape Effects menu to display the Glow gallery.

3 Point to Brown, 11 pt glow, Accent color 4 in the Glow Variations area (fourth glow in third row) to display a live preview of the selected glow effect applied to the selected shape in the document window (Figure 11–30).

4 Click Brown, 11 pt glow, Accent color 4 in the Glow gallery (fourth variation in third row) to apply the shape effect to the selected shape.

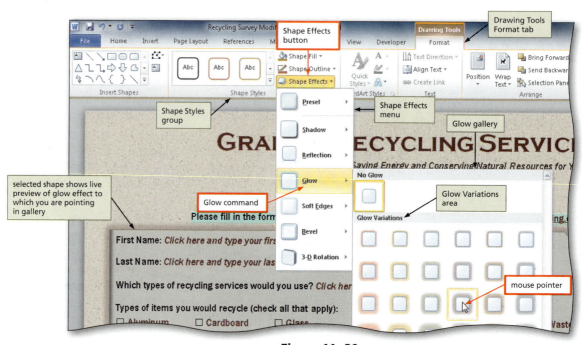

Figure 11–30

To Apply a Shadow Shape Effect

The rectangle in this online form has a shadow that is in the same color as the company name. The following steps apply a shadow effect and change its color.

1

• With the rectangle shape still selected, click the Shape Effects button (Drawing Tools Format tab | Shape Styles group) again to display the Shape Effects menu.

• Point to Shadow in the Shape Effects menu to display the Shadow gallery.

• Scroll to the Perspective area at the bottom of the gallery and then point to Perspective Diagonal Upper Right in the Shadow gallery to display a live preview of that shadow applied to the shape in the document (Figure 11–31).

🔎 **Experiment**

• Point to various shadows in the Shadow gallery and watch the shadow on the selected shape change.

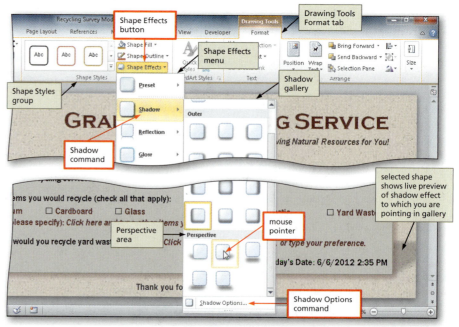

Figure 11–31

- Click Perspective Diagonal Upper Right in the Shadow gallery to apply the selected shadow to the selected shape.

- Click the Shape Effects button (Drawing Tools Format tab | Shape Styles group) again to display the Shape Effects menu.

- Point to Shadow in the Shape Effects menu to display the Shadow gallery.

- Click Shadow Options in the Shadow gallery to display the Format Shape dialog box.

- Click the Color button arrow (Format Shape dialog box) and then click Tan, Accent 1, Darker 50% (fifth color in sixth row) in the Color gallery to change the shadow color.

- Click the Transparency box down arrow as many times as necessary until the Transparency box displays 60% to change the amount of transparency in the shadow (Figure 11–32).

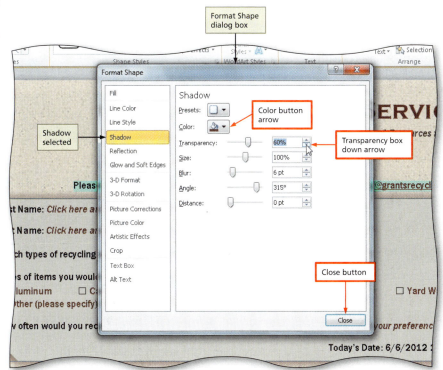

Figure 11–32

- Click the Close button to close the dialog box.

To Fill a Shape with a Picture

The rectangle in this online form contains a picture of the recycle symbol. The picture, called Recycle Symbol, is located on the Data Files for Students. See the inside back cover of this book for instructions on downloading the Data Files for Students, or contact your instructor for information about accessing the required files. The following steps fill a shape with a picture.

- With the rectangle shape still selected, click the Shape Fill button arrow (Drawing Tools Format tab | Shape Styles group) to display the Shape Fill gallery (Figure 11–33).

Q&A

My Shape Fill gallery did not display. Why not?

You clicked the Shape Fill button instead of the Shape Fill button arrow. Repeat Step 1.

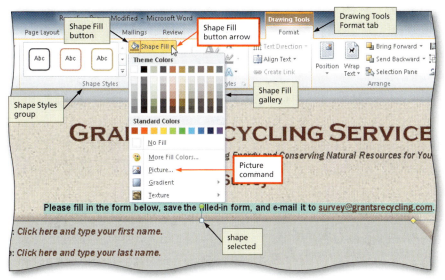

Figure 11–33

2

- Click Picture in the Shape Fill gallery to display the Insert Picture dialog box.

- Locate and then click the file called Recycle Symbol (Insert Picture dialog box) to select the file.

- Click the Insert button (Insert Picture dialog box) to fill the rectangle shape with the picture (Figure 11–34).

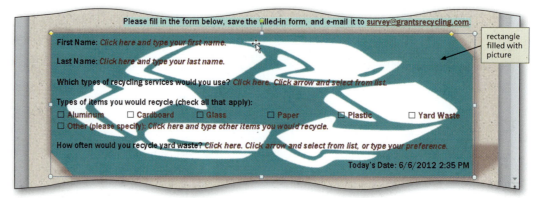

Figure 11–34

To Change the Color of a Picture

The text in the rectangle shape is difficult to read because the picture just inserted is too colorful. You can experiment with adjusting the brightness, contrast, and color of a picture so that the text is readable. In this project, the color is changed to the washout setting so that the text is easier to read. The following steps change the color of the picture to washout.

1 Display the Picture Tools Format tab.

2 With the rectangle shape still selected, click the Color button (Picture Tools Format tab | Adjust group) to display the Color gallery.

3 Point to Washout in the Color gallery (fourth color in first row) to display a live preview of the selected color applied to the selected picture (Figure 11–35).

4 Click Washout in the Color gallery to apply the selected color to the selected picture.

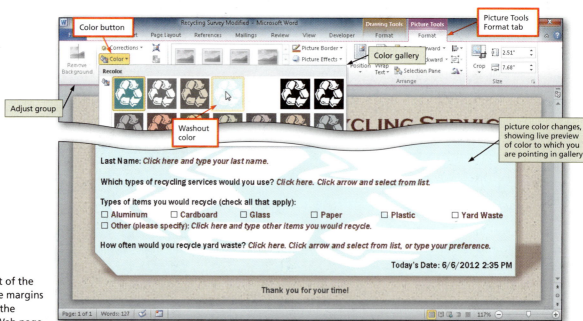

BTWs

For a complete list of the BTWs found in the margins of this book, visit the Word 2010 BTW Web page (scsite.com/wd2010/btw).

Figure 11–35

To Insert, Change Wrapping Style, and Resize a Picture

The top of the online form in this chapter contains a picture of a recycle bin. The picture, called Recycle Bin, is located on the Data Files for Students. See the inside back cover of this book for instructions on downloading the Data Files for Students, or contact your instructor for information about accessing the required files.

You will change the wrapping style of the inserted picture so that it can be positioned in front of the text. Because the graphic's original size is too large, you also will resize it. The following steps insert a picture, change its wrapping style, and resize it.

1 Position the insertion point in a location near where the picture will be inserted, in this case, near the top of the online form.

2 Display the Insert tab. Click the Insert Picture from File button (Insert tab | Illustrations group) to display the Insert Picture dialog box.

3 Locate and then click the file called Recycle Bin (Insert Picture dialog box) to select the file.

4 Click the Insert button to insert the picture at the location of the insertion point.

5 With the picture selected, click the Wrap Text button (Picture Tools Format tab | Arrange group) and then click In Front of Text so that the graphic can be positioned on top of text.

6 Change the value in the Shape Height box (Picture Tools Format tab | Size group) to 1.9" and the value in the Shape Width box (Picture Tools Format tab | Size group) to 2.85".

7 If necessary, scroll to display the online form in the document window (Figure 11–36).

BTW

Drawing Canvas
Some users prefer inserting graphics on a drawing canvas, which is a rectangular boundary between a shape and the rest of the document; it also is a container that helps you resize and arrange shapes on the page. To insert a drawing canvas, click the Shapes button (Insert tab | Illustrations group) and then click New Drawing Canvas. You can use the Drawing Tools Format tab to insert objects in the drawing canvas or format the appearance of the drawing canvas.

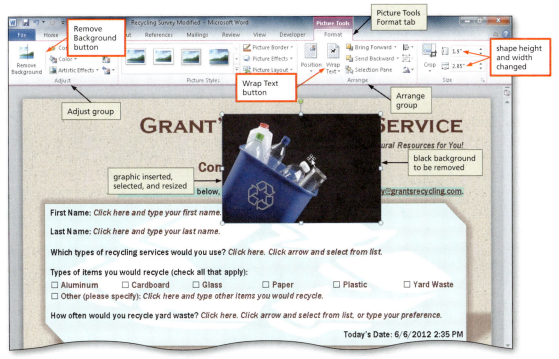

Figure 11–36

To Remove a Background

Notice in Figure 11–36 that the picture of the recycle bin is surrounded by a large black background. In Word, you can remove a background from a picture. The steps on the next page remove a background.

1

● Click the Remove Background button (Picture Tools Format tab | Adjust group), shown in Figure 11–36 on the previous page, to display the Background Removal tab and show the proposed area to be deleted in purple (Figure 11–37).

Q&A

What is the Background Removal tab?

You can draw around areas to keep or areas to remove by clicking the respective buttons on the Background Removal tab. If you mistakenly mark too much, use the Delete Mark button. You also can drag the proposed rectangle to adjust the proposed removal area. When finished marking, click the Close Background Removal and Keep Changes button, or to start over, click the Close Background Removal and Discard Changes button.

Figure 11–37

2

● Drag the proposed marking lines to the left and bottom edges of the picture, as shown in Figure 11–38, so that the entire recycle bin shows and the entire black background is shaded purple. If necessary, drag the top line up to include the tops of all containers.

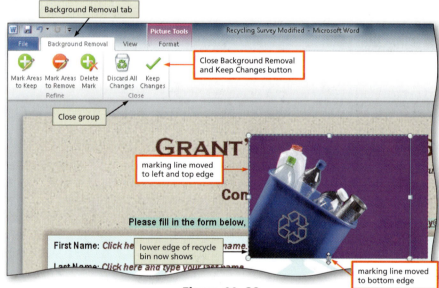

Figure 11–38

3

● Click the Close Background Removal and Keep Changes button (Background Removal tab | Close group) to remove the area shaded purple and close the Background Removal tab (Figure 11–39).

Figure 11–39

To Apply an Artistic Effect

The next step is to apply an artistic effect to the picture. Word provides several different artistic effects, such as blur, line drawing, and paint brush, that alter the appearance of a picture. The following steps apply an artistic effect.

 • Click the Artistic Effects button (Picture Tools Format tab | Adjust group) to display the Artistic Effects gallery.

• Point to Paint Brush (third effect in second row) in the Artistic Effects gallery to display a live preview of the effect applied to the selected picture in the document window (Figure 11–40).

2 • Click Paint Brush in the Artistic Effects gallery to apply the selected effect to the selected picture.

Figure 11–40

To Change the Color of a Graphic and Move the Graphic

In this project, the color of the recycle bin is changed to match the colors in the company name. Then, the recycle bin graphic is to be positioned on the left edge of the form with the bottom edge aligned with the top of the data entry area. The following steps change the color of the picture and then move it.

1 With the picture still selected, click the Color button (Picture Tools Format tab | Adjust group) to display the Color gallery.

2 Click Tan, Accent color 1 Light in the Color gallery (second color in last row) to apply the selected color to the selected picture.

3 Position the mouse pointer in the graphic so that the mouse pointer has a four-headed arrow attached to it and then drag the graphic to the location shown in Figure 11–41 on the next page.

To Draw a Text Box

The recycle bin image in this form has a text box with the word, Recycle!, positioned on top of the bin. The first step in creating the text box is to draw its perimeter. You draw a text box using the same procedure as you do to draw a shape. The steps on the next page draw a text box.

- Position the insertion point somewhere in the top of the online form.

- Display the Insert tab.

- Click the Text Box button (Insert tab | Text group) to display the Text Box gallery (Figure 11–41).

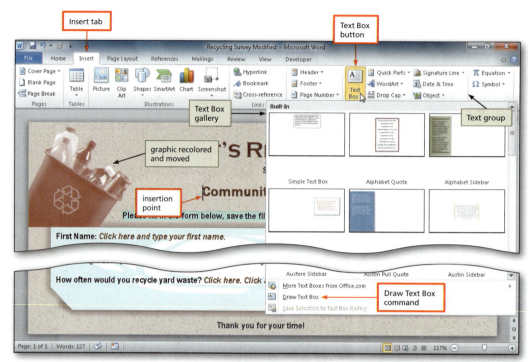

Figure 11–41

- Click Draw Text Box in the Text Box gallery, which removes the gallery and changes the mouse pointer to the shape of a crosshair.

- Drag the mouse to the right and downward to form the boundaries of the text box, as shown in Figure 11–42.

Figure 11–42

- Release the mouse button so that Word draws the text box according to your drawing in the document window.

- Verify your shape is the same approximate height and width as the one in this project by clicking the Size button (Drawing Tools Format tab | Size group) and then, if necessary, changing the values in the Shape Height and Shape Width boxes to 0.4" and 0.8", respectively (Figure 11–43). When finished, click the Size button again to remove the Shape Height and Shape Width boxes.

Figure 11–43

To Add Text to a Text Box and Format the Text

The next step is to add the word, Recycle!, centered in the text box using a text effect. You add text to a text box using the same procedure you do when adding text to a shape. The following steps add text to a text box.

1 Display the Home tab. With the text box selected, click the Center button (Home tab | Paragraph group) so that the text you enter is centered in the text box.

2 With the text box selected, click the Text Effects button (Home tab | Font group) and then click Gradient Fill – Tan, Accent 1 (fourth effect in third row) in the Text Effects gallery to specify the format for the text in the text box.

3 If your insertion point is not positioned in the text box (shape), right-click the shape to display a shortcut menu and the Mini toolbar and then click Edit Text on the shortcut menu to place an insertion point centered in the text box.

4 Type `Recycle!` as the text for the text box (shown in Figure 11–44). (If necessary, adjust the width of the text box to fit the text.)

To Change Text Direction in a Text Box

The next step is to change the direction of the text in the text box from horizontal to vertical. The following steps change text direction in a text box.

1

- Display the Drawing Tools Format tab.

- With the shape still selected, click the Text Direction button (Drawing Tools Format tab | Text group) to display the Text Direction gallery (Figure 11–44).

Q&A What if my text box is no longer selected?

Click the text box to select it.

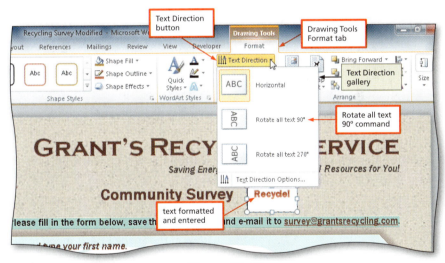

Figure 11–44

2

- Click 'Rotate all text 90°' in the Text Direction gallery to display the text in the text box vertically from top to bottom (Figure 11–45).

Q&A What happened to the text?

With the text displaying vertically, it does not fit in the current text box height and width. Thus, the next step is to resize the text box.

Figure 11–45

3

- Click the Size button (Drawing Tools Format tab | Size group) and then change the values in the Shape Height and Shape Width boxes to 0.8" and 0.4", respectively (Figure 11–46). When finished, click the Size button again to remove the Shape Height and Shape Width boxes.

Q&A

What if my text does not show in the text box?

Click the Align Text button (Drawing Tools Format tab | Text group) and then change the alignment of the text in the text box to the alignment that causes the text to be displayed correctly in the text box.

Figure 11–46

Other Ways

1. Click Format Shape Dialog Box Launcher (Drawing Tools Format tab | Shape Styles group), click Text Box button in left pane (Format Shape dialog box), select desired direction, click Close button

2. Right-click text box, click Format Shape on shortcut menu, click Text Box button in left pane (Format Shape dialog box), select desired direction, click Close button

To Apply a Shadow Shape Effect to a Text Box

The text box in this online form has an inside shadow that is in the same color as the company name. The following steps apply a shadow effect and change its color.

1 With the text box shape still selected, click the Shape Effects button (Drawing Tools Format tab | Shape Styles group) to display the Shape Effects menu.

2 Point to Shadow in the Shape Effects menu to display the Shadow gallery and then click Inside Left in the Shadow gallery to apply the selected shadow to the selected shape.

3 Click the Shape Effects button (Drawing Tools Format tab | Shape Styles group) again to display the Shape Effects menu.

4 Point to Shadow in the Shape Effects menu to display the Shadow gallery and then click Shadow Options in the Shadow gallery to display the Format Shape dialog box.

5 Click the Color button arrow (Format Shape dialog box) and then click Tan, Accent 1, Darker 50% (fifth color in sixth row) in the Color gallery to change the shadow color.

6 Click the Transparency box up or down arrow as many times as necessary until the Transparency box displays 60% to change the amount of transparency in the shadow (shown in Figure 11–47).

7 Click the Close button to close the dialog box.

To Change a Shape Outline of a Text Box

The text box in this form has no outline. You change an outline on a text box (shape) using the same procedure as you do with a picture. The next steps remove the shape outline on the text box.

1

- With the text box still selected, click the Shape Outline button arrow in the Shape Styles gallery (Drawing Tools Format tab | Shape Styles group) to display the Shape Outline gallery (Figure 11–47).

Q&A

The Shape Outline gallery did not display. Why not?

You clicked the Shape Outline button instead of the Shape Outline button arrow. Repeat Step 1.

 Experiment

- Point to various colors in the Shape Outline gallery and watch the color of the outline on the text box change in the document.

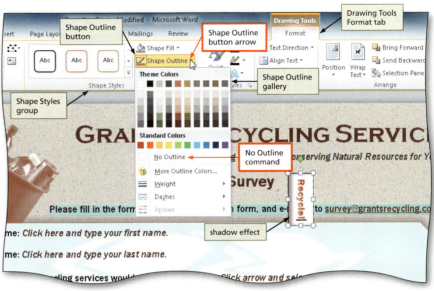

Figure 11–47

2

- Click No Outline in the Shape Outline gallery to remove the outline from the selected shape.

Other Ways		
1. Click Format Shape Dialog Box Launcher (Drawing Tools Format tab | Shape Styles group), click Line Color button in left pane (Format Shape dialog box),	select desired option in right pane, click Close button 2. Right-click shape, click Format Shape on shortcut menu, click Line Color	button in left pane (Format Shape dialog box), select desired option in right pane, click Close button

To Apply a 3-D Effect to a Text Box

Word provides 3-D effects for shapes (such as text boxes) that are similar to those it provides for pictures. In this form, the text box is rotated using a 3-D rotation effect. The following steps apply a 3-D rotation effect to a text box.

1

- With the text box selected, click the Shape Effects button (Drawing Tools Format tab | Shape Styles group) to display the Shape Effects gallery.

- Point to 3-D Rotation in the Shape Effects gallery to display the 3-D Rotation gallery.

- Point to Isometric Top Up in the Parallel area (third rotation in first row) to display a live preview of the selected 3-D effect applied to the text box in the document window (Figure 11–48).

 Experiment

- Point to various 3-D rotation effects in the 3-D Rotation gallery and watch the text box change in the document window.

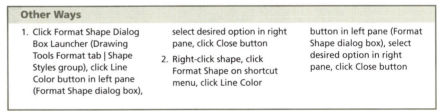

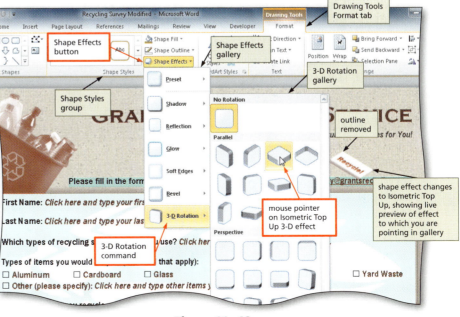

Figure 11–48

- Click Isometric Top Up in the 3-D Rotation gallery to apply the selected 3-D effect.

Other Ways		
1. Right-click shape, click Format Shape on shortcut menu, click 3-D Rotation in left pane (Format Shape dialog box), select	desired options, click Close button 2. Click Format Shape Dialog Box Launcher (Drawing Tools Format tab | Shape	Styles group), click 3-D Rotation in left pane (Format Shape dialog box), select desired options, click Close button

To Move the Graphic

In this project, the text box is to be positioned on top of the recycle bin graphic. The following step moves the text box.

Position the mouse pointer in the selected graphic so that the mouse pointer has a four-headed arrow attached to it and then drag the graphic to the location shown in Figure 11–49. (You may need to drag the text box a couple of times to position it as shown in the figure.)

Figure 11–49

To Group Objects

When you have multiple graphics, such as pictures, clip art, and shapes, positioned on a page, you can group them so that they are a single graphic instead of separate graphics. Grouping the graphics makes it easier to move them because they all move together as a single graphic. The following steps group the recycle bin graphic and the text box together.

- With the text box selected, hold down the CTRL key while clicking the recycle bin picture (that is, CTRL+click), so that both graphics are selected at the same time.

Q&A

What if I had more than two graphics that I wanted to group?

For each subsequent graphic to select, CTRL+click the graphic, which enables you to select multiple objects at the same time.

- Click the Group button (Drawing Tools Format tab | Arrange group) to display the Group menu (Figure 11–50).

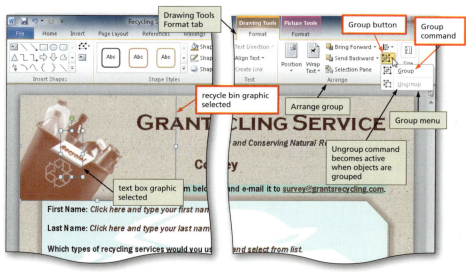

Figure 11–50

2

- Click Group on the Group menu to group the selected objects into a single selected object (Figure 11–51).

Q&A

What if I wanted to ungroup grouped objects?

Select the object to ungroup, click the Group button (Drawing Tools Format tab | Arrange group), and then click Ungroup on the Group menu.

3

- Click outside of the graphic to position the insertion point in the document and deselect the graphic.

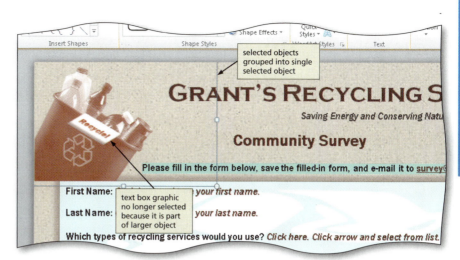

Figure 11–51

To Save an Existing Template with the Same File Name

You have made several modifications to the template since you last saved it. Thus, you should save it again. The following step saves the template again.

1 Click the Save button on the Quick Access Toolbar to overwrite the previously saved file.

Break Point: If you wish to take a break, this is a good place to do so. You can quit Word now. To resume at a later time, start Word, open the file called Recycling Survey Modified, and continue following the steps from this location forward.

Using a Macro to Automate a Task

A **macro** consists of a series of Word commands or instructions that are grouped together as a single command. This single command is a convenient way to automate a difficult or lengthy task. Macros often are used to simplify formatting or editing activities, to combine multiple commands into a single command, or to select an option in a dialog box using a shortcut key.

To create a macro, you can use the macro recorder or the Visual Basic Editor. With the macro recorder, Word generates the VBA instructions associated with the macro automatically as you perform actions in Word. If you wanted to write the VBA instructions yourself, you would use the Visual Basic Editor. This chapter uses the macro recorder to create a macro and the Visual Basic Editor to modify it.

The **macro recorder** creates a macro based on a series of actions you perform while the macro recorder is recording. The macro recorder is similar to a video camera: after you start the macro recorder, it records all actions you perform while working in a document and stops recording when you stop the macro recorder. To record a macro, you follow this sequence of steps:

1. Start the macro recorder and specify options about the macro.
2. Execute the actions you want recorded.
3. Stop the macro recorder.

After you record a macro, you can execute the macro, or play it, any time you want to perform the same set of actions.

BTW

Naming Macros
If you give a new macro the same name as an existing built-in command in Microsoft Word, the new macro actions will replace the existing actions. Thus, you should be careful not to name a macro FileSave (see Table 11–1 on page WD 711) or after any Word commands. To view a list of built-in macros in Word, click the View Macros button (View tab | Macros group) to display the Macros dialog box. Click the Macros in box arrow and then click Word commands.

To Record a Macro and Assign It a Shortcut Key

Assume you find that you are repeatedly hiding the formatting marks and rulers while designing the online form. To simplify this task, the macro in this project hides these screen elements. In Word, you can assign a shortcut key to a macro so that you can execute the macro by pressing the shortcut key instead of using a dialog box to execute it. The following steps record a macro that hides formatting marks and the rulers; the macro is assigned the shortcut key, ALT+H.

1
- Display formatting marks and the rulers on the screen.
- Display the Developer tab.
- Click the Record Macro button (Developer tab | Code group) to display the Record Macro dialog box.
- Type **HideScreenElements** in the Macro name text box (Record Macro dialog box).

Q&A Do I have to name a macro?

If you do not enter a name for the macro, Word assigns a default name. Macro names can be up to 255 characters in length and can contain only numbers, letters, and the underscore character. A macro name cannot contain spaces or other punctuation.

- Click the 'Store macro in' box arrow and then click Documents Based On Recycling Survey Modified.

Q&A What is the difference between storing a macro with the document template versus the Normal template?

Macros saved in the Normal template are available to all future documents; macros saved with the document template are available only with a document based on the template.

- In the Description text box, type this sentence (Figure 11–52): **Hide formatting marks and the rulers.**

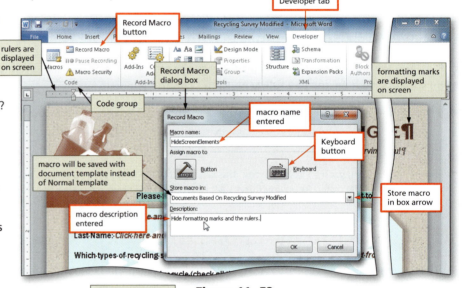

Figure 11–52

2
- Click the Keyboard button to display the Customize Keyboard dialog box.

- Press ALT+H to display the characters ALT+H in the 'Press new shortcut key' text box (Customize Keyboard dialog box) (Figure 11–53).

Q&A Can I type the letters in the shortcut key (ALT+H) in the text box instead of pressing them?

No. Although typing the letters places them in the text box, the shortcut key is valid only if you press the shortcut key combination itself.

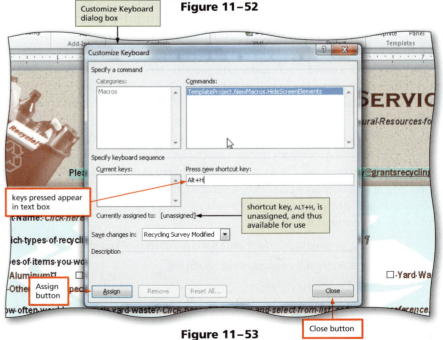

Figure 11–53

3

- Click the Assign button (Customize Keyboard dialog box) to assign the shortcut key, ALT+H, to the macro named, HideScreenElements.

- Click the Close button, which closes the dialog box, places a Macro Recording button on the status bar, and starts the macro recorder (Figure 11–54).

Q&A How do I record the macro?

While the macro recorder is running, any action you perform in Word will be part of the macro — until you stop or pause the macro.

Q&A What is the purpose of the Pause Recording button (Developer tab | Code group)?

If, while recording a macro, you want to perform some actions that should not be part of the macro, click the Pause Recording button to suspend the macro recorder. The Pause Recording button changes to a Resume Recorder button that you click when you want to continue recording.

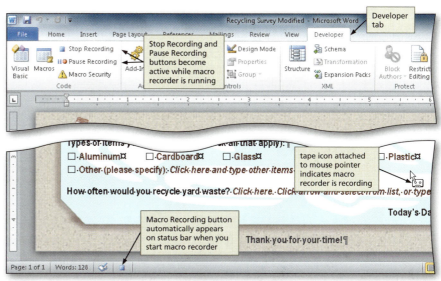

Figure 11–54

4

- Display the Home tab.

Q&A What happened to the tape icon?

While recording a macro, the tape icon might disappear from the mouse pointer when the mouse pointer is in a menu, on the Ribbon, or in a dialog box.

- Click the Show/Hide ¶ button (Home tab | Paragraph group) to hide formatting marks.

- Click the View Ruler button at the top of the vertical scroll bar to hide the rulers (Figure 11–55).

Figure 11–55

5

- Click the Macro Recording button on the status bar to turn off the macro recorder, that is, to stop recording actions you perform in Word.

Q&A What if I made a mistake while recording the macro?

Delete the macro and record it again. To delete a macro, click the View Macros button (Developer tab | Code group), select the macro name in the list (Macros dialog box), click the Delete button, and then click the Yes button.

Q&A What if I wanted to assign the macro to a button instead of a shortcut key?

You would click the Button button in the Record Macro dialog box (Figure 11–52) and then follow Steps 4 through 6 on pages WD 709 and WD 710.

Other Ways

1. Click View Macros button arrow (View tab | Macros group), click Record Macros on Macros menu

2. Press ALT+F8

BTW

Running Macros
You can run a macro by clicking the View Macros button (Developer tab | Code group or View tab | Macros group) or by pressing ALT+F8 to display the Macros dialog box, selecting the macro name in the list, and then clicking the Run button (Macros dialog box).

To Run a Macro

The next step is to execute, or run, the macro to ensure that it works. Recall that this macro hides formatting marks and the rulers, which means you must be sure the formatting marks and rulers are displayed on the screen before running the macro. Because you created a shortcut key for the macro in this project, the following steps show formatting marks and the rulers so that you can run the HideScreenElements macro using the shortcut key, ALT+H.

1 Display formatting marks on the screen.

2 Display rulers on the screen.

3 Press ALT+H, which causes Word to perform the instructions stored in the HideScreenElements macro, that is, to hide formatting marks and rulers.

To Add a Command and a Macro as Buttons on the Quick Access Toolbar

Word allows you to add buttons to and delete buttons from the Quick Access Toolbar. You also can assign a command, such as a macro, to a button on the Quick Access Toolbar. This chapter shows how to add an existing command to the Quick Access Toolbar and also shows how to create a button for the HideScreenElements macro so that instead of pressing the shortcut keys, you can click the button to hide formatting marks and the rulers.

The following steps add the New command to the Quick Access Toolbar and assign the HideScreenElements macro to a new button on the Quick Access Toolbar.

1
• Click the Customize Quick Access Toolbar button on the Quick Access Toolbar to display the Customize Quick Access Toolbar menu (Figure 11–56).

Q&A
What happens if I click the commands listed on the Customize Quick Access Toolbar menu?

If the command does not have a check mark beside it and you click it, Word places the button associated with the command on the Quick Access Toolbar. If the command has a check mark beside it and you click (deselect) it, Word removes the command from the Quick Access Toolbar.

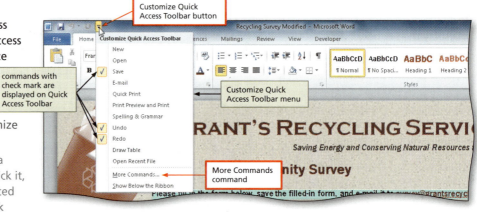

Figure 11–56

2
• Click More Commands on the Customize Quick Access Toolbar menu to display the Word Options dialog box with Quick Access Toolbar selected in the left pane.

• Scroll through the list of popular commands (Word Options dialog box) and then click New to select the command.

• Click the Add button to add the selected command (New, in this case) to the Customize Quick Access Toolbar list (Figure 11–57).

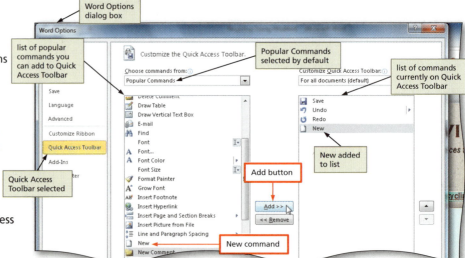

Figure 11–57

• Click the 'Choose commands from' box arrow to display a list of categories of commands (Figure 11–58).

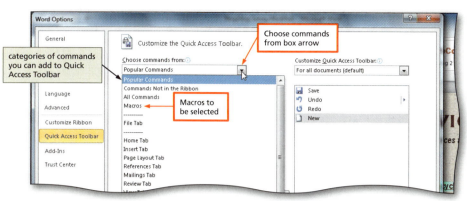

Figure 11–58

• Click Macros in the 'Choose commands from' list to display the macro in this document.

• If necessary, click the macro to select it.

• Click the Add button (Word Options dialog box) to display the selected macro in the Customize Quick Access Toolbar list.

• Click the Modify button to display the Modify Button dialog box.

• Change the name in the Display name text box to **Hide Screen Elements** (Modify Button dialog box), which will be the text that appears in the ScreenTip for the button.

• In the list of symbols, click the screen icon as the new face for the button (Figure 11–59).

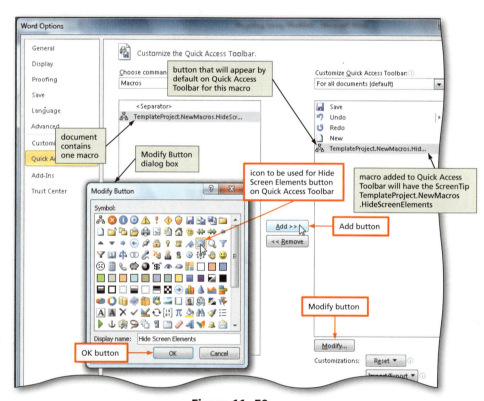

Figure 11–59

5

• Click the OK button (Modify Button dialog box) to change the button characteristics in the Customize Quick Access Toolbar list (Figure 11–60).

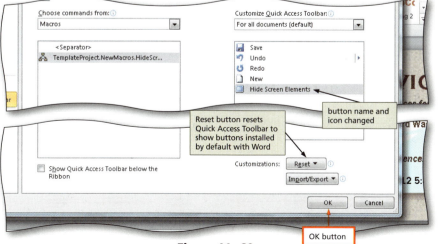

Figure 11–60

6
- Click the OK button (Word Options dialog box) to add the buttons to the Quick Access Toolbar (Figure 11–61).

Figure 11–61

Other Ways

1. Right-click Quick Access Toolbar, click Customize Quick Access Toolbar on shortcut menu

To Use the New Buttons on the Quick Access Toolbar

The next step is to test the new buttons on the Quick Access Toolbar, that is, the New button and the Hide Screen Elements button, which will execute, or run, the macro that hides formatting marks and the rulers. The following steps use buttons on the Quick Access Toolbar.

1 Click the New button on the Quick Access Toolbar to display a new blank document window. Close the new blank document window.

2 Display formatting marks on the screen.

3 Display rulers on the screen.

4 Click the Hide Screen Elements button on the Quick Access Toolbar, which causes Word to perform the instructions stored in the HideScreenElements macro, that is, to hide formatting marks and the rulers.

To Delete Buttons from the Quick Access Toolbar

If you no longer plan to use a button on the Quick Access Toolbar, you can delete it. The following steps delete the New button and the Hide Screen Elements button from the Quick Access Toolbar.

- Right-click the button to be deleted from the Quick Access Toolbar, in this case the Hide Screen Elements button, to display a shortcut menu (Figure 11–62).

2
- Click Remove from Quick Access Toolbar on the shortcut menu to remove the button from the Quick Access Toolbar.

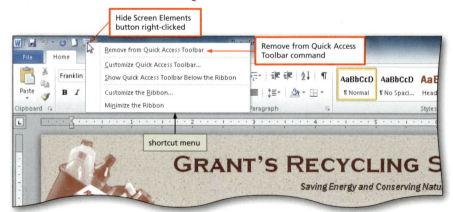

Figure 11–62

- Repeat Steps 1 and 2 for the New button on the Quick Access Toolbar.

TO RENAME A MACRO

If you wanted to rename a macro, you would perform the following steps.

1. Click the View Macros button (Developer tab | Code group) to display the Macros dialog box.

2. Click the Organizer button (Macros dialog box) to display the Organizer dialog box.

3. Click the macro to rename (Organizer dialog box) and then click the Rename button to display the Rename dialog box.

4. Enter the new macro name in the New name text box (Rename dialog box) and then click the OK button to rename the macro.

5. Close the Organizer dialog box.

TO DELETE A MACRO

If you wanted to delete a macro, you would perform the following steps.

1. Click the View Macros button (Developer tab | Code group) to display the Macros dialog box.

2. Click the macro to delete and then click the Delete button (Macros dialog box) to display a dialog box asking if you are sure you want to delete the macro. Click the Yes button in the dialog box.

3. Close the Macros dialog box.

Automatic Macros

The previous section showed how to create a macro, assign it a unique name (HideScreenElements) and a shortcut key, and then add a button that executes the macro on the Quick Access Toolbar. This section creates an **automatic macro**, which is a macro that executes automatically when a certain event occurs. Word has five prenamed automatic macros. Table 11–1 lists the name and function of these automatic macros.

Table 11–1 Automatic Macros	
Macro Name	**Event That Causes Macro to Run**
AutoClose	Closing a document that contains the macro
AutoExec	Starting Word
AutoExit	Quitting Word
AutoNew	Creating a new document based on a template that contains the macro
AutoOpen	Opening a document that contains the macro

BTW

Automatic Macros
A document can contain only one AutoClose macro, one AutoNew macro, and one AutoOpen macro. The AutoExec and AutoExit macros, however, are not stored with the document; instead, they must be stored in the Normal template. Thus, only one AutoExec macro and only one AutoExit macro can exist for all Word documents.

The automatic macro you choose depends on when you want certain actions to occur. In this chapter, when a user creates a new Word document that is based on the Recycling Survey template, you want to be sure that the zoom is set to page width. Thus, the AutoNew automatic macro is used in this online form.

To Create an Automatic Macro

The online form in this chapter is displayed properly when the zoom is set to page width. Thus, you will record the steps to zoom to page width in the AutoNew macro. The steps on the next page create an AutoNew macro, using the macro recorder.

- Display the Developer tab.

- Click the Record Macro button (Developer tab | Code group) to display the Record Macro dialog box.

- Type **AutoNew** in the Macro name text box (Record Macro dialog box).

- Click the 'Store macro in' box arrow and then click Documents Based On Recycling Survey Modified.

- In the Description text box, type this sentence (Figure 11–63): **Specifies how the form initially is displayed.**

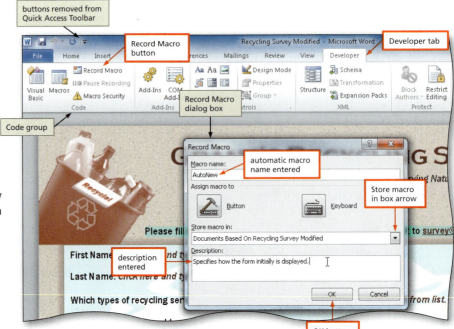

Figure 11–63

- Click the OK button to close the Record Macro dialog box and start the macro recorder.

- Display the View tab.

- Click the Page Width button (View tab | Zoom group) to zoom page width (Figure 11–64).

❸

- Click the Macro Recording button on the status bar to turn off the macro recorder, that is, stop recording actions you perform in Word.

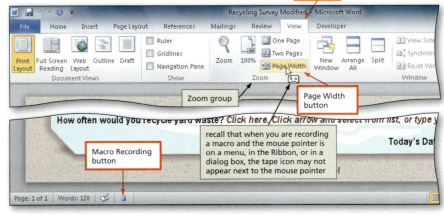

Figure 11–64

Q&A How do I test an automatic macro?

Activate the event that causes the macro to execute. For example, the AutoNew macro runs whenever you create a new Word document that is based on the template.

To Run the AutoNew Macro

The next step is to execute, or run, the AutoNew macro to ensure that it works. To run the AutoNew macro, you need to create a new Word document that is based on the Recycling Survey Modified template. This macro contains instructions to zoom page width. To verify that the macro works as intended, you will change the zoom to 100% before testing the macro. The following steps run a macro.

❶ Use the Zoom Out button on the status bar to change the zoom to 100%.

❷ Save the template with the same name, Recycling Survey Modified.

❸ Click the Windows Explorer button on the taskbar to open the Windows Explorer window.

4 Locate and then double-click the file named Recycling Survey Modified to display a new document window that is based on the contents of the Recycling Survey Modified template, which should be zoomed to page width as shown in Figure 11–1a on page WD 675. (If Word displays a dialog box about disabling macros, click its OK button. If the Message Bar displays a security warning, click the Enable Content button.)

5 Close the new document that displays the form in the Word window. Click the Don't Save button when Word asks if you want to save the changes to the new document.

6 Close the Windows Explorer window.

7 Change the zoom back to page width.

To Edit a Macro's VBA Code

In addition to zooming page width when the online form is displayed in a new document window, you would like to be sure that the Developer tab is hidden. As mentioned earlier, a macro consists of VBA instructions. To edit a recorded macro, you use the Visual Basic Editor.

The following steps use the Visual Basic Editor to add VBA instructions to the AutoNew macro. These steps are designed to show the basic composition of a VBA procedure and illustrate the power of VBA code statements.

1

• Display the Developer tab.

• Click the View Macros button (Developer tab | Code group) to display the Macros dialog box.

• If necessary, select the macro to be edited, in this case, AutoNew (Figure 11–65).

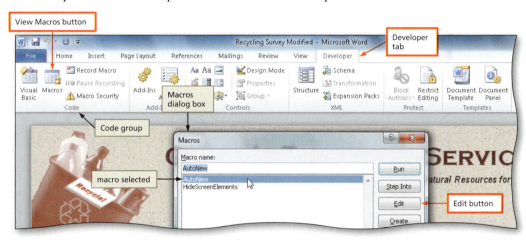

Figure 11–65

2

• Click the Edit button (Macros dialog box) to start the Visual Basic Editor and display the VBA code for the AutoNew macro in the Code window — your screen may appear differently depending on previous Visual Basic Editor settings (Figure 11–66).

Q&A What if the Code window does not appear in the Visual Basic Editor?

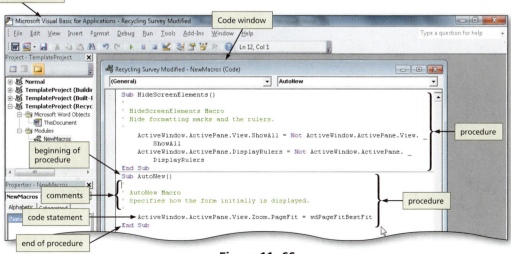

Figure 11–66

In the Visual Basic Editor, click View on the menu bar and then click Code. If it still does not appear and you are in a network environment, this feature may be disabled for some users.

Q&A What are the lines of text (instructions) in the Code window?

The named set of instructions associated with a macro is called a **procedure**. It is this set of instructions — beginning with the words Sub and continuing sequentially to the line with the words End Sub — that executes when you run the macro. The instructions within a procedure are called **code statements**.

 3

- Position the insertion point at the end of the second-to-last line in the AutoNew macro and then press the ENTER key to insert a blank line for a new code statement.

- On a single line, type `Options .ShowDevTools = False` and then press the ENTER key, which enters the VBA code statement that hides the Developer tab (Figure 11–67).

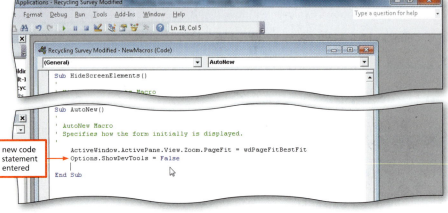

Figure 11–67

Q&A What are the lists that appear in the Visual Basic Editor as I enter code statements?

The lists present valid statement elements to assist you with entering code statements. Because they are beyond the scope of this chapter, ignore them.

4

- Click the Close button on the right edge of the Microsoft Visual Basic window title bar.

To Run the AutoNew Macro

The next step is to execute, or run, the AutoNew macro again to ensure that it works. To be sure the macro works as intended, ensure the Developer tab is displayed on the Ribbon. The AutoNew macro should hide the Developer tab. The following steps run the automatic macro.

1 If necessary, display the Developer tab.

2 Save the template with the same file name, Recycling Survey Modified.

3 Click the Windows Explorer button on the taskbar to open the Windows Explorer window.

4 Locate and then double-click the file named Recycling Survey Modified to display a new document window that is based on the contents of the Recycling Survey Modified template, which should be zoomed to page width and display no Developer tab. (If Word displays a dialog box about disabling macros, click its OK button. If the Message Bar displays a security warning, click the Enable Content button.)

5 Close the new document that displays the form in the Word window. Click the Don't Save button when Word asks if you want to save the changes to the new document.

6 Close the Windows Explorer window.

BTW

VBA
VBA includes many more statements than those presented in this chapter. You may need a background in computer programming if you plan to write VBA code instructions in macros you develop and if the VBA code instructions are beyond those instructions presented in this chapter.

VBA

As shown in the steps on pages WD 713 and WD 714, a VBA procedure begins with a Sub statement and ends with an End Sub statement. The Sub statement is followed by the name of the procedure, which is the macro name (AutoNew). The parentheses following the macro name in the Sub statement are required. They indicate that arguments can be passed from one procedure to another. Passing arguments is beyond the scope of this chapter, but the parentheses still are required. The End Sub statement signifies the end of the procedure and returns control to Word.

Comments often are added to a procedure to help you remember the purpose of the macro and its code statements at a later date. Comments begin with an apostrophe (') and appear in green in the Code window. The macro recorder, for example, placed four comment lines below the Sub statement. These comments display the name of the macro and its description, as entered in the Record Macro dialog box. Comments have no effect on the execution of a procedure; they simply provide information about the procedure, such as its name and description, to the developer of the macro.

For readability, code statement lines are indented four spaces. Table 11–2 explains the function of each element of a code statement.

Table 11–2 Elements of a Code Statement

Code Statements

Element	Definition	Examples
Keyword	Recognized by Visual Basic as part of its programming language. Keywords appear in blue in the Code window.	Sub End Sub
Variable	An item whose value can be modified during program execution.	ActiveWindow.ActivePane.View.Zoom.PageFit
Constant	An item whose value remains unchanged during program execution.	False
Operator	A symbol that indicates a specific action.	=

To Protect a Form Using the Backstage View

You now are finished enhancing the online form and adding macros to it. Because the last macro hid the Developer tab on the Ribbon, you will use the Backstage view to protect the form. The following steps protect the online form so that users are restricted to entering data only in content controls using the Backstage view.

1. Open the Backstage view and then, if necessary, display the Info gallery.

2. Click the Protect Document button to display the Protect Document menu.

3. Click Restrict Editing on the Protect Document menu to display the Restrict Formatting and Editing task pane.

4. In the Editing restrictions area, if necessary, place a check mark in the 'Allow only this type of editing in the document' check box, click its box arrow, and then select 'Filling in forms' in the list.

5. Click the Yes, Start Enforcing Protection button and then click the OK button (Start Enforcing Protection dialog box) to protect the document without a password.

6. Close the Restrict Formatting and Editing task pane.

To Save an Existing Template with the Same File Name

You have made several modifications to the template since you last saved it. Thus, you should save it again. The following step saves the template again.

1. Click the Save button on the Quick Access Toolbar to overwrite the previously saved file.

BTW
Set Exceptions to Editing Restrictions
You can use the Restrict Formatting and Editing task pane to allow editing in just certain areas of the document, a procedure called adding users excepted from restrictions. To do this, place a check mark in the 'Allow only this type of editing in the document' check box and then change the associated text box to No changes (Read only), which instructs Word to prevent any editing to the document. Next, select the placeholder text for which you want to except users from restrictions and place a check mark in the Everyone check box in the Exceptions (optional) area to instruct Word that the selected item can be edited — the rest of the form will be read only.

BTW

Certification
The Microsoft Office Specialist (MOS) program provides an opportunity for you to obtain a valuable industry credential — proof that you have the Word 2010 skills required by employers. For more information, visit the Word 2010 Certification Web page (scsite.com/wd2010/cert).

Adding a Digital Signature to a Document

Some users attach a **digital signature** to a document to verify its authenticity. A digital signature is an electronic, encrypted, and secure stamp of authentication on a document. This signature confirms that the file originated from the signer (file creator) and that it has not been altered.

A digital signature references a digital certificate. A **digital certificate** is an attachment to a file, macro project, or e-mail message that vouches for its authenticity, provides secure encryption, or supplies a verifiable signature. Many users who receive online forms enable the macros based on whether they are digitally signed by a developer on the user's list of trusted sources.

You can obtain a digital certificate from a commercial certification authority or from your network administrator, or you can create a digital certificate yourself. A digital certificate you create yourself is not issued by a formal certification authority. Documents using such a certificate are referred to as self-signed documents. Certificates you create yourself are considered unauthenticated and still will generate a warning when opened at certain security levels. Many users, however, consider self-signed documents safer to open than those with no certificates at all.

Once a digital signature is added, the document becomes a read-only document, which means that modifications cannot be made to it. Thus, you should create a digital signature only when the document is final. In Word, you can add two types of digital signatures to a document: (1) an invisible digital signature or (2) a signature line.

To Add an Invisible Digital Signature to a Document

An invisible digital signature does not appear as a tangible signature in the document. If the status bar displays a Signatures button, the document has an invisible digital signature. The following steps add an invisible digital signature to a document.

1

- Open the Backstage view and then, if necessary, display the Info gallery.

- Click the Protect Document button to display the Protect Document menu (Figure 11–68).

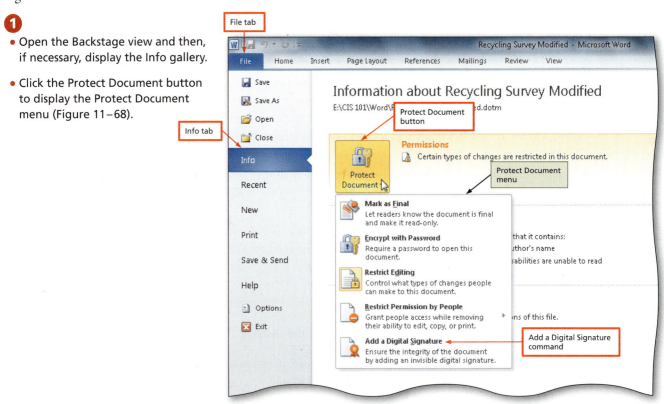

Figure 11–68

2

- Click Add a Digital Signature on the Protect Document menu to display the Sign dialog box.

- If a dialog box about signature services appears, click its OK button.

What if a dialog box appears indicating I need a digital ID?

If necessary, select the 'Get your own digital ID' option button, click the OK button, and then follow the on-screen instructions.

- In the 'Purpose for signing this document' text box (Sign dialog box), type **Verify its authenticity.** (Figure 11–69).

Figure 11–69

3

- Click the Sign button to add the digital signature, show the Signatures button on the status bar, and display Marked as Final on a Message Bar.

- If a dialog box appears asking if you want to use the certificate, click its Yes button.

- If a dialog box appears indicating the signature has been saved successfully, click its OK button.

- Click the File tab to close the Backstage view (Figure 11–70).

Figure 11–70

How can I view the digital signatures in a document?

Click the Signatures button on the status bar or open the Backstage view, display the Info tab, and then click the View Signatures button to display the Signatures task pane.

4

- Click the Edit Anyway button on the Message Bar to remove the digital signature from the template. When Word displays a dialog box about removing the signatures, click the Yes button. If Word displays another dialog box confirming this action, click its OK button.

TO ADD A SIGNATURE LINE TO A DOCUMENT

A digital signature line, which resembles a printed signature placeholder, allows a recipient of the electronic file to type a signature, include an image of his or her signature, or write a signature using the ink feature on a Tablet PC. Digital signature lines enable organizations to use paperless methods of obtaining signatures on official documents such as contracts. If you wanted to add a digital signature line to a document, you would perform the following steps.

1. Position the insertion point at the location for the digital signature.

2. Display the Insert tab. Click the Signature Line button (Insert tab | Text group) to display the Signature Setup dialog box. (If a dialog box appears about signature services, click its OK button.)

3. Type the name of the person who should sign the document.

4. If available, type the signer's e-mail address.

5. Place a checkmark in the 'Allow the signer to add comments in the Sign dialog' check box so that the recipient can send a response back to you.

6. Click the OK button (Signature Setup dialog box) to insert a signature line in the document at the location of the insertion point.

Q&A How does a recipient insert his or her digital signature?

When the recipient opens the document, a Message Bar appears that contains a View Signatures button. The recipient can click the View Signatures button to display the Signatures task pane, click the requested signature box arrow, and then click Sign on the menu (or double-click the signature line in the document) to display a dialog box that the recipient then completes.

BTW

Quick Reference
For a table that lists how to complete the tasks covered in this book using the mouse, Ribbon, shortcut menu, and keyboard, see the Quick Reference Summary at the back of this book, or visit the Word 2010 Quick Reference Web page (scsite.com/wd2010/qr).

To Quit Word

The following steps quit Word and close the Windows Explorer window.

1 Quit Word.

2 If the Windows Explorer window is still open, close it.

Chapter Summary

In this chapter, you learned how to enhance the look of text and graphics; automate a series of tasks with a macro; secure a document with digital signatures. The items listed below include all the new Word skills you have learned in this chapter.

1. Save a Macro-Enabled Template (WD 677)
2. Unprotect a Document (WD 678)
3. Specify Macro Settings in Word (WD 679)
4. Convert a Table to Text (WD 682)
5. Insert a Date Field (WD 685)
6. Edit a Field (WD 686)
7. Modify a Style Using the Styles Task Pane (WD 687)
8. Create a Character Style (WD 689)
9. Use a Fill Effect for the Page Color (WD 691)
10. Change a Shape (WD 693)
11. Apply a Shadow Shape Effect (WD 694)
12. Fill a Shape with a Picture (WD 695)
13. Remove a Background (WD 697)
14. Apply an Artistic Effect (WD 699)
15. Draw a Text Box (WD 699)
16. Change Text Direction in a Text Box (WD 701)
17. Change a Shape Outline of a Text Box (WD 702)
18. Apply a 3-D Effect to a Text Box (WD 703)
19. Group Objects (WD 704)
20. Record a Macro and Assign It a Shortcut Key (WD 706)
21. Run a Macro (WD 708)
22. Add a Command and a Macro as Buttons on the Quick Access Toolbar (WD 708)
23. Delete Buttons from the Quick Access Toolbar (WD 710)
24. Rename a Macro (WD 711)
25. Delete a Macro (WD 711)
26. Create an Automatic Macro (WD 711)
27. Edit a Macro's VBA Code (WD 713)
28. Add an Invisible Digital Signature to a Document (WD 716)
29. Add a Signature Line to a Document (WD 717)

If you have a SAM 2010 user profile, your instructor may have assigned an autogradable version of this assignment. If so, log into the SAM 2010 Web site at www.cengage.com/sam2010 to download the instruction and start files.

Learn It Online

Test your knowledge of chapter content and key terms.

Instructions: To complete the Learn It Online exercises, start your browser, click the Address bar, and then enter the Web `scsite.com/wd2010/learn`. When the Word 2010 Learn It Online page is displayed, click the link for the exercise you want to complete and then read the instructions.

Chapter Reinforcement TF, MC, and SA
A series of true/false, multiple choice, and short answer questions that test your knowledge of the chapter content.

Flash Cards
An interactive learning environment where you identify chapter key terms associated with displayed definitions.

Practice Test
A series of multiple choice questions that test your knowledge of chapter content and key terms.

Who Wants To Be a Computer Genius?
An interactive game that challenges your knowledge of chapter content in the style of a television quiz show.

Wheel of Terms
An interactive game that challenges your knowledge of chapter key terms in the style of the television show *Wheel of Fortune*.

Crossword Puzzle Challenge
A crossword puzzle that challenges your knowledge of key terms presented in the chapter.

Apply Your Knowledge

Reinforce the skills and apply the concepts you learned in this chapter.

Working with Graphics, Shapes, and Fields
Note: To complete this assignment, you will be required to use the Data Files for Students. See the inside back cover of this book for instructions on downloading the Data Files for Students, or contact your instructor for information about accessing the required files.

Instructions: Start Word. Open the template, Apply 11-1 TechConnections Survey, from the Data Files for Students. In this assignment, you add an artistic effect to pictures, group images, change a shape, use a texture fill effect, and insert a date field (Figure 11–71).

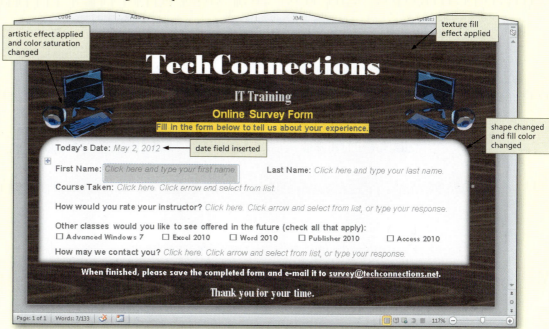

Figure 11–71

Continued >

Apply Your Knowledge *continued*

Perform the following tasks:

1. Unprotect the template.

2. Apply the Cutout artistic effect to both of the computer images. Change the color saturation of each image to Saturation: 400%.

3. Group the two computer images together. Move the grouped images down so that their keyboards just cross into the data entry area.

4. Change the page color to the Walnut fill effect.

5. Change the shape around the data entry area from Rectangle to Round Same Side Corner Rectangle.

6. Change the fill color of the rectangle shape to White, Background 2.

7. Apply the Inside Center shadow to the rectangle shape.

8. Display the Developer tab. Change the properties of the date picker content control so that its contents can be deleted and then delete the content control. Insert a date field after the Today's Date: label in the format month day, year (i.e., May 2, 2012). Change the format of the displayed date field to Subtle Emphasis. Hide the Developer tab.

9. Protect the form. Save the modified form using the file name, Apply 11-1 TechConnections Survey Modified.

10. Submit the file in the format specified by your instructor.

Extend Your Knowledge

Extend the skills you learned in this chapter and experiment with new skills. You may need to use Help to complete the assignment.

Working with Document Security

Note: To complete this assignment, you will be required to use the Data Files for Students. See the inside back cover of this book for instructions on downloading the Data Files for Students, or contact your instructor for information about accessing the required files.

Instructions: Start Word. Open the document, Extend 11-1 Welcome Letter Draft, from the Data Files for Students. You will create your own digital ID, add a digital signature line, add an invisible digital signature, and encrypt the document with a password.

Perform the following tasks:

1. Use Help to review and expand your knowledge about these topics: creating a digital ID, signature lines, invisible digital signatures, passwords, and document encryption.

2. Create your own digital ID.

3. Add a digital signature line to the document (Figure 11–72). Use your personal information in the signature line.

4. Add an invisible digital signature to the document.

5. Encrypt the document. Be sure to use a password you will remember.

6. Save the document with a new file name. Then, close the document and reopen it. Enter the password when prompted.

7. View the signatures in the document.

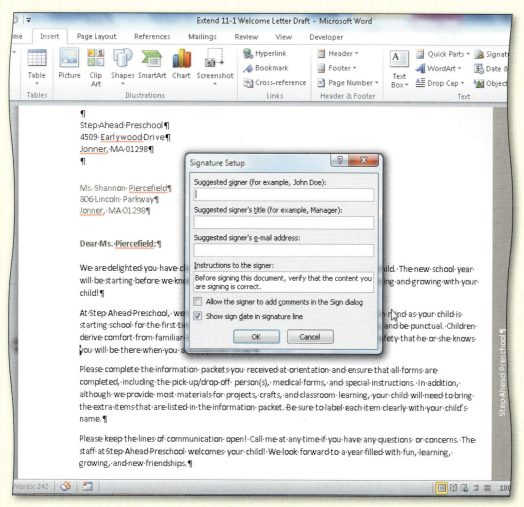

Figure 11–72

8. Sign the document; that is, enter your digital signature (type it or select an image).

9. Mark the document as final.

10. Change the document properties as specified by your instructor. Submit the document in the format specified by your instructor.

Make It Right

Analyze a document and correct all errors and/or improve the design.

Formatting an Online Form

Note: To complete this assignment, you will be required to use the Data Files for Students. See the inside back cover of this book for instructions on downloading the Data Files for Students, or contact your instructor for information about accessing the required files.

Continued >

Make It Right *continued*

Instructions: Start Word. Open the template, Make It Right 11-1 Fix-It Crew Survey Draft, from the Data Files for Students. In this assignment, you change fill effects and a shape, modify a style, ungroup graphics, and format a text box (Figure 11–73).

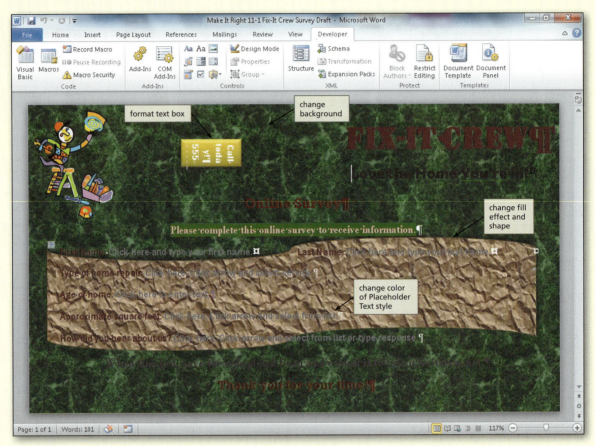

Figure 11–73

Perform the following tasks:

1. Unprotect the template.
2. Change the fill effect to a texture that does not compete with the colors of the text on the form.
3. Change the shape covering the data entry area to one of the rectangle shapes.
4. Change the fill effect of the rectangle shape to a color instead of a texture.
5. Change the color of the Placeholder Text style from the default. *Hint*: Click the Manage Styles button in the Styles task pane to edit the Placeholder Text style.
6. Ungroup the graphic and text box.
7. Add a Glow effect to the graphic.
8. Change the size of the text box to fit the rotated text. Change the shape style of the text box so that the text in the text box is easier to see. Apply a 3-D rotation effect to the text box. Position the text box in a noticeable location on the form.
9. Make any necessary adjustments to the form so that it fits on a single page. Adjust the formats of text and objects so that the form is easy to read.
10. Protect the form, changing the editing restrictions from Tracked changes to Filling in forms.
11. Change the document properties as specified by your instructor.
12. Save the revised form with a new file name. Test the form. Submit the form in the format specified by your instructor.

In the Lab

Design and/or create a document using the guidelines, concepts, and skills presented in this chapter. Labs are listed in order of increasing difficulty.

Lab 1: Enhancing the Graphics and Shapes on an Online Form

Problem: You created the online form shown in Figure 10–78 on page WD 667 for the Performing Arts Center. Your supervisor has asked you to change the form's appearance. You modify the form so that it looks like the one shown in Figure 11–74.

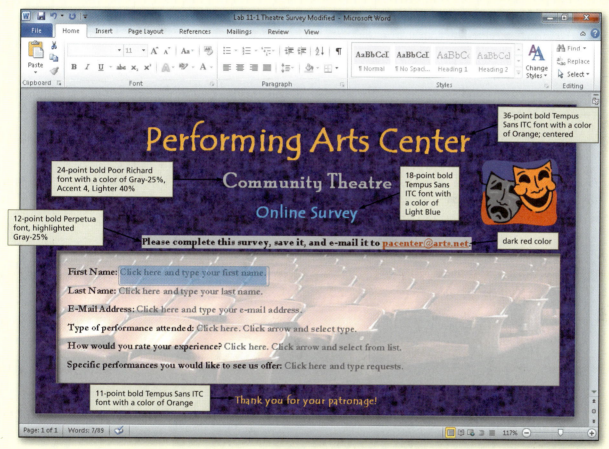

Figure 11–74

Perform the following tasks:

1. Open the template called Lab 10-1 Theatre Survey that you created in Lab 1 of Chapter 10. Save the template with a new file name of Lab 11-1 Theatre Survey Modified. If you did not complete the lab in Chapter 10, see your instructor for a copy. Unprotect the template.

2. Use the Purple mesh fill effect for the page color.

3. Change the document theme to Couture.

4. Modify the formats of the company name, business tag line, form title, user instruction, and thank you lines as shown in Figure 11–74 (or with similar fonts).

5. Convert the table to text for the 2 × 1 table containing the First Name and Last Name content controls. Extend the rectangle to cover the entire data entry area.

6. Add the Inside Diagonal Top Left shadow to the rectangle shape.

Continued >

In the Lab *continued*

7. Modify the Normal style to include the bold format so that the labels in the data entry area are bold.

8. Use the picture fill effect to place a picture in the rectangle shape. Use the picture called Theatre from the Data Files for Students. Change the color of the picture in the rectangle to washout.

9. Remove the current clip art and insert the one shown in the figure (or a similar image). Format the image as floating In Front of Text. Resize the clip art.

10. Adjust spacing as necessary so that the entire form fits on a single page.

11. Protect the form.

12. Save the form again and submit it in the format specified by your instructor.

13. Access the template through Windows Explorer. Fill in the form and submit the filled-in form in the format specified by your instructor.

In the Lab

Lab 2: Enhancing the Graphics, Shapes, and Text Boxes on an Online Form

Problem: You created the online form shown in Figure 10–79 on page WD 668 for Capital Investments, Inc. Your supervisor has asked you to change the form's appearance and add a text box. You modify the form so that it looks like the one shown in Figure 11–75.

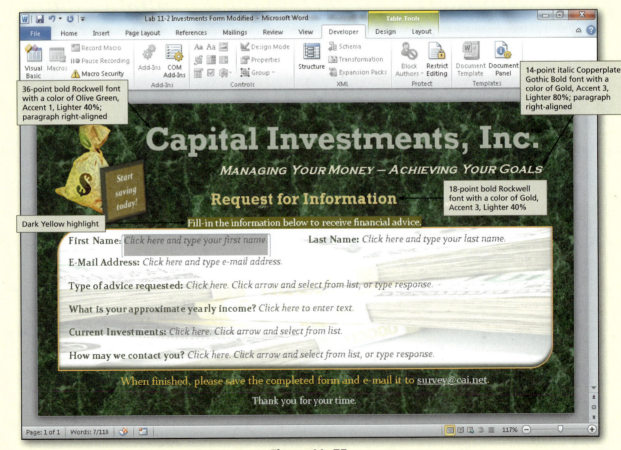

Figure 11–75

Perform the following tasks:

1. Open the template called Lab 10-2 Investments Form that you created in Lab 2 of Chapter 10. Save the template with a new file name of Lab 11-2 Investments Form Modified. If you did not complete the lab in Chapter 10, see your instructor for a copy. Unprotect the template.

2. Change the document theme to Paper.

3. Use the Green marble fill effect for the page color.

4. Modify the formats of the company name, business tag line, form title, and user instruction lines as shown in Figure 11–75 (or with similar fonts).

5. Use the picture fill effect to place a picture in the rectangle shape. Use the picture called Money from the Data Files for Students. Change the color of the picture in the rectangle to washout.

6. Create a character style, with the name Data Entry Labels, for all labels in the data entry that starts with the current format and applies the bold format with a color of Olive Green, Accent 1, Darker 50%.

7. Change the shape of the rectangle to Round Diagonal Corner Rectangle. Change the shape outline color (border) to Orange, Accent 2.

8. Apply the Inside Bottom shadow effect to the rectangle shape. Change the shadow color to Dark Green, Text 2. Change the transparency of the shade in the rectangle to 20%.

9. Remove the current clip art and insert the picture called Money Bag from the Data Files for Students. Format the image as floating In Front of Text. Resize the image. Remove the background, as shown in the figure. Apply the Watercolor sponge artistic effect to the picture. Position the image as shown in the figure.

10. Draw a text box that is approximately 0.8" × 0.9" that contains the text, Start saving today!, centered in the text box. Apply the Intense Effect — Gold, Accent 3 shape style to the text box. Change the shape outline to 4½ pt Olive Green, Accent 1, Darker 50%. Apply the Perspective Contrasting Right 3-D Rotation to the text box. Position the text box on the graphic as shown in the figure and then group the two images together.

11. Protect the form.

12. Save the form again and submit it in the format specified by your instructor.

13. Access the template through Windows Explorer. Fill in the form and submit the filled-in form in the format specified by your instructor.

In the Lab

Lab 3: Enhancing the Look of an Online Form and Adding Macros to the Form

Problem: You created the online form shown in Figure 10–80 on page WD 669 for Monrovia Country Club. Your supervisor has asked you to change the form's appearance, add a field, and add some macros. You modify the form so that it looks like the one shown in Figure 11–76.

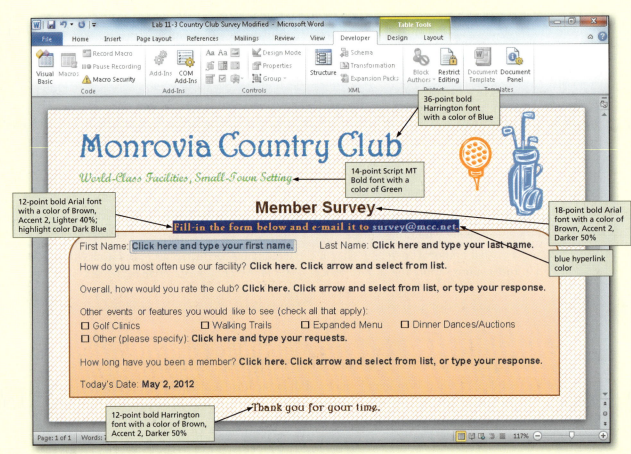

Figure 11–76

Perform the following tasks:

1. Open the template called Lab 10-3 Country Club Survey that you created in Lab 3 of Chapter 10. Save the template as a macro-enabled template with a new file name of Lab 11-3 Monrovia Country Club Modified. If you did not complete the lab in Chapter 10, see your instructor for a copy. Unprotect the template.

2. Change the document theme to Perspective.

3. Change the page color to Brown, Accent 2, Lighter 60%. Apply the Diagonal brick pattern fill effect to the page color.

4. Change the fill color in the rectangle shape to Brown, Accent 2, Lighter 40%. Apply the Linear Up gradient fill effect to the rectangle shape.

5. Modify the formats of the company name, business tag line, form title, user instruction, and thank you lines as shown in Figure 11–76 (or with similar fonts).

6. Remove the Today's Date content control. Insert a date field from the Quick Parts gallery in the format May 2, 2012.

7. Modify the Emphasis style to the color Gray-50%, Accent 6, Darker 50% and change the italic format to a bold format.

8. Remove the current clip art and insert two images from the Web similar to those shown in the figure. Format the images as floating In Front of Text. Resize the images and position them as shown. Group them together.

9. Record a macro that hides the formatting marks and the rulers. Name it HideScreenElements. Assign it the shortcut key, ALT+H. Run the macro to test it.

10. Add a button to the Quick Access Toolbar for the macro created in Step 9. Test the button and then delete the button from the Quick Access Toolbar.

11. Create an automatic macro called AutoNew using the macro recorder. The macro should change the view to page width.

12. Edit the AutoNew macro so that it also hides the Developer tab.

13. Protect the form.

14. Save the form again and submit it in the format specified by your instructor.

15. Access the template through Windows Explorer. Fill in the form and submit the filled-in form in the format specified by your instructor.

Cases and Places

Note: To complete these assignments, you may be required to use the Data Files for Students. See the inside back cover of this book for instructions on downloading the Data Files for Students, or contact your instructor for information about accessing the required files.

1: Modify an Online Form for the Student Tutoring Center

Academic

You created the online form for the Student Tutoring Center that was defined in Cases and Places Assignment 1 in Chapter 10 on page WD 671. Your supervisor was pleased with the initial design. You and your supervisor, however, believe the form can be improved by enhancing its appearance. Make the following modifications to the form: Change the company name, slogan, and title to a different font and color; change the page color to a texture; change the highlight color; and change the font and color of the last line. Change the rectangle shape around the data entry area. In the rectangle, add a picture fill effect using the Books file on the Data Files for Students (or a similar image) and recolor it using the Washout color. Change the color of the shadow in the rectangle. Delete the existing clip art, replace it with the picture called Tutoring on the Data Files for Students (or a similar image), and apply an artistic effect to the picture. Draw a text box with the text, Your opinion counts!, and apply a 3-D effect to the text box.

Specify the appropriate macro security level. Record a macro that hides screen elements and then assign the macro to a button on the Quick Access Toolbar. Record another macro for a task you would like to automate. Add another button to the Quick Access Toolbar for any Word command not on the Ribbon.

Use the concepts and techniques presented in this chapter to modify the online form. Be sure to save it as a macro-enabled template. Protect the form, test it, and submit it in the format specified by your instructor.

Continued >

Cases and Places *continued*

2: Modify an Online Form for a Children's Party Place

Personal

You created the online form for Cool Kidz Parties that was defined in Cases and Places Assignment 2 in Chapter 10 on page WD 671. Your aunt was pleased with the initial design. You and your aunt, however, believe the form can be improved by enhancing its appearance. Make the following modifications to the form: Change the font and color of the business name, business tag line, and form title; change the page color to a texture; change the highlight color; and change the font and color of the last line. Change the rectangle shape around the data entry area. In the rectangle, add a picture fill effect using the Party Hats file on the Data Files for Students (or a similar image) and recolor it using the Washout color. Change the color of the shadow in the rectangle. Delete the existing clip art, replace it with the picture called Kid Party on the Data Files for Students (or a similar image), and apply an artistic effect to the picture. Draw a text box with the text, Great Prices!, and apply a 3-D effect to the text box.

Specify the appropriate macro security level. Record a macro that hides screen elements and then assign the macro to a button on the Quick Access Toolbar. Record another macro for a task you would like to automate. Add another button to the Quick Access Toolbar for any Word command not on the Ribbon.

Use the concepts and techniques presented in this chapter to modify the online form. Be sure to save it as a macro-enabled template. Protect the form, test it, and submit it in the format specified by your instructor.

3: Modify an Online Form for an Environment-Friendly Business

Professional

You created the online form for Naturally Good that was defined in Cases and Places Assignment 3 in Chapter 10 on page WD 672. Your boss was pleased with the initial design. You and your boss, however, believe the form can be improved by enhancing its appearance. Make the following modifications to the form: Change the font and color of the business name, business tag line, and form title; change the page color to a texture; change the highlight color; and change the font and color of the last line. Change the rectangle shape around the data entry area. In the rectangle, add a picture fill effect using the Green Leaf file on the Data Files for Students (or a similar image) and recolor it using the Washout color. Change the color of the shadow in the rectangle. Delete the existing clip art, replace it with the picture called Wheat on the Data Files for Students (or a similar image), and apply an artistic effect to the picture. Draw a text box with the text, Member Discounts!, and apply a 3-D effect to the text box.

Specify the appropriate macro security level. Record a macro that hides screen elements and then assign the macro to a button on the Quick Access Toolbar. Record another macro for a task you would like to automate. Add another button to the Quick Access Toolbar for any Word command not on the Ribbon.

Use the concepts and techniques presented in this chapter to modify the online form. Be sure to save it as a macro-enabled template. Protect the form, test it, and submit it in the format specified by your instructor.

NOTES

NOTES

NOTES

NOTES

Appendix A
Project Planning Guidelines

Using Project Planning Guidelines

The process of communicating specific information to others is a learned, rational skill. Computers and software, especially Microsoft Office 2010, can help you develop ideas and present detailed information to a particular audience.

Using Microsoft Office 2010, you can create projects such as Word documents, PowerPoint presentations, Excel spreadsheets, and Access databases. Productivity software such as Microsoft Office 2010 minimizes much of the laborious work of drafting and revising projects. Some communicators handwrite ideas in notebooks, others compose directly on the computer, and others have developed unique strategies that work for their own particular thinking and writing styles.

No matter what method you use to plan a project, follow specific guidelines to arrive at a final product that presents information correctly and effectively (Figure A–1). Use some aspects of these guidelines every time you undertake a project, and others as needed in specific instances. For example, in determining content for a project, you may decide that a chart communicates trends more effectively than a paragraph of text. If so, you would create this graphical element and insert it in an Excel spreadsheet, a Word document, or a PowerPoint slide.

Determine the Project's Purpose

Begin by clearly defining why you are undertaking this assignment. For example, you may want to track monetary donations collected for your club's fund-raising drive. Alternatively, you may be urging students to vote for a particular candidate in the next election. Once you clearly understand the purpose of your task, begin to draft ideas of how best to communicate this information.

Analyze Your Audience

Learn about the people who will read, analyze, or view your work. Where are they employed? What are their educational backgrounds? What are their expectations? What questions do they have?

PROJECT PLANNING GUIDELINES

1. DETERMINE THE PROJECT'S PURPOSE
Why are you undertaking the project?

2. ANALYZE YOUR AUDIENCE
Who are the people who will use your work?

3. GATHER POSSIBLE CONTENT
What information exists, and in what forms?

4. DETERMINE WHAT CONTENT TO PRESENT TO YOUR AUDIENCE
What information will best communicate the project's purpose to your audience?

Figure A–1

Design experts suggest drawing a mental picture of these people or finding photos of people who fit this profile so that you can develop a project with the audience in mind.

By knowing your audience members, you can tailor a project to meet their interests and needs. You will not present them with information they already possess, and you will not omit the information they need to know.

Example: Your assignment is to raise the profile of your college's nursing program in the community. How much do they know about your college and the nursing curriculum? What are the admission requirements? How many of the applicants admitted complete the program? What percent pass the state board exams?

Gather Possible Content

Rarely are you in a position to develop all the material for a project. Typically, you would begin by gathering existing information that may reside in spreadsheets or databases. Web sites, pamphlets, magazine and newspaper articles, and books could provide insights of how others have approached your topic. Personal interviews often provide perspectives not available by any other means. Consider video and audio clips as potential sources for material that might complement or support the factual data you uncover.

Determine What Content to Present to Your Audience

Experienced designers recommend writing three or four major ideas you want an audience member to remember after reading or viewing your project. It also is helpful to envision your project's endpoint, the key fact you wish to emphasize. All project elements should lead to this ending point.

As you make content decisions, you also need to think about other factors. Presentation of the project content is an important consideration. For example, will your brochure be printed on thick, colored paper or posted on the Web? Will your PowerPoint presentation be viewed in a classroom with excellent lighting and a bright projector, or will it be viewed on a notebook computer monitor? Determine relevant time factors, such as the length of time to develop the project, how long readers will spend reviewing your project, or the amount of time allocated for your speaking engagement. Your project will need to accommodate all of these constraints.

Decide whether a graph, photo, or artistic element can express or emphasize a particular concept. The right hemisphere of the brain processes images by attaching an emotion to them, so audience members are more apt to recall these graphics long term rather than just reading text.

As you select content, be mindful of the order in which you plan to present information. Readers and audience members generally remember the first and last pieces of information they see and hear, so you should place the most important information at the top or bottom of the page.

Summary

When creating a project, it is beneficial to follow some basic guidelines from the outset. By taking some time at the beginning of the process to determine the project's purpose, analyze the audience, gather possible content, and determine what content to present to the audience, you can produce a project that is informative, relevant, and effective.

Appendix B

Publishing Office 2010 Web Pages Online

With Office 2010 programs, you use the Save As command in the Backstage view to save a Web page to a Web site, network location, or FTP site. **File Transfer Protocol (FTP)** is an Internet standard that allows computers to exchange files with other computers on the Internet.

You should contact your network system administrator or technical support staff at your Internet access provider to determine if their Web server supports Web folders, FTP, or both, and to obtain necessary permissions to access the Web server.

Using an Office Program to Publish Office 2010 Web Pages

When publishing online, someone first must assign the necessary permissions for you to publish the Web page. If you are granted access to publish online, you must obtain the Web address of the Web server, a user name, and possibly a password that allows you to connect to the Web server. The steps in this appendix assume that you have access to an online location to which you can publish a Web page.

To Connect to an Online Location

To publish a Web page online, you first must connect to the online location. To connect to an online location using Windows 7, you would perform the following steps.

1. Click the Start button on the Windows 7 taskbar to display the Start menu.
2. Click Computer in the right pane of the Start menu to open the Computer window.
3. Click the 'Map network drive' button on the toolbar to display the Map Network Drive dialog box. (If the 'Map network drive' button is not visible on the toolbar, click the 'Display additional commands' button on the toolbar and then click 'Map network drive' in the list to display the Map Network Drive dialog box.)
4. Click the 'Connect to a Web site that you can use to store your documents and pictures' link (Map Network Drive dialog box) to start the Add Network Location wizard.
5. Click the Next button (Add Network Location dialog box).
6. Click 'Choose a custom network location' and then click the Next button.
7. Type the Internet or network address specified by your network or system administrator in the text box and then click the Next button.
8. Click 'Log on anonymously' to deselect the check box, type your user name in the User name text box, and then click the Next button.
9. If necessary, enter the name you want to assign to this online location and then click the Next button.
10. Click to deselect the Open this network location when I click Finish check box, and then click the Finish button.

11. Click the Cancel button to close the Map Network Drive dialog box.

12. Close the Computer window.

To Save a Web Page to an Online Location

The online location now can be accessed easily from Windows programs, including Microsoft Office programs. After creating a Microsoft Office file you wish to save as a Web page, you must save the file to the online location to which you connected in the previous steps. To save a Microsoft Word document as a Web page, for example, and publish it to the online location, you would perform the following steps.

1. Click File on the Ribbon to display the Backstage view and then click Save As in the Backstage view to display the Save As dialog box.

2. Type the Web page file name in the File name text box (Save As dialog box). Do not press the ENTER key because you do not want to close the dialog box at this time.

3. Click the 'Save as type' box arrow and then click Web Page to select the Web Page format.

4. If necessary, scroll to display the name of the online location in the navigation pane.

5. Double-click the online location name in the navigation pane to select that location as the new save location and display its contents in the right pane.

6. If a dialog box appears prompting you for a user name and password, type the user name and password in the respective text boxes and then click the Log On button.

7. Click the Save button (Save As dialog box).

The Web page now has been published online. To view the Web page using a Web browser, contact your network or system administrator for the Web address you should use to connect to the Web page.

Appendix C

Saving to the Web Using Windows Live SkyDrive

Introduction

Windows Live SkyDrive, also referred to as **SkyDrive**, is a free service that allows users to save files to the Web, such as documents, presentations, spreadsheets, databases, videos, and photos. Using SkyDrive, you also can save files in folders, providing for greater organization. You then can retrieve those files from any computer connected to the Internet. Some Office 2010 programs including Word, PowerPoint, and Excel can save files directly to an Internet location such as SkyDrive. SkyDrive also facilitates collaboration by allowing users to share files with other SkyDrive users (Figure C–1).

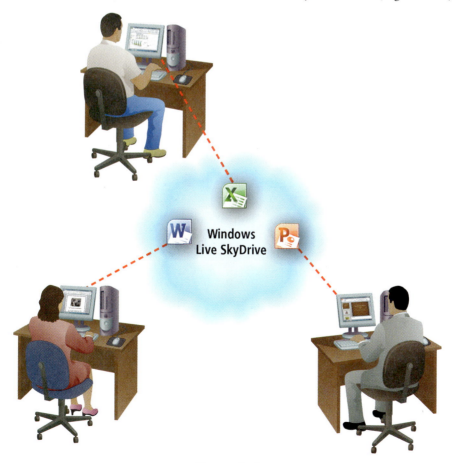

Figure C–1

Note: An Internet connection is required to perform the steps in this appendix.

To Save a File to Windows Live SkyDrive

You can save files directly to SkyDrive from within Word, PowerPoint, and Excel using the Backstage view. The following steps save an open Word document (Koala Exhibit Flyer, in this case) to SkyDrive. These steps require you to have a Windows Live account. Contact your instructor if you do not have a Windows Live account.

1

- Start Word and then open a document you want to save to the Web (in this case, the Koala Exhibit Flyer).

- Click File on the Ribbon to display the Backstage view (Figure C–2).

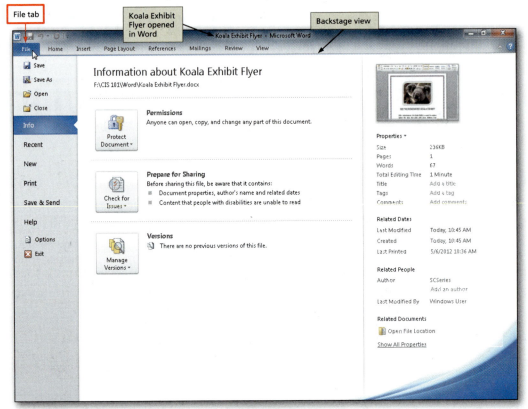

Figure C–2

2

- Click the Save & Send tab to display the Save & Send gallery (Figure C–3).

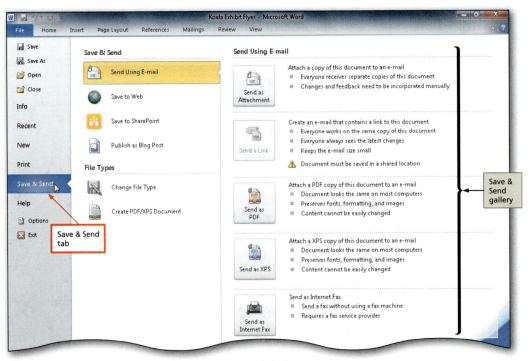

Figure C–3

3

- Click Save to Web in the Save & Send gallery to display information about saving a file to the Web (Figure C–4).

Save to Web command

Save & Send

Send Using E-mail

Save to Web

Save to SharePoint

Publish as Blog Post

File Types

Change File Type

Create PDF/XPS Document

Save to Windows Live

Save to Web to access this document from any computer or to share it with other people.

Learn more about Windows Live

Sign in with: Windows Live ID (Hotmail/Messenger/Xbox LIVE)

Sign In

Sign up for Windows Live

information about saving to Web in right pane (contents of your pane may differ)

Sign In button

clicking this link displays a Web page allowing you to sign up for a Windows Live account

Figure C–4

4

- Click the Sign In button to display a Windows Live login dialog box that requests your e-mail address and password (Figure C–5).

Q&A

What if the Sign In button does not appear?

If you already are signed into Windows Live, the Sign In button will not be displayed. Instead, the contents of your Windows Live SkyDrive will be displayed. If you already are signed into Windows Live, proceed to Step 6.

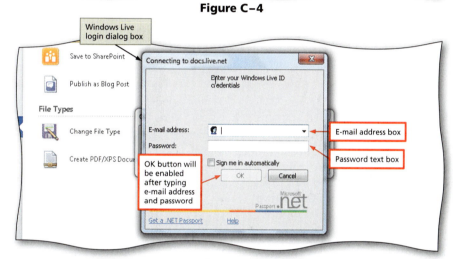

Windows Live login dialog box

Save to SharePoint

Publish as Blog Post

File Types

Change File Type

Create PDF/XPS Docu

Connecting to docs.live.net

Enter your Windows Live ID credentials

E-mail address:

Password:

Sign me in automatically

OK   Cancel

Microsoft
.net
Passport

Get a .NET Passport   Help

OK button will be enabled after typing e-mail address and password

E-mail address box

Password text box

Figure C–5

5

- Enter your Windows Live e-mail address in the E-mail address box (Windows Live login dialog box).
- Enter your Windows Live password in the Password text box.
- Click the OK button to sign into Windows Live and display the contents of your Windows Live SkyDrive in the right pane of the Save & Send gallery.
- If necessary, click the My Documents folder to set the save location for the document (Figure C–6).

Q&A

What if the My Documents folder does not exist?

Click another folder to select it as the save location. Record the name of this folder so that you can locate and retrieve the file later in this appendix.

Q&A

My SkyDrive shows personal and shared folders. What is the difference?

Personal folders are private and are not shared with anyone. Shared folders can be viewed by SkyDrive users to whom you have assigned the necessary permissions.

Koala Exhibit Flyer - Microsoft Word

References   Mailings   Review   View

Save to Windows Live SkyDrive

Save to Web to access this document from any computer or to share it with other peopl

Carol Jones's SkyDrive (Not Carol Jones?)

Windows Live SkyDrive

Personal Folders

My Documents
Shared with: Just me

Save As

New

My Documents folder selected

clicking this button refreshes the list of folders on SkyDrive

clicking this button creates a new folder on SkyDrive

folders contained on SkyDrive (your list may differ)

Save As button

Figure C–6

6

● Click the Save As button in the right pane of the Save & Send gallery to contact the SkyDrive server (which may take some time, depending on the speed of your Internet connection) and then display the Save As dialog box (Figure C–7).

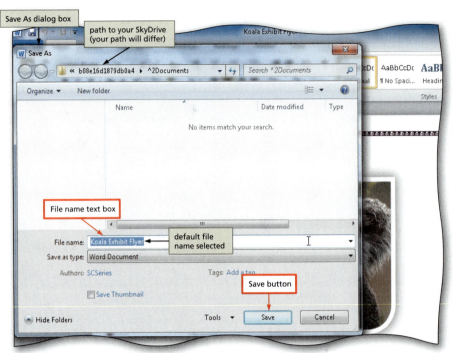

Figure C–7

7

● Type **Koala Exhibit Web** in the File name text box to enter the file name and then click the Save button (Save As dialog box) to save the file to Windows Live SkyDrive (Figure C–8).

Q&A

Is it necessary to rename the file?

It is good practice to rename the file. If you download the file from SkyDrive to your computer, having a different file name will preserve the original file.

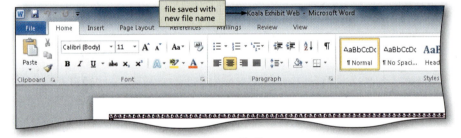

Figure C–8

8

● If you have one Word document open, click the Close button on the right side of the title bar to close the document and quit Word; or if you have multiple Word documents open, click File on the Ribbon to open the Backstage view and then click Exit in the Backstage view to close all open documents and quit Word.

Web Apps

Microsoft has created a scaled-down, Web-based version of its Microsoft Office suite, called **Microsoft Office Web Apps,** or **Web Apps**. Web Apps contains Web-based versions of Word, PowerPoint, Excel, and OneNote that can be used to view and edit files that are saved to SkyDrive. Web Apps allows users to continue working with their files even while they are not using a computer with Microsoft Office installed. In addition to working with files located on SkyDrive, Web Apps also enables users to create new Word documents, PowerPoint presentations, Excel spreadsheets, and OneNote notebooks. After returning to a computer with the Microsoft Office suite, some users choose to download files from SkyDrive and edit them using the associated Microsoft Office program.

Note: As with all Web applications, SkyDrive and Office Web Apps are subject to change. Consequently, the steps required to perform the actions in this appendix might be different from those shown.

To Download a File from Windows Live SkyDrive

Files saved to SkyDrive can be downloaded from a Web browser using any computer with an Internet connection. The following steps download the Koala Exhibit Web file using a Web browser.

- Click the Internet Explorer program button pinned on the Windows 7 taskbar to start Internet Explorer.

- Type **skydrive.live.com** in the Address bar and then press the ENTER key to display a SkyDrive Web page requesting you sign in to your Windows Live account (Figure C–9). (If the contents of your SkyDrive are displayed instead, you already are signed in and can proceed to Step 3 on the next page.)

Q&A

Why does the Web address change after I enter it in the Address bar?

The Web address changes because you are being redirected to sign into Windows Live before you can access SkyDrive.

Q&A

Can I open the file from Microsoft Word instead of using the Web browser?

If you are opening the file on the same computer from which you saved it to the SkyDrive, click File on the Ribbon to open the Backstage view. Click the Recent tab and then click the desired file name (Koala Exhibit Web, in this case) in the Recent Documents list, or click Open and then navigate to the location of the saved file (for a detailed example of this procedure, refer to the Office 2010 and Windows 7 chapter at the beginning of this book).

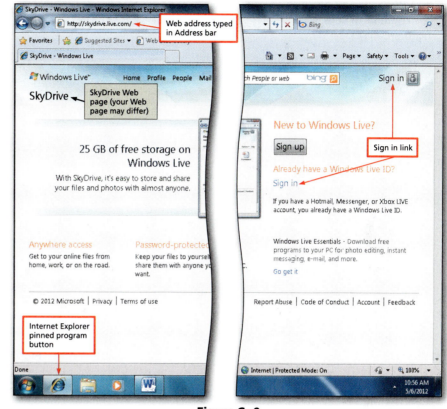

Figure C–9

- Click the Sign in link to display the Windows Live ID and Password text boxes (Figure C–10).

Q&A

Why can I not locate the Sign in link?

If your computer remembers your Windows Live sign in credentials from a previous session, your e-mail address already may be displayed on the SkyDrive Web page. In this case, point to your e-mail address to display the Sign in button, click the Sign in button, and then proceed to Step 3. If you cannot locate your e-mail address or Sign in link, click the Sign in with a different Windows Live ID link and then proceed to Step 3.

Figure C–10

3

- If necessary, enter your Windows Live ID and password in the appropriate text boxes and then click the Sign in button to sign into Windows Live and display the contents of your SkyDrive (Figure C–11).

Q&A

What if my screen shows the contents of a particular folder, instead of all folders?

To display all folders on your SkyDrive, point to Windows Live in the upper-left corner of the window and then click SkyDrive on the Windows Live menu.

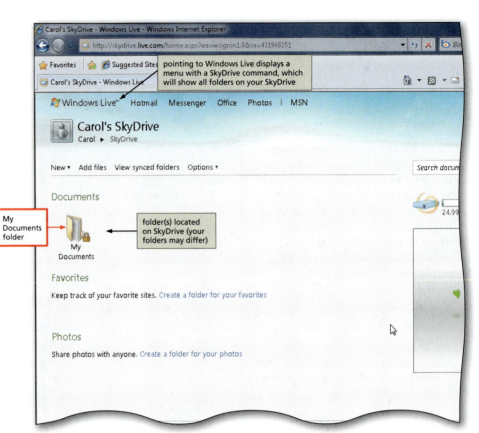

Figure C–11

4

- Click the My Documents folder, or the link corresponding to the folder containing the file you wish to open, to select the folder and display its contents (Figure C–12).

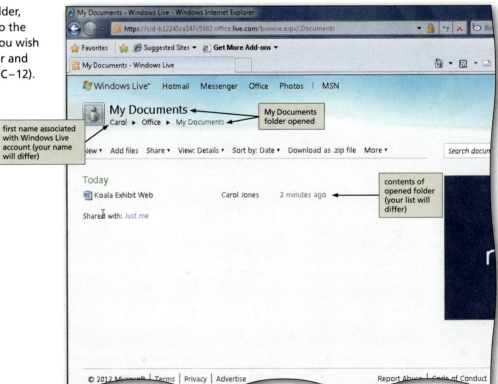

Figure C–12

- Point to the Koala Exhibit Web file to select the file and display commands associated with the file.

- Click the More link to display the More menu (Figure C–13).

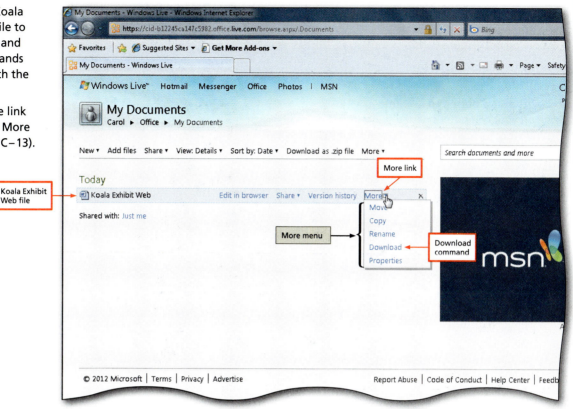

Figure C–13

6

- Click Download on the More menu to display the File Download dialog box (Figure C–14).

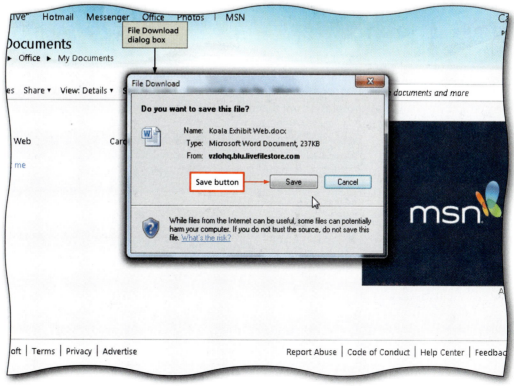

Figure C–14

- Click the Save button (File Download dialog box) to display the Save As dialog box (Figure C–15).

- Navigate to the desired save location.

- Click the Save button to save the file on your computer's hard disk or other storage device connected to the computer.

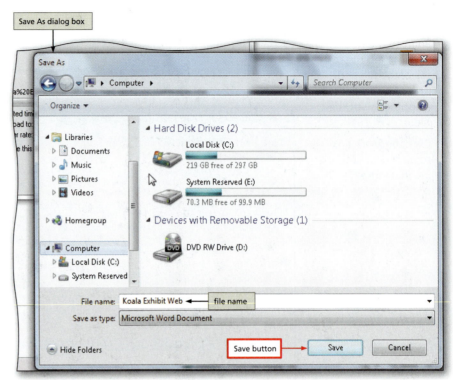

Figure C–15

Collaboration

In today's workplace, it is common to work with others on projects. Collaborating with the members of your team often requires sharing files. It also can involve multiple people editing and working with a certain set of files simultaneously. Placing files on SkyDrive in a public or shared folder enables others to view or modify the files. The members of the team then can view and edit the files simultaneously using Web Apps, enabling the team to work from one set of files (Figure C–16). Collaboration using Web Apps not only enables multiple people to work together, it also can reduce the amount of time required to complete a project.

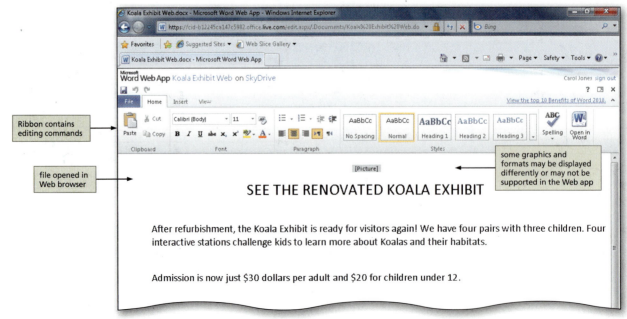

Figure C–16

Appendix D

APA Research Paper — Chapter 2 Supplement

Project — Research Paper Based on APA Documentation Style

As described in Chapter 2, two popular documentation styles for research papers are the Modern Language Association of America (MLA) and American Psychological Association (APA). This appendix creates the same research paper shown in Chapter 2, except it uses the APA documentation style instead of the MLA documentation style (Figure D–1 on the next page).

This appendix is intended as a supplement for Chapter 2. It assumes you have completed the Chapter 2 project and thus presents only the steps required to create the research paper following the APA guidelines. That is, this appendix does not repeat background, explanations, boxes, or steps from Chapter 2 that are not required specifically to create the APA version of the research paper. For example, this appendix does not present proofing tools, citation placeholders, footnotes, copy and paste, Research task pane, etc. You should know the material presented in Chapter 2 because it will help you to complete later chapters in the book successfully and if you intend to take the Word Certification exam.

APA Documentation Style

The research paper in this appendix follows the guidelines presented by the APA. To follow the APA documentation style, format the text to 12-point Times New Roman or a similar font. Double-space text on all pages of the paper using one-inch top, bottom, left, and right margins. Indent the first word of each paragraph in the body of the paper, and in footnotes if they are used, one-half inch from the left margin. At the top of each page, place a left-aligned running head and a right-aligned page number. The **running head** consists of the text, Running head:, followed by an abbreviated paper title (no more than 50 characters) in all capital letters.

The APA documentation style requires a title page. In addition to the running head and page number at the top of the page, the title page contains the complete paper title, author name, and institutional affiliation, all centered on separate lines in the upper-half of the page. The paper title should not exceed 12 words and should be written so that it easily can be shortened to an abbreviated title for the running head. The author name, also

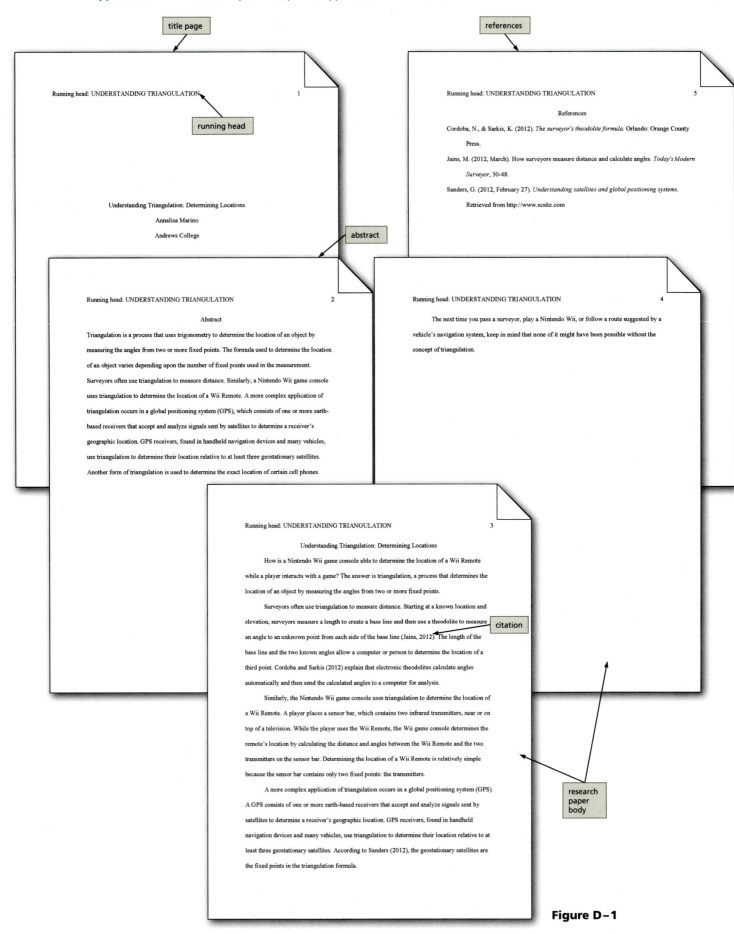

title page

running head

references

abstract

citation

research paper body

Figure D–1

called an author byline, should not contain any title (e.g., Professor) or degrees (e.g., PhD). If the author is not affiliated with an institution, list the author's city and state of residence. The title page also can include an author note centered at the bottom of the page, which can contain separate paragraphs identifying the author's departmental affiliation, changes in affiliation during research, acknowledgments, and contact information. If the title page contains an author note, the text, Author Note, should be centered above the notes.

Research papers that follow the APA documentation style include an abstract. The **abstract** is a one-paragraph summary (usually 250 words or fewer) of the most important topics in the paper. The abstract appears after the title page on its own numbered page, which includes the running head. The title, Abstract, is centered above a single paragraph that is double-spaced and not indented.

The APA documentation style cites references in the text of the paper, called **citations**, instead of noting each source at the bottom of the page or at the end of the paper. This documentation style uses the term, **references,** to refer to the bibliographic list of sources at the end of the paper. The references page alphabetically lists sources that are cited in the paper. Place the list of sources on a separate numbered page. Center the title, References, one inch from the top margin. Double-space all entries and format them with a **hanging indent**, in which the first line of a paragraph begins at the left margin and subsequent lines in the same paragraph are indented. The APA guidelines specify the hanging indent should be one-half inch from the left margin. List each source by the author's last name, or, if the author's name is not available, by the title of the source. Capitalize only the first letter of the first word in a title, along with any proper nouns.

To Start Word

If you are using a computer to step through the project in this appendix and you want your screens to match the figures in this appendix, you should change your screen's resolution to 1024×768. For information about how to change a computer's resolution, refer to the Office 2010 and Windows 7 chapter at the beginning of this book.

The following steps, which assume Windows 7 is running, start Word based on a typical installation. You may need to ask your instructor how to start Word for your computer.

1 Click the Start button on the Windows 7 taskbar to display the Start menu.

2 Type `Microsoft Word` as the search text in the 'Search programs and files' text box and watch the search results appear on the Start menu.

3 Click Microsoft Word 2010 in the search results on the Start menu to start Word and display a new blank document in the Word window.

4 If the Word window is not maximized, click the Maximize button next to the Close button on its title bar to maximize the window.

5 If the Print Layout button on the status bar is not selected (shown in Figure D–2 on the next page), click it so that your screen is in Print Layout view.

6 If Normal (Home tab | Styles group) is not selected in the Quick Style gallery (shown in Figure D–2), click it so that your document uses the Normal style.

7 If your zoom percent is not 100, click the Zoom Out or Zoom In button on the status bar as many times as necessary until the Zoom button displays 100% on its face (shown in Figure D–2).

To Display Formatting Marks

As discussed in Chapter 1, it is helpful to display formatting marks that indicate where in the document you press the ENTER key, SPACEBAR, and other keys. The following steps display formatting marks.

1 If the Home tab is not the active tab, click Home on the Ribbon to display the Home tab.

2 If the Show/Hide ¶ button (Home tab | Paragraph group) is not selected already, click it to display formatting marks on the screen.

To Modify the Normal Style for the Current Document

The APA documentation style requires that all text in the research paper use 12-point Times New Roman, or a similar, font. If you change the font and font size using buttons on the Ribbon, you may need to make the change many times during the course of creating the paper because Word formats different areas of a document using the Normal style, which uses 11-point Calibri font. By changing the Normal style, you ensure that all text in the document will use the format required by the APA. The following steps change the Normal style.

1

• Right-click Normal in the Quick Style gallery (Home tab | Styles group) to display a shortcut menu (Figure D–2).

Home tab

Show/Hide ¶ button selected

Normal style selected and right-clicked

Quick Style gallery

Modify command

current font and font size for Normal style

Paragraph group

Styles group

shortcut menu

Note: To help you locate screen elements that are referenced in the step instructions, such as buttons and commands, this book uses red boxes to point to these screen elements.

Print Layout button

zoom percent

Figure D–2

- Click Modify on the shortcut menu to display the Modify Style dialog box.

- Click the Font box arrow (Modify Style dialog box) to display the Font list. Scroll to and then click Times New Roman in the Font list to change the font for the selected style.

- Click the Font Size box arrow (Modify Style dialog box) and then click 12 in the Font Size list to change the font size for the selected style.

- Ensure that the 'Only in this document' option button is selected (Figure D–3).

- Click the OK button (Modify Style dialog box) to update the selected style (in this case, the Normal style) to the specified settings.

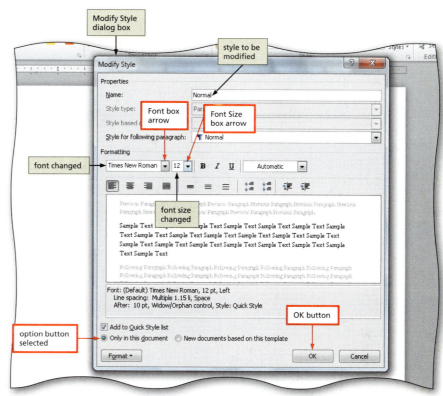

Figure D–3

To Change Line Spacing to Double

The APA documentation style requires that you double-space the entire research paper. That is, the amount of vertical space between each line of text and above and below paragraphs should be equal to one blank line. The following steps change the line spacing to 2.0, which double-spaces the lines in the research paper.

- Click the Line and Paragraph Spacing button (Home tab | Paragraph group) to display the Line and Paragraph Spacing gallery (Figure D–4).

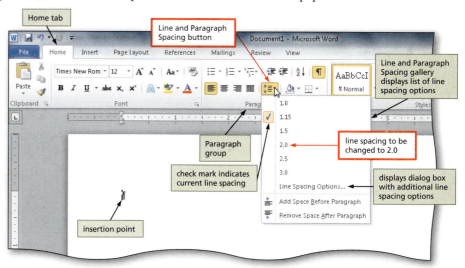

- Click 2.0 in the Line and Paragraph Spacing gallery to change the line spacing for the paragraph containing the insertion point.

Figure D–4

To Remove Space after a Paragraph

The research paper should not have additional blank space after each paragraph. The following steps remove the blank space after a paragraph.

 Click the Line and Paragraph Spacing button (Home tab | Paragraph group) to display the Line and Paragraph Spacing gallery (Figure D–5).

 Click Remove Space After Paragraph in the Line and Paragraph Spacing gallery so that no blank space appears after paragraphs.

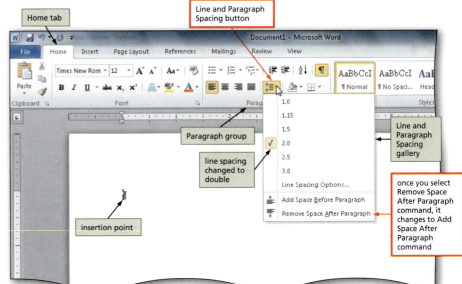

Figure D–5

To Update a Style to Match a Selection

To ensure that all paragraphs in the paper will be double-spaced and do not have space after the paragraphs, you want the Normal style to include the line and paragraph spacing changes made in the previous two sets of steps. Because no text has yet been typed in the research paper, you do not need to select text prior to updating the Normal style. The following steps update the Normal style.

 Right-click Normal in the Quick Style gallery (Home tab | Styles group) to display a shortcut menu (Figure D–6).

❷ Click Update Normal to Match Selection on the shortcut menu to update the current style to reflect the settings at the location of the insertion point.

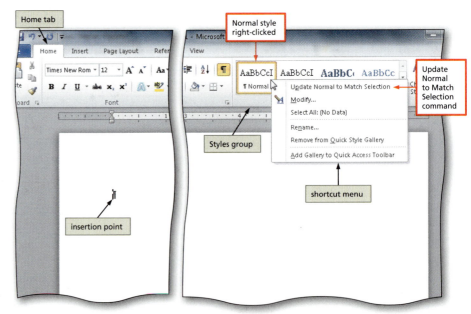

Figure D–6

To Insert a Formatted Header and Switch to the Header

In this research paper, the running head is to be placed at the left margin and the page number at the right margin, both on the same line one-half inch from the top of each page. Because the APA documentation style requires text at both the left and right margins, you can insert a formatted header that contains placeholders for text at the left, center, and right locations of the header. The following steps insert a formatted header and then switch from editing the document text to editing the header.

1
- Click Insert on the Ribbon to display the Insert tab.

- Click the Header button (Insert tab | Header & Footer group) to display the Header gallery (Figure D–7).

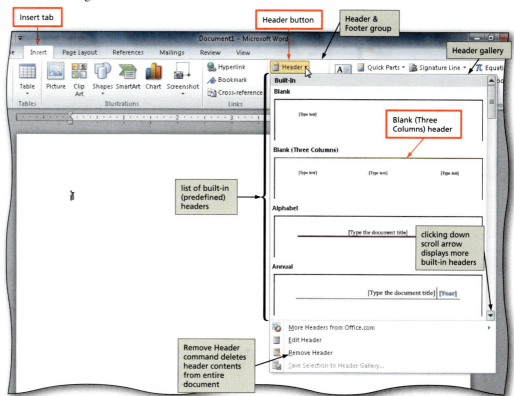

Figure D–7

2
- Click Blank (Three Columns) in the Header gallery to insert the selected header design in the document and switch from the document text to the header, which allows you to edit the contents of the header (Figure D–8).

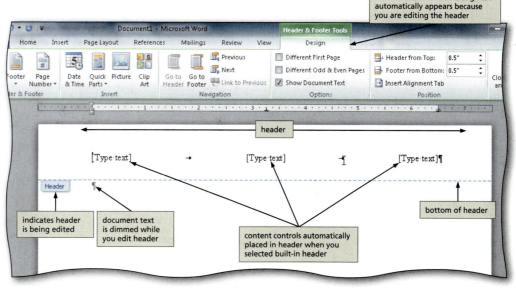

Figure D–8

To Enter Text in a Header Content Control

The formatted header contains three content controls (one at the left margin, one centered, and one at the right margin) with a tab character between each content control. A **content control** contains instructions for filling areas of text or graphics. The tab characters, which are formatting marks that indicate the TAB key has been pressed, are displayed because Word uses tab stops to align these content controls. Chapter 3 discusses tab stops in more depth.

To select a content control, you click it. As soon as you begin typing in a selected content control, the text you type replaces the instruction in the control. For this reason, you do not need to delete the selection unless you wish to remove the content control and not enter any replacement text. The following steps delete the centered content control and then enter the running head at the location of the leftmost content control in the header.

- Click the centered content control in the header to select the content control.

- Press the DELETE key to delete the selected content control.

- Click the leftmost content control in the header to select the content control (Figure D–9).

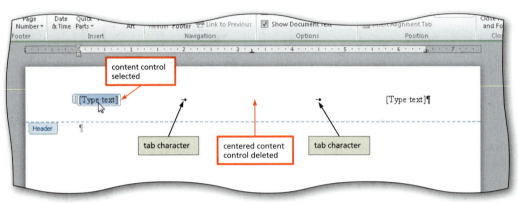

Figure D–9

- Type **Running head: UNDERSTANDING TRIANGULATION** as the text in the leftmost content control and then press the DELETE key twice to remove one of the tab characters so that the running head text fits on the same line as the rightmost content control, which will contain the page number (Figure D–10).

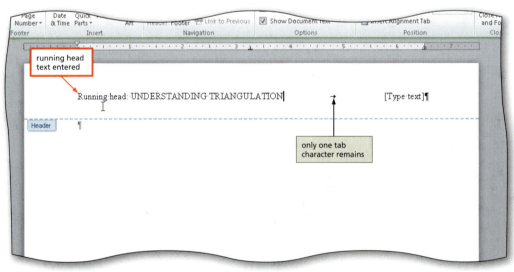

Figure D–10

To Count Characters

The running head should be no more than 50 characters, according to the APA documentation style. The next steps count the characters in the running head.

1

- Drag through the running head text, UNDERSTANDING TRIANGULATION, to select the text.

- With the running head selected, click the Word Count indicator on the status bar to display the Word Count dialog box (Figure D–11).

2

- Click the Close button (Word Count dialog box) to close the dialog box.

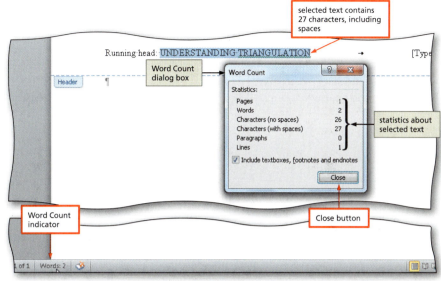

Figure D–11

To Insert a Page Number in a Header Content Control

The next task is to insert the current page number in the header. The following steps insert a page number at the location of the rightmost content control in the header.

1

- Click the rightmost content control in the header to select the content control.

- Click the Insert Page Number button (Header & Footer Tools Design tab | Header & Footer group) to display the Insert Page Number menu.

- Point to Current Position on the Insert Page Number menu to display the Current Position gallery (Figure D–12).

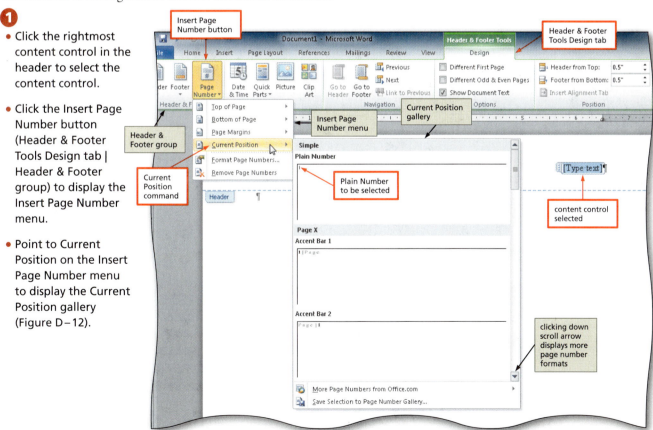

Figure D–12

- Click Plain Number in the Current Position gallery to insert an unformatted page number at the location of the selected content control in the header (Figure D–13).

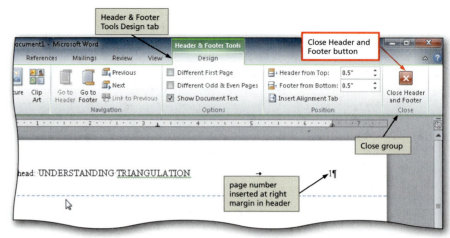

Figure D–13

To Close the Header

The header is complete. Thus, the next task is to switch back to the document text. The following step closes the header.

- Click the Close Header and Footer button (Header & Footer Tools Design tab | Close group) (shown in Figure D–13) to close the header and switch back to the document text (Figure D–14).

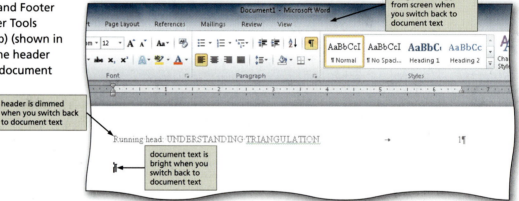

Figure D–14

To Type the Title Page Text

In addition to the header, which appears on every page in the paper, the title page for this research paper should contain the complete paper title, author name, and institutional affiliation, all centered on separate lines in the upper-half of the page. The following steps type the title page text.

1 With the insertion point at the top of the document, press the ENTER key six times.

2 Click the Center button (Home tab | Paragraph group) to center the insertion point.

3 Type **Understanding Triangulation: Determining Locations** and then press the ENTER key.

4 Type **Annalisa Marino** and then press the ENTER key.

5 Type **Andrews College** and then press the ENTER key (Figure D–15).

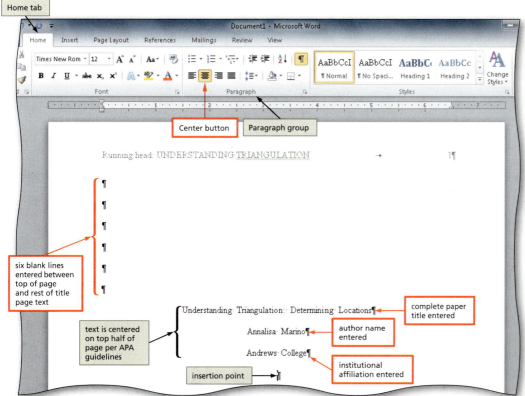

Figure D–15

To Page Break Manually

The title page is complete, and the abstract for the research paper will begin on a new page. To move the insertion point to the next page, you insert a manual page break. A **manual page break**, or **hard page break**, is one that you force into the document at a specific location.

Word never moves or adjusts manual page breaks; however, Word adjusts any automatic page breaks that follow a manual page break. Word inserts manual page breaks immediately above or to the left of the location of the insertion point. The following step inserts a manual page break after the title page.

1

- Verify the insertion point is positioned below the college name on the title page (shown in Figure D–15), which is the location for the page break.

- Click Insert on the Ribbon to display the Insert tab.

- Click the Page Break button (Insert tab | Pages group) to insert a manual page break immediately to the left of the insertion point and position the insertion point immediately below the manual page break (Figure D–16).

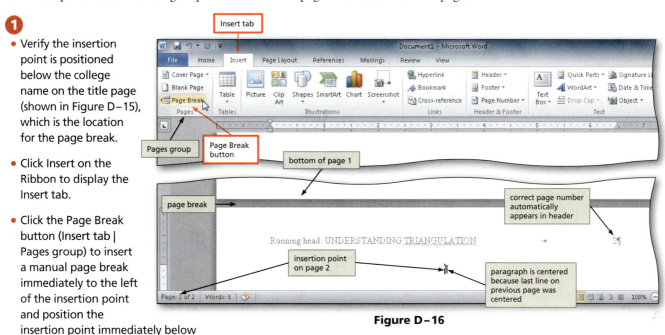

Figure D–16

To Type the Abstract

The abstract is a one-page summary of the most important points in the research paper. The title should be centered, and the paragraph below the title should be left-aligned. The following steps type the title centered, left-align a paragraph, and then type the abstract in the research paper.

1 Type **Abstract** and then press the ENTER key to enter the title for the page containing the abstract.

2 Press CTRL+L to left-align the current paragraph, that is, the paragraph containing the insertion point. (Recall from Chapter 1 that a notation such as CTRL+L means to press the letter L on the keyboard while holding down the CTRL key.)

3 Type the abstract text as shown in Figure D–17.

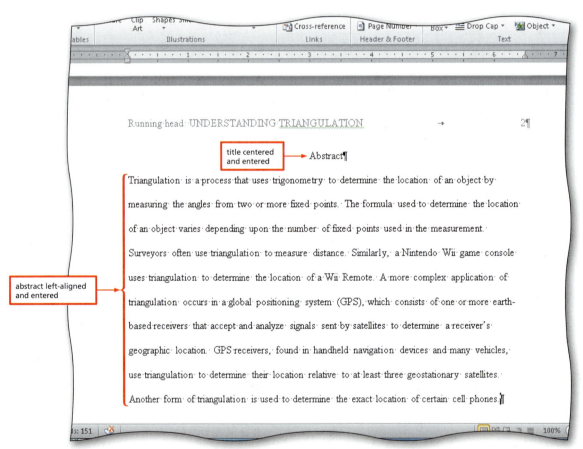

Figure D–17

To Count Words

When you write papers, you often are required to compose the papers with a minimum number of words. In addition, the APA documentation style specifies that the abstract in a research paper should contain no more than 250 words, sometimes no more than 150 words. The next steps verify the number of words in the abstract.

1

- Position the mouse pointer in the paragraph containing the abstract and then triple-click to select the paragraph.

- Verify the number of words in the selected text by looking at the Word Count indicator on the status bar (Figure D–18).

2

- Click anywhere in the abstract to remove the selection from the text.

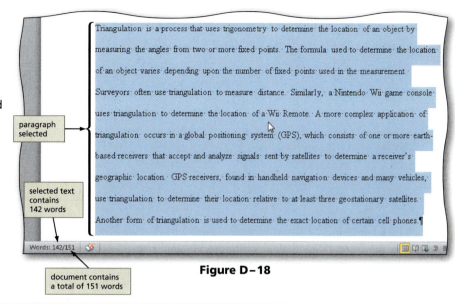

paragraph selected

selected text contains 142 words

document contains a total of 151 words

Figure D–18

To Page Break Manually

The abstract is complete, and the text for the research paper should begin on a new page. The following steps insert a manual page break after the abstract.

1 Press CTRL+END to position the insertion point at the end of the document, which is the end of the abstract in this case.

2 Click the Page Break button (Insert tab | Pages group) to insert a manual page break immediately to the left of the insertion point and position the insertion point immediately below the manual page break.

To Enter the Paper Title

The following steps enter the title of the research paper centered between the page margins.

1 Center the insertion point.

2 Type **Understanding Triangulation: Determining Locations** and then press the ENTER key to enter the title of the paper (Figure D–19).

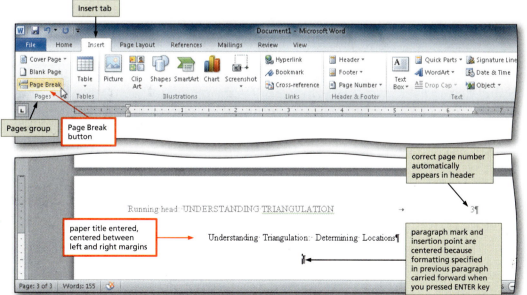

Insert tab

Pages group

Page Break button

correct page number automatically appears in header

paper title entered, centered between left and right margins

paragraph mark and insertion point are centered because formatting specified in previous paragraph carried forward when you pressed ENTER key

Running head: UNDERSTANDING TRIANGULATION   3

Understanding Triangulation: Determining Locations¶

Figure D–19

To Format Text

The paragraphs below the paper title should be left-aligned, instead of centered. Thus, the following step left-aligns the paragraph below the paper title.

1 Press CTRL+L to left-align the current paragraph, that is, the paragraph containing the insertion point.

To First-Line Indent Paragraphs

The first line of each paragraph in the research paper is to be indented one-half inch from the left margin. You can use the horizontal ruler, usually simply called the **ruler**, to indent just the first line of a paragraph, which is called a **first-line indent**.

The left margin on the ruler contains two triangles above a square. The **First Line Indent marker** is the top triangle at the 0" mark on the ruler (Figure D–20). The small square at the 0" mark is the Left Indent marker. The **Left Indent marker** allows you to change the entire left margin, whereas the First Line Indent marker indents only the first line of the paragraph. The following steps first-line indent paragraphs in the research paper.

- If the rulers are not displayed, click the View Ruler button on the vertical scroll bar to display the horizontal and vertical rulers on the screen.

- With the insertion point on the paragraph mark below the research paper title, point to the First Line Indent marker on the ruler (Figure D–20).

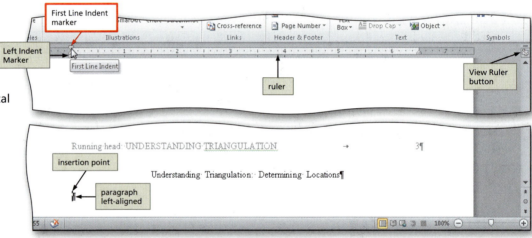

Figure D–20

- Drag the First Line Indent marker to the .5" mark on the ruler to display a vertical dotted line in the document window, which indicates the proposed location of the first line of the paragraph (Figure D–21).

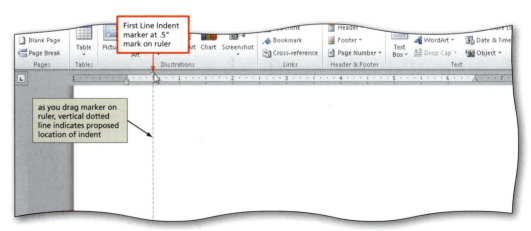

Figure D–21

- Release the mouse button to place the First Line Indent marker at the .5" mark on the ruler, or one-half inch from the left margin (Figure D–22).

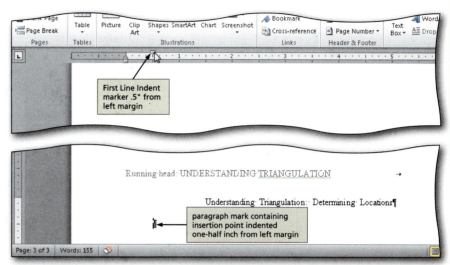

Figure D–22

To Type the First and Second Paragraphs

The following steps type the first and second paragraphs of the research paper.

1. Type the first paragraph of the research paper as shown in Figure D–23 and then press the ENTER key.

2. Type the second paragraph of the research paper as shown in Figure D–23.

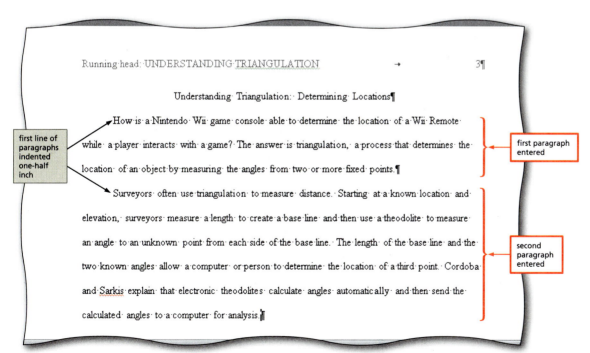

Figure D–23

To Save a Document

You have performed several tasks while creating this research paper and do not want to risk losing work completed thus far. Accordingly, you should save the document. The following steps save the document on a USB flash drive using the file name, Triangulation Paper.

1 With a USB flash drive connected to one of the computer's USB ports, click the Save button on the Quick Access Toolbar to display the Save As dialog box.

2 Type **Triangulation Paper** in the File name text box to change the file name. Do not press the ENTER key after typing the file name because you do not want to close the dialog box at this time.

3 Navigate to the desired save location (in this case, the Word folder in the CIS 101 folder [or your class folder] on the USB flash drive). For a detailed example of this procedure, refer to Steps 3a – 3c in the To Save a File in a Folder section in the Office 2010 and Windows 7 chapter at the beginning of this book.

4 Click the Save button (Save As dialog box) to save the document in the selected folder on the selected drive with the entered file name.

To Change the Bibliography Style

The APA guidelines suggest the use of in-text citations instead of footnoting each source of material in a paper. These parenthetical acknowledgments guide the reader to the end of the paper for complete information about the source.

The first step in inserting a citation is to be sure the citations and sources will be formatted using the correct documentation style, called the bibliography style in Word. The following steps change the specified documentation style.

- Click References on the Ribbon to display the References tab.

- Click the Bibliography Style box arrow (References tab | Citations & Bibliography group) to display a gallery of predefined documentation styles (Figure D–24).

- Click APA Fifth Edition in the Bibliography Style gallery to change the documentation style to APA.

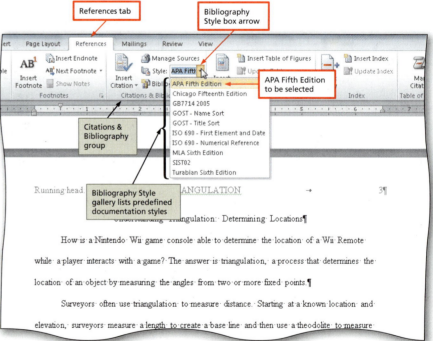

Figure D–24

To Insert a Citation and Create Its Source

With the documentation style selected, the next task is to insert a citation placeholder and enter the source information. You can accomplish these steps at once by instructing Word to add a new source. The following steps add a new source for a magazine (periodical) article.

• Position the insertion point to the right of the word, line, at the end of the second sentence in the second paragraph, before the period, and then press the SPACEBAR because you want a space between the end of the sentence and the citation.

• Click the Insert Citation button (References tab | Citations & Bibliography group) to display the Insert Citation menu (Figure D–25).

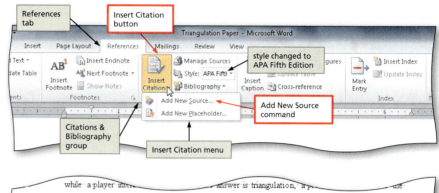

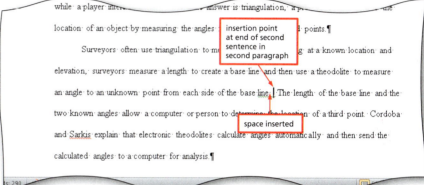

Figure D–25

• Click Add New Source on the Insert Citation menu to display the Create Source dialog box (Figure D–26).

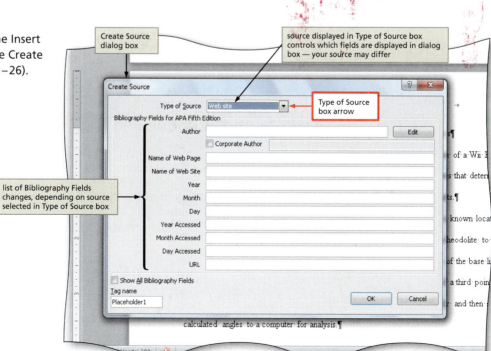

Figure D–26

3

- If necessary, click the Type of Source box arrow (Create Source dialog box) and then click Article in a Periodical, so that the list shows fields required for a magazine (periodical).

- Type **Jains, M.** in the Author text box.

- Type **How surveyors measure distance and calculate angles** in the Title text box.

- Type **Today's Modern Surveyor** in the Periodical Title text box.

- Type **2012** in the Year text box.

- Type **March** in the Month text box.

- Type **30-48** in the Pages text box (Figure D–27).

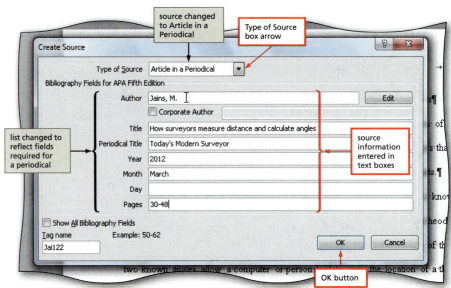

Figure D–27

4

- Click the OK button to close the dialog box, create the source, and insert the citation in the document at the location of the insertion point (Figure D–28).

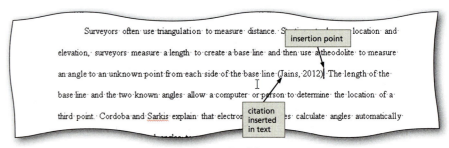

Figure D–28

To Insert Another Citation and Create Its Source

The following steps add a new source for a book.

1 Position the insertion point at the location for the citation (in this case, after the name, Sarkis, in the last sentence of the second paragraph) and then press the SPACEBAR (shown in Figure D–29).

2 Click the Insert Citation button (References tab | Citations & Bibliography group) to display the Insert Citation menu.

3 Click Add New Source on the Insert Citation menu to display the Create Source dialog box.

4 If necessary, click the Type of Source box arrow (Create Source dialog box) and then click Book, so that the list shows fields required for a Book.

5 Type **Cordoba, N.; Sarkis, K.** in the Author text box.

6 Type **The surveyor's theodolite formula** in the Title text box.

7 Type **2012** in the Year text box.

8 Type `Orlando` in the City text box.

9 Type `Orange County Press` in the Publisher text box (Figure D–29).

10 Click the OK button to close the dialog box, create the source, and insert the citation in the document at the location of the insertion point.

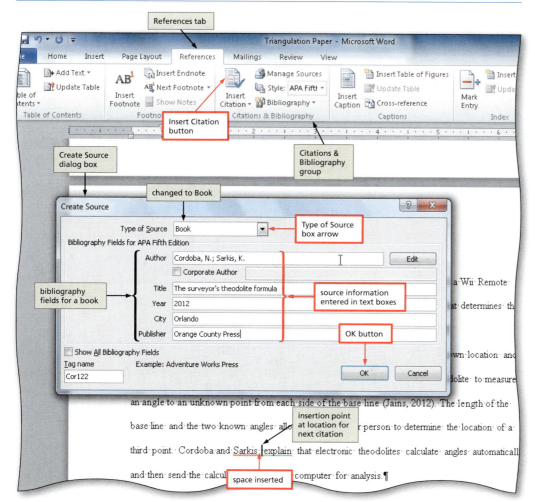

Figure D–29

To Edit a Citation

In the APA documentation style, if you reference the author's name in the text, you should not list it again in the citation. Instead, just list the publication year in the citation. To do this, instruct Word to suppress the author and title. The following steps edit the citation, suppressing the author and title but displaying the page numbers.

1

• Click somewhere in the citation to be edited, in this case somewhere in (Cordoba & Sarkis, 2012), which selects the citation and displays the Citation Options box arrow.

• Click the Citation Options box arrow to display the Citation Options menu (Figure D–30).

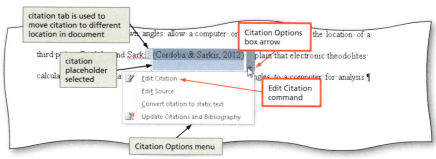

Figure D–30

2

- Click Edit Citation on the Citation Options menu to display the Edit Citation dialog box.

- In the Suppress area (Edit Citation dialog box), click the Author check box to place a check mark in it.

- In the Suppress area, click the Title check box to place a check mark in it (Figure D–31).

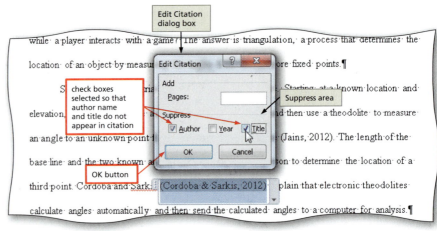

Figure D–31

3

- Click the OK button to close the dialog box, remove the author name from the citation, and suppress the title from showing.

- Press CTRL+END to move the insertion point to the end of the document, which also removes the selection from the citation (Figure D–32).

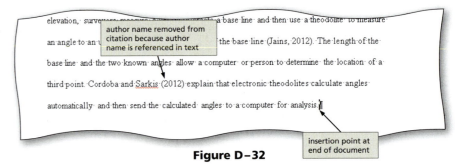

Figure D–32

To Type the Third and Fourth Paragraphs

The following steps continue typing text in the research paper.

1 With the insertion point positioned as shown in Figure D-32, press the ENTER key and then type the third paragraph of the research paper as shown in Figure D–33.

2 Press the ENTER key and then type the fourth paragraph of the research paper as shown in Figure D–33.

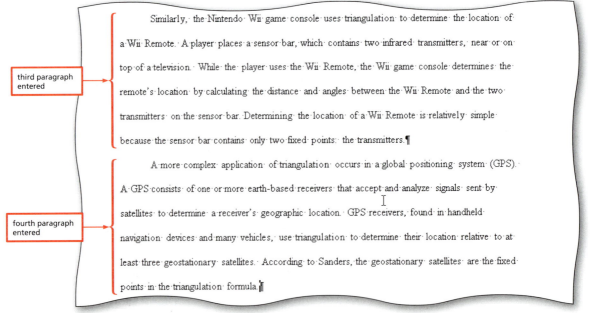

Figure D–33

To Insert Another Citation and Create Its Source

The following steps add a new source for a Web site.

1 Position the insertion point at the location for the citation (in this case, after the name, Sanders, in the last sentence of the fourth paragraph) and then press the SPACEBAR to insert a space before the comma.

2 Click the Insert Citation button (References tab | Citations & Bibliography group) to display the Insert Citation menu.

3 Click Add New Source on the Insert Citation menu to display the Create Source dialog box.

4 If necessary, click the Type of Source box arrow (Create Source dialog box) and then click Web site, so that the list shows fields required for a Web site.

5 Type `Sanders, G.` in the Author text box.

6 Type `Understanding satellites and global positioning systems` in the Name of Web Page text box.

7 Type `2012` in the Year text box.

8 Type `February` in the Month text box.

9 Type `27` in the Day text box.

10 Type `http://www.scsite.com` in the URL text box (Figure D–34).

11 Click the OK button to close the dialog box, create the source, and insert the citation in the document at the location of the insertion point.

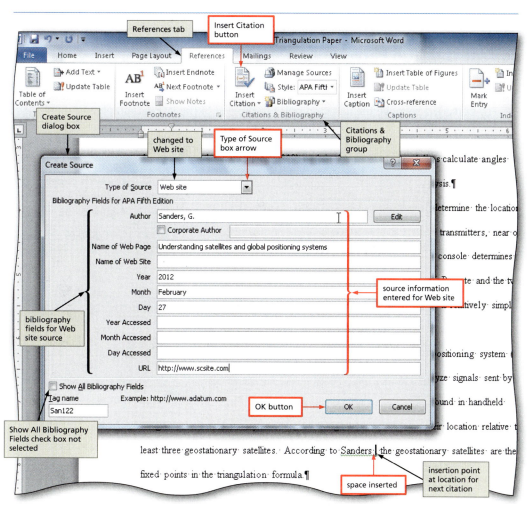

Figure D–34

To Edit a Citation

As previously mentioned, if you reference the author's name in the text, you should not list it again in the citation. Instead, just list the page number in the citation. The following steps edit the citation, suppressing the author but displaying the year.

1 If necessary, click somewhere in the citation to be edited, in this case somewhere in (Sanders, 2012), to select the citation and display the Citation Options box arrow.

2 Click the Citation Options box arrow to display the Citation Options menu.

3 Click Edit Citation on the Citation Options menu to display the Edit Citation dialog box.

4 In the Suppress area (Edit Citation dialog box), click the Author check box to place a check mark in it.

5 In the Suppress area, click the Title check box to place a check mark in it (Figure D–35).

6 Click the OK button to close the dialog box and remove the author name from the citation.

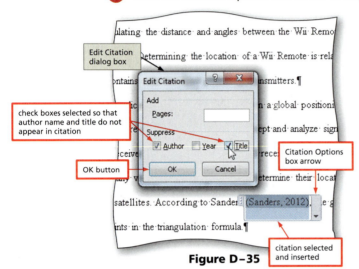

Figure D–35

To Type the Fifth Paragraph

The following steps type the last paragraph in the research paper.

1 Press CTRL+END to move the insertion point to the end of the last paragraph and then press the ENTER key.

2 Type the fifth paragraph of the research paper as shown in Figure D–36.

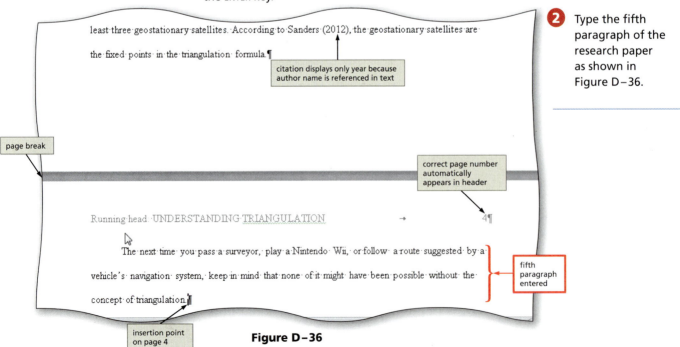

Figure D–36

To Save an Existing Document with the Same File Name

You have made several modifications to the research paper since you last saved it. Thus, you should save it again. The following step saves the document again.

1 Click the Save button on the Quick Access Toolbar to overwrite the previously saved file.

To Page Break Manually

The research paper text is complete. The next step is to create the references on a separate numbered page. The following steps insert a manual page break.

1 Click Insert on the Ribbon to display the Insert tab.

2 Click the Page Break button (Insert tab | Pages group) to insert a manual page break immediately to the left of the insertion point and position the insertion point immediately below the manual page break (shown in Figure D–37).

To Apply the Normal Style

The references title is to be centered between the margins of the paper. If you simply issue the Center command, the title will not be centered properly. Instead, it will be one-half inch to the right of the center point because earlier you set the first-line indent for paragraphs to one-half inch from the left margin.

So that you can properly center the title of the reference page, you will apply the Normal style to the location of the insertion point. Recall that you modified the Normal style for this document to 12-point Times New Roman with double-spaced, left-aligned paragraphs that have no space after the paragraphs.

To apply a style to a paragraph, first position the insertion point in the paragraph and then apply the style. The following step applies the modified Normal style to the location of the insertion point.

1

- Click Home on the Ribbon to display the Home tab.

- With the insertion point on the paragraph mark at the top of page 5, as shown in Figure D–37, even if Normal is selected, click Normal in the Quick Style gallery (Home tab | Styles group) to apply the selected style to the paragraph containing the insertion point (Figure D–37).

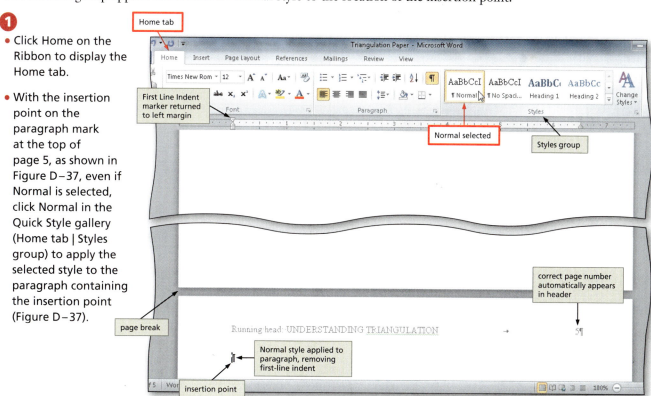

Figure D–37

To Enter the References Page Title

The next step is to enter the title, References, centered between the margins of the paper. The following steps use shortcut keys to format the title.

1 Press CTRL+E to center the paragraph mark.

2 Type **References** as the title.

3 Press the ENTER key.

4 Press CTRL+L to left-align the paragraph mark (shown in Figure D–38).

To Create the Bibliographical List

While typing the research paper, you created several citations and their sources. Word can format the list of sources and alphabetize them in a **bibliographical list**, which spares you the task of looking up style guidelines. That is, Word will create a bibliographical list with each element of the source placed in its correct position with proper punctuation, according to the specified style. For example, in this research paper, the book source will list, in this order, the author name(s), publication year, book title, publisher city, and publishing company name with the book title italicized and the correct punctuation between each element according to the specified APA documentation style. The following steps create an APA-styled bibliographical list from the sources previously entered.

- Click References on the Ribbon to display the References tab.

- With the insertion point positioned as shown in Figure D–38, click the Bibliography button (References tab | Citations & Bibliography group) to display the Bibliography gallery (Figure D–38).

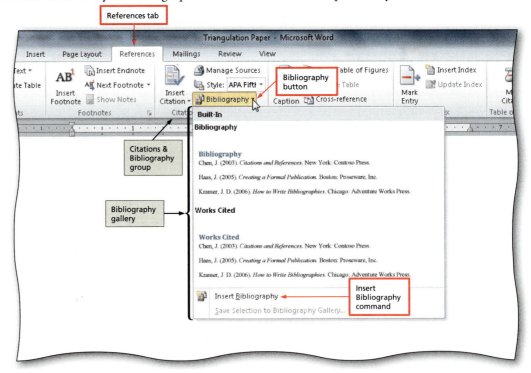

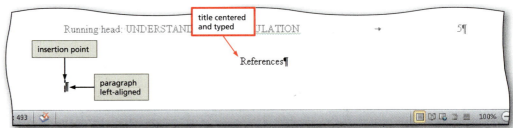

Figure D–38

2

• Click Insert Bibliography in the Bibliography gallery to insert a list of sources at the location of the insertion point.

• If necessary, scroll to display the entire list of sources in the document window (Figure D–39).

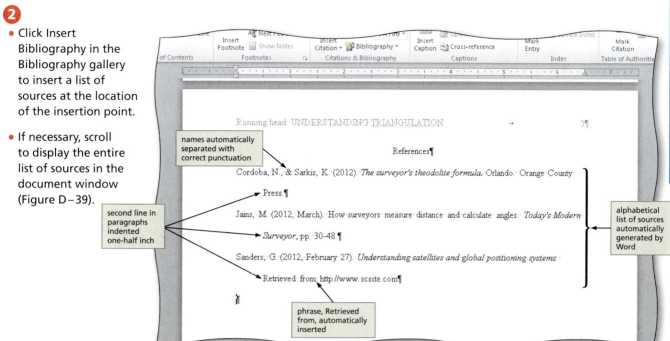

Figure D–39

To Convert a Field to Regular Text

Word may use an earlier version of the APA documentation style to format the bibliography. The latest guidelines for the APA documentation style, for example, state that the page number in magazine articles should not be preceded with the pp. notation. If you edit the bibliography, Word automatically will change it back to the Bibliography style's predetermined text and formats when the bibliography field is updated. To preserve modifications you make to the format of the bibliography, you can convert the bibliography field to regular text. Keep in mind, though, once you convert the field to regular text, it no longer is a field that can be updated. The following step converts a field to regular text.

1

• Click somewhere in the field to select it, in this case, somewhere in the bibliography (Figure D–40).

2

• Press CTRL+SHIFT+F9 to convert the selected field to regular text.

• Click anywhere in the document to remove the selection from the text.

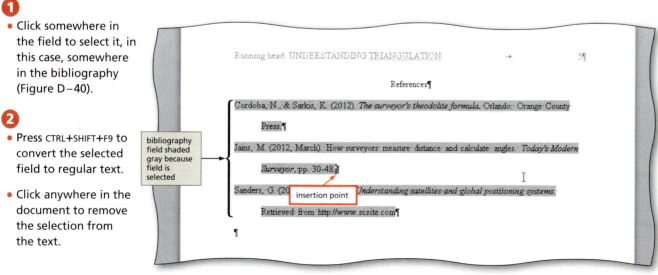

Figure D–40

To Format the References as Specified by the Latest APA Documentation Style

The following steps remove the pp. notation in front of the page number, as specified by the latest APA guidelines.

1 Drag through the pp. notation in the magazine entry to select it.

2 Press the DELETE key to delete the selected text (Figure D–41).

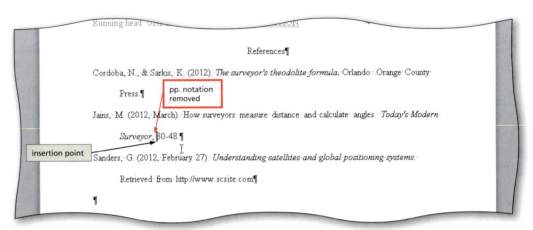

Figure D–41

To Change Document Properties

Before saving the research paper again, you will add your name, course information, and some keywords as document properties. The following steps use the Document Information Panel to change document properties.

1 Click File on the Ribbon to open the Backstage view and, if necessary, select the Info tab.

2 Click the Properties button in the right pane of the Info gallery to display the Properties menu and then click Show Document Panel on the Properties menu to close the Backstage view and display the Document Information Panel in the Word document window.

3 Click the Author text box, if necessary, and then type your name as the Author property. If a name already is displayed in the Author text box, delete it before typing your name.

4 Click the Subject text box, if necessary delete any existing text, and then type your course and section as the Subject property.

5 Click the Keywords text box, if necessary delete any existing text, and then type `surveyor, Wii, GPS` as the Keywords property.

6 Click the Close the Document Information Panel button so that the Document Information Panel no longer is displayed.

To Save an Existing Document, Print the Document, and Quit Word

The document now is complete. You should save the research paper again before quitting Word. The next steps save the document again and then quit Word.

1 Click the Save button on the Quick Access Toolbar to overwrite the previously saved file.

2 Click File on the Ribbon to open the Backstage view and then click the Print tab in the Backstage view to display the Print gallery.

3 Verify the printer name that appears on the Printer Status button will print a hard copy of the document. If necessary, click the Printer Status button to display a list of available printer options and then click the desired printer to change the currently selected printer.

4 Click the Print button in the Print gallery to print the research paper on the currently selected printer (shown in Figure D–1 on page APP 14).

5 If you have one Word document open, click the Close button on the right side of the title bar to close the document and quit Word; or if you have multiple Word documents open, click File on the Ribbon to open the Backstage view and then click Exit in the Backstage view to close all open documents and quit Word.

6 If a Microsoft Word dialog box appears, click the Save button to save any changes made to the document since the last save.

Appendix Summary

In this appendix, you have learned how to create the same research paper as the one shown in Chapter 2, except you used the APA documentation style instead of the MLA documentation style. This appendix presented only the steps required to create this research paper.

Learn It Online

Test your knowledge of chapter content and key terms.

Instructions: To complete the Learn It Online exercises, start your browser, click the Address bar, and then enter the Web address **scsite.com/wd2010/learn**. When the Word 2010 Learn It Online page is displayed, click the link for the exercise you want to complete and then read the instructions.

Chapter Reinforcement TF, MC, and SA
A series of true/false, multiple choice, and short answer questions that test your knowledge of the chapter content.

Flash Cards
An interactive learning environment where you identify chapter key terms associated with displayed definitions.

Practice Test
A series of multiple choice questions that test your knowledge of chapter content and key terms.

Who Wants To Be a Computer Genius?
An interactive game that challenges your knowledge of chapter content in the style of a television quiz show.

Wheel of Terms
An interactive game that challenges your knowledge of chapter key terms in the style of the television show *Wheel of Fortune*.

Crossword Puzzle Challenge
A crossword puzzle that challenges your knowledge of key terms presented in the chapter.

Apply Your Knowledge

Reinforce the skills and apply the concepts you learned in Chapter 2.

Revising Text and Paragraphs in a Document

Note: This exercise covers tasks presented in Chapter 2 and assumes you completed the Chapter 2 project. To complete this assignment, you will be required to use the Data Files for Students. See the inside back cover of this book for instructions on downloading the Data Files for Students, or contact your instructor for information about accessing the required files.

Instructions: Start Word. Open the document, Apply D-1 Space Paragraph Draft, from the Data Files for Students. The document you open contains a paragraph of text. You are to revise the document as follows: move a word, move another word and change the format of the moved word, change paragraph indentation, change line spacing, find all occurrences of a word, replace all occurrences of a word with another word, locate a synonym, and edit the header.

Perform the following tasks:

1. Copy the word, exploration, from the first sentence and paste it in the last sentence after the word, space, so that it is the eighth word in the sentence.

2. Select the underlined word, safe, in the paragraph. Use drag-and-drop editing to move the selected word, safe, so that it is before the word, mission, in the same sentence. Click the Paste Options button that displays to the right of the moved word, safe. Remove the underline format from the moved sentence by clicking the Keep Text Only button on the Paste Options menu.

3. Display the ruler, if necessary. Use the ruler to indent the first line of the paragraph one-half inch.

4. Change the line spacing of the paragraph to double.

5. Use the Navigation Pane to find all occurrences of the word, sensors. How many are there?

6. Use the Find and Replace dialog box to replace all occurrences of the word, issues, with the word, problems. How many replacements were made?

7. Use Word to find the word, height. Use Word's thesaurus to change the word, height, to the word, altitude.

8. Switch to the header so that you can edit it. In the first line of the header, change the word, Draft, to the word, Modified, so that it reads: Space Paragraph Modified.

9. In the second line of the header, insert the page number (with no formatting) one space after the word, Page.

10. Change the alignment of both lines of text in the header from left-aligned to right-aligned. Switch back to the document text.

11. Change the document properties, as specified by your instructor.

12. Click File on the Ribbon and then click Save As. Save the document using the file name, Apply D-1 Space Paragraph Modified.

13. Print the document properties and then print the revised document, shown in Figure D–42.

14. Use the Research task pane to look up the definition of the word, NASA, in the paragraph. Handwrite the definition of the word on your printout.

15. Change the Search for box to All Research Sites. Print an article from one of the sites.

16. Display the Research Options dialog box and, on your printout, handwrite the currently active Reference Books, Research Sites, and Business and Financial Sites. If your instructor approves, activate one of the services.

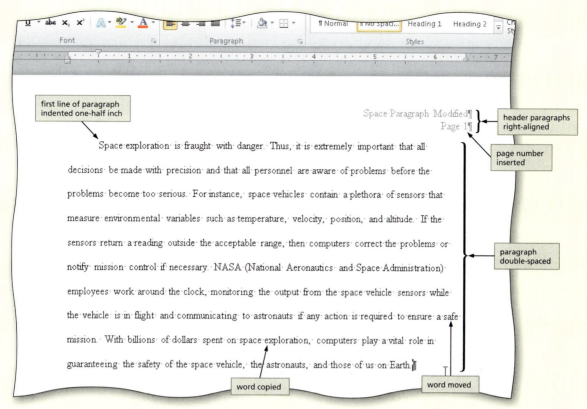

Figure D–42

Extend Your Knowledge

Extend the skills you learned in Chapter 2 and Appendix D, and experiment with new skills. You may need to use Help to complete the assignment.

Working with References and Proofing Tools

Note: To complete this assignment, you will be required to use the Data Files for Students. See the inside back cover of this book for instructions on downloading the Data Files for Students, or contact your instructor for information about accessing the required files.

Instructions: Start Word. Open the document, Extend D-1 Digital Camera Paper Draft, from the Data Files for Students. You will add a footnote, convert the footnote to an endnote, modify the Endnote Text style, use the thesaurus, and translate the document to another language.

Perform the following tasks:

1. Use Help to learn more about footers, footnotes and endnotes, bibliography styles, AutoCorrect, and the Mini Translator.

2. Delete the footer from the document.

3. Determine the APA guidelines for footnotes. Insert the following footnote at an appropriate place in the research paper: For instance, Cass states that digital cameras can last well beyond five years if maintained properly, so consider this a longer-term investment that will create memories lasting you a lifetime.

4. Insert this second footnote at an appropriate place in the research paper: For instance, Adams states that you may be able to crop photos, change the brightness, or remove red eye effects.

Continued >

Extend Your Knowledge *continued*

5. Convert the footnotes to endnotes, so that the footnotes are on a separate numbered page after the references. Place the title, Footnotes, at the top of the page.

6. Modify the Endnote Text style to 12-point Times New Roman font, double-spaced text with a hanging indent.

7. Use the Find and Replace dialog box to find the word, small, in the document and then replace it with a word of your choice.

8. Add an AutoCorrect entry that replaces the word, camora, with the word, camera. Add this sentence, A field camora usually is more than sufficient for most users., to the end of the second paragraph, misspelling the word camera as written to test the AutoCorrect entry. Delete the AutoCorrect entry just added that replaces camora with the word, camera.

9. Display readability statistics. What are the Flesch-Kincaid Grade Level, the Flesch Reading Ease score, and the percent of passive sentences?

10. Save the document with a new file name and then print it. On the printout, write the number of words, characters without spaces, characters with spaces, paragraphs, and lines in the document. Be sure to include footnote text in the statistics.

11. If you have an Internet connection, translate the research paper into a language of your choice using the Translate button (Review tab | Language group). Figure D–43 shows a sample translated document. Print the translated document. Use the Mini Translator to hear how to pronounce three words in your paper.

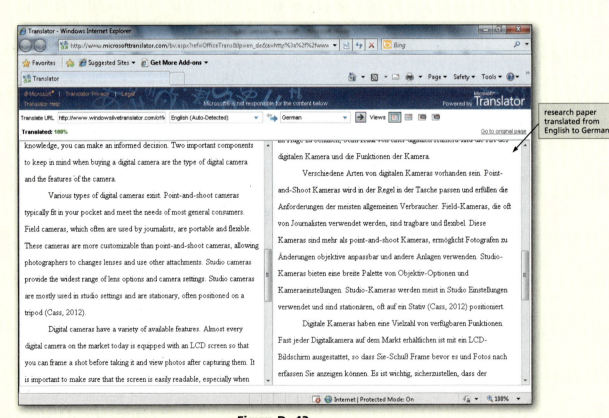

Figure D–43

Make It Right

Analyze a document and correct all errors and/or improve the design.

Inserting Missing Elements in an APA-Styled Research Paper

Note: To complete this assignment, you will be required to use the Data Files for Students. See the inside back cover of this book for instructions on downloading the Data Files for Students, or contact your instructor for information about accessing the required files.

Instructions: Start Word. Open the document, Make It Right D-1 Biometrics Paper Draft, from the Data Files for Students. The document is a research paper that is missing several elements. You are to insert these missing elements, all formatted according to the APA documentation style: title page, header with a running head and page number, manual page breaks, paper title, citations, and source information for the citations.

Perform the following tasks:

1. Insert a header with a running head (Running head: BIOMETRIC TECHNOLOGY) and a page number, formatted according to the APA documentation style.

2. Insert a title page that contains the header, along with the complete paper title (Biometric Technology: No Two the Same), author name (use your name), and school affiliation (use your school). If necessary, insert a manual page break after the end of the title page.

3. On the Abstract page, center the title and then remove the first-line indent from the paragraph below the title.

4. On the first page of the body of the paper, type and center the research paper title above the first paragraph.

5. The Jenkins placeholder (tag name) is missing its source information (Figure D–44). Use the following source information to edit the source: magazine article titled "Fingerprint Readers" written by A. D. Jenkins and M. K. Weavers, magazine name is *Security Today*, publication date is February 2012, article is on pages 55 – 60. The citation should display the author name and publication year.

6. Modify the source of the book authored by Carolina Doe, so that the publisher city is Chicago instead of Dallas.

7. Use the Navigation Pane to display page 5. Use Word to insert the bibliographical list (bibliography). Convert the works cited to regular text. Remove the pp. notation from the magazine entry.

8. Change the document properties, as specified by your instructor. Save the revised document with the file name, Make It Right D-1 Biometrics Paper Modified, and then submit it in the format specified by your instructor.

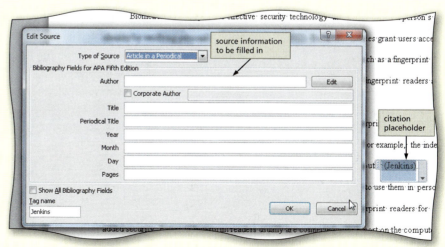

Figure D–44

In the Lab

Design and/or create a document using the guidelines, concepts, and skills presented in this appendix. Labs are listed in order of increasing difficulty.

Lab 1: Preparing a Short Research Paper

Problem: You are a college student currently enrolled in an introductory business class. Your assignment is to prepare a short research paper (275 – 300 words) about video or computer games. The requirements are that the paper be presented according to the APA documentation style and have three references. One of the three references must be from the Web. You prepare the paper shown in Figure D–45 on pages APP 45 – APP 47, which discusses game controllers.

Instructions: Perform the following tasks:

1. Start Word. If necessary, display formatting marks on the screen.

2. Modify the Normal style to 12-point Times New Roman font.

3. Adjust line spacing to double.

4. Remove space below (after) paragraphs.

5. Update the Normal style to reflect the adjusted line and paragraph spacing.

6. Create a header that includes the running head (Running head: GAME CONTROLLERS) at the left margin and the page number at the right margin.

7. Insert the title page as shown in Figure D–45a, ensuring it includes a header, along with the complete paper title (Game Controllers: Enriching the Gaming Experience), author name, and school affiliation. Insert a manual page break after the last line on the title page.

8. Type the Abstract as shown in Figure D–45b. Insert a manual page break after the last line of the abstract.

9. Set a first-line indent to one-half inch for paragraphs in the body of the research paper.

10. Type the research paper as shown in Figure D–45c on page APP 46. Change the bibliography style to APA. As you insert citations, enter their source information (shown in Figure D–45d on page APP 47). If necessary, edit the citations so that they appear as shown in Figure D–45c.

11. At the end of the research paper text, insert a manual page break so that the References page begins on a new page. Enter and format the references title (Figure D–45d). Use Word to insert the references list (bibliography). Convert the bibliography field to text. Remove the pp. notation from the page numbers in the magazine article entry (shown in Figure D–45d).

12. Check the spelling and grammar of the paper at once.

13. Change the document properties, as specified by your instructor. Save the document using Lab D-1 Game Controllers Paper as the file name.

14. Print the research paper. Handwrite the number of words, paragraphs, and characters in the research paper above the title of your printed research paper.

Running head: GAME CONTROLLERS   1

Game Controllers: Enriching the Gaming Experience

Harley Kimble

Longherst University

Figure D–45 (a) Page 1

Running head: GAME CONTROLLERS   2

Abstract

Video games and computer games use a game controller as the input device that directs

movements and actions of on-screen objects. Two commonly used game controllers are

gamepads and motion-sensing game controllers. A gamepad is held by the player with both

hands, allowing the player to control the movement or actions of the objects in the video or

computer games. Motion-sensing game controllers allow the user to guide on-screen elements or

trigger events by moving a handheld input device in predetermined directions through the air.

Game controllers not only enrich the gaming experience but also aid in the movements and

actions of players.

Figure D–45 (b) Page 2

Continued >

Running head: GAME CONTROLLERS   3

Game Controllers: Enriching the Gaming Experience

Video games and computer games use a game controller as the input device that directs movements and actions of on-screen objects. Two commonly used game controllers are gamepads and motion-sensing game controllers (Joyce, 2012). Game controllers not only enrich the gaming experience but also aid in the movements and actions of players.

A gamepad is held by the player with both hands, allowing the player to control the movement or actions of the objects in the video or computer games. Players press buttons on the gamepad, often with their thumbs, to carry out actions. Some gamepads have swiveling sticks that also can trigger events during game play (Cortez & Matthews, 2012). Some gamepads include wireless capabilities; others connect via a cable directly to the game console or a personal computer.

Motion-sensing game controllers allow the user to guide on-screen elements or trigger events by moving a handheld input device in predetermined directions through the air. These controllers communicate with a game console or personal computer via wired or wireless technology. A variety of games, from sports to simulations, use motion-sensing game controllers. Some of these controllers, such as baseball bats and golf clubs, are designed for only one specific kind of game; others are general purpose. A popular general-purpose, motion-sensing game controller is Nintendo's Wii Remote. Shaped like a television remote control and operated with one hand, the Wii Remote uses Bluetooth wireless technology to communicate with the Wii game console (Bloom, 2012).

Game controllers are used primarily to direct movement and actions of on-screen objects. Two popular types are gamepads and motion-sensing game controllers. Games become more enjoyable every day with the use of new and exciting game controllers. What will be next?

Running head: GAME CONTROLLERS   4

References

Bloom, J. (2012). *The gaming experience*. New York: Buffalo Works Press.

Cortez, D., & Matthews, M. (2012, January). Today's game controllers. *Gaming, Gaming, Gaming*, 12-34.

Joyce, A. (2012, February 15). *What gamers want*. Retrieved from http://www.scsite.com

In the Lab

Lab 2: Preparing a Research Paper

Problem: You are a college student enrolled in an introductory English class. Your assignment is to prepare a short research paper in any area of interest to you. The requirements are that the paper be presented according to the APA documentation style and have three references. One of the three references must be from the Internet. You prepare a paper about trends in agriculture. The abstract and body of the research paper, the second and third pages, are shown in Figure D – 46.

Running head: COMPUTERS IN AGRICULTURE   2

Abstract

Although people have worked in agriculture for more than 10,000 years, advances in technology assist with maintaining and protecting land, crops, and animals. The demand to keep food prices affordable encourages those working in the agriculture industry to operate as efficiently as possible. Many farmers use technology on a daily basis to regulate soil moisture and to keep their crops pest free. In addition to keeping the soil moist and reducing maintenance costs, computers also can utilize sensors to analyze the condition of crops in the field and determine whether pests or diseases are affecting the crops. With technology, farming can be much more convenient and efficient.

Figure D – 46 (a) Abstract

Instructions: Perform the following tasks:

1. Start Word. Modify the Normal style to 12-point Times New Roman font. Adjust line spacing to double and remove space below (after) paragraphs. Update the Normal style to include the adjusted line and paragraph spacing. Create a header that includes the running head (Running head: COMPUTERS IN AGRICULTURE) at the left margin and the page number at the right margin. Create an appropriate title page (page 1). Create the abstract (page 2) as shown in Figure D – 46a. Center and type the title. Set a first-line indent for paragraphs in the body of the research paper.

2. Type the research paper (page 3) as shown in Figure D – 46b. Change the bibliography style to APA. As you insert citations, use the source information on page APP 50, making certain you enter them properly formatted according to the APA guidelines.

Running head: COMPUTERS IN AGRICULTURE   3

Computers in Agriculture: Farming on a New Level

Although people have worked in agriculture for more than 10,000 years, advances in technology assist with maintaining and protecting land, crops, and animals. The demand to keep food prices affordable encourages those working in the agriculture industry to operate as efficiently as possible (Newman & Ruiz, 2012).

Almost all people and companies in this industry have many acres of land they must maintain, and it is not always feasible for farmers to take frequent trips around the property to perform basic tasks such as watering soil in the absence of rain. The number of people-hours required to water soil manually on several thousand acres of land might result in businesses spending thousands of dollars in labor and utility costs. If the irrigation process is automated, sensors detect how much rain has fallen recently, as well as whether the soil is in need of watering. According to Barton (2012), the sensors then send this data to a computer that processes it and decides when and how much to water. Brewster (2012) also points out that many automated home irrigation systems are programmable and use rain sensors.

In addition to keeping the soil moist and reducing maintenance costs, computers also can utilize sensors to analyze the condition of crops in the field and determine whether pests or diseases are affecting the crops. If sensors detect pests and/or diseases, computers send a notification to the appropriate individual to take corrective action. In some cases, according to Brewster (2012), the discovery of pests might trigger a pesticide to discharge in the affected area automatically.

Many farmers use technology on a daily basis to regulate soil moisture and to keep their crops pest free. With technology, farming can be much more convenient and efficient.

Figure D–46 (b) Body of Research Paper

Continued >

In the Lab *continued*

    a. Type of Source: Article in a Periodical

       Author: B. Barton

       Title: Computers in Agriculture

       Periodical Title: Agriculture Today and Tomorrow

       Year: 2012

       Month: Feb.

       Pages: 53 – 86

    b. Type of Source: Book

       Authors: A. Newman and C. Ruiz

       Title: The Agricultural Industry Today

       Year: 2012

       City: New York

       Publisher: Alabama Press

    c. Type of Source: Web site

       Author: L. Brewster

       Name of Web page: Agriculture: Expanding and Growing

       Year: 2012

       Month: January

       Day: 3

       Web site: http://www.scsite.com

3. At the end of the research paper text, press the ENTER key once and insert a manual page break so that the References page begins on a new page (page 4). Enter and format the references title. Use Word to insert the bibliographical list. Convert the bibliography field to text. Remove the pp. notation from the page numbers in the magazine article entry.

4. Check the spelling and grammar of the paper.

5. Save the document using Lab D-2 Agriculture Paper as the file name.

6. Print the research paper. Handwrite the number of words in the research paper above the title of your printed research paper.

In the Lab

Lab 3: Composing a Research Paper from Notes

Problem: You have drafted the notes shown in Figure D–47. Your assignment is to prepare a short research paper from these notes.

Instructions: Perform the following tasks:

1. Start Word. Review the notes in Figure D–47 and then rearrange and reword them. Embellish the paper as you deem necessary. Present the paper according to the APA documentation style. Create an AutoCorrect entry that automatically corrects the spelling of the misspelled word, digtal, to the correct spelling, digital. Be sure to add a title page and abstract page. Enter citations and their sources as shown, ensuring they are formatted according to the APA documentation style. Create the references page (bibliography) from the listed sources. Convert the bibliography field to text. Remove the pp. notation from the page numbers in the magazine article entry.

2. If necessary, set the default dictionary. Add the word, Flickr, to the dictionary. Check the spelling and grammar of the paper.

3. Use the Research task pane to look up a definition of a word in the paper. Copy and insert the definition into the document. Be sure to quote the definition and cite the source.

4. Save the document using Lab D-3 Cloud Storage Paper as the file name. Print the research paper. Handwrite the number of words, including the footnotes, in the research paper above the title of the printed research paper.

Cloud Storage:
- When storing data using cloud storage, the user must locate the appropriate Web site. Some sites support only certain file types. Other sites provide more than just storage.
- Cloud storage is one of the many different features available on the Internet.
- Cloud storage allows users to store files on Web sites.
- Computer users may use this type of storage if they do not want to store their data locally on a hard disk or other type of media.

Different Web sites provide different types of cloud storage. Three are Google's Gmail, YouTube, and Windows Live SkyDrive (source: "Cloud Storage and the Internet," an article on pages 23-37 in March 2012 issue of *Internet Usage and Trends* by Leona Carter).
- Google's e-mail program, Gmail, is cloud storage that stores e-mail messages.
- YouTube is different from Gmail, however, because it stores only digital videos (source: pages 22-24 in a book called *Working with the Internet: Cloud Storage* by Robert M. Gaff, published at Jane Lewis Press in New York in 2012).
- Windows Live SkyDrive is a cloud storage provider that accepts any type of file. This type of Web site is used mainly for backup or additional storage space.

Some cloud storage Web sites also provide other services (source: a Web site titled *The Internet: Cloud Storage* by Rebecca A. Ford and Harry I. Garland of Course Technology dated January 2, 2012, viewed on March 7, 2012).
- Flickr provides cloud storage for digital photos and also enables users to manage their photos and share them with others.
- Facebook provides cloud storage for a number of different file types including digital photos, digital videos, messages, and personal information. Facebook also provides a means of social networking.
- Google Docs not only stores documents, spreadsheets, and presentations in its cloud, it also enables its users to create these documents.

Figure D–47

Cases and Places

Apply your creative thinking and problem solving skills to design and implement a solution.

Note: To complete these assignments, you may be required to use the Data Files for Students. See the inside back cover of this book for instructions on downloading the Data Files for Students, or contact your instructor for information about accessing the required files.

1: Create a Research Paper about Preparing for a Career in the Computer Industry

Academic

As a student in an introductory computer class, your instructor has assigned a research paper that discusses educational options available for students pursuing a career in the computer industry. The source for the text in your research paper is in a file called Preparing for a Career in the Computer Industry, which is located on the Data Files for Students. In addition to this source, if your instructor requests, use the Research task pane to obtain information from another source. Add an AutoCorrect entry to correct a word you commonly mistype.

Using the concepts and techniques presented in Chapter 2 and this appendix, along with the text in the file on the Data Files for Students, create and format this research paper according to the APA documentation style. Be sure to check spelling and grammar of the finished paper. Submit your assignment in the format specified by your instructor.

2: Create a Research Paper about Computer Viruses

Personal

The computer you recently purchased included an antivirus program. Because you need practice writing research papers and you want to learn more about computer viruses, you decide to write a paper about computer viruses. The source for the text in your research paper is in a file called Computer Viruses, which is located on the Data Files for Students. In addition to this source, if your instructor requests, use the Research task pane to obtain information from another source. Add an AutoCorrect entry to correct a word you commonly mistype.

Using the concepts and techniques presented in Chapter 2 and this appendix, along with the text in the file on the Data Files for Students, create and format this research paper according to the APA documentation style. Be sure to check spelling and grammar of the finished paper. Submit your assignment in the format specified by your instructor.

3: Create a Research Paper about a Disaster Recovery Plan

Professional

Your boss has asked you to research the components of a disaster recovery plan. Because you learned in college how to write research papers, you decide to present your findings in a research paper. The source for the text in your research paper is in a file called Disaster Recovery Plan, which is located on the Data Files for Students. In addition to this source, if your instructor requests, use the Research task pane to obtain information from another source. Add an AutoCorrect entry to correct a word you commonly mistype.

Using the concepts and techniques presented in Chapter 2 and this appendix, along with the text in the file on the Data Files for Students, create and format this research paper according to the APA documentation style. Be sure to check spelling and grammar of the finished paper. Submit your assignment in the format specified by your instructor.

Appendix E

Microsoft Office 2010 Specialist and Expert Certifications

What Are Microsoft Office Specialist and Expert Certifications?

Microsoft Corporation has developed a set of standardized, performance-based examinations that you can take to demonstrate your overall expertise with Microsoft Office 2010 programs, including Microsoft Word 2010, Microsoft PowerPoint 2010, Microsoft Excel 2010, Microsoft Access 2010, and Microsoft Outlook 2010. When you successfully complete an examination for one of these Office programs, you will have earned the designation as a specialist or as an expert in that particular Office program.

These examinations collectively are called the Microsoft Office 2010 Specialist and Microsoft Office 2010 Expert certification exams. The information in Table E–1 identifies each of these examinations.

Table E–1 Microsoft Office Specialist and Expert Certifications			
Certification Exam	**Description**	**Requirement**	**Credential Earned**
Microsoft Word 2010 Specialist	Indicates you have proficiency in using at least 80 percent of the features and capabilities of Word 2010	Successfully complete Exam 77-881	Microsoft Office Specialist: Microsoft Word 2010
Microsoft Word 2010 Expert	Indicates you have proficiency in using Word 2010 at the feature and functionality levels, together with advanced features of Word 2010	Successfully complete Exam 77-887	Microsoft Office Specialist: Microsoft Word 2010 Expert
Microsoft PowerPoint 2010 Specialist	Indicates you have proficiency in using PowerPoint 2010 by creating complex slide shows using sophisticated data presented in visual formats	Successfully complete Exam 77-883	Microsoft Office Specialist: Microsoft PowerPoint 2010

Table E–1 Microsoft Office Specialist and Expert Certifications *(continued)*			
Certification Exam	**Description**	**Requirement**	**Credential Earned**
Microsoft Excel 2010 Expert	Indicates you have proficiency in using Excel 2010 at the feature and functionality levels, together with advanced features of Excel 2010	Successfully complete Exam 77-888	Microsoft Office Specialist: Microsoft Excel 2010 Expert
Microsoft Access 2010	Indicates you have proficiency in using Access 2010 by creating, modifying, and extending functionality of basic database objects	Successfully complete Exam 77-885	Microsoft Office Specialist: Microsoft Access 2010
Microsoft Outlook 2010	Indicates you have proficiency in using Outlook 2010 by formatting message content, creating contact records and appointments, scheduling meetings, and sharing schedules	Successfully complete Exam 77-884	Microsoft Office Specialist: Microsoft Outlook 2010

You will notice in Table E–1 that Word and Excel have an Expert certification. The other programs do not.

Microsoft provides one other level of Office certification: 2010 Microsoft Office Master certification. To be certified as a 2010 Microsoft Office Master, you must successfully complete the following exams:

- 77-887: Word 2010 Expert
- 77-888: Excel 2010 Expert
- 77-883: PowerPoint 2010

and either

- 77-885: Access 2010

or

- 77-884: Outlook 2010

Why Should You Be Certified?

Microsoft Office 2010 certification provides a number of benefits for both you and your potential employer. The benefits for you include the following:

- You can differentiate yourself in the employment marketplace from those who are not Microsoft Office Specialist or Expert certified.
- You have proved your skills and expertise when using Microsoft Office 2010.
- You will be able to perform at a higher skill level in your job.
- You will be working at a higher professional level than those who are not certified.
- You will broaden your employment opportunities and advance your career more rapidly.

For employers, Microsoft Office 2010 certification offers the following advantages:

- When hiring or promoting employees, employers have immediate verification of employees' skills.
- Companies can maximize their productivity and efficiency by employing Microsoft Office 2010 certified individuals.

Taking the Microsoft Office 2010 Certification Exams

The Certiport Company administers the Microsoft Office 2010 Specialist and Expert certification exams. You can contact Certiport at 888-999-9830 x138 or at the Web site http://www.certiport.com. On the Web site, click the Microsoft Office 2010 Specialist link. Be sure to explore the links on these Certiport pages to obtain a thorough understanding of the Microsoft Office 2010 certification exams.

To take an exam, you must register and pay a fee. The fee varies depending on the test and the testing center. Each exam requires that you complete specified tasks using the program on which you are being tested, that is, tasks you would perform while at work. Remember — these are performance-based exams, so you will be using the software, not answering questions about the software.

You can find testing centers by following the links on the Certiport Web site and then clicking Find a Testing Center.

How Do I Prepare for the Microsoft Office 2010 Specialist Exam?

The Shelly Cashman Series offers Microsoft-approved textbooks for the certification exams listed in Table E–1 on pages APP 53 and APP 54. These textbooks can be found by visiting the Web site, www.cengagebrain.com, and then entering the search topic, Shelly. Using any of the approved textbooks will prepare you to take and pass the indicated Microsoft Office 2010 Specialist or Expert exam. For a list of skill sets specific to this book, see Table E–2 on pages APP 56 through APP 61 and Table E–3 on pages APP 61 through APP 63. The use of all appropriate Shelly Cashman Series Office 2010 textbooks will prepare you for the 2010 Microsoft Office Master certification.

For further information from Microsoft regarding Microsoft Office 2010 certification, please visit http://www.microsoft.com/learning/en/us/certification/mos.aspx and http://office.microsoft.com/en-us/word-help/should-you-become-a-microsoft-office -specialist-HA001211101.aspx.

Table E–2 Specialist-Level Skill Sets and Locations in Book for Microsoft Word 2010

Skill Set	Page Number(s)
Sharing and Maintaining Documents	
Apply Different Views to a Document	
Select Zoom Options	WD 5, WD 33, WD 36, WD 40, WD 257, WD 362, WD 615
Split Windows	WD 438, WD 440
Arrange Windows	WD 439
View Side by Side	WD 517
Synchronous Scrolling	WD 519
Arrange Document Views	OFF 12, WD 5, WD 311, WD 561, WD 562, WD 563, WD 566
Reorganize a Document Outline	WD 561, WD 562, WD 563, WD 584, WD 596
Master Documents	WD 561, WD 565, WD 566
Subdocuments	WD 564, WD 565, WD 566
Web Layout	WD 313
Draft	WD 591
Switch between Windows	OFF 24, WD 454
Open a Document in a New Window	OFF 34, OFF 35, OFF 37, OFF 38, WD 70, WD 165, WD 277, WD 279, WD 300, WD 301, WD 658
Apply Protection to a Document	
Apply Protection by Using the Microsoft Office Backstage View Commands	
Apply Controls and Restrictions to Document Access	WD 490, WD 656, WD 657, WD 660, WD 678, WD 715, WD 716
Password-Protect a Document	WD 656, WD 657, WD 660
Mark as Final	WD 490, WD 717
Applying Protection by Using Ribbon Commands	WD 655, WD 656, WD 657, WD 660, WD 678, WD 717
Manage Document Versions	
Recover Draft Versions	WD 560
Delete All Draft Versions	WD 561
Share Documents	
Send Documents via E-Mail	WD 310
Send Documents via SkyDrive	WD 314, APP 5, APP 6, APP 9
Send Documents via Internet Fax	WD 311
Change File Types	WD 164, WD 301, WD 303, WD 304, WD 306, WD 308, WD 312, WD 614, WD 677
Create PDF Documents	WD 51, WD 301, WD 302, WD 308, WD 310, WD 311
Create Shared Documents	WD 51, WD 162, WD 301, WD 302, WD 303, WD 304, WD 305, WD 308, WD 309, WD 310, WD 311, WD 312, WD 314, APP 5, APP 6, APP 8
Publish a Blog Post	WD 520, WD 521, WD 524, WD 525
Register a Blog Account	WD 520
Save a Document	OFF 19, OFF 25, OFF 39, WD 308, WD 312, WD 338, WD 614, WD 677, APP 4, APP 6
Use Compatibility Mode	WD 305, WD 306, WD 308
Use Protected Mode	WD 554
Use Save As Options	OFF 25, OFF 39, WD 164, WD 303, WD 305, WD 306, WD 308, WD 312, WD 338, WD 558, WD 614, WD 657, WD 677, APP 4, APP 6, APP 9

Table E–2 Specialist-Level Skill Sets and Locations in Book for Microsoft Word 2010 *(continued)*

Skill Set	Page Number(s)
Apply a Template to a Document	
Find Templates	
Locate a Template on Your Disk	WD 164, WD 165, WD 277, WD 301, WD 334, WD 657, WD 660
Find Templates on the Web	WD 277, WD 300, WD 301
Formatting Content	
Apply Font and Paragraph Attributes	
Apply Character Attributes	WD 12, WD 16, WD 17, WD 18, WD 19, WD 24, WD 25, WD 26, WD 27, WD 28, WD 81, WD 161, WD 217, WD 225, WD 651
Apply Styles	WD 28, WD 70, WD 106, WD 107, WD 166, WD 167, WD 206, WD 226, WD 227, WD 567
Use Format Painter	WD 233, WD 234
Navigate and Search through a Document	
Use the Navigation Pane	
Headings	WD 115, WD 580, WD 582, WD 583
Pages	WD 115, WD 117, WD 555, WD 556, WD 557
Results	WD 115, WD 550
Use Go To	WD 112, WD 117, WD 370, WD 486, WD 548, WD 593
Use Browse by Button	WD 112, WD 115, WD 116, WD 117, WD 486, WD 547, WD 548, WD 577
Use Highlight Features	WD 115, WD 358, WD 490, WD 577, WD 651
Set Find and Replace Options	WD 115, WD 116
Format	WD 117, WD 575, WD 576, WD 577
Special	WD 117, WD 577
Apply Indentation and Tab Settings to Paragraphs	
Apply Indents	WD 81, WD 210, WD 211, WD 290
First Line	WD 83, WD 96
Hanging	WD 109
Set Tabs	WD 168, WD 169, WD 170, WD 192, WD 413, WD 414, WD 445
Use the Tabs Dialog Box	WD 168, WD 170, WD 413, WD 414, WD 445
Set Tabs on the Ruler	WD 169, WD 170
Clear Tab	WD 168, WD 170, WD 462
Set Tab Stops	WD 168, WD 170, WD 414
Move Tab Stops	WD 170, WD 193
Apply Spacing Settings to Text and Paragraphs	
Set Line Spacing	WD 72, WD 73, WD 81, WD 96, WD 166
Set Paragraph Spacing	WD 43, WD 72, WD 74, WD 81, WD 166
Create Tables	
Use the Insert Table Dialog Box	WD 177, WD 462, WD 623
Use Draw Table	WD 178, WD 247, WD 262
Insert a Quick Table	WD 523, WD 531
Convert Text to Table	WD 382
Use a Table to Control Page Layout	WD 622

Table E–2 Specialist-Level Skill Sets and Locations in Book for Microsoft Word 2010 *(continued)*

Skill Set	Page Number(s)
Manipulate Tables in a Document	
Sort Content	WD 248, WD 385
Add a Row to a Table	WD 176, WD 177, WD 178, WD 184
Add a Column to a Table	WD 185, WD 251
Manipulate Rows	
Split	WD 186, WD 249
Merge	WD 252
Move	WD 185, WD 249, WD 286
Resize	WD 181, WD 241, WD 242, WD 250, WD 251
Delete	WD 185, WD 247
Manipulate Columns	
Split	WD 186, WD 249, WD 261
Merge	WD 185
Move	WD 185
Resize	WD 180, WD 181, WD 240, WD 246, WD 250, WD 251, WD 253
Delete	WD 185, WD 247
Define the Header Row	WD 179, WD 184, WD 193, WD 243, WD 339, WD 384
Convert Tables to Text	WD 682
View Gridlines	WD 239
Apply Bullets to a Document	
Apply Bullets	WD 22, WD 187
Select a Symbol Format	WD 158, WD 159, WD 235, WD 236, WD 558, WD 559
Define a Picture to be Used as a Bullet	WD 235
Use AutoFormat	WD 162, WD 186, WD 187
Promote and Demote Bullet Levels	WD 236, WD 237, WD 238, WD 451
Applying Page Layout and Reusable Content	
Apply and Manipulate Page Setup Settings	
Set Margins	WD 141, WD 221, WD 281, WD 405, WD 406, WD 570, WD 589, WD 590, WD 617
Insert Non-Breaking Spaces	WD 175
Add Hyphenation	WD 430, WD 462
Add Columns	WD 425, WD 426, WD 429, WD 434, WD 435, WD 443, WD 447
Remove a Break	WD 221, WD 225
Force a Page Break	WD 106, WD 242
Insert a Section Break	
Continuous	WD 425, WD 570
Next Page	WD 220, WD 433, WD 563
Next Odd	WD 592
Next Even	WD 592
Insert a Blank Page into a Document	WD 572
Apply Themes	
Use a Theme to Apply Formatting	WD 12, WD 28, WD 29, WD 226, WD 279, WD 453, WD 618
Customize a Theme	WD 295, WD 296, WD 453, WD 653, WD 654, WD 679

Table E–2 Specialist-Level Skill Sets and Locations in Book for Microsoft Word 2010 *(continued)*

Skill Set	Page Number(s)
Construct Content in a Document by Using the Quick Parts Tool	
Add Built-In Building Blocks	
Quotes	WD 436, WD 437
Text Boxes	WD 437, WD 551, WD 552, WD 699
Header	WD 75, WD 76, WD 78, WD 220, WD 221, WD 229, WD 230, WD 551, WD 588, APP 19
Footer	WD 75, WD 77, WD 220, WD 221, WD 230, WD 551, WD 587
Cover Page	WD 551, WD 567, WD 568
Watermark	WD 258, WD 551, WD 559
Equations	WD 551, WD 553, WD 597
Create and Manipulate Page Backgrounds	
Format a Document's Background	WD 316, WD 317, WD 560, WD 691, WD 692
Set a Colored Background	WD 316, WD 317, WD 618
Add a Watermark	WD 258, WD 551, WD 559
Set Page Borders	WD 41, WD 53, WD 457, WD 458
Create and Modify Headers and Footers	
Insert Page Numbers	WD 75, WD 77, WD 551, APP 21
Format Page Numbers	WD 231, WD 574
Insert the Current Date and Time	WD 75, WD 170, WD 588, WD 589, WD 685
Insert a Built-In Header or Footer	WD 77, WD 229, WD 230, WD 551, WD 587, APP 19
Add Content to a Header or Footer	
Custom Dialog Box	WD 553
Manual Entry	WD 77, WD 78, WD 229, WD 230, WD 588, WD 589, APP 20, APP 21
Delete a Header or Footer	WD 75, WD 230
Change Margins	WD 228, WD 589
Apply a Different First Page Attribute	WD 220, WD 231, WD 589
Including Illustrations and Graphics in a Document	
Insert and Format Pictures in a Document	WD 31, WD 697, WD 698
Add Captions	WD 544, WD 545, WD 548
Apply Artistic Effects	WD 699
Apply Picture Styles	WD 37, WD 38, WD 39, WD 154
Compress Pictures	WD 558
Modify a Shape	WD 693
Adjust Position and Size	WD 34, WD 35, WD 36, WD 147, WD 697, WD 699
Insert Screenshots	WD 321, WD 542
Insert and Format Shapes, WordArt, and SmartArt	WD 142, WD 213, WD 215, WD 407, WD 410, WD 450, WD 456, WD 647
Add Text to a Shape	WD 145, WD 214, WD 408, WD 451
Modify Text on a Shape	WD 146, WD 147, WD 409, WD 413, WD 451, WD 452
Add Captions	WD 544, WD 548
Set Shape Styles	WD 144, WD 216, WD 449, WD 651, WD 693, WD 694, WD 695
Border	WD 154, WD 515, WD 650, WD 703

Table E–2 Specialist-Level Skill Sets and Locations in Book for Microsoft Word 2010 *(continued)*	
Skill Set	**Page Number(s)**
Text	WD 146, WD 147, WD 409, WD 413, WD 451, WD 452, WD 582
Adjust Position and Size	WD 144, WD 147, WD 148, WD 216, WD 408, WD 409, WD 452, WD 455, WD 456, WD 649
Insert and Format Clip Art	WD 148, WD 417
Organize Clip Art	WD 154, WD 193
Add Captions	WD 544, WD 548
Apply Artistic Effects	WD 151, WD 152, WD 153, WD 154
Compress Pictures	WD 558
Adjust Position and Size	WD 150, WD 151, WD 154, WD 155, WD 156, WD 157, WD 418, WD 420, WD 421, WD 621
Apply and Manipulate Text Boxes	WD 437, WD 552, WD 699
Format Text Boxes	WD 440, WD 441, WD 442, WD 554, WD 701, WD 702, WD 703, WD 704
Save a Selection to the Text Box Gallery	WD 441
Apply Text Box Styles	WD 441, WD 702
Change Text Direction	WD 440, WD 701, WD 702
Apply Shadow Effects	WD 441, WD 702
Apply 3-D Effects	WD 441, WD 703
Proofreading Documents	
Validate Content by Using Spelling and Grammar Checking Options	WD 9, WD 86, WD 119, WD 120
Set Grammar	WD 57, WD 122
Set Style Options	WD 9, WD 122
Configure AutoCorrect Settings	
Add or Remove Exceptions	WD 86, WD 88
Turn On and Off AutoCorrect	WD 86, WD 87, WD 88, WD 162, WD 163, WD 187, WD 288
Insert and Modify Comments in a Document	
Insert a Comment	WD 477, WD 478, WD 479, WD 481
Edit a Comment	WD 480
Delete a Comment	WD 486, WD 487
View a Comment	
View Comments from Another User	WD 479, WD 480, WD 486, WD 496
View Comments Inline	WD 483, WD 484, WD 485
View Comments as Balloons	WD 483, WD 478, WD 486
Applying References and Hyperlinks	
Apply a Hyperlink	
Apply a Hyperlink to Text or Graphic	WD 546, WD 594
Use a Hyperlink as a Bookmark	WD 593, WD 594
Link a Hyperlink to an E-Mail Address	WD 161, WD 162, WD 314, WD 315
Create Endnotes and Footnotes in a Document	WD 93
Demonstrate the Difference between Endnotes and Footnotes	WD 69, WD 93
Manage Footnote and Endnote Locations	WD 100, WD 128

Table E–2 Specialist-Level Skill Sets and Locations in Book for Microsoft Word 2010 *(continued)*

Skill Set	Page Number(s)
Configure Footnote and Endnote Format	WD 95, WD 129
Presentation	WD 100, WD 548
Change Footnote and Endnote Numbering	WD 100, WD 129
Create a Table of Contents in a Document	
Use Default Formats	WD 573, WD 578, WD 579
Set Levels	WD 574
Set Alignment	WD 579
Set Tab Leader	WD 445, WD 579
Modify Styles	WD 574
Update a Table of Contents	
Page Numbers	WD 575
Entire Table	WD 578
Performing Mail Merge Operations	
Set Up Mail Merge	WD 330–WD 386
Perform a Mail Merge Using the Mail Merge Wizard	WD 330, WD 333, WD 339, WD 340, WD 346, WD 360, WD 361, WD 362, WD 363, WD 371
Perform a Mail Merge Manually	WD 335, WD 344, WD 364, WD 366, WD 379, WD 381
Use Auto Check for Errors	WD 361
Execute Mail Merge	
Preview and Print a Mail Merge Operation	WD 361, WD 362, WD 364, WD 365, WD 370

Table E–3 Expert-Level Skill Sets and Locations in Book for Microsoft Word 2010

Skill Set	Page Number(s)
Sharing and Maintaining Documents	
Configure Word Options	
Change Default Program Options	WD 110, WD 162, WD 241, WD 259, WD 288, WD 311, WD 314, WD 335, WD 359, WD 480, WD 481, WD 542, WD 545, WD 626, WD 679
Change Spelling Options	WD 9, WD 57, WD 120, WD 122
Change Grammar Checking Options	WD 9, WD 57, WD 120, WD 122
Apply Protection to a Document	
Restrict Editing	WD 655, WD 656, WD 660, WD 715
Apply Controls or Restrictions to Document Access	WD 656, WD 657, WD 679, WD 715, WD 716, WD 717
Apply a Template to a Document	
Modify an Existing Template	WD 283, WD 284, WD 285, WD 286, WD 291, WD 627, WD 628, WD 630, WD 634, WD 636, WD 637, WD 640, WD 642, WD 645, WD 678, WD 680, WD 681, WD 684
Create a New Template	WD 164, WD 613, WD 614, WD 624, WD 626, WD 633, WD 637, WD 639, WD 641, WD 644, WD 655, WD 677
Apply a Template to an Existing Document	WD 164, WD 277, WD 300, WD 301, WD 344, WD 345, WD 477, WD 521, WD 658, WD 660
Manage Templates by Using the Organizer	OFF 35, WD 164, WD 165, WD 277, WD 278, WD 300, WD 301, WD 477, WD 521, WD 613, WD 660

Table E–3 Expert-Level Skill Sets and Locations in Book for Microsoft Word 2010 *(continued)*

Skill Set	Page Number(s)
Formatting Content	
Apply Advanced Font and Paragraph Attributes	
Use Character Attributes	WD 12, WD 16, WD 17, WD 18, WD 19, WD 24, WD 25, WD 26, WD 27, WD 28, WD 81, WD 161, WD 217, WD 225, WD 651
Use Character-Specific Styles	WD 12, WD 689, WD 690
Create Tables and Charts	WD 498, WD 512
Insert Tables by Using Microsoft Excel Data in Tables	WD 504, WD 505, WD 507, WD 508, WD 509
Apply Formulas or Calculations on a Table	WD 192, WD 254, WD 255, WD 256
Modify Chart Data	WD 499, WD 509, WD 514
Save a Chart as a Template	WD 517
Modify Chart Layout	WD 499, WD 500, WD 501, WD 502, WD 503, WD 514, WD 515, WD 516, WD 517
Construct Reusable Content in a Document	
Create Customized Building Blocks	WD 171, WD 172
Save a Selection as a Quick Part	WD 172
Save Quick Parts after a Document is Saved	WD 172, WD 173, WD 190
Insert Text as a Quick Part	WD 174, WD 291, WD 551
Add Content to a Header or Footer	WD 229, WD 230, WD 551, WD 558, WD 587, WD 588, WD 589, APP 19
Link Sections	
Link Text Boxes	WD 556
Break Links between Text Boxes	WD 510, WD 557
Link Different Sections	WD 229, WD 230, WD 505, WD 507, WD 508, WD 565, WD 587, WD 594
Tracking and Referencing Documents	
Review, Compare, and Combine Documents	WD 484, WD 486, WD 487, WD 488, WD 489, WD 490, WD 491
Apply Tracking	WD 482, WD 483,
Merge Different Versions of a Document	WD 493
Track Changes in a Combined Document	WD 482, WD 493, WD 496
Review Comments in a Combined Document	WD 488, WD 489, WD 493, WD 496
Create a Reference Page	
Add Citations	WD 88, WD 90, WD 91, WD 94, WD 99, WD 104, WD 108
Manage Sources	WD 92, WD 97, WD 103, WD 109
Compile a Bibliography	WD 89, WD 105, WD 108, WD 109, WD 110
Apply Cross-References	WD 546, WD 548
Create a Table of Authorities in a Document	WD 586, WD 587, APP 65
Apply Default Formats	WD 586, WD 587, APP 66
Adjust Alignment	WD 586, WD 587, APP 66
Apply a Tab Leader	WD 586, WD 587, APP 66
Modify Styles	WD 586, WD 587, APP 66
Mark Citations	WD 586, WD 587, APP 64
Use Passim (Short Form)	APP 65

Table E–3 Expert-Level Skill Sets and Locations in Book for Microsoft Word 2010 *(continued)*

Skill Set	Page Number(s)
Create an Index in a Document	WD 583
Specify Index Type	WD 583, WD 586
Specify Columns	WD 583
Specify Language	WD 584
Modify an Index	WD 585, WD 586
Mark Index Entries	WD 549, WD 550, WD 551, WD 584
Performing Mail Merge Operations	
Execute Mail Merge	
Merge Rules	WD 354, WD 355, WD 356, WD 357
Send Personalized E-Mail Messages to Multiple Recipients	WD 333, WD 339, WD 363
Create a Mail Merge by Using Other Data Sources	
Use Microsoft Outlook Tables as the Data Source for a Mail Merge Operation	WD 332, WD 340, WD 346
Use Access Tables as the Data Source for a Mail Merge Operation	WD 332, WD 345, WD 346, WD 373, WD 377, WD 380
Use Excel Tables as the Data Source for a Mail Merge Operation	WD 332, WD 346
Use Word Tables as the Data Source for a Mail Merge Operation	WD 346
Create Labels and Forms	
Prepare Data	WD 364, WD 365, WD 366, WD 368, WD 369, WD 371
Create Mailing Labels	WD 190, WD 332, WD 371, WD 372, WD 378
Create Envelope Forms	WD 189, WD 332, WD 371, WD 377
Create Label Forms	WD 371, WD 372, WD 374, WD 376
Managing Macros and Forms	
Apply and Manipulate Macros	
Record a Macro	WD 705, WD 706, WD 707
Run a Macro	WD 708
Apply Macro Security	WD 677, WD 679
Apply and Manipulate Macro Options	
Run Macros When a Document Is Opened	WD 711, WD 712, WD 714
Run Macros When a Button Is Clicked	WD 708, WD 710
Assign a Macro to a Command Button	WD 707, WD 708
Create a Custom Macro Button on the Quick Access Toolbar	WD 708, WD 710
Create Forms	
Use the Controls Group	WD 624, WD 625, WD 626, WD 627, WD 628, WD 631, WD 633, WD 634, WD 637, WD 639, WD 640, WD 641, WD 643, WD 644, WD 645
Add Help Content to Form Fields	WD 627, WD 628, WD 631, WD 634, WD 639, WD 642, WD 645
Link a Form to a Database	WD 660, APP 66, APP 67, APP 68
Lock a Form	WD 655, WD 656, WD 715
Manipulate Forms	
Unlock a Form	WD 660, WD 678
Add Fields to a Form	WD 685
Remove Fields from a Form	WD 631, WD 685

Table of Authorities

Legal documents often include a **table of authorities** to list references to cases, rules, statutes, etc., along with the page number(s) on which the references appear. To create a table of authorities, mark the citations first and then build the table of authorities.

To Mark a Citation

If you wanted to mark a citation, creating a citation entry, you would perform the following steps.

1. Select the long, full citation that you wish to appear in the table of authorities (for example, State v. Smith 220 J.3d 167 (UT, 1997)).
2. Click the Mark Citation button (References tab | Table of Authorities group) or press ALT+SHIFT+I to display the Mark Citation dialog box.
3. If necessary, click the Category box arrow (Mark Citation dialog box) and then select a new category type.
4. If desired, enter a short version of the citation in the Short citation text box.
5. Click the Mark button to mark the selected text in the document as a citation.

Q&A Why do formatting marks now appear on the screen?

When you mark a citation, Word automatically shows formatting marks (if they are not showing already) so that you can see the citation field. The citation entry begins with the letters, TA.

6. Click the Close button (Mark Citation dialog box).

Q&A How could I see all marked citation entries in a document?

With formatting marks displaying, you could scroll through the document, scanning for all occurrences of TA, or you could use the Navigation Pane (that is, place a check mark in the Navigation Pane check box (View tab | Show group)) to find all occurrences of TA.

To Mark Multiple Citations

Word leaves the Mark Citation dialog box open until you close it, which allows you to mark multiple citations without having to redisplay the dialog box repeatedly. To mark multiple citations, you would perform the following steps.

1. With the Mark Citation dialog box displayed, click in the document window; scroll to and then select the next citation.
2. If necessary, click the Selected text text box (Mark Citation dialog box) to display the selected text in the Selected text text box.
3. Click the Mark button.
4. Repeat Steps 1 through 3 for all citations you wish to mark. When finished, click the Close button in the dialog box.

To Edit a Citation Entry

At some time, you may want to change a citation entry after you have marked it. For example, you may need to change the case of a letter. If you wanted to change a citation entry, you would perform the following steps.

1. Display formatting marks.
2. Locate the TA field for the citation entry you wish to change.
3. Change the text inside the quotation marks.
4. Update the table of authorities as described in the steps on page APP 65.

To Delete a Citation Entry

If you wanted to delete a citation entry, you would perform the following steps.

1. Display formatting marks.

2. Select the TA field for the citation entry you wish to delete.

3. Press the DELETE key, or click the Cut button (Home tab | Clipboard group), or right-click the field and then click Cut on the shortcut menu.

4. Update the table of authorities as described in the steps at the bottom of this page.

To Build a Table of Authorities

Once all citations are marked, Word can build a table of authorities from the citation entries in the document. Recall that citation entries begin with TA; the citation entries appear on the screen when formatting marks are displayed. When citation entries show on the screen, the document's pagination probably will be altered because of the extra text in the citation entries. Thus, be sure to hide formatting marks before building a table of authorities. To build a table of authorities, you would perform the following steps.

1. Position the insertion point at the location for the table of authorities.

2. Ensure that formatting marks are not displayed.

3. Click the Insert Table of Authorities button (References tab | Table of Authorities group) to display the Table of Authorities dialog box.

4. If necessary, select the category to appear in the table of authorities by clicking the desired option in the Category list, or leave the default selection of All so that all categories will be displayed in the table of authorities.

5. If necessary, click the Formats box arrow (Table of Authorities dialog box) and then select the desired format for the table of authorities.

6. If necessary, click the Tab leader box arrow and then select the desired leader character in the list to specify the leader character to be displayed between the marked citation and the page number.

7. If you wish to display the word, passim, instead of page numbers for citations with more than four page references, select the Use passim check box.

Q&A What does the word, passim, mean?
Here and there.

8. Click the OK button (Table of Authorities dialog box) to create a table of authorities using the specified settings at the location of the insertion point.

To Update a Table of Authorities

If you add, delete, or modify citation entries, you must update the table of authorities to display the new or modified citation entries. If you wanted to update a table of authorities, you would perform the following steps.

1. In the document window, click the table of authorities to select it.

2. Click the Update Table of Authorities button (References tab | Table of Authorities group) or press the F9 key to update the table of authorities.

TO CHANGE THE FORMAT OF THE TABLE OF AUTHORITIES

If you wanted to change the format of the table of authorities, you would perform the following steps.

1. Click the table of authorities to select it.

2. Click the Insert Table of Authorities button (References tab | Table of Authorities group) to display the Table of Authorities dialog box.

3. Change settings in the dialog box as desired. To change the style of headings, alignment, etc., click the Formats box arrow and then click From template; next, click the Modify button to display the Style dialog box, make necessary changes and then click the OK button (Style dialog box).

4. Click the OK button (Table of Contents dialog box) to apply the changed settings.

5. Click the OK button when Word asks if you want to replace the selected category of the table of authorities.

TO DELETE A TABLE OF AUTHORITIES

If you wanted to delete a table of authorities, you would perform the following steps.

1. Click the table of authorities to select it.

2. Press SHIFT+F9 to display field codes.

3. Drag through the entire field code, including the braces, and then press the DELETE key, or click the Cut button (Home tab | Clipboard group), or right-click the field and then click Cut on the shortcut menu.

Working with XML

You can convert an online form to the XML format so that the data in the form can be shared with other programs, such as Microsoft Access. XML is a popular format for structuring data, which allows the data to be reused and shared. **XML**, which stands for eXtensible Markup Language, is a language used to encapsulate data and a description of the data in a single text file, the **XML file**. XML uses **tags** to describe data items. Each data item is called an **element**. Businesses often create standard XML file layouts and tags to describe commonly used types of data.

In Word, you can save a file in a default XML format, in which Word parses the document into individual components that can be used by other programs. Or, you can identify specific sections of the document as XML elements; the elements then can be used in other programs, such as Microsoft Access. This feature is available only in the stand-alone version of Microsoft Word and in Microsoft Office Professional.

TO SAVE A DOCUMENT IN THE DEFAULT XML FORMAT

If you wanted to save a document in the XML format, you would perform the following steps.

1. Open the file to be saved in the XML format (for example, a form containing content controls).

2. Open the Backstage view and then click Save As to display the Save As dialog box.

3. Click the 'Save as type' box arrow (Save As dialog box), click Word XML Document in the list, and then click the Save button to save the template as an XML document.

Q&A

How can I identify an XML document?

XML documents typically have an .xml extension.

To Attach a Schema File

To identify sections of a document as XML elements, you first attach an XML schema to the document, usually one that contains content controls. An **XML schema** is a special type of XML file that describes the layout of elements in other XML files. Word users typically do not create XML schema files. Computer programmers or other technical personnel create an XML schema file and provide it to Word users. XML schema files, often simply called schema files, usually have an extension of .xsd. If you wanted to attach a schema file to a document, such as an online form, you would perform the following steps.

1. Open the file to which you wish to attach the schema, such as an online form that contains content controls.
2. Open the Backstage view and then use the Save As command to save the file with a new file name, to preserve the contents of the original file.
3. Click the Schema button (Developer tab | XML group) to display the Templates and Add-ins dialog box.
4. Click the Add Schema button (Templates and Add-ins dialog box) to display the Add Schema dialog box.
5. Locate and select the schema file (Add Schema dialog box) and then click the Open button to display the Schema Settings dialog box.
6. Enter the URI and alias in the appropriate text boxes (Schema Settings dialog box) and then click the OK button to add the schema to the Schema Library and to add the namespace alias to the list of available schemas in the XML Schema sheet (Templates and Add-ins dialog box).

Q&A
What are a URI and an alias?

Word uses the URI, also called a **namespace**, to refer to the schema. Because these names are difficult to remember, you can define a namespace alias. In a setting outside of an academic environment, a computer administrator would provide you with the appropriate namespace entry.

7. If necessary, place a check mark in the desired schema's check box.
8. Click the OK button, which causes Word to attach the selected schema to the open document and display the XML Structure task pane in the Word window.

To Delete a Schema from the Schema Library

To delete a schema from a document, you would remove the check mark from the schema name's check box in the XML Schema sheet in the Templates and Add-ins dialog box. If you wanted to delete a schema altogether from the Schema Library, you would do the following.

1. Click the Schema button (Developer tab | XML group) to display the Templates and Add-ins dialog box.
2. Click the Schema Library button (Templates and Add-ins dialog box) to display the Schema Library dialog box.
3. Click the schema you want to delete in the 'Select a schema' list (Schema Library dialog box) and then click the Delete Schema button.
4. When Word displays a dialog box asking if you are sure you wish to delete the schema, click the Yes button.
5. Click the OK button (Schema Library dialog box) and then click the Cancel button (Templates and Add-ins dialog box).

To Add a Parent and a Child XML Element

After a schema has been attached to a document, the next step is to add XML elements to the document. XML elements are data items whose value often changes, such as values entered in content controls on an online form. The first step is to add the entire online form XML element, called the **parent element**, to the document and then add the elements subordinate to the parent, called the **child elements**. First, you select the item to be tagged and then you add the desired XML element to apply the tag, which is called tagging the text. If you wanted to add parent and child elements to an online form, for example, you would perform the following steps.

1. Position the insertion point at the top of the document.

2. In the 'Choose an element to apply to your current selection' list in the XML Structure task pane, click the desired schema name to display the 'Apply to entire document' dialog box.

3. Click the Apply to Entire Document button ('Apply to entire document' dialog box) to place start and end tags on the entire document, that is, to tag the parent element, so that all content control names also appear in the XML Structure task pane.

4. Be sure the 'Show XML tags in the document' check box contains a check mark so that the parent and child tags appear in the document window.

5. Click a content control and then click its label to select the content control.

Q&A   What if the item to select is not a content control?
Drag through the item to which you want to assign the child element.

6. In the XML Structure task pane, click the associated control name in the 'Choose an element to apply to your current selection' list, which places start and end tags on the item selected in the document and moves the selected child element below the parent element in the 'Elements in the document' list.

7. Repeat Steps 5 and 6 for the remaining content controls in the document.

8. In the XML Structure task pane, remove the check mark from the 'Show XML tags in the document' check box so that the tags no longer appear in the document window.

To Remove a Tag

If you wanted to remove a tag that was added to a document, you would perform the following steps.

1. Right-click the start or end tag in the document window and then click Remove [tag name] tag on the shortcut menu, which instructs Word to remove both the start and end tag.

   or

   Right-click the element name in the 'Elements in the document' area in the XML Structure task pane and then click Remove [tag name] tag on the shortcut menu.

Index

Quick Reference Summary

Microsoft Word 2010 Quick Reference Summary

Task	Page Number	Mouse	Ribbon	Shortcut Menu	Keyboard Shortcut
AddressBlock Merge Field, Add	WD 349		Address Block button (Mailings tab | Write & Insert Fields group) or Address block link in Mail Merge task pane		
AddressBlock Merge Field, Edit	WD 349			Edit Address Block	
All Caps	WD 81		Change Case button (Home tab | Font group), UPPERCASE	Font, Font tab (Font dialog box)	CTRL+SHIFT+A
Arrange All Open Word Documents on Screen	WD 439		Arrange All button (View tab | Window group)		
Artistic Effect, Apply	WD 699		Artistic Effects button (Picture Tools Format tab | Adjust group)		
AutoCorrect Entry, Create	WD 86		Options (File tab), Proofing (Word Options dialog box)		
AutoCorrect Options button, Use	WD 85	Point to AutoCorrect Options button in flagged word			
Background Color, Add	WD 316		Page Color button (Page Layout tab | Page Background group)		
Background, Remove from Graphic	WD 697		Remove Background button (Picture Tools Format tab | Adjust group)		
Bibliographical List, Create	WD 108		Bibliography button (References tab | Citations & Bibliography group)		
Bibliography Style, Change	WD 89		Bibliography Style box arrow (References tab | Citations & Bibliography group)		
Blank Page, Insert	WD 572		Blank Page button (Insert tab | Pages group)		
Blog Account, Register	WD 520		Manage Accounts button (Blog Post tab | Blog group), New button (Blog Accounts dialog box)		
Blog Category, Insert	WD 524		Insert Category button (Blog Post tab | Blog group)		

Microsoft Word 2010 Quick Reference Summary *(continued)*

Task	Page Number	Mouse	Ribbon	Shortcut Menu	Keyboard Shortcut
Blog Post, Create Blank Document For	WD 521		File tab | New tab, Blog post button (Available Templates area), Create button		
Blog Post, Open Existing	WD 526		Open Existing button (Blog Post tab | Blog group), select title of post to open (Open Existing Post dialog box)		
Blog Post, Publish	WD 525		Publish button (Blog Post tab | Blog group)		
Blog Web Page, Display in Browser Window	WD 526		Home Page button (Blog Post tab | Blog group)		
Bold	WD 28	Bold button on Mini toolbar	Bold button (Home tab | Font group)	Font, Font tab (Font dialog box)	CTRL+B
Bookmark, Create	WD 592		Bookmark button (Insert tab | Links group)		
Bookmark, Go To	WD 593		Bookmark button (Insert tab | Links group), select bookmark name (Bookmark dialog box), Go To button		F5
Border Paragraph	WD 160, WD 206, WD 415		Border button arrow (Home tab | Paragraph group) or Page Borders button (Page Layout tab | Page Background group), Borders tab (Borders and Shading dialog box)		
Building Block, Create	WD 171		Quick Parts button (Insert tab | Text group)		ALT+F3
Building Block, Edit Properties	WD 553		Quick Parts button (Insert tab | Text group), Building Blocks Organizer, Edit Properties button (Building Blocks Organizer dialog box)		
Building Block, Insert	WD 174, WD 291, WD 551		Quick Parts button (Insert tab | Text group		F3
Building Block, Modify	WD 173		Quick Parts button (Insert tab | Text group), right-click building block, Edit Properties		
Building Blocks, Sort	WD 552		Quick Parts button (Insert tab | Text group), Building Blocks Organizer, click desired heading (Building Blocks Organizer dialog box)		
Bullets, Apply	WD 22, WD 162		Bullets button (Home tab | Paragraph group)	Bullets	* (ASTERISK), SPACEBAR
Bullets, Change Level	WD 559		Bullets button arrow (Home tab | Paragraph group), Change List Level (Bullets gallery)		
Bullets, Customize	WD 235, WD 558		Bullets button arrow (Home tab | Paragraph group), Define New Bullet in Bullets gallery		

Microsoft Word 2010 Quick Reference Summary *(continued)*

Task	Page Number	Mouse	Ribbon	Shortcut Menu	Keyboard Shortcut
Buttons, Add to Quick Access Toolbar	WD 708	Customize Quick Access Toolbar button on Quick Access Toolbar, More Commands, select command, Add button (Word Options dialog box)		Customize Quick Access Toolbar	
Buttons, Delete from Quick Access Toolbar	WD 710			Right-click button to be deleted, Remove from Quick Access Toolbar	
Callout, Add	WD 514		Shapes button (Chart Tools Layout tab | Insert group), select desired shape (Shapes gallery), draw shape in desired location, enter text in and format callout		
Caption, Insert	WD 544		Insert Caption button (References tab | Captions group)		
Caption, Remove Field Codes	WD 545		Options (File tab), Options		ALT+F9
Center	WD 14	Center button on Mini toolbar	Center button (Home tab | Paragraph group)	Paragraph, Indents and Spacing tab (Paragraph dialog box)	CTRL+E
Change Case	WD 18		Change Case button (Home tab | Font group)		SHIFT+F3
Change Spacing before or after Paragraph	WD 43		Spacing Before or Spacing After box arrow (Page Layout tab | Paragraph group)	Paragraph, Indents and Spacing tab (Paragraph dialog box)	
Character Spacing, Modify	WD 216		Font Dialog Box Launcher (Home tab | Font group), Advanced tab (Font dialog box)	Font, Advanced tab (Font dialog box)	
Character Style, Create	WD 689		Styles Dialog Box Launcher (Home tab | Styles group), Manage Styles button (Styles task pane), New Style button (Manage Styles dialog box)		
Chart, Graph by Column	WD 499	By Column button (Standard toolbar) or Series in Columns (Data menu)			
Chart, Move Legend Using Graph	WD 500	Chart Objects box arrow (Standard toolbar), Legend, Format Legend button (Standard toolbar) Placement tab, Bottom (Format Legend dialog box)		Format Legend	

Microsoft Word 2010 Quick Reference Summary *(continued)*

Task	Page Number	Mouse	Ribbon	Shortcut Menu	Keyboard Shortcut
Chart, Move Legend Using Office Chart Tools	WD 514		Legend button (Chart Tools Layout tab | Labels group)	Format Legend	
Chart, Resize	WD 500	Drag sizing handle			
Chart, Save as Template	WD 517		Save As Template button (Chart Tools Design tab | Type group)		
Chart, Use Saved Template	WD 517		Change Chart Type button (Chart Tools Design tab | Type group), Templates (Change Chart Type dialog box), click desired saved template		
Chart Area, Format Text Using Graph	WD 502	Chart Objects box arrow (Standard toolbar), Chart Area, Format Chart Area button (Standard toolbar), Font tab (Format Chart Area dialog box)			
Chart Axis, Format Using Graph	WD 502	Chart Objects box arrow (Standard toolbar), Category Axis, Format Axis button (Standard toolbar), Scale tab (Format Axis dialog box)		Format Axis	
Chart Axis, Format Using Office Chart Tools	WD 516	Right-click axis, Chart Elements box arrow on Mini toolbar	Chart Elements box arrow (Chart Tools Format tab | Current Selection group), specify object to be formatted in Chart Elements gallery, Format Selection button (Chart Tools Format tab | Current Selection group)		
Chart Table, Using Graph	WD 498		Insert Object button (Insert tab | Text group), Create New tab (Object dialog box), Microsoft Graph Chart		
Chart Table, Using Office Chart Tools	WD 511		Select table, Copy button (Home tab | Clipboard group), Insert Chart button (Insert tab | Illustrations group), specify chart type (Insert Chart dialog box)		
Chart Type, Change Using Graph	WD 501	Chart (menu bar), Chart Type, Standard Types tab, select chart type (Chart Type dialog box)			
Citation, Edit	WD 91	Click citation, Citation Options box arrow, Edit Citation			
Citation, Insert	WD 90		Insert Citation button (References tab | Citations & Bibliography group), Add New Source		

Microsoft Word 2010 Quick Reference Summary *(continued)*

Task	Page Number	Mouse	Ribbon	Shortcut Menu	Keyboard Shortcut
Citation, Mark	APP 64		Mark Citation button (References tab | Table of Authorities group)		ALT+SHIFT+I
Citation, Mark Multiple	APP 64		Mark Citation button (References tab | Table of Authorities group), Selected text text box (Mark Citation dialog box), Mark button		
Citation Entry, Delete	APP 65		Select field, Cut button (Home tab | Clipboard group)	Select field, Cut	Select field, DELETE
Citation Entry, Edit	APP 64	Edit text inside quotation marks in citation entry			
Citation Placeholder, Insert	WD 94		Insert Citation button (References tab | Citations & Bibliography group), Add New Placeholder		
Clear Formatting	WD 161		Clear Formatting button (Home tab | Font group)		CTRL+SPACEBAR, CTRL+Q
Click and Type	WD 80	Position mouse pointer until desired icon appears, then double-click			
Clip Art, Insert	WD 148		Clip Art button (Insert tab | Illustrations group)		
Color Text	WD 25	Font Color button arrow on Mini toolbar	Font Color button arrow (Home tab | Font group)	Font, Font tab (Font dialog box)	
Column Break, Insert	WD 434		Insert Page and Section Breaks button (Page Layout tab | Page Setup group)		CTRL+SHIFT+ENTER
Column, Increase Width	WD 429	Double-click space between columns on ruler or drag column boundaries on ruler	Columns button (Page Layout tab | Page Setup group), More Columns, Width box up arrow (Columns dialog box)		
Columns, Balance	WD 447		Insert Page and Section Breaks button (Page Layout tab | Page Setup group), Continuous in Insert Page and Section Breaks gallery		
Columns, Change Number of	WD 426		Columns button (Page Layout tab | Page Setup group)		
Columns, Insert Vertical Rule between	WD 429		Columns button (Page Layout tab | Page Setup group), More Columns, Line between check box (Columns dialog box) or Borders button arrow (Home tab | Paragraph group)		
Commands, Add to Quick Access Toolbar	WD 708		Customize Quick Access Toolbar button on Quick Access Toolbar, More Commands, select command, 'Choose commands from' box arrow	Customize Quick Access Toolbar	
Comment, Insert	WD 477		Insert Comment button (Review tab | Comments group)		CTRL+ALT+M

Microsoft Word 2010 Quick Reference Summary *(continued)*

Task	Page Number	Mouse	Ribbon	Shortcut Menu	Keyboard Shortcut
Comment, Reply to	WD 481		Insert Comment button (Review tab | Comments group)		
Comments, Change Display	WD 483		Show Markup button (Review tab | Tracking group), Balloons (Show Markup menu), select desired markup appearance		
Comments, Delete All	WD 487		Delete Comment button arrow (Review tab | Comments group), Delete All Comments in Document (Delete Comment menu)		
Comments, View or Delete	WD 485		Next Comment button (Review tab | Comments group), Delete Comment button (Review tab | Comments group)	Delete Comment	
Compare and Merge	WD 493		Compare button (Review tab | Compare group), Original document box arrow (Compare Documents dialog box) or Revised document box arrow (Compare Documents dialog box)		
Compare Documents	WD 491		Compare button (Review tab | Compare group), Compare		
Compare Revisions, Multiple Authors	WD 493		Compare button (Review tab | Compare group), Combine, Original document box arrow (Combine Documents dialog box), select files		
Compatibility Checker	WD 305		Check for Issues button (File tab | Info tab), Check Compatibility		
Compress Pictures	WD 558	Tools button (Save As dialog box), Compress Pictures	Compress Pictures button (Picture Tools Format tab | Adjust group)		
Content Control, Change Properties, Combo Box	WD 642		Control Properties button (Developer tab | Controls group)		
Content Control, Change Properties, Date Picker	WD 645		Control Properties button (Developer tab | Controls group)		
Content Control, Change Properties, Drop-Down List	WD 634		Control Properties button (Developer tab | Controls group)		
Content Control, Change Properties, Plain Text	WD 628		Control Properties button (Developer tab | Controls group)		
Content Control, Delete	WD 284		Cut button (Home tab | Clipboard group)	Remove Content Control	CTRL+X, DELETE, or BACKSPACE

Microsoft Word 2010 Quick Reference Summary *(continued)*

Task	Page Number	Mouse	Ribbon	Shortcut Menu	Keyboard Shortcut
Content Control, Edit Placeholder Text	WD 627		Design Mode button (Developer tab | Controls group), edit text, Design Mode button (Developer tab | Controls group)		
Content Control, Format	WD 283	Select content control, apply formats			
Content Control, Insert Check Box	WD 637		Check Box Content Control button (Developer tab | Controls group)		
Content Control, Insert Combo Box	WD 641		Combo Box Content Control button (Developer tab | Controls group)		
Content Control, Insert Date Picker	WD 644		Date Picker Content Control button (Developer tab | Controls group)		
Content Control, Insert Drop-Down List	WD 633		Drop-Down List Content Control button (Developer tab | Controls group)		
Content Control, Insert Plain Text	WD 626		Plain Text Content Control button (Developer tab | Controls group)		
Content Control, Insert Rich Text	WD 639		Rich Text Content Control button (Developer tab | Controls group)		
Content Control, Modify Text	WD 283	Select content control, type new text			
Control Layout Using a Table	WD 622		Table button (Insert tab | Tables group) or Table button (Insert tab | Tables group), Insert Table in Table gallery, enter number of columns		
Convert Text to a Table	WD 382		Table button (Insert tab | Tables group), Convert Text to Table in Table gallery		
Copy	WD 113, WD 439, WD 453		Copy button (Home tab | Clipboard group)	Copy	CTRL+C
Count Words	WD 101	Word Count indicator on status bar	Word Count button (Review tab | Proofing group)		CTRL+SHIFT+G
Cover Page, Delete	WD 568		Cover Page button (Insert tab | Pages group), Remove Current Cover Page (Cover Page gallery)		
Cover Page, Insert	WD 567		Cover Page button (Insert tab | Pages group) or Quick Parts button (Insert tab | Text group)		
Cross-Reference	WD 546		Cross-reference button (References tab | Captions group)		
Cross-Reference, Update	WD 547			Update Field	F9

Microsoft Word 2010 Quick Reference Summary *(continued)*

Task	Page Number	Mouse	Ribbon	Shortcut Menu	Keyboard Shortcut
Custom Dictionary, Set Default, View or Modify Entries	WD 120		Options (File tab), Proofing (Word Options dialog box), Custom Dictionaries button		
Data Source, Create	WD 340		'Type a new list' in Select recipients area in Mail Merge task pane, Create link in 'Type new list' area, Customize Columns button (New Address List dialog box) or Select Recipients button (Mailings tab | Start Mail Merge group), Type New List		
Data Source, Find and Display Data	WD 370		Find Recipient button (Mailings tab | Preview Results group), enter search text, Find Next button (Find Entry dialog box)		
Data Source, Save	WD 345		Enter file name in File name text box (Save Address List dialog box), navigate to save location, Save button		
Data Source, Sort Records	WD 368		Edit Recipient List button (Mailings tab | Start Mail Merge group), button arrow to right of field on which to sort		
Data Source, Use Access Table, Excel Worksheet, or Word Table	WD 346	Use Existing List (Mail Merge task pane)	Select Recipients button (Mailings tab | Start Mail Merge group), Use Existing List, select desired data source (Select Data Source dialog box), Open button		
Data Source, Use Existing	WD 346	Select appropriate option in Select recipients area (Mail Merge task pane)	Select Recipients button (Mailings tab | Start Mail Merge group)		
Data Source, Use Microsoft Outlook Contacts	WD 346	Click Select from Outlook contacts (Mail Merge task pane), select desired contact folder (Select Contacts dialog box)	Select Recipients button (Mailings tab | Start Mail Merge group), select desired contact folder (Select Contacts dialog box)		
Date, Insert Current	WD 170, WD 348	Click content control box arrow, click desired date or type date in content control	Insert Date and Time button (Insert tab | Text group)		
Date Field, Insert	WD 685		Quick Parts button (Insert tab | Text group), Field (Quick Parts menu), Date (Field dialog box) or Insert Date and Time button (Insert tab | Text group), select date format		
Developer Tab, Remove from Ribbon	WD 657		Options (File tab), Customize Ribbon, Developer check box (Word Options dialog box)		

Microsoft Word 2010 Quick Reference Summary *(continued)*

Task	Page Number	Mouse	Ribbon	Shortcut Menu	Keyboard Shortcut
Developer Tab, Show on Ribbon	WD 625		Options (File tab), Customize Ribbon, Developer check box (Word Options dialog box)		
Digital Signature, Add Invisible	WD 716		File tab | Info tab, Protect Document button, Add a Digital Signature (Protect Document menu), enter signature's purpose, Sign button (Sign dialog box)		
Digital Signature, Insert	WD 718	View Signatures button on Message Bar			
Digital Signature Line, Add	WD 717		Signature Line button (Insert tab | Text group)		
Digital Signatures, View	WD 717	Signatures button on status bar	File tab | Info tab, View Signatures button		
Document, Create New	WD 70, WD 279		Blank document (File tab | New tab), Create button		CTRL+N
Document, Create from Template	WD 277		File tab | New tab		
Document Inspector	WD 311, WD 497		Check for Issues button (File tab | Info tab), Inspect Document, make selections, Inspect button (Document Inspector dialog box)		
Document Properties, Change	WD 49		Properties button (File tab | Info tab)		
Document Properties, Print	WD 123		File tab | Print tab, first button in Settings area		
Document Theme, Change	WD 279		Themes button (Page Layout tab | Themes group)		
Double-Space	WD 73		Line and Paragraph Spacing button (Home tab | Paragraph group), 2.0	Paragraph, Indents and Spacing tab (Paragraph dialog box), Line spacing box arrow, 2.0	CTRL+2
Double-Underline	WD 27, WD 81		Underline button arrow (Home tab | Font group)	Font, Font tab (Font dialog box), Underline style box arrow	CTRL+SHIFT+D
Draft Versions, Delete	WD 561		Manage Versions button (File tab | Info tab), Delete All Unsaved Documents		
Draft Versions, Recover	WD 560		Recover Unsaved Documents (File tab | Recent tab) or Manage Versions button (File tab | Info tab), Recover Unsaved Documents		
Draft View	WD 591	Draft button on status bar	Draft View button (View tab | Document Views group)		
Drop Cap	WD 431		Drop Cap button (Insert tab | Text group)		

Microsoft Word 2010 Quick Reference Summary *(continued)*

Task	Page Number	Mouse	Ribbon	Shortcut Menu	Keyboard Shortcut
Editing Restrictions, Set to Tracked Changes or Comments or No Edits	WD 657		Restrict Editing button (Developer tab | Protect group), 'Allow only this type of editing in the document' check box (Restrict Formatting and Editing task pane), Yes, Start Enforcing Protection button		
E-Mail Attachments, Customize How Word Opens	WD 311		Options (File tab), General (Word Options dialog box)		
E-Mail, Send Document as	WD 310		Send Using E-Mail (File tab | Save & Send tab), Send as Attachment		
Embed Excel Object in a Word Document	WD 509		In Excel, Copy button (Home tab | Clipboard group), switch to Word, Paste button arrow (Home tab | Clipboard group Paste Special in Paste gallery, Paste option button (Paste Special dialog box), select object		
Embedded Object, Edit	WD 509	Double-click embedded object			
Envelope, Address and Print	WD 189		Create Envelopes button (Mailings tab | Create group), Envelopes tab (Envelopes and Labels dialog box)		
Equation, Insert	WD 553		Quick Parts button (Insert tab | Text group) or Equation button (Insert tab | Symbols group)		
Field, Convert to Regular text	WD 110				Click field, CTRL+SHIFT+F9
Field, Delete	WD 685		Cut (Home tab | Clipboard group)	Cut	DELETE or BACKSPACE
Field, Edit	WD 686			Edit Field	
Field Code, Display	WD 358			Toggle Field Codes	SHIFT+F9
Field Codes, Print	WD 359		Options (File tab), Advanced (Word Options dialog box), Print area		
Fill Effect, Add to Background	WD 316		Page Color button (Page Layout tab | Page Background group), Fill Effects in Page Color gallery		
Find Format	WD 575	Select Browse Object button on vertical scroll bar, Find icon	Find button arrow (Home tab | Editing group), Advanced Find, Format button (Find and Replace dialog box)		CTRL+F
Find Text	WD 115	Select Browse Object button on vertical scroll bar, Find button, or Page Number indicator on status bar, Find tab (Find and Replace dialog box)	Find button (Home tab | Editing group)		CTRL+F

Microsoft Word 2010 Quick Reference Summary *(continued)*

Task	Page Number	Mouse	Ribbon	Shortcut Menu	Keyboard Shortcut
Folder, Create while Saving	WD 338		Save button on Quick Access Toolbar, navigate to new location (Save As dialog box), New folder button		F12, New folder button
Font, Change	WD 17	Font box arrow on Mini toolbar	Font box arrow (Home tab | Font group)	Font, Font tab (Font dialog box)	CTRL+D
Font Settings, Modify Default	WD 225		Font Dialog Box Launcher (Home tab | Font group), Font tab (Font dialog box), Set As Default button		
Font Size, Change	WD 16	Font Size box arrow on Mini toolbar	Font Size box arrow (Home tab | Font group)	Font, Font tab (Font dialog box)	CTRL+D
Font Size, Decrease	WD 81, WD 146	Shrink Font button on Mini toolbar	Shrink Font button (Home tab | Font group)		CTRL+SHIFT+<
Font Size, Decrease 1 point	WD 81				CTRL+[
Font Size, Increase	WD 81, WD 146	Grow Font button on Mini toolbar	Grow Font button (Home tab | Font group)		CTRL+SHIFT+>
Font Size, Increase 1 point	WD 81				CTRL+]
Footnote, Insert	WD 93		Insert Footnote button (References tab | Footnotes group)		
Format Characters	WD 216		Font Dialog Box Launcher (Home tab | Font group), Font tab (Font dialog box)	Font, Font tab (Font dialog box)	
Format Painter	WD 233		Format Painter button (Home tab | Clipboard group)		
Formatting Marks, Show or Hide	WD 7		Show/Hide ¶ button (Home tab | Paragraph group)		CTRL+SHIFT+*
Formatting Restrictions, Set	WD 656		Restrict Editing button (Developer tab | Protect group), select restrictions (Restrict Formatting and Editing task pane), Yes, Start Enforcing Protection button		
Go to a Page	WD 117	'Browse the pages in your document' tab in Navigation Pane	Find button arrow (Home tab | Editing group)		CTRL+G
Grammar and Style Options	WD 122		Options button (File tab), Proofing (Word Options dialog box)		
Graph, Quit	WD 504	Click outside graph			
Graphic, Adjust Brightness and Contrast	WD 153		Corrections button (Picture Tools Format tab | Adjust group)	Format Picture, Picture Corrections button (Format Picture dialog box)	
Graphic, Change Border Color	WD 154		Picture Border button arrow (Picture Tools Format tab | Picture Styles group)		
Graphic, Change Color	WD 151		Color button (Picture Tools Format tab | Adjust group)	Format Picture, Picture Color button (Format Picture dialog box)	

Microsoft Word 2010 Quick Reference Summary *(continued)*

Task	Page Number	Mouse	Ribbon	Shortcut Menu	Keyboard Shortcut
Graphic, Crop	WD 418		Crop button (Picture Tools Format tab | Size group)		
Graphic, Flip	WD 157		Rotate button (Picture Tools Format tab | Arrange group)		
Graphic, Move	WD 155	Drag graphic			
Graphic, Resize	WD 34	Drag sizing handle	Shape Height and Shape Width text boxes (Picture Tools Format tab | Size group)	Size and Position, Size tab (Layout dialog box)	
Graphic, Rotate	WD 421	Drag graphic's rotate handle			
Graphic, Send behind Text	WD 649		Send Backward button arrow (Drawing Tools Format tab | Arrange group)	Send to Back, Send Behind Text	
Graphic, Set Transparent Color	WD 152		Color button (Picture Tools Format tab | Adjust group)		
GreetingLine Merge Field, Add	WD 349		Greeting Line button (Mailings tab | Write & Insert Fields group) or Greeting line link in Mail Merge task pane		
GreetingLine Merge Field, Edit	WD 351			Edit Greeting Line	
Group Objects	WD 704		Group button (Drawing Tools Format tab | Arrange group), Group		
Gutter Margin	WD 590		Margins button (Page Layout tab | Page Setup group), Custom Margins		
Hanging Indent, Create	WD 81, WD 109	Drag Hanging Indent marker on ruler	Paragraph Dialog Box Launcher (Home tab or Page Layout tab | Paragraph group), Indents and Spacing tab (Paragraph dialog box)	Paragraph, Indents and Spacing tab (Paragraph dialog box)	CTRL+T
Hanging Indent, Remove	WD 81, WD 109	Drag Hanging Indent marker on ruler	Paragraph Dialog Box Launcher (Home tab or Page Layout tab | Paragraph group), Indents and Spacing tab (Paragraph dialog box)	Paragraph, Indents and Spacing tab (Paragraph dialog box)	CTRL+SHIFT+T
Header, Different from Previous	WD 229		Deselect Link to Previous button (Header & Footer Tools Design tab | Navigation group) or Quick Parts button (Insert tab | Text group), Building Blocks Organizer (Quick Parts menu), select desired header (Building Blocks Organizer dialog box), Insert button		
Header, Switch to	WD 75	Double-click dimmed header	Header button (Insert tab | Header & Footer group)	Edit Header	

Microsoft Word 2010 Quick Reference Summary *(continued)*

Task	Page Number	Mouse	Ribbon	Shortcut Menu	Keyboard Shortcut
Header and Footer, Change Margins	WD 589		Header Position from Top or Footer Position from Bottom boxes (Header & Footer Tools Design tab | Position group) or Page Setup Dialog Box Launcher (Page Layout tab | Page Setup group), Layout sheet (Page Setup dialog box) or Insert Alignment Tab button (Header & Footer Tools Design tab | Position group)		
Header and Footer, Close	WD 78	Double-click dimmed document text	Close Header and Footer button (Header & Footer Tools Design tab | Close group)		
Header and Footer, Create Alternating	WD 587		Header button or Footer button (Insert tab | Header & Footer group), Edit Header or Edit Footer, Different Odd & Even Pages check box (Header & Footer Tools Design tab | Options group)		
Header and Footer, Different First Page	WD 589		Different First Page check box (Header & Footer Tools Design tab | Options group)		
Header and Footer, Insert Building Block	WD 587		Quick Parts button (Header & Footer Tools Design tab | Insert group), Building Blocks Organizer		
Header and Footer, Insert Date	WD 588		Insert Date and Time button (Header & Footer Tools Design tab | Insert group)		
Header and Footer, Link Sections	WD 230		Link to Previous button (Header & Footer Tools Design tab | Navigation group)		
Highlight Text	WD 651		Text Highlight Color button arrow (Home tab | Font group)		
Hyperlink, Convert to Regular Text	WD 163	Undo Hyperlink (AutoCorrect Options menu)	Hyperlink button (Insert tab | Links group)	Remove Hyperlink	
Hyperlink, Edit	WD 315		Insert Hyperlink button (Insert tab | Links group)	Edit Hyperlink	CTRL+K
Hyperlink, Format Text as	WD 314		Insert Hyperlink button (Insert tab | Links group)	Hyperlink	CTRL+K
Hyperlink, Insert	WD 594		Insert Hyperlink button (Insert tab | Links group), Place in This Document (Insert Hyperlink dialog box)		
Hyphenate	WD 430		Hyphenation button (Page Layout tab | Page Setup group)		
If Field, Insert	WD 355		Rules button (Mailings tab | Write & Insert Fields group)		

Microsoft Word 2010 Quick Reference Summary *(continued)*

Task	Page Number	Mouse	Ribbon	Shortcut Menu	Keyboard Shortcut
Indent, Decrease	WD 81, WD 290	Drag Left Indent Indent marker on horizontal ruler	Decrease Indent button (Home tab | Paragraph group) or Paragraph Dialog Box Launcher (Home tab | Paragraph group), Indents and Spacing tab (Paragraph dialog box)	Paragraph, Indents and Spacing tab (Paragraph dialog box)	CTRL+SHIFT+M
Indent, First-Line	WD 83	Drag First Line Indent marker on ruler	Paragraph Dialog Box Launcher (Home tab or Page Layout tab | Paragraph group), Indents and Spacing tab (Paragraph dialog box)	Paragraph, Indents and Spacing tab (Paragraph dialog box)	TAB
Indent, Increase	WD 81, WD 290	Drag Left Indent marker on horizontal ruler	Increase Indent button (Home tab | Paragraph group) or Paragraph Dialog Box Launcher (Home tab | Paragraph group), Indents and Spacing tab (Paragraph dialog box)	Paragraph, Indents and Spacing tab (Paragraph dialog box)	CTRL+M
Indent Paragraph	WD 210, WD 290	Drag Left Indent and Right Indent markers on ruler	Indent Left or Indent Right box arrow (Page Layout tab | Paragraph group) or Paragraph Dialog Box Launcher (Home tab | Paragraph group), Indents and Spacing tab (Paragraph dialog box)	Paragraph, Indents and Spacing tab (Paragraph dialog box)	
Index, Build	WD 583		Insert Index button (References tab | Index group)		
Index, Change Format	WD 586		Insert Index button (References tab | Index group), select options (Index dialog box)		
Index, Change Language	WD 584		Insert Index button (References tab | Index group), Language box arrow (Index dialog box)		
Index, Delete	WD 586				Select index, SHIFT+F9, select field code, DELETE
Index, Update	WD 586		Update Index button (References tab | Index group)		Select index, F9
Index Entry, Delete	WD 585				Select field, DELETE
Index Entry, Edit	WD 585				Change text inside quotation marks
Index Entry, Mark	WD 549		Mark Entry button (References tab | Index group)		ALT+SHIFT+X
Index Entry, Mark Multiple	WD 551	Select entry, Main entry text box (Mark Index Entry dialog box), Mark button			
Insert Word Document in Existing Document	WD 222, WD 428		Insert Object button arrow (Insert tab | Text group), Text from File		

Microsoft Word 2010 Quick Reference Summary *(continued)*

Task	Page Number	Mouse	Ribbon	Shortcut Menu	Keyboard Shortcut
Insertion Point, Move Down/Up One Line	WD 11				DOWN ARROW/ UP ARROW
Insertion Point, Move Down/Up One Paragraph	WD 11				CTRL+DOWN ARROW/ CTRL+UP ARROW
Insertion Point, Move Down/Up One Screen	WD 11				PAGE DOWN/ PAGE UP
Insertion Point, Move Left/ Right One Character	WD 11				LEFT ARROW/ RIGHT ARROW
Insertion Point, Move Left/ Right One Word	WD 11				CTRL+LEFT ARROW/ CTRL+RIGHT ARROW
Insertion Point, Move to Beginning/End of Document	WD 11				CTRL+HOME/ CTRL+END
Insertion Point, Move to Beginning/End of Line	WD 11				HOME/ END
Insertion Point, Move to Bottom/Top of Document Window	WD 11				ALT+CTRL+PAGE DOWN/ ALT+CTRL+PAGE UP
Italicize	WD 24, WD 81	Italic button on Mini toolbar	Italic button (Home tab | Font group)	Font, Font tab (Font dialog box)	CTRL+I
Justify Paragraph	WD 81, WD 427		Justify button (Home tab | Paragraph group) or Paragraph Dialog Box Launcher (Home tab or Page Layout tab | Paragraph group), Indents and Spacing tab (Paragraph dialog box)	Paragraph, Indents and Spacing tab (Paragraph dialog box)	CTRL+J
Left-Align Paragraph	WD 14, WD 81		Align Text Left button (Home tab | Paragraph group)	Paragraph, Indents and Spacing tab (Paragraph dialog box)	CTRL+L
Line Break, Insert	WD 289				SHIFT+ENTER
Line Spacing, Change	WD 73		Line and Paragraph Spacing button (Home tab | Paragraph group)	Paragraph, Indents and Spacing tab (Paragraph dialog box)	CTRL+[number of desired line spacing, i.e., 2 for double-spacing]
Link, Break	WD 509			Right-click linked object, Linked Worksheet Object, Links, select source file, Break Link button (Links dialog box)	CTRL+SHIFT+F9
Link Entire Source File	WD 508		Insert Object button (Insert tab | Text group), Create from File tab, locate file, 'Link to file' check box (Object dialog box)		

Microsoft Word 2010 Quick Reference Summary *(continued)*

Task	Page Number	Mouse	Ribbon	Shortcut Menu	Keyboard Shortcut
Link Excel Worksheet in a Word Document	WD 507		In Excel, Copy button (Home tab | Clipboard group), switch to Word, Paste button arrow (Home tab | Clipboard group), Link & Keep Source Formatting button in Paste gallery or Paste button arrow (Home tab | Clipboard group), Paste Special, Paste link (Paste Special dialog box), select object to link		
Link to a Graphic	WD 594		Hyperlink button (Insert tab | Links group), enter Web address in Address text box (Insert Hyperlink dialog box)		
Linked Object, Edit	WD 509			Right-click linked object, Linked Worksheet Object, Edit Link	
Linked Object Source File, Locate	WD 507		File tab	Info tab, Edit Links to Files, select source file, Change Source button, locate source file (Links dialog box)		
Macro, Assign to Button	WD 707		Record Macro button (Developer tab | Code group), Button button (Record Macro dialog box)		
Macro, Create Automatic	WD 711		Record Macro button (Developer tab | Code group)		
Macro, Delete	WD 711		View Macros button (Developer tab | Code group), select macro to delete, Delete button (Macros dialog box)		
Macro, Edit VBA Code	WD 713		View Macros button (Developer tab | Code group), select macro to edit, Edit button (Macros dialog box)		
Macro, Record and Assign Shortcut Key	WD 706		Record Macro button (Developer tab | Code group) or View Macros button arrow (View tab | Macros group), Record Macros		ALT+F8
Macro, Rename	WD 711		View Macros button (Developer tab | Code group), Organizer button (Macros dialog box), select macro to rename (Organizer dialog box), enter new name (Rename dialog box), Rename button		

Microsoft Word 2010 Quick Reference Summary *(continued)*

Task	Page Number	Mouse	Ribbon	Shortcut Menu	Keyboard Shortcut
Macro Settings, Specify	WD 679		Macro Security button (Developer tab | Code group), specify setting (Trust Center dialog box) or Options (File tab), Trust Center (Word Options dialog box), Trust Center Settings button, Macro Settings (Trust Center dialog box), select desired setting		
Macro-Enabled Template, Save	WD 677		Save As (File tab), Save as type box arrow, Word Macro-Enabled Template (Save As dialog box)		
Mail Merge, Envelopes	WD 377		Create button (File tab | New tab), Start Mail Merge button (Mailings tab | Start Mail Merge group)		
Mail Merge, Labels	WD 371		Create button (File tab | New tab), Start Mail Merge button (Mailings tab | Start Mail Merge group)		
Mailing Label, Print	WD 190, WD 371		Create Labels button (Mailings tab | Create group)		
Main Document, Identify for Form Letter	WD 333		Start Mail Merge button (Mailings tab | Start Mail Merge group)		
Margin Settings, Change	WD 141, WD 405	Drag margin boundary on ruler	Margins button (Page Layout tab | Page Setup group)		
Mark as Final	WD 490		File tab | Info tab, Protect Document button, Mark as Final		
Markups, Change Display	WD 483		Show Markup button (Review tab | Tracking group), Balloons on Show Markup menu, select desired markup appearance		
Markups, Print	WD 485		File tab | Print tab, first button in Settings area		
Merge, Select Records	WD 365		Edit Recipient List button (Mailings tab | Start Mail Merge group)		
Merge Condition, Remove	WD 368		Edit Recipient List button (Mailings tab | Start Mail Merge group), Filter link (Mail Merge Recipients dialog box), Clear All button (Filter and Sort dialog box)		
Merge Errors, Check for	WD 361		Auto Check for Errors button (Mailings tab | Preview Results group)		
Merge Field, Insert	WD 353		Insert Merge Field button arrow (Mailings tab | Write & Insert Fields group)		

Microsoft Word 2010 Quick Reference Summary *(continued)*

Task	Page Number	Mouse	Ribbon	Shortcut Menu	Keyboard Shortcut
Merge Fields, Highlight	WD 358		Highlight Merge Fields button (Mailings tab | Write & Insert Fields group)		
Merge Form Letters to New Document	WD 361		Finish & Merge button (Mailings tab | Finish group), Edit Individual Documents, All (Merge to New Document dialog box)		
Merge Form Letters to Printer	WD 364		Finish & Merge button (Mailings tab | Finish group), Print Documents, or Print link in Mail Merge task pane		
Merge to a Directory	WD 379		Start Mail Merge button (Mailings tab | Start Mail Merge group), Select Recipients button (Mailings tab | Start Mail Merge group), select merge fields		
Merge to E-Mail Addresses	WD 333		Start Mail Merge button (Mailings tab | Start Mail Merge group)		
Merged Data, View in Main Document	WD 349		Preview Results button (Mailings tab | Preview Results group)		
Move Text	WD 47	Drag and drop selected text	Cut button (Home tab | Clipboard group); Paste button (Home tab | Clipboard group)	Cut; Paste	CTRL+X; CTRL+V
Multilevel Numbered List	WD 236		Numbering button (Home tab | Paragraph group)	Numbering	Type 1., SPACEBAR
Navigation Pane, Go To Heading	WD 580		'Browse the headings in your document' tab (Navigation Pane)		
New File, Create from Existing	WD 165		'New from existing' button (File tab | New tab)		
Nonbreaking Space, Insert	WD 175		Symbol button (Insert tab | Symbols group), More Symbols, Special Characters tab (Symbol dialog box)		CTRL+SHIFT+ SPACEBAR
Normal Style, Apply	WD 106		Normal in Quick Style gallery (Home tab | Styles group)		CTRL+SHIFT+S
Normal Style, Modify	WD 70		Styles Dialog Box Launcher (Home tab | Styles group), style box arrow, Modify	Right-click style (Home tab | Styles group), Modify	ALT+CTRL+ SHIFT+S
Open a Document	WD 45		Open (File tab)		CTRL+O
Open a New Document Based on a Template, Using Windows Explorer	WD 658	Double-click template name in Windows Explorer window			
Outline, Add Entries	WD 561		Promote or Demote button (Outlining tab | Outline Tools group)		

Microsoft Word 2010 Quick Reference Summary *(continued)*

Task	Page Number	Mouse	Ribbon	Shortcut Menu	Keyboard Shortcut
Outline, Add to Chart	WD 515		Shape Outline button arrow (Chart Tools Format tab | Shape Styles group)	Right-click chart edge, Shape Outline on Mini toolbar	
Outline, Show First Line Only	WD 563		Show First Line Only check box (Outlining tab | Outline Tools group)		
Outline View	WD 561	Outline button on status bar	Outline View button (View tab | Document Views group)		
Outline View, Exit	WD 566		Close Outline View button (Outlining tab | Close group)		
Page Border, Add	WD 41, WD 458		Page Borders button (Page Layout tab | Page Background group)		
Page Break, Insert	WD 106		Page Break button (Insert tab | Pages group)		CTRL+ENTER
Page Color, Fill Effect	WD 691		Page Color button (Page Layout tab | Page Background group), Fill Effects in Page Color gallery		
Page Color, Remove	WD 692		Page Color button (Page Layout tab | Page Background group) No Color in Page Color gallery		
Page Number, Insert	WD 77		Insert Page Number button (Header & Footer Tools Design tab | Header & Footer group), or (Insert tab | Header & Footer group)		
Page Numbers, Start at Different	WD 231		Insert Page Number button (Header & Footer Tools Design tab | Header & Footer group) or Insert Page Number button (Insert tab | Header & Footer group), Format Page Numbers, Start at option button (Page Number Format dialog box)		
Page Orientation, Change	WD 379		Page Orientation button (Page Layout tab | Page Setup group)		
Paper Size, Change	WD 615		Page Size button (Page Layout tab | Page Setup group)		
Paste	WD 113, WD 439, WD 455		Paste button (Home tab | Clipboard group) or Clipboard Dialog Box Launcher (Home tab | Clipboard group)	Paste	CTRL+V
Paste Options	WD 156		Paste button arrow (Home tab | Clipboard group)		
Paste Options Menu, Display	WD 114	Paste Options button by moved/copied text			
PDF Document, Create	WD 301		Create PDF/XPS Document (File tab | Save & Send tab)		

Microsoft Word 2010 Quick Reference Summary *(continued)*

Task	Page Number	Mouse	Ribbon	Shortcut Menu	Keyboard Shortcut
Picture, Change	WD 569		Change Picture button (Picture Tools Format tab | Adjust group)	Change Picture	
Picture, Fill a Shape with	WD 695		Shape Fill button arrow (Drawing Tools Format tab | Shape Styles group), Picture in Shape Fill gallery, select file, Insert button (Insert Picture dialog box)		
Picture, Insert	WD 31		Insert Picture from File button (Insert tab | Illustrations group)		
Picture, Save in Other Format	WD 558			Save as Picture	
Picture Effects, Apply	WD 38		Picture Effects button (Picture Tools Format tab | Picture Styles group)	Format Picture	
Picture Style, Apply	WD 37		More button in Picture Styles gallery (Picture Tools Format tab | Picture Styles group)		
Placeholder Text, Replace	WD 284	Select placeholder text, type new text			
Preview a Document	WD 124		File tab | Print tab, Next Page and Previous Page buttons		CTRL+P
Print Document	WD 51		Print button (File tab | Print tab)		CTRL+P, ENTER
Print Specific Pages	WD 223		Print tab | File tab, type desired page numbers in Pages text box		CTRL+P
Protect a Form	WD 655		Restrict Editing button (Developer tab | Protect group), select restrictions (Restrict Formatting and Editing task pane), Yes, Start Enforcing Protection button		
Protected View	WD 554		Options button (File tab) Trust Center (Word Options dialog box), Trust Center Settings button		
Quick Style, Apply	WD 166		[style name] in Quick Style gallery (Home tab | Styles group)		CTRL+SHIFT+S, style name box arrow
Quick Style, Create	WD 296		More button in Quick Styles gallery (Home tab | Styles group), Save Selection as a New Quick Style in Quick Styles gallery	Save Selection as a New Quick Style	
Quick Table	WD 523		Table button (Insert tab | Tables group), Quick Tables in Table gallery		
Quit Word	WD 44	Close button on title bar	Exit (File tab)		ALT+F4

Microsoft Word 2010 Quick Reference Summary *(continued)*

Task	Page Number	Mouse	Ribbon	Shortcut Menu	Keyboard Shortcut
Quotation, Format in Running Text	WD 436		More button (Home tab | Styles group)		
Rectangle, Draw	WD 648		Shapes button (Insert tab | Illustrations group), Rectangle in Shapes gallery		
Redo	WD 23	Redo button on Quick Access Toolbar			CTRL+Y
Remove Character Formatting	WD 81				CTRL+SPACEBAR
Remove Paragraph Formatting	WD 81				CTRL+Q
Remove Space after Paragraph	WD 74, WD 81		Line and Paragraph Spacing button (Home tab | Paragraph group)	Paragraph, Indents and Spacing tab (Paragraph dialog box)	
Replace Text	WD 116	Select Browse Object button on vertical scroll bar, Find button, Replace tab (Find and Replace dialog box), or Page Number indicator on status bar, Replace tab (Find and Replace dialog box)	Replace button (Home tab | Editing group)		CTRL+H
Research Task Pane, Look Up Information	WD 120	ALT+click desired word	Research button (Review tab | Proofing group)		
Reset Original Theme Colors	WD 654		Theme Colors button (Page Layout tab | Themes group), Create New Theme Colors in Theme Colors gallery, Reset button (Create New Theme Colors dialog box)		
Reveal Formatting	WD 298				SHIFT+F1
Reviewer Information, Change	WD 480		Track Changes button arrow (Review tab | Tracking group), Change User Name (Track Changes menu) or Options (File tab), General, enter name in User name text box (Word Options dialog box)		
Reviewing Pane	WD 484		Reviewing Pane button arrow (Review tab | Tracking group)		
Right-Align	WD 76		Align Text Right button (Home tab | Paragraph group)	Paragraph, Indents and Spacing tab (Paragraph dialog box)	CTRL+R
Rows, Move	WD 185	Drag selected row(s) to new location	Cut button (Home tab | Clipboard group); Paste button (Home tab | Clipboard group)		

Microsoft Word 2010 Quick Reference Summary *(continued)*

Task	Page Number	Mouse	Ribbon	Shortcut Menu	Keyboard Shortcut
Rulers, Display	WD 82	View Ruler button on vertical scroll bar	View Ruler check box (View tab | Show group)		
Save Document, Same File Name	WD 30	Save button on Quick Access toolbar	Save (File tab)		CTRL+S
Save Document as Template	WD 613		File tab | Save & Send tab, Change File Type in Save & Send gallery, Template, Save As button; or Save As (File tab), 'Save as type' box arrow (Save As dialog box), Word Template		F12
Save Location, Set Default	WD 314		Options (File tab), Save (Word Options dialog box)		
Save New Document	WD 12	Save button on Quick Access Toolbar	Save or Save As (File tab)		F12 or CTRL+S
Save Word 2010 Document in Earlier Format	WD 306		Change File Type (File tab | Save & Send tab), Word 97-2003 Document		F12
Save Word Document as Different File Type	WD 308		Change File Type (File tab | Save & Send tab)		
Save Word Document as Web Page	WD 312		Change File Type (File tab | Save & Send tab)		F12
Screenshot, Insert	WD 542		Screenshot button (Insert tab | Illustrations group)		
Scroll, Page by Page	WD 112	Previous Page/Next Page button on vertical scroll bar			CTRL+PAGE UP or CTRL+PAGE DOWN
Scroll, Up/Down One Line	WD 11	Click scroll arrow at top/bottom of vertical scroll bar			UP ARROW/ DOWN ARROW
Scroll, Up/Down One Screen	WD 11	Click above/below scroll box on vertical scroll bar			PAGE UP/ PAGE DOWN
Scroll through Documents Side by Side	WD 517		View Side by Side button (View tab | Window group)		
Section Break, Continuous	WD 425		Insert Page and Section Breaks button (Page Layout tab | Page Setup group), Continuous		
Section Break, Delete	WD 221			Cut	BACKSPACE or DELETE
Section Break, Next Page	WD 220, WD 433		Insert Page and Section Breaks button (Page Layout tab | Page Setup group), Next Page		
Select Block of Text	WD 30	Click beginning, SHIFT-click end, or drag through text			
Select Browse Object Menu	WD 547	Select Browse Object button on vertical scroll bar or Page Number indicator on status bar		ALT+CTRL+HOME	
Select Character(s)	WD 30	Drag through character(s)			SHIFT+RIGHT ARROW or SHIFT+LEFT ARROW
Select Entire Document	WD 30	In left margin, triple-click	Select button arrow (Home tab | Editing group), Select All		CTRL+A

Microsoft Word 2010 Quick Reference Summary *(continued)*

Task	Page Number	Mouse	Ribbon	Shortcut Menu	Keyboard Shortcut
Select Graphic	WD 30	Click graphic			
Select Group of Words	WD 27, WD 30	Drag mouse pointer through words			CTRL+SHIFT+RIGHT ARROW or CTRL+SHIFT+LEFT ARROW
Select Line	WD 15, WD 30	Click in left margin			SHIFT+DOWN ARROW or SHIFT+UP ARROW, or HOME, SHIFT+END or END, SHIFT+HOME
Select Multiple Lines	WD 21, WD 30	Drag mouse pointer in left margin			SHIFT+DOWN ARROW or SHIFT+UP ARROW
Select Nonadjacent Items	WD 15, WD 244	Select first item, hold down CTRL key while selecting additional item(s)			
Select Paragraph	WD 30	Triple-click paragraph, or double-click in left margin			CTRL+SHIFT+DOWN ARROW or CTRL+SHIFT+UP ARROW
Select Sentence	WD 30	CTRL-click			
Select Word	WD 30	Double-click word			CTRL+SHIFT+RIGHT ARROW or CTRL+SHIFT+LEFT ARROW
Selection Pane	WD 421		Selection Pane button (Drawing Tools Format tab or Picture Tools Format tab | Arrange group)		
Shade Paragraph	WD 20		Shading button arrow (Home tab | Paragraph group)		
Shape, Add 3-D or Shadow Effects	WD 650		Shape Effects button (Drawing Tools Format tab | Shape Styles group)		
Shape, Add Border (Outline)	WD 650		Shape Outline button (Drawing Tools Format tab | Shape Styles group)		
Shape, Add Text	WD 145			Add Text	
Shape, Apply Shadow Effect	WD 650		Shape Effects button (Drawing Tools Format tab | Shape Styles group), Shadow		
Shape, Apply Style	WD 144		More button in Shape Styles gallery (Drawing Tools Format tab | Shape Styles group)	Format Shape, Fill button in left pane (Format Shape dialog box)	
Shape, Change	WD 693		Edit Shape button (Drawing Tools Format tab | Insert Shapes group), Change Shape		
Shape, Change Shadow Color	WD 695		Shape Effects button (Drawing Tools Format tab | Shape Styles group), Shadow, Shadow Options		
Shape, Fill	WD 650		Shape Fill button (Drawing Tools Format tab | Shape Styles group)		

Microsoft Word 2010 Quick Reference Summary *(continued)*

Task	Page Number	Mouse	Ribbon	Shortcut Menu	Keyboard Shortcut
Shape, Insert	WD 142		Shapes button (Insert tab | Illustrations group)		
Single-Space Lines	WD 73, WD 81		Line and Paragraph Spacing button (Home tab | Paragraph group)	Paragraph, Indents and Spacing tab (Paragraph dialog box)	CTRL+1
Small Caps	WD 81, WD 216		Font Dialog Box Launcher (Home tab | Font group), Font tab (Font dialog box)		CTRL+SHIFT+K
SmartArt Graphic, Add Shape	WD 216		Add Shape button (SmartArt Tools Design tab | Create Graphic group)		
SmartArt Graphic, Add Text	WD 214, WD 451	Select shape, enter text, or click Text Pane control, enter text in Text Pane	Text Pane button (SmartArt Tools Design tab | Create Graphic group), enter text in Text Pane		
SmartArt Graphic, Adjust Shape Size	WD 452		Smaller button or Larger button (SmartArt Tools Format tab | Shapes group)		
SmartArt Graphic, Apply Style	WD 216		More button in SmartArt Styles gallery (SmartArt Tools Design tab | SmartArt Styles group)		
SmartArt Graphic, Change Color	WD 215		Change Colors button (SmartArt Tools Design tab | SmartArt Styles group)		
SmartArt Graphic, Change Layout	WD 449		Layouts gallery (SmartArt Tools Design tab | Layouts group)		
SmartArt Graphic, Delete Shape	WD 214				Select shape, DELETE
SmartArt Graphic, Insert	WD 213		Insert SmartArt Graphic button (Insert tab | Illustrations group)		
SmartArt Graphic, Layer in Front of Text	WD 456		Arrange button (SmartArt Tools Format tab | Arrange group), Bring Forward button arrow		
Sort Paragraphs	WD 232		Sort button (Home tab | Paragraph group)		
Source, Edit	WD 97		Click citation, Citation Options box arrow, Edit Source		
Source, Modify	WD 109		Manage Sources button (References tab | Citations & Bibliography group), Edit button		
Spelling and Grammar, Check at Once	WD 118	Spelling and Grammar Check icon on status bar, Spelling	Spelling & Grammar button (Review tab | Proofing group)	Spelling	F7
Spelling, Check as You Type	WD 9	Click word, Spelling and Grammar Check icon on status bar		Correct word on shortcut menu	

Microsoft Word 2010 Quick Reference Summary *(continued)*

Task	Page Number	Mouse	Ribbon	Shortcut Menu	Keyboard Shortcut
Split Window	WD 438	Double-click resize pointer on split box at top of vertical scroll bar	Split button (View tab | Window group)		ALT+CTRL+S, ENTER
Status Bar, Customize	WD 481			Right-click status bar, click item on Status Bar menu	
Style, Add New Style to Quick Parts Gallery	WD 690		Styles Dialog Box Launcher (Home tab | Styles group), Manage Styles button (Styles task pane), New Style button (Manage Styles dialog box), Add to Quick Style list check box (Create New Style from Formatting dialog box)		
Style, Modify	WD 299		Styles Dialog Box Launcher (Home tab | Styles group), click [style name], Modify	Modify	
Style, Modify Using Styles Task Pane	WD 687		Styles Dialog Box Launcher (Home tab | Styles group), select style (Styles task pane), style box arrow, Modify		
Style, Update to Match Selection	WD 74		Right-click style in Quick Style gallery (Home tab | Styles group)	Styles	
Style Set, Change	WD 567		Change Styles button (Home tab | Styles group)		
Subdocument, Convert to Master Document	WD 566		Unlink button (Outlining tab | Master Document group)		
Subdocument, Delete	WD 565				Select subdocument icon, DELETE
Subdocument, Expand	WD 565		Expand Subdocuments button (Outlining tab | Master Document group)		
Subdocument, Insert	WD 564		Insert Subdocument button (Outlining tab | Master Document group)		
Subscript	WD 81		Subscript button (Home tab | Font group)	Font, Font tab (Font dialog box)	CTRL+EQUAL SIGN
Superscript	WD 81		Superscript button (Home tab | Font group)	Font, Font tab (Font dialog box)	CTRL+SHIFT+PLUS SIGN
Switch from One Open Document to Another	WD 454	Click live preview on Windows taskbar	Switch Windows button (View tab | Window group)		ALT+TAB
Symbol, Insert	WD 158		Insert Symbol button (Insert tab | Symbols group)		
Synonym, Find and Insert	WD 118		Thesaurus (Review tab | Proofing group)	Synonyms	SHIFT+F7
Tab Stops, Set Custom	WD 169, WD 413	Click desired tab stop on ruler	Paragraph Dialog Box Launcher (Home tab or Page Layout tab | Paragraph group), Tabs button (Paragraph dialog box)		

Task	Page Number	Mouse	Ribbon	Shortcut Menu	Keyboard Shortcut
Table, Align Data in Cells	WD 182		Align [location] button (Table Tools Layout tab | Alignment group)		
Table, Apply Style	WD 179		More button in Table Styles gallery (Table Tools Design tab | Table Styles group)		
Table, Border	WD 254		Borders button arrow (Table Tools Design tab | Table Styles group)		
Table, Center	WD 183	Select table, Center button on Mini toolbar	Select table, Center button (Home tab | Font group)		
Table, Change Cell Spacing	WD 245		Cell Margins button (Table Tools Layout tab | Alignment group) or Table Properties button (Table Tools Layout tab | Table group)	Table Properties	
Table, Change Column Width	WD 240	Drag Move Table Column marker on horizontal ruler or double-click column boundary	Table Column Width box (Table Tools Layout tab | Cell Size group or Table Properties button (Table Tools Layout tab | Table group)		
Table, Change Row Height	WD 241	Drag row boundary or Adjust Table Row marker on vertical ruler	Table Row Height box up or down arrows (Table Tools Layout tab | Cell Size group) or Table Properties button (Table Tools Layout tab | Table group)	Table Properties	
Table, Convert to Text	WD 682		Convert to Text button (Table Tools Layout tab | Data group)		
Table, Copy and Paste Item	WD 293		Copy button (Home tab | Clipboard group), then Paste button (Home tab | Clipboard group)	Copy, then Paste	CTRL+C, then CTRL+V
Table, Delete Cell Contents	WD 185		Cut button (Home tab | Clipboard group)		Select cell contents, DELETE or BACKSPACE or CTRL+X
Table, Delete Entire	WD 185		Delete button (Table Tools Layout tab | Rows & Columns group)		
Table, Delete Row or Column	WD 185, WD 247		Delete button (Table Tools Layout tab | Rows & Columns group)	Select row/column, Delete Rows or Delete Columns	
Table, Display Text Vertically in Cell	WD 252		Text Direction button (Table Tools Layout tab | Alignment group)		
Table, Distribute Columns	WD 250		Distribute Columns button (Table Tools Layout tab | Cell Size group)		
Table, Distribute Rows	WD 251		Distribute Rows button (Table Tools Layout tab | Cell Size group)		
Table, Insert	WD 176		Table button (Insert tab | Tables group)		

Microsoft Word 2010 Quick Reference Summary *(continued)*

Task	Page Number	Mouse	Ribbon	Shortcut Menu	Keyboard Shortcut
Table, Insert Column	WD 185		Insert Columns to the Left/Right button (Table Tools Layout tab | Rows & Columns group)	Insert	
Table, Insert Row	WD 184		Insert Rows Above/Below button (Table Tools Layout Tab | Rows & Columns group)	Insert	
Table, Merge Cells	WD 185		Merge Cells button (Table Tools Layout tab | Merge group)	Merge Cells	
Table, Move Cell Boundary	WD 250	Drag cell boundary or Move Table Column marker on horizontal ruler			
Table, Move Columns	WD 185	Drag selected column(s) to new location	Cut button (Home tab | Clipboard group); Paste button (Home tab | Clipboard group)		
Table, Move Rows	WD 286	Drag selected row(s) to new location	Cut button (Home tab | Clipboard group); Paste button (Home tab | Clipboard group)	Cut; Keep Source Formatting	CTRL+X; CTRL+V
Table, Repeat Header Rows	WD 384		Repeat Header Rows button (Table Tools Layout tab | Data group)		
Table, Resize Columns to Fit Table Contents	WD 180	Double-click column boundary	AutoFit button (Table Tools Layout tab | Cell Size group)	AutoFit	
Table, Select Cell	WD 181	Click left edge of cell	Select button (Table Tools Layout tab | Table group)		
Table, Select Column	WD 181	Click top border of column	Select button (Table Tools Layout tab | Table group)		
Table, Select Entire	WD 181	Click table move handle	Select button (Table Tools Layout tab | Table group)		
Table, Select Multiple Cells, Rows, or Columns, Adjacent	WD 181	Drag through cells, rows, or columns			
Table, Select Next Cell	WD 181				TAB
Table, Select Previous Cell	WD 181				SHIFT+TAB
Table, Select Row	WD 181	Click to left of row	Select button (Table Tools Layout tab | Table group)		
Table, Show/Hide Gridlines	WD 239		View Table Gridlines button (Table Tools Layout tab | Table group)		
Table, Sort	WD 248		Sort button (Table Tools Layout tab | Data group)		
Table, Sort by Multiple Columns	WD 385		Sort button (Table Tools Layout tab | Data group), Sort by box arrow (Sort dialog box), Then by box arrow (Sort dialog box)		
Table, Split Cells	WD 186, WD 249		Split Cells button (Table Tools Layout tab | Merge group)	Split Cells	
Table, Sum Columns	WD 254		Formula button (Table Tools Layout tab | Data group)		

Microsoft Word 2010 Quick Reference Summary *(continued)*

Task	Page Number	Mouse	Ribbon	Shortcut Menu	Keyboard Shortcut
Table Cell, Shade	WD 243		Shading button arrow (Table Tools Design tab | Table Styles group)		
Table of Authorities, Build	APP 65		Insert Table of Authorities button (References tab | Table of Authorities group)		
Table of Authorities, Change Format	APP 66		Insert Table of Authorities button (References tab | Table of Authorities group), Formats box arrow, Modify button		
Table of Authorities, Delete	APP 66		Select table, Cut button (Home tab | Clipboard group)	Select table, Cut	Select table, DELETE or BACKSPACE
Table of Authorities, Update	APP 65		Select table, Update Table of Authorities button (References tab | Table of Authorities group)		Select table, F9
Table of Contents, Change Format	WD 579		Table of Contents button (References tab | Table of Contents group), Insert Table of Contents, Formats box arrow (Table of Contents dialog box)		
Table of Contents, Change Style	WD 574		Table of Contents button (References tab | Table of Contents group), Insert Table of Contents (Table of Contents gallery), Options button (Table of Contents dialog box)		
Table of Contents, Create	WD 573		Table of Contents button (References tab | Table of Contents group) or Quick Parts button (Insert tab | Text group), Building Blocks Organizer		
Table of Contents, Delete	WD 573		Table of Contents button (References tab | Table of Contents group), Remove Table of Contents (Table of Contents gallery)		
Table of Contents, Retain Formatting when Adding Text	WD 578		With insertion point in the paragraph of text to add to table of contents, Add Text button (References tab | Table of Contents group)		
Table of Contents, Update	WD 575	Select table of contents, Update Table button	Select table of contents, Update Table button (References tab | Table of Contents group)		F9
Table of Figures, Change Format	WD 582		Insert Table of Figures button (References tab | Captions group), select formats (Table of Figures dialog box)		

Microsoft Word 2010 Quick Reference Summary *(continued)*

Task	Page Number	Mouse	Ribbon	Shortcut Menu	Keyboard Shortcut
Table of Figures, Create	WD 581		Insert Table of Figures button (References tab | Captions group)		
Table of Figures, Update	WD 582		Update Table of Figures button (References tab | Captions group)		Select table, F9
Text Box, Apply 3-D Effect	WD 703		Shape Effects button (Drawing Tools Format tab | Shape Styles group), 3-D Rotation or Format Shape Dialog Box Launcher (Drawing Tools Format tab | Shape Styles group), 3-D Rotation (Format Shape dialog box), select desired options	Format Shape on shortcut menu, click 3-D Rotation in left pane (Format Shape dialog box), select desired options	
Text Box, Break Link	WD 557		Break Link button (Drawing Tools Format tab | Text group)		
Text Box, Change Outline	WD 702		Shape Outline button in Shape Styles gallery (Drawing Tools Format tab | Shape Styles group) or Format Shape Dialog Box Launcher (Drawing Tools Format tab | Shape Styles group), Line Color button (Format Shape dialog box), select desired option	Format Shape, Line Color button (Format Shape dialog box), select desired option	
Text Box, Change Text Direction	WD 701		Text Direction button (Drawing Tools Format tab | Text group) or Format Shape Dialog Box Launcher (Drawing Tools Format tab | Shape Styles group), Text Box button (Format Shape dialog box), select desired direction	Format Shape, Text Box button (Format Shape dialog box), select desired direction	
Text Box, Draw	WD 699		Text Box button (Insert tab | Text group), Draw Text Box in Text Box gallery		
Text Box, Insert	WD 437		Text Box button (Insert tab | Text group)		
Text Box, Link	WD 556		Create Link button (Drawing Tools Format tab | Text group)		
Text Box, Position	WD 442	Drag to new location			
Text Box Gallery, Saving To	WD 441		Text Box button (Insert tab | Text group), Save Selection to Text Box Gallery		
Text Effect, Apply	WD 19		Text Effects button (Home tab | Font group)		
Text Wrapping, Change	WD 148		Wrap Text button (Drawing Tools format tab or Picture Tools Format tab | Arrange group)	Wrap Text	

Microsoft Word 2010 Quick Reference Summary *(continued)*

Task	Page Number	Mouse	Ribbon	Shortcut Menu	Keyboard Shortcut
Theme Color, Customize	WD 653		Theme Colors button (Page Layout tab | Themes group), Create New Theme Colors in Theme Colors gallery, select colors (Create New Theme Colors dialog box) or Make changes, Themes button (Page Layout tab | Themes group), Save Current Theme in Themes gallery		
Theme Colors, Change	WD 28		Change Styles button (Home tab | Styles group), Colors, or Theme Colors button (Page Layout tab | Themes group)		
Theme Effects, Modify	WD 453		Theme Effects button (Page Layout tab | Themes group)		
Theme Fonts, Change	WD 226		Change Styles button (Home tab | Styles group) or Theme Fonts button (Page Layout tab | Themes group)		
Theme Fonts, Customize	WD 295		Change Styles button (Home tab | Styles group), Fonts, Create New Theme Fonts in Fonts gallery or Theme Fonts button arrow (Page Layout tab | Themes group), Create New Theme Fonts in Fonts gallery		
Themes, Save Customized	WD 453		Themes button (Page Layout tab | Themes group), Save Current Theme in Themes gallery		
Track Changes	WD 483				With Track Changes enabled, type text
Tracked Changes, Accept All	WD 489		Accept and Move to Next button arrow (Review tab | Comments group), Accept All Changes in Document		
Tracked Changes, Disable	WD 483	Track Changes indicator on status bar	Track Changes button (Review tab | Tracking group)		CTRL+SHIFT+E
Tracked Changes, Enable	WD 482	Track Changes indicator on status bar	Track Changes button (Review tab | Tracking group) or Track Changes button arrow (Review tab | Tracking group), Track Changes		CTRL+SHIFT+E
Tracked Changes, Reject All	WD 489		Reject and Move to Next button arrow (Review tab | Comments group), Reject All Changes in Document		
Tracked Changes, Review	WD 487		Next Change button (Review tab | Changes group), Accept and Move to Next button or Reject and Move to Next button (Review tab | Changes group)	Right-click comment, click desired change	

Microsoft Word 2010 Quick Reference Summary *(continued)*

Task	Page Number	Mouse	Ribbon	Shortcut Menu	Keyboard Shortcut
Tracked Changes, Show by Single Reviewer	WD 496		Show Markup button (Review tab | Tracking group), point to Reviewers (Show Markup menu), select reviewer (Reviewers submenu)		
Tracked Changes, View without Accepting	WD 486		Display for Review button arrow (Review tab | Tracking group), Final		
Tracking Options, Change	WD 490		Track Changes button arrow (Review tab | Tracking group), Change Tracking Options		
Underline	WD 27, WD 81	Underline button on Mini toolbar	Underline button (Home tab | Font group)	Font, Font tab (Font dialog box)	CTRL+U
Underline Words, Not Spaces	WD 81		Font Dialog Box Launcher (Home tab | Font group), Font tab (Font dialog box), Underline style box arrow		CTRL+SHIFT+W
Undo	WD 23	Undo button on Quick Access Toolbar			CTRL+Z
Ungroup Objects	WD 705		Group button (Drawing Tools Format tab | Arrange group), Ungroup		
Unprotect a Document	WD 678		Restrict Editing button (Developer tab | Protect group), Stop Protection button (Restrict Formatting and Editing task pane) or File tab | Info tab, Protect Document button, Restrict Editing, Stop Protection button (Restrict Formatting and Editing task pane)		
User Name and Initials, Change	WD 335		Options (File tab), General (Word Options dialog box)		
Vertical Alignment	WD 571		Page Setup Dialog Box Launcher (Page Layout tab | Page Setup group), Layout tab (Page Setup dialog box)		
Watermark, Create	WD 258		Watermark button (Page Layout tab | Page Background group) or Quick Parts button (Insert tab | Text group), Building Blocks Organizer (Quick Parts menu), select desired watermark (Building Blocks Organizer dialog box), Insert button		
Watermark, Remove	WD 560		Watermark button (Page Layout tab | Page Background group), Remove Watermark		
Web Layout View	WD 315	Web Layout View button on status bar			

Task	Page Number	Mouse	Ribbon	Shortcut Menu	Keyboard Shortcut
White Space, Hide/Show	WD 241	Double-click space between pages	Options (File tab), Display (Word Options dialog box), Page display options		
WordArt, Change Fill Color	WD 410		Text Fill button arrow (Drawing Tools Format tab | WordArt Styles group)		
WordArt, Change Shape	WD 413		Text Effects button (Drawing Tools Format tab | WordArt Styles group), Transform in Text Effects gallery		
WordArt, Insert	WD 407		WordArt button (Insert tab | Text group)		
XML, Add Parent and Child Elements	APP 68	Click desired schema name in 'Choose an element to apply to your current selection' list (XML Structure task pane), Apply to Entire Document button ('Apply to entire document' dialog box), select content control, select associated control name in 'Choose an element to apply to your current selection' list (XML Structure task pane)			
XML, Attach Schema	APP 67		Schema button (Developer tab | XML group), Add Schema button (Templates and Add-ins dialog box), select schema file (Add Schema dialog box), Open button, enter URI and alias in text boxes (Schema Settings dialog box)		
XML, Delete Schema from Library	APP 67		Schema button (Developer tab | XML group), Schema Library button (Templates and Add-ins dialog box), select schema in 'Select a schema' list (Schema Library dialog box), Delete Schema button		
XML Document, Save As	APP 66		Save As (File tab), 'Save as type' box arrow (Save As dialog box), Word XML Document, Save button		
XML Tag, Remove	APP 68	Right click element name in 'Elements in the document' area (XML Structure task pane), Remove [tag name] tag		Remove [tag name] tag	
XPS Document, Create	WD 303		Create PDF/XPS Document (File tab | Save & Send tab)		

Microsoft Word 2010 Quick Reference Summary *(continued)*

Task	Page Number	Mouse	Ribbon	Shortcut Menu	Keyboard Shortcut
Zoom Document	WD 33	Zoom Out or Zoom In button or drag Zoom slider on status bar	Zoom button (View tab | Zoom group)		
Zoom One Page	WD 41		One Page button (View tab | Zoom group)		
Zoom Page Width	WD 615		Page Width button (View tab | Zoom group)		